THE COLUMBIA
GRANGER'S®
INDEX TO
AFRICAN-AMERICAN
POETRY

OTHER COLUMBIA UNIVERSITY PRESS PUBLICATIONS

The Columbia Granger's® Index to Poetry in Anthologies, 11th edition.
Nicholas Frankovich, ed. (1997)

The Columbia Granger's® Index to Poetry in Collected and Selected Works.
Nicholas Frankovich, ed. (1996)

The Columbia Granger's® World of Poetry 1995 (CD-ROM)

The Columbia Granger's® Dictionary of Poetry Quotations.
Edith P. Hazen, ed. (1992)

The Columbia Granger's® Guide to Poetry Anthologies, 2d edition.
William Katz, Linda Sternberg Katz, and Esther Crain, eds. (1994)

THE COLUMBIA
GRANGER'S®
INDEX TO
AFRICAN-AMERICAN
POETRY

EDITED BY

NICHOLAS FRANKOVICH

AND

DAVID LARZELERE

COLUMBIA UNIVERSITY PRESS

NEW YORK

THE COLUMBIA GRANGER'S® INDEX TO AFRICAN-AMERICAN POETRY

Copyright 1999

by Columbia University Press

All Rights Reserved

Library of Congress Cataloging-in-Publication Data

The Columbia Granger's index to African-American poetry / edited
by Nicholas Frankovich and David Larzelere.
p.   cm.
Includes bibliographical references.
ISBN 0-231-11234-3 (alk. paper)
    1. American poetry—Afro-American authors—Indexes.
2. Afro-Americans in Literature—Indexes.
I. Frankovich, Nicholas.   II. Larzelere, David.   III. Title: Index to
African-American poetry.
    Z1229.N39C65   1999
    [PS153.N5]   98-46181
    016.811008'0896073—dc21   CIP

Casebound editions of Columbia University Press books are
printed on permanent and durable acid-free paper.

Printed in the United States of America

c 10 9 8 7 6 5 4 3 2 1

PREFACE

When deciding which poems they would select to be indexed, the editors of what has come to be known as *The Columbia Granger's® Index to Poetry* have always taken care to identify the poetry books most likely to be found on library shelves. That has been the aim since the first edition, in 1904.

In recent years we have called on consultants, specialists in the various fields to which this poetry index is relevant. Their knowledge of poetry publishing is deep, and so they help to insure that our list of anthologies in any given edition is a good, accurate snapshot of what the core of a library's poetry collection should be at that point in time.

The librarians, teachers, poets, and anthologists who in the role of consultant have advised us in this matter have impressed on us the continuing boom in African-American poetry, which also, of course, has a long tradition. It would be hard to identify a category of English-language poetry that has a larger or more enthusiastic audience. African-American poetry is the subject of extensive scholarship, of seminars and colloquia, of college and high-school courses. Certain anthologies of African-American literature are eagerly awaited. Once published, they become the object of strong opinions expressed by expert reviewers in prominent journals, newspapers, and magazines.

Moreover, all this has been directed to our attention not only by our consultants but also by unsolicited comments that users of Granger's® have sent to us over the years. So we concluded that the interest in and demand for poetry by African Americans is great enough to warrant an index devoted to it.

The Columbia Granger's® Index to African-American Poetry cites 7,983 poems in 33 anthologies and 32 volumes of collected or selected works by individual authors. In the main section of this index, all of these poems are listed by title or first line; most are listed by both. And 2,500 of the most frequently anthologized poems are listed by last line as well.

Of the 65 books indexed here, 33 have not been indexed in any edition of Granger's® previously. They are new to this edition.

We index 659 authors, who write on 1,958 subjects, ranging from Abandonment to Zen Buddhism. Some new subject headings have been added for this edition. These include Integration, Segregation, Race, Hip-Hop, and several leading figures—Rosa Parks, for example, and Ralph Ellison—in African-American history and culture.

When assigning subjects to poems, we strive for precision and accuracy as well as for completeness. Inevitably there are judgment calls. The best example is the distinction to be made between Blacks and African Americans. The former category is broader, including black people in Africa, Europe, and other places outside the United States. A poem may have as its subject black people generally, not just in the United States, even though the author happens to be African American.

Often, of course, the definition of a poem's subject is ambiguous. Poets write about what they write about. It does not always fit neatly into one of the subject headings used in Granger's®. For this reason many of the subject headings here, as in previous editions, are cross-referenced. We trust that users will find the cross references to be helpful.

Our selection of books for this edition was informed by the valuable advice of three knowledgeable and helpful consultants—Joanne Braxton of The College of William and Mary, Charles James of Swarthmore College, and Genette McLaurin of the Schomburg Center for Research in Black Culture. We are grateful for their assistance.

HOW TO USE THE INDEXES

This volume is divided into three sections:
— Title, First Line, and Last Line Index
— Author Index
— Subject Index

Each section is arranged alphabetically.

Every poem covered here is cited at least once in each of the three sections (except for those that are too abstract to be assigned to any heading in the Subject Index). Every poem cited here appears in at least one anthology or volume of collected and selected works listed on pages xv–xvii.

See also the explanatory notes at the beginning of each of the three sections, pages 1, 179, and 217.

Title, First Line, and Last Line Index

The clearest way to explain the Title, First Line, and Last Line Index is to begin by showing how it answers specific questions brought to it.

Where can I find a poem called "Through the Varied Patterned Lace"? Go to the Title, First Line, and Last Line Index. The citation for "Through the Varied Patterned Lace" is followed by the name of the poem's author, Margaret Danner, and by the letter code Klds. Look up Klds in the List of Anthologies, where the codes, not the titles of the anthologies, are arranged alphabetically. There you learn that you can read "Through the Varied Patterned Lace" in *Kaleidoscope; Poetry by American Negro Poets,* edited by Robert Hayden and published by Harcourt, Brace & World in 1967.

What is the title of the poem that begins "Mæcenas, you, beneath the myrtle shade"? The first-line citation is followed by the title, "To Mæcenas," and then by the author, Phillis Wheatley, and the letter codes NAAAL and CP-WheaP. The List of Anthologies and Collected and Selected Works indicates that the books in which this poem can be found are *The Norton Anthology of African American Literature* (Henry Louis Gates, Jr., et al., editors; 1987) and *The Collected Poems of Phillis Wheatley* (Julian D. Mason, Jr., editor; University of North Carolina Press, 1989).

What poem ends with the line "This is my page for English B"? This last-line citation is followed by the title, "Theme for English B," and then by the author, Langston Hughes, and four letter codes. The List of Anthologies and Collected and Selected Works indicates that the title of the anthology coded BALP is *Black American Literture; Poetry* (Darwin Turner, editor; Charles E. Merrill, 1969).

Titles, First Lines, and Last Lines.
Initial capitals in the important words usually indicate that the citation is the title of the poem. "Kadava Kumbis Devise a Way to Marry for Love, The," for example, by Rita Dove, is a title.

First-line and last-line citations are followed by the title (except where the poem has no title). The sign (LL) following last-line citations distinguishes them from first lines.

You know, for example, that "Of a morning sun" is not a title because the title, "Four Glimpses of Night," follows it, and because the initial letters of all the words (except the first one) are lowercase. You know that the citation is a last line and not a first line because it is followed by (LL).

When the first line or the last line of a poem is the same as or slightly longer than the

title, only the title is listed. The poem listed under the title "They Went Home" for example, has no listing for first line because that is the beginning of the first line.

Brackets. Brackets usually indicate variant spellings or slight variations in wording. For example, see the title citation "Listen, Lord—[a Prayer]." In the two books (BANP, BPo) in which that title appears, the wording may vary as indicated in brackets.

Capitalization. The first letter of the first word in every citation is capitalized, even when in its published form it appears as lowercase.

Initial Articles. An article—"a," "an," or "the"—that begins a title or a line is transposed to the end of the citation. "The Ballad of Joe," for example, by Sterling Brown, is listed as "Ballad of Joe, The."

Parentheses. When an entire citation is enclosed by parentheses, it usually means that it is a variant title, first line, or last line. Parentheses are used instead of brackets when it is necessary to indicate a version that varies widely from the standard version, with the result that, in this alphabetized index, it can also be found in a place far from where the standard version is listed.

Indentation. Indentation of a citation indicates that it is a selection. See, for example, "New Orleans Haiku" by Kalamu ya Salaam.

> New Orleans Haiku. Kalamu ya Salaam. SpiFl
> > All Nite Long.
> > Everywhere You Eat.
> > French Quarter Intimacies.

"'All Nite Long," "Everywhere You Eat," and "French Quarter Intimacies" are indented because they are selections from "New Orleans Haiku."

The letter code SpiFl in the top line of this entry refers to the anthology *Spirit & Flame* and indicates that the entire longer work, including each of the selections in the indented list under that top line, can be found there.

Each of the indented selections of the longer work has its own entry in its alphabetical place in the Title, First Line, and Last Line Index. For example, you can also find "All Nite Long" under the *A*'s, where it is identified as a selection of "New Orleans Haiku" and the letter code SpiFl appears.

Author Index

Under each author's name, poems are listed alphabetically by title or, where the poem has no title, by first line.

What poems can I find by Derrick I. M. Gilbert? The Author Index lists three poems by him.

Does he write under a pseudonym? The Author Index indicates that he uses the pen name D-Knowledge.

Subject Index

Under each subject heading, poems are listed alphabetically by author's name.

What poems can I find about marriage? The subject index shows that there are 36 poems

about marriage, by 27 different authors, including Claude McKay and Marilyn Nelson. Citations for all these poems can be found in the Title, First Line, and Last Line Index, where the letter codes, which refer to the List of Anthologies and Collected and Selected Works, indicate in which books the poems are published.

Did Paul Laurence Dunbar write poems about God? Go to the heading for "God" and locate "Dunbar" in the list of poems alphabetized by author.

The Columbia Granger's® Index
to African-American Poetry

PUBLISHER
WILLIAM STRACHAN

PROJECT DIRECTOR
JAMES RAIMES

DIRECTOR OF DESIGN AND PRODUCTION
AUDREY SMITH

EDITORS
NICHOLAS FRANKOVICH
DAVID LARZELERE

CONSULTANTS

The Columbia Granger's® Index
to African-American Poetry

JOANNE M. BRAXTON

Professor of American Studies and English
The College of William and Mary

CHARLES L. JAMES

Professor of English
Swarthmore College

GENETTE M. McLAURIN

Curator
General Research and Reference,
Schomburg Center for Research in Black Culture

ABBREVIATIONS

abr.	abridged		*mod.*	modernized *or* modern
ad.	adapted		*N.T.*	New Testament
add.	additional		*O.T.*	Old Testament
arr.	arranged		*orig.*	original
at.	attributed		*par.*	paraphrase *or* paraphrased
bk.	book		*pr.*	prose
br.	brief		*pt.*	part *or* parts
ch.	chapter		*rev.*	revised
comp.	compiled *or* compiler		*sc.*	scene
comps.	compilers		*sec.*	section
cond.	condensed		*sel.*	selection
diff.	different		*sels.*	selections
fr.	from		*sl.*	slightly
frag.	fragment		*st.*	stanza
incl.	included *or* including		*sts.*	stanzas
introd.	introduction *or* introductory		*tr.*	translator, translation, *or* translated
ll.	lines		*trs.*	translators *or* translations
LL	last line		*var.*	various
med.	medieval		*vers.*	version *or* versions
misc.	miscellaneous		*wr.*	wrong *or* wrongly

CONTENTS

PREFACE   v

HOW TO USE THE INDEXES   vii

ABBREVIATIONS   xii

LIST OF ANTHOLOGIES AND COLLECTED AND SELECTED WORKS   xv

TITLE, FIRST LINE, AND LAST LINE INDEX   1

AUTHOR INDEX   179

SUBJECT INDEX   217

LIST OF ANTHOLOGIES
AND COLLECTED AND SELECTED WORKS

AAP   African-American Poetry of the Nineteenth Century; an Anthology. *Joan R. Sherman, ed.* (1992) University of Illinois Press. 506p., pap., o.p.

AfAmPo   African-American Poetry; an Anthology, 1773–1927. *Joan R. Sherman, ed.* (1997) Dover. 82p., pap.

AmNP   American Negro Poetry. *Arna Bontemps, ed.* (Rev. ed., 1974) Hill and Wang. 252p., pap., o.p.

BALP   Black American Literature: Poetry. *Darwin T. Turner, ed.* (1969) Charles E. Merrill. 132p.

BANP   The Book of American Negro Poetry. *James Weldon Johnson, ed.* (Rev. ed., 1931) Harcourt Brace Jovanovich. 300p., pap.

BPo   The Black Poets. *Dudley Randall, ed.* (1971) Bantam Books. 355p., pap.

BkSV   Black Southern Voices; an Anthology of Fiction, Poetry, Drama, Nonficiton, and Critical Essays. *John Oliver Killens and Jerry W. Ward, eds.* (1992) Meridian. 608p., pap.

BlFi   Black Fire; an Anthology of Afro-American Writing. *LeRoi Jones and Larry Neal, eds.* (1968) William Morrow and Company. 670p.

BlSi   Black Sister; Poetry by Black American Women, 1746–1980. *Erlene Stetson, ed.* (1981) Indiana University Press. 312p., pap.

BrTr   A Broadside Treasury. *Gwendolyn Brooks* (1971) Broadside Press. 188p., pap.

CBWP-1   Collected Black Women's Poetry. Vol. I. *Joan R. Sherman, ed.* (1988) Oxford University Press.

CBWP-2   Collected Black Women's Poetry. Vol. II. *Joan R. Sherman, ed.* (1988) Oxford University Press.

CBWP-3   Collected Black Women's Poetry. Vol. III. *Joan R. Sherman, ed.* (1988) Oxford University Press.

CBWP-4   Collected Black Women's Poetry. Vol. IV. *Joan R. Sherman, ed.* (1988) Oxford University Press.

CDC   Caroling Dusk; an Anthology of Verse by Negro Poets. *Countee Cullen, ed.* (1927) Harper & Brothers. 237p., o.p.

CP-AngeM   The Complete Collected Poems of Maya Angelou. (1994) Random House. 273p.

CP-BrowS   The Collected Poems of Sterling A. Brown. *Michael S. Harper, ed.* (1980) TriQuarterly Books / Northwestern University Press. 267p., pap.

CP-CullC   My Soul's High Song; the Collected Writings of Countee Cullen, Voice of the Harlem Renaissance. *Gerald Early, ed.* (1991) Doubleday. 618p., pap.

CP-DunbP   The Collected Poetry of Paul Laurence Dunbar. *Joanne M. Braxton, ed.* (1993) University Press of Virginia. 396p., pap.

CP-HarpF   A Brighter Coming Day; a Frances Ellen Watkins Harper Reader. *Frances Smith Foster, ed.* (1990) The Feminist Press at The City University of New York. 416p., pap.

CP-HaydR   Collected Poems [Robert Hayden]. *Frederick Glaysher, ed.* (1985) Liveright. 205p., pap.

CP-HughL   The Collected Poems of Langston Hughes. *Arnold Rampersad and David Roessel, eds.* (1994) Alfred A. Knopf. 708p.

CP-LordA   The Collected Poems of Audre Lorde. (1997) W. W. Norton. 489p.

CP-ReedI   New and Collected Poems [Ishmael Reed]. (1988) Atheneum. 233p.

CP-ToomJ   The Collected Poems of Jean Toomer. *Robert B. Jones and Margery Toomer Latimer, eds.* (1988) University of North Carolina Press. 111p., pap.

CP-WalkA   Her Blue Body Everything We Know; Earthling Poems, 1965–1990 [Alice Walker]. (1991) Harcourt Brace. 459p., pap.

CP-WalkM   This Is My Century; New and Collected Poems [Margaret Walker]. (1989) University of Georgia Press. 209p., pap.

CP-WheaP   The Poems of Phillis Wheatley. *Julian D. Mason, Jr., ed.* (1989) University of North Carolina Press. 235p., pap.

CP-YounA   Heaven; Collected Poems 1956–1990 [Al Young]. (1992) Creative Arts Book Company. 348p., pap.

CrDW   Crossing the Danger Water. *Deirdre Mullane, ed.* (1993) Doubleday. 769p., pap.

Crnst   Cornerstones; an Anthology of African American Literature. *Melvin Donaldson, ed.* (1996) St. Martin's Press. 1,001p.

CtF   Catch the Fire!!!; a Cross-Generational Anthology of Contemporary African-American Poetry. *Derrick I. M. Gilbert, ed.* (1998) Riverhead Books. 288p., pap.

EBAP   Early Black American Poets. *William H. Robinson, Jr., ed.* (1971) Wm. C. Brown Company. 309p., pap.

ESEAA   Every Shut Eye Ain't Asleep; an Anthology of Poetry by African Americans Since 1945. *Michael S. Harper and Anthony Walter, eds.* (1994) Little, Brown and Company. 327p., pap.

FB   The Forerunners; Black Poets in America. *Woodie King, Jr., ed.* (1975) Howard University Press. 126p.

GT   The Garden Thrives; Twentieth-Century African-American Poetry. *Clarence Major, ed.* (1996) HarperCollins. 470p., pap.

GetYo   Get Your Ass in the Water and Swim Like Me; Narrative Poetry from Black Oral Tradition. *Bruce Jackson, ed.* (1974) Harvard University Press. 243p.

IDB   I Am the Darker Brother; an Anthology of Modern Poems by NegroAmericans. *Arnold Adoff, ed.* (1968) Macmillan. 128p.

IHS   I Hear a Symphony; African Americans Celebrate Love. *Paula L. Woods and Felix H. Liddell, eds.* (1994) Anchor / Doubleday. 334p., pap.

JB   Jump Bad; a New Chicago Anthology. *Gwendolyn Brooks, ed.* (1971) Broadside Press. 190p., pap.

Klds   Kaleidoscope; Poems by American Negro Poets. *Robert Hayden, ed.* (1967) Harcourt, Brace & World. 231p.

NAAAL   The Norton Anthology of African American Literature. *Henry Louis Gates, Jr., and Nellie Y. McKay, eds.* (1997) W. W. Norton. 2,665p.

NBP   The New Black Poetry. *Clarence Major, ed.* (1969) International Publishers. 156p.

NBV   New Black Voices; an Anthology of Contemporary Afro-American Literature. *Abraham Chapman, ed.* (1972) Mentor. 606p., pap.

NNP   New Negro Poets U.S.A. *Langston Hughes, ed.* (1964) Indiana University Press. 127p., o.p.

PoBA   The Poetry of Black America; Anthology of the 20th Century. *Arnold Adoff, ed.* (1973) Harper & Row. 552p.

SP-AngeM   Maya Angelou; Poems. (1986) Bantam Books / Random House. 209p., pap.

SP-BaraA   Transbluesency; Selected Poems 1961–1995 [Amiri Baraka]. *Paul Vangelisti, ed.* (1995) Marsilio Publishers. 271p., pap.

SP-BrooG   Selected Poems by Gwendolyn Brooks. (1963) Harper & Row. 127p., pap.

SP-ClifL   Good Woman; Poems and a Memoir, 1969–1980 [Lucille Clifton]. (1987) BOA Editions. 276p., pap.

SP-CortJ   Coagulations: New and Selected Poems [Jayne Cortez]. (1984) Thunder's Mouth Press. 112p.

SP-DoveR   Selected Poems [Rita Dove]. (1993) Vintage Books. 207p., pap.

SP-GiovN   The Selected Poems of Nikki Giovanni. (1996) William Morrow and Company. 292p.

SP-HarpM   Images of Kin; New and Selected Poems [Michael S. Harper]. (1977) University of Illinois Press. 213p., pap.

SP-HortG   The Black Bard of North Carolina; George Moses Horton and His Poetry. *Joan R. Sherman* (1997) University of North Carolina Press. 158p., pap.

SP-HughL   Selected Poems of Langston Hughes. (1959) Vintage Books. 297p., pap.

SP-JordJ   Naming Our Destiny; New and Selected Poems [June Jordan]. (1989) Thunder's Mouth Press. 211p., pap.

SP-KaufB   Cranial Guitar; Selected Poems by Bob Kaufman. *Gerald Nicosia, ed.* (1996) Coffee House Press. 163p., pap.

SP-KnigE   The Essential Etheridge Knight. (1986) University of Pittsburgh Press. 114p., pap.

SP-KomuY   Neon Vernacular; New and Selected Poems [Yusef Komunyakaa]. (1993) Wesleyan University Press / University Press of New England. 178p., pap.

SP-LordA   Undersong; Chosen Poems, Old and New [Audre Lorde]. (1992) W. W. Norton. 206p., pap.

SP-McKaC   Selected Poems of Claude McKay. *Max Eastman, ed.* (1953) Bookman Associates. 112p.

SP-NelsM   The Fields of Praise; New and Selected Poems [Marilyn Nelson] (1997) Louisiana State University Press. 209p.

LIST OF ANTHOLOGIES AND COLLECTED AND SELECTED WORKS

SP-SancS   I've Been a Woman; New and Selected Poems [Sonia Sanchez] (1985) Third World Press. 101p., pap.

SpiFl   Spirit of Flame; an Anthology of African-American Poetry. *Keith Gilyard, ed.* (1997) Syracuse University Press. 304p., pap.

SSLK   Shimmy Shimmy Shimmy like My Sister Kate. *Nikki Giovanni, ed.* (1996) Henry Holt and Company. 188p.

ShDr   Shadowed Dreams; Women's Poetry of the Harlem Renaissance. *Maureen Honey, ed.* (1989) Rutgers University Press. 238p., pap.

TtW   Trouble the Water; 250 Years of African-American Poetry. *Jerry W. Ward, Jr., ed.* (1997) Mentor. 566p., pap.

TITLE, FIRST LINE, AND LAST LINE INDEX

Titles, first lines, and last lines are arranged in one alphabetical listing in the Title, First Line, and Last Line Index. Titles are distinguished by initial capital letters on the important words. All first-line entries are followed by the title of the poem, if there is a title. When the title and the first line of a poem are identical, or nearly so, only one of them is listed, although occasionally, for purposes of clarity, the first line has been added in quotation marks and in parentheses to the title entry.

Anthology codes are listed after titles, first lines, and last lines. Last lines are distinguished from first lines by the symbol (LL). However, more complete information as to translators, acts and scenes, abridgments, and various titles is given in the title entry.

An indented citation indicates that the poem is a selection from the work listed one level above. A citation indented and inside parentheses indicates a variant title, variant first line, or variant last line as used in the anthologies that follow.

Generic title entries, such as Ode, Song, Sonnet, are followed by the first line in quotation marks for easy identification. Such entries, of course, may also be located by first-line listing.

Titles and first lines beginning with "O" and "Oh" are filed separately, with cross-references where necessary. Names beginning "Mac," "Mc," and "M'" are filed in alphabetical order.

A

A-way-up out of the way. (LL) The Signifying Monkey. *Unknown.* CrDW; NAAAL

Abandoned for a time their long pursuit. (LL) The Islands. Robert Hayden. CP-HaydR; ESEAA

Abba Jacob and Miracles. Marilyn Nelson. SP-NelsM

Abba Jacob and St. Francis. Marilyn Nelson. SP-NelsM

Abba Jacob and the Angel. Marilyn Nelson. SP-NelsM

Abba Jacob and the Businessman. Marilyn Nelson. SP-NelsM

Abba Jacob and the Theologian. Marilyn Nelson. SP-NelsM

Abba Jacob at Bat. Marilyn Nelson. SP-NelsM

Abba Jacob closes the prayer book. At Prayer. Marilyn Nelson. SP-NelsM

Abba Jacob Gets Down. Marilyn Nelson. SP-NelsM

Abba Jacob hums quietly, negotiating traffic. Fish and Floor-Dust Bouquet. Marilyn Nelson. SP-NelsM

Abba Jacob in the Well. Marilyn Nelson. SP-NelsM

Abba Jacob, on the word. The Fruit of Faith. Marilyn Nelson. SP-NelsM

Abba Jacob said: / Did I ever tell you about the time. Blessing the Boats. Marilyn Nelson. SP-NelsM

Abba Jacob said: / Do you know anything about Zen? Laughter as the Highest Form of Contemplation. Marilyn Nelson. SP-NelsM

Abba Jacob said: I pray for Lucifer. May Your Love Convert Lucifer. Marilyn Nelson. SP-NelsM

Abba Jacob said: / I scooped some dying fish. Men in the Kitchen. Marilyn Nelson. SP-NelsM

Abba Jacob said: / I wonder if souls are unhappy. Abba Jacob's Aside on Hell. Marilyn Nelson. SP-NelsM

Abba Jacob said: / I'm sorry; I forgot. I'm always forgetting things. Post-Prandial Conversation. Marilyn Nelson. SP-NelsM

Abba Jacob said: / It's amazing: The old nun has been resurrected! Leaving the Hospice. Marilyn Nelson. SP-NelsM

Abba Jacob said: / The older I get, the more clearly I believe. Aches and Pains. Marilyn Nelson. SP-NelsM

Abba Jacob said: / There was once a Desert Father. Abba Jacob Gets Down. Marilyn Nelson. SP-NelsM

Abba Jacob said: / There's a big difference between. The Simple Wisdom. Marilyn Nelson. SP-NelsM

Abba Jacob said: When I was in grad school, I house-sat. Don't Throw Out Wine Bottles. Marilyn Nelson. SP-NelsM

Abba Jacob with his invention. Abba Jacob and St. Francis. Marilyn Nelson. SP-NelsM

Abba Jacob's Aside on Hell. Marilyn Nelson. SP-NelsM

Abba Jacob's Seven Devils. Marilyn Nelson. SP-NelsM

Abduction, The. Rita Dove. SP-DoveR

Abduction of Saints, The. Alice Walker. CP-WalkA

Abe Lincoln. Langston Hughes. CP-HughL

Ablaze / with candles sconced. Dawnbreaker. Robert Hayden. CP-HaydR

Abolished, and its weeks spent walking aimlessly. Where When Was. Reginald Shepherd. GT

Abomunist Manifesto. Bob Kaufman. SP-KaufB

Abortions will not let you forget. The Mother. Gwendolyn Brooks. CrDW; Crnst; ESEAA; NAAAL; TtW *Fr.* A Street in Bronzeville. BPo; BlSi; SP-BrooG

About Enrique's Drawing. June Jordan. SP-JordJ

About its head. (LL) City. Langston Hughes. CP-HughL

About Long Distances on Saturday. June Jordan. SP-JordJ

About love. If it's so tough, / forget it. (LL) Blues. Derek Walcott. Crnst

About me young and careless feet. On Broadway. Claude McKay. SP-McKaC

About Our Hips. Harriet Jacobs. SpiFl

About Poetry and South Africa. Samuel Allen. Crnst

About Religion. Audre Lorde. CP-LordA

Absence. Paul Laurence Dunbar. CP-DunbP

Absence. Claude McKay. CDC; SP-McKaC

Absent from the United States. Al Young. CP-YounA

Abu / 's a stone black revolutionary. Dudley Randall. BPo

Abundantly. In His Name / Phillis. (LL) A Letter from Phillis Wheatley. Robert Hayden. CP-HaydR; ESEAA; NAAAL

Accept the university of death. (LL) The Children of the Poor. Gwendolyn Brooks. Crnst; SP-BrooG, *sect.* I, *pt.* 1-5

Acceptance. Langston Hughes. CP-HughL

Acceptance Speech. Jayne Cortez. SP-CortJ

Accident. Maya Angelou. SP-AngeM

("Black-White truth.") (LL) CP-AngeM

Accidents. Companion Pieces. Niama Leslie JoAnn Williams. CtF

Accompanying a Gift ("From thy patient, who while here"). Lizelia Augusta Jenkins Moorer. CBWP-3

Accompanying a Gift ("One whose love will never end"). Lizelia Augusta Jenkins Moorer. CBWP-3

According to my Teachers. Kojo; I Am a Black. Gwendolyn Brooks. ESEAA; TtW *Fr.* Children Coming Home.

According to reports, I entered the third car. To Emerge from the Shadows. Sekou Sundiata. *Fr.* Notes from the Defense of Colin Ferguson. SpiFl

Accountability. Paul Laurence Dunbar. CP-DunbP

Aches and Pains. Marilyn Nelson. SP-NelsM

Across an autumn freezing everywhere. (LL) What shall I give my children? who are poor. Gwendolyn Brooks. BPo; Crnst; SP-BrooG; TtW

Across lunar wastes of wind and snow. Robert Hayden. CP-HaydR

Across our backs. (LL) Hard Rock Returns to Prison from the Hospital for the Criminal Insane. Etheridge Knight. ESEAA; GT; TtW

Across the dewy lawn she treads. Paean. Jonathan Henderson Brooks. CDC

Across the flesh and feeling of soledad. Orisha. Jayne Cortez. BlSi

Across the hills and down the narrow ways. A Winter's Day. Paul Laurence Dunbar. CP-DunbP

Across the wide green water. (LL) A Poem of Attrition. Etheridge Knight. GT; SP-KnigE; TtW

Acrostics. George Moses Horton. AAP; SP-HortG

Adagio. Gerald William Barrax. GT

Adam and Eve. Lucille Clifton. SP-ClifL

Addenda to the Papal Bull. June Jordan. SP-JordJ

Addendum. Yusef Komunyakaa. SP-KomuY

Addition: "Put 5 and 5 together." Langston Hughes. CP-HughL

Addition: "7 + 7 + love =." Langston Hughes. CP-HughL

Address to Ethiopia. Priscilla Jane Thompson. CBWP-2

Address to Miss Phillis Wheatly, Ethiopian Poetess, An. Jupiter Hammon. EBAP; TtW

Address to the Atheist, By P. Wheatley at the Age of 14 Years—1767. Phillis Wheatley. CP-WheaP

Address to the Deist—1767, An. Phillis Wheatley. CP-WheaP

Adelina Patti. Adah Isaacs Menken. CBWP-1

Adieu. Camille Thierry. TtW

Adieu. Mary E. Tucker. CBWP-1

Adieu, Adieu, Forever. Priscilla Jane Thompson. CBWP-2

Adieu New England's smiling Meads. Farewell to America. Phillis Wheatley. CP-WheaP

Adieu New England's smiling Meads. Phillis Wheatley. CP-WheaP

Adieu to the land of my birth. The Emigrant. Benjamin Clark. EBAP

Adieu, you haughty maiden! Adieu, Adieu, Forever. Priscilla Jane Thompson. CBWP-2

Adios, Carenage. Derek Walcott. *Fr.* The Schooner *Flight.* ESEAA

Adjuration. Charles Enoch Wheeler. AmNP

Admiration. Josephine D. Henderson Heard. CBWP-4

Admonitions. Lucille Clifton. BPo; SP-ClifL

Adolescence. Claude McKay. SP-McKaC

Adolescence—I. Rita Dove. SP-DoveR

Adolescence—II. Rita Dove. SP-DoveR

Adolescence—III. Rita Dove. SP-DoveR

Adown the heights of Ages. Priscilla Jane Thompson. CBWP-2

Adown the west a golden glow. At Sunset Time. Paul Laurence Dunbar. CP-DunbP

Adulthood. Nikki Giovanni. SP-GiovN

Adulthood II. Nikki Giovanni. Crnst; SP-GiovN; SP-GiovN

Adupe. Lucille Clifton. ESEAA

Advance of Education, The. Josephine D. Henderson Heard. CBWP-4

Advertisement for the Waldorf-Astoria. Langston Hughes. CP-HughL

Advice. Gwendolyn B. Bennett. BlSi; CDC

Advice. Paul Laurence Dunbar. CP-DunbP

Advice. Langston Hughes. *Fr.* Montage of a Dream Deferred. CP-HughL; SP-HughL

Advice to a Beauty. Countee Cullen. CP-CullC

Advice to the Girls. Frances Ellen Watkins Harper. CP-HarpF; TtW

Advice to Young Ladies. Ann Plato. AAP; TtW

Aerolingual Poet of Prey. Eugene B. Redmond. SpiFl

Aesthete in Harlem. Langston Hughes. *See* Esthete in Harlem.

Afar though near the silence waxes. The Cloak. Norman Henry, II Pritchard. GT

Affirmation. Helen Armstead Johnson. AmNP

Affirmative Action Blues. Elizabeth Alexander. IHS

Afraid. Langston Hughes. CP-HughL

Afraid. Al Young. CP-YounA

Afraid is a country with no exit visas. Diaspora. Audre Lorde. CP-LordA

Afresh'd with paint the shop had glare. New Storefront. Russell Atkins. FB; GT

Africa. Lewis Alexander. CDC

Africa. Maya Angelou. CP-AngeM; SP-AngeM

Africa. Lucille Clifton. SP-ClifL

Africa. Nikki Giovanni. SP-GiovN

Africa. Langston Hughes. CP-HughL; SP-HughL

Africa. Claude McKay. BALP; NAAAL; SP-McKaC

Africa. Lizelia Augusta Jenkins Moorer. CBWP-3

Africa. Margaret Abigail Walker. CP-WalkM

Africa. / don't let them. Change Is Not Always Progress. Haki R. Madhubuti. BrTr

Africa I. Nikki Giovanni. SP-GiovN

Africa II. Nikki Giovanni. SP-GiovN

Africa is a young man bathing. Africa II. Nikki Giovanni. SP-GiovN

Africa Thing, The. Adam David Miller. NBV

African Affair, The. Bruce McM. Wright. AmNP; PoBA

African blues / does not know me. Her steps, in sands. Notes for a Speech. Amiri Baraka. SP-BaraA

African China. Melvin Beaunearus Tolson. Klds; PoBA

African Dream. Bob Kaufman. AmNP; GT; PoBA; SP-KaufB

African Guardian of Souls. Conversion. Jean Toomer. CP-ToomJ

African Images, Glimpses from a Tiger's Back. Alice Walker. CP-WalkA

African Sculpture. Christopher Gilbert. ESEAA

African Village, The. Margaret Abigail Walker. CP-WalkM

Africland. Oliver La Grone. FB

Afrikan name, An. (LL) Light / on my mother's tongue. Lucille Clifton. ESEAA; SP-ClifL

Afro-American. Henry L. Dumas. Crnst

Afro-American Fragment. Langston Hughes. CP-HughL; SP-HughL ("Little yellow / Bastard boy, A.") (LL) Crnst

Afrocentricity. Niama Leslie JoAnn Williams. SpiFl

Aft' them white trash any mo'. (LL) Mrs. Johnson Objects. Clara Ann Thompson. BlSi; CBWP-2

After. Maya Angelou. CP-AngeM; SP-AngeM

After a First Book. Audre Lorde. *See* Paperweight.

After a month or so. And Jonah Began to Stroke a Tentative Rhythm. Marilyn Nelson. *Fr.* I Dream the Book of Jonah. SP-NelsM

After a Visit. Countee Cullen. CP-CullC

After a Visit. Paul Laurence Dunbar. CP-DunbP

After all and after all. Donald Jeffrey Hayes. CDC

After all, there's no need. Flirtation. Rita Dove. SP-DoveR

After Church. Samuel Alfred Beadle. AAP

After church meeting. Tanka: "After church meeting." Lenard D. Moore. SpiFl

After church / on Sundays. About Religion. Audre Lorde. CP-LordA

After each quake. Crack in the Wall Holds Flowers. Adam David Miller. PoBA

After Eli Whitney's gin. Southeast Arkansia. Maya Angelou. CP-AngeM; SP-AngeM

After explanations and regulations, he. A WASP Woman Visits a Black Junkie in Prison. Etheridge Knight. NBV; SP-KnigE

After-Glow of Pain, The. Clara Ann Thompson. CBWP-2

After Hearing a Radio Announcement: a Comment on Some Conditions. Quincy Troupe. Crnst

After Her Man Had Left Her for the Sixth Time That Year / (An Uncommon Occurrence). Haki R. Madhubuti. Crnst

After Kent State. Lucille Clifton. SP-ClifL

After lunch, they would bathe in fire. (LL) Aircraft. Rita Dove. SP-DoveR

After Many Days. Paul Laurence Dunbar. CP-DunbP

After Many Springs. Langston Hughes. CP-HughL

After midnight they load up. Boat People. Yusef Komunyakaa. SP-KomuY

After our fierce loving. The Profile on the Pillow. Dudley Randall. BPo; BrTr; PoBA

After Reading Bryant's Lines to a Waterfowl. Eloise Bibb. ShDr

After Reading *Mickey in the Night Kitchen* for the Third Time Before Bed. Rita Dove. Crnst

After sickness and a begging. On the Spirit of Mildred Jordan. June Jordan. SP-JordJ

After Summer Fell Apart. Yusef Komunyakaa. SP-KomuY

After the all been done and i. Island Mary. Lucille Clifton. SP-ClifL

After the cloud embankments. Reconnaissance. Arna Bontemps. AmNP; BPo; Klds

After the Dance. Reuben Jackson. GT

After the Japanese. Mae V. Cowdery. ShDr

After the murder. The Last Quatrain of the Ballad of Emmett Till. Gwendolyn Brooks. PoBA; SP-BrooG

After the Quarrel. Paul Laurence Dunbar. CDC; CP-DunbP

After the Quarrel. Priscilla Jane Thompson. CBWP-2

After the Shrink. Alice Walker. CP-WalkA

After the Storm. Henrietta Cordelia Ray. CBWP-3

After the Storm. Derek Walcott. *Fr.* The Schooner *Flight*. ESEAA

After the Verdict. Tony Medina. SpiFl

After the war when rationing was over. Aunt Agnes Hatcher Tells. Lucille Clifton. SP-ClifL

After the Winter. Claude McKay. BANP; IDB; PoBA; SP-McKaC

After their afternoon walk to the sheepfold. Clown Nose. Marilyn Nelson. SP-NelsM

After they sawed through the bone. Daughter, That Picture of You. Keith Gilyard. SpiFl

After twenty years of nods. The Katskills Kiss Romance Goodbye. Ishmael Reed. CP-ReedI

After Visiting Arl at the Hospital. Al Young. CP-YounA

After While. Paul Laurence Dunbar. CP-DunbP

After Winter. Sterling A. Brown. CP-BrowS; GT; PoBA

After working through, all day. Conferences with the Unknown. Michael S. Harper. SP-HarpM

Afterglow. Georgia Douglas Johnson. ShDr

Afterglow, The. Henrietta Cordelia Ray. CBWP-3

Afterimages. Audre Lorde. CP-LordA; SP-LordA

Afterlove. Audre Lorde. CP-LordA

Aftermath. June Jordan. SP-JordJ

Afternoon After, The. Al Young. CP-YounA

Afternoon Gossip, An. Priscilla Jane Thompson. CBWP-2

Afternoon sun/ somewhere in the South, The. Landscapes. Harris Duriel. SpiFl

Afterwards, They Shall Dance. Bob Kaufman. SP-KaufB

Afterword: a Film. Michael S. Harper. SP-HarpM

Afterword: For Gwen Brooks, An. Don L. Lee. JB

Again. Lenard D. Moore. GT

Again he strode forward. One Year Ago. David Llorens. BrTr

Again heavy rain drives him home. Stepfather: A Girl's Song. Yusef Komunyakaa. SP-KomuY

Again the day. If the Stars Should Fall. Samuel Allen. IDB; NNP; PoBA

Again we drift back to these mountains, these. In Marin Again. Al Young. CP-YounA

Again / Who am I? Al Young. CP-YounA

Against a feathery sky. (LL) Adolescence—I. Rita Dove. SP-DoveR

Against our puny sound and sight. For Helen Keller. Countee Cullen. CP-CullC

Against That Day. Sterling A. Brown. CP-BrowS

Against the day of sorrow. Trifle. Georgia Douglas Johnson. AmNP

Against the potent poison of your hate. (LL) The White House. Claude McKay. AmNP; Crnst; NAAAL; PoBA; SP-McKaC; TtW

Against the striking students. (LL) The Workers Rose on May Day or Postscript to Karl Marx. Audre Lorde. CP-LordA; SP-LordA

Against what light / is false what breath. Black Dada Nihilismus. Amiri Baraka. SP-BaraA; TtW

Against your ear. (LL) The Distant Drum. Calvin C. Hernton. GT; NNP; TtW

Age. Nikki Giovanni. Crnst; SP-GiovN

Age / requires this task, The. A Different Image. Dudley Randall. BPo

Agonies confirm His hour. Bahá'u'lláh in the Garden of Ridwan. Robert Hayden. CP-HaydR; PoBA

Agony. As Now, An. Amiri Baraka. BALP; BPo; SP-BaraA

Agosta the Winged Man and Rasha the Black Dove. Rita Dove. SP-DoveR

Ah blow! thou art the last, the last! Broken Heart. Henrietta Cordelia Ray. CBWP-3

Ah, Douglass, we have fall'n on evil days. Douglass. Paul Laurence Dunbar. AAP; CP-DunbP; NAAAL; TtW

Ah, how poets sing and die! Dunbar. Anne Spencer. AfAmPo; BANP; CDC; Klds; NAAAL

Ah! I could curse them in my woe. Revenge. Mary E. Tucker. CBWP-1

Ah, I have changed, I do not know. A Lost Dream. Paul Laurence Dunbar. CP-DunbP

Ah, I know what happiness is! Poem. Blanche Taylor Dickinson. CDC

Ah, is there no, no place on earth. Weariness. Mary E. Tucker. CBWP-1

Ah, little road, all whirry in the breeze. The Road. Helene Johnson. AmNP; BANP; BlSi; CDC; ShDr

Ah, love, my love is like a cry in the night. A Love Song. Paul Laurence Dunbar. CP-DunbP

Ah me, it is cold and chill. The Wraith. Paul Laurence Dunbar. CP-DunbP

Ah, Momma, / Did the house ever know. June Jordan. SP-JordJ

Ah, / My black one. Poem: "Ah, / My black one." Langston Hughes. CP-HughL

Ah, my daughter: / which of this throng of griefs. Hecuba Mourns. Euripides. SP-NelsM, *tr. by* Marilyn Nelson. *Fr.* Hecuba.

Ah, my race. My Race. Helene Johnson. ShDr

Ah, Nora, my Nora, the light fades away. Nora: A Serenade. Paul Laurence Dunbar. CP-DunbP

Ah, pink tip of sixth sense. Passions. Yusef Komunyakaa. SP-KomuY

Ah! the year is slowly dying. Passing of the Old Year. Mary Weston Fordham. CBWP-2

Ah, yes, 't is sweet still to remember. Ione. Paul Laurence Dunbar. CP-DunbP

Ah, yes, the chapter ends to-day. The End of the Chapter. Paul Laurence Dunbar. CP-DunbP

Ah, you are cruel. Neighbors. Anne Spencer. CDC

Ahab's gaily clad fisherfriends. Evil Is No Black Thing. Sarah Webster Fabio. PoBA; TtW

Ah'm sick, doctor-man, Ah'm sick! Calling the Doctor. John Wesley Holloway. BANP

Aido Hwedo is coming. (LL) Call. Audre Lorde. CP-LordA

Ailey, Baldwin, Floyd, Killens, and Mayfield. Maya Angelou. CP-AngeM; IHS

Aim get your sights and its sound. Canto 7: First Thesis. Tom Weatherly. PoBA

Ain't been on Market Street for nothing. Ballad of the Hoppy-Toad. Margaret Abigail Walker. BlSi; CP-WalkM; FB; NBV; TtW

Ain't Gonna Let Nobody Turn Me Round. *Unknown.* CrDW

Ain't got a reason. The Slave's Critique of Practical Reason. Rita Dove. SP-DoveR

Ain't I a Woman? Sojourner Truth. BlSi

Ain't It a Bitch? *African-American Oral Tradition.* GetYo

Ain't it nice to have a mammy. Scamp. Paul Laurence Dunbar. CP-DunbP

Ain't No Spring Chicken. Ahmos, II Zu-Bolton. TtW

Ain't nobody better'n my Daddy. Little Girl Speakings. Maya Angelou. CP-AngeM; SP-AngeM

Ain't / nobody / heard me. The Hurt of It All. Sarah Webster Fabio. TtW

Ain't nobody nevah tol' you not a wo'd a-tall. Critters' Dance, De. Paul Laurence Dunbar. CP-DunbP

Aint Rachel was an ex-slave. Ribbons and Lace. Elma Stuckey. TtW

Ain't That Bad. Maya Angelou. CP-AngeM; SP-AngeM

Air. Jean Toomer. CP-ToomJ

Air a-gittin' cool an' coolah. Signs of the Times. Paul Laurence Dunbar. CP-DunbP

Air is dark, the sky is gray, The. A Drowsy Day. Paul Laurence Dunbar. CP-DunbP

Air Raid: Barcelona. Langston Hughes. CP-HughL

Air Raid over Harlem. Langston Hughes. CP-HughL

Air, the dream-inspiring air, The. An Idyl of Spring. Henrietta Cordelia Ray. CBWP-3

Aircraft. Rita Dove. SP-DoveR

Ajax' Conclusion. Frank Barbour Coffin. AAP

Akosua selling palm wine. The Palm Wine Seller. Gladys May Casely Hayford. ShDr

Al Capone in Alaska. Ishmael Reed. CP-ReedI

Al Fitnah Muhajir. Nazzam Al-Sudan. NBP

Alabama. Julia Fields. PoBA

Alabama Centennial. Naomi Long Madgett. BALP; BPo

Alabama Earth. Langston Hughes. CP-HughL

Alabama Poem. Nikki Giovanni. BkSV; SP-GiovN

Alafia. Odaro. BlFi

Alarm and time clock still intrude too early. And on This Shore. M. Carl Holman. AmNP; PoBA

Alas! and am I born for this. On Liberty and Slavery. George Moses Horton. AAP; AfAmPo; Klds; SP-HortG; TtW

Alas! that such a soul should taste of death. In Memory of Arthur Clement Williams. Eloise Bibb. CBWP-4

Alas! the time has come, old dress. Lines to an Old Dress. Mary E. Tucker. CBWP-1

Alaska. Mary Weston Fordham. CBWP-2

Alaska's rape. Untitled: "Alaska's rape." Ishmael Reed. CP-ReedI

Alba. Al Young. CP-YounA

Albert Ayler: Eulogy for a Decomposed Saxophone Player. Stanley Crouch. PoBA

Albert, don't you play in dat road. (LL) Baby. Langston Hughes. CP-HughL; SP-HughL

Albert! / Hey, Albert! Baby. Langston Hughes. CP-HughL; SP-HughL

Alberta, lovely little dame. Priscilla Jane Thompson. CBWP-2

Albuquerque Graveyard, The. Jay Wright. ESEAA

Aleta mentions in her tender letters. Wild May. Claude McKay. SP-McKaC

Alexander Crummel—Dead. Paul Laurence Dunbar. CP-DunbP

Alfonso, Dressing to Wait at Table. Claude McKay. SP-McKaC

Alfonso is a handsome bronze-hued lad. Alfonso, Dressing to Wait at Table. Claude McKay. SP-McKaC

Algernon Charles Swinburne. Joseph Seamon Cotter, Sr. AAP

Ali. Lloyd M., Jr. Corbin. PoBA

Alice. Paul Laurence Dunbar. CP-DunbP

Alice. Michael S. Harper. SP-HarpM

Alice. Gale Jackson. SpiFl

Alice Braxton Johnson. Michael S. Harper. SP-HarpM

Alice Flips the Script. Ta-Nehisi Coates. CtF

Alien. Donald Jeffrey Hayes. AmNP

Alien winds sweeping the highway. Bob Kaufman. SP-KaufB

Alive / between the Panther News and Zabar's. Do You Remember Laura. Audre Lorde. CP-LordA

All Alone. Mary E. Tucker. CBWP-1

All along the rail. In Texas Grass. Quincy Troupe. GT; NAAAL; PoBA

All Are Gay. Sterling A. Brown. CP-BrowS

All around old Chattanooga. Freedom at McNealy's. Priscilla Jane Thompson. CBWP-2

All beginnings start right here. The Move Continuing. Al Young. CP-YounA; PoBA

All by itself. (LL) One. Langston Hughes. CP-HughL; SP-HughL

All Cana was abuzz next day with stories. Epithalamium and Shivaree. Marilyn Nelson. IHS; SP-NelsM

All-conquering Death! by thy resistless pow'r. To His Honour the Lieutenant-Governor, on the Death of His Lady, March 24, 1773. Phillis Wheatley. CP-WheaP

All day in the sun. The Consumptive. Langston Hughes. CP-HughL

All day subdued, polite. Negro Servant. Langston Hughes. CP-HughL

All day Sunday didn't even dress up. Sunday. Langston Hughes. Fr. Seven Moments of Love. CP-HughL

All day we scrubbing scrubbing. (LL) Anna Speaks of the Childhood of Mary Her Daughter. Lucille Clifton. SP-ClifL

All Day We've Longed for Night. Sarah Webster Fabio. BlSi

All de night long twell de moon goes down. Twell de Night Is Pas'. Paul Laurence Dunbar. CP-DunbP

All dream, all whim. Joy/Spring. Al Young. CP-YounA

All eager-lipped I kissed the mouth of Death. (LL) Sonnet: "He came in silvern armor, trimmed with black." Gwendolyn B. Bennett. AmNP; CDC; PoBA; TtW

All earth is a poet. Algernon Charles Swinburne. Joseph Seamon Cotter, Sr. AAP

All for ourselves and all for nothing. (LL) Champagne. Rita Dove. SP-DoveR

All god's SPADES got SPADES. (LL) The Truth. Ted Joans. AmNP

All God's spades wear dark shades. Its Curtains. Ted Joans. PoBA

All hail! thou gorgeous sunset. Sunset. Mary Weston Fordham. CBWP-2

All hail! thou truly noble chief. To Cinque. James M. Whitfield. EBAP; TtW

All Hallows Eve. Audre Lorde. CP-LordA

All her black words of fire and blood. (LL) For Gwen, 1969. Margaret Abigail Walker. CP-WalkM

All hot and grimy from the road. The Fount of Tears. Paul Laurence Dunbar. CP-DunbP

All i gotta do. Nikki Giovanni. SP-GiovN

All I wanted / was your / love. To Mother and Steve. Mari E. Evans. BPo; PoBA

All in a literary parleur. Bootie Black and the Seven Giants. Mike Cook. JB

All life is but the climbing of a hill. Search. Langston Hughes. CP-HughL

All meet here with us, finally: the. Ostriches and Grandmothers! Amiri Baraka. SP-BaraA

All men are locked in their cells. Fall Down. Calvin C. Hernton. GT; PoBA

All morning, I watch him. Sunday. Carl Phillips. GT

All my life/ they have told me. To You. Frank Horne. BPo Fr. Letters [or Notes] Found near a Suicide. AmNP; CDC; PoBA

All Nashville is a chill. And everywhere. A January Dandelion. George Marion McClellan. AAP; AfAmPo; EBAP

All night I walked among your spirits, Richard. A Mourning Letter from Paris. Conrad Kent Rivers. BPo

All-Night Issue, The. Jackie Warren-Moore. SpiFl

All night they whine upon their ropes and boom. Nocturne of the Wharves. Arna Bontemps. BANP; BPo; GT

All night, through the eternity of night. Through Agony. Claude McKay. SP-McKaC

All Nite Long. Kalamu ya Salaam. Fr. New Orleans Haiku. SpiFl

All of those sensuous bodies. Landscape with Nymphs and Satyrs. Norman Henry, II Pritchard. GT

All over the world. Shall the Good Go Down? Langston Hughes. CP-HughL

All problems being / as personal as they are. Forced Retirement. Nikki Giovanni. SP-GiovN

All right with me, / You are. (LL) Poem: "Little brown boy." Helene Johnson. AmNP; BANP; CDC; PoBA; ShDr

All round about, the clouds encompassed me. To Dr. James Newton Matthews, Mason, Ill. Paul Laurence Dunbar. CP-DunbP

All silence says music will follow. Onion Bucket. Lorenzo Thomas. BlFi; GT; PoBA; TtW

All Singing in a Pie. Alvin Aubert. TtW

All that I ran from. The Mood. Quandra Prettyman. PoBA

All that night / I prayed for eyes to see again. South: The Name of Home. Alice Walker. CP-WalkA

All that night I walked alone and wept. Gethsemane. Arna Bontemps. CDC

All the best minds. Wise: Having the Ability to Perceive and Adopt the Best Means for Accomplishing an End. Lucille Clifton. SP-ClifL

All the children on this ward are dying of AIDS. The Sacrament of Poverty. Marilyn Nelson. GT; SP-NelsM

All the corners that are left. (LL) Final Curve. Langston Hughes. CP-HughL; SP-HughL

All the craziness. Dixie South Africa. Langston Hughes. CP-HughL

All the long way from Jamaica. To Market. Marilyn Nelson. SP-NelsM

All the old folks say the fourth a May was a hell of a day. Titanic: "All the old folks say the fourth a May was a hell of a day." African-American Oral Tradition. GetYo

All the things. The objects. Cold Term. Amiri Baraka. BPo

All the time the teacher. Fights After School. Norman J. Loftis. SpiFl

All the time they were praying. The Death Bed. Waring Cuney. CDC

All the tom-toms of the jungles beat in my blood. Poem: "All the tom-toms of the jungles beat in my blood." Langston Hughes. CP-HughL

All the toothy Fräuleins are left behind. The Son. Rita Dove. SP-DoveR

All the while I was quite happy. (LL) Nikki-Rosa. Nikki Giovanni. AmNP; BlSi; GT; NAAAL; NBP; PoBA; SP-GiovN; SSLK; TtW

All the world is so sweet, dear. To Alice Dunbar. Paul Laurence Dunbar. CP-DunbP

All the World Moved. June Jordan. GT; NBP; PoBA

All these girls licking & sucking. Leaving Syracuse. Al Young. CP-YounA; ESEAA

All things come to pass. My Name Is Afrika. Keorapetse W. Kgositsile. PoBA

All things confirm me in the thought that dust. In Spite of Death. Countee Cullen. CP-CullC

All Things Insensible. Kathleen Tankersley Young. ShDr

All this happened around fifteen. Life of a Junkie. African-American Oral Tradition. GetYo

All those ships that never sailed. Bob Kaufman. SP-KaufB

All We Ask Is Justice. Mrs. Henry Linden. CBWP-4

All week she's cleaned. Domestic Work, 1937. Natasha Trethewey. SpiFl

All who have and have all can cry: "Peace!" Editorial Poem on an Incident of Effects Far-reaching. Russell Atkins. NBP

All wines are / Not the same. The Vachel Lindsay Fault. Ishmael Reed. CP-ReedI

All winter long. Confession. Alice Walker. CP-WalkA

All ye nations, pause a moment! listen to the Negro's voice. The Voice of the Negro. Lizelia Augusta Jenkins Moorer. CBWP-3

All yesterday it poured, and all night long. Summer Morn in New Hampshire. Claude McKay. SP-McKaC

All you cool cats, bop daddies, and pennyweight pimps who think you know the score. Herman from the Shark-Tooth Shore. African-American Oral Tradition. GetYo

All you tough guys that thinks you're wise. African-American Oral Tradition. GetYo

All you violated ones with gentle hearts. For Malcolm X. Margaret Abigail Walker. BPo; CP-WalkM; NAAAL; PoBA

Alla Tha's All Right, But. June Jordan. SP-JordJ

Allegheny Shadows. Michael S. Harper. SP-HarpM

Allegory in Black. Carl Clark. JB

All's Well. Amiri Baraka. SP-BaraA

Alone. Maya Angelou. CP-AngeM; SP-AngeM

Alone. Nikki Giovanni. BrTr; SP-GiovN

Alone again but happeeee. O! Al Young. CP-YounA

Alone. I remember now. (LL) In Retrospect. Maya Angelou. CP-AngeM; SP-AngeM

Alone I tiptoe through the stars. Star Journey. Naomi Long Madgett. BPo

Alone on the hill of storms. Battle of the Stars. Adah Isaacs Menken. CBWP-1

Along by the river of ruin. The River of Ruin. Paul Laurence Dunbar. CP-DunbP

Along Lenox Avenue folk said. Old Pettigrew. Melvin B. Tolson. GT

Along the lake the bugle rings. Echo Reverie. Henrietta Cordelia Ray. CBWP-3

Alphabet, The. *African-American Oral Tradition.* GetYo

Already I am no longer looked at with lechery or love. A Sunset of the City. Gwendolyn Brooks. GT; SP-BrooG

Already it's been years. Dancing Together. Al Young. CP-YounA

Altars and Sacrifice. Jay Wright. FB

Although it is night, I sit in the bathroom, waiting. Adolescence—II. Rita Dove. SP-DoveR

Although she feeds me bread of bitterness. America. Claude McKay. BALP; CDC; Crnst; IHS; NAAAL; PoBA; SP-McKaC; TtW

Although she had lain. (LL) Africa. Maya Angelou. CP-AngeM; SP-AngeM

Alvin Cash/Keep on Dancin', *to the children of intermediate school 55, ocean hill-brownsville.* David Henderson. GT

Always at dusk, the same tearless experience. The Eyes of My Regret. Angelina Weld Grimké. CDC

Always / Etheridge Knight. (LL) A Poem to Galway Kinnell. Etheridge Knight. SP-KnigE

Always first to rise. In My Father's House. George Barlow. ESEAA

Always for your never named sake. (LL) The Lost Baby Poem. Lucille Clifton. ESEAA; SP-ClifL

Always / in the middle. Love, Maybe. Audre Lorde. CP-LordA; SP-LordA

Always it's either / a beginning. Al Young. CP-YounA; TtW   *Fr.* The Song Turning Back into Itself.

Always Know. Kalamu ya Salaam. SpiFl

Always Lei of Ginger Blossoms for the First Lady of Hawai'i: Queen Lili'uokalani, An. June Jordan. SP-JordJ

Always the Same. Langston Hughes. CP-HughL

Always the same, sweet hurt. Why Do So Few Blacks Study Creative Writing? Cornelius Eady. GT

Always this waking dream of palmtrees. The Islands. Robert Hayden. CP-HaydR; ESEAA

Always your heart, atomic symbol. Honey of Being. Jean Toomer. CP-ToomJ

Am Driven Mad. Allen Polite. NNP

Am gonna take me seriously. A Needed/Poem/ for My Salvation. Sonia Sanchez. BrTr

Am I a ho. Rhetorically Speaking. Nikkia Billingsley. CtF

Am I sadly cast aside. The Slave's Complaint. George Moses Horton. AAP; CrDW; EBAP; SP-HortG

Am I to be cursed forever with becoming. Change of Season. Audre Lorde. CP-LordA; SP-LordA

Am/trak. Amiri Baraka. SP-BaraA

Amazon. Ojenke. CtF

Amazon peeled back to gold and rubber, The. Cutting a Road from Manaus to Belém. Colleen J. McElroy. TtW

Ambition. Maggie Pogue Johnson. CBWP-4

Ambition. Henrietta Cordelia Ray. CBWP-3

Ambush. Yusef Komunyakaa. SP-KomuY

Amen. Richard W. Thomas. BlFi; PoBA

Amen. Amen. James Weldon Johnson. *See* The Creation.

America. Maya Angelou. CP-AngeM; SP-AngeM

America. Henry L. Dumas. PoBA

America. Langston Hughes. CP-HughL

America. Claude McKay. BALP; CDC; Crnst; IHS; NAAAL; PoBA; SP-McKaC; TtW

America. Phillis Wheatley. CP-WheaP

America Bleeds. Angelo Lewis. PoBA

America calling. Haki R. Madhubuti. NAAAL

America Calls! Michael S. Harper. SP-HarpM

America, here is your son, born of your iron heel. The True American. Georgia Douglas Johnson. ShDr

America, it is to thee. From America. James M. Whitfield. BPo, *ll.* 1–14; EBAP; NAAAL

America, lost in tall grass', serene idyll. (LL) A Village Life. Derek Walcott. GT

American Airlines Sutra. Ishmael Reed. CP-ReedI

American Cancer Society Or There Is More Than One Way to Skin a Coon. Audre Lorde. CP-LordA; SP-LordA

American deputy assistant secretary of defense, The. Equal Opportunity. Audre Lorde. CP-LordA

American Dialogue. Victor E. Blue. CtF

American Ecstasy. Amiri Baraka. SP-BaraA

American Glamour. Al Young. CP-YounA

American Gothic. Samuel Allen. *See* To Satch.

American Heartbreak. Langston Hughes. BPo; CP-HughL; SP-HughL

American History. Michael S. Harper. BPo; ESEAA; SP-HarpM

[American Journal]. Robert Hayden. CP-HaydR
 ("Here among them the americans this baffling.") ESEAA
 ("Quiddity i cannot penetrate or name.") (LL) ESEAA

American Sonnet (10). Wanda Coleman. NAAAL

American that 's me. (LL) Madam's Calling Cards. Langston Hughes. SP-HughL

American Time. Al Young. CP-YounA

America's Young Black Joe! Langston Hughes. CP-HughL

Amid dancing and. All Nite Long. Kalamu ya Salaam. *Fr.* New Orleans Haiku. SpiFl

Amid the noncommitted compounds of the mind. Metagnomy. Norman Henry, II Pritchard. NBP

Amoeba is lucky it's so small, An. Love: Is a Human Condition. Nikki Giovanni. Crnst

Amoebaean for Daddy. Maya Angelou. CP-AngeM; SP-AngeM

Among the Berkshire Hills. Henrietta Cordelia Ray. CBWP-3

Among the dear old friends we people cherish. Memory of Lincoln and the Yankees. James Ephriam McGirt. AAP

Among the sayings of our race. We Are Rising. George Clinton Rowe. AAP

Among things with souls, find me. The Success. Amiri Baraka. SP-BaraA

Amos, 1963. Margaret Abigail Walker. CP-WalkM; TtW

Amos (Postscript, 1968). Margaret Abigail Walker. CP-WalkM

Amp light on the station, The. Crossing Lake Michigan. Michael S. Harper. SP-HarpM

Amused contempt, is it, that scintillates. Juan de Pareja: Painted by Velazquez. Richard A. Long. AmNP

An' ain't we fine? (LL) Ain't That Bad. Maya Angelou. CP-AngeM; SP-AngeM

An' calls me to my qua'ters in de sky. (LL) The Deserted Plantation. Paul Laurence Dunbar. CP-DunbP

An' de co'n pone's hot. (LL) When de Co'n Pone's Hot. Paul Laurence Dunbar. AAP; BANP; CP-DunbP; TtW

An' de walls come tumblin' down. (LL) Joshua fit de battle of Jericho [*or* ob Jerico]. *Unknown.* BPo; CrDW

An' dey ain't no use in talkin', we jes had one scrumptious time! (LL) The Party. Paul Laurence Dunbar. AmNP; CP-DunbP

An' I'm a-layin' neah huh! (LL) Song of Summer. Paul Laurence Dunbar. CP-DunbP

An' it's too nigh Chris'mus mo'nin, now fu' me. (LL) Soliloquy of a Turkey. Paul Laurence Dunbar. BPo; CP-DunbP

An' raise dat rucus to-night. (LL) Raise a "Rucus" To-Night. *Unknown.* BPo

An' so ole Tho'nton bounced you. The Turncoat. Priscilla Jane Thompson. CBWP-2

Analysands. Dudley Randall. BPo

Ancestors. Dudley Randall. BPo

Ancestral Messengers/Composition 13. Ntozake Shange. GT

Ancestral pearls so deep, so blue. Baptism. Alvin Aubert. BkSV

Anchored. Paul Laurence Dunbar. CP-DunbP

Ancient Rain, The. Bob Kaufman. SP-KaufB

And afraid / of nothing. (LL) New Year's Day. Audre Lorde. CP-LordA; SP-LordA

And ages long of troubles end. (LL) At Harper's Ferry Just before the Attack. Edward W. Williams. AAP

And all my days are dying. (LL) The Memory. Maya Angelou. CP-AngeM; SP-AngeM

And all the host of heaven. (LL) An Address to Miss Phillis Wheatly, Ethiopian Poetess. Jupiter Hammon. EBAP; TtW

And all the love he had. (LL) Judas Iscariot. Countee Cullen. CP-CullC

And answered thunder with his thunder back. (LL) Frederick Douglass. Paul Laurence Dunbar. BALP; CP-DunbP; PoBA

And anybody's daughter. (LL) Country Lover. Maya Angelou. CP-AngeM; SP-AngeM

And are strong. (LL) Upon Your Leaving. Etheridge Knight. GT; SP-KnigE

And ask them for your name again. (LL) 'Mystery Boy' Looks for Kin in Nashville. Robert Hayden. CP-HaydR

And at night light upon his back. (LL) For Freckle-Faced Gerald. Etheridge Knight. BPo; Crnst; ESEAA; SP-KnigE

And be buried in the dust of marching feet. (LL) For Black Poets Who Think of Suicide. Etheridge Knight. Crnst; NAAAL; PoBA; SP-KnigE

And beating the land's / Edge into a swoon. Langston Hughes. *See* Moonlight Night: Carmel.

And bided my time. (LL) The Ballad of Nat Turner. Robert Hayden. BALP; BPo; CP-HaydR

And blood hangs in the pine-soaked air. (LL) Adolescence—III. Rita Dove. SP-DoveR

And bouffants that bustle, and rustle. (LL) Empty woman took toys! The. Gwendolyn Brooks. SP-BrooG

And break your motherfucken neck. (LL) And may your life become unlivable, boy. *African-American Oral Tradition*. GetYo

And break your motherfucken neck. (LL) You Told Me a Lie. *African-American Oral Tradition*. GetYo

And, brother, what shall you say? (LL) And What Shall You Say? Joseph Seamon Cotter, Sr. BANP; CDC; PoBA

And brought forth music sweet and strong, An. (LL) The Master-Player. Paul Laurence Dunbar. CP-DunbP

And buzzed / when she died. (LL) Emily Dickinson's Defunct. Marilyn Nelson. ESEAA; SP-NelsM

And by *we* I mean The Community! (LL) The Old O.O. Blues. Al Young. CP-YounA

And can't explode? (LL) Sherbet. Cornelius Eady. GT

And classic bronze of Benin. (LL) A Different Image. Dudley Randall. BPo

And comes out reason. (LL) Change of Season. Audre Lorde. CP-LordA; SP-LordA

And constellations catch the long refrain. (LL) The Lute of Afric's Tribe. Albery Allson Whitman. EBAP; TtW

And curl forever in some far-off farmyard flower. (LL) Beehive. Jean Toomer. CP-ToomJ; GT; IDB; PoBA

And curse the moon and fear the rising of the sun. (LL) The Wheel. Robert Hayden. BPo; CP-HaydR

And dance this / boneharp tree. "Dance the Orange." Robert Hayden. CP-HaydR

And dart from world to world. (LL) George Moses Horton, Myself. George Moses Horton. AAP; AfAmPo; Klds; NAAAL; SP-HortG; TtW

And dig all plays. (LL) Flatted Fifths. Langston Hughes. CP-HughL

And dish water gives back no images. (LL) No Images. Waring Cuney. AmNP; BANP; CDC; SSLK

And Don't Think I Won't Be Waiting. Audre Lorde. CP-LordA; SP-LordA

And dreams, like me. (LL) Water-Front Streets. Langston Hughes. CP-HughL; SP-HughL

And dripped their juice / On you? (LL) Midnight Dancer. Langston Hughes. CP-HughL; SP-HughL

And drop like firebrands on the fragrant hearth. (LL) Church Burning: Mississippi. James A. Emanuel. PoBA

And end the date of snaps. (LL) Snaps for Dinner, Snaps for Breakfast and Snaps for Supper. George Moses Horton. SP-HortG; TtW

And every now and them I think. Poem (No Name No. 1). Nikki Giovanni. SP-GiovN

And Fall Shall Sit in Judgment. Audre Lorde. NNP

And far more lethal than emphysema. (LL) American Cancer Society Or There Is More Than One Way to Skin a Coon. Audre Lorde. CP-LordA; SP-LordA

And feel, and die. (LL) War Memoir: Jazz, Don't Listen to It at Your Own Risk. Bob Kaufman. SP-KaufB

And felt my heart forebear, my pulse grow still. (LL) Brown Boy to Brown Girl. Countee Cullen. CP-CullC; PoBA

And final notices from the Finances company. (LL) Arthur Ridgewood, M.D. Frank Marshall Davis. Klds; TtW

And find an unburnt picture. (LL) Women gather, The. Nikki Giovanni. SP-GiovN

And find another lover. (LL) Song in Spite of Myself. Countee Cullen. BALP; CP-CullC

And find redress from God. (LL) Ethiopia. Frances Ellen Watkins Harper. CP-HarpF; NAAAL

And footsteps in the dark. (LL) Oakland Blues. Ishmael Reed. CP-ReedI; NAAAL

And for hours used no hot words. (LL) A WASP Woman Visits a Black Junkie in Prison. Etheridge Knight. NBV; SP-KnigE

And found Life stepping on my feet! (LL) Esthete in Harlem. Langston Hughes. CP-HughL

And found my senses lost. (LL) Senses of Insecurity. Maya Angelou. CP-AngeM; SP-AngeM

And, friend, in your buying, remember poor me! (LL) Upon Receipt of a Pound of Coffee in 1863. Mary E. Tucker. CBWP-1

And gave away her heart. (LL) The Ballad of Aunt Geneva. Marilyn Nelson. GT; SP-NelsM

And gave me / five! (LL) Roach / came struttin, A. John Raven. BPo

And go home to my Lord and be free. (LL) O Freedom! / O Freedom! *Unknown*. CrDW

And, God knows, / It's mine! (LL) Argument. Langston Hughes. SP-HughL

And God stepped out on space. The Creation. James Weldon Johnson. BALP; BANP; CDC; NAAAL; PoBA; SSLK; TtW

And God, who sometimes spits right in its face. (LL) I look with awe upon the human race. Langston Hughes. CP-HughL; Klds

And grateful hail fair Luna's tender light. (LL) Wordsworth. Charlotte L. Forten Grimké. AAP; AfAmPo

And grinning. Still / Grinning. (LL) Through the Inner City to the Suburbs. Maya Angelou. CP-AngeM; SP-AngeM

And hateful wrath / quickly. (LL) Artful Pose. Maya Angelou. CP-AngeM; SP-AngeM

And having no need to let myself be robbed / a second time. (LL) Nomen. Naomi Long Madgett. BlSi

And he couldn't porter. (LL) Giles Johnson, Ph.D. Frank Marshall Davis. BPo; Klds; PoBA; TtW

And he took your hands. Love. Sabah As-Sabah. CtF

And Heavenly *Freedom* spread her golden Ray. (LL) Liberty and Peace. Phillis Wheatley. BlSi; CP-WheaP

And here is / Old Picasso and the dove. The Dove. Langston Hughes. CP-HughL

And here's to the duck that swim the pond. *African-American Oral Tradition*. GetYo

And his slow strut moves him on again. (LL) Harlem Freeze Frame. Lebert Bethune. BlFi; GT

& hope to see you soon Yrs Cal. (LL) The Dream. Robert Hayden. CP-HaydR; NBV

And I a beginner. Answer to Yo / Question. Sonia Sanchez. BPo

And i am turning. (LL) Perhaps. Lucille Clifton. SP-ClifL

And I and I / must admit. Belly Song. Etheridge Knight. BkSV; SP-KnigE; TtW

And I and your eyes. I And Your Eyes. Etheridge Knight. SP-KnigE

And I bear witness--all praise is due Allah! (LL) Malcolm X—an Autobiography. Larry Neal. AmNP; BPo; BlFi; BrTr; TtW

And I can Remember still your first lies America. Q. R. Hand. BlFi

... And I come out of it. Scenario VI. Amiri Baraka. SP-BaraA

And I don't want no Bail. (LL) Girl Held without Bail. Margaret Abigail Walker. BPo; CP-WalkM; PoBA

And I doubt all. You. Or a violet. (LL) Love Note I: Surely. Gwendolyn Brooks. SP-BrooG

And i entered into young. Young Womanhood. Sonia Sanchez. TtW

And i guess nobody ever does. (LL) Legacies. Nikki Giovanni. SP-GiovN

And I have broken down before the wind. (LL) Nocturne of the Wharves. Arna Bontemps. BANP; BPo; GT

And I have no pity. (LL) No No No No. Maya Angelou. CP-AngeM; SP-AngeM

And I know where sleeps Holofernes. (LL) Judith. Adah Isaacs Menken. CBWP-1

And I let her bleed, Lord, I let her bleed. (LL) The Country Midwife: A Day. Ai. SP-AiAi

And I love the rain. (LL) April Rain Song. Langston Hughes. CP-HughL

And I mean I really hate to lose something. (LL) No Loser, No Weeper. Maya Angelou. CP-AngeM; SP-AngeM; TtW

And I set forth upon the southern road. (LL) The Southern Road. Dudley Randall. BrTr; NNP; PoBA

And I shall die an old Parisian. (LL) Four Sheets to the Wind and a One-Way Ticket to France. Conrad Kent Rivers. AmNP; BPo; IDB; NNP; PoBA

And I to my wife or mistress flee. (LL) The Poet's Shuffle. Calvin Forbes. GT

And I was born with you, wasn't I, Blues? The Blues Don't Change. Al Young. CP-YounA; ESEAA; GT; TtW

And I went up to that chandeliered place. Poem. Calvin C. Hernton. GT

And I, woman, cracked in blues. I, Woman. Irma McClaurin. BlSi

And if it's not askin' too much, pleeease. B.B. Blues. Mary Weems. SpiFl

And if sun comes. Truth. Gwendolyn Brooks. SP-BrooG

& I'm from Look Back. (LL) Black Is a Soul. Joseph Blanco White. IDB; PoBA

And imagined her. She Had Known Brothers. Sherley Anne Williams. GT

And in her smile there is a blight. (LL) The White Witch. James Weldon Johnson. AfAmPo; TtW

And in immense perdition sinks the soul. (LL) To the University of Cambridge, in New-England. Phillis Wheatley. BALP; CP-WheaP; EBAP; NAAAL; TtW

And into the majors. (LL) Turning Pro. Ishmael Reed. CP-ReedI

And is you. (LL) Effendi. Michael S. Harper. PoBA; SP-HarpM

And it was almost a boy who undid. First Kiss. Rita Dove. SP-DoveR

And it's familiar. Flame. Jayne Cortez. SP-CortJ

And Jonah Began to Stroke a Tentative Rhythm. Marilyn Nelson. *Fr.* I Dream the Book of Jonah. SP-NelsM

And just what the fuck else were we supposed to do. (LL) Rape. Jayne Cortez. GT; SP-CortJ

And kindly pays expenses. (LL) Dilettante, The: A Modern Type. Paul Laurence Dunbar. CP-DunbP

And laid them away in a box of gold. (LL) For a Poet. Countee Cullen. CP-CullC

And landing upon their heads. (LL) Between Ourselves. Audre Lorde. CP-LordA

And laughs at each eviction notice. / Come! (LL) Starvation. Maya Angelou. CP-AngeM; SP-AngeM

And less terror / for our children. (LL) Release Time. Audre Lorde. CP-LordA; SP-LordA

And let my fool-self fall. (LL) Lament over Love. Langston Hughes. CP-HughL; NAAAL; SP-HughL

And let the woman live. (LL) Women's Locker Room. Marilyn Nelson. SP-NelsM

And let your full lips laugh at Fate! (LL) To a Dark Girl. Gwendolyn B. Bennett. BANP; BlSi; CDC; NAAAL; PoBA; ShDr

And let's heave it down. (LL) One More Round. Maya Angelou. CP-AngeM; SP-AngeM

And letting them out again. (LL) The Vacant Lot. Gwendolyn Brooks. NAAAL

And life for me ain't been no crystal stair. (LL) Mother to Son. Langston Hughes. AfAmPo; AmNP; CDC; CP-HughL; Crnst; NAAAL; SP-HughL; TtW

And lightly weight the air. (LL) Three Modes of History and Culture. Amiri Baraka. ESEAA; SP-BaraA

And lo! the earth was filled with lights. (LL) After the Storm. Henrietta Cordelia Ray. CBWP-3

And love was a burning fence about my house. (LL) Gemini. Audre Lorde. CP-LordA; SP-LordA

And make America again! (LL) Let America Be American Again. Langston Hughes. CP-HughL

And man became a living soul. / Amen. (LL) The Creation. James Weldon Johnson. BALP; BANP; CDC; NAAAL; PoBA

And may your life become unlivable, boy. *African-American Oral Tradition.* GetYo

And mayst thou find a home at last in heaven's celestial bowers. (LL) Wail of the Divorced. Mary E. Tucker. CBWP-1

And, moon, the darkness you float in. Moon, How Do I Measure Up? Al Young. CP-YounA

And moved his feet in the dark. (LL) The Wind Bloweth Where It Listeth. Countee Cullen. CP-CullC; GT

And much more painful. (LL) Insomniac. Maya Angelou. CP-AngeM; SP-AngeM

And no curtain drapes the door. (LL) On Diverse Deviations. Maya Angelou. BlSi; CP-AngeM; SP-AngeM

And not afraid to dare. (LL) Interim. Clarissa Scott Delany. CDC; ShDr

And not be / one. (LL) From the House of Yemanjá. Audre Lorde. CP-LordA

And now i know. Always Know. Kalamu ya Salaam. SpiFl

And now she knows: The big fist shattering her face. The Female and the Silence of a Man. June Jordan. NAAAL; SP-JordJ

And now to overcome what? Acceptance Speech. Jayne Cortez. SP-CortJ

... And now / When the rumble of death. Sunday Morning Prophecy. Langston Hughes. SP-HughL

And o'er your happy songs its plaudits rang. (LL) Paul Laurence Dunbar. James David Corrothers. AfAmPo; BANP; NAAAL

And of her blood. (LL) Breaded Meat, Breaded Hands. Michael S. Harper. SP-HarpM

And of moons and maidens at midnight. (LL) Apology for Apostasy? Etheridge Knight. SP-KnigE

And on This Shore. M. Carl Holman. AmNP; PoBA

And one morning while in the woods I stumbled suddenly upon the thing. Between the World and Me. Richard Wright. AmNP; IDB; PoBA; TtW

And only bitter land was washed away. (LL) Childhood. Margaret Abigail Walker. CP-WalkM; Klds; PoBA

And our ordinary garments decent in the dead one's eyes. (LL) Journey to the Place of Ghosts. Jay Wright. Crnst; GT

And Pass. Jean Toomer. CP-ToomJ

And plagues me to my heart. (LL) Troubled with the Itch and Rubbing with Sulphur. George Moses Horton. AAP; AfAmPo; SP-HortG

And pluck gems from graves. (LL) Haiku: "To write a blues song." Etheridge Knight. ESEAA; TtW

And poor old Caste there end her feeble days. (LL) The End of the Whole Matter. Albery Allson Whitman. AAP

And poor old Caste there end her feeble days. (LL) Free schools, free press, free speech and equal laws. Albery Allson Whitman. AfAmPo

And poplars stand there still as death. (LL) Southern Mansion. Arna Bontemps. AmNP; BALP; BANP; FB; GT; IDB; Klds; NAAAL; PoBA

And relieve us from the burden of that made to order smile. (LL) The Made to Order Smile. Paul Laurence Dunbar. CP-DunbP; GT

And rent day's here again. (LL) Contemporary Announcement. Maya Angelou. CP-AngeM; SP-AngeM

And salvage mostly / The leaning. (LL) In These Dissenting Times. Alice Walker. CP-WalkA; PoBA

And say dat's good enough for nigger. (LL) Song: "We raise de wheat." *Unknown.* BPo; CrDW; NAAAL

And several strengths from drowsiness campaigned. The Sermon on the Warpland. Gwendolyn Brooks. BPo; PoBA

And shall I prime my children, pray, to pray? Gwendolyn Brooks. *Fr.* The Children of the Poor. Crnst; SP-BrooG; *sect.* I, *pt.* 1-5; NAAAL.

And shall it not fade? (LL) And on This Shore. M. Carl Holman. AmNP; PoBA

And shall we ever seek in vain. All Alone. Mary E. Tucker. CBWP-1

And She Was Bad. Marvin, Jr. Wyche. AmNP

And shone that smile on us and sang. (LL) Homage to the Empress of the Blues. Robert Hayden. CP-HaydR; ESEAA; NAAAL; PoBA; TtW

And show him the little unpainted arrows. (LL) Unhistorical Events. Bob Kaufman. SP-KaufB

And silence / which proves but. The End of Man Is His Beauty. Amiri Baraka. AmNP; BALP; TtW

And Sin is the consort of Woe. (LL) An Appeal to My Countrywomen. Frances Ellen Watkins Harper. SP-HarpF; NAAAL

And so becoming pretension / concretized. (LL) Moving Out Or the End of Cooperative Living. Audre Lorde. CP-LordA; SP-LordA

And so for nights. The Night-Blooming Cereus. Robert Hayden. CP-HaydR; ESEAA; IDB

And so the seed. For Russell and Rowena Jelliffe. Langston Hughes. CP-HughL

And so / we lick our chops at Birmingham. Northern Liberal. Langston Hughes. CP-HughL

And sold them to a magazine. (LL) Then and Now. Paul Laurence Dunbar. CP-DunbP

And some were they, which one by one have set. Albery Allson Whitman. EBAP *Fr.* Leelah Misled.

And some where distantly. A Beginning for New Beginnings. Angela Jackson. TtW

And Sometimes I Hear This Song in My Head. Harriet Jacobs. SpiFl

And sometimes i sit. Nikki Giovanni. SP-GiovN

And speeding toward the light. (LL) Recovery. Maya Angelou. CP-AngeM; SP-AngeM

And still we wear our uniforms, follow. The Progress. Gwendolyn Brooks. SP-BrooG

And stone will shove the softness from my face. (LL) Piano after War. Gwendolyn Brooks. AmNP; ESEAA; Klds; SP-BrooG

And strut down the streets with paint on my face. (LL) A Song in the Front Yard. Gwendolyn Brooks. ESEAA; IDB; NAAAL; PoBA

& sudden inexplicable bliss. (LL) Birthday Poem. Al Young. CP-YounA

And Syllables Grow Wings There. Quincy Trethewey. SpiFl

And tell me not the secret that I ask. (LL) The Mystery. Paul Laurence Dunbar. CP-DunbP

And Tell Me Poet, Can Love Exist in Slavery? Etheridge Knight. SP-KnigE

And that is life! (LL) Life. Paul Laurence Dunbar. AmNP; CDC; CP-DunbP

And that one is my love. (LL) Many and More. Maya Angelou. CP-AngeM

And that they are superior. Heathens Think Fascism Is Civilization. Amiri Baraka. SP-BaraA

And that's what's the matter with you. (LL) Old Cods. *African-American Oral Tradition.* GetYo

And the absence of despair / over yonder? (LL) Southeast Arkanasia. Maya Angelou. CP-AngeM; SP-AngeM

And the back that wears it. (LL) The Militance of a Photograph in the Passbook of a Bantu under Detention. Michael S. Harper. TtW

And the *blood* / of warriors. (LL) Granny Blak Poet (in Pastel). Arthur Pfister. BrTr

And the blues, I tell you, they blew up. The James Cotton Band at Keystone. Al Young. CP-YounA

And the Devil Sent a Ford Pinto Which She Also Routed. Ishmael Reed. CP-ReedI

And the dying Negro moan. (LL) Southern Cop. Sterling A. Brown. CP-BrowS

And the gods are laughing at us. (LL) Lenox Avenue. Langston Hughes. CP-HughL

And the Gods will too. (LL) Don't Cry, Scream. Haki R. Madhubuti. BrTr

And the grasses will still be / Singing? (LL) Prologue: "Haunted by poems beginning with I." Audre Lorde. CP-LordA; ESEAA

And the joy. feeling. Sonia Sanchez. SP-SancS

And the last beam of hope was almost gone. (LL) On Hearing of the Intention of a Gentleman to Purchase the Poet's Freedom. George Moses Horton. AAP; EBAP; NAAAL; SP-HortG

And the light is broken / clear. (LL) Naming the Stories. Audre Lorde. CP-LordA

And the naked / Black-White truth. (LL) Accident. Maya Angelou. SP-AngeM

And the old river rolls on, sleepily to the gulf. (LL) Foreclosure. Sterling A. Brown. CP-BrowS; GT

And the Old Women Gathered. Mari E. Evans. BlSi; Klds; NNP; PoBA

And the open gashes. (LL) The Pruning. Adam David Miller. NBV

And the pink's in us. (LL) After Reading *Mickey in the Night Kitchen* for the Third Time Before Bed. Rita Dove. Crnst

And the Power is therein. (LL) Black and White. Umar Abd Rahim Hasson. BrTr

And the seething streets of Selma and of bitter Birmingham. (LL) Amos, 1963. Margaret Abigail Walker. CP-WalkM; TtW

And the song / and me. (LL) Mystery. Langston Hughes. CP-HughL

And the spray-bright, spume-chill, bladed air. (LL) Sand wet and cool, The. Dennis Brutus. GT

And the subway gives such refinement. The Subway. Conrad Kent Rivers. Klds

And the two make up the whole! (LL) Mors et Vita. James Edwin Campbell. AAP; AfAmPo

And the Verb / be / a Woman. (LL) Genesis 11. Etheridge Knight. SP-KnigE

And the voices dropped. T. C. Walter Bradford. BrTr

And the wonderful *star* of a wonderful age! (LL) Modern Moses, or "My Policy" Man. James Madison Bell. AAP; EBAP

And the woods run mad with riot. (LL) Summer in the South. Paul Laurence Dunbar. CP-DunbP; GT

And then, come back to me! (LL) To a Young Wife. Georgia Douglas Johnson. ShDr

And then I smile and title it. If I Write a Poem. A. Van Jordan. SpiFl

And then / our lives full of streetcar clamor. Dream Orpheum Balcony. Tom Dent. BkSV

And then to pay the tax. (LL) Telly Boob-Tube on the Idiot Box. Margaret Abigail Walker. CP-WalkM

And there are so few / left. (LL) Eulogy for Alvin Frost. Audre Lorde. CP-LordA

And there are stars, but none of you, to spare. (LL) Sunflower Sonnet Number Two. June Jordan. TtW

And there they were: with fire everywhere. A New Dance. S. E. Anderson. NBP

And there was nothing startling in the weather. (LL) White Troops Had Their Orders but the Negroes Looked Like Men. Gwendolyn Brooks. SP-BrooG

And these failures are my job. (LL) The Making of Poems. Lucille Clifton. SP-ClifL

And these will last not overlong. (LL) Against That Day. Sterling A. Brown. CP-BrowS

And they lay my soul in strips. (LL) Remembering. Maya Angelou. CP-AngeM; SP-AngeM

And they were not afraid. (LL) Belsen, Day of Liberation. Robert Hayden. CP-HaydR

And They were there in the City of Fire, enflamed. JuJu. Askia Muhammad Touré. PoBA

And they weren't even / sisters. (LL) For the Record. Audre Lorde. CP-LordA; ESEAA

And they're deaf! (LL) Second Generation: New York. Langston Hughes. CP-HughL

And things that go with Spring. (LL) I'm running for the office of love. Ishmael Reed. CP-ReedI

And think of nightly slumbers with surprise. (LL) Meditation on a Cold, Dark and Rainy Night. George Moses Horton. SP-HortG

And this chair empty. (LL) Alice Braxton Johnson. Michael S. Harper. SP-HarpM

And this poor little fly, he was smothered to death. (LL) The Fly. *African-American Oral Tradition.* GetYo

And this silly wire. Poem (For PCH). Nikki Giovanni. SP-GiovN

And this was in the 19th century! (LL) Wise 4. Amiri Baraka. SP-BaraA

And this we did to "serve him right." (LL) The Dismissal of Tyng. Frances Ellen Watkins Harper. CP-HarpF

And through the Caribbean Sea. Margaret Else Danner. BPo; TtW

And thunders, let the slave be free! (LL) Slavery, thou peace-disturbing thief. George Moses Horton. SP-HortG

And to die bleeding—consummate with Life. (LL) Fulfillment. Helene Johnson. CDC; ShDr

And to his progeny with rage aspire? (LL) The Slave. George Moses Horton. SP-HortG; TtW

And to our Promised Land? (LL) At the Lincoln Monument in Washington, August 28, 1963. Margaret Abigail Walker. CP-WalkM

And to thy father tune the praise divine. (LL) To a Lady on the Death of Three Relations. Phillis Wheatley. CP-WheaP

And to your God immortal anthems raise. (LL) To a Lady and Her Children, on the Death of Her Son and Their Brother. Phillis Wheatley. CP-WheaP

And took the children of the future to join the cosmic race. (LL) Children of the Future. Jalaluddin Mansur Nuriddin. SpiFl

And took the robber chief to worlds on high. (LL) Great God! and yet shall feeble man presume. Albery Allson Whitman. EBAP

And took the Voodoo Queen to be his wife. (LL) The Voodoo Queen. *African-American Oral Tradition.* GetYo

And touches my eyes like rain. (LL) Wind Thoughts. Pinkie Gordon Lane. GT

And trace him to the bosom of his God. (LL) On the Death of a Young Gentleman. Phillis Wheatley. CP-WheaP; Crnst

And transcribe him with deeds of love. (LL) To-day Is a King in Disguise. Frances Ellen Watkins Harper. CP-HarpF

And trembling for me. (LL) A Zorro Man. Maya Angelou. CP-AngeM; SP-AngeM

And truce don't last / but temporarily. (LL) Poem for Benjamin Franklin. June Jordan. SP-JordJ

And turn for home. (LL) The Albuquerque Graveyard. Jay Wright. ESEAA

And turn myself in. (LL) Away from you these. Sonia Sanchez. SP-SancS

And turns her auburn locks to gray. (LL) October is the treasurer of the year. Paul Laurence Dunbar. CP-DunbP

And twice as easy / to take. (LL) Something to be Said for Silence. Nikki Giovanni. SP-GiovN

And two birdchildren. Poem for Thel—the Very Tops of Trees. Joseph Major. NBP

And universals / are not that world. Ron Welburn. NBV

And up and left his yellow bride. (LL) Long John Nelson and Sweetie Pie. Margaret Abigail Walker. CP-WalkM

And very old. (LL) When the Saints Come Marching In. Audre Lorde. SP-LordA

And victory will be complete. (LL) Law! what is law? The wise and sage. Elymas Payson Rogers. AAP

And wait, and tend our agonizing seeds. (LL) From the Dark Tower. Countee Cullen. AfAmPo; BALP; BANP; BPo; CDC; CP-CullC; CrDW; IDB; Klds; NAAAL; PoBA; TtW

And walk the sordid ways of men. (LL) The Song: "My soul, lost in the music's mist." Paul Laurence Dunbar. CP-DunbP

And warthogs / waving flags. (LL) There were palm trees. Alice Walker. CP-WalkA

And was carried forth to that promised land. (LL) Emmett Till. Wanda Coleman. NAAAL

And Was Not Improved. Lerone, Jr. Bennett. PoBA

And watch my children / grow. (LL) Elegy: "I lay down in my grave." Maya Angelou. CP-AngeM; SP-AngeM

And waved a bit of crape. (LL) For a Pessimist. Countee Cullen. CP-CullC

And we all sing. (LL) Summer Words of a Sistuh Addict. Sonia Sanchez. BPo; BlSi; Crnst; NAAAL; SP-SancS

And we are the universe of their time free at last. (LL) Now the Time Is Ripe to Be. Jon Goncalves. BlFi

And we cannot hear the guns / across the river. (LL) Big Apple Circus. Audre Lorde. CP-LordA

And We Conquered. Rob Penny. PoBA

And we don't miss. (LL) Knock on Wood. Henry L. Dumas. BlFi

And we feel / And live. Bob Kaufman. *See* War Memoir: Jazz, Don't Listen to It at Your Own Risk.

And we forest forever with recitation. (LL) Recitation. Saul Stacey Williams. CtF

And we own / the night. (LL) We Own the Night. Amiri Baraka. CrDW; PoBA

And we sing. (LL) The Chicago Picasso. Gwendolyn Brooks. NAAAL

And we sing Hallelujah. (LL) Ulysses "Religion." Gwendolyn Brooks. TtW

And we went to bed / without replacing them. (LL) All Hallows Eve. Audre Lorde. CP-LordA

"And we were black," three shades reply, "but kings." (LL) Black Majesty. Countee Cullen. CP-CullC; PoBA

And we will lace the. God Send Easter. Lucille Clifton. SP-ClifL

And we're afraid. (LL) Afraid. Langston Hughes. CP-HughL

And were at one. (LL) The Dogwood Trees. Robert Hayden. CP-HaydR

And were content. (LL) Big John. Norman J. Loftis. SpiFl

And What About the Children. Audre Lorde. CP-LordA; PoBA ("We've made a child.") SP-LordA

And what do you say. Lightning, Divine Lightning. Al Young. CP-YounA

And what I have learned. Duncan Spoke of a Process. Amiri Baraka. SP-BaraA

And what love as the elephant chimes. (LL) The Dance of the Elephants. Michael S. Harper. SP-HarpM

And What Shall You Say? Joseph Seamon Cotter, Sr. BANP; CDC; PoBA

And what song to sing to vacationers returning to Michigan. (LL) Crossing Lake Michigan. Michael S. Harper. SP-HarpM

And what the blessings of maternal care! (LL) To a Lady on Her Remarkable Preservation in an Hurricane in North-Carolina. Phillis Wheatley. CP-WheaP

And what would I do in heaven, pray. She of the Dancing Feet Sings. Countee Cullen. CP-CullC

And when i was all alone. For Theresa. Nikki Giovanni. SP-GiovN

And when it came down to Negro nights. A Poem for Lena Horne. Al Young. CP-YounA

And when it was over / only pain. (LL) Hard Love Rock. Audre Lorde. CP-LordA; SP-LordA

And when that ballad lady went. A Road in Kentucky. Robert Hayden. CP-HaydR

And when / the cold white ness. Query. Ebon Dooley. PoBA

And When the Revolution Came. Carolyn M. Rodgers. TtW

And when you have forgotten the bright bedclothes. When You Have Forgotten Sunday: The Love Story. Gwendolyn Brooks. BPo

And when you learn I left you this is how you'll feel. (LL) Joe Turner Blues. William Christopher Handy. CrDW

And While We Are Waiting. Carolyn M. Rodgers. JB

And while we're on our knees, at that. (LL) And When the Revloution Came. Carolyn M. Rodgers. TtW

And who shall separate the dust. Common Dust. Georgia Douglas Johnson. AmNP; PoBA; ShDr

And why and how and what, and sometimes even if. (LL) The Reckoning. Naomi Long Madgett. Klds

And why are you pointing upwards? (LL) The Black Finger. Angelina Weld Grimké. NAAAL; TtW

And will be taken to the landfill, and filled, and filled. (LL) Landfill. Michael S. Harper. SP-HarpM

And will love thee, yes, forever and aye! (LL) From the German of Uhland. Ludwig Uhland, *German, tr. by* James Weldon Johnson. CDC

And will they weep for us. For Owen Dodson, 1983. Margaret Abigail Walker. CP-WalkM

And will want to be remembered / as realpeople. (LL) We Walk the Way of the New World. Haki R. Madhubuti. ESEAA; TtW

And wilt thou, love, my soul display. The Lover's Farewell. George Moses Horton. EBAP; NAAAL

And win a martyr's crown. (LL) A Mother's Heroism. Frances Ellen Watkins Harper. CP-HarpF

And with a little piece of string, and a sharp stone / invented suicide. (LL) Suicide. Bob Kaufman. SP-KaufB

And write about daybreak / In Alabama. (LL) Daybreak in Alabama. Langston Hughes. CP-HughL; SP-HughL

And write about romance. (LL) Impeccable Conception. Maya Angelou. CP-AngeM; SP-AngeM

And wrote thee down among her treasured few! (LL) Lincoln. Paul Laurence Dunbar. CP-DunbP

And, yeah, brothers. Dark Prophecy: I Sing of Shine. Etheridge Knight. BPo; Crnst; ESEAA; SP-KnigE

And, Yes, Those Spiritual Matters. Christopher Gilbert. ESEAA

And, yes, we'd like to get shut of the sight of him. (LL) The Rag Man. Robert Hayden. CP-HaydR

And yet 'tis given to thankless man. (LL) Ocean. John Boyd. EBAP

And you are always here. (LL) For Owen Dodson, 1983. Margaret Abigail Walker. CP-WalkM

And you are welcome, welcome. (LL) Invitation to Love. Paul Laurence Dunbar. CP-DunbP; IHS

And you become immortal. (LL) The Sacrifice. Gerald William Barrax. Klds

And you did. (LL) Daughter, That Picture of You. Keith Gilyard. SpiFl

And you have come. The Year of the Child. Robert Hayden. CP-HaydR

And you know you can't buy potlicker at the AandP. (LL) Potlicker Blues. Calvin Forbes. GT

And you will be amazed. (LL) Instructions to a Princess. Ishmael Reed. CP-ReedI; PoBA

And you will understand / My hatred. (LL) Hatred. Gwendolyn B. Bennett. AmNP; BANP; BlSi; CDC; PoBA; ShDr

And your eyes peel to red mud. (LL) Babylon Revisited. Amiri Baraka. BPo

And your growth into martyrdom. (LL) For Malcolm: After Mecca. Gerald William Barrax. PoBA

And your money, too. (LL) 50–50. Langston Hughes. CP-HughL; SP-HughL

And your namesakes, / in the chambers. (LL) Mr. P. C. Michael S. Harper. SP-HarpM

Andy Warhol, / there are empty cans of Campbell soup. First Essay on the Art of the U. S. Ron Welburn. BlFi

A-ness never / Had a chance. (LL) The Negro. James A. Emanuel. BrTr; Klds

Angel of Mercy's, The. Red Cross. Langston Hughes. CP-HughL

Angel, robed in spotless white, An. Dawn. Paul Laurence Dunbar. AmNP; CP-DunbP

Angel with a voice like summer show'rs, An. Repose. Henrietta Cordelia Ray. CBWP-3

Angela Davis. Alice S. Cobb. BlSi

Angelic Eve. Jean Toomer. CP-ToomJ

Angelina. Paul Laurence Dunbar. CP-DunbP

Angels. Lucille Clifton. SP-ClifL

Angels gather. Arrival. Maya Angelou. CP-AngeM; SP-AngeM

Angels is a-mindin' you, my baby. Jack Frost at Bedtime. Paul Laurence Dunbar. CP-DunbP

Angel's Message, The. Clara Ann Thompson. CBWP-2

Angels Prayer, An. Lefty Sims. BlFi

Angel's Visit, The. Charlotte L. Forten Grimké. AAP

Angels wings is white as snow, The. Langston Hughes. CP-HughL; SP-HughL

Angle of ascent / achieved, The. (LL) For a Young Artist. Robert Hayden. CP-HaydR

Angola Question Mark. Langston Hughes. BPo; CP-HughL

Anita and Giovanni. Henrietta Cordelia Ray. CBWP-3

Anna Speaks of the Childhood of Mary Her Daughter. Lucille Clifton. SP-ClifL

Anne Boleyn. Eloise Bibb. CBWP-4

Anne Spencer's Table. Langston Hughes. CP-HughL

Annette came through the meadows. Pastoral. Henrietta Cordelia Ray. CBWP-3

Anniad, The. Gwendolyn Brooks. BlSi; SP-BrooG

Annie, my first-born, gentle child. To Annie. Mary E. Tucker. CBWP-1

Annie Pearl Smith Discovers Moonlight. Patricia Smith. GT

Anniversary. Rita Dove. SP-DoveR

Anniversary. Audre Lorde. CP-LordA

Announcement. Langston Hughes. CP-HughL

Announcement. James T. Stewart. BlFi

Anointing, An. Thylias Moss. GT

Anon. Poster. Ishmael Reed. CP-ReedI

Anonymous water can slide under the ground. Explanations. Lucille Clifton. SP-ClifL

Another brother gone. Biafra Blues. Michael S. Harper. SP-HarpM

Another brother gone. (LL) Dead-Day: Malcolm, Feb. 21. Michael S. Harper. SP-HarpM

Another / by / assassination. (LL) Malcolm's Messasge. Al Young. CP-YounA

Another conference year has passed. To the Conference. Mrs. Henry Linden. CBWP-4

Another Man Done Gone. *Unknown.* NAAAL

Another miracle / comes knocking at his door. Abba Jacob's Seven Devils. Marilyn Nelson. SP-NelsM

Another mule kicking. Sterling Plumpp. GT

Another of my new black angels. You Don't Know What Love Is. Al Young. CP-YounA

Another Poem about the Man. June Jordan. SP-JordJ

Another Poem for Me (after Recovering from an O.D.). Etheridge Knight. SP-KnigE

Another sate near him, whose harp of gold. Fenton Johnson. BANP

Another weaver of black dreams has gone. (LL) For Langston Hughes. Etheridge Knight. NBV; SP-KnigE

Another youthful advocate of truth and right has gone. To the Memory of J. Horace Kimball. "Ada." BlSi

Answer, The, *see also* To a Gentleman of the Navy *and* Philis's Reply *by* Phillis Wheatley. *Unknown.* CP-WheaP

Answer Me. Adah Isaacs Menken. CBWP-1

Answer to Dunbar's "A Choice." Joseph Seamon Cotter, Sr. EBAP

Answer to Dunbar's "After a Visit." Joseph Seamon Cotter, Sr. AAP; EBAP

Answer to the *Rebus*, by the Author of These Poems, An, *see also* A Rebus *by* Unknown. Phillis Wheatley. CP-WheaP

Answer to Yo / Question. Sonia Sanchez. BPo

Ante-bellum Negro prayed, The. Must Be Freed. Lizelia Augusta Jenkins Moorer. CBWP-3

Ante-Bellum Sermon, An. Paul Laurence Dunbar. AAP; BALP; BPo; CP-DunbP; NAAAL; TtW

   ("We is gathahed hyeah, my brothah.") AfAmPo

Anti-Father. Rita Dove. SP-DoveR

Anti-Semanticist, The. Everett Hoagland. BPo; NBV

Antigone and Oedipus. Henrietta Cordelia Ray. AAP; BlSi; CBWP-3; EBAP

Antigone I. Herbert Martin. PoBA

Antigone, This Is It. Ishmael Reed. CP-ReedI

Antigone VI. Herbert Martin. PoBA

Ants of Argos, The. Rita Dove. SP-DoveR

Any fool knows a Br'er in a rocker. Br'er Sterling and the Rocker. Michael S. Harper. NAAAL; SP-HarpM

Any Human to Another. Countee Cullen. CP-CullC

Any Inner City Blues. Al Young. CP-YounA

Any of the several names. Eulogy for Populations. Ron Welburn. BlFi; PoBA

Anybody / Better than / Nobody. Desert. Langston Hughes. CP-HughL; Klds; SP-HughL

Anything he wants out of it. (LL) Buddy. Langston Hughes. CP-HughL

Ape-Gods. Marilyn Nelson. SP-NelsM

Ape to angel under the influence of star-gazing is the Dream. (LL) Moon Watching by Lake Chapala. Al Young. CP-YounA

Aphorisms. Joel Chandler Harris. CrDW

Apollinaire / never knew about rock gut charlie. Unhistorical Events. Bob Kaufman. SP-KaufB

Apollo's wrath to man the dreadful spring. Niobe in Distress for Her Children Slain by Apollo, from Ovid's Metamorphoses, Book VI, and from a View of the Painting of Mr. Richard Wilson. Phillis Wheatley. CP-WheaP

Apologies to All the People in Lebanon. June Jordan. SP-JordJ

Apology for Apostasy? Etheridge Knight. SP-KnigE

Apology (to the Panthers). Lucille Clifton. SP-ClifL

Apostrophe to the Land. Countee Cullen. CP-CullC

Appaloosa, The. Michael S. Weaver. GT

Appeal to My Countrywomen, An. Frances Ellen Watkins Harper. BlSi; CP-HarpF; NAAAL

Appeal to the American People, An. Frances Ellen Watkins Harper. CP-HarpF

Appearance of a Lost Goddess, The. Jay Wright. Crnst

Appendix to the Anniad. Gwendolyn Brooks. BlSi; SP-BrooG

Applauding youths laughed with young prostitutes. The Harlem Dancer. Claude McKay. AfAmPo; BALP; BANP; BPo; CrDW; SP-McKaC

Apple blossoms falling o'er thee. Come and Kiss Me Sweet and Twenty. Paul Laurence Dunbar. CP-DunbP

Apple Core. Clarence Major. GT

Apple Dumplings. Mary E. Tucker. CBWP-1

Apples are still as sweet, The. Everywhere. Al Young. CP-YounA

Appoggiatura. Donald Jeffrey Hayes. AmNP; PoBA

Appreciation. Paul Laurence Dunbar. CP-DunbP

Apprenticeship. Yusef Komunyakaa. SP-KomuY

Approaching night her mantle flings. To ———. James M. Whitfield. AAP

Approximations. Robert Hayden. CP-HaydR

April. Cornelius Eady. ESEAA

April. Henrietta Cordelia Ray. CBWP-3

4/30/92; for Rodney King. Lucille Clifton. ESEAA

April Blue. Al Young. CP-YounA

April Day, An. Joseph Seamon Cotter, Sr. CDC

April Fools' Day. Yusef Komunyakaa. GT; SP-KomuY

April in Coolwell. Sterling A. Brown. CP-BrowS

April is on the way! Alice Moore Dunbar-Nelson. NAAAL

April of Alabama, The. George Marion McClellan. EBAP

April Rain Song. Langston Hughes. CP-HughL

April Rape. Marilyn Nelson. SP-NelsM

Arabella Johnson and the Texas Kid. Death in Harlem. Langston Hughes. CP-HughL

Arabesque. Fred Johnson. PoBA

Arabia it's so fine so hot. Al Young. CP-YounA

/ arabs / ain't got no, The. Sonia Sanchez. SP-SancS

Ardella. Langston Hughes. CP-HughL; SP-HughL

Are being hunted down the federal canyons / of Yellowstone Park. (LL) Relevant Is Different Points on the Circle. Audre Lorde. CP-LordA; SP-LordA

Are known beyond death's door. (LL) Threnody: "Only quiet death." Waring Cuney. AmNP; BANP

Are merged in Paradise. (LL) The Litany of the Dark People. Countee Cullen. CP-CullC

Are one with all the dead, since she is gone. (LL) Glory of the Day Was in Her Face, The. James Weldon Johnson. BANP; CDC; IDB; PoBA

Are sudden tear-drops in your eyes. (LL) Some things are very dear to me. Gwendolyn B. Bennett. TtW; NAAAL

Are sweet like wanton loves because I hate. (LL) The White City. Claude McKay. BPo; CrDW; SP-McKaC

Are Their Blues Singers in Russia? Amiri Baraka. SP-BaraA

Are walking towards me. Five Elephants. Rita Dove. SP-DoveR

Are you an ethnic poet? After the Dance. Reuben Jackson. GT

Are you not the light. When Brown Is Black. Keorapetse W. Kgositsile. BrTr

Are You the Lover or Loved? Al Young. CP-YounA

Aretha. Deep butter dipt, burnt pot liquor, twisted sugarcane. Asking for a Heart Attack. Patricia Smith. CtF

Argument. Langston Hughes. SP-HughL *Fr.* Montage of a Dream Deferred. CP-HughL

Argument: "Now lookahere, gal." Langston Hughes. CP-HughL

Arise, my soul, on wings enraptured, rise. Thoughts on the Works of Providence. Phillis Wheatley. EBAP

Aristocrat among patriarchs, This. The Copper Beech. Rita Dove. SP-DoveR

Ark, The. Noah Calwell Cannon. AAP

Arkansas Chant. Sterling A. Brown. CP-BrowS

Arkansas twilight, An. (LL) Kin. Maya Angelou. CP-AngeM; SP-AngeM

Armageddon. Georgia Douglas Johnson. ShDr

Armah: October 12, 1990. Alice Walker. CP-WalkA

Armed Men. Marilyn Nelson. SP-NelsM

Armored in oxygen. Astronauts. Robert Hayden. CP-HaydR; ESEAA

Army. I cannot even dream, The. Clinton. Sterling Plumpp. BkSV

Around me roar and crash the pagan isms. The Pagan Isms. Claude McKay. BPo; SP-McKaC

Around the church. Julius Lester. *Fr.* Poems. Klds

Arria to Poetus. Mary E. Tucker. CBWP-1

Arrival. Maya Angelou. CP-AngeM; SP-AngeM

Arrive. The Ladies from the Ladies' Betterment League. The Lovers of the Poor. Gwendolyn Brooks. ESEAA; NAAAL

Arrow rides upon the sky, An. Love Song. Samuel Allen. NNP

Arrows of rain. Dark Dreaming. Dorothy Kruger. ShDr

Arroyo. Tom Weatherly. PoBA

Ars Longa. Which is crueller. The Peacock Room. Robert Hayden. CP-HaydR; FB

Ars Poetica. Al Young. CP-YounA

Arson and Cold Lace. Worth Long. NBP

Art of a Poet, The. George Moses Horton. EBAP; SP-HortG

Art of Benny Carter, The. Al Young. CP-YounA

Art of Charles White is like making love, The. Charles White. Nikki Giovanni. SP-GiovN

Art of Response, The. Audre Lorde. CP-LordA

Art of the Nickname, The. Dominique Parker. SpiFl

Artful Pose. Maya Angelou. CP-AngeM; SP-AngeM

Arthur Ridgewood, M.D. Frank Marshall Davis. Klds; TtW

Artichoke Pickle Passion: Sonnet. Beverly Fields Burnette. CtF

Artina. Langston Hughes. *See* To Artina.

Artisan. Audre Lorde. CP-LordA

Artist, The. Frances Ellen Watkins Harper. CP-HarpF

As a child / I bought a red scarf. Four Sheets to the Wind and a One-Way Ticket to France. Conrad Kent Rivers. BPo; IDB; NNP; PoBA

As a child I was. Woman. Elouise Loftin. PoBA

As a Masai warrior. Black Music Man. Lethonia Gee. BlFi

As a Possible Lover. Amiri Baraka. SP-BaraA; TtW

   ("Practices / silence, they way of wind.") AmNP

As a quiet little seedling. The Seedling. Paul Laurence Dunbar. CP-DunbP

As Befits a Man. Langston Hughes. CP-HughL; SP-HughL

As facing mirrors clarify each other. Union Apprehended. Marilyn Nelson. *Fr.* The Plotinus Suite. SP-NelsM

As far as possible, she strove. Born That Way. Maya Angelou. CP-AngeM

As for the hawk, what grander bird. Sentience. Al Young. CP-YounA

As ghost, double, alter ego then? (LL) Names. Robert Hayden. CP-HaydR; GT

As he sinks two into the chains. (LL) Makin' Jump Shots. Michael S. Harper. SP-HarpM

As I am, / I should be able to. Missing Beat. Carolyn M. Rodgers. JB

As i conclude this work. Introducing a New Loa. Ishmael Reed. CP-ReedI

As I dig my spoon into the belly of a melon. (LL) The Dancer. Al Young. CP-YounA; PoBA

As I Grew Older. Langston Hughes. BANP; CP-HughL; Crnst; SP-HughL

As I Grew Up Again. Audre Lorde. SP-LordA

   (As I Grow Up Again.) CP-LordA

As I had been taught to do. (LL) In the Old Neighborhood. Rita Dove. SP-DoveR; SpiFl

As I lie in bed. Prayer. Joseph Seamon Cotter, Sr. BANP

As I look into each different face. Through the Varied Patterned Lace. Margaret Else Danner. Klds

As I love you. (LL) Dear Toni Instead of a Letter of Congratulation. Audre Lorde. CP-LordA; SP-LordA

As I sat one evening in sweet meditation. The Twilight Hour. Joshua McCarter Simpson. AAP

As I see I must. (LL) On Stripping Bark from Myself. Alice Walker. CP-WalkA; NAAAL

As I sit by the ruddy oak fire. Nestle-down Cottage. Mary Weston Fordham. CBWP-2

As I talk with learned people. A Spade Is Just a Spade. Walter Everette Hawkins. PoBA

As I was going to town. Me Alone. Lula Lowe Weeden. CDC

As I was putting away the groceries. Bali Hai Calls Mama. Marilyn Nelson. SP-NelsM

As I was walkin down L.A. Street. L.A. Street. *African-American Oral Tradition.* GetYo

As if it were some noble thing. Mother in Wartime. Langston Hughes. CP-HughL

As if looks were everything. (LL) A Hill of Beans. Rita Dove. SP-DoveR

As in some dim baronial hall restrained. Behind the Arras. Paul Laurence Dunbar. CP-DunbP

As it is / in my country. We Have a Map of the World. Alice Walker. CP-WalkA

As it was with Christ, so it is with Malcolm. The Abduction of Saints. Alice Walker. CP-WalkA

As keeps this young nymph, Joy! (LL) Joy. Langston Hughes. CP-HughL; SP-HughL

As King grew cold on a Memphis slab. Samuel Allen. *Fr.* Paul Vesey's Ledger. TtW

As lone I sat one summer's day. Love Despoiled. Paul Laurence Dunbar. CP-DunbP

As my blood was drawn. Robert Hayden. CP-HaydR

As my heart burned. Memorial IV. Audre Lorde. CP-LordA

As my mind in fancy wanders. The Negro Has a Chance. Maggie Pogue Johnson. CBWP-4

As o'er thy loved one now in grief ye bendeth. Solace. Josephine D. Henderson Heard. CBWP-4

As once in her fire-lit heart I felt the furies / Beating, beating. (LL) Lines to a Nasturtium. Anne Spencer. AmNP; CDC; ShDr

As possible as yeast. I Am Not Done Yet. Lucille Clifton. SP-ClifL

As riper years approach us. Glimpses of Infancy. Priscilla Jane Thompson. CBWP-2

As round the rose's heart the golden threads. Soul Incense. Henrietta Cordelia Ray. CBWP-3

As she beats her ordinary bread. (LL) In Salem. Lucille Clifton. ESEAA; SP-ClifL

As she pulled it down. (LL) Christmas Eve: My Mother Dressing. Toi Derricotte. CtF

As shines the sunbeam through dark clouds. Hope. Mary E. Tucker. CBWP-1

As simple an act. Way Out West. Amiri Baraka. PoBA; SP-BaraA

As Simple as That. Marilyn Nelson. SP-NelsM

As some rapt gazer on the lowly earth. Love's Humility. Paul Laurence Dunbar. CP-DunbP

As surely as I hold your hand in mine. Brown Boy to Brown Girl. Countee Cullen. CP-CullC; PoBA

As the Eagle Soars. Jean Toomer. CP-ToomJ

As the gook woman howls. In the Mourning Time. Robert Hayden. BPo

As the queen upon her throne. (LL) Learning to Read. Frances Ellen Watkins Harper. AfAmPo; CP-HarpF; EBAP; NAAAL

As the sun that lights creation. Africa. Lizelia Augusta Jenkins Moorer. CBWP-3

As the Word came to the prophets of old. Prophets for a New Day. Margaret Abigail Walker. BPo; BrTr; NAAAL

As they lean over the beans in their rented back room that is full of beads and receipts and dolls and cloths, tobacco crumbs, vases and fringes.

(LL) The Bean Eaters. Gwendolyn Brooks. BlSi; Crnst; ESEAA; PoBA; SP-BrooG

As they wave their tongues. (LL) Song: I Want a Witness. Michael S. Harper. SP-HarpM

As things be / come. Word Poem (Perhaps Worth Considering). Nikki Giovanni. PoBA

As though her lips. To Dorothy Maynor. Langston Hughes. CP-HughL

As though they did not care. (LL) Old Black Men. Georgia Douglas Johnson. CDC; PoBA

As through earth's garden once I strayed. The Crushed Flower. Mary E. Tucker. CBWP-1

As to harden the unhard and unhard / the hardened. (LL) It's Here In The. Russell Atkins. AmNP; PoBA

As usual, legend got it all. Nestor's Bathtub. Rita Dove. SP-DoveR

As warm as bread or as a homecoming. (LL) Upstate. Derek Walcott. GT

As we go about the toils of life. As We Sow We Shall Reap. Maggie Pogue Johnson. CBWP-4

As we got. Julius Lester. *Fr.* Poems. Klds

As we have borne the pains. (LL) Mothers. Nikki Giovanni. SP-GiovN

As We Sow We Shall Reap. Maggie Pogue Johnson. CBWP-4

As well as by my side. (LL) Hard Love Rock #II. Audre Lorde. CP-LordA; SP-LordA

"As When Emotion Too Far Exceeds Its Cause." Gloria C. Oden. AmNP; Klds

As Women of Our Race. Mrs. Henry Linden. CBWP-4

As You Leave Me. Etheridge Knight. BrTr; SP-KnigE

As you read your comics. No. 24. Michael S. Harper. SP-HarpM

As you search over this year. To Martha: a New Year. Audre Lorde. CP-LordA

As your own birthmark of his scream. (LL) Kin. Michael S. Harper. SP-HarpM; TtW

Asante Sana, Te Te. Thadious M. Davis. BlSi

Ascendancy. Herbert A. Simmons. NBP

Ashes, Lord— / But warm still from the fire that cheered us. Nat Turner in the Clearing. Alvin Aubert. TtW

Ashes to ashes, dust to dust. Mortality. Paul Laurence Dunbar. CP-DunbP

Ashkelon is not cut off with the remnant of a valley. Judith. Adah Isaacs Menken. CBWP-1

Ask Your Mama; 12 Moods for Jazz. Langston Hughes. CP-HughL

   Ask Your Mama.

   Bird in Orbit.

   Blues in Stereo.

   Cultural Exchange.

   Gospel Cha-Cha.

   Horn of Plenty.

   If You Would.

   Is It True?

   Jazztet Muted.

   Ode to Dinah.

   Ride, Red, Ride.

   Shades of Pigmeat.

   Show Fare, Please.

Asked me for a kiss. (LL) Suicide's Note. Langston Hughes. CDC; CP-HughL; SP-HughL

Asking for a Heart Attack. Patricia Smith. CtF

Aspect of Love, Alive in the Ice and Fire, An. Gwendolyn Brooks. BPo

Aspiration. Langston Hughes. CP-HughL

Aspiration. Adah Isaacs Menken. AAP; CBWP-1

Aspiration. Henrietta Cordelia Ray. CBWP-3

Assailant. John Raven. BPo

Assassination. Don L. Lee. AmNP; PoBA

Assassination. Haki R. Madhubuti. BrTr; GT

Assurance. Josephine D. Henderson Heard. CBWP-4

Assuredly, that fissured face. Eulogy to W. H. Auden. Derek Walcott. ESEAA

Astrologer Predicts at Mary's Birth, The. Lucille Clifton. SP-ClifL

Astronauts. Robert Hayden. CP-HaydR; ESEAA

Aswelay. Norman Henry, II Pritchard. PoBA

At 29. Speculations on the Present through the Prism of the Past. June Jordan. GT

At a Parting. Countee Cullen. CP-CullC

At a VA Hospital in the Middle of the United States of America: An Act in a Play. Etheridge Knight. SP-KnigE

At a woman's bedroom window. (LL) The Thorn Merchant's Son. Yusef Komunyakaa. SP-KomuY

At an English conference presentation. Dancing in the Dark. Demetrice A. Worley. SpiFl

At Ann's place, even before you arrive. Available Light. Al Young. CP-YounA

At April. Angelina Weld Grimké. BlSi; GT

At break of another dawn. (LL) Remnant Ghosts at Dawn. Oliver La Grone. FB; NBV

At Candle-Lightin' Time. Paul Laurence Dunbar. CP-DunbP

At Cheshire Cheese. Paul Laurence Dunbar. CP-DunbP

At Christmas-Tide. Henrietta Cordelia Ray. CBWP-3

At Dunbar, Castle or Arcade. Double Feature. Robert Hayden. CP-HaydR

At fifteen / pain / called me. A Brief Synopsis. Carolyn M. Rodgers. TtW

At first I did not fight it. Alice Walker. CP-WalkA

At First I Thought You Were Talking about . Audre Lorde. CP-LordA

At first nothing is. Nothing Is. Sun-Ra. BlFi; PoBA

At first we see the tiny leaves. The Strawberry. Maggie Pogue Johnson. CBWP-4

At first you'll joy to see the playful snow. To One Coming North. Claude McKay. SP-McKaC

At fourteen you crawl through a hole. Gerry's Jazz. Yusef Komunyakaa. SP-KomuY

At General Electric, Where They Eat Their/Young. Robert Farr. SpiFl

At Harper's Ferry Just before the Attack. Edward W. Williams. AAP

At his cramped desk. Star-Fix. Marilyn Nelson. ESEAA; SP-NelsM

At Home in Dakar. Margaret Else Danner. BlSi; FB

At home / in the countryside. Pagan. Alice Walker. CP-WalkA

At home we pray every morning, we. Ulysses "Religion." Gwendolyn Brooks. TtW

At Jonestown. Lucille Clifton. NAAAL

At just that moment in history. (LL) Ocean Springs Missippy. Al Young. CP-YounA

At Kisheneff two wicked men. Russia's Resentment. Lizelia Augusta Jenkins Moorer. CBWP-3

At last I am acquitted. Where Is the Guilt. May Miller. TtW

At last we killed the roaches. Lucille Clifton. SP-ClifL

At least has common sense. (LL) Advice to the Girls. Frances Ellen Watkins Harper. CP-HarpF; TtW

At least I can offer that. / Com'mere, boy! (LL) Brass Spittoons. Langston Hughes. AmNP; BANP

At Loafing-Holt. Paul Laurence Dunbar. CP-DunbP

AT LYNCHINGS / HEATHENS WEAR. Christ Was Never in Europe! Amiri Baraka. SP-BaraA

At Nature's Shrine. Henrietta Cordelia Ray. CBWP-3

At Night. Paul Laurence Dunbar. CP-DunbP

At night the wide and level stretch of wold. Morning Joy. Claude McKay. SP-McKaC

At night while / whitey sleeps. Black Warrior. Norman Jordan. BlFi; PoBA

At our hearts? (LL) At April. Angelina Weld Grimké. GT

At our Redeemer's feet. (LL) My mother's kiss, my mother's kiss. Frances Ellen Watkins Harper. CP-HarpF

At our Redeemer's feet. (LL) To Bishop Payne. Frances Ellen Watkins Harper. CP-HarpF

At Prayer. Marilyn Nelson. SP-NelsM

At Sea. Jean Toomer. BALP; CP-ToomJ

At seventeen your. Maryuma. Frank Lamont Phillips. AmNP

At some moment the confidence snaps. June Jordan. SP-JordJ

At Sunset. Henrietta Cordelia Ray. CBWP-3

At Sunset Time. Paul Laurence Dunbar. CP-DunbP

At That Moment. Raymond R. Patterson. BrTr; PoBA; TtW

At the back fence calling. Peace Conference in an American Town. Langston Hughes. CP-HughL

At the Border of Constant Disaster. Jerry W., Jr. Ward. CtF

At the bottom of the sea. (LL) Dinosaur Spring. Marilyn Nelson. SP-NelsM

At the Carnival. Anne Spencer. BANP; BlSi; CDC; Klds; NAAAL; ShDr; TtW

At the Cascade. Henrietta Cordelia Ray. CBWP-3

At the Cemetery. Michael S. Harper. SP-HarpM

At the center of. Sonia Sanchez. SP-SancS

At the ceremony of Emobo. Ceremony. Kattie M. Cumbo. BlSi

At the Closed Gate of Justice. James David Corrothers. AfAmP; BANP; NAAAL; TtW

At the Colonial Y They Are Aesthetically and Culturally Deprived (Y's Later) (31). Amiri Baraka. SP-BaraA

At the dinner table, before the baked eggplant. The Boast. Rita Dove. SP-DoveR

At the dinner table where you sat with Peabody. Dining from a Treed Condition, an Historical Survey. Michael S. Harper. SP-HarpM

At the edge of the mariner's. Primer for the Nuclear Age. Rita Dove. SP-DoveR

At the feet o' Jesus. Feet O' Jesus. Langston Hughes. CP-HughL; SP-HughL

At the foot of the steps a forest. Speechless. Audre Lorde. CP-LordA

At the German Writers Conference in Munich. Rita Dove. SP-DoveR

At the golden gate of song. Inspiration. Paul Laurence Dunbar. CP-DunbP

At the illusion world that has come into existence. The Ancient Rain. Bob Kaufman. SP-KaufB

At the Lincoln Monument in Washington, August 28, 1963. Margaret Abigail Walker. CP-WalkM

At the motorpool / across the street. (LL) Freeman Field. Marilyn Nelson. ESEAA; SP-NelsM

At the outset, hysteria. Cholera. Rita Dove. SP-DoveR

At the Portals of the Future. Lines. Frances Ellen Watkins Harper. CP-HarpF

At the Record Hop. Wanda Coleman. NAAAL

At the rifle factory. Dreams: American. Michael S. Harper. SP-HarpM

At the Screen Door. Yusef Komunyakaa. SP-KomuY

At the Spring Dawn. Angelina Weld Grimké. ShDr

At the Tavern. Paul Laurence Dunbar. CP-DunbP

At the throat of Soweto. A Song for Soweto. June Jordan. SP-JordJ

At the top. (LL) To Be Somebody. Langston Hughes. CP-HughL; SP-HughL

At the tray / she looks in the heart. Trays: a Portfolio. Michael S. Harper. SP-HarpM

At the vehemence / of my negative / reply. (LL) My husband says. Alice Walker. CP-WalkA

At the Wailing Wall in Jerusalem. Countee Cullen. CP-CullC

At those same words cried in the English tongue? (LL) Karenge Ya Marenge. Countee Cullen. CP-CullC; TtW

At times she thought to commit suicide. Albery Allson Whitman. *Fr.* Leelah Misled. EBAP

At two, the barnyard settled. Pamela. Rita Dove. SP-DoveR

At War. Russell Atkins. AmNP

Atheism. Phillis Wheatley. CP-WheaP

Athelstane. Priscilla Jane Thompson. CBWP-2

Atlanta Exposition Ode. Mary Weston Fordham. AAP; CBWP-2

("Cast down your bucket where you are.") AfAmPo

Atlantic City Waiter. Countee Cullen. CP-CullC

Atlantic is a sea of bones. Lucille Clifton. ESEAA

Atlantic Monthly, December 1970, The. Ishmael Reed. CP-ReedI

Atrocities. Nikki Giovanni. SP-GiovN

Attend my lays, ye ever honour'd nine. An Hymn to the Morning. Phillis Wheatley. CP-WheaP

Attentiveness. Alice Walker. CP-WalkA

Audacity of the Lower Gods. Yusef Komunyakaa. SP-KomuY

Audubon, Drafted. Amiri Baraka. Klds; SP-BaraA

Auf Wiedersehen. Donald Jeffrey Hayes. CDC

August. Henrietta Cordelia Ray. CBWP-3

August 19th. Langston Hughes. CP-HughL

August the 12th. Lucille Clifton. SP-ClifL

August. The mums nod past, each a prickly heart on a sleeve. (LL) Teach Us to Number Our Days. Rita Dove. ESEAA; SP-DoveR

August 'twas the twenty-fifth. Bar[']s Fight[, August 28, 1746]. Lucy Terry. BPo; BlSi; CrDW; EBAP; NAAAL; TtW

August 2. Norman Jordan. PoBA

Aunt. Al Young. CP-YounA

Aunt Agnes Hatcher Tells. Lucille Clifton. SP-ClifL

Aunt Annie's Prayer. Marilyn Nelson. SP-NelsM

Aunt Chloe. Frances Ellen Watkins Harper. CP-HarpF

Aunt Chloe's Lullaby. Daniel Webster Davis. AAP; AfAmPo; EBAP

Aunt Chloe's Politics. Frances Ellen Watkins Harper. CP-HarpF; NAAAL

Aunt Jane Allen. Fenton Johnson. IDB; PoBA

Aunt Jemima of the Ocean Waves. Robert Hayden. CP-HaydR; PoBA

Aunt Jessie. Wanda Coleman. GT

Aunt Martha bustles. Old Houses. Melvin B. Tolson. GT

Aunt Sue's Stories. Langston Hughes. CP-HughL; SP-HughL

Aurora Borealis. Rita Dove. SP-DoveR

Author Reflects on His 35th Birthday, The. Ishmael Reed. CP-ReedI

Autobiography. Tom Weatherly. NBV

Autograph on the Soul, The. Adah Isaacs Menken. CBWP-1

Autumn ("List to the sad wind, drearily moaning"). Priscilla Jane Thompson. CBWP-2

Autumn. Marjorie Marshall. ShDr

Autumn. Helen G. Quigless. BkSV

Autumn ("Sun shines bright, but sadly, The"). Priscilla Jane Thompson. CBWP-2
Autumn. a bonfire. Sonia Sanchez. SP-SancS
Autumn Day, An. Clara Ann Thompson. CBWP-2
Autumn God. Eugene B. Redmond. TtW
Autumn Leaves. Clara Ann Thompson. CBWP-2
Autumn leaves / Are too heavy with color, The. Poème d'Automne. Langston Hughes. CP-HughL
Autumn moon, The. (LL) Haiku: "Black woman, A." Lenard D. Moore. CtF; TtW
Autumn Note. Langston Hughes. CP-HughL
Autumn Prison. Nikki Giovanni. SP-GiovN
Autumn Thought. Langston Hughes. CP-HughL
Autumn Thoughts. Mary E. Tucker. CBWP-1
Available Light. Al Young. CP-YounA
Avalanche. Quincy Troupe. SpiFl
Avec Merci, Mother. Maya Angelou. CP-AngeM; SP-AngeM
Avoidances. Ron Welburn. PoBA
Awake all night with loving. Fired. Langston Hughes. CP-HughL; SP-HughL
Awake! arise! Oh, men of my race. Daybreak. George Marion McClellan. AAP
AWAKE! For the morning. Boston 5:00 A.M.—10/74. Etheridge Knight. SP-KnigE
Awaken us to the long day of the spirit. Our Growing Day. Jean Toomer. CP-ToomJ
Awakening, The. Paul Laurence Dunbar. CP-DunbP
Awakening, The. Keorapetse W. Kgositsile. BlFi
Awakening. Henrietta Cordelia Ray. CBWP-3
Awakening, The. Alice Walker. CP-WalkA
Awakening, / rumours of necessity for your death. A Woman/Dirge for Wasted Children. Audre Lorde. CP-LordA
Awaking in New York. Maya Angelou. CP-AngeM; SP-AngeM
Award. Ray Durem. BPo; IDB; NNP; PoBA
Awareness. Don L. Lee. PoBA
Awareness. Haki R. Madhubuti. BrTr
Away down into the shadowy depths of the Real I once lived. Myself. Adah Isaacs Menken. CBWP-1
Away from earth and its cares set free. Eternity. Josephine D. Henderson Heard. CBWP-4
Away from this toward fair Georgia's plain. Albery Allson Whitman. Fr. Leelah Misled. EBAP
Away from you these. Sonia Sanchez. SP-SancS
Away to Canada. Joshua McCarter Simpson. AAP; AfAmPo
Axes has been ringin' in de woods de blessid day, De. A Back-Log Song. Paul Laurence Dunbar. CP-DunbP
Aye, lay him in his grave, the old dead year! The King is Dead. Paul Laurence Dunbar. CP-DunbP
Azikiwe in Jail. Langston Hughes. CP-HughL
Azuri. Askia M. Toure. SpiFl

B

B.B. Blues. Mary Weems. SpiFl
Baby. Langston Hughes. CP-HughL; SP-HughL
Baby Cobina. Gladys May Casely Hayford. CDC; ShDr
Baby, dance with me! (LL) Sunday by the Combination. Langston Hughes. CP-HughL
Baby, how come you can't see me. Ultimatum. Langston Hughes. SP-HughL Fr. Montage of a Dream Deferred. CP-HughL
Baby I hold in my arms is a black baby, The. Black Baby. Anita Scott Coleman. ShDr
Baby, / I just want you to. Shades of Pharoah Sanders Blues for My Baby. John O'Neal. NBV
Baby, if you love me. Down and Out. Langston Hughes. CP-HughL; SP-HughL
Baby. you are sweet. Sonia Sanchez. SP-SancS
Babylon Revisited. Amiri Baraka. BPo
Back Again, Home. Don L. Lee. BALP; BPo
Back Again, Home. Haki R. Madhubuti. NAAAL
Back & forth between us like / borrowed breath. (LL) When Black People Are. Alfred B. Spellman. BPo; PoBA
Back down in the jungle up under the stick. Signifying Monkey: "Back down in the jungle up under the stick." African-American Oral Tradition. GetYo
Back home the black women are all beautiful. W. W. Amiri Baraka. NBP; PoBA

Back in chi/ / all the blackwomen. Reflections on a Lost Love. Haki R. Madhubuti. BrTr
Back in forty-nine when times was hard. Stackolee: "Back in forty-nine when times was hard." African-American Oral Tradition. GetYo
Back in the day. Too Many. Derrick I. M. Gilbert. CtF
Back into the Garden. Sarah Webster Fabio. BlSi
Back-Log Song, A. Paul Laurence Dunbar. CP-DunbP
Back on the nineteenth of June. Partytime Monkey. African-American Oral Tradition. GetYo
Back Then. Yusef Komunyakaa. GT; SP-KomuY
Back to Africa. Ishmael Reed. CP-ReedI
Back to Back: 3rd Eye. Ishmael Reed. CP-ReedI
Back to our theme, McLambert's "ev'ning rides." Albery Allson Whitman. Fr. Leelah Misled. EBAP
Back to the breast of thy mother. Alexander Crummel—Dead. Paul Laurence Dunbar. CP-DunbP
Back up in the room they snap on. Making Love After Hours. Al Young. CP-YounA
Background: / a reckoning has left. Off d Pig. Ishmael Reed. CP-ReedI
Backlash Blues, The. Langston Hughes. BPo; CP-HughL
Backtracking. Al Young. CP-YounA
Backwater Blues. Bessie Smith. NAAAL
Backwater Blues. Unknown. Crnst
Bad, Bad Man, A. Sterling A. Brown. CP-BrowS
Bad Luck Card. Langston Hughes. CP-HughL; SP-HughL
Bad Man. Langston Hughes. CP-HughL; NAAAL
Bad-Man Stagolee. Margaret Abigail Walker. CP-WalkM
Bad Morning. Langston Hughes. CP-HughL; SP-HughL
Bad that way, / Daddy-o. (LL) Migrant. Langston Hughes. CP-HughL; SP-HughL
Bad town, I see a white-faced bull. Clinton. Sterling Plumpp. BkSV
Badman of the Guest Professor. Ishmael Reed. BPo; SSLK ("U worry me whoever u are.") CP-ReedI
Bagel Shop Jazz. Bob Kaufman. SP-KaufB
Bahá'u'lláh in the Garden of Ridwan. Robert Hayden. CP-HaydR; PoBA
Bakar, Atul, and Clancy lower a bucket. Abba Jacob in the Well. Marilyn Nelson. SP-NelsM
Baker's boy delivers loaves, The. Mary Effie Lee Newsome. CDC; ShDr
Balance. Marilyn Nelson. SP-NelsM
Balances. Nikki Giovanni. SP-GiovN
Balboa, the Entertainer. Amiri Baraka. SP-BaraA
Bali Hai Calls Mama. Marilyn Nelson. SP-NelsM
Ballad: "I know my love is true." Paul Laurence Dunbar. CP-DunbP
Ballad for Ashes. Audre Lorde. CP-LordA
Ballad for Phillis Wheatley. Margaret Abigail Walker. CP-WalkM
Ballad for Stirling Street, A. Sonia Sanchez. BrTr
Ballad from Childhood. Audre Lorde. CP-LordA; SP-LordA
Ballad of Aunt Geneva, The. Marilyn Nelson. GT; SP-NelsM
Ballad of Badmen. Owen Dodson. FB
Ballad of Birmingham. Dudley Randall. BPo; BrTr
Ballad of Booker T. Langston Hughes. CP-HughL
Ballad of Charlie James, The. Ishmael Reed. CP-ReedI
Ballad of Gin Mary. Langston Hughes. CP-HughL
Ballad of Harry Moore. Langston Hughes. CP-HughL
Ballad of Joe, The. Sterling A. Brown. CP-BrowS
Ballad of Little Sallie. Langston Hughes. CP-HughL
Ballad of Margie Polite. Langston Hughes. CP-HughL
Ballad of Mary's Son. Langston Hughes. CP-HughL
Ballad of Nat Turner, The. Robert Hayden. BALP; BPo; CP-HaydR
Ballad of Negro History, A. Langston Hughes. CP-HughL
Ballad of Ozie Powell. Langston Hughes. CP-HughL
Ballad of Remembrance, A. Robert Hayden. AmNP; BPo; CP-HaydR; ESEAA; IDB; NAAAL; PoBA
Ballad of Roosevelt. Langston Hughes. CP-HughL
Ballad of Rudolph Reed, The. Gwendolyn Brooks. SP-BrooG
Ballad of Sam Solomon. Langston Hughes. CP-HughL
Ballad of Sue Ellen Westerfield, The. Robert Hayden. CP-HaydR; ESEAA; Klds
Ballad of the Black Sheep. Langston Hughes. CP-HughL
Ballad of the Brown Girl, The. Countee Cullen. CP-CullC
Ballad of the Brown Girl. Alice Walker. CP-WalkA
Ballad of the Fool. Langston Hughes. CP-HughL
Ballad of the Fortune Teller. Langston Hughes. CP-HughL; SP-HughL
Ballad of the Free, The. Margaret Abigail Walker. CP-WalkM
Ballad of the Girl Whose Name Is Mud. Langston Hughes. CP-HughL; SP-HughL
Ballad of the Gypsy. Langston Hughes. CP-HughL; SP-HughL

Ballad of the Hoppy-Toad. Margaret Abigail Walker. BlSi; CP-WalkM; FB; NBV; TtW

Ballad of the Killer Boy. Langston Hughes. CP-HughL

Ballad of the Landlord. Langston Hughes. NAAAL; SP-HughL   *Fr.* Montage of a Dream Deferred. CP-HughL

Ballad of the Light-Eyed Little Girl, The. Gwendolyn Brooks. SP-BrooG

Ballad of the Man Who's Gone. Langston Hughes. CP-HughL; SP-HughL

Ballad of the Miser. Langston Hughes. CP-HughL

Ballad of the Pawnbroker. Langston Hughes. CP-HughL

Ballad of the Seven Songs. Langston Hughes. CP-HughL

Ballad of the Sinner. Langston Hughes. CP-HughL

Ballad of the Two Thieves. Langston Hughes. CP-HughL

Ballad of Walter White. Langston Hughes. CP-HughL

Ballade: "By Mystic's banks I held my dream." Paul Laurence Dunbar. CP-DunbP

Ballade des Belles Milatraisses. Rosalie Jonas. BlSi

Ballads of Lenin. Langston Hughes. CP-HughL

Banana leaves are burning. "Containing Communism." Charlie Cobb. PoBA

Bananas ripe and green, and ginger-root. Claude McKay. *See* The Tropics in New York.

Bananas ripe and green, and gingerroot. The Tropics in New York. Claude McKay. AfAmPo; AmNP; CrDW; GT; PoBA

Band of Gideon roam the sky, The. Joseph Seamon Cotter, Sr. BANP; CDC; TtW

Band plays an intro. Lady's Way. Reuben Jackson. GT

Banjo done commence de shune, De. A Virginia Reel. Paul Laurence Dunbar. CP-DunbP

Banjo Player, The. Fenton Johnson. BANP; TtW

   ("But I fear that I am a failure. Last night a woman called me a troubadour. What is a troubadour?") (LL)   Klds

Banjo Song, A. Paul Laurence Dunbar. CP-DunbP

Banking Coal. Jean Toomer. CP-ToomJ

Banking Potatoes. Herbert Asquith. NAAAL

Banneker. Rita Dove. ESEAA; SP-DoveR

Bantamweight King of, The. Petite Kid Everett. Ishmael Reed. CP-ReedI

Baptism. Alvin Aubert. BkSV

Baptism. Claude McKay. SP-McKaC

Baptism. Alice Walker. CP-WalkA

Bar. Langston Hughes. SP-HughL   *Fr.* Montage of a Dream Deferred. CP-HughL

Barcelona. Claude McKay. SP-McKaC

Bare pecan tree, A. Haiku: "Bare pecan tree, A." Etheridge Knight. ESEAA; TtW

Barefoot Blues. Langston Hughes. CP-HughL

Baroness and the Black Musician, The. Larry Neal. BlFi

Barren. Audre Lorde. CP-LordA; SP-LordA

Barren cross-ties of penny-whistle twigs. Affirmation. Helen Armstead Johnson. AmNP

Barren days come, too, The. (LL)   Wisdom Cometh with the Years. Countee Cullen. CP-CullC; Klds

Barricades hammered into place. Michael S. Harper. PoBA; SP-HarpM

Barrier, The. Paul Laurence Dunbar. CP-DunbP

Barrier, The. Claude McKay. BANP; SP-McKaC

Bars Fight, August 28, 1746. Lucy Terry Prince. TtW

Bar[']s Fight[, August 28, 1746]. Lucy Terry. BPo; BlSi; CrDW; EBAP; NAAAL

Bars on Eighth Avenue in Harlem, The. Harlem Gallery: From the Inside. Larry Neal. BPo; NBV

Bartender, make it straight and make it two—. An Ex-Judge at the Bar. Melvin Beaunearus Tolson. NAAAL

Bartow Black. Timothy Thomas Fortune. AAP

Baseball. Christopher Stanard. SpiFl

Bathed Is My Blood. Oliver La Grone. NNP

Battle Ground. Langston Hughes. CP-HughL

Battle of Saratoga (Springs) Revisited, The. Michael S. Harper. SP-HarpM

Battle of the Stars. Adah Isaacs Menken. CBWP-1

Battle Report. Bob Kaufman. AmNP

Battle waged strong, The. The Release. Adah Isaacs Menken. CBWP-1

Battle waxed (battle wax, good night!), The. War Poem. Amiri Baraka. SP-BaraA

Battling gods of Milton's epic page, The. Albery Allson Whitman. *Fr.* Leelah Misled. EBAP

Bay breeze, The. Salt. George Barlow. GT

Bazaar. Audre Lorde. CP-LordA

Be Active. Frances Ellen Watkins Harper. CP-HarpF

Be-Bop Boys. Langston Hughes. *Fr.* Montage of a Dream Deferred. CP-HughL

Be Cool, Baby. Rob Penny. PoBA

Be Daedalus. Nanina Alba. PoBA

Be ever our desires. (LL)   Advice to Young Ladies. Ann Plato. AAP; TtW

Be going home. (LL)   .05. Ishmael Reed. CP-ReedI; ESEAA

Be good! / Be good! (LL)   Silhouette. Langston Hughes. CP-HughL; SP-HughL

Be me a Pharaoh. For Us, Who Dare Not Dare. Maya Angelou. CP-AngeM; SP-AngeM

Be my stillborn son my son. Mulatto Lullaby. Ralph Dickey. ESEAA

Be never. (LL)   No Regrets. Langston Hughes. CP-HughL; SP-HughL

Be nobody's darling; / Be an outcast. Outcast. Alice Walker. CP-WalkA; NAAAL; TtW

Be quiet awful woman. Calming Kali. Lucille Clifton. SP-ClifL

Be Quiet, Go Away. Wanda Coleman. NAAAL

Be Somebody Fragrant. Peter Harris. IHS

Be still, heart, cease those measured strokes. The Foolish Heart. Countee Cullen. CP-CullC

Be Sunday. (LL)   Summer Evening (Calumet Avenue). Langston Hughes. CP-HughL; SP-HughL

Be who you are and will be. For Each of You. Audre Lorde. CP-LordA; SP-LordA

Be with Me. Jean Toomer. CP-ToomJ

Be You. Norman Jordan. NBV

Beads around / my neck / Mt. Kenya away. African Images, Glimpses from a Tiger's Back. Alice Walker. CP-WalkA

Beale Street. Langston Hughes. CP-HughL; SP-HughL

Beale Street Blues. William Christopher Handy. CrDW; NAAAL

Beale Street Love. Langston Hughes. CP-HughL

Beale Street, Memphis. Thurmond Snyder. NNP

Beams. Audre Lorde. CP-LordA; ESEAA

Bean Eaters, The. Gwendolyn Brooks. BlSi; Crnst; ESEAA; PoBA; SP-BrooG

   ("Dolls and cloths, tobacco crumbs, vases and fringes.") (LL)   Klds

Bear Gulch Road. Al Young. CP-YounA

Bear in mind. Drum. Langston Hughes. SP-HughL

Bear the rhythm of. Sonia Sanchez. SP-SancS

Bearded "TEACH" : walking. pissing thots. on church, The. Pome. For Weird. Hearts. and All. Ahmed Legraham Alhamisi. BlFi

Beast. Alice Walker. CP-WalkA

Beast & Burden: Seven Improvisations, The. Yusef Komunyakaa. SP-KomuY

Beast Section, The. Welton Smith. *Fr.* Malcolm. BlFi

Beast with Chrome Teeth, The. Thurmond Snyder. NNP

Beast's backing up. his ass, The. The Beautiful Day #9. Alfred B. Spellman. BlFi

Beat the drums of tragedy for me. Fantasy in Purple. Langston Hughes. BANP; CDC; CP-HughL; SP-HughL

Beating a way for the rising sun. (LL)   The Day-Breakers [or Daybreakers]. Arna Bontemps. AmNP; CDC; IDB; PoBA

Beating hearts / Untidily wrapped in raw flesh, nestled in the rain on highways. Untitle. Kuwasi Balagon. BlFi

Beating wind with a stick. Chair Gallows. Yusef Komunyakaa. SP-KomuY

Beaufort, fair Beaufort, thou art a favored spot. General Robert Smalls. Josephine D. Henderson Heard. CBWP-4

Beaumont to Detroit: 1943. Langston Hughes. CP-HughL

Beautiful, also, are the souls of my people. (LL)   My People. Langston Hughes. CDC; CP-HughL; SP-HughL

Beautiful Black Men. Nikki Giovanni. BPo; BrTr; NAAAL; SP-GiovN

Beautiful, BLACK womanhood; / reaching inward to open the soul. Death of Days and Nights of Life. Clarence Franklin. BlFi

Beautiful Black Women. Amiri Baraka. BPo

Beautiful Day #9, The. Alfred B. Spellman. BlFi

Beautiful Sea, The. Mary E. Tucker. CBWP-1

Beautiful, The! what is not perfect here below. Mary E. Tucker. CBWP-1

Beauty. Langston Hughes. CP-HughL

Beauty. Octavia Beatrice Wynbush. ShDr

Beauty and the Beast. Rita Dove. ESEAA; SP-DoveR

Beauty of Milwaukee cold with rain, The. Al Young. CP-YounA

Beauty Shoppe. Marilyn Nelson. SP-NelsM

Beauty so sudden for that time of year. (LL)   November Cotton Flower. Jean Toomer. CDC; CP-ToomJ

Bebopper in his soul, he sends, A. Dexter Gordon at Keystone Korner. Al Young. CP-YounA

Because a burning sword notches both of my doorposts. Sequelae. Audre Lorde. CP-LordA

Because beer tingles. Beer Drops. Melba Joyce Boyd. BlSi

Because I had loved so deeply. Compensation. Paul Laurence Dunbar. AmNP; BPo; CP-DunbP

Because I have wandered long through my own darkness. "Stephany." *Fr.* Moving Deep. BrTr

Because I know deep in my own heart. Song. Pauli Murray. BlSi

Because I love to live. (LL) The Lesson. Maya Angelou. CP-AngeM; SP-AngeM

Because love they say / never dies. (LL) Rose Solitude. Jayne Cortez. SP-CortJ; TtW

Because man is not virtuous in himself. Tribute. Countee Cullen. CP-CullC

Because my mouth / Is wide with laughter. Minstrel Man. Langston Hughes. CP-HughL

Because no man would taste you. To Thelma Who Worried Because I Couldn't Cook. Lucille Clifton. SP-ClifL

Because there was a man somewhere in a candystripe silk shirt. Homage to the Empress of the Blues. Robert Hayden. CP-HaydR; ESEAA; NAAAL; PoBA; TtW

Because we go on / loving. (LL) Grand Army Plaza. June Jordan. SP-JordJ

Because women are expected to keep silent about. On Stripping Bark from Myself. Alice Walker. CP-WalkA; NAAAL

Because you are to me a song. Passing Love. Langston Hughes. CP-HughL

Because you love me I have much achieved. Encouraged. Paul Laurence Dunbar. CP-DunbP

Beck'ning vision, fair, illusive, sweet!, A. (LL) Ambition. Henrietta Cordelia Ray. CBWP-3

Bed calls. i sit in the dark in the living room. Bedtime Story. Wanda Coleman. NAAAL

Bed Time. Langston Hughes. *Fr.* Seven Moments of Love. CP-HughL

Bedtime Story. Wanda Coleman. NAAAL

Bedtime Story. Nayo-Barbara Watkins. NBV

Bedtime's come fu' little boys. Lullaby. Paul Laurence Dunbar. CP-DunbP

Bee hit sip some honey f'om de matermony vine, De. Song. Paul Laurence Dunbar. CP-DunbP

Bee that was searching for sweets one day, A. Two Songs. Paul Laurence Dunbar. CP-DunbP

Beehive. Jean Toomer. CP-ToomJ; GT; IDB; PoBA

Been in the Storm So Long. *Unknown.* NAAAL

Been workin' on de levee. Mississippi Levee. Langston Hughes. CP-HughL

BEEP ... bEEP / joy ... / BEEP! (LL) Christmas 1959 Et Cetera. Gerald William Barrax. Klds

Beep Beep Poem, The. Nikki Giovanni. SP-GiovN

Beer Drops. Melba Joyce Boyd. BlSi

Bees, The. Audre Lorde. CP-LordA; SP-LordA

Bees work, The. Black Workers. Langston Hughes. CP-HughL

Beethoven. Henrietta Cordelia Ray. CBWP-3

Beetles, / noisy bumble bees. Come Visit My Garden. Tom Dent. NNP

Before a Painting. James Weldon Johnson. GT

Before / and After. Jewel C. Latimore. JB

Before I cry. (LL) Ultimatum: Kid to Kid. Langston Hughes. CP-HughL

Before I destroy us. (LL) Oya. Audre Lorde. CP-LordA; SP-LordA

Before i travel. Sonia Sanchez. SP-SancS

Before me / taut pallets of smoke. Clinton. Sterling Plumpp. BkSV

Before she let me love her. Brief Encounter. Norman J. Loftis. SpiFl

Before the early dawn / Bops bright. (LL) Chord. Langston Hughes. SP-HughL

Before the Feast of Shushan. Anne Spencer. BANP; BlSi; NAAAL; ShDr

Before the mind can soar. (LL) The Art of a Poet. George Moses Horton. EBAP; SP-HortG

Before the world, I hold that none of these. Albery Allson Whitman. AAP

Before we shall both be slain. (LL) Meet. Audre Lorde. CP-LordA

Before You Leave. Ai. GT

Beg Song. Yusef Komunyakaa. SP-KomuY

Beggar Boy. Langston Hughes. CP-HughL

Begin to talk / of HYenaaaAAS. (LL) Hospital/Poem. Sonia Sanchez. BPo; PoBA

Beginning by Value. Christopher Gilbert. GT

Beginning for New Beginnings, A. Angela Jackson. TtW

Beginning of a Long Poem on Why I Burned the City, The. Lawrence Benford. NBP

Beginnings. Robert Hayden. CP-HaydR

Behind a Descartes Bumpersticker. Marilyn Nelson. *Fr.* The Plotinus Suite. SP-NelsM

Behind him a picture. Class Room. Virginia A. Houston. ShDr

Behind his dinner jacket. He's Doing Natural Life. Conyus. PoBA

Behind my side of the headboard. Lobengula: Having a Son at 38. Nikky Finney. SpiFl

Behind the Arras. Paul Laurence Dunbar. CP-DunbP

Behind you, now. Schwerner, Chaney, Goodman. Raymond R. Patterson. NBV

Behold the lilies of the field. Frances Ellen Watkins Harper. CP-HarpF

Behold young Raphael coming back. Raphael. Priscilla Jane Thompson. CBWP-2

Beige sailors with large noses. Seashore through Dark Glasses (Atlantic City). Langston Hughes. CP-HughL; SP-HughL

Bein' Back Home. Paul Laurence Dunbar. CP-DunbP

Being a colored poet. Jacket Notes. Ishmael Reed. CP-ReedI

Being always / Poor. (LL) Ennui. Langston Hughes. CP-HughL; SP-HughL

Being and Nothingness. Nikki Giovanni. SP-GiovN

Being beat down, / I would fly away on the wings of a hawk. Nightdreams (Black). Tom Dent. TtW

Being black in America. Lonely Eagles. Marilyn Nelson. ESEAA; SP-NelsM

Being neither white nor black? (LL) Cross. Langston Hughes. AmNP; BANP; CP-HughL; GT; IDB; PoBA; SP-HughL

Being Old. Langston Hughes. CP-HughL

Being property once myself. Lucille Clifton. SP-ClifL

Being walkers with the dawn and morning. Walkers with the Dawn. Langston Hughes. CP-HughL

Being you, you cut your poetry from wood. The Egg Boiler. Gwendolyn Brooks. PoBA; TtW

Belated wanderer of the ways of spring. To a Violet Found on All Saints' Day. Paul Laurence Dunbar. CP-DunbP

Belgrade moon, where are you. Al Young. CP-YounA

Believe, Believe. Bob Kaufman. SP-KaufB

Believe in this. Young apple seeds. Believe, Believe. Bob Kaufman. SP-KaufB

Believe it love / believe. Roman Poem Number Fourteen. June Jordan. SP-JordJ

Believe me, I knew you, though faintly, and I loved, I loved you / All. (LL) The Mother. Gwendolyn Brooks. CrDW; ESEAA; NAAAL; TtW

Believe my love / believe / believe it. (LL) Roman Poem Number Fourteen. June Jordan. SP-JordJ

Belinda's Petition. Rita Dove. SP-DoveR

Belle de grâce et belle de jeunesse. A Malvina. B. Valcour. TtW

Belligerent and beautiful as a trapped ibis. Parting. Audre Lorde. CP-LordA

Bells. bells. bells. / let the bells ring. Earth Mother. Sonia Sanchez. *Fr.* Past. SP-SancS

Bells of St. Michael. Mary Weston Fordham. CBWP-2

Bells, the cannons, the houses black with crepe, The. The Abduction. Rita Dove. SP-DoveR

Bells Toll Kindly, The. Langston Hughes. CP-HughL

Belly Song. Etheridge Knight. BkSV; SP-KnigE

("That nearly swallowed you— / and me too.") (LL) TtW

Beloved, / In what other lives or lands. Refusal. Maya Angelou. CP-AngeM; SP-AngeM

Belsen, Day of Liberation. Robert Hayden. CP-HaydR

Belshazzer's Feast. Eloise Bibb. CBWP-4

Bend your back when I say "Go." *African-American Oral Tradition.* GetYo

Beneath its breast my mother lies asleep. (LL) My Mother. Claude McKay. GT; NAAAL; SP-McKaC

Beneath my head. (LL) Fired. Langston Hughes. CP-HughL; SP-HughL

Beneath spring snow. (LL) Late-Winter Blues and Promises of Love. Houston A., Jr. Baker. TtW

Beneath the better part. (LL) Apple Dumplings. Mary E. Tucker. CBWP-1

Beneath the burden of our joy. Fifteenth Amendment. Frances Ellen Watkins Harper. CP-HarpF

Beneath the carving drag of wood. Oaxaca. Audre Lorde. CP-LordA; SP-LordA

Beneath the grain. No Strings Attached. Al Young. CP-YounA

Beneath the moon. (LL) Nostalgia. Marjorie Marshall. ShDr

Beneath the poinsettia's red in war December. (LL) Flame-Heart. Claude McKay. AmNP; BALP; BANP; CDC

Beneath the pointsettia's red in warm December. Claude McKay. *See* Flame-Heart.

Benediction. Donald Jeffrey Hayes. AmNP

Benediction. Bob Kaufman. SP-KaufB

Benefits of Sorrow. Lizelia Augusta Jenkins Moorer. CBWP-3

Benevolent step / mother America. (LL) Hymn for Lanie Poo. Amiri Baraka. SP-BaraA

Benign Neglect / Mississippi, 1970. Primus St. John. PoBA

Benin Bronze. Samuel Allen. Crnst

Benison given. Unused, A. The Singer Will Not Sing. Maya Angelou. CP-AngeM; SP-AngeM

Benjamin Banneker Helps to Build a City. Jay Wright. Crnst

Bent on our conjugating business. (LL) Bloodbirth. Audre Lorde. CP-LordA; SP-LordA

Bereft. Josephine D. Henderson Heard. CBWP-4

Berkeley Pome. Al Young. CP-YounA

Berlin again after chemotherapy. Restoration. Audre Lorde. CP-LordA

Berlin Is Hard on Colored Girls. Audre Lorde. CP-LordA

Bernice said she wanted. Ballad of the Killer Boy. Langston Hughes. CP-HughL

Beside our way the streams are dried. To Booker T. Washington. Paul Laurence Dunbar. CP-DunbP

Beside you, prone. Prelude to a Parting. Maya Angelou. CP-AngeM; SP-AngeM

Bessie. Sterling A. Brown. CP-BrowS

Bessie Altmann is home again. April Rape. Marilyn Nelson. SP-NelsM

Best Loved of Africa. Margaret Else Danner. PoBA

Betancourt. Amiri Baraka. SP-BaraA

Bête Noire. Harryette Mullen. TtW

Better. For they existed. (LL) Ailey, Baldwin, Floyd, Killens, and Mayfield. Maya Angelou. CP-AngeM; IHS

Better in the quiet night. Langston Hughes. CP-HughL

Better save me some. (LL) A Message for Langston. "Kush." NBV

Better than nobody / In this lonely / Land. (LL) Desert. Langston Hughes. CP-HughL; Klds; SP-HughL

Betty's Ball Blues. Ishmael Reed. CP-ReedI

Between Days. Yusef Komunyakaa. ESEAA

Between Me and Anyone Who Can Understand. Sharon Scott. JB

Between Ourselves. Audre Lorde. CP-LordA

Between the little clouds of heaven. Pastoral. Langston Hughes. CP-HughL

Between the world and me. The Meaning of Protest. Michael S. Harper. SP-HarpM

Between the World and Me. Richard Wright. AmNP; IDB; PoBA; SSLK; TtW

Between the world, and me, and you. (LL) The Meaning of Protest. Michael S. Harper. SP-HarpM

Between two rivers. Island: "Between two rivers." Langston Hughes. *Fr.* Lenox Avenue Mural. AmNP; SP-HughL *Fr.* Montage of a Dream Deferred. CP-HughL

Between us, always, loved one. Troubled Water. Langston Hughes. CP-HughL

Beverly Hills, Chicago. Gwendolyn Brooks. ESEAA; SP-BrooG

Beverly's Poem. Audre Lorde. CP-LordA

Bewailing mid the ruthless wave. The Poet's Feeble Petition. George Moses Horton. CP-HortG

Beware: Do Not Read This Poem. Ishmael Reed. BPo; PoBA

("Space in the lives of their friends, A.") (LL) CP-ReedI; GT

("Tonite, *thriller* was / abt an old woman, so vain she.") CP-ReedI; GT

Beyond the cornfields and the wood. Parted. Paul Laurence Dunbar. CP-DunbP

Beyond the Nigger. Sterling Plumpp. PoBA

Beyond the people. The Escape Artist. Kevin Young. GT

Beyond the turning sea's far foam. At War. Russell Atkins. AmNP

Beyond the years the answer lies. Paul Laurence Dunbar. CP-DunbP

Beyond What. Alice Walker. CP-WalkA

Biafra. L. V. Mack. PoBA

Biafra Blues. Michael S. Harper. SP-HarpM

Bible, The. Lizelia Augusta Jenkins Moorer. CBWP-3

Bible Belt. Langston Hughes. CP-HughL

Bible Defence of Slavery. Frances Ellen Watkins Harper. CP-HarpF

Bible Study. Gloria C. Oden. ESEAA; GT

Bicentennial Poem #21,000,000. Audre Lorde. CP-LordA

Bid me from servitude ascend, / Forever! (LL) The Slave's Complaint. George Moses Horton. AAP; CrDW; EBAP; SP-HortG

Bien loin de tes parens, sur la rive étrangère. Un Frère au Tombeau de Son Frère. Armand Lanusse. EBAP; TtW

Big Apple Circus. Audre Lorde. CP-LordA

Big Bell in Zion, The. Theodore Henry Shackleford. BANP

Big Ben, I'm gonna bust you bang up side the wall! Daybreak. Langston Hughes. *Fr.* Seven Moments of Love. CP-HughL

Big Boy came. Catch. Langston Hughes. CP-HughL; SP-HughL

Big Buddy, Big Buddy. Langston Hughes. CP-HughL

Big Fanny and stromin vinnie deal. Suicide. Bob Kaufman. SP-KaufB

Big Gate, The. Elma Stuckey. TtW

Big Harpe, Little Harpe. Theory of Evil. Robert Hayden. CP-HaydR

Big House Revisited, The. Tony Medina. SpiFl

Big Jess fired on the Alabama Central. Break of Day. Sterling A. Brown. CP-BrowS

Big John. Norman J. Loftis. SpiFl

Big John Henry. Margaret Abigail Walker. CP-WalkM

Big Mac, french fries, Cokes and ketchup to go. (LL) For Janet Kafka, Dead at 30. Al Young. CP-YounA

Big Momma. Haki R. Madhubuti. BPo; TtW

Big muddy daddy my daddys gris-gris to the world, A. Mud Water Shango. "Weatherly." GT; NBV

Big ocean-waving, woman-pulling moon. Al Young. CP-YounA

Big 'possum clime little tree. Plantation Proverbs. Joel Chandler Harris. CrDW

Big ships shudder. Worker's Song. Maya Angelou. CP-AngeM

Big Sur. Langston Hughes. CP-HughL

Big Sur. Al Young. CP-YounA

Big-Timer, The. Langston Hughes. CP-HughL

Big yellow woman. Laurel Street, 1950. Dorothy Perry Thompson. SpiFl

Big Zeb Johnson. Everett Hoagland. GT

Bigger thomas / wasn't suppose. The Big House Revisited. Tony Medina. SpiFl

Biggest Fisherman, The. Bob Kaufman. SP-KaufB

Bill / exists. A Personality Sketch: Bill. Ronda M. Davis. JB

Billie. Al Young. CP-YounA

Billie Holiday's burned voice. Canary. Rita Dove. ESEAA

Billion dollar behind. (LL) Aunt Agnes Hatcher Tells. Lucille Clifton. SP-ClifL

Billy Eckstine, now I. Soul Proprietorship. Ishmael Reed. CP-ReedI

Biological Didn't Bother. Shaquille, O'Neal. CtF

Bird delicious to the taste, A. A Rebus. *Unknown.* CP-WheaP

Bird Frau, The. Rita Dove. SP-DoveR

Bird in Orbit. Langston Hughes. *Fr.* Ask Your Mama; 12 Moods for Jazz. CP-HughL

Bird in the Cage, The. Mary Effie Lee Newsome. ShDr

Bird is lost, The. Yardbird's Skull. Owen Dodson. AmNP; IDB; PoBA

"Bird Lives": Charles Parker. Michael S. Harper. SP-HarpM

Bird of the woodland, sing me a song. To the Mock-Bird. Mary Weston Fordham. CBWP-2

Bird Song, The. Mrs. Henry Linden. CBWP-4

Bird with Painted Wings. Bob Kaufman. SP-KaufB; TtW

Birds and sunlight. Yellow. De Leon Harrison. PoBA

Birds flew south, The. Hampton, Virginia. Nikki Giovanni. SP-GiovN

Birds flit / in the blue palms, The. Village Blues. Michael S. Harper. SP-HarpM

Birds flying / away. (LL) Roman Poem Number Five. June Jordan. SP-JordJ

Birds follow the sun / rain coming on / we drive South. Lady's Days. Larry Neal. NBV

Birds on a Powerline. Herbert Asquith. NAAAL

Birds on a Powerline. Yusef Komunyakaa. SP-KomuY

Birmingham. Margaret Abigail Walker. CP-WalkM; PoBA

Birmingham, 1963. Margaret Abigail Walker. CP-WalkM

Birmingham 1963. Raymond R. Patterson. PoBA; TtW

Birmingham Sunday. Langston Hughes. CP-HughL

Birth. Langston Hughes. CP-HughL

Birth in a Narrow Room, The. Gwendolyn Brooks. BlSi

Birth of a new world, The. (LL) Childhood. Sharan Strange. GT

Birth of an idea is violent, The. Afrocentricity. Niama Leslie JoAnn Williams. SpiFl

Birth of Jesus, The. Josephine D. Henderson Heard. CBWP-4

Birth of John Henry, The. Melvin Beaunearus Tolson. BPo; NAAAL

Birth of Time, The. Josephine D. Henderson Heard. CBWP-4

Birthday greetings / From a friend. Birthday Wishes to a Physician. Lizelia Augusta Jenkins Moorer. CBWP-3

Birthday Memorial to Seventh Street, A. Audre Lorde. CP-LordA; SP-LordA

Birthday Poem. Etheridge Knight. SP-KnigE

Birthday Poem. Al Young. CP-YounA

Birthday Wishes to a Husband. Lizelia Augusta Jenkins Moorer. CBWP-3

Birthday Wishes to a Minister of the Gospel. Lizelia Augusta Jenkins Moorer. CBWP-3

Birthday Wishes to a Physician. Lizelia Augusta Jenkins Moorer. CBWP-3

Bishop James A. Shorter. Josephine D. Henderson Heard. CBWP-4

Bishop of Atlanta: Ray Charles, The. Julian Bond. AmNP

Bishop seduces the world with his voice, The. The Bishop of Atlanta: Ray Charles. Julian Bond. AmNP

Bitch. Ishmael Reed. CP-ReedI

Biting Back. Patricia Smith. GT

Bitter black bitterness. Poem (No Name No. 2). Nikki Giovanni. SP-GiovN

Bitter bullshit rotten white parts / alone, The. (LL) Leroy. Amiri Baraka. BPo; PoBA

Bitter Chocolate. Ishmael Reed. CP-ReedI

Bitter Fruit of the Tree. Sterling A. Brown. CP-BrowS

Bitter note makes the song so sweet, The. (LL) Detroit 1958. Al Young. CP-YounA; ESEAA

Bitter River, The. Langston Hughes. CP-HughL

Bitter Spring Again, The. Al Young. CP-YounA

Bitter tears are stone, The. Anniversary. Audre Lorde. CP-LordA

Bitterness of days like these we know, The. Salutamus. Sterling A. Brown. CDC; CP-BrowS

Bizarre? / mysterioso? Thelonious. Reuben Jackson. ESEAA

Black All Day. Raymond R. Patterson. PoBA

Black / and live. (LL) After Kent State. Lucille Clifton. SP-ClifL

Black and tan—yeah, black and tan. Dancing Gal. Frank Marshall Davis. FB

Black and White. Umar Abd Rahim Hasson. BrTr

Black Angel, The. Michael S. Harper. SP-HarpM

Black Angel / Doing what she's gotta do. The Singer. Gerald William Barrax. ESEAA

Black Art. Amiri Baraka. BPo; BlFi; ESEAA; NAAAL; SP-BaraA

Black / As the gentle night. Me and My Song. Langston Hughes. CP-HughL

Black Baby. Anita Scott Coleman. ShDr

Black banana / can make you high, A. From the Files of Agent 22. Ishmael Reed. CP-ReedI

Black Bourgeoisie. Amiri Baraka. BPo; ESEAA

Black boy / let me get up from the white man's table of fifty sounds. Melvin Beaunearus Tolson. PoBA

Black Boys Play the Classics. Toi Derricotte. SpiFl

Black brother, think you life so sweet. Time to Die. Ray Garfield Dandridge. BANP; PoBA

Black chest hairs, soft sudden mass. Lines Muttered in Sleep. Rita Dove. SP-DoveR

Black Christ, The. Countee Cullen. CP-CullC

Black Christ, The. Haki R. Madhubuti. TtW

Black Church on Sunday. Joseph M., Jr. Mosley. NBP

Black Cock, The. Ishmael Reed. CP-ReedI

Black Crispus Attucks taught. Dark Symphony. Melvin Beaunearus Tolson. AmNP; BALP; NAAAL; SSLK

Black Crown, The. Langston Hughes. CP-HughL

Black Dada Nihilismus. Amiri Baraka. SP-BaraA; TtW

Black Dancers. Langston Hughes. CP-HughL

Black Draftee from Dixie, The. Carrie Williams Clifford. BlSi

Black Ethics. Sterling Plumpp. TtW

Black Faces. Anita Scott Coleman. ShDr

Black Finger, The. Angelina Weld Grimké. AmNP; PoBA; ShDr; TtW ("I have just seen a beautiful thing.") NAAAL

Black Gal. Langston Hughes. CP-HughL

Black girl black girl. Blackberry Sweet. Dudley Randall. NBP; PoBA

Black girl going, A. Generation II. Audre Lorde. CP-LordA; SP-LordA

Black Gold, blackgold . . . aint no oil. Blackgoldblueswoman. Kirk Hall. NBV

Black Henry. Tejumola Ologboni. NBV

Black history. The Living Truth. Sterling Plumpp. PoBA

Black human photograph: apple tree. (LL) History as Apple Tree. Michael S. Harper. SP-HarpM

Black Intellectual, The. Kenneth A. McClane. TtW

Black Is a Soul. Joseph Blanco White. IDB; PoBA

Black is beautiful. Ron Welburn. NBV

Black Is Best. Larry Thompson. PoBA

Black is not / all inclusive. A Poem Looking for a Reader. Haki R. Madhubuti. BrTr

Black is; slavery was; I am. This Child Is the Mother. Gloria C. Oden. BlSi

Black is the first nail I ever stepped on. Negritude. James A. Emanuel. BPo; IHS

Black is what the prisons are. The African Affair. Bruce McM. Wright. AmNP; PoBA

Black Jam for Dr. Negro. Mari E. Evans. BPo; PoBA

Black Joe Harmon has lost his job. Episode. Sterling A. Brown. CP-BrowS

Black Judgements. Nikki Giovanni. BrTr

Black like me. Langston Hughes. See Dream Variations.

Black like the depths of my Africa. (LL) Negro. Langston Hughes. CP-HughL; SP-HughL

Black Lotus. Alicia Loy Johnson. NBP

Black Madonna, The. Albert Rice. CDC

Black Magdalens. Countee Cullen. BANP; CP-CullC

Black Magic. Dudley Randall. See Blackberry Sweet.

Black Magic. Sonia Sanchez. BPo; BrTr; SP-SancS

Black Magic. Margaret Abigail Walker. CP-WalkM

Black Mail. Alice Walker. CP-WalkA

Black Majesty. Countee Cullen. CP-CullC; PoBA

Black Mammies. John Wesley Holloway. BANP

Black Man, A. Sam Cornish. PoBA

Black Man, 13th Floor. James A. Emanuel. NBV

Black Man Go Back To The Old Country. High Modes: Vision as Ritual: Confirmation. Michael S. Harper. NBV; SP-HarpM

Black man: I'm a black man. Brother John. Michael S. Harper. SP-HarpM

Black man o' mine. Anne Spencer. Crnst

Black Man Speaks, The. Langston Hughes. CP-HughL

Black man straddling the unbalanced scale. Split Standard. Hart Leroi Bibbs. BlFi

Black Man Talks of Reaping, A. Arna Bontemps. AmNP; BANP; BPo; CDC; FB; IDB; Klds; NAAAL; PoBA; SSLK; TtW

Black Manhood: Toward a Definition. Haki R. Madhubuti. Crnst

Black Man's Feast. Sarah Webster Fabio. PoBA

Black Maria. Langston Hughes. CP-HughL; SP-HughL

Black Mary Janes, white-ruffled sox. Yesterday. Mary Weems. SpiFl

Black men? (LL) Black Woman. Naomi Long Madgett. GT

Black men are oaks cut down. Debridement. Michael S. Harper. SP-HarpM

Black men are the tall trees that remain. Portraiture. Anita Scott Coleman. ShDr

Black men bleeding to death inside themselves. Eulogy for Alvin Frost. Audre Lorde. CP-LordA

Black men holding up the earth. The Soldiers of the Dusk. Fenton Johnson. EBAP

Black men with outasight afros. (LL) Beautiful Black Men. Nikki Giovanni. BPo; BrTr; NAAAL; SP-GiovN

Black Monday: *I must go down to de ole man.* (LL) "Emperor": Shields Green: Fugitives. Michael S. Harper. SP-HarpM

Black Mother Woman. Audre Lorde. CP-LordA; SP-LordA

Black Music Man. Lethonia Gee. BlFi

Black Narcissus. Gerald William Barrax. Klds; PoBA

Black Ode. Maya Angelou. CP-AngeM; SP-AngeM

Black Orpheus. Frederick, Jr. Bryant. BlFi

Black Panther. Langston Hughes. CP-HughL

Black Paramour. Margaret Abigail Walker. CP-WalkM

Black pendulum, a dark tree unexplained, inexplicable, A. No No, Bad Daddy. Marilyn Nelson. SP-NelsM

Black People! Amiri Baraka. BPo

Black people fishing the causeway. Florida. Audre Lorde. CP-LordA

BLACK PEOPLE THINK. Awareness. Haki R. Madhubuti. BrTr; PoBA

Black People: This Is Our Destiny. Amiri Baraka. TtW

Black people, we rainclouds. We Rainclouds. Marvin, Jr. Wyche. AmNP

Black Pierrot, A. Langston Hughes. CP-HughL; SP-HughL

Black poems will / feed Black minds but. Just Us. Kwame Alexander. CtF

Black Poet Leaps to His Death, A. Etheridge Knight. SP-KnigE

Black Poet, White Critic. Dudley Randall. BPo

Black Poets should live—not leap. For Black Poets Who Think of Suicide. Etheridge Knight. NAAAL; PoBA; SP-KnigE

Black Power. Nikki Giovanni. BrTr; SP-GiovN

Black Power. Raymond R. Patterson. NBV

Black Power. Alvin Saxon. PoBA

Black Power Poem. Ishmael Reed. BPo; CP-ReedI

Black Pride. Margaret Goss Burroughs. BlSi

Black Prince, The. Alice Walker. CP-WalkA

Black Queen for More Than a Day. Al Young. CP-YounA

Black reapers with the sound of steel on stones. Reapers. Jean Toomer. BPo; CDC; CP-ToomJ; GT; Klds; PoBA

Black relatives / you are always. Some Things I Like about My Triple Bloods. Alice Walker. CP-WalkA

Black Revolution is passing you bye, The. Poem (No Name No. 3). Nikki Giovanni. BrTr; SP-GiovN

Black Revolutionary Woman. Revolutionary Love. Amiri Baraka. CtF

Black Sampson, The. Josephine D. Henderson Heard. CBWP-4

Black Sampson of Brandywine. Paul Laurence Dunbar. CP-DunbP; NAAAL

Black Seed. Langston Hughes. CP-HughL

Black Separatism. Nikki Giovanni. SP-GiovN

Black sergeant first class, The. To Have Danced with Death. Yusef Komunyakaa. SP-KomuY

Black Sister. Kattie M. Cumbo. BlSi

Black skin against bright green. Black Sister. Kattie M. Cumbo. BlSi

Black smoke of sound. Air Raid: Barcelona. Langston Hughes. CP-HughL

Black Soul of the Land. Lance Jeffers. BlFi; FB

Black Spring. Michael S. Harper. SP-HarpM

Black Star Line. Henry L. Dumas. Crnst; PoBA

Black Stick with a Ball of Cotton for a Head and a Running Machine for a Mouth, A. Calvin C. Hernton. BlFi

Black String of Days. Yusef Komunyakaa. SP-KomuY

Black Students. Julia Fields. NBP

Black Taffy. Peggy Susberry Kenner. JB

Black teenager strapped to, A. Manhattan March, The 1970s. Al Young. CP-YounA

Black the way a hero dies. (LL) Negritude. James A. Emanuel. IHS

Black Trumpeter. Henry L. Dumas. PoBA

Black unicorn is greedy, The. Audre Lorde. CP-LordA

Black universe. sky. / embrace. (LL) For Our Women. Larry Neal. BlFi

Black Warrior. Norman Jordan. BlFi; PoBA

Black Wedding Song, A. Gwendolyn Brooks. IHS

Black-White truth. Maya Angelou. See Accident.

Black woman, A. Haiku: "Black woman, A." Lenard D. Moore. CtF; TtW

Black Woman. Georgia Douglas Johnson. BALP

Black Woman. Naomi Long Madgett. BlSi; FB; GT; PoBA

Black Woman, Queen of the World. (LL) Alafia. Odaro. BlFi

Black Woman Throws a Tantrum. Nayo-Barbara Watkins. NBV; TtW

Black Workers. Langston Hughes. CP-HughL

Blackberry Sweet. Dudley Randall. NBP

(Black Magic.) Negro.

Blackboard in my mind holds words eye dream, A. And Syllables Grow Wings There. Quincy Tretheway. SpiFl

Blackbottom. Toi Derricotte. GT

Blacker de berry, sweeter is de juice. (LL) St. Louis Blues. *Unknown.* BkSV; Crnst

Blackgoldblueswoman. Kirk Hall. NBV

BLACKIE Speaks on Campus: a Valentine for Vachel Lindsay. Stanley Crouch. BlFi

Blackie Thinks of His Brothers. Stanley Crouch. BlFi; GT; PoBA

Blackjack. Michael S. Harper. SP-HarpM

Blackjack moses / returning from the war. The Seeker. Ahmos, II Zu-Bolton. TtW

Blacklash Blues. Langston Hughes. CP-HughL

Blackmusic / a Beginning. Haki R. Madhubuti. BrTr

Blacks in frame houses. Song: I Want a Witness. Michael S. Harper. SP-HarpM

Blackstone Rangers, The. Gwendolyn Brooks. ESEAA; PoBA

Blackstudies. Audre Lorde. CP-LordA; SP-LordA

Blackwoman. Haki R. Madhubuti. BrTr

Blade in the bed of a child, A. On the Edge. Audre Lorde. CP-LordA

Blam! Blam! Blam! Pow! Blam! Pow! For a Black Poet. Gerald William Barrax. NBV; TtW

Blame not the world for your troubles, blame yourself. Proverbs. Marvin X. BrTr

Blank fish-eyes. (LL) Smelt Fishing. Robert Hayden. CP-HaydR

Blasphemy. Yusef Komunyakaa. SP-KomuY

Blazing from outstretched palms, a skunk bagged and eaten in tears. (LL) Corduroy Road. Rita Dove. CP-DoveR

Bleached white in / blazing napalm sun. (LL) Death of the Moonshine Supermen. Reginald Lockett. BlFi

Bleeding hearts talk of happy days. Today Is Not Like They Said. Kirk Hall. NBV

Bleeding themselves of others. (LL) Blue Slanted into Blueness. Bob Kaufman. SP-KaufB

Blessed are the dehumanized. Mandela's Sermon. Keorapetse W. Kgositsile. BrTr

Blessed Hope, The. Frances Ellen Watkins Harper. CP-HarpF

Blessed Rhett, the Martyr. (LL) Miss Scarlet, Mr. Rhett and other Latter-Day Saints. Maya Angelou. CP-AngeM; SP-AngeM

Blessing the Boats. Marilyn Nelson. SP-NelsM

Blessing without Company. *Unknown.* BPo

Blight. Arna Bontemps. BANP; CDC

Blight of Love, The. Mary E. Tucker. CBWP-1

Blight rests in your face, The. To a Publisher ... Cut-out. Amiri Baraka. SP-BaraA

Blind. Langston Hughes. CP-HughL

Blind Old Woman. Clarence Major. PoBA

Blistering, / the lone black jockey's. Race Results, U.S.A., 1966. Sarah Webster Fabio. BrTr

Blk/Rhetoric. Sonia Sanchez. Crnst; SP-SancS

Block the cannon; let no trumpets sound! Sunset Horn. Myron O'Higgins. AmNP

Blonde White Women. Patricia Smith. GT

Blood and cathedrals / and—. (LL) Lisbon. Russell Atkins. GT

Blood dripping note by note. (LL) Colored Blues Singer. Countee Cullen. CP-CullC

Blood hounds, long upon the trail, The. Jefferson in a Tight Place. George Moses Horton. SP-HortG

Blood in our pockets. (LL) The Subway Witnesses. Lorenzo Thomas. GT

Blood, / Or a flag. Hero—International Brigade. Langston Hughes. CP-HughL

Blood-red flower of revolution, The. (LL) Roses and Revolutions. Dudley Randall. BPo; BrTr; PoBA; TtW

Blood-stained, continue cutting weeds and shade. (LL) Reapers. Jean Toomer. BPo; CDC; CP-ToomJ; GT; Klds; PoBA

Blood strepped, The. Memo #2. Etheridge Knight. SP-KnigE

Blood Suckers. Jayne Cortez. CortJ

Blood, Sweat, and Fears. Marlon C. Williams. CtF

Bloodbirth. Audre Lorde. CP-LordA; SP-LordA

Bloodstorm. Kiarri T-H Cheatwood. TtW

Blow, bugles! Armageddon has begun! (LL) Selassie at Geneva. Marcus B. Christian. TtW

Blowing away from him. (LL) My Grandfather Walks in the Woods. Marilyn Nelson. ESEAA; SP-NelsM

Blown up with painful care and hard to light. Man, a Torch. George Moses Horton. SP-HortG

Bludoo Baby, Want Money, and Alligator Got It to Give. Amiri Baraka. BlFi

Blue. Paul Laurence Dunbar. CP-DunbP

Blue Bayou. Langston Hughes. CP-HughL; SP-HughL

Blue-bell springs upon the ledge, A. Spring Song. Paul Laurence Dunbar. CP-DunbP

Blue Clay. Ellease Southerland. GT

Blue Deep. Quo Vadis Gex-Breaux. TtW

Blue Horses. Ed Roberson. GT; PoBA

Blue is this night of stars. Inquietude. Pauli Murray. BlSi

Blue Light Lounge Sutra for the Performance Poets at Harold Park Hotel. Yusef Komunyakaa. SP-KomuY

Blue Meridian, The. Jean Toomer. See Brown River, Smil.

Blue mists surround the mountains now. Lines Written on a Farewell View of the Franconia Mountains at Twilight. Henrietta Cordelia Ray. CBWP-3

Blue Monday. Calvin Forbes. ESEAA

Blue Monday. Langston Hughes. CP-HughL; SP-HughL

Blue Monday. Al Young. SpiFl

Blue O'Clock. Bob Kaufman. SP-KaufB

Blue Ruth: America. Michael S. Harper. PoBA; SP-HarpM

Blue sky arching overhead, The. The Change. Frances Ellen Watkins Harper. CP-HarpF

Blue sky blue water. Home. Calvin Forbes. GT

Blue Slanted into Blueness. Bob Kaufman. SP-KaufB

Blue smoke eclipsed, The. Eclipse. Amir Rashidd. NBP

Blue Tanganyika. Lebert Bethune. BlFi; PoBA

Blue, the most beautiful of afternoons. Falling Asleep in a Darkening Room. Al Young. CP-YounA

Blues. Edward Kamau Brathwaite. GT

Blues, The. Langston Hughes. CP-HughL

Blues. Sonia Sanchez. BlFi; GT; SP-SancS

Blues. Derek Walcott. Crnst

("Forget it.") (LL) GT

Blues ain't culture. Liberation / Poem. Sonia Sanchez. NBV

Blues Alabama. Michael S. Harper. SP-HarpM

Blues and Bitterness. Lerone, Jr. Bennett. NNP; PoBA

Blues and blues. Remembered. Sterling Plumpp. GT

Blues at 1. Dorothy Perry Thompson. SpiFl

Blues at Dawn. Langston Hughes. SP-HughL *Fr.* Montage of a Dream Deferred. CP-HughL

Blues blow in their purity, The. Blue Monday. Al Young. SpiFl

Blues Chant Hoodoo Revival. Yusef Komunyakaa. SP-KomuY

Blues Don't Change, The. Al Young. CP-YounA; ESEAA; GT

("Love the only / possible / end.") (LL) TtW

Blues Fantasy. Langston Hughes. CP-HughL

Blues for Franks Wooten; House of the Lifting of the Head. Tom Weatherly. GT; NBV

Blues in December. Al Young. CP-YounA

Blues in Stereo. Langston Hughes. *Fr.* Ask Your Mama; 12 Moods for Jazz. CP-HughL

Blues (in Two Parts), The. Val Ferdinand. NBV

Blues lady / with the beaded face. Grinding Vibrato. Jayne Cortez. BlSi

Blues may be the life you've led, The. A Good Woman Feeling Bad. Maya Angelou. CP-AngeM; SP-AngeM

Blues meant Swiss-Up, The. Riding Across John Lee's Finger. Stanley Crouch. GT; PoBA

Blues / Never climb a hill. Get Up, Blues. James A. Emanuel. AmNP; PoBA

Blues Note. Bob Kaufman. PoBA

Blues on a Box. Langston Hughes. CP-HughL

Blues Today, The. Mae Jackson. PoBA

Blues walk weeps ragtime. In the Tradition. Amiri Baraka. SP-BaraA

Blunts. Major L. Jackson. SpiFl

Boarding House. Langston Hughes. CP-HughL

Boast, The. Rita Dove. SP-DoveR

Boat People. Yusef Komunyakaa. SP-KomuY

Boat Song. Henrietta Cordelia Ray. CBWP-3

Boatman sang it over in the willows' shade, The. (LL) "Come now, my love, the moon is on the lake;." Albery Allson Whitman. AAP

Bob Hope's on stage, but we want the Gold Diggers. Communique. Yusef Komunyakaa. SP-KomuY

Bob-ing split-able heads. Solitary Visions of a Kaufmanoid. James Cunningham. JB

Bobby-soxers exchange clandestine feels. At the Record Hop. Wanda Coleman. NAAAL

Bocas: A Daughter's Geography. Ntozake Shange. NAAAL

Boccaccio: The Plague Years. Rita Dove. SP-DoveR

/ Bodacious / Black / Bad / Beautiful, A. Little Black Girls, The Original Eve (Spreadin' More Beautiful Brown Around). Karen Williams. SpiFl

Bodies broken on, The. Lucille Clifton. ESEAA; NAAAL; SP-ClifL

Bohemian, The. Paul Laurence Dunbar. CP-DunbP

Bold champion of a noble race. The Seminole. Benjamin Clark. EBAP

Bold Nat Turner by the blood of God. The Ballad of the Free. Margaret Abigail Walker. CP-WalkM

Bolero, silk-tassled, the fuchsia, The. For Kazuko. Rita Dove. SP-DoveR

Boll-weevil's coming, and the winter's cold. November Cotton Flower. Jean Toomer. CDC; CP-ToomJ

Bombings in Dixie. Langston Hughes. CP-HughL

"Bon soir, monsieur," they called to me. The Street Called Crooked. Countee Cullen. CP-CullC

Bond of live things everywhere, The. (LL) Cutting Greens. Lucille Clifton. ESEAA; SP-ClifL

Bonding, A. Haki R. Madhubuti. CtF

Bonds for All. Langston Hughes. CP-HughL

Bonds: In Memoriam. Langston Hughes. CP-HughL

Bondsman's gloomy night has passed, The. James Madison Bell. AAP ("Though slavery's dead, yet there remains.") AfAmPo

Bone-Flower Elegy. Robert Hayden. CP-HaydR

Bones a-gittin' achy. Chrismus Is A-Comin'. Paul Laurence Dunbar. CP-DunbP

Bones do not connect with bones. (LL) A Black Stick with a Ball of Cotton for a Head and a Running Machine for a Mouth. Calvin C. Hernton. BlFi

Bones float in raised stone. St. Louis Cemetery Crypt. Kalamu ya Salaam. *Fr.* New Orleans Haiku. SpiFl

Bones of My Father, The. Etheridge Knight. SP-KnigE

Boni Boni Boni Boni Boni. (LL) The Red Pepper Poet. Jayne Cortez. SP-CortJ

Boogah Man, The. Paul Laurence Dunbar. CP-DunbP

Boogie: 1 A.M. Langston Hughes. *Fr.* Montage of a Dream Deferred. CP-HughL

Boogie With O.O. Gabugah. Al Young. CP-YounA

Book that, if we could / read, would change our lives, The. (LL) Kentucky, 1833. Rita Dove. SP-DoveR

Booker T. and W. E. B. Dudley Randall. Klds

Booker T. / Was a practical man. Ballad of Booker T. Langston Hughes. CP-HughL

Booker T. Washington. Paul Laurence Dunbar. CP-DunbP

Book's Creed, The. Joseph Seamon Cotter, Sr. AAP

Boothill McCoy. *African-American Oral Tradition.* GetYo

Bootie Black and the Seven Giants. Mike Cook. JB

Boppin' is Safer than Grindin'. Thulani Davis. GT

Border Ballad, A. Paul Laurence Dunbar. CP-DunbP

Border Line. Langston Hughes. CP-HughL; SP-HughL

Borders. Michael S. Weaver. GT

Bored, confused actually. have started several letters. Four Lines of a Black Love Letter Between Teachers. Ed Roberson. NBV

Born like the pines to sing. James Ephriam McGirt. AAP

Born of the sorrowful of heart. For Paul Laurence Dunbar. Countee Cullen. *Fr.* Four Epitaphs. AmNP; CDC; CP-CullC; PoBA; SSLK

Born That Way. Maya Angelou. CP-AngeM

Born two thousand years ago. (LL) Kid Stuff. Frank Horne. AmNP; Klds; PoBA

Borning Room, The. Michael S. Harper. SP-HarpM

Boston 5:00 A.M.—10/74. Etheridge Knight. SP-KnigE

Boston Road Blues. David Henderson. BlFi

Boston Year. Elizabeth Alexander. GT

Both at once / Are sounded. (LL) Pair in One. Langston Hughes. CP-HughL

BOTH HITLER—AND JIM CROW. (LL) Beaumont to Detroit: 1943. Langston Hughes. CP-HughL

Bothers, i / under/overstand. The Revolutionary Screw. Haki R. Madhubuti. BrTr

Bottled [New York]. Helene Johnson. BlSi; CDC; PoBA; ShDr

Bound No'th Blues. Langston Hughes. AfAmPo; AmNP; CP-HughL; SP-HughL

Bound on a voyage of awful length. Henry Highland Garnet. CrDW

Bouquet. Langston Hughes. CP-HughL

Bow down my soul in worship very low. St. Isaac's Church, Petrograd. Claude McKay. AmNP; CDC; Klds; NAAAL; PoBA; SP-McKaC

Bow to her footsteps on the dusty Alabama road. (LL) When She Spoke of God. Lance Jeffers. BrTr

Bowed down for one flame hour my pride to prove. (LL) The City's Love. Claude McKay. SP-McKaC

Bowery Street. Jayne Cortez. SP-CortJ

Bowl he starts with, The. The Man. His Bowl. His Raspberries. Claudia Rankine. GT

Boxes. Nikki Giovanni. SP-GiovN

Boxing Day. Yusef Komunyakaa. SP-KomuY

Boy and his body, A. Christian's Box Seat: So What! Michael S. Harper. SP-HarpM

Boy Breaking Glass. Gwendolyn Brooks. ESEAA

Boy died in my alley, The. Gwendolyn Brooks. Crnst

Boy is born in hard time Mississippi, A. Living for the City. Stevie Wonder. Crnst

Boy long years ago, The. (LL) Mother's Songs. Frank Barbour Coffin. AAP

Boy walks out, A. The Saint Leaves His Father's House. Marilyn Nelson. *Fr.* The Life of a Saint. SP-NelsM

Boy Wearing a Dead Man's Clothes. Yusef Komunyakaa. SP-KomuY

Boys forget about women. The Excuse. Carl H. Greene. NBV

Boys have to slash their fingers to become brothers. Girls trade. An Anointing. Thylias Moss. GT

Boys / I don't promise you nothing. Admonitions. Lucille Clifton. BPo; SP-ClifL

Boys, I used to live the life of a millionaire. Down and Out. *African-American Oral Tradition.* GetYo

Boys in the Park. Marilyn Nelson. SP-NelsM

Boys of Summer, The. Kelly Norman Ellis. SpiFl

Boys of Summer, The. E. Ethelbert Miller. SpiFl

Boy's Summer Song, A. Paul Laurence Dunbar. CP-DunbP

Boys, you know it's a damned shame when you have been fucked and also framed. They Can't Do That. *African-American Oral Tradition.* GetYo

Boys, you remember way back on the day of the eighth of May. Titanic: "Boys, you remember way back on the day of the eighth of May." *African-American Oral Tradition.* GetYo

Boys, you're subject to a fall and trip to the Walls. Subject to a Fall: "Boys, you're subject to a fall and trip to the Walls." *African-American Oral Tradition.* GetYo

Brahms / stabbed me in the ear. St. Julien's Eve. James Cunningham. JB

Brain to the Heart, The. Yusef Komunyakaa. SP-KomuY

Brand New Clothes. Langston Hughes. CP-HughL

Brand New Morning Love Song, A. Al Young. CP-YounA

Branded with jefferson hair. (LL) Monticello. Lucille Clifton. SP-ClifL

Brass Spittoons. Langston Hughes. AmNP; BANP ("Come 'ere, boy!") (LL) CP-HughL

Brave Grant, thou hero of the war. General Grant—the Hero of the War. George Moses Horton. AAP; SP-HortG

Brave Man and Brave Woman. Mrs. Henry Linden. CBWP-4

Brazilian butterflies, static and perfect as. Butterfly Piece. Robert Hayden. CP-HaydR

Bread Man, The. Lucinda Roy. GT

Bread-oh, bread-oh, ten-cent bread. . . . The Bread Man. Lucinda Roy. GT

Breaded Meat, Breaded Hands. Michael S. Harper. SP-HarpM

Break from the Bush, A. Yusef Komunyakaa. SP-KomuY

Break / Its jail. (LL) Oppression. Langston Hughes. CP-HughL

Break me my bounds, and let me fly. A Career. Paul Laurence Dunbar. CP-DunbP

Break me no bread however white it be. Hunger. Countee Cullen. CP-CullC

Break of Day. Sterling A. Brown. CP-BrowS

Break, or / be broken. (LL) Eldridge. Lucille Clifton. SP-ClifL

Break refulgent on the sight. (LL) President Lincoln's Proclamation of Freedom. Frances Ellen Watkins Harper. CP-HarpF

Break wind with me. (LL) I Am New York City. Jayne Cortez. SP-CortJ

Breaking of mind / upon darkness and / tide. (LL) Lake Murry. Pinkie Gordon Lane. GT

Breaking the Charm. Paul Laurence Dunbar. CP-DunbP

Breaklight. Lucille Clifton. SP-ClifL

Breaks very close to me my love. (LL) Roman Poem Number Thirteen. June Jordan. SP-JordJ

Breakthrough. Carolyn M. Rodgers. BPo

Breakthrough. John Sinclair. NBP

Breast Examination. Wanda Coleman. GT

Breast under breast when you shall lie. Ghosts. Countee Cullen. CP-CullC

Breath of a Rose. Langston Hughes. CP-HughL

Breath of life imbued those few dim days, The. Fragment. Jessie Redmond Fauset. CDC; ShDr

Breathe in. Breathe out. (LL) Heartbeats. Melvin Dixon. ESEAA

Breathe unshackled dreams. (LL) Round Midnight, Place de Congo. Kalamu ya Salaam. SpiFl

Breathing in morning. Song Turning Back Into Itself 1. Al Young. CP-YounA

Breathless she stood, her graceful head bent low. Listening Nydia. Henrietta Cordelia Ray. CBWP-3

Breeze is blowin' 'cross de bay, De. Parted. Paul Laurence Dunbar. CP-DunbP

Breeze is narcotic. (LL) Our Natures Rise. Kalamu ya Salaam. SpiFl

Breezes blowin' middlin' brisk. Speakin' o' Christmas. Paul Laurence Dunbar. CP-DunbP

Br'er Sterling and the Rocker. Michael S. Harper. NAAAL; SP-HarpM

Bress mah life! why, dis hain't Trussey? Trussy's Visit. Elliot B. Henderson. EBAP

Bridal Measure, A. Paul Laurence Dunbar. CP-DunbP

Bride of Death, The. Frances Ellen Watkins Harper. CP-HarpF

Bridge, The. Amiri Baraka. SP-BaraA

Bridge through My Windows. Audre Lorde. CP-LordA; SP-LordA

Brief Encounter. Langston Hughes. CP-HughL

Brief Encounter. Norman J. Loftis. SpiFl

Brief Innocence. Maya Angelou. CP-AngeM; SP-AngeM

Brief Synopsis, A. Carolyn M. Rodgers. TtW

Bright and beautiful art thou. October. Mary Weston Fordham. CBWP-2

Bright as the light that burns at night. Venetia. Adah Isaacs Menken. CBWP-1

Bright Bindings. Countee Cullen. CP-CullC

Bright, jolly sunshine and clear blue skies. Signs of Spring. Langston Hughes. CP-HughL

Bright uncanny music was beating through the room. The Fallen. Audre Lorde. CP-LordA

Bright white street lights, The. Allegory in Black. Carl Clark. JB

Brighter than crisp new money. Jonestown: More Eyes for *Jadwiga's Dream.* Yusef Komunyakaa. SP-KomuY

Brilliant-bellied newt flashes, The. Helene Johnson. BlSi; CDC ("Summer matures. Brilliant Scorpion.") ShDr

Bring back the life / of Claude Reece Jr. Give Me the Red on the Black of the Bullet. Jayne Cortez. SP-CortJ

Bring dreams of Christ to dusky cane-lipped throngs. (LL) Georgia Dusk. Jean Toomer. AfAmPo; AmNP; BPo; CDC; CP-ToomJ; Klds; PoBA; TtW

Bring forth the balance, let the weight be gold! The Soul. Frances Ellen Watkins Harper. CP-HarpF

Bring me all your dreams. The Dream Keeper. Langston Hughes. CP-HughL

Bring me knowledge of my hunger. (LL) Harvest Song. Jean Toomer. CP-ToomJ

Bring me the livery of no other man. The Bohemian. Paul Laurence Dunbar. CP-DunbP

Bring me those needles, Martha. Owen Dodson. *Fr.* The Confession Stone. Klds

Bristol: Bicentenary Remembrances of Trade. Michael S. Harper. SP-HarpM

Britannia's isles proclaim. To the First of August. Ann Plato. BlSi; TtW

British said to Azikiwe, The. Azikiwe in Jail. Langston Hughes. CP-HughL

Brittania's isles proclaim. Ann Plato. *See* To the First of August.

Bro Duncanson. C. S. Giscombe. GT

Bro, they been calling that sister by the wrong name. (LL) Gwendolyn Brooks Elizabeth. Haki R. Madhubuti. ESEAA

Broadcast on Ethiopia. Langston Hughes. CP-HughL

Broadcast to the West Indies. Langston Hughes. CP-HughL

Brock Hankton. *African-American Oral Tradition.* GetYo

Broke. Langston Hughes. CP-HughL

Broken Dark, The. Robert Hayden. CP-HaydR; GT

Broken Heart. Henrietta Cordelia Ray. CBWP-3

Broken Heart, Broken Machine. Richard E. Grant. PoBA

Brokenhearted / brown girl / blues, The. (LL) Brown Girl Blues. Kysha N. Brown. CtF

Bronze Bodhisattva's ancient smile, A. (LL) The Peacock Room. Robert Hayden. CP-HaydR; FB

Bronze Buckaroo, The. Amiri Baraka. SP-BaraA

Bronze / in the bright sun. (LL) Warning. Alice Walker. CP-WalkA

Bronze Legacy, The. Mary Effie Lee Newsome. ShDr

Bronzeville Man with a Belt in the Back. Gwendolyn Brooks. IDB; PoBA; SP-BrooG

Bronzeville Mother Loiters in Mississippi. / Meanwhile, a Mississippi Mother Burns Bacon. Gwendolyn Brooks. Crnst; ESEAA; SP-BrooG ("Through a red prairie.") (LL) SSLK

Bronzeville Woman in a Red Hat. Gwendolyn Brooks. SP-BrooG; GT

Brooding. Jayne Cortez. SP-CortJ

Brook glides on to the river, The. Reverie. Henrietta Cordelia Ray. CBWP-3

Brooklyn. Michael S. Weaver. SpiFl

Brothah, wid yo'se'f. (LL) Advice. Paul Laurence Dunbar. CP-DunbP

Brother. Jewel C. Latimore. JB

Brother Alvin. Audre Lorde. CP-LordA

Brother Baptis' on Woman Suffrage. Rosalie Jonas. BlSi

Brother, come! And What Shall You Say? Joseph Seamon Cotter, Sr. BANP; CDC; PoBA

Brother Harlem Bedford Watts Tells Mr. Charlie Where ITs At. Bobb Hamilton. BlFi

Brother John. Michael S. Harper. SP-HarpM

Brother Malcolm's Echo. Keorapetse W. Kgositsile. BrTr

Brother to the firefly. Morning Light. Mary Effie Lee Newsome. AmNP; CDC; PoBA; ShDr

Brotherly Love. Langston Hughes. CP-HughL

Brothers. Solomon Edwards. NNP

Brothers. Langston Hughes. SP-HughL *Fr.* Montage of a Dream Deferred. CP-HughL

Brothers. James Weldon Johnson. BANP; NAAAL

Brothers and Sisters, I will weep no more. Disillusion for Flower Children of Long Ago. Margaret Abigail Walker. CP-WalkM

Brothers at the Bar. Naomi Long Madgett. NBV

Brothers / brothers / everywhere. Utopia. Jewel C. Latimore. BPo

Brothers, let us discover our hearts again. Open Letter. Owen Dodson. BALP

Brothers—you and I. (LL) Brothers. Langston Hughes. CP-HughL; SP-HughL

Brought here in slave ships and pitched over board. Love Your Enemy. Yusef Iman. BlFi

Brown Aesthete Speaks, A. Mae V. Cowdery. ShDr

Brown Autumn came, and at her solemn close. In the House of the Aylors. Albery Allson Whitman. AAP

Brown Baby Cobina, with his large black velvet eyes. Baby Cobina. Gladys May Casely Hayford. CDC; ShDr

Brown Boy to Brown Girl. Countee Cullen. CP-CullC; PoBA

Brown Girl Blues. Kysha N. Brown. CtF

Brown Girl Dead, A. Countee Cullen. CP-CullC; GT; Klds

Brown has mighty things to do. (LL) The Bronze Legacy. Mary Effie Lee Newsome. ShDr

Brown Menace or Poem to the Survival of Roaches, The. Audre Lorde. CP-LordA; SP-LordA

Brown River, Smile. Jean Toomer. AmNP; PoBA (Blue Meridian, The.) CP-ToomJ

Bruddah Mocking Bird. Uncle Ned an' de Mockin' Bird. Elliot B. Henderson. EBAP

Brushes and paints are all I have. Quatrains. Gwendolyn B. Bennett. CDC

Bubble, clearheaded man. Flying High. Lana C. Williams. CtF

Buck. Michael S. Harper. SP-HarpM

Buckdanced on the midnight air. (LL) Sam Smiley. Sterling A. Brown. CP-BrowS; NAAAL

Buddhist experience, A. Bob Kaufman. SP-KaufB

Buddy. Langston Hughes. *Fr.* Montage of a Dream Deferred. CP-HughL

Buddy, have you heard? (LL) Deferred. Langston Hughes. CP-HughL

Buds from winter's frost-work lift, The. The Coming of Spring. Henrietta Cordelia Ray. CBWP-3

Buffalo. Henry L. Dumas. PoBA

Buffalo War. Lucille Clifton. SP-ClifL

"Build me a house," said the Master. The Building. Frances Ellen Watkins Harper. CP-HarpF

"Build me a nation," said the Lord. Then and Now. Frances Ellen Watkins Harper. CP-HarpF

Building, The. Frances Ellen Watkins Harper. CP-HarpF

Building. Audre Lorde. CP-LordA

Building Nicole's Mama. Patricia Smith. SpiFl

Buildings in Harlem are brick and stone, The. The Heart of Harlem. Langston Hughes. CP-HughL

Bulddaggers' Hall, *see also* Freaks' Ball *and* Twenty-Two-Twenty. *African-American Oral Tradition.* GetYo

"Bullshit," said I. (LL) I said to Poetry: "I'm finished." Alice Walker. CP-WalkA

Bumi. Amiri Baraka. PoBA

Bump d'Bump. Maya Angelou. CP-AngeM; SP-AngeM

Bump d'bump bump d'bump. (LL) Bump d'Bump. Maya Angelou. CP-AngeM; SP-AngeM

Buona notte, goodnight-goodnight-wherever-you-are! (LL) Coastal Moon. Al Young. CP-YounA

Burden. Langston Hughes. CP-HughL

Burdens of All, The. Frances Ellen Watkins Harper. CP-HarpF

Burgundy Street. David Henderson. TtW

Burial. Alice Walker. CP-WalkA

Burial of a Fairy Queen. Mary E. Tucker. CBWP-1

Burial of Moses, The. Frances Ellen Watkins Harper. CP-HarpF

Burial of Srah. Frances Ellen Watkins Harper. CP-HarpF

Burial of the Young Love. Waring Cuney. BANP

Buried alive with me. (LL) For Myself. Countee Cullen. CP-CullC

Buried down there in North Carolina. (LL) A Poem for a Poet. Audre Lorde. CP-LordA; SP-LordA

Burly fading one beside the engine, The. Robert Hayden. CP-HaydR

Burn, Baby, Burn. Marvin E. Jackmon. BlFi

Burn white with stars. (LL) Young Negro Girl. Langston Hughes. CP-HughL

Burn your bridges! Come away! (LL) At Loafing-Holt. Paul Laurence Dunbar. CP-DunbP

Burned - black by birth. A White Friend Flies in from the Coast. Michael S. Harper. SP-HarpM

Burning General, The. Amiri Baraka. SP-BaraA

Burning the Water Hyacinth. Audre Lorde. CP-LordA

Burns and fades and burns. (LL) Veracruz. Robert Hayden. AmNP

Burnt out year, The. New Year Letter. Edward Kamau Brathwaite. GT

Burnt Sienna. Norman Henry, II Pritchard. GT

Burros are all heehawed out, The. Going Back Home. Al Young. CP-YounA

Burst from sorghum lips. (LL) Clinton. Sterling Plumpp. BkSV

Burst of light, A. (LL) Never to Dream of Spiders. Audre Lorde. CP-LordA

Bury Me in a Free Land. Frances Ellen Watkins Harper. AAP; BPo; CrDW; Crnst; EBAP; NAAAL

("Is bury me not in a land of slaves.") (LL) AfAmPo; CP-HarpF; Crnst; TtW

Bush Mama. Kalamu ya Salaam. TtW

Businessman heard about Abba Jacob, A. Abba Jacob and the Businessman. Marilyn Nelson. SP-NelsM

But a chappie needs diverting. A Chappie. Paul Laurence Dunbar. CP-DunbP

But a red headed woman make a boy slap his papa down. (LL) St. Louis Blues. William Christopher Handy. NAAAL

But a tom cat wouldn't let it / stay. (LL) A Robin's Poem. Nikki Giovanni. BrTr

But after all—once you were mine. (LL) Poem (For BMC No. 1). Nikki Giovanni. BrTr; SP-GiovN

But ain't I lucky I can still breathe in. (LL) On Aging. Maya Angelou. CP-AngeM; SP-AngeM

But as advancing fast, prepare for equal Joy. (LL) To the Hon'ble Thomas Hubbard, Esq.; on the Death of Mrs. Thankfull Leonard. Phillis Wheatley. CP-WheaP

But as love. Bob Kaufman. SP-KaufB

But, baby, I feel blue. (LL) Yesterday and Today. Langston Hughes. CP-HughL

But, baby, where are you? (LL) Ballad of Birmingham. Dudley Randall. BPo; BrTr

But beyond the / anxiety. No Poem Because Time Is Not a Name. June Jordan. SP-JordJ

But bring her to me, Wind,—my little March girl. (LL) My Little March Girl. Paul Laurence Dunbar. CP-DunbP

But burning blind. (LL) Black Mail. Alice Walker. CP-WalkA

But by the grace and sufferance of Death. (LL) Sonnet Dialogue. Countee Cullen. CP-CullC

But can see better there, and laughing there. Gwendolyn Brooks. *Fr.* Notes from the Childhood and the Girlhood. Kids; SP-BrooG

But Can You Kill the Nigga in You? Chuck D. CtF

But cannot. (LL) Locust Trees. Margaret L. Thomas. ShDr

But cart me up to number eleven. (LL) I used to could diddle all night long. *African-American Oral Tradition.* GetYo

But change the bloody gauze. (LL) The Ballad of Rudolph Reed. Gwendolyn Brooks. SP-BrooG

But death. / I am I. (LL) The Tattooed Man. Robert Hayden. CP-HaydR

But does not self-destruct. (LL) Do You Remember Laura. Audre Lorde. CP-LordA

But drains the fount of pleasure. (LL) Song of Liberty and Parental Advice. George Moses Horton. SP-HortG

But expect nothing. Live frugally / On surprise. (LL) Expect nothing. Live frugally. Alice Walker. CP-WalkA

But He Was Cool. Haki R. Madhubuti. AmNP; BPo; BrTr; Crnst; PoBA

But he'd entered the music, safely, his mansion. (LL) No Trespassing. Al Young. CP-YounA

But Hitler, you lied to me. (LL) Hitler, You Lied to Me. *African-American Oral Tradition.* GetYo

But hit's mighty ha'd to giggle w'en dey's nuffin' in de pot. (LL) Philosophy. Paul Laurence Dunbar. BPo; CP-DunbP; NAAAL

But I fear that I am a failure. Last night a woman called me a troubadour. What is a troubadour? Fenton Johnson. The Banjo Player.

But I had called the office. Poem (For BMC No. 3). Nikki Giovanni. SP-GiovN

But I hear the beating of dead boughs. (LL) Blight. Arna Bontemps. BANP; CDC

But I Know That Unseen Anger Runs a Raft. Lance Jeffers. TtW

But I *sure* ain't gonna pay! (LL) Madam and the Phone Bill. Langston Hughes. CP-HughL; SP-HughL

But I thought it was Tangiers I wanted. (LL) I Thought It Was Tangiers I Wanted. Langston Hughes. CP-HughL; IHS

But I was hoppin mad. (LL) Then Jonah Took Out His Guitar. Marilyn Nelson. SP-NelsM

But I'd be satisfied with one. (LL) One to Love. Alfred Islay Walden. AAP

But, "if a man die, shall he live again?" Albery Allson Whitman. AAP

But if I tell you how my heart swings wide. Sunflower Sonnet Number One. June Jordan. TtW

But I'm gonna break your goddamned neck about that 'switch it, Mr. Bear. (LL) Poolshooting Monkey: "It was in Speero's poolroom in the year eighteen-ten." *African-American Oral Tradition.* GetYo

But I'm sober again. (LL) Drinkin'. *African-American Oral Tradition.* GetYo

But I'm talking about / Harlem to you! (LL) Comment on Curb. Langston Hughes. AmNP; SP-HughL

But in my devotion to snot / we resemble. (LL) Bowery Street. Jayne Cortez. SP-CortJ

But in the crowding darkness not a word did they say. The Old-Marrieds. Gwendolyn Brooks. AmNP; PoBA

But isn't talking. The Hill Has Something to Say. Rita Dove. SP-DoveR

But Jess done gone, baby he done gone. (LL) Break of Day. Sterling A. Brown. CP-BrowS

But just come out and tell him so. (LL) On Hearing James W. Riley Read. Joseph Seamon Cotter, Sr. AAP; EBAP

But knows the heart, 'tis but a word for pain. (LL) Love is a flame that burns with sacred fire. George Marion McClellan. AAP; EBAP

But leave you safe within a living land. (LL) To One Not There. Countee Cullen. CP-CullC

But lif' up yo' haid w'en de King go by! (LL) A Spiritual. Paul Laurence Dunbar. BPo; CP-DunbP

But lightning comes. (LL) Oaxaca. Audre Lorde. CP-LordA; SP-LordA

But look a trial down from some far height. Full Vision. Henrietta Cordelia Ray. CBWP-3

But look on me with smile or sigh. (LL) Response. Paul Laurence Dunbar. CP-DunbP

But look well to the life that you daily lead. (LL) Go ponder at that faithful mother's grave. Albery Allson Whitman. EBAP

But Lucifer was tall, his wings were long? (LL) Dictum. Countee Cullen. CP-CullC

But mother and child / Thought it fun. (LL) S-sss-ss-sh! Langston Hughes. SP-HughL

But my brother is bitter, and he does not hear. (LL) Bitter Fruit of the Tree. Sterling A. Brown. CP-BrowS

But my father brings fresh glazed donuts in a white bag. (LL) Love from My Father. Carole C. Gregory Clemmons. PoBA

But my life is not portable now. The Trollop Maiden. Audre Lorde. CP-LordA

But nevermore the May! (LL) Youth. Georgia Douglas Johnson. BANP; NAAAL

But, nevertheless / A dud. (LL) The Vachel Lindsay Fault. Ishmael Reed. CP-ReedI

But night in their brains. (LL) Jonestown: More Eyes for *Jadwiga's Dream*. Yusef Komunyakaa. SP-KomuY

But Nobody Was There. Ishmael Reed. CP-ReedI

But not even you, wolf, can bring me down. (LL) Before You Leave. Ai. GT

But not really / anywhere. (LL) Kid in the Park. Langston Hughes. CP-HughL; SP-HughL

But not the anger of that day. (LL) For Malcolm, a Year After. Etheridge Knight. SP-KnigE

But nothing happens. (LL) Execution. James A., Jr. Randall. BrTr

But now a glimpse of Leelah checks him up. Albery Allson Whitman. Fr. Leelah Misled. EBAP

But now, the deal was closing in her eyes. (LL) They Never Lose. Lorenzo Thomas. TtW

But of course you were. Nothing Much. Maya Angelou. CP-AngeM

But often now the youthful eye cuts down its. God Works in a Mysterious Way. Gwendolyn Brooks. SP-BrooG

But one of these Wednesdays everything could work. A Sonnet for A.B.T. June Jordan. SP-JordJ

But only seeks release. (LL) Worn Out. Paul Laurence Dunbar. CP-DunbP; NAAAL

But partly bread and butter. (LL) Wish for an Overcoat. Alfred Islay Walden. AAP; AfAmPo

But pass the time / playing cards. (LL) The Sailor in Africa. Rita Dove. SP-DoveR

But reaching is his rule. (LL) Life for my child is simple, and is good. Gwendolyn Brooks. SP-BrooG

But see the heart. (LL) See the Heart. Jean Toomer. CP-ToomJ; IHS

But seen from the angle of her /death death. (LL) Burial. Alice Walker. CP-WalkA

But she and I have come this way / before. (LL) Barren. Audre Lorde. CP-LordA; SP-LordA

But Since You Finally Asked. Nikki Giovanni. CtF; SP-GiovN

But, sir, I may not, till you abdicate. (LL) To a Captious Critic. Paul Laurence Dunbar. BPo; CP-DunbP; Klds

But that some doubted, you may well judge why. (LL) But why he'd ride "ride" so certainly each eve. Albery Allson Whitman. EBAP

But the air cannot stand my singing long. (LL) The Violent Space. Etheridge Knight. BPo; SP-KnigE

But the men who are now dying. Breakthrough. John Sinclair. NBP

But the next time you see a gentleman, keep your motherfucken mouth shut. (LL) Hobo Ben. *African-American Oral Tradition*. GetYo

But the whole thing is a miracle—See? Black Power. Nikki Giovanni. BrTr; SP-GiovN

But the wind is our teacher. (LL) Hugo I. Audre Lorde. CP-LordA

But There Are Miles. Harris Duriel. CtF

But there will be less to say. (LL) Length of Moon. Arna Bontemps. CDC

"But they come by tens." (LL) Old Lem. Sterling A. Brown. BPo; FB; IDB; PoBA

But they have raised no cry. / I wonder why. (LL) Scottsboro, Too, Is Worth Its Song. Countee Cullen. CP-CullC; PoBA

But was just as if they'd left. (LL) Crossing. Langston Hughes. CP-HughL; SP-HughL

But What Can You Teach My Daughter. Audre Lorde. CP-LordA

But what we are / together. (LL) A Poem of Friendship. Nikki Giovanni. IHS; SP-GiovN

But when will we love ourselves? (LL) Love Your Enemy. Yusef Iman. BPo; BlFi

But where's the joke? (LL) Misapprehension. Paul Laurence Dunbar. BPo; CP-DunbP

But who sees? (LL) Faces and more remember. Maya Angelou. CP-AngeM; SP-AngeM

But who would miss me if I left? (LL) Reverie on the Harlem River. Langston Hughes. CP-HughL; SP-HughL

But why he'd ride "ride" so certainly each eve. Albery Allson Whitman. Fr. Leelah Misled. EBAP

But will stay for ever, / Crystal Sukee River. (LL) Sukee River. Claude McKay. SP-McKaC

"But worse, for thou art mire." (LL) Distinction. Paul Laurence Dunbar. CP-DunbP

But would not bend to shame. (LL) Vashti. Frances Ellen Watkins Harper. AAP; BlSi; EBAP

But yet my love and yet my hate shall civilize this land, / this land's salvation. Lance Jeffers. *See* My Blackness Is the Beauty of This Land.

But you can straighten 'em out in a jiff, old pal, just tell 'em they met Hophead Willie. (LL) Hophead Willie. *African-American Oral Tradition*. GetYo

But you can't get rid of that funky smell. (LL) Pussy ain't nothin' but a hairy split. *African-American Oral Tradition*. GetYo

But you do. (LL) Low to High. Langston Hughes. CP-HughL

But you got to love again. (LL) Love Again Blues. Langston Hughes. CP-HughL

But you have to *feel* for it. (LL) My life, the quality of which. Etheridge Knight. SP-KnigE

But you lak to made me sin! (LL) Temptation. Paul Laurence Dunbar. CP-DunbP

But you still love Trane. (LL) No matter where you travel. Houston A., Jr. Baker. TtW

But you thought you would. (LL) Maybe. Langston Hughes. CP-HughL; SP-HughL

But you wait for Jones nex' week. (LL) Speakin' at de Cou't-House. Paul Laurence Dunbar. CP-DunbP

But you were not there at all! (LL) Dream. Langston Hughes. CP-HughL; SP-HughL

But you'd have to carry me to get me back there. (LL) Carry Me Back to Old Virginny. Elma Ehrlich Levinger. ShDr

But your heart has become perfect. (LL) Desire's Persistence. Jay Wright. ESEAA

But your poor heart breaks, too, and you, too, die. (LL) Nonette. Langston Hughes. CP-HughL

But you're wel / come here. (LL) On the Birth of a Black / Baby / Boy. Etheridge Knight. SP-KnigE

Butterflies, white butterflies, in the sunshine. Angelina Weld Grimké. GT

Butterfly, The. Nikki Giovanni. SP-GiovN

Butterfly in Church, A. George Marion McClellan. BANP

Butterfly Piece. Robert Hayden. CP-HaydR

Button on my last year / Ragdoll. (LL) Christmas Morning I. Carol Freeman. BlFi; PoBA

Buy a Bond for Grandma. Bonds for All. Langston Hughes. CP-HughL

Buy a drink for me. (LL) Jazz Girl. Langston Hughes. CP-HughL

Buy "burgers" and sticky sweets! (LL) Television Speaks. Etheridge Knight. SP-KnigE

Bwagamoyo. Lebert Bethune. BlFi; PoBA

By a cliff of limestone that leaves chalk on my breasts. (LL) The Secret Garden. Rita Dove. SP-DoveR

By a definite reason. (LL) For Jose and Regina. Audre Lorde. CP-LordA

By a good ol' hick'ry fiah. (LL) The Suitor. Paul Laurence Dunbar. CP-DunbP

By and by. (LL) Hope: "Sometimes when I'm lonely." Langston Hughes. CP-HughL; SP-HughL

By angel fingers strung. (LL) The Lost Bells. Frances Ellen Watkins Harper. CP-HarpF

By bayonets, forever falling. (LL) Crispus Attucks. Robert Hayden. CP-HaydR; ESEAA

By fifty, you know who you are and, more. Fifty-Fifty. Al Young. SpiFl

By glistening, dancing seas. Lethonia Gee. BlFi

By Heart. Al Young. CP-YounA

By her arriving immigrant bees. (LL) Blue Horses. Ed Roberson. GT

By hitching your thanks for God's love to my plow. (LL) Sermon in the Ruined Garden. Marilyn Nelson. SP-NelsM

By letting the strength of his arm go to waist. (LL) Confirmation. Paul Laurence Dunbar. CP-DunbP

By mirrors, horoscopes, / and blood. (LL) Family Jewels. Essex Hemphill. GT

By Mystic's banks I held my dream. Ballade. Paul Laurence Dunbar. CP-DunbP

By Nebo a lonely mountain. The Burial of Moses. Frances Ellen Watkins Harper. CP-HarpF

By noon we'll be deep into it—. Conjugal Visits. Al Young. NAAAL

By rivers dream / they are immortal. (LL) St. Louis Out of Time. Audre Lorde. SP-LordA

By rugged ways and thro' the night. Paul Laurence Dunbar. CP-DunbP

By sightseers day & night. (LL) Grizzly Peak. Al Young. CP-YounA

By sound that shimmers— / Where? (LL) Song for Billie Holiday. Langston Hughes. SP-HughL

By steppin' dis Vahginia reel. (LL) A Virginia Reel. Paul Laurence Dunbar. CP-DunbP

By the 5th Generation Louisiana, After Slavery. Ahmos, II Zu-Bolton. BkSV

By the frost . . . (LL) Poem . . . For a Lover. Mae V. Cowdery. ShDr

By the life that I tried / to live. (LL) The Life I Led. Nikki Giovanni. SP-GiovN

By the miraculous sun turned glad and warm. (LL) To One Coming North. Claude McKay. SP-McKaC

By the pool that I see in my dreams, dear love. The Pool. Paul Laurence Dunbar. CP-DunbP

By the resurrection's might. (LL) The Resurrection of Jesus. Frances Ellen Watkins Harper. CP-HarpF

By the rising sea. (LL) The Seventh Sign. Audre Lorde. CP-LordA; SP-LordA

"By the Rivers of Babylon." Mary Weston Fordham. CBWP-2

By the sea, brown now with alien debris? (LL) Watsonville after the Quake. Al Young. CP-YounA

By the sea it was, the Pacific. Whatever Become of the Living. Al Young. CP-YounA

By the side of the road. (LL) Growing into My Name. Harriet Jacobs. SpiFl

By the stream I dream in calm delight, and watch as in a glass. Paul Laurence Dunbar. CP-DunbP

By then the poetry is written. Not What Was. Langston Hughes. CP-HughL

By this narcotic thought: I know my soul. (LL) I Know My Soul. Claude McKay. SP-McKaC

By this, New England will increase like thee. (LL) America. Phillis Wheatley. CP-WheaP

By what sends. Children's Rhymes. Langston Hughes. BPo

Byron's Oak at Newstead Abbey. Timothy Thomas Fortune. AAP; EBAP

Byways and bygone. The Traveler. Maya Angelou. CP-AngeM; SP-AngeM

C

C. C. Rider. Lucille Clifton. GT

"C" ing in Colors: Blue. Safiya Henderson-Holmes. SpiFl

"C" ing in Colors: Red. Safiya Henderson-Holmes. SpiFl

Cabaret. Sterling A. Brown. NAAAL ("Dee da dee DAAAAH.") (LL) CP-BrowS

Cabaret. Langston Hughes. CP-HughL

Cabaret, cabaret! Minnie Sings Her Blues. Langston Hughes. CP-HughL

Cabaret Girl Dies on Welfare Island. Langston Hughes. CP-HughL

Cabin Tale, A. Paul Laurence Dunbar. CP-DunbP; NAAAL

Cables to Rage or I've Been Talking on This Street Corner a Hell of a Long Time. Audre Lorde. CP-LordA; SP-LordA

Cadences of dead flesh / obscure the vowels. (LL) There Are No Honest Poems about Dead Women. Audre Lorde. CP-LordA

Café: 3 A.M. Langston Hughes. Fr. Montage of a Dream Deferred. CP-HughL

Cage Walker, The. Yusef Komunyakaa. SP-KomuY

Caged Bird. Maya Angelou. CP-AngeM; SP-AngeM

Caged in the circus of civilization. (LL) Lament for Dark Peoples. Langston Hughes. CP-HughL

Cain. Lucille Clifton. SP-ClifL

Calabash wherein she served my food, The. The Serving Girl. Gladys May Casely Hayford. CDC; ShDr

Caledonia. Colleen J. McElroy. BlSi; NAAAL

Calico summer, The. Moon/Light Quarter/Back Sack. Samuel F. Reynolds. SpiFl

California Peninsula: El Camino Real. Al Young. CP-YounA; GT

California Prodigal. Maya Angelou. CP-AngeM; SP-AngeM

Ca'line's Prayer. Lucille Clifton. SP-ClifL

Call. Audre Lorde. CP-LordA

Call Boy. Sterling A. Brown. CP-BrowS

Call for Barnum. Sterling A. Brown. CP-BrowS

Call him deluded, say that he. Homage to Paul Robeson. Robert Hayden. CP-HaydR

Call it anything. (LL) Roots. Lucille Clifton. SP-ClifL

Call it love. (LL) Beyond What. Alice Walker. CP-WalkA

Call it neither love nor spring madness. Without Name. Pauli Murray. AmNP; PoBA

Call it our craziness even. Roots. Lucille Clifton. SP-ClifL

Call Letters: Mrs. V.B. Maya Angelou. CP-AngeM; SP-AngeM

Call me / your deepest urge. The Brown Menace or Poem to the Survival of Roaches. Audre Lorde. CP-LordA; SP-LordA

Call of Ethiopia. Langston Hughes. CP-HughL

Call out the colored girls. For the Record. Audre Lorde. CP-LordA; ESEAA

Call to Creation. Langston Hughes. CP-HughL

Called. Michael S. Harper. SP-HarpM

Called out of Egypt. America Calls! Michael S. Harper. SP-HarpM

Calling all black people, come in, black people, come / on in. (LL) SOS. Amiri Baraka. BPo; NAAAL; PoBA

Calling back. (LL) What We Have Lost. Harris Duriel. SpiFl

Calling black people. SOS. Amiri Baraka. BPo; NAAAL; PoBA

Calling Dreams. Georgia Douglas Johnson. ShDr

Calling him Son. (LL) Variation on Gaining a Son. Rita Dove. SP-DoveR

Calling life anew. (LL) Rain Music. Joseph Seamon Cotter, Sr. TtW

Calling life / To come! / Come! / Come! (LL) Drum. Langston Hughes. SP-HughL

Calling of Names, The. Maya Angelou. CP-AngeM; SP-AngeM

Calling of the Disciples, The. Lucille Clifton. SP-ClifL

Calling on All Silent Minorities. June Jordan. SP-JordJ

Calling the Chippewa in. (LL) The Ice-Fishing House. Michael S. Harper. SP-HarpM

Calling the Doctor. John Wesley Holloway. BANP

Calm after Storm. Frank Yerby. AmNP

Calm and cloudless features / of Benin, The. (LL) Benin Bronze. Samuel Allen. Crnst

Calm / Cool face of the river, The. Suicide's Note. Langston Hughes. CDC; CP-HughL; SP-HughL

Calmest joy she'll yield to thee. (LL) Fancy and Imagination. Henrietta Cordelia Ray. CBWP-3

Calming Kali. Lucille Clifton. SP-ClifL

Calvary Way. May Miller. TtW

Calv'ry's tragedy is ended. The Empty Tomb. Clara Ann Thompson. CBWP-2

Camcorder clicking in memories, and just be still?, The. (LL) The Jesus Prayer. Marilyn Nelson. SP-NelsM

Came a stranger late among us. In Memory of James M. Rathel. Josephine D. Henderson Heard. CBWP-4

Came the wild cry of geese. (LL) Bali Hai Calls Mama. Marilyn Nelson. SP-NelsM

Came upstairs either. (LL) Mystery 1st Lady. Ishmael Reed. CP-ReedI

Cameo No. II. June Jordan. BPo

Cameras are rolling, The. (LL) The Domino Theory (Or Snoop Dogg Rules the World). Kenneth Carroll. CtF; SpiFl

Camouflaging the Chimera. Yusef Komunyakaa. SP-KomuY

Can America be reckoned as the country of the free? The Negro Ballot. Lizelia Augusta Jenkins Moorer. CBWP-3

Can be found. (LL) Expendable. Langston Hughes. CP-HughL

Can be pronounced the same. (LL) On the Death of Allen's Son. Lucille Clifton. SP-ClifL

Can claim the hands of the son? (LL) To Mother. Keorapetse W. Kgositsile. GT

Can fan into a fire. (LL) Youth Sings a Song of Rosebuds. Countee Cullen. BANP; CP-CullC

Can handle. Snap a picture & let's go! (LL) Process. Al Young. CP-YounA

Can I forget thee? No, while mem'ry lasts. On Parting with a Friend. Mary Weston Fordham. CBWP-2

Can I go home wid yuh, sweetie? / Sure. (LL) Jazz Band in a Parisian Cabaret. Langston Hughes. CP-HughL

Can—I—poet. For Some Poets. Mae Jackson. PoBA

Can it be true, that we can meet. Slumbering Passion. Josephine D. Henderson Heard. CBWP-4

Can life's best consciousness of joy. Questioning. Henrietta Cordelia Ray. CBWP-3

Can make it out here alone. (LL) Alone. Maya Angelou. CP-AngeM; SP-AngeM

Can persess the self-same soul? (LL) The Lawyers' Ways. Paul Laurence Dunbar. CP-DunbP

Can reach your elbow. (LL) Pineapple is armored flower. Harryette Mullen. TtW

Can redwhite & blue I enter. Self World. Clarence Major. NBV

Can take a person's life. (LL) Little Old Letter. Langston Hughes. CP-HughL; SP-HughL

Can tha congregation/ pleaze sai/ AMEN. (LL) Familee reunion tyme iz a special tyme. Roni Walter. CtF

Can the baby inside you take hot sauce? (LL) The Night before Michael Was Born. Al Young. CP-YounA

Can they buy each other? (LL) Keyfoods. Audre Lorde. CP-LordA; SP-LordA

Can this sin live. (LL) Slaveship. Lucille Clifton. ESEAA

Can u walk away from ugly. Positives for Sterling Plumpp. Don L. Lee. JB; PoBA

Can violate or circumvent His plan. (LL) The Pagan Isms. Claude McKay. SP-McKaC

Can we go back home? (LL) Out of Pocket. Kevin Powell. CtF

Can you dance? Shall / you? (LL) From an Almanac (2). Amiri Baraka. SP-BaraA

Can you hear it/ a *faint echo/ vespers from the book of ancestry/ once bound.* What We Have Lost. Harris Duriel. SpiFl

Can you Remember / or did you ever know. Future Shock. Abiodun Oyewole. GT

Can you say Teotacacinte? First Poem from Nicaragua Libre: *Teotcacinte.* June Jordan. SP-JordJ

Canal Carondelet, le vent du nord me chasse. Adieu. Camille Thierry. TtW

Canary. Rita Dove. ESEAA

Cancers are a serious condition. Nikki Giovanni. SP-GiovN

Cane-Brake-Blues. Eugene B. Redmond. TtW

Cannon Arrested. Michael S. Harper. SP-HarpM

Cannot by these low promptings be confined. (LL) To care for others is the God in man. Albery Allson Whitman. EBAP

Can't afford that much. (LL) Puzzlement. Langston Hughes. CP-HughL

Can't C.P.T. / a show. (LL) Dancer. Langston Hughes. CP-HughL

Can't come, so there. (LL) Telegram to Alex/Bagel Shop, North Beach SF. Bob Kaufman. SP-KaufB

Can't erase the sign of the beast. (LL) 1984. Yusef Komunyakaa. SP-KomuY

Can't find what you can't see / can you? (LL) American History. Michael S. Harper. BPo; ESEAA; SP-HarpM

Can't see! And don't know! And won't ever care! (LL) The Colored Soldier. Langston Hughes. CP-HughL

Can't you hear me when i call. (LL) His Eminence Plays the Soular System. Eugene B. Redmond. TtW

Cant you / hear / the drummer? (LL) July. Daniel Gray-Kontar. SpiFl

Can't You Line It? *Unknown.* NAAAL

Can't you see I'm lonely. (LL) Poem (For BMC No. 2). Nikki Giovanni. SP-GiovN

Can't you see the dawn appears? (LL) Armageddon. Georgia Douglas Johnson. ShDr

Canticle for Abba Jacob, A. Marilyn Nelson. SP-NelsM

Canto 7: First Thesis. Tom Weatherly. PoBA

Cantos. Tom Weatherly. PoBA

Cape Coast Castle Revisted. Jo Ann Hall-Evans. BlSi

Capitalism Is a Brutal Motherfucker. Tony Medina. CtF

Capt. Smith and Pocahontas. Eloise Bibb. CBWP-4

Capture, The. Paul Laurence Dunbar. CP-DunbP

Car no more. (LL) Announcement. Langston Hughes. CP-HughL

Car seat and a lot of used condoms, A. (LL) Diverne's House. Marilyn Nelson. SP-NelsM

Career, A. Paul Laurence Dunbar. CP-DunbP

Carefully, in a clip. (LL) "Word to the Wise Is Enough, A." Raymond R. Patterson. NBV

Carefully / the leaves of autumn. Late October. Maya Angelou. CP-AngeM; SP-AngeM

Careless Word, The. Frances Ellen Watkins Harper. CP-HarpF

Caressing the black breast / of Jezebel. (LL) A Day in the Life of. . . . Conyus. GT

Caribbean Sunset. Langston Hughes. CP-HughL

Carl Chessman interviews San Quentin P.T.A. before leaving. The Enormous Gas Bill at the Dwarf Factory. A Horror Movie to be Shot with Eyes. Bob Kaufman. SP-KaufB

Carl Chessman Interviews the P.T.A. in His Swank Gas Chamber Before Leaving on His Annual Inspection of Capital, Tour of Northern California Death Universities, Happy. Bob Kaufman. SP-KaufB

Carlton, Patrick and I. The Boys of Summer. E. Ethelbert Miller. SpiFl

Carma. Jean Toomer. Klds

"Wind is in the cane. Come along."

Carmen. Victor Hernandez Cruz. PoBA

Carmencita loves Patrick. Little Song. Langston Hughes. CP-HughL

Carnival. Primus St. John. GT

Carol of the Brown King. Langston Hughes. CP-HughL

Carolina Cabin. Langston Hughes. CP-HughL

Carolina, in which he was killed. (LL) Robert G. Shaw. Henrietta Cordelia Ray. AAP; BlSi; CBWP-3

Carolina Moon. Al Young. CP-YounA

Carolina mourns to-day. For he, the gifted. Tribute to Capt. F. W. Dawson. Mary Weston Fordham. CBWP-2

Caroling softly souls of slavery. (LL) Song of the Son. Jean Toomer. AmNP; CDC; CP-ToomJ; CrDW; Klds; PoBA; TtW

Carousel, The. Gloria C. Oden. AmNP; GT; Klds; PoBA

Carpets cover many floors where I come from. To Vietnam. Charlie Cobb. PoBA

Carried away on the stream of your might, / Dionysos. (LL) Hail, Dionysos. Dudley Randall. BrTr

Carried her unprotesting out the door. The Rites for Cousin Vit. Gwendolyn Brooks. BPo; NAAAL; SP-BrooG

Carried lonely up the aisle. Funeral. Langston Hughes. CP-HughL

Carried me to de court. Ballad of Gin Mary. Langston Hughes. CP-HughL

Carried out assignment / with precision. (LL) The Family of Debridement. Michael S. Harper. SP-HarpM

Carry Me Back to Old Virginny. Elma Ehrlich Levinger. ShDr

Carver, The. Lucille Clifton. SP-ClifL

Carver / Brother, The. (LL) The Carver. Lucille Clifton. SP-ClifL

Case in Point. June Jordan. SP-JordJ

Case through the Looking Glass, The. Sekou Sundiata. *Fr.* Notes from the Defense of Colin Ferguson. SpiFl

Casey Jones. *African-American Oral Tradition.* GetYo

Cassandra and Friend. Norman Henry, II Pritchard. GT

"Cast down your bucket where you are." Atlanta Exposition Ode. Mary Weston Fordham. AAP; CBWP-2

Cast / out of rainclouds. Sheila. Bob Kaufman. SP-KaufB

Castaways, The. Claude McKay. SP-McKaC

Casting. Kevin Young. GT

Casual. Langston Hughes. CP-HughL

Casualty. Langston Hughes. *Fr.* Montage of a Dream Deferred. CP-HughL

Cat, The. Charles Baudelaire, *French.* CP-CullC, *tr. by* Countee Cullen

Cat and the Saxophone (2 a.m.), The. Langston Hughes. CP-HughL

Cat Is Sleeping on a Poem, The. Bob Kaufman. SP-KaufB

Cat said / on the corner, A. Vietnam #4. Clarence Major. NBV; PoBA

Catch. Langston Hughes. CP-HughL; SP-HughL

Catch him coming off the thing after a state of the union. Strategies. Welton Smith. NBP; PoBA

Catch of Shy Fish, A. Gwendolyn Brooks. SP-BrooG

Catch the faint spring fragrance of longing. (LL) Behind a Descartes Bumpersticker. Marilyn Nelson. SP-NelsM

Catch the Fire. Sonia Sanchez. CtF

Catches the soul of what you send. (LL) Tell me, dear beauty of the dusk. Jean Toomer. CP-ToomJ

Catechism of d Neoamerican Hoodoo Church. Ishmael Reed. NBV
("Little red wagon for the black bureaucrat, A.") CP-ReedI

Categories. Nikki Giovanni. SP-GiovN

Catharine of Arragon. Eloise Bibb. CBWP-4

Cathedrals sway in the blue face of the steel. Citizen. Julia Fields. GT

Catherine of Alexandria. Rita Dove. SP-DoveR

Catherine of Siena. Rita Dove. SP-DoveR

Cathexis. Frederick, Jr. Bryant. NBV; PoBA

Cats, *see also* Lovers, Scholars—the fervent, the austere. Charles Baudelaire, *French.* CP-CullC, *tr. by* Countee Cullen

Caught in a vastness beyond our sight to see? (LL) Thoughts in a Zoo. Countee Cullen. CP-CullC

Caught Susanner whistlin'; well. Breaking the Charm. Paul Laurence Dunbar. CP-DunbP

Cause he spit right in my eye. (LL) Prayer to the White Man's God. Charles Anderson. BlFi

Cause her "French" folks is "French"—same as mine! (LL) Cofaire? Sybil Klein. TtW

Cause I don't want to be blue. (LL) Young Gal's Blues. Langston Hughes. CP-HughL

Cause if I don't they'll cut down my pay. (LL) Supper Time. Langston Hughes. CP-HughL

'Cause I'm going to Kansas City. (LL) Parker's Mood. Clarence Beeks. NAAAL

Cause I'm still here kickin'! (LL) Madam and the Wrong Visitor. Langston Hughes. CP-HughL; SP-HughL

Cause I'm the general! See? (LL) Battle Ground. Langston Hughes. CP-HughL

Cause nobody deals with Aretha—a mother with four. Poem for Aretha. Nikki Giovanni. BPo; BrTr; PoBA; SP-GiovN

Cause sam cooke said, "a change is gonna come." (LL) Revolutionary Music. Nikki Giovanni. SP-GiovN

Cause she didn't know where it was. (LL) Mississippi. E. Ethelbert Miller. GT

Cause she my Sat. nite drinking partner and she deserves it done right. (LL) Sat. Nite. Jamal. CtF

Cause we are carving. Sonia Sanchez. SP-SancS

Cause you don't love me. Bad Luck Card. Langston Hughes. CP-HughL; SP-HughL

Causing her heart to rend, and leave it rent. (LL) Time passed away, and Leelah downcast grew. Albery Allson Whitman. EBAP

Cauterized me home. (LL) I paraplegic. Sonia Sanchez. SP-SancS

Cautious and Incantatory. Gwensways. Eugene B. Redmond. SpiFl

Cavalier. Richard Bruce. CDC

Caves. Michael S. Harper. SP-HarpM

Caw, caw, caw. Poem/Ditty-Bop. Carolyn M. Rodgers. JB

Cayenne in our blood. The Spice of Life. Kalamu ya Salaam. *Fr.* New Orleans Haiku. SpiFl

Cease then, my song, cease the unequal lay. (LL) On Imagination. Phillis Wheatley. BlSi; CP-WheaP; CrDW; NAAAL; TtW

Cecil County. Ron Welburn. PoBA

Celebrated Return. Clarence Major. AmNP

Celestial choir! enthron'd in realms of light. To His Excellency General Washington. Phillis Wheatley. CP-WheaP; Klds; NAAAL; TtW

Celestial muse! for sweetness fam'd inspire. To a Gentleman of the Navy. Phillis Wheatley. CP-WheaP

Celestial muse! sublimest of the nine. The Answer. *Unknown.* CP-WheaP

Cell Song. Etheridge Knight. PoBA; SP-KnigE

Cellophanes his future. (LL) Interne at Provident. Langston Hughes. CP-HughL; SP-HughL

Cemeteries are places for departed souls. Lines Written at the Grave of Alexander [*or* Alexandre] Dumas. Gwendolyn B. Bennett. CDC

Censure yourselves as well as the advisor. (LL) Prologue to a Supposed Play. Joseph Seamon Cotter, Sr. EBAP

Census man, The. Madam and the Census Man. Langston Hughes. CP-HughL; SP-HughL

Centaurian smoke blower / shyly smoking my breast. Prayer: "Centaurian smoke blower / shyly smoking my breast." Shonda Buchanan. CtF

Centipede. Rita Dove. SP-DoveR

Century Prayer, The. James Ephriam McGirt. AAP

Century Quilt, The. Marilyn Nelson. SP-NelsM

Ceremonial hill, this oak. (LL) Dead Oaks. Michael S. Harper. SP-HarpM

Ceremony. Kattie M. Cumbo. BlSi

Ceremony. Jewel C. Latimore. BlSi

Certain man had seven sons, A. On the Death of Allen's Son. Lucille Clifton. SP-ClifL

Certain Peace, A. Nikki Giovanni. SP-GiovN

Certain person wondered why, A. They Ask Why. Maya Angelou. CP-AngeM

Certainly they are the same weathered trees. From the Field. Lenard D. Moore. GT

'Cession's stahted on de gospel way, De. A Spiritual. Paul Laurence Dunbar. BPo; CP-DunbP

Cha-cha ... cha-cha / cha. (LL) Gospel Cha-Cha. Langston Hughes. CP-HughL

Chagall's chickens / ALIVE / WAKING! (LL) Get that feeling sometimes. Al Young. CP-YounA

Chain. Audre Lorde. BlSi; CP-LordA

Chain gangs keep me from my own?, The. (LL) Sorrow Home. Margaret Abigail Walker. CP-WalkM

Chained to her side by uncertainty! (LL) Insatiate. Mae V. Cowdery. ShDr

Chains are loosed, and at a smack, The. Flight of Leeona. Albery Allson Whitman. AAP

Chains that bind my thinking, The. The Searching. Alice S. Cobb. BlSi

Chair Gallows. Yusef Komunyakaa. SP-KomuY

Chalk-Dust. Lillian Byrnes. ShDr

Chalk mark sex of the nation, on walls we drummers. Three Modes of History and Culture. Amiri Baraka. ESEAA; SP-BaraA

Challenge. Sterling A. Brown. CDC; CP-BrowS

Champagne. Rita Dove. SP-DoveR

Change, The. Paul Laurence Dunbar. CP-DunbP

Change, The. Frances Ellen Watkins Harper. CP-HarpF

Change. Langston Hughes. CP-HughL

Change. Audre Lorde. CP-LordA

Change has come, The. (LL) Change has come, and Helen sleeps, The. Paul Laurence Dunbar. CP-DunbP

Change has come, and Helen sleeps, The. Paul Laurence Dunbar. CP-DunbP

Change Is Not Always Progress. Haki R. Madhubuti. BrTr

Change is thy other name. (LL) Dear lovely Death. Langston Hughes. CP-HughL

Change. / like if u were a match i wd light u into something. A Poem to Compliment Other Poems. Haki R. Madhubuti. BPo; BrTr; NAAAL; NBV; TtW

Change of Season. Audre Lorde. CP-LordA; SP-LordA

Change-up. Don L. Lee. PoBA

Changed Mind (or the Day I Woke Up). Tejumola Ologboni. NBV

Changes. Maya Angelou. CP-AngeM; SP-AngeM

Changes: or, Reveries at a Window Overlooking a Country Road, with Two Women Talking Blues in the Kitchen. Yusef Komunyakaa. SP-KomuY

Changing. Maya Angelou. CP-AngeM

Changing my name. (LL) Clinton. Sterling Plumpp. BkSV

Changing Time. Paul Laurence Dunbar. CP-DunbP

Chant for May Day. Langston Hughes. CP-HughL

Chant for Tom Mooney. Langston Hughes. CP-HughL

Chant for Young/Brothas and Sistuhs, A. Sonia Sanchez. BPo

Chanting / to the 1st fire. (LL) Speech #38 (or Y We Say It This Way). Amiri Baraka. SP-BaraA

Chappie, A. Paul Laurence Dunbar. CP-DunbP

Charge, The. Jay Wright. FB

Charity. Paul Laurence Dunbar. CP-DunbP

Charity. Henrietta Cordelia Ray. CBWP-3

Charles Sumner. Charlotte L. Forten Grimké. AAP

Charles Sumner. Henrietta Cordelia Ray. CBWP-3

Charles White. Nikki Giovanni. SP-GiovN

Charleston, / mamma! / ! (LL) The Cat and the Saxophone (2 a.m.). Langston Hughes. CP-HughL

Charley du Bignon. Mary E. Tucker. CBWP-1

Charm, The. Rita Dove. SP-DoveR

Charmante Emma, je vole sur tes pas. (LL) Le Retour au Village aux Perles. Nelson Desbrosses. EBAP; TtW

Charmed. Yusef Komunyakaa. SP-KomuY

Charmion's Lament. Eloise Bibb. CBWP-4

Charting the Night Winds. Nikki Giovanni. SP-GiovN

Charting tomorrow. (LL) Migration. Langston Hughes. CP-HughL

Chase, The. Paul Laurence Dunbar. CP-DunbP

Chase, The. Jean Toomer. CP-ToomJ

Chateaux en Espagne. Henrietta Cordelia Ray. CBWP-3

Chattanooga. Ishmael Reed. CP-ReedI; NAAAL

Chaucer. Benjamin Brawley. BANP

Cheap little rhymes. Sliver. Langston Hughes. *Fr.* Montage of a Dream Deferred. CP-HughL

Cheapest boarding house! (LL) Boarding House. Langston Hughes. CP-HughL

Checkers. Sterling A. Brown. CP-BrowS

Checking out burros! (LL) Absent from the United States. Al Young. CP-YounA

Checking the traps. The Ice-Fishing House. Michael S. Harper. SP-HarpM

Checks the wild pigeons taking them to breast. (LL) Letter across Doubt and Distance. M. Carl Holman. AmNP

Cheerless Condition of Bachelorship, The. George Moses Horton. SP-HortG

Chemical bliss of/or flesh, waiting for nothing less than The / Real Thing. (LL) The Problem of Identity. Al Young. CP-YounA

Chemistry. Al Young. CP-YounA

Cherokee, The. Mary Weston Fordham. CBWP-2

Chic Freedom's Reflection. Alice Walker. CP-WalkA

Chicago. Margaret Abigail Walker. CP-WalkM; GT

Chicago Blues. Langston Hughes. CP-HughL

Chicago *Defender* Sends a Man to Little Rock, The. Gwendolyn Brooks. AmNP; CrDW; NAAAL; PoBA; SP-BrooG

Chicago Exposition Ode. Mary Weston Fordham. CBWP-2

Chicago is a town. Chicago Blues. Langston Hughes. CP-HughL

Chicago Picasso, The. Gwendolyn Brooks. BPo

(Two Dedications.) NAAAL

Chicken-Licken. Maya Angelou. SP-AngeM

("Dead of acute peoplessness.") (LL) CP-AngeM

Chicken thaws, blood, A. Eden. Claudia Rankine. GT

Chieftan's light canoe, in which his maid you see, A. Albery Allson Whitman. *See* "Come now, my love, the moon is on the lake;"

City has no will but yours! The. (LL) Welcome Address. Paul Laurence Dunbar. CP-DunbP

City Home Detroit. Al Young. CP-YounA

City is a jealous bitch, The. J'Accuse. Bob Kaufman. SP-KaufB

City of tense and stricken faces. Jackson, Mississippi. Margaret Abigail Walker. BrTr; CP-WalkM; FB

City planners. To the New Annex to the Detroit County Jail. Richard W. Thomas. PoBA

City Rises, The. James Cunningham. JB

City rises / in color, our sad, The. A Poem for Democrats. Amiri Baraka. SP-BaraA

City's Love, The. Claude McKay. SP-McKaC

Civil Rights Bill #666. Amiri Baraka. SP-BaraA

Civil Rights / included Nathan. History on Wheels. Amiri Baraka. SP-BaraA

Claflin's Alumni. Lizelia Augusta Jenkins Moorer. CBWP-3

Clamb ape mountain backwards. To Be Quicker. Don L. Lee. JB

Clan Meeting: Births and Nations: A Blood Song. Michael S. Harper. SP-HarpM

Clark's Way Out West: Another Version. Michael S. Harper. SP-HarpM

Class Room. Virginia A. Houston. ShDr

Class Song of '91. Eloise Bibb. CBWP-4

Clay. Amiri Baraka. ESEAA

Clean an' bright. (LL) Judgment Day. Langston Hughes. CP-HughL; SP-HughL

Clean de ba'n an' sweep de flo'. Uncle Eph's Banjo Song. James Edwin Campbell. BANP

Clean jeans and comfortable shoes. Syracuse Airport. Audre Lorde. CP-LordA

Clean the spittoons, boy. Brass Spittoons. Langston Hughes. AmNP; BANP; CP-HughL

Clean until he can / possess me. (LL) Africa II. Nikki Giovanni. SP-GiovN

Clean up your room. (LL) If mama / could see. Lucille Clifton. NAAAL; SP-ClifL

Clear. Angelo Lewis. PoBA

Climb / into a jar. Pithos. Rita Dove. SP-DoveR

Climbing. Lucille Clifton. GT

Climbing to greet minstrel poles. (LL) Clinton. Sterling Plumpp. BkSV

Clinging / to lost / horizons / i. (LL) Upon Leaving the Parole Board Hearing. Conyus. GT

Clinton. Sterling Plumpp. BkSV

Clipped / separated / piled up. Mulch. Adam David Miller. NBV

Cloak, The. Norman Henry, II Pritchard. GT

Cloak of night and the midnight sun lit his way along the / Lively streets. (LL) Ghetto Waif. B. Felton. BrTr

Close of Day, The. Wesley Curtright. CDC

Close of Life, The. George Moses Horton. SP-HortG

Close the dim eyes, for expression hath left them. Lines on a Dead Girl. Priscilla Jane Thompson. CBWP-2

Close their eyes / and snap. (LL) Wishbone. Frank X. Walker. SpiFl

"Close Your Eyes!" Arna Bontemps. AmNP; CDC; FB; GT; Klds; PoBA

Close your eyes. Ascend into yourself. (LL) Union Apprehended. Marilyn Nelson. SP-NelsM

Close your eyes; walk bravely through. (LL) "Close Your Eyes!" Arna Bontemps. AmNP; CDC; FB; GT; Klds; PoBA

Close your sleepy eyes, or the pale moonlight will steal you. Lullaby. Aqua Laluah. ShDr

Closed against his icy breath. (LL) Youth in Heaven. Frances Ellen Watkins Harper. CP-HarpF

Closed window looks down, A. Ka 'Ba. Amiri Baraka. BPo; CrDW; NBV

Closer in. Bro Duncanson. C. S. Giscombe. GT

Closer to escaping into day / trams. (LL) Electricity of Blossoms. Lorenzo Thomas. GT

Closing Time. Langston Hughes. CP-HughL

Cloteel: / Rampart Street knows you now: the golden. Sterling A. Brown. CP-BrowS

Clother with the rich aspect of this fair clime. Albery Allson Whitman. Fr. Leelah Misled. EBAP

Cloud. Jean Toomer. CP-ToomJ

Cloud Fantasy. Henrietta Cordelia Ray. CBWP-3

Cloud fell down from the heavens, A. A Starry Night. Paul Laurence Dunbar. CP-DunbP

Cloud looked in at the window, The. Changing Time. Paul Laurence Dunbar. CP-DunbP

Cloud Song. Henrietta Cordelia Ray. CBWP-3

Cloudless summer day. Haiku: "Cloudless summer day." Lenard D. Moore. SpiFl

Clouds fill the sky. The Morning after. . . Love. Kattie M. Cumbo. BlSi

Clouds grow thickest when the summit's nigh, The. (LL) Slow Through the Dark. Paul Laurence Dunbar. CP-DunbP

Clouds weave a shawl, The. Garment. Langston Hughes. CP-HughL

Clown, The. D. L. Graham. BlFi

Clown Nose. Marilyn Nelson. SP-NelsM

Clutching at trees and clawing rocks. For an Indian Screen. Langston Hughes. CP-HughL

Clutter-up People. Alice Walker. CP-WalkA

Coach after raging coach. (LL) True we are two grown men. Ed Roberson. GT

Coal. Audre Lorde. BlSi; NBV; PoBA

("I is the total black.") ESEAA; SP-LordA

("I / Is the total black, being spoken.") CP-LordA

("Take my word for jewel in your open light.") (LL) CP-LordA; NAAAL

Coastal Moon. Al Young. CP-YounA

Cocaine Nell. African-American Oral Tradition. GetYo

Cocaine Shorty. African-American Oral Tradition. GetYo

Cock is a crickly creature. African-American Oral Tradition. GetYo

Cock my pistol before I shoot. (LL) Ringo. African-American Oral Tradition. GetYo

Cockroach / who is dying, The. Kitchen Linoleum. Audre Lorde. CP-LordA

Cocktails / no / more / toms. (LL) Illusions. Kirk Hall. BlFi

Cocoa Morning. Bob Kaufman. AmNP; NBV; SP-KaufB

Cocumscussoc is my village. History as Apple Tree. Michael S. Harper. SP-HarpM

Coeur cassé. My life is settling in a cup of. Fragments from the Diary of Amelie Patiné, Quadroon Mistress of Monsieur Jacques R-------. Sybil Klein. TtW

Cofaire? Sybil Klein. TtW

Coiling at your toes for granite peace. (LL) Clinton. Sterling Plumpp. BkSV

Cold and dark street. (LL) Samantha Is My Negro Cat. William J. Harris. GT

Cold chain of life presseth heavily on me tonight, The. Fragment. Adah Isaacs Menken. CBWP-1

Cold grey walls. San Francisco County Jail Cell B-6. Conyus. PoBA

Cold hands to my hotheadedness. (LL) Self-Portrait: Holding On. Al Young. CP-YounA

Cold has put blue horses where lambs were, The. Blue Horses. Ed Roberson. GT; PoBA

Cold in a chair. (LL) The 26th Person. Dolores Kendrick. GT

Cold morning early. Two Mornings. Lawrence McGaugh. PoBA

Cold, smoldering, The. A Love Dirge to the Whitehouse. Bob Fletcher. NBP

Cold Term. Amiri Baraka. BPo

Coleridge Jackson had nothing. Maya Angelou. CP-AngeM

Collage. Quincy Troupe. CtF

Collage for Richard Davis—Two Short Forms, A. De Leon Harrison. PoBA

Collars, billowing, for lift off. (LL) Soul Proprietorship. Ishmael Reed. CP-ReedI

Collection Day. Natasha Trethewey. SpiFl

College Formal: Renaissance Casino. Langston Hughes. Fr. Montage of a Dream Deferred. CP-HughL

Colloquy. Sterling A. Brown. CP-BrowS

Color. Langston Hughes. CP-HughL

Color ain't no faucet. Within the Veil. Michelle Cliff. NAAAL

Color Bane, The. George Marion McClellan. EBAP

Color of violence is black, The. Endangered Species. Ai. ESEAA

Color Sergeant, The, (On an Incident at the Battle of San Juan Hill). James Weldon Johnson. GT

Colored Band, The. Paul Laurence Dunbar. CP-DunbP

Colored Blues Singer. Countee Cullen. CP-CullC

Colored Heroes, Hark the Bugle. Robert Charles O'Hara Benjamin. AAP

Colored heroes seek your standard. Colored Heroes, Hark the Bugle. Robert Charles O'Hara Benjamin. AAP

Colored Soldier, The. Langston Hughes. CP-HughL

Colored Soldiers, The. Paul Laurence Dunbar. AAP; CP-DunbP; NAAAL

Colorless apartheid? (LL) Where? When? Which? Langston Hughes. Klds

Colors. Countee Cullen. CP-CullC

Colors for Mama. Barbara Mahone. PoBA

Coltrane must understand how. Soul. D. L. Graham. Klds; PoBA

Columbia. Ishmael Reed. CP-ReedI

Columbia, all hail! Chicago Exposition Ode. Mary Weston Fordham. CBWP-2

Columbia! be thine. (LL) Chicago Exposition Ode. Mary Weston Fordham. CBWP-2

Columbia, / My dear girl. Langston Hughes. CP-HughL

Columbia on the battle-ground. The Soliloquy. Francis A. Boyd. *Fr.* Columbiana. EBAP

Columbia, still be free. (LL) Liberty. George Moses Horton. SP-HortG

Columbian Ode. Paul Laurence Dunbar. CP-DunbP

Columbiana. Francis A. Boyd. EBAP
Dream, The.
Soliloquy, The.

Column six, page thirty-six. Photographs of the Medusa. Marilyn Nelson. SP-NelsM

Comb their hair for dinner. (LL) The English. Langston Hughes. CP-HughL

Come alive in her ears. (LL) Studs. Michael S. Harper. ESEAA

Come all ye Colonizationists. Old Liberia Is Not the Place for Me. Joshua McCarter Simpson. AAP

Come all you people whilst you present at hand. Jesse James. *African-American Oral Tradition.* GetYo

Come along ten million strong. (LL) Harriet Tubman. Margaret Abigail Walker. CP-WalkM; TtW

Come, And Be My Baby. Maya Angelou. CP-AngeM; SP-AngeM

Come and get that memory. (LL) Egyptian Book of the Dead. David Henderson. TtW

Come and Kiss Me Sweet and Twenty. Paul Laurence Dunbar. CP-DunbP

Come and listen to the chiming. Bells of St. Michael. Mary Weston Fordham. CBWP-2

Come away to dreamin' town. Dreamin' Town. Paul Laurence Dunbar. CP-DunbP

Come Back Blues. Michael S. Harper. PoBA; SP-HarpM

Come back to find himself / a Black Man / again. (LL) There he stands, see? Carl Wendell, Jr. Hines. Klds

Come back to me! my life is young. Karazah to Karl. Adah Isaacs Menken. CBWP-1

Come back to me, O ye, my children. Mother's Recall. Mary Weston Fordham. CBWP-2

Come back to seek the girl she was in these familiar stones. (LL) To a Young Girl Leaving the Hill Country. Arna Bontemps. GT; Klds

Come between— / Or men. (LL) Addition: "Put 5 and 5 together." Langston Hughes. CP-HughL

Come, brother, come. Let's lift it. Cotton Song. Jean Toomer. BPo; CDC; CP-ToomJ

Come Celebrate Me. (LL) Lynch Fragment 2. Jayne Cortez. SP-CortJ

Come, children, hear the joyful sound. The Big Bell in Zion. Theodore Henry Shackleford. BANP

Come, claim your wings. Mumble the Magic Words. Jabari Asim. CtF

Come dance with me. (LL) II. Song of the Reverend Gatemouth Moore. Etheridge Knight. BkSV

Come down. (LL) Down Where I Am. Langston Hughes. CP-HughL

Come, drink a stirrup cup with me. The Stirrup Cup. Paul Laurence Dunbar. CP-DunbP

Come 'ere, boy! Langston Hughes. *See* Brass Spittoons.

Come, essay a sprightly measure. A Bridal Measure. Paul Laurence Dunbar. CP-DunbP

Come, gather around me, children. The Jewish Grandfather's Story. Frances Ellen Watkins Harper. CP-HarpF

Come, help flatten a raindrop. (LL) Jail Poems. Bob Kaufman. NAAAL

Come help me sing the morning song. Song of Liberty and Parental Advice. George Moses Horton. SP-HortG

Come here, I want to show you something. Sightseeing. Rita Dove. GT; SP-DoveR

Come home from the movies. Lucille Clifton. SP-ClifL

Come home i need you. (LL) Make Up. Nikki Giovanni. SP-GiovN

Come home to die! (LL) Lover's Return. Langston Hughes. CP-HughL; SP-HughL

Come home with me a little space. Christmas at Melrose. Leslie Pinckney Hill. BANP

Come in, Aunt Jemima. Wintah Styles, De. Maggie Pogue Johnson. CBWP-4

Come in hyeah, you scamp! (LL) A Grievance. Paul Laurence Dunbar. CP-DunbP

Come in sweet grief. Tricked Again. Ridhiana. NBP

Come in to dinner, squalls the dame. Snaps for Dinner, Snaps for Breakfast and Snaps for Supper. George Moses Horton. SP-HortG; TtW

Come into Black geography. Sonia Sanchez. *Fr.* Past. SP-SancS

"Come Juju come." (LL) A Juju of My Own. Lebert Bethune. PoBA

Come, let us join this festal lay. Rally Song. Mary Weston Fordham. CBWP-2

Come let us journey to. Bob Kaufman. SP-KaufB

Come, let us plant our love as farmers plant. The Love Tree. Countee Cullen. CP-CullC

Come, / Let us roam the night together. Harlem Night Song. Langston Hughes. CP-HughL; SP-HughL

Come love, / Love come. (LL) Come let us journey to. Bob Kaufman. SP-KaufB

Come nearer to me, husband. The Dying Mother. Frances Ellen Watkins Harper. CP-HarpF

Come now, all you who are singers. Song of Spain. Langston Hughes. CP-HughL

"Come now, my love, the moon is on the lake." Albery Allson Whitman. AAP; AfAmPo *Fr.* Twasinta's Seminoles; Or Rape of Florida

Come on baby, take off your clothes, / Round about Midnight. (LL) Round about Midnight. Bob Kaufman. SP-KaufB

Come On Home. Sharon Scott. JB

Come on home girl. (LL) Tougaloo Blues. Kelly Norman Ellis. SpiFl

Come on out of there with your hands up, Charlie. Patriotic Ode on the Fourteenth Anniversary of the Persecution of Charlie Chaplin. Bob Kaufman. PoBA

COME ON! They killed Martin Luther thingabob. (LL) Oh shit a riot! Jacques Wakefield. BlFi

Come on walkin' wid me, Lucy. A Spring Wooing. Paul Laurence Dunbar. CP-DunbP

Come out, come out, wherever you are. Sarajevo Moon. Al Young. CP-YounA

Come Peace, on snowy pinions. Ode to Peace. Mary Weston Fordham. CBWP-2

Come rain or shining moon. (LL) Belgrade moon, where are you. Al Young. CP-YounA

Come ride my birth, earth mother. Woman. Sonia Sanchez. *Fr.* Past. SP-SancS

Come right in this house, Will Johnson! Mrs. Johnson Objects. Clara Ann Thompson. BlSi; CBWP-2

Come! rouse ye brothers, rouse! a peal now breaks. Spirit Voice; or Liberty Call to the Disfranchised (State of New York), The. Charles Lewis Reason. AAP; EBAP

Come, / says the master. / Partake. (LL) The Fruit of Faith. Marilyn Nelson. SP-NelsM

Come sing, come sing, come sing sing / And sing. (LL) Yardbird's Skull. Owen Dodson. AmNP; IDB; PoBA

Come singing in your chains. Faith Healer. Yusef Komunyakaa. SP-KomuY

Come speak to me of Jesus. Jesus. Frances Ellen Watkins Harper. CP-HarpF

Come, the young dawn bringing! (LL) Tell me, ye sad winds sighing. Timothy Thomas Fortune. EBAP

Come then Poet, and sing. And Tell Me Poet, Can Love Exist in Slavery? Etheridge Knight. SP-KnigE

Come there to me in words. (LL) Winter in the Country. Claude McKay. SP-McKaC

Come to guard us, come to bless us. The Triple Benison. Henrietta Cordelia Ray. CBWP-3

Come to me / be mine to love / over and over again. (LL) A Cultural Trip. Opal Palmer Adisa. GT

Come to me broken dreams and all. The Still Voice of Harlem. Conrad Kent Rivers. IDB; Klds; NNP; PoBA

Come to rest at quiet time. (LL) Motion and Rest. Jean Toomer. CP-ToomJ

Come to the pane, draw the curtain apart. My Little March Girl. Paul Laurence Dunbar. CP-DunbP

Come to the road! (LL) To the Road. Paul Laurence Dunbar. CP-DunbP

Come to your Wedding Song. (LL) A Black Wedding Song. Gwendolyn Brooks. IHS

Come true. (LL) Passing. Langston Hughes. CP-HughL

Come Visit My Garden. Tom Dent. NNP

Come weep with us. (LL) Lonely Woman. Jayne Cortez. NBV

Come when the nights are bright with stars. Invitation to Love. Paul Laurence Dunbar. CP-DunbP; IHS

Come, why not don my spangled jacket? (LL) The Bohemian. Paul Laurence Dunbar. CP-DunbP

Come, "Will," let's be good friends again. Sunshine after Cloud. Josephine D. Henderson Heard. CBWP-4

Come with me. Parker's Mood. Clarence Beeks. NAAAL

Come with me. (LL) Port Town. Langston Hughes. CP-HughL; SP-HughL

Come woman be my wife, come woman be my wife. (LL) I Am Open. Michael Datcher. CtF

Come. . . have do with dillying. Shrine to What Should Be. Mari E. Evans. NNP

Comes now / Taste of firecrackers. Duke Ellington. Frank Marshall Davis. TtW

Coming and Going: Gabriel's Song. George Barlow. *Fr.* Gabriel. TtW

Coming [or Comin'] for [or fer] to carry me home. (LL) Swing low, sweet chariot. *Unknown.* CrDW

Coming from flat-bed bones of the funky funky / nighttrains. (LL) Nighttrains. Jayne Cortez. SP-CortJ

Coming from the south. Six Ten Sixty-Nine. Conyus. GT; PoBA

Coming home. Langston Hughes. *See* Seascape.

Coming in and out of cities. Touring. Audre Lorde. CP-LordA

Coming of Kali, The. Lucille Clifton. SP-ClifL

Coming of Spring, The. Henrietta Cordelia Ray. CBWP-3

Coming out of that mouth. (LL) First, they said we were savages. Alice Walker. CP-WalkA

Coming to the Net. Brian G. Gilmore. SpiFl

Coming together / it is easier to work. Recreation. Audre Lorde. CP-LordA

Coming Woman, The. Mary Weston Fordham. CBWP-2

Comme la vaste mer grondant sous la tropique. Le Retour de Napoléon. Victor Séjour. EBAP

Commemoration. Claude McKay. BANP; SP-McKaC

Comment. Langston Hughes. CP-HughL

Comment on Curb. Langston Hughes. *Fr.* Lenox Avenue Mural. AmNP; SP-HughL *Fr.* Montage of a Dream Deferred. CP-HughL

Comment on War. Langston Hughes. CP-HughL

Comments. Peggy Susberry Kenner. JB

Committee's fat, The. Un-American Investigators. Langston Hughes. BPo; CP-HughL

Common Dust. Georgia Douglas Johnson. AmNP; PoBA; ShDr

Common hands' destiny, The. (LL) Zimbabwe. Sterling Plumpp. TtW

Common Occurrence, A. Priscilla Jane Thompson. CBWP-2

Common Things. Paul Laurence Dunbar. CP-DunbP; GT

Commonwealth of God, The. (LL) The Present Age. Frances Ellen Watkins Harper. CP-HarpF

Communication. Nikki Giovanni. SP-GiovN

Communication I. Maya Angelou. CP-AngeM; SP-AngeM

Communication II. Maya Angelou. CP-AngeM; SP-AngeM

Communication in Whi-te. Don L. Lee. BPo

Communion. Paul Laurence Dunbar. CP-DunbP

Communion. Langston Hughes. CP-HughL

Communiqué. Langston Hughes. CP-HughL

Communique. Yusef Komunyakaa. SP-KomuY

Companion Pieces. Niama Leslie JoAnn Williams. CtF

Companion's Progress, A. Paul Laurence Dunbar. CP-DunbP; GT

Company. Rita Dove. SP-DoveR

Comparison. Paul Laurence Dunbar. CP-DunbP

Compass points. (LL) Seashore through Dark Glasses (Atlantic City). Langston Hughes. CP-HughL; SP-HughL

Compassionate art. All else fades. (LL) Homage to Paul Robeson. Robert Hayden. CP-HaydR

Compassion's Bird. Jay Wright. ESEAA

Compendium. Rita Dove. SP-DoveR

Compensation. James Edwin Campbell. BANP

Compensation. Paul Laurence Dunbar. AmNP; BPo; CP-DunbP

Compensation. Henrietta Cordelia Ray. CBWP-3

Complaint of these / green hills, The. (LL) Turning Thirty, I Contemplate Students Bicycling Home. Rita Dove. ESEAA

Complicity. Jayne Cortez. SP-CortJ

Compose for Red a proper verse. For Malcolm, a Year After. Etheridge Knight. SP-KnigE

Compressed into a slither of the bed. Out-of-Body Experience. Jenoyne Adams. CtF

Compulsory Chapel. Alice Walker. CP-WalkA

Comrade. Paul Laurence Dunbar. CP-DunbP

Comrade Lenin of Russia. Ballads of Lenin. Langston Hughes. CP-HughL

Conceit, A. Maya Angelou. CP-AngeM; SP-AngeM

Conception. Waring Cuney. BANP

Concerning One Responsible Negro with Too Much Power. Nikki Giovanni. BPo

Concert, The. Paul Laurence Dunbar. CP-DunbP

Concert. Helen G. Quigless. NBP

Conclusion. Audre Lorde. CP-LordA; SP-LordA

Concrete beneath our feet, The. (LL) For Brother Malcolm. Edward S. Spriggs. BrTr

Condemned to be like God? (LL) The Negro Laughs Back. Mary Jenness. ShDr

Condition Blue/ Dress. Ron Welburn. NBV

Conduct your blooming in the noise and whip of the whirlwind. (LL) The Second Sermon on the Warpland. Gwendolyn Brooks. BPo; PoBA

Conferences with the Unknown. Michael S. Harper. SP-HarpM

Confession. Lucille Clifton. SP-ClifL; TtW

Confession. Donald Jeffrey Hayes. CDC

Confession. Alice Walker. CP-WalkA

Confession Stone, The. Owen Dodson. Klds

Confession to Malcolm. Conyus. NBV

Confessional. Paul Laurence Dunbar. CP-DunbP

Confessional Poem. Marilyn Nelson. SP-NelsM

Confessions of a blood cake / it's nothing. (LL) It's nothing / this tragedy in our arms. Jayne Cortez. SP-CortJ

Confetti & cheers in Havana. (LL) Boxing Day. Yusef Komunyakaa. SP-KomuY

Confidence, A. Paul Laurence Dunbar. CP-DunbP

Confirmation. Paul Laurence Dunbar. CP-DunbP

Confront ourselves / in our past. (LL) Reverses. Maya Angelou. CP-AngeM

Coniagui women / wear their flesh like war, The. Audre Lorde. CP-LordA

Conies had their hiding-place, The. He "Had Not Where to Lay His Head." Frances Ellen Watkins Harper. CP-HarpF

Conjugal Visits. Al Young. NAAAL

Conjure up the spell for motion. (LL) Blue Deep. Quo Vadis Gex-Breaux. TtW

Conjured. Sterling A. Brown. CP-BrowS

Conjurer. And of himself of God. (LL) Witch Doctor. Robert Hayden. AmNP; CP-HaydR

Connections. Stephen Dobyns. SP-DoveR

Connoisseur of pearl, A. African China. Melvin Beaunearus Tolson. Klds; PoBA

Connubial Felicity. George Moses Horton. SP-HortG

Conquerors, The. Paul Laurence Dunbar. CP-DunbP

Conquest. Georgia Douglas Johnson. AmNP

Conquest. Pauli Murray. GT

Conscience and Remorse. Paul Laurence Dunbar. CP-DunbP

Conservatory Student Struggles with Higher Instrumentation. Langston Hughes. CP-HughL

Consider her now, glowing, light-worn. A Sunday Sonnet for My Mother's Mother. Al Young. CP-YounA

Consider me, / A colored boy. Langston Hughes. CP-HughL; SP-HughL

Consider me a memory, a dream that passed away. Recessional. Georgia Douglas Johnson. CDC

Consider the eternal Cat. Homage. Naomi Long Madgett. TtW

Consider them both in paradise. W. H. Auden & Mantan Moreland. Al Young. CP-YounA

Constant Labor, A. James W. Thompson. BPo

Construction. Audre Lorde. CP-LordA

Consultation. Jayne Cortez. SP-CortJ

Consumes your name. (LL) The Fireplace. Michael S. Harper. GT

Consumptive, The. Langston Hughes. CP-HughL

Consumptive, The. Priscilla Jane Thompson. CBWP-2

Contact Lenses. Audre Lorde. CP-LordA

"Containing Communism." Charlie Cobb. PoBA

Contemporary Announcement. Maya Angelou. CP-AngeM; SP-AngeM

Content. Paul Laurence Dunbar. CP-DunbP

Contest ends at midnight. (LL) My Brothers. Ishmael Reed. CP-ReedI

Contest of Song and Love, The. George Marion McClellan. *Fr.* The Legend of Tannhauser and Elizabeth. EBAP

Continuing. Al Young. CP-YounA

Continuous Visit. Michael S. Harper. SP-HarpM

Con/tin/u/way/shun Blues. Etheridge Knight. SP-KnigE

Contract. (For The Destruction and Rebuilding of Paterson), A. Amiri Baraka. SP-BaraA

Contradiction. Joseph Seamon Cotter, Sr. EBAP

Contrary to / tales you told us. Anti-Father. Rita Dove. SP-DoveR

Contrast, The. Frances Ellen Watkins Harper. CP-HarpF

Conundrum. Carl Clark. JB

Convent. Langston Hughes. CP-HughL

Conversation. Nikki Giovanni. SP-GiovN

Conversation in Crisis. Audre Lorde. *See* Conversations in Crisis.

Conversation in the smoker. Call for Barnum. Sterling A. Brown. CP-BrowS

Conversation on V. Owen Dodson. Klds

Conversation Overheard. Quincy Troupe. NAAAL

Conversation with My Grandson, Waiting to Be Conceived. Lucille Clifton. SP-ClifL

Conversations in Crisis. Audre Lorde. SP-LordA
  (Conversation in Crisis.) CP-LordA

Converse with heav'n, and taste the promis'd joy. (LL) To the Honourable T.H. Esq.; on the Death of His Daughter. Phillis Wheatley. CP-WheaP

Conversion. Jean Toomer. CP-ToomJ

Convert, The. Margaret Else Danner. BPo; BrTr

Convict. Sterling A. Brown. CP-BrowS

Convict strolled into the prison administration building to, The. Rehabilitation & Treatment in the Prisons of America. Etheridge Knight. SP-KnigE

Convicted in this / country / of Slavery! / -Coyt's Son. (LL) The Turn Around Y36. Amiri Baraka. SP-BaraA

Convict's Prayer. *African-American Oral Tradition.* GetYo

Cool beneath melon-colored cloth, your belly. For Arl in Her Sixth Month. Al Young. CP-YounA

Cool is the wind, for the summer is waning. To the Road. Paul Laurence Dunbar. CP-DunbP

Cool shadows blanked dead cities, falling. Falling. Bob Kaufman. PoBA; SP-KaufB

Cool-slick-fly— / a whole generation of. Impressions. Kirk Hall. BlFi

Cool to cool to cool. (LL) Making Poems. Sekou Sundiata. SpiFl

Coolwell Vignette. Sterling A. Brown. CP-BrowS

Cop-Out Session. Etheridge Knight. SP-KnigE

Cop / with a cold, The. High-cool/2. James Cunningham. JB

Copacetic Mingus. Yusef Komunyakaa. SP-KomuY

Coping. Audre Lorde. CP-LordA

Copper Beech, The. Rita Dove. SP-DoveR

Coquette Conquered, A. Paul Laurence Dunbar. CP-DunbP

Cor cordium is written there. Countee Cullen. CP-CullC

Cora. Langston Hughes. CP-HughL; SP-HughL

Coral Atoll. Dudley Randall. TtW

Coral stone at the edge of Bufano Road, A. Hugo I. Audre Lorde. CP-LordA

Corduroy Road. Rita Dove. SP-DoveR

Core of conversations we never had, A. Sister, Morning Is a Time for Miracles. Audre Lorde. SP-LordA

Corktown. Michael S. Harper. SP-HarpM

Corn-Song, A. Paul Laurence Dunbar. CP-DunbP

Corn Song, The. John Wesley Holloway. BANP

Corn-Stalk Fiddle, THe. Paul Laurence Dunbar. AAP; CP-DunbP

Corner Meeting. Langston Hughes. *Fr.* Montage of a Dream Deferred. CP-HughL

Corner of 47th and South Park, *see also* Little Old Wicked Nell. *African-American Oral Tradition.* GetYo

Cornered and trapped, The. For Mack C. Parker. Pauli Murray. PoBA

Corners / Of South Parkway. Jitney. Langston Hughes. CP-HughL

Corrected Review. Michael S. Harper. SP-HarpM

Corrigenda. Yusef Komunyakaa. SP-KomuY

Corrupt madness of the individual. You cannot live, The. Red Eye. Amiri Baraka. SP-BaraA

Cos, Kelly M——, I bets on you. (LL) To Kelly Miller, Jr. Paul Laurence Dunbar. CP-DunbP

Co'se you knows dat possum's mine! (LL) A Coquette Conquered. Paul Laurence Dunbar. CP-DunbP

Cosmic Age, The. Sun-Ra. BlFi

Cosmic-Timelessness of the Cosmic Age. (LL) The Cosmic Age. Sun-Ra. BlFi

Cotton blouse you wear, your mother said, The. McDonogh Day in New Orleans. Marcus B. Christian. AmNP

Cotton Candy on a Rainy Day. Nikki Giovanni. SP-GiovN

Cotton Club, The. Clarence Major. TtW

Cotton eyes soaking up blood. Blue Monday. Calvin Forbes. ESEAA

Cotton rows crisscross the world. The Memory. Maya Angelou. SP-AngeM

Cotton Song. Jean Toomer. BPo; CDC; CP-ToomJ

Cough of a mortar tube, The. (LL) Ambush. Yusef Komunyakaa. SP-KomuY

Could be Hastings Street. Langston Hughes. CP-HughL; SP-HughL

Could better make and use / Black bread. (LL) Naturally. Audre Lorde. CP-LordA

Could break death's adamantine law. (LL) For an Anarchist. Countee Cullen. CP-CullC

Could find a Heav'n, a bright, golden sphere. (LL) I love the symphony of nature's chords. Albery Allson Whitman. EBAP

Could I but find the words. (LL) A Song to a Negro Wash-woman. Langston Hughes. CP-HughL

Could I but retrace. Tanka (I–VIII). Lewis Alexander. CDC

Could it be, Bud. For Bud. Michael S. Harper. ESEAA; SP-HarpM

Could weep just once again. (LL) December, 1919. Claude McKay. SP-McKaC

Count Basie's place. Ted Wilson. BlFi

Count it anyway he wants. Variation on Guilt. Rita Dove. SP-DoveR

Count Your Blessings. Mrs. Henry Linden. CBWP-4

Counter Mood. Countee Cullen. CP-CullC

Countess Erica Blaise: Chorus. Bob Kaufman. SP-KaufB

Counting. Fenton Johnson. AmNP

Counting the eyes that see. (LL) The Message on Cape Cod. Michael S. Weaver. GT

Country. Langston Hughes. CP-HughL

Country kid in Mississippi I drew water, A. A Little More Traveling Music. Al Young. CP-YounA; NBV

Country Lover. Maya Angelou. CP-AngeM; SP-AngeM

Country Midwife: A Day, The. Ai. GT

Couple, The. Maya Angelou. CP-AngeM; SP-AngeM

Courage. Claude McKay. SP-McKaC

Courtesy, A Trenchant Grace, A. Cyrus Cassells. GT

Courtship. Rita Dove. SP-DoveR

Courtship, Diligence. Rita Dove. SP-DoveR

Cousin Mary. Wanda Coleman. GT

Covenant, The. James Cunningham. JB

Cover him over with daisies white. The Death of the First Born. Paul Laurence Dunbar. CP-DunbP

Cover Photograph. Marilyn Nelson. SP-NelsM

Covers me with day. (LL) When i return home. Sonia Sanchez. SP-SancS

Covetous Nebraskaites, Fr. Elymas Payson Rogers. *Fr.* The Repeal of the Missouri Compromise Considered. AAP; EBAP

Cow-hoof imprint, A. Skyline. Jean Toomer. CP-ToomJ

Cowards they, who turn and fly. (LL) Colored Heroes, Hark the Bugle. Robert Charles O'Hara Benjamin. AAP

Cowering true believers would have said. (LL) Electrical Storm. Robert Hayden. CP-HaydR

Cowrie shells / St. Louis Woman. (LL) St. Louis Woman. Ishmael Reed. CP-ReedI

Crack has overtaken your immune defenses. Sandra. Demetrice A. Worley. SpiFl

Crack in the Wall Holds Flowers. Adam David Miller. PoBA

Cracked teacup screams, The. (LL) Haiku: "In the August grass." Etheridge Knight. ESEAA; TtW

Craftsman, The. Marcus B. Christian. TtW

Craftsman the gift of peace. (LL) Eulogy to W. H. Auden. Derek Walcott. ESEAA

Cramps from her developing tank. (LL) Utility Room. Michael S. Harper. SP-HarpM

Crap Game. Langston Hughes. CP-HughL

Crated coffin, A. (LL) Approximations. Robert Hayden. CP-HaydR

Craving for infinity, The. A Singular Yen. Al Young. CP-YounA

Craving of Samuel Rouse for clearance to create, The. The Slave and the Iron Lace. Margaret Else Danner. AmNP; BPo

Crawl, and wait. (LL) This Is an African Worm. Margaret Else Danner. TtW

Crawling down headfirst into the hole. Tunnels. Yusef Komunyakaa. SP-KomuY; TtW

Crazed. Mary E. Tucker. CBWP-1

Crazy pigeon strutting outside my cell. Etheridge Knight. NBV

Crazy Woman, The. Gwendolyn Brooks. SP-BrooG

Cream eaters—it was a hot Roman summer. (LL) Green arbor that I once knew, A. Linda Beatrice Brown. GT

Create new green. (LL) Mulch. Adam David Miller. NBV

Creation. Mary Weston Fordham. CBWP-2

Creation, The. James Weldon Johnson. BALP; BANP; CDC; NAAAL; PoBA; TtW

("Amen. Amen.") (LL) SSLK

Creation fires my tongue. Praise of Creation. George Moses Horton. AAP; SP-HortG

Creation is perfect. (LL) The Poet. Bob Kaufman. SP-KaufB

Creditor to His Proud Debtor, The. George Moses Horton. AAP; NAAAL; SP-HortG

Credo. Georgia Douglas Johnson. BALP; PoBA

Creed. Anne Spencer. CDC; ShDr

Crept towards Canada. (LL) Ice Age. Ishmael Reed. CP-ReedI

Crescent moon, naturally, A. (LL) To a Suitor. Maya Angelou. CP-AngeM; SP-AngeM

Crickets and gardenias attempted to fill my senses, The. Summer. Helen G. Quigless. BkSV

Crisis, The. Paul Laurence Dunbar. CP-DunbP

Crispus Attacks McKoy. Sterling A. Brown. BPo; CP-BrowS

Crispus Attucks. Robert Hayden. CP-HaydR; ESEAA

Criss-crossed pile of / sun-bleached bones, A. (LL) Evil Is No Black Thing. Sarah Webster Fabio. TtW

Critic advises, A. Black Poet, White Critic. Dudley Randall. BPo

Critics cry unfair, The. In Defense of Black Poets. Conrad Kent Rivers. BPo

Critters' Dance, De. Paul Laurence Dunbar. CP-DunbP

Crocodiles. Ishmael Reed. CP-ReedI

Crocuses, The. Frances Ellen Watkins Harper. BlSi; CP-HarpF

Crooked Afro. Frank X. Walker. SpiFl

Crooked / beneath a denim. Dreams. Charles Cooper. PoBA

Croon. Langston Hughes. *Fr.* Montage of a Dream Deferred. CP-HughL

Croon softly, Baby it's you. (LL) On Hearing "The Girl with the Flaxen Hair." Nikki Giovanni. SP-GiovN

Crootey Songo. Bob Kaufman. SP-KaufB

Cross. Langston Hughes. AmNP; BANP; CP-HughL; GT; IDB; PoBA; SP-HughL

Cross Winds. Bob Kaufman. SP-KaufB

Cross your tongue's dance floor. (LL) MAke You Go Oohhh! Kalamu ya Salaam. SpiFl

Crossed, and the florid black found. (LL) Oregon. Bob Kaufman. GT

Crossed over, on. (LL) It Is Deep. Carolyn M. Rodgers. NAAAL; SSLK

Crossing. Sterling A. Brown. CP-BrowS; TtW

Crossing. Langston Hughes. CP-HughL; SP-HughL

Crossing Lake Michigan. Michael S. Harper. SP-HarpM

Crostic for touch, A. (LL) Horse casts a shoe, The. Audre Lorde. CP-LordA

Crow dot sat a-squawkin', "I's a mockin'-bird," A. (LL) Limitations. Paul Laurence Dunbar. CP-DunbP

Crow Goes, Too. Langston Hughes. CP-HughL

Crow Jane in High Society. Amiri Baraka. SP-BaraA

Crow Jane the Crook. Amiri Baraka. SP-BaraA

Crow Jane's Manner. Amiri Baraka. SP-BaraA

Crow the Sioux and the Kickapoo, The. (LL) Once Upon a Road. Jayne Cortez. SP-CortJ

Crowd at the foot / of the gallows. (LL) Blues Chant Hoodoo Revival. Yusef Komunyakaa. SP-KomuY

Crowded Out. Rosalie Jonas. ShDr

Crowded with longings to be drunker than drunk? (LL) Hangover. Al Young. CP-YounA

Crowing Hen Blues. Langston Hughes. CP-HughL

Crowning glory of the Negro Woman Beautiful!, The. (LL) Madame Alpha Devine she made a million. Melvin B. Tolson. TtW

Crowns and Garlands. Langston Hughes. CP-HughL

Crowns from the south. "Rescue Work": Dues. Michael S. Harper. SP-HarpM

Crows in a Strong Wind. Cornelius Eady. ESEAA

Crucifixion. Waring Cuney. BANP

Crucifixion, The. Mary Weston Fordham. CBWP-2

Crucifixion. *Unknown.* BPo

Cruel in vengeance, reckless in wrath. Death of Zombi. Frances Ellen Watkins Harper. CP-HarpF

Crum Appointment, The. Lizelia Augusta Jenkins Moorer. CBWP-3

Crumb, a crumb, and a little seed, A. Paul Laurence Dunbar. CP-DunbP

Crushed Flower, The. Mary E. Tucker. CBWP-1

Crushed marigold or / a child's hand. Poem for Jan. June Jordan. SP-JordJ

Crushing caresses in the head. (LL) The Bitter Spring Again. Al Young. CP-YounA

Crust of bread and a corner to sleep in, A. Life. Paul Laurence Dunbar. AmNP; CDC; CP-DunbP

Crutches. Nikki Giovanni. SP-GiovN

Cry I bring down from the hills, The. You and I Are Disappearing. Yusef Komunyakaa. SP-KomuY

Cry "Infidel!" Alfred Gibbs Campbell. AAP

Crying, "Doors of Death, fly wide." (LL) Communion. Paul Laurence Dunbar. CP-DunbP

Crying to paint me blue, in the california afternoon. (LL) Alien winds sweeping the highway. Bob Kaufman. SP-KaufB

Crystal Palace used to be, The. Margaret Abigail Walker. CP-WalkM

Cuba could be heard crying / in the mountains. (LL) Grenada. E. Ethelbert Miller. TtW

Cuba, 1962. Ai. ESEAA

Cubes. Langston Hughes. CP-HughL

Cuckoo, glad cuckoo, Oh! where wilt thou rest to-night? Cuckoo Song. Henrietta Cordelia Ray. CBWP-3

Cuckoo is a funny bird, A. Ishmael Reed. CP-ReedI

Cuckoo Song. Henrietta Cordelia Ray. CBWP-3

Culling his rarest blossom. (LL) Thoughts of death / Crowd over my happiness. Sterling A. Brown. CP-BrowS

Cultivation. Mrs. Henry Linden. CBWP-4

Cultural Exchange. Langston Hughes. *Fr.* Ask Your Mama; 12 Moods for Jazz. BPo; CP-HughL; PoBA

Cultural Trip, A. Opal Palmer Adisa. GT

Cum here, Mandy, what's you chewin'. When Daddy Cums from Wuk. Maggie Pogue Johnson. CBWP-4

Cum, listen w'ile yore Unkel sings. 'Ittle Touzle Head. Ray Garfield Dandridge. BANP

Curative Powers of Silence, The. Al Young. CP-YounA ("Suddenly.") GT

Curb you! (LL) Warning. Langston Hughes. CP-HughL

Cure All, The. Haki R. Madhubuti. BrTr

Curiosity. Paul Laurence Dunbar. CP-DunbP

Curious. Langston Hughes. CP-HughL

Curious twists, The. Energy for a New Thang. Ernie Mkalimoto. NBP

Curious White Boy. Cree Summer. CtF

Curling them around. Cutting Greens. Lucille Clifton. ESEAA; GT; SP-ClifL

Current Events. June Jordan. SP-JordJ

Current Trends in California. (LL) The Robbie's Dance. Al Young. CP-YounA

Curse our children who became junk. (LL) To My Daughter the Junkie on a Train. Audre Lorde. SP-LordA

Cursing the trees for their teeth. (LL) Biting Back. Patricia Smith. GT

Curtain. Paul Laurence Dunbar. CP-DunbP

Curtains forcing their will. Awaking in New York. Maya Angelou. CP-AngeM; SP-AngeM

Custer's Last Ride. Albery Allson Whitman. EBAP

Customs and Culture? Ted Joans. TtW

Cut a cane that once. In the Bulrush. Rita Dove. SP-DoveR

Cut—with no music—on her smile. (LL) Notes for a Movie Script. M. Carl Holman. Klds

Cuttin Down to Size. Henry L. Dumas. BlFi

Cutting a Road from Manaus to Belém. Colleen J. McElroy. TtW

Cutting back / wherever the weather. The Pruning. Adam David Miller. NBV

Cutting Greens. Lucille Clifton. ESEAA; GT; SP-ClifL

Cutting off the edge of time, falling, endlessly. (LL) Falling. Bob Kaufman. SP-KaufB

Cuz' Mama Played Jazz. Daniel Gray-Kontar. SpiFl

Cymbals clash. Harlem Sounds: Hallelujah Corner. William Browne. AmNP

Cymbals trembling. (LL) Haiku: "Spring moonrise." Lenard D. Moore. SpiFl

Czechoslovakia lynched on a swastika cross! Song for Ourselves. Langston Hughes. CP-HughL

D

D Blues. Calvin C. Hernton. PoBA

D fuck would you know. (LL) Dragon's Blood. Ishmael Reed. CP-ReedI

Da 9 is a lost and found. Out of Pocket. Kevin Powell. CtF

Daddy. Lucille Clifton. SP-ClifL

Daddy' ain't you heard? (LL) Good morning, daddy! Langston Hughes. CP-HughL; SP-HughL

Daddy at the stove or sink. Large. War and Memory. June Jordan. SP-JordJ

Daddy, / don't let your dog. Warning. Langston Hughes. *Fr.* Montage of a Dream Deferred. CP-HughL

Daddy don't smile. Crooked Afro. Frank X. Walker. SpiFl

Daddy / is hot butter corn bread in the winter. Waitin on Summer. Ruth Forman. SpiFl

Daddy-o / Buddy-o. Migrant. Langston Hughes. CP-HughL; SP-HughL

Daddy Poem, A. William J. Harris. NBV

Daddy sits / in his brown. Sunflowers and Saturdays. Melba Joyce Boyd. BlSi

Daddy would drop purple-veined vines. Banking Potatoes. Herbert Asquith. NAAAL

Daddy's Friends. Esther Iverem. GT

Dah you been daihin' me. (LL) Reluctance. Paul Laurence Dunbar. CP-DunbP

Dahomey. Audre Lorde. CP-LordA

Daih's a moughty soothin' feelin'. 'Long To'ds Night. Paul Laurence Dunbar. CP-DunbP

Daily Grind, The. Fenton Johnson. AmNP

Daisy, dead and dry. (LL) For the Candle Light. Angelina Weld Grimké. BlSi; CDC; NAAAL

Da'kest hour, dey allus say, De. Joggin' Erlong. Paul Laurence Dunbar. CP-DunbP

Damit blackman. Domestics. Kattie M. Cumbo. BlSi

Damn if I don't believe you pushing me. (LL) Poolshooting Monkey. *African-American Oral Tradition.* GetYo

Damn the snow. Elegy for Thelonious. Yusef Komunyakaa. ESEAA; SP-KomuY

Dan to evah git born. (LL) Johnny Thomas. Sterling A. Brown. CP-BrowS

Dance, The. Paul Laurence Dunbar. CP-DunbP

Dance, The. Cornelius Eady. GT

Dance. Lula Lowe Weeden. CDC

Dance for Aging Hipsters, A. Al Young. CP-YounA

Dance for Li Po, A. Al Young. CP-YounA

Dance For Ma Rainey, A. Al Young. CP-YounA; NBP; NBV ("To prove that we're still here.") (LL) NAAAL

Dance for Militant Dilettantes, A. Al Young. CP-YounA; NBV; PoBA

Dance grows, The. The Dead. Jay Wright. FB

Dance Lesson, A. A. Van Jordan. SpiFl

Dance: Nicaragua. June Jordan. SP-JordJ

Dance of the Elephants, The. Michael S. Harper. SP-HarpM

Dance of the Freaks: "It was a cool and mystic rain." *African-American Oral Tradition.* GetYo

Dance of the Freaks: "It was cold and mist and rain in old Spokane." *African-American Oral Tradition.* GetYo

Dance of the Infidels. Al Young. CP-YounA; ESEAA; NBV; PoBA

"Dance the Orange." Robert Hayden. CP-HaydR

Dance they call / "The Our Turn", A. (LL) Introducing a New Loa. Ishmael Reed. CP-ReedI

Dance with me ... dance with me ... we are the song. Three/Quarters Time. Nikki Giovanni. SP-GiovN

Dance with you, my sweet brown Harlem girl. (LL) Juke Box Love Song. Langston Hughes. CP-HughL

Danced in the evenin'. Jenny in Love. Dolores Kendrick. ESEAA

Danced round the dreadful thing in fiendish glee. (LL) The Lynching. Claude McKay. BALP; BANP; CrDW; GT; IDB; PoBA; SP-McKaC

Dancer. Langston Hughes. *Fr.* Montage of a Dream Deferred. CP-HughL

Dancer, The. Al Young. CP-YounA; PoBA

Dancers. Langston Hughes. CP-HughL

Dancin' the funky chicken. Ain't That Bad. Maya Angelou. CP-AngeM; SP-AngeM

Dancing. (LL) They say that black people. Patricia Smith. GT

Dancing. Al Young. CP-YounA

Dancing All Alone. Al Young. CP-YounA

Dancing, / around her head. (LL) Inside Connie. Bob Kaufman. SP-KaufB

Dancing Day to Day. Al Young. CP-YounA

Dancing Gal. Frank Marshall Davis. FB

Dancing in Menopause. Dorothy Perry Thompson. SpiFl

Dancing in the Dark. Demetrice A. Worley. SpiFl

Dancing in the Laundromat [or] Dust: an Ordinary Song. Al Young. CP-YounA

Dancing in the Street. Al Young. CP-YounA

Dancing Naked. Al Young. CP-YounA

Dancing Pierrot. Al Young. CP-YounA

Dancing Together. Al Young. CP-YounA

Dandelion stares, The. The Little Dandelion. Lula Lowe Weeden. CDC

Dandelions. Frances Ellen Watkins Harper. CP-HarpF

Dangerous / Are the western waters now. To Captain Mulzac. Langston Hughes. CP-HughL

Dangerous Carnival, The. Marilyn Nelson. SP-NelsM

Dangerous rock in the mouth of this century's history. (LL) I live in the mouth of history. Kalamu ya Salaam. SpiFl

Daniel. Lucille Clifton. SP-ClifL

Dannemora Contraband. Jackie Warren-Moore. SpiFl

Danny Banjo / wry great griot elegance. Danny Barker/Danny Banjo. Kalamu ya Salaam. TtW

Danny Barker/Danny Banjo. Kalamu ya Salaam. TtW

Danse Africaine. Langston Hughes. CP-HughL; NAAAL; SP-HughL

Dante. Henrietta Cordelia Ray. CBWP-3

Dar isn't no use o' talkin': when er man lets loose o' evil. The Devil and Sis' Viney. J. Mord Allen. EBAP

Dare. Langston Hughes. CP-HughL

Dare a mighty *row* in Zion an' de *debbil's gittin' high*,. Linin' ub De Hymns, De. Daniel Webster Davis. AAP

Dares keep down the children of the Negro mother. (LL) The Negro Mother. Langston Hughes. CP-HughL; SP-HughL

Dares the dark / To stand. (LL) Dare. Langston Hughes. CP-HughL

Dark Actress—Somewhere, A. Blanche Taylor Dickinson. ShDr

Dark an' stormy may come de wedder. Slave Marriage Ceremony Supplement. *Unknown.* BPo; CrDW

Dark Area. Russell Atkins. FB; GT

Dark, black robe. Invitation (To the Night and All Other Things Dark). Ronda M. Davis. JB

Dark Blood. Margaret Abigail Walker. CP-WalkM

Dark Brother, The. Lewis Alexander. CDC

Dark Dreaming. Dorothy Kruger. ShDr

Dark gray / the stone wall hangs. This Urn Contains Earth from German Concentration Camps. Audre Lorde. CP-LordA

Dark is the face of Harriet. Harriet Tubman. Margaret Abigail Walker. CP-WalkM; TtW

Dark Mirror. Calvin Forbes. GT

Dark of the Moon. Sterling A. Brown. CP-BrowS

Dark Phrases. Ntozake Shange. BlSi

Dark Prophecy: I Sing of Shine. Etheridge Knight. BPo; Crnst; ESEAA; SP-KnigE

Dark rock-road, The. Haiku: "Dark rock-road, The." Maiisha L. Moore. CtF

Dark rose the walls, a church and prison joined. Albery Allson Whitman. AAP *Fr.* Twasinta's Seminoles; Or Rape of Florida

Dark Symphony. Melvin Beaunearus Tolson. AmNP; BALP; NAAAL; SSLK

Dark Testament. Pauli Murray. AmNP; AmNP; BlSi

Dark Way Home: Survivors, The. Michael S. Harper. SP-HarpM

Dark Youth of the U.S.A. Langston Hughes. CP-HughL

Darkened bedroom, the double bed, The. Driving Wheel. Sherley Anne Williams. BlSi

Darkening prairie surf / like stars, The. (LL) A Richland County Lyric for Elizabeth Asleep. June Jordan. SP-JordJ

Darkmistress / of wounded love, The. (LL) Sister Blues with Livewire Davis. Ahmos, II Zu-Bolton. TtW

Darling girl, The. (LL) Lucy one-eye. Lucille Clifton. SP-ClifL

"Darling," he said, "I never meant." Forgetfulness! Josephine D. Henderson Heard. CBWP-4

Darling, how long before this breath will cease? Evanishings. Mary E. Tucker. CBWP-1

Darling, I come, I come. (LL) A Love Song: "Ah, love, my love is like a cry in the night." Paul Laurence Dunbar. CP-DunbP

Darling, my darling, my heart is on the wing. Morning Song of Love. Paul Laurence Dunbar. CP-DunbP

Darling, the plates have been cleared away. Beauty and the Beast. Rita Dove. ESEAA; SP-DoveR

Dar's a lazy, sorta hazy. Sprin' Fevah. Ray Garfield Dandridge. BANP

Dar's a skool in West Virginny. To Professor Byrd Prillerman. Maggie Pogue Johnson. CBWP-4

Dar's plenty t'ings to write erbout. Dat Mule ob Brudder Wright's. Maggie Pogue Johnson. CBWP-4

Darts, touches much—flies, soars, hovers, puffs, breezes, blasts. Air. Jean Toomer. CP-ToomJ

Das Kapital. Amiri Baraka. SP-BaraA

Dat des drizzle all de day. (LL) Drizzle. Paul Laurence Dunbar. CP-DunbP

Dat Mule ob Brudder Wright's. Maggie Pogue Johnson. CBWP-4

Dat nigger tore his shirt in two. (LL) Run, Nigger, Run! *Unknown.* NAAAL

Dat Ol' Mare o' Mine. Paul Laurence Dunbar. CP-DunbP

Dat you gits in spring. (LL) Spring Fever. Paul Laurence Dunbar. CP-DunbP

Dat's de reason I's a-sighin' an' a-singin' now fu' you, Li'l' gal. (LL) Li'l' Gal. Paul Laurence Dunbar. CP-DunbP

Dat's enuff 'uligion. (LL) Dely. Paul Laurence Dunbar. CP-DunbP

"Dat's my only son, Lawd, Lawd, dat's my only son." (LL) Poor Lazarus. *Unknown.* NAAAL

Datsun's Death. Ishmael Reed. CP-ReedI

Daufuskie. Mari E. Evans. BlSi

Daughter, That Picture of You. Keith Gilyard. SpiFl

Daughter to pick the whitest rose, A. (LL) Pathway: From Son to Father. Lenard D. Moore. IHS

Daughters, 1900. Marilyn Nelson. SP-NelsM

Daughters—and live / with diabetes. (LL) Big Zeb Johnson. Everett Hoagland. GT

Dave Garroway's Mr. J. Fred Muggs often thumps. These Beasts and the Benin Bronze. Margaret Else Danner. Klds

David and Goliath. Priscilla Jane Thompson. CBWP-2

David Justice turns at him and winks as he signs autographs for all the kids. (LL) Baseball. Christopher Stanard. SpiFl

David Walker (1785–1830). Rita Dove. NAAAL; SP-DoveR

Dawn. Paul Laurence Dunbar. AmNP; CP-DunbP

Dawn. Angelina Weld Grimké. ShDr

Dawn again / and no sleep. White Blues: the Master's Song. George Barlow. *Fr.* Gabriel. TtW

Dawn came at six today. To the Man in the Yellow Terry. Alice Walker. CP-WalkA

Dawn in New York. Claude McKay. SP-McKaC

Dawn of Love, The. Henrietta Cordelia Ray. BlSi; CBWP-3; EBAP

Dawn offers / innocence to a half-mad city. Brief Innocence. Maya Angelou. CP-AngeM; SP-AngeM

Dawn! The Dawn! The crimson-tinted, comes, The. Dawn in New York. Claude McKay. SP-McKaC

Dawn, the gulls weep for the Jews. I Decide Not to Have Children. Marilyn Nelson. SP-NelsM

Dawnbreaker. Robert Hayden. CP-HaydR

Dawn's a-comin'!, The. (LL) Prayer Meeting. Langston Hughes. CP-HughL; SP-HughL

Dawn's Awake, The! Otto Leland Bohanan. BANP

Dawn's Carol. Henrietta Cordelia Ray. CBWP-3

Day. Paul Laurence Dunbar. CP-DunbP

Day. Langston Hughes. CP-HughL

Day a Dancer Learned to Sing of Dreamless Escapades, The. L. Goodwin. BlFi

Day after Conference, The. Josephine D. Henderson Heard. CBWP-4

Day after day I sit and write. Advice to Young Ladies. Ann Plato. AAP; TtW

Day and Night. Lewis Alexander. CDC

Day befo' Thanksgibin', De. Maggie Pogue Johnson. CBWP-4

Day-Breakers [*or* Daybreakers], The. Arna Bontemps. AmNP; CDC; IDB; PoBA

Day breaks without thanks or caution. A Small Slaughter. Audre Lorde. CP-LordA

Day / drunk with the nectar of, A. Wonder. Maya Angelou. CP-AngeM; SP-AngeM

Day feels put together hastily, The. Audre Lorde. *See* New Year's Day.

Day hangs heavy, The. Greyday. Maya Angelou. CP-AngeM; SP-AngeM

Day I was sentenced to the rest of my life, The. The Week in Review. Sekou Sundiata. *Fr.* Notes from the Defense of Colin Ferguson. SpiFl

Day in, Day out, you just kept belching. (LL) To a Publisher ... Cut-out. Amiri Baraka. SP-BaraA

Day in the Life of. . . , A. Conyus. GT

Day in the Life of a Poet, A. Quincy Troupe. NBV

Day is a Negro, The. Day and Night. Lewis Alexander. CDC

Day is o'er and twilight's shade, The. Gerarda. Eloise Bibb. AAP; CBWP-4

Day Kennedy Died. Al Young. CP-YounA

Day? Memorial, The. Grape Sherbet. Rita Dove. SP-DoveR

Day of long ergo, De. (LL) Long Ago. Paul Laurence Dunbar. CP-DunbP

Day of the vernal winds / 1967. (LL) Do Nothing Till You Hear from Me. David Henderson. GT; TtW

Day prior to: Two Brothers killing. Days Prior to. Jacques Wakefield. BlFi

Day rides the hills of death. (LL) Death. Paul Laurence Dunbar. CP-DunbP

Day that they stole her tiger's-eye ring, The. On Becoming a Tiger. Lorna Goodison. GT

Day they eulogized Mahalia, The. Audre Lorde. SP-LordA

("Day they eulogized Mahalia, The.") (LL) CP-LordA

Daybreak. Langston Hughes. *Fr.* Seven Moments of Love. CP-HughL

Daybreak. George Marion McClellan. AAP

Daybreak in Alabama. Langston Hughes. CP-HughL; SP-HughL

Days git wa'm an' wa'mah. Wadin' in de Crick. Paul Laurence Dunbar. CP-DunbP

Days have kept on coming, The. Daddy. Lucille Clifton. SP-ClifL

Days of my childhood I woo you not back. Frances Ellen Watkins Harper. CP-HarpF

Days Prior to. Jacques Wakefield. BlFi

Daystar. Rita Dove. NAAAL; SP-DoveR; TtW

De Black Cat Crossed His Luck. James David Corrothers. AfAmPo

De Cunjah Man. James Edwin Campbell. AAP; AfAmPo; BANP; EBAP; TtW

De-daddy-dy! / De-dop! (LL) What? So Soon! Langston Hughes. CP-HughL

De— / delight— / delighted! Introduce me to Eartha. Bird in Orbit. Langston Hughes. *Fr.* Ask Your Mama; 12 Moods for Jazz. CP-HughL

De fence they keep on talking 'bout. Defense. Elma Stuckey. TtW

De Gospel train am er scootin' down de rail! Git on Board, Chillun. Elliot B. Henderson. EBAP

De lady I work for. Present. Langston Hughes. CP-HughL

De nex' day de hide drap off'n yŏ' back. (LL) Jack and Dinah Want Freedom. *Unknown.* NAAAL

De railroad bridge's. Homesick Blues. Langston Hughes. CDC; NAAAL

De toi, près du foyer! (LL) Adieu. Camille Thierry. TtW

De Two-Nineteen done took mah baby away. Mamie's Blues. *Unknown.* Crnst

Deacon Jones' Grievance. Paul Laurence Dunbar. AAP; CP-DunbP

Deacon Morgan. Naomi Long Madgett. BlSi

Dead. Paul Laurence Dunbar. CP-DunbP

Dead, The. Jay Wright. FB

Dead bird be reborn, The. (LL) That bright chimeric beast. Countee Cullen. AmNP; CP-CullC

Dead-Day: Malcolm, Feb. 21. Michael S. Harper. SP-HarpM

Dead / Dead / DEAD! (LL) Too Many. Derrick I. M. Gilbert. CtF

Dead Fires. Jessie Redmond Fauset. BANP

Dead flowers. (LL) The Poet the Dreamer. Norman Jordan. NBV

Dead. He died in Detroit, his beard. Etheridge Knight. *Fr.* 2 Poems for Black Relocation Centers. BrTr

Dead in There. Langston Hughes. *Fr.* Montage of a Dream Deferred. CP-HughL

Dead Lady Canonized, The. Amiri Baraka. SP-BaraA

Dead leaves before splintered doors. (LL) The Wrong Side of the Morning. May Miller. TtW

Dead Man Dragged from the Sea, The. Carl Gardner. PoBA

Dead man lives, and none perceives him slain, The. (LL) The Proud Heart. Countee Cullen. CP-CullC

Dead men are wisest, for they know. The Wise. Countee Cullen. CP-CullC; Crnst

Dead Oaks. Michael S. Harper. SP-HarpM

Dead of acute peoplelessness. (LL) Chicken-Licken. Maya Angelou. SP-AngeM

Dead rising from the boiling seas, The. (LL) Fears of the Eighth Grade. Toi Derricotte. GT

Dead shall rise again, The. The Raising of Lazarus. Lucille Clifton. SP-ClifL

Dead, slavery can only end in blood. (LL) Sojourner Truth: Black Sybil in Salem. Michael S. Harper. SP-HarpM

Dead Spaniard who wanted to live forever. (LL) Ponce de León: A Morning Walk. Al Young. CP-YounA

Dead! when last we met his lips were fresh. Obituary for J. Edwards Barnes. Frances Ellen Watkins Harper. CP-HarpF

Deadly certain, death takes its time. Dirge for J. A. Rogers. Hart Leroi Bibbs. BlFi

Deadness was threatening us—15 Nigerians and 1 Mississippi nigger, The. Ilu, the Talking Drum. Etheridge Knight. SP-KnigE

Deafen his ears to the butcher's song? (LL) Vietnam: I Need More Than This Crust of Salt. Lance Jeffers. BrTr

Dear Alex, tomorrow i am going to eat all of the Suez. Telegram to Alex/ Bagel Shop, North Beach SF. Bob Kaufman. SP-KaufB

Dear are the names that charmed me in my youth. Margaret Abigail Walker. CP-WalkM

Dear Arl. Al Young. CP-YounA

Dear Bess, / He'll have rings and linen things. Rime for the Christmas Baby. Anne Spencer. ShDr

Dear Brother at home. Letter from Spain. Langston Hughes. CP-HughL

Dear brothers and sisters, we love one another. The Ark. Noah Calwell Cannon. AAP

Dear Cassie: Yes, I got your letter. Letter. Langston Hughes. *Fr.* Seven Moments of Love. CP-HughL

Dear critic, who my lightness so deplores. To a Captious Critic. Paul Laurence Dunbar. BPo; CP-DunbP; Klds

Dear Death: / I got your message. Official Notice. Langston Hughes. CP-HughL

Dear father, I hear a whisper. The Dying Child to Her Blind Father. Frances Ellen Watkins Harper. CP-HarpF

Dear Fellow Americans. Will V-Day Be Me-Day Too? Langston Hughes. CP-HughL

Dear Folks at home. Postcard from Spain. Langston Hughes. CP-HughL

Dear Frère Jacques. Letter to a Benedictine Monk. Marilyn Nelson. GT

Dear Friend, since you have chosen to associate. Tennyson's Poems. Josephine D. Henderson Heard. CBWP-4

Dear Friends and Gentle Hearts. Countee Cullen. CP-CullC

Dear friends, we are gathered together. A Tribute to the Bride and Groom. Priscilla Jane Thompson. CBWP-2

Dear heart, good-night! Premonition. Paul Laurence Dunbar. CP-DunbP

Dear Joe. Audre Lorde. CP-LordA

Dear John, Dear Coltrane. Michael S. Harper. NAAAL; SP-HarpM; TtW

Dear Jonno / there are pigeons who nest. A Trip on the Staten Island Ferry. Audre Lorde. CP-LordA; SP-LordA

Dear Kelly, when I was a kid. To Kelly Miller, Jr. Paul Laurence Dunbar. CP-DunbP

Dear Lela is my joy and crown. Lela's Charms. Lizelia Augusta Jenkins Moorer. CBWP-3

Dear letters, fond letters. Love Letters. Josephine D. Henderson Heard. CBWP-4

Dear Liza, I is bin down town. Nigger's Got to Go, De. Daniel Webster Davis. AAP

Dear lovely Death. Langston Hughes. CP-HughL

Dear Mama. Wanda Coleman. Crnst

Dear Mama, / Time I pay rent and get my food. Letter. Langston Hughes. *Fr.* Lenox Avenue Mural. AmNP; SP-HughL *Fr.* Montage of a Dream Deferred. CP-HughL

Dear Miss Lucy: I been t'inkin' dat I'd write you long fo' dis. A Letter. Paul Laurence Dunbar. CP-DunbP

Dear Miss Nettie, / The School is in a spinney. Letters from a New England Negro. Sherley Anne Williams. ESEAA

Dear Mr. President. Langston Hughes. CP-HughL

Dear, Mother-Father God. Pardon Me. Oktavi. CtF

Dear murdered comrades, not in vain. Tulips from Their Blood. Edwin Brooks. NBP

Dear muse, to thee I lift mine eyes. To the Muse. George Moses Horton. SP-HortG

Dear Obour / Our crossing was without. A Letter from Phillis Wheatley. Robert Hayden. CP-HaydR; ESEAA; NAAAL

Dear Old Stockholm. Al Young. CP-YounA

Dear Ravi Shankar. Al Young. CP-YounA

Dear Samson, / I put your hair. Love Letter. Carole C. Gregory Clemmons. BlSi

Dear school of my childhood. Lines to an Old School-House. Priscilla Jane Thompson. CBWP-2

Dear Sirs: / I have been enjoying the law and order of our. Letter to the Local Police. June Jordan. SP-JordJ

Dear sister / love / dear sister. (LL) Lane Is the Pretty One. Lucille Clifton. SP-ClifL

Dear Toni Instead of a Letter of Congratulation. Audre Lorde. CP-LordA; SP-LordA

Dear, when we sit in that high, placid room. Touché. Jessie Redmond Fauset. BlSi; CDC; ShDr

Dearer destiny than dirgeful death, A. (LL) Memorial Day. Paul Laurence Dunbar. CP-DunbP

Dearest one, thou art my star. (LL) Over the hills and the valleys of dreaming. Paul Laurence Dunbar. CP-DunbP

Death. Paul Laurence Dunbar. CP-DunbP

Death ain't / No jive. (LL) Death in Yorkville. Langston Hughes. CP-HughL

Death and Resurrection. Priscilla Jane Thompson. CBWP-2

Death as History. Jay Wright. ESEAA; PoBA

Death Bed, The. Waring Cuney. CDC

Death Dance, The. Haki R. Madhubuti. BrTr

Death Dance for a Poet. Audre Lorde. CP-LordA

Death don't ring no doorbells. Casual. Langston Hughes. CP-HughL

Death in Africa. Langston Hughes. CP-HughL

Death in Harlem. Langston Hughes. CP-HughL

Death in Yorkville. Langston Hughes. CP-HughL; PoBA

Death is a five o'clock door forever changing time. Kwa Mama Zetu Waliotuzaa. Sonia Sanchez. SP-SancS

Death is a tower. Tower. Langston Hughes. CP-HughL

Death is not a disease. (LL) Mawu. Audre Lorde. CP-LordA

Death is not a dream; death lives. Darwin T. Turner. BALP

Death Is Not as Natural as You Fags Seem to Think. Amiri Baraka. SP-BaraA

Death knocks all night at my door. Journey to the Place of Ghosts. Jay Wright. Crnst; GT

Death notes, busily unnaming themselves. (LL) Audacity of the Lower Gods. Yusef Komunyakaa. SP-KomuY

Death of a Friend. Pauli Murray. PoBA

Death of a Grandparent. Mrs. Jennette Bonneau. Mary Weston Fordham. CBWP-2

Death of a Negro Poet, The. Conrad Kent Rivers. BPo

Death of a Squirrel in McKinley Park, The. Gerald William Barrax. Klds

Death of an Old Carriage Horse. George Moses Horton. SP-HortG

Death of an Old Seaman. Langston Hughes. CP-HughL

Death of Days and Nights of Life. Clarence Franklin. BlFi

Death of Do Dirty: A Rounder's Song. Langston Hughes. CP-HughL

Death of Dr. King. Sam Cornish. PoBA

Death of Justice, The. Walter Everette Hawkins. PoBA

Death of Moses, The. Frances Ellen Watkins Harper. *Fr.* Moses: A Story of the Nile. AAP; CP-HarpF

Death of Polyxena, The. Euripides, *Greek. Fr.* Hecuba. SP-NelsM, *tr. by* Marilyn Nelson

Death of the First Born, The. Paul Laurence Dunbar. CP-DunbP

Death of the Moonshine Supermen. Reginald Lockett. BlFi

Death of the Old Sea King. Frances Ellen Watkins Harper. CP-HarpF; EBAP

Death of Zombi. Frances Ellen Watkins Harper. CP-HarpF

Death Song[, A]. Paul Laurence Dunbar. BANP; CDC; CP-DunbP

Death Songs. L. V. Mack. PoBA

Death surrounds itself with the living. Mississippi. E. Ethelbert Miller. GT

Death to the klan! (LL) In the Tradition. Amiri Baraka. SP-BaraA

Death to the Poor. Charles Baudelaire, *French.* CP-CullC, *tr. by* Countee Cullen

Death wore out your boot heels. (LL) 1938. Yusef Komunyakaa. SP-KomuY

Deathwatch. Michael S. Harper. NAAAL; PoBA; SP-HarpM

Debridement. Michael S. Harper. SP-HarpM

Debridement: Operation Harvest Moon: *On Repose.* Michael S. Harper. SP-HarpM

Debt, The. Paul Laurence Dunbar. AmNP; BANP; CDC; CP-DunbP; Klds

Decade That Screamed, The. Ishmael Reed. CP-ReedI

Decay in my voice. (LL) The Measure of Memory (The Navigator). Amiri Baraka. SP-BaraA

Deceased. Langston Hughes. CP-HughL

December. Josephine D. Henderson Heard. CBWP-4

December. Henrietta Cordelia Ray. CBWP-3

December, 1919. Claude McKay. SP-McKaC

December 15, 1811. Poem for My Family: Hazel Griffin and Victor Hernandez Cruz. June Jordan. BPo

December of My Springs, The. Nikki Giovanni. GT; SP-GiovN

December Portrait. Kathleen Tankersley Young. ShDr

December/ no signs of a Chicago winter/ no boulder-sized clumps of snow. For My Father. Harris Duriel. SpiFl

Deception. Josephine D. Henderson Heard. CBWP-4

Decked, stacked, pillaged from. The Middle Passage and After. Larry Neal. NBV

Declaration. Langston Hughes. CP-HughL

Declined to outmode / the / hug? (LL) Nothing is right. Alice Walker. CP-WalkA

Decoration Day. Josephine D. Henderson Heard. CBWP-4

Dedicated to a Young Lady Representing the Indian Race at Howard University. Alfred Islay Walden. AAP

Dedicated to Dr. W. H. Sheppard. Maggie Pogue Johnson. CBWP-4

Dedicated to the Right Rev'd D. A. Payne. Mary Weston Fordham. CBWP-2

Dedication. Alice Walker. CP-WalkA

Dedication Day. Maggie Pogue Johnson. CBWP-4

Dedication Day Poem. Lizelia Augusta Jenkins Moorer. CBWP-3

Dedication Poem. Frances Ellen Watkins Harper. CP-HarpF

Dedication to the Final Confrontation. Lloyd M., Jr. Corbin. PoBA

Dee da dee D A A A A H. (LL) Cabaret. Sterling A. Brown. NAAAL

Dee dee dee dee dee wee weee eeeeee wee we. Communication in Whi-te. Don L. Lee. BPo

Deed perfidious, and the Hero's fate, The. On the Capture of General Lee. Phillis Wheatley. CP-WheaP

Deems robin still the sweetest bird. (LL) Comparison. Paul Laurence Dunbar. CP-DunbP

Deep down in the jungle in the coconut grove. Signifying Monkey: "Deep down in the jungle in the coconut grove." *African-American Oral Tradition.* GetYo

Deep down in the stick. Poolshooting Monkey. *African-American Oral Tradition.* GetYo

Deep echo, of open fear: the field drawn in, A. Green Lantern's Solo. Amiri Baraka. SP-BaraA

Deep in Alabama earth. Alabama Earth. Langston Hughes. CP-HughL

Deep in knowledge. (LL) Drapery Factory, Gulfport, Mississippi, 1956. Natasha Trethewey. SpiFl

Deep in my heart that aches with the repression. Unexpressed. Paul Laurence Dunbar. CP-DunbP

Deep in my soul there roared the crashing thunder. Calm after Storm. Frank Yerby. AmNP

Deep in the hearts and minds of men. (LL) Whittier. Paul Laurence Dunbar. CP-DunbP

Deep in this grave her bones remain. Reflections, Written on Visiting the Grave of a Venerated Friend. Ann Plato. BlSi; EBAP

Deep in your cheeks. Origins. Keorapetse W. Kgositsile. PoBA

Deep into the midst of a great, dark, wood. The Snail's Lesson. Priscilla Jane Thompson. CBWP-2

Deep river, my home is over Jordan. *Unknown*. BPo; BkSV; CrDW

Deeper than solitudes of birth. (LL) Kin. Naomi Long Madgett. TtW

Deer feed on. Upon Leaving the Parole Board Hearing. Conyus. GT; PoBA

Defense. Elma Stuckey. TtW

Defense Rests, The. Sekou Sundiata. *Fr.* Notes from the Defense of Colin Ferguson. SpiFl

Deferred. Langston Hughes. *Fr.* Montage of a Dream Deferred. CP-HughL

Defiant in the cannon's mouth. Stonewall Jackson, 1886. Albery Allson Whitman. EBAP

Define their being; oh sing, Etheridge, ease the spirit. (LL) Message to Etheridge Knight. Lenard D. Moore. TtW

Definition for Blk/Children. Sonia Sanchez. PoBA

Definition in the Face of Unnamed Fury. Rita Dove. SP-DoveR

Definition of Nature. Eugene B. Redmond. NBV; PoBA

Definitionless in this strict atmosphere. (LL) A Lovely Love. Gwendolyn Brooks. BPo; NAAAL; SP-BrooG

Defy him! Tear his organ off! Strike him. Good Friday Prayer. Marilyn Nelson. *Fr.* Thus Far by Faith. SP-NelsM

Degree Four. Nathaniel Mackey. ESEAA

Deify the room/space/drive ... mass control. Jazz. Kenneth A. McClane. TtW

Deism. Phillis Wheatley. CP-WheaP

Del Cascar, Del Cascar. William Stanley Braithwaite. BANP; CDC; TtW

Delft. Rita Dove. SP-DoveR

Delicate embroideries / of bone, The. (LL) Ethiopia. Audre Lorde. CP-LordA

Delicious, *fine* Sugar Hill. (LL) Harlem Sweeties. Langston Hughes. CP-HughL

Delinquent, The. Paul Laurence Dunbar. CP-DunbP

Delinquent. Langston Hughes. CP-HughL; SP-HughL

Delirium. Norman J. Loftis. SpiFl

Deliverance, The. Frances Ellen Watkins Harper. CP-HarpF

Deliverance. Frances Ellen Watkins Harper. CP-HarpF

Delivered at the Knighting of Lord Durgling by Great Bruce-Jean. Jean Toomer. CP-ToomJ; GT

DeLiza and the TV News. June Jordan. SP-JordJ

DeLiza Come to London Town; a Birthday Poem for Mark. June Jordan. SP-JordJ

DeLiza laugh out loud. (LL) Sometimes DeLiza. June Jordan. SP-JordJ

Deliza Questioning Perplexities. June Jordan. SP-JordJ

DeLiza walk across the Waterloo. DeLiza Come to London Town; a Birthday Poem for Mark. June Jordan. SP-JordJ

DeLiza watch one hostage then. DeLiza and the TV News. June Jordan. SP-JordJ

Delta. Margaret Abigail Walker. CP-WalkM

Dely. Paul Laurence Dunbar. CP-DunbP

Demand. Langston Hughes. CP-HughL; SP-HughL

Demanding that I explain / my treachery. (LL) Blonde White Women. Patricia Smith. GT

Demanding / work schedule, The. (LL) Gas Station Attendant. Brian G. Gilmore. SpiFl

Demerol. Al Young. CP-YounA

Demeter Mourning. Rita Dove. NAAAL

Demeter's Prayer to Hades. Rita Dove. NAAAL

Democracy will not come. Langston Hughes. Crnst; SP-HughL

Democratic Order, The: Such Things in Twenty Years I Understood. Alice Walker. CP-WalkA

Demon, Demon, you have dumped me. Her Love Poem. Lucille Clifton. SP-ClifL

Demon vanishes before a prayer, The. (LL) Full Vision. Henrietta Cordelia Ray. CBWP-3

Demonstration. Langston Hughes. CP-HughL

Den pass on! (LL) A Plantation Portrait. Paul Laurence Dunbar. CP-DunbP

Den we'll go an' thrash sum wheat. (LL) Trussy's Visit. Elliot B. Henderson. EBAP

Denounce us. (LL) Generations. Lucille Clifton. SP-ClifL

Departure. Langston Hughes. CP-HughL

Dependable, from a physical point of view. (LL) Earth. Jean Toomer. CP-ToomJ

Deplorable abortion / more and / more. (LL) In Memoriam: Martin Luther King, Jr. June Jordan. SP-JordJ

Depreciation. Audre Lorde. CP-LordA

Depression. Sonia Sanchez. ESEAA

Deprived of learning and. Catherine of Alexandria. Rita Dove. SP-DoveR

Der Rabbit's Foot. James David Corrothers. EBAP

Dere's no hidin' place down dere. *Unknown*. BPo

DERRAT SLEGELATIONS, FLOR GOOF BABER. Crootey Songo. Bob Kaufman. SP-KaufB

Derringer Youngblood, the jet-black nigger. *African-American Oral Tradition*. GetYo

Des a little cabin. A Little Cabin. Charles Bertram Johnson. BANP

Des a-noddin' by de fiah. (LL) Noddin' by de Fire. Paul Laurence Dunbar. CP-DunbP

Des 'lasses an' watah, 'lasses an' watah. (LL) A Preference. Paul Laurence Dunbar. CP-DunbP

Des Moines Iowa Rap. June Jordan. SP-JordJ

Describing my pain. (LL) Walker. Alice Walker. CP-WalkA

Desert. Langston Hughes. CP-HughL; Klds; SP-HughL

Desert dreamer, telepathic. The Man Who Carries the Desert Around Inside Himself: For Wally. Yusef Komunyakaa. SP-KomuY

Desert moon has veiled its pale-gold face, The. (LL) To a Dark Dancer. Marjorie Marshall. ShDr

Deserted Plantation, The. Paul Laurence Dunbar. CP-DunbP

Deserter, The. Joseph Seamon Cotter, Sr. CDC

Design, The. Clarence Major. PoBA

Desire. Marjorie Marshall. ShDr

Desire. Jean Toomer. CP-ToomJ

Desire, and the freedom to imagine it. (LL) Pastoral. Rita Dove. NAAAL

Desire to us. Langston Hughes. CP-HughL; SP-HughL

Desire weaves its fantasy of dreams. Spring for Lovers. Langston Hughes. CP-HughL

Desire's Persistence. Jay Wright. ESEAA

Desolate. Claude McKay. CDC; SP-McKaC

Despair. Paul Laurence Dunbar. CP-DunbP

Desperate days / Of life. (LL) Dancers. Langston Hughes. CP-HughL

Desperate retellings of the thin-lipped Nebraska / pogroms. (LL) The Enormous Gas Bill at the Dwarf Factory. A Horror Movie to be Shot with Eyes. Bob Kaufman. SP-KaufB

Destiny. Eloise Bibb. CBWP-4

Destiny of this earth, The. (LL) To a Woman Poet That I Know. Pinkie Gordon Lane. TtW

Detached, The. Maya Angelou. CP-AngeM; SP-AngeM

Detective fingers of the moon. (LL) My little 'bout-town gal has gone. Gwendolyn Brooks. SP-BrooG

Detectives from the vice squad. Café: 3 A.M. Langston Hughes. *Fr.* Montage of a Dream Deferred. CP-HughL

Determination. John Henrik Clarke. PoBA

Detroit Conference of Unity and Art. Nikki Giovanni. SP-GiovN

Detroit 1958. Al Young. ESEAA

Devil and Sis' Viney, The. J. Mord Allen. EBAP

Devil is a rider, The. Arkansas Chant. Sterling A. Brown. CP-BrowS

Devil Worship. Amiri Baraka. SP-BaraA

Devil's Music in Hell, The. Julius E. Thompson. TtW

Devil's own rag babydoll, The. (LL) Elegies for Paradise Valley. Robert Hayden. CP-HaydR

Dew is on the grasses, dear, The. Youth. Georgia Douglas Johnson. BANP; NAAAL

Dewdrop's / Mystery, The. (LL) Snail. Langston Hughes. CP-HughL; SP-HughL

Dexter Gordon at Keystone Korner. Al Young. CP-YounA

Dexter Gordon's tenor sax. February in Sydney. Yusef Komunyakaa. ESEAA; NAAAL; SP-KomuY

Dey been speakin' at de cou't-house. Speakin' at de Cou't-House. Paul Laurence Dunbar. CP-DunbP

Dey had a gread big pahty down to Tom's de othah night. The Party. Paul Laurence Dunbar. AmNP; CP-DunbP

Dey is snow upon de meddahs. Snowin'. Paul Laurence Dunbar. CP-DunbP

Dey is times in life when Nature. When de Co'n Pone's Hot. Paul Laurence Dunbar. AAP; BANP; CP-DunbP; TtW

Dey sent John Thomas. Johnny Thomas. Sterling A. Brown. CP-BrowS

Dey want me to help score d ambush. (LL) Badman of the Guest Professor. Ishmael Reed. CP-ReedI; SSLK

Dey was hard times jes 'fo' Christmas round our neighborhood one year. An Indignation Dinner. James David Corrothers. AfAmPo; BANP; NAAAL

Dey was oncet a awful quoil. Trouble in de Kitchen. Paul Laurence Dunbar. CP-DunbP

Dey was talkin' in de cabin, dey was talkin' in de hall. When Dey 'Listed Colored Soldiers. Paul Laurence Dunbar. BPo; CP-DunbP

Dey's a so't o' threatenin' feelin' in de blowin' of de breeze. Soliloquy of a Turkey. Paul Laurence Dunbar. BPo; CP-DunbP

Dey's many'll weep wid me. (LL) A Christmas Folksong. Paul Laurence Dunbar. CP-DunbP

Deze eatin' folks may tell me ub de gloriz ub spring lam'. Hog Meat. Daniel Webster Davis. BANP

Dialect Quatrain. Marcus B. Christian. AmNP

Dialog outside the Lakeside Grocery. Ishmael Reed. CP-ReedI

Dialogue, A. Frances Ellen Watkins Harper. CP-HarpF

Dialogue, A. Lizelia Augusta Jenkins Moorer. CBWP-3

Diamond body of his being, The. (LL) The Lost Dancer. Jean Toomer. CP-ToomJ

Diamond Canady / Was stabbed in bed by Little Eva Winn. Harlem. Melvin B. Tolson. TtW

Diamonds are mined ... oil is discovered. A Poem for Langston Hughes. Nikki Giovanni. SP-GiovN; SSLK

Diamonds / Decadence / and / Disease. (LL) Count Basie's place. Ted Wilson. BlFi

Diamonds on Liz's bosom, The. Alice Walker. CP-WalkA

Diaspora. Audre Lorde. CP-LordA

Dichtung. Amiri Baraka. SP-BaraA

Dick Tracy chases Eighty-Eight Keys. Clinton. Sterling Plumpp. BkSV

Dictum. Countee Cullen. CP-CullC

Did Fear and Danger so perplex your Mind. On Messrs. Hussey and Coffin. Phillis Wheatley. CP-WheaP

Did I / completely. (LL) On the Yard. Etheridge Knight. SP-KnigE

Did I evah tell you, Sonny. Uncle Jimmie's Yarn. Priscilla Jane Thompson. CBWP-2

Did i ever live / up your / way? / ??? / ?? / ? (LL) Stokely Malcolm Me. Langston Hughes. CP-HughL

Did John's Music Kill Him? Alfred B. Spellman. NAAAL

Did not fire because he saw a girl. (LL) The Same Death Over and Over or Lullabies Are for Children. Audre Lorde. CP-LordA

Did / Somebody / Die? (LL) World War II. Langston Hughes. CP-HughL

Did This Happen to Your Mother? Did Your Sister Throw Up a Lot? Alice Walker. CP-WalkA

Did ya ever cry. Haiku: "Did ya ever cry." Sonia Sanchez. SP-SancS

"Did You Call Me, Father?" Mary E. Tucker. CBWP-1

Did you ever go down to the river. Reverie on the Harlem River. Langston Hughes. CP-HughL; SP-HughL

Did you ever walk into a firehose. Demonstration. Langston Hughes. CP-HughL

Did you hear? The Old Warrior Terror. Alice Walker. CP-WalkA

Didn't like jazz, he once claimed. William Carlos Williams. Cornelius Eady. GT

Didn't my Lord Deliver Daniel. *Unknown.* NAAAL

Die / Big Red. (LL) One Year Ago. David Llorens. BrTr

Die Black Pervert. Reginald Lockett. BlFi

Die is cast, and we must part, The. The Parting. Josephine D. Henderson Heard. CBWP-4

Die is cast, come weal, come woe, The. Marriage. Mary Weston Fordham. CBWP-2

Died of Starvation. Frances Ellen Watkins Harper. CP-HarpF

Dies Irae. Margaret Abigail Walker. CP-WalkM

Difference between / my heart and your, The. Untitled IV. Ishmael Reed. CP-ReedI

Difference between poetry and rhetoric, The. Power. Audre Lorde. CP-LordA; TtW

Differences. Paul Laurence Dunbar. CP-DunbP

Different Image, A. Dudley Randall. BPo

Different in persons. Men. Jean Toomer. CP-ToomJ

Dig And Be Dug / In Return. (LL) Motto. Langston Hughes. CP-HughL

Digging. Audre Lorde. CP-LordA

Digging our poetry with our nails. (LL) Lovely's Daughters: Visitors. Michael S. Harper. SP-HarpM

Digging the grave / through black dirt. Called. Michael S. Harper. SP-HarpM

Digging up dirt on the folks that put us here. (LL) Pardon Me. Oktavi. CtF

Dilettante, The: A Modern Type. Paul Laurence Dunbar. CP-DunbP

Dime. Langston Hughes. *Fr.* Montage of a Dream Deferred. CP-HughL

Dime after Dime. Mary Weems. SpiFl

Dimmed too soon. (LL) Gypsy Melodies. Langston Hughes. CP-HughL; SP-HughL

Dimout in Harlem. Langston Hughes. CP-HughL

Dinah Kneading Dough. Paul Laurence Dunbar. CP-DunbP; NAAAL

Dinah stan' befo' de glass. The Looking-Glass. Paul Laurence Dunbar. CP-DunbP

Dining at 8 and 6:30. Psychophotos of Hampton. Michael S. Harper. SP-HarpM

Dining from a Treed Condition, an Historical Survey. Michael S. Harper. SP-HarpM

Dinner Guest: Me. Langston Hughes. BPo; CP-HughL; SSLK

Dinosaur Spring. Marilyn Nelson. SP-NelsM

Dip into this river with your ebony cups. (LL) Black Star Line. Henry L. Dumas. Crnst; PoBA

Diplomacy. Paul Laurence Dunbar. CP-DunbP

Directions, The. Christopher Gilbert. GT

Dirge: "It is the endless dance of the dead." Quincy Troupe. PoBA

Dirge: "Place this bunch of mignonette." Paul Laurence Dunbar. CP-DunbP

Dirge for a Soldier. Paul Laurence Dunbar. CP-DunbP

Dirge for J. A. Rogers. Hart Leroi Bibbs. BlFi

Dis is gospel weathah sho'. Song of Summer. Paul Laurence Dunbar. CP-DunbP

Dis is Ned dat am er-speakin'. Ned's Psalm of Life for the Negro. Joseph Seamon Cotter, Sr. AAP

Dis sun are hot. This Sun Is Hot. *Unknown.* BPo

Disappearing around the corner. Foggy Morning. Al Young. CP-YounA

Disappearing from Kansas. (LL) Forty Days Looking Backwards: Notes from a Surveyor. Michael S. Harper. SP-HarpM

Disappearing into bush— / Now—sweet singing. (LL) Blue Tanganyika. Lebert Bethune. BlFi

Disappointed. Paul Laurence Dunbar. CP-DunbP

Disappointment. Mary E. Tucker. CBWP-1

Disarticulated / arm torn out. Last Affair: Bessie's Blues Song. Michael S. Harper. ESEAA; SP-HarpM

Discard the fear and what. The Couple. Maya Angelou. CP-AngeM; SP-AngeM

Discover Me, *for Pam, Rosa and Joan.* Opal Palmer Adisa. GT

Discover this country. (LL) America. Maya Angelou. CP-AngeM; SP-AngeM

Discovered. Paul Laurence Dunbar. CP-DunbP

Discoveries of Fire, The. Lucille Clifton. SP-ClifL

Discovering. Sharon Scott. JB

Discovers one as fair. (LL) A Song of Praise. Countee Cullen. CP-CullC

Discovery, The. Paul Laurence Dunbar. CP-DunbP

Disease, now, is / continuous! (LL) 1929: Y you ask? (26). Amiri Baraka. SP-BaraA

Disguised / as a baboon. (LL) Wood Has No Mouth. Audre Lorde. CP-LordA

Disguised in my mouth as a swampland. In the Morning. Jayne Cortez. BlSi; SP-CortJ

Disillusion. Langston Hughes. CP-HughL

Disillusion for Flower Children of Long Ago. Margaret Abigail Walker. CP-WalkM

Dismissal of Tyng, The. Frances Ellen Watkins Harper. CP-HarpF

Distant Drum, The. Calvin C. Hernton. GT; NNP; TtW

Distinction. Paul Laurence Dunbar. CP-DunbP

Disturbed by consciousness. Satori. Gayl Jones. BlSi

Disturber, The. Paul Laurence Dunbar. CP-DunbP

Dium was empty, and Sugar was / on the train. (LL) The Atlantic Monthly, December 1970. Ishmael Reed. CP-ReedI

Dive. Langston Hughes. *Fr.* Montage of a Dream Deferred. CP-HughL

Diver, The. Robert Hayden. BPo; CP-HaydR; Klds; NAAAL

Diverne stands in the kitchen as they dance. Diverne's Waltz. Marilyn Nelson. SP-NelsM

Diverne wanted to die, that August night. Chosen. Marilyn Nelson. SP-NelsM

Diverne's House. Marilyn Nelson. SP-NelsM

Diverne's Waltz. Marilyn Nelson. SP-NelsM

Diversity in stock? (LL) Take them out! June Jordan. SP-JordJ

Divided by 2? (LL) Problems. Langston Hughes. CP-HughL

Divided States of America, The. Roland Poet X. CtF

Divine approval is thy sweetest praise. (LL) To My Father. Henrietta Cordelia Ray. AAP; BlSi; CBWP-3; EBAP; TtW

Divine Mission, The. Alfred Gibbs Campbell. AAP

Division of an Estate. George Moses Horton. NAAAL; SP-HortG

Dixie Man to Uncle Sam. Langston Hughes. CP-HughL

Dixie South Africa. Langston Hughes. CP-HughL

Do' a-stan'in' on a jar, fiah a-shinin' thoo. Howdy, Honey, Howdy! Paul Laurence Dunbar. CP-DunbP

Do blk do blk do blk do blk do blk. (LL) 2 B BLK. Val Ferdinand. NBV

Do drop a line or telephone. (LL) The Lie. Maya Angelou. CP-AngeM; SP-AngeM

Do, Jesus! / Lord! / Amen! (LL) Not Else—But. Langston Hughes. CP-HughL

Do, Jesus! / Lord! / Amen! (LL) Shades of Pigmeat. Langston Hughes. CP-HughL

Do, Lawd. *African-American Oral Tradition*. TtW

Do not call me Dr. Poem for an Intellectual on the Way Up to Submit to His Lady. Langston Hughes. CP-HughL

Do not call me out of my name. (LL) Kojo; I Am a Black. Gwendolyn Brooks. ESEAA; TtW

"Do Not Cheer, Men Are Dying," Said Capt. Phillips, in the Spanish-American War. Frances Ellen Watkins Harper. CP-HarpF

Do not climb too high. (LL) Love Song for Lucinda. Langston Hughes. CP-HughL

Do not hesitate / move / away. (LL) Move. Lucille Clifton. NAAAL

Do not hesitate to call me into consultation / Respectfully yours. (LL) Letter to the Local Police. June Jordan. SP-JordJ

Do not hold my few years / against me. So We've Come at Last to Freud. Alice Walker. CP-WalkA

Do not hunger. (LL) All Things Insensible. Kathleen Tankersley Young. ShDr

Do not sell me out, baby. In a Troubled Key. Langston Hughes. CP-HughL

Do not speak to me of martyrdom. Malcolm. Sonia Sanchez. BrTr; SP-SancS

Do not stifle me with the strange scent. Alien. Donald Jeffrey Hayes. AmNP

Do Nothing Till You Hear from Me, *for Langston Hughes*. David Henderson. GT; TtW

  ("Last time blues / with no hesitations., The.") (LL) PoBA

Do-right man? Langston Hughes. *See* Early Evening Quarrel.

Do sumpin' fu' to comfo't dad! (LL) Puttin' the Baby Away. Paul Laurence Dunbar. CP-DunbP

Do they miss me at home. Benjamin Clark. EBAP

Do, writing books, she also said that he smiles a lot and kinda got good teeth. (LL) Poet: What Ever Happened to Luther? Haki R. Madhubuti. SpiFl

Do you blame me that I loved him? A Double Standard. Frances Ellen Watkins Harper. AAP; BlSi; CP-HarpF; CrDW; Crnst; EBAP; NAAAL

Do you dream of me to-night? (LL) The Spanish Needle. Claude McKay. SP-McKaC

Do You Know Me? Nayo-Barbara Watkins. TtW

Do' you know Thanksgibbin's hyeah? (LL) Signs of the Times. Paul Laurence Dunbar. CP-DunbP

Do You Reckon? Langston Hughes. CP-HughL

Do you remember/ How you won. To James. Frank Horne. *Fr.* Letters [*or* Notes*]* Found near a Suicide. AmNP; BPo; CDC; Klds; PoBA

Do You Remember Laura. Audre Lorde. CP-LordA

Do you see this cup—this tempting cup. Signing the Pledge. Frances Ellen Watkins Harper. CP-HarpF

Do you see this grain of sand. A Grain of Sand. Frances Ellen Watkins Harper. CP-HarpF

Do you see this ragged stocking. The Ragged Stocking. Frances Ellen Watkins Harper. CP-HarpF

Do You Think? Josephine D. Henderson Heard. CBWP-4

Do you think a revolution is what I need. (LL) I'm A Worker. Jayne Cortez. NBV

Do you think inasmuch as. At First I Thought You Were Talking about . Audre Lorde. CP-LordA

Do you think this is a sad day. Jayne Cortez. SP-CortJ; TtW

"Do you think you will hug the shore, Captain, to-day?" Hugging the Shore. Mary E. Tucker. CBWP-1

Do you understand? (LL) Bush Mama. Kalamu ya Salaam. TtW

Do Your Best. Mrs. Henry Linden. CBWP-4

Dock Song Crazy. Al Young. CP-YounA

Doctor Dan doth wed to-day. (LL) To Dan. Paul Laurence Dunbar. CP-DunbP

Doctor, doctor, it fits real fine. Vet's Rehabilitation. Ray Durem. PoBA

Does a first draft on your / breath. (LL) Paul Laurence Dunbar in the Tenderloin. Ishmael Reed. CP-Reed; ESEAA

Does a jazz-band ever sob? Cabaret. Langston Hughes. CP-HughL

Does he think of me in the merry throng. The Question. Josephine D. Henderson Heard. CBWP-4

Does man love Art? Man visits Art, but squirms. The Chicago Picasso. Gwendolyn Brooks. BPo; NAAAL

Does not feed you. (LL) Attentiveness. Alice Walker. CP-WalkA

Does not show his. His Shirt. Rita Dove. SP-DoveR

Does that *sound* / right / to you? (LL) Some people despise me be-. June Jordan. SP-JordJ

Does the Secret Mind Whisper? Bob Kaufman. SP-KaufB

Dog Act, The. Yusef Komunyakaa. SP-KomuY

Dog go howlin' 'long de road, De. Hope. Paul Laurence Dunbar. CP-DunbP

Dog howled, A. Suburban Evening. Langston Hughes. CP-HughL

Dog lover, A. On Seeing Diana Go Maddddddddd. Haki R. Madhubuti. BrTr

Dog ran away, The. (LL) Untitled: "I know of a man who treated his body like a dog." Ishmael Reed. CP-ReedI

Dog ran down the street, The. Silly Animals. Langston Hughes. CP-HughL

Dogass Pimp. *African-American Oral Tradition*. GetYo

Dogon iguana / one eye openseeing me, A. The Lizard Series. Ntozake Shange. CtF

Dogs are random. (LL) Probability and Birds in the Yard. Russell Atkins. GT

Dogs, but people / stop anyway. (LL) Untitled: "Law isn't all." Ishmael Reed. CP-ReedI

Dogs have nothing better, The. Three Days of Forest, a River, Free. Rita Dove. SP-DoveR

Dogwood Blossoms. George Marion McClellan. BANP

Dogwood Trees, The. Robert Hayden. CP-HaydR

Doing Battle with the Wolf. Wanda Coleman. TtW

Doing what they've gotta do / Black Angels. (LL) The Singer. Gerald William Barrax. ESEAA

Doleful moon breaks against my window. Or did my shadow move?, The. (LL) Fragments from the Diary of Amelie Patiné, Quadroon Mistress of Monsieur Jacques R------. Sybil Klein. TtW

Dollars, they bring me back. (LL) A Suite for Augustus. Rita Dove. SP-DoveR

Dolls and cloths, tobacco crumbs, vases and fringes. Gwendolyn Brooks. *See* The Bean Eaters.

Dolly sits a-quilting by her mother, stitch by stitch. The Quilting. Paul Laurence Dunbar. CP-DunbP

Dolomite: "Some folks say that Willie Green." *African-American Oral Tradition*. GetYo

Dolomite first originated in San Antone. *African-American Oral Tradition*. GetYo

Domestic Storm, A. Priscilla Jane Thompson. CBWP-2

Domestic Tranquility. Gerald William Barrax. GT

Domestic Work, 1937. Natasha Trethewey. SpiFl

Domestics. Kattie M. Cumbo. BlSi

Domino. Audre Lorde. CP-LordA

Domino Theory (Or Snoop Dogg Rules the World), The. Kenneth Carroll. CtF; SpiFl

Don José Gorostiza Encounters El Cordobés. Jay Wright. ESEAA

Don Pullen at the Zanzibar Blue Jazz Cafe, 1994. Major L. Jackson. SpiFl

Done are the toils and the wearisome marches. Ode for Memorial Day. Paul Laurence Dunbar. CP-DunbP

Done begun! (LL) Black Maria. Langston Hughes. CP-HughL

Done by walking thru mirrors to the other side. (LL) The Prestidigitator 2. Al Young. CP-YounA; NBV

Done just 'bout wore 'em out. (LL) This Is It. Elma Stuckey. TtW

Don't abuse your drum. (LL) If the drum is a woman. Jayne Cortez. SP-CortJ; TtW

Don't Ask Me Who I Am. James A., Jr. Randall. BPo

Don't Be Fourteen (In Mississippi). Jerry W. Ward, Jr. BkSV

Don't believe the hype. Public Enemy. NAAAL

Don't-Care Negro, The. Joseph Seamon Cotter, Sr. AAP; AfAmPo

Don't care to know / the / truth. (LL) Pledge of Allegiance. Carl Hancock Rux. SpiFl

Don't Cry, Scream. Haki R. Madhubuti. BrTr

Don't Estimate! June Jordan. SP-JordJ

Don't Feel So Downhearted, Buddy, *see also* Don't Look So Downhearted, Buddy. *African-American Oral Tradition*. GetYo

Don't fight, honey. Mama's Report. Michael S. Harper. SP-HarpM

Dont forget to fly. (LL) For Poets. Al Young. CP-YounA; PoBA

Don't get enough of. (LL) I Want Aretha to Set This to Music. Sherley Anne Williams. NAAAL

Don't go, don't go, don't go! (LL) Sing a Song of Singapore. Al Young. CP-YounA

Don't go. if you go. Sonia Sanchez. SP-SancS

Don't hate me cause my skin is smooth like fine lustrous fiber forming a tuft. Poetri. CtF

Don't it make you wanna cry? (LL) Petite Kid Everett. Ishmael Reed. CP-ReedI

Don't it make you want to cry? (LL) Those Boys That Ran Together. Lucille Clifton. PoBA; SP-ClifL

Don't knock at my door, little child. Black Woman. Georgia Douglas Johnson. BALP

Don't knock on my door, little child. Motherhood. Georgia Douglas Johnson. ShDr

Don't know why I. Angola Question Mark. Langston Hughes. BPo; CP-HughL

Don't let them die out. Now Poem. For Us. Sonia Sanchez. PoBA

Don't let your dog curb you! Warning: Augmented. Langston Hughes. *Fr.* Montage of a Dream Deferred. CP-HughL; SP-HughL

Don't look now / I'm fading away. Cotton Candy on a Rainy Day. Nikki Giovanni. SP-GiovN

Don't Look So Downhearted, Buddy, *see also* Don't Feel So Downhearted, Buddy. *African-American Oral Tradition.* GetYo

Don't make waves / is good advice. Lightly. Audre Lorde. CP-LordA

Don't never come to no good end. (LL) Aphorisms. Joel Chandler Harris. CrDW

Don't prick your finger. (LL) The Geni in the Jar. Nikki Giovanni. SP-GiovN

Don't rise up. (LL) Cain. Lucille Clifton. SP-ClifL

Don't say goodbye to the Porkpie Hat that rolled. Larry Neal. GT; TtW

Don't start none won't be none. (LL) My Woman. Malcolm-Jamal Warner. CtF

Don't stop rummaging, through sacred silence. Message to Etheridge Knight. Lenard D. Moore. TtW

Don't take daddy away! (LL) As Befits a Man. Langston Hughes. SP-HughL

Don't the moon look lonesome shining through the trees? Sent for You Yesterday. Jimmy Rushing. NAAAL

Don't Throw Out Wine Bottles. Marilyn Nelson. SP-NelsM

Don't turn out like I am. (LL) Evening Song. Langston Hughes. CP-HughL

Don't want no yaller gal, dat's a color will not stay. Choices. Sterling A. Brown. CP-BrowS

Don't worry baby. Broken Heart, Broken Machine. Richard E. Grant. PoBA

Don't you fool wid me! (LL) Jealous. Paul Laurence Dunbar. CP-DunbP

Don't you hear this hammer ring? (LL) Big Buddy, Big Buddy. Langston Hughes. CP-HughL

Don't you see? (LL) I got a home in dat Rock. *Unknown.* BPo; CrDW

Donut Man. Adwin Brown. CtF

Door burst open into a cathedral, The. Sneak Preview. Marilyn Nelson. *Fr.* The Plotinus Suite. SP-NelsM

Door of Hope, The. Lizelia Augusta Jenkins Moorer. CBWP-3

Doorknobs. Langston Hughes. CP-HughL

Doretha wore the short blue lace last night. The Reception. June Jordan. SP-JordJ

Doris. Angela Shannon. CtF

Doth far 'bove nature gaze. (LL) On the Poetic Muse. George Moses Horton. SP-HortG

Double-conscious brother in the veil. (LL) Afterword: a Film. Michael S. Harper. SP-HarpM

Double-conscious brother in the veil. (LL) Paul Laurence Dunbar: 1872-1906. Michael S. Harper. SP-HarpM

Double-conscious sister in the veil. Madimba. Michael S. Harper. SP-HarpM

Double Elegy. Michael S. Harper. ESEAA

Double Feature. Robert Hayden. CP-HaydR

Double I, / The cleft sky, The. Mended. Jean Toomer. CP-ToomJ

Double Standard, A. Frances Ellen Watkins Harper. AAP; BlSi; CP-HarpF; CrDW; Crnst; EBAP; NAAAL

Double Standard Lifestyle Studies: #1. June Jordan. SP-JordJ

Double Take at Relais de L'Espadon. Thadious M. Davis. BlSi

Doubt crept into a heart one day, A. Clara Ann Thompson. CBWP-2

Doubt no longer miracles. Miracles. Arna Bontemps. NAAAL

Dough I knows dat Lizy's waitin' wid de skillet w'en I's done. (LL) Fishing. Paul Laurence Dunbar. CP-DunbP

Dough lone de way, my dearie. (LL) On the Road. Paul Laurence Dunbar. CP-DunbP

Douglass. Paul Laurence Dunbar. AAP; CP-DunbP; NAAAL; TtW

Douglass, Du Bois, Garvey, King, and Malcolm X. Five Black Men. Margaret Abigail Walker. CP-WalkM

Douglass was someone who. Frederick Douglass: 1817–1895. Langston Hughes. BPo; CP-HughL

'Dout a lovah's lane. (LL) Lover's Lane. Paul Laurence Dunbar. BANP; CP-DunbP

Dove, The. Paul Laurence Dunbar. CP-DunbP

Dove, The. Langston Hughes. CP-HughL

Down and Out. *African-American Oral Tradition.* GetYo

Down and Out. Langston Hughes. CP-HughL; SP-HughL

Down at the barbershop. Slim Hears "The Call." Sterling A. Brown. CP-BrowS

Down at the hall at midnight sometimes. Dance. Lula Lowe Weeden. CDC

Down, down, in millions, blending. The Snow-Flakes. Priscilla Jane Thompson. CBWP-2

Down / Down into the fathomless depths. Black Is a Soul. Joseph Blanco White. IDB; PoBA

Down-Hearted Blues. Albert Hunter *and* Louie Austin. NAAAL

Down home / he sets on a stoop. Neighbor. Langston Hughes. *Fr.* Montage of a Dream Deferred. CP-HughL

Down I came to wash my soul. Tuskegee, Tuskegee! Lance Jeffers. BkSV

Down in Alabama. (LL) Uncle Rufus. Melvin B. Tolson. TtW

Down in Atlanta, / De whitefolks got laws. Slim in Atlanta. Sterling A. Brown. CP-BrowS

Down in history we find it and in grandest works of art. Negro Heroines. Lizelia Augusta Jenkins Moorer. CBWP-3

Down in Natchitoches there is a statue in a public square. The Sévignés. Anne Spencer. ShDr

Down in Puerto Rico, when. Datsun's Death. Ishmael Reed. CP-ReedI

Down in the bass. Easy Boogie. Langston Hughes. *Fr.* Montage of a Dream Deferred. CP-HughL

Down in the bottom built for comfort. (LL) Impressions / of Chicago; For Howlin' Wolf. Quincy Troupe. NAAAL; NBV

Down in the cabin all things were gay. Thwarted. Priscilla Jane Thompson. CBWP-2

Down in the dell. Sunrise. Henrietta Cordelia Ray. *Fr.* Idyl. CBWP-3; EBAP

Down in the jungle about treetop deep. Signifying Monkey: "Down in the jungle about treetop deep." *African-American Oral Tradition.* GetYo

Down in the Lonesome Garden. *Unknown.* BPo

Down in the Valley. *Unknown.* CrDW

Down in West Texas where the sun. West Texas. Langston Hughes. CP-HughL; SP-HughL

Down into the candle of the blood. (LL) Poem about the Head of a Negro. June Jordan. TtW

Down let the shrine of Moloch sink. Henry Highland Garnet. CrDW

Down on '33rd Street. Statement. Langston Hughes. CP-HughL

Down our street. (LL) The Palm Wine Seller. Gladys May Casely Hayford. ShDr

Down the falls to the basin below. (LL) Clark's Way Out West: Another Version. Michael S. Harper. SP-HarpM

Down the Freeway to freedom? (LL) Suicide. Al Young. CP-YounA

Down the imperturbable street. (LL) An Aspect of Love, Alive in the Ice and Fire. Gwendolyn Brooks. BPo

Down the stream of memory? (LL) To Pfrimmer. Paul Laurence Dunbar. CP-DunbP

Down the street the ground is feeling so. The Directions. Christopher Gilbert. GT

Down the street young Harlem. Dimout in Harlem. Langston Hughes. CP-HughL

Down the streets. (LL) Boston 5:00 A.M.—10/74. Etheridge Knight. SP-KnigE

Down Wall Street / the students marched for peace. The Workers Rose on May Day or Postscript to Karl Marx. Audre Lorde. CP-LordA; SP-LordA

Down Where I Am. Langston Hughes. CP-HughL

Down where the birds call, / Marie, Marie. (LL) Diplomacy. Paul Laurence Dunbar. CP-DunbP

Down where the Dream Woman dwells. (LL) The Paradox. Paul Laurence Dunbar. AAP; CP-DunbP; Klds; PoBA

Down Wind against the Highest Peaks. Clarence Major. NBP

Downright American little dude, A. (LL) Dude in Denver. Al Young. CP-YounA

Downtown-Boy Uptown. David Henderson. NNP

Doxology. Josephine D. Henderson Heard. CBWP-4

Dozens, The. Audre Lorde. CP-LordA; SP-LordA

Dr. Booker T. Washington to the National Negro Business League. Joseph Seamon Cotter, Sr. AAP

("'Tis strange indeed to hear us plead.") AfAmPo

Dr. King's photograph. Report from the Skull's Diorama. Yusef Komunyakaa. SP-KomuY

Draft of love was cool and sweet, The. Love's Draft. Paul Laurence Dunbar. CP-DunbP

Draftees. Langston Hughes. CP-HughL

Dragon's Blood. Ishmael Reed. CP-ReedI

Drama, The. Suliaman El-Hadi. SpiFl

Drama for Winter Night (Fifth Avenue). Langston Hughes. CP-HughL

Drapery Factory, Gulfport, Mississippi, 1956. Natasha Trethewey. SpiFl

Draw a little closer, comrades! The Fisherman's Story. Henrietta Cordelia Ray. CBWP-3

Drawing. Al Young. CP-YounA

Dream, The. Francis A. Boyd. *Fr.* Columbiana. EBAP

Dream. Solomon Edwards. NNP

Dream, The. Robert Hayden. CP-HaydR; ESEAA; NBV

Dream. Langston Hughes. CP-HughL; SP-HughL

Dream, A. Maggie Pogue Johnson. CBWP-4

Dream and the Song. James David Corrothers. BANP

Dream Boogie. Langston Hughes. *Fr.* Montage of a Dream Deferred. CP-HughL; NAAAL; SP-HughL; SSLK

Dream Boogie: Variation. Langston Hughes. *Fr.* Montage of a Dream Deferred. CP-HughL

Dream days of fond delight and hours. A Madrigal. Paul Laurence Dunbar. CP-DunbP

Dream Deferred. Langston Hughes. *See* Harlem.

Dream deferred. (LL) Likewise. Langston Hughes. CP-HughL

Dream Dust. Langston Hughes. CP-HughL; SP-HughL

Dream Fix. Sonja Marie. CtF

Dream is a cocktail at Sloppy Joe's, The. Havana Dreams. Langston Hughes. CP-HughL; SP-HughL

Dream is vague, The. Beale Street. Langston Hughes. CP-HughL; SP-HughL

Dream Keeper, The. Langston Hughes. CP-HughL

Dream of Elfland, A. Henrietta Cordelia Ray. CBWP-3

Dream of Freedom. Langston Hughes. CP-HughL

Dream of Pairing. Ntozake Shange. GT

Dream of the Ring: the Great Jack Johnson, A. George Barlow. ESEAA

Dream of yesterday. Motherland. Langston Hughes. CP-HughL

Dream on, for dreams are sweet. Dreams. Paul Laurence Dunbar. CP-DunbP

Dream Orpheum Balcony. Tom Dent. BkSV

Dream Sequence, Part 9. Naomi Long Madgett. BPo

Dream-singers / Story-tellers. Laughers. Langston Hughes. CP-HughL

Dream Song. Lewis Alexander. PoBA

Dream Song I. Paul Laurence Dunbar. CP-DunbP

Dream Song II. Paul Laurence Dunbar. CP-DunbP

Dream Take: 22. Al Young. CP-YounA

Dream / they are immortal. Audre Lorde. *See* St. Louis Out of Time.

Dream they saw a free future. (LL) They clapped when we landed. Nikki Giovanni. SP-GiovN

Dream Thief. Nathaniel Mackey. GT

Dream Variations. Langston Hughes. AmNP; BALP; CDC; CP-HughL; IDB; PoBA; SP-HughL
    ("Black like me.") (LL) NAAAL; SSLK

Dream within a Song, A. Henrietta Cordelia Ray. CBWP-3

Dream/eaters on the edge. Shirley Bradley LeFlore. SpiFl

Dream/Songs from the Moon of Beulah Land. Audre Lorde. CP-LordA

Dreambook Bestiary. Yusef Komunyakaa. SP-KomuY

Dreamer, The. Paul Laurence Dunbar. CP-DunbP

Dreamer. Langston Hughes. CP-HughL

Dreamin' Town. Paul Laurence Dunbar. CP-DunbP

Dreaming / Colorado where the whole earth rises. Poem for Joy. June Jordan. SP-JordJ

Dreaming is still on the house. (LL) The Katskills Kiss Romance Goodbye. Ishmael Reed. CP-ReedI

Dreamjot: 1962. Al Young. CP-YounA

Dreams. Charles Cooper. PoBA

Dreams. Paul Laurence Dunbar. CP-DunbP

Dreams. Nikki Giovanni. PoBA; SP-GiovN

Dreams. Langston Hughes. CP-HughL

Dreams: American. Michael S. Harper. SP-HarpM

Dreams bite. Audre Lorde. CP-LordA; SP-LordA

Dreams have a way. The Wonder Woman. Nikki Giovanni. SP-GiovN

Dreams of Beauty. Adah Isaacs Menken. CBWP-1

Dreams of Life. Timothy Thomas Fortune. EBAP
    "Fontaine no longer cared to live."
    "O, Life of Dreams! O, Dreams of Life!"

Dreams of Paradise. Al Young. CP-YounA

Dreams of the Dreamer, The. Georgia Douglas Johnson. CDC

Dream's Wisdom, The. Marilyn Nelson. SP-NelsM

Dress Rehearsal Paranoia #2. Ishmael Reed. CP-ReedI

Dressed Up. Langston Hughes. CP-HughL

Dressed up in my melancholy. Song. M. Carl Holman. AmNP; Klds

Dressed up in pain. Milestone: The Birth of an Ancestor. Eugene B. Redmond. SpiFl

Drift-Wood. Clara Ann Thompson. CBWP-2

Drifters are in Harlem, The. Neon Diaspora. David Henderson. BlFi

Drifting night in the Georgia pines. O Daedalus, Fly Away Home. Robert Hayden. CP-HaydR; IDB; NAAAL; PoBA; TtW

Drifts on noonday heat. (LL) Haiku: "Family reunion." Lenard D. Moore. SpiFl

Drifts That Bar My Door. Adah Isaacs Menken. CBWP-1

Driftwood gathered here and there. To Pfrimmer. Paul Laurence Dunbar. CP-DunbP

Drink of my / juice. (LL) Discover Me. Opal Palmer Adisa. GT

Drink On. Mary E. Tucker. CBWP-1

Drinkin'. *African-American Oral Tradition.* GetYo

Drinks, the enormous lie, and love, The. (LL) Old Woman. Al Young. CP-YounA

Dripping down candles in sacred places. (LL) Raising a Humid Flag. Thylias Moss. GT

Drive In, The. Michael S. Harper. SP-HarpM

Driven by a godawful wind. (LL) You and I Are Disappearing. Yusef Komunyakaa. SP-KomuY

Driving through New England. Lucille Clifton. ESEAA; SP-ClifL

Driving Wheel. Sherley Anne Williams. BlSi

Drizzle. Paul Laurence Dunbar. CP-DunbP

Drizzle hangs in the air, A. Rocks Push. Yusef Komunyakaa. SP-KomuY

Droning a drowsy syncopated tune. The Weary Blues. Langston Hughes. BALP; CP-HughL; NAAAL; SP-HughL

Droops in the grassy pen. (LL) The Wild Goat. Claude McKay. SP-McKaC

Drowning of the Facts of a Life, The. Michael S. Harper. ESEAA

Drowning yesterday? (LL) Poem for Youth. Langston Hughes. CP-HughL

Drowsy Day, A. Paul Laurence Dunbar. CP-DunbP

Drowsy with beauty, I bathe &. The Afternoon After. Al Young. CP-YounA

Drugstore theater / can- / not / cure / ? (LL) Hallucinogenic Halleluuuu. Al Young. CP-YounA

Drum. Langston Hughes. SP-HughL

Drum Majah, De. Ray Garfield Dandridge. BANP

Drumdrumdrum, A. The Wall. Gwendolyn Brooks. PoBA

Drums. Langston Hughes. CP-HughL

Drums ... Pa-Rum ... the rat-tat-tat ... of drums, The. Nikki Giovanni. SP-GiovN

Drunk long / Ago. (LL) Sport. Langston Hughes. CP-HughL

Drunk Time. Bob Kaufman. SP-KaufB

Drunkard. Langston Hughes. *Fr.* Montage of a Dream Deferred. CP-HughL

Drunkard's Child, The. Frances Ellen Watkins Harper. CP-HarpF

Drunkard's Wife, The. Mary E. Tucker. CBWP-1

Drunken laughter escapes. Moonshine. Yusef Komunyakaa. SP-KomuY

Drunken Lover. Owen Dodson. AmNP

Dry brown coughing beneath their feet, The. Beverly Hills, Chicago. Gwendolyn Brooks. ESEAA; SP-BrooG

Dry dreams. (LL) Communication II. Maya Angelou. CP-AngeM; SP-AngeM

Dry feathers on my lover's step. (LL) Feathers. Jayne Cortez. SP-CortJ

Dry tablets without token. (LL) We saw beyond our seeming. Maya Angelou. CP-AngeM; SP-AngeM

Dryness is upon the house, A. In Honor of David Anderson Brooks, My Father. Gwendolyn Brooks. SP-BrooG

Dualism in Ralph Ellison's Invisible Man. Ishmael Reed. CP-ReedI; NAAAL
    (Dualism.) ESEAA; TtW

Duck come switchin' 'cross de lot. The Capture. Paul Laurence Dunbar. CP-DunbP

DUCK SISTERS. don't get hit. yet. either way you die. (LL) Uhuru (freedom. now. swahili. east african lango). Ahmed Legraham Alhamisi. BlFi

Dude in Denver. Al Young. CP-YounA

Due meed for your endeavor. (LL) To Miss Mary Britton. Paul Laurence Dunbar. CP-DunbP

Duke Checks Out Ella as She Scats Like That. Michael War. CtF

Duke Ellington. Frank Marshall Davis. TtW

Duke look at you. The Cotton Club. Clarence Major. TtW

Duke's World / is the explanation. Amiri Baraka. SpiFl

Dull unwashed windows of eyes. A Poem Some People Will Have to Understand. Amiri Baraka. BPo; GT; SP-BaraA

Dumb / figure / skater per, A. Columbia. Ishmael Reed. CP-ReedI

Dumb prancing pigeon, mourning for your love. (LL) Crazy pigeon strutting outside my cell. Etheridge Knight. NBV

Dumb with her wet bowels. (LL) Poem: "Look at me 8th / grade." Sonia Sanchez. SP-SancS

Dunbar. Anne Spencer. AfAmPo; BANP; CDC; Klds; NAAAL

Duncan Spoke of a Process. Amiri Baraka. SP-BaraA

Durban, Birmingham, / Cape Town, Atlanta. Question and Answer. Langston Hughes. BPo; CP-HughL

During the season of cut organs we. Initiation. Jayne Cortez. PoBA

Dusk. Mae V. Cowdery. ShDr

Dusk. Angelina Weld Grimké. CDC; ShDr

Dusk. Langston Hughes. CP-HughL

Dusk dark / On Railroad Avenue. Railroad Avenue. Langston Hughes. CP-HughL; SP-HughL

Dusk / no dawns, and silver linings. No Dawns. Julianne Perry. PoBA

Dusk Song. William H. A. Moore. BANP

Dusk. The *Flight* passing Blanchisseuse. The *Flight*, Passing Blanchisseuse. Derek Walcott. *Fr.* The Schooner Flight. ESEAA

Dusky children tease, / "African China!", The. (LL) African China. Melvin B. Tolson. Klds

Dust, as they say, settled, The. (LL) The Third Sermon on the Warpland. Gwendolyn Brooks. NAAAL

Dust Bowl. Robert A. Davis. IDB

Dust of ancient pages, The. Communication II. Maya Angelou. CP-AngeM; SP-AngeM

Dust, / Through which. Waring Cuney. CDC

Dustbowl. Langston Hughes. CP-HughL

Dusting. Rita Dove. SP-DoveR

   ("Every day a wilderness—no.") ESEAA

   ("Maurice.") (LL) ESEAA

Dusting. Marilyn Nelson. SP-NelsM

Duty, or Truth at Work. Lizelia Augusta Jenkins Moorer. CBWP-3

Dying. Adah Isaacs Menken. CBWP-1

Dying. (LL) Today Is Not Like They Said. Kirk Hall. NBV

Dying Beast. Langston Hughes. CP-HughL

Dying Bondman, The. Frances Ellen Watkins Harper. CP-HarpF

Dying Child to Her Blind Father, The. Frances Ellen Watkins Harper. CP-HarpF

Dying Christian, The. Frances Ellen Watkins Harper. CP-HarpF

Dying Fugitive, The. Frances Ellen Watkins Harper. CP-HarpF; TtW

Dying Girl, The. Mary Weston Fordham. CBWP-2

Dying in the dark. (LL) Love is a wild wonder. Langston Hughes. CP-HughL; SP-HughL

Dying Mother, The. Frances Ellen Watkins Harper. CP-HarpF

Dying Queen, The. Frances Ellen Watkins Harper. CP-HarpF

Dying Year, The. Clara Ann Thompson. CBWP-2

Dylan, Two Days, *for Dylan Corbett*. Patricia Smith. GT

Dylan, Who Is Dead. Samuel Allen. PoBA

E

Each blade sings aobut desire. (LL) Rocks Push. Yusef Komunyakaa. SP-KomuY

Each body has its art, its precious prescribed. Still Do I Keep My Look, My Identity. . . . Gwendolyn Brooks. SP-BrooG

Each hour has some glory all its own. The Hour's Glory. Henrietta Cordelia Ray. CBWP-3

Each hurt swallowed. Promises. Rita Dove. SP-DoveR

Each known mile comes late. The Train Runs Late to Harlem. Conrad Kent Rivers. IDB; PoBA

Each laugh bedded with blood. (LL) Trays: a Portfolio. Michael S. Harper. SP-HarpM

Each little room. Room. Langston Hughes. CP-HughL

Each man on this slow train. Farewell to You. Elizabeth Alexander. GT

Each morning / I go down. Amiri Baraka. ESEAA *Fr.* Hymn for Lanie Poo. SP-BaraA

Each One, Pull One. Alice Walker. CP-WalkA

Each other. So riots are boss outlets. (LL) Days Prior to. Jacques Wakefield. BlFi

Each other? Why are the beautiful sick and divided / like myself? (LL) Cold Term. Amiri Baraka. BPo

Each silently, but not alone. (LL) In Time of Crisis. Raymond R. Patterson. IDB; NBP; PoBA

Each Sunday. Nikki Giovanni. SP-GiovN

Each time I order her to go. Forgiveness. Alice Walker. CP-WalkA

Each to our separate house. (LL) Mentor. Audre Lorde. CP-LordA; SP-LordA

Eagerly / Like a woman hurrying to her lover. Four Glimpses of Night. Frank Marshall Davis. AmNP; PoBA

Eagle Rock. Alice Walker. CP-WalkA

Eagles are a majestic species ... living in the thin searing air. Nikki Giovanni. SP-GiovN

Ear Training. Sekou Sundiata. SpiFl

Early Affection. George Moses Horton. AAP; AfAmPo; SP-HortG

Early blue evening. Langston Hughes. *Fr.* Montage of a Dream Deferred. CP-HughL

Early blue evening. Wonder. Langston Hughes. SP-HughL

Early Evening Quarrel. Langston Hughes. SP-HughL

   ("Do-right man?") (LL) CP-HughL

Early Losses: a Requiem. Alice Walker. BlSi; CP-WalkA

Early Loves. Bob Kaufman. SP-KaufB

Early Morning on the Tel Aviv-Haifa Freeway. Rita Dove. SP-DoveR

Early one morning. Voodoo on the Un-Assing of Janis Joplin. Carolyn M. Rodgers. JB

Early spring's sweet blush, The. Eloise Bibb. CBWP-4

Earth. Lucille Clifton. SP-ClifL

Earth. Rolland Snellings. BlFi

Earth. Jean Toomer. CP-ToomJ

Earth. Askia Muhammad Touré. BrTr

Earth eyes. breathing me. Sonia Sanchez. SP-SancS

Earth is a beautiful place, The. The Third Sermon on the Warpland. Gwendolyn Brooks. BPo; NAAAL

Earth / is a wonderful, The. Poem for Friends. Quincy Troupe. PoBA

Earth-meaning, The. Fulfilment. Langston Hughes. CP-HughL; SP-HughL

Earth Mother. Sonia Sanchez. *Fr.* Past. SP-SancS

Earth moves / the sirens flare, The. Good Nights. Saundra Sharp. SpiFl

Earth Screaming. Esther Iverem. GT

Earth Song. Langston Hughes. CP-HughL

Earth turns / like a rainbow, The. When You Read This Poem. Pinkie Gordon Lane. BlSi

Earth was young, the world was fair, The. The Saxon Legend of Language. Mary Weston Fordham. AAP; CBWP-2

Earthquake Blues. Ishmael Reed. CP-ReedI

Earthquake of 1886, The. Josephine D. Henderson Heard. CBWP-4

Easily, almost matter-of-factly they step. The Performers. Robert Hayden. CP-HaydR

East Berlin. Audre Lorde. CP-LordA

East Boston. Al Young. CP-YounA

Easter Bonnet, The. Clara Ann Thompson. CBWP-2

Easter Bunny Blues or All I Want for Xmas Is the Loop, The. Ebon Dooley. PoBA

Easter Carol. Henrietta Cordelia Ray. CBWP-3

Easter Flower, The. Claude McKay. SP-McKaC

Easter Light, The. Clara Ann Thompson. CBWP-2

Easter Morn. Josephine D. Henderson Heard. CBWP-4

Easter Ode, An. Paul Laurence Dunbar. CP-DunbP

Easter; or, Spring-Time. Lizelia Augusta Jenkins Moorer. CBWP-3

Easter Sermon, 1866. Marilyn Nelson. *Fr.* Thus Far by Faith. SP-NelsM

Easter Sunday. Lucille Clifton. SP-ClifL

Eastern European Eclogues. Rita Dove. SP-DoveR

Eastern guard tower. Haiku: "Eastern guard tower." Etheridge Knight. BPo; ESEAA; SP-KnigE; TtW

Easy Boogie. Langston Hughes. *Fr.* Montage of a Dream Deferred. CP-HughL

Easy-Goin' Feller, An. Paul Laurence Dunbar. CP-DunbP

Easy Living. Michael S. Weaver. SpiFl

Easy rider, see what you done done, Lawd, Lawd. *Unknown.* CrDW

Easy to forget the little lies: I'll call you. Is She Okay? Marilyn Nelson. SP-NelsM

Easy way out. Nayo-Barbara Watkins. NBV

Eat and lay their heads! (LL) Sather Tower Mystery. Ishmael Reed. CP-ReedI

Eat Helen B Happy (a Found Poem). Etheridge Knight. SP-KnigE

Eat, Helen, / Be happy! Eat Helen B Happy (a Found Poem). Etheridge Knight. SP-KnigE

Eat it all, / Die! (LL) Bird with Painted Wings. Bob Kaufman. SP-KaufB; TtW

Ebb / with the flow. Daufuskie. Mari E. Evans. BlSi

Echo. Audre Lorde. CP-LordA; SP-LordA

Echo Reverie. Henrietta Cordelia Ray. CBWP-3

Echoes. Audre Lorde. CP-LordA

Echo's Complaint. Henrietta Cordelia Ray. CBWP-3

Eclipse. Albert E., Jr. Haynes. BlFi

Eclipse. Amir Rashidd. NBP

Eclipse. Ed Roberson. GT

Ecstasy. Virginia A. Houston. ShDr

Eddie and Charlie and Jack and Ted. Bonds: In Memoriam. Langston Hughes. CP-HughL

Eddie Ledoux: "There's some strange and queer tales that come through all jails." *African-American Oral Tradition.* GetYo

Eddie Ledoux: "Wise and queer tales float through all the jails." *African-American Oral Tradition.* GetYo

Eden. Claudia Rankine. GT

Edgar Allan Poe. Timothy Thomas Fortune. AAP

Edge into a swoon. (LL) Moonlight Night: Carmel. Langston Hughes. CP-HughL; GT

Edge of our bed was a wide grid, The. Sisters in Arms. Audre Lorde. CP-LordA

Edge / of this, The. Eldridge. Lucille Clifton. SP-ClifL

Editorial Poem on an Incident of Effects Far-reaching. Russell Atkins. NBP

Education. Don L. Lee. AmNP; BALP

E'en as the sculptor chisels patiently. The Tireles Sculptor. Henrietta Cordelia Ray. CBWP-3

Een de mighty fine house on de mighty high hill! (LL) Ol' Doc' Hyar. James Edwin Campbell. AfAmPo; EBAP; TtW

E'en John the Baptist did not know. On the Truth of the Saviour. George Moses Horton. SP-HortG

E'er yet the morning heav'd its Orient head. On the Death of the Rev'd Dr. Sewall, 1769. Phillis Wheatley. CP-WheaP

Ef dey's anyt'ing dat riles me. Possum. Paul Laurence Dunbar. CP-DunbP

Ef I's layin' 'mong de t'ings I's allus knowed. (LL) Death Song[, A]. Paul Laurence Dunbar. CP-DunbP

Ef you's only got de powah fe' to blow a little whistle. Limitations. Paul Laurence Dunbar. CP-DunbP

Effendi. Michael S. Harper. PoBA; SP-HarpM

Efficiency Apartment. Gerald William Barrax. PoBA

Effie. Sterling A. Brown. BANP; CP-BrowS

Egg Boiler, The. Gwendolyn Brooks. PoBA; TtW

Ego Tripping. Nikki Giovanni. GT; SP-GiovN

Egyptian Book of the Dead. David Henderson. TtW

Egyptian collection, The. (LL) The Return of Julian the Apostate to Rome. Ishmael Reed. CP-ReedI

8 black boys in a Southern jail. Scottsboro. Langston Hughes. CP-HughL

Eight of 'em hyeah all tol' an' yet. Puttin' the Baby Away. Paul Laurence Dunbar. CP-DunbP

Eighth a May was a hell of a day, The. Titanic: "Eighth a May was a hell of a day, The." *African-American Oral Tradition.* GetYo

Either heard or taught. Song for a Thin Sister. Audre Lorde. CP-LordA; SP-LordA

El Beso. Angelina Weld Grimké. ShDr

El-Hajj Malik El-Shabazz. Robert Hayden. BrTr; CP-HaydR; Crnst; ESEAA; NAAAL; PoBA

El Paso Monologue. Ishmael Reed. SpiFl

Elder Mistletoe. Sterling A. Brown. CP-BrowS

Elderly Leaders. Langston Hughes. CP-HughL

Eldridge. Lucille Clifton. SP-ClifL

Elected virgins, The. Wedding in Hanover. Lorna Goodison. GT

Election Day. Amiri Baraka. BlFi

Election Night Pome. Al Young. CP-YounA

Electric Cop, The. Victor Hernandez Cruz. PoBA

Electric Slide Boogie, The. Audre Lorde. CP-LordA

Electrical Storm. Robert Hayden. CP-HaydR

Electricity of Blossoms, *for Janet.* Lorenzo Thomas. GT

Elegance in the extreme. Ntozake Shange. TtW

Elegiac Poem on the Death of George Whitefield, An. Phillis Wheatley. *See* On the Death of the Rev. Mr. George Whitefield, 1770.

Elegies for Paradise Valley. Robert Hayden. CP-HaydR

Elegy: "Good morning! / Good morning!" Al Young. CP-YounA

Elegy: "I lay down in my grave." Maya Angelou. SP-AngeM ("I lie down in my grave.") CP-AngeM

Elegy: "Strange summer sun shines round our globe of circumstance." Margaret Abigail Walker. CP-WalkM

Elegy for a Lady. Walt Delegall. BlFi

Elegy for a Martyred Poet. El Rivera. CtF

Elegy for David Diop. Keorapetse W. Kgositsile. BrTr

Elegy for Etheridge. Pinkie Gordon Lane. TtW

Elegy (for MOVE and Philadelphia). Sonia Sanchez. Crnst; ESEAA; TtW

Elegy for Thelonious. Yusef Komunyakaa. ESEAA; SP-KomuY

Elegy on Leaving —, An. Phillis Wheatley. CP-WheaP

Elegy, Sacred to the Memory of That Great Divine, the Reverend and Learned Dr. Samuel Cooper, Who Departed This Life December 29, 1783, Ætatis 59, An. Phillis Wheatley. CP-WheaP

Elegy, to Miss Mary Moorhead, An. Phillis Wheatley. CP-WheaP

Elements of Grammar. Calvin C. Hernton. NBP

Elephant Rock. Primus St. John. PoBA

Elevator Boy. Langston Hughes. CP-HughL; SP-HughL

Elevator Man Adheres to Form, The. Margaret Else Danner. PoBA

Elevator music from a Tokyo radio. The Sad Hour of Your Peace. Al Young. CP-YounA

1100 Exposition. Newletter from My Mother. Michael S. Harper. PoBA

11/10 Again. Lucille Clifton. GT

Eliza Harris. Frances Ellen Watkins Harper. AAP; CP-HarpF; NAAAL

Eliza in Uncle Tom's Cabin. Eloise Bibb. CBWP-4

Eliza, tell thy lover why. To Eliza. George Moses Horton. EBAP; SP-HortG; TtW

Elle folâtre en ces lieux pleins de charmes. Le Retour au Village aux Perles. Nelson Desbrosses. EBAP; TtW

Else they cannot eat. (LL) A Contract. (For The Destruction and Rebuilding of Paterson). Amiri Baraka. SP-BaraA

Else we might as well lay down and die. (LL) Within the Veil. Michelle Cliff. NAAAL

Elsewhere. Derek Walcott. Crnst

Elvin's Blues. Michael S. Harper. BPo; SP-HarpM

Emancipation. Paul Laurence Dunbar. CP-DunbP

Emancipation. Priscilla Jane Thompson. CBWP-2

Emancipation: 1865. Long View: Negro. Langston Hughes. CP-HughL

Emancipation Day. Lizelia Augusta Jenkins Moorer. CBWP-3

Emancipation of George-Hector (a Colored Turtle), The. Mari E. Evans. AmNP

Emblem of blasted hope and lost desire. Sonnet. Paul Laurence Dunbar. CP-DunbP

Embryonic or symphonic. Hot House. Al Young. CP-YounA

Emerges now a hero new. Epitome. Ruth G. Dixon. ShDr

Emerson. Joseph Seamon Cotter, Sr. EBAP

Emerson. Henrietta Cordelia Ray. CBWP-3

Emigrant, The. Benjamin Clark. EBAP

Emily Dickinson's Defunct. Marilyn Nelson. ESEAA; SP-NelsM

Emmett Till. Wanda Coleman. NAAAL

Emmett Till. James A. Emanuel. PoBA

Emmett's mother is a pretty-faced thing. Gwendolyn Brooks. *See* The Last Quatrain of the Ballad of Emmett Till.

Emperor Haile Selassie. Langston Hughes. CP-HughL

"Emperor": Shields Green: Fugitives. Michael S. Harper. SP-HarpM

Empress Brand Trim: Ruby Reminisces, The. Sherley Anne Williams. BlSi

Empty carousel in a deserted place, An. The Carousel. Gloria C. Oden. AmNP; PoBA

Empty House. Langston Hughes. CP-HughL

Empty Tomb, The. Clara Ann Thompson. CBWP-2

Empty woman took toys! The. Gwendolyn Brooks. SP-BrooG

En Passant. June Jordan. SP-JordJ

En route to the picnic they drive through their history. Picnic: the Liberated. M. Carl Holman. PoBA

Enacting someone's notion of themselves. Aunt Jemima of the Ocean Waves. Robert Hayden. CP-HaydR; PoBA

Enchanted Shell, The. Henrietta Cordelia Ray. CBWP-3

Enchantment. Lewis Alexander. PoBA

Enclave where new mythologies. Zeus over Redeye. Robert Hayden. CP-HaydR

Encounter. Langston Hughes. CP-HughL

Encouraged. Paul Laurence Dunbar. CP-DunbP

Encouragement. Paul Laurence Dunbar. CP-DunbP

Encouragement. Mrs. Henry Linden. CBWP-4

End. Langston Hughes. CP-HughL; SP-HughL

End of Ethnic Dream, The. Jay Wright. BlFi

End of Man Is His Beauty, The. Amiri Baraka. AmNP; BALP; TtW

End of the Chapter, The. Paul Laurence Dunbar. CP-DunbP

End of the Whole Matter, The. Albery Allson Whitman. AAP *Fr.* Not a Man, and Yet a Man

Endangered Species. Ai. ESEAA

Ending. Alice Walker. CP-WalkA

Endymion, your star is steadfast now. To Endymion. Countee Cullen. CP-CullC

Enemy. Langston Hughes. CP-HughL

Enemy, The. Alice Walker. CP-WalkA; GT

Enemy far away on the other side of the sea, The. (LL) A Poem for Black Relocation Centers. Etheridge Knight. ESEAA; SP-KnigE

Energy. Victor Hernandez Cruz. PoBA

Energy for a New Thang. Ernie Mkalimoto. NBP

England, cannot thy shores boast bards as great. Ye Bards of England. Albery Allson Whitman. EBAP

England, I thought, will look like Africa. Poem for Mark. June Jordan. SP-JordJ

English, The. Langston Hughes. CP-HughL

English Lace. Cheryl Boyce Taylor. CtF

Engraved on / our chains. (LL) The Thing Itself. Alice Walker. CP-WalkA

Enigmatic moon has at long last died, The. Stevedore. Leslie Morgan Collins. AmNP

Enneads, I, vi. Marilyn Nelson. *Fr.* The Plotinus Suite. SP-NelsM

Ennui. Langston Hughes. SP-HughL

("Is's such a.") CP-HughL

Enormous Gas Bill at the Dwarf Factory. A Horror Movie to be Shot with Eyes, The. Bob Kaufman. SP-KaufB

Enough for you. (LL) For Bud. Michael S. Harper. ESEAA; SP-HarpM

Enough talk about bleeding Kansas. Manual for the Patriotic Volunteer. Michael S. Harper. SP-HarpM

Enough to hold us aloft by heart and by ear. (LL) Sweet Sixteen Lines. Al Young. CP-YounA

Enough women over thirty are at Redbones. Raising a Humid Flag. Thylias Moss. GT

Enslaved. Claude McKay. AfAmPo; BALP; BPo; NAAAL; SP-McKaC

Enter Harlem. Walk with de Mayor of Harlem. David Henderson. PoBA

Entered the conquering dark. (LL) Jackie Robinson. Lucille Clifton. SP-ClifL

Enthralling me like the cataract of a cosmic orgasm. (LL) The Awakening. Keorapetse W. Kgositsile. BlFi

Enthroned upon the mighty truth. Justice. Paul Laurence Dunbar. CP-DunbP

Envied us our thunder? (LL) Spring Reminiscence. Countee Cullen. CP-CullC

Envoy to Africa. Langston Hughes. CP-HughL

Enybody else wanna cop-out? (LL) Cop-Out Session. Etheridge Knight. SP-KnigE

Epilogue: "Lily, being white not red, The." Countee Cullen. CP-CullC

Epilogue to the Opera of Dead on Arrival. Yusef Komunyakaa. SP-KomuY

Episode. Sterling A. Brown. CP-BrowS

Epistolary Monologue. Ishmael Reed. CP-ReedI

Epistrophe. Amiri Baraka. Klds; NNP

Epitaph: "She leans across a golden table." Countee Cullen. CP-CullC

Epitaph: "Uncle Tom, / When he was alive." Langston Hughes. CP-HughL

Epitaph, An: "When I am gone." Josephine D. Henderson Heard. AAP; CBWP-4

Epitaph: "Within this grave lie." Langston Hughes. CP-HughL

Epitaph for My Father. Margaret Abigail Walker. CP-WalkM

Epithalamium and Shivaree. Marilyn Nelson. IHS; SP-NelsM

Epitome. Ruth G. Dixon. ShDr

Equal Opportunity. Audre Lorde. CP-LordA

Equality. Maya Angelou. CP-AngeM

Equinox. Audre Lorde. CP-LordA; SP-LordA

Equipment. Paul Laurence Dunbar. CP-DunbP

Ere sleep comes down to soothe the weary eyes. Paul Laurence Dunbar. BALP; BANP; CDC; CP-DunbP; NAAAL

Ere yet the morn its lovely blushes spread. On the Death of the Rev. Dr. Sewell, 1769. Phillis Wheatley. CP-WheaP

Erect in the movies. Afterword: a Film. Michael S. Harper. SP-HarpM

Erica Blaise began her life with several established truths. Countess Erica Blaise: Chorus. Bob Kaufman. SP-KaufB

Erosong. Al Young. CP-YounA

Escape. Georgia Douglas Johnson. PoBA; ShDr; TtW

Escape Artist, The. Kevin Young. GT

Essence, the center, home. (LL) Poem with Orange. Al Young. CP-YounA

Essentially description, night. (1978, Remembering 1962). C. S. Giscombe. GT

Essentially, it allows more Negroes to become. Civil Rights Bill #666. Amiri Baraka. SP-BaraA

Estate bird / sits on the water, The. Loon. Michael S. Harper. ESEAA

Esteville fire begins to burn. On Summer. George Moses Horton. AAP; SP-HortG

Esther say I drink too much. Various Protestations From Various People. Etheridge Knight. SP-KnigE

Esthete in Harlem. Langston Hughes. BANP; BPo

(Aesthete in Harlem.) CP-HughL

Estimable Mable. Gwendolyn Brooks. FB

Etch in the memory of your bones. For Mark James Robert Essex d. 1973. Alvin Aubert. BkSV

Eternal *dénouement*, The. (LL) Particulars. Rita Dove. Crnst

Eternal Landscape, The. Lenard D. Moore. GT

Eternal spirit / of dead dried. Black Lotus. Alicia Loy Johnson. NBP

Eternal spring of boundless grace! Heavenly Love. George Moses Horton. SP-HortG

Eternal unit of forever. (LL) The Imitation Dance. Al Young. CP-YounA

Eternities now numbering six or seven. Saint Peter Relates an Incident of the Resurrection Day. James Weldon Johnson. Klds

Eternity. Josephine D. Henderson Heard. CBWP-4

Eternity. George Marion McClellan. EBAP

Eternity. Al Young. CP-YounA

Ethel in her crimson row boat. Chateaux en Espagne. Henrietta Cordelia Ray. CBWP-3

Ethel Waters sleeps in the stable. The Devil's Music in Hell. Julius E. Thompson. TtW

Ethical schizophrenia you called it. Goin' to the Territory. Michael S. Harper. NAAAL

Ethiopia. Frances Ellen Watkins Harper. CP-HarpF; NAAAL

Ethiopia. Fenton Johnson. EBAP

Ethiopia. Audre Lorde. CP-LordA

Ethiopia / Lift your night-dark face. Call of Ethiopia. Langston Hughes. CP-HughL

Ethiopia—tragi-song. (LL) Broadcast on Ethiopia. Langston Hughes. CP-HughL

Ethiopian's Song, The. Fenton Johnson. Crnst

Etta Moten's Attic. Margaret Else Danner. BrTr

Eulogy. Audre Lorde. CP-LordA

Eulogy for Alvin Frost. Audre Lorde. CP-LordA

Eulogy for Populations. Ron Welburn. BlFi; PoBA

Eulogy to W. H. Auden. Derek Walcott. ESEAA

Euphony. Yusef Komunyakaa. ESEAA

Europe / Is endowed with the first move. Calvin Forbes. NBV

Eutawville Lynching, The. Lizelia Augusta Jenkins Moorer. CBWP-3

Evahmo'. . . . Sterling A. Brown. *See* Southern Road.

Evanescent hue whose pearly gleam, An. An Ideal. Henrietta Cordelia Ray. CBWP-3

Evangeline made her. Straight Talk from Plain Women. Sherley Anne Williams. GT

Evanishings. Mary E. Tucker. CBWP-1

Eva's Farewell. Frances Ellen Watkins Harper. CP-HarpF

Eve of Christmas had arrived, The. A Christmas Ghost. Priscilla Jane Thompson. CBWP-2

Eve (Rachel). Michael S. Harper. ESEAA; SP-HarpM

Evelyn. Priscilla Jane Thompson. CBWP-2

Even. Audre Lorde. CP-LordA

Even a hair. Sea Level. Al Young. CP-YounA

Even as I hold you. Alice Walker. CP-WalkA

Even as we kill. On the Birth of My Son, Malcolm Coltrane. Julius Lester. PoBA

Even at 26, the hush when. Paul Laurence Dunbar in the Tenderloin. Ishmael Reed. CP-Reed; ESEAA

Even at night the air rang and rang. Boccaccio: The Plague Years. Rita Dove. SP-DoveR

Even being able to get a glimpse of moon. Fun City Samba. Al Young. CP-YounA

Even here, dwelling in chaos. Ecstasy. Virginia A. Houston. ShDr

Even if it is my home. (LL) Croon. Langston Hughes. CP-HughL

Even if you forgot. (LL) Your Hands. Angelina Weld Grimké. CDC; PoBA

Even sunlight dares. Prisoner. Maya Angelou. CP-AngeM; SP-AngeM

Even the most die-hard liberals. A Lonely Affair. Reuben Jackson. GT

Even the roots of grass / quicken. (LL) The Winds of Orisha. Audre Lorde. CP-LordA

Even then / in the attenuated light. Solidarity. June Jordan. SP-JordJ

Even this is movement. Altars and Sacrifice. Jay Wright. FB

Even this laughter, even your tears. (LL) Twenty-Six Ways of Looking at a Blackman. Raymond R. Patterson. ESEAA

Even tonight and I need to take a walk and clear. Poem About My Rights. June Jordan. NAAAL; SP-JordJ

Evenin' Air Blues. Langston Hughes. CP-HughL

Evening. Paul Laurence Dunbar. CP-DunbP

Evening. Helen G. Quigless. BkSV

Evening came, a child was missing. Little Bell. Mary E. Tucker. CBWP-1

Evening, ending, The. Guest Lecturer. Darwin T. Turner. BALP

Evening is the Fourth of July. Summer. Al Young. CP-YounA

Evening isnt so much a playland as it is. Groupie. Al Young. CP-YounA

Evening News, The. Audre Lorde. CP-LordA; NAAAL; SP-LordA

Evening Prayer. Henrietta Cordelia Ray. CBWP-3

Evening Song. Langston Hughes. *Fr.* Montage of a Dream Deferred. CP-HughL

Evening Song. Jean Toomer. BPo; CDC; CP-ToomJ; GT

Evening Thought, An [: Salvation by Christ with Penetential Cries]. Jupiter Hammon. CrDW

("Salavation comes by Christ alone.") EBAP

Evenings I hear. A Plague of Starlings. Robert Hayden. CP-HaydR; ESEAA

Event, The. Rita Dove. ESEAA; NAAAL

("Where the wheel turned the water / gently shirred.") (LL) SP-DoveR

Ever and ever anon. The Road to the Bow. James David Corrothers. BANP

Ever been kidnapped. Kidnap Poem. Nikki Giovanni. AmNP; BPo; BrTr; SP-GiovN

Ever since I realized there was someone callt. No More Love Poems #1. Ntozake Shange. BlSi

Ever since Miss Susan Johnson lost her jockey, Lee. Yellow Dog Blues. William Christopher Handy. NAAAL

Ever since they'd left the Tennessee ridge. The Event. Rita Dove. ESEAA; NAAAL; SP-DoveR

Ever want to crawl. Nikki Giovanni. SP-GiovN

Every day a wilderness—no. Dusting. Rita Dove. SP-DoveR

Every Harlem Face Is AFROMANISM Surviving. Edward S. Spriggs. BlFi

Every Man a King. Timothy Thomas Fortune. EBAP

Every morning I exercise. Alice Walker. CP-WalkA

Every night Winnie Mandela. To Free Nelson Mandela. June Jordan. SP-JordJ

Every one simpler than before. (LL) Nothing Lovely as a Tree. Frederick, Jr. Bryant. BlFi

Every planet is a small plane. The Plane: Earth. Sun-Ra. PoBA

Every Traveler Has One Vermont Poem. Audre Lorde. CP-LordA

Everybody but Me. Margaret Goss Burroughs. BlSi; FB

EVERYBODY / Half-pint. The Cat and the Saxophone (2 a.m.). Langston Hughes. CP-HughL

Everybody in columbia. Untitled III. Ishmael Reed. CP-ReedI

Everybody knows her, for they see her every day. Pay Your Debts. Mrs. Henry Linden. CBWP-4

Everybody wants to know. Poem for Two Daughters. Ishmael Reed. CP-ReedI

Everyday. Indian Girl. Lenard D. Moore. GT

Everyday I need my shit done in a special way. Lana Moorer. CtF

Everyone wants to know. The Old Days. Audre Lorde. CP-LordA

Everything changes the old. The News. Lucille Clifton. SP-ClifL

Everything is nothingness. (LL) Prayer for a Winter Night. Langston Hughes. CP-HughL

Everything is, once was not. Life after Death. Richard W. Thomas. PoBA

Everything is stopped. Stopped. Allen Polite. NNP

Everything Is Wonderful. Jayne Cortez. SP-CortJ

Everything / we know. (LL) We have a beautiful / mother. Alice Walker. CP-WalkA

Everything's a metaphor, some wise. History. Rita Dove. NAAAL

Everywhere. Al Young. CP-YounA

Everywhere You Eat. Kalamu ya Salaam. *Fr.* New Orleans Haiku. SpiFl

Evicted from sleep's mute palace. Shaker, Why Don't You Sing? Maya Angelou. CP-AngeM; SP-AngeM

Evil. Langston Hughes. CP-HughL; SP-HughL

Evil Is No Black Thing. Sarah Webster Fabio. PoBA; TtW

Evil-mannered, underfed, underbred, restless, godless rule of light. Satan's Playground of Hell. *African-American Oral Tradition.* GetYo

Evil Morning. Langston Hughes. CP-HughL

Evil That Men Do, The. Queen Latifah. NAAAL

Evil Woman. Langston Hughes. CP-HughL

Evil word it is, / This Love, An. (LL) In Memory of Radio. Amiri Baraka. NAAAL; SP-BaraA

Evolutionary Poem No. 1. Etheridge Knight. SP-KnigE

Evolutionary Poem No. 2. Etheridge Knight. SP-KnigE

Ex-Judge at the Bar, An. Melvin Beaunearus Tolson. NAAAL

Ex-Slave. Margaret Abigail Walker. CP-WalkM

Exactly the same. (LL) Memo to Non-White People. Langston Hughes. CP-HughL

Examination, The. Priscilla Jane Thompson. CBWP-2

Exchange in greed the ungraceful signs. Thrust. The Violent Space. Etheridge Knight. BPo; BrTr; SP-KnigE

Excite my breasts. Feathers. Jayne Cortez. SP-CortJ

Excited from Reading the Obedience of Nature to her Lord in the Vessel on the Sea. George Moses Horton. SP-HortG

Excuse, The. Carl H. Greene. NBV

Excuse. Alice Walker. CP-WalkA

Execution. James A., Jr. Randall. BPo; BrTr

Execution of Private Henry Anderson. George Moses Horton. SP-HortG

Exercises on Themes from Life. Alice Walker. CP-WalkA

Exeunt the Viols. Rita Dove. SP-DoveR

Exhaustion among rocks. The Mirages. Robert Hayden. CP-HaydR

Exhortation: Summer, 1919. Claude McKay. CDC

Exile lingering here, An. (LL) Infelix. Adah Isaacs Menken. AAP; CBWP-1

Exiled from places of honor about the Throne of Grace. Black Church on Sunday. Joseph M., Jr. Mosley. NBP

Exiled from this earth. (LL) The Couple. Maya Angelou. CP-AngeM; SP-AngeM

Exile's Reverie, The. Mary Weston Fordham. CBWP-2

Exist, without a man cook. (LL) The Coming Woman. Mary Weston Fordham. CBWP-2

Exits. Langston Hughes. CP-HughL

Exits and Entrances. Naomi Long Madgett. BlSi; TtW

Exodus. Mary Effie Lee Newsome. ShDr

Expect nothing. Live frugally. Alice Walker. CP-WalkA

Expectation. Paul Laurence Dunbar. CP-DunbP

Expected, the handsome, the one who needs us? The. (LL) Beauty and the Beast. Rita Dove. ESEAA; SP-DoveR

Expecting to see him anytime. Between Days. Yusef Komunyakaa. ESEAA

Expendable. Langston Hughes. CP-HughL

Expenditures; Economic Love Song 1. Jayne Cortez. SP-CortJ

Explain It, Please. Langston Hughes. CP-HughL

Explaining to me that my mind. Friends Come. Lucille Clifton. SP-ClifL

Explanations. Lucille Clifton. SP-ClifL

Expulsion of Hagar, The. Eloise Bibb. CBWP-4

Extravagantly rosy her fair cheeks. Albery Allson Whitman. *Fr.* Leelah Misled. EBAP

Exult in glorious liberty. (LL) How long, oh gracious God! how long. James M. Whitfield. AAP; AfAmPo

Exultation. Mae V. Cowdery. ShDr

Eye and eye. Eric Priestley. CtF

Eye follows, the land, The. California Prodigal. Maya Angelou. CP-AngeM; SP-AngeM

Eye of Love, The. George Moses Horton. BALP

Eye of this storm is not quiet, The. To a Gone Era. Irma McClaurin. BlSi

Eye sit here, now, inside my fast thickening breath. Reflections on Growing Older. Quincy Troupe. GT

Eye we are told, The. Photography. Nikki Giovanni. SP-GiovN

Eyes of My Regret, The. Angelina Weld Grimké. CDC

Eyes / That are frozen. Grief. Langston Hughes. CP-HughL

Eyes that see past self. Oseola McCarty. Evelyn E. Shockley. CtF

Ez Malindy sings. (LL) When Malindy Sings. Paul Laurence Dunbar. AAP; AfAmPo; CP-DunbP; NAAAL; PoBA

F

Fable: "Once upon a today and yesterday and nevermore there were 7 men." Etheridge Knight. SP-KnigE

Face. Jean Toomer. CDC; CP-ToomJ

Face in the window ... is not the face in the mirror, The. Mirrors. Nikki Giovanni. SP-GiovN

Face it. The stars have their own lives and care. Twelve Gates. Lorenzo Thomas. BlFi

Face like a chocolate bar. 125th Street. Langston Hughes. *Fr.* Montage of a Dream Deferred. CP-HughL; SP-HughL

Face of Poverty. Lucy Smith. NNP

Face of war is my face, The. War. Langston Hughes. CP-HughL

Face sings, alone, The. A Poem for Wille Best. Amiri Baraka. SP-BaraA

Faces and more remember. Maya Angelou. CP-AngeM; SP-AngeM

Faces surround me that have no smell or color no time. Chain. Audre Lorde. BlSi; CP-LordA

Facing a single doom. (LL) Day. Langston Hughes. CP-HughL

Facing It. Yusef Komunyakaa. ESEAA; NAAAL; SP-KomuY

Facing the Way. Alice Walker. CP-WalkA

Fact. Langston Hughes. *Fr.* Montage of a Dream Deferred. CP-HughL

Fade in the sound of summer music. Notes for a Movie Script. M. Carl Holman. AmNP; Klds; PoBA

Fading Skiff, The. Henrietta Cordelia Ray. CBWP-3

Failure. Henrietta Cordelia Ray. CBWP-3

Fain would I rival thee. To the Eagle. Mary Weston Fordham. CBWP-2

Faint-flushed buds awake within the cup, The. Awakening. Henrietta Cordelia Ray. CBWP-3

Fair Alabama, "Here we rest," thy name. The April of Alabama. George Marion McClellan. EBAP

Fair, fragile Una, golden-haired. The Enchanted Shell. Henrietta Cordelia Ray. CBWP-3

Fair Hope with lucent light in her glad eyes. The Quest of the Ideal. Henrietta Cordelia Ray. CBWP-3

Fair London by his side. (LL) The Ballad of the Brown Girl. Countee Cullen. CP-CullC

Fair Mildred wide her lattice threw. Mildred's Doves. Henrietta Cordelia Ray. CBWP-3

Fair morn unbars her gates of gold. Dawn's Carol. Henrietta Cordelia Ray. CBWP-3

Fair Musidora starry-eyed. Musidora's Vision. Henrietta Cordelia Ray. CBWP-3

Fair nights beneath the mellow moon. The Maid of Ehrenthal. Henrietta Cordelia Ray. CBWP-3

Fairer Hope, a Brighter Morn, A. Frances Ellen Watkins Harper. CP-HarpF

Fairest one of all, The. (LL) For the Fair Miss M. M. McLean. George Moses Horton. SP-HortG

Fairest soonest fade, The. Connubial Felicity. George Moses Horton. SP-HortG

Fairies. Langston Hughes. CP-HughL

Faith. Paul Laurence Dunbar. CP-DunbP

Faith hasn't got no eyes, but she long-legged. Zora Neale Hurston. NAAAL

Faith Healer. Yusef Komunyakaa. SP-KomuY

Faithful Frances Ellen Harper! Mrs. Francis Ellen Harper. George Clinton Rowe. AAP

Faithful One. Langston Hughes. CP-HughL

Faithful watcher sits alone, A. The Watcher. Clara Ann Thompson. CBWP-2

Fall Down, (in Memory of Eric Dolphy). Calvin C. Hernton. GT; PoBA

Fall, I cool my heels and let go, A. (LL) Houston in October. Al Young. CP-YounA

Fall Is Here, The. Mrs. Henry Linden. CBWP-4

Fall of / velvet plum points and umber aureolae, The. Mastectomy. Wanda Coleman. NAAAL

Fall To. Howard Jones. NBP

Fallen, The. Audre Lorde. CP-LordA

Falling. Bob Kaufman. PoBA; SP-KaufB

Falling. Yusef Komunyakaa. SP-KomuY

Falling Asleep in a Darkening Room. Al Young. CP-YounA

Falling from the sky. (LL) On a bright day, next week. Maya Angelou. CP-AngeM; SP-AngeM

Falling in love again. (LL) Boccaccio: The Plague Years. Rita Dove. SP-DoveR

Falling snow flakes, The. Haiku: "Falling snow flakes, The." Etheridge Knight. ESEAA; TtW

False Leads. Yusef Komunyakaa. SP-KomuY

Falso Brilhante. Nathaniel Mackey. NAAAL

Fame. Josephine D. Henderson Heard. CBWP-4

Familee reunion tyme iz a special tyme. Roni Walter. CtF

Familiarize your. Sonia Sanchez. SP-SancS

Families Album, The. Michael S. Harper. SP-HarpM

Family Affairs. Maya Angelou. CP-AngeM; SP-AngeM

Family Jewels, for Washington, D.C. Essex Hemphill. GT

Family Of. Alice Walker. CP-WalkA

Family of Debridement, The. Michael S. Harper. SP-HarpM

Family Portraits. Mary E. Tucker. CBWP-1

Family Resemblance, A. Audre Lorde. CP-LordA; SP-LordA

Family reunion. Haiku: "Family reunion." Lenard D. Moore. SpiFl

Family Secrets. Toi Derricotte. SpiFl

Famine. June Jordan. SP-JordJ

Fancy and Imagination. Henrietta Cordelia Ray. CBWP-3

Fancy halts my feet at the way-side well, A. The Way-Side Well. Joseph Seamon Cotter, Sr. CDC; TtW

Fanfare, Coda, and Finale. Margaret Abigail Walker. CP-WalkM

Fantasy. Gwendolyn B. Bennett. BlSi; CDC; ShDr

Fantasy and Conversation. Audre Lorde. CP-LordA; SP-LordA

Fantasy in Purple. Langston Hughes. BANP; CDC; CP-HughL; SP-HughL

Far away from my heart. (LL) Nobody Riding the Roads Today. June Jordan. SP-JordJ

Far away, I suppose you could say. What Is the Blues? Al Young. CP-YounA

Far Cry from Africa, A. Derek Walcott. ESEAA

Far down, down through the city's great gaunt gut. Subway Wind. Claude McKay. SP-McKaC

Far, far above this world I soar. On the Poetic Muse. George Moses Horton. SP-HortG

Far, far out lie the white sails all at rest. An Ocean Musing. Henrietta Cordelia Ray. CBWP-3

Far from Africa: Four Poems. Margaret Else Danner. AmNP; NNP; PoBA
    Garnishing the Aviary. BPo

Far from this foreign Easter damp and chilly. The Easter Flower. Claude McKay.

Far in the land of sunny South. A Southern Scene. Priscilla Jane Thompson. CBWP-2

Farewell! ye friendly bowers, ye streams adieu. An Elegy on Leaving —. Phillis Wheatley. CP-WheaP

Farewell: "No more / The feel of your hand." Mae V. Cowdery. ShDr

Farewell, A: "With gypsies and sailors." Langston Hughes. CP-HughL

Farewell, farewell, my love Irene. My Love Irene. Paul Laurence Dunbar. CP-DunbP

Farewell, father! I am dying. Eva's Farewell. Frances Ellen Watkins Harper. CP-HarpF

Farewell! If ne'er I see thee more. Farewell to Frances. George Moses Horton. SP-HortG

Farewell Song. Paul Laurence Dunbar. CP-DunbP

Farewell to Allen University. Josephine D. Henderson Heard. CBWP-4

Farewell to America. Phillis Wheatley. CP-WheaP

Farewell to Arcady. Paul Laurence Dunbar. CP-DunbP

Farewell to Frances. George Moses Horton. SP-HortG

Farewell to Morocco, A. Claude McKay. SP-McKaC

Farewell to You. Elizabeth Alexander. GT

Farm Child's Lullaby, The. Paul Laurence Dunbar. CP-DunbP

Farmer's Soliloquy, The. Robert Charles O'Hara Benjamin. AAP

Farther up the mountainside. (LL) Remember Mexico. Michael S. Harper. ESEAA; SP-HarpM

Fascination. Langston Hughes. CP-HughL

Fashion to form one all-inclusive gap. (LL) Jolt. Al Young. CP-YounA

Fast fly the faces through our blood-years. The Narrative of Black Magicians. Larry Neal. BlFi

Faster ... / after dark. (LL) Dive. Langston Hughes. CP-HughL

Fat Grass and Slow Rain. Merilene M. Murphy. CtF

Fatal Pledge, The. Frances Ellen Watkins Harper. CP-HarpF

Fate of an Innocent Dog, The. George Moses Horton. SP-HortG

Fates, burn these novels that young ladies read. Albery Allson Whitman. Fr. Leelah Misled. EBAP

Father. Ralph Dickey. ESEAA

Father and Daughter. Sonia Sanchez. GT
    ("We talk of light things you and I in this.") SP-SancS

Father and mother, authors of my birth. The Mournful Lute or the Preceptor's Farewell. Daniel Alexander Payne. EBAP; TtW

Father, how sharp you stand. Pathway: From Son to Father. Lenard D. Moore. IHS

Father / I am not equal to the faith required. Confession. Lucille Clifton. SP-ClifL; TtW

Father, / I wait for you in oceans. Child Dead in Old Seas. Maya Angelou. CP-AngeM; SP-AngeM

Father John's bread was made of rye. Rye Bread. William Stanley Braithwaite. CDC; GT

Father Missouri takes his own. Foreclosure. Sterling A. Brown. CP-BrowS; GT; PoBA

Father of love! Evening Prayer. Henrietta Cordelia Ray. CBWP-3

Father out Walking on the Lawn, A. Rita Dove. SP-DoveR

Father Son and Holy Ghost. Audre Lorde. CP-LordA; ESEAA; NAAAL; PoBA; SP-LordA

Father the year has fallen. Audre Lorde. SP-LordA

Father, the Year Is Fallen. Audre Lorde. CP-LordA; PoBA

Father's Love, The. Mary E. Tucker. CBWP-1

Father's seed. (LL) Lines to the Black Oak. Oliver La Grone. NBV

Favorite Slave's Story, The. Priscilla Jane Thompson. AAP; CBWP-2

Fear threads its song. The Beast & Burden: Seven Improvisations. Yusef Komunyakaa. SP-KomuY

Fearful Traveller in the Haunted Castle, The. George Moses Horton. SP-HortG

Fears of the Eighth Grade. Toi Derricotte. GT

Feathers. Jayne Cortez. SP-CortJ

February. Henrietta Cordelia Ray. CBWP-3

February 13, 1980. Lucille Clifton. SP-ClifL

February in Sydney. Yusef Komunyakaa. ESEAA; NAAAL; SP-KomuY

Feeble Old Man. African-American Oral Tradition. GetYo

Feeble Old Man and a Kid Named Dan. African-American Oral Tradition. GetYo

Feed him arrogant prophets. (LL) There's a whale in my thigh. at. Ishmael Reed. CP-ReedI

Feeding the Lions. Norman Jordan. NBP; PoBA

Feeding us mortality in such small portions. (LL) In the Restaurant. Gerald William Barrax. GT

Feel free. / like my daddy. To Bobby Seale. Lucille Clifton. PoBA; SP-ClifL

Feel its terror. (LL) For a Black Poet. Gerald William Barrax. NBV; TtW

Feeling Fucked/Up Up. Etheridge Knight. GT; SP-KnigE

Feeling swell. (LL) Enemy. Langston Hughes. CP-HughL

Feeling Through. Alvin Aubert. BkSV

Feet flat like white tiles. (LL) Woman. rocking her. Sonia Sanchez. SP-SancS

Feet O' Jesus. Langston Hughes. CP-HughL; SP-HughL

Feet of Judas, The. George Marion McClellan. AAP; AfAmPo; BANP

Feet unbound / walk the Earth. Praise Song for Katherine Dunham: A Choreopoem. Chezia Thompson-Cager. CtF

Fell the leader and. Haitians. Ishmael Reed. CP-ReedI

Felt my freedom deep / My signature! (LL) Index to a Black Catharsis. Richard W. Thomas. BlFi

Felt negatives work the pores. Photographs. Michael S. Harper. SP-HarpM

Female and the Silence of a Man, The. June Jordan. NAAAL; SP-JordJ

Feminism. Carolyn M. Rodgers. TtW

Feral Pioneers, The. Ishmael Reed. CP-ReedI; PoBA

Ferrets are out!, The. George Barlow. Fr. Gabriel. TtW

Festus Conrad. Melvin B. Tolson. GT

Fever. Yusef Komunyakaa. SP-KomuY

Few Sirens, A. Alice Walker. CP-WalkA

Few years back and they told me Black, A. A Poem about Intelligence for My Brothers and Sisters. June Jordan. SP-JordJ

Fiammetta Breaks Her Peace. Rita Dove. SP-DoveR

Fickle comfort steals away. Changes. Maya Angelou. CP-AngeM; SP-AngeM

Fickle layers to endure, the worth standing in, The. (LL) (1962 At the Edge of Town). C. S. Giscombe. GT

Field Trip. Kevin Young. GT

Fields are white, The. Nothing to Do. James Ephriam McGirt. AAP

Fifty cents more an hour would get me. Financial Planning. June Jordan. SP-JordJ

Fifteen years up & her tongue's still flapping. Not Her, She Aint No Gypsy. Al Young. CP-YounA

Fifteenth Amendment. Frances Ellen Watkins Harper. CP-HarpF

50–50. Langston Hughes. CP-HughL; SP-HughL

Fifty-Fifty. Al Young. SpiFl

Fifty or maybe just five flies eat at the chin. Famine. June Jordan. SP-JordJ

Fifty Years. James Weldon Johnson. BANP; NAAAL

Fight the Power. Public Enemy. Crnst

Fight was at its hottest, The. Rev. Andrew Brown, over the Hill to Rest. Josephine D. Henderson Heard. CBWP-4

Fight with the Crew. Derek Walcott. Fr. The Schooner Flight. ESEAA

Fightin' was natural. Maya Angelou. CP-AngeM

Fighting My Homophobia. Gloria Wade-Gayles. IHS

Fights After School. Norman J. Loftis. SpiFl

Figurine / De-dop! (LL) Question. Langston Hughes. SP-HughL

Filled with gems of crystal thought. (LL) Alice. Paul Laurence Dunbar. CP-DunbP

Filling my eyes with flowers of no name. Out in the Country of My Country (Peterborough, New Hampshire). June Jordan. SP-JordJ

Final Call. Langston Hughes. CP-HughL

Final Curve. Langston Hughes. CP-HughL; SP-HughL

Finally retired pensionless. Big Momma. Haki R. Madhubuti. BPo; TtW

Finally you sit. Poem with Orange. Al Young. CP-YounA

Financial Planning. June Jordan. SP-JordJ

Find nothing to do? (LL) Nothing to Do. James Ephriam McGirt. AAP

Finding His Fist. Saundra Sharp. SpiFl

Finding the black way back to what we've lost. (LL) Churchgoing. Marilyn Nelson. SP-NelsM

Fine and Mellow. Billie Holiday. NAAAL

Fine evening may I have. Courtship. Rita Dove. SP-DoveR

Fine living .. à la carte?? Advertisement for the Waldorf-Astoria. Langston Hughes. CP-HughL

Finger Pop'in. Charles Anderson. BlFi

Fingers counting the roses / in the wallpaper. (LL) Born That Way. Maya Angelou. CP-AngeM

Fingers smelling always of onions. (LL) I Am Becoming My Mother. Lorna Goodison. GT

Finis. Waring Cuney. AmNP; BANP

Finished now the weary throbbing. Gone to God. Frances Ellen Watkins Harper. CP-HarpF

Fire. Jean Toomer. CP-ToomJ

Fire-Caught. Langston Hughes. CP-HughL

Fire, / Fire, Lord! Langston Hughes. CP-HughL; SP-HughL

Fire, Hair, Meat and Bone. Fred Johnson. PoBA

Fire in the Drum, The. Derrick I. M. Gilbert. CtF

Fire Keeper. Bahiyyih Maroon. SpiFl

Fire more priceless than diamonds rare. The Father's Love. Mary E. Tucker. CBWP-1

Fireblade / Flame scimitar's cutting edge. Suncoming. Oliver La Grone. NBV

Fired. Langston Hughes. CP-HughL; SP-HughL

Fireflies [or Fire-flies] come stagg'ring down the dark, The. (LL) A Summer's Night. Paul Laurence Dunbar. CP-DunbP

Fireplace, The. Michael S. Harper. GT

Firespitters / spitting across the desert. Jayne Cortez. SP-CortJ

First a fable, and then the truth. We sensed. Greenhouse. Gerald William Barrax. TtW

First answer was incorrect, The. The Art of Response. Audre Lorde. CP-LordA

First blow hurt, The. Freedom Rider: Washout. James A. Emanuel. BrTr

First Claims Poem. Victor Hernandez Cruz. NBV

First day I shot dope, The. Summer Words of a Sistuh Addict. Sonia Sanchez. BPo; BlSi; Crnst; NAAAL; SP-SancS

First Essay on the Art of the U. S. Ron Welburn. BlFi

First, feel, then feel, then. Young Soul. Amiri Baraka. BPo

First fight. Then fiddle. Ply the slipping string. Gwendolyn Brooks. Fr. The Children of the Poor. Crnst, sect. I, 1-5; NAAAL; SP-BrooG, sect. I, 1-5.

First Grey Hair, The. Mary E. Tucker. CBWP-1

First horn lifts its arm over the dew-lit grass, The. The House Slave. Rita Dove. SP-DoveR

First Kiss. Rita Dove. SP-DoveR

First light of day in Mississippi. Birthday Poem. Al Young. CP-YounA

First Man. Naomi Long Madgett. IHS

First light of day in Mississippi. Birthday Poem. Al Young. CP-YounA

First Monday Scottsboro Alabama. Tom Weatherly. PoBA

First of August in Jamaica, The. Joshua McCarter Simpson. AAP

First of May, The. Chant for May Day. Langston Hughes. CP-HughL

First of May. Langston Hughes. CP-HughL

First poem ... ever written ... was probably carved, The. Charting the Night Winds. Nikki Giovanni. SP-GiovN

First Poem from Nicaragua Libre: Teotcacinte. June Jordan. SP-JordJ

First rule of road: attend quiet victims first. The Evening News. Audre Lorde. CP-LordA; NAAAL; SP-LordA

First sign was your hair, The. I'm Just a Stranger Here, Heaven Is My Home. Carole C. Gregory Clemmons. PoBA

First, suicide notes should be. Suicide. Alice Walker. GT

First / take the first. Symphony Sid. Amiri Baraka. SP-BaraA

1st, The. Lucille Clifton. SP-ClifL

First the melody, clean and hard. How High the Moon. Lance Jeffers. PoBA

First the plumbing breaks down. Depreciation. Audre Lorde. CP-LordA

First they said I was too light. A Short Note to My Very Critical and Well-Beloved Friends and Comrades. June Jordan. SP-JordJ

First, they said we were savages. Alice Walker. CP-WalkA

First thing tied to last. (LL) Dreambook Bestiary. Yusef Komunyakaa. SP-KomuY

First time I got high I stood in a circle, The. Blunts. Major L. Jackson. SpiFl

First time I was sweet sixteen. Nayo-Barbara Watkins. NBV

First World. Haki R. Madhubuti. TtW

First, worms begin with a man's mind. In the Background of Silence. Yusef Komunyakaa. SP-KomuY

First you must have. Instructions for Building Straw Huts. Yusef Komunyakaa. GT

Firstly Inclined to Take What It Is Told. Gwendolyn Brooks. SP-BrooG

Fish and Floor-Dust Bouquet. Marilyn Nelson. SP-NelsM

Fish in the Stone, The. Rita Dove. GT; SP-DoveR

Fish like sunlight from the afternoon sky. (LL) Fish and Floor-Dust Bouquet. Marilyn Nelson. SP-NelsM

Fisher Child's Lullaby, The. Paul Laurence Dunbar. CP-DunbP

Fisher Street. Thylias Moss. GT

Fisherman's Story, The. Henrietta Cordelia Ray. CBWP-3

Fishermen. James A. Emanuel. BrTr

Fishermen. Song. Primus St. John. GT

Fishers of Men. Frances Ellen Watkins Harper. CP-HarpF

Fishes and the Poet's Hands, The. Frank Yerby. AmNP

Fishing. Paul Laurence Dunbar. CP-DunbP

Fishing among the Learned. Nikky Finney. SpiFl

Fishing the White Water. Audre Lorde. CP-LordA; GT

Fisk is / a / a / negroid / institution. Sharon Scott. JB

Fist clenched round my heart, The. The Fist. Derek Walcott. ESEAA

Fit fer a hoppin' toad. (LL) Bound No'th Blues. Langston Hughes. AfAmPo; AmNP; CP-HughL; SP-HughL

Fit to be loved. (LL) First time I was sweet sixteen. Nayo-Barbara Watkins. NBV

5 before 2/22 i am. The Last Week in 30. Ishmael Reed. CP-ReedI

Five Black Men. Margaret Abigail Walker. CP-WalkM

Five buds were on the parent tree. Family Portraits. Mary E. Tucker. CBWP-1

.05. Ishmael Reed. CP-ReedI; ESEAA

Five daughters, in the slant light on the porch. Daughters, 1900. Marilyn Nelson. SP-NelsM

Five Elephants. Rita Dove. SP-DoveR

Five men pull straws. Fragging. Yusef Komunyakaa. ESEAA

Five men shaped this century. Giants of My Century. Margaret Abigail Walker. CP-WalkM

"5 Minutes, Mr. Salam." Kalamu ya Salaam. SpiFl

Five rings light your approach across. A Father out Walking on the Lawn. Rita Dove. SP-DoveR

Five Sense. Marvin, Jr. Wyche. AmNP

5 shirts / 2 blouses. On the Real World: Meditation #1. June Jordan. SP-JordJ

Five thousand lovers I would have taken. Madness. Al Young. CP-YounA

Five Vignettes. Jean Toomer. CP-ToomJ

Fivetenfifteentwenty. Young/Black/Girl. Sonia Sanchez. Fr. Past. SP-SancS

Fixed in the fireplace. The Fireplace. Michael S. Harper. GT

Fixing Certificates: Dog Tags: Letters Home. Michael S. Harper. SP-HarpM

Fixing my eyes downward. Coming and Going: Gabriel's Song. George Barlow. Fr. Gabriel. TtW

Fizz into boom. (LL) Little and Big. Frank Marshall Davis. TtW

Flags. Gwendolyn Brooks. AmNP
   (Love Note II: Flags.) SP-BrooG

Flame. Jayne Cortez. SP-CortJ

Flame-flower, day-torch, Mauna Loa. Lines to a Nasturtium. Anne Spencer. AmNP; CDC; ShDr

Flame-Heart. Claude McKay. AmNP; BALP; BANP; CDC; SP-McKaC
   ("Beneath the pointsettia's red in warm December.") (LL) AfAmPo
   ("So much I have forgotten in ten years.") GT

Flames around him spread, The. (LL) Death of the Old Sea King. Frances Ellen Watkins Harper. EBAP

Flames from sun. Magnificent Tomorrows. Haki R. Madhubuti. SpiFl

Flamiing in the sun. (LL) For Malcolm Who Walks in the Eyes of Our Children. Quincy Troupe. PoBA

Flash Cards. Rita Dove. ESEAA

Flat with variations. Not. Delft. Rita Dove. SP-DoveR

Flatted Fifths. Langston Hughes. Fr. Montage of a Dream Deferred. CP-HughL

Fledgling Bard and the Poetry Society, The, much abr. George Reginald Margetson. BANP

Fleeing love / to stay, A. (LL) Prelude to a Parting. Maya Angelou. CP-AngeM; SP-AngeM

Flesh, and cars, tar, dug holes beneath stone. A Contract. (For The Destruction and Rebuilding of Paterson). Amiri Baraka. SP-BaraA

Flesh of the Young Men Is Burning, The. Lance Jeffers. BkSV

Fleshing his dream of the beautiful, needful thing. (LL) Frederick Douglass. Robert Hayden. AmNP; CP-HaydR; IDB; Klds; NAAAL; PoBA

Fleshlessness and bloodlessness, was helpless when it came to dirty jokes. (LL) I wish that whoever is inside of me. Bob Kaufman. SP-KaufB

Flickering-sputtering-speaking-stuttering-strutting. Visions ... Leaders. Clarence Franklin. BlFi

Flickers, flames, burns. Fire. Jean Toomer. CP-ToomJ

'Flicted Arm Pete: "It was way down in this little town that they call Louisville." African-American Oral Tradition. GetYo

Flight. Langston Hughes. CP-HughL

Flight 828, now boarding at Gate 17. (LL) Vacation. Rita Dove. SpiFl

Flight Anchors in Castries Harbor, The. Derek Walcott. Fr. The Schooner Flight. ESEAA

Flight into Midian. Frances Ellen Watkins Harper. Fr. Moses: A Story of the Nile. AAP; SP-HarpF

Flight of Leeona. Albery Allson Whitman. AAP Fr. Not a Man, and Yet a Man.

Flight, Passing Blanchisseuse, The. Derek Walcott. Fr. The Schooner Flight. ESEAA

Fling out your banners, your honors be bringing. Emancipation. Paul Laurence Dunbar. CP-DunbP

Flirt. Al Young. CP-YounA

Flirtation. Rita Dove. SP-DoveR

Flirtation. Claude McKay. SP-McKaC

Float up / to / silence. (LL) Koto Music/Singing. Al Young. CP-YounA

Floating thru morning. Friday the 12th. Al Young. CP-YounA

Floods the womb until I drown. (LL) Malcolm. Sonia Sanchez. BrTr; SP-SancS

Floodtide. Askia Muhammad Touré. PoBA; TtW

Floorwax Mother. Harryette Mullen. TtW

Florida. Audre Lorde. CP-LordA

Florida means land of flowers. Ballad of Harry Moore. Langston Hughes. CP-HughL

Florida Night, A. Paul Laurence Dunbar. CP-DunbP

Florida Road Workers. Langston Hughes. CP-HughL

Flotsam. Langston Hughes. CP-HughL

Flower no scent encloses, The. (LL) Rememberance. Langston Hughes. CP-HughL

Flower of Love. Claude McKay. BALP; SP-McKaC

Flowers. Lucille Clifton. SP-ClifL

Flowers are dead, The. Scenery. Ted Joans. PoBA

Flowers are happy in summer. Autumn Thought. Langston Hughes. CP-HughL

Flowers of Darkness. Frank Marshall Davis. AmNP; IDB; PoBA

Flows—on and on. Soaks, bathes, slops, gushes. Water. Jean Toomer. CP-ToomJ

Flu. Al Young. CP-YounA

Flukum couldn't stand the strain. Flukum. A Poem for Black Relocation Centers. Etheridge Knight. Fr. Two Poems for Black Relocation Centers. BrTr; ESEAA; SP-KnigE

Flushed with the hope of high desire. My Hero. Benjamin Brawley. BANP

Fly, The. African-American Oral Tradition. GetYo

Fly away birdies, fly away home. Small Black World. Margaret Abigail Walker. CP-WalkM

Fly is dying hard, The. Mayday. Ed Roberson. PoBA

Fly on into my poem. The John Coltrane Dance. Al Young. CP-YounA

Fly whispering in absolute silence. (LL) My poems have holes sewn into them. Quincy Troupe. TtW

Flying High. Lana C. Williams. CtF

"Fo' to stay up here." (LL) Slim in Hell ("Slim Greer went to heaven"). Sterling A. Brown. BPo; CP-BrowS; FB

Fog. Langston Hughes. CP-HughL

Fog Galleon. Yusef Komunyakaa. SP-KomuY

Fog Report. Audre Lorde. CP-LordA

Foggy Morning. Al Young. CP-YounA

Fold their wings upon fulfillment. (LL) Honey of Being. Jean Toomer. CP-ToomJ

Folks ain't got no right to censuah othah [or uthah] folks about dey habits. Accountability. Paul Laurence Dunbar. CP-DunbP

Folks downstairs brought him home, The. Dylan, Two Days. Patricia Smith. GT

Folks, I come up North. Evenin' Air Blues. Langston Hughes. CP-HughL

Folks, I'm telling you. Advice. Langston Hughes. Fr. Montage of a Dream Deferred. CP-HughL; SP-HughL

Folks is talkin' 'bout de money. The Real Question. Paul Laurence Dunbar. CP-DunbP

Folks with no titles in front of their names, The. In Explanation of Our Times. Langston Hughes. CP-HughL; SP-HughL

Follow the dreaming see, but follow! (LL) Intimacy. Al Young. CP-YounA

Follow the train full of bodies. Judge Every One with Perfect Calm. Alice Walker. CP-WalkA

Following minutes were, The. A Secretary to the Spirits. Ishmael Reed. CP-ReedI

Following the hands. (LL) Parish Doctor. Sterling A. Brown. CP-BrowS

F'om one dat raaly needs to eat. (LL) Way T'ings Come, De. Paul Laurence Dunbar. CP-DunbP

Fondle me. Marrow of My Bone. Mari E. Evans. BPo

Fontaine no longer cared to live. Timothy Thomas Fortune. Fr. Dreams of Life. EBAP

Food for Thought. Val Ferdinand. NBV

Foolhearted mindreader, / help us see how. Beg Song. Yusef Komunyakaa. SP-KomuY

Foolin' wid de Seasons. Paul Laurence Dunbar. CP-DunbP

Foolish Heart, The. Countee Cullen. CP-CullC

Foolology. Ishmael Reed. CP-ReedI

Footnote to a Gray Bird's Pause, A. James Cunningham. JB

Footnote to a Pretentious Book. Amiri Baraka. SP-BaraA

Footsteps of the superlative fair, The. (LL) On Friendship. Phillis Wheatley. CP-WheaP; EBAP

For a Black Poet. Gerald William Barrax. NBV; TtW

For a Brookline Lady I Love. Etheridge Knight. SP-KnigE

For a colored man. (LL) A Daddy Poem. William J. Harris. NBV

For a creed that will not let you dance? (LL) Magalu. Helene Johnson. BlSi; CDC; PoBA; ShDr

For a former Macon waiter. (LL) Robert Whitmore. Frank Marshall Davis. BPo; Klds; PoBA; TtW

For a Friend Who Considers Suicide. Gloria Wade-Gayles. IHS

For a kid that's black? (LL) Merry-Go-Round. Langston Hughes. CP-HughL; SP-HughL

For a Lady I Know. Countee Cullen. Fr. Four Epitaphs. AmNP; CDC; CP-CullC; IDB; PoBA; SSLK
   ("She even thinks that up in heaven.") Klds

For a Lady of Pleasure Now Retired. Nikki Giovanni. BrTr; SP-GiovN

For a man to go crazy. (LL) The Cage Walker. Yusef Komunyakaa. SP-KomuY

For a Mouthy Woman. Countee Cullen. CP-CullC; PoBA

For a Pessimist. Countee Cullen. CP-CullC

For a Poet. Countee Cullen. CP-CullC

For a single beautiful word. (LL) Parsley. Rita Dove. ESEAA; NAAAL; SP-DoveR; TtW

For / A Voice / like a star. Why I Must Make Language. Angela Jackson. TtW

For a Young Artist. Robert Hayden. CP-HaydR

For all our noble heritage. A Litany of Black History for Black People. Margaret Abigail Walker. CP-WalkM

For an Anarchist. Countee Cullen. CP-CullC

For an Atheist. Countee Cullen. CP-CullC

For an Evolutionist and His Opponent. Countee Cullen. CP-CullC

For an Indian Screen. Langston Hughes. CP-HughL

For an Intellectual Audience. Nikki Giovanni. SP-GiovN

For an old possum. (LL) Clinton. Sterling Plumpp. BkSV

For Andy Goodman—Michael Schwerner—and James Chaney. Margaret Abigail Walker. BPo; BrTr; CP-WalkM

For Angela. Zack Gilbert. PoBA

For Arl in Her Sixth Month. Al Young. CP-YounA

For Assata. Audre Lorde. CP-LordA

For Backwards Buppies. Karen Williams. SpiFl

For Bill Hawkins, a Black Militant. William J. Harris. PoBA

For Black People. Haki R. Madhubuti. BrTr

For Black Poets Who Think of Suicide. Etheridge Knight. BrTr; Crnst; NAAAL; PoBA; SP-KnigE

For Both of Us at Fisk. Sharon Scott. JB

For Brother Malcolm. Edward S. Spriggs. BrTr

For Bud. Michael S. Harper. ESEAA; SP-HarpM

For Cal. James Cunningham. JB

For Cardinal Spellman Who Hated Voo Doo. Ishmael Reed. CP-ReedI

For Craig. Audre Lorde. CP-LordA

For Crow Jane (Mama Death). Amiri Baraka. SP-BaraA

For Dancer. Ishmael Reed. CP-ReedI

For Daughters of Magdalen. Countee Cullen. CP-CullC

For Dave: 1976. June Jordan. SP-JordJ

For dawn, wind / off the river. Wind. For Crow Jane (Mama Death). Amiri Baraka. SP-BaraA

For de Lawd. Lucille Clifton. PoBA
   (For DeLawd.) SP-ClifL

For Dead Mimes. Langston Hughes. CP-HughL

For deeds of guilt and wrong. (LL) Free Labor. Frances Ellen Watkins Harper. CP-HarpF

For DeLawd. Lucille Clifton. See For de Lawd.

For Duke Ellington. Reuben Jackson. ESEAA

For each as each, we lose no Paradise. (LL) One Day We Played a Game. Countee Cullen. CP-CullC

For Each of You. Audre Lorde. CP-LordA; SP-LordA

For Ethelbert. June Jordan. SP-JordJ

For Etheridge Knight. Jackie Warren-Moore. SpiFl

For Eusi, Ayi Kwei and Gwen Brooks. Keorapetse W. Kgositsile. PoBA

For ever havin' a daughter. (LL) A Ruined Gal. Langston Hughes. CP-HughL

For example I would slit. Double Standard Lifestyle Studies: #1. June Jordan. SP-JordJ

For Freckle-Faced Gerald. Etheridge Knight. BPo; Crnst; ESEAA; SP-KnigE

For freedom's birth. (LL) Tomorrow's Seed. Langston Hughes. CP-HughL

For Gwen, 1969. Margaret Abigail Walker. CP-WalkM

For H. W. Fuller. Carolyn M. Rodgers. BPo

For heart's ease, May and I. (LL) After Church. Samuel Alfred Beadle. AAP

For Helen Keller. Countee Cullen. CP-CullC

For hell itself respects a fearless manly man! (LL) 'T is hard to judge if hatred's of one's race. Albery Allson Whitman. AfAmPo

For her hiding place. Lucille Clifton. SP-ClifL

For her misery. (LL) Misery. Langston Hughes. CP-HughL; SP-HughL

For Hettie. Amiri Baraka. GT

For hours I stood upon the bridge. Loew's Bridge: A Broadway Idyl. Mary E. Tucker. CBWP-1

For I am rightful fellow of their band. Mentors. Gwendolyn Brooks. ESEAA; Klds; SP-BrooG

For I am still in town. (LL) To Mary Church Terrell. Paul Laurence Dunbar. CP-DunbP

For I have known that. (LL) Demeter Mourning. Rita Dove. NAAAL

For instance / if the sea should break. If Something Should Happen. Lucille Clifton. SP-ClifL

For it will be. (LL) Because I have wandered long through my own darkness. "Stephany." BrTr

For Janet Kafka, Dead at 30. Al Young. CP-YounA

For Jim, Easter Eve. Anne Spencer. AmNP

For Joanne in Poland. Al Young. CP-YounA

For John Keats. Countee Cullen. Fr. Four Epitaphs. AmNP; CDC; CP-CullC; Klds; PoBA

For Jose and Regina. Audre Lorde. CP-LordA

For Joseph Conrad. Countee Cullen. CP-CullC

For Judith. Audre Lorde. CP-LordA

For Kazuko. Rita Dove. SP-DoveR

For Kenneth & Miriam Patchen. Al Young. CP-YounA

For King, for Robert Kennedy. Words in the Mourning Time. Robert Hayden. CP-HaydR

For Kinte. Oliver La Grone. FB

For Langston Hughes. Etheridge Knight. NBV; SP-KnigE

For Langston Hughes. (LL) Langston Blues. Dudley Randall. FB

For laughter. / And nothing hereafter. (LL) Young Sailor. Langston Hughes. CP-HughL; SP-HughL

For Lil Louis. Tom Dent. BkSV

For Lover Man, and All the Other Young Men Who Failed to Return from World War II. Nance Williams. NNP

For Mack C. Parker. Pauli Murray. PoBA

For Malcolm. Joyce Whitsitt Lawrence. BrTr

For Malcolm, a Year After. Etheridge Knight. SP-KnigE

For Malcolm: After Mecca. Gerald William Barrax. PoBA

For Malcolm Who Walks in the Eyes of Our Children. Quincy Troupe. PoBA

For Malcolm X. Nanina Alba. PoBA

For Malcolm X. Margaret Abigail Walker. BPo; CP-WalkM; NAAAL; PoBA

For Malcolm's eyes, when they broke. A Poem for Black Hearts. Amiri Baraka. BrTr; IDB; NAAAL; PoBA

For Malcolm's eyes, when they broke. A Poem for Black Hearts. LeRoi Jones and Imamu Amiri Baraka. SSLK

For many years I did not make migration. Tougaloo Blues. Kelly Norman Ellis. SpiFl

For Mark James Robert Essex d. 1973. Alvin Aubert. BkSV

For Mary Ellen McAnally. Etheridge Knight. SP-KnigE

For Mary, Fourth Month. Marilyn Nelson. SP-NelsM

For Mary McLeod Bethune. Margaret Abigail Walker. CP-WalkM

For me and ol Slim Greer. (LL) Once on a Night in the Delta: A Report From Hell. Etheridge Knight. SP-KnigE

For / Me / ONCE. (LL) Here's to Adhering. Maya Angelou. CP-AngeM; SP-AngeM

For Michael Angelo Thompson. June Jordan. SP-JordJ

For miracles. (LL) I have seen them trying. Norman Jordan. NBV

For "Mr. Dudley," a Black Spy. James A. Emanuel. BPo; NBV

For moisture / cactus tongued. (LL) Parting. Audre Lorde. CP-LordA

For My Brother. June Jordan. SP-JordJ

For my coming, for my coming. (LL) Song of the Whirlwind. Fenton Johnson. NAAAL

For My Father. Harris Duriel. SpiFl

For my grandchildren. (LL) Scrapbooks. Nikki Giovanni. SP-GiovN

For My Grandmother. Countee Cullen. Fr. Four Epitaphs. AmNP; CDC; CP-CullC; PoBA; SSLK

For my hand. (LL) Grandmother: Crossing Jordan. Melvin Dixon. ESEAA

For My Jamaican Sister a Little Bit Lost on the Island of Manhattan. June Jordan. SP-JordJ

For my love. (LL) Dirge: "Place this bunch of mignonette." Paul Laurence Dunbar. CP-DunbP

For my people everywhere singing their slave songs repeatedly. Margaret Abigail Walker. AmNP; BALP; CP-WalkM; IDB; Klds; PoBA; SSLK; TtW

For My Singing Sister. Audre Lorde. CP-LordA; SP-LordA

For My Sister Molly Who in the Fifties. Alice Walker. CP-WalkA; TtW

FOR MY SISTER MOLLY WHO IN THE FIFTIES / Left us. (LL) For My Sister Molly Who in the Fifties. Alice Walker. CP-WalkA; TtW

For My Unborn and Wretched Children. Alfred B. Spellman. PoBA

For my unborn son. Two Poems, II. Robert J. Abrams. NNP

For Myself. Countee Cullen. CP-CullC

For none have time to wait. (LL) They're Leaving Memphis in Droves. *Unknown.* CrDW

For now, that's life enough. (LL) So is there life on you, moon? Al Young. CP-YounA

For one brief day, did Queenie stay. Queenie. Mary Weston Fordham. CBWP-2

For one brief golden moment rare like wine. The City's Love. Claude McKay. SP-McKaC

For one bright moment, heavenly goddess! shine. Philis's Reply to the Answer in Our Last by the Gentleman in the Navy. Phillis Wheatley. CP-WheaP

For one damn / voting day. (LL) Democratic Order, The: Such Things in Twenty Years I Understood. Alice Walker. CP-WalkA

For one little wrong poke you take nowadays will cause your ship to sink. (LL) Limpty Lefty McCree. *African-American Oral Tradition.* GetYo

For only either you are neither. (LL) Are You the Lover or Loved? Al Young. CP-YounA

For openers, the Federal Government. How to Change the U.S.A. Harry Edwards, *arr. in verse by* Walter Lowenfels. NBP

For Our Lady. Sonia Sanchez. NAAAL

For our Transgressions he did bear the curse. (LL) Deism. Phillis Wheatley. CP-WheaP

For Our Women. Larry Neal. BlFi

For Owen Dodson, 1983. Margaret Abigail Walker. CP-WalkM

For Paul Laurence Dunbar. Countee Cullen. *Fr.* Four Epitaphs. AmNP; CDC; CP-CullC; PoBA; SSLK

   ("Born of the sorrowful of heart.") Klds

For Paul Laurence Dunbar. Margaret Abigail Walker. CP-WalkM

For Paula Cooper (The 18 Year Old Who Waits on Death Row). Jackie Warren-Moore. SpiFl

For Poets. Al Young. CP-YounA; PoBA

For profit or for pleasure. (LL) The Deliverance. Frances Ellen Watkins Harper. CP-HarpF

For Real. Jayne Cortez. PoBA

For Russell and Rowena Jelliffe. Langston Hughes. CP-HughL

For Salome. Langston Hughes. CP-HughL

For Sammy Younge. Charlie Cobb. PoBA

For Saundra. Nikki Giovanni. BPo; BrTr; NAAAL; SP-GiovN; TtW

For she still has the box that the cherry came in. (LL) Here's to the lady with the little red shoes. *African-American Oral Tradition.* GetYo

For sin today. (LL) Madam and the Minister. Langston Hughes. CP-HughL; SP-HughL

For Singing In Good Mood. Lebert Bethune. GT

For Sistuhs Wearin' Straight Hair. Carolyn M. Rodgers. NAAAL

For smoking carnivores. (LL) The Health-Food Diner. Maya Angelou. CP-AngeM; SP-AngeM

For so long / We looked into mirrors. Us. Julius Lester. PoBA

For Some Poets. Mae Jackson. PoBA

For some wild faun. (LL) Young Singer. Langston Hughes. CP-HughL

For something, ere in vain you die. (LL) Time to Die. Ray Garfield Dandridge. BANP; PoBA

For Stephen Dixon. Zack Gilbert. PoBA

For 10.95. (LL) Memo #9. Etheridge Knight. SP-KnigE

For that hour he is enkindled. Hermitage Breakfast. Marilyn Nelson. *Fr.* The Plotinus Suite. SP-NelsM

For the aging hipster. A Dance for Aging Hipsters. Al Young. CP-YounA

For the Bird Who Flew against Our Window One Morning and Broke His Natural Neck. Lucille Clifton. SP-ClifL

For the Blind. Lucille Clifton. SP-ClifL

For the Brave Young Students in Soweto. Jayne Cortez. SP-CortJ

For the bread for the children. Street Car Gang. Sterling A. Brown. CP-BrowS

For the caged bird / sings of freedom. (LL) Caged Bird. Maya Angelou. CP-AngeM; SP-AngeM

For the Candle Light. Angelina Weld Grimké. BlSi; CDC; NAAAL

For the child of her love is no longer a slave! (LL) Eliza Harris. Frances Ellen Watkins Harper. AAP; CP-HarpF; NAAAL

For the child of her love is no longer a slave. (LL) She's Free! Frances Ellen Watkins Harper. BlSi

For the coming winter. (LL) Winter. Nikki Giovanni. SP-GiovN

For the Dancer. Niama Leslie JoAnn Williams. SpiFl

For the days when the coffee grounds refuse to settle. Out of the Wind. Audre Lorde. CP-LordA

For the dim regions whence my fathers came. Outcast. Claude McKay. AmNP; BALP; PoBA; SP-McKaC

For the Fair Miss M. M. McLean. George Moses Horton. SP-HortG

For the first time. A Poem for Positive Thinkers. Barbara Mahone. PoBA

For the 500th time? (LL) Identities. Al Young. CP-YounA

For the Freedom Train. (LL) Dream Boogie: Variation. Langston Hughes. CP-HughL

For the Good of the Pythian Order. Mrs. Henry Linden. CBWP-4

For the King and Queen of Summer. Audre Lorde. CP-LordA

For the Lame. Lucille Clifton. SP-ClifL

For the Mad. Lucille Clifton. SP-ClifL

For the Man Who Fails. Paul Laurence Dunbar. CP-DunbP

For the Mute. Lucille Clifton. SP-ClifL

For the Negro Nurse there's been no easy way. Where Service Is Needed. Langston Hughes. CP-HughL

For the Poets. Jayne Cortez. SP-CortJ

For the Record. Audre Lorde. CP-LordA; ESEAA

For the same reason you probably stopped shufflin. (LL) W. H. Auden & Mantan Moreland. Al Young. CP-YounA

For the sun that shone at the dawn of spring. A Song of Thanks. Edward Smyth Jones. BANP

For the tropic traveler! (LL) Morning Light. Mary Effie Lee Newsome. AmNP; CDC; PoBA; ShDr

For the Truth (Because It Is Necessary). Edward S. Spriggs. BlFi; BrTr

For the Twenty-Fifth Anniversary of the "Old Folks' Home." Frances Ellen Watkins Harper. CP-HarpF

For the vanished mother / of a Black girl. Audre Lorde. *See* Story Books on a Kitchen Table.

For the Walking Dead. Yusef Komunyakaa. SP-KomuY

For the withered body / Of despair! (LL) How Thin a Blanket. Langston Hughes. CP-HughL

For the woman / African in ancestry. A Freedom Song for the Black Woman. Carole C. Gregory Clemmons. BlSi

For Theodore Roosevelt. Paul Laurence Dunbar. CP-DunbP

For Theresa. Nikki Giovanni. SP-GiovN

For they have made me / wise. (LL) Solomon. Lucille Clifton. SP-ClifL

For they who fashion songs must live too close to pain. Weltschmerz. Frank Yerby. AmNP

For this is from whence we came. (LL) S, C, M. Ted Wilson. BlFi

For this man / I first read. Tribute to Robert Hayden. Margaret Abigail Walker. CP-WalkM

For this peculiar tint that paints my house. My House. Claude McKay. CDC

For this spring's seeding. (LL) Walking Our Boundaries. Audre Lorde. CP-LordA

For those of us who live at the shoreline. A Litany for Survival. Audre Lorde. CP-LordA; NAAAL

For Tiger Flowers. (LL) Free Fantasia: Tiger Flowers. Robert Hayden. CP-HaydR; ESEAA

For to praise my Lord! (LL) Testimonial. Langston Hughes. CP-HughL

For Tommy. Nikki Giovanni. SP-GiovN

For Two Jameses. Nikki Giovanni. SP-GiovN

For two who. Dedication. Alice Walker. CP-WalkA

For us to be / happy. (LL) Walking down park. Nikki Giovanni. SP-GiovN

For Us, Who Dare Not Dare. Maya Angelou. CP-AngeM; SP-AngeM

For Walter Washington. Tom Dent. NBV

For war-scarred veterans, God's sweet welcome home. (LL) The Negro Meets to Pray. Daniel Webster Davis. AAP

For we spirit to spirit will embrace / this world. (LL) Poem (For Nina). Nikki Giovanni. SP-GiovN

For what flower, plucked, / Lingers long? (LL) Flowers of Darkness. Frank Marshall Davis. AmNP; IDB; PoBA

For what's in a heart. (LL) Water Buffalo. Yusef Komunyakaa. SP-KomuY

For when He crows they quiver and when He comes they frown. (LL) The Black Cock. Ishmael Reed. CP-ReedI

For Who? Mary Weston Fordham. CBWP-2

For William Edward Burghardt Du Bois on His Eightieth Birthday. Bette Darcie Latimer. PoBA

For women / perspective is more easily maintained. To Marie, in Flight. Audre Lorde. CP-LordA

For you and me / There's / Woe. (LL) Angola Question Mark. Langston Hughes. CP-HughL

For you are dead. (LL) To a Dead Friend. Langston Hughes. CP-HughL

For you I wept, and now for you I pray. (LL) The Mournful Lute or the Preceptor's Farewell. Daniel Alexander Payne. EBAP; TtW

For you— / Or me. (LL) Dixie Man to Uncle Sam. Langston Hughes. CP-HughL

For You, Sweetheart, I'll Sell Plutonium Reactors. Yusef Komunyakaa. SP-KomuY

For you'll find him hell to handle when he gets in fightin' trim. (LL) For Theodore Roosevelt. Paul Laurence Dunbar. CP-DunbP

For your sleep-song lullaby. (LL) Lullaby: "My little dark baby." Langston Hughes. CP-HughL

Forbidden Things. Alice Walker. CP-WalkA

Forced Retirement. Nikki Giovanni. SP-GiovN

Ford, The. African-American Oral Tradition. GetYo

Fore it is too late! (LL) Evil Morning. Langston Hughes. CP-HughL

'Fore they jine the heavenly choir. (LL) Deacon Jones' Grievance. Paul Laurence Dunbar. AAP; CP-DunbP

Foreclosure. Sterling A. Brown. CP-BrowS; GT

("And the old river rolls on, slowly to the gulf.") (LL) PoBA

Forest Greeting, The. Paul Laurence Dunbar. CP-DunbP

Forever. Paul Laurence Dunbar. CP-DunbP

Forever let there be shouting Sisters. In a Harlem Store Front Church. Clarence Reed. BlFi

Forever, life-long. (LL) To O.E.A E. A. Claude McKay. GT; SP-McKaC

Forever ruling everywhere. (LL) The Dream. Francis A. Boyd. EBAP

Forever with the Lord. (LL) Saved at Last. Frances Ellen Watkins Harper. CP-HarpF

Forget about your Jesse James. A Bad, Bad Man. Sterling A. Brown. CP-BrowS

Forget / and drown easily. (LL) Coping. Audre Lorde. CP-LordA

Forget it. Derek Walcott. See Blues.

Forget Me Not. Bob Kaufman. AmNP

Forget Me Not. Ann Plato. EBAP

Forgetfulness! Josephine D. Henderson Heard. CBWP-4

Forgetting—flowers wither in an hour. (LL) Spring for Lovers. Langston Hughes. CP-HughL

Forgive. Maya Angelou. CP-AngeM

Forgive life for happening / to them. (LL) Old Folks Laugh. Maya Angelou. CP-AngeM

Forgive me if I have not sent you. Valentines. Henry L. Dumas. IHS

Forgive me if my praises. Alice Walker. CP-WalkA

Forgive me, soldier. Please. Yusef Komunyakaa. SP-KomuY

"Forgive these nigguhs that know not what they do." Gwendolyn Brooks. See The Rites for Cousin Vit.

Forgive us for all the torture, for all the pain. (LL) In Memoriam; for James Baldwin (1924–1987). Quincy Troupe. IHS

Forgiveness. Alice Walker. CP-WalkA

Forgiving My Father. Lucille Clifton. SP-ClifL

Formula. Langston Hughes. CP-HughL

Fort Collins, Colorado. Al Young. CP-YounA

Forth on the fatal morn. Custer's Last Ride. Albery Allson Whitman. EBAP

Fortunate Spill, The. Marilyn Nelson. SP-NelsM

Fortune Teller Blues. Langston Hughes. CP-HughL

Fortune teller looked in my hand. Madam and the Fortune Teller. Langston Hughes. CP-HughL; SP-HughL

Forty Days Looking Backwards: Notes from a Surveyor. Michael S. Harper. SP-HarpM

Forty-nine Ford and a tank full of gas. African-American Oral Tradition. GetYo

Forward abrupt. Night and a Distant Church. Russell Atkins. PoBA

Fossil, fuchsia, mantis, man. Theme and Variation. Robert Hayden. CP-HaydR

'Foun' dis rabbit's foot, you see. Der Rabbit's Foot. James David Corrothers. EBAP

Found—Who Lost? Mary E. Tucker. CBWP-1

Founding Fathers in Philadelphia, The. Michael S. Harper. SP-HarpM

Fount of Tears, The. Paul Laurence Dunbar. CP-DunbP

Four Epitaphs. Countee Cullen. AmNP; CDC; PoBA

  For a Lady I Know. CP-CullC; IDB; Klds; SSLK

  For John Keats. CP-CullC; Klds

  For My Grandmother. CP-CullC; SSLK

  For Paul Laurence Dunbar. CP-CullC; Klds; SSLK

Four Glimpses of Night. Frank Marshall Davis. AmNP; PoBA

Four great walls have hemmed me in. Four Walls. Blanche Taylor Dickinson. CDC; ShDr

Four hundred years ago a tangled waste. Columbian Ode. Paul Laurence Dunbar. CP-DunbP

Four Lines of a Black Love Letter Between Teachers. Ed Roberson. NBV

Four little girls. Birmingham Sunday. Langston Hughes. CP-HughL

Four M-48 tank platoons ambushed. Caves. Michael S. Harper. SP-HarpM

403 Blues. Langston Hughes. CP-HughL

Four Questions Addressed to His Excellency, the Prime Minister. James P. Vaughn. AmNP

Four Sheets to the Wind and a One-Way Ticket to France. Conrad Kent Rivers. BPo; IDB; NNP; PoBA

("As a Black child I was a dreamer.") AmNP

Four stories high / i viz both waterways of new o. Burgundy Street. David Henderson. TtW

Four Walls. Blanche Taylor Dickinson. CDC; ShDr

Four walls can hold. Walls. Langston Hughes. CP-HughL

Four Worthies: Souls of Black Folk. Michael S. Harper. SP-HarpM

Fourth Dance Poem. Gerald William Barrax. PoBA

Fourth of July Thought. Langston Hughes. CP-HughL

Foxfire. Dominique Parker. SpiFl

Fragging. Yusef Komunyakaa. ESEAA

Fragile and / ordinary. (LL) His Shirt. Rita Dove. SP-DoveR

Fragment: "Breath of life imbued those few dim days, The." Jessie Redmond Fauset. CDC; ShDr

Fragment: "Cold chain of life presseth heavily on me tonight, The." Adah Isaacs Menken. CBWP-1

Fragment, A: "Our fancies are but joys all unexprest." Henrietta Cordelia Ray. CBWP-3

Fragment Reflection I. Doris Turner. JB

Fragments. Langston Hughes. CP-HughL

Fragments from a Parable. June Jordan. SP-JordJ

Fragments from the Diary of Amelie Patiné, Quadroon Mistress of Monsieur Jacques R-------. Sybil Klein. TtW

Frail children of sorrow, dethroned by a hue. Hope. Georgia Douglas Johnson. CDC

Frail woman dead, we are alone. (LL) A Poem for Democrats. Amiri Baraka. SP-BaraA

France! How shall we call her belle again? La Belle, La Douce, La Grande. Countee Cullen. CP-CullC

Frank Albert and Viola Benzena Owens. Ntozake Shange. BlSi

Frankie and Johnny. Sterling A. Brown. CP-BrowS

Frankie and Johnny were lovers. Unknown. NAAAL

Frankie was a halfwit, Johnny was a nigger. Frankie and Johnny. Sterling A. Brown. CP-BrowS

Franklin pierce's wife never. Mystery 1st Lady. Ishmael Reed. CP-ReedI

Freaks' Ball, see also Bulldaggers' Hall and Twenty-Two-Twenty. African-American Oral Tradition. GetYo

Frederick Douglass. Sam Cornish. PoBA

Frederick Douglass. Joseph Seamon Cotter, Sr. AAP; AfAmPo; EBAP

Frederick Douglass. Paul Laurence Dunbar. BALP; CP-DunbP; PoBA

Frederick Douglass. Robert Hayden. AmNP; CP-HaydR; ESEAA; IDB; Klds; NAAAL; PoBA

("Fleshing dreams of the beautiful, needful thing.") (LL) TtW

Frederick Douglass: 1817–1895. Langston Hughes. BPo; CP-HughL

Frederick, is God Dead? Sojourner Truth: Black Sybil in Salem. Michael S. Harper. SP-HarpM

Free at last [or las'], free at last [or las']. I Thank God I'm Free at Las'. Unknown. BPo; CrDW

Free bird leaps, A. Caged Bird. Maya Angelou. CP-AngeM; SP-AngeM

Free Fantasia: Tiger Flowers. Robert Hayden. CP-HaydR; ESEAA

Free Flight. June Jordan. SP-JordJ

Free from the ball-and-chain of circumstance! (LL) Festus Conrad. Melvin B. Tolson. GT

Free Labor. Frances Ellen Watkins Harper. CP-HarpF

Free Man. Langston Hughes. CP-HughL

Free reeds drift in the weeping morning. Drunk Time. Bob Kaufman. SP-KaufB

Free schools, free press, free speech and equal laws. Albery Allson Whitman. AAP Fr. "Hail dawning Peace! Speed on thy glorious rise!" AfAmPo Fr. Not a Man, and Yet a Man.

Free to travel, he still couldn't be shown how lucky. David Walker (1785–1830). Rita Dove. NAAAL; SP-DoveR

Freedom. Langston Hughes. CP-HughL

Freedom: "Some folks think." Langston Hughes. CP-HughL

Freedom at McNealy's. Priscilla Jane Thompson. CBWP-2

Freedom Bell, The. Frances Ellen Watkins Harper. CP-HarpF

Freedom Hair. Raymond Washington. NBV

Freedom in the Air. Unknown. NAAAL

Freedom is a dream. Dark Testament. Pauli Murray. AmNP; BlSi

Freedom / Is just frosting. Frosting. Langston Hughes. CP-HughL

Freedom never dies! (LL) Ballad of Harry Moore. Langston Hughes. CP-HughL

Freedom Rider: Washout. James A. Emanuel. BrTr

Freedom Seeker. Langston Hughes. CP-HughL

Freedom Song for the Black Woman, A. Carole C. Gregory Clemmons. BlSi

Freedom Train. Langston Hughes. CP-HughL; SP-HughL

Freedom will not come. Langston Hughes. CP-HughL; PoBA

Freedom's Plow. Langston Hughes. CP-HughL; SP-HughL

Freeman Field. Marilyn Nelson. ESEAA; SP-NelsM

French Leave. Claude McKay. SP-McKaC

French Quarter Intimacies. Kalamu ya Salaam. *Fr.* New Orleans Haiku. SpiFl

Fresh and fair the morn awaketh. Morn. Josephine D. Henderson Heard. CBWP-4

Friday in berkeley. the crippled. Untitled I. Ishmael Reed. CP-ReedI

Friday night / the bullet ripped. Keith Antar Mason. CtF

Friday the 12th. Al Young. CP-YounA

Friend of mine who raised six daughters and, A. Case in Point. June Jordan. SP-JordJ

Friendly in a Friendly Way. Langston Hughes. CP-HughL

Friends. Ray Durem. PoBA

Friends—burst through the cavity / like flame. (LL) The Ride. Lucinda Roy. GT

Friends Come. Lucille Clifton. SP-ClifL

Friends i am   like you   tied. Alfred B. Spellman. BlFi

Friends warned of moose that. The Moose Wallow. Robert Hayden. CP-HaydR

Frightened Lover's Sleep, The. Jay Wright. BlFi

Frogs burrow the mud. Winter. Nikki Giovanni. SP-GiovN

Frolic, A. Paul Laurence Dunbar. CP-DunbP

From a Brother Dreaming in the Rye. James Cunningham. JB

From a brown and brimming gourd! (LL) The Gourd. Paul Laurence Dunbar. CP-DunbP

From a Bus. Malaika Ayo Wangara. NBP

From a distance, I watch. Practical Concerns. William J. Harris. PoBA

From a Letter: About Snow. Toi Derricotte. SpiFl

From a pit of bones. The Poet. Bob Kaufman. SP-KaufB

From a Town in Minnesota. Michael S. Harper. SP-HarpM

From a vision red with war I awoke and saw the Prince of Peace. The New Day. Fenton Johnson. BANP

From America. James M. Whitfield. BPo

From an Almanac. Amiri Baraka. SP-BaraA

From an Almanac (2). Amiri Baraka. SP-BaraA

From an Almanac (3). Amiri Baraka. SP-BaraA

From behind closed doors. (LL) Progress Report. Audre Lorde. CP-LordA; SP-LordA

From Bowling Green. Al Young. CP-YounA; ESEAA

From breasts / Of Africland. Africland. Oliver La Grone. FB

From bright West Indies' seas. Stanzas for the First of August. James M. Whitfield. EBAP

From bright West Indies' sunny seas. Stanzas for the First of August. James M. Whitfield. TtW

From buttered gold to. New Orleans Rainbow. Kalamu ya Salaam. *Fr.* New Orleans Haiku. SpiFl

From cavities of bones. From the Cavities of Bones. Patricia Parker. BlSi

From Christ to Gandhi. Wealth. Langston Hughes. CP-HughL

From dark abodes to fair etherial light. On the Death of a Young Lady of Five Years of Age. Phillis Wheatley. CP-WheaP

From deep sleep. Nightmare. James A. Emanuel. BPo

From fair Jamaica's fertile plains. Lines. "Ada." BlSi

From fathers nursed on blueberry hills. (LL) Clinton. Sterling Plumpp. BkSV

From Fort Scott I met Jim Daniels. Jim Daniels: Hamilton Massacre: Parable. Michael S. Harper. SP-HarpM

From her perch of beauty. Avec Merci, Mother. Maya Angelou. CP-AngeM; SP-AngeM

From hill to hill let Freedom ring! Every Man a King. Timothy Thomas Fortune. EBAP

From him came the Sea. Visions of the Sea. Kiarri T-H Cheatwood. TtW

From ignorance and darkness, stupidity, and fears. A Litany from the Dark People. Margaret Abigail Walker. CP-WalkM

From Inside an Empty Purse. Audre Lorde. CP-LordA

From ivory towers they come. Soul. Austin Black. NBP

From looking at things Navajo. Al Young. CP-YounA

From Macon out, 'twas just a "pleasant ride." Albery Allson Whitman. *Fr.* Leelah Misled. EBAP

From Montgomery to Memphis he marches. Amos (Postscript, 1968). Margaret Abigail Walker. CP-WalkM

From my personal album. For Malcolm X. Nanina Alba. PoBA

From Nicaragua Libre: Photograph of Managua. June Jordan. SP-JordJ

From other-greater-worlds. (LL) Of the Cosmic-Blueprints. Sun-Ra. BlFi

From partial bondage to a life indeed. (LL) Spirit Voice, The; or Liberty Call to the Disfranchised (State of New York). Charles Lewis Reason. AAP; EBAP

From regions ever fair and bright. His Name. Frances Ellen Watkins Harper. CP-HarpF

From Rome's palaces and villas. The Hermit's Sacrifice. Frances Ellen Watkins Harper. CP-HarpF

From Sea to Shining Sea. June Jordan. SP-JordJ

From Selma. Langston Hughes. CP-HughL

From Spain to Alabama. Langston Hughes. CP-HughL

From stages into aisles. (LL) Tune. Al Young. CP-YounA

From that all-perfect place. (LL) She of the Dancing Feet Sings. Countee Cullen. CP-CullC

From that same hour. (LL) After While. Paul Laurence Dunbar. CP-DunbP

From the Cave. Audre Lorde. CP-LordA

From the Cavities of Bones. Patricia Parker. BlSi

From the corpse woodpiles, from the ashes. Robert Hayden. CP-HaydR

From the crash. (LL) Black Man, 13th Floor. James A. Emanuel. NBV

From the Dark Tower. Countee Cullen. AfAmPo; BALP; BANP; BPo; CDC; CP-CullC; CrDW; IDB; Klds; PoBA; TtW

("And wait, and tend our agonizing seed.") (LL) Crnst

("We shall not always plant what others reap.") NAAAL

From the Field. Lenard D. Moore. GT

From the Files of Agent 22. Ishmael Reed. CP-ReedI

From the first it had been like a. Bronzeville Mother Loiters in Mississippi. / Meanwhile, a Mississippi Mother Burns Bacon. Gwendolyn Brooks. Crnst; ESEAA; SP-BrooG; SSLK

From the German of Uhland. Ludwig Uhland, *German*. CDC, *tr.* by James Weldon Johnson

From the Greenhouse. Audre Lorde. CP-LordA

From the House of Yemanjá. Audre Lorde. CP-LordA

From the / Mystery. (LL) Consider me, / A colored boy. Langston Hughes. CP-HughL; SP-HughL

From the obscurity of the past, we saw. Nat Turner. Samuel Allen. FB

From the ocean filled with sand inside of me. Man with a Furnace in His Hand. Lance Jeffers. BlFi

From the old slave shack I chose my lady. Trellie. Lance Jeffers. FB; NBV; TtW

From the peaceful heights of a higher life. A Fairer Hope, a Brighter Morn. Frances Ellen Watkins Harper. CP-HarpF

From the Porch at Runnymede. Paul Laurence Dunbar. CP-DunbP

From the Saviour's wounded side. (LL) The Washerwoman. Mary Weston Fordham. CBWP-2

From the shadows of the quarter. Ask Your Mama. Langston Hughes. *Fr.* Ask Your Mama; 12 Moods for Jazz. CP-HughL

From the shadows of the quarter. Is It True? Langston Hughes. *Fr.* Ask Your Mama; 12 Moods for Jazz. CP-HughL

From the shiny iron stove. Easy Living. Michael S. Weaver. SpiFl

From the sleeping calendar I have stolen a month. Results of a Lie Detector. Bob Kaufman. SP-KaufB

From the sombre clouds fell slow. Snow Song. Henrietta Cordelia Ray. CBWP-3

From the soothing distance. The Orchard at Night in Rain Light. Al Young. CP-YounA

From the *source* comes the imagery and language. Corrected Review. Michael S. Harper. SP-HarpM

From the void / into the / sky. (LL) At General Electric, Where They Eat Their/Young. Robert Farr. SpiFl

From this low-lying valley, oh, how sweet. Two Points of View. Lucian B. Watkins. BANP

From this the muse rich consolation draws. On the Death of General Wooster. Phillis Wheatley. CP-WheaP

From thy patient, who while here. Accompanying a Gift. Lizelia Augusta Jenkins Moorer. CBWP-3

From time to time, McLambert came and went. Albery Allson Whitman. *Fr.* Leelah Misled. EBAP

From walking hot seasons, through unmasked years of light. Walking Hot Seasons. Bob Kaufman. SP-KaufB

From what great sleep. Watts. Alvin Saxon. PoBA

From what i've been hearing. Letter. Keith Gilyard. SpiFl

From where she stood the air she craved, *see also* "He rode across like a cavalier." Two Who Croseed a Line (She Crosses). Countee Cullen. CP-CullC

From which we spring. (LL) American Sonnet (10). Wanda Coleman. NAAAL

From world to world, unknown we speed. One Generation Passeth Away and Another Cometh. George Moses Horton. SP-HortG

Front of the head, The. If into Love the Image Burdens. Amiri Baraka. SP-BaraA

Frosting. Langston Hughes. CP-HughL

Frozen with snow. (LL) Dreams. Langston Hughes. CP-HughL

Fruit of Faith, The. Marilyn Nelson. SP-NelsM

Fruit of the Flower. Countee Cullen. CP-CullC

Fruit of the orchard is over-ripe, Elaine, The. Lancelot. Arna Bontemps. CDC

Fu' de peace o' my eachin' heels, set down. Itching Heels. Paul Laurence Dunbar. CP-DunbP

Fu' hit's Chrismus an' de back-log's bu'nin' thoo! (LL) A Back-Log Song. Paul Laurence Dunbar. CP-DunbP

Fugitive, The. Priscilla Jane Thompson. CBWP-2

Fugitive Paths. Michael S. Harper. SP-HarpM

Fugitive returned on New Year's Eve, The. Festus Conrad. Melvin B. Tolson. GT

Fugitive Slaves. Gale Jackson. SpiFl

Fugitive's Wife, The. Frances Ellen Watkins Harper. CP-HarpF

Fulfillment. Helene Johnson. CDC; ShDr

Fulfilment. Paul Laurence Dunbar. CP-DunbP

Fulfilment. Langston Hughes. CP-HughL; SP-HughL

Full day—. Today Tutu Is Beating the Same Burru As Me. Lebert Bethune. GT

Full many a time, in life's fair spring, I've strolled. Albery Allson Whitman. Fr. Leelah Misled. EBAP

Full many lift and sing. Negro Poets. Charles Bertram Johnson. BANP

Full Moon. Robert Hayden. BPo; CP-HaydR; GT; Klds

Full moon rises, A. Hurrah, Hurrah. Marilyn Nelson. SP-NelsM

Full moon rising on the waters of my heart. Evening Song. Jean Toomer. BPo; CDC; CP-ToomJ; GT

Full September moon sheds floods of light, The. A September Night. George Marion McClellan. AAP; AfAmPo; EBAP

Full Vision. Henrietta Cordelia Ray. CBWP-3

Fullmoon night hog maws fell, The. Spring 1937/ for Honoré Roussell. Alvin Aubert. TtW

Fully reckoned, time-honed / hour of triumph. (LL) Race Results, U.S.A., 1966. Sarah Webster Fabio. BrTr

Fumes of city bus. (LL) Haiku: "Morning fog / my daughter dropped off at camp." Lynn G. Moore. CtF

Fun City Samba. Al Young. CP-YounA

Fundamental question about revolution, The. Facing the Way. Alice Walker. CP-WalkA

Funeral. Sterling A. Brown. CP-BrowS

Funeral. Langston Hughes. CP-HughL

Funeral of Martin Luther King, Jr, The. Nikki Giovanni. AmNP; BPo; SP-GiovN

Funeral Poem on the Death of C.E., an Infant of Twelve Months, A. Phillis Wheatley. CP-WheaP

Funeraled Fare Well. Kalamu ya Salaam. Fr. New Orleans Haiku. SpiFl

Funk. Mary Weems. SpiFl

Funky blues / Keen toed shoes. Country Lover. Maya Angelou. CP-AngeM; SP-AngeM

Funky Football. Ruby C. Saunders. BlSi

Funny about best friends. Judas. Ishmael Reed. CP-ReedI

Futile of me to offer you my hand. Last Prince of the East. Langston Hughes. CP-HughL

Futile to chide the stinging shower. Perspectives. Dudley Randall. AmNP

Futility. Claude McKay. SP-McKaC

Future as we see the now and here, The. (LL) Here and Now. Catharine Cater. AmNP

Future is possible, The. (LL) Spring Song. Lucille Clifton. SP-ClifL

Future Promise. Audre Lorde. CP-LordA

Future Shock. Abiodun Oyewole. CtF

G

Gabriel. George Barlow. TtW

    Coming and Going: Gabriel's Song.

    "Ferrets are out!, The."

    History Is Thunder and Rain.

    Life and Death: The Bitch's Brew / The Readiness Is ALL.

    October, 1800: A Son in the Continuum.

    Rainbow, The.

    Spirit in the Dark.

    Trumpeter, The.

    White Blues: the Master's Song.

    Will and the Swan, The.

Gabriel's glory, openended. (LL) Fugitive Paths. Michael S. Harper. SP-HarpM

Gains. Michael S. Harper. SP-HarpM

Gala, holding on. Zinnias. Robert Hayden. CP-HaydR

Gal's Cry for a Dying Lover. Langston Hughes. NAAAL ("Hear de owl a hootin'.") CP-HughL

Game of Game, The. Nikki Giovanni. BrTr

Gamut, The. Maya Angelou. CP-AngeM; SP-AngeM

Gangster Goes Legit. Ishmael Reed. CP-ReedI

Gangsters. Langston Hughes. CP-HughL

Gangster's Death, The. Ishmael Reed. CP-ReedI; PoBA

Gansters of the world, The. Gangsters. Langston Hughes. CP-HughL

Garden. Langston Hughes. CP-HughL; SP-HughL

Garden is very quiet tonight, The. Dusk Song. William H. A. Moore. BANP

Garden of Shushan! Before the Feast of Shushan. Anne Spencer. BANP; BlSi; NAAAL; ShDr

Garden we walked in, The. Green Grass and Yellow Balloons. Etheridge Knight. GT; SP-KnigE

Garment. Langston Hughes. CP-HughL

Garnish of the world's acclaim, The. Funeral. Sterling A. Brown. CP-BrowS

Garnishing the Aviary. Margaret Else Danner. Fr. Far from Africa: Four Poems. AmNP; BPo; NNP; PoBA

Garret, The. Paul Laurence Dunbar. CP-DunbP

Gas Station Attendant. Brian G. Gilmore. SpiFl

Gatemouth Moore. II. Song of the Reverend Gatemouth Moore. Etheridge Knight. BkSV

Gather out of star-dust. Dream Dust. Langston Hughes. CP-HughL; SP-HughL

Gather quickly. Bouquet. Langston Hughes. CP-HughL

Gather round me, fellas, I have a story to tell. Lady Liberty. African-American Oral Tradition. GetYo

Gather up / In the arms of your pity. Litany. Langston Hughes. CP-HughL; SP-HughL

Gathering, The. Charlie R. Braxton. CtF

Gathering of the Grand Army, The. Charlotte L. Forten Grimké. AAP

Gatsby's Theory of Aesthetics. Amiri Baraka. SP-BaraA

Gauge. Langston Hughes. Fr. Montage of a Dream Deferred. CP-HughL

Gaunt thing, The. Babylon Revisited. Amiri Baraka. BPo

Gave me things I. Swallow the Lake. Clarence Major. ESEAA; GT; NAAAL; PoBA

Gawd only know! (LL) Old King Cotton. Sterling A. Brown. CP-BrowS

Gay Chaps at the Bar. Gwendolyn Brooks. SP-BrooG

Gay little devils / That hide in gin. Nocturne for the Drums. Langston Hughes. CP-HughL

Gay little Girl-of-the-Diving-Tank. At the Carnival. Anne Spencer. BANP; BlSi; CDC; Klds; NAAAL; ShDr; TtW

Gaze not upon my outside, friend. Apple Dumplings. Mary E. Tucker. CBWP-1

Gee, but it's hard to love someone, when that someone don't love you. Down-Hearted Blues. Albert Hunter and Louie Austin. NAAAL

Gem-like stars, The. Midnight. Henrietta Cordelia Ray. Fr. Idyl. EBAP

Gemini. Audre Lorde. CP-LordA; SP-LordA

Gems. Defari Herut. CtF

Gen. Grant—the Hero of the War. George Moses Horton. See General Grant—the Hero of the War.

Genealogy. Frank Lamont Phillips. AmNP

Geneology. Bob Kaufman. NBV; SP-KaufB

General Grant—the Hero of the War. George Moses Horton. AAP (Gen. Grant—the Hero of the War.) SP-HortG

General Robert Smalls. Josephine D. Henderson Heard. CBWP-4

General Science. Ishmael Reed. CP-ReedI

Generation. Audre Lorde. CP-LordA; NBV; SP-LordA

Generation Gap, The. Ruby C. Saunders. BlSi

Generation II. Audre Lorde. CP-LordA; SP-LordA

Generation III. Audre Lorde. CP-LordA

Generations. Lucille Clifton. SP-ClifL

Generations 1. Sam Cornish. GT

Generations 2. Sam Cornish. GT

Generations lost to be found, / to be found. (LL) The House on Moscow Street. Marilyn Nelson. SP-NelsM

Genes confessing. (LL) The Weakness. Toi Derricotte. GT

Genesis. Etheridge Knight. SP-KnigE

Genesis 11. Etheridge Knight. SP-KnigE

Geneva was the wild one. The Ballad of Aunt Geneva. Marilyn Nelson. GT; SP-NelsM

Genevieve / what are you seeing. Memorial II. Audre Lorde. CP-LordA; SP-LordA

Geni in the Jar, The. Nikki Giovanni. SP-GiovN

Genius Child. Langston Hughes. CP-HughL; SP-HughL

Genius is power. Adah Isaacs Menken. CBWP-1

Gen'l Tubman, as We Call Her. Michael S. Harper. SP-HarpM

Genocide doesn't only mean bombs. Vietnam Addenda. Audre Lorde. CP-LordA; SP-LordA

Gentle and smiling as before. The Wheel. Robert Hayden. BPo; CP-HaydR

Gentle as a maiden's dream. The Snow Storm. Mary Weston Fordham. CBWP-2

Gentlemen who have got to be classics and are now old with beards (or dead and in their graves) will kindly come forward and speak upon the subject. Letter to the Academy. Langston Hughes. CP-HughL

Gently shirred. (LL) The Event. Rita Dove. ESEAA; NAAAL

Geography of the Near Past. Al Young. CP-YounA

Geometry. Rita Dove. SP-DoveR; TtW

George. Dudley Randall. BPo; Klds

George: / Don't be no Chinaman. The Law for George. Sterling A. Brown. CP-BrowS

George-Hector. The Emancipation of George-Hector (a Colored Turtle). Mari E. Evans. AmNP

George Moses Horton, Myself. George Moses Horton. AAP; AfAmPo; Klds; NAAAL; SP-HortG; TtW

Georgia Dusk. Langston Hughes. CP-HughL; Crnst; SP-HughL

Georgia Dusk. Jean Toomer. AfAmPo; AmNP; BPo; CDC; CP-ToomJ; Klds; PoBA; TtW

Georgia—It's the Gospel Truth. Everett Hoagland. BrTr

Georgia Song, A. Maya Angelou. CP-AngeM; SP-AngeM

Georgie Grimes, with a red suitcase. Sterling A. Brown. CP-BrowS

Gerarda. Eloise Bibb. AAP; CBWP-4

Gerry's Jazz. Yusef Komunyakaa. SP-KomuY

Get away, they're all gone. Chops Are Flyin. Stanley Crouch. GT; NBP

Get In Out of the Rain. *African-American Oral Tradition.* GetYo

Get on board our Freedom Train! (LL) Freedom Train. Langston Hughes. CP-HughL; SP-HughL

Get on top. On Top of It All. Keith Gilyard. SpiFl

Get out the lunch-box of your dreams. Lunch in a Jim Crow Car. Langston Hughes. CP-HughL; SP-HughL

Get over double trouble, Juber boys, Juber. (LL) Juber up and Juber down. *African-American Oral Tradition.* TtW

Get that feeling sometimes. Al Young. CP-YounA

Get this now! Index to a Black Catharsis. Richard W. Thomas. BlFi

Get Up, Blues. James A. Emanuel. AmNP; PoBA

Get Up off That Old Jive. Langston Hughes. CP-HughL

Gethsemane. Arna Bontemps. CDC

Gets the idea / that you don't. (LL) Poem from Taped Testimony in the Tradition of Bernard Goetz. June Jordan. SP-JordJ

Gets you all the way back there— / to your first scene. (LL) Painting Drunken Twilight. George Barlow. GT

Gettin Down to Get over. June Jordan. SP-JordJ

Gettin to the next town / Baby. (LL) Pickin Em Up and Layin Em Down. Maya Angelou. CP-AngeM; SP-AngeM

Getting up in the morning lonesome and sad? (LL) Daybreak. Langston Hughes. CP-HughL

Ghandhi Is Fasting. Langston Hughes. CP-HughL

Ghastly, ghoulish, grinning skull. To a Skull. Joshua Henry Jones. BANP

Ghazal at Full Moon. June Jordan. SP-JordJ

Ghetto Lovesong—Migration. Carole C. Gregory Clemmons. NBP (Migration.) PoBA

Ghetto Waif. B. Felton. BrTr

Ghost. Audre Lorde. CP-LordA

Ghost appears in the dark of winter, The. The Ghost of Soul-making. Michael S. Harper. NAAAL

Ghost / Ghost / Watch out, The. So the King Sold the Farmer #39. Amiri Baraka. SP-BaraA

Ghost in Birmingham, The. Ishmael Reed. CP-ReedI

Ghost of Soul-making, The. Michael S. Harper. NAAAL

Ghost-Who-Walks, The. Colleen J. McElroy. GT

Ghosts. Countee Cullen. CP-CullC

Ghosts of 1619. Langston Hughes. CP-HughL

Ghosts of all too solid flesh. Ghosts of 1619. Langston Hughes. CP-HughL

Ghosts snare us with the past & future. Jungle Surrender. Yusef Komunyakaa. SP-KomuY

Giant Red Woman. Clarence Major. GT

Giant stopper in my throat, A. (LL) Now that the book is finished. Alice Walker. CP-WalkA

Giants of My Century. Margaret Abigail Walker. CP-WalkM

Gift. Alice Walker. CP-WalkA

Gift from Kenya. May Miller. BlSi

Gift Horse. Yusef Komunyakaa. GT

Gifts. Lenard D. Moore. SpiFl

Giles Johnson, Ph.D. Frank Marshall Davis. BPo; Klds; PoBA; TtW

Gimme $25.00. Request. Langston Hughes. *Fr.* Montage of a Dream Deferred. CP-HughL

Gimme six-bits' worth o' ticket. Six-Bits Blues. Langston Hughes. CP-HughL

Gin is better than the water in Lethe. (LL) The Scarlet Woman. Fenton Johnson. BANP; PoBA

"Gin us peace an' joy. Amen!" (LL) In the Morning. Paul Laurence Dunbar. BPo; CP-DunbP

Ginger Bread Mama. Doughtry Long. BPo; PoBA

Girdle the world with peace. (LL) Songs for the People. Frances Ellen Watkins Harper. AfAmPo; CP-HarpF; EBAP; NAAAL; TtW

Girl. Kelly Norman Ellis. SpiFl

Girl. Langston Hughes. CP-HughL

Girl, a community of believers, A. (LL) Some Kind of Crazy. Major L. Jackson. SpiFl

Girl at the Window. Pinkie Gordon Lane. GT

Girl from the realm of birds florid and fleet. Something Like a Sonnet for Phillis Miracle Wheatley. June Jordan. SP-JordJ

Girl Held without Bail. Margaret Abigail Walker. BPo; CP-WalkM; PoBA

Girl in my sister's house, A. Eulogy. Audre Lorde. CP-LordA

Girl of fifteen. James Weldon Johnson. GT

Girl told me, A. *African-American Oral Tradition.* GetYo

Girl Who Died #1, The. Alice Walker. CP-WalkA

Girl Who Died #2, The. Alice Walker. CP-WalkA

Girl with all that raising, A. Ballad of the Girl Whose Name Is Mud. Langston Hughes. CP-HughL; SP-HughL

Girl with no arms. (LL) Poem for Guatemala. June Jordan. NAAAL; SP-JordJ

Girl with the Afro, The. (Title.) Bob Bennett. BlFi

Girlfriend. Audre Lorde. CP-LordA

Girls fragrant in their beds, The. (LL) Compendium. Rita Dove. SP-DoveR

Girls love deceivers, as true hearts, the same. (LL) 'Twas said by some, that Leelah was too fast. Albery Allson Whitman. EBAP

Git on Board, Chillun. Elliot B. Henderson. EBAP

Git out o' bed, you rascals. Call Boy. Sterling A. Brown. CP-BrowS

Give a damn. (LL) Impasse. Langston Hughes. CP-HughL

Give back the life I gave. Generation III. Audre Lorde. CP-LordA

Give me a happy heart and suasive tongue. A Happy Heart. Josephine D. Henderson Heard. CBWP-4

Give me again the flaming torch of truth. Ode on the Occasion of the Inauguration of the Sixth President of Jackson State College. Margaret Abigail Walker. CP-WalkM

Give me fire and I will sing you morning. A Lover's Song. Audre Lorde. CP-LordA

Give Me Jesus. *Unknown.* BPo

Give me no days more brilliant than I know. Content. Paul Laurence Dunbar. CP-DunbP

Give Me the Red on the Black of the Bullet. Jayne Cortez. SP-CortJ

Give me your hand. A Conceit. Maya Angelou. CP-AngeM; SP-AngeM

Give My Love to the World. Frances Ellen Watkins Harper. CP-HarpF

Give over to high things the fervent thought. To Lovers of Earth: Fair Warning. Countee Cullen. CDC

Give Us Our Peace. Langston Hughes. CP-HughL

Given to love. (LL) Agony, An. As Now. Amiri Baraka. BALP; BPo

Given to the dust. (LL) Suffer the Children. Audre Lorde. CP-LordA; SP-LordA

Glamour of this moment too will pass, The. Demerol. Al Young. CP-YounA

Glass of sweet milk, A. Rediscovered Diary Entry. Al Young. CP-YounA

Gleamed a resplendent star. At Christmas-Tide. Henrietta Cordelia Ray. CBWP-3

Glimpse. Pearl Cleage Lomax. PoBA

Glimpses. Christopher Gilbert. GT

Glimpses of Infancy. Priscilla Jane Thompson. CBWP-2

Gloom of night had overspread the land, The. The Nativity. Mary Weston Fordham. CBWP-2

Gloria has a permit. Building. Audre Lorde. CP-LordA

Gloria's Clues. Yusef Komunyakaa. SP-KomuY

Glorified and undefiled. (LL) The Mother's Blessing. Frances Ellen Watkins Harper. CP-HarpF

Glorious, nourishing, flourishing moon, swollen with. The Moon, the Whole Moon, and Nothing but the Moon. Al Young. CP-YounA

Glory falls around us. Maya Angelou. CP-AngeM

Glory, Glory. Sterling A. Brown. CP-BrowS

Glory! Hallelujah! / The dawn's a-comin'! Prayer Meeting. Langston Hughes. CP-HughL; SP-HughL

Glory of the Day Was in Her Face, The. James Weldon Johnson. BANP; CDC; IDB; PoBA

Glory Trumpeter, The. Derek Walcott. GT

Gnawing the highway's edges, its black mouth. The Swamp. Derek Walcott. GT

Go ahead—see where it gets you. (LL) Demeter's Prayer to Hades. Rita Dove. NAAAL

Go and see Carlowitz the Carthusian. Poem in C. Jean Toomer. CP-ToomJ

Go chanting away. (LL) Imploring to Be Resigned at Death. George Moses Horton. AAP; AfAmPo

Go count the stars! Counting. Fenton Johnson. AmNP

Go Down Death. James Weldon Johnson. AmNP; PoBA ("Weep not, weep not, / She is not dead.") BkSV

Go Down, Moses! Marcus B. Christian. TtW

Go down, Moses. *Unknown.* BPo; BkSV; CrDW; Crnst; NAAAL

Go Down, Old Hannah. *Unknown.* NAAAL

Go;—for 'tis Memorial morning. Memorial Day. Clara Ann Thompson. CBWP-2

Go forth my little volume. God Speed. George Clinton Rowe. AAP

Go hmmmp hmmmmp hmmmmmp. (LL) Tapping. Jayne Cortez. SP-CortJ

Go home and make love to my woman. (LL) Conversation Overheard. Quincy Troupe. NAAAL

Go home, stupid. Ultimatum: Kid to Kid. Langston Hughes. CP-HughL

Go look for beauty where you least. More Than a Fool's Song. Countee Cullen. CP-CullC

Go opaque with confusion and shame, like a child's. (LL) Motherhood. Rita Dove. NAAAL; SP-DoveR

Go ponder at that faithful mother's grave. Albery Allson Whitman. *Fr.* Leelah Misled. EBAP

Go, ponder at that mansion desolate. Albery Allson Whitman. *Fr.* Leelah Misled. EBAP

Go *slow*, they say. Langston Hughes. CP-HughL

Go through the gates with closed eyes. "Close Your Eyes!" Arna Bontemps. AmNP; CDC; FB; GT; Klds; PoBA

Go to the moon / white folks going to the moon / going to. Moon Bound. Raymond Washington. NBV

Go 'way from dat window, "My Honey, My Love." Song to the Runaway Slave. *Unknown.* NAAAL

Go where you will. No Fixed Place. Alice Walker. CP-WalkA

Go with me to Paradise. (LL) Ballad of the Two Thieves. Langston Hughes. CP-HughL

Go work in my vineyard, said the Lord. Frances Ellen Watkins Harper. CP-HarpF

God. Langston Hughes. CP-HughL

God. *Unknown.* NAAAL

God and the devil still are wrangling. For a Mouthy Woman. Countee Cullen. CP-CullC; PoBA

God Bless Our Native Land. Frances Ellen Watkins Harper. CP-HarpF

God! but the interest! (LL) The Debt. Paul Laurence Dunbar. AmNP; BANP; CDC; CP-DunbP; Klds

God cannot let it come to naught. (LL) Fifty Years. James Weldon Johnson. NAAAL

God curtained from thy vision. To Mr. and Mrs. W. F. Johnson on Their Twenty-Fifth Wedding Anniversary. Frances Ellen Watkins Harper. CP-HarpF

God declares no independence. Monticello. Lucille Clifton. SP-ClifL

God gave the word, and woman heard. Woman's Work. Frances Ellen Watkins Harper. CP-HarpF

God Give to Men. Arna Bontemps. BANP; BPo; CDC

God got his eye on. (LL) Moses. Lucille Clifton. SP-ClifL

God grant some day your dreams come true. (LL) A City Garden. William Stanley Braithwaite. GT

God has his plans, and what if we. To the Memory of Mary Young. Paul Laurence Dunbar. CP-DunbP

God having a hemorrhage. Caribbean Sunset. Langston Hughes. CP-HughL

God, in His infinite wisdom. Acceptance. Langston Hughes. CP-HughL

God is above grammar. The Piping Down of God. Ishmael Reed. CP-ReedI

God / Is kind. Mae V. Cowdery. ShDr

God is on the side of the right! (LL) Be Active. Frances Ellen Watkins Harper. CP-HarpF

God is the Old Repair Man. The Old Repair Man. Fenton Johnson. AmNP

God knows / We have our troubles, too. High to Low. Langston Hughes. *Fr.* Montage of a Dream Deferred. CP-HughL

God never planted a garden. Anne Spencer. ShDr

God of my father discovered at midnight. Oya. Audre Lorde. CP-LordA; SP-LordA

God of the right, arise. To Miss Mary Britton. Paul Laurence Dunbar. CP-DunbP

God Reigns. Paul Laurence Dunbar. CP-DunbP

God Rest Ye Merry, Gentlemen. Derek Walcott. GT

God said, "Let there be light, and there was light." Mysteries of Life. Mary E. Tucker. CBWP-1

God Send Easter. Lucille Clifton. SP-ClifL

God slumbers in a back alley. A Christian Country. Langston Hughes. CP-HughL

God Speed. George Clinton Rowe. AAP

God— / they fear you, they hold you so. Testimony. Carolyn M. Rodgers. BPo

God, this mud. Fear's habit. Water Buffalo. Yusef Komunyakaa. SP-KomuY

God to Hungry Child. Langston Hughes. CP-HughL

God waits for the wandering world. Lucille Clifton. SP-ClifL

God, why have you ruined me. Job's Ancient Lament. Owen Dodson. FB

God Works in a Mysterious Way. Gwendolyn Brooks. SP-BrooG

God / you aint. I Wonta Thank Ya. Tejumola Ologboni. NBV

Goddamn! who taught jews how to lynch niggers? (LL) Cuttin Down to Size. Henry L. Dumas. BlFi

Gods. Langston Hughes. CP-HughL

God's A-Gonna Trouble the Water. *Unknown.* NAAAL

God's angry with the world again. Electrical Storm. Robert Hayden. CP-HaydR

Gods Are Here, The. Jean Toomer. CP-ToomJ

God's armies of Heaven, with pinions extended. Pro Patria—America, 1861. Adah Isaacs Menken. CBWP-1; EBAP

God's blessings all are uniform. They Are the Same. Priscilla Jane Thompson. CBWP-2

God's Electric Power. Mrs. Henry Linden. CBWP-4

God's Glory and my country's shame. The Black Christ. Countee Cullen. CP-CullC

Gods in Vietnam. Eugene B. Redmond. NBP; PoBA

God's Mood. Lucille Clifton. SP-ClifL

Gods their god-like fun, The. (LL) Letter to My Sister. Anne Spencer. AfAmPo; AmNP; BlSi; NAAAL; PoBA; ShDr; TtW

God's Trombone. Sarah Webster Fabio. TtW

God's Ways, Not Our Ways. Henrietta Cordelia Ray. AAP; CBWP-3

Gods Wrote, The. Keorapetse W. Kgositsile. GT

Goes way back to the days/my father a young man. Cousin Mary. Wanda Coleman. GT

Goggled mother with her children. The Families Album. Michael S. Harper. SP-HarpM

Goin' Back. Paul Laurence Dunbar. CP-DunbP

Goin' down the road, Lawd. Bound No'th Blues. Langston Hughes. AfAmPo; AmNP; CP-HughL; SP-HughL

Goin' Home. Paul Laurence Dunbar. CP-DunbP

Goin' to Chicago Blues. *Unknown.* NAAAL

Goin' to the Territory. Michael S. Harper. NAAAL

Going Back Home. Al Young. CP-YounA

Going back to D.F. Mexico City Lover. Al Young. CP-YounA

Going East. Frances Ellen Watkins Harper. CP-HarpF

Going to Chicago, sorry that I can't take you. Goin' to Chicago Blues. *Unknown.* NAAAL

Going to praise God till I die. (LL) Slavery chain done broke at last, broke at last, broke at last. *Unknown.* BkSV

Gold and brown. (LL) College Formal: Renaissance Casino. Langston Hughes. CP-HughL

Gold dust of your voice, The. Letter to Bob Kaufman. Yusef Komunyakaa. SP-KomuY

Gold moth did not love him, The. Fire-Caught. Langston Hughes. CP-HughL

Gold of heaven, The. Love. Tom Dent. NNP

Gold of her promise, The. America. Maya Angelou. CP-AngeM; SP-AngeM

Gold will not buy this voyage. Looking for a Country under Its Original Name. Colleen J. McElroy. BlSi

Golden Day, A. Paul Laurence Dunbar. CP-DunbP

Golden girl. College Formal: Renaissance Casino. Langston Hughes. *Fr.* Montage of a Dream Deferred. CP-HughL

Golden Jubilee of Wilberforce. Mrs. Henry Linden. CBWP-4

Golden mists o'er Cloudland wreathing. Fancy and Imagination. Henrietta Cordelia Ray. CBWP-3

Golden Moonrise. William Stanley Braithwaite. PoBA

Golden wings of time, The. The Transition—S.M. Alfred Islay Walden. AAP

Golgotha Is a Mountain. Arna Bontemps. AmNP; CDC

("Golgotha is a mountain, a purple mound.") NAAAL; TtW

Goliath of Gath. Phillis Wheatley. BALP; CP-WheaP

Gollygog / The Bingbuffer, The. Monsters from the Ozarks. Ishmael Reed. CP-ReedI

Gombo Févi / A whole chicken—if chicken cannot be. The Neo-HooDoo Aesthetic. Ishmael Reed. CP-ReedI

Gone are the sensuous stars, and manifold. Chaucer. Benjamin Brawley. BANP

Gone beyond the realities of life. (LL) Solomon Mahlangu, Freedom Fighter from Mamelodi. Jayne Cortez. SP-CortJ

Gone Boy. Langston Hughes. CP-HughL; SP-HughL

Gone   Gone / Another weaver of black dreams has gone. For Langston Hughes. Etheridge Knight. NBV; SP-KnigE

Gone out West, / Gone! (LL) One-Way Ticket. Langston Hughes. CP-HughL; SP-HughL

Gone to God. Frances Ellen Watkins Harper. CP-HarpF

Gone, with all her sparkling beauty. Mary E. Tucker. CBWP-1

Gonna be so slammin. This Poem. Ruth Forman. SpiFl

Gonna get lowdown tonight. (LL) Annabelle. Yusef Komunyakaa. SP-KomuY

Gonna talk about you when I get on my knees. (LL) I been rebuked and I been scorned. *Unknown.* BkSV; NAAAL

Goo'-by, Jinks, I got to hump. The Delinquent. Paul Laurence Dunbar. CP-DunbP

Good and gracious Nazarene, The. (LL) Sir, We Would See Jesus. Frances Ellen Watkins Harper. AAP; AfAmPo; CP-HarpF

Good Bluffers. Langston Hughes. CP-HughL

Good-by, my son, good-by. The Wayward Son. Mrs. Henry Linden. CBWP-4

Good-by, sweetheart, our days of bliss. The Parting Lovers. Mrs. Henry Linden. CBWP-4

Good-bye, good-bye, good- / bye. (LL) Elegy for Etheridge. Pinkie Gordon Lane. TtW

Good Bye, Honey—Good Bye. Elliot B. Henderson. EBAP

"Good-bye," I said to my conscience. Conscience and Remorse. Paul Laurence Dunbar. CP-DunbP

Good-bye! Off for Kansas. John Willis Menard. AAP

Good come out of / prison. (LL) Cell Song. Etheridge Knight. PoBA; SP-KnigE

Good evening, daddy! Boogie: 1 A.M. Langston Hughes. *Fr.* Montage of a Dream Deferred. CP-HughL

Good excuse. (LL) The Excuse. Carl H. Greene. NBV

Good Friday. Lucille Clifton. SP-ClifL

Good Friday Prayer. Marilyn Nelson. *Fr.* Thus Far by Faith. SP-NelsM

Good glory, give a look at Sporting Beasley. Sporting Beasley. Sterling A. Brown. CP-BrowS; Klds; NAAAL

Good hunting!—aye, good hunting. The Forest Greeting. Paul Laurence Dunbar. CP-DunbP

Good Joe. Yusef Komunyakaa. SP-KomuY

Good Lady / I have corn and beets. A Negro Peddler's Song. Fenton Johnson. AmNP

Good luck is money. (LL) The New Yorkers. Nikki Giovanni. SP-GiovN

Good Memory, A. Yusef Komunyakaa. SP-KomuY

Good Mirrors are Not Cheap. Audre Lorde. SP-LordA

("It is a waste of time hating a mirror.") CP-LordA

Good Morning, Blues. Jimmy Rushing. NAAAL

Good morning, Daddy! Dream Boogie. Langston Hughes. NAAAL; SP-HughL; SSLK *Fr.* Montage of a Dream Deferred. CP-HughL

Good morning, daddy! Langston Hughes. *Fr.* Lenox Avenue Mural. AmNP; SP-HughL

Good morning, daddy! / Ain't you heard? (LL) Island. Langston Hughes. SP-HughL

Good morning! / Good morning! Elegy. Al Young. CP-YounA

Good morning, Miss Lookingood. Miss Lookingood. *African-American Oral Tradition.* GetYo

Good-morning, Revolution. Langston Hughes. CP-HughL

Good Morning, Stalingrad. Langston Hughes. CP-HughL

Good morning, Ted. (LL) Elegy: "Good morning! / Good morning!" Al Young. CP-YounA

Good news about the earth. (LL) Bodies broken on, The. Lucille Clifton. ESEAA; NAAAL; SP-ClifL

Good news from the windy city: Thomas Edison's. Muddy Waters & the Chicago Blues. Cornelius Eady. ESEAA

Good-Night. Paul Laurence Dunbar. CP-DunbP

Good-night, my love, for I have dreamed of thee. Absence. Paul Laurence Dunbar. CP-DunbP

Good Night, Willie Lee, I'll See You in the Morning. Alice Walker. CP-WalkA; NAAAL

Good Nights. Saundra Sharp. SpiFl

Good Samaritan Hospital. Michael S. Harper. SP-HarpM

Good Times. Lucille Clifton. AmNP; BPo; PoBA; SP-ClifL

Good Woman Feeling Bad, A. Maya Angelou. CP-AngeM; SP-AngeM

Goodbye Christ. Langston Hughes. CP-HughL

Goodbye David Tamunoemi West. Margaret Else Danner. BPo

Goodmorning, Stalingrad! Good Morning, Stalingrad. Langston Hughes. CP-HughL

"Goodnight, lad." "Goodnight, dad." "Good night." (LL) Feeble Old Man. *African-American Oral Tradition.* GetYo

Goree. Harriet Jacobs. SpiFl

Gorée ten miles offshore beckons. Everett Hoagland. GT

Gospel. Rita Dove. SP-DoveR

Gospel Cha-Cha. Langston Hughes. *Fr.* Ask Your Mama; 12 Moods for Jazz. CP-HughL

Gossip. Mrs. Henry Linden. CBWP-4

Got me son canebrake blues / baby / this sugarpain sho is bad. Cane-Brake-Blues. Eugene B. Redmond. TtW

Got my man and gone. (LL) Joe Turner. *Unknown.* CrDW

Got to be / Kidding, / Son. (LL) Sunday Night at Grandfather's. Rita Dove. SP-DoveR

Got up / this morning at 2:45, breakfast at 3:30. The Passage. Rita Dove. ESEAA

Gourd, The. Paul Laurence Dunbar. CP-DunbP

Governor Fires Dean. Langston Hughes. CP-HughL

Governor has sent out, The. Tyrone (3). Lucille Clifton. SP-ClifL

Governor of the Ollie Street, The. Ahmos, II Zu-Bolton. BkSV

Grace / to mourn for / me? (LL) Mourning Grace. Maya Angelou. SP-AngeM

Gracious Saviour let me make. Thou Lovest Me. Josephine D. Henderson Heard. CBWP-4

Graduate Leaving College, The. George Moses Horton. SP-HortG

Graduation. Langston Hughes. CP-HughL; SP-HughL

Grafted Bud, The. Mary Weston Fordham. CBWP-2

Grain of Sand, A. Frances Ellen Watkins Harper. CP-HarpF

Grand Army Plaza. June Jordan. SP-JordJ

Granddaughters' bright smiles, chili dogs, and lemonade in the shade start old men to. Baseball. Christopher Jennings. SpiFl

Grandfather. Michael S. Harper. ESEAA; NAAAL; SP-HarpM

Grandfather Poem, A. William J. Harris. PoBA

Grandfather Was Queer, Too. Bob Kaufman. NAAAL; SP-KaufB

Grandma sleeps with / my sick. Medicine. Alice Walker. CP-WalkA

Grandmama frying / black skillet full of catfish. Tanka. Lenard D. Moore. CtF

Grandmother: Crossing Jordan. Melvin Dixon. ESEAA

Grandpa's Stories. Langston Hughes. CP-HughL

Grandson Is a Hoticeberg, A. Margaret Else Danner. BlSi; FB

Granite air, A. (LL) The Carousel. Gloria C. Oden. GT

Granite-colored gulls unlocked, The. 1938. Yusef Komunyakaa. SP-KomuY

Granny Blak Poet (in Pastel). Arthur Pfister. BrTr

Granny's gone a-visitin'. Opportunity. Paul Laurence Dunbar. CP-DunbP

Grant Park. Langston Hughes. CP-HughL

Grape Sherbet. Rita Dove. SP-DoveR

Grapes: Still-Life. Anne Spencer. ShDr

Grass bends low, the pregnant trees, The. Singing in the Rain. Countee Cullen. CP-CullC

Grass commence a-comin'. Spring Fever. Paul Laurence Dunbar. CP-DunbP

Grass Fingers. Angelina Weld Grimké. CDC; ShDr; TtW

Grateful grave, each whitened skull / Will grin, The. (LL) Harlem Street Walkers. Sterling A. Brown. CP-BrowS

Gratitude. George Moses Horton. SP-HortG

Grave Yard. Langston Hughes. CP-HughL

Gravel rattles against the fenders of the van. Once on a Night in the Delta: A Report From Hell. Etheridge Knight. SP-KnigE

Graveyard is the, The. Boarding House. Langston Hughes. CP-HughL

Gray. Alice Walker. CP-WalkA

Gray are the pages of record. Black Samson of Brandywine. Paul Laurence Dunbar. CP-DunbP; NAAAL

Gray-blue shadows lift. Starlight Scope Myopia. Yusef Komunyakaa. SP-KomuY

Gray dawn on the mountain top, The. Day. Paul Laurence Dunbar. CP-DunbP

Gray is the palace where she dwells. My Lady of Castle Grand. Paul Laurence Dunbar. CP-DunbP

Gray of the sea, and the gray of the sky, The. Her Thought and His. Paul Laurence Dunbar. CP-DunbP; NAAAL

Gray suit. / Blue day. Wrong Color. Christopher Stanard. SpiFl

Great Amazon of God behold your bread. For Mary McLeod Bethune. Margaret Abigail Walker. CP-WalkM

Great God accept our gratitude. Doxology. Josephine D. Henderson Heard. CBWP-4

Great God! and yet shall feeble man presume. Albery Allson Whitman. *Fr.* Leelah Misled. EBAP

Great-Grandfathers, blessed by great-grandmothers. Geneology. Bob Kaufman. NBV; SP-KaufB

Great lonely hills. Big Sur. Langston Hughes. CP-HughL

Great mob that knows no fear. Revolution. Langston Hughes. CP-HughL

Great Painter! to thy soul aglow with thought. Raphael. Henrietta Cordelia Ray. CBWP-3

Great Palaces of Versailles, The. Rita Dove. ESEAA

Great Pax Whitie, The. Nikki Giovanni. SP-GiovN

Great Santa Barbara Oil Disaster OR, The. Conyus. NBV

Great swart cheek and the gleam of tears, A. The Washer-Woman. Otto Leland Bohanan. BANP

Great Uncle Beefheart. Rita Dove. SP-DoveR

Great white race, The. (LL) Ku Klux. Langston Hughes. BPo; CP-HughL; SP-HughL

Greater Friendship Baptist Church, The. Carole C. Gregory Clemmons. BlSi

Greatest self-made man in the world today, The. Our Noble Booker T. Washington. Mrs. Henry Linden. CBWP-4

Greek Room, The. James W. Thompson. BPo

Green Apples. Dudley Randall. FB

Green arbor that I once knew, A. Linda Beatrice Brown. GT

Green as an afterthought. (LL) Weathering Out. Rita Dove. ESEAA; SP-DoveR

Green Boots n Lil Honeys. Ruth Forman. SpiFl

Green Grass and Yellow Balloons, *(for Alexandria Keller, a poet at four).* Etheridge Knight. GT; SP-KnigE

Green Is a Feeling, Not a Color. Al Young. CP-YounA

Green is the color of everything. One West Coast. Al Young. CP-YounA

Green lamp flares on the table, The. This Life. Rita Dove. GT; SP-DoveR

Green Lantern's Solo. Amiri Baraka. SP-BaraA

Green lawn / a picket fence. Once. Alice Walker. BlSi; CP-WalkA

Green Memory. Langston Hughes. *Fr.* Montage of a Dream Deferred. CP-HughL

Green of Jesus, The. Spring Song. Lucille Clifton. SP-ClifL

Green screams enfold my night. (LL) African Dream. Bob Kaufman. GT; SP-KaufB

Green sludge of a riverbank. One Volume Missing. Rita Dove. SP-DoveR

Greenhouse. Gerald William Barrax. TtW

Greenness. Angelina Weld Grimké. CDC

Greeting. Henrietta Cordelia Ray. CBWP-3

Grenada. E. Ethelbert Miller. TtW

Grenudita. A(e)rin Wilson. CtF

Grew hair for fun. Ike. Rita Dove. SP-DoveR

Grey trees, grey skies, and not a star. Dawn. Angelina Weld Grimké. ShDr

Greyday. Maya Angelou. CP-AngeM; SP-AngeM

Grief. Langston Hughes. CP-HughL

Grief is not apparel. Homocide. Essex Hemphill. GT

Grief Streams Down My Chest. Lance Jeffers. PoBA

Grievance, A. Paul Laurence Dunbar. CP-DunbP

Grim monarch! see, depriv'd of vital breath. To a Lady on the Death of Her Husband. Phillis Wheatley. CP-WheaP

Grim Monarch! see depriv'd of vital breath. To Mrs. Leonard, on the Death of Her Husband. Phillis Wheatley. CP-WheaP

Grinding Vibrato. Jayne Cortez. BlSi

Griots Who Know Brer Fox, The. Colleen J. McElroy. NAAAL

Grizzly. Ishmael Reed. CP-ReedI

Grizzly Peak. Al Young. CP-YounA

Groceries ring / in my intestines. Corktown. Michael S. Harper. SP-HarpM

Grocery had provided him with, The. Dialog outside the Lakeside Grocery. Ishmael Reed. CP-ReedI

Grocery Store. Langston Hughes. CP-HughL

Group of Musings, A. Henrietta Cordelia Ray. CBWP-3

Groupie. Al Young. CP-YounA

Grow dim or cease to be! (LL) I Want to Die While You Love Me. Georgia Douglas Johnson. AmNP; BANP; BlSi; CDC; NAAAL; ShDr; TtW

Grow high above my head. (LL) Invocation: "Let me be buried in the rain." Helene Johnson. NAAAL

Growin' Gray. Paul Laurence Dunbar. CP-DunbP

Growing into My Name. Harriet Jacobs. SpiFl

Growth can sit there from. Regenesis. Ron Welburn. NBP

Guerilla Handbook, A. Amiri Baraka. PoBA; SP-BaraA

Guerrilla-Cong, The. Michael S. Harper. NBV

Guess I'll quit now. (LL) Elevator Boy. Langston Hughes. CP-HughL; SP-HughL

Guess we'll give it one mo' try. (LL) Strange Legacies. Sterling A. Brown. Klds

Guest Lecturer. Darwin T. Turner. BALP

Guilty, the New York Philharmonic Signs up a Whale. Ishmael Reed. CP-ReedI

Gulf Coast Blues. Clarence Williams. NAAAL

Gulls. Robert Hayden. CP-HaydR

Gum. Jean Toomer. CP-ToomJ

Guns of war are silenced, The. Peace Be with You. Bob Kaufman. SP-KaufB

Gurgling waters foam and play, The. On the rapids of the St. Lawrence. Henrietta Cordelia Ray. CBWP-3

Gus. Nikki Giovanni. SP-GiovN

Gus, the lineman / Route forty-nine. Margaret Abigail Walker. CP-WalkM

Guys who own, The. What I Think. Langston Hughes. CP-HughL

G'way an' quit dat noise, Miss Lucy—. When Malindy Sings. Paul Laurence Dunbar. AAP; CP-DunbP; NAAAL; PoBA

Gwendolyn Brooks Elizabeth. Haki R. Madhubuti. ESEAA

Gwensways. Eugene B. Redmond. SpiFl

Gwine to leeb his dear ol' place. Good Bye, Honey—Good Bye. Elliot B. Henderson. EBAP

Gypsy Man. Langston Hughes. CP-HughL; NAAAL

Gypsy Melodies. Langston Hughes. CP-HughL; SP-HughL

Gypsy woman told my mother, The. Hoochie Coochie. Muddy Waters. NAAAL

Gyre's Galax. Norman Henry, II Pritchard. PoBA

H

H₂O. Al Young. CP-YounA

Ha! tott'ring Johnny strut and boast. The Creditor to His Proud Debtor. George Moses Horton. AAP; NAAAL; SP-HortG

Habana. Julian Bond. NNP

Habits. Nikki Giovanni. SP-GiovN

Habits of the soul. (LL) A Plague of Starlings. Robert Hayden. CP-HaydR; ESEAA

Had closed his eyes in death. (LL) The Artist. Frances Ellen Watkins Harper. CP-HarpF

Had cut deep bloody grooves / Across our backs. Etheridge Knight. *See* Hard Rock Returns to Prison from the Hospital for the Criminal Insane.

Had cut grooves too deeply across our backs. Etheridge Knight. *See* Hard Rock Returns to Prison from the Hospital for the Criminal Insane.

Had I not known that the heart. Prescience. Maya Angelou. CP-AngeM; SP-AngeM

Had I the wings of a bird. Thoughts. Maggie Pogue Johnson. CBWP-4

Had reported / A panther / Missing. (LL) Black Power. Nikki Giovanni. BrTr; SP-GiovN

Had to come by / this. (LL) Prayer. Lucille Clifton. NAAAL; SP-ClifL

Haiku: "Bare pecan tree, A." Etheridge Knight. ESEAA; TtW

Haiku: "Black woman, A." Lenard D. Moore. CtF; TtW

Haiku: "Cloudless summer day." Lenard D. Moore. SpiFl

Haiku: "Dark rock-road, The." Maisha L. Moore. CtF

Haiku: "Did ya ever cry." Sonia Sanchez. SP-SancS

Haiku: "Eastern guard tower." Etheridge Knight. BPo; ESEAA; SP-KnigE; TtW

Haiku: "Falling snow flakes, The." Etheridge Knight. ESEAA; TtW

Haiku: "Family reunion." Lenard D. Moore. SpiFl

Haiku: "I am now in the." Sonia Sanchez. SP-SancS

Haiku: "I saw you today." Sonia Sanchez. SP-SancS

Haiku: "If i had known, if." Sonia Sanchez. SP-SancS

Haiku: "In the August grass." Etheridge Knight. ESEAA; TtW

Haiku: "Jazz is / the way brown sugar." DJ Renegade. CtF

Haiku: "Making jazz swing in." Etheridge Knight. ESEAA; TtW

Haiku: "Morning fog / my daughter dropped off at camp." Lynn G. Moore. CtF

Haiku: "Morning sun slants cell." Etheridge Knight. ESEAA; TtW

Haiku: "O i am so sad, i." Sonia Sanchez. SP-SancS

Haiku: "O i was wide and." Sonia Sanchez. SP-SancS

Haiku: "Piano man, The." Etheridge Knight. ESEAA; TtW

Haiku: "Sipping the new tea." Lenard D. Moore. TtW

Haiku: "Spring moonrise." Lenard D. Moore. SpiFl

Haiku: "Summer evening sun." Lenard D. Moore. TtW

Haiku: "To write a blues song." Etheridge Knight. ESEAA; TtW

Haiku: "Two hours I've walked." Etheridge Knight. SP-KnigE

Haiku: "Under moon shadows." Etheridge Knight. ESEAA; TtW

Haiku: "Was it yesterday." Sonia Sanchez. SP-SancS

Haiku: "Winter stillness." Lenard D. Moore. TtW

Haiku 1: "Slender finger of light, A." Etheridge Knight. SP-KnigE

Hail dawning Peace! Speed on thy glorious rise! Albery Allson Whitman. AfAmPo *Fr.* Not a Man, and Yet a Man.

(End of the Whole Matter, The.) AAP

"Free schools, free press and equal laws." AAP

Hail, Dionysos. Dudley Randall. BPo; BrTr

Hail Flag of the Union! Hail Flag of the free! Stars and Stripes. Mary Weston Fordham. CBWP-2

Hail, happy day, when, smiling like the morn. To the Right Honourable William, Earl of Dartmouth, His Majesty's Principal Secretary of State for North-America, Etc. Phillis Wheatley. CP-WheaP; CrDW; NAAAL

Hail, happy saint, on thine immortal throne. On the Death of the Rev. Mr. George Whitefield, 1770. Phillis Wheatley. CP-WheaP; EBAP; NAAAL

Hail Happy Saint, on thy Immortal Throne! An Ode of Verses on the Death of George Whitefield. Phillis Wheatley. CP-WheaP

Hail! home of exiles and of Seminoles! Albery Allson Whitman. AAP *Fr.* Twasinta's Seminoles; Or Rape of Florida

Hail thou sweet and welcome day. The First of August in Jamaica. Joshua McCarter Simpson. AAP

Hail to the black! (LL) The Song of the Smoke. William Edward Burghardt DuBois. SSLK

Hain't no use to weep, hain't no use to moan. Down in the Lonesome Garden. *Unknown.* BPo

Hain't you see my Mandy Lou. A Plantation Portrait. Paul Laurence Dunbar. CP-DunbP

Hair—braided chestnut. Portrait in Georgia. Jean Toomer. CP-ToomJ

Hair- / silver-gray, / like streams of stars. Face. Jean Toomer. CDC; CP-ToomJ

Hair slicked back as if. Child's Play. Yusef Komunyakaa. SP-KomuY

Haitians. Ishmael Reed. CP-ReedI

Half Black, Half Blacker. Sterling Plumpp. PoBA; TtW

Half-built / your greathouse looms. Judith's Fancy. Audre Lorde. CP-LordA

Half girl / To marry. (LL) Catch. Langston Hughes. CP-HughL; SP-HughL

Half in the dim light from the hall. To ———. William Stanley Braithwaite. BALP; PoBA

Half of his / body hung in. Spirits. Victor Hernandez Cruz. PoBA

Half-past eight Don Pullen just arrived. Don Pullen at the Zanzibar Blue Jazz Cafe, 1994. Major L. Jackson. SpiFl

Halfnaked children / met us singing for coins. Kodachromes of the Island. Robert Hayden. CP-HaydR

Halfway between the rain and Washington. My Fifth Trip to Washington Ended in Northeast Delaware. Audre Lorde. CP-LordA; SP-LordA

Halfway through an afternoon. Hot Comb. Natasha Trethewey. SpiFl

Hallowe'en. Lizelia Augusta Jenkins Moorer. CBWP-3

Hallucinogenic Halleluuuu. Al Young. CP-YounA

Hampton, Virginia. Nikki Giovanni. SP-GiovN

Hand Me Down Blues, *for my brother George 1933–1971.* Calvin Forbes. GT

Hand over hungry hand. (LL) Climbing. Lucille Clifton. GT

Hand waves gracefully, The. For the Dancer. Niama Leslie JoAnn Williams. SpiFl

Hands and arms and legs and mouths. The Bitter Spring Again. Al Young. CP-YounA

Hands; For Mother's Day. Nikki Giovanni. IHS; SP-GiovN

Hands make love to thigh, breast, clavicle. Euphony. Yusef Komunyakaa. ESEAA

Hands she can trust. (LL) To my Friend, Jerina. Lucille Clifton. ESEAA

Hanged Man, The. I Die for All Mysterious Things. Audre Lorde. CP-LordA

Hanging Fire. Audre Lorde. CP-LordA

Hanging from a tree—I see a body! (LL) I Know I'm Not Sufficiently Obscure. Ray Durem. BPo; PoBA

Hanging from fresh trees. Lemons, Lemons. Al Young. CP-YounA

Hanging on the wall, an iron face watches me. The Mask. Irma McClaurin. BlSi

Hanging out / means being. For Judith. Audre Lorde. CP-LordA

Hangover. Al Young. CP-YounA

Hanoi Hannah. Yusef Komunyakaa. SP-KomuY

Happen you will rise. For the Lame. Lucille Clifton. SP-ClifL

Happenstance. Rita Dove. SP-DoveR

Happy Day (or Independence Day). James Cunningham. JB

Happy Heart, A. Josephine D. Henderson Heard. CBWP-4

Happy moments tell me, pray. The Birth of Time. Josephine D. Henderson Heard. CBWP-4

Happy Pair, A. Priscilla Jane Thompson. CBWP-2

Hard core nights are so. Our Natures Rise. Kalamu ya Salaam. *Fr.* New Orleans Haiku. SpiFl

Hard Daddy. Langston Hughes. BANP; CP-HughL; NAAAL; SP-HughL

Hard Love Rock. Audre Lorde. SP-LordA

("Today I heard my heart screeching like a subway train.") CP-LordA

Hard Love Rock #II. Audre Lorde. CP-LordA; SP-LordA

Hard Luck. Langston Hughes. CP-HughL

Hard Rock Returns to Prison from the Hospital for the Criminal Insane. Etheridge Knight. ESEAA; GT; TtW

("Had cut deep bloody grooves / Across our backs.") (LL) SP-KnigE

("Had cut grooves too deeply across our backs.") (LL) BrTr; NAAAL

Hard Rock / was / known not to take no shit. Hard Rock Returns to Prison from the Hospital for the Criminal Insane. Etheridge Knight. BrTr; ESEAA; GT; NAAAL; SP-KnigE; TtW

Hard sex. The silken, honeyed twang of parting. No Jazz. Marilyn Nelson. *Fr.* The Plotinus Suite. SP-NelsM

Hard Times A' Coming. "Nayo." BkSV

Hard Times Blues. *Unknown.* Crnst

Harlem. Langston Hughes. *Fr.* Lenox Avenue Mural. AmNP; CrDW; GT; NAAAL; SP-HughL; SSLK *Fr.* Montage of a Dream Deferred. CP-HughL

(Dream Deferred.) PoBA

Harlem. Langston Hughes. *See* Puzzled.

Harlem. Melvin B. Tolson. TtW

Harlem '67. Clarence Reed. BlFi

Harlem Advocate fell between his legs, The. Uncle Rufus. Melvin B. Tolson. TtW

Harlem Dance Hall. Langston Hughes. CP-HughL

Harlem Dancer, The. Claude McKay. AfAmPo; BALP; BANP; BPo; CrDW; SP-McKaC

Harlem dud. For "Mr. Dudley," a Black Spy. James A. Emanuel. BPo; NBV

Harlem Freeze Frame. Lebert Bethune. BlFi; GT; PoBA

Harlem Gallery. Melvin B. Tolson. Klds

"Strange but true is the story."

Harlem Gallery: From the Inside. Larry Neal. BPo; NBV

Harlem Happiness. Sterling A. Brown. CP-BrowS

Harlem Hopscotch. Maya Angelou. CP-AngeM; SP-AngeM

Harlem is on parade. While Poets Are Watching. Colleen J. McElroy. TtW

Harlem is vicious / modernism. BangClash. Return of the Native. Amiri Baraka. BPo

Harlem / Knows a song. Harlem Night. Langston Hughes. CP-HughL

Harlem Night. Langston Hughes. CP-HughL

Harlem Night Club. Langston Hughes. CP-HughL

Harlem Night Song. Langston Hughes. CP-HughL; SP-HughL

Harlem Riot, 1943. Pauli Murray. PoBA

Harlem / wasn't him home. Deceased. Langston Hughes. CP-HughL

Harlem Shadows. Claude McKay. BANP; NAAAL; SP-McKaC; TtW

Harlem Sounds: Hallelujah Corner. William Browne. AmNP

Harlem Street Walkers. Sterling A. Brown. CP-BrowS

Harlem Sweeties. Langston Hughes. CP-HughL

Harlem. Where once I trailed the rivers edge. The Invaders. Clarence Reed. BlFi

Harriet Beecher Stowe. Paul Laurence Dunbar. AAP; BPo; CP-DunbP; Klds

Harriet Beecher Stowe's Works. Frank Barbour Coffin. AAP

Harriet / if i be you. Lucille Clifton. SP-ClifL

Harriet there was always somebody calling us crazy. Audre Lorde. BlSi; CP-LordA

Harriet Tubman. Samuel Allen. Crnst; TtW

Harriet Tubman. Margaret Abigail Walker. CP-WalkM; TtW

Harsh World that lashest me each day. Countee Cullen. CP-CullC

Harvest. Nikki Giovanni. SP-GiovN

Harvest Song. Jean Toomer. CP-ToomJ

Harwood Alley Song. Bob Kaufman. SP-KaufB

Has a gold tooth, sits long hours. Black Bourgeoisie. Amiri Baraka. BPo; ESEAA

Has had enough to do. (LL) Piggy-back. Langston Hughes. CP-HughL

Hast thou no mercy, wind, that thou should'st tear from me. The Mother's Lament. Mary E. Tucker. CBWP-1

Haste to the mighty ocean. August. Henrietta Cordelia Ray. CBWP-3

Hat on the table, The. Headdress. Rita Dove. SP-DoveR

Hatchet's shadow on the / Rippling green, The. (LL) Receiving the Stigmata. Rita Dove. SP-DoveR

Hatred. Gwendolyn B. Bennett. AmNP; BANP; BlSi; CDC; PoBA; ShDr ("My hatred.") (LL) NAAAL

Haunted by poems beginning with I. Prologue: "Haunted by poems beginning with I." Audre Lorde. CP-LordA; ESEAA

Haunted Oak, The. Paul Laurence Dunbar. AAP; AfAmPo; BANP; CP-DunbP; Klds; NAAAL

Haunting face of poverty, The. Grant Park. Langston Hughes. CP-HughL

Havana Dreams. Langston Hughes. CP-HughL; SP-HughL

Have danced in ecstasy. Poem for the Liberation of Southern Africa. Etheridge Knight. SP-KnigE

Have died, the Present teaches, but in vain! (LL) Robert Gould Shaw. Paul Laurence Dunbar. CP-DunbP; Klds

Have found a quiet needed for so long. (LL) Return. Sterling A. Brown. CP-BrowS; Crnst

Have mercy, Lord! Sinner. Langston Hughes. CP-HughL; SP-HughL

Have seared his own with flame. (LL) For John Keats. Countee Cullen. CP-CullC; Klds

Have sheltered for the night. (LL) After the Winter. Claude McKay. BANP; IDB; PoBA

Have the bright and glowing visions. Lines to Hon. Thaddeus Stevens. Frances Ellen Watkins Harper. CP-HarpF

Have to work after all. (LL) Necessity. Langston Hughes. CP-HughL

Have you dug the spill. Harlem Sweeties. Langston Hughes. CP-HughL

Have you ever heard of lynching in the great United States? Lynching. Lizelia Augusta Jenkins Moorer. CBWP-3

Have you ever seen the moon. Have You Seen It. Lula Lowe Weeden. CDC

Have you heard, my friend, the slander that the Negro has to face? Immortality. Lizelia Augusta Jenkins Moorer. CBWP-3

Have you heard the news? (LL) Leaving Syracuse. Al Young. CP-YounA; ESEAA

Have You Seen It. Lula Lowe Weeden. CDC

Haven. Donald Jeffrey Hayes. AmNP

Having attained success in business. Robert Whitmore. Frank Marshall Davis. BPo; Klds; PoBA; TtW

Having eaten two pillows. Alice Walker. CP-WalkA

Having given up hope for a high-wire act. Learning to Swim at Forty-Five. Colleen J. McElroy. GT

Having had you once. Mae V. Cowdery. ShDr

Having known robins on the window sill. Old Age. Langston Hughes. CP-HughL

Having never been. On Trying to Imagine the Kiwi Pregnant. Clarence Major. GT

Having reached perfection. Perfection. Alice Walker. CP-WalkA

Having tried to use the. It Is Deep. Carolyn M. Rodgers. NAAAL; SSLK; TtW

Hawk Lawler: Chorus. Bob Kaufman. SP-KaufB

Hawk Revsited, The. Al Young. CP-YounA

Hazing. Brian G. Gilmore. CtF

He ain't gone. (LL) Gone Boy. Langston Hughes. CP-HughL; SP-HughL

He always had pretty legs. Gus. Nikki Giovanni. SP-GiovN

He always pulled himself on. Grizzly. Ishmael Reed. CP-ReedI

He avoided the empty millyards. Under the Viaduct, 1932. Rita Dove. SP-DoveR

He bad. The Pusher. Maya Angelou. CP-AngeM; SP-AngeM

He bought some more. (LL) In Uganda an early king chose. Alice Walker. CP-WalkA

He calls me from his house and. About Long Distances on Saturday. June Jordan. SP-JordJ

He came, a dark youth, singing in the dawn. James David Corrothers. See Paul Laurence Dunbar.

He came—a wanderer; years of sin. The Prodigal's Return. Frances Ellen Watkins Harper. CP-HarpF

He came, a youth, singing in the dawn. Paul Laurence Dunbar. James David Corrothers. AfAmPo; BANP

He came apart in the open. Martin's Blues. Michael S. Harper. PoBA; SP-HarpM

He came / in flowing robes. Armah: October 12, 1990. Alice Walker. CP-WalkA

He came in silvern armor, trimmed with black. Sonnet. Gwendolyn B. Bennett. AmNP; CDC; PoBA Fr. Sonnets. TtW

He can climb vulgar. Swift, Tiny and Fine. Ishmael Reed. CP-ReedI

He carries / His own strength. Young Sailor. Langston Hughes. CP-HughL; SP-HughL

He Comes Not To-night. Josephine D. Henderson Heard. CBWP-4

He comes toward me with lashless eyes. Upon Meeting Don L. Lee, in a Dream. Rita Dove. SP-DoveR

He debated whether / as a poet. Arthur Ridgewood, M.D. Frank Marshall Davis. Klds; TtW

He did not! Current Events. June Jordan. SP-JordJ

He didn't say / wear yr/blackness in. Malcolm Spoke / Who Listened? Haki R. Madhubuti. BrTr; ESEAA; NAAAL

He dines alone surrounded by reflections. Witch Doctor. Robert Hayden. AmNP; CP-HaydR

He drums the piano wood. Shakespeare Say. Rita Dove. SP-DoveR

He frightens all the witches and the dragons in the air. The Black Cock. Ishmael Reed. CP-ReedI

He-frog told the she-frog, The. African-American Oral Tradition. GetYo

He gave up fine cordials and. Compendium. Rita Dove. SP-DoveR

He glides so swiftly. Snake. Langston Hughes. CP-HughL

He had a name. Generations 1. Sam Cornish. GT

He had been coming a very long time. For Malcolm Who Walks in the Eyes of Our Children. Quincy Troupe. PoBA

He had got, finally. A Poem for Speculative Hipsters. Amiri Baraka. SP-BaraA

He had his dream, and all through life. Paul Laurence Dunbar. CP-DunbP

He "Had Not Where to Lay His Head." Frances Ellen Watkins Harper. CP-HarpF

He had plunged into our sorrows. Christ's Entry into Jerusalem. Frances Ellen Watkins Harper. CP-HarpF

He has a girl who has flaxen hair. On Hearing "The Girl with the Flaxen Hair." Nikki Giovanni. SP-GiovN

He has been. Old Sailor. Langston Hughes. CP-HughL

"He has no enemies!" you say. No Enemies. Benjamin Clark. EBAP

He has the sign. Portrait of Malcolm X. Etheridge Knight. PoBA

He Hath Need of Rest. Josephine D. Henderson Heard. CBWP-4

He heard the chant of unseen lips. Words for the Hour. Frances Ellen Watkins Harper. CP-HarpF

He is as salt. Salt. Lucille Clifton. SP-ClifL

He is bound to make something happen. The Revolutionary. Alvin Aubert. TtW

He is coming, she said, to Simon's feast. Simon's Feast. Frances Ellen Watkins Harper. CP-HarpF

He is death / in life. Life and Death: The Bitch's Brew / The Readiness Is ALL. George Barlow. Fr. Gabriel. TtW

He is forever trapped. Audre Lorde. See Suffer the Children.

He is Gabriel; / black man and slave. The Trumpeter. George Barlow. Fr. Gabriel. TtW

He is gone, the strong base of the nation. Lincoln Is Dead. George Moses Horton. SP-HortG

He is murdered upright in the day. Vaticide. Myron O'Higgins. IDB; PoBA

He is not dead. (LL) Frederick Douglass: 1817–1895. Langston Hughes. BPo; CP-HughL

He is sun-bright myth and Cosmic Light. O Mystic Light! A Mystic Sage Returns to Realms of Eternity. Askia M. Toure. SpiFl

He is very busy with his looking. Young Heroes. Gwendolyn Brooks. BPo; NAAAL

He is wasted now. Dylan, Who Is Dead. Samuel Allen. PoBA

He jumped me while I was asleep. Assailant. John Raven. BPo

He lets her pick the color. Nothing Down. Rita Dove. SP-DoveR

He lifted up his pleading eyes. The Martyr of Alabama. Frances Ellen Watkins Harper. CP-HarpF; TtW

He liked to joke and all of his jokes were practical. Sunday Night at Grandfather's. Rita Dove. SP-DoveR

He looks back at me. The Guerrilla-Cong. Michael S. Harper. NBV

He loved her, and through many years. Then and Now. Paul Laurence Dunbar. CP-DunbP

He mounts the stand &. Your Basic Black Poet. Al Young. CP-YounA

He never spoke a word to me. Simon the Cyrenian Speaks. Countee Cullen. AmNP; BPo; CP-CullC

He never was a silly boy. Ph.D. Langston Hughes. CP-HughL

He ordered a beer. Roman Poem Number Eight. June Jordan. SP-JordJ

He Paid Me Seven. *Unknown.* BPo

He pins the hems of Angels and. The Wardrobe Master of Paradise. Ishmael Reed. CP-ReedI

He prayed for patience; Care and Sorrow came. His Answer. Clara Ann Thompson. BlSi; CBWP-2

He ran his hands thru her hair. Some Recent Fiction. Al Young. CP-YounA

He raped / she wept. In the Tradition of Bobbitt. Saundra Sharp. SpiFl

He rode across like a cavalier, *see also* "From where she stood the air she craved." Two Who Crossed a Line. Countee Cullen. CP-CullC

He rose up on his dying bed. Hope: "He rose up on his dying bed." Langston Hughes. SP-HughL *Fr.* Montage of a Dream Deferred. CP-HughL

He said come. Alice Walker. CP-WalkA

He said he loved another. (LL) Communication I. Maya Angelou. CP-AngeM; SP-AngeM

He said: Here is my soul. Gift. Alice Walker. CP-WalkA

He said: I want you to be happy. Alice Walker. CP-WalkA

He said, then calmly died. (LL) The Cherokee. Mary Weston Fordham. CBWP-2

He sang of life, serenely sweet. The Poet. Paul Laurence Dunbar. AAP; AfAmPo; BPo; CP-DunbP; CrDW; Klds; NAAAL

He sat there / on the porch of eternity. Mississippi Griot. Sterling Plumpp. TtW

He sat upon the rolling deck. Sailor. Langston Hughes. CP-HughL

He saw the rope, the moving mob. The Lynching. Dorothea Matthews. ShDr

He says: / "Only the black mind can project." Moving. Helen G. Quigless. BkSV

He scans the world with calm and fearless eyes. The New Negro. James Edward McCall. CDC

He scribbles some in prose and verse. Dilettante, The: A Modern Type. Paul Laurence Dunbar. CP-DunbP

He sees through stone. Etheridge Knight. BALP; GT; NBP; PoBA; SP-KnigE

He shot Katlian in the back. (LL) Points of View. Ishmael Reed. CP-ReedI; TtW

He shoves the .38. The Cage Walker. Yusef Komunyakaa. SP-KomuY

He sits at the bar in the Alhambra. Simple. Naomi Long Madgett. FB; GT; PoBA

He sits in front of the bright, blazing grate. The Old Freedman. Priscilla Jane Thompson. CBWP-2

He sits on a hill. Jaime. Langston Hughes. CP-HughL

He slept like a rock or a man that's dead. (LL) The Weary Blues. Langston Hughes. BALP; CP-HughL; NAAAL; SP-HughL

He snuggles his fingers. After Winter. Sterling A. Brown. CP-BrowS; GT; PoBA

He speaks of voyages. Tour Guide: La Maison des Esclaves. Melvin Dixon. ESEAA

He stepped into the night aware. The Tired Man. Suliaman El-Hadi. SpiFl

He stood before her. Dreamjot: 1962. Al Young. CP-YounA

He stood before his finished work. The Artist. Frances Ellen Watkins Harper. CP-HarpF

He stood before my heart's closed door. The Refiner's Gold. Frances Ellen Watkins Harper. CP-HarpF

He stood before the savage throng. The Tennessee Hero. Frances Ellen Watkins Harper. CP-HarpF

He stood before the sons of Heth. Burial of Srah. Frances Ellen Watkins Harper. CP-HarpF

He stood beside his dying child. The Drunkard's Child. Frances Ellen Watkins Harper. CP-HarpF

He stood beside the station rail. Goin' Back. Paul Laurence Dunbar. CP-DunbP

He stoops down eating sunflowers. Healing Song. Michael S. Harper. SP-HarpM

He strolled from door to door. Ghetto Waif. B. Felton. BrTr

He takes his love much as he takes his wine. Nordic. Lillian Byrnes. ShDr

He tells many bad things. Young Training. Lawrence McGaugh. PoBA

He, through the eyes of the first marauder. To a Girl Who Knew What Side Her Bread Was Buttered On. Audre Lorde. CP-LordA; SP-LordA

He tilled the old deserted fields with zeal. Emerson. Joseph Seamon Cotter, Sr. EBAP

He took all his money. Ballad of the Miser. Langston Hughes. CP-HughL

He walks the blistered boulevards for hours. In This Waking. Wanda Coleman. Crnst

He waltzes into the lane. Makin' Jump Shots. Michael S. Harper. SP-HarpM

He was a good man. Wake Cry. Waring Cuney. BANP

He Was a Man. Sterling A. Brown. CP-BrowS

He was a man who lived a peaceful life. Contradiction. Joseph Seamon Cotter, Sr. EBAP

He was a poet who wrote clever verses. Confirmation. Paul Laurence Dunbar. CP-DunbP

He was a soldier in the army. Casualty. Langston Hughes. *Fr.* Montage of a Dream Deferred. CP-HughL

He was arrested and detained. Soft Targets. Essex Hemphill. GT

He was born in Alabama. Of De Witt Williams on His Way to Lincoln Cemetery. Gwendolyn Brooks. *Fr.* A Street in Bronzeville. BPo; BlSi; ESEAA; SP-BrooG

He was dreaming of the factories across the water's fog. What Cannot Be Kept. Reginald Shepherd. GT

He was first seen in a Louisiana bayou. Grandfather Was Queer, Too. Bob Kaufman. NAAAL; SP-KaufB

He was holding clean globes in his hands. (LL) Medgar Evers. Gwendolyn Brooks. ESEAA

He was just back. Vietnam. Clarence Major. PoBA

He was married / for a short time. Pains with a Light Touch. Haki R. Madhubuti. BrTr

He was so pure. Seducing the Saint. Marilyn Nelson. *Fr.* The Life of a Saint. SP-NelsM

He was still Uncle. The Empress Brand Trim: Ruby Reminisces. Sherley Anne Williams. BlSi

He was strange weather, this luther, he read books, mainly poetry and sometimes. Poet: What Ever Happened to Luther? Haki R. Madhubuti. SpiFl

He was the only one of us. The Governor of the Ollie Street. Ahmos, II Zu-Bolton. BkSV

He watch her like a coonhound watch a tree. Balance. Marilyn Nelson. SP-NelsM

He went to being called a Colored man. The Calling of Names. Maya Angelou. CP-AngeM; SP-AngeM

He who thinks immortality. Elegy for David Diop. Keorapetse W. Kgositsile. BrTr

He wore his coffin for a hat. For a Pessimist. Countee Cullen. CP-CullC

He wrote upon his heart. Inscription. Donald Jeffrey Hayes. CDC

Head bent, walking through snow. 125th Street and Abomey. Audre Lorde. CP-LordA

Head of a Woman. Al Young. CP-YounA

Head of Lincoln looks down from the wall, The. Lincoln Theatre. Langston Hughes. CP-HughL

Headdress. Rita Dove. SP-DoveR

Heading North, straw hat. Jiving. Rita Dove. SP-DoveR

Headline: / Another Church Is Burned! Miracle. Derrick I. M. Gilbert. CtF

Healing Song. Michael S. Harper. SP-HarpM

Health-Food Diner, The. Maya Angelou. CP-AngeM; SP-AngeM

Hear de owl a hootin'. Langston Hughes. *See* Gal's Cry for a Dying Lover.

Hear me / don't you hear me. Tambourine. James Cunningham. SpiFl

Hear, O Israel! and plead my cause against the ungodly nation. Adah Isaacs Menken. AAP; CBWP-1

Hear the dreary, dreary rain. Voices of the Rain. Henrietta Cordelia Ray. CBWP-3

Hear the sound. Listen. Charles Patterson. NBP

Hear this prayer from a Plaquemine jail! Hosea. Margaret Abigail Walker. CP-WalkM

Hear ye not how, from all high points of Time. Henry Highland Garnet. CrDW

Heard de owl a hootin'. Gal's Cry for a Dying Lover. Langston Hughes. NAAAL

Heard you that shriek? It rose. Slave Mother, The: "Heard you that shriek? It rose." Frances Ellen Watkins Harper. CP-HarpF; CrDW; EBAP; NAAAL; TtW

Hearing James Brown at the Café des Nattes. Richard A. Long. AmNP

Heart. Langston Hughes. CP-HughL

Heart free, hand free. Sic Vita. William Stanley Braithwaite. BANP; NAAAL

Heart has need of some deceit, The. Only the Polished Skeleton. Countee Cullen. CP-CullC

Heart-Hungry. Josephine D. Henderson Heard. CBWP-4

Heart of a Woman, The. Georgia Douglas Johnson. BlSi; CDC; ShDr ("Heart of a woman goes forth with the dawn, The.") NAAAL; TtW

Heart of Harlem, The. Langston Hughes. CP-HughL

Heart of my heart, the day is chill. A Misty Day. Paul Laurence Dunbar. CP-DunbP

Heart of the soft, wild rose. Two Questions. William Stanley Braithwaite. BALP

Heart of the Southland, heed me pleading now. To the South. Paul Laurence Dunbar. CP-DunbP

Heartbeats. Melvin Dixon. ESEAA

Heartblow: Messages. Michael S. Harper. SP-HarpM

Heartbreak October moon of sun. Where the Danube and Sava Rivers Meet. Al Young. CP-YounA

Heart's Ease. Mary E. Tucker. CBWP-1

Heart's Graveyard Shift, The. Yusef Komunyakaa. SP-KomuY

Heartstring. Blessed wood. Copacetic Mingus. Yusef Komunyakaa. SP-KomuY

Heat of the oven, The. Breaded Meat, Breaded Hands. Michael S. Harper. SP-HarpM

Heat / you left with me, The. Autumn Prison. Nikki Giovanni. SP-GiovN

Heathen Bliss. Amiri Baraka. SP-BaraA

Heathen Technology & Media. Amiri Baraka. SP-BaraA

Heathens. Amiri Baraka. SP-BaraA

Heathens in Evolution. Amiri Baraka. SP-BaraA

Heathens Think Fascism Is Civilization. Amiri Baraka. SP-BaraA

Heather Bell. Bob Kaufman. SP-KaufB

Heaven aint the only H in the dictionary. (LL) Ho. Al Young. CP-YounA

Heaven is / The place where. Langston Hughes. CP-HughL; SP-HughL

Heavenly Love. George Moses Horton. SP-HortG

Heavy Water Blues. Bob Kaufman. NBV ("Radio is teaching my goldfish Jujutsu, The.") SP-KaufB

Hecuba. Euripides. SP-NelsM, *tr. by* Marilyn Nelson
   Death of Polyxena, The.
   Hecuba Mourns.

Hecuba Mourns. Euripides. *Fr.* Hecuba. SP-NelsM, *tr. by* Marilyn Nelson

He'd divided his days into. (LL) April Fools' Day. Yusef Komunyakaa. GT; SP-KomuY

He'd play, after the bawdy songs and blues. When de Saints Go Ma'ching Home. Sterling A. Brown. AmNP; CP-BrowS

He'd rather dance than rule. (LL) Why I Often Allude to Osiris. Ishmael Reed. CP-ReedI; GT

HEEEYYYSOOUUL / SISS-TERS / Your deepest concern for. This Poem for Black Women. Reginald Lockett. BlFi

Heel and toe, heel and toe. The Dance. Paul Laurence Dunbar. CP-DunbP

Height, Breadth, Depth. Kalamu ya Salaam. *Fr.* New Orleans Haiku. SpiFl

Held in / waiting, / waiting. (LL) Breathing in morning. Al Young. CP-YounA

Held in / waiting, / waiting. (LL) Song Turning Back Into Itself 1. Al Young. CP-YounA

Held me virgin and. Southern Roads/City Pavement. Virgia Brocks-Shedd. TtW

Helen Keller. Langston Hughes. CP-HughL

Heliotropic moth looked up, A. Parable of the Moth. Marilyn Nelson. *Fr.* The Plotinus Suite. SP-NelsM

Hell, Mary / Bell Jones. Jon Eckels. BrTr

Hellhound on My Trail. Robert Johnson. NAAAL

Hello dar, Miss Melerlee! Miss Melerlee. John Wesley Holloway. BANP

Hello. / I'm sorry. / I can't talk to you. What Is This in Reference To? or We Must Get Together Sometime Soon! June Jordan. SP-JordJ

Hello, Jamaica! / Hello, Haiti! Broadcast to the West Indies. Langston Hughes. CP-HughL

Hello, Mister Jack / The Ripper, come on in. Light on the Subject. Yusef Komunyakaa. SP-KomuY

Hello, ole man, you're a-gittin' gray. Growin' Gray. Paul Laurence Dunbar. CP-DunbP

Hello, sailor boy. Port Town. Langston Hughes. CP-HughL; SP-HughL

Hello, young sailor. Martial Choreograph. Maya Angelou. CP-AngeM; SP-AngeM

Help us brother turn this wheel. Sister Brother Don't You Stumble. Jon Goncalves. BlFi

Hemlock in the Furrows. Adah Isaacs Menken. CBWP-1

Hemp ... / A stick. Gauge. Langston Hughes. *Fr.* Montage of a Dream Deferred. CP-HughL

Her arms semaphore fat triangles. Momma Welfare Roll. Maya Angelou. CP-AngeM; SP-AngeM

Her body was on fire beneath his. Moses. E. Ethelbert Miller. TtW

Her counsel was accepted: the times are grave. Lady Luncheon Club. Maya Angelou. CP-AngeM; SP-AngeM

Her Cruising Car. Nikki Giovanni. SP-GiovN

Her dark brown face. Young Prostitute. Langston Hughes. CP-HughL

Her exquisite yellow youth. . . . (LL) Jessie Mitchell's Mother. Gwendolyn Brooks. SP-BrooG

Her eyes are bright as sparkling stars. Mine. Mary E. Tucker. CBWP-1

Her eyes? Dark pools of deepest shade. Portrait. George Leonard Allen. CDC

Her eyes were gentle; her voice was for soft singing. An Old Woman Remembers. Sterling A. Brown. CP-BrowS; PoBA

Her going through changes. Seth Bingham. William W. Cook. SpiFl

Her grandmother called her from the playground. Legacies. Nikki Giovanni. SP-GiovN

Her great adventure ended. S-sss-ss-sh! Langston Hughes. CP-HughL; SP-HughL

Her hair is a brilliant red, and her voice like a bumblebee's hum. My Best Girl. Paul Laurence Dunbar. CP-DunbP

Her leg flies open like a dictionary dropped. Mama's Murders. Marilyn Nelson. SP-NelsM

Her Lips Are Copper Wire. Jean Toomer. AfAmPo; CP-ToomJ; GT

Her lips on my breasts. (LL) She said: "When I was with him." Alice Walker. CP-WalkA

Her long / un- / braided / hair. (LL) Medicine. Alice Walker. CP-WalkA

Her love is true I know. True Love. Waring Cuney. CDC

Her Love Poem. Lucille Clifton. SP-ClifL

Her magnified voice reverberates. Aunt Annie's Prayer. Marilyn Nelson. SP-NelsM

Her only treasure, / and never spent. (LL) Early Losses: a Requiem. Alice Walker. BlSi; CP-WalkA

Her own clasped hands. (LL) Preface to a Twenty Volume Suicide Note. Amiri Baraka. AmNP; CrDW; ESEAA; NAAAL; NNP; PoBA; SP-BaraA; TtW

Her parents and her dolls destroyed. Belsen, Day of Liberation. Robert Hayden. CP-HaydR

Her ringlets glistened like the gold of morn. A Picture. Henrietta Cordelia Ray. CBWP-3

Her roots bound. A Woman Is Not a Potted Plant. Alice Walker. CP-WalkA

Her skin is like dusk on the eastern horizon. Jean Toomer. *Fr.* Karintha. Klds

Her skin so brown. (LL) Mexican Market Woman. Langston Hughes. CP-HughL; SP-HughL

Her sleeping head with its great gelid mass. Perseus. Robert Hayden. CP-HaydR

Her song to me across years. (LL) Cousin Mary. Wanda Coleman. GT

Her Story. Naomi Long Madgett. PoBA

Her teeth are as white as the meat of an apple. Fascination. Langston Hughes. CP-HughL

Her Thought and His. Paul Laurence Dunbar. CP-DunbP; NAAAL

Her veins run mogen david. Lane Is the Pretty One. Lucille Clifton. SP-ClifL

Herbert Hoover. *African-American Oral Tradition*. GetYo

Here, Adam, take back your God damn rib. (LL) Geneology. Bob Kaufman. NBV; SP-KaufB

Here am I with my head held high! Sister Johnson Marches. Langston Hughes. CP-HughL

Here among them the americans   this baffling. [American Journal]. Robert Hayden. CP-HaydR

Here and Now. Catharine Cater. AmNP

Here I am. Falling. Yusef Komunyakaa. SP-KomuY

Here / I am cutting you. For Kenneth & Miriam Patchen. Al Young. CP-YounA

Here I come! Little Song on Housing. Langston Hughes. CP-HughL

Here I set with a bitter old thought. Twilight Reverie. Langston Hughes. *Fr.* Seven Moments of Love. CP-HughL

Here I sit. Bad Morning. Langston Hughes. CP-HughL; SP-HughL

Here I sit with my belly full. Success. Langston Hughes. CP-HughL

Here in a Chicago museum, these small bells of. The Small Bells of Benin. Margaret Else Danner. BrTr

Here in the newspaper—the wreck of the East Bound. It's Here In The. Russell Atkins. AmNP; PoBA

Here / in the wombed room. A Zorro Man. Maya Angelou. CP-AngeM; SP-AngeM

Here in violet light. Al Young. CP-YounA

Here is a place that is no place. Madhouse. Calvin C. Hernton. IDB; Klds; NNP; PoBA

Here / is America's killing. The Rainbow. George Barlow. *Fr.* Gabriel. TtW

Here is that sleeping place. Grave Yard. Langston Hughes. CP-HughL

Here is the shadow of its joy. (LL) Monet's "Waterlilies." Robert Hayden. CP-HaydR; GT

Here is the spirit in the dark. Spirit in the Dark. George Barlow. *Fr.* Gabriel. TtW

Here is where it was dry. Earth. Lucille Clifton. SP-ClifL

Here its like that. Blue Tanganyika. Lebert Bethune. BlFi; PoBA

Here lies the Pariah of his race. (LL) The Misanthropist. James M. Whitfield. AAP; AfAmPo; EBAP

Here on the edge of hell. Puzzled. Langston Hughes. CP-HughL; SP-HughL

Here redbuds like momentary trees. Locus. Robert Hayden. CP-HaydR

Here we are / running with the weeds. Flowers. Lucille Clifton. SP-ClifL

Here we have watched ten thousand. View from Rosehill Cemetery: Vicksburg. Alice Walker. CP-WalkA

Here we raise the dead. Secondline Send Off. Kalamu ya Salaam. *Fr.* New Orleans Haiku. SpiFl

Here Where Coltrane Is. Michael S. Harper. ESEAA; NAAAL; PoBA; SP-HarpM

Here's how you put your enemy. Rough Trade Slumlord Totem. Ishmael Reed. CP-ReedI

Here's the story about a young guy named Ping Pong Joe. Ping Pong Joe. *African-American Oral Tradition.* GetYo

Here's to Adhering. Maya Angelou. CP-AngeM; SP-AngeM

Here's to the lady with the little red shoes. *African-American Oral Tradition.* GetYo

Here's to you, Mag, you dirty hag. *African-American Oral Tradition.* GetYo

Here's to your eyes. Toast. Frank Horne. BANP

Here's to your soul as yet unborn. (LL) Toast. Frank Horne. BANP

Heritage. Gwendolyn B. Bennett. AmNP; BANP; BlSi; NAAAL; PoBA; ShDr

Heritage. Mae V. Cowdery. ShDr

Heritage. Countee Cullen. AmNP; BANP; BPo; CP-CullC; CrDW; Crnst; NAAAL; PoBA; SSLK; TtW

Heritage. Claude McKay. SP-McKaC

Herman from the Shark-Tooth Shore. *African-American Oral Tradition.* GetYo

Hermit, The. Eloise Bibb. CBWP-4

Hermit and the Soul, The. Henrietta Cordelia Ray. CBWP-3

Hermit in his cave beside the sea, The. The Hermit and the Soul. Henrietta Cordelia Ray. CBWP-3

Hermitage Breakfast. Marilyn Nelson. *Fr.* The Plotinus Suite. SP-NelsM

Hermit's Sacrifice, The. Frances Ellen Watkins Harper. CP-HarpF

Hero—International Brigade. Langston Hughes. CP-HughL

Herrick Hospital, Fifth Floor. Al Young. CP-YounA

Herring run / in the silver morning. Michael S. Harper. SP-HarpM

Herself slowly rolling down the sides of the earth. (LL) Pomade. Rita Dove. SP-DoveR

He's Doing Natural Life. Conyus. PoBA

He's gone, alas! I know not whither. The Horse Stolen from the Camp. George Moses Horton. SP-HortG

He's just an ordinary guy. Just an Ordinary Guy. Langston Hughes. CP-HughL

He's so much like his daddy / when he cries. (LL) Avec Merci, Mother. Maya Angelou. CP-AngeM; SP-AngeM

He's so romantic, he's kissed both my arms. The Marriage Nightmare. Marilyn Nelson. SP-NelsM

He's struttin' sho ernuff. Drum Majah, De. Ray Garfield Dandridge. BANP

He's tucked his feet into corduroy scuffs. Recovery. Rita Dove. SP-DoveR

Hesh! my baby; stop yer fuss. Aunt Chloe's Lullaby. Daniel Webster Davis. AAP; AfAmPo; EBAP

Hesitant door chain, The. Into Blackness Softly. Mari E. Evans. PoBA

Hey! Langston Hughes. CP-HughL

Hey bop hey bop re re bop. (LL) A Poem for Langston Hughes. Nikki Giovanni. SP-GiovN; SSLK

Hey, Buddy! / Look at me! Florida Road Workers. Langston Hughes. CP-HughL

HEY / C'MON / COME OUT. Calling on All Silent Minorities. June Jordan. SP-JordJ

Hey! Hey! Langston Hughes. CP-HughL

Hey-Hey Blues. Langston Hughes. CP-HughL

Hey! Hey! / That's what the. Blues Fantasy. Langston Hughes. CP-HughL

Hey, little yellow boy. From a Bus. Malaika Ayo Wangara. NBP

Hey Mama, what's revolution? Bedtime Story. Nayo-Barbara Watkins. NBV

Hey! Mister Bloodhound Boss. False Leads. Yusef Komunyakaa. SP-KomuY

Hey ninny neigh! Shakespeare in Harlem. Langston Hughes. CP-HughL

Hey Shabaka. Song of Winnie. Gwendolyn Brooks. *Fr.* Winnie. ESEAA

Hey! That's the wrong goal post, traitor. Liberalissimo. Hart Leroi Bibbs. BlFi

Hey there poleece / Black skin in blue mask. Poem to a Nigger Cop. Bobb Hamilton. BlFi

Hi! Miss Liza's got er banjer. Miss Liza's Banjer. Daniel Webster Davis. AAP; EBAP

Hickory wood is the best of wood. *African-American Oral Tradition.* GetYo

Hid in a close and lowly nook. A City Garden. William Stanley Braithwaite. GT

Hidden by a minstrel-smile. (LL) Heritage. Gwendolyn B. Bennett. AmNP; BANP; BlSi; NAAAL; PoBA; ShDr

Hidden Essence. Henrietta Cordelia Ray. CBWP-3

Hidden in a forest of questions. Death Dance for a Poet. Audre Lorde. CP-LordA

High / above this desert. Sahara. Audre Lorde. CP-LordA; TtW

High and Haughty. Marilyn Nelson. SP-NelsM

High-cool/2. James Cunningham. JB

High in the darkening heavens. Harriet Tubman. Samuel Allen. Crnst; TtW

High Modes: Vision as Ritual: Confirmation. Michael S. Harper. NBV; SP-HarpM

High on the Hog. Julia Fields. TtW

High sheriff tol' de deputy, "Go out an' bring me Laz'us." Poor Lazarus. *Unknown.* NAAAL

High to Low. Langston Hughes. *Fr.* Montage of a Dream Deferred. CP-HughL

High-yellow lawyer woman, A. What You Mean I Can't Irony? Ishmael Reed. CP-ReedI

Highland Mary. Mary Weston Fordham. CBWP-2

Highway is full of big cars, The. Come, And Be My Baby. Maya Angelou. CP-AngeM; SP-AngeM

Hill Has Something to Say, The. Rita Dove. SP-DoveR

Hill of Beans, A. Rita Dove. SP-DoveR

Hills are wroth; the stones have scored you bitterly, The. To a Young Girl Leaving the Hill Country. Arna Bontemps. GT; Klds

Hills in emerald robes of richest dye, The. Among the Berkshire Hills. Henrietta Cordelia Ray. CBWP-3

Hills of Sewanee, The. George Marion McClellan. BANP

Hills of this tractor, The. Bear Gulch Road. Al Young. CP-YounA

Hint of gold where the moon will be, A. The Want of You. Angelina Weld Grimké. ShDr

Hip boots / Deep in the blues. Not Else—But. Langston Hughes. CP-HughL

Hip hitting riffs / split my brain on past. Jazzy St. Walk. Charlie R. Braxton. TtW

His All-Mind bids us keep this sacred place! (LL) Substitution. Anne Spencer. BlSi; CDC; ShDr

His Ancestry. George Clinton Rowe. AAP

His Answer. Clara Ann Thompson. BlSi; CBWP-2

His artificial feet calumped in holy rhythm. Deacon Morgan. Naomi Long Madgett. BlSi

His Boyhood. George Clinton Rowe. AAP

His brother after dinner. Uncle Bull-Boy. June Jordan. PoBA

His country seared its conscience through its gain. William Lloyd Garrison. Joseph Seamon Cotter, Sr. AAP

His desires, growing. Black Man's Feast. Sarah Webster Fabio. PoBA

His eldest son, Arradas' heir. His Boyhood. George Clinton Rowe. AAP

His Eminence Plays the Soular System. Eugene B. Redmond. TtW

His fingernails are black. Apprenticeship. Yusef Komunyakaa. SP-KomuY

His fingers leaned. Sun House. Haki R. Madhubuti. ESEAA

His Fingers Seem to Sing. Sam Cornish. GT

His friends went off and left Him dead. The Resurrection. Jonathan Henderson Brooks. AmNP; CDC; TtW

His headstone said. The Funeral of Martin Luther King, Jr. Nikki Giovanni. AmNP; BPo; SP-GiovN

His heart's upwelling of its own accord. Sermon in the Cotton Field. Marilyn Nelson. *Fr.* Thus Far by Faith. SP-NelsM

His Horn. Bob Kaufman. SP-KaufB

His Manhood. George Clinton Rowe. AAP

His mother whisper my son my son. (LL) How He Is Coming Then. Lucille Clifton. SP-ClifL

His Name. Frances Ellen Watkins Harper. CP-HarpF

His name is / Rubin. Rubin. Charles Cooper. PoBA

His photograph, yellowed by the years. Big John. Norman J. Loftis. SpiFl

His Prime. George Clinton Rowe. AAP

His Shirt. Rita Dove. SP-DoveR

His songs drop like plum. (LL) Haiku: "Piano man, The." Etheridge Knight. ESEAA; TtW

His sons—and / you / know it. (LL) Report to the Mother. Etheridge Knight. SP-KnigE

His soul curdled. John J. Maya Angelou. CP-AngeM; SP-AngeM

His Spirit in smoke ascended to high heaven. The Lynching. Claude McKay. BALP; BANP; CrDW; GT; IDB; PoBA; SP-McKaC

His tan and golden self. Known to Eve and Me. Maya Angelou. CP-AngeM

His voice soothes. Gains. Michael S. Harper. SP-HarpM

His voice used to sing. Sonia Sanchez. SP-SancS

His wet nose pushing at the screen. A Richland County Lyric for Elizabeth Asleep. June Jordan. SP-JordJ

His whole world revolves around light dark. Michael At Sixteen Months. Al Young. CP-YounA

His wife looked it up in her dream book / and played it. (LL) Hope. Langston Hughes. SP-HughL

His work was done; his blessing lay. The Death of Moses. Frances Ellen Watkins Harper. Fr. Moses: A Story of the Nile. AAP; CP-HarpF

Historiography. Lorenzo Thomas. TtW

History. Rita Dove. NAAAL

History. Langston Hughes. CP-HughL

History as Apple Tree. Michael S. Harper. SP-HarpM

History as Bandages: Polka Dots and Moonbeams. Michael S. Harper. SP-HarpM

History as Cap'n Brown. Michael S. Harper. SP-HarpM

History as Trash. Michélle T. Clinton. SpiFl

History / bless me with my children's growing rebellion. Relevant Is Different Points on the Circle. Audre Lorde. CP-LordA; SP-LordA

History Is Thunder and Rain. George Barlow. Fr. Gabriel. TtW

History of blackie is put down in the motions, The. The Sound of Afroamerican History Chapt I. S. E. Anderson. BlFi; PoBA

History on Wheels. Amiri Baraka. SP-BaraA

History-Wise #22. Amiri Baraka. SP-BaraA

History's long page. Prelude to Our Age. Langston Hughes. CP-HughL

Hit me! Jab me! Third Degree. Langston Hughes. BPo; CP-HughL; SP-HughL

Hitler, You Lied to Me. African-American Oral Tradition. GetYo

Hit's been drizzlin' an' been sprinklin'. Drizzle. Paul Laurence Dunbar. CP-DunbP

Ho. Al Young. CP-YounA

Hobo Ben. African-American Oral Tradition. GetYo

Hoboes' Convention. African-American Oral Tradition. GetYo

Hoboken Broken Down: A Hasty Recollection. Al Young. CP-YounA

Hog Meat. Daniel Webster Davis. BANP

Hokku: In the Falling Snow. Richard Wright. IDB Fr. Hokku Poems. AmNP; PoBA

Hokku Poems. Richard Wright. AmNP; PoBA
  Hokku: In the Falling Snow. IDB

Hold fast to dreams. Dreams. Langston Hughes. CP-HughL

Hold hard then, heart. This way at least you live. (LL) The Fist ("The Fist clenched round my heart"). Derek Walcott. ESEAA

Hold on sweet mama; Br'er Sterling's rocker glows. (LL) Br'er Sterling and the Rocker. Michael S. Harper. NAAAL; SP-HarpM

Holding the bandage ready for your eyes. (LL) And shall I prime my children, pray, to pray? Gwendolyn Brooks. Crnst; SP-BrooG

Holes in my arms. For Real. Jayne Cortez. PoBA

Holographs. Audre Lorde. CP-LordA

Holy ghost woman / stolen out of your name. Call. Audre Lorde. CP-LordA

Holy haloes. Lord, in My Heart. Maya Angelou. CP-AngeM; SP-AngeM

"Holy, holy, holy!" the choir chants sweet and low. An Opening Service. Clara Ann Thompson. CBWP-2

Holy Night. Lucille Clifton. SP-ClifL

Homage. Naomi Long Madgett. TtW

Homage to My Hair. Lucille Clifton. SP-ClifL

Homage to My Hips. Lucille Clifton. NAAAL; SP-ClifL

Homage to Paul Robeson. Robert Hayden. CP-HaydR

Homage to the Empress of the Blues. Robert Hayden. CP-HaydR; ESEAA; NAAAL; PoBA; TtW

Homage to the New World. Michael S. Harper. ESEAA; SP-HarpM

Home. Calvin Forbes. GT

Home. Audre Lorde. CP-LordA

Home agin, an' home to stay. Bein' Back Home. Paul Laurence Dunbar. CP-DunbP

Home Greeting, A. Priscilla Jane Thompson. CBWP-2

Home: January 29, 1984. June Jordan. SP-JordJ

Home Longings. Paul Laurence Dunbar. CP-DunbP

Home / oh / home. Africa. Lucille Clifton. SP-ClifL

Home Sweet Earth. Ishmael Reed. CP-ReedI

Home, Sweet Home. Frances Ellen Watkins Harper. CP-HarpF

Home Thoughts. Claude McKay. SP-McKaC

Home/the land the landless. Sanders Bottom. Sterling Plumpp. TtW

Homecoming. Mawiyah Kai El-Jamah Bomani. CtF

Homecoming. Langston Hughes. CP-HughL; SP-HughL

Homecoming. Sonia Sanchez. NAAAL; PoBA; SP-SancS

Homecoming Singer, The. Jay Wright. PoBA

Homeplace, The. Lenard D. Moore. GT

Homesick Blues. Langston Hughes. CDC; NAAAL

Homing. Arna Bontemps. CDC

Homing Swallows. Claude McKay. SP-McKaC

Homocide, for Ronald Gibson. Essex Hemphill. GT

Homophobia / racism / self-definition. Meta-Rhetoric. June Jordan. SP-JordJ

Honey babe, / You braid your hair too tight. Langston Hughes. CP-HughL

Honey Mah Love. Sterling A. Brown. CP-BrowS

Honey of Being. Jean Toomer. CP-ToomJ

Honey people murder mercy U.S.A. In Memoriam: Martin Luther King, Jr. June Jordan. NAAAL; PoBA

Honey, take yo' bressed time. (LL) Sister Lou. Sterling A. Brown. AmNP; BkSV; CP-BrowS; PoBA

Honey / When de man. Sister Lou. Sterling A. Brown. AmNP; BkSV; CP-BrowS; PoBA

Honeystain / the rhetoricians of blackness. The Anti-Semanticist. Everett Hoagland. BPo; NBV

"Honeysuckle Was the Saddest Odor of All, I Think." Thadious M. Davis. BlSi

Hoochie Coochie. Muddy Waters. NAAAL

Hoochie Route. Kalunda-rae. CtF

Hoodoo. DJ Renegade. CtF

Hoodoo Poem in Transient. Ishmael Reed. CP-ReedI

Hope. Paul Laurence Dunbar. CP-DunbP

Hope. Langston Hughes. SP-HughL Fr. Montage of a Dream Deferred. CP-HughL

Hope. Georgia Douglas Johnson. CDC

Hope: "Sometimes when I'm lonely." Langston Hughes. CP-HughL; SP-HughL

Hope. Clara Ann Thompson. CBWP-2

Hope. Mary E. Tucker. CBWP-1

Hope Deferred. Clara Ann Thompson. CBWP-2

Hope for Harlem. Langston Hughes. CP-HughL

Hope is a crushed stalk. Dark Testament. Pauli Murray. AmNP

Hope Thou in God. Josephine D. Henderson Heard. CBWP-4

Hope! Thou vain, delusive maiden. Josephine D. Henderson Heard. CBWP-4

Hophead Willie. African-American Oral Tradition. GetYo

Horatio Alger Uses Scag. Amiri Baraka. SP-BaraA

Horeb's mountain top of old. Mountain Tops. Lizelia Augusta Jenkins Moorer. CBWP-3

Horizon Blues. David Henderson. GT

Horn of Plenty. Langston Hughes. Fr. Ask Your Mama; 12 Moods for Jazz. CP-HughL

Horns protruded from the. The Rising. Jayne Cortez. NBV

Horoscope. Colleen J. McElroy. GT

Horse casts a shoe, The. Audre Lorde. CP-LordA

Horse-headed clouds. Fog Galleon. Yusef Komunyakaa. SP-KomuY

Horse Stolen from the Camp, The. George Moses Horton. SP-HortG

Horton, Smith, Rose, are the landmarks. At the Cemetery. Michael S. Harper. SP-HarpM

Hosannah! Christus natus est. (LL) Christus Natus Est. Countee Cullen. CP-CullC

Hosea. Margaret Abigail Walker. CP-WalkM

Hospital/Poem. Sonia Sanchez. BPo; PoBA

Host of loves is the city, and its memory, A. Tone Poem. Amiri Baraka. SP-BaraA

Hot Comb. Natasha Trethewey. SpiFl

Hot House. Al Young. CP-YounA

Hot the tears Del Cascar wept. (LL) Del Cascar, Del Cascar. William Stanley Braithwaite. BANP; CDC; TtW

Hotel Ameridemocratogrando. Black Man, 13th Floor. James A. Emanuel. NBV

Hour, the spot, are here at last, The. At Harper's Ferry Just before the Attack. Edward W. Williams. AAP

Hour's Glory, The. Henrietta Cordelia Ray. CBWP-3

House in Taos, A. Langston Hughes. CDC; SP-HughL
  ("Of our house in Taos.") (LL) CP-HughL; NAAAL

House in the World. Langston Hughes. CP-HughL

House of Desire, The. Sherley Anne Williams. BlSi

House of Falling Leaves, The. William Stanley Braithwaite. NAAAL

House of myth, The. Diverne's House. Marilyn Nelson. SP-NelsM

House of Prayer, The. Margaret Abigail Walker. CP-WalkM

House on Bishop Street, The. Rita Dove. SP-DoveR

House on Moscow Street, The. Marilyn Nelson. SP-NelsM

House Slave, The. Rita Dove. SP-DoveR

Housecleaning. Nikki Giovanni. BrTr; SP-GiovN

Household of Ruth, The. Mrs. Henry Linden. CBWP-4

Houston in October. Al Young. CP-YounA

How about It, Dixie. Langston Hughes. CP-HughL

How about that! (LL) To Satch. Samuel Allen. AmNP; IDB; Klds; PoBA; TtW

How Are the Mighty Fallen! Frances Ellen Watkins Harper. CP-HarpF

How beautiful you are. Seventh April. Al Young. CP-YounA

How beautiful you are, my love. A Canticle for Abba Jacob. Marilyn Nelson. SP-NelsM

How can I give thee up, my child, my dearest, earliest born. Wail of the Divorced. Mary E. Tucker. CBWP-1

How can I turn from Africa and live? (LL) A Far Cry from Africa. Derek Walcott. ESEAA

How can love heal. Safe Subjects. Yusef Komunyakaa. SP-KomuY

How can you. Dixie Man to Uncle Sam. Langston Hughes. CP-HughL

How can you comfort. Sonia Sanchez. SP-SancS

How can you forget me? Low to High. Langston Hughes. Fr. Montage of a Dream Deferred. CP-HughL

How can you stand there and. Ju-Ju Man. Art Nixon. CtF

How comest thou, O flower so fair. The Snowdrop. Mary Weston Fordham. CBWP-2

How dear comes beauty when a skin is black. (LL) McDonogh Day in New Orleans. Marcus B. Christian. AmNP

How did he die / O if I told you. The Gangster's Death. Ishmael Reed. PoBA

How did it happen that we quarreled? Words! Words! Jessie Redmond Fauset. CDC

How did you feel, Mary. Calvary Way. May Miller. TtW

How do poets write. A Poem Off Center. Nikki Giovanni. SP-GiovN

How do we embrace a blazing revolutionary spirit. The Fire in the Drum. Derrick I. M. Gilbert. CtF

How do we get to that promised motherland? Enneads, I, vi. Marilyn Nelson. Fr. The Plotinus Suite. SP-NelsM

How do you spell change brother like frayed slogan underwear. New York City 1970. Audre Lorde. NBV

How do you write a poem. Nikki Giovanni. SP-GiovN

How does it feel to be. Nude Woman Spotted in Cappuccino Cup as Advertising Dollar Co-Opts Another Life. Bahiyyih Maroon. SpiFl

How easily my heart falls back into habits. It's All in Your Head. Marilyn Nelson. SP-NelsM

How He Is Coming Then. Lucille Clifton. SP-ClifL

How High the Moon. Lance Jeffers. PoBA

How his red blood / decorates the snow. (LL) Separation. Audre Lorde. CP-LordA; SP-LordA

How I Can Lie to You. Maya Angelou. CP-AngeM; SP-AngeM

How I Discovered Poetry. Marilyn Nelson. SP-NelsM

How I Got Ovah. Carolyn M. Rodgers. TtW

How I love country you have heard. Lines. Samuel Alfred Beadle. AAP

How I miss my father. Poem at Thirty-nine. Alice Walker. CP-WalkA

How I See Things. Yusef Komunyakaa. ESEAA; SP-KomuY

How is the word made flesh made steel made shit. A Sewerplant Grows in Harlem or I'm a Stranger Here Myself When Does the Next Swan Leave. Audre Lorde. CP-LordA; SP-LordA

How it hurts / a whole country arrested. Still Life, Stealing Life / Caught Red-Handed. Kalamu ya Salaam. TtW

How Long Blues. Leroy Carr. NAAAL

How Long Has Trane Been Gone. Joe Corrie. NAAAL

How long, how long, has that evenin' train gone? How Long Blues. Leroy Carr. NAAAL

How long, O God! how long must I remain. The Negro's Lament. John Willis Menard. AAP

How long, oh gracious God! how long. James M. Whitfield. AAP; AfAmPo

How Lucy Backslid. Paul Laurence Dunbar. CP-DunbP

How many bullets does it take. Death in Yorkville. Langston Hughes. CP-HughL; PoBA

How many Indians? Poem for Derrick Gilbert. June Jordan. CtF

How many other dark young men at 33. Dear Joe. Audre Lorde. CP-LordA

How many scenes, O sun. Ode to the Sun. Eloise Bibb. CBWP-4

How many silent centuries sleep in my sultry veins? Margaret Abigail Walker. CP-WalkM

How many years since 1619 have I been singing Spirituals? Since 1619. Margaret Abigail Walker. CP-WalkM

How much living have you done? The Poet Speaks. Georgia Douglas Johnson. AmNP

How much love can I pour into you I said. Dream/Songs from the Moon of Beulah Land. Audre Lorde. CP-LordA

How much of me is sandwiches radio beer? Lonesome in the Country. Al Young. CP-YounA

How often must we. Reverses. Maya Angelou. CP-AngeM; SP-AngeM

How overwhelming / that Lester tune. Topsy: Part 2. Al Young. CP-YounA

How Poems Are Made: A Discredited View. Alice Walker. CP-WalkA

How quickly morphology. Old Light. Al Young. CP-YounA

How quiet and how still to-day old Bethel's corners 'round. The Day after Conference. Josephine D. Henderson Heard. CBWP-4

How quiet / It is in this sick room. Sick Room. Langston Hughes. CP-HughL

How sad it must be. A Poem for My Father. Sonia Sanchez. BPo; BrTr; SP-SancS

How say that by law we may torture and chase. She's Free! Frances Ellen Watkins Harper. BlSi

How shall I hold my spirit, that it not. Lovesong. Marilyn Nelson. SP-NelsM

How shall I woo thee to win thee, mine own? Paul Laurence Dunbar. CP-DunbP

How shall your name go down in history. To Youth. Josephine D. Henderson Heard. CBWP-4

How silently the years have sped away. To My Dead Brother. Clara Ann Thompson. CBWP-2

How slowly glide the hours by, the minutes hours seem. The Drunkard's Wife. Mary E. Tucker. CBWP-1

How Stars Start. Al Young. CP-YounA; ESEAA

How still, / How strangely still. Sea Calm. Langston Hughes. CP-HughL; SP-HughL

How strange that grass should sing. Quatrain 2. Gwendolyn B. Bennett. ShDr

How strangely blind is prejudice, the Negro's greatest foe! Prejudice. Lizelia Augusta Jenkins Moorer. CBWP-3

How sweet the music sounded. An Old Memory. Paul Laurence Dunbar. CP-DunbP

How the days went. Now That I Am Forever with Child. Audre Lorde. CP-LordA; IHS; NAAAL; PoBA; SP-LordA

How the fruit lay at your feet. Oshun's Table. Audre Lorde. CP-LordA

How the majestic stellar lights of Heav'n. Compensation. Henrietta Cordelia Ray. CBWP-3

How the Rainbow Works. Al Young. CP-YounA; ESEAA

How the young attempt and are broken. Generation. Audre Lorde. CP-LordA; NBV; SP-LordA

How Thin a Blanket. Langston Hughes. CP-HughL

How thin and sharp is the moon tonight! Winter Moon. Langston Hughes. CP-HughL; SP-HughL

How to burn up discreetly. (LL) Elegance in the extreme. Ntozake Shange. TtW

How to Change the U.S.A. Harry Edwards, arr. in verse by Walter Lowenfels. NBP

How to "cut the nut." (LL) On Seeing the Black Male as #1 Sex Object in America. Etheridge Knight. SP-KnigE

How to say No. (LL) The Thorn Merchant's Mistress. Yusef Komunyakaa. SP-KomuY

How we have strained at our dark works. Prayer (I): "How we have strained at our dark works." Jean Toomer. CP-ToomJ

How will it go, crumbling earthquake, towering inferno, juggernaut, volcano, smashup. New Reality Is Better Than a New Movie, A! Amiri Baraka. SP-BaraA

How Will You Call Me, Brother. Mari E. Evans. BlSi

"How'd I solve de Negro Problum?" Uncle Rube on the Race Problem. Clara Ann Thompson. CBWP-2

Howdy, Honey, Howdy! Paul Laurence Dunbar. CP-DunbP

However the image enters. Afterimages. Audre Lorde. CP-LordA; SP-LordA

How's a man to write a sonnet, can you tell. The Poet and the Baby. Paul Laurence Dunbar. CP-DunbP

Huge and beautifully black as he ever was / But dead. (LL) Best Loved of Africa. Margaret Else Danner. PoBA

Hugging the Shore. Mary E. Tucker. CBWP-1

Hugo I. Audre Lorde. CP-LordA

Huh!—For All?. (LL) Children's Rhymes. Langston Hughes. BPo

Huh uh! Chillun, let us pray! (LL) An Ante-Bellum Sermon. Paul Laurence Dunbar. AAP; BALP; BPo; CP-DunbP; NAAAL; TtW

Human face becoming locked insect face. Richard Hunt's "Arachne." Robert Hayden. CP-HaydR; FB

Human Family. Maya Angelou. CP-AngeM

Human Love is all electrical, a whirring. Jolt. Al Young. CP-YounA

Humming-Bird, The. Mary E. Tucker. CBWP-1

Humming like a hawk in motion. Poem for Omar Khayyam (1050?-1123? A.D.). Al Young. CP-YounA

Hunchback Girl: She Thinks of Heaven. Gwendolyn Brooks. *Fr.* A Street in Bronzeville. BlSi; BPo; Klds; SP-BrooG

Hunched, hump-backed, gigantic. Blues. Edward Kamau Brathwaite. GT

Hunger. Countee Cullen. CP-CullC

Hunger. Kathleen Tankersley Young. ShDr

Hungrier than I / thot. (LL) Dualism in Ralph Ellison's Invisible Man. Ishmael Reed. CP-ReedI; ESEAA; NAAAL; TtW

Hungry Black Child, The. Adam David Miller. NBV; PoBA

Hungry cancer will not let him rest, A. A Thorn Forever in the Breast. Countee Cullen. CP-CullC

Hungry child, / I didn't make this world for you. God to Hungry Child. Langston Hughes. CP-HughL

Hunters are back, The. Audre Lorde. *See* The Woman Thing.

Hunters are back / from beating the winter's face, The. The Woman Thing. Audre Lorde. BlSi; CP-LordA; SP-LordA

Hunters mount menacing as they go, The. Albery Allson Whitman. AfAmPo *Fr.* Not a Man, and Yet a Man.

(Saville in Trouble) AAP

Hunter's Point: Might. The Ballad of Charlie James. Ishmael Reed. CP-ReedI

Hunting Song. Paul Laurence Dunbar. CP-DunbP

Hurrah, Hurrah. Marilyn Nelson. SP-NelsM

Hurray! Hurry! / Come through the keyhole. Starvation. Maya Angelou. CP-AngeM; SP-AngeM

Hurt. Langston Hughes. CP-HughL

Hurt of It All, The. Sarah Webster Fabio. TtW

Hurt. / U worried abt a. To All Sisters. Sonia Sanchez. BlFi; PoBA

Hurt was the Nation with a mighty wound. Lincoln. Paul Laurence Dunbar. CP-DunbP

Husband's Return, The. Priscilla Jane Thompson. CBWP-2

Hush Honey. Ruby C. Saunders. BlSi

Hush is over all the teeming lists, A. Frederick Douglass. Paul Laurence Dunbar. BALP; CP-DunbP; PoBA

Hush little Lily. Chillen Get Shoes. Sterling A. Brown. CP-BrowS

Hush ye, hush ye! honey, darlin'. Lullaby. Clara Ann Thompson. CBWP-2

Hush! Yo' mouth. Hush Honey. Ruby C. Saunders. BlSi

Hushaby, hushaby, dark one at my knee. A Negro Mother's Lullaby. Countee Cullen. CP-CullC

Hushed by the Hands of Sleep. Angelina Weld Grimké. CDC

Hustlin' Dan. *African-American Oral Tradition.* GetYo

Hv merci on d po wrm who dares go it alone. Of Puddles, Worms, Slimy Things. Sarah Webster Fabio. TtW

Hydromel and Rue. George Marion McClellan. AAP

Hyeah come Cæesar Higgins. Jealous. Paul Laurence Dunbar. CP-DunbP

Hyeah dat singin' in de medders. When Sam'l Sings. Paul Laurence Dunbar. CP-DunbP

Hymn: "I well remember / A time when." Alice Walker. CP-WalkA

Hymn, A: "Lead gently, Lord, and slow." Paul Laurence Dunbar. CP-DunbP

Hymn: "Lord, within thy fold I be." Priscilla Jane Thompson. CBWP-2

Hymn: "O li'l lamb out in de col'." Paul Laurence Dunbar. CP-DunbP

Hymn: "When storms arise." Paul Laurence Dunbar. CP-DunbP

Hymn, a snare, and an exceeding sun. (LL) Boy Breaking Glass. Gwendolyn Brooks. ESEAA

Hymn for Lanie Poo. Amiri Baraka. SP-BaraA

"Each morning / I go down." ESEAA

Hymn for the Slain in Battle. William Stanley Braithwaite. BALP

Hymn to Humanity, An. Phillis Wheatley. CP-WheaP

Hymn to the Evening, An. Phillis Wheatley. AfAmPo; CP-WheaP

Hymn to the Morning, An. Phillis Wheatley. CP-WheaP

Hymn to the Nation. Albery Allson Whitman. EBAP

Hymn to the Thousand Islands. Henrietta Cordelia Ray. CBWP-3

Hymn Written after Jeremiah Preached to Me in a Dream. Owen Dodson. AmNP; Klds

Hypocrites shed tears. On Watching Politicians Perform at Martin Luther King's Funeral. Etheridge Knight. SP-KnigE

I

I ain't gonna mistreat ma. Evil Woman. Langston Hughes. CP-HughL

I ain't got long to stay here. (LL) Steal Away to Jesus. *Unknown.* BPo; BkSV; CrDW; Crnst; NAAAL

I ain't got nobody. Evolutionary Poem No. 1. Etheridge Knight. SP-KnigE

I ain't never been scared of hard work. Monologue. Margaret Abigail Walker. CP-WalkM

I ain't seen no poems stop a .38. Haki R. Madhubuti. *Fr.* Two Poems (from "Sketches from a Black-Nappy-Headed Poet"). BrTr

I ain't seen the light. Georgia—It's the Gospel Truth. Everett Hoagland. BrTr

I ain't superstitious. Superstitions. Maggie Pogue Johnson. CBWP-4

I almost remember. Maya Angelou. CP-AngeM; SP-AngeM

I always like summer. Knoxville, Tennessee. Nikki Giovanni. AmNP; BPo; BlSi; BrTr; PoBA; SP-GiovN

I always liked house cleaning. Housecleaning. Nikki Giovanni. BrTr; SP-GiovN

"I always think that when I see you you." Estimable Mable. Gwendolyn Brooks. FB

I always wanted to be a bridesmaid. Rituals. Nikki Giovanni. SP-GiovN

I am a black Pierrot. A Black Pierrot. Langston Hughes. CP-HughL; SP-HughL

I Am a Black Woman. Mari E. Evans. NAAAL; TtW

I am a Black woman. Jessehelms. Audre Lorde. CP-LordA

I am a Black Woman. My Truth and My Flame. Margaret Abigail Walker. CP-WalkM

I am a child of the valley. Delta. Margaret Abigail Walker. CP-WalkM

I Am a Cowboy in the Boat of Ra. Ishmael Reed. CP-ReedI; ESEAA; NAAAL; NBP; PoBA; TtW

I am a displaced person. My Heart Has Reopened to You. Alice Walker. CP-WalkA

I am a little orphan girl. An Orphan Girl. Mrs. Henry Linden. CBWP-4

I am a moody woman. Moody. Alice Walker. CP-WalkA

I am a Negro. Negro. Langston Hughes. CP-HughL; SP-HughL

I am a poor pilgrim of sorrow. City Called Heaven. *Unknown.* NAAAL

I am a reaper whose muscles set at sundown. All my oats are. Harvest Song. Jean Toomer. CP-ToomJ

I am a river. No More. Carl Clark. JB

I am a soul in the world: in. The Invention of Comics. Amiri Baraka. AmNP; GT; NAAAL; PoBA

I am a teller of tales. Africa. Nikki Giovanni. SP-GiovN

I am a wandering child. Women at the Crossroad / (May Elegba Forever Guard the Right Doors). Opal Palmer Adisa. GT

I am a woman controlled. The Scream. May Miller. TtW

I Am / are you / Ready? (LL) NOW. Audre Lorde. CP-LordA; SP-LordA

I Am as Happy as a Queen on Her Throne. Mrs. Henry Linden. CBWP-4

I am as old as sin. Ain't No Spring Chicken. Ahmos, II Zu-Bolton. TtW

I am astounded at their mouthful names. Building Nicole's Mama. Patricia Smith. SpiFl

I am at a retreat house, Still Point, not too far from Yaddo. From a Letter: About Snow. Toi Derricotte. SpiFl

I Am Becoming My Mother. Lorna Goodison. GT

I am black and I have seen black hands. I Have Seen Black Hands. Richard Wright. PoBA; TtW

I am bleed mouth nod. Lynch Fragment 2. Jayne Cortez. SP-CortJ

I am blind. Blind. Langston Hughes. CP-HughL

"I am but clay," the sinner plead. Distinction. Paul Laurence Dunbar. CP-DunbP

I am driven mad with the printed word. Am Driven Mad. Allen Polite. NNP

I am eating. Smash the Church. June Jordan. SP-JordJ

I am essence of Rose Solitude. Rose Solitude. Jayne Cortez. SP-CortJ; TtW

I Am Fashion's Toy. Mary E. Tucker. CBWP-1

I am for sleeping and forgetting. Requiescam. Countee Cullen. CP-CullC

I / am / forced. Jackie McLean: Alto Saxophone. Al Young. CP-YounA

I am fourteen / and my skin has betrayed me. Hanging Fire. Audre Lorde. CP-LordA

I am glad daylong for the gift of song. Rhapsody. William Stanley Braithwaite. AmNP; BALP; BANP; TtW

I am God— / Without one friend. God. Langston Hughes. CP-HughL

I am going blind. Perhaps. Lucille Clifton. SP-ClifL

I / am going to rise. Vive Noir! Mari E. Evans. PoBA

I am here again / pox marks have obscured my dimples. I Would Be a Painter Most of All. Len Chandler. NBP

I am here in / my usual place. Poem No. 4. Sonia Sanchez. SP-SancS

I am high on the man called crazy. Lucille Clifton. SP-ClifL

I am in a box. Boxes. Nikki Giovanni. SP-GiovN

I am in a quiet place. But There Are Miles. Harris Duriel. CtF

I am in mourning. Natural Star. Alice Walker. CP-WalkA

I Can Trust. Daniel Webster Davis. AAP; AfAmPo

I cannot hold my peace, John Keats. To John Keats, Poet, at Springtime. Countee Cullen. AfAmPo; BANP; CDC; CP-CullC; NAAAL

I cannot move / from your voice. Welton Smith. *Fr.* Malcolm. BlFi; BPo

I cannot recall you gentle. Black Mother Woman. Audre Lorde. CP-LordA; SP-LordA

I cannot sing, with loves I cannot speak. (LL) A September Night. George Marion McClellan. AAP; AfAmPo; EBAP

I Can't Get Started, *for Ira Hayes.* Ai. GT

I can't hear myself think in America no more! Spearo's Blues (or: Ode to a Grecian Yearn). Eugene B. Redmond. NBV

I can't help but think. Lost Wax. Yusef Komunyakaa. TtW

I can't just sit here. Today Is Not the Day. Audre Lorde. CP-LordA

I can't keep up with your love anymore. The Only Race There Is. Al Young. CP-YounA

I can't touch you. After Summer Fell Apart. Yusef Komunyakaa. SP-KomuY

I catch myself trying. Untitled Blues. Yusef Komunyakaa. ESEAA; GT; SP-KomuY

I catch the pattern. Silence. Langston Hughes. CP-HughL

I caught the American bull. Buffalo. Henry L. Dumas. PoBA

I celebrate the power in your eyes. Troy. Wendy L. James. CtF

I charge you, O chaste lasses! all beware. Albery Allson Whitman. *Fr.* Leelah Misled. EBAP

I choose not to walk among ghosts. Antigone VI. Herbert Martin. PoBA

I climb a red thread. Slight Alterations. Bob Kaufman. SP-KaufB

I cling to the funk. Funk. Mary Weems. SpiFl

I closed my book to listen. Church Bells. Clara Ann Thompson. CBWP-2

I come crying / dry leaves. Clinton. Sterling Plumpp. BkSV

I come down too hard on myself sometimes. That Picture in the Paper. Sekou Sundiata. *Fr.* Notes from the Defense of Colin Ferguson. SpiFl

I come quietly. Tree Stillness. Karen L. Mitchell. GT

I conclude that for. Report of the Reed Commission. Ishmael Reed. CP-ReedI

I could love her with a love so warm. The World Is a Mighty Ogre. Fenton Johnson. AmNP

I could not disappoint you and so prevailed. (LL) Encouraged. Paul Laurence Dunbar. CP-DunbP

I could not swallow the lake. (LL) Swallow the Lake. Clarence Major. ESEAA; GT; NAAAL; PoBA

I could recite the grass on a hill. Recitation. Saul Stacey Williams. CtF

I could remember more familiar sights. (LL) Iowa Farmer. Margaret Abigail Walker. CP-WalkM; GT; Klds

I could take the Harlem night. Juke Box Love Song. Langston Hughes. *Fr.* Montage of a Dream Deferred. CP-HughL

I could tell you. Impasse. Langston Hughes. CP-HughL

I couldnt ever tell you. Paris. Al Young. CP-YounA

I couldn't tell fact from fiction. Senses of Insecurity. Maya Angelou. CP-AngeM; SP-AngeM

I count black-lipped. Come Back Blues. Michael S. Harper. PoBA; SP-HarpM

I cradle my four-year-old daughter. Mississippi Winter III. Alice Walker. CP-WalkA

I crisscrossed with Monk. Jazz Fan Looks Back. Jayne Cortez. ESEAA

I danced on "Shop Around." Boppin' is Safer than Grindin'. Thulani Davis. GT

I Decide Not to Have Children. Marilyn Nelson. SP-NelsM

I did not fall from the sky. The Women of Dan Dance with Swords in Their Hands to Mark the Time When They Were Warriors. Audre Lorde. CP-LordA

I did not hear him. (LL) Monkeyman. Audre Lorde. CP-LordA; SP-LordA

I did not know that life could be so sweet. The Awakening. Paul Laurence Dunbar. CP-DunbP

I didn't know and nobody told me and what. Apologies to All the People in Lebanon. June Jordan. SP-JordJ

I Die for All Mysterious Things. Audre Lorde. CP-LordA

I do crazy things when. Memo #5. Etheridge Knight. SP-KnigE

I do my best to smile at spring, small flowers. White Days. Reginald Shepherd. GT

I do not ask for love, ah! no. Lethe. Georgia Douglas Johnson. CDC

I do not dare to reject the quarter moon. In Paris. June Jordan. SP-JordJ

I do not expect the spirit of Penelope. Love Poem, A: "I do not expect the spirit of Penelope." Etheridge Knight. BrTr

I do not hate you. The White Ones. Langston Hughes. CP-HughL

I do not know. (LL) Echoes. Audre Lorde. CP-LordA

I do not know if the color of the day. A Poem of Attrition. Etheridge Knight. GT; SP-KnigE; TtW

I do not know the power of my black hand. When I Know the Power of My Black Hand. Lance Jeffers. NBV; TtW

I do not like my uncle anymore. (LL) Merle; Uncle Seagram. Gwendolyn Brooks. ESEAA; TtW

I do not need to know. (LL) As I Grew Up Again. Audre Lorde. CP-LordA; SP-LordA

I do not sleep at night. Night-Piece. Raymond R. Patterson. PoBA

I do not want to stand. My Own Hallelujahs. Zack Gilbert. PoBA

I do not want to turn away. Two Poems, I. Robert J. Abrams. NNP

I do not wish to speak about the bulldozer and the. Moving Towards Home. June Jordan. SP-JordJ

I Done Got So Thirsty That My Mouth Waters at the Thought of Rain. Patricia Jones. BlSi

I done got 'uligion, honey, an' I's happy ez a king. Temptation. Paul Laurence Dunbar. CP-DunbP

I done shot dope, been to jail, swilled. Cop-Out Session. Etheridge Knight. SP-KnigE

I don't ask the Foreign Legion. On Working White Liberals. Maya Angelou. CP-AngeM; SP-AngeM

I don't ask to be forgiven. How Stars Start. Al Young. CP-YounA; ESEAA

I don't believe a single bit. John and Jacob—a Dialogue on Woman's Rights. Frances Ellen Watkins Harper. CP-HarpF

I don't believe in 'ristercrats. My Sort o' Man. Paul Laurence Dunbar. AmNP; CP-DunbP

I don't dare start thinking in the morning. Blues at Dawn. Langston Hughes. *Fr.* Montage of a Dream Deferred. CP-HughL; SP-HughL

I don't fatten frogs to feed snakes. (LL) Ballad from Childhood. Audre Lorde. CP-LordA; SP-LordA

I don't give a damn. Croon. Langston Hughes. *Fr.* Montage of a Dream Deferred. CP-HughL

I don't know about anything sometimes. Between Me and Anyone Who Can Understand. Sharon Scott. JB

I don't know but I was told. Poolshooting Monkey: "I don't know but I was told." *African-American Oral Tradition.* GetYo

I don't know, but my folks say. Titanic: "I don't know, but my folks say." *African-American Oral Tradition.* GetYo

I don't know how you died. The Singer. James Danner. BlFi

I don't know if I helped him up. The Transport or Slaves From Maryland to Mississippi. Rita Dove. SP-DoveR

I don't know what the final buzzer means. Triple Overtime. Lucinda Roy. GT

I don't know why. Puzzlement. Langston Hughes. CP-HughL

I don't know why but. On Moral Leadership as a Political Dilemma. June Jordan. SP-JordJ

I don't love you. Amiri Baraka. NAAAL

I don't mind dying. As Befits a Man. Langston Hughes. CP-HughL; SP-HughL

I don't need to be rich. Beverly's Poem. Audre Lorde. CP-LordA

I don't pretend to drink. A Welcome for Etheridge. James Cunningham. JB

I don't remember being very, very good or horrid. "C" ing in Colors: Red. Safiya Henderson-Holmes. SpiFl

I don't think it important. The Beast Section. Welton Smith. *Fr.* Malcolm. BlFi

I don't want a drought to feed on itself. Push Back the Catastrophes. Jayne Cortez. SP-CortJ

I don't want no woman that's gonna rob and steal. Sweet Lovin' Rose. *African-American Oral Tradition.* GetYo

I doubt not God is good, well-meaning, kind. Yet Do I Marvel. Countee Cullen. AfAmPo; AmNP; BANP; BPo; CDC; CP-CullC; CrDW; IDB; NAAAL; PoBA; SSLK

I draw hats on rabbits, sew women back. The Prestidigitator 2. Al Young. CP-YounA; NBV

I dream a world where man. Langston Hughes. AmNP; CP-HughL

I dream of a place between your breasts. Woman. Audre Lorde. CP-LordA

I dream of coupling. Dream of Pairing. Ntozake Shange. GT

I dream of Serenity. I'm a Dreamer. Kattie M. Cumbo. BlSi

I dream of the drums. Drums. Langston Hughes. CP-HughL

I Dream the Book of Jonah. Marilyn Nelson. SP-NelsM

    And Jonah Began to Stroke a Tentative Rhythm.

    I Fell Asleep on the Couch.

    I Woke Up and Wrote About It.

    Jonah Begins His Story.

    Now His Fingers Found the Melody.

    Now Jonah Began to Tune His Guitar.

    So Jonah Sang the Blues.

    Then Jonah Took Out His Guitar.

I dreamed a dream, and in my dream, I heard. The Snapping of the Bow. James David Corrothers. NAAAL

I dreamed all my fortitude screamed. Letter across Doubt and Distance. M. Carl Holman. AmNP

I dreamed / Mama came back. The Dream's Wisdom. Marilyn Nelson. SP-NelsM

I dreamed that the sky was tight and. Two Dreams (for M. L. K.'s one). Clarence Franklin. BlFi

I drip blood / on my way to and from work. Doing Battle with the Wolf. Wanda Coleman. TtW

I drive west from the old dump. The Drive In. Michael S. Harper. SP-HarpM

I dug you / off red and brown. To the "J F K" Quintet. Al Fraser. BlFi

I dun already seen. (LL) U Name This One. Carolyn M. Rodgers. BlSi; PoBA

I eat on all fours. Dead Oaks. Michael S. Harper. SP-HarpM

I entered my parlor one bright summer morn. The Humming-Bird. Mary E. Tucker. CBWP-1

I envy the sleep. All Things Insensible. Kathleen Tankersley Young. ShDr

I feel like a Zulu. Inaugural Day, 1981. Ishmael Reed. CP-ReedI

I feel like dancin', baby. Sunday by the Combination. Langston Hughes. Fr. Montage of a Dream Deferred. CP-HughL

I feel myself in need. George Moses Horton, Myself. George Moses Horton. AAP; AfAmPo; Klds; NAAAL; SP-HortG; TtW

I fell asleep, and had a dream. An Unromantic Awakening. Priscilla Jane Thompson. CBWP-2

I Fell Asleep on the Couch. Marilyn Nelson. Fr. I Dream the Book of Jonah. SP-NelsM

I first saw you in a trance. Erosong. Al Young. CP-YounA

I floated on a cloud one day. Cloud Fantasy. Henrietta Cordelia Ray. CBWP-3

I Followed a Path. Patricia Parker. BlSi

I forgot / to send a card to Jennie. Madam's Christmas (or Merry Christmas Everybody). Langston Hughes. CP-HughL

I forgotten who. Bumi. Amiri Baraka. PoBA

I found his wool face, I went away. Reading Walt Whitman. Calvin Forbes. ESEAA; NBV; PoBA

I found me a cranny of perpetual dusk. Idyll: "I found me a cranny of perpetual dusk." Sterling A. Brown. CP-BrowS

I found you and I lost you. A Golden Day. Paul Laurence Dunbar. CP-DunbP

I, from my chamber window, mark. Autumn Thoughts. Mary E. Tucker. CBWP-1

I from my window looked at early dawning. Bereft. Josephine D. Henderson Heard. CBWP-4

I gather up / each sound. Poem No. 3. Sonia Sanchez. SP-SancS

I gaze at you. The Tattooed Man. Robert Hayden. CP-HaydR

I gazed at Steppin Fetchit. Benin Bronze. Samuel Allen. Crnst

I get my degree. Lawd, Dese Colored Chillum. Ruby C. Saunders. BlSi

I go for voting clean. (LL) Aunt Chloe's Politics. Frances Ellen Watkins Harper. CP-HarpF; NAAAL

I go out to totem street. Knock on Wood. Henry L. Dumas. BlFi; PoBA

I go through my rooms. In the Evenings. Lucille Clifton. SP-ClifL

I go to the movies. Madam and the Movies. Langston Hughes. CP-HughL

I got a friend named Percy. Percy / 68. Glenn Myles. NBP

I got a home in dat Rock. Unknown. BPo; CrDW

I got a job down in Florida for Croft. African-American Oral Tradition. GetYo

I got a job now. Elevator Boy. Langston Hughes. CP-HughL; SP-HughL

I got a piece of a job on the waterfront. Me and My Work. Maya Angelou. CP-AngeM

I got high / last night. Sinner. Norman Jordan. BlFi

I got me a Ford since you seen me last. The Ford. African-American Oral Tradition. GetYo

I got me a question. Ruminations of Luke Johnson. Sterling A. Brown. CP-BrowS

I got the middle class blues. The Middle Class Blues. Ishmael Reed. CP-ReedI

I got those sad old weary blues. Too Blue. Langston Hughes. CP-HughL

I got to keep on dancing. Alvin Cash/Keep on Dancin'. David Henderson. GT

I got to leave this town. Lonesome Place. Langston Hughes. CP-HughL

I gots to be gon now; we ding potaht. Louisiana Pastoral. Sterling A. Brown. CP-BrowS

I grew a rose once more to please mine eyes. Fulfilment. Paul Laurence Dunbar. CP-DunbP

I grew a rose within a garden fair. Promise. Paul Laurence Dunbar. CP-DunbP

I guess DEMOCRACY'S meant to be. Song After Lynching. Langston Hughes. CP-HughL

I guess. this is what. Sonia Sanchez. SP-SancS

I had a dream. Nightmare Boogie. Langston Hughes. Fr. Montage of a Dream Deferred. CP-HughL

I had a dream, a varied dream. Fishers of Men. Frances Ellen Watkins Harper. CP-HarpF

I had a dream one winter's night. A Dream. Maggie Pogue Johnson. CBWP-4

I had a gal. Announcement. Langston Hughes. CP-HughL

I had a good teacher. Education. Don L. Lee. AmNP; BALP

I had all but one of the family pictures. The True Magic. Marilyn Nelson. Fr. The Plotinus Suite. SP-NelsM

I had an uncle once who kept a rock in his pocket. I've Got a Home in That Rock. Raymond R. Patterson. PoBA

I had become callous like most. On the Death of Lisa Lyman. Della Burt. BlSi

I had imagined you. Brown Girl Blues. Kysha N. Brown. CtF

I had ma clothes cleaned. Dressed Up. Langston Hughes. CP-HughL

I had no nation now but the imagination. Shabine Leaves the Republic. Derek Walcott. Fr. The Schooner Flight. ESEAA

I had no thought of violets of late. Sonnet. Alice Moore Dunbar-Nelson. BANP; BlSi; CDC; PoBA

I had not known before. Forever. Paul Laurence Dunbar. CP-DunbP

I had some cards printed. Madam's Calling Cards. Langston Hughes. CP-HughL; SP-HughL

I had thought of putting an / altar. Prayer. Isabella Maria Brown. NNP

I had to kick their law into their teeth in order to save them. "Negro" Hero. Gwendolyn Brooks. Klds; SP-BrooG

I had two husbands. Madam and Her Might-Have-Been. Langston Hughes. CP-HughL; SP-HughL

I hang on the edge. Sky Diving. Nikki Giovanni. SP-GiovN

I hardly remember my mother's face. Phillis. Naomi Long Madgett. TtW

I has always laked good eatin's. Sweeten 'Tatahs. James David Corrothers. EBAP

I has hyeahd o' people dancin' an' I's hyeahd o' people singin'. Paul Laurence Dunbar. CP-DunbP

I hate to die this way with the quiet. Cabaret Girl Dies on Welfare Island. Langston Hughes. CP-HughL

I hate to die this way with the quiet. Mazie Dies Alone in the City Hospital. Langston Hughes. CP-HughL

I hate to lose something. No Loser, No Weeper. Maya Angelou. CP-AngeM; SP-AngeM; TtW

I hate to see de evenin' sun go down. St. Louis Blues. Unknown. BkSV; Crnst

I hate to see de ev'nin' sun go down, longer vers. St. Louis Blues. William Christopher Handy. CrDW

I have a bottle and a pen. Thoughts from a Bottle. Carl Clark. JB

I have a child. A Child Shall Lead. Audre Lorde. CP-LordA

I have a daughter / mozambique. Bocas: A Daughter's Geography. Ntozake Shange. NAAAL

I have a delicious problem. Giant Red Woman. Clarence Major. GT

I have a dream of where (when I grow old. To France. Countee Cullen. CP-CullC

I have a friend. Gray. Alice Walker. CP-WalkA

I have a friend. My Friend. Samuel Allen. FB

I Have a Friend. Anne Spencer. CDC

I have a new home. a roaring Sparring Partner like a sunspot. The Newark Public Library Reading Room. Sotère Torregian. NBV

I have a rendezvous with Life. Life's Rendezvous. Countee Cullen. CDC; CP-CullC

I have all / my mother's habits. Mother's Habits. Nikki Giovanni. BlSi

I / Have Arrived. Status Symbol. Mari E. Evans. IDB; NAAAL

I have awakened from the unknowing to the knowing. For William Edward Burghardt Du Bois on His Eightieth Birthday. Bette Darcie Latimer. PoBA

I have been a seeker. Star Seeker. Langston Hughes. CP-HughL

I have been a / way so long. Homecoming. Sonia Sanchez. NAAAL; PoBA; SP-SancS

I have been seeking. Stokely Malcolm Me. Langston Hughes. CP-HughL

I have been waiting to speak to you. Eve (Rachel). Michael S. Harper. ESEAA; SP-HarpM

I have built my tower on the wings of a spider. My Tower. Nikki Giovanni. SP-GiovN

I have but four, the treasures of my soul. Slave Mother, The: "I have but four, the treasures of my soul." Frances Ellen Watkins Harper. CP-HarpF

I have come home. (LL) Pirouette. Audre Lorde. NNP; SP-LordA

I have come through the maze and the mystery of living. The Labyrinth of Life. Margaret Abigail Walker. CP-WalkM

I have come to you tonite out of the depths. Reflections After the June 12th March for Disarmament. Sonia Sanchez. ESEAA

I have considered / my reluctance. Poem: "I have considered / my reluctance." Nikki Giovanni. SP-GiovN

I have darker hair. Turk. Sam Cornish. BlFi

I have done so little. Poet to Bigot. Langston Hughes. CP-HughL

I Have Folded My Sorrows. Bob Kaufman. AmNP; PoBA

I have forgotten the head. The Bridge. Amiri Baraka. SP-BaraA

I have forgotten you as one forgets at dawning. Words. Helen Morgan Brooks. NNP

I have given my answer. (LL) Personal. Langston Hughes. AmNP; CP-HughL; SP-HughL

I have gone back in boyish wonderment. Return. Sterling A. Brown. BALP; CDC; CP-BrowS; Crnst

I have gone into my eyes. Depression. Sonia Sanchez. ESEAA

I have got old. Ca'line's Prayer. Lucille Clifton. SP-ClifL

I have heard your voice floating, royal and real. To Dinah Washington. Etheridge Knight. PoBA

I have just seen a most beautiful thing. The Black Finger. Angelina Weld Grimké. AmNP; PoBA; ShDr; TtW

I have known nights rain-washed and crystal-clear. Wisdom. Frank Yerby. AmNP

I have known what it is to love. Love. Darwin T. Turner. BALP

I have learned. Daniel. Lucille Clifton. SP-ClifL

I have learned not to worry about love. New Face. Alice Walker. CP-WalkA

I have learned this winter that, yes. 1971. Alice Walker. CP-WalkA

I have lived in circles of solitude. Consultation. Jayne Cortez. SP-CortJ

I have looked into. Sonia Sanchez. SP-SancS

I have no answer to the blank inequity. Mama's Promise. Marilyn Nelson. SP-NelsM

I have no fancy for that ancient cant. The Right to Die. Paul Laurence Dunbar. CP-DunbP

I have no right to ask you to live. For a Friend Who Considers Suicide. Gloria Wade-Gayles. IHS

I have not entered the raga. Dear Ravi Shankar. Al Young. CP-YounA

I have not ever seen my father's grave. Father Son and Holy Ghost. Audre Lorde. CP-LordA; ESEAA; NAAAL; PoBA; SP-LordA

I have not loved you in the noblest way. Sonnet. Countee Cullen. CP-CullC

I have pined for the sight of the sea for years. The Beautiful Sea. Mary E. Tucker. CBWP-1

I have sailed the south rivers of China and prayed to hillside Buddhas. In Search of Aunt Jemima. Crystal A. Williams. CtF

I have seen a hawk chase white pigeons. The Chase. Jean Toomer. CP-ToomJ

I have seen a lovely thing. Blight. Arna Bontemps. BANP; CDC

I Have Seen Black Hands. Richard Wright. PoBA; TtW

I have seen full many a sight. Dinah Kneading Dough. Paul Laurence Dunbar. CP-DunbP; NAAAL

I have seen lines on a paper. Borders. Michael S. Weaver. GT

I have seen peoples come and go. Old. Paul Laurence Dunbar. CP-DunbP

I have seen the robins. Memory. Mary Effie Lee Newsome. ShDr

I have seen the smallest minds of my generation. Problem in Social Geometry—the Inverted Square! Ray Durem. NBP; PoBA

I have seen them trying. Norman Jordan. NBV

I have sown beside all waters in my day. A Black Man Talks of Reaping. Arna Bontemps. AmNP; BANP; BPo; CDC; FB; IDB; Klds; NAAAL; PoBA; SSLK; TtW

I have spent my life. "Stephany." NBV

I have studied the tight curls on the back of your neck. Movement Song. Audre Lorde. CP-LordA; SP-LordA

I have taken / this self-appointed priest. The Appearance of a Lost Goddess. Jay Wright. Crnst

I have the greatest fun at night. The Quilt. Mary Effie Lee Newsome. CDC

I have this / Strange small memory. Small Memory. Langston Hughes. CP-HughL

I have traveled, I have traveled. The Consumptive. Priscilla Jane Thompson. CBWP-2

I have walked a long time. Sonia Sanchez. TtW

I have watched you dancing. Theme Brown Girl. Elton Hill-Abu Ishak. NBP

I have wrapped my dreams in a silken cloth. For a Poet. Countee Cullen. CP-CullC

I haven't done anything. Being and Nothingness. Nikki Giovanni. SP-GiovN

I haven't written a poem in so long. Habits. Nikki Giovanni. SP-GiovN

I hear a rumbling underground. Margaret Abigail Walker. CP-WalkM; TtW

I hear a whistling. Emmett Till. James A. Emanuel. PoBA

I hear folks talking. Speaking of Food. Langston Hughes. CP-HughL

I hear it in your breath. (LL) To a Freedom Fighter. Maya Angelou. CP-AngeM; SP-AngeM

I hear myself drought caught. Echo. Audre Lorde. CP-LordA; SP-LordA

I hear people waiting for the riot to begin in their hearts. Ray Charles at Mississippi State. Tom Dent. NBV

I hear the halting footsteps of a lass. Harlem Shadows. Claude McKay. BANP; NAAAL; SP-McKaC; TtW

I hear the man downstairs slapping the hell out of his stupid wife again. The .38. Ted Joans. NNP

I hear voices. i hear them often. I've heard them. Be Quiet, Go Away. Wanda Coleman. NAAAL

I hear you were. How I See Things. Yusef Komunyakaa. ESEAA; SP-KomuY

I heard a crying child in the other room. But Nobody Was There. Ishmael Reed. CP-ReedI

I Heard a Young Man Saying. Julia Fields. NNP

I heard my heart screeching like a subway train. Hard Love Rock. Audre Lorde. SP-LordA

I heard, my young friend. Report. Frances Ellen Watkins Harper. CP-HarpF

"I heeard da ole folks talkin' in our house da other night." Why Adam Sinned. Alex Rogers. BANP

I held my heart so far from harm. Kidnaped. Paul Laurence Dunbar. CP-DunbP

I hold my honey and I store my bread. My Dreams, My Works Must Wait Till after Hell. Gwendolyn Brooks. SP-BrooG; TtW

I hold not with the fatalist creed. Ultimatum. Countee Cullen. CP-CullC

I holler hallelujah. This Is It. Elma Stuckey. TtW

I honor you. Dancing Naked. Al Young. CP-YounA

I hope my child'll. Lament over Love. Langston Hughes. CP-HughL; NAAAL

I hope when I am dead that I shall lie. Oblivion. Jessie Redmond Fauset, fr. the French of Massillon Coicou. BANP

I hoped that you. Be with Me. Jean Toomer. CP-ToomJ

I hunt / the black puritan. Death Is Not as Natural as You Fags Seem to Think. Amiri Baraka. SP-BaraA

I imagine driving across country. Marilyn Nelson. SP-NelsM

I imagine her couplings and uncouplings. Foxfire. Dominique Parker. SpiFl

I implore Neptune to claim his child to-day! (LL) At the Carnival. Anne Spencer. BANP; BlSi; CDC; ShDr; TtW

I is the total black. Audre Lorde. See Coal.

I / Is the total black, being spoken. Audre Lorde. See Coal.

I joined them, whispering / yes. (LL) Mary's Dream. Lucille Clifton. SP-ClifL

I jump between the cat. Charmed. Yusef Komunyakaa. SP-KomuY

I Just Heard John Buffington Died. Kalamu ya Salaam. SpiFl

I keep him waiting, tuck in the curtains. Planning the Perfect Evening. Rita Dove. Fr. A Suite for Augustus. GT; SP-DoveR

I keep Life's rendezvous. (LL) I have a rendezvous with Life. Countee Cullen. CDC; CP-CullC

I keep on dying again. The Lesson. Maya Angelou. CP-AngeM; SP-AngeM

I keep thinking that there is. The Frightened Lover's Sleep. Jay Wright. BlFi

I killed you Malcolm. Confession to Malcolm. Conyus. NBV

I kissed a kiss in youth. Scintilla. William Stanley Braithwaite. AmNP; BANP; CDC; TtW

I kneel down like a. Sonia Sanchez. SP-SancS

I knew her self was not in that strange place. (LL) The Harlem Dancer. Claude McKay. AfAmPo; BALP; BANP; BPo; CrDW; SP-McKaC

I knew not who had wrought with skill so fine. Before a Painting. James Weldon Johnson. GT

I knew something was wrong. I. Slim's Song. Etheridge Knight. BkSV

I Knew That. Marilyn Nelson. SP-NelsM

I know a man. The Sand-Man. Paul Laurence Dunbar. CP-DunbP

I know de moonlight, I know de starlight. Unknown. BPo

I know her story-telling eye. The Eye of Love. George Moses Horton. BALP

I know I am / The Negro Problem. Dinner Guest: Me. Langston Hughes. BPo; CP-HughL; SSLK

I know i haven't grown. The Rose Bush. Nikki Giovanni. SP-GiovN

I Know I'm Not Sufficiently Obscure. Ray Durem. BPo; PoBA

I know it's an unfortunate way to say it, but. Nightline: September 20, 1982. June Jordan. SP-JordJ

I know moon-rise, I know star-rise. Unknown. CrDW; NAAAL

I know my love is true. Ballad. Paul Laurence Dunbar. CP-DunbP

I Know My Soul. Claude McKay. BPo; SP-McKaC

I know my upper arms will grow. The Life I Led. Nikki Giovanni. GT; SP-GiovN

I know not why, but it is true—it may. Edgar Allan Poe. Timothy Thomas Fortune. AAP

I know not why or whence he came. The Deserter. Joseph Seamon Cotter, Sr. CDC

I know now how a man whose blood is hot. Sonnet. Countee Cullen. CP-CullC

I know now / That Notre Dame is in Paris. I Thought It Was Tangiers I Wanted. Langston Hughes. CP-HughL; IHS

I know of a man who treated his body like a dog. Untitled: "I know of a man who treated his body like a dog." Ishmael Reed. CP-ReedI

I know salt marshes that move along like one big. Audacity of the Lower Gods. Yusef Komunyakaa. SP-KomuY

I know that his eyes look into mine. Assurance. Josephine D. Henderson Heard. CBWP-4

I know that I shall never see the rain. April in Coolwell. Sterling A. Brown. CP-BrowS

I know that it must be pleasant. Thine Eyes Shall See the King in His Beauty. Frances Ellen Watkins Harper. CP-HarpF

I know / the boundaries of my nation lie. Bicentennial Poem #21,000,000. Audre Lorde. CP-LordA

I know the incapacity of dream. Compassion's Bird. Jay Wright. ESEAA

I know the limitations of my body. The Realist. Carl H. Greene. NBV

I know the mighty power of my hand! (LL) When I Know the Power of My Black Hand. Lance Jeffers. TtW

I know these trees. Upper Marlboro. Kenneth Carroll. SpiFl

I know thou art a senseless thing. The Old Crib. Mary E. Tucker. CBWP-1

I know what the caged bird feels, alas! Sympathy. Paul Laurence Dunbar. AAP; AfAmPo; AmNP; CDC; CP-DunbP; CrDW; Crnst; GT; IDB; NAAAL; PoBA; SSLK; TtW

I know why the caged bird sings! (LL) Sympathy. Paul Laurence Dunbar. AAP; AfAmPo; AmNP; CDC; CP-DunbP; CrDW; Crnst; GT; IDB; NAAAL; PoBA; SSLK; TtW

I lafs und sings, und shumps aroundt. Lager Beer. Paul Laurence Dunbar. CP-DunbP

I laks yo' kin' of lovin'. Long Gone. Sterling A. Brown. BALP; BANP; BPo; CDC; NAAAL

I lay down in my grave. Elegy. Maya Angelou. SP-AngeM

I lay on the great shadow. Cloud. Jean Toomer. CP-ToomJ

I lay paralyzed. Suppression. Jayne Cortez. NBV

I lean back and feel. Sonia Sanchez. SP-SancS

I learned of your death over spiced tea. For Etheridge Knight. Jackie Warren-Moore. SpiFl

I learned the spoons from. The Musician Talks about "Process." Rita Dove. ESEAA

I learned to be honest. A Question of Climate. Audre Lorde. CP-LordA

I learned to shoot. Casting. Kevin Young. GT

I leave their fields. The Long Night Home. Charles F. Gordon. NBP

I leave to forgive me. (LL) I am running into a new year. Lucille Clifton. SP-ClifL

I leave you on that downtown street of. Roland Navarro (1939-1961). Al Young. CP-YounA

I lie down in my grave. Maya Angelou. *See* Elegy: "I lay down in my grave."

I like it here just fine. Girl Held without Bail. Margaret Abigail Walker. BPo; CP-WalkM; PoBA

I like love anonymous. Uhuru in the O.R. June Jordan. SP-JordJ

I like movies because. Why I Like Movies. Patricia Jones. BlSi

I like this quiet place. Interlude. Mae V. Cowdery. ShDr

I like to hear of wealth and gold. Common Things. Paul Laurence Dunbar. CP-DunbP; GT

I like to walk down Fisher Street. Fisher Street. Thylias Moss. GT

I likes a woman. Preference. Langston Hughes. *Fr.* Montage of a Dream Deferred. CP-HughL

I likes to take it real slow. (LL) The Reactionary Poet. Ishmael Reed. CP-ReedI; ESEAA; GT; TtW

I listen for the sounds of cannon, cries. On Lookout Mountain. Robert Hayden. CP-HaydR

I listen for yo. Sonia Sanchez. SP-SancS

I live alone, like pith in a tree. "Michelangelo" the Elder. Bob Kaufman. SP-KaufB

I live in a town. Family Jewels. Essex Hemphill. GT

I live in the mouth of history. Kalamu ya Salaam. SpiFl

I live on a park bench. Park Bench. Langston Hughes. CP-HughL

I live quietly and go nowhere. My Father's House. Calvin Forbes. ESEAA

I lived there too. (LL) Pachuta, Mississippi/a /Memoir A Memoir. Al Young. CP-YounA

I long for purple kisses. Merging. Niama Leslie JoAnn Williams. SpiFl

I long not now, a little while at least. Protest. Countee Cullen. CDC; CP-CullC

I long to spread my tiny wings. A Wreath of Holly. Joseph Cephas Holly. AAP

I look at life like. A Philosophical Perspective on Everyday Shit. Nadir Lasana Bomani. CtF

I look in the kettle, the kettle is dry. Supper Time. Langston Hughes. *Fr.* Seven Moments of Love. CP-HughL

I look out into the Yonder. Last Call. Langston Hughes. CP-HughL

I look with awe upon the human race. *Fr.* Two Somewhat Different Epigrams. CP-HughL; Klds

I looked and I saw. Who But the Lord? Langston Hughes. BPo; CP-HughL; SP-HughL

I Looked and Saw History Caught. Alfred B. Spellman. NBP

I looked at their black faces. Negro Ghetto. Langston Hughes. CP-HughL

I looked down 31st Street. Midnight Chippie's Lament. Langston Hughes. CP-HughL

I lose faith in my left hand. The Heart's Graveyard Shift. Yusef Komunyakaa. SP-KomuY

I lov'd thee from the earliest dawn. Early Affection. George Moses Horton. AAP; AfAmPo; SP-HortG

I love a man who is not worth / my love. Did This Happen to Your Mother? Did Your Sister Throw Up a Lot? Alice Walker. CP-WalkA

I love beautiful things. The Proletariat Speaks. Alice Moore Dunbar-Nelson. ShDr

I love black faces. Black Faces. Anita Scott Coleman. ShDr

I love Kentucky; tho' she merit scorn. Albery Allson Whitman. AAP *Fr.* "Thrice hail! proud land, whose genius boasts a clay!" AfAmPo *Fr.* Not a Man, and Yet a Man.

I love the dear old ballads best. Songs. Paul Laurence Dunbar. CP-DunbP

I love the hour before takeoff. Vacation. Rita Dove. SpiFl

I love the man whose lofty mind. Self-Reliance. James M. Whitfield. NAAAL

I love the quiet, hard. Eternity. Al Young. CP-YounA

I love the symphony of nature's chords. Albery Allson Whitman. *Fr.* Leelah Misled. EBAP

I love the way Janie Crawford. Janie Crawford. Alice Walker. CP-WalkA

I Love Thee. Josephine D. Henderson Heard. CBWP-4

I Love Those Little Booths at Benvenuti's. Gwendolyn Brooks. SP-BrooG

I love to see the big white moon. My Loves. Langston Hughes. CP-HughL

I love *you*. (LL) Dance of the Infidels. Al Young. CP-YounA; NBV; PoBA

I love you / because the Earth turns round the sun. Resignation. Nikki Giovanni. SP-GiovN

I love you for your brownness. To a Dark Girl. Gwendolyn B. Bennett. BANP; BlSi; CDC; NAAAL; PoBA; ShDr

I love you ginger bread mama. Ginger Bread Mama. Doughtry Long. BPo; PoBA

I love you / I need you. Dancing in the Laundromat [or] Dust: an Ordinary Song. Al Young. CP-YounA

I love your hands. Your Hands. Angelina Weld Grimké. CDC; PoBA

I loved my friend. Poem. Langston Hughes. CP-HughL

I Loved You Once. Aleksandr Sergeyevich Pushkin, *Russian.* AmNP, *tr. by* Dudley Randall

I make my children promises in wintry afternoons. Teacher. Audre Lorde. CP-LordA; SP-LordA

I marveled at the sight of you who without knowing. A Whole Two Weeks After the Million Man March; and Still, if You Asked Me about It, This Is All I Could Say about It. Richard Rykard. SpiFl

I mastered pastoral theology, the Greek of the Apostles, and all the difficult subjects in a minister's curriculum. The Minister. Fenton Johnson. Klds

I may be following you! (LL) Award. Ray Durem. BPo; IDB; NNP; PoBA

I mean / if I didn't know. Discovering. Sharon Scott. JB

I mean. / we bees real. We a BadddDDD PEOPLE. Sonia Sanchez. BrTr

I met a Lady Poet. Impeccable Conception. Maya Angelou. CP-AngeM; SP-AngeM

I met You on Your way to death. Encounter. Langston Hughes. CP-HughL

I might not have known his voice. Last Letter. Gerald William Barrax. ESEAA

I mind me how when first I looked at her. Medusa. Countee Cullen. CP-CullC

I mingle with the young and gay. I Smile, but Oh! My Heart Is Breaking. Mary E. Tucker. CBWP-1

I miss that red clay, Lawd, I. Red Clay Blues. Langston Hughes. CP-HughL

I miss that red clay, Lawd, I. Red Clay Blues. Richard Wright. TtW

I mix my men and booze. Sally: Twelfth Street. Naomi Long Madgett. NBV

I move on feeling and have learned to distrust those who don't. Poem of Angela Yvonne Davis. Nikki Giovanni. PoBA; SP-GiovN

I must be careful about such things as these. Sonnet. Ed Roberson. GT

I Must Become a Menace to My Enemies. June Jordan. NAAAL; TtW

I must love the questions. Reassurance. Alice Walker. CP-WalkA

I must not dare to sleep. (LL) Tinsel Marie; the Coora Flower. Gwendolyn Brooks. ESEAA

I must not gaze at them although. The Barrier. Claude McKay. BANP; SP-McKaC

I must remove you / from my life. (LL) Housecleaning. Nikki Giovanni. BrTr; SP-GiovN

I must say I never liked. Boy Wearing a Dead Man's Clothes. Yusef Komunyakaa. SP-KomuY

I must say / Yes, sir. Porter. Langston Hughes. CP-HughL; SP-HughL

I need a ritual to perform, / clean and sane, for this perfect washday. Domestic Tranquility. Gerald William Barrax. GT

I need kai kai ah. For the Poets. Jayne Cortez. SP-CortJ

I need me a house like that. Where the Heart Is. Ntozake Shange. GT

I need more than this crust of salt upon my eye. Vietnam: I Need More Than This Crust of Salt. Lance Jeffers. BrTr

I need to know / exactly. Don't Estimate! June Jordan. SP-JordJ

I never learned to spell it. / Not Failure. (LL) Call Letters: Mrs. V.B. Maya Angelou. CP-AngeM; SP-AngeM

I/ never liked/ white folks. Alice Walker. Fr. Once. BlSi; CP-WalkA; PoBA

I never seen such real hard times befo'. Hard Times Blues. Unknown. Crnst

I never shall furgit that night when father hitched up Dobbin. The Spellin'-Bee. Paul Laurence Dunbar. CP-DunbP

I never thought that I would live forever. Poem at the Midnight of My Life. June Jordan. SP-JordJ

I never was a slave—a robber took. Albery Allson Whitman. AfAmPo st. VII and VIII only; AAP Fr. Twasinta's Seminoles; Or Rape of Florida

I nodded at the sun. Friendly in a Friendly Way. Langston Hughes. CP-HughL

I note the obvious differences. Human Family. Maya Angelou. CP-AngeM

I offer my. She Insists on Me. Lucille Clifton. SP-ClifL

I once knew a man who had wild horses killed. Lucille Clifton. SP-ClifL; TtW

I once knowed an ole Sexion Boss but he done been laid low. The Old Section Boss. Unknown. BPo

I once pledged / my father's fraternity. Hazing. Brian G. Gilmore. CtF

I once read a poem. There's History in My Hair. Karen Williams. SpiFl

I only want to. My House. Nikki Giovanni. SP-GiovN

I opens ma mouth an' laughs. (LL) Homesick Blues. Langston Hughes. CDC; NAAAL

I owe him for pictures. Buck. Michael S. Harper. SP-HarpM

I owe you this picture. Total Incandescence. Al Young. CP-YounA

I paraplegic. Sonia Sanchez. SP-SancS

I park the car because I'm happy. Now. Christopher Gilbert. GT

I peer adown a shining group. Tribute. Eloise Bibb. CBWP-4

I pick up my life. One-Way Ticket. Langston Hughes. CP-HughL; SP-HughL

I place these numbed wrists to the pane. Nightmare Begins Responsibility. Michael S. Harper. ESEAA; GT; SP-HarpM

I play it cool. Motto. Langston Hughes. Fr. Montage of a Dream Deferred. CP-HughL

I playact three monkeys. Touch-up Man. Yusef Komunyakaa. SP-KomuY

I plucked my soul out of its secret place. I Know My Soul. Claude McKay. BPo; SP-McKaC

I ply with all the cunning of my art. The Craftsman. Marcus B. Christian. TtW

I poet. (LL) Sisters. Lucille Clifton. SP-ClifL

I pray to God another love you so. (LL) I Loved You Once. Aleksandr Sergeyevich Pushkin, Russian. AmNP, tr. by Dudley Randall

I proposed a Negro school in Hudson: 1828. Plans: 2. Michael S. Harper. SP-HarpM

I prove a theorem and the house expands. Geometry. Rita Dove. SP-DoveR; TtW

I put my nickel. Midnight Raffle. Langston Hughes. CP-HughL; SP-HughL

I ran, / from what, I didn't remember. The Whipping. Samuel F. Reynolds. SpiFl

I reach from pain. Reuben, Reuben. Michael S. Harper. SP-HarpM

I read in the papers about the / Freedom Train. Freedom Train. Langston Hughes. SP-HughL

I reckon they must have. Southern Negro Speaks. Langston Hughes. CP-HughL

I rememba / Rayboy blu/blk bug-eyed wid yo chocolate smile. Rayboy Blk and Bluz. Shirley Bradley LeFlore. SpiFl

I Remember ("I remember / January, / 1968"). Mae Jackson. PoBA

I remember 1983. Mendi Lewis. CtF

I remember bathing with you. Lovesong to My Father. Rohan B. Preston. CtF

I remember hiding in the hall closet. Light under the Door. Marilyn Nelson. SP-NelsM

I Remember How She Sang. Rob Penny. PoBA

I remember / January, / 1968. I Remember. Mae Jackson. PoBA

I remember learning you jump. Nikki Giovanni. SP-GiovN

I remember Memorial Day Massacre. On Police Brutality. Margaret Abigail Walker. CP-WalkM

I remember that time. That Was Then. Kupenda Auset. CtF

I remember the night. Somebody Call. Carolyn M. Rodgers. JB

I remember the time. A Little Girl's Dream World. Della Burt. BlSi

I remember Wednesday was the day. Two Lean Cats. Myron O'Higgins. PoBA

I remember, well remember. Aunt Chloe. Frances Ellen Watkins Harper. CP-HarpF

I resound in your wide halls. Clinton. Sterling Plumpp. BkSV

I rested in my mother's womb. Wild Pansies. Marilyn Nelson. SP-NelsM

I retrace your path in my bare feet. Letter from a Wife. S. Carolyn Reese. BrTr

I return the bitterness. Transformation. Lewis Alexander. CDC

I ride through Queens. An Invitation to Madison County. Jay Wright. ESEAA; PoBA

I rise at 2 a.m. these mornings. The Feral Pioneers. Ishmael Reed. CP-ReedI; PoBA

I rise / I rise / I rise. (LL) Still I Rise. Maya Angelou. BlSi; CP-AngeM; NAAAL; SP-AngeM

I rise up above my self. Good Friday. Lucille Clifton. SP-ClifL

I rode with Geronimo. Conyus. NBV

I run my fingers over a photo. Le Xuan, Beautiful Spring. Yusef Komunyakaa. SP-KomuY

I said, I believe. Madam and the Crime Wave. Langston Hughes. CP-HughL

I said: I cannot tell you. The Instant of Our Parting. Alice Walker. CP-WalkA

I said, in drunken pride of youth and you. Challenge. Sterling A. Brown. CDC; CP-BrowS

I said: / Now will the poets sing. Scottsboro, Too, Is Worth Its Song. Countee Cullen. CP-CullC; PoBA; TtW

I said to my baby. Same in Blues. Langston Hughes. SP-HughL; SSLK Fr. Lenox Avenue Mural. AmNP Fr. Montage of a Dream Deferred. CP-HughL

I said to Poetry: "I'm finished." Alice Walker. CP-WalkA

I sailed in my dreams to the Land of Night. Fantasy. Gwendolyn B. Bennett. BlSi; CDC; ShDr

I sat alone at my window. Retrospect. Josephine D. Henderson Heard. CBWP-4

I sat in the door of our cottage. An Autumn Day. Clara Ann Thompson. CBWP-2

I sat on my stool. Father. Ralph Dickey. ESEAA

I sat there singing her. Songs. Langston Hughes. CP-HughL

I sat with John Brown. That night moonlight framed. Narrative. Russell Atkins. GT; PoBA

I save your grace inside. Fire Keeper. Bahiyyih Maroon. SpiFl

I saw a dark boy. A Prayer. Mae V. Cowdery. ShDr

I saw a maiden, fairest of the fair. Charity. Henrietta Cordelia Ray. CBWP-3

I saw an old black man walk down the road. Black Soul of the Land. Lance Jeffers. BlFi; FB

I saw her in a cluttered basement store. The Note. Melvin B. Tolson. GT

I saw him there riddled. My Brother and Me. Clarence Reed. BlFi

I saw him yesterday. The Quarrel. Josephine D. Henderson Heard. CBWP-4

I saw myself leaving. Reflections. Carl Gardner. NNP; PoBA

I saw them lynch festus whiteside and. Carol Freeman. BlFi; PoBA

I saw / wet clothes hanging from a clothes line dripping with. Vision from the Ghetto. Raymond Washington. NBV

I saw you. Near Miss. "Nayo." BkSV

I saw you / on my walk last. Glimpse. Pearl Cleage Lomax. PoBA

I saw you today. Haiku: "I saw you today." Sonia Sanchez. SP-SancS

I saw your drumming lover. To a Daughter of Isaiah. Ishmael Reed. CP-ReedI

I saw / Your hands on my lips like blind needles. Pirouette. Audre Lorde. CP-LordA; NNP

I say things to myself. Phraseology. Jayne Cortez. BlSi

I says to my baby. Rent Day Blues. Sterling A. Brown. CP-BrowS

I see a tree. (LL) Mary. Lucille Clifton. SP-ClifL

I see a woman with wings. Freedom Seeker. Langston Hughes. CP-HughL

I see by the papers. Explain It, Please. Langston Hughes. CP-HughL

I see by the papers. Governor Fires Dean. Langston Hughes. CP-HughL

I see by the papers. The Mitchell Case. Langston Hughes. CP-HughL

I see by the papers. NAACP. Langston Hughes. CP-HughL

I See Chano Pozo. Jayne Cortez. SP-CortJ

I see hard times. Hard Times A' Coming. "Nayo." BkSV

I See Her Lovely There. Jean Toomer. CP-ToomJ

I see her yet, that dark-eyed one. A Memory. Adah Isaacs Menken. CBWP-1

I see it zooming down. New Orleans Intermissiom. Al Young. CP-YounA

"I see the good in others," answered she. (LL) Charity. Henrietta Cordelia Ray. CBWP-3

I see them coming up the road. A Happy Pair. Priscilla Jane Thompson. CBWP-2

I see them / Puerto Ricans. You're Nothing but a Spanish Colored Kid. Felipe Luciano. PoBA

I see You / Brown-skinned. Thank You, Lord. Maya Angelou. CP-AngeM; SP-AngeM

I see'd her in de springtime. She Hugged Me and Kissed Me. Unknown. BPo

I / seek / integration. The New Integrationist. Haki R. Madhubuti. BrTr

I seem to remember / Smiling. (LL) I almost remember. Maya Angelou. CP-AngeM; SP-AngeM

I seldom see / A kangaroo. Not Often. Langston Hughes. CP-HughL

I send a message, my worthy chief. A Message to a Loved One Dead. Josephine D. Henderson Heard. CBWP-4

I Send Mama Home. Marilyn Nelson. SP-NelsM

I send you down the road from Paden. I Send Mama Home. Marilyn Nelson. SP-NelsM

I set the bowl of raw vegetables on the table. Before You Leave. Ai. GT

I shall come this way again. Auf Wiedersehen. Donald Jeffrey Hayes. CDC

I shall ever call / you. (LL) Memorial III from a Phone Booth on Broadway. Audre Lorde. CP-LordA; SP-LordA

I shall go forth from here. Nostalgia. Marjorie Marshall. ShDr

I shall hate you. Hatred. Gwendolyn B. Bennett. AmNP; BANP; BlSi; CDC; NAAAL; PoBA; ShDr

I shall make a song like your hair. Secret. Gwendolyn B. Bennett. BlSi; CDC; ShDr

I shall not sing a May song. The Crazy Woman. Gwendolyn Brooks. SP-BrooG

I shall recall / As a sinister omen. Revelations. Sterling A. Brown. CP-BrowS; Klds

I shall return again. I shall return. Claude McKay. SP-McKaC

I shall save my poems. You Are There. Nikki Giovanni. SP-GiovN

I shall write of the old men I knew. In These Dissenting Times. Alice Walker. CP-WalkA; PoBA

I shelter a song for you / Secretly. (LL) Secret. Gwendolyn B. Bennett. BlSi; CDC; ShDr

I should have known if you gave me flowers. Then Came Flowers. Rita Dove. SP-DoveR

I should like to creep. A Mona Lisa. Angelina Weld Grimké. BlSi; CDC; ShDr; TtW

I should write a poem. The Beep Beep Poem. Nikki Giovanni. SP-GiovN

I Sigh a Marbled Sigh Ah, at Last. Bob Kaufman. SP-KaufB

I Sing No New Songs. Frank Marshall Davis. PoBA

I sing of a hero. Crispus Attacks McKoy. Sterling A. Brown. BPo; CP-BrowS

I sing of slum scabs on city. Today. Margaret Abigail Walker. CP-WalkM; FB

I sing you release. (LL) A Black Poet Leaps to His Death. Etheridge Knight. SP-KnigE

I sit a throne upon the times. Let's Majeste. Maya Angelou. CP-AngeM; SP-AngeM

I sit and sew—a useless task it seems. Alice Moore Dunbar-Nelson. BlSi; CDC; NAAAL; ShDr

I Sit and Wait for Beauty. Mae V. Cowdery. BlSi

I sit at my lathe. Lathe: Shirl's Tree. Michael S. Harper. SP-HarpM

I sit crotch high. Under the Oak Table. Colleen J. McElroy. GT

I sit for hours staring at my own right hand. January 10, 1973. Alice Walker. CP-WalkA

I sit in cubbyhole. Heartblow: Messages. Michael S. Harper. SP-HarpM

I sit in my room. Jean Toomer. CP-ToomJ; GT

I sit upon the old sea wall. On the Sea Wall. Paul Laurence Dunbar. CP-DunbP

I. Slim's Song. Etheridge Knight. BkSV

I Smile, but Oh! My Heart Is Breaking. Mary E. Tucker. CBWP-1

I smiling an ordinary smile. (LL) A Song of Mary. Lucille Clifton. SP-ClifL

I so admired you then. Ending. Alice Walker. CP-WalkA

I sometimes feel that life contains. We Know No More. Timothy Thomas Fortune. EBAP

I speak in the name of the black millions. A New Song. Langston Hughes. CP-HughL

I speak no polite. Turf Song. Sterling Plumpp. GT

I speak skimpily to. Personal Letter No. 2. Sonia Sanchez. SP-SancS

I speak to you as a friend speaks. Conversations in Crisis. Audre Lorde. CP-LordA; SP-LordA

I staggered in a place called the Bucket a Blood. Stackoloee: "I staggered in a place called the Bucket a Blood." African-American Oral Tradition. GetYo

I stand above the city's rush and din. From the Porch at Runnymede. Paul Laurence Dunbar. CP-DunbP

I stand already condemned. (LL) What my child learns of the sea. Audre Lorde. CP-LordA; GT; NBP; PoBA; SP-LordA

I stand beside the window here. The Old Story. Paul Laurence Dunbar. CP-DunbP

I stand in moonlight. The Borning Room. Michael S. Harper. SP-HarpM

I stand most humbly. Wisdom. Langston Hughes. CP-HughL

I stand to-day on this historic ground. The National Cemetery, Beaufort, South Carolina. Josephine D. Henderson Heard. CBWP-4

I stand up. (LL) Miss Rosie. Lucille Clifton. BlSi; ESEAA; PoBA; SP-ClifL

I start no / wars, raining poison. Son to Mother. Maya Angelou. CP-AngeM

I stepped from black to black. Black Power. Raymond R. Patterson. NBV

I stepped on the black winter seeds. Seeds. Thurmond Snyder. NNP

I still will trust. (LL) I Can Trust. Daniel Webster Davis. AAP; AfAmPo

I stomp about these rooms in an old overcoat. Sketch for an Aesthetic Project. Jay Wright. GT

I stood at 6 a.m. on the wharf. Someone's Blood. Rita Dove. SP-DoveR

I stood by the shore at the death of day. The Wind and the Sea. Paul Laurence Dunbar. CP-DunbP

I stood still and was a mushroom on the forest green. Poem (For BMC No. 1). Nikki Giovanni. BrTr; SP-GiovN

I suffer now from stress. Old Age. Margaret Abigail Walker. CP-WalkM

I suppose living. Luxury. Nikki Giovanni. SP-GiovN

I surprise girlhood. I Want Aretha to Set This to Music. Sherley Anne Williams. NAAAL

I swear I ain't done what Richard. Say Hello to John. Sherley Anne Williams. BlSi

I swear to the Lord. The Black Man Speaks. Langston Hughes. CP-HughL

I take it. (LL) Momma Welfare Roll. Maya Angelou. CP-AngeM

I take it back. Corrigenda. Yusef Komunyakaa. SP-KomuY

I take my dreams. Dreamer. Langston Hughes. CP-HughL

I take them with me to the fights. Martine's Keen Eyes. Ishmael Reed. CP-ReedI

I takes up for my colored men. The Generation Gap. Ruby C. Saunders. BlSi

I talk to rocks. Parting. Audre Lorde. CP-LordA

I talked to a farmer one day in Iowa. Iowa Farmer. Margaret Abigail Walker. CP-WalkM; GT; Klds

I talked to old Lem. Old Lem. Sterling A. Brown. BPo; CP-BrowS; FB; IDB; PoBA

I tarry in days shaped like the high staired street. A Birthday Memorial to Seventh Street. Audre Lorde. CP-LordA; SP-LordA

I tell you, Chickadee. S M. Alice Walker. CP-WalkA

I tell you how dat hypocrite do. That Hypocrite. Unknown. BPo

I Thank God I'm Free at Las'. Unknown. BPo; CrDW

I thank thee for thy pleading. To Mrs. Harriet Beecher Stowe. Frances Ellen Watkins Harper. CP-HarpF

I that had found the way so smooth. The Return. Jessie Redmond Fauset. CDC

I think an impulse stronger than my mind. Mood. Countee Cullen. CP-CullC

I think Archie Shepp played hambone hambone. Suite Repose. Carl Hancock Rux. SpiFl

I think at a distance I hear a loud voice. The Missionary. Mrs. Henry Linden. CBWP-4

I think hands must be very important. Hands; For Mother's Day. Nikki Giovanni. IHS; SP-GiovN

I think I see her sitting bowed and black. Oriflamme. Jessie Redmond Fauset. BANP; BlSi; PoBA; ShDr

I Think I See Him There. Waring Cuney. CDC

I think it must be lonely to be God. The Preacher: Ruminates Behind the Sermon. Gwendolyn Brooks. *Fr.* A Street in Bronzeville. BPo; BlSi; NAAAL; SP-BrooG

I think it will be Golgotha. (LL) Golgotha Is a Mountain. Arna Bontemps. NAAAL; TtW

I think my days are numbered. Numbered. Langston Hughes. CP-HughL

I think of a coffin's quiet. A Poem for a Poet. Audre Lorde. CP-LordA; SP-LordA

I think that man hath made no beauteous thing. To Melody. George Leonard Allen. CDC

I think that though the clouds be dark. After While. Paul Laurence Dunbar. CP-DunbP

I think there is in this the stuff for many lyrics. Harlem Happiness. Sterling A. Brown. CP-BrowS

I think when Judas' mother heard. Judas Iscariot. Countee Cullen. CP-CullC

I thirst, but earth cannot allay. Frances Ellen Watkins Harper. CP-HarpF

I thirst for / the Kool-Aid. Black Queen for More Than a Day. Al Young. CP-YounA

I thought I saw an angel flying low. Nocturne at Bethesda. Arna Bontemps. AmNP; BALP; BANP; CDC; NAAAL; TtW

I Thought It Was Tangiers I Wanted. Langston Hughes. CP-HughL; IHS

I, thy King, so say! (LL) Before the Feast of Shushan. Anne Spencer. BANP; BlSi; NAAAL; ShDr

I Told Jesus. Sterling Plumpp. PoBA

I told my brothers I heard. Songs for my Father. Yusef Komunyakaa. SP-KomuY

I, too am America. (LL) I too, sing America. Langston Hughes. AfAmPo; AmNP; CDC; CrDW; IDB; Klds; NAAAL; PoBA; SP-HughL; SSLK

I too am moved by passing winds. To a Weathercock. Raymond R. Patterson. TtW

I, Too, Know What I Am Not. Bob Kaufman. GT; NBP

I too / once lived / in the country. Pachuta, Mississippi/a /Memoir A Memoir. Al Young. CP-YounA

I too, sing America. Langston Hughes. AfAmPo; AmNP; CDC; CP-HughL; CrDW; IDB; Klds; NAAAL; PoBA; SP-HughL; SSLK

I too will unmask my dark / hard rock sand. (LL) Sahara. Audre Lorde. CP-LordA; TtW

I took orders, made my trail. Fever. Yusef Komunyakaa. SP-KomuY

I took up the burden of life anew. To My Mother. Mary Weston Fordham. CBWP-2

I tore down my thoughts. If My Enemy Is a Clown, a Natural Born Clown. Ishmael Reed. CP-ReedI

I tried to tell her. Offspring. Naomi Long Madgett. FB; GT

I tried to tell the doctor. Oh, I'm 10 Months Pregnant. Ntozake Shange. GT

I try to describe how this aching begins or how it began. Ghazal at Full Moon. June Jordan. SP-JordJ

I turn to my Rand McNally Atlas. Problems of Translation: Problems of Language. June Jordan. SP-JordJ

I turned aside and bowed my head and wept. (LL) The Tropics in New York. Claude McKay. AfAmPo; AmNP; CrDW; GT; Klds; PoBA; SP-McKaC

I understand. In the Restaurant. Gerald William Barrax. GT

I used to be a cowboy. *African-American Oral Tradition.* GetYo

I used to could diddle all night long. *African-American Oral Tradition.* GetYo

I used to dream militant. Revolutionary Dreams. Nikki Giovanni. SP-GiovN

I used to read the funny papers. On Youth and Age II. Margaret Abigail Walker. CP-WalkM

I used to sign my name with a flourish. No more. The Defense Rests. Sekou Sundiata. *Fr.* Notes from the Defense of Colin Ferguson. SpiFl

I used to wonder. Border Line. Langston Hughes. CP-HughL; SP-HughL

I usta wonder who i'd be. Adulthood. Nikki Giovanni. SP-GiovN

I violinize peace. Al Young. CP-YounA

I vision God standing. God. *Unknown.* NAAAL

I wait on your carved ugly stool. In the Interest of Personal Appearance. Clarence Major. TtW

I waited full two hours, or more. The Tryst. Mary E. Tucker. CBWP-1

I wake to the sound of a soft, low patter. Night Rain. Countee Cullen. CP-CullC; GT

I wake up / and hells around me. The Clown. D. L. Graham. BlFi

I wake up chasing my breath, my. Falso Brilhante. Nathaniel Mackey. NAAAL

I wake up dreaming I'm forty years in. Winged Abyss. Nathaniel Mackey. ESEAA

I wake up standing before a scene I stood. The Phantom Light of All Our Day. Nathaniel Mackey. GT

I walk across noon with you today. A Song of Names and Faces. Audre Lorde. CP-LordA

I walk down the aisles of my local video store. What Do I Want from Men and Love? Lisa B. Thompson. CtF

I walk on bones. Moses. Lucille Clifton. SP-ClifL

I walk out in the first. The Night of Frost. Michael S. Harper. SP-HarpM

I walked all over the zoo and the park. Stranger in Town. Langston Hughes. CP-HughL

I walked de streets till. Out of Work. Langston Hughes. CP-HughL

I wanna be somebody. Be Somebody Fragrant. Peter Harris. IHS

I Want Aretha to Set This to Music. Sherley Anne Williams. NAAAL

I want freedom / Just as you. (LL) Democracy will not come. Langston Hughes. Crnst; SP-HughL

I want it to be clear for us. On My Stand. Sharon Scott. JB

I want me a home. Black Woman Throws a Tantrum. Nayo-Barbara Watkins. NBV; TtW

I want my body bathed again by southern suns, my soul. Southern Song. Margaret Abigail Walker. CP-WalkM

I want to be / like that. Nikki Giovanni. *See* Poem for Flora.

I want to be remembered. Cover Photograph. Marilyn Nelson. SP-NelsM

I want to be with you. Telling. Alice Walker. CP-WalkA

I want to bust out. Bush Mama. Kalamu ya Salaam. TtW

I Want to Die While You Love Me. Georgia Douglas Johnson. AmNP; BANP; BlSi; CDC; Klds; NAAAL; ShDr; TtW

I want to make justice for the blackness / of Claude Reece Jr. (LL) Give Me the Red on the Black of the Bullet. Jayne Cortez. SP-CortJ

I want to scream into the pink hearing aid nestled. Finding His Fist. Saundra Sharp. SpiFl

I want to see my mother. Ride, Red, Ride. Langston Hughes. *Fr.* Ask Your Mama; 12 Moods for Jazz. CP-HughL

I want to see the slim palm-trees. Heritage. Gwendolyn B. Bennett. AmNP; BANP; BlSi; NAAAL; PoBA; ShDr

I want to sing. Nikki Giovanni. SP-GiovN

I want to take down with my hands. Want. Mae V. Cowdery. ShDr

I want to tell you 'bout that woman. Only Woman Blues. Langston Hughes. CP-HughL

I want to thank You. (LL) Thank You, Lord. Maya Angelou. CP-AngeM; SP-AngeM

I want to write. Margaret Abigail Walker. CP-WalkM

I want to write an image. A Very Simple Wish. Nikki Giovanni. SP-GiovN

I wanta say just gotta say something. Beautiful Black Men. Nikki Giovanni. BPo; BrTr; NAAAL; SP-GiovN

I wanted to be a nature poet. "Honeysuckle Was the Saddest Odor of All, I Think." Thadious M. Davis. BlSi

I wanted to know my mother when she sat. Leroy. Amiri Baraka. BPo; PoBA

I wanted to start the story. We Are Going to Be Here Now. Primus St. John. GT

I wanted to take. Just a New York Poem. Nikki Giovanni. SP-GiovN

I wanted to write / a poem. For Saundra. Nikki Giovanni. BPo; NAAAL; SP-GiovN

I was a boy then. Man. Langston Hughes. CP-HughL

I was a fool to dream that you. To a Young Wife. Georgia Douglas Johnson. ShDr

I was a harness horse. Death of an Old Carriage Horse. George Moses Horton. SP-HortG

I was a pretty baby. Amoebaean for Daddy. Maya Angelou. CP-AngeM; SP-AngeM

I was a red man one time. Lament for Dark Peoples. Langston Hughes. CP-HughL

"I Was a Stranger and Ye Took Me In." Mary E. Tucker. CBWP-1

I was born here. New Yorkers. Langston Hughes. *Fr.* Montage of a Dream Deferred. CP-HughL

I was born in a hotel. Lucille Clifton. SP-ClifL

I was born in Mississippi;. A Poem for Myself (Or Blues for a Mississippi Black Boy). Etheridge Knight. BkSV; SP-KnigE

I was born in the Congo. Ego Tripping. Nikki Giovanni. GT; SP-GiovN

I was born in the gut of Blackness. To the Poet Who Happens to Be Black and the Black Poet Who Happens to Be a Woman. Audre Lorde. CP-LordA

I was born with twelve fingers. Lucille Clifton. SP-ClifL

I was dealing short coin in the Golden West. Little Girl in the Gambler's Nest. *African-American Oral Tradition.* GetYo

I was ill, lying on my bed of old papers. The Secret Garden. Rita Dove. SP-DoveR

I was kissed once. The Kiss. Alice Walker. CP-WalkA; GT

I was lookin' for a sandwich, Judge. Brief Encounter. Langston Hughes. CP-HughL

I Was Looking at Miles. Honorée F. Jeffers. CtF

I Was Looking for the University. Clarence Major. GT

I was mindless. The Potter's Wheel. Calvin Forbes. GT

I was never the light lad. The Spawn of Slums. James W. Thompson. BPo

I was not; now I am—a few days hence. The Mystery. Paul Laurence Dunbar. CP-DunbP

I was of people. Wise 2. Amiri Baraka. SP-BaraA

I was offered roses. Temptation. Elma Stuckey. TtW

I was on my high. The Thorn Merchant's Mistress. Yusef Komunyakaa. SP-KomuY

I was parading the Côte d'Azur. My Father's Geography. Michael S. Weaver. GT

I was seated in a poolroom on one cold December day. Toledo Slim. *African-American Oral Tradition.* GetYo

I was servin' time in a Southern town. Feeble Old Man and a Kid Named Dan. *African-American Oral Tradition.* GetYo

I was setting on the hen-house steps. Crowing Hen Blues. Langston Hughes. CP-HughL

I was sick. Jesus Was Crucified or: It Must Be Deep. Carolyn M. Rodgers. BlSi; PoBA

I was sittin' in the jail to do a stretch of time. *African-American Oral Tradition.* GetYo

I was sleeping / on his breath. (LL) Lonely Eagles. Marilyn Nelson. ESEAA; SP-NelsM

I was so sick last night I. Morning After. Langston Hughes. CP-HughL; SP-HughL

I was spinning with Earth and a foul wind was blowing. Finger Pop'in. Charles Anderson. BlFi

I was trying to figure out. Communion. Langston Hughes. CP-HughL

I was twelve, and did not. Lesson on Braces. Valerie Jean. SpiFl

I watch the calligraphy of shadows. Philodendron. Helen Armstead Johnson. AmNP

I watched little black boys. Nayo-Barbara Watkins. NBV

I watched the dawn come. At the Spring Dawn. Angelina Weld Grimké. ShDr

I wear an easy garment. Free Labor. Frances Ellen Watkins Harper. CP-HarpF

I weep. It is not yet daylight. (LL) The House Slave. Rita Dove. SP-DoveR

I weep / Not as the young do noisily. Angelina Weld Grimké. CDC; ShDr

I well remember / A time when. Hymn. Alice Walker. CP-WalkA

I went back in the alley. Homecoming. Langston Hughes. CP-HughL; SP-HughL

I went down the road. Ballad of the Sinner. Langston Hughes. CP-HughL

I went down to Jordan. Singing Hallelujia. Fenton Johnson. NAAAL

I went down to malcolmland. Half Black, Half Blacker. Sterling Plumpp. PoBA; TtW

I went down to the corner. Lonesome Corner. Langston Hughes. CP-HughL

I went down to the river. Life Is Fine. Langston Hughes. CP-HughL; SP-HughL

I went into my mother as. To the Unborn and Waiting Children. Lucille Clifton. SP-ClifL

I went to a party. Here's to Adhering. Maya Angelou. CP-AngeM; SP-AngeM

I went to ch'ch, 'tother night. Sister Johnson's Speech. Maggie Pogue Johnson. CBWP-4

I went to Chicago. Poor Girl's Ruination. Langston Hughes. CP-HughL

I went to court last night. Puck Goes to Court. Fenton Johnson. CDC

I went to de gypsy. Fortune Teller Blues. Langston Hughes. CP-HughL

I went to look for Joy. Joy. Langston Hughes. CP-HughL; SP-HughL

I went to ma daddy. Hard Daddy. Langston Hughes. BANP; CP-HughL; NAAAL; SP-HughL

I went to San Francisco. Trip: San Francisco. Langston Hughes. CP-HughL

I went to the Gypsy's. Ballad of the Gypsy. Langston Hughes. CP-HughL; SP-HughL

I went to the valley. Lucille Clifton. SP-ClifL

I went walkin' / By the blue bayou. Blue Bayou. Langston Hughes. CP-HughL; SP-HughL

I who employ a poet's tongue. Timid Lover. Countee Cullen. BANP

I will be God when it comes to you. (LL) To Artina. Langston Hughes. CP-HughL; SP-HughL

I will be patient while my Lord. Cinderella. Ruby C. Saunders. BlSi

I will bring you big things. A Wooing. Langston Hughes. CP-HughL

I will build you a house. Tou Wan Speaks to Her Husband Liu Sheng. Rita Dove. ESEAA; SP-DoveR

I will have to forget. To Ms. Ann. Lucille Clifton. ESEAA; SP-ClifL

I will hide my soul and its mighty love. In the Heart of a Rose. George Marion McClellan. EBAP

I Will Look Up. Josephine D. Henderson Heard. CBWP-4

I will look with detachment. On Being Head of the English Department. Pinkie Gordon Lane. BlSi; GT

I will marry this clump of flowers. The Kadava Kumbis Devise a Way to Marry for Love. Rita Dove. SP-DoveR

I will never again. The Promise. Toi Derricotte. GT

I will no longer lightly walk behind. I Must Become a Menace to My Enemies. June Jordan. NAAAL; TtW

I will not deign to die. (LL) Refusal. Maya Angelou. CP-AngeM; SP-AngeM

I Will Not Let Them Take You. Opal Palmer Adisa. IHS

I will not reason, wrestle here with you. Tormented. Claude McKay. SP-McKaC

I will not toy with it nor bend an inch. The White City. Claude McKay. BPo; CrDW; SP-McKaC

I will outlive oppressors. (LL) Determination. John Henrik Clarke. PoBA

I will remember thee. (LL) Away to Canada. Joshua McCarter Simpson. AAP; AfAmPo

I will sing in the rising. The Song Poem. Lenard D. Moore. SpiFl

I will take your heart. To Artina. Langston Hughes. CP-HughL; SP-HughL

I will / touch stone. A Visit to Gettysburg. Lucille Clifton. SP-ClifL

I will track you down the years. Quest. Naomi Long Madgett. BPo

I wish de day was neah at han'. Goin' Home. Paul Laurence Dunbar. CP-DunbP

I wish I could be. Water of Your Bath. Ahmasi. IHS

I wish I could still stay. The Peacock Poems: 1. Sherley Anne Williams. NAAAL

I Wish I Was a Grown Up Man. Maggie Pogue Johnson. CBWP-4

I wish I'd never been born. (LL) Po' Boy Blues. Langston Hughes. CP-HughL; NAAAL

I wish it were mid. Sonia Sanchez. SP-SancS

I wish that I were dead. (LL) La Vie C'est la Vie. Jessie Redmond Fauset. BANP; CDC

I wish that whoever it is inside of me. Bob Kaufman. SP-KaufB

I wish the rent. Little Lyric (of Great Importance). Langston Hughes. CP-HughL; SP-HughL

I wish them cramps. Wishes for Sons. Lucille Clifton. NAAAL

I wish to own only the warmth. Thief. Alice Walker. CP-WalkA

I wish your body were in the grave. A Song of Sour Grapes. Countee Cullen. CP-CullC

I wist not that I had the pow'r to sing. A Question. Paul Laurence Dunbar. CP-DunbP

I Woke Up and Wrote About It. Marilyn Nelson. *Fr.* I Dream the Book of Jonah. SP-NelsM

I woke up this mornin'. Sylvester's Dying Bed. Langston Hughes. CP-HughL; SP-HughL

I woke up this morning with a hard on. *African-American Oral Tradition.* GetYo

I, Woman. Irma McClaurin. BlSi

I wonder. Q. R. Hand. BlFi

I wonder about / the brother. Come On Home. Sharon Scott. JB

I wonder could she have been thinking the same? (LL) Her Thought and His. Paul Laurence Dunbar. CP-DunbP; NAAAL

I wonder how it feels. Aspiration. Langston Hughes. CP-HughL

I wonder is there nowhere a / Do-right man? (LL) Early Evening Quarrel. Langston Hughes. SP-HughL

I wonder what become of my mama. If He Ask You Was I Laughing. Lucille Clifton. SP-ClifL

I wonder why. Tom Poole. NBP

I wondered at the huge blockade. Negro Improvement League. Sterling A. Brown. CP-BrowS

I won't look at her. Work. Yusef Komunyakaa. SP-KomuY

I Wonta Thank Ya. Tejumola Ologboni. NBV

I wore a baseball cap, so like my brothers. Sunny. Naomi Long Madgett. BrTr

I work all day. Pierrot. Langston Hughes. CP-HughL

I work up this mornin'. Langston Hughes. *See* Sylvester's Dying Bed.

I worked for a woman. Madam and Her Madam. Langston Hughes. BALP; CP-HughL; SP-HughL

I works all day. Workin' Man. Langston Hughes. CP-HughL

I Would Be a Painter Most of All. Len Chandler. NBP

I would be for you rain. Sarah Webster Fabio. TtW

I would be one with the morning. Desire. Marjorie Marshall. ShDr

I would be simple again. Disillusion. Langston Hughes. CP-HughL

I would be thine when morning breaks. Lines to My—. George Moses Horton. SP-HortG

I would be wandering in distant fields. In Bondage. Claude McKay. PoBA; SP-McKaC

I would give you. Poem . . . For a Lover. Mae V. Cowdery. ShDr

I would like to be a sinner. It Gives Me Pause. Langston Hughes. CP-HughL

I would like to be a white man, wouldn't you? Song of Adoration. Langston Hughes. CP-HughL

I would like / to make. Oh—Yeah! Sharon Scott. JB

I would like to scream but there is no one to hear. Setting / Slow Drag. Carolyn M. Rodgers. JB

I would liken you. Ardella. Langston Hughes. CP-HughL; SP-HughL

I would not tell them why I had smashed the window. "In This House, There Shall Be No Idols." Carolyn M. Rodgers. JB

I would risk ticks. Romance in Irony. June Jordan. SP-JordJ

I would take your money, too. (LL) Ballad of the Gypsy. Langston Hughes. CP-HughL; SP-HughL

I wouldn't coax the plant if I were you. Woman with Flower. Naomi Long Madgett. AmNP; FB; GT

I write my God in blue. Meta-A and the A of Absolutes. Jay Wright. ESEAA

I wrote a good omelet ... and ate a hot poem. Nikki Giovanni. SP-GiovN

I wrote stubbornly into the evening. Nexus. Rita Dove. SP-DoveR

I/ am going to rise. Vive Noir! Mari E. Evans. NBV

Ian. Al Young. CP-YounA

Icarus Dream. Marilyn Nelson. Fr. The Plotinus Suite. SP-NelsM

Ice Age. Ishmael Reed. CP-ReedI

Ice-cold passion / And a bitter breath. Poem to a Dead Soldier. Langston Hughes. CP-HughL

Ice-Fishing House, The. Michael S. Harper. SP-HarpM

Ice Storm. Robert Hayden. CP-HaydR; ESEAA

Ice tinkled in glasses. Blues and Bitterness. Lerone, Jr. Bennett. NNP; PoBA

Icicles upon the pane, The. February. Henrietta Cordelia Ray. CBWP-3

Icy evil that struck his father down, The. El-Hajj Malik El-Shabazz. Robert Hayden. BrTr; CP-HaydR; Crnst; ESEAA; NAAAL; PoBA

I'd scratch out both his eyes. (LL) Hard Daddy. Langston Hughes. BANP; CP-HughL; NAAAL; SP-HughL

Idea of Ancestry, The. Etheridge Knight. BALP; BPo; BrTr; ESEAA; GT; NAAAL; PoBA; SP-KnigE; TtW

Ideal, An. Henrietta Cordelia Ray. CBWP-3

Ideals are like the stars. Teacher. Langston Hughes. CP-HughL

Identities. Al Young. CP-YounA

Idiot, The. Dudley Randall. BPo

Idolatry. Arna Bontemps. AmNP

Idyl. Henrietta Cordelia Ray. CBWP-3; EBAP

Midnight.

Noontide.

Sunrise. BlSi;

Sunset. BlSi;

Idyl of Spring, An. Henrietta Cordelia Ray. CBWP-3

Idyll: "I found me a cranny of perpetual dusk." Sterling A. Brown. CP-BrowS

If a city / takes its rhythms. St. Louis Out of Time. Audre Lorde. SP-LordA

If Ah evah git to glory, an' Ah hop to mek it thoo. Black Mammies. John Wesley Holloway. BANP

If an eagle be imprisoned. America. Henry L. Dumas. PoBA

If an old board laid out in a field. Praising Dark Places. Yusef Komunyakaa. SP-KomuY

If Blood is Black Then Spirit Neglects My Unborn Son. Conrad Kent Rivers. BrTr; PoBA

If dead men died abruptly by a blow. Our Need. Margaret Abigail Walker. CP-WalkM

If Death should claim me for her own to-day. Love-Song. Paul Laurence Dunbar. CP-DunbP

If Dustin Hoffaman prove. Deliza Questioning Perplexities. June Jordan. SP-JordJ

If ever a garden was a Gethsemane. For Jim, Easter Eve. Anne Spencer. AmNP

If He Ask You Was I Laughing. Lucille Clifton. SP-ClifL

If he could solve the riddle. Sphinx. Robert Hayden. CP-HaydR; GT

If here and now be but a timely span. Here and Now. Catharine Cater. AmNP

If I bring back. For My Unborn and Wretched Children. Alfred B. Spellman. PoBA

If I call you son and not brother. For Craig. Audre Lorde. CP-LordA

If I can't do. Choices. Nikki Giovanni. SP-GiovN

If I cda known youd be real. For Ethelbert. June Jordan. SP-JordJ

If I could but forget. Paul Laurence Dunbar. CP-DunbP

If I Could Touch. William Stanley Braithwaite. BALP

If I ever hit for a dollar. Numbers. Langston Hughes. Fr. Montage of a Dream Deferred. CP-HughL

If I had a heart of gold. Vari-Colored Song. Langston Hughes. CP-HughL

If I had a nickel. .05. Ishmael Reed. CP-ReedI; ESEAA

If I had erased my life there. Mississippi Winter I. Alice Walker. CP-WalkA

If i had known, if. Haiku: "If i had known, if." Sonia Sanchez. SP-SancS

If I had some small change. If-ing. Langston Hughes. CP-HughL

If I have run my course and seek the pearls. The Marathon Runner. Fenton Johnson. CDC

If I just had a piano. Testimonial. Langston Hughes. Fr. Montage of a Dream Deferred. CP-HughL

If I lived in sight of the lake. A Matter of Locality. Paul Laurence Dunbar. CP-DunbP

If I love you! (LL) Madam and Her Madam. Langston Hughes. BALP; CP-HughL; SP-HughL

If I may borrow your ear, I promise you'll hear. The Voodoo Queen. African-American Oral Tradition. GetYo

If I must know sorrow. Mae V. Cowdery. ShDr

If I remember correctly. London. Maya Angelou. CP-AngeM

If I Ride This Train. Joe Johnson. PoBA

If I should sing. Long Song for Antonia. Langston Hughes. CP-HughL

If I speek good english. Changed Mind (or the Day I Woke Up). Tejumola Ologboni. NBV

If i stand in my window. Lucille Clifton. BPo; SP-ClifL

If i stretch my neck all the way. Goree. Harriet Jacobs. SpiFl

If I think myself. The Insidious Dr. Fu Man Chu. Amiri Baraka. SP-BaraA

If I was a sea-lion. Declaration. Langston Hughes. CP-HughL

If I was you. (LL) Bad Luck Card. Langston Hughes. CP-HughL; SP-HughL

If I were from Timbuktu, perhaps. Dark Mirror. Calvin Forbes. GT

If I were sitting. Midnight Song. Pinkie Gordon Lane. GT; TtW

If I Write a Poem. A. Van Jordan. SpiFl

If-ing. Langston Hughes. CP-HughL

If into Love the Image Burdens. Amiri Baraka. SP-BaraA

If it be shame to love a pretty woman. Albery Allson Whitman. AAP

If it was not slavery. Of the Cosmic-Blueprints. Sun-Ra. BlFi

If life were but a dream, my love. Paul Laurence Dunbar. CP-DunbP

If Loup Garou means change into. Loup Garou Means Change Into. Ishmael Reed. CP-ReedI

If mama / could see. Lucille Clifton. NAAAL; SP-ClifL

If Margie Polite. Ballad of Margie Polite. Langston Hughes. CP-HughL

If Mary came again. (LL) A Penitent Considers Another Coming of Mary. Gwendolyn Brooks. SP-BrooG

If Mary came would Mary. A Penitent Considers Another Coming of Mary. Gwendolyn Brooks. SP-BrooG

If music is the most universal language. Communication. Nikki Giovanni. SP-GiovN

If My Enemy Is a Clown, a Natural Born Clown. Ishmael Reed. CP-ReedI

If my garden oak spares one bare ledge. Creed. Anne Spencer. CDC; ShDr

If my love were meat and bread. Insatiate. Mae V. Cowdery. ShDr

If Nature says to you. The Daily Grind. Fenton Johnson. AmNP

If not a so-called Negro bought a bottle. Racist Psychotherapy. Isaac J. Black. NBV

If orange chiffon sadness. Orange Chiffon. Jayne Cortez. BlSi

If Randi Could Write. Elaine Brown. CtF

If she wore her dresses. Each Sunday. Nikki Giovanni. SP-GiovN

If Something Should Happen. Lucille Clifton. SP-ClifL

If St. Louis / took its rhythms. Audre Lorde. See St. Louis Out of Time.

If the Black Frog Will Not Ring. Ed Roberson. PoBA

If the blues would let me. Miss Blues'es Child. Langston Hughes. CP-HughL; SP-HughL

If the drum is a woman. Jayne Cortez. SP-CortJ; TtW

If the muse were mine to tempt it. The Colored Soldiers. Paul Laurence Dunbar. AAP; CP-DunbP; NAAAL

If the Stars Should Fall. Samuel Allen. IDB; NNP; PoBA

If there be sorrow. Mari E. Evans. Klds; NNP

If there was any justice. Alice Walker. CP-WalkA

If there were not, where would my neighbours go? (LL) Theology. Paul Laurence Dunbar. CP-DunbP

If there were seven blind men. XXII. Essex Hemphill. NAAAL

If they ever find their way / back home. (LL) A Trip on the Staten Island Ferry. Audre Lorde. CP-LordA; SP-LordA

If they put you in a jack-in-the-box poet. Toy Poem. Nikki Giovanni. BrTr

If this country is a bastard. Request. Maya Angelou. CP-AngeM; SP-AngeM

If this is peace, this dead and leaden thing. Dead Fires. Jessie Redmond Fauset. BANP

If this is showbiz, then am I. Ian. Al Young. CP-YounA

If this radio was good I'd get KDQ. Bed Time. Langston Hughes. *Fr.* Seven Moments of Love. CP-HughL

If "those people" like you. Alice Walker. CP-WalkA

If Thou Shouldst Return. Clara Ann Thompson. CBWP-2

If thro' the sea of night which here surrounds me. Anchored. Paul Laurence Dunbar. CP-DunbP

If today, I follow death. Mourning Grace. Maya Angelou. CP-AngeM; SP-AngeM

If trees could talk. Alabama Poem. Nikki Giovanni. BkSV; SP-GiovN

If 'twere fair to suppose. Suppose. Paul Laurence Dunbar. CP-DunbP

If we all knew where. The Rainbow. Opal Palmer Adisa. GT

If We Cannot Live People as People. Charles Lynch. PoBA

If we could know the mystery. Our Task. Henrietta Cordelia Ray. CBWP-3

If we don't listen. (LL) Malcolm Spoke / Who Listened? Haki R. Madhubuti. BrTr; ESEAA; NAAAL

If we hate the rush hour subways. One Year to Life on the Grand Central Shuttle. Audre Lorde. CP-LordA

If we must die—let it not be like hogs. Claude McKay. AmNP; BALP; BANP; BPo; CrDW; IDB; NAAAL; PoBA; SSLK

  ("If we must die, let it not be like hogs.") AfAmPo; Crnst; Klds; SP-McKaC; TtW

  ("Pressed to the wall, dying, but fighting back!") (LL) AfAmPo; Crnst; Klds; SP-McKaC; TtW

If within the cruel Southland you have chanced to take a ride. Jim Crow Cars. Lizelia Augusta Jenkins Moorer. CBWP-3

If you are a revolutionary. The Reactionary Poet. Ishmael Reed. CP-ReedI; ESEAA; GT; TtW

If you are Black and for me. To a Suitor. Maya Angelou. CP-AngeM; SP-AngeM

If you can't be free, be a mystery. (LL) Canary. Rita Dove. ESEAA

If you can't finance it undercover. Romance Without Finance. Al Young. CP-YounA

If you come as softly. Memorial I. Audre Lorde. CP-LordA; SP-LordA

If You Come Softly. Audre Lorde. AmNP

  ("If you come as softly.") CP-LordA

If you could sit with me beside the sea to-day. Longing. Paul Laurence Dunbar. CP-DunbP

If you ever find. Wise 1. Amiri Baraka. SP-BaraA

If you find a man who does not receive. Cry "Infidel!" Alfred Gibbs Campbell. AAP

If you have a word of cheer. Tell Her So. Mrs. Henry Linden. CBWP-4

If you plant grain. A Robin's Poem. Nikki Giovanni. AmNP; BrTr

If You Saw a Negro Lady. June Jordan. GT; SP-JordJ

If you see a cycle of heavy breezes. The Red Pepper Poet. Jayne Cortez. SP-CortJ

If You See My Little Girl in Denver, *see also* Lady Liberty. *African-American Oral Tradition.* GetYo

If You Should Go. Countee Cullen. CP-CullC

If you should see/ a man/ walking. The Truth. Ted Joans. AmNP; Klds

If you want to save some money. Mossy. Ishmael Reed. CP-ReedI

If You Would. Langston Hughes. *Fr.* Ask Your Mama; 12 Moods for Jazz. CP-HughL

If you would only stop to count your blessings. Count Your Blessings. Mrs. Henry Linden. CBWP-4

If you'll listen for a moment, I will tell you now, my friends. What We Teach at Claflin. Lizelia Augusta Jenkins Moorer. CBWP-3

If your reputation. Snob. Langston Hughes. CP-HughL

If you're great enough. Shame on You. Langston Hughes. *Fr.* Montage of a Dream Deferred. CP-HughL

If you're not home, where. Numbers, Letters. Amiri Baraka. BPo; SP-BaraA

If you've got the key. That Day. Nikki Giovanni. SP-GiovN

II. Song of the Reverend Gatemouth Moore. Etheridge Knight. BkSV

III. Healing Song. Etheridge Knight. BkSV

Ike. Rita Dove. SP-DoveR

Ikhnaton looked like. Why I Often Allude to Osiris. Ishmael Reed. CP-ReedI; GT

I'll be a lady forever. How Are the Mighty Fallen! Frances Ellen Watkins Harper. CP-HarpF

I'll be the first. A Dream of the Ring: the Great Jack Johnson. George Barlow. ESEAA

I'll build a house of arrogance. Haven. Donald Jeffrey Hayes. AmNP

I'll faint no more beneath the burden. Submission. Clara Ann Thompson. CBWP-2

I'll Follow Thee. Clara Ann Thompson. CBWP-2

I'll read your other palm. (LL) Madam and the Fortune Teller. Langston Hughes. CP-HughL; SP-HughL

I'll sign the / Paper. (LL) Third Degree. Langston Hughes. BPo; CP-HughL; SP-HughL

I'll sink my roots far down. Returning Spring. Pauli Murray. GT

I'll strike back. (LL) Lord, in My Heart. Maya Angelou. CP-AngeM; SP-AngeM

I'll think of thee, mine own, dear one. To a Loved One. Mary Weston Fordham. CBWP-2

I'll walk the tightrope that's been stretched for me. Margaret Else Danner. Klds

I'll Wear Me a Cotton Dress. *Unknown.* BPo

Ills I sorrow at, The. Any Human to Another. Countee Cullen. CP-CullC

Ills of all the human race, The. Misunderstood. Lizelia Augusta Jenkins Moorer. CBWP-3

Illusions. Kirk Hall. BlFi

Ilu, the Talking Drum. Etheridge Knight. SP-KnigE

I'm a bad, bad man. Bad Man. Langston Hughes. CP-HughL; NAAAL

I'm a bone roller. Addendum. Yusef Komunyakaa. SP-KomuY

I'm a cap'tilist, can you dig it? / (pow pow). (LL) Times-Square-Shoeshine-Composition. Maya Angelou. SP-AngeM; TtW

I'm a Dreamer. Kattie M. Cumbo. BlSi

I'm a Dreamer in Ready Stance. Dream Fix. Sonja Marie. CtF

I'm a hammer / you see some lame thing to do. Announcement. James T. Stewart. BlFi

I'm a happy *moile.* For an Intellectual Audience. Nikki Giovanni. SP-GiovN

I'm a river hip daddy mama dig a muddy hole. (LL) Mud Water Shango. "Weatherly." GT; NBV

I'm a-rollin', I'm a-rollin', I'm a-rollin', through an unfriendly world. *Unknown.* NAAAL

I'm A Worker. Jayne Cortez. NBV

I'm all alone in this world, she said. 50–50. Langston Hughes. CP-HughL; SP-HughL

I'm black / AND / beautiful. (LL) On Getting a Natural. Dudley Randall. FB; PoBA

I'm folding up my little dreams. My Little Dreams. Georgia Douglas Johnson. BANP; BlSi; CDC; NAAAL

I'm goin' to whoop you, Sammy Taylor. A Domestic Storm. Priscilla Jane Thompson. CBWP-2

I'm goin' where de shingles covers people mo' my kind. (LL) Tin Roof Blues. Sterling A. Brown. CP-BrowS; NAAAL

I'm goin' where de Southern crosses top de C. & O. Tin Roof Blues. Sterling A. Brown. NAAAL

I'm going out and get something. Riot Act, April 29, 1992. Ai. ESEAA

I'm going to be just like you, Ma. A Dance For Ma Rainey. Al Young. CP-YounA; NAAAL; NBP; NBV

I'm going where de Southern crosses top de C. and O. Sterling A. Brown. *See* Tin Roof Blues.

I'm gonna get me some mummy tape for your love. A Love Poem Written for Sterling Brown. Sonia Sanchez. SP-SancS

I'm gonna make a change, for once in my life. Man in the Mirror. Michael Jackson. Crnst

I'm gonna tell you a story about a hell of a bitch. Hustlin' Dan. *African-American Oral Tradition.* GetYo

I'm gonna wake up some mornin'. So Tired Blues. Langston Hughes. CP-HughL

I'm gonna walk to the graveyard. Young Gal's Blues. Langston Hughes. CP-HughL; SP-HughL

I'm in deep trouble. Moan. Langston Hughes. CP-HughL

I'm in the middle. Sonia Sanchez. SP-SancS

I'm Just a Stranger Here, Heaven Is My Home. Carole C. Gregory Clemmons. PoBA

I'm just going to school. (LL) Soul Make A Path Through Shouting. Cyrus Cassells. GT

I'm just happy to be being. New Moon Over Grove Street. Al Young. CP-YounA

I'm just Miss Blues'es child! (LL) Miss Blues'es Child. Langston Hughes. CP-HughL; SP-HughL

I'm Kentucky born. Kentucky Blues. Sterling A. Brown. CP-BrowS

I'm looking for a house. House in the World. Langston Hughes. CP-HughL

I'm looking out of the window. The Invention of a Garden. Jay Wright. GT

I'm *Madam* to you! (LL) Madam and the Census Man. Langston Hughes. CP-HughL; SP-HughL

I'm not lonely. Nikki Giovanni. BrTr; SP-GiovN

I'm on my way to Canada. Away to Canada. Joshua McCarter Simpson. AAP; AfAmPo

I'm out to find the new, the modern school. The Fledgling Bard and the Poetry Society. George Reginald Margetson. BANP

I'm raising CHILDREN. V. Kali Nurigan. CtF

I'm really very fond of you. Alice Walker. CP-WalkA

I'm running for the office of love. Ishmael Reed. CP-ReedI

I'm sitting by the hearthstone now. Twilight Musings. Mary Weston Fordham. CBWP-2

I'm sorry for you. Communiqué. Langston Hughes. CP-HughL

I'm sporting a floppy existential sky-blue hat. Woman, I Got the Blues. Yusef Komunyakaa. SP-KomuY

I'm stepping out on Your word. (LL) Just like Job. Maya Angelou. CP-AngeM; SP-AngeM

I'm still here! (LL) Still Here. Langston Hughes. BPo; CP-HughL; SP-HughL

I'm the best that ever done it. Times-Square-Shoeshine-Composition. Maya Angelou. CP-AngeM; SP-AngeM; TtW

I'm the one. Willie B (4). Lucille Clifton. SP-ClifL

I'm the warm-up act. The Dog Act. Yusef Komunyakaa. SP-KomuY

I'm tired of pacing the petty round of the ring of the thing I know. Wishes. Georgia Douglas Johnson. ShDr

I'm upward boun'. (LL) Northboun'. Lucy Ariel Williams Holloway. BANP; BlSi; CDC; ShDr

I'm waitin' for de springtime. Red Roses. Langston Hughes. CP-HughL

I'm waiting for ma mammy. Mammy. Langston Hughes. CP-HughL

I'm what has gone out blithely and with noise. A Man of the Middle Class. Gwendolyn Brooks. SP-BrooG

Image in the Mirror. Peggy Susberry Kenner. JB

Image of Myself 3. Ira B. Jones. IHS

Image Reach, The. Sun-Ra. BlFi

Images cast against the eternally shifting / heavens. (LL) Study Peace. Amiri Baraka. PoBA

Imagination in Flight: an Improvisational Duet. Harriet Jacobs. SpiFl

Imagine! / They are afraid of you. Langston Hughes. CP-HughL

Imitation Dance, The. Al Young. CP-YounA

Immani in Sunburst Summer: a Chant. Askia M. Toure. SpiFl

Immortality. Frank Horne. BANP

Immortality. Lizelia Augusta Jenkins Moorer. CBWP-3

Imogene. Eloise Bibb. CBWP-4

Impala. Marilyn Nelson. SP-NelsM

Impasse. Langston Hughes. CP-HughL

Impeccable Conception. Maya Angelou. CP-AngeM; SP-AngeM

Impeccable is possible, The. Selectric II. Al Young. CP-YounA

Imperial Thumbprint. Tom Weatherly. PoBA

Imploring Mecca. Be-Bop Boys. Langston Hughes. *Fr.* Montage of a Dream Deferred. CP-HughL

Imploring to Be Resigned at Death. George Moses Horton. AAP; AfAmPo; SP-HortG

Impressions. Kirk Hall. BlFi

Impressions / of Chicago; For Howlin' Wolf. Quincy Troupe. NAAAL; NBV

Imprint for Rio Grande. Jean Toomer. CP-ToomJ; TtW

Improvisation. Al Young. CP-YounA

In 1928 Langston Hughes published in the *Crisis* an anti-poem. About Poetry and South Africa. Samuel Allen. Crnst

In a back room. Resonance. George Barlow. ESEAA

In a Charleston, South Carolina gift store. 1994 Inventory. Toi Derricotte. SpiFl

In / a / cove. The Signs. Norman Henry, II Pritchard. NBV

In a dream / she is not allowed. A Meeting of Minds. Audre Lorde. CP-LordA

In a English Garden. Paul Laurence Dunbar. CP-DunbP

In a far far land where men are men. The Snow King. Rita Dove. SP-DoveR

In a far off hamlet near the sea. Uranne. Mary Weston Fordham. CBWP-2

In a few moments. The Death of a Negro Poet. Conrad Kent Rivers. BPo

In a Grave-Yard. William Stanley Braithwaite. PoBA

In a greatbig...night . . . big . . . night. (LL) Sylvester's Dying Bed. Langston Hughes. NAAAL; SP-HughL

In a Harlem Store Front Church. Clarence Reed. BlFi

In a homemade field / of love. (LL) 1977: Poem for Mrs. Fannie Lou Hamer. June Jordan. SP-JordJ

In a hotel in Tashkent. Political Relations. Audre Lorde. CP-LordA

In a land that's mine. (LL) Black Woman Throws a Tantrum. Nayo-Barbara Watkins. NBV; TtW

In a land whose novelty was speech. (LL) California Peninsula: El Camino Real. Al Young. CP-YounA; GT

In a lovely garden, filled with fair and blooming flowers. The Mission of the Flowers. Frances Ellen Watkins Harper. BlSi

In a morning coat, / hands locked behind your back. Benjamin Banneker Helps to Build a City. Jay Wright. Crnst

In a naked / Room. (LL) Desire to us. Langston Hughes. CP-HughL; SP-HughL

In a package of minutes there is this We. An Aspect of Love, Alive in the Ice and Fire. Gwendolyn Brooks. BPo

In a Period of Growth. Haki R. Madhubuti. TtW

In a press conference this afternoon the Secretary. Poem Towards a Final Solution. June Jordan. SP-JordJ

In a small and lonely cabin out of noisy traffic's way. The Voice of the Banjo. Paul Laurence Dunbar. CP-DunbP

In a spiral of lights. (LL) Banneker. Rita Dove. ESEAA; SP-DoveR

In a Stream of Ink. Jayne Cortez. SP-CortJ

In a time of secret wooing. Maya Angelou. CP-AngeM; SP-AngeM

In a tobacco trance. Life at the Back of the Plane. Al Young. CP-YounA

In a Troubled Key. Langston Hughes. CP-HughL

In a twinkling, the green. Al Young. CP-YounA

In a wooden barrel. (LL) Salt. Yusef Komunyakaa. SP-KomuY

In africa night walks. Night. Nikki Giovanni. SP-GiovN

In ages past ere wisdom's height. God Reigns. Paul Laurence Dunbar. CP-DunbP

In Alabama / Stars hang down so low. Stars in Alabama. Jessie Redmond Fauset. ShDr

In america. XXIV. Essex Hemphill. NAAAL

In an age of napalmed children. Atrocities. Nikki Giovanni. SP-GiovN

In an envelope marked. Personal. Langston Hughes. AmNP; CP-HughL; SP-HughL

In Answer to Your Silly Question. Alice Walker. CP-WalkA

In Arlesheim /the solstice smelled like hair pomade. A Question of *Essence.* Audre Lorde. CP-LordA

In Atlanta, Gee A. (LL) Slim in Atlanta. Sterling A. Brown. CP-BrowS

In audible dreams I'm forever going back. My Spanish Heart. Al Young. CP-YounA

In August. Paul Laurence Dunbar. CP-DunbP

In balmy / iconic / prague. The Smell of Lebanon. Alice Walker. CP-WalkA

In Barcelona city they dance the nights. Barcelona. Claude McKay. SP-McKaC

In berkeley whenever. My Thing abt Cats. Ishmael Reed. CP-ReedI

In Bethlehem on a Christmas night. On a Christmas Night. Langston Hughes. CP-HughL

In Bethlehem / On Christmas morn. Christus Natus Est. Countee Cullen. CP-CullC

In black core of night, it explodes. African Dream. Bob Kaufman. AmNP; GT; PoBA; SP-KaufB

In Bondage. Claude McKay. PoBA; SP-McKaC

In California / The day looks as though it's seen a ghost. Nov 22, 1988. Ishmael Reed. ESEAA

In calm fellowship they sleep. In a Grave-Yard. William Stanley Braithwaite. PoBA

In childhood's sunny day my heart was taught to love. To Whittier. Josephine D. Henderson Heard. AAP; CBWP-4

In college once I climbed the tree. Sickle Pears. Owen Dodson. AmNP

In Commemoration of the Centennial of the A.M.E. Church. Frances Ellen Watkins Harper. CP-HarpF

In cuba / a dark skin woman asks me. Spanish Conversation. E. Ethelbert Miller. TtW

In curve scooped out and necklaced with light. Bridge through My Windows. Audre Lorde. CP-LordA; SP-LordA

In days of old, when our fond mother earth. The Negro Meets to Pray. Daniel Webster Davis. AAP

In de dead of night I sometimes. The Old Cabin. Paul Laurence Dunbar. CP-DunbP

In dead of winter. Approximations. Robert Hayden. CP-HaydR

In death alone is what consoles; and life. Death to the Poor. Charles Baudelaire, *French*. CP-CullC, *tr. by* Countee Cullen

In Defense of Black Poets. Conrad Kent Rivers. BPo

In dese hard times. (LL) Negro Soldier's Civil War Chant. *Unknown*. BPo

In detention / in concentration camps. Intifada. June Jordan. NAAAL; SP-JordJ

In Emanuel's Nightmare: Another Coming of Christ. Gwendolyn Brooks. SP-BrooG

In every town and village. Where We Belong, A Duet. Maya Angelou. CP-AngeM; SP-AngeM

In ev'ry race, in ev'ry clime. Lines to a Graduate. Lizelia Augusta Jenkins Moorer. CBWP-3

In Explanation of Our Times. Langston Hughes. CP-HughL; SP-HughL

In far-off England, years ago. Destiny. Eloise Bibb. CBWP-4

In feeling I was but a child. One Year Ago. Adah Isaacs Menken. CBWP-1

In 15 minutes. California Peninsula: El Camino Real. Al Young. CP-YounA; GT

In fragrant Dixie's arms. Church Burning: Mississippi. James A. Emanuel. PoBA

In from the night. Answer Me. Adah Isaacs Menken. CBWP-1

In front of the bank building. The New Yorkers. Nikki Giovanni. SP-GiovN

In front of the City Hotel in Kumasi. A Rock Thrown into the Water Does Not Fear the Cold. Audre Lorde. CP-LordA

In front of their names. (LL) In Explanation of Our Times. Langston Hughes. CP-HughL; SP-HughL

In Germany the fabled Venusburg. The Venusburg. George Marion McClellan. *Fr.* The Legend of Tannhauser and Elizabeth. EBAP

In glassy, incandescent glory. The Indiana Gig. Al Young. CP-YounA

In gray, battle-scarred Leningrad. The Enemy. Alice Walker. CP-WalkA; GT

In great Berlin, each weary night on night. Go Down, Moses! Marcus B. Christian. TtW

In groves of green trees. Black Students. Julia Fields. NBP

In Harlem wandering from street to street. (LL) Harlem Shadows. Claude McKay. NAAAL; SP-McKaC; TtW

In hasty praise / of lemon / light. (LL) Lemons, Lemons. Al Young. CP-YounA

In Hayden's Collage. Michael S. Harper. ESEAA; NAAAL

In heavens eternal court it was decreed. On the Death of Mr. Snider Murder'd by Richardson. Phillis Wheatley. CP-WheaP

In his kitchen / STANDING TALL. Saturday Morning Pancakes. Paula White-Jackson. CtF

In his miraculously fixed. I Knew That. Marilyn Nelson. SP-NelsM

In homes all green, but cold in death. Our Martyred Soldiers. Paul Laurence Dunbar. CP-DunbP

In Honor of David Anderson Brooks, My Father. Gwendolyn Brooks. SP-BrooG

In idle August, while the sea soft. Adios, Carenage. Derek Walcott. *Fr.* The Schooner *Flight*. ESEAA

In jest, to hide a heart that bled. (LL) For Paul Laurence Dunbar. Countee Cullen. CDC; CP-CullC; SSLK

In Jimmy's Garden, *for James Baldwin (1924–1987)*. Quincy Troupe. GT

In joy, that our lives / are so familiar. (LL) Return of the Native. Amiri Baraka. BPo; SP-BaraA

In july of 19 somethin. With All Deliberate Speed. Don L. Lee. JB

In Kenscoff Market the breeze brought spices. Kenscoff. Lorna Goodison. GT

In Kyoto. And the windows of 5th street / scream. (LL) A Poem for Neutrals. Amiri Baraka. BPo; SP-BaraA

In life / one is always. Balances. Nikki Giovanni. SP-GiovN

In Life's Red Sea with faith I plant my feet. Mare Rubrum. Paul Laurence Dunbar. CP-DunbP

In line of what my folks say in Montgomery. Brotherly Love. Langston Hughes. CP-HughL

In Little Rock the people bear. The Chicago *Defender* Sends a Man to Little Rock. Gwendolyn Brooks. AmNP; CrDW; NAAAL; PoBA; SP-BrooG

In looking o'er the prospects. The Prospect of the Future. Mrs. Henry Linden. CBWP-4

In Los Angeles / while the mountains cleared of smog. Tongue-tied in Black and White. Michael S. Harper. SP-HarpM

In man's cannot be right. (LL) A Double Standard. Frances Ellen Watkins Harper. AAP; BlSi; CP-HarpF; CrDW; Crnst; EBAP; NAAAL

In Margaret's Garden. Audre Lorde. CP-LordA

In Marin Again. Al Young. CP-YounA

In math I was the whiz kid, keeper. Flash Cards. Rita Dove. ESEAA

In May. Paul Laurence Dunbar. CP-DunbP

In me there is a rage to defy. Rage. Alice Walker. CP-WalkA

In Memoriam. Alphonse Campbell Fordham. Mary Weston Fordham. AAP; CBWP-2

In Memoriam; for James Baldwin (1924–1987). Quincy Troupe. IHS

In Memoriam Frederick Douglass. Eloise Bibb. CBWP-4

In Memoriam Frederick Douglass. Henrietta Cordelia Ray. CBWP-3

In Memoriam: Martin Luther King, Jr. June Jordan. NAAAL; PoBA ("Honey people murder mercy U.S.A.") SP-JordJ

In Memoriam of E. B. Clark. Lizelia Augusta Jenkins Moorer. CBWP-3

In Memoriam Paul Laurence Dunbar. Henrietta Cordelia Ray. CBWP-3

In Memoriam. Susan Eugenia Bennett. Mary Weston Fordham. CBWP-2

In Memorium: Robert Hayden. Norman J. Loftis. SpiFl

In Memory of Arthur Clement Williams. Eloise Bibb. CBWP-4

In Memory of James M. Rathel. Josephine D. Henderson Heard. CBWP-4

In Memory of Radio. Amiri Baraka. NAAAL; SP-BaraA

In Memphis—in Tennessee. On the Birth of a Black / Baby / Boy. Etheridge Knight. SP-KnigE

In Mem'ry's fairest court a shrine is set. To Laura. Henrietta Cordelia Ray. CBWP-3

In Miami / the blood suckers came sucking in full speed. Blood Suckers. Jayne Cortez. SP-CortJ

In Mississippi / balloons of hunger. No New Music. Stanley Crouch. PoBA

In my bein' dead. (LL) Wake. Langston Hughes. CP-HughL; SP-HughL

In my dry cell. The Riven Quarry. Gloria C. Oden. GT; PoBA

In My Father's House. George Barlow. ESEAA

In My Grandmother's Living Room. Karen Williams. SpiFl

In my mind's eye. Julius E. Thompson. TtW

In my Missouri. Maya Angelou. CP-AngeM

In My Mother's Room, *(for Vanessa)*. Colleen J. McElroy. GT

In my own season / at last. (LL) Turning into my own. Lucille Clifton. SP-ClifL

In my street. Dancing Day to Day. Al Young. CP-YounA

In my younger years. Dreams. Nikki Giovanni. PoBA; SP-GiovN

In / New York / my mother opens. My Father's Girlfriend. E. Ethelbert Miller. SpiFl

In 1915 my grandfather's. Grandfather. Michael S. Harper. ESEAA; NAAAL; SP-HarpM

In nineteen thirty-two when the times was hard. Nineteen Thirty-Two. *African-American Oral Tradition*. GetYo

In One Battle. Amiri Baraka. BPo

In one hand / I hold the tragedy. The Jester. Langston Hughes. CP-HughL

In Orangeburg My Brothers Did. Alfred B. Spellman. BPo; PoBA

In order to blow what it's like being born. (LL) Lester Leaps In. Al Young. CP-YounA; ESEAA

In order to go on living. (LL) Equinox. Audre Lorde. CP-LordA; SP-LordA

In other destinies of choice. Timepiece. Audre Lorde. CP-LordA

In our beginning our Blackness was not thought so beautiful. The African Village. Margaret Abigail Walker. CP-WalkM

In our community everything was kept quiet. A Kiss in the Dark. Thomas Sayers Ellis. GT

In our infancy of action we were women of peace. Timing. Audre Lorde. CP-LordA

In Paris. June Jordan. SP-JordJ

In perfect printed breath. Leaving Rochester. Al Young. CP-YounA

In places like / Selma, Alabama. From Selma. Langston Hughes. CP-HughL

In populated air. Lucille Clifton. SP-ClifL

In raging fires of Love. (LL) Walking Parker Home. Bob Kaufman. NAAAL; SP-KaufB

"In Rama," here was truly heard "a voice." Albery Allson Whitman. *Fr.* Leelah Misled. EBAP

In Retrospect. Maya Angelou. CP-AngeM; SP-AngeM

In rev'rent love we guard thy memory. Henrietta Cordelia Ray. *See* Robert G. Shaw.

In Salem. Lucille Clifton. ESEAA; SP-ClifL

In san francisco they are. Dress Rehearsal Paranoia #2. Ishmael Reed. CP-ReedI

In sandblows once green. Ntarama (Rwanda) Chronicles. Karen Williams. SpiFl

In scarecrow patches and tatters, face. The Rag Man. Robert Hayden. CP-HaydR

In Search of Aunt Jemima. Crystal A. Williams. CtF

In ships all over the world. The English. Langston Hughes. CP-HughL

In solitude. Without a hand to hold. (LL) The Preacher: Ruminates Behind the Sermon. Gwendolyn Brooks. NAAAL

In some pilgrmiage. Crow Jane's Manner. Amiri Baraka. SP-BaraA

In southern springs we dug for artichokes. Artichoke Pickle Passion: Sonnet. Beverly Fields Burnette. CtF

In Spite of Death. Countee Cullen. CP-CullC

In spite of her raw terror. And his whip. (LL) Chosen. Marilyn Nelson. SP-NelsM

In stained barn drenched. Paysagesque. Norman Henry, II Pritchard. GT

In stony / Lonesome / Ground! (LL) Stony Lonesome. Langston Hughes. CP-HughL; SP-HughL

In such an armor he may rise and raid. Bronzeville Man with a Belt in the Back. Gwendolyn Brooks. IDB; PoBA; SP-BrooG

In Summer. Paul Laurence Dunbar. CP-DunbP

In Summer Time. Paul Laurence Dunbar. CP-DunbP

In sun or cold the weather picks scarecrow bones clean. The Long Blues. Calvin C. Hernton. GT

In sun-whetted / morning. Gulls. Robert Hayden. CP-HaydR

In suspicious silence. (LL) Gods in Vietnam. Eugene B. Redmond. NBP; PoBA

In Texas Grass. Quincy Troupe. GT; NAAAL; PoBA

In that gathering / that water. (LL) October 23, 1983. June Jordan. SP-JordJ

In that same beginning winter. Poem for Buddy. June Jordan. SP-JordJ

In the afternoon sun. Beams. Audre Lorde. CP-LordA; ESEAA

In the antique forest dreary. Rhyme of the Antique Forest. Henrietta Cordelia Ray. CBWP-3

In the August grass. Haiku: "In the August grass." Etheridge Knight. ESEAA; TtW

In the Background of Silence. Yusef Komunyakaa. SP-KomuY

In the basement of the opera house. Nuns in the Basement of God. T'Kalla. CtF

In the beginning, God, the great schoolmaster. The Autograph on the Soul. Adah Isaacs Menken. CBWP-1

In the beginning, in the wet. War Memoir: Jazz, Don't Listen to It at Your Own Risk. Bob Kaufman. NAAAL; SP-KaufB

In the beginning was the word. The Great Pax Whitie. Nikki Giovanni. SP-GiovN

In the beginning / was the word. Testament. Lucille Clifton. SP-ClifL

In the branches of your nerves. Green Is a Feeling, Not a Color. Al Young. CP-YounA

In the Bulrush. Rita Dove. SP-DoveR

In the center of a harsh and spectrumed city. Outside. Audre Lorde. CP-LordA

In the center of the bloodvein. My Uncle is My Honor and a Guest in My House. Etheridge Knight. SP-KnigE

In the city of St. Francis they have taken down the statue of St. Francis. Afterwards, They Shall Dance. Bob Kaufman. SP-KaufB

In the city, under the saw-toothed leaves of an oak. Straw Hat. Rita Dove. SP-DoveR

In the clearing stands. Missionaries in the Jungle. Linda Piper. BlSi

In the clutter and clatter of the Bronx. Providence Journal V: Israel of Puerto Rico. Michael S. Weaver. SpiFl

In the cold spring night. Smelt Fishing. Robert Hayden. CP-HaydR

In the dark. Night Song. Langston Hughes. CP-HughL

In the dark corners of buildings. White Powder! Victor Hernandez Cruz. BlFi

In the dark they fell a-crying. Irish Wake. Langston Hughes. CP-HughL

In the days of the broken cubes of Picasso. Cubes. Langston Hughes. CP-HughL

In the dead hour of night. The Silent Night. Mrs. Henry Linden. CBWP-4

In the december of my springs. The December of My Springs. Nikki Giovanni. GT; SP-GiovN

In the dream, I am burning the rice. Offering. Sharan Strange. GT

In the dream I became 2 men my age. (1980). C. S. Giscombe. GT

In the dream I enter the house. Bone-Flower Elegy. Robert Hayden. CP-HaydR

In the early days of my visitation. The Visitation. Sun-Ra. BlFi

In the earnest path of duty. Poem. Charlotte Forten. BlSi

In the east the morning comes. Dirge for a Soldier. Paul Laurence Dunbar. CP-DunbP

In the end Abba Jacob gave up. Abba Jacob and the Angel. Marilyn Nelson. SP-NelsM

In the era of raining boys, a steady downpour. La Peste. Marilyn Nelson. SP-NelsM

In the Evenings. Lucille Clifton. SP-ClifL

In the face of / What we remember. (LL) Puzzled. Langston Hughes. CP-HughL; SP-HughL

In the falling snow. Hokku: In the Falling Snow. Richard Wright. Fr. Hokku Poems. AmNP; IDB; PoBA

In the forenoon's restful quiet. When the Old Man Smokes. Paul Laurence Dunbar. CP-DunbP

In the furrows of the world. Nation. Charlie Cobb. PoBA

In the gutter. Up-Beat. Langston Hughes. Fr. Montage of a Dream Deferred. CP-HughL; SP-HughL

In the hall of the Hofbräuhaus. At the German Writers Conference in Munich. Rita Dove. SP-DoveR

In the Heart of a Rose. George Marion McClellan. EBAP

In the heartbeat / of the talking drum. (LL) Back Then. Yusef Komunyakaa. GT; SP-KomuY

In the heavy earth the miner. The Gourd. Paul Laurence Dunbar. CP-DunbP

In the House Blues. Bessie Smith. NAAAL

In the House of the Aylors. Albery Allson Whitman. AAP Fr. Not a Man, and Yet a Man

In the / in the quarter. Cultural Exchange. Langston Hughes. Fr. Ask Your Mama; 12 Moods for Jazz. CP-HughL

In the Inner City. Lucille Clifton. SP-ClifL; TtW

In the Interest of Black Salvation. Haki R. Madhubuti. BrTr

In the Interest of Personal Appearance. Clarence Major. TtW

In the Johannesburg mines. Johannesburg Mines. Langston Hughes. CP-HughL

In the Keyfood Market on Broadway. Keyfoods. Audre Lorde. CP-LordA; SP-LordA

In the kitchen / making dishes with a brush. A Plea to My Sister. James Cunningham. JB

In the land of God. Cecil County. Ron Welburn. PoBA

In the lives of their friends. (LL) Beware: Do Not Read This Poem. Ishmael Reed. BPo; PoBA

In the love of home and country and the flag of Uncle Sam. Loyalty to the Flag. Lizelia Augusta Jenkins Moorer. CBWP-3

In "The Masque of the Red Death." 1929: Y you ask? (26). Amiri Baraka. SP-BaraA

In the Matter of Two Men. James David Corrothers. BANP; TtW

In the men's room. (LL) Do you think this is a sad day. Jayne Cortez. SP-CortJ; TtW

In the middle of everything I'm not doing. The Subtle Art of Breathing. Asha Bandele. CtF

In the middle of the winter. Midwinter Blues. Langston Hughes. CP-HughL; SP-HughL

In the mist of the moon I saw you. Langston Hughes. CP-HughL

In the moment's centrifuge of dying / becoming. (LL) Richard Hunt's "Arachne." Robert Hayden. CP-HaydR; FB

In the Morning. Jayne Cortez. BlSi; SP-CortJ

In the Morning. Paul Laurence Dunbar. BPo; CP-DunbP

In the morning part. Did John's Music Kill Him? Alfred B. Spellman. NAAAL

In the morning the city. City. Langston Hughes. CP-HughL

In the Mourning Time. Robert Hayden. BPo

In the nature / of flesh, these clown gods. From an Almanac. Amiri Baraka. SP-BaraA

In the Negores of the quarter. Jazztet Muted. Langston Hughes. Fr. Ask Your Mama; 12 Moods for Jazz. CP-HughL

In the night / in my half hour. Blues. Sonia Sanchez. BlFi; GT; SP-SancS

In the ol'-fashioned way. (LL) The Ol' Tunes. Paul Laurence Dunbar. CP-DunbP

In the Old Neighborhood. Rita Dove. SP-DoveR; SpiFl

In the old neighborhood, each funeral parlor. Teach Us to Number Our Days. Rita Dove. ESEAA; SP-DoveR

In the old testament. Bible Study. Gloria C. Oden. ESEAA; GT

In the open light. (LL) Coal. Audre Lorde. BlSi; ESEAA; NBV; PoBA; SP-LordA

In the palm / the seed. A Guerilla Handbook. Amiri Baraka. PoBA; SP-BaraA

In the Projects. Michael S. Harper. SP-HarpM

In the push of time, it's all too easy. Why a Hush Should Not Be Rushed. Al Young. CP-YounA

In the quarter of the Negroes. Cultural Exchange: "In the quarter of the Negroes." Langston Hughes. BPo; PoBA

In the quarter of the Negroes. Gospel Cha-Cha. Langston Hughes. Fr. Ask Your Mama; 12 Moods for Jazz. CP-HughL

In the quarter of the Negroes. Ode to Dinah. Langston Hughes. Fr. Ask Your Mama; 12 Moods for Jazz. CP-HughL

In the quarter of the Negroes. Shades of Pigmeat. Langston Hughes. Fr. Ask Your Mama; 12 Moods for Jazz. CP-HughL

In the region of rain and cloud. Desire's Persistence. Jay Wright. ESEAA

In the Restaurant. Gerald William Barrax. GT

In the ribs of an ugly school building. Three Brown Girls Singing. M. Carl Holman. Klds

In the rusty pages of Gray's Anatomy. Digging. Audre Lorde. CP-LordA

In the seat we shared in the second grade. Brother Alvin. Audre Lorde. CP-LordA

In the shadows of the waiting room. On Declining Values. June Jordan. SP-JordJ

In the shower naked. Breast Examination. Wanda Coleman. GT

In the Silence. Stephany Fuller. BPo

In the silence and the dark. Armageddon. Georgia Douglas Johnson. ShDr

In the silence of my heart. Communion. Paul Laurence Dunbar. CP-DunbP

In the slave quarters. The Will and the Swan. George Barlow. *Fr.* Gabriel. TtW

In the small old barn. The Eternal Landscape. Lenard D. Moore. GT

In the soft air perfumed with blooming May. Lines to Mount Glen. George Marion McClellan. AAP

In the South. His Fingers Seem to Sing. Sam Cornish. GT

In the south, sleeping against. Legacy. Amiri Baraka. PoBA

In the State of "Old Palmetto," from the town of Eutawville. The Eutawville Lynching. Lizelia Augusta Jenkins Moorer. CBWP-3

In the street outside a school. The Bees. Audre Lorde. CP-LordA; SP-LordA

In the tea rooms. For the Truth (Because It Is Necessary). Edward S. Spriggs. BlFi; BrTr

In the tender woodland. Al Young. CP-YounA

In the tents of Akbar. Paul Laurence Dunbar. CP-DunbP

In the Time of Revolution. Julius Lester. PoBA

In the town where I was born. Eagle Rock. Alice Walker. CP-WalkA

In the Tradition. Amiri Baraka. SP-BaraA

In the Tradition of Bobbitt. Saundra Sharp. SpiFl

In the Twilight. A. K. Toney. CtF

In the Valley. Priscilla Jane Thompson. CBWP-2

In the Void, in the Storm, in the Wastelands of our hearts. Sunrise!! Rolland Snellings. BlFi

In the warm mud of alcoholic gloom. Old Woman. Al Young. CP-YounA

In the winter of 1966 Pablo Neruda. Poem Delivered Before Assembly of Colored People Held at Glide Memorial Church, Oct. 4, 1973 and Called to Protest Recent Events in the Sovereign Republic of Chile. Ishmael Reed. CP-ReedI

In the wondrous light of a pair of brown eyes. Admiration. Josephine D. Henderson Heard. CBWP-4

In the / Wrong / Direction. (LL) Assassination. Don L. Lee. AmNP; PoBA

In the yard / the truck sits stuck in the mud. Mountain Wife. E. Ethelbert Miller. CtF

In the year of eighteen-twelve. Titanic: "In the year of eighteen-twelve." *African-American Oral Tradition.* GetYo

In the Year of the Dragon. (LL) Lonesome in the Country. Al Young. CP-YounA

In the yellow pickup. The Weekend Equestrian. Michael S. Weaver. GT

In their own order. I. At Nagasaki. Lucille Clifton. ESEAA

In these bodies of soiled, broken, mending hands. (LL) Eve (Rachel). Michael S. Harper. ESEAA; SP-HarpM

In These Dissenting Times. Alice Walker. CP-WalkA; PoBA
Women. NAAAL; TtW

In this garden. Lucille Clifton. SP-ClifL

In this green month when resurrected flowers. Memorial Wreath. Dudley Randall. IDB; NNP; PoBA

"In This House, There Shall Be No Idols." Carolyn M. Rodgers. JB

In this misty place where hunger finds us. Fog Report. Audre Lorde. CP-LordA

In this new picture your smile has been to war. For Assata. Audre Lorde. CP-LordA

In this old garden, fair, I walk to-day. In a English Garden. Paul Laurence Dunbar. CP-DunbP

In this old house. (LL) Sadie and Maud. Gwendolyn Brooks. ESEAA; NAAAL

In this place of helmets and tar. On Being Asked to Leave a Place of Honor for One of Comfort, Preferably in the Northern Suburbs. Alice Walker. CP-WalkA

In this room, holding hands. All Day We've Longed for Night. Sarah Webster Fabio. BlSi

In this sombre garden close. The Monk's Walk. Paul Laurence Dunbar. CP-DunbP

In this stoned and. Definition of Nature. Eugene B. Redmond. NBV; PoBA

In this stucco house there is nothing but air. Night Watch. Rita Dove. SP-DoveR

In this the hour of new reckonings! This Hour. Oliver La Grone. NNP

In This Waking. Wanda Coleman. Crnst

In this white room full of strangers. Mawu. Audre Lorde. CP-LordA

In tight pants, tight skirts. The Young Ones, Flip Side. James A. Emanuel. KIds

In Time of Crisis. Raymond R. Patterson. IDB

In time of silver rain. Langston Hughes. CP-HughL; SP-HughL

In times of stormy weather. Strange Hurt. Langston Hughes. CP-HughL; GT; SP-HughL

In town to do good works, filled with our own. Boys in the Park. Marilyn Nelson. SP-NelsM

In Uganda an early king chose. Alice Walker. CP-WalkA

In us and into us and ours. For Eusi, Ayi Kwei and Gwen Brooks. Keorapetse W. Kgositsile. PoBA

In Vain. Adah Isaacs Menken. CBWP-1

In vain! In vain! My pleading all in vain! Arria to Poetus. Mary E. Tucker. CBWP-1

In vain thou bid'st me strike the lyre. The Misanthropist. James M. Whitfield. AAP; AfAmPo; EBAP

In water-heavy nights behind grandmother's porch. Adolescence—I. Rita Dove. SP-DoveR

In western skies. Sunset. Henrietta Cordelia Ray. *Fr.* Idyl. CBWP-3; EBAP

In what had been a pathway. Afterlove. Audre Lorde. CP-LordA

In whirlwinds of God's wrath. (LL) The Martyr of Alabama. Frances Ellen Watkins Harper. CP-HarpF; TtW

In whose bed / did I lie asweat. Change. Audre Lorde. CP-LordA

In wintertime I have such fun. Quoits. Mary Effie Lee Newsome. CDC

In workshops without light. Artisan. Audre Lorde. CP-LordA

In yonder halls reclining. The Revel. Frances Ellen Watkins Harper. CP-HarpF

In your thighs. (LL) Africa. Langston Hughes. CP-HughL; SP-HughL

INAMORATAS, with an approbation. The Sundays of Satin-Legs Smith. Gwendolyn Brooks. NAAAL; SP-BrooG

Inaugural Day, 1981. Ishmael Reed. CP-ReedI

Inauguration. Lorenzo Thomas. NBV

Incandescence / formless form. Lucille Clifton. SP-ClifL

Incense of the Lucky Virgin. Robert Hayden. CP-HaydR

Incentive / born in ancient. On Riots. Cy Leslie. NBP

Incident. Countee Cullen. BPo; CDC; CP-CullC; IDB; NAAAL; PoBA; SSLK

Incidental Pieces to a Walk. James Cunningham. JB

Incompleteness. Henrietta Cordelia Ray. CBWP-3

Inconvenience, An. John Raven. BPo

Incredibly bright blue almost white open sky, An. I Just Heard John Buffington Died. Kalamu ya Salaam. SpiFl

Index to a Black Catharsis. Richard W. Thomas. BlFi

Indian Girl. Lenard D. Moore. GT

Indiana Gig, The. Al Young. CP-YounA

Indiana Haiku. Etheridge Knight. SP-KnigE

Indiana Haiku—2. Etheridge Knight. SP-KnigE

Indianapolis/Summer/1969/Poem. Sonia Sanchez. SP-SancS

Indians Aren't Attacking, The. (LL) My Fifth Trip to Washington Ended in Northeast Delaware. Audre Lorde. CP-LordA; SP-LordA

Indians beat drums, sing and dance to assert themselves as human beings (or to surrender themselves?) in the vast universe that comes to earth in New Mexico, The. Imprint for Rio Grande. Jean Toomer. CP-ToomJ; TtW

Indignation Dinner, An. James David Corrothers. AfAmPo; BANP; NAAAL

Indulgent muse! my grov'ling mind inspire. To a Lady on Her Coming to North-America with Her Son, for the Recovery of Her Health. Phillis Wheatley. CP-WheaP

Infants of Summer. Lennox Raphael. NBP

Infelicia. Adah Isaacs Menken. EBAP
Resurgam.

Infelix. Adah Isaacs Menken. AAP; CBWP-1

Inference of Mexico, An. Robert Hayden. CP-HaydR
Veracruz. AmNP

Infinity doesn't interest me. On a New Year's Eve. June Jordan. SP-JordJ

Infirm and aged, doth he sit. The Old Year. Priscilla Jane Thompson. CBWP-2

Inflation blues is what we got. Margaret Abigail Walker. CP-WalkM

Inherent nonchalance. (LL) To Sallie, Walking. Sterling A. Brown. CP-BrowS; GT

Inheritance—His. Audre Lorde. CP-LordA

Initiation. Jayne Cortez. PoBA

Injustice of the Courts. Lizelia Augusta Jenkins Moorer. CBWP-3

Inner lit, twisted trees. Inside Connie. Bob Kaufman. SP-KaufB

Inner Realm, The. Priscilla Jane Thompson. CBWP-2

Innocence. Anne Spencer. CDC; ShDr

Inquietude. Pauli Murray. BlSi

Inquiry. Ntozake Shange. TtW

Insatiate. Mae V. Cowdery. ShDr

Inscription: "He wrote upon his heart." Donald Jeffrey Hayes. CDC

Inside beyond our craziness is reality. People rushing through life. Reggae or Not! Amiri Baraka. SP-BaraA

Inside Connie. Bob Kaufman. SP-KaufB

Inside its own mystery, the poetic line circles back and forth. Collage. Quincy Troupe. CtF

Inside out, the police announce. Molasses and the Three Witches. Michael S. Harper. SP-HarpM

Inside Track, The. Ishmael Reed. CP-ReedI

Insidious Dr. Fu Man Chu, The. Amiri Baraka. SP-BaraA

Insignificant. Maya Angelou. CP-AngeM

Insomnia. Cornelius Eady. ESEAA

Insomniac. Maya Angelou. CP-AngeM; SP-AngeM

Inspiration. Paul Laurence Dunbar. CP-DunbP

Inspire our sons to seek their man-shadows. If We Cannot Live People as People. Charles Lynch. PoBA

Instability. Henrietta Cordelia Ray. CBWP-3

Instant of Our Parting, The. Alice Walker. CP-WalkA

Instantaneous ("Instantaneously!"). Vivian Ayers. NNP

Instead of icepacks. Dancing in Menopause. Dorothy Perry Thompson. SpiFl

Instinct leads me to another flow. U.N.I.T.Y. Queen Latifah. Crnst

Instructions for Building Straw Huts. Yusef Komunyakaa. GT

Instructions to a Princess. Ishmael Reed. CP-ReedI; PoBA

Instructor said, The. Theme for English B. Langston Hughes. BALP; SSLK *Fr.* Montage of a Dream Deferred. CP-HughL; SP-HughL

Insulted. Priscilla Jane Thompson. CBWP-2

Insurance man, / I heard his knock. Madam and the Insurance Man. Langston Hughes. CP-HughL

Intellectualism. Nikki Giovanni. SP-GiovN

Intellectuals, The. Dudley Randall. PoBA

Intelligence Quotients. Dorothy Perry Thompson. SpiFl

Intemperance Club, The. George Moses Horton. SP-HortG

Intent and thrilled I have watched birds fly. Motion and Rest. Jean Toomer. CP-ToomJ

Interim. Clarissa Scott Delany. CDC; ShDr; TtW

Interlinked is truth to duty, have you had the precious thought. Duty, or Truth at Work. Lizelia Augusta Jenkins Moorer. CBWP-3

Interlude. Mae V. Cowdery. ShDr

Interlude. Welton Smith. PoBA *Fr.* Malcolm. BlFi

Interne at Provident. Langston Hughes. CP-HughL; SP-HughL

Interrupted Reproof, The. Priscilla Jane Thompson. CBWP-2

Intifada. June Jordan. NAAAL; SP-JordJ

Intimacy. Al Young. CP-YounA

Into a rainbow! (LL) Little Song. Langston Hughes. CP-HughL

Into a thousand whirling dreams / Of sun! (LL) As I Grew Older. Langston Hughes. BANP; CP-HughL; Crnst; SP-HughL

Into Blackness Softly. Mari E. Evans. PoBA

Into cropped and fragrant air. (LL) Every Traveler Has One Vermont Poem. Audre Lorde. CP-LordA

Into her mother's bedroom to wash the ballooning body. Jessie Mitchell's Mother. Gwendolyn Brooks. SP-BrooG

Into his rosy chamber stepped the Sun. At Sunset. Henrietta Cordelia Ray. CBWP-3

Into space-time walks bass strings of charlie mingus. One for Charlie Mingus. Quincy Troupe. SpiFl

Into the commonest ash. (LL) To be in love. Gwendolyn Brooks. GT; SP-BrooG

Into the Depths. Adah Isaacs Menken. CBWP-1

Into the furnace let me go alone. Baptism. Claude McKay. SP-McKaC

Into the laps. Mellow. Langston Hughes. *Fr.* Montage of a Dream Deferred. CP-HughL

Into the sixties / a trane. Don't Cry, Scream. Haki R. Madhubuti. BrTr

Into the soil a seed is sown. Mors et Vita. James Edwin Campbell. AAP; AfAmPo

Into the toxic tears / of this stockpile. (LL) Stockpiling of frozen trees, The. Jayne Cortez. SP-CortJ

Into the whitecaps, / laughing. (LL) A Break from the Bush. Yusef Komunyakaa. SP-KomuY

Into the windlessness / Of our house in Taos. (LL) A House in Taos. Langston Hughes. CDC; SP-HughL

Into this door of sun forever. (LL) Myself When I Am Real. Al Young. CP-YounA; PoBA

Intro to My Final Book of Poems. Ahmos, II Zu-Bolton. TtW

Introduce me first as a man. Unnatural State of the Unicorn. Yusef Komunyakaa. SP-KomuY

Introducing a New Loa. Ishmael Reed. CP-ReedI

Introductory to Second Edition. Alfred Islay Walden. AAP

Introspection. Nikki Giovanni. SP-GiovN

Invaders, The. Clarence Reed. BlFi

Invasion. Ishmael Reed. CP-ReedI

Invention of a Garden, The. Jay Wright. GT

Invention of Comics, The. Amiri Baraka. AmNP; GT; NAAAL; PoBA

Invention of the wheel was long ago, The. Power to the People. Margaret Abigail Walker. CP-WalkM

Invisible Man, The. Conrad Kent Rivers. Klds

Invitation. Al Young. CP-YounA

Invitation to Love. Paul Laurence Dunbar. CP-DunbP; IHS

Invitation to Madison County, An. Jay Wright. ESEAA; PoBA

Invitation (To the Night and All Other Things Dark). Ronda M. Davis. JB

Invocation: "Let me be buried in the rain." Helene Johnson. AmNP; BANP; NAAAL; ShDr

Invocation to the Muse. Henrietta Cordelia Ray. CBWP-3

Involv'd in Clouds of Wo, Maria mourns. An Elegy, to Miss Mary Moorhead. Phillis Wheatley. CP-WheaP

Ione. Paul Laurence Dunbar. CP-DunbP

Iowa Farmer. Margaret Abigail Walker. CP-WalkM; GT; Klds

Irish Wake. Langston Hughes. CP-HughL

Iron Flowers. Kalamu ya Salaam. TtW

Ironic: LL.D. William Stanley Braithwaite. BANP

Irritable Song. Russell Atkins. AmNP

Is a deliberate attempt. The Trip, Dharma Trip, Sangha Trip. Bob Kaufman. SP-KaufB

I's a-gittin' weary of de way dat people do. Faith. Paul Laurence Dunbar. CP-DunbP

Is a turn of the mirror / Time's question only. (LL) Generation. Audre Lorde. CP-LordA; NBV; SP-LordA

Is Africa's / Dark face. (LL) Afro-American Fragment. Langston Hughes. CP-HughL; SP-HughL

I's always been a workin' girl. Black Gal. Langston Hughes. CP-HughL

Is Bakuba memory / (from Lumumba's region). Every Harlem Face Is AFROMANISM Surviving. Edward S. Spriggs. BlFi

I's boun' to see my gal to-night. On the Road. Paul Laurence Dunbar. CP-DunbP

Is breaking in despair. (LL) Slave Mother, The: "Heard you that shriek! It rose." Frances Ellen Watkins Harper. CP-HarpF; CrDW; NAAAL; TtW

Is—*Bury me not in a land of slaves!* (LL) Bury Me in a Free Land. Frances Ellen Watkins Harper. AAP; BPo; CrDW; NAAAL

I's feelin kin o' lonesome in my little room to-night. To the Eastern Shore. Paul Laurence Dunbar. CP-DunbP

Is for ass, upon it we sit, A. The Alphabet. *African-American Oral Tradition.* GetYo

I's frustrated! (LL) Bad Morning. Langston Hughes. CP-HughL; SP-HughL

Is / georgia grown / georgia bruised. My Beige Mom. Edward S. Spriggs. BlFi

Is Heathen. Devil Worship. Amiri Baraka. SP-BaraA

Is it an idle fantasy. The Mist Maiden. Henrietta Cordelia Ray. CBWP-3

Is It Because I Am Black? Joseph Seamon Cotter, Sr. BANP; TtW

Is It True? Langston Hughes. *Fr.* Ask Your Mama; 12 Moods for Jazz. CP-HughL

Is it true the ribs can tell. A Kind of Love, Some Say. Maya Angelou. CP-AngeM; SP-AngeM

Is Life itself but many ways of thought. Substitution. Anne Spencer. BlSi; CDC; ShDr

Is Love. Maya Angelou. CP-AngeM

Is love, / Is life. (LL) O-Jazz-O. Bob Kaufman. SP-KaufB

Is manhood less because man's face is black? Albery Allson Whitman. AAP *Fr.* Twasinta's Seminoles; Or Rape of Florida

"'Tis hard to judge if hatred of one's race." AfAmPo

Is merry glory. Langston Hughes. Gwendolyn Brooks. SP-BrooG

Is my dress appropriate? American Glamour. Al Young. CP-YounA

Is not that slight tossing dead Leander? (LL) A Private Letter to Brazil. Gloria C. Oden. ESEAA; GT; Klds

Is not to live at all. (LL) To Richard Wright. Conrad Kent Rivers. AmNP; IDB; PoBA

Is nowhere. (LL) Border Line. Langston Hughes. CP-HughL; SP-HughL

Is / red beans. Energy. Victor Hernandez Cruz. PoBA

Is She Okay? Marilyn Nelson. SP-NelsM

Is something like the rest. The Politics of Rich Painters. Amiri Baraka. SP-BaraA

Is that dream. (LL) Powell; March 1991. Lucille Clifton. ESEAA

Is that you sistah Harris? An Afternoon Gossip. Priscilla Jane Thompson. CBWP-2

Is the age of pisces / check it out. (LL) 12 Gates to the City. Nikki Giovanni. PoBA

Is the alphabet responsible. Learning to Write. Audre Lorde. CP-LordA; GT

Is the eternal voice, Coltrane is. Orishas. Larry Neal. NBP

Is the fire out? Is the fire out? Self-Doubt. Lance Jeffers. TtW

Is the right of every race. (LL) To the Union Savers of Cleveland. Frances Ellen Watkins Harper. AAP; AfAmPo; CP-HarpF

Is the sacrifice of desire. (LL) Sacrifice. Audre Lorde. CP-LordA; SP-LordA

Is the slim curved crook of the moon tonight! (LL) Winter Moon. Langston Hughes. CP-HughL; SP-HughL

Is the total black, being spoken. Coal. Audre Lorde. BlSi; NAAAL; NBV; PoBA

Is this dancing sunlight. Symphony. Frank Horne. AmNP

Is this the way my Father. Matin Hymn. Josephine D. Henderson Heard. CBWP-4

Is thy sun obscured to-day. My Grace Is Sufficient. Josephine D. Henderson Heard. CBWP-4

Is / to be / very-hot. (LL) But He Was Cool. Haki R. Madhubuti. BrTr; Crnst

Is what side yall gon be on. (LL) A Poem for Deep Thinkers. Amiri Baraka. SP-BaraA

Is yo eye so empty. Signals. Jewel C. Latimore. PoBA

Isaiah LXIII, 1–8. Phillis Wheatley. CP-WheaP

Isaiah to Mandy. Sterling A. Brown. CP-BrowS

Isaiah was a man of the court. Margaret Abigail Walker. CP-WalkM

I'se been upon de karpet. Old Maid's Soliloquy. Maggie Pogue Johnson. CBWP-4

I'se wild Nigger Bill. Wild Negro Bill. *Unknown*. BPo; NAAAL

Island. Langston Hughes. CP-HughL; SP-HughL

Island. Langston Hughes. *Fr*. Lenox Avenue Mural. AmNP; SP-HughL *Fr*. Montage of a Dream Deferred. CP-HughL

Island Mary. Lucille Clifton. SP-ClifL

Island within Island. Henry L. Dumas. GT

Islands, The. Robert Hayden. CP-HaydR; ESEAA

Israel á la Begin, begins: "We." A Poem on the Middle East "Peace Process." Etheridge Knight. SP-KnigE

Is's such a. Langston Hughes. *See* Ennui.

Issue, with cold feet, jumped in bed with us, An. The All-Night Issue. Jackie Warren-Moore. SpiFl

Is't here the fairies haunt the place. On a Nook Called Fairyland. Henrietta Cordelia Ray. CBWP-3

It be be the last time I'm snuffin' candles in the cold dark. Sadie Snuffs a Candle. Dolores Kendrick. ESEAA

It began with A—years before in a room. Robert Schumann, Or: Musical Genius Begins with Affliction. Rita Dove. SP-DoveR

It came / Out of the blackness of the spaces between galaxies. The Second Coming. Carl Clark. JB

It came upon the noontide air. Bishop James A. Shorter. Josephine D. Henderson Heard. CBWP-4

IT CAN BE beautiful this sitting by oneself all alone except for. Moon Watching by Lake Chapala. Al Young. CP-YounA

It can put you in the hospital! (LL) Who Has Seen the Wind? Bob Kaufman. Klds; SP-KaufB

It cannot come / except you make it. Balboa, the Entertainer. Amiri Baraka. SP-BaraA

It comes in black. The Telephone. Maya Angelou. CP-AngeM; SP-AngeM

It comes over him sometimes, he can't help. Like Father, Like Son. Marilyn Nelson. SP-NelsM

It cost me a lot. Elegy for a Lady. Walt Delegall. BlFi

It crawled away from 'neath my feet. That Hill. Blanche Taylor Dickinson. CDC

It does, it does, I have seen it. America Bleeds. Angelo Lewis. PoBA

It does not happen. That love, removes. Audubon, Drafted. Amiri Baraka. Klds; SP-BaraA

It does not impress me that I have. Will. Alice Walker. CP-WalkA

It doesn't matter if you can't see. Some Kind of Crazy. Major L. Jackson. SpiFl

It Don't Mean a Thing (If It Ain't Got That Swing). *Unknown*. NAAAL

It feels dangerous now. East Berlin. Audre Lorde. CP-LordA

It Gives Me Pause. Langston Hughes. CP-HughL

It got me up. The Monster. Karen L. Mitchell. GT

It had already happened. (LL) At That Moment. Raymond R. Patterson. BrTr; TtW

It had gotten so bad. By the 5th Generation Louisiana, After Slavery. Ahmos, II Zu-Bolton. BkSV

It had no dignity before. Harlem Dance Hall. Langston Hughes. CP-HughL

It had one bitch on board, like he had me mark. Fight with the Crew. Derek Walcott. *Fr*. The Schooner *Flight*. ESEAA

It has been so long oshun. The Meaning of the Smell of Sweat. Niama Leslie JoAnn Williams. SpiFl

It has rained for five days. Coping. Audre Lorde. CP-LordA

It is a blessed heritage. Heritage. Mae V. Cowdery. ShDr

It is a new America. Brown River, Smile. Jean Toomer. AmNP; CP-ToomJ; PoBA

It is a normal day. Poem Found Emptying Out My Pockets. Al Young. CP-YounA

It is a waste of time to hate a mirror. Good Mirrors are Not Cheap. Audre Lorde. SP-LordA

It is again. "Stephany." NBV

It is all blood and breaking. She Understands Me. Lucille Clifton. SP-ClifL

It is All Souls' Day, then, a reverential day in Portugal. Lisbon. Russell Atkins. GT

It is as if a silver chord. To a Dead Friend. Paul Laurence Dunbar. CP-DunbP

It is beginning oh. Robert Hayden. CP-HaydR

It is dangerous for a woman to defy the gods;. Letter to My Sister. Anne Spencer. AfAmPo; AmNP; BlSi; NAAAL; PoBA; ShDr; TtW

It Is Deep. Carolyn M. Rodgers. NAAAL; SSLK; TtW

It is difficult to believe that we. Father and Daughter. Sonia Sanchez. GT; SP-SancS

It is essential I remember. Man White, Brown Girl and All That Jazz. Gloria C. Oden. GT; PoBA

It is essential that Summer be grafted to. Poem for July 4, 1994. Sonia Sanchez. SpiFl

It is Everywhere. Jean Toomer. CP-ToomJ; GT

It is fitting that you be here. On Seeing Two Brown Boys in a Catholic Church. Frank Horne. BANP; CDC; PoBA

It is fitting that you be here. (LL) On Seeing Two Brown Boys in a Catholic Church. Frank Horne. BANP; CDC; PoBA

It is friday. We have come. Forgiving My Father. Lucille Clifton. SP-ClifL

It Is God that Moves in Your Heart. Al Young. CP-YounA

It is like lao tse's dream, my. Man or Butterfly. Ishmael Reed. CP-ReedI

It is like the plot of an ol. Instructions to a Princess. Ishmael Reed. CP-ReedI; PoBA

It is midnight / no magical bewitching. Poem at Thirty. Sonia Sanchez. BPo; BlFi; BlSi; BrTr; NAAAL; PoBA; SP-SancS

It is midnite. The room is blue. Death Songs. L. V. Mack. PoBA

It is New Year's Day. Best Loved of Africa. Margaret Else Danner. PoBA

It is not enough. The Prophet's Warning or Shoot to Kill. Ebon Dooley. PoBA

It is not weariness. Burden. Langston Hughes. CP-HughL

It is not who or what. Quincy Troupe. TtW

It is nothing to me, the beauty said. Nothing and Something. Frances Ellen Watkins Harper. CP-HarpF; EBAP

It is overdue time. Ron Welburn. NBV

It is possible to rest here. Poetry. Al Young. CP-YounA

It is so clear / now. The Domino Theory (Or Snoop Dogg Rules the World). Kenneth Carroll. CtF; SpiFl

It is Sunday, day of roughhousing. We are let out in the woods. Kentucky, 1833. Rita Dove. SP-DoveR

It is the black God, Kali. The Coming of Kali. Lucille Clifton. SP-ClifL

It is the color of light. Lyric: I Am Looking at Music. Pinkie Gordon Lane. IHS

It is the endless dance of the dead. Dirge. Quincy Troupe. PoBA

It is the eve of battle. The Reason Why. George Clinton Rowe. AAP

It is the Negro's tragedy I feel. The Negro's Tragedy. Claude McKay. BPo; SP-McKaC

It is the same everywhere for me. Always the Same. Langston Hughes. CP-HughL

It is the silver seeking salvation. The Plight. James W. Thompson. BPo

It is the sink of the afternoon. Sowing. Audre Lorde. CP-LordA; SP-LordA

It is Thursday, October 23rd. Ocean of the Streams of Story. Primus St. John. GT

It is time for action. Bob Bennett. BlFi

It is time for the United States to spend money on education so that every American would be hipper, *thus no war!* Ted Joans. Klds; NNP

It is time to make our way home. (LL) Moving Towards Home. June Jordan. SP-JordJ

It is too easy not to like. J, My Good Friend (Another Foolish Innocent). Alice Walker. CP-WalkA

It is true--/ I've always loved. Alice Walker. *Fr.* Once. BlSi; CP-WalkA; PoBA

It is we who are liars. Liars. Langston Hughes. CP-HughL

It is whatever day, whatever time it is. Sunday Morning. Wayne Moreland. PoBA

It isn't nice to be naked? (LL) March Moon. Langston Hughes. CP-HughL; SP-HughL

It just don't/flood. Poem on the Second Consecutive Day of Rain. June Jordan. SP-JordJ

It lifts the poor man from his cell. The Powers of Love. George Moses Horton. BALP

It lives for those who once upon a time had a dream. (LL) There Is a Woman in This Town. Patricia Parker. BlSi

It looks like to me. Little Green Tree. Langston Hughes. CP-HughL; SP-HughL

It may be misery not to sing at all. Life's Tragedy. Paul Laurence Dunbar. CP-DunbP

It must be / deeeeep. (LL) Jesus Was Crucified or: It Must Be Deep. Carolyn M. Rodgers. BlSi; PoBA

It must be nice to be a sheep. Shearing Time. Langston Hughes. CP-HughL

It must have been a year. Fire, Hair, Meat and Bone. Fred Johnson. PoBA

It must have been something like. Jazz to Jackson to John. Jerry W. Ward, Jr. BkSV

It must have been that the fellow was tongue-tied. Transfer. Sterling A. Brown. CP-BrowS; TtW

It must have been yesterday. Evil Morning. Langston Hughes. CP-HughL

It occurs to me now. Changing. Maya Angelou. CP-AngeM

It pours. Night Rain. Karen L. Mitchell. GT

It seems to be the time of bad gigs. Written in Bracing, Gray L.A. Rainlight. Al Young. SpiFl

"It seems to me," said Booker T. Booker T. and W. E. B. Dudley Randall. Klds

It shall flash through coming ages. President Lincoln's Proclamation of Freedom. Frances Ellen Watkins Harper. CP-HarpF

It Shall Not Come Nigh Thee. Frances Ellen Watkins Harper. CP-HarpF

It should have a woman's name. The Lake in Central Park. Jay Wright. ESEAA; GT

It showed at baseball. What it showed in school. (LL) Still Do I Keep My Look, My Identity. . . . Gwendolyn Brooks. SP-BrooG

It sits lopsided. The Nazi Doll. Yusef Komunyakaa. SP-KomuY

It starts with a hand. Black Separatism. Nikki Giovanni. SP-GiovN

It stifles me—God, must I sit and sew? (LL) I sit and sew—a useless task it seems. Alice Moore Dunbar-Nelson. NAAAL

It takes a well-spent lifetime, and perhaps more, to crystallize in us. As the Eagle Soars. Jean Toomer. CP-ToomJ

It took 27 years to write this poem. Ruth. Colleen J. McElroy. BlSi

It trails always behind me. Jamaica 1980. Lorna Goodison. GT

It uproots trees! (LL) Warning. Langston Hughes. BPo; CP-HughL; SP-HughL

It was a cool and mystic rain. Dance of the Freaks: "It was a cool and mystic rain." *African-American Oral Tradition.* GetYo

It was a cool evening. Freeman Field. Marilyn Nelson. ESEAA; SP-NelsM

It was a drab street. The Shining Parlor. Anita Scott Coleman. ShDr

It was a foreign night. Thin Water. Nadir Lasana Bomani. CtF

It was a funky deal. Etheridge Knight. BPo; BrTr; NBV; PoBA; SP-KnigE

It was a glorious May morning. Victor Garibaldi. Melvin B. Tolson. GT

It was a long time ago. As I Grew Older. Langston Hughes. BANP; CP-HughL; Crnst; SP-HughL

It was as if Gauguin. Etta Moten's Attic. Margaret Else Danner. BrTr

It was as though we met at McDonald's. For Janet Kafka, Dead at 30. Al Young. CP-YounA

It was as though you struggled against. Letter. Robert Hayden. CP-HaydR

It was at the town convention. "Chronic Kicker," The. Paul Laurence Dunbar. CP-DunbP

It was back in the time of nineteen hundred and two. Stackolee: "It was back in the time of nineteen hundred and two." *African-American Oral Tradition.* GetYo

It was back in the year of forty-one when the times was hard. Stackolee: "It was back in the year of forty-one when the times was hard." *African-American Oral Tradition.* GetYo

It was Chrismus Eve, I mind hit fu' a mighty gloomy day. Chrismus on the Plantation. Paul Laurence Dunbar. CP-DunbP

It was cold and mist and rain in old Spokane. Dance of the Freaks: "It was cold and mist and rain in old Spokane." *African-American Oral Tradition.* GetYo

It was done, the deed of horror. The Resurrection of Jesus. Frances Ellen Watkins Harper. CP-HarpF

It was early in the morning one bright summer day. Signifying Monkey: "It was early in the morning one bright summer day." *African-American Oral Tradition.* GetYo

It was fun / traveling through the heart of this country. Once Upon a Road. Jayne Cortez. SP-CortJ

It was Hackensack, no, Hoboken, the town. Hoboken Broken Down: A Hasty Recollection. Al Young. CP-YounA

It was held in God's great temple. The Concert. Paul Laurence Dunbar. CP-DunbP

It was in Abomey that I felt. Dahomey. Audre Lorde. CP-LordA

It was in Speero's poolroom back in nineteen-ten. Poolshooting Monkey: "It was in Speero's poolroom back in nineteen-ten." *African-American Oral Tradition.* GetYo

It was in Speero's poolroom in the year eighteen-ten. Poolshooting Monkey: "It was in Speero's poolroom in the year eighteen-ten." *African-American Oral Tradition.* GetYo

It was in the empty house. Empty House. Langston Hughes. CP-HughL

It was in the Spring. Ballad of Mary's Son. Langston Hughes. CP-HughL

It was in the year of eighteen hundred and sixty-one. Stackalee. *Unknown, comp. by* Onah L. Spencer. CrDW

It was just about sundown in a border town. Boothill McCoy. *African-American Oral Tradition.* GetYo

It was late one day and I was on my way. Junkies' Ball. *African-American Oral Tradition.* GetYo

It was like soul-kissing, the way the words. How I Discovered Poetry. Marilyn Nelson. SP-NelsM

It was my father who loved you first. Poem for Tracy (Chapman). Candice M. Jenkins. CtF

It was my sad and weary lot. The Fugitive's Wife. Frances Ellen Watkins Harper. CP-HarpF

It was 1912 when the awful news got around. Shine and the Titanic. *Unknown.* CrDW; NAAAL

It was not as if he didn't try. Great Uncle Beefheart. Rita Dove. SP-DoveR

It Was Not Fate. William H. A. Moore. BANP

It was not that you were pure. Possibilities: Remembering Malcolm X. Haki R. Madhubuti. SpiFl

It was perhaps no accident. Vague Opening. Jean Toomer. CP-ToomJ

It was running down to the great Atlantic. The Stream. Lula Lowe Weeden. CDC

It was sad indeed, it was sad in mind. Titanic: "It was sad indeed, it was sad in mind." *African-American Oral Tradition.* GetYo

It was Summer, all the time. When Mark Deloach Ruled the World. Dominique Parker. SpiFl

It was that lonely day, folks. Crossing. Langston Hughes. CP-HughL; SP-HughL

It was the beginning of me. Look at My Face, a Collage. Carolyn M. Rodgers. JB

It was the night before Christmas and all through the pad. Junkies' Heaven. *African-American Oral Tradition.* GetYo

It was the silver, heart-enveloping view. The Plateau. Claude McKay. SP-McKaC

It was the Southern drifting over the flats on a hundred low trestles. (The Recent Past). C. S. Giscombe. GT

It was thy noble soul and high desert. To the Hon. Commodore Hood on His Pardoning a Deserter. Phillis Wheatley. CP-WheaP

It was Tiny's habit. Sketches of Harlem. David Henderson. Klds; NNP

It was very pleasant. A Certain Peace. Nikki Giovanni. SP-GiovN

It was water I was trying to think of all the time. Appoggiatura. Donald Jeffrey Hayes. AmNP; PoBA

It was way back in old Frisco, that was where I first saw the light. Little Old Wicked Nell. *African-American Oral Tradition.* GetYo

It was way down in this little town that they call Louisville. 'Flicted Arm Pete: "It was way down in this little town that they call Louisville." *African-American Oral Tradition.* GetYo

It was wild. Assassination. Haki R. Madhubuti. AmNP; BrTr; GT; PoBA

It was yesterday morning. Little Old Letter. Langston Hughes. CP-HughL; SP-HughL

It wasn't about no woman. He Was a Man. Sterling A. Brown. CP-BrowS

It well bespeaks a man beheaded, quite. Division of an Estate. George Moses Horton. NAAAL; SP-HortG

It will break her eye. (LL) The Astrologer Predicts at Mary's Birth. Lucille Clifton. SP-ClifL

It will go on. (LL) My Poem. Nikki Giovanni. BrTr; SP-GiovN; TtW

"It will mean me." (LL) Everybody but Me. Margaret Goss Burroughs. BlSi; FB

It would be easier. The Albuquerque Graveyard. Jay Wright. ESEAA

It would be nice. Enemy. Langston Hughes. CP-HughL

It would be so easy. Any Inner City Blues. Al Young. CP-YounA

It would be too bad if Jesus. Bible Belt. Langston Hughes. CP-HughL

It would never end. (LL) Dear Old Stockholm. Al Young. CP-YounA

Itching Heels. Paul Laurence Dunbar. CP-DunbP

It'll hurt worse if you don't. (LL) Dear Mama. Wanda Coleman. Crnst

It's 5 after 4 a.m. and nothing but my own. Relativity. June Jordan. SP-JordJ

It's a good way to live and. Sky Diving. Ishmael Reed. CP-ReedI; Ttw

It's a grand thing when you're old, love. Life's Golden Sunset. Mrs. Henry Linden. CBWP-4

It's a hell / creeping back into. Back into the Garden. Sarah Webster Fabio. BlSi

It's a journey ... that I propose ... I am not the guide. A Journey. Nikki Giovanni. SP-GiovN

It's a Low Down Dirty Shame. Ollie Shepard. NAAAL

It's a lowdown shame how some of you cocksuckin' lames. The Lame and the Whore. *African-American Oral Tradition.* GetYo

It's a slow, slow process. On Watching a Caterpillar Become a Butterfly. Clarence Major. NAAAL

It's a Terrible Thing! Everett Hoagland. BPo

It's about style. The Place Where He Arose. George Barlow. GT

It's About You: on the Beach. June Jordan. SP-JordJ

It's all a farce,—these tales they tell. Merry Autumn. Paul Laurence Dunbar. CP-DunbP

It's All in Your Head. Marilyn Nelson. SP-NelsM

It's All the Same. Thadious M. Davis. BlSi

It's almost a year and I still. Girlfriend. Audre Lorde. CP-LordA

It's always been like this with me. The Hawk Revsited. Al Young. CP-YounA

It's an earth song. Earth Song. Langston Hughes. CP-HughL

It's because you are so young. Being Old. Langston Hughes. CP-HughL

It's been 50 years since. My Father's Retirement. A. Van Jordan. SpiFl

It's been a long time since we got together, Sam. Colloquy. Sterling A. Brown. CP-BrowS

Its brightness harsh as bloodstained swords. (LL) Tour 5. Robert Hayden. CP-HaydR

Its Curtains. Ted Joans. PoBA

It's funny that smells and sounds return. Scrapbooks. Nikki Giovanni. SP-GiovN

It's getting / to be a thing. Be You. Norman Jordan. NBV

It's good enough / for me! (LL) Sermonette. Ishmael Reed. CP-ReedI; PoBA

It's great to be able to call you. Starting All Over Again. Audre Lorde. CP-LordA

It's hard being / folded/licked. Paul Calderón. CtF

It's hard to make clothes fit a miserable man. Aphorisms. Joel Chandler Harris. CrDW

It's Here In The. Russell Atkins. AmNP; PoBA

It's hot to-day. The bees is buzzin'. A Summer Pastoral. Paul Laurence Dunbar. CP-DunbP

It's India. Al Young. CP-YounA

It's intriguing to me that "bookmaker" is a gambling. Lorraine Hansberry: an Emotional View. Nikki Giovanni. SP-GiovN

It's just no use. Execution. James A., Jr. Randall. BPo; BrTr

It's like a gray, dreary day, wet with tears and mourning. In Memoriam; for James Baldwin (1924–1987). Quincy Troupe. IHS

It's like a jungle sometimes, it makes me wonder. The Message. Grandmaster Flash *and* the Furious Five. NAAAL

It's like a terrible dream designed to make you scream. The Drama. Suliaman El-Hadi. SpiFl

It's me / bathed and ashy. Me, in Kulu Se and Karma. Carolyn M. Rodgers. PoBA

It's moughty tiahsome layin' 'roun'. W'en I Gits Home. Paul Laurence Dunbar. CP-DunbP

It's not enough to mourn. Bombings in Dixie. Langston Hughes. CP-HughL

It's Not so Good to be Born a Girl/ Sometimes. Ntozake Shange. SSLK

It's not the crutches we decry. Crutches. Nikki Giovanni. SP-GiovN

It's nothing / this tragedy in our arms. Jayne Cortez. SP-CortJ

It's one thing to sing lovesongs. Another. Rilke's Third Elegy. Rainer Maria Rilke. SP-NelsM, *tr. by* Marilyn Nelson

Its secret life as if a fortune were yours. (LL) My Father's House. Calvin Forbes. ESEAA

It's spring again. Providence, Rhode Island. Al Young. CP-YounA

It's such a / Bore. Ennui. Langston Hughes. SP-HughL

It's such a static reference; looking. Epistrophe. Amiri Baraka. Klds; NNP

Its sudden dash from the huddled trees. The Death of a Squirrel in McKinley Park. Gerald William Barrax. Klds

It's Sunday evening. Pomp holds the receipts. Chopin. Marilyn Nelson. SP-NelsM

It's the ragged source of memory. The House on Moscow Street. Marilyn Nelson. SP-NelsM

"It's the small deaths in the supermarket" she said. The Same Death Over and Over or Lullabies Are for Children. Audre Lorde. CP-LordA

It's time for bloody Watusi to romp through the streets. Time Poem. Quentin Hill. NBP

It's time the clock got thrown out the window. April Blue. Al Young. CP-YounA

It's time you learned something. Roses. Rita Dove. SP-DoveR

It's too dark to see black. A Mother Speaks: The Algiers Motel Incident, Detroit. Michael S. Harper. BPo; NBV; SP-HarpM

It's true Mattie Lee. Unidentified Flying Object. Robert Hayden. CP-HaydR

Its wednesday night baby. Master Charge Blues. Nikki Giovanni. SP-GiovN

'Ittle Touzle Head. Ray Garfield Dandridge. BANP

I've a humble little motto. Keep A-Pluggin' Away. Paul Laurence Dunbar. CP-DunbP

Ive already told you about the dance. Backtracking. Al Young. CP-YounA

I've always been a faithful man. After Many Days. Paul Laurence Dunbar. CP-DunbP

I've been a woman. Poem No. 8. Sonia Sanchez. SP-SancS

I've been blue all day, my gal's gone away. Gulf Coast Blues. Clarence Williams. NAAAL

I've been here fur many days. Home Longings. Paul Laurence Dunbar. CP-DunbP

I've been in an open field. A Day in the Life of. . . . Conyus. GT

I've been in the storm so long. Been in the Storm So Long. *Unknown.* NAAAL

I've been list'nin' to them lawyers. The Lawyers' Ways. Paul Laurence Dunbar. CP-DunbP

I've been prayin' for centuries. Prayer to the White Man's God. Charles Anderson. BlFi

I've been scarred and battered. Still Here. Langston Hughes. BPo; CP-HughL; SP-HughL

I've been watchin' of 'em, parson. Deacon Jones' Grievance. Paul Laurence Dunbar. AAP; CP-DunbP

I've come back many times today. Gift from Kenya. May Miller. BlSi

I've come this far to freedom and I won't turn back. Midway. Naomi Long Madgett. BPo; BlSi; NNP

I've cropped the black hair Diego loves. Painting / (Frida Kahlo). Elizabeth Alexander. GT

I've eaten handfuls of fire. Back Then. Yusef Komunyakaa. GT; SP-KomuY

I've ever lost were. For Both of Us at Fisk. Sharon Scott. JB

I've fought off the octopi and the Great White Shark. The Prayer of Silence. Marilyn Nelson. SP-NelsM

Ive found peace & it's good sleeping late today—head full of. Sunday Illumination. Al Young. CP-YounA

I've Got a Home in That Rock. Raymond R. Patterson. PoBA

I've got the children to tend. Woman Work. Maya Angelou. CP-AngeM; SP-AngeM

I've got to keep moving. Hellhound on My Trail. Robert Johnson. NAAAL

I've got two / hundred / dollars. Ballad of the Brown Girl. Alice Walker. CP-WalkA

Ive had dreams of Paradise where all you do is open your heart. Dreams of Paradise. Al Young. CP-YounA

I've had tangled feelings lately. Breakthrough. Carolyn M. Rodgers. BPo

I've journeyed 'roun' consid'able. Possum Trot. Paul Laurence Dunbar. CP-DunbP

I've known rivers. The Negro Speaks of Rivers. Langston Hughes. AfAmPo; AmNP; BANP; BPo; CDC; CP-HughL; CrDW; IDB; NAAAL; PoBA; SP-HughL; SSLK; TtW

I've noticed i'm happier. The Way I Feel. Nikki Giovanni. SP-GiovN

I've sat on the park benches in Paris. Park Benching. Langston Hughes. CP-HughL

I've seen the lights of gay Broadway. Beale Street Blues. William Christopher Handy. CrDW; NAAAL

I've / seen the Mississippi River. Mississippi Blues. Lamont B. Steptoe. SpiFl

I've spent the last 10 years. My Office. Lorenzo Thomas. TtW

I've stayed in the front yard all my life. A Song in the Front Yard. Gwendolyn Brooks. *Fr.* A Street in Bronzeville. BPo; BlSi; ESEAA; IDB; NAAAL; PoBA; SP-BrooG

I've watched them mother, and I know. Fiammetta Breaks Her Peace. Rita Dove. SP-DoveR

Ivory gods, / And the ebony gods, The. Gods. Langston Hughes. CP-HughL

Ivory Masks in Orbit. Keorapetse W. Kgositsile. BlFi; PoBA ("These new night.") BrTr

J

J, My Good Friend (Another Foolish Innocent). Alice Walker. CP-WalkA

JA ZZ : (The "Say what?") IS IS JA LIVES. Amiri Baraka. SpiFl

J'Accuse. Bob Kaufman. SP-KaufB

Jack and Dinah Want Freedom. *Unknown.* BPo; NAAAL

Jack Frost at Bedtime. Paul Laurence Dunbar. CP-DunbP

Jack, if you got to be a rounder. Street Song. Langston Hughes. *Fr.* Montage of a Dream Deferred. CP-HughL

Jack Johnson Does the Eagle Rock. Thylias Moss. ESEAA

Jack johnson licked. White Hope. Ishmael Reed. CP-ReedI

Jack Johnson / was convicted. The Turn Around Y36. Amiri Baraka. SP-BaraA

Jackal-Headed Cowboy, The. Ishmael Reed. CP-ReedI

Jacket Notes. Ishmael Reed. CP-ReedI

Jackie McLean: Alto Saxophone. Al Young. CP-YounA

Jackie Robinson. Lucille Clifton. SP-ClifL

Jackson, Mississippi. Margaret Abigail Walker. BrTr; CP-WalkM; FB

Jackson State, May 15, 1970. Margaret Abigail Walker. CP-WalkM

Jail Poems. Bob Kaufman. NAAAL

Jaime. Langston Hughes. CP-HughL

Jalapeña Gypsies. Jay Wright. NBV

Jam Session. Langston Hughes. *Fr.* Montage of a Dream Deferred. CP-HughL

Jamaica 1980. Lorna Goodison. GT

Jamaica is an Island full of Bays. Epitaph for My Father. Margaret Abigail Walker. CP-WalkM

Jamal; Nineteen Cows in a Slow Line Walking. Gwendolyn Brooks. *Fr.* Children Coming Home. ESEAA

Jamal's Lamentation. Reuben Jackson. GT

Jambangle / and a black body. BLACKIE Speaks on Campus: a Valentine for Vachel Lindsay. Stanley Crouch. BlFi

James Cotton Band at Keystone, The. Al Young. CP-YounA

James Hugo Johnston. Maggie Pogue Johnson. CBWP-4

James Powell on Imagination. Larry Neal. BPo

James Whitcomb Riley. Paul Laurence Dunbar. CP-DunbP

Jamie's Puzzle. Frances Ellen Watkins Harper. CP-HarpF

Janie Crawford. Alice Walker. CP-WalkA

January. Henrietta Cordelia Ray. CBWP-3

January. Al Young. CP-YounA

January Dandelion, A. George Marion McClellan. AAP; AfAmPo; EBAP

January 10, 1973. Alice Walker. CP-WalkA

January 3, 1970. Mae Jackson. PoBA

Japanese Hokku. Lewis Alexander. CDC

Japanese neon landscape blinks, A. A Poem for Neutrals. Amiri Baraka. BPo; SP-BaraA

Jasmine. Claude McKay. GT; SP-McKaC

Jasmine. E. Ethelbert Miller. GT

Jazz. Kenneth A. McClane. TtW

Jazz. Carolyn M. Rodgers. JB

JAZZ (a New Interpretation). Karen Williams. SpiFl

Jazz as Was. Al Young. CP-YounA; ESEAA

Jazz Band in a Parisian Cabaret. Langston Hughes. BANP; CP-HughL

Jazz Chick. Bob Kaufman. SP-KaufB

Jazz Fan Looks Back. Jayne Cortez. ESEAA

Jazz Girl. Langston Hughes. CP-HughL

JAZZ is my religion. Ted Joans. TtW

Jazz is / the way brown sugar. Haiku: "Jazz is / the way brown sugar." DJ Renegade. CtF

Jazz June. We / Die soon. (LL) We real cool. We. Gwendolyn Brooks. CrDW; ESEAA; IDB; NAAAL; PoBA; SP-BrooG

Jazz radio on a midnight kick. Round about Midnight. Bob Kaufman. SP-KaufB

Jazz? / Remember that song. Jazz Girl. Langston Hughes. CP-HughL

Jazz to Jackson to John. Jerry W. Ward, Jr. BkSV

Jazzonia. Langston Hughes. AfAmPo; AmNP; BANP; CP-HughL; Klds ("O, silver tree!") NAAAL

Jazztet Muted. Langston Hughes. *Fr.* Ask Your Mama; 12 Moods for Jazz. CP-HughL

Jazzy St. Walk. Charlie R. Braxton. TtW

Jazzy Vanity. Richard W. Thomas. BlFi

Jealous. Paul Laurence Dunbar. CP-DunbP

Jefferson in a Tight Place. George Moses Horton. SP-HortG

Jelly Roll Morton. Sybil Klein. TtW

Jenny in Love. Dolores Kendrick. ESEAA

Jenny in Sleep. Dolores Kendrick. ESEAA

Jeremiah, prophet of Jerusalem. Margaret Abigail Walker. CP-WalkM

Jericho is on the inside. The Walls of Jericho. Blanche Taylor Dickinson. CDC

Jes' beyan a clump o' pines. The Corn Song. John Wesley Holloway. BANP

Jes' lak toddy wahms you thoo'. Dely. Paul Laurence Dunbar. CP-DunbP

Jesse James. *African-American Oral Tradition.* GetYo

Jessehelms. Audre Lorde. CP-LordA

Jessie Mitchell's Mother. Gwendolyn Brooks. SP-BrooG

Jest finished readen a book. A Ballad for Stirling Street. Sonia Sanchez. BrTr

Jester, The. Langston Hughes. CP-HughL

Jesus. Frances Ellen Watkins Harper. CP-HarpF

Jesús, Estrella, Esperanza, Mercy. Middle Passage. Robert Hayden. AmNP; BPo; CP-HaydR; IDB; PoBA

Jesus' mother never had no man. Conception. Waring Cuney. BANP

Jesus Prayer, The. Marilyn Nelson. *Fr.* The Plotinus Suite. SP-NelsM

Jesus, The. Langston Hughes. CP-HughL

Jesus Was Crucified or: It Must Be Deep. Carolyn M. Rodgers. BlSi; PoBA

Jet that was screeching over the *Flight,* The. Maria Concepcion & the Book of Dreams. Derek Walcott. *Fr.* The Schooner *Flight.* ESEAA

Jew. James A., Jr. Randall. BPo

Jeweled entrails of pomegranates, The. The Last Feast of Belshazzar. Langston Hughes. CP-HughL

Jewish Grandfather's Story, The. Frances Ellen Watkins Harper. CP-HarpF

Jews: / Groceries, The. Likewise. Langston Hughes. *Fr.* Montage of a Dream Deferred. CP-HughL

Jews: / Groceries / Suits, The. Likewise. Langston Hughes. SP-HughL

Jilted. Paul Laurence Dunbar. CP-DunbP

Jim Crow Car. Langston Hughes. *See* Lunch in a Jim Crow Car.

Jim Crow Cars. Lizelia Augusta Jenkins Moorer. CBWP-3

Jim Crow's Last Stand. Langston Hughes. CP-HughL

Jim Daniels: Hamilton Massacre: Parable. Michael S. Harper. SP-HarpM

Jim is on the gang. Convict. Sterling A. Brown. CP-BrowS

Jim never had no luck wid de women. Pardners. Sterling A. Brown. CP-BrowS

Jimmy, go / To the store, please. Grocery Store. Langston Hughes. CP-HughL

Jingle in a broken tongue, A. (LL) The Poet. Paul Laurence Dunbar. AAP; AfAmPo; BPo; CP-DunbP; CrDW; Klds; NAAAL

Jitney. Langston Hughes. CP-HughL

Jitterbugging in the Streets. Calvin C. Hernton. BlFi; PoBA

Jitterbugging on shimmering air. (LL) Epithalamium and Shivaree. Marilyn Nelson. IHS; SP-NelsM

Jiving. Rita Dove. SP-DoveR

Joan / did you never hear. To Joan. Lucille Clifton. SP-ClifL

Job easy / is the pride. Lucille Clifton. SP-ClifL

Job's Ancient Lament. Owen Dodson. FB

Joe, Gus, Sham. Changes: or, Reveries at a Window Overlooking a Country Road, with Two Women Talking Blues in the Kitchen. Yusef Komunyaaka. SP-KomuY

Joe Louis. Langston Hughes. SP-HughL *Fr.* Montage of a Dream Deferred. CP-HughL

Joe Louis is a man. Langston Hughes. CP-HughL

Joe the Grinder and G.I. Joe. *African-American Oral Tradition.* GetYo

Joe Turner. *Unknown.* CrDW

Joe Turner Blues. William Christopher Handy. CrDW

JOE WILLIAMS is. Memo #32. Etheridge Knight. SP-KnigE

Joel, that young prophet-son of Pethuel! Margaret Abigail Walker. CP-WalkM

Joggin' Erlong. Paul Laurence Dunbar. CP-DunbP

Johann. Alice Walker. CP-WalkA

Johannesburg Mines. Langston Hughes. CP-HughL

John. Lucille Clifton. SP-ClifL

John and Jacob—a Dialogue on Woman's Rights. Frances Ellen Watkins Harper. CP-HarpF

John Boyle O'Reilly. Paul Laurence Dunbar. CP-DunbP

John Brown. Robert Hayden. CP-HaydR

John Cabot, out of Wilma, once a Wycliffe. The Rites for Cousin Vit. Gwendolyn Brooks. BPo; NAAAL; NBV; PoBA

John Coltrane: An Impartial Review. Alfred B. Spellman. NNP; PoBA

John Coltrane Dance, The. Al Young. CP-YounA

John Henry. *Unknown.* BPo; CrDW

John J. Maya Angelou. CP-AngeM; SP-AngeM

John Keats, keep revel with me, too. (LL) To John Keats, Poet, at Springtime. Countee Cullen. AfAmPo; BANP; CDC; CP-CullC; NAAAL

John, look what Mis' Nelson give me. The Easter Bonnet. Clara Ann Thompson. CBWP-2

Johnny Speaks. Paul Laurence Dunbar. CP-DunbP

Johnny Thomas. Sterling A. Brown. CP-BrowS

Johnny's Pet Superstition. Clara Ann Thompson. CBWP-2

Joined again into its / greedy arms. (LL) A Plagued Journey. Maya Angelou. CP-AngeM; SP-AngeM

Jolly fat widows, The. Julia Fields. GT

Jolt. Al Young. CP-YounA

Jonah. Lucille Clifton. SP-ClifL

Jonah Begins His Story. Marilyn Nelson. *Fr.* I Dream the Book of Jonah. SP-NelsM

Jonestown: More Eyes for *Jadwiga's Dream.* Yusef Komunyakaa. SP-KomuY

Joseph. Lucille Clifton. SP-ClifL

Joseph, i afraid of stars. Holy Night. Lucille Clifton. SP-ClifL

Joseph to His Brothers. Amiri Baraka. SP-BaraA

Joshua fit de battle of Jericho [*or ob* Jerico]. *Unknown.* BPo; CrDW

Journey, A. Nikki Giovanni. SP-GiovN

Journey to the Place of Ghosts. Jay Wright. Crnst; GT

Journeystones. Audre Lorde. CP-LordA

Joy. Langston Hughes. CP-HughL; SP-HughL

Joy kindles by thy vital gale. Gratitude. George Moses Horton. SP-HortG

Joy shakes me like the wind that lifts a sail. Clarissa Scott Delany. CDC; ShDr

Joy to my bosom! rest to my fear! The Syrophenician Woman. Frances Ellen Watkins Harper. CP-HarpF

Joy/Spring. Al Young. CP-YounA

Ju-Ju Man. Art Nixon. CtF

Juan de Pareja: Painted by Velazquez. Richard A. Long. AmNP

JUba dis and JUba dat an. *African-American Oral Tradition.* TtW

Juber up and Juber down. *African-American Oral Tradition.* TtW

Judas. Ishmael Reed. CP-ReedI

Judas Iscariot. Countee Cullen. CP-CullC

Judeebug's Country. Joe Johnson. PoBA

Judge Every One with Perfect Calm. Alice Walker. CP-WalkA

JUDGE GIVES NEGRO 90 DAYS IN COUNTY JAIL. (LL) Ballad of the Landlord. Langston Hughes. CP-HughL; NAAAL; SP-HughL

Judge Not. Josephine D. Henderson Heard. CBWP-4

Judge William Hastie. Langston Hughes. CP-HughL

Judgement Day: For Big Red the Darwinian Doge. R.I.P. Kent Foreman. BrTr

Judging your roundness / delightful. (LL) On a Night of the Full Moon. Audre Lorde. CP-LordA; SP-LordA

Judgment Day. Langston Hughes. CP-HughL; SP-HughL

Judgment day will come by and by, The. (LL) To the White People of America. Joshua McCarter Simpson. AAP; AfAmPo

Judgment of God is upon us, The. Dies Irae. Margaret Abigail Walker. CP-WalkM

Judgment slumbered. God in mercy. Retribution. Frances Ellen Watkins Harper. CP-HarpF

Judith. Eloise Bibb. CBWP-4

Judith. Adah Isaacs Menken. CBWP-1

Judith's Fancy. Audre Lorde. CP-LordA

Juice Joint: Northern City. Langston Hughes. CP-HughL

Juice of a Lemon on the Trail of a Little Yellow. June Jordan. SP-JordJ

JuJu. Askia Muhammad Touré. PoBA

Juju of My Own, A. Lebert Bethune. BlFi; PoBA

Juke Box Love Song. Langston Hughes. *Fr.* Montage of a Dream Deferred. CP-HughL

Julian / Come back. The Return of Julian the Apostate to Rome. Ishmael Reed. CP-ReedI

Juliet. Langston Hughes. CP-HughL; SP-HughL

July. Daniel Gray-Kontar. SpiFi

July. Henrietta Cordelia Ray. CBWP-3

July. Sonia Sanchez. GT; SP-SancS

July 1st, 1982. Ishmael Reed. CP-ReedI

July 2, 1982—Juneau. Going the Rotterdam is in port. The Smiley School. Ishmael Reed. CP-ReedI

July 27. Norman Jordan. NBV

July 31. Norman Jordan. PoBA

Jump back, honey, jump back. (LL) A Negro Love Song. Paul Laurence Dunbar. AAP; BANP; CP-DunbP; CrDW; NAAAL; SSLK; TtW

Jump bigness upward. Mwilu / or Poem for the Living. Don L. Lee. JB

Jump down, turn around to pick a bale of cotton. Pick a Bale of Cotton. *Unknown.* NAAAL

Jump stop shake. (LL) Blackberry Sweet. Dudley Randall. NBP; PoBA

June. Mary Weston Fordham. CBWP-2

June. Henrietta Cordelia Ray. CBWP-3

June at Truro Beach the joyous bathers. Kite-Flying. Christopher Gilbert. GT

June or July—I'm not really sure—In. The Way It Is. Jon Goncalves. BlFi

Juneteenth. Marilyn Nelson. SP-NelsM

Jungle Strut. Al Young. CP-YounA

Jungle Surrender. Yusef Komunyakaa. SP-KomuY

Jungle Taste. Edward S. Silvera. CDC

Junglegrave. S. E. Anderson. PoBA

Junior Addict. Langston Hughes. BPo; CP-HughL

Junkie Monkey Reel. Maya Angelou. CP-AngeM; SP-AngeM

Junkies' Ball. *African-American Oral Tradition.* GetYo

Junkies' Heaven. *African-American Oral Tradition.* GetYo

Junkies loved Charles Parker and the sports, The. Historiography. Lorenzo Thomas. TtW

Jus get your beautiful black behind. Up Sister. Ruth Forman. IHS

Just a herd of Negroes. Share-Croppers. Langston Hughes. CP-HughL; SP-HughL

Just a New York Poem. Nikki Giovanni. SP-GiovN

Just ain't got no heart. (LL) Southern Mammy Sings. Langston Hughes. CP-HughL; SP-HughL

Just an Ordinary Guy. Langston Hughes. CP-HughL

Just as the twilight's holy hour. To an Infant. Mary Weston Fordham. CBWP-2

Just back from Minnesota/North Dakota. Letter to My Friend the Poet Ntozake Shange. June Jordan. SP-JordJ

Just because I love you. Reasons Why. Langston Hughes. CP-HughL

Just because you. Dragon's Blood. Ishmael Reed. CP-ReedI

Just because you wear a natural baby. Dancing in the Street. Al Young. CP-YounA

Just before sunlight / burns off morning fog. At the Screen Door. Yusef Komunyakaa. SP-KomuY

Just Beyond my reaching. Slave Coffle. Maya Angelou. CP-AngeM; SP-AngeM

Just for a Time. Maya Angelou. CP-AngeM; SP-AngeM

Just How It Happened. Priscilla Jane Thompson. CBWP-2

Just last friday. Jamal's Lamentation. Reuben Jackson. GT

Just like a rose in early spring. Requiescat in Pace. Benjamin Clark. EBAP

Just like Job. Maya Angelou. CP-AngeM; SP-AngeM

Just like me. (LL) Poor Girl. Maya Angelou. CP-AngeM; SP-AngeM

Just like the cedar of Lebanon. (LL) Taking in Wash. Rita Dove. SP-DoveR

Just look, 'tis a quarter past six, love. The Coming Woman. Mary Weston Fordham. CBWP-2

Just Taking Note. Sharon Scott. JB

Just the two of us. Sonia Sanchez. SP-SancS

Just to look at me. (LL) Amoebaean for Daddy. Maya Angelou. CP-AngeM; SP-AngeM

Just Us. Kwame Alexander. CtF

Just when I think I've got you nailed. The Battle of Saratoga (Springs) Revisited. Michael S. Harper. SP-HarpM

Just whistle a bit, if the day be dark. Paul Laurence Dunbar. CP-DunbP

Just you. just me. must. Sonia Sanchez. SP-SancS

Justice. Paul Laurence Dunbar. CP-DunbP

Justice. Langston Hughes. BPo; CP-HughL

K

Ka 'Ba. Amiri Baraka. BPo; CrDW; NBV

Kadava Kumbis Devise a Way to Marry for Love, The. Rita Dove. SP-DoveR

Kali / queen of fertility. Lucille Clifton. NAAAL; SP-ClifL

Kali's Galaxy. Ishmael Reed. CP-ReedI

Kansas and America. Michael S. Harper. SP-HarpM

Karamojongs. Alice Walker. CP-WalkA

Karazah to Karl. Adah Isaacs Menken. CBWP-1

Kardek Method, The. Ishmael Reed. CP-ReedI

Karenge Ya Marenge. Countee Cullen. CP-CullC; TtW

Karintha. Jean Toomer. Klds
"Her skin is like dusk on the eastern horizon."

Karma's Footsteps. Mariahadessa "Ekere" Tallie. CtF

"Kat" can play ball, Man, The. Funky Football. Ruby C. Saunders. BlSi

Katherine is warm. Why? Melba Joyce Boyd. BlSi

Katskills Kiss Romance Goodbye, The. Ishmael Reed. CP-ReedI

Keep A-Pluggin' Away. Paul Laurence Dunbar. CP-DunbP

Keep a Song Up on de Way. Paul Laurence Dunbar. CP-DunbP

Keep Me, Jesus, Keep Me ("Keep me 'neath Thy mighty wing"). Waverly Turner Carmichael. BANP

Keep on Pushing. David Henderson. BlFi; PoBA

Keep Your Eyes on the Prize. Unknown. CrDW

Keep your hand on the plow! / Hold on! (LL) Freedom's Plow. Langston Hughes. CP-HughL; SP-HughL

Keeper, (for Washington, D.C.). Esther Iverem. GT

Keeping of a Promise, The. Etheridge Knight. SP-KnigE

Keith, the white man who lived. I Was Looking at Miles. Honorée F. Jeffers. CtF

Kenscoff. Lorna Goodison. GT

Kentucky Blues. Sterling A. Brown. CP-BrowS

Kentucky, 1833. Rita Dove. SP-DoveR

Key and bar, key and bar. Love's Castle. Paul Laurence Dunbar. CP-DunbP

Keyfoods. Audre Lorde. SP-LordA
(Keyfood.) CP-LordA

Kicking. Al Young. CP-YounA

Kid, The. Ai. GT

Kid in the Park. Langston Hughes. CP-HughL; SP-HughL

Kid Sleepy. Langston Hughes. CP-HughL; SP-HughL

Kid Stuff. Frank Horne. AmNP; Klds; PoBA

Kidnap Poem. Nikki Giovanni. AmNP; BPo; SP-GiovN
("Yeah if i were a poet i'd kid / nap you.") (LL) BrTr

Kidnaped. Paul Laurence Dunbar. CP-DunbP

Kids in School with Me, The. Langston Hughes. CP-HughL

Kids Who Die. Langston Hughes. CP-HughL

Kill him—and let his soul run wild! (LL) Genius Child. Langston Hughes. SP-HughL

Killed / by a white woman. Clay. Amiri Baraka. ESEAA

Killers. Alice Walker. CP-WalkA

Killing Memory. Haki R. Madhubuti. TtW

Killing summer heat wraps up the city, A. A Poem for Women in Rage. Audre Lorde. CP-LordA; SP-LordA

Killing the Calves. Robert Hayden. CP-HaydR

Kin. Maya Angelou. CP-AngeM; SP-AngeM

Kin. Michael S. Harper. SP-HarpM; TtW

Kin. Naomi Long Madgett. TtW

Kind and gracious princess, more than friend. Moses: A Story of the Nile. Frances Ellen Watkins Harper. CP-HarpF

Kind of Love, Some Say, A. Maya Angelou. CP-AngeM; SP-AngeM

Kind of Man He Is, The. Lucille Clifton. SP-ClifL

Kindly Deed, A. Priscilla Jane Thompson. CBWP-2

Kindness. Mary E. Tucker. CBWP-1

King: April 4, 1968, For Eva Ray. Gerald William Barrax. ESEAA; GT

King is Dead, The. Paul Laurence Dunbar. CP-DunbP

King Oliver of New Orleans. Satchmo. Melvin Beaunearus Tolson. BPo; NAAAL

King, once summoned his favorites, A. The King's Favorites. Priscilla Jane Thompson. CBWP-2

King Saul was disconcerted. David and Goliath. Priscilla Jane Thompson. CBWP-2

King's Favorites, The. Priscilla Jane Thompson. CBWP-2

King's X—no fairs to use it anymore! (LL) U. S. 1946 King's X. Robert Frost. CrDW

Kiss, The. Alice Walker. CP-WalkA; GT

Kiss. Al Young. CP-YounA; PoBA

Kiss? A. Pray tell me, what is in a kiss. Mary E. Tucker. CBWP-1

Kiss in the Dark, A. Thomas Sayers Ellis. GT

Kiss me good night. A Kiss Requested. Eda Lou Walton. ShDr

Kiss me, Miami, thou most constant one. To the Miami. Paul Laurence Dunbar. CP-DunbP

Kiss Requested, A. Eda Lou Walton. ShDr

Kissie Lee. Margaret Abigail Walker. BlSi; CP-WalkM

Kissing Keys. Karen Williams. CtF

Kissinger has made it, yall. He's the secretary. Horatio Alger Uses Scag. Amiri Baraka. SP-BaraA

Kitchen is its readiness, The. This Winter Day. Maya Angelou. CP-AngeM; SP-AngeM

Kitchen Linoleum. Audre Lorde. CP-LordA

Kitchenette Building. Gwendolyn Brooks. Fr. A Street in Bronzeville. BPo; BlSi; BPo; GT; NAAAL; SP-BrooG

Kite-Flying. Christopher Gilbert. GT

Kiver up yo' haid, my little lady. Lullaby. Paul Laurence Dunbar. CP-DunbP

Kneading. Michael S. Harper. SP-HarpM

Kneegrows niggas. Be Cool, Baby. Rob Penny. PoBA

Knees of a Natural Man, (for Jay Wright). Henry L. Dumas. GT

Knife blade of cold air keeps prying, A. Upstate. Derek Walcott. GT

Knight, The. Paul Laurence Dunbar. CP-DunbP

Knight of My Maiden Love. Priscilla Jane Thompson. CBWP-2

Knight of "silver tongue" and stately grace, A. Wendell Phillips. Henrietta Cordelia Ray. CBWP-3

Knitting. Mary E. Tucker. CBWP-1

Knock is at her door, but she is weak, A. Dead. Paul Laurence Dunbar. CP-DunbP

Knock on Wood. Henry L. Dumas. BlFi; PoBA

Knockin' down chairs and slammin' doors. African-American Oral Tradition. GetYo

Know me / Africa. (LL) For Us, Who Dare Not Dare. Maya Angelou. CP-AngeM; SP-AngeM

Know that more than white is missing. (LL) Lessons from a Mirror. Thylias Moss. ESEAA

Know ye the man whom God has blessed. Lines to the Hon. George L. Knox. Eloise Bibb. CBWP-4

Know you, winds that blow your course. Alice. Paul Laurence Dunbar. CP-DunbP

Knowing her is not knowing her. An Afterword: For Gwen Brooks. Don L. Lee. JB

Known to Eve and Me. Maya Angelou. CP-AngeM

Knoxville, Tennessee. Nikki Giovanni. AmNP; BPo; BlSi; BrTr; PoBA; SP-GiovN

Kodachromes of the Island. Robert Hayden. CP-HaydR

Kojo; I Am a Black. Gwendolyn Brooks. TtW Fr. Children Coming Home. ESEAA

Koky Taylor sang. Blues at 1. Dorothy Perry Thompson. SpiFl

Kora kora hear the strings attached. His Eminence Plays the Soular System. Eugene B. Redmond. TtW

Koto Music/Singing. Al Young. CP-YounA

Krismas Dinnah. Maggie Pogue Johnson. CBWP-4

Ku Klux. Langston Hughes. BPo; CP-HughL; SP-HughL

Kwa Mama Zetu Waliotuzaa. Sonia Sanchez. SP-SancS

L

L. A. (Lost Assholes). Madd Vibe. CtF

L.A. Street. African-American Oral Tradition. GetYo

La Belle, La Douce, La Grande. Countee Cullen. CP-CullC

La Peste. Marilyn Nelson. SP-NelsM

La Vie C'est la Vie. Jessie Redmond Fauset. BANP; CDC

Labor Storm. Langston Hughes. CP-HughL

Labyrinth of Life, The. Margaret Abigail Walker. CP-WalkM

Lacking what they want to see. Contact Lenses. Audre Lorde. CP-LordA

Lacrimas or There Is a Need to Scream. K. Curtis Lyle. NBV; PoBA

Ladder, flag, and amplifier. Corner Meeting. Langston Hughes. Fr. Montage of a Dream Deferred. CP-HughL

Lady cigarette fixed in the ash trays of history, A. The Cat Is Sleeping on a Poem. Bob Kaufman. SP-KaufB

Lady in Cabaret. Langston Hughes. CP-HughL

Lady, Lady, I saw your face. Anne Spencer. BlSi; NAAAL; PoBA; ShDr

Lady Liberty, see also If You See My Little Girl in Denver. African-American Oral Tradition. GetYo

Lady Luncheon Club. Maya Angelou. CP-AngeM; SP-AngeM

Lady, my lady, come from out the garden. To a Certain Lady, in Her Garden. Sterling A. Brown. CDC; CP-BrowS

Lady of the Night star-breathed. The Night-Blooming Jasmine. Audre Lorde. CP-LordA

Lady, tell me, will you, pray. Found—Who Lost? Mary E. Tucker. CBWP-1

Lady / when ya purple heels hit concrete. You So Woman. Ruth Forman. SpiFl

Lady with thine eyes of beauty. The Valentine. Mary Weston Fordham. CBWP-2

Lady's Boogie. Langston Hughes. SP-HughL *Fr.* Montage of a Dream Deferred. CP-HughL

Lady's Days. Larry Neal. NBV

Lady's love is gained, A. The Price of Disrespect. Lizelia Augusta Jenkins Moorer. CBWP-3

Lady's Way. Reuben Jackson. GT

Lager Beer. Paul Laurence Dunbar. CP-DunbP

Lake Bud. Ishmael Reed. CP-ReedI

Lake City Tragedy, The. Frances Ellen Watkins Harper. CP-HarpF

Lake in Central Park, The. Jay Wright. ESEAA; GT

Lake Merritt is Bud Powell's piano. Lake Bud. Ishmael Reed. CP-ReedI

Lake Michigan / (like so much hearsay). The Madison Experience. June Jordan. SP-JordJ

Lake Murry. Pinkie Gordon Lane. GT

Lakefront, Cleveland. Russell Atkins. GT

Lake's dark breast, The. The Rising of the Storm. Paul Laurence Dunbar. CP-DunbP

Lame and the Whore, The. *African-American Oral Tradition.* GetYo

Lament: "Now let all lovely things embark." Countee Cullen. CP-CullC

Lament for Dark Peoples. Langston Hughes. CP-HughL

Lament of a Vanquished Beau, The. Langston Hughes. CP-HughL

Lament over Love. Langston Hughes. CP-HughL; NAAAL; SP-HughL

Lamenting thru gipsies his fast suicide. (LL) Political Poem. Amiri Baraka. SP-BaraA

Lancelot. Arna Bontemps. CDC

Land is cold and its men gather earth for no reason, The. A Woman's Song. Colleen J. McElroy. BlSi

Land o' Used to Be, The. Paul Laurence Dunbar. CP-DunbP

Land of flowers is dusty, The. For the King and Queen of Summer. Audre Lorde. CP-LordA

Land of nod, The. Cain. Lucille Clifton. SP-ClifL

Land of Pharoah. Whichway. Ron Welburn. NBV

Land / Wants me to come back, The. Dustbowl. Langston Hughes. CP-HughL

Land was there before us, The. Inauguration. Lorenzo Thomas. NBV

Landfill. Michael S. Harper. SP-HarpM

Landgrave's gilded hall was all bedecked, The. The Contest of Song and Love. George Marion McClellan. *Fr.* The Legend of Tannhauser and Elizabeth. EBAP

Landlady, landlady, lock all your doors. Cocaine Nell. *African-American Oral Tradition.* GetYo

Landlord, landlord. Ballad of the Landlord. Langston Hughes. NAAAL; SP-HughL *Fr.* Montage of a Dream Deferred. CP-HughL

Land's end. And sound and river come. The Point. Robert Hayden. CP-HaydR; ESEAA

Landscape for the Disappeared. Yusef Komunyakaa. SP-KomuY

Landscape with Nymphs and Satyrs. Norman Henry, II Pritchard. GT

Landscape with Saxophonist. Thylias Moss. ESEAA

Landscapes. Harris Duriel. SpiFl

Lane Is the Pretty One. Lucille Clifton. SP-ClifL

Langston Blues. Dudley Randall. FB

Langston Hughes. Gwendolyn Brooks. SP-BrooG

Language of past seasons, The. Thaw. Audre Lorde. CP-LordA

Languages We Are, The. Frederick, Jr. Bryant. NBP

Lapse, The. Paul Laurence Dunbar. CP-DunbP

Large Room with Wood Floor. Clarence Major. GT

Large supply of golden grain, A. (LL) On Summer. George Moses Horton. AAP; SP-HortG

Lark is silent in his nest, The. Good-Night. Paul Laurence Dunbar. CP-DunbP

Las Flores para una Niña Negra. Demetrice A. Worley. SpiFl

Las Turistas Negras Grande. Wanda Coleman. TtW

Last Affair: Bessie's Blues Song. Michael S. Harper. ESEAA; SP-HarpM

Last Call. Langston Hughes. CP-HughL

Last comfore in Gethsemane. (LL) For Jim, Easter Eve. Anne Spencer. AmNP

Last Day of the Year; or, New Year's Eve, The. Mrs. Henry Linden. CBWP-4

Last Decision, The. Maya Angelou. CP-AngeM; SP-AngeM

Last episode / left her holding it, The. She Should Have Called 911. Pam Ward. CtF

Last Feast of Belshazzar, The. Langston Hughes. CP-HughL

Last Letter. Gerald William Barrax. ESEAA

Last Letter to the Western Civilization. D. T. Ogilvie. NBP

Last love, / proper in conclusion, A. Recovery. Maya Angelou. CP-AngeM; SP-AngeM

Last Man Living, The. Langston Hughes. CP-HughL

Last night an old man warned me. From the Cave. Audre Lorde. CP-LordA

Last night I danced on the rim of the moon. Ethel M. Caution. ShDr

Last night, I dreamed of America. More. Ai. GT

Last night I dreamt. Dream. Langston Hughes. CP-HughL; SP-HughL

Last night I heard your voice, mother. December, 1919. Claude McKay. SP-McKaC

Last night I lay upon my bed and would have slept. After a Visit. Countee Cullen. CP-CullC

Last night / I played Kirk Douglas to. Poison Light. Ishmael Reed. CP-ReedI

Last night I watched the moon go out. Lunar Eclipse. Audre Lorde. CP-LordA

Last night you were a river. Conquest. Pauli Murray. GT

Last Note to My Girls. Lucille Clifton. SP-ClifL; TtW

Last on legs, last on sax. "Bird Lives": Charles Parker. Michael S. Harper. SP-HarpM

Last Poem I'm Gonna Write Bout Us. Sonia Sanchez. SP-SancS

Last Poem on Bell's Theorem. June Jordan. SP-JordJ

Last Prince of the East. Langston Hughes. CP-HughL

Last Quarter Moon of the Dying Year, The. Jonathan Henderson Brooks. CDC; TtW

Last quatrain, The. (LL) Bronzeville Mother Loiters in Mississippi. / Meanwhile, a Mississippi Mother Burns Bacon. Gwendolyn Brooks. Crnst; ESEAA; SP-BrooG

Last Quatrain of the Ballad of Emmett Till, The. Gwendolyn Brooks. PoBA; SP-BrooG

("Emmett's mother is a pretty-faced thing.") ESEAA

Last Ride of Wild Bill. Sterling A. Brown. CP-BrowS

Last time, The. Alice Walker. CP-WalkA

Last time blues / with no hesitations., The. David Henderson. *See* Do Nothing Till You Hear from Me.

Last time i was home, The. Mothers. Nikki Giovanni. SP-GiovN

Last Week in 30, The. Ishmael Reed. CP-ReedI

Last week / my mother died. Haki R. Madhubuti. *Fr.* Two Poems (from "Sketches from a Black-Nappy-Headed Poet"). BrTr

Last Words By "Slick." Etheridge Knight. SP-KnigE

Last year changed its seasons. In Retrospect. Maya Angelou. CP-AngeM; SP-AngeM

Late at night. Raid. Langston Hughes. CP-HughL

Late Corner. Langston Hughes. CP-HughL; Klds

Late in the day when light is sandwiched. New Autumn, New York. Al Young. CP-YounA

Late Lamented Wind, Burned in Indignation, The. Bob Kaufman. SP-KaufB

Late last night I. Langston Hughes. CP-HughL; SP-HughL

Late October. Maya Angelou. CP-AngeM; SP-AngeM

Late that mad Monday evening. Madness One Monday Evening. Julia Fields. Klds; NNP

Late-Winter Blues and Promises of Love. Houston A., Jr. Baker. TtW

Lately / everybody i meet. Lucille Clifton. SP-ClifL

Lately, I've become accustomed to the way. Preface to a Twenty Volume Suicide Note. Amiri Baraka. AmNP; CrDW; ESEAA; Klds; NAAAL; NNP; PoBA; SP-BaraA; TtW

Later he'll say Death stepped right up. The Stroke. Rita Dove. SP-DoveR

Later i'll say / i spent my life. Lucille Clifton. SP-ClifL

Lathe: Shirl's Tree. Michael S. Harper. SP-HarpM

Laughed in our furnished room. (LL) Heavy Water Blues. Bob Kaufman. NBV; SP-KaufB

Laughers. Langston Hughes. CP-HughL

Laughing eyes followed. Asante Sana, Te Te. Thadious M. Davis. BlSi

Laughing, merry, childish voices, woke us in their eager glee. Christmas, South, 1866. Mary E. Tucker. CBWP-1

Laughing, with a TV's blue-static figures. When Loneliness Is a Man. Yusef Komunyakaa. SP-KomuY

Laughter as the Highest Form of Contemplation. Marilyn Nelson. SP-NelsM

Laughter tumbled over laughter. Spring. Helen G. Quigless. BkSV

Laurel Street, 1950. Dorothy Perry Thompson. SpiFl

Law, The. Albert E., Jr. Haynes. NBP

Law for George, The. Sterling A. Brown. CP-BrowS

Law isn't all. Untitled. "Law isn't all." Ishmael Reed. CP-ReedI

Law! What is law! The wise and sage. Elymas Payson Rogers. AAP *Fr.* On the Fugitive Slave Law. EBAP

Lawd, Dese Colored Chillum. Ruby C. Saunders. BlSi

Lawd I saw the sun go down! (LL) Blue Bayou. Langston Hughes. CP-HughL; SP-HughL

Lawd Zambesi! For Singing In Good Mood. Lebert Bethune. GT

Lawyer had a legal mouse, A. A Legal Mouse. Lizelia Augusta Jenkins Moorer. CBWP-3

Lawyers' Ways, The. Paul Laurence Dunbar. CP-DunbP

Lay back women are cooking, The. Bazaar. Audre Lorde. CP-LordA

Lay me down beneaf de willers in de grass. Death Song[, A]. Paul Laurence Dunbar. BANP; CDC; CP-DunbP

Lazy Day, A. Paul Laurence Dunbar. CP-DunbP

Lazy, laughing South, The. The South. Langston Hughes. CP-HughL; SP-HughL

Le Carnaval. Armand Lanusse. TtW

Le Retour au Village aux Perles. Nelson Desbrosses. EBAP; TtW

Le Retour de Napoléon. Victor Séjour. EBAP

Le Xuan, Beautiful Spring. Yusef Komunyakaa. SP-KomuY

Lead. Jayne Cortez. PoBA

Lead gently, Lord, and slow. A Hymn. Paul Laurence Dunbar. CP-DunbP

Leadbelly. Cornelius Eady. ESEAA

Leadbelly Song, The. Al Young. CP-YounA

Leading to the underworld. (LL) Tu Do Street. Yusef Komunyakaa. SP-KomuY; TtW

Leaf from freedom's golden chaplet fair, A. To My Father. Henrietta Cordelia Ray. AAP; BlSi; CBWP-3; EBAP; TtW

"League of Gileadites": Messages. Michael S. Harper. SP-HarpM

Lean and hungry and tired of my dry bones and years? (LL) Since 1619. Margaret Abigail Walker. CP-WalkM

Lean bird circles, A. (LL) Legacy: My South. Dudley Randall. NNP; PoBA; TtW

Lean is the ghost of Molly Means. (LL) Molly Means. Margaret Abigail Walker. AmNP; BlSi; CP-WalkM; Klds

Lean pinchbeck housewives pointed their fingers. Memories of Salem. Sterling A. Brown. CP-BrowS

Leanna's Poem. Lucille Clifton. SP-ClifL

Leap Yeah Party, De. Maggie Pogue Johnson. CBWP-4

Lear Is Gay. Robert Hayden. CP-HaydR

Learn how to fall. (LL) Sky Diving. Ishmael Reed. CP-ReedI; TtW

Learn to be Black men. (LL) True Import of Present Dialogue, Black vs. Negro. Nikki Giovanni. BrTr; Crnst

Learn to Count. Unknown. NAAAL

Learning to Dance. Rudy Bee Graham. BlFi

Learning to Read. Frances Ellen Watkins Harper. AAP; AfAmPo; BlSi; CP-HarpF; NAAAL

(Learning to Read (Sketches of a Southern Life, 1872).) EBAP

Learning to Swim at Forty-Five, I could not whistle and walk in storms along Lake Michigan's shore. . . I could not swallow the lake.. Colleen J. McElroy. GT

Learning to Write. Audre Lorde. CP-LordA; GT

Leave me: oh! leave me. Dying. Adah Isaacs Menken. CBWP-1

Leave your Coras. Draftees. Langston Hughes. CP-HughL

Leaves. Countee Cullen. GT

Leaves are sere, The. November. Henrietta Cordelia Ray. CBWP-3

Leaves believe, The. The Lesson of the Falling Leaves. Lucille Clifton. SP-ClifL

Leaves in for space so light can get thru. (LL) The Prestidigitator 1. Al Young. CP-YounA; NBV

Leaves nothing / The same. (LL) Beale Street. Langston Hughes. CP-HughL; SP-HughL

Leaves on the trees, The. By Heart. Al Young. CP-YounA

Leaves turned red and brown as my Father, The. Autumn. Helen G. Quigless. BkSV

Leaving Eden. Ralph Dickey. ESEAA

Leaving Home for Home. Al Young. CP-YounA

Leaving   leaving / the bridged water. On My Way Out I passed You and the Varrazano Bridge. Audre Lorde. CP-LordA

Leaving Rochester. Al Young. CP-YounA

Leaving Syracuse. Al Young. CP-YounA; ESEAA

Leaving the Hospice. Marilyn Nelson. SP-NelsM

Leaving the known for another city. Women on Trains. Audre Lorde. CP-LordA

Leaving you. A Courtesy, A Trenchant Grace. Cyrus Cassells. GT

Lee-ers of Hew. James Cunningham. JB

Lee of Leesburg in this place, A. Roberta Lee. Sterling A. Brown. CP-BrowS

Leelah looked up and, sobbed. "McLambert, ma." Albery Allson Whitman. Fr. Leelah Misled. EBAP

Leelah Misled. Albery Allson Whitman. EBAP
  "And some were they, which one by one have set."
  "At times she thought to commit suicide."
  "Away from this toward fair Georgia's plain."
  "Back to our theme, McLambert's 'ev'ning rides'."
  "Battling gods of Milton's epic page, The."
  "But now a glimpse of Leelah checks him up."
  "But why he'd ride 'ride' so certainly each eve."
  "Clother with the rich aspect of this fair clime."
  "Extravagantly rosy her fair cheeks."
  "Fates, burn these novels that young ladies read."
  "From Macon out, 'twas just a 'pleasant ride'."
  "From time to time, McLambert came and went."
  "Full many a time, in life's fair spring, I've strolled."
  "Go ponder at that faithful mother's grave."
  "Go, ponder at that mansion desolate."
  "Great God! and yet shall feeble man presume."
  "I charge you, O chaste lasses! all beware."
  "I love the symphony of nature's chords."
  "'In Rama,' here was truly heard 'a voice'."
  "Leelah looked up and, sobbed. 'McLambert, ma'."
  "McLambert long had gone from home away."
  "McLambert now upon Leelah looked down."
  "My fetters borken, I begin to sing."
  "My Leelah's ruined, and her mother's grief."
  "My muse is mournful, and I turn away."
  "'My shell is broken,' but I once again."
  "Nor sing to me of distant climes, O muse!"
  "Not beautiful, but very prepossessing."
  "Not of imputed Heroes, nor of ghosts."
  "Now, reader, pardon me for having sung."
  "Now, reader, this digression you'll excuse."
  "O, seems it not to other eyes as sweet."
  "Only child was she of a rich pair, The."
  "Servant met him at the outer gate, A."
  "'Sitr, cooks,' the mistress whispers, in a rage."
  "There lived a dashing gentleman of worth."
  "There's one, who never will her own forsake."
  "Though slaves, a thousand come at her command."
  "Time passed away, and Leelah downcast grew."
  "To care for others is the God in man."
  "'Twas eve, ah fatal eve! and no one near."
  "'Twas eve, and far and near deep quiet reigned."
  "'Twas eve, and there no parent's eye could see."
  "'Twas said by some, that Leelah was too fast."
  "'Twill hope and fear, this condition's a war."
  "When he, his heart had pledged, to full fifteen."
  "With hands behind him clasped, that father walked."

Left-Handed Cellist, The. Rita Dove. SP-DoveR

Left like water in glasses overnight. Love from My Father. Carole C. Gregory Clemmons. PoBA

Leg-acy of a Blue Capricorn. James Cunningham. JB

Legacies. Nikki Giovanni. SP-GiovN

Legacy. Amiri Baraka. PoBA

Legacy—Hers. Audre Lorde. CP-LordA

Legacy: My South. Dudley Randall. NNP; PoBA; TtW

Legacy of a Brother. Renaldo Fernandez. NBV

Legal Mouse, A. Lizelia Augusta Jenkins Moorer. CBWP-3

Legend. Sterling A. Brown. CP-BrowS

Legend of Tannhauser and Elizabeth, The. George Marion McClellan. EBAP
  Contest of Song and Love, The.
  Pilgrimage and Staff, The.
  Venusburg, The.

Legend of Versailles, A. Melvin Beaunearus Tolson. BPo; NAAAL

Lela's Charms. Lizelia Augusta Jenkins Moorer. CBWP-3

Lemme be wid Casey Jones. Odyssey of Big Boy. Sterling A. Brown. BANP; CDC; CP-BrowS; NAAAL

Lemme roll 'em, boy. Crap Game. Langston Hughes. CP-HughL

Lemons, Lemons. Al Young. CP-YounA

Lena Lovelace. Melvin B. Tolson. GT

Lend me your ears if you want to hear. Treacherous Breast. African-American Oral Tradition. GetYo

Length of Moon. Arna Bontemps. CDC

Lenin walks around the world. Langston Hughes. CP-HughL

Lenox Avenue. Langston Hughes. CP-HughL

Lenox Avenue / by daylight. Dive. Langston Hughes. Fr. Montage of a Dream Deferred. CP-HughL

Lenox Avenue is a big street. Keep on Pushing. David Henderson. BlFi; PoBA

Lenox Avenue Mural. AmNP

Comment on Curb. SP-HughL

"Good morning, daddy!" SP-HughL

Harlem: "What happens to a dream deferred?". CrDW; GT; NAAAL; SP-HughL; SSLK

(Dream Deferred.) PoBA

Island: "Between two rivers." SP-HughL

Letter. SP-HughL

Same in Blues. SP-HughL; SSLK

Leona, dear, twelve months ago. Eloise Bibb. CBWP-4

Leroy. Amiri Baraka. BPo; PoBA

Leslie. Marvin, Jr. Wyche. AmNP

Lesson, The. Maya Angelou. CP-AngeM; SP-AngeM

Lesson, The. Paul Laurence Dunbar. CP-DunbP

Lesson. Al Young. CP-YounA

Lesson of the Falling Leaves, The. Lucille Clifton. SP-ClifL

Lesson on Braces. Valerie Jean. SpiFl

Lessons from a Mirror. Thylias Moss. ESEAA

Lessons of the Street. Frances Ellen Watkins Harper. CP-HarpF

Lester Leaps In. Al Young. CP-YounA; ESEAA

Lester Young. Ted Joans. AmNP

Let a race of men now rise and take control. (LL) For my people everywhere singing their slave songs repeatedly. Margaret Abigail Walker. CP-WalkM; Klds; NAAAL; SSLK; TtW

Let all who will. Militant. Langston Hughes. CP-HughL; PoBA

Let America Be American Again. Langston Hughes. CP-HughL

Let Amicitia in her ample reign. On Friendship. Phillis Wheatley. CP-WheaP; EBAP

Let darkness / Gather up its roses. Dare. Langston Hughes. CP-HughL

Let happy throats be mute. Threnody. Donald Jeffrey Hayes. AmNP

Let him come. (LL) Nat Turner. Samuel Allen. FB

Let him have his spats and cane. (LL) Sporting Beasley. Sterling A. Brown. CP-BrowS; Klds; NAAAL

Let it be alleys. Let it be a hall. A Lovely Love. Gwendolyn Brooks. BPo; NAAAL; SP-BrooG

Let love be / at the end. (LL) Let There Be New Flowering. Lucille Clifton. SP-ClifL

Let me be buried in the rain. Invocation. Helene Johnson. AmNP; BANP; NAAAL; ShDr

Let Me Be Held When the Longing Comes. Stephany Fuller. BPo

Let me be your flute. Sonia Sanchez. SP-SancS

Let me become dead eyed. Wise Men. Langston Hughes. CP-HughL

Let me close the eyes of my soul. Despair. Paul Laurence Dunbar. CP-DunbP

Let me die and not tremble at death. Imploring to Be Resigned at Death. George Moses Horton. AAP; AfAmPo; SP-HortG

Let me hip you to the streets. Letter to an Aspiring Junkie. Maya Angelou. CP-AngeM; SP-AngeM

Let me learn now where Beauty is. Questing. Anne Spencer. CDC

Let me look and see love's. Soul-Smiles. S. E. Anderson. BlFi

Let me make songs for the people. Songs for the People. Frances Ellen Watkins Harper. AfAmPo; CP-HarpF; EBAP; TtW

Let me open mama your 3 corner box. Blues for Franks Wooten; House of the Lifting of the Head. Tom Weatherly. GT; NBV

Let none ignobly halt because. Joseph Seamon Cotter, Sr. EBAP

Let not the proud of heart condemn. Little Sonnet to Little Friends. Countee Cullen. CP-CullC

Let scoffers mock, let unbelief deny. Albery Allson Whitman. AAP

Let the band play Dixie. Song of Triumph. Sterling A. Brown. CP-BrowS

Let the knowing speak. Adjuration. Charles Enoch Wheeler. AmNP

Let the Light Enter! Frances Ellen Watkins Harper. CP-HarpF

Let the rain kiss you. April Rain Song. Langston Hughes. CP-HughL

Let them come / As they usually do by night. Elma Stuckey. TtW

Let them keep it. And Was Not Improved. Lerone, Jr. Bennett. PoBA

"Let there be light," a joyous thrill. Frances Ellen Watkins Harper. CP-HarpF

Let There Be New Flowering. Lucille Clifton. SP-ClifL

Let this be scattered far and wide, laid low. Counter Mood. Countee Cullen. CP-CullC

Let those who will stride on their barren roads. A Roadway. Paul Laurence Dunbar. CP-DunbP

Let uh revolution come. U Name This One. Carolyn M. Rodgers. BlSi; PoBA

Let us be still. To Usward. Gwendolyn B. Bennett. BlSi; ShDr

Let us begin the real work. Sonia Sanchez. BrTr

Let us call her footnote, oddity, heart tug. The Woman Who Died in Line. Saundra Sharp. SpiFl

Let us forgive Ty Kendricks. Southern Cop. Sterling A. Brown. CP-BrowS

Let us give thanks to God above. Thanksgiving. Lizelia Augusta Jenkins Moorer. CBWP-3

Let us kill off youth. Comment on War. Langston Hughes. CP-HughL

Let us not turn for this aside to die. At a Parting. Countee Cullen. CP-CullC

Let us roam the night together / Singing. (LL) Harlem Night Song. Langston Hughes. CP-HughL; SP-HughL

Let us stiffen. The Covenant. James Cunningham. JB

Let Us Strive to Do Something. Mrs. Henry Linden. CBWP-4

Let us suppose him differently placed. Sterling A. Brown. CP-BrowS

Let us with Angels share. (LL) Evening Thought, An [: Salvation by Christ with Penetential Cries]. Jupiter Hammon. CrDW; EBAP

Lethe. Georgia Douglas Johnson. CDC

Let's call him *Jim Crow*. A Reconsideration of the Blackbird. Thylias Moss. ESEAA

Let's go see Old Abe. Lincoln Monument: Washington. Langston Hughes. CP-HughL

Let's Majeste. Maya Angelou. CP-AngeM; SP-AngeM

Let's Take All the Blame. Peter Harris. CtF

Let's talk of Judas for a while. Judas Iscariot. Countee Cullen. CP-CullC

Letter, A. Paul Laurence Dunbar. CP-DunbP

Letter. Keith Gilyard. SpiFl

Letter. Robert Hayden. CP-HaydR

Letter. Langston Hughes. SP-HughL *Fr.* Lenox Avenue Mural. AmNP *Fr.* Montage of a Dream Deferred. CP-HughL

Letter. Langston Hughes. *Fr.* Seven Moments of Love. CP-HughL

Letter across Doubt and Distance. M. Carl Holman. AmNP

Letter for Jan. Audre Lorde. CP-LordA

Letter from a Wife. S. Carolyn Reese. BrTr

Letter from Phillis Wheatley, A. Robert Hayden. CP-HaydR; ESEAA; NAAAL

Letter from Spain. Langston Hughes. CP-HughL

Letter in my mailbox says you've made it, A. To the Girl Who Lives In a Tree. Audre Lorde. CP-LordA; SP-LordA

Letter in Winter. Raymond R. Patterson. PoBA

Letter to a Benedictine Monk. Marilyn Nelson. GT

("Dear Frère Jacques.") SP-NelsM

Letter to an Aspiring Junkie. Maya Angelou. CP-AngeM; SP-AngeM

Letter to Anne, A. Langston Hughes. CP-HughL

Letter to Bob Kaufman. Yusef Komunyakaa. SP-KomuY

Letter to E. Franklin Frazier. Amiri Baraka. BPo; PoBA; SP-BaraA

Letter to Madame Lindé from Justine, Her Creole Servant. Sybil Klein. TtW

Letter to My Friend the Poet Ntozake Shange. June Jordan. SP-JordJ

Letter to My Sister. Anne Spencer. AfAmPo; AmNP; BlSi; NAAAL; PoBA; ShDr; TtW

Letter to the Academy. Langston Hughes. CP-HughL

Letter to the Local Police. June Jordan. SP-JordJ

Letters [*or* Notes] Found near a Suicide. Frank Horne. AmNP; CDC; Klds; PoBA

To "Chick". BPo

To James. BPo;

To Mother. BPo

To You. BPo

Letters from a New England Negro. Sherley Anne Williams. ESEAA

Letters from friends used to be an art form. Pages for a Friend. Ntozake Shange. IHS

Letting go / in order to hold on. How Poems Are Made: A Discredited View. Alice Walker. CP-WalkA

Letting midnight / out on bail. Jam Session. Langston Hughes. *Fr.* Montage of a Dream Deferred. CP-HughL

Levitation with Baby. Marilyn Nelson. SP-NelsM

L'hiver, sémillante Palmyre. Le Carnaval. Armand Lanusse. TtW

Liar, The. Amiri Baraka. SP-BaraA

Liars. Langston Hughes. CP-HughL

'Lias! 'Lias! Bless de Lawd! In the Morning. Paul Laurence Dunbar. BPo; CP-DunbP

Libation. / Hey sisters, we the color of our men. Ceremony. Jewel C. Latimore. BlSi

Liberalissimo. Hart Leroi Bibbs. BlFi

Liberation / Poem. Sonia Sanchez. NBV

Liberty. George Moses Horton. SP-HortG

Liberty and Peace. Phillis Wheatley. CP-WheaP

Liberty and Slavery. George Moses Horton. *See* On Liberty and Slavery.

Lie, The. Maya Angelou. CP-AngeM; SP-AngeM

Lie bedridden. Spring. Clinton. Sterling Plumpp. BkSV

Lies of young boys are to be heard about, or read about, The. Election Day. Amiri Baraka. BlFi

Life. Paul Laurence Dunbar. AmNP; CDC; CP-DunbP

Life. Henrietta Cordelia Ray. CBWP-3

Life. Mary E. Tucker. CBWP-1

Life after Death. Richard W. Thomas. PoBA

Life aint all beer and skittles. Bête Noire. Harryette Mullen. TtW

Life and Death: The Bitch's Brew / The Readiness Is ALL. George Barlow. *Fr. Gabriel.* TtW

Life at the Back of the Plane. Al Young. CP-YounA

Life! Ay, as best, 'tis but a mystery! (LL) Life. Henrietta Cordelia Ray. CBWP-3

Life Cycles. Nikki Giovanni. SP-GiovN

Life Doesn't Frighten Me. Maya Angelou. CP-AngeM; SP-AngeM

Life for a Life. Mary E. Tucker. CBWP-1

Life / For him / Must be. Sport. Langston Hughes. CP-HughL

Life for my child is simple, and is good. Gwendolyn Brooks. SP-BrooG

Life I Led, The. Nikki Giovanni. GT; SP-GiovN

Life is a glass wherein we dimly see. Life's Boundary. Henrietta Cordelia Ray. CBWP-3

Life is a screwball comedy. Ishmael Reed. CP-ReedI

Life / is at 2 playing. Childhood. Jewel C. Latimore. JB

Life Is Fine. Langston Hughes. CP-HughL; SP-HughL

Life is fine! (LL) Life Is Fine. Langston Hughes. CP-HughL; SP-HughL

Life is for the living. Note in Music. Langston Hughes. CP-HughL

Life is full of mirth and pleasure. Adieu. Mary E. Tucker. CBWP-1

Life is made for earnest action. Something to Do. Frances Ellen Watkins Harper. CP-HarpF

Life is ours like the real. Theme One: The Variations. August Wilson. PoBA

Life-long, Poor Browning. Anne Spencer. CDC

Life of a Junkie. *African-American Oral Tradition.* GetYo

Life of a Saint, The. Marilyn Nelson. SP-NelsM

   Saint Leaves His Father's House, The.

   Saint Preaches, The.

   Saint's Dream, The.

   Seducing the Saint.

Life of Lincoln West, The. Gwendolyn Brooks. BrTr; FB

Life / Poem. Sonia Sanchez. BrTr

Life to her no brightness brought. Saved by Faith. Frances Ellen Watkins Harper. CP-HarpF

Life was mine full of the close concern, A. Love. Paul Laurence Dunbar. CP-DunbP

Life was trembling, faintly trembling. The Dying Bondman. Frances Ellen Watkins Harper. CP-HarpF

Life we find is nevermore. Deception. Josephine D. Henderson Heard. CBWP-4

Life's a funny old proposition. *African-American Oral Tradition.* GetYo

Life's Boundary. Henrietta Cordelia Ray. CBWP-3

Life's Golden Sunset. Mrs. Henry Linden. CBWP-4

Life's pathway to me is dreary. The Opium-Eater. Mary E. Tucker. CBWP-1

Life's Rendezvous. Countee Cullen. CP-CullC

Life's stormy surge had scarcely touched. The Grafted Bud. Mary Weston Fordham. CBWP-1

Life's Tragedy. Paul Laurence Dunbar. CP-DunbP

Lift Ev'ry Voice and Sing. James Weldon Johnson. AfAmPo; CrDW; NAAAL; TtW

Lift Me Higher. Mary E. Tucker. CBWP-1

Light, The. Paul Laurence Dunbar. CP-DunbP

Light and diplomatic bird, A. Gwendolyn Brooks. SP-BrooG

Light Baggage. Alice Walker. CP-WalkA

Light for the midnight that is mine and theirs. (LL) Mentors. Gwendolyn Brooks. ESEAA; Klds; SP-BrooG

Light in Darkness. Frances Ellen Watkins Harper. CP-HarpF

Light in Darkness. Mary E. Tucker. CBWP-1

Light keeps on breaking. Breaklight. Lucille Clifton. SP-ClifL

Light. Love. Freedom. Like a Blessing. Stanley Crouch. GT

Light! more light! the shadows deepen. Let the Light Enter! Frances Ellen Watkins Harper. CP-HarpF

Light / on my mother's tongue. Lucille Clifton. ESEAA; SP-ClifL

Light on the Subject. Yusef Komunyakaa. SP-KomuY

Light that came to lucille clifton, The. Lucille Clifton. SP-ClifL

Light under the Door. Marilyn Nelson. SP-NelsM

Light was faintly streaming, the. The Dying Christian. Frances Ellen Watkins Harper. CP-HarpF

Light was on the golden sands, The. Paul Laurence Dunbar. CP-DunbP

Lighten up. Prayer. Lucille Clifton. NAAAL; SP-ClifL

Lightly. Audre Lorde. CP-LordA

Lightnin' Blues. Rita Dove. SP-DoveR

Lightning, Divine Lightning. Al Young. CP-YounA

Like a bird in the sky. (LL) Ego Tripping. Nikki Giovanni. SP-GiovN

Like a Blessing. Stanley Crouch. GT

Like a fawn from the arrow, startled and wild. Eliza Harris. Frances Ellen Watkins Harper. AAP; CP-HarpF; NAAAL

Like a gargantuan tongue. Ice Age. Ishmael Reed. CP-ReedI

Like a man overboard. The White Boy. Lucille Clifton. SP-ClifL

Like a pot turned on the straw. How He Is Coming Then. Lucille Clifton. SP-ClifL

Like a quail. Clinton. Sterling Plumpp. BkSV

Like a rising Blackening sun. (LL) The Woman Thing. Audre Lorde. BlSi; CP-LordA; GT; SP-LordA

Like a strong tree that in the virgin earth. Claude McKay. SP-McKaC

Like a will-o'-the-wisp in the night. Poem: "Like a will-o'-the-wisp in the night." Nikki Giovanni. SP-GiovN

Like an otter, but warm. Pastoral. Rita Dove. NAAAL

Like aunt jemima. (LL) The Kiss. Alice Walker. CP-WalkA; GT

Like bigger thomas. Sonia Sanchez. SP-SancS

Like dat one upon de wall. (LL) A Banjo Song. Paul Laurence Dunbar. CP-DunbP

Like dives in the deeps of hell. Save the Boys. Frances Ellen Watkins Harper. AAP; CP-HarpF

Like Father, Like Son. Marilyn Nelson. SP-NelsM

Like good unprocessed. Spiritual. William W. Cook. SpiFl

Like he always said. Poem for My Sisters. Lucille Clifton. SP-ClifL

Like I am. Langston Hughes. *See* Me and the Mule.

Like. / i mean. / don't it all come down. Indianapolis/Summer/1969/Poem. Sonia Sanchez. SP-SancS

Like, / if he had da called me. In a Period of Growth. Haki R. Madhubuti. TtW

Like it used to be, not even the future. (LL) Ö. Rita Dove. SP-DoveR

Like lizards on rocks. (LL) Haiku: "Eastern guard tower." Etheridge Knight. BPo; ESEAA; SP-KnigE; TtW

Like memories in the mind of God. (LL) The Point. Robert Hayden. CP-HaydR; ESEAA

Like my mother and her grandmother before. Once a Lady Told Me. Nikki Giovanni. SP-GiovN

Like plump green floor plans. Rotation. Julian Bond. NNP

Like priceless treasures sinking in the sand. (LL) America. Claude McKay. BALP; CDC; Crnst; IHS; NAAAL; PoBA; SP-McKaC; TtW

Like right now it's the summertime. The Old O.O. Blues. Al Young. CP-YounA

Like rivers in conflux, let parties now blend. The Union of Parties. George Moses Horton. SP-HortG

Like sea-washed sand upon the shore. On a Clean Book. Paul Laurence Dunbar. CP-DunbP

Like sheep from the rains and thunders. (LL) Rhapsody. William Stanley Braithwaite. AmNP; BALP; BANP; TtW

Like so many other young men in those troubled. For Lover Man, and All the Other Young Men Who Failed to Return from World War II. Nance Williams. NNP

Like some lost part of a model kit. Dreambook Bestiary. Yusef Komunyakaa. SP-KomuY

Like somebody's ass in a Friday Nite Video. Flirt. Al Young. CP-YounA

Like that. (LL) Poem for Flora. Nikki Giovanni. BPo; PoBA

Like the arms of dancers / and dying swans. (LL) Martial Choreograph. Maya Angelou. CP-AngeM; SP-AngeM

Like the blush upon the rose. Love's Pictures. Paul Laurence Dunbar. CP-DunbP

Like the cadence of an old love song. Child Life. Mary E. Tucker. CBWP-1

Like the quiver of a Negro woman's eye-lids cupping tears. (LL) Negro Woman. Lewis Alexander. CDC; PoBA

Like the shark who feels low but. Sleepy Day at Half Moon Bay. Al Young. CP-YounA

Like Venus / My spin is retrograde. Sputin. Ishmael Reed. CP-ReedI

Like warm beer. (LL) July. Sonia Sanchez. GT; SP-SancS

Like we call it / home. (LL) In the Inner City. Lucille Clifton. SP-ClifL; TtW

Like you / Letting down your. Dusk. Mae V. Cowdery. ShDr

Likewise. Langston Hughes. SP-HughL *Fr.* Montage of a Dream Deferred. CP-HughL

Likewise / in all these years. One More Time. Amiri Baraka. SP-BaraA

Li'l' Gal. Paul Laurence Dunbar. CP-DunbP

Lilies swinging censers fair. Easter Carol. Henrietta Cordelia Ray. CBWP-3

Lilt and a swing, A. At the Tavern. Paul Laurence Dunbar. CP-DunbP

Lily, being white not red, The. Epilogue. Countee Cullen. CP-CullC

Lily of the Valley, The. Paul Laurence Dunbar. CP-DunbP

Limitations. Paul Laurence Dunbar. CP-DunbP

Limitations. Henrietta Cordelia Ray. CBWP-3

Limpty Lefty McCree. *African-American Oral Tradition.* GetYo

Lincoln. Paul Laurence Dunbar. CP-DunbP

Lincoln. Henrietta Cordelia Ray. CBWP-3

Lincoln Is Dead. George Moses Horton. SP-HortG

Lincoln Monument: Washington. Langston Hughes. CP-HughL

Lincoln Theatre. Langston Hughes. CP-HughL

Lincoln University: 1954. Langston Hughes. CP-HughL

Lindie, chile, fo' Lawd sake, tell me. After the Quarrel. Priscilla Jane Thompson. CBWP-2

Lineage. Margaret Abigail Walker. BlSi; CP-WalkM; Klds; PoBA; TtW

Lines. "Ada." BlSi

   (Lines Suggested on Reading "An Appeal to Christian Women of the South," by A. E. Grimke.) NAAAL

   ("My spirit leaps in joyousness tow'rd thine.") NAAAL

Lines: "At the Portals of the Future." Frances Ellen Watkins Harper. CP-HarpF

Lines: "From fair Jamaica's fertile plains." "Ada." BlSi

Lines: "How I love country you have heard." Samuel Alfred Beadle. AAP

Lines: "Singularly and in pairs the decade has been ripped by bullets." Herbert Martin. PoBA

Lines: "Wake not again the cannon's thundrous voice." Alfred Gibbs Campbell. AAP

Lines for a Hospital. Countee Cullen. CP-CullC

Lines Muttered in Sleep. Rita Dove. SP-DoveR

Lines on a Dead Girl. Priscilla Jane Thompson. CBWP-2

Lines, On Hearing of the Intention of a Gentleman to Purchase the Poet's Freedom. George Moses Horton. *See* On Hearing of the Intention of a Gentleman to Purchase the Poet's Freedom.

Lines on the Death of the Rev. S. K. Talmage. Mary E. Tucker. CBWP-1

Lines parallel. The Room. De Leon Harrison. PoBA

Lines Suggested on Reading "An Appeal to Christian Women of the South," by A. E. Grimke. "Ada." *See* Lines.

Lines to————. Mary Weston Fordham. CBWP-2

Lines to a Graduate. Lizelia Augusta Jenkins Moorer. CBWP-3

Lines to a Nasturtium. Anne Spencer. AmNP; CDC; ShDr

Lines to a Sophisticate. Mae V. Cowdery. ShDr

Lines to an Old Dress. Mary E. Tucker. CBWP-1

Lines to an Old School-House. Priscilla Jane Thompson. CBWP-2

Lines to Caste. Samuel Alfred Beadle. AAP

Lines to Charles Sumner. Frances Ellen Watkins Harper. CP-HarpF

Lines to Emma. Priscilla Jane Thompson. CBWP-2

Lines to Florence. Mary Weston Fordham. CBWP-2

Lines to Garcia Lorca. Amiri Baraka. NNP

Lines to Hon. Thaddeus Stevens. Frances Ellen Watkins Harper. CP-HarpF

Lines to M.A.H. Frances Ellen Watkins Harper. CP-HarpF

Lines to Miles O'Reiley. Frances Ellen Watkins Harper. CP-HarpF

Lines to Mrs. Isabel Peace. Mary Weston Fordham. CBWP-2

Lines to Mrs. M. C. Turner. Eloise Bibb. CBWP-4

Lines to Mount Glen. George Marion McClellan. AAP

Lines to My—. George Moses Horton. SP-HortG

Lines to My Father. Countee Cullen. CP-CullC

Lines to Our Elders. Countee Cullen. CDC

Lines to the Black Oak. Oliver La Grone. NBV

Lines to the Hon. George L. Knox. Eloise Bibb. CBWP-4

Lines Written at the Grave of Alexander [*or* Alexandre] Dumas. Gwendolyn B. Bennett. CDC

Lines Written on a Farewell View of the Franconia Mountains at Twilight. Henrietta Cordelia Ray. CBWP-3

Linin' ub De Hymns, De. Daniel Webster Davis. AAP

Linkage. Nikki Giovanni. SP-GiovN

Lions, The. Robert Hayden. CP-HaydR

Lips pressed against my heart. (LL) Evening Song. Jean Toomer. BPo; CDC; CP-ToomJ; GT

Lisa, Leona, Loretta? Salt. Yusef Komunyakaa. SP-KomuY

Lisbon. Russell Atkins. GT

List, I hear the church bells ring. The Church Bells. Mrs. Henry Linden. CBWP-4

List! list! the sleigh bells peal across the snow. December. Henrietta Cordelia Ray. CBWP-3

List to the sad wind, drearily moaning. Autumn. Priscilla Jane Thompson. CBWP-2

Listen. Charles Patterson. NBP

Listen / after I have set the table. Patricia's Poem. June Jordan. SP-JordJ

Listen! / All you beauty-makers. Call to Creation. Langston Hughes. CP-HughL

Listen brother love you. Hard Love Rock #II. Audre Lorde. CP-LordA; SP-LordA

Listen children / keep this in the place. Lucille Clifton. IHS; PoBA; SP-ClifL

Listen, Christ, / You did alright in your day, I reckon. Goodbye Christ. Langston Hughes. CP-HughL

Listen! / Dear dream of utter aliveness. Demand. Langston Hughes. CP-HughL; SP-HughL

Listen Here Blues. Langston Hughes. CP-HughL

Listen here, Joe. Without Benefit of Declaration. Langston Hughes. AmNP; CP-HughL

Listen, / I never dreamed. Alice Walker. CP-WalkA

Listen, John Cracker; hear me, Joe Nigg. Side by Side. Sterling A. Brown. CP-BrowS

Listen, Kid Sleepy. Kid Sleepy. Langston Hughes. CP-HughL; SP-HughL

Listen, Lord—[a Prayer]. James Weldon Johnson. BANP; BPo

Listen, / stop tanning yourself. Without Commercials. Alice Walker. CP-WalkA

Listen to the tale. Slim Greer. Sterling A. Brown. BALP; BANP; CP-BrowS; NAAAL

Listen to yo' prophets. Shout. Langston Hughes. CP-HughL; SP-HughL

Listen to yo' saints! (LL) Shout. Langston Hughes. CP-HughL; SP-HughL

Listen, / when i found there was no safety. To my Friend, Jerina. Lucille Clifton. ESEAA

Listen, / you a wonder. What the Mirror Said. Lucille Clifton. SP-ClifL

Listen, you drawing men. Snapshots of the Cotton South. Frank Marshall Davis. PoBA

Listenen to Big Black at S. F. State. Sonia Sanchez. BPo

Listening for the sound. Nocturne. Pinkie Gordon Lane. BlSi

Listening Nydia. Henrietta Cordelia Ray. CBWP-3

Listening to Aunt Sue's stories. (LL) Aunt Sue's Stories. Langston Hughes. CP-HughL; SP-HughL

Listening winds / overhear my privacies. Love Letter. Maya Angelou. CP-AngeM

Litany: "Gather up / In the arms of your pity." Langston Hughes. SP-HughL

   (Prayer.) CP-HughL

Litany for Survival, A. Audre Lorde. CP-LordA; NAAAL

Litany from the Dark People, A. Margaret Abigail Walker. CP-WalkM

Litany of [*or* at] Atlanta, A. William Edward Burghardt DuBois. BANP; CDC

Litany of Black History for Black People, A. Margaret Abigail Walker. CP-WalkM

Litany of the Dark People, The. Countee Cullen. CP-CullC

Little and Big. Frank Marshall Davis. TtW

Little Bell. Mary E. Tucker. CBWP-1

Little bird, a tender bird, A. The Siren Bird. Henrietta Cordelia Ray. CBWP-3

Little bird sits in the nest and sings, The. Preparation. Paul Laurence Dunbar. CP-DunbP

Little bird, with plumage brown, A. The Sparrow. Paul Laurence Dunbar. CP-DunbP

Little bird with tuneful throat. My Canary. Josephine D. Henderson Heard. CBWP-4

Little birds warble their song in the tree, The. The Bird Song. Mrs. Henry Linden. CBWP-4

Little Black boy. Nigger. Frank Horne. BANP; CDC

Little Black Girls, The Original Eve (Spreadin' More Beautiful Brown Around). Karen Williams. SpiFl

Little boy wears my mistakes, A. As I Grew Up Again. Audre Lorde. CP-LordA; SP-LordA

Little boy / who sticks a needle in his arm, The. Junior Addict. Langston Hughes. BPo; CP-HughL

Little brown baby wif spa'klin' eyes. Paul Laurence Dunbar. BANP; CP-DunbP; NAAAL

Little brown boy. Poem. Helene Johnson. AmNP; BANP; CDC; NAAAL; PoBA; ShDr

Little brown face full of smiles. Liza May. Paul Laurence Dunbar. CP-DunbP

Little Builders, The. Frances Ellen Watkins Harper. CP-HarpF

Little Cabin, A. Charles Bertram Johnson. BANP

Little Cats. Langston Hughes. CP-HughL

Little child sat on the floor, A. Where Do School Days End? Josephine D. Henderson Heard. CBWP-4

Little Child Shall Lead Them, A. Frances Ellen Watkins Harper. CP-HarpF

Little Christmas Basket, A. Paul Laurence Dunbar. CP-DunbP

Little cullud boys with beards. Flatted Fifths. Langston Hughes. *Fr.* Montage of a Dream Deferred. CP-HughL

Little cullud boys / with fears. Tag. Langston Hughes. SP-HughL *Fr.* Montage of a Dream Deferred. CP-HughL

Little Dandelion, The. Lula Lowe Weeden. CDC

Little dark baby. America. Langston Hughes. CP-HughL

Little dreaming by the way, A. The Sum. Paul Laurence Dunbar. CP-DunbP

Little dreams / Of springtime. Slum Dreams. Langston Hughes. CP-HughL

Little Fay's Thanksgiving. Henrietta Cordelia Ray. CBWP-3

Little flowers of yesterday, The. Autumn Note. Langston Hughes. CP-HughL

Little fox is still, The. Broadcast on Ethiopia. Langston Hughes. CP-HughL

Little girl / Dreaming of a baby grand piano. To Be Somebody. Langston Hughes. CP-HughL; SP-HughL

Little Girl in the Gambler's Nest, *see also* While Playing Short Coin. *African-American Oral Tradition.* GetYo

Little Girl Speakings. Maya Angelou. CP-AngeM; SP-AngeM

Little Girl's Dream World, A. Della Burt. BlSi

Little Green Tree. Langston Hughes. CP-HughL; SP-HughL

Little grey dreams. Angelina Weld Grimké. ShDr

Little house with a broken stair, A. Promenade. Sam Cornish. BlFi

Little Julie / Has grown quite tall. Delinquent. Langston Hughes. CP-HughL; SP-HughL

Little lady at de do'. The Visitor. Paul Laurence Dunbar. CP-DunbP

Little loving / in between, A. (LL) Advice. Langston Hughes. CP-HughL; SP-HughL

Little Lucy Landman. Paul Laurence Dunbar. CP-DunbP

Little Lyric (of Great Importance). Langston Hughes. CP-HughL; SP-HughL

Little Man around the House. Yusef Komunyakaa. SP-KomuY

Little More about the Brothers and Sisters, A. Sharon Scott. JB

Little More Traveling Music, A. Al Young. CP-YounA; NBV

Little Old Letter. Langston Hughes. CP-HughL; SP-HughL

Little Old Wicked Nell, *see also* Corner of 47th and South Park. *African-American Oral Tradition.* GetYo

Little people often make big heroes. Little and Big. Frank Marshall Davis. TtW

Little Poem About Jazz, A. Al Young. CP-YounA

Little red wagon for d black bureaucrat, A. Catechism of d Neoamerican Hoodoo Church. Ishmael Reed. NBV

Little Robin red breast / I hear you sing your song. Robin Red Breast. Lula Lowe Weeden. CDC

Little Sallie, Little Sallie. Ballad of Little Sallie. Langston Hughes. CP-HughL

Little seed, in weakness sown, A. In Commemoration of the Centennial of the A.M.E. Church. Frances Ellen Watkins Harper. CP-HarpF

Little sister, not all Black. For My Singing Sister. Audre Lorde. CP-LordA; SP-LordA

Little snail, / Dreaming you go. Snail. Langston Hughes. CP-HughL; SP-HughL

Little Son. Georgia Douglas Johnson. CDC

Little Song. Langston Hughes. CP-HughL

Little Song on Housing. Langston Hughes. CP-HughL

Little Sonnet to Little Friends. Countee Cullen. CP-CullC

Little Southern colored child, A. Migration. Langston Hughes. CP-HughL

Little twig that Byron planted here, The. Byron's Oak at Newstead Abbey. Timothy Thomas Fortune. AAP; EBAP

little while spring will claim its own, A. My Heart has Known its Winter. Arna Bontemps. GT

Little Wren, A. Priscilla Jane Thompson. CBWP-2

Little yellow / Bastard boy, A. Langston Hughes. *See* Afro-American Fragment.

Little yellow / Bastard boy, A. (LL) Mulatto. Langston Hughes. CP-HughL; SP-HughL

Little Yellow looked at the banana tree and. Juice of a Lemon on the Trail of a Little Yellow. June Jordan. SP-JordJ

Live and Let Live. Langston Hughes. *Fr.* Montage of a Dream Deferred. CP-HughL

Live happily ever after. (LL) Grandfather Was Queer, Too. Bob Kaufman. NAAAL; SP-KaufB

"Live like the wind," he said, "unfettered." The Wind Bloweth Where It Listeth. Countee Cullen. CP-CullC; GT

Living Earth. Jean Toomer. CP-ToomJ

Living for the City. Stevie Wonder. Crnst

Living Truth, The. Sterling Plumpp. PoBA

Liza! call dat chile. Meal Time. Maggie Pogue Johnson. CBWP-4

Liza May. Paul Laurence Dunbar. CP-DunbP

Lizard Series, The. Ntozake Shange. CtF

Lloyd George and Woodrow Wilson and Clemenceau—. A Legend of Versailles. Melvin Beaunearus Tolson. BPo; NAAAL

Lo & behold. Yes, peat bogs. Landscape for the Disappeared. Yusef Komunyakaa. SP-KomuY

Lo! for this dark terrestrial ball. An Hymn to Humanity. Phillis Wheatley. CP-WheaP

Lo! Freedom comes. Th' prescient Muse foretold. Liberty and Peace. Phillis Wheatley. BlSi; CP-WheaP

"Lo, I am black but I am comely too." The Dark Brother. Lewis Alexander. CDC

Lo! the glorious dawn is breaking. Easter Morn. Josephine D. Henderson Heard. CBWP-4

Loaded like spoons. Slaveship. Lucille Clifton. ESEAA

Loaded on an oxcart. (LL) Starlight Scope Myopia. Yusef Komunyakaa. SP-KomuY

Loads of trash and we light the match. Landfill. Michael S. Harper. SP-HarpM

Lobengula: Having a Son at 38. Nikky Finney. SpiFl

Locked arm in arm they cross the way. Tableau. Countee Cullen. BANP; CP-CullC; Klds; NAAAL; PoBA

Locked up in one) was aging and tasty. Bottoms up! (LL) Jungle Strut. Al Young. CP-YounA

Locus. Robert Hayden. CP-HaydR

Locust Trees. Margaret L. Thomas. ShDr

Loew's Bridge: A Broadway Idyl. Mary E. Tucker. CBWP-1

Lolotte, who attires my hair. Noblesse Oblige. Jessie Redmond Fauset. CDC

London. Maya Angelou. CP-AngeM

Loneliness, A. Haki R. Madhubuti. GT

Loneliness. Al Young. CP-YounA; PoBA

Loneliness terrific beats on my heart. Refugee. Langston Hughes. CP-HughL

Lonely Affair, A. Reuben Jackson. GT

Lonely and dreary was the day. Heart's Ease. Mary E. Tucker. CBWP-1

Lonely / As the wind. One. Langston Hughes. CP-HughL; SP-HughL

Lonely Eagles. Marilyn Nelson. ESEAA; SP-NelsM

Lonely little question mark. Kid in the Park. Langston Hughes. CP-HughL; SP-HughL

Lonely Mother, The. Fenton Johnson. NAAAL

Lonely Nocturne. Langston Hughes. CP-HughL

Lonely Particular. Alice Walker. CP-WalkA

Lonely people / In the lonely night. Little Song. Langston Hughes. CP-HughL

Lonely Woman. Jayne Cortez. NBV

Lonely World. Mrs. Henry Linden. CBWP-4

Lonesome. Paul Laurence Dunbar. CP-DunbP

Lonesome Corner. Langston Hughes. CP-HughL

Lonesome in the Country. Al Young. CP-YounA

Lonesome Place. Langston Hughes. CP-HughL

Long Ago. Paul Laurence Dunbar. CP-DunbP

Long Blues, The. Calvin C. Hernton. GT

Long Cotton Row. Elma Stuckey. TtW

Long de cool o' night w'en day am daid. Fenton Johnson. EBAP

Long, dream night with me, A. (LL) Natcha, offering love. Langston Hughes. CP-HughL; SP-HughL

Long Gone. Sterling A. Brown. BALP; BANP; BPo; CDC; CP-BrowS; NAAAL

Long had I grieved at what I deemed abuse. Resignation. Paul Laurence Dunbar. CP-DunbP

Long hast thou slumber'd, O, my sounding lyre! Daniel Alexander Payne. AAP *Fr.* The Pleasures. EBAP

Long have I beat with timid hands upon life's leaden door. The Suppliant. Georgia Douglas Johnson. BALP; CDC; PoBA; ShDr

Long have I yearned and sought for beauty. I Sit and Wait for Beauty. Mae V. Cowdery. BlSi

Long Island sound, the pitiless clamor, The. The Penitential Cries of Jupiter Hammond. Gary Smith. GT

Long John Nelson and Sweetie Pie. Margaret Abigail Walker. CP-WalkM

Long Night Home, The. Charles F. Gordon. NBP

Long Reality, The. Haki R. Madhubuti. NAAAL

Long since, in sore distress, I heard one pray. The Warrior's Prayer. Paul Laurence Dunbar. CP-DunbP

Long Song for Antonia. Langston Hughes. CP-HughL

Long time ago, we two set out. Vagrants. Paul Laurence Dunbar. CP-DunbP

Long time yet, because you're strong as a mule, A. (LL) George. Dudley Randall. BPo; Klds

'Long To'ds Night. Paul Laurence Dunbar. CP-DunbP

Long Track Blues. Sterling A. Brown. CP-BrowS

Long Trip. Langston Hughes. CP-HughL; SP-HughL

Long View: Negro. Langston Hughes. CP-HughL

Long ways from home, A. (LL) Sometimes I feel like a motherless child. *Unknown.* BkSV; Crnst

Long years ago, within a distant clime. Dream Song I. Paul Laurence Dunbar. CP-DunbP

Long years have passed since first a merry child. To One Who Sleepeth. Mary E. Tucker. CBWP-1

Longfellow. Henrietta Cordelia Ray. AAP; CBWP-3

Longing. Paul Laurence Dunbar. CP-DunbP

Longings. Mae V. Cowdery. ShDr

Longshot if he cracks up in, A. The Inside Track. Ishmael Reed. CP-ReedI

Look at me 8th / grade. Poem: "Look at me 8th / grade." Sonia Sanchez. PoBA; SP-SancS

Look at My Face, a Collage. Carolyn M. Rodgers. JB

Look at old Scrappy puttin' on dog. Puttin' on Dog. Sterling A. Brown. CP-BrowS

Look at them fly. Sister Roll. Sabah As-Sabah. CtF

Look at yo' legs. (LL) Red Silk Stockings. Langston Hughes. CP-HughL; NAAAL

Look for You Yesterday, Here You Come Today. Amiri Baraka. SP-BaraA; SSLK

Look Good, Smell Good, Feel. Al Young. CP-YounA

Look here, Petah! whut's dis here. The Examination. Priscilla Jane Thompson. CBWP-2

Look hyeah, Molly, ain't it jolly. To Mary Church Terrell. Paul Laurence Dunbar. CP-DunbP

Look of him, The. The Kind of Man He Is. Lucille Clifton. SP-ClifL

Look on that form, once fit for the sculptor! Working and Waiting. Adah Isaacs Menken. CBWP-1

"Look!" she cried. The Girl Who Died #1. Alice Walker. CP-WalkA

Look there at the star! Shepherd's Song at Christmas. Langston Hughes. CP-HughL

Look up, dear one, nor be cast down. Truth. Josephine D. Henderson Heard. CBWP-4

Look Within. Claude McKay. SP-McKaC

Looking. Gwendolyn Brooks. SP-BrooG

Looking a Mad Dog Dead in the Eyes. Yusef Komunyakaa. SP-KomuY

Looking back, we cannot see. Traveling through Fog. Robert Hayden. CP-HaydR

Looking down into my father's / dead face. Good Night, Willie Lee, I'll See You in the Morning. Alice Walker. CP-WalkA; NAAAL

Looking for a Country under Its Original Name. Colleen J. McElroy. BlSi

Looking-Glass, The. Paul Laurence Dunbar. CP-DunbP

Looking into the blue. Horizon Blues. David Henderson. GT

Looking into your eyes. Ndebele. Alice Walker. CP-WalkA

Looking over my shoulder at you this morning, I'm listening to. Sarajevo Moonlight. Al Young. CP-YounA

Looking thru the commercial. A Loneliness. Haki R. Madhubuti. GT

Looks like what drives me crazy. Evil. Langston Hughes. CP-HughL; SP-HughL

Looky here, America. Beaumont to Detroit: 1943. Langston Hughes. CP-HughL

Loon. Michael S. Harper. ESEAA

Loose in the brush pines. Tango. Ntozake Shange. GT

Lord, all I am and hope to be. An Offering. Eloise Bibb. CBWP-4

"Lord, being dark," I said, "I cannot bear." The Shroud of Color. Countee Cullen. CP-CullC; NAAAL

Lord, don't set that sun. Long Cotton Row. Elma Stuckey. TtW

Lord / forgive me / if I twist the sunset. The Hungry Black Child. Adam David Miller. NBV; PoBA

Lord God, / I do not know. (LL) Prayer: "I ask you this: / Which way to go." Langston Hughes. CDC; CP-HughL; SP-HughL

Lord, God of all in Life and Death. Hymn for the Slain in Battle. William Stanley Braithwaite. BALP

Lord God of Hosts incline thine ear. The Century Prayer. James Ephriam McGirt. AAP

Lord had a job for me, but I had so much to do, The. Too Busy. Paul Laurence Dunbar. CP-DunbP

Lord Haw Haw (as Pygmy) #37. Amiri Baraka. SP-BaraA

Lord Himself was tested, Brother Mule, The. Sermon in the Woodlot. Marilyn Nelson. *Fr.* Thus Far by Faith. SP-NelsM

Lord, in My Heart. Maya Angelou. CP-AngeM; SP-AngeM

Lord is my Shepherd and I do want, The. Show Me Lord Show Me. Yusef Iman. BlFi

Lord, let me live to serve and make a loan. Hydromel and Rue. George Marion McClellan. AAP

Lord, let me not be silent while we fight. Look Within. Claude McKay. SP-McKaC

Lord, Lord, an East Virginia man. (LL) John Henry. *Unknown.* BPo; NAAAL

Lord, Lord, sweet Mama. So Jonah Sang the Blues. Marilyn Nelson. *Fr.* I Dream the Book of Jonah. SP-NelsM

Lord, shall I find it in Thy Holy Church. Truth. Claude McKay. BPo; SP-McKaC

Lord she's gone done left me done packed/up and split. Feeling Fucked/Up Up. Etheridge Knight. GT; SP-KnigE

Lord take her to a distant place. I See Her Lovely There. Jean Toomer. CP-ToomJ

Lord, who am I to teach the way. The Teacher. Leslie Pinckney Hill. BANP

Lord will see us through some day, The. (LL) We shall overcome. *Unknown.* CrDW

Lord, within thy fold I be. Hymn. Priscilla Jane Thompson. CBWP-2

Lord's lost Him His mockingbird. Mourning Poem for the Queen of Sunday. Robert Hayden. CP-HaydR; NAAAL; PoBA

Lorraine Hansberry: an Emotional View. Nikki Giovanni. SP-GiovN

Loss of Life and Both Feet of Both Hands or Both Eyes ... The Principal Sum. American Ecstasy. Amiri Baraka. SP-BaraA

Loss of love and youth, The. Maya Angelou. CP-AngeM

Lost Baby Poem, The. Lucille Clifton. BlSi; ESEAA; NAAAL; SP-ClifL

Lost Bells, The. Frances Ellen Watkins Harper. CP-HarpF

Lost Dancer, The. Jean Toomer. BALP; CP-ToomJ; PoBA

Lost Daughter, The. Marilyn Nelson. SP-NelsM

Lost Dream, A. Paul Laurence Dunbar. CP-DunbP

Lost Illusions. Georgia Douglas Johnson. NAAAL

Lost! lost! lost! Anne Boleyn. Eloise Bibb. CBWP-4

Lost—lost—lost! Into the Depths. Adah Isaacs Menken. CBWP-1

Lost Moment. Hoyt W. Fuller. PoBA

Lost My Voice? Of Course. Alice Walker. CP-WalkA

Lost Opportunities. Henrietta Cordelia Ray. CBWP-3

Lost Teddy Bear, The. Maggie Pogue Johnson. CBWP-4

Lost Wax. Yusef Komunyakaa. TtW

Lost Window. Bob Kaufman. SP-KaufB

Louis i'm trying to understand what you were here. For Lil Louis. Tom Dent. BkSV

Louisiana Pastoral. Sterling A. Brown. CP-BrowS

Louisiana Weekly #4, The. David Henderson. PoBA

Loup Garou Means Change Into. Ishmael Reed. CP-ReedI

Love. Sabah As-Sabah. CtF

Love. Benjamin Clark. EBAP

Love. Tom Dent. NNP

Love. Paul Laurence Dunbar. CP-DunbP

Love. George Moses Horton. SP-HortG

Love. Darwin T. Turner. BALP

Love Again Blues. Langston Hughes. CP-HughL

Love and Grief. Paul Laurence Dunbar. CP-DunbP

Love Child—a Black Aesthetic. Everett Hoagland. BPo

Love Despoiled. Paul Laurence Dunbar. CP-DunbP

Love Dirge to the Whitehouse, A. Bob Fletcher. NBP

Love for you. (LL) Portrait of Malcolm X. Etheridge Knight. PoBA

Love from My Father. Carole C. Gregory Clemmons. PoBA

Love hath the wings of the butterfly. Love's Phases. Paul Laurence Dunbar. CP-DunbP

Love in the Weather's Bells. Jay Wright. ESEAA

Love / Is a brown man's fist. Beale Street Love. Langston Hughes. CP-HughL

Love is a flame that burns with sacred fire. George Marion McClellan. AAP; EBAP

Love: Is a Human Condition. Nikki Giovanni. Crnst

Love / Is a ripe plum. Love Song for Lucinda. Langston Hughes. CP-HughL

Love is a star that lights the night. Paul Laurence Dunbar. CP-DunbP

Love is a wild wonder. Langston Hughes. CP-HughL; SP-HughL

"Love is enough," I read somewhere. To an Unknown Poet. Countee Cullen. CP-CullC

Love is internal. (LL) The Detached. Maya Angelou. CP-AngeM; SP-AngeM

Love is like dew. Breath of a Rose. Langston Hughes. CP-HughL

Love is not concerned. Alice Walker. CP-WalkA

Love is not love demanding all, itself. Love's Way. Countee Cullen. CP-CullC

Love is the light of the world, my dear. Paul Laurence Dunbar. CP-DunbP

Love is the master of the ring. The Ring. Langston Hughes. CP-HughL

Love, leave me like the light. If You Should Go. Countee Cullen. CP-CullC

Love Letter. Maya Angelou. CP-AngeM

Love Letter. Carole C. Gregory Clemmons. BlSi

Love Letter, A. Paul Laurence Dunbar. CP-DunbP

Love-letter, A. Mary E. Tucker. CBWP-1

Love Letters. Josephine D. Henderson Heard. CBWP-4

Love, Maybe. Audre Lorde. CP-LordA; SP-LordA

Love me. I care not what the circling years. Love's Apotheosis. Paul Laurence Dunbar. CP-DunbP

Love Medley: Patrice Cuchulain. Michael S. Harper. SP-HarpM

Love Note I: Surely. Gwendolyn Brooks. SP-BrooG

Love Note II: Flags. Gwendolyn Brooks. *See* Flags.

Love of Moses for his race soon found, The. Flight into Midian. Frances Ellen Watkins Harper. *Fr.* Moses: A Story of the Nile. CP-HarpF; AAP

Love opened a vista rare with stars. Love's Vista. Henrietta Cordelia Ray. CBWP-3

Love person / from love people, A. My Poem. Lucille Clifton. SP-ClifL

Love Pictures You as Black and Long-faced. Lance Jeffers. FB

Love plays a lute, and Thought an organ grand. The Two Musicians. Henrietta Cordelia Ray. CBWP-3

Love Poem. Audre Lorde. CP-LordA; SP-LordA

Love Poem. Norman Henry, II Pritchard. GT

Love Poem, A: "I do not expect the spirit of Penelope." Etheridge Knight. BrTr

Love Poem Written for Sterling Brown, A. Sonia Sanchez. SP-SancS

Love rejected / hurts so much more. Lucille Clifton. BPo; SP-ClifL

Love Song, A: "Ah, love, my love is like a cry in the night." Paul Laurence Dunbar. CP-DunbP

Love Song. Samuel Allen. NNP

Love-Song: "If Death should claim me for her own to-day." Paul Laurence Dunbar. CP-DunbP

Love Song for Alex, 1979. Margaret Abigail Walker. CP-WalkM

Love Song for Lucinda. Langston Hughes. CP-HughL

Love supreme, a love supreme, A. (LL) Dear John, Dear Coltrane. Michael S. Harper. SP-HarpM; TtW

Love the only / possible / end. (LL) Always it's either. Al Young. CP-YounA; TtW

Love the only / possible / end. Al Young. *See* The Blues Don't Change.

Love thee? Yes, I'm sure I love thee. The City by the Sea. Josephine D. Henderson Heard. CBWP-4

Love Tree, The. Countee Cullen. CP-CullC

Love twists. The Pressures. Amiri Baraka. BPo

Love used to carry a bow, you know. The Change. Paul Laurence Dunbar. CP-DunbP

Love withheld... / ...restrained. (LL) If there be sorrow. Mari E. Evans. NNP

Love. you are. you are. Sonia Sanchez. SP-SancS

Love Your Enemy. Yusef Iman. BPo; BlFi

Loved feared hated. John Brown. Robert Hayden. CP-HaydR

Loveliest lynchee was our Lord, The. (LL) The Chicago *Defender* Sends a Man to Little Rock. Gwendolyn Brooks. AmNP; CrDW; NAAAL; PoBA; SP-BrooG

Lovelight. Georgia Douglas Johnson. AmNP

Lovely dainty Spanish needle. The Spanish Needle. Claude McKay. SP-McKaC

Lovely, dark, and lonely one. Song: "Lovely, dark, and lonely one." Langston Hughes. CP-HughL

Lovely girl protected by her cruel/incandescent energies, A. (LL) The Female and the Silence of a Man. June Jordan. NAAAL

Lovely Love, A. Gwendolyn Brooks. BPo; NAAAL; SP-BrooG

Lovely's Daughters: Visitors. Michael S. Harper. SP-HarpM

Lover and the Moon, The. Paul Laurence Dunbar. CP-DunbP

Lover whom duty called over the wave, A. The Lover and the Moon. Paul Laurence Dunbar. CP-DunbP

Lover's Farewell, The. George Moses Horton. EBAP; NAAAL

Lover's Lane. Paul Laurence Dunbar. BANP; CP-DunbP

Lovers of the Poor, The. Gwendolyn Brooks. ESEAA; NAAAL
("Arrive. The Ladies from the Ladies'.") SSLK
("Arrive. The Ladies from the Ladies' Betterment /League League.") SP-BrooG

Lover's Return. Langston Hughes. CP-HughL; SP-HughL

Lover's Song, A. Audre Lorde. CP-LordA

Lovers that burn and learnéd scholars cold. Cats. Charles Baudelaire, *French.* CP-CullC, *tr.* by Countee Cullen

Love's Apotheosis. Paul Laurence Dunbar. CP-DunbP

Love's Castle. Paul Laurence Dunbar. CP-DunbP

Love's Chastening. Paul Laurence Dunbar. CP-DunbP

Love's Draft. Paul Laurence Dunbar. CP-DunbP

Love's Humility. Paul Laurence Dunbar. CP-DunbP

Love's Phases. Paul Laurence Dunbar. CP-DunbP

Love's Pictures. Paul Laurence Dunbar. CP-DunbP

Love's Seasons. Paul Laurence Dunbar. CP-DunbP

Love's true, and triumphs; and God's actual. (LL) One wants a Teller in a time like this. Gwendolyn Brooks. SP-BrooG

Love's Vista. Henrietta Cordelia Ray. CBWP-3

Love's Way. Countee Cullen. CP-CullC

Lovesong. Marilyn Nelson. SP-NelsM

Lovesong of O. O. Gabugah. Al Young. CP-YounA

Lovesong to My Father. Rohan B. Preston. CtF

Low beating of the tom-toms, The. Danse Africaine. Langston Hughes. CP-HughL; NAAAL; SP-HughL

Low-burning moon of moons, The. Grizzly Peak. Al Young. CP-YounA

Low to High. Langston Hughes. *Fr.* Montage of a Dream Deferred. CP-HughL

Lower the flags. Special Bulletin. Langston Hughes. CP-HughL; PoBA

Loyal subject, thou, to that bright Queen, A. To W. L. G. on Reading His "Chosen Queen." Charlotte Forten. BlSi

Loyalty to the Flag. Lizelia Augusta Jenkins Moorer. CBWP-3

Lucent lake was lit with sheen, The. A Thought of Lake Ontario. Henrietta Cordelia Ray. CBWP-3

Lucid night effulgent grows, The. Sketch of a Verying Evening Sky. John Boyd. EBAP

Lucindy, who you 'spose I seed. A Common Occurrence. Priscilla Jane Thompson. CBWP-2

Luck. Langston Hughes. CP-HughL; SP-HughL

Lucky One, The. Reginald Shepherd. GT

Lucy and Her Girls. Lucille Clifton. SP-ClifL

Lucy / by sam. New Year. Lucille Clifton. SP-ClifL

Lucy done gone back on me. Jilted. Paul Laurence Dunbar. CP-DunbP

Lucy is the ocean. Lucy and Her Girls. Lucille Clifton. SP-ClifL

Lucy one-eye. Lucille Clifton. SP-ClifL

Lullaby: "Bedtime's come fu' little boys." Paul Laurence Dunbar. CP-DunbP

Lullaby: "Close your sleepy eyes, or the pale moonlight will steal you." Aqua Laluah. ShDr

Lullaby: "Hush ye, hush ye! honey, darlin'." Clara Ann Thompson. CBWP-2

Lullaby: "Kiver up yo' haid, my little lady." Paul Laurence Dunbar. CP-DunbP

Lullaby: "My little dark baby." Langston Hughes. CP-HughL

Lullaby for Ann-Lucian. Calvin Forbes. NBV; PoBA

Lulu walked forlornly in late April twilight. Seeking Religion. Sterling A. Brown. CP-BrowS

"Luminously indiscreet; / Complete; continuous." (LL) The Sermon on the Warpland. Gwendolyn Brooks. BPo; PoBA

Lumumba's Grave ("Lumumba was black"). Langston Hughes. CP-HughL

Lunar Eclipse. Audre Lorde. CP-LordA

Lunch in a Jim Crow Car. Langston Hughes. SP-HughL
(Jim Crow Car.) CP-HughL

Lute of Afric's Tribe, The. Albery Allson Whitman. EBAP; TtW

Lutherans sit stolidly in rows, The. Churchgoing. Marilyn Nelson. SP-NelsM

Luxembourg Garden. Michael S. Weaver. GT

Luxuriant, clustered round your cottage door! (LL) Jasmine. Claude McKay. GT; SP-McKaC

Luxury. Nikki Giovanni. SP-GiovN

Luxury, then, is a way of. Political Poem. Amiri Baraka. SP-BaraA

Lying in wait. for honor and peace. / one day. (LL) Elegy (for MOVE and Philadelphia). Sonia Sanchez. Crnst; ESEAA; TtW

Lying, thinking. Alone. Maya Angelou. CP-AngeM; SP-AngeM

Lynch Fragment 2. Jayne Cortez. SP-CortJ

Lynching, The. Dorothea Matthews. ShDr

Lynching, The. Claude McKay. BALP; BANP; CrDW; GT; IDB; PoBA; SP-McKaC

Lynching. Lizelia Augusta Jenkins Moorer. CBWP-3

Lynching, The. Thylias Moss. GT

Lynching and Burning. Primus St. John. PoBA

Lynching for Skip James, A. Rudy Bee Graham. BlFi

Lynching Song. Langston Hughes. CP-HughL

Lyric, A: "My lady love lives far away." Paul Laurence Dunbar. CP-DunbP

Lyric: I Am Looking at Music. Pinkie Gordon Lane. IHS

Lyrics shimmy like. Ron Welburn. NBV

M

Ma baby lives across de river. Wide River. Langston Hughes. CP-HughL

Ma cousine Tee-Ta, she say she Cajun. Cofaire? Sybil Klein. TtW

Ma Jesus. Troubled Jesus. Waring Cuney. BANP

Ma Lord ain't no stuck-up man. Langston Hughes. CP-HughL

Ma Man. Langston Hughes. CP-HughL

Ma man's a gypsy / Cause he never does come home. Gypsy Man. Langston Hughes. CP-HughL; NAAAL

Ma Rainey. Sterling A. Brown. CP-BrowS; TtW

   ("When Ma Rainey.") NAAAL

Ma sweet good man has. Suicide. Langston Hughes. CP-HughL

Maceo dead! a thrill of sorrow. Frances Ellen Watkins Harper. CP-HarpF

Madam and Her Madam. Langston Hughes. BALP; CP-HughL; SP-HughL

Madam and Her Might-Have-Been. Langston Hughes. CP-HughL; SP-HughL

Madam and the Army. Langston Hughes. CP-HughL

Madam and the Census Man. Langston Hughes. CP-HughL; SP-HughL

Madam and the Charity Child. Langston Hughes. CP-HughL; SP-HughL

Madam and the Crime Wave. Langston Hughes. CP-HughL

Madam and the Fortune Teller. Langston Hughes. CP-HughL; SP-HughL

Madam and the Insurance Man. Langston Hughes. CP-HughL

Madam and the Minister. Langston Hughes. CP-HughL; SP-HughL

Madam and the Movies. Langston Hughes. CP-HughL

Madam and the Newsboy. Langston Hughes. CP-HughL

Madam and the Number Writer. Langston Hughes. CP-HughL; SP-HughL

Madam and the Phone Bill. Langston Hughes. SP-HughL

   ("You say I O.K.ed.") CP-HughL

Madam and the Rent Man. Langston Hughes. CP-HughL; SP-HughL

Madam and the Wrong Visitor. Langston Hughes. CP-HughL; SP-HughL

Madam could look in your hand. Ballad of the Fortune Teller. Langston Hughes. CP-HughL; SP-HughL

Madam to you. (LL) Madam's Past History. Langston Hughes. CP-HughL; SP-HughL

Madame Alpha Devine she made a million. Melvin B. Tolson. TtW

Madam's Calling Cards. Langston Hughes. CP-HughL; SP-HughL

Madam's Christmas (or Merry Christmas Everybody). Langston Hughes. CP-HughL

Madam's Past History. Langston Hughes. CP-HughL; SP-HughL

Made Connections. Michael S. Harper. SP-HarpM

Made hair? The girls here. Naolo Beauty Academy, New Orleans, Louisiana, 1943. Natasha Trethewey. SpiFl

Made it blossom Black? (LL) Haiku: "Was it yesterday." Sonia Sanchez. SP-SancS

Made long ago. (LL) American Heartbreak. Langston Hughes. BPo; CP-HughL; NAAAL

Made of stone, round, and very ugly. (LL) Audubon, Drafted. Amiri Baraka. Klds; SP-BaraA

Made to Order Smile, The. Paul Laurence Dunbar. CP-DunbP; GT

Madhouse. Calvin C. Hernton. IDB; Klds; NNP

   (Patient: Rockland County Sanitarium, The.) PoBA

Madimba. Michael S. Harper. SP-HarpM

Madison Experience, The. June Jordan. SP-JordJ

Madness. Al Young. CP-YounA

Madness One Monday Evening. Julia Fields. Klds; NNP

Madrid. Jay Wright. ESEAA

Madrid 1963: Some Changes. Al Young. CP-YounA

Madrigal, A: "Dream days of fond delight and hours." Paul Laurence Dunbar. CP-DunbP

Mæcenas, you, beneath the myrtle shade. To Mæcenas. Phillis Wheatley. NAAAL

Magalu. Helene Johnson. BlSi; CDC; PoBA; ShDr

Maggie came up from Spartansburg. Mecca. Sterling A. Brown. CP-BrowS

Magic. Rita Dove. SP-DoveR

Magic. Sonia Sanchez. SP-SancS

Magic / my man / is you. Black Magic. Sonia Sanchez. BPo; BrTr; SP-SancS

Magnets. Countee Cullen. BALP; CP-CullC

Magnificent Tomorrows. Haki R. Madhubuti. SpiFl

Magnolia. Mary Weston Fordham. CBWP-2

Magnolia Flowers. Langston Hughes. CP-HughL; SP-HughL

Magnolia trees, The. Genealogy. Frank Lamont Phillips. AmNP

Maid of Ehrenthal, The. Henrietta Cordelia Ray. CBWP-3

Maiden, The. Audre Lorde. CP-LordA; SP-LordA

Maiden and River. Mary Weston Fordham. CBWP-2

Maiden wept and, as a comforter, A. Passion and Love. Paul Laurence Dunbar. CP-DunbP

Mail Has Come, The. Mary E. Tucker. CBWP-1

Make a garland of Leontynes and Lenas. Crowns and Garlands. Langston Hughes. CP-HughL

Make even feathered wings. (LL) Be Daedalus. Nanina Alba. PoBA

Make heathens at your doors! (LL) Bible Defence of Slavery. Frances Ellen Watkins Harper. CP-HarpF

Make me a grave where'er you will. Bury Me in a Free Land. Frances Ellen Watkins Harper. AAP; AfAmPo; BPo; CP-HarpF; CrDW; EBAP; TtW

Make our hosannas incense on the wind. Palm Sunday, 1866. Marilyn Nelson. *Fr.* Thus Far by Faith. SP-NelsM

Make Up. Nikki Giovanni. SP-GiovN

Make way for the beast with chrome teeth. The Beast with Chrome Teeth. Thurmond Snyder. NNP

Makes You Go Oohhh! Kalamu ya Salaam. *Fr.* New Orleans Haiku. SpiFl

Maker-of-Sevens in the scheme of things. The Wife-Woman. Anne Spencer. BANP; NAAAL

Makin' Jump Shots. Michael S. Harper. SP-HarpM

Makin' me die this way? (LL) Cabaret Girl Dies on Welfare Island. Langston Hughes. CP-HughL

Makin' me die this way? (LL) Mazie Dies Alone in the City Hospital. Langston Hughes. CP-HughL

Makin' rounds at night. (LL) Street Song. Langston Hughes. CP-HughL

Making It. Audre Lorde. CP-LordA

Making jazz swing in. Haiku: "Making jazz swing in." Etheridge Knight. ESEAA; TtW

Making Love After Hours. Al Young. CP-YounA

Making Love to Concrete. Audre Lorde. CP-LordA

Making of Poems, The. Lucille Clifton. SP-ClifL

Making pilgrimage to herself. walking. (LL) Present. Sonia Sanchez. NAAAL; SP-SancS

Making Poems. Sekou Sundiata. SpiFl

Malagueña Salerosa. Al Young. CP-YounA

Malcolm. Lucille Clifton. NAAAL; SP-ClifL

Malcolm. Sonia Sanchez. BrTr; SP-SancS

Malcolm. Welton Smith. BlFi; BPo

   Beast Section, The.

   "I cannot move / from your voice."

   Interlude: "Screams / screams / malcolm / does not hear my screams." PoBA

   Interlude: "We never spent time in the mountains."

   Malcolm.

   Nigga Section, The.

   Special Section for the Niggas on the Lower Eastside or: Invert the Divisor and Multiply.

Malcolm. Alice Walker. CP-WalkA

Malcolm Spoke / Who Listened? Haki R. Madhubuti. BrTr; ESEAA; NAAAL

Malcolm. / The Saint / behind our skulls. That Old Time Religion. Marvin E. Jackmon. BlFi

Malcolm X. Gwendolyn Brooks. BALP; NAAAL; PoBA; TtW

Malcolm X—an Autobiography. Larry Neal. AmNP; BPo; BlFi; BrTr; TtW

MALCOLM X SPOKE TO ME and sounded you. My Ace of Spades. Ted Joans. BrTr

Malcolm's Blues. Michael S. Harper. SP-HarpM

Malcolm's Messasge. Al Young. CP-YounA

Malika / What is this. Till the Sun Goes Down. Marvin X. BrTr

Malocclusions, the inconditions of love, The. (LL) People who have no children can be hard. Gwendolyn Brooks. Crnst; SP-BrooG

Malvina, A. B. Valcour. TtW

Mama and Daughter. Langston Hughes. CP-HughL; SP-HughL

Mama, don't cry. (LL) Without Benefit of Declaration. Langston Hughes. AmNP; CP-HughL

Mama Elsie's ninety now. Little Man around the House. Yusef Komunyaka. SP-KomuY

Mama, I found this soldier's cap. When the Armies Passed. Langston Hughes. CP-HughL

Mama I remember. Marilyn Nelson. SP-NelsM

Mama Knows. Sharon Scott. JB

Mama Mary's counting them. Birds on a Powerline. Yusef Komunyakaa. SP-KomuY

Mama Mary's counting them. Birds on a Powerline. Herbert Asquith. NAAAL

Mama, / papa, / and us. An Inconvenience. John Raven. BPo

Mama, please brush off my coat. Mama and Daughter. Langston Hughes. CP-HughL; SP-HughL

Mama / Remembers the four-leaf clover. Second Generation: New York. Langston Hughes. CP-HughL

Mama say / he was a black hero. Wille B (3). Lucille Clifton. SP-ClifL

Mama say / i got no business out here. Willie B (1). Lucille Clifton. SP-ClifL

Mama's Murders. Marilyn Nelson. SP-NelsM

Mama's Promise. Marilyn Nelson. SP-NelsM

Mama's Report. Michael S. Harper. SP-HarpM

Mamie's Blues. *Unknown.* Crnst

Mamma! Frank Horne. BPo

Mammy. Langston Hughes. CP-HughL

Mammy / Sun shines east, sun shines west. Real Mammy Song. Sterling A. Brown. CP-BrowS

Mammy's baby, Lou. (LL) Aunt Chloe's Lullaby. Daniel Webster Davis. AAP; AfAmPo

Mammy's in de kitchen, an' de do' is shet. Curiosity. Paul Laurence Dunbar. CP-DunbP

Man. Langston Hughes. CP-HughL

Man, a Torch. George Moses Horton. SP-HortG

Man Bigot. Maya Angelou. CP-AngeM

Man git his feet set in a sticky mudbank, A. Riverbank Blues. Sterling A. Brown. CP-BrowS

Man. His Bowl. His Raspberries, The. Claudia Rankine. GT

Man, i am trying. Sonia Sanchez. SP-SancS

Man, I brisk in the galley first thing next dawn. Shabine Encounters the Middle Passage. Derek Walcott. *Fr.* The Schooner *Flight.* ESEAA

Man in the Mirror. Michael Jackson. Crnst

Man inside the mandolin, The. Refrain. Rita Dove. SP-DoveR

Man into Men. Langston Hughes. CP-HughL

Man / is an alien in this world. A Poem of Praise. Sonia Sanchez. SP-SancS

Man is not cute, The. From Nicaragua Libre: Photograph of Managua. June Jordan. SP-JordJ

Man Is What He Wills to Be. Mrs. Henry Linden. CBWP-4

Man knocked three times, A. Madam and the Wrong Visitor. Langston Hughes. CP-HughL; SP-HughL

Man of low degree was sore oppressed, A. The Crisis. Paul Laurence Dunbar. CP-DunbP

Man of the Middle Class, A. Gwendolyn Brooks. SP-BrooG

Man or Butterfly. Ishmael Reed. CP-ReedI

Man rejects imprisonment. Fall To. Howard Jones. NBP

Man, standing in the shadows of a, A. For H. W. Fuller. Carolyn M. Rodgers. BPo

Man, them revolutionary niggers is all. Just Taking Note. Sharon Scott. JB

Man went forth with gifts, A. Martin Luther King, Jr. Gwendolyn Brooks. BrTr; PoBA

Man White, Brown Girl and All That Jazz. Gloria C. Oden. GT; PoBA

Man who brought you the garbage can, The. Another Poem about the Man. June Jordan. SP-JordJ

Man Who Carries the Desert Around Inside Himself: For Wally, The. Yusef Komunyakaa. SP-KomuY

Man who is a bigot, The. Man Bigot. Maya Angelou. CP-AngeM

Man who puts his armor on, The. Respectfully Dedicated to Dr. Alexander Crummell on the Fiftieth Anniversary of His Pastorate. Frances Ellen Watkins Harper. CP-HarpF

Man who tried to, The. Julius Lester. *Fr.* Poems. Klds

Man whose height his fear improved he, The. Medgar Evers. Gwendolyn Brooks. ESEAA; PoBA

Man whose life wasl ike a candle's flame, A. For Paul Laurence Dunbar. Margaret Abigail Walker. CP-WalkM

Man with a Furnace in His Hand. Lance Jeffers. BlFi

Man with the blood in his sight, The. To Strike for Night. Lebert Bethune. NBP

Man, your whole history. Brother Harlem Bedford Watts Tells Mr. Charlie Where ITs At. Bobb Hamilton. BlFi

Mandarin / in a silent film. The Yellow Bird. James W. Thompson. PoBA

Mandela's Sermon. Keorapetse W. Kgositsile. BrTr

Manhattan March, The 1970s. Al Young. CP-YounA

Manual for the Patriotic Volunteer. Michael S. Harper. SP-HarpM

Many a year is in its grave. The Passage. Paul Laurence Dunbar. CP-DunbP

Many and More. Maya Angelou. CP-AngeM

Many are thy tones, O Ocean. Sea Cadences. Henrietta Cordelia Ray. AAP; CBWP-3

Many clocks in many towers. The Bells Toll Kindly. Langston Hughes. CP-HughL

Many Die Here. Gayl Jones. BlSi

Many long years ago, I loved a youth. The Blight of Love. Mary E. Tucker. CBWP-1

Many poets great and gifted whom the muse's touch had blessed. My Childhood's Happy Days. Daniel Webster Davis. AAP

Many sow, but only the chosen reap, The. Lines to My Father. Countee Cullen. CP-CullC

Many thousand gone. (LL) No more auction block for me. *Unknown.* BPo; NAAAL

Many Thousand Gone. *Unknown.* CrDW

Many whiskey ads. More even than *The.* The Atlantic Monthly, December 1970. Ishmael Reed. CP-ReedI

Map, The. Gloria C. Oden. AmNP; NNP

Map shows me where it is you are. I, The. A Private Letter to Brazil. Gloria C. Oden. ESEAA; GT; Klds

Marathon Runner, The. Fenton Johnson. CDC

March. Henrietta Cordelia Ray. CBWP-3

March Moon. Langston Hughes. CP-HughL; SP-HughL

3-31-70. Gayl Jones. BlSi

Marching up to freedom land. (LL) Ain't Gonna Let Nobody Turn Me Round. *Unknown.* CrDW

Mare Rubrum. Paul Laurence Dunbar. CP-DunbP

Maria Concepcion & the Book of Dreams. Derek Walcott. *Fr.* The Schooner *Flight.* ESEAA

Maria, she said. No city river. The Scuba Diver Recovers the Body of a Drowned Child. Gerald William Barrax. GT; NBV

Marie. *African-American Oral Tradition.* GetYo

Market Street woman is known fuh to have dark days. New St. Louis Blues. Sterling A. Brown. CP-BrowS

Markings on a shitter wall. Legacy of a Brother. Renaldo Fernandez. NBV

Marks / of the mother are. The Stretching of the Belly. Etheridge Knight. SP-KnigE

Marriage. Mary Weston Fordham. CBWP-2

Marriage Nightmare, The. Marilyn Nelson. SP-NelsM

Marriage Vow. Mrs. Henry Linden. CBWP-4

Marrie dear. When in Rome. Mari E. Evans. AmNP

Married to rural goldmines. The Dark Way Home: Survivors. Michael S. Harper. SP-HarpM

Marrow of My Bone. Mari E. Evans. BPo

Martha / Mary passed this morning. Mary Passed This Morning. Owen Dodson. PoBA

Martha this is a catalog of days. Audre Lorde. CP-LordA; SP-LordA

Martial Choreograph. Maya Angelou. CP-AngeM; SP-AngeM

Martin Luther King, Jr. Gwendolyn Brooks. BrTr; PoBA

Martine's Keen Eyes. Ishmael Reed. CP-ReedI

Martin's Blues. Michael S. Harper. PoBA; SP-HarpM

Martyr of Alabama, The. Frances Ellen Watkins Harper. CP-HarpF; TtW

Martyrdom. Richard W. Thomas. PoBA

Mary. Lucille Clifton. SP-ClifL

Mary at the Feet of Christ. Frances Ellen Watkins Harper. CP-HarpF

Mary, don you weep an Marthie don you moan. *African-American Oral Tradition.* TtW

Mary had a little lamb for which she cared no particle. *African-American Oral Tradition.* GetYo

Mary mary astonished by God. Lucille Clifton. SP-ClifL

Mary Passed This Morning. Owen Dodson. PoBA

Mary's Dream. Lucille Clifton. SP-ClifL

Maryuma. Frank Lamont Phillips. AmNP

Mask, The. Clarissa Scott Delany. CDC; ShDr; TtW

Mask, The. Irma McClaurin. BlSi

Masquerade. Carolyn M. Rodgers. BlSi

Mastah drink his ol' Made'a. A Preference. Paul Laurence Dunbar. CP-DunbP

Mastectomy. Wanda Coleman. NAAAL

Master and Man. Sterling A. Brown. CP-BrowS

Master Charge Blues. Nikki Giovanni. SP-GiovN

Master only left old Mistus. The Deliverance. Frances Ellen Watkins Harper. CP-HarpF

Master-Player, The. Paul Laurence Dunbar. CP-DunbP

Master, the tempest is raging. Peace Be Still. *Unknown.* NAAAL

Master, we perish if thou sleep. Excited from Reading the Obedience of Nature to her Lord in the Vessel on the Sea. George Moses Horton. SP-HortG

Masters, The. Paul Laurence Dunbar. CP-DunbP

Match the steel stillness. (LL) Haiku: "Falling snow flakes, The." Etheridge Knight. ESEAA; TtW

Matin Hymn. Josephine D. Henderson Heard. CBWP-4

Matter of Locality, A. Paul Laurence Dunbar. CP-DunbP

Mattie dear / the box is full. Mari E. Evans. *See* When in Rome.

Mattinata. Mary Effie Lee Newsome. ShDr

Maud went to college. Sadie and Maud. Gwendolyn Brooks. *Fr.* A Street in Bronzeville. BPo; BlSi; ESEAA; NAAAL; SP-BrooG

Maumee Ruth. Sterling A. Brown. CDC; CP-BrowS

Maurice. Rita Dove. *See* Dusting.

Mawu. Audre Lorde. CP-LordA

Maxie Allen always taught her. Gwendolyn Brooks. NAAAL

Maxine / I used to admire your talent. Journeystones. Audre Lorde. CP-LordA

May. Mrs. Henry Linden. CBWP-4

May. Henrietta Cordelia Ray. CBWP-3

May be refin'd, and join th' angelic train. (LL) On Being Brought from Africa to America. Phillis Wheatley. AfAmPo; CP-WheaP; NAAAL; TtW

May de Devil Preach 'is fůner'l song. (LL) Promises of Freedom. *Unknown.* BPo; CrDW; NAAAL

May escape the spell of the South. (LL) The South. Langston Hughes. CP-HughL; SP-HughL

May God bless your home. Marriage Vow. Mrs. Henry Linden. CBWP-4

May he have new life like the fall. John Coltrane: An Impartial Review. Alfred B. Spellman. NNP; PoBA

May I not love the beauteous flow'rs. Daniel Alexander Payne. EBAP

May it ain't right. Live and Let Live. Langston Hughes. *Fr.* Montage of a Dream Deferred. CP-HughL

May Saraswati give thee. Saraswati. Bob Kaufman. SP-KaufB

May the Saddest Memory. Birthday Wishes to a Husband. Lizelia Augusta Jenkins Moorer. CBWP-3

May this inspired acrostic prove. For the Fair Miss M. M. McLean. George Moses Horton. SP-HortG

May very well cost you your life. (LL) Poem About My Rights. June Jordan. NAAAL; SP-JordJ

May Your Love Convert Lucifer. Marilyn Nelson. SP-NelsM

Maya. Al Young. CP-YounA

Mayakovsky was right. Kiss. Al Young. CP-YounA; PoBA

Maybe. Langston Hughes. CP-HughL; SP-HughL

Maybe I shouldn't but I must tell you. A Brand New Morning Love Song. Al Young. CP-YounA

Maybe it was the Bichot. Poetry Makes Rhythm in Philosophy. Ishmael Reed. CP-ReedI

Mayday. Ed Roberson. PoBA

May's Invocation after a Tardy Spring. Henrietta Cordelia Ray. CBWP-3

Mazie Dies Alone in the City Hospital. Langston Hughes. CP-HughL

McDonogh Day in New Orleans. Marcus B. Christian. AmNP

McLambert long had gone from home away. Albery Allson Whitman. *Fr.* Leelah Misled. EBAP

McLambert now upon Leelah looked down. Albery Allson Whitman. *Fr.* Leelah Misled. EBAP

Me Alone. Lula Lowe Weeden. CDC

Me an' ma baby's / Got two mo' ways. Negro Dancers. Langston Hughes. CP-HughL

Me an my captain don't agree. Me and My Captain. *Unknown.* NAAAL

Me and My Captain. *Unknown.* NAAAL

Me and My Song. Langston Hughes. CP-HughL

Me and My Work. Maya Angelou. CP-AngeM

Me and the Mule. Langston Hughes. IDB; SP-HughL
("Like I am.") (LL) CP-HughL

Me and tuko go down to the jew. Cuttin Down to Size. Henry L. Dumas. BlFi

Me and you be sisters. Sisters. Lucille Clifton. SP-ClifL

Me early one morning? (LL) Prelude to Nothing. Sonia Sanchez. GT; SP-SancS

Me? / I never could keep my edges and kitchen. For Sistuhs Wearin' Straight Hair. Carolyn M. Rodgers. NAAAL

Me?—I / was / peeing. (LL) Talking in the Woods with Karl Amorelli. Etheridge Knight. SP-KnigE

Me, in Kulu Se and Karma. Carolyn M. Rodgers. PoBA

Me 'n' Dunbar. James David Corrothers. NAAAL

Me nappy hair dream child. Image in the Mirror. Peggy Susberry Kenner. JB

Meadow Lark, The. Paul Laurence Dunbar. CP-DunbP

Meal Time. Maggie Pogue Johnson. CBWP-4

Mean mean mean to be free. (LL) Runagate Runagate. Robert Hayden. BALP; BPo; CP-HaydR; ESEAA; IDB; NAAAL; PoBA; SSLK; TtW

Mean old murderous Leadbelly. The Midnight Special Revisited. Al Young. CP-YounA

Mean Old Yesterday. Langston Hughes. CP-HughL

Meaning of Protest, The. Michael S. Harper. SP-HarpM

Meaning of the Smell of Sweat, The. Niama Leslie JoAnn Williams. SpiFl

Meanwhile, in Rwanda. Saundra Sharp. SpiFl

Measure of Memory (The Navigator), The. Amiri Baraka. SP-BaraA

Mecca. Sterling A. Brown. CP-BrowS

Mechanical / Oracles dot the sky. Gods in Vietnam. Eugene B. Redmond. NBP; PoBA

Mechanics have always been the same. Politics As History. Al Young. CP-YounA

Medgar Evers. Gwendolyn Brooks. ESEAA; PoBA

Medgar Evers, 1925-1963. Margaret Abigail Walker. CP-WalkM

Medicine. Alice Walker. CP-WalkA

Medicine Man. Calvin C. Hernton. TtW

Meditation on a Cold, Dark and Rainy Night. George Moses Horton. SP-HortG

Meditation over the Washtub. Marilyn Nelson. *Fr.* Thus Far by Faith. SP-NelsM

Medley goes like this, The. Time for Tyner: Folksong. Michael S. Harper. SP-HarpM

Medusa. Countee Cullen. CP-CullC

Meet. Audre Lorde. CP-LordA

Meeting After the Savior Gone, The. Lucille Clifton. SP-ClifL

Meeting in secret, with my great. The Founding Fathers in Philadelphia. Michael S. Harper. SP-HarpM

Meeting of Minds, A. Audre Lorde. CP-LordA

Meetings meetings meetings. Yuh Lookin Good. Carolyn M. Rodgers. BPo

Mel, I dreamed this. I Woke Up and Wrote About It. Marilyn Nelson. *Fr.* I Dream the Book of Jonah. SP-NelsM

Melancholia. Paul Laurence Dunbar. CP-DunbP

Mellow. Langston Hughes. *Fr.* Montage of a Dream Deferred. CP-HughL

Mellow moon hangs golden in the sky, The. October. Henrietta Cordelia Ray. CBWP-3

Mellow sunlight, soothing, warm. Autumn. Marjorie Marshall. ShDr

Melting Pot, The. Dudley Randall. BALP; BPo; NBV

Melvin's dead, / a cloud-nine moves. Return to Temptation. Mary Weems. SpiFl

Memento. Marilyn Nelson. SP-NelsM

Memo. June Jordan. SP-JordJ

Memo. Charles Lynch. PoBA

Memo: For the Race Orators. Sterling A. Brown. CP-BrowS

Memo #2. Etheridge Knight. SP-KnigE

Memo #5. Etheridge Knight. SP-KnigE

Memo #9. Etheridge Knight. SP-KnigE

Memo #32. Etheridge Knight. SP-KnigE

Memo #43. Etheridge Knight. SP-KnigE

Memo to Non-White People. Langston Hughes. CP-HughL

Memorial. Claude McKay. SP-McKaC

Memorial. Sonia Sanchez. BlSi

Memorial Day. Paul Laurence Dunbar. CP-DunbP

Memorial Day. Clara Ann Thompson. CBWP-2

Memorial I. Audre Lorde. CP-LordA; SP-LordA

Memorial II. Audre Lorde. CP-LordA; SP-LordA

Memorial III from a Phone Booth on Broadway. Audre Lorde. CP-LordA; SP-LordA

Memorial IV. Audre Lorde. CP-LordA

Memorial Wreath. Dudley Randall. IDB; NNP; PoBA

Memories of Salem. Sterling A. Brown. CP-BrowS

Memory, The. Maya Angelou. SP-AngeM
("Cotton rows criscross the world.") CP-AngeM

Memory, A. Adah Isaacs Menken. CBWP-1

Memory. Mary Effie Lee Newsome. ShDr

Memory. Margaret Abigail Walker. CP-WalkM; GT

Memory / carved on stelae of, A. Two Egyptian Portrait Masks. Robert Hayden. CP-HaydR

Memory of June, A. Claude McKay. SP-McKaC

Memory of Lincoln and the Yankees. James Ephriam McGirt. AAP

Memory of Martha, The. Paul Laurence Dunbar. CP-DunbP

Memory of your profile on the pillow, The. (LL) The Profile on the Pillow. Dudley Randall. BPo; BrTr; PoBA

Memphis Blues. Sterling A. Brown. BANP; CP-BrowS; NAAAL

Men. Maya Angelou. CP-AngeM; SP-AngeM

Men. Jean Toomer. CP-ToomJ

Men choose a crystal goblet filled with wine. God's Ways, Not Our Ways. Henrietta Cordelia Ray. AAP; CBWP-3

Men claim the easiest spots. Fishing the White Water. Audre Lorde. CP-LordA; GT

Men Folks ob Today, De. Maggie Pogue Johnson. CBWP-4

Men in the Kitchen. Marilyn Nelson. SP-NelsM

Men lean toward the wood. Lynching and Burning. Primus St. John. PoBA

Men may sing of their Havanas, elevating to the stars. My Corn-Cob Pipe. Paul Laurence Dunbar. CP-DunbP

Men never know. The Radical. Waring Cuney. CDC

Men of careful turns, haters of forks in the road. Gwendolyn Brooks. SP-BrooG

Men of Cleveland, had a vulture. To the Union Savers of Cleveland. Frances Ellen Watkins Harper. AAP; AfAmPo; CP-HarpF

Men of the North! it is no time. Words for the Hour. Frances Ellen Watkins Harper. CP-HarpF

Men saw the blush and called it Dawn. (LL) Dawn. Paul Laurence Dunbar. AmNP; CP-DunbP

Men start digging in the ground. Missing in Action. Yusef Komunyakaa. SP-KomuY

Men who ride strange wild horses. Tapestry. Langston Hughes. CP-HughL

Mended. Jean Toomer. CP-ToomJ

Mentor. Audre Lorde. CP-LordA; SP-LordA

Mentors. Gwendolyn Brooks. ESEAA; Klds; SP-BrooG

Menu. June Jordan. SP-JordJ

Mercedes is a jungle-lily in a death house. To the Dark Mercedes of "El Palacio de Amor." Langston Hughes. CP-HughL

"Merely a Negro"—in a day like this! (LL) At the Closed Gate of Justice. James David Corrothers. TtW

Merging. Niama Leslie JoAnn Williams. SpiFl

Merl. Jean Toomer. CP-ToomJ; GT

Merle "Uncle Seagram." Gwendolyn Brooks. TtW

Merle; Uncle Seagram. Gwendolyn Brooks. Fr. Children Coming Home. ESEAA

Merry Autumn. Paul Laurence Dunbar. CP-DunbP

Merry Christmas, China. Langston Hughes. CP-HughL

Merry-Go-Round. Langston Hughes. CP-HughL; SP-HughL

Merry voices chatterin'. Two-an'-Six. Claude McKay. BANP

Message, The. Grandmaster Flash and the Furious Five. NAAAL

Message All Black People Can Dig, A. Haki R. Madhubuti. BrTr

Message for Langston, A. "Kush." NBV

Message on Cape Cod, The. Michael S. Weaver. GT

Message to a Loved One Dead, A. Josephine D. Henderson Heard. CBWP-4

Message to Etheridge Knight. Lenard D. Moore. TtW

Message to the President. Langston Hughes. CP-HughL

Messengers, The. Henrietta Cordelia Ray. CBWP-3

Meta-A and the A of Absolutes. Jay Wright. ESEAA

Meta-Rhetoric. June Jordan. SP-JordJ

Metagnomy. Norman Henry, II Pritchard. NBP

Metal door groans, The. Re-creating the Scene. Yusef Komunyakaa. SP-KomuY

Methought the Moon, pale regent of the sky. The Vision. John Boyd. EBAP

Metropolitan Museum. Langston Hughes. CP-HughL

Mexican Market Woman. Langston Hughes. CP-HughL; SP-HughL

Mexico City Lover. Al Young. CP-YounA

Mexico needs mahogany. El Paso Monologue. Ishmael Reed. SpiFl

Micah was a young man of the people. Margaret Abigail Walker. CP-WalkM

Michael At Sixteen Months. Al Young. CP-YounA

"Michelangelo" the Elder. Bob Kaufman. SP-KaufB

Mid-Life Crises: A Critical Review. Al Young. CP-YounA

'Mid the discordant noises of the day I hear thee calling. Prayer, A: "'Mid the discordant noises of the day I hear thee calling." Claude McKay. SP-McKaC

Middle-aged white man in a beat-up blue Pinto, The. The Lucky One. Reginald Shepherd. GT

Middle Class Blues, The. Ishmael Reed. CP-ReedI

Middle Passage. Frederick Douglass. CrDW

Middle Passage. Robert Hayden. AmNP; BPo; CP-HaydR; IDB; PoBA ("Sails falshing to the wind like weapons.") NAAAL

Middle Passage and After, The. Larry Neal. NBV

Midnight. Henrietta Cordelia Ray. Fr. Idyl. EBAP

Midnight Chippie's Lament. Langston Hughes. CP-HughL

Midnight Dancer. Langston Hughes. CP-HughL; SP-HughL

Midnight is no time for. No Time for Poetry. Julia Fields. AmNP

Midnight Raffle. Langston Hughes. CP-HughL; SP-HughL

Midnight Song. Pinkie Gordon Lane. GT; TtW

Midnight Special Revisited, The. Al Young. CP-YounA

Midnight wooed the Morning-Star, The. The Barrier. Paul Laurence Dunbar. CP-DunbP

Midway. Naomi Long Madgett. BPo; BlSi; NNP

Midwinter Blues. Langston Hughes. CP-HughL; SP-HughL

Midwives and winding sheets. Is Love. Maya Angelou. CP-AngeM

Might as well bury her. Maumee Ruth. Sterling A. Brown. CDC; CP-BrowS

Might Britain, tremble! Ghandhi Is Fasting. Langston Hughes. CP-HughL

Mightier than the sword thou art. The Pen. Mary Weston Fordham. CBWP-2

Mighty drums echoing the voices. S, C, M. Ted Wilson. BlFi

Mighty Soviet armies marching on the West. Salute to Soviet Armies. Langston Hughes. CP-HughL

Mignon. Henrietta Cordelia Ray. CBWP-3

Migrant. Langston Hughes. CP-HughL; SP-HughL

Migration. Carole C. Gregory Clemmons. See Ghetto Lovesong—Migration.

Migration. Langston Hughes. CP-HughL

Migration. Pinkie Gordon Lane. BlSi

Mike 65. Lennox Raphael. PoBA

Mildred's Doves. Henrietta Cordelia Ray. CBWP-3

Milestone: The Birth of an Ancestor. Eugene B. Redmond. SpiFl

Milestones: September 28, 1991. Askia M. Toure. CtF

Militance of a Photograph in the Passbook of a Bantu under Detention, The. Michael S. Harper. TtW

Militant. Langston Hughes. CP-HughL; PoBA

Military spending huge profits and death. Expenditures; Economic Love Song 1. Jayne Cortez. SP-CortJ

Mill Mountain. Sterling A. Brown. CP-BrowS

Mills / That grind and grind, The. Steel Mills. Langston Hughes. CP-HughL

Milton. Henrietta Cordelia Ray. BlSi; CBWP-3; EBAP; TtW

Mind for All Its Reasoning, The. Bob Kaufman. SP-KaufB

Mind knows no death. Life is the "first and last." Albery Allson Whitman. AAP

Mind of a Madman kills. Eddie Griffin. CtF

Mine. Mary E. Tucker. CBWP-1

Mingled / breath and smell. Subway Rush Hour. Langston Hughes. Fr. Montage of a Dream Deferred. CP-HughL

Mingus. Bob Kaufman. PoBA

Minister, The. Fenton Johnson. Klds

Minnie Sings Her Blues. Langston Hughes. CP-HughL

Minor Miracle. Marilyn Nelson. SP-NelsM

Minstrel Man. Langston Hughes. CP-HughL

Minuets of memory, The. (LL) The Anniad. Gwendolyn Brooks. BlSi; SP-BrooG

Minutely Hurt. Countee Cullen. CP-CullC

Miracle. Derrick I. M. Gilbert. CtF

Miracles. Arna Bontemps. NAAAL

Mirages, The. Robert Hayden. CP-HaydR

Mirrors. Nikki Giovanni. SP-GiovN

Misanthropist, The. James M. Whitfield. AAP; AfAmPo; EBAP

Misapprehension. Paul Laurence Dunbar. BPo; CP-DunbP

Miscellaneous Verses. Gustavus Vassa. EBAP

Miserimus. Adah Isaacs Menken. CBWP-1

Misery. Langston Hughes. CP-HughL; SP-HughL

Miss Blues'es Child. Langston Hughes. CP-HughL; SP-HughL

Miss Gardner's in her garden. Southern Mammy Sings. Langston Hughes. CP-HughL; SP-HughL

Miss Jones. Wanda Coleman. IHS

Miss Liza's Banjer. Daniel Webster Davis. AAP; EBAP

Miss Lookingood. African-American Oral Tradition. GetYo

Miss Marfy sco'n young Issac so. The Suitor. Paul Laurence Dunbar. CP-DunbP

Miss Melerlee. John Wesley Holloway. BANP

Miss Muffett in a runaway ugly machine. I mean. Like that. (LL) W. W. Amiri Baraka. NBP; PoBA

Miss Rosie. Lucille Clifton. BlSi; ESEAA; PoBA; SP-ClifL

Miss Scarlet, Mr. Rhett and other Latter-Day Saints. Maya Angelou. CP-AngeM; SP-AngeM

Missing Beat. Carolyn M. Rodgers. JB

Missing in Action. Yusef Komunyakaa. SP-KomuY

Missing you is like. Sonia Sanchez. SP-SancS

Mission. Michael S. Harper. SP-HarpM

Mission of the Flowers, The. Frances Ellen Watkins Harper. BlSi

Missionaries in the Jungle. Linda Piper. BlSi

Missionary, The. Mrs. Henry Linden. CBWP-4

Missions and Magnolias. Nayo-Barbara Watkins. TtW

Mississippi. Langston Hughes. CP-HughL

Mississippi. E. Ethelbert Miller. GT

Mississippi Blues. Lamont B. Steptoe. SpiFl

Mississippi Concerto. Rolland Snellings. BlFi

Mississippi Griot. Sterling Plumpp. TtW

Mississippi Levee. Langston Hughes. CP-HughL

Mississippi Winter I. Alice Walker. CP-WalkA

Mississippi Winter II. Alice Walker. CP-WalkA

Mississippi Winter III. Alice Walker. CP-WalkA

Mississippi Winter IV. Alice Walker. CP-WalkA

Missouri Haiku. Etheridge Knight. SP-KnigE

Mist has left the greening plain, The. Morning. Paul Laurence Dunbar. CP-DunbP

Mist Maiden, The. Henrietta Cordelia Ray. CBWP-3

Mistah Rabbit, Mistah Rabbit, yo tale's mighty white. *African-American Oral Tradition.* TtW

Mister Backlash, Mister Backlash. Blacklash Blues, The. Langston Hughes. BPo; CP-HughL

Mr. Danny. Sterling A. Brown. CP-BrowS

Mr. Edward Fordham. Mary Weston Fordham. CBWP-2

Mister Minister, I found. Why I Turned Vegetarian. Rita Dove. SP-DoveR

Mr. P. C. Michael S. Harper. SP-HarpM

Mr. President, kindly please. Message to the President. Langston Hughes. CP-HughL

Mr. Roosevelt Regrets. Pauli Murray. PoBA

Mister Samuel and Sam. Sterling A. Brown. CP-BrowS

Mister Samuel, he belong to Rotary. Mister Samuel and Sam. Sterling A. Brown. CP-BrowS

Mister Sandman. Langston Hughes. CP-HughL

Mr. Tut's House A Recollection. Julia Fields. BkSV

Mr. White Man, White Man. Do You Reckon? Langston Hughes. CP-HughL

Mr. Z. M. Carl Holman. Klds

Mistletoe. Mary E. Tucker. CBWP-1

Mrs. Coley's three-flat brick. The Vacant Lot. Gwendolyn Brooks. *Fr.* A Street in Bronzeville. BPo; BlSi; NAAAL; SP-BrooG

Mrs. E. Cohrs Brown. Mary Weston Fordham. CBWP-2

Mrs. Francis Ellen Harper. George Clinton Rowe. AAP

Mrs. Hobart-Constantine awakens. Two Ladies Bidding Us "Good Morning." James P. Vaughn. NNP

Mrs. Johnson Objects. Clara Ann Thompson. BlSi; CBWP-2

Mrs. Louise B. Weston. Mary Weston Fordham. CBWP-2

Mrs. Mary Furman Weston Byrd. Mary Weston Fordham. CBWP-2

Mrs. Myrick's Lecture. Mary E. Tucker. CBWP-1

Mistress of green in flowers arrayed. Acrostics. George Moses Horton. AAP; SP-HortG

Mrs. Rebecca Weston. Mary Weston Fordham. CBWP-2

Mrs. Small went to the kitchen for her pocketbook. Gwendolyn Brooks. GT; SP-BrooG

Mrs. Williams' face was pleading when she spoke of her God to me. When She Spoke of God. Lance Jeffers. BrTr

Misty Day, A. Paul Laurence Dunbar. CP-DunbP

Misunderstood. Lizelia Augusta Jenkins Moorer. CBWP-3

Mitchell Case, The. Langston Hughes. CP-HughL

Mixed Sketches. Haki R. Madhubuti. BPo; BrTr

Mneme begin. Inspire, ye sacred Nine. On Recollection. Phillis Wheatley. CP-WheaP; EBAP

Mneme, begin; inspire, ye sacred Nine! Recollection. Phillis Wheatley. CP-WheaP

Moan. Langston Hughes. CP-HughL

Mobile-Buck. James Edwin Campbell. AAP

Modern Moses, or "My Policy" Man. James Madison Bell. AAP; EBAP

Mojo Pete is bad. Checkers. Sterling A. Brown. CP-BrowS

Mojo Queen of the Feathery Plumes. Ishmael Reed. CP-ReedI

Molasses and the Three Witches. Michael S. Harper. SP-HarpM

Molly Means. Margaret Abigail Walker. AmNP; BlSi; CP-WalkM; Klds

Moment 9/The Woman. John W. Love, Jr. CtF

Moment comes to me, A. This Bridge Across. Christopher Gilbert. GT

Moment comes to me, A. This Bridge Across. George Barlow. ESEAA

Moment Please, A. Samuel Allen. AmNP; IDB; PoBA; SSLK

   ("When I gaze at the sun.") Klds

Moment's rest, and peace of mind, A. (LL) The Opium-Eater. Mary E. Tucker. CBWP-1

Momma a carrot grows underground. Potlicker Blues. Calvin Forbes. GT

Momma had words for us. Momma Sayings. Harryette Mullen. TtW

Momma Momma Momma. Gettin Down to Get over. June Jordan. SP-JordJ

Momma Sayings. Harryette Mullen. TtW

Momma Welfare Roll. Maya Angelou. CP-AngeM; SP-AngeM

Mommy mommy come and see. Ballad from Childhood. Audre Lorde. CP-LordA; SP-LordA

Mon sa me el kirimoor. Sound Poem (I). Jean Toomer. CP-ToomJ

Mona Lisa, A. Angelina Weld Grimké. BlSi; CDC; ShDr; TtW

Monet whispered softly. Bird with Painted Wings. Bob Kaufman. SP-KaufB; TtW

Monet's "Waterlilies", *(for Bill and Sonja).* Robert Hayden. CP-HaydR; GT

Money and art. Paint. Langston Hughes. CP-HughL

Money cannot buy you. From Inside an Empty Purse. Audre Lorde. CP-LordA

Money, Honey, Money. Margaret Abigail Walker. CP-WalkM

Money was near. (LL) Green Memory. Langston Hughes. CP-HughL

Mongolian Sunset in Gobi Desert. Bob Kaufman. SP-KaufB

Monkey and the Lion, The. The Signifying Monkey. *Unknown.* CrDW; NAAAL

Monkey Island. Ishmael Reed. CP-ReedI

Monkeyman. Audre Lorde. CP-LordA; SP-LordA

Monk's Walk, The. Paul Laurence Dunbar. CP-DunbP

Monologue. Margaret Abigail Walker. CP-WalkM

Monotony. Langston Hughes. CP-HughL

Monroe's Blues. Langston Hughes. CP-HughL; SP-HughL

Monroe's fell on evil days. Monroe's Blues. Langston Hughes. CP-HughL; SP-HughL

Monsoon Season. Yusef Komunyakaa. SP-KomuY

Monster, The. Karen L. Mitchell. GT

Monsters from the Ozarks. Ishmael Reed. CP-ReedI

Montage of a Dream Deferred. Langston Hughes. CP-HughL; SP-HughL

   Advice.

   Argument: "White is right."

   Ballad of the Landlord. NAAAL

   Bar.

   Be-Bop Boys.

   Blues at Dawn.

   Boogie: 1 A.M.

   Brothers.

   Buddy.

   Café: 3 A.M.

   Casualty.

   Children's Rhymes. BPo

   Chord.

   College Formal: Renaissance Casino.

   Comment on Curb.

   Corner Meeting.

   Croon.

   Dancer.

   Dead in There.

   Deferred.

   Dime.

   Dive.

   Dream Boogie. NAAAL; SSLK

   Dream Boogie: Variation.

   Drunkard.

   "Early blue evening."

   Easy Boogie.

   Evening Song.

   Fact.

   Flatted Fifths.

   Gauge.

   "Good morning, daddy!"

   Green Memory.

   Harlem: "What happens to a dream deferred?"

      (Dream Defferred.)

   High to Low.

   Hope: "He rose up on his dying bed."

   Island: "Between two rivers."

   Jam Session.

   Joe Louis: "They worshipped Joe."

   Juke Box Love Song.

   Lady's Boogie.

   Letter.

Likewise.

Live and Let Live.

Low to High.

Mellow.

Motto.

Movies.

Mystery.

Necessity.

Neighbor.

Neon Signs.

New Yorkers.

"Night funeral / In Harlem."

Nightmare Boogie.

Not a Movie.

Numbers.

125th Street.

Parade.

Passing.

Preference.

Projection.

Question: "Said the lady, *Can you do.*"

Relief.

Request.

Same in Blues.

Shame on You.

Sister.

Situation.

Sliver.

Sliver of Sermon.

"*So long* / is in the song."

Street Song.

Subway Rush Hour.

Sunday by the Combination.

Tag.

Tell Me.

Testimonial.

Theme for English B.   BALP; SSLK

"Tomorrow may be."

Ultimatum.

Up-Beat.

Warning.

Warning: Augmented.

What? So Soon!

Wine-O.

World War II.

Montgomery.   Sam Cornish.   PoBA

Month of rain ends.   Tanka: "Month of rain ends."   Lenard D. Moore.   SpiFl

Monticello.   Lucille Clifton.   SP-ClifL

Montmartre.   Langston Hughes.   CP-HughL; Klds

Mood.   Countee Cullen.   CP-CullC

Mood, The.   Quandra Prettyman.   PoBA

Moody.   Alice Walker.   CP-WalkA

Moon beams and yams.   Rapping Along with Ronda Davis.   James Cunningham.   JB

Moon begins her stately ride, The.   Evening.   Paul Laurence Dunbar.   CP-DunbP

Moon Bound.   Raymond Washington.   NBV

Moon has left the sky, love, The.   Night of Love.   Paul Laurence Dunbar.   CP-DunbP

Moon, How Do I Measure Up?   Al Young.   CP-YounA

Moon hung low 'mid clouds enshrined, The.   The Fading Skiff.   Henrietta Cordelia Ray.   CBWP-3

Moon is but a lantern set by some, The.   Mill Mountain.   Sterling A. Brown.   CP-BrowS

Moon is fat and old tonight, The.   Change.   Langston Hughes.   CP-HughL

Moon is naked, The.   March Moon.   Langston Hughes.   CP-HughL; SP-HughL

Moon marked and touched by sun.   A Woman Speaks.   Audre Lorde.   CP-LordA

Moon minded the sun goes farther from us.   Gemini.   Audre Lorde.   CP-LordA; SP-LordA

Moon, moon, me go now but.   Pidgin Moon.   Al Young.   CP-YounA

Moon of moon & quintessential moonness.   Coastal Moon.   Al Young.   CP-YounA

Moon of no return, never the same.   Al Young.   CP-YounA

Moon Over Matter.   Al Young.   CP-YounA

Moon shines down, The.   Nikki Giovanni.   SP-GiovN

Moon still sends its mellow light.   To a Dead Friend.   Langston Hughes.   CP-HughL

Moon, the Whole Moon, and Nothing but the Moon, The.   Al Young.   CP-YounA

Moon Up Close in Winter by the Telescope, The.   Al Young.   CP-YounA

Moon / Was an old, old woman tonight, The.   Theft.   Esther Popel.   ShDr

Moon Watching by Lake Chapala.   Al Young.   CP-YounA

Moon/Light Quarter/Back Sack.   Samuel F. Reynolds.   SpiFl

Moonlessness.   Al Young.   CP-YounA

Moonlight breaks upon the city's domes, The.   A Song of the Moon.   Claude McKay.   SP-McKaC

Moonlight in Valencia.   Moonlight in Valencia: Civil War.   Langston Hughes.   CP-HughL

Moonlight in Valencia: Civil War.   Langston Hughes.   CP-HughL

Moonlight Night: Carmel.   Langston Hughes.   CP-HughL; GT
  ("And beating the land's / Edge into a swoon.")   (LL)   SP-HughL

Moonlight, The: Juice flowing from an overripe pomegranate.   Enchantment.   Lewis Alexander.   PoBA

Moonlight's a slow rain.   Fat Grass and Slow Rain.   Merilene M. Murphy.   CtF

Moonlit snow slope, A.   (LL)   Haiku: "Bare pecan tree, A."   Etheridge Knight.   ESEAA; TtW

Moonshine.   Yusef Komunyakaa.   SP-KomuY

Moose Wallow, The.   Robert Hayden.   CP-HaydR

More, *for James Wright*.   Ai.   GT

More Clues to the Blues.   Al Young.   CP-YounA

More Girl Than Boy.   Yusef Komunyakaa.   SP-KomuY

More Letters Found near a Suicide.   Frank Horne.   BANP

More Love to His Life.   Alice Walker.   CP-WalkA

More Than a Fool's Song.   Countee Cullen.   CP-CullC

More than once.   Lucille Clifton.   SP-ClifL

Morn.   Josephine D. Henderson Heard.   CBWP-4

Morn hath risen clear and bright, The.   The Expulsion of Hagar.   Eloise Bibb.   CBWP-4

Morning.   Paul Laurence Dunbar.   CP-DunbP

Morning After.   Langston Hughes.   CP-HughL; SP-HughL

Morning after. . . Love, The.   Kattie M. Cumbo.   BlSi

Morning. / and she awoke to.   Five Sense.   Marvin, Jr. Wyche.   AmNP

Morning Duke Ellington Praised the Lord and Six Little Black Davids Tapped Danced Unto, The.   Owen Dodson.   FB

Morning fog / my daughter dropped off at camp.   Haiku: "Morning fog / my daughter dropped off at camp."   Lynn G. Moore.   CtF

Morning glories.   Clinton.   Sterling Plumpp.   BkSV

Morning Joy.   Bob Kaufman.   SP-KaufB

Morning Joy.   Claude McKay.   SP-McKaC

Morning Light.   Mary Effie Lee Newsome.   AmNP; CDC; PoBA; ShDr

Morning of sleeplessness up to heckle wife as jokes.   Day Kennedy Died.   Al Young.   CP-YounA

Morning on the mountains where the mist, The.   June Jordan.   SP-JordJ

Morning Poem for Michael, A.   Al Young.   CP-YounA

Morning Raga for Malcolm.   Larry Neal.   BrTr

Morning snow falling.   Sonia Sanchez.   SP-SancS

Morning Song of Love.   Paul Laurence Dunbar.   CP-DunbP

Morning Star, The.   Primus St. John.   PoBA

Morning sun heats up the young beech tree.   Aftermath.   June Jordan.   SP-JordJ

Morning sun slants cell.   Haiku: "Morning sun slants cell."   Etheridge Knight.   ESEAA; TtW

Mornings / I got up early.   The Way It Was.   Lucille Clifton.   SP-ClifL

Mornings / of an impossible love.   Alice Walker.   CP-WalkA

Morocco conquering homage paid to Spain.   Tetuan.   Claude McKay.   SP-McKaC

Mors et Vita.   James Edwin Campbell.   AAP; AfAmPo

Mortality.   Paul Laurence Dunbar.   CP-DunbP

Mortality.   Naomi Long Madgett.   NNP; PoBA; TtW

Mosaic Harlem.   Henry L. Dumas.   BlFi

Moscow for many loving her was dead.   Claude McKay.   SP-McKaC

Mose is black and evil.   Sterling A. Brown.   CP-BrowS; Klds

Moses.   Lucille Clifton.   SP-ClifL

Moses.   E. Ethelbert Miller.   TtW

Moses: A Story of the Nile.   Frances Ellen Watkins Harper.   CP-HarpF
  Death of Moses, The.   AAP
  Flight into Midian.   AAP
  "Moses sought again the presence of the king."   AfAmPo

Moss.   Al Young.   CP-YounA

Mossy. Ishmael Reed. CP-ReedI

Most people in the world stumble. Conversation Overheard. Quincy Troupe. NAAAL

Most popular "act" in, The. Black Boys Play the Classics. Toi Derricotte. SpiFl

Most royal / affluent / advertisement. Wig. Kirk Hall. BlFi

Most things are colorful things—the sky, earth, and sea. White Things. Anne Spencer. ShDr

Mostly we occupy ocular zones, clinging. How the Rainbow Works. Al Young. CP-YounA; ESEAA

Mother, The. Gwendolyn Brooks. *Fr.* A Street in Bronzeville. BPo; BlSi; CrDW; Crnst; ESEAA; NAAAL; SP-BrooG; TtW

Mother. Josephine D. Henderson Heard. CBWP-4

"Mother dear, may I go downtown." Ballad of Birmingham. Dudley Randall. BPo; BrTr

Mother, for months a mist has been before me. Light in Darkness. Mary E. Tucker. CBWP-1

Mother, i am mad. Lucille Clifton. SP-ClifL

Mother in Wartime. Langston Hughes. CP-HughL

Mother, mother / there's too many of you crying. What's Going On. Marvin Gaye. Crnst

Mother Speaks: The Algiers Motel Incident, Detroit, A. Michael S. Harper. BPo; NBV; SP-HarpM

Mother to Son. Langston Hughes. AfAmPo; AmNP; CDC; CP-HughL; Crnst; NAAAL; SP-HughL; TtW

Mother was a wolf; snarled her long. Recollection. Donald D. Govan. NBP

Motherfuck a woman lay flat on her back. *African-American Oral Tradition.* GetYo

Motherhood. Rita Dove. NAAAL; SP-DoveR

Motherhood. Georgia Douglas Johnson. ShDr

Mothering Blackness, The. Maya Angelou. CP-AngeM; SP-AngeM

Motherland. Langston Hughes. CP-HughL

Motherless Child. *African-American Oral Tradition.* TtW

Mothers. Nikki Giovanni. SP-GiovN

Mother's Blessing, The. Frances Ellen Watkins Harper. CP-HarpF

Mothers / cranking the machine. The Greater Friendship Baptist Church. Carole C. Gregory Clemmons. BlSi

Mother's face looked tired and worn, The. The Skeptic. Clara Ann Thompson. CBWP-2

Mother's father. Big Zeb Johnson. Everett Hoagland. GT

Mother's gone a-visitin' to spend a month er two. Lonesome. Paul Laurence Dunbar. CP-DunbP

Mother's Habits. Nikki Giovanni. BlSi

Mother's Heroism, A. Frances Ellen Watkins Harper. CP-HarpF

Mother's Lament, The. Mary E. Tucker. CBWP-1

Mother's Love, A. Josephine D. Henderson Heard. CBWP-4

Mothers pass. Summer Evening (Calumet Avenue). Langston Hughes. CP-HughL; SP-HughL

Mother's Recall. Mary Weston Fordham. CBWP-2

Mother's Songs. Frank Barbour Coffin. AAP

Mother's Treasures. Frances Ellen Watkins Harper. CP-HarpF

Motion and Rest. Jean Toomer. CP-ToomJ

Motto. Langston Hughes. *Fr.* Montage of a Dream Deferred. CP-HughL

Mountain / Is earth's mouth, A. Of Earth. Mae V. Cowdery. ShDr

Mountain Tops. Lizelia Augusta Jenkins Moorer. CBWP-3

Mountain Wife. E. Ethelbert Miller. CtF

Mountains call me, The. Allegheny Shadows. Michael S. Harper. SP-HarpM

Mountains cover me like rain. For an Atheist. Countee Cullen. CP-CullC

Mountains of California: Part 1, The. Al Young. CP-YounA

Mountains of California: Part 2, The. Al Young. CP-YounA

Mourn not, friends, mourn not, bereaved. Lines on the Death of the Rev. S. K. Talmage. Mary E. Tucker. CBWP-1

Mournful Lute or the Preceptor's Farewell, The. Daniel Alexander Payne. EBAP; TtW

Mourning Grace. Maya Angelou. CP-AngeM; SP-AngeM

Mourning Letter from Paris, A. Conrad Kent Rivers. BPo

Mourning Poem for the Queen of Sunday. Robert Hayden. CP-HaydR; NAAAL; PoBA

Mouthing the ocean names of light. (LL) The Maiden. Audre Lorde. CP-LordA; SP-LordA

Move. Lucille Clifton. NAAAL

Move Continuing, The. Al Young. CP-YounA; PoBA

Move, into our own, not theirs. Move Un-noticed to Be Noticed: a Nationhood Poem. Haki R. Madhubuti. BrTr

Move Un-noticed to Be Noticed: a Nationhood Poem. Haki R. Madhubuti. BrTr

Movement Song. Audre Lorde. CP-LordA; SP-LordA

Movie Queen. James P. Vaughn. NNP

Movies. Langston Hughes. *Fr.* Montage of a Dream Deferred. CP-HughL

Moving. Helen G. Quigless. BkSV

Moving Deep. "Stephany." BrTr; NBV

"Because I have wandered long through my own darkness."

"My love when this is past."

"Who collects the pain."

"Who is not a stranger still."

"You are instantly enfolded."

Moving In. Audre Lorde. CP-LordA

Moving, Merging, Fading, Standing Still. Al Young. CP-YounA

Moving Out Or the End of Cooperative Living. Audre Lorde. CP-LordA; SP-LordA

Moving Towards Home. June Jordan. SP-JordJ

Much more than there was time for him to be. (LL) El-Hajj Malik El-Shabazz. Robert Hayden. BrTr; CP-HaydR; Crnst; ESEAA; NAAAL; PoBA

Mud turkle settin' on de end of a log. The Turtle's Song. *Unknown.* BPo

Mud Water Shango. "Weatherly." GT; NBV

Muddy Waters & the Chicago Blues. Cornelius Eady. ESEAA

Mulatto. Langston Hughes. CP-HughL; SP-HughL

Mulatto Lullaby. Ralph Dickey. ESEAA

Mulch. Adam David Miller. NBV

Mule meanders into sunshine from the wood, A. Sermon in the Ruined Garden. Marilyn Nelson. *Fr.* Thus Far by Faith. SP-NelsM

Mumble the Magic Words. Jabari Asim. CtF

Murder self slowly. And die like ants shuffling up under. Reckoning A.M. Thursday. Doris Turner. JB

Murdered Lover, The. Paul Laurence Dunbar. CP-DunbP

Murderers / of Emmet Till / I salute you. Salute. Oliver Pitcher. Klds; PoBA

Murmur. Esther Iverem. GT

Murmurs of a distant strife, The. A Mother's Heroism. Frances Ellen Watkins Harper. CP-HarpF

Muse bumped / against my window this morning, The. Levitation with Baby. Marilyn Nelson. SP-NelsM

Muse of Poetry came down one day, The. In Memoriam Paul Laurence Dunbar. Henrietta Cordelia Ray. CBWP-3

Muse! where shall I begin the spacious feild. Address to the Atheist, By P. Wheatley at the Age of 14 Years—1767. Phillis Wheatley. CP-WheaP

Muse's Favor, The. Priscilla Jane Thompson. AAP; AfAmPo; CBWP-2

Music. Josephine D. Henderson Heard. CBWP-4

Music: a pattern etched into time. Billie. Al Young. CP-YounA

Music and its harmony, The. The Design. Clarence Major. PoBA

Music divides the evening. Tu Do Street. Yusef Komunyakaa. SP-KomuY; TtW

Music from her breast vibrating. Jazz Chick. Bob Kaufman. SP-KaufB

Music is your mistress. For Duke Ellington. Reuben Jackson. ESEAA

Music, *jazz,* comes in. (LL) Reuben, Reuben. Michael S. Harper. SP-HarpM

Music! Lilting, soft and languorous. Alice Moore Dunbar-Nelson. BlSi

Music of Broadswords, The. Michael S. Harper. SP-HarpM

Music of the Other World. Ted Wilson. BlFi

Music That Hurts, The. Yusef Komunyakaa. SP-KomuY

Musical, A. Paul Laurence Dunbar. CP-DunbP

Musician Talks about "Process", The. Rita Dove. ESEAA

Musidora's Vision. Henrietta Cordelia Ray. CBWP-3

Musing on roses and revolutions. Roses and Revolutions. Dudley Randall. BPo; BrTr; PoBA; TtW

Must Be Freed. Lizelia Augusta Jenkins Moorer. CBWP-3

Must be the Black Maria. Black Maria. Langston Hughes. CP-HughL; SP-HughL

Must Ethiopians be imploy'd for you? An Address to the Deist—1767. Phillis Wheatley. CP-WheaP

Must Ethiopians be imploy'd for you. Deism. Phillis Wheatley. CP-WheaP

Must fust be in de soul. (LL) Miss Liza's Banjer. Daniel Webster Davis. AAP; EBAP

Must I shoot the. Watts. Conrad Kent Rivers. PoBA

Mwilu / or Poem for the Living. Don L. Lee. JB

My 200 inch eyes are trained. Kali's Galaxy. Ishmael Reed. CP-ReedI

My Ace of Spades. Ted Joans. BrTr

My America. Oliver La Grone. NNP

My Arkansas. Maya Angelou. BlSi; CP-AngeM; NAAAL; SP-AngeM

My army cross over. *Unknown.* CrDW

My baby / loves flowers. William J. Harris. NBV

My beautiful wife. Two A.M. Al Young. CP-YounA

My Beige Mom. Edward S. Spriggs. BlFi

My Beloved. Langston Hughes. CP-HughL

My beloved hath a vineyard. The Vineyard of My Beloved. Priscilla Jane Thompson. AAP; CBWP-2

My Best Girl. Paul Laurence Dunbar. CP-DunbP

My black face fades. Facing It. Yusef Komunyakaa. ESEAA; NAAAL; SP-KomuY

My black mother birthed me. Afro-American. Henry L. Dumas. Crnst

My black mothers I hear them singing. Black Star Line. Henry L. Dumas. Crnst; PoBA

My Blackness Is the Beauty of This Land. Lance Jeffers. BlFi; IHS; NBP; PoBA; TtW

My body & my self. Tiny Self-Portrait. Al Young. CP-YounA

My body arcing across your white place. Making It. Audre Lorde. CP-LordA

My body breaking. (LL) Later i'll say / i spent my life. Lucille Clifton. SP-ClifL

My body is a torn mattress. Would You Wear My Eyes? Bob Kaufman. GT; TtW

My body is opaque to the soul. Prayer. Jean Toomer. CP-ToomJ; NAAAL

My body waiting. Sonia Sanchez. SP-SancS

My book is largely growing. Introductory to Second Edition. Alfred Islay Walden. AAP

My boy Alec is a smart bootlegger. No More Worlds to Conquer. Sterling A. Brown. CP-BrowS

My boys beauty is. Lucille Clifton. SP-ClifL

My Brother. James Danner. BlFi

My Brother and Me. Clarence Reed. BlFi

My brother died in France—but I came back. The Colored Soldier. Langston Hughes. CP-HughL

My brother, / He never left the old fireside. Ballad of the Black Sheep. Langston Hughes. CP-HughL

My Brothers. Ishmael Reed. CP-ReedI

My Canary. Josephine D. Henderson Heard. CBWP-4

My Childhood's Happy Days. Daniel Webster Davis. AAP

My children play with skulls. School Note. Audre Lorde. CP-LordA

My City. James Weldon Johnson. BANP; CDC; IHS; NAAAL

My city slept. The Beginning of a Long Poem on Why I Burned the City. Lawrence Benford. NBP

My Corn-Cob Pipe. Paul Laurence Dunbar. CP-DunbP

My cot was down by a cypress grove. The Lesson. Paul Laurence Dunbar. CP-DunbP

My Daddy has paid the rent. Good Times. Lucille Clifton. AmNP; BPo; PoBA; SP-ClifL

My Daddy, Mr. Franklin, my truculent. Poem for Benjamin Franklin. June Jordan. SP-JordJ

My daddy rides me piggy-back. Piggy-back. Langston Hughes. CP-HughL

My daddy's fingers move among the couplers. Lucille Clifton. SP-ClifL

My dark and sultry / love. (LL) The Invention of Comics. Amiri Baraka. AmNP; GT; NAAAL; PoBA

My daughter is coming! Alice Walker. CP-WalkA

My daughter marks the day that spring begins. Equinox. Audre Lorde. CP-LordA; SP-LordA

My daughter spreads her legs. After Reading *Mickey in the Night Kitchen* for the Third Time Before Bed. Rita Dove. Crnst

My daughter / tosses a dime in lake Erie. Dime after Dime. Mary Weems. SpiFl

My Dear Khomeini: / I read your fourteen thousand dollar. The Pope Replies to the Ayatollah Khomeini. Ishmael Reed. CP-ReedI

My dear love died last night. Paul Laurence Dunbar. CP-DunbP

My Dearest Michael: / My favorite lady-in-waiting is so loyal. Epistolary Monologue. Ishmael Reed. CP-ReedI

My Dreams, My Works Must Wait Till after Hell. Gwendolyn Brooks. SP-BrooG; TtW

My eager waiting heart can bear no more. He Comes Not To-night. Josephine D. Henderson Heard. CBWP-4

My Easter Dove. Henrietta Cordelia Ray. CBWP-3

My empty steps mashed. The Death Dance. Haki R. Madhubuti. BrTr

My face resembles your face. Inheritance—His. Audre Lorde. CP-LordA

My father and mother both. Mississippi Winter IV. Alice Walker. CP-WalkA

My father / (back blistered). Democratic Order, The: Such Things in Twenty Years I Understood. Alice Walker. CP-WalkA

My father came back regularly, to see. Recurrent Dream. Marilyn Nelson. SP-NelsM

My father is a hand-/ some guy. A Daddy Poem. William J. Harris. NBV

My father is a quiet man. Fruit of the Flower. Countee Cullen. CP-CullC

My Father, it is surely a blue place. Hunchback Girl: She Thinks of Heaven. Gwendolyn Brooks. *Fr.* A Street in Bronzeville. BPo; BlSi; Klds; SP-BrooG

My father lies black and hushed. The Worker. Richard W. Thomas. BlFi; PoBA

My father was a dictator. Revolution. Brian G. Gilmore. SpiFl

My father! when I saw thee last. To Father. Mary E. Tucker. CBWP-1

My Father's Geography. Michael S. Weaver. GT

My Father's Girlfriend. E. Ethelbert Miller. SpiFl

My Father's House. Calvin Forbes. ESEAA

My Father's Retirement. A. Van Jordan. SpiFl

My Fathers sit on benches. Song for the Old Ones. Maya Angelou. CP-AngeM; SP-AngeM

My Father's Story. Priscilla Jane Thompson. CBWP-2

My Father's Telescope. Rita Dove. SP-DoveR

My feet have felt the sands. Determination. John Henrik Clarke. PoBA

My feet kiss the pavement on castillo. Las Turistas Negras Grande. Wanda Coleman. TtW

My feet two hundred years old. (LL) Montgomery. Sam Cornish. PoBA

My fetters borken, I begin to sing. Albery Allson Whitman. *Fr.* Leelah Misled. EBAP

My Fifth Trip to Washington Ended in Northeast Delaware. Audre Lorde. CP-LordA; SP-LordA

My first week in Cambridge a car full of white boys. Boston Year. Elizabeth Alexander. GT

My folks could beg or borrow. (LL) Saturday's Child. Countee Cullen. CP-CullC; Klds; NAAAL; PoBA

My Friend. Samuel Allen. FB

My friend / they don't care. There It Is. Jayne Cortez. SP-CortJ

My friend, your face. Who Is My Brother? Pinkie Gordon Lane. BlSi

My Friends. Lucille Clifton. SP-ClifL

My friends, our race is ostracised. Ajax' Conclusion. Frank Barbour Coffin. AAP

My girlfriend, you know, she. Reggie's Version. Al Young. CP-YounA

My girls / my girls. Last Note to My Girls. Lucille Clifton. SP-ClifL; TtW

My God in Heaven said to me. Fenton Johnson. NAAAL

My God, sometimes I cannot pray. Unuttered Prayer. Josephine D. Henderson Heard. CBWP-4

My God, than they? (LL) Ice Storm. Robert Hayden. CP-HaydR; ESEAA

My Grace Is Sufficient. Josephine D. Henderson Heard. CBWP-4

My Grandfather Walks in the Woods. Marilyn Nelson. ESEAA; SP-NelsM

My Grandmama / dont believe they walked in space. It's All the Same. Thadious M. Davis. BlSi

My Grandmother is waiting for me to come home. Novelle; My Grandmother Is Waiting for Me to Come Home. Gwendolyn Brooks. *Fr.* Children Coming Home. ESEAA

My grandmothers were strong. Lineage. Margaret Abigail Walker. BlSi; CP-WalkM; Klds; PoBA; TtW

My greater, guiding star! (LL) A Hymn: "Lead gently, Lord, and slow." Paul Laurence Dunbar. CP-DunbP

My guilt is "slavery's chains," too long. Maya Angelou. CP-AngeM; SP-AngeM

My hair is springy like the forest grasses. Black Woman. Naomi Long Madgett. BlSi; FB; GT; PoBA

My hand by chance. The Web. Robert Hayden. CP-HaydR

My hand moved furiously. Short Poem. Kenneth Carroll. SpiFl

My hands are wrinkled from the cold. Pale Ant. Ellease Southerland. GT

My hands ooze over you. Portraits of a Moment. Keith Gilyard. SpiFl

My hatred. Gwendolyn B. Bennett. *See* Hatred.

My head hangs. / It's all to do with. Annabelle. Yusef Komunyakaa. SP-KomuY

My head so big. Narrative: Ali. Elizabeth Alexander. ESEAA

My Heart has Known its Winter. Arna Bontemps. GT

My Heart Has Reopened to You. Alice Walker. CP-WalkA

My heart / in / another. (LL) Where Have You Gone? Mari E. Evans. BPo; NNP; TtW

My heart is aching. Relief. Langston Hughes. *Fr.* Montage of a Dream Deferred. CP-HughL

My heart that was so passionless. Rencontre. Jessie Redmond Fauset. CDC

My heart to bust. (LL) Madam and Her Might-Have-Been. Langston Hughes. CP-HughL; SP-HughL

My heart to thy heart. Song. Paul Laurence Dunbar. CP-DunbP

My heart wamrs under snow. My Mississippi Spring. Margaret Abigail Walker. CP-WalkM

"My heritage!" It is to live within. Adah Isaacs Menken. AAP; CBWP-1; EBAP

My sister and I. Plans. Helen Morgan Brooks. NNP

My sister and I were in love. The Century Quilt. Marilyn Nelson. SP-NelsM

My sister has my hair my mouth my eyes. A Family Resemblance. Audre Lorde. CP-LordA; SP-LordA

My sister rubs the doll's face in mud. The Kid. Ai. GT

My sleep was like a prenatal death. The Awakening. Keorapetse W. Kgositsile. BlFi

My Song. James Ephriam McGirt. AAP

My sons and daughters are like the first twinkling of the stars. Image of Myself 3. Ira B. Jones. IHS

My sons / sometimes I can. Efficiency Apartment. Gerald William Barrax. PoBA

My Sort o' Man. Paul Laurence Dunbar. AmNP; CP-DunbP

My soul has grown deep like the rivers. (LL) The Negro Speaks of Rivers. Langston Hughes. AmNP; BANP; BPo; CDC; CrDW; IDB; NAAAL; PoBA; SP-HughL; SSLK; TtW

My soul is a witness for my Lord. Who'll Be a Witness for My Lord? Unknown. CrDW

My soul, lost in the music's mist. The Song. Paul Laurence Dunbar. CP-DunbP

My Spanish Heart. Al Young. CP-YounA

My spirit is a pestilential city. Desolate. Claude McKay. CDC; SP-McKaC

My spirit leans in joyousness tow'rd thine. Lines. "Ada." BlSi

My spirit wails for water, water now! Thirst. Claude McKay. SP-McKaC

My Spirit's Complement. Henrietta Cordelia Ray. AAP; CBWP-3

My Spring Thing. Everett Hoagland. BPo

My stock has gone down and my tailor has sent. A Companion's Progress. Paul Laurence Dunbar. CP-DunbP; GT

My story is / how deep the heart runs. Blues Chant Hoodoo Revival. Yusef Komunyakaa. SP-KomuY

My sunlight came pre-packaged. Nomen. Naomi Long Madgett. BlSi

My Sweet Brown Gal. Paul Laurence Dunbar. CP-DunbP

"My sweet," you sang, and, "Sweet," I sang. Spring Reminiscence. Countee Cullen. CP-CullC

My Thing abt Cats. Ishmael Reed. CP-ReedI

My Tower. Nikki Giovanni. SP-GiovN

My true love is leaving. (LL) The Gamut. Maya Angelou. CP-AngeM; SP-AngeM

My Truth and My Flame. Margaret Abigail Walker. CP-WalkM

My uncle had a old gray horse. African-American Oral Tradition. GetYo

My Uncle is My Honor and a Guest in My House. Etheridge Knight. SP-KnigE

My uncle likes me too much. Merle; Uncle Seagram. Gwendolyn Brooks. TtW Fr. Children Coming Home. ESEAA

My Uncle Sam was a good old man. African-American Oral Tradition. GetYo

My way is from woe to wonder. The Near-Johannesburg Boy. Gwendolyn Brooks. ESEAA; TtW

My Way's Cloudy. Unknown. CrDW

My wife is left-handed. For Hettie. Amiri Baraka. GT

My wife sleeps. Portrait of Mary. Etheridge Knight. SP-KnigE

My window and the soup. (LL) This Winter Day. Maya Angelou. CP-AngeM; SP-AngeM

My window / is his wall. For the Bird Who Flew against Our Window One Morning and Broke His Natural Neck. Lucille Clifton. SP-ClifL

My window opens out into the trees. Solace. Clarissa Scott Delany. AmNP; CDC; PoBA; ShDr

My Woman. Malcolm-Jamal Warner. CtF

My woman and my friend is dead. (LL) Monroe's Blues. Langston Hughes. CP-HughL; SP-HughL

My woman has picked. New Season. Michael S. Harper. SP-HarpM

My worthy hearers, have you come tonight. Prologue to a Supposed Play. Joseph Seamon Cotter, Sr. EBAP

Myself. Adah Isaacs Menken. CBWP-1

Myself When I Am Real. Al Young. CP-YounA; PoBA

Mysteries. Alice Walker. CP-WalkA

Mysteries of Life. Mary E. Tucker. CBWP-1

Mystery, The. Paul Laurence Dunbar. CP-DunbP

Mystery. Langston Hughes. Fr. Montage of a Dream Deferred. CP-HughL

Mystery 1st Lady. Ishmael Reed. CP-ReedI

'Mystery Boy' Looks for Kin in Nashville. Robert Hayden. CP-HaydR

Mystery here in this paperweight world, The. People of Letters. Al Young. CP-YounA

Mystery that surely is present, The. Lucille Clifton. SP-ClifL

Mystic Sea, The. Paul Laurence Dunbar. CP-DunbP

Myth Science of Our Time, The. Al Young. CP-YounA

N

N i'm waiting for the light to turn green. Green Boots n Lil Honeys. Ruth Forman. SpiFl

NAACP. Langston Hughes. CP-HughL

Naked, he lies in the blinded room. Soledad. Robert Hayden. CP-HaydR; NAAAL

Name in a footnote. Faceless name. Crispus Attucks. Robert Hayden. CP-HaydR; ESEAA

Name of the beast is, The. Small Comment. Sonia Sanchez. NBP

Name of this poem is, The. Cameo No. II. June Jordan. BPo

Named and unnamed and renamed. Leaving Eden. Ralph Dickey. ESEAA

Names. Robert Hayden. CP-HaydR; GT

Names / of the things, The. Adam and Eve. Lucille Clifton. SP-ClifL

Naming the Stories. Audre Lorde. CP-LordA

Naolo Beauty Academy, New Orleans, Louisiana, 1943. Natasha Trethewey. SpiFl

Nappy Edges. Ntozake Shange. NAAAL

Nappy Edges (A Cross Country Sojourn). Ntozake Shange. BlSi

Narrative. Russell Atkins. GT; PoBA

Narrative: Ali. Elizabeth Alexander. ESEAA

Narrative of Black Magicians, The. Larry Neal. BlFi

Narrator's Trance, The. James Cunningham. JB

Narrow Path, The. Norman Henry, II Pritchard. GT

Nat Turner. Samuel Allen. FB

Nat Turner in the Clearing. Alvin Aubert. TtW

Natcha, offering love. Langston Hughes. CP-HughL; SP-HughL

Nation. Charlie Cobb. PoBA

National Cemetery, Beaufort, South Carolina, The. Josephine D. Henderson Heard. CBWP-4

National Federation is a grand and glorious band, The. All We Ask Is Justice. Mrs. Henry Linden. CBWP-4

Nation's Friend, The. Alfred Islay Walden. AAP

Natives here have given up their backyards, The. Champagne. Rita Dove. SP-DoveR

Natives of America, The. Ann Plato. BlSi ("Tell me a story, father, please.") EBAP

Nativity, The. Mary Weston Fordham. CBWP-2

Nativity. Gladys May Casely Hayford. CDC

Natural order is being restored. From Sea to Shining Sea. June Jordan. SP-JordJ

Natural Star. Alice Walker. CP-WalkA

Naturally. Audre Lorde. BlSi; CP-LordA

Nature and Art. Paul Laurence Dunbar. CP-DunbP

Nature of the beast is the, The. Sonia Sanchez. See Small Comment.

Nature of This Flower Is to Bloom, The. Alice Walker. CP-WalkA

Nature's Minor Chords. Henrietta Cordelia Ray. CBWP-3

Nature's Uplifting. Henrietta Cordelia Ray. CBWP-3

Naught's a naught. Learn to Count. Unknown. NAAAL

Naughty child / Who ventured to go cut flowers, The. Langston Hughes. CP-HughL

Naw, / naw, little brotha. Rip-Off. Ronda M. Davis. BrTr

Nay, do not blush! I only heard. Advice to the Girls. Frances Ellen Watkins Harper. CP-HarpF; TtW

Nay, why reproach each other, be unkind. Polarity. Claude McKay. SP-McKaC

Nazi Doll, The. Yusef Komunyakaa. SP-KomuY

Ndebele. Alice Walker. CP-WalkA

Near-Johannesburg Boy, The. Gwendolyn Brooks. ESEAA; TtW

Near Miss. "Nayo." BkSV

Near the beach / grenada enjoyed taking long baths. Grenada. E. Ethelbert Miller. TtW

Near the City of Petersburg. The V. N. and C. I. Maggie Pogue Johnson. CBWP-4

Nearest you've come to living yourself, The. (LL) Martha this is a catalog of days. Audre Lorde. CP-LordA; SP-LordA

Nearly gone. (LL) Song. Cornelius Eady. ESEAA; GT

Nearly ripe for worms. (LL) Face. Jean Toomer. CDC; CP-ToomJ

'Neath the old apple tree. (LL) The Old Apple-Tree. Paul Laurence Dunbar. CP-DunbP

Neber min' what's in your cran'um. The Don't-Care Negro. Joseph Seamon Cotter, Sr. AAP; AfAmPo

Necessity. Langston Hughes. Fr. Montage of a Dream Deferred. CP-HughL

Ned's Psalm of Life for the Negro. Joseph Seamon Cotter, Sr. AAP

Need: A Chorale for Black Woman Voices. Audre Lorde. SP-LordA (Need: a Choral of Black Women's Voices.) CP-LordA

Need gotta be / so deep words can't, The. Blue Light Lounge Sutra for the Performance Poets at Harold Park Hotel. Yusef Komunyakaa. SP-KomuY

Needed/Poem/ for My Salvation, A. Sonia Sanchez. BrTr

Needing someone. Discover Me. Opal Palmer Adisa. GT

Needing to be stranger. (LL) October. Audre Lorde. CP-LordA; SP-LordA

Negatives, The. Michael S. Harper. SP-HarpM

Negritude. James A. Emanuel. BPo; IHS

Negro, The. James A. Emanuel. Klds

   ("Never saw him.") BrTr

Negro. Langston Hughes. CP-HughL; SP-HughL

Negro Ballot, The. Lizelia Augusta Jenkins Moorer. CBWP-3

Negro Dancers. Langston Hughes. CP-HughL

Negro Dreams. Doughtry Long. PoBA

Negro Ghetto. Langston Hughes. CP-HughL

Negro Has a Chance, The. Maggie Pogue Johnson. CBWP-4

"Negro" Hero. Gwendolyn Brooks. Klds; SP-BrooG

Negro Heroines. Lizelia Augusta Jenkins Moorer. CBWP-3

Negro Improvement League. Sterling A. Brown. CP-BrowS

Negro Laughs Back, The. Mary Jenness. ShDr

Negro laughter. Anita Scott Coleman. ShDr

Negro Love Song, A. Paul Laurence Dunbar. AAP; BANP; CP-DunbP; CrDW; NAAAL; SSLK; TtW

Negro Meets to Pray, The. Daniel Webster Davis. AAP

Negro Mother, The. Langston Hughes. CP-HughL; SP-HughL

Negro Mother's Lullaby, A. Countee Cullen. CP-CullC

Negro Peddler's Song, A. Fenton Johnson. AmNP

Negro Poets. Charles Bertram Johnson. BANP

Negro Schools, The. Lizelia Augusta Jenkins Moorer. CBWP-3

Negro Serenade. James Edwin Campbell. BANP

Negro Servant. Langston Hughes. CP-HughL

Negro Singer, The. James David Corrothers. BANP

Negro Soldiers, The. Roscoe Conkling Jamison. BANP

Negro Soldier's Civil War Chant. *Unknown.* BPo

Negro Soldier's Viet Nam Diary, A. Herbert Martin. PoBA

Negro Speaks of Rivers, The. Langston Hughes. AmNP; BANP; BPo; CDC; CrDW; IDB; NAAAL; PoBA; SP-HughL; SSLK; TtW

   ("My soul has grown deep like rivers.") (LL) AfAmPo; CP-HughL

Negro Steven found Kansas. Forty Days Looking Backwards: Notes from a Surveyor. Michael S. Harper. SP-HarpM

Negro, / With the trumpet at his lips, The. Trumpet Player. Langston Hughes. CP-HughL; SP-HughL

Negro Woman. Lewis Alexander. CDC; PoBA

Negroes, / Sweet and docile. Warning. Langston Hughes. BPo; CP-HughL; SP-HughL

Negro's Friend, The. Claude McKay. SP-McKaC

Negro's Lament, The. John Willis Menard. AAP

Negro's Tragedy, The. Claude McKay. BPo; SP-McKaC

Neighbor. Langston Hughes. *Fr.* Montage of a Dream Deferred. CP-HughL

Neighbor. Bahiyyih Maroon. SpiFl

Neighborhood House, The. Jay Wright. NBV

Neighbors. Audre Lorde. CP-LordA; SP-LordA

Neighbors. Anne Spencer. CDC

Neo-HooDoo Aesthetic, The. Ishmael Reed. CP-ReedI

Neo-HooDoo is a litany seeking its text. Neo-HooDoo Manifesto. Ishmael Reed. CP-ReedI

Neo-HooDoo Manifesto. Ishmael Reed. CP-ReedI

Neon Diaspora. David Henderson. BlFi

Neon glitter of night. Beale Street, Memphis. Thurmond Snyder. NNP

Neon sign blinked red, A. Something Old, Something New. Carl H. Greene. NBV

Neon Signs. Langston Hughes. *Fr.* Montage of a Dream Deferred. CP-HughL

Neon stripes tighten my wall. The Zebra Goes Wild Where the Sidewalk Ends. Henry L. Dumas. GT

Nestle-down Cottage. Mary Weston Fordham. CBWP-2

Nestor's Bathtub. Rita Dove. SP-DoveR

Never love with all your heart. Song in Spite of Myself. Countee Cullen. BALP; CP-CullC

Never may my thirst. Sonia Sanchez. SP-SancS

Never mind / Even the Be-Still tree will never stop. An Always Lei of Ginger Blossoms for the First Lady of Hawai'i: Queen Lili'uokalani. June Jordan. SP-JordJ

Never Offer Your Heart to Someone Who Eats Hearts. Alice Walker. CP-WalkA

Never saw him. / Never can. The Negro. James A. Emanuel. Klds

Never Take Fire for a Woman. Audre Lorde. CP-LordA

Never to Dream of Spiders. Audre Lorde. CP-LordA

Never would I seek. Lines to a Sophisticate. Mae V. Cowdery. ShDr

NEVER YOUR CAPTIVE! (LL) Blues Note. Bob Kaufman. PoBA

NEVER YOUR CAPTIVE! (LL) How High the Moon. Lance Jeffers. PoBA

New Autumn, New York. Al Young. CP-YounA

New Bones. Lucille Clifton. SP-ClifL

New Cabaret Girl, The. Langston Hughes. CP-HughL

New Chief of police, The. Last Ride of Wild Bill. Sterling A. Brown. CP-BrowS

New clowns / at cut rate. (LL) Good Mirrors are Not Cheap. Audre Lorde. CP-LordA; SP-LordA

New Congo, The. Sterling A. Brown. CP-BrowS

New Dance, A. S. E. Anderson. NBP

New Day, The. Fenton Johnson. BANP

New Day. Naomi Long Madgett. BlSi

New England first a wilderness was found. America. Phillis Wheatley. CP-WheaP

New Face. Alice Walker. CP-WalkA

New Fashions. George Moses Horton. SP-HortG

New Flowers. Langston Hughes. CP-HughL

New House, The. Maya Angelou. CP-AngeM

New Integrationist, The. Haki R. Madhubuti. BrTr

New man in the ovens., the. (LL) Black Man, A. Sam Cornish. PoBA

New Mode of Production, The. Al Young. CP-YounA

New Moon. Langston Hughes. CP-HughL

New Moon Over Grove Street. Al Young. CP-YounA

New Mystic, The. Al Young. CP-YounA

New Negro, The. James Edward McCall. CDC

New Organ, The. Josephine D. Henderson Heard. CBWP-4

New Orleans Haiku. Kalamu ya Salaam. SpiFl

   All Nite Long.

   Everywhere You Eat.

   French Quarter Intimacies.

   Funeraled Fare Well.

   Height, Breadth, Depth.

   Makes You Go Oohhh!

   New Orleans Rainbow.

   Our Natures Rise.

   Quarter Moon Rise.

   Round Midnight, Place de Congo.

   Secondline Send Off.

   Spice of Life, The.

   Spiritual Geography.

   St. Louis Cemetery Crypt.

   Sunrise on the River.

   Till Death Do Us Part.

New Orleans Intermissiom. Al Young. CP-YounA

New Orleans Rainbow. Kalamu ya Salaam. *Fr.* New Orleans Haiku. SpiFl

New Pietà: For the Mothers and Children of Detroit, The. June Jordan. PoBA

New Reality Is Better Than a New Movie, A! Amiri Baraka. SP-BaraA

New Season. Michael S. Harper. SP-HarpM

New Sheriff, The. Amiri Baraka. SP-BaraA

New Song, A. Langston Hughes. CP-HughL

New St. Louis Blues. Sterling A. Brown. CP-BrowS

New steps / O my Lawd. Sterling A. Brown. CP-BrowS

New Storefront. Russell Atkins. FB; GT

New Windows. Claudia Rankine. GT

New World, The. Amiri Baraka. SP-BaraA

New Year. Lucille Clifton. SP-ClifL

New Year. Langston Hughes. CP-HughL

New year has dawned and we meet it with gladness, The. New Year's Morning; or, the First Day of the Year. Mrs. Henry Linden. CBWP-4

New Year Letter. Edward Kamau Brathwaite. GT

New Year's Day. Audre Lorde. SP-LordA

   ("Day feels put together hastily, The.") CP-LordA

New Year's Day 1:16 A.M. The Electric Slide Boogie. Audre Lorde. CP-LordA

New Year's Morning; or, the First Day of the Year. Mrs. Henry Linden. CBWP-4

New York City 1970. Audre Lorde. NBV

   ("How do you spell change like frayed slogan underwear.") CP-LordA

   (New York City.) SP-LordA

New york / won't you confess. Bowery Street. Jayne Cortez. SP-CortJ

New Yorkers, The. Nikki Giovanni. SP-GiovN

New Yorkers. Langston Hughes. *Fr.* Montage of a Dream Deferred. CP-HughL

Newark, for Now (68). Carolyn M. Rodgers. PoBA

Newark Public Library Reading Room, The. Sotère Torregian. NBV

Newletter from My Mother. Michael S. Harper. PoBA

Newport Beach, 1979. Yusef Komunyakaa. SP-KomuY

Newport Jazz Festival: Saratoga Springs and Especially about George Benson and Everyone Who Was Listening. June Jordan. SP-JordJ

News, The. Lucille Clifton. SP-ClifL

News, The. Paul Laurence Dunbar. CP-DunbP

Newsboy knocks. Madam and the Newsboy. Langston Hughes. CP-HughL

Newspapers printed in secret report. Party Time. Audre Lorde. CP-LordA

Next day, dark sea. A arse-aching dawn. Out of the Depths. Derek Walcott. *Fr.* The Schooner *Flight.* ESEAA

Nexus. Rita Dove. SP-DoveR

NI SE RINDE NI SE VENDE. Dance: Nicaragua. June Jordan. SP-JordJ

Nigga Section, The. Welton Smith. *Fr.* Malcolm. BlFi

Nigger. Frank Horne. BANP; CDC

Nigger. Sonia Sanchez. BPo

Nigger / Can you kill. True Import of Present Dialogue, Black vs. Negro. Nikki Giovanni. BPo; BrTr; Crnst; PoBA

Nigger comes home from work, A. Man into Men. Langston Hughes. CP-HughL

Nigger-Lover is a song, spat out. Song. Cornelius Eady. ESEAA; GT

Nigger . . . nigger. (LL) Nigger. Frank Horne. BANP; CDC

Nigger Song: An Odyssey. Rita Dove. SP-DoveR

Nigger's Got to Go, De. Daniel Webster Davis. AAP

Nigguh, I ain't playin' this time. (LL) The Calling of Names. Maya Angelou. CP-AngeM; SP-AngeM

Nigguhs with naturrrals. So This Is Our Revolution. Sonia Sanchez. BrTr

Night. Paul Laurence Dunbar. CP-DunbP

Night. Nikki Giovanni. SP-GiovN

Night. Josephine D. Henderson Heard. CBWP-4

Night and a Distant Church. Russell Atkins. PoBA

Night and a starless sky. Shipwreck. Mary Weston Fordham. CBWP-2, *tr. by* Mary Ann Caws

Night / And death rides fast on foul breath. Night Slivers. Darwin T. Turner. NBP

Night / and in the warm blackness. Upon Your Leaving. Etheridge Knight. GT; SP-KnigE

Night and the hood. Prelude. Conrad Kent Rivers. PoBA

Night before Michael Was Born, The. Al Young. CP-YounA

Night Before the First Day of School, The. E. Ethelbert Miller. SpiFl

Night— / blackbright with shadows that caress, The. To Our First Born or the Prophet Arrives. Ebon. BrTr

Night-Blooming Cereus, The. Robert Hayden. CP-HaydR; ESEAA; FB

Night-Blooming Jasmine, The. Audre Lorde. CP-LordA

Night closed o'er the battl'ing army. The Sin of Achar. Frances Ellen Watkins Harper. CP-HarpF

Night comes walking out our way. Esther Popel. ShDr

Night coming tenderly / Black like me. (LL) Dream Variations. Langston Hughes. AmNP; BALP; CDC; CP-HughL; IDB; PoBA; SP-HughL

Night creep down erlong de lan, De. The Tryst. Paul Laurence Dunbar. CP-DunbP

Night, Death, Mississippi. Robert Hayden. CP-HaydR; Crnst

Night, dim night, and it rains, my love, it rains. Paul Laurence Dunbar. CP-DunbP

Night: Four Songs. Langston Hughes. CP-HughL; SP-HughL

Night funeral / In Harlem. Langston Hughes. *Fr.* Montage of a Dream Deferred. CP-HughL

Night grows no flower children. Ascendancy. Herbert A. Simmons. NBP

Night has secreted us. Amen. Richard W. Thomas. BlFi; PoBA

Night hung o'er Virginia's forest wild, The. Capt. Smith and Pocahontas. Eloise Bibb. CBWP-4

Night, I know you are powerful and artistic. For Bill Hawkins, a Black Militant. William J. Harris. PoBA

Night in Nigeria. Ellease Southerland. GT

Night Interpreted. Everett Hoagland. NBP

Night is beautiful, The. My People. Langston Hughes. CDC; CP-HughL; SP-HughL

Night is cold and frosty, The. A Winter Night. Priscilla Jane Thompson. CBWP-2

Night is dewy as a maiden's mouth, The. A Summer's Night. Paul Laurence Dunbar. CP-DunbP

Night is for sorrow and dawn is for joy. With the Lark. Paul Laurence Dunbar. CP-DunbP

Night is like an avalanche. Bessie Mayle. ShDr

Night John Henry is born an ax, The. The Birth of John Henry. Melvin Beaunearus Tolson. BPo; NAAAL

Night like purple flakes of snow. Donald Jeffrey Hayes. CDC

Night music slanted. Cell Song. Etheridge Knight. PoBA; SP-KnigE

Night of Death, The. Frances Ellen Watkins Harper. CP-HarpF

Night of Frost, The. Michael S. Harper. SP-HarpM

Night of Love. Paul Laurence Dunbar. CP-DunbP

Night of the two moons. Night: Four Songs. Langston Hughes. CP-HughL; SP-HughL

Night on the Chesapeake. Paul Laurence Dunbar. CP-DunbP

Night-Piece. Raymond R. Patterson. PoBA

Night pumping like an. Sonia Sanchez. SP-SancS

Night Rain. Countee Cullen. CP-CullC; GT

Night Rain. Karen L. Mitchell. GT

Night rests like a ball of fur on my tongue. (LL) Adolescence—II. Rita Dove. SP-DoveR

Night Slivers. Darwin T. Turner. NBP

Night Song. Langston Hughes. CP-HughL

Night Sung Sailor's Prayer. Bob Kaufman. SP-KaufB

Night that Lorca Comes, The. Bob Kaufman. SP-KaufB; TtW

Night town, strange winds of mystery. Clinton. Sterling Plumpp. BkSV

Night turned over. After the Japanese. Mae V. Cowdery. ShDr

Night was made for rest and sleep, The. Interim. Clarissa Scott Delany. CDC; ShDr; TtW

Night was white. There was nowhere to hide, The. (LL) God Rest Ye Merry, Gentlemen. Derek Walcott. GT

Night Watch. Rita Dove. SP-DoveR

Night wears a garment. Street Lamps in Early Spring. Gwendolyn B. Bennett. ShDr

Nightdreams (Black). Tom Dent. TtW

Nightline: September 20, 1982. June Jordan. SP-JordJ

Nightmare. Rita Dove. SP-DoveR

("She's dreaming.") GT

Nightmare. James A. Emanuel. BPo

Nightmare Begins Responsibility. Michael S. Harper. ESEAA; GT; SP-HarpM

Nightmare Boogie. Langston Hughes. *Fr.* Montage of a Dream Deferred. CP-HughL

Night's Protégé. Marjorie Marshall. ShDr

Nightstone. Audre Lorde. CP-LordA

Nighttrains. Jayne Cortez. SP-CortJ

Nikki-Rosa. Nikki Giovanni. GT; NAAAL; SP-GiovN; SSLK; TtW

("Childhood remembrances [*or* memories] are always a drag.") AmNP; BlSi; NBP; PoBA

Nineteen. Elizabeth Alexander. GT

1929: Y you ask? (26). Amiri Baraka. SP-BaraA

Nineteen Thirty-Two, *see also* Stackolee. *African-American Oral Tradition.* GetYo

1933. Margaret Abigail Walker. CP-WalkM

1938. Yusef Komunyakaa. SP-KomuY

(1962 At the Edge of Town). C. S. Giscombe. GT

1963; / we march. Blackjack. Michael S. Harper. SP-HarpM

1971. Alice Walker. CP-WalkA

1973. Reuben Jackson. GT

1977: Poem for Mrs. Fannie Lou Hamer. June Jordan. SP-JordJ

(1978, Remembering 1962). C. S. Giscombe. GT

(1980). C. S. Giscombe. GT

1981 and / I did not find Nicolás Guillén. Adupe. Lucille Clifton. ESEAA

1984. Yusef Komunyakaa. SP-KomuY

1989 the number another summer (get down). Fight the Power. Public Enemy. Crnst

1994 Inventory. Toi Derricotte. SpiFl

Nineteenth century, like a hurricane lamp, The. The Storm Figure. Derek Walcott. Crnst

Nineveh, Tyre, / Babylon. Memphis Blues. Sterling A. Brown. BANP; CP-BrowS; NAAAL

Niobe. Henrietta Cordelia Ray. CBWP-3

Niobe in Distress for Her Children Slain by Apollo, from Ovid's Metamorphoses, Book VI, and from a View of the Painting of Mr. Richard Wilson. Phillis Wheatley. CP-WheaP

No. 24. Michael S. Harper. SP-HarpM

No Bargains Today. Peggy Susberry Kenner. JB

No boy chooses war. Sailors on Leave. Owen Dodson. AmNP

No business to die. (LL) Ballad of the Man Who's Gone. Langston Hughes. CP-HughL; SP-HughL

No coat has I got. Wise 4. Amiri Baraka. SP-BaraA

No Dawns. Julianne Perry. PoBA

No, dere ain't no use r workin' in de blazin' summertime. When de Sun Shines Hot. James Ephriam McGirt. AAP

No doubt I will end my life as poor as you. Talking to My Grandmother Who Died Poor. Alice Walker. CP-WalkA

No doubt she was a singer. The Girl Who Died #2. Alice Walker. CP-WalkA

No Enemies. Benjamin Clark. EBAP

No Fixed Place. Alice Walker. CP-WalkA

No flowers from the store. (LL) Midwinter Blues. Langston Hughes. CP-HughL; SP-HughL

No forward soul, ambition stung. After Reading Bryant's Lines to a Waterfowl. Eloise Bibb. ShDr

No friend to wipe the sweat of death. The Pauper's Grave. Benjamin Clark. EBAP

No front yard to speak of. The House on Bishop Street. Rita Dove. SP-DoveR

No Good Whore, *see also* Sweet Lovin' Rose *and* Whores Are No Good. *African-American Oral Tradition.* GetYo

No Good Whore and Crime Don't Pay, *see also* Sweet Lovin' Rose *and* Whores Are no Good. *African-American Oral Tradition.* GetYo

No gorgeous coat has he. My Mocking Bird. Josephine D. Henderson Heard. CBWP-4

No: I am neither seeking to change nor keep myself. A Brown Aesthete Speaks. Mae V. Cowdery. ShDr

No, I am not death wishes of sacred rapists. I, Too, Know What I Am Not. Bob Kaufman. NBP

No, / I cannot / turn from love. To Turn from Love. Sarah Webster Fabio. BlSi; TtW

No: / I did not buy this sweatshirt with. Last Poem on Bell's Theorem. June Jordan. SP-JordJ

No I don't think you wree chicken not to speak. Letter for Jan. Audre Lorde. CP-LordA

No Images. Waring Cuney. AmNP; BANP; CDC; SSLK

No Jazz. Marilyn Nelson. *Fr.* The Plotinus Suite. SP-NelsM

No lady cookinger than my Mommy. (LL) Little Girl Speakings. Maya Angelou. CP-AngeM; SP-AngeM

No, let it stay. It speaks but truth. The First Grey Hair. Mary E. Tucker. CBWP-1

No Letter. Mary E. Tucker. CBWP-1

No locust grows alone. Locust Trees. Margaret L. Thomas. ShDr

No longer throne of a goddess to whom we pray. Full Moon. Robert Hayden. BPo; CP-HaydR; GT; Klds

No Loser, No Weeper. Maya Angelou. CP-AngeM; SP-AngeM; TtW

No love from above. (LL) Litany: "Gather up / In the arms of your pity." Langston Hughes. CP-HughL; SP-HughL

No man is robbed of stone, of a dead root. Nightstone. Audre Lorde. CP-LordA

No man knows. When A Woman Gets Blue. Norman Jordan. NBV

"No, Master, Never!" Joshua McCarter Simpson. AAP

No matter how loudly I call you the sound of your name. Poem for Guatemala. June Jordan. NAAAL; SP-JordJ

No matter what you call it. James Whitcomb Riley. Paul Laurence Dunbar. CP-DunbP

No matter where I turn, she is there. Statistic: The Witness. Rita Dove. NAAAL

No matter where you travel. Houston A., Jr. Baker. TtW

No mo meetings. Listenen to Big Black at S. F. State. Sonia Sanchez. BPo

No money to bury him. Ballad of the Man Who's Gone. Langston Hughes. CP-HughL; SP-HughL

No moon floods the memory of that night. Etheridge Knight. SP-KnigE

No More. Carl Clark. JB

No more auction block for me. *Unknown.* BPo; BkSV; NAAAL

No More Doors Tonight. Al Young. CP-YounA

No more for you the city's thorny ways. Rest in Peace. Claude McKay. SP-McKaC

No more jazz. No More Jazz at Alcatraz. Bob Kaufman. SP-KaufB

No More Jazz at Alcatraz. Bob Kaufman. SP-KaufB

No More Love Poems #1. Ntozake Shange. BlSi

No more peck o' corn for me. Many Thousand Gone. *Unknown.* CrDW

No more the chicken and the egg come. On the Loss of Energy. June Jordan. SP-JordJ

No more / The feel of your hand. Farewell. Mae V. Cowdery. ShDr

No more the flow'ry scenes of pleasure rise. On the Death of J.C. an Infant. Phillis Wheatley. CP-WheaP

No More Worlds to Conquer. Sterling A. Brown. CP-BrowS

No New Music. Stanley Crouch. GT; PoBA

No No, Bad Daddy. Marilyn Nelson. SP-NelsM

No / No / No / I am not doing. Our Lives. Sharon Scott. JB

No No No No. Maya Angelou. CP-AngeM; SP-AngeM

No one asked us ... what we thought of Jamestown. But Since You Finally Asked. Nikki Giovanni. CtF; SP-GiovN

No one can communicate to you. Face of Poverty. Lucy Smith. NNP

No one can help him anymore. Company. Rita Dove. SP-DoveR

No One Can Watch the Wasichu. Alice Walker. CP-WalkA

No one could have a blacker tail. Othello Jones Dresses for Dinner. Ed Roberson. PoBA

No one else on earth / has ever / seen. (LL) New Face. Alice Walker. CP-WalkA

No one is left to eat by my fire. Signs. Audre Lorde. SP-LordA

No one knows where the undertaker lives. The Owl In Daytime. Thylias Moss. GT

No one's going to read. A Dance for Militant Dilettantes. Al Young. CP-YounA; NBV; PoBA

No Poem Because Time Is Not a Name. June Jordan. SP-JordJ

No Regrets. Langston Hughes. CP-HughL; SP-HughL

No Reservations. Nikki Giovanni. BrTr; SP-GiovN

No rest! No rest on this bleak earth for me;. Crazed. Mary E. Tucker. CBWP-1

No rock along the road but knows. Poet. Donald Jeffrey Hayes. AmNP

No room for fear. (LL) Subway Rush Hour. Langston Hughes. CP-HughL

No Sebastian, not again, nor a first time either. Blue Slanted into Blueness. Bob Kaufman. SP-KaufB

No, señora rodriguez. Ancestral Messengers/Composition 13. Ntozake Shange. GT

No servile little fear shall daunt my will. French Leave. Claude McKay. SP-McKaC

No, she's brushing a boy's hair. (LL) Facing It. Yusef Komunyakaa. ESEAA; NAAAL; SP-KomuY

No Simple Explanations, *(to the Memory of Larry Neal).* Jayne Cortez. GT; SP-CortJ

No sleep tonight / not even after all. Summary. Sonia Sanchez. BPo; BlFi; BrTr

No Smiles. Frank Lamont Phillips. AmNP

No son, I dont wanta draw. The Kardek Method. Ishmael Reed. CP-ReedI

No sound falls. After. Maya Angelou. CP-AngeM; SP-AngeM

No sprouted wheat and soya shoots. The Health-Food Diner. Maya Angelou. CP-AngeM; SP-AngeM

No square poet's job. (LL) Haiku: "Making jazz swing in." Etheridge Knight. ESEAA; TtW

No Strings Attached. Al Young. CP-YounA

No, suh! no, suh! dat'll do. (LL) A Cabin Tale. Paul Laurence Dunbar. CP-DunbP; NAAAL

No sun these months. Ice-dark and cold. Robert Hayden. CP-HaydR

No / the two legg'd beasts. No No No No. Maya Angelou. CP-AngeM; SP-AngeM

No they will not understand. My Friends. Lucille Clifton. SP-ClifL

No thing / no-thing. Cathexis. Frederick, Jr. Bryant. NBV; PoBA

No Time for Poetry. Julia Fields. AmNP

No Trespassing. Al Young. CP-YounA

No trumpets announce. Rebellion Suite. Askia Muhammad Touré. TtW

No unh-unh no hot sauce for me. The Rundown at Ned's Bar B.Q. Al Young. CP-YounA

No use in my going. Blue Monday. Langston Hughes. CP-HughL; SP-HughL

No wedding ring of doges, this white cirque that lies. Coral Atoll. Dudley Randall. TtW

No West Indians that I could see at my grandfather's funeral. (1962 At the Edge of Town). C. S. Giscombe. GT

No wonder the vampire. Vamp. Ishmael Reed. CP-ReedI

No Worst. Marilyn Nelson. SP-NelsM

No worthy deeds to emulate? (LL) Bondsman's gloomy night has passed, The. James Madison Bell. AAP; AfAmPo

Noblesse Oblige. Jessie Redmond Fauset. CDC

Nobody ain't Christmas shoppin'. Crowded Out. Rosalie Jonas. ShDr

Nobody but Lester let Lester leap. Lester Leaps In. Al Young. CP-YounA; ESEAA

Nobody else can do the work that God's marked out for you. (LL) Too Busy. Paul Laurence Dunbar. CP-DunbP

Nobody else can have as much fun as. The Twenty Grand (Saturday Night on the Block). Naomi Long Madgett. NBV

Nobody Knows Da Trubble Ah See. *African-American Oral Tradition.* TtW

Nobody lives! / cried the thin man. Ballad for Ashes. Audre Lorde. CP-LordA

Nobody mentioned war. Malcolm. Lucille Clifton. NAAAL; SP-ClifL

Nobody planted roses, he recalls. Summertime and the Living. Robert Hayden. CP-HaydR; Klds; PoBA

Nobody Riding the Roads Today. June Jordan. BPo

Nobody wants to die on the way. A Song for Many Movements. Audre Lorde. CP-LordA

Nocturnal Sounds. Kattie M. Cumbo. BlSi

Nocturne: "Listening for the sound." Pinkie Gordon Lane. BlSi

Nocturne. Naomi Long Madgett. BALP

Nocturne: "Softly blow lightly." Donald Jeffrey Hayes. CDC

Nocturne: "This cool night is strange." Gwendolyn B. Bennett. BANP; ShDr

Nocturne at Bethesda. Arna Bontemps. AmNP; BALP; BANP; CDC; NAAAL; TtW

Nocturne for the Drums. Langston Hughes. CP-HughL

Nocturne of the Wharves. Arna Bontemps. BANP; BPo; GT

Nocturne Varial. Lewis Alexander. PoBA

Noddin' by de Fire. Paul Laurence Dunbar. CP-DunbP

Noise outside. Spring. Pinkie Gordon Lane. GT

Nomen. Naomi Long Madgett. BlSi

None of this makes any sense. The Ghost-Who-Walks. Colleen J. McElroy. GT

Nonette. Langston Hughes. CP-HughL

Nook. George Barlow. GT

Noon. Paul Laurence Dunbar. CP-DunbP

Noonday April Sun, The. George Love. IDB; NNP

Noontide. Henrietta Cordelia Ray. *Fr.* Idyl. EBAP

Nor a single day begun in light. (LL) How Stars Start. Al Young. CP-YounA; ESEAA

Nor can any ever be, at any time in time to come. (LL) To My Son Parker, Asleep in the Next Room. Bob Kaufman. Klds; SP-KaufB; TtW

Nor cherrying in Michigan or Maine. (LL) Old Mary. Gwendolyn Brooks. SP-BrooG

Nor fleeting time, nor space, can change. The Savage Dreamer. Timothy Thomas Fortune. EBAP

Nor sing to me of distant climes, O muse! Albery Allson Whitman. *Fr.* Leelah Misled. EBAP

Nor speaks nor sings. (LL) Lines Written at the Grave of Alexander [*or* Alexandre] Dumas. Gwendolyn B. Bennett. CDC

Nor, will anyone dare say to. Sharon Will Be No/Where on Nobody's Best-selling List. Sharon Scott. JB

Nora: A Serenade. Paul Laurence Dunbar. CP-DunbP

Nordic. Lillian Byrnes. ShDr

North and South. Claude McKay. SP-McKaC

North of Dark / North from Shango. Medicine Man. Calvin C. Hernton. TtW

North Star, The. James M. Whitfield. TtW

Northboun'. Lucy Ariel Williams Holloway. BANP; BlSi; CDC; ShDr

Northern Liberal. Langston Hughes. CP-HughL

Nostalgia. Marjorie Marshall. ShDr

Not a Man, and Yet a Man. Albery Allson Whitman.
   Flight of Leeona. AAP
   "Hail dawning Peace! Speed on thy glorious rise!" AfAmPo
   (End if the Whole Matter, The.) AAP
   "Free schools, free press and equal laws." AAP
   "Hunters mount menacing as they go, The." AfAmPo
   (Saville in Trouble.) AAP
   In the House of the Aylors. AAP
   Old Sac Village, The. AAP
   "Thrice hail! proud land, whose genius boasts a clay!" AfAmPo
   "I love Kentucky; tho' she merit scorn." AAP
   (Runaway. The). AAP

Not a Movie. Langston Hughes. *Fr.* Montage of a Dream Deferred. CP-HughL

Not a new thing. Black Ethics. Sterling Plumpp. TtW

Not a word, not a word, not a word. (LL) Crucifixion. *Unknown.* BPo

Not all rats live in sewers. Sixth Street Corporate War. Ishmael Reed. CP-ReedI

Not as the white nations. The Black Madonna. Albert Rice. CDC

Not beautiful, but very prepossessing. Albery Allson Whitman. *Fr.* Leelah Misled. EBAP

Not beca'se we was dishonest, but *indignant,* sah. Dat's all. (LL) An Indignation Dinner. James David Corrothers. AfAmPo; NAAAL

Not by hammering the furious word. Harlem Riot, 1943. Pauli Murray. PoBA

Not by wayout hairdos, bulbous Afro blowouts and certainly. Only in This Way. Margaret Goss Burroughs. BlSi

Not Dead, but Sleeping. Clara Ann Thompson. CBWP-2

Not Else—But. Langston Hughes. CP-HughL

Not enough. Field Trip. Kevin Young. GT

Not for me—and may nothing enhance. Jean Toomer. CP-ToomJ

Not for myself I make this prayer. Pagan Prayer. Countee Cullen. CP-CullC

Not for sale. (LL) Dream Dust. Langston Hughes. CP-HughL; SP-HughL

Not for them the length'ning shadows. Youth in Heaven. Frances Ellen Watkins Harper. CP-HarpF

Not hear them / Anymore. (LL) Sweet Words on Race. Langston Hughes. CP-HughL

Not Her, She Aint No Gypsy. Al Young. CP-YounA

Not me alone. Union. Langston Hughes. CP-HughL

Not more than we can bear ... more than we should have to. This Is Not for John Lennon. Nikki Giovanni. SP-GiovN

Not No Socialism/Communism classical, but Some Power to the People Jazz. Daniel Gray-Kontar. SpiFl

Not o'er thy dust let there be spent. Whittier. Paul Laurence Dunbar. CP-DunbP

Not of imputed Heroes, nor of ghosts. Albery Allson Whitman. *Fr.* Leelah Misled. EBAP

Not of the dust, but of the wave. For Joseph Conrad. Countee Cullen. CP-CullC

Not Often. Langston Hughes. CP-HughL

Not once in all our days of poignant love. One Year After. Claude McKay. SP-McKaC

Not only were you waiting. H$_2$O. Al Young. CP-YounA

Not only when you go to bed / And sleep. (LL) Knoxville, Tennessee. Nikki Giovanni. AmNP; BPo; BlSi; BrTr; PoBA; SP-GiovN

Not Sacco and Vanzetti. Countee Cullen. CP-CullC

Not That Far. May Miller. BlSi

Not they who soar! (LL) Not they who soar, but they who plod. Paul Laurence Dunbar. CP-DunbP; NAAAL

Not they who soar, but they who plod. Paul Laurence Dunbar. CP-DunbP; NAAAL

Not to dance with her. A Triviality. Waring Cuney. CDC

Not to the midnight of the gloomy past. On the Dedication of Dorothy Hall. Paul Laurence Dunbar. CP-DunbP

Not What Was. Langston Hughes. CP-HughL

Not when leaves are brown and sere. When I Would Die. Josephine D. Henderson Heard. CBWP-4

Not with my hands. Benediction. Donald Jeffrey Hayes. AmNP

Not writ in water, nor in mist. For John Keats. Countee Cullen. *Fr.* Four Epitaphs. AmNP; CDC; CP-CullC; Klds; PoBA

Notable Dinner, A. Lizelia Augusta Jenkins Moorer. CBWP-3

Note, The. Melvin B. Tolson. GT

Note in Music. Langston Hughes. CP-HughL

Note on Commercial Theatre. Langston Hughes. CP-HughL; SP-HughL
   (Notes on the Broadway Theatre.) SSLK
   ("You've done taken my blues and gone—.") SSLK

Note to All Nazis Fascists and Klansmen. Langston Hughes. CP-HughL

Notes for a Movie Script. M. Carl Holman. AmNP; Klds; PoBA

Notes for a Poem from the Middle Passage of Years. Lamont B. Steptoe. SpiFl

Notes for a Speech. Amiri Baraka. SP-BaraA

Notes from a Tunisian Journal. Rita Dove. SP-DoveR

Notes from the Childhood and the Girlhood. Gwendolyn Brooks. SP-BrooG
   "But can see better there, and laughing there." Klds

Notes from the Defense of Colin Ferguson. Sekou Sundiata. SpiFl
   Case through the Looking Glass, The.
   Defense Rests, The.
   That Picture in the Paper.
   Time Leading Up To, The.
   To Emerge from the Shadows.
   Week in Review, The.

Notes on the Broadway Theatre. Langston Hughes. *See* Note on Commercial Theatre.

Nothin' be as terrible. Jenny in Sleep. Dolores Kendrick. ESEAA

Nothing and Something. Frances Ellen Watkins Harper. CP-HarpF; EBAP

Nothing but a plain black boy. (LL) Of De Witt Williams on His Way to Lincoln Cemetery. Gwendolyn Brooks. ESEAA

Nothing can console me. You may bring silk. Demeter Mourning. Rita Dove. NAAAL

Nothing Down. Rita Dove. SP-DoveR

Nothing endures, / Not even love. Countee Cullen. CP-CullC

Nothing fills me up at night. Free Flight. June Jordan. SP-JordJ

Nothing happening. (LL) Letter to an Aspiring Junkie. Maya Angelou. CP-AngeM; SP-AngeM

Nothing happens only once. Circle One. Owen Dodson. Klds

Nothing if not utterly in death. So? James P. Vaughn. AmNP

Nothing Is. Sun-Ra. BlFi; PoBA

Nothing is right. Alice Walker. CP-WalkA

Nothing / is sorry / sameness. Even. Audre Lorde. CP-LordA

Nothing Lovely as a Tree. Frederick, Jr. Bryant. BlFi

Nothing Much. Maya Angelou. CP-AngeM

Nothing nastier than a white person! The Great Palaces of Versailles. Rita Dove. ESEAA

Nothing out there that I didn't already see. A dump, an overpopulated. Children of the Cosmos. Kuwasi Balagon. BlFi

Nothing says that you must see me in the street. The Dozens. Audre Lorde. CP-LordA; SP-LordA

Nothing so charms the American. "League of Gileadites": Messages. Michael S. Harper. SP-HarpM

Nothing to Do. James Ephriam McGirt. AAP

Nothing to it, man. Kicking. Al Young. CP-YounA

Nothing will keep. Personal Letter No. 3. Sonia Sanchez. ESEAA; SP-SancS; SSLK

Nous n'irons plus au bois. Sterling A. Brown. CP-BrowS

Nov 22, 1988. Ishmael Reed. ESEAA

Novelle; My Grandmother Is Waiting for Me to Come Home. Gwendolyn Brooks. *Fr.* Children Coming Home. ESEAA

November. Henrietta Cordelia Ray. CBWP-3

November Cotton Flower. Jean Toomer. CDC; CP-ToomJ

November for Beginners. Rita Dove. SP-DoveR

November sun invites me, The. Nutting Song. Paul Laurence Dunbar. CP-DunbP

Novitiates sing Ave. Miss Scarlet, Mr. Rhett and other Latter-Day Saints. Maya Angelou. CP-AngeM; SP-AngeM

Now. Christopher Gilbert. GT

NOW. Audre Lorde. CP-LordA; SP-LordA

Now. Margaret Abigail Walker. CP-WalkM

Now Ain't That Love? Carolyn M. Rodgers. BPo; BrTr

Now, Alex, you know the T. B. Bee have been my complaint. T. B. Bees. *African-American Oral Tradition.* GetYo

Now as I watch you, strong of arm and endurance, battling and struggling. To the Swimmer. Countee Cullen. CP-CullC

Now dreams / Are not avaliable. Oppression. Langston Hughes. CP-HughL

Now Elder Johnson's name been changed. Elder Mistletoe. Sterling A. Brown. CP-BrowS

Now for my story. For many years. Delirium. Norman J. Loftis. SpiFl

Now full of hope and deep repentance too. The Pilgrimage and Staff. George Marion McClellan. *Fr.* The Legend of Tannhauser and Elizabeth. EBAP

Now gypsy fires burn bright in every tree. October. Vittoria Aganoor Pompili. ShDr

Now His Fingers Found the Melody. Marilyn Nelson. *Fr.* I Dream the Book of Jonah. SP-NelsM

Now I am dry bones and my face a stony skull staring in yellow surprise at the sun. (LL) Between the World and Me. Richard Wright. AmNP; IDB; PoBA; TtW

Now I am going. The Thing Itself. Alice Walker. CP-WalkA

Now I am young and credulous. Wisdom Cometh with the Years. Countee Cullen. CP-CullC; Klds

Now I don't know whether it's true or not. Old Cods. *African-American Oral Tradition.* GetYo

Now i find my arms. Sassafras Memories. Edward S. Spriggs. BlFi

Now I invest the world. What is Beautiful. Jay Wright. GT

Now I'm where I belong. (LL) Where We Belong, A Duet. Maya Angelou. CP-AngeM; SP-AngeM

Now, / In June. After Many Springs. Langston Hughes. CP-HughL

Now is the time to. Thelonious: An Intro. Al Young. CP-YounA

Now it is time. Labor Storm. Langston Hughes. CP-HughL

Now it was getting dark in the Eastwood Park. Marie. *African-American Oral Tradition.* GetYo

Now Jonah Began to Tune His Guitar. Marilyn Nelson. *Fr.* I Dream the Book of Jonah. SP-NelsM

Now let all lovely things embark. Lament. Countee Cullen. CP-CullC

Now Long Ago. Maya Angelou. CP-AngeM; SP-AngeM

Now lookahere, gal. Argument: "Now lookahere, gal." Langston Hughes. CP-HughL

Now must I grieve and fret my little way. Solace. Margaret Abigail Walker. CP-WalkM

Now my first wife never did come out of her room. Lucille Clifton. SP-ClifL

Now peoples, as I gaze tonight at the pale moonlight. My Reflection. *African-American Oral Tradition.* GetYo

Now Poem. For Us. Sonia Sanchez. PoBA

Now, reader, pardon me for having sung. Albery Allson Whitman. *Fr.* Leelah Misled. EBAP

Now, reader, this digression you'll excuse. Albery Allson Whitman. *Fr.* Leelah Misled. EBAP

Now rock the boat to a fare-thee-well. Rite of Passage. Audre Lorde. PoBA

Now seals the fair creation from my sight. (LL) To S. M., a Young African Painter, on Seeing His Works. Phillis Wheatley. BlSi; CP-WheaP; Crnst; EBAP; NAAAL

Now that death has fled these quiet corridors. (LL) Another Poem for Me (after Recovering from an O.D.). Etheridge Knight. SP-KnigE

Now That I Am Forever with Child. Audre Lorde. CP-LordA; IHS; NAAAL; PoBA; SP-LordA

Now that nothing has worked out. Ars Poetica. Al Young. CP-YounA

Now that our love has drifted. Finis. Waring Cuney. AmNP; BANP

Now that the book is finished. Alice Walker. CP-WalkA

Now the bitter pangs of hope deferred. The Mail Has Come. Mary E. Tucker. CBWP-1

Now the children of the future tried to come to terms. Children of the Future. Jalaluddin Mansur Nuriddin. SpiFl

Now the dead past seems vividly alive. Heritage. Claude McKay. SP-McKaC

Now the thing the Negro has GOT to do—. View from the Corner. Samuel Allen. SSLK

Now the Time Is Ripe to Be. Jon Goncalves. BlFi

Now there will be nobody, you say. The Thorn. Langston Hughes. CP-HughL

Now thread my voice. How I Can Lie to You. Maya Angelou. CP-AngeM; SP-AngeM

Now Walter White. Ballad of Walter White. Langston Hughes. CP-HughL

Now we must come to the net. Coming to the Net. Brian G. Gilmore. SpiFl

Now we've made a child. And What About the Children. Audre Lorde. CP-LordA; PoBA

Now what I can't understand is your plan to leave me be. My Woman. Malcolm-Jamal Warner. CtF

Now, when I / die, don't bury me. Last Words By "Slick." Etheridge Knight. SP-KnigE

Now would I tread my darkness down. When I Am Dead. Owen Dodson. Klds

"Now you all must die," the young one said. The Rite. Dudley Randall. BrTr

Now you are gone, and with your unreturning goes. Therefore, Adieu. Countee Cullen. CP-CullC

Now you, John Henry, 'tain't no use. Charity. Paul Laurence Dunbar. CP-DunbP

Now you take ol Rufus. He beat drums. For Freckle-Faced Gerald. Etheridge Knight. BPo; Crnst; ESEAA; SP-KnigE

Now you take / This Bill Hastie guy. Judge William Hastie. Langston Hughes. CP-HughL

Now you wanna kill me. But Can You Kill the Nigga in You? Chuck D. CtF

Nowhere are we safe. Hymn Written after Jeremiah Preached to Me in a Dream. Owen Dodson. AmNP; Klds

Now's the Time. Al Young. CP-YounA

Ntarama (Rwanda) Chronicles. Karen Williams. SpiFl

Nude Woman Spotted in Cappuccino Cup as Advertising Dollar Co-Opts Another Life. Bahiyyih Maroon. SpiFl

Nude Young Dancer. Langston Hughes. CP-HughL

Nudge their draftee years. / Pop-a-da! (LL) Tag. Langston Hughes. CP-HughL; SP-HughL

Nullo. Jean Toomer. CP-ToomJ

Number. Langston Hughes. CP-HughL

Number Four. Doughtry Long. PoBA

Number runner / Come to my door. Madam and the Number Writer. Langston Hughes. CP-HughL; SP-HughL

Numbered. Langston Hughes. CP-HughL

Numbers. Langston Hughes. *Fr.* Montage of a Dream Deferred. CP-HughL

Numbers, Letters. Amiri Baraka. BPo; SP-BaraA

Nuns in the Basement of God. T'Kalla. CtF

Nursing the tough skins of figs. (LL) This Life. Rita Dove. GT; SP-DoveR

Nutting Song. Paul Laurence Dunbar. CP-DunbP

Nyanu was appointed. Early Losses: a Requiem. Alice Walker. BlSi; CP-WalkA

O

Ö. Rita Dove. SP-DoveR

O! Al Young. CP-YounA

O Africa, know thou not my call? Song of Innocence. Julius E. Thompson. TtW

O Africa, where I baked my bread. Lance Jeffers. TtW

O Allah ... receive him, a morning god. Morning Raga for Malcolm. Larry Neal. BrTr

O antique city on St. Lawrence shore. Quebec. Henrietta Cordelia Ray. CBWP-3

O apple blossoms. Japanese Hokku. Lewis Alexander. CDC

O bards! weak heritors of passion and of pain! Miserimus. Adah Isaacs Menken. CBWP-1

O Black and unknown bards of long ago. James Weldon Johnson. AfAmPo; AmNP; BANP; BPo; CrDW; NAAAL; PoBA; TtW

O boy the blues! The Old Fashioned Cincinnati Blues. Al Young. CP-YounA

O, bretheren, my way, my way's cloudy, my way. My Way's Cloudy. *Unknown.* CrDW

O brothers mine, take care! Take care! The White Witch. James Weldon Johnson. AfAmPo; BANP; CDC; TtW

O brothers mine, today we stand. Fifty Years. James Weldon Johnson. BANP

O children of the tropics. The Rallying Cry. Frances Ellen Watkins Harper. CP-HarpF

O chillen, run, de Cunjah man. De Cunjah Man. James Edwin Campbell. AAP; AfAmPo; BANP; EBAP; TtW

O Christ, who in Gethsemane. Prayer. Henrietta Cordelia Ray. CBWP-3

O, come erlong, come erlong. Mobile-Buck. James Edwin Campbell. AAP

O come to me in my dreams love! Lines to———. Mary Weston Fordham. TtW

O come, you pious youth! adore. An Address to Miss Phillis Wheatly, Ethiopian Poetess. Jupiter Hammon. EBAP; TtW

O, comrades! to-morrow we try. A Slave's Reflections the Eve before His Sale. George Moses Horton. SP-HortG

O crownless soul of Ishmael! Hemlock in the Furrows. Adah Isaacs Menken. CBWP-1

O Daedalus, Fly Away Home. Robert Hayden. CP-HaydR; IDB; NAAAL; PoBA; TtW

O day!/ With sun glowing. Exultation. Mae V. Cowdery. ShDr

O, de birds ar' sweetly singin'. 'Weh Down Souf. Daniel Webster Davis. BANP

O, de Black Cat cotch ole Sambo Lee. De Black Cat Crossed His Luck. James David Corrothers. AfAmPo

O, de light-bugs glimmer down de lane. Negro Serenade. James Edwin Campbell. BANP

O' de wurl' ain't flat! Northboun'. Lucy Ariel Williams Holloway. BANP; BlSi; CDC; ShDr

O Death! whose sceptre, trembling realms obey. To Mr. and Mrs. —, on the Death of Their Infant Son. Phillis Wheatley. CP-WheaP

O Death! Why dost thou steal the great. In Memoriam Frederick Douglass. Eloise Bibb. CBWP-4

O do, Lawd, remember me! Do, Lawd. *African-American Oral Tradition.* TtW

O Earth, adore creative power. Creation. Mary Weston Fordham. CBWP-2

O eloquent and caustic sage. Frederick Douglass. Joseph Seamon Cotter, Sr. AAP; AfAmPo; EBAP

O fly away home fly away. (LL) O Daedalus, Fly Away Home. Robert Hayden. CP-HaydR; IDB; NAAAL; PoBA

O foolish tears, go back! In Vain. Adah Isaacs Menken. CBWP-1

O Freedom! Freedom! O! how oft. Charles Lewis Reason. AAP

O Freedom! / O Freedom! *Unknown.* CrDW

O God of my salvation. (LL) Hymn: "When storms arise." Paul Laurence Dunbar. CP-DunbP

O, Great God of Cold and Winter. Prayer for a Winter Night. Langston Hughes. CP-HughL

O great tone-master! low thy massive head. Beethoven. Henrietta Cordelia Ray. CBWP-3

O, hits time fur de plantin' ur de co'n. Song of the Corn. James Edwin Campbell. AAP

"O hoppy-toad," he cried. (LL) Ballad of the Hoppy-Toad. Margaret Abigail Walker. CP-WalkM; TtW

O, hungry heart. Heart-Hungry. Josephine D. Henderson Heard. CBWP-4

O i am so sad, i. Haiku: "O i am so sad, i." Sonia Sanchez. SP-SancS

O i was wide and. Haiku: "O i was wide and." Sonia Sanchez. SP-SancS

O, I wish that yesterday. Yesterday and Today. Langston Hughes. CP-HughL

O, insatiable monster! Could'st thou not. Requiem. Mary Weston Fordham. CBWP-2

O islets green, Nature's immortal gems. Hymn to the Thousand Islands. Henrietta Cordelia Ray. CBWP-3

O-Jazz-O. Bob Kaufman. SP-KaufB

O-JAZZ-O War Memoir: Jazz, Don't Listen To It At Your Own Risk. Bob Kaufman. *See* War Memoir: Jazz, Don't Listen to It at Your Own Risk.

O. K. / you scat taking. Victor Hernandez Cruz. BlFi

O land of mine, O land I love. Apostrophe to the Land. Countee Cullen. CP-CullC

O, Liberty, thou dove of peace. Liberty. George Moses Horton. SP-HortG

O, Life of Dreams! O, Dreams of Life! Timothy Thomas Fortune. AAP *Fr.* Dreams of Life. EBAP

O li'l lamb out in de col'. Hymn. Paul Laurence Dunbar. CP-DunbP

O, little tree! (LL) Little Green Tree. Langston Hughes. CP-HughL; SP-HughL

O lonely heart so timid of approach. Courage. Claude McKay. SP-McKaC

O Lord, the hard-won miles. A Prayer. Paul Laurence Dunbar. CP-DunbP

O Lord, we come this morning. Listen, Lord—[a Prayer]. James Weldon Johnson. BANP; BPo

O Man, behold your destiny. This Is My Century. Margaret Abigail Walker. CP-WalkM

O minstrel lyre of ancient Ethiop. Ethiopia. Fenton Johnson. EBAP

O mongrel land! My America. Oliver La Grone. NNP

O Mother-heart! when fast the arrows flew. Niobe. Henrietta Cordelia Ray. CBWP-3

O Mother Race! to thee I bring. Ode to Ethiopia. Paul Laurence Dunbar. BALP; CP-DunbP; NAAAL; TtW

O my brother I heard u. Before / and After. Jewel C. Latimore. JB

O Mystic Light! A Mystic Sage Returns to Realms of Eternity. Askia M. Toure. SpiFl

O night betrayed by darkness not its own. (LL) Night, Death, Mississippi. Robert Hayden. CP-HaydR; Crnst

O.O. Gabugah writes that he "was born in a taxicab right." Boogie With O.O. Gabugah. Al Young. CP-YounA

O peerless marble marvel! what of grace. The Venus of Milo. Henrietta Cordelia Ray. CBWP-3

O, po' sinner, O, now is yo' time. What Yo' Gwine to [*or* t'] Do When Yo' [*or* de] Lamp Burn Down? *Unknown.* BPo

O poet gifted with the sight divine! Milton. Henrietta Cordelia Ray. BlSi; CBWP-3; EBAP; TtW

O rare Narcissus! sunny-haired! Echo's Complaint. Henrietta Cordelia Ray. CBWP-3

O Restless Heart, Be Still! Henrietta Cordelia Ray. CBWP-3

O, rich young lord, thou ridest by. Compensation. James Edwin Campbell. BANP

O rocking boat, rocking boat poised on the wave. Boat Song. Henrietta Cordelia Ray. CBWP-3

O sailing stars! Star Song. Henrietta Cordelia Ray. CBWP-3

O San Francisco lighting the truth of. Berkeley Pome. Al Young. CP-YounA

O say can u see. On Watching a World Series Game. Sonia Sanchez. NBV

O, seems it not to other eyes as sweet. Albery Allson Whitman. *Fr.* Leelah Misled. EBAP

O Silent God, Thou whose voice afar in mist and mystery. A Litany of [*or* at] Atlanta. William Edward Burghardt DuBois. BANP; CDC

O silver splendor, marvelous! A Vision of Moonlight. Henrietta Cordelia Ray. CBWP-3

O, silver tree! Langston Hughes. *See* Jazzonia.

O! sing ye a dirge for the loved and the lost. Tribute to a Lost Steamer. Mary Weston Fordham. CBWP-2

O snowflake clouds, O feath'ry clouds. Cloud Song. Henrietta Cordelia Ray. CBWP-3

O soldiers, soldiers, get ye back, I pray! Saved. Adah Isaacs Menken. CBWP-1

O soul, why shouldst thou downcast be? Hope Thou in God. Josephine D. Henderson Heard. CBWP-4

O Spirits of whom my soul is but a little finger. (LL) Prayer. Jean Toomer. CP-ToomJ; NAAAL

O, sweep of stars over Harlem streets. Stars. Langston Hughes. CP-HughL; SP-HughL

O sweet are tropic lands for waking dreams. North and South. Claude McKay. SP-McKaC

O sweet, sad, singing river. Song. Henrietta Cordelia Ray. CBWP-3

O sylvan priest of nature! rightly thou. A Thought at Walden. Henrietta Cordelia Ray. CBWP-3

O, that the Holy Angels would indite. The Quarto Centennial. Josephine D. Henderson Heard. CBWP-4

O, that the years had language! time would / tell. Judith. Eloise Bibb. CBWP-4

O there's a laughy light. Absent from the United States. Al Young. CP-YounA

O, / these wild trees. Hymn for Lanie Poo. Amiri Baraka. SP-BaraA

O thou bright jewel in my aim I strive. On Virtue. Phillis Wheatley. CP-WheaP; TtW

O Thou, enthron'd with Cherubs in the realms of day! (LL) On Virtue. Phillis Wheatley. CP-WheaP

O thou who never harbored fear. Sonnet. Eloise Bibb. CBWP-4

O thou whose exit wraps in boundless woe. An Elegy, Sacred to the Memory of That Great Divine, the Reverend and Learned Dr. Samuel Cooper, Who Departed This Life December 29, 1783, Ætatis 59. Phillis Wheatley. CP-WheaP

O tremble! O tremble, O tremble. Six Sunday. Hart Leroi Bibbs. NBP

O whisper, O my soul! The afternoon. The Tired Worker. Claude McKay. BANP; BPo; SP-McKaC

O white-face mimes. For Dead Mimes. Langston Hughes. CP-HughL

O White Mistress. Don Allen Johnson. NNP

O, wondrous depth to which my soul is stirr'd. Music. Josephine D. Henderson Heard. CBWP-4

O word I love to sing! thou art too tender. Claude McKay. SP-McKaC

O, you can't find a buddy. Death of Do Dirty: A Rounder's Song. Langston Hughes. CP-HughL

O you that strike will never flinch. Secret. Mary Jenness. ShDr

O you would clothe me in silken frocks. The Wild Goat. Claude McKay. CDC; SP-McKaC

Oak. Michael S. Harper. SP-HarpM

Oakland Blues. Ishmael Reed. CP-ReedI; NAAAL

Oaxaca. Audre Lorde. CP-LordA; SP-LordA

Ob all de subjicts I kin read. Men Folks ob Today, De. Maggie Pogue Johnson. CBWP-4

Obedience. Rita Dove. SP-DoveR

Obituary for J. Edwards Barnes. Frances Ellen Watkins Harper. CP-HarpF

Oblivion. Jessie Redmond Fauset, fr. the French of Massillon Coicou. BANP

Oblivion—the shroud and envelope of happiness. (LL) Oblivion. Jessie Redmond Fauset, fr. the French of Massillon Coicou. BANP

Obstruction of Genius, The. George Moses Horton. SP-HortG

Ocean. John Boyd. EBAP

Ocean Musing, An. Henrietta Cordelia Ray. CBWP-3

Ocean of the Streams of Story. Primus St. John. GT

Ocean Springs Missippy. Al Young. CP-YounA

October. Mary Weston Fordham. CBWP-2

October. Audre Lorde. CP-LordA; SP-LordA

October. Vittoria Aganoor Pompili. ShDr

October. Henrietta Cordelia Ray. CBWP-3

October, 1800: A Son in the Continuum. George Barlow. Fr. Gabriel. TtW

October 23, 1983. June Jordan. SP-JordJ

October 31st 1994 7:30 am. "C" ing in Colors: Blue. Safiya Henderson-Holmes. SpiFl

October Is Here. Mrs. Henry Linden. CBWP-4

October is the treasurer of the year. Paul Laurence Dunbar. CP-DunbP

October— / its plangency, its glow. Robert Hayden. CP-HaydR; ESEAA

October Journey. Margaret Abigail Walker. AmNP; CP-WalkM; GT; IDB; PoBA

October 16: The Raid. Langston Hughes. CP-HughL; PoBA; SP-HughL

October slows thru me. The October Variations. Al Young. CP-YounA

October XXIX, 1795. William Stanley Braithwaite. CDC

October Variations, The. Al Young. CP-YounA

October Window. Al Young. CP-YounA

Odd stillness of your body, The. Clutter-up People. Alice Walker. CP-WalkA

Odds, The. Al Young. CP-YounA

Ode. Elizabeth Alexander. GT

Ode for Memorial Day. Paul Laurence Dunbar. CP-DunbP

Ode of Verses on the Death of George Whitefield, An. Phillis Wheatley. CP-WheaP

Ode on the Birthday of Pompey Stockbridge, An. Phillis Wheatley. EBAP

Ode on the Occasion of the Inauguration of the Sixth President of Jackson State College. Margaret Abigail Walker. CP-WalkM

Ode on the Twentieth Century. Henrietta Cordelia Ray. CBWP-3

Ode to a Beautiful Woman. Carl Clark. JB

Ode to Dinah. Langston Hughes. Fr. Ask Your Mama; 12 Moods for Jazz. CP-HughL

Ode to Ethiopia. Paul Laurence Dunbar. BALP; CP-DunbP; NAAAL; TtW

Ode to Neptune. Phillis Wheatley. CP-WheaP

Ode to Peace. Mary Weston Fordham. CBWP-2

Ode to Tenochtitlan. Michael S. Harper. SP-HarpM

Ode to the Sun. Eloise Bibb. CBWP-4

Odyssey of Big Boy. Sterling A. Brown. BANP; CDC; CP-BrowS; NAAAL

O'er all my song the image of a face. The Negro Singer. James David Corrothers. BANP

O'er this wide extended country. To the White People of America. Joshua McCarter Simpson. AAP; AfAmPo

O'erwhelming sorrow now demands my song. To a Lady and Her Children, on the Death of Her Son and Their Brother. Phillis Wheatley. CP-WheaP

Of a Black girl. (LL) Story Books on a Kitchen Table. Audre Lorde. CP-LordA; SP-LordA

Of a dying dream. (LL) Tears / The crystal rags. Maya Angelou. CP-AngeM; SP-AngeM

Of a lady fair to see. Lines to Mrs. M. C. Turner. Eloise Bibb. CBWP-4

Of a morning sun. (LL) Four Glimpses of Night. Frank Marshall Davis. AmNP; PoBA

Of all grandeur that was Solomon's. At the Wailing Wall in Jerusalem. Countee Cullen. CP-CullC

Of all the mighty nations of the sun. (LL) Africa. Claude McKay. NAAAL; SP-McKaC

Of all the nights, yours were greenest, Gene. Jungle Strut. Al Young. CP-YounA

Of all the ways in which this country. American Cancer Society Or There Is More Than One Way to Skin a Coon. Audre Lorde. CP-LordA; SP-LordA

Of all things, lady, be not proud. Advice to a Beauty. Countee Cullen. CP-CullC

Of all those / yester- / days. (LL) The Move Continuing. Al Young. CP-YounA; PoBA

Of black flesh after flame. (LL) Portrait in Georgia. Jean Toomer. CP-ToomJ

Of both their angers. (LL) Generation II. Audre Lorde. CP-LordA; SP-LordA

Of cat-gut lace. (LL) Boogie: 1 A.M. Langston Hughes. CP-HughL

Of cat-gut lace. (LL) Nightmare Boogie. Langston Hughes. CP-HughL

Of childish pranks with / angels. (LL) Brief Innocence. Maya Angelou. CP-AngeM; SP-AngeM

Of course, I don't know very much. Aunt Chloe's Politics. Frances Ellen Watkins Harper. CP-HarpF; NAAAL

Of course it is snowing. Dear Old Stockholm. Al Young. CP-YounA

Of course you will always want to be. Mid-Life Crises: A Critical Review. Al Young. CP-YounA

Of De Witt Williams on His Way to Lincoln Cemetery. Gwendolyn Brooks. Fr. A Street in Bronzeville. BPo; BlSi; ESEAA; SP-BrooG

Of Earth. Mae V. Cowdery. ShDr

Of Ethiopia spreading her gorgeous wings. (LL) Summertime and the Living. Robert Hayden. CP-HaydR; PoBA

Of Ethiopia's glory. (LL) Ode to Ethiopia. Paul Laurence Dunbar. BALP; CP-DunbP; NAAAL; TtW

Of falling leaves and melting. Artful Pose. Maya Angelou. CP-AngeM; SP-AngeM

Of green grass. (LL) Green Grass and Yellow Balloons. Etheridge Knight. GT; SP-KnigE

Of happiness, haply hysterics. Is. (LL) The Rites for Cousin Vit. Gwendolyn Brooks. BPo; NAAAL; SP-BrooG

Of his gastronomical past. (LL) Black Man's Feast. Sarah Webster Fabio. PoBA

Of iron feet again. And again wild. (LL) The Progress. Gwendolyn Brooks. SP-BrooG

Of love's austere and lonely offices? (LL) Those Winter Sundays. Robert Hayden. CP-HaydR; ESEAA; IDB; PoBA; SSLK

Of man's Divinity alive in stone. (LL) St. Isaac's Church, Petrograd. Claude McKay. Klds; NAAAL; SP-McKaC

Of Nightsong and Flight. June Jordan. SP-JordJ

Of noble minds and noble hearts. John Boyle O'Reilly. Paul Laurence Dunbar. CP-DunbP

Of once beautiful children. (LL) New York City 1970. Audre Lorde. CP-LordA; NBV; SP-LordA

Of 125th Street and Lenox. (LL) Cables to Rage or I've Been Talking on This Street Corner a Hell of a Long Time. Audre Lorde. CP-LordA; SP-LordA

Of our absent selves. (LL) After. Maya Angelou. CP-AngeM; SP-AngeM

Of our house in Taos. Langston Hughes. See A House in Taos.

Of our own enslavements. But Bird was a junkie! (LL) Historiography. Lorenzo Thomas. TtW

Of our return / At the end. (LL) Good Night, Willie Lee, I'll See You in the Morning. Alice Walker. CP-WalkA; NAAAL

Of Puddles, Worms, Slimy Things. Sarah Webster Fabio. TtW

Of Robert Frost. Gwendolyn Brooks. SP-BrooG

Of sad and wise / decisions. (LL) How I Can Lie to You. Maya Angelou. CP-AngeM; SP-AngeM

Of Southern peace. (LL) A Georgia Song. Maya Angelou. CP-AngeM; SP-AngeM

Of the Cosmic-Blueprints. Sun-Ra. BlFi

Of the ills we daily see. The Social Life. Lizelia Augusta Jenkins Moorer. CBWP-3

Of the night / of the rain, she. Crow Jane the Crook. Amiri Baraka. SP-BaraA

Of the tall rocks. (LL) Your soul shines. Alice Walker. CP-WalkA

Of the Tallahatchie. (LL) The Bones of My Father. Etheridge Knight. SP-KnigE

Of the three Wise Men. Carol of the Brown King. Langston Hughes. CP-HughL

Of the world. (LL) Light Baggage. Alice Walker. CP-WalkA

Of the world's business. (LL) Mrs. Small went to the kitchen for her pocketbook. Gwendolyn Brooks. GT; SP-BrooG

Of these men and their music. (LL) Here Where Coltrane Is. Michael S. Harper. ESEAA; NAAAL; SP-HarpM

Of time— / Old Abe. (LL) Lincoln Monument: Washington. Langston Hughes. CP-HughL

Of us naked women. (LL) In My Mother's Room. Colleen J. McElroy. GT

Of violets, and my soul's forgotten gleam. (LL) Sonnet: "I had no thought of violets of late." Alice Moore Dunbar-Nelson. BANP; BlSi; CDC; PoBA

Of warring shades whose weapons kill. (LL) Locus. Robert Hayden. CP-HaydR

Of What Use Is Poetry? (Babalu Meets the Wolfman). Amiri Baraka. CtF

Of winter branches, wonders read as signs. (LL) Elsewhere. Derek Walcott. Crnst

Off-color eyes tht shine through lobes. Studs. Michael S. Harper. ESEAA

Off d Pig. Ishmael Reed. CP-ReedI

Off go the crows from the roof. Crows in a Strong Wind. Cornelius Eady. ESEAA

Off our New England coast the sea to-night. The House of Falling Leaves. William Stanley Braithwaite. NAAAL

Off the coast of Ireland. Seascape. Langston Hughes. CP-HughL; GT; SP-HughL

Off the track / I blew. Phoenix. Carolyn M. Rodgers. JB

Off to Philadelphia in the morning. Dennis Brutus. GT

Offering, An. Eloise Bibb. CBWP-4

Offering. Sharan Strange. GT

Offers the boon of Death. (LL) Compensation. Paul Laurence Dunbar. AmNP; BPo; CP-DunbP

Office Building: Evening. Langston Hughes. CP-HughL

"Officer, I broke your gun." (LL) A Mother Speaks: The Algiers Motel Incident, Detroit. Michael S. Harper. BPo; NBV

Official Notice. Langston Hughes. CP-HughL

Offspring. Naomi Long Madgett. FB; GT

Oft do I hear those windows ope. The Fearful Traveller in the Haunted Castle. George Moses Horton. SP-HortG

Often times / parents. Wishbone. Frank X. Walker. SpiFl

Oftimes I wish that I could be. Poplar Tree. Mae V. Cowdery. ShDr

Oh, a hidden power is in my breast. Song of the Moon. Priscilla Jane Thompson. CBWP-2

Oh Achilles of the moleskins. To "Chick." Frank Horne. Fr. Letters [or Notes] Found near a Suicide. AmNP; BPo; CDC; PoBA

Oh angels! will ye never sweep the drifts from my door? Drifts That Bar My Door. Adah Isaacs Menken. CBWP-1

Oh, Athelstane, the faithful! Athelstane. Priscilla Jane Thompson. CBWP-2

Oh beautiful, black martyr. For Malcolm. Joyce Whitsitt Lawrence. BrTr

Oh children think about the Good times. (LL) Good Times. Lucille Clifton. AmNP; BPo; PoBA

Oh, comrade, comrade, I have missed you so! Comrade. Paul Laurence Dunbar. CP-DunbP

Oh, Congo brother. We, Too. Langston Hughes. CP-HughL

Oh, could I but sing as the minstrels of old! Lines to Emma. Priscilla Jane Thompson. CBWP-2

Oh! crush it not, that hope so blest. The Blessed Hope. Frances Ellen Watkins Harper. CP-HarpF

Oh, Danny got a goat to ride. Mr. Danny. Sterling A. Brown. CP-BrowS

Oh, de clouds is mighty heavy. Keep a Song Up on de Way. Paul Laurence Dunbar. CP-DunbP

Oh, de grubbin'-hoe's a-rustin' in de co'nah. The Deserted Plantation. Paul Laurence Dunbar. CP-DunbP

Oh, de ole sheep, dey know de road. Ole Sheep Dey Know de Road, De. Unknown. BPo

Oh de wagon keeps a rollin'. Isaiah to Mandy. Sterling A. Brown. CP-BrowS

Oh, de weathah it is balmy an' de breeze is sighin' low. Li'l' Gal. Paul Laurence Dunbar. CP-DunbP

Oh, dere's lots o' keer an' trouble. A Banjo Song. Paul Laurence Dunbar. CP-DunbP

Oh! Erin my country, my ancestor's home! Song to Erin. Mary Weston Fordham. CBWP-2

Oh, fields of wonder. Birth. Langston Hughes. CP-HughL

Oh, for a drink, to-night. Charmion's Lament. Eloise Bibb. CBWP-4

"Oh! for a thousand tongues to sing." The Farmer's Soliloquy. Robert Charles O'Hara Benjamin. AAP

Oh for the breath of the briny deep. A Sailor's Song. Paul Laurence Dunbar. CP-DunbP

Oh, for the veils of my far away youth. Lost Illusions. Georgia Douglas Johnson. NAAAL

Oh, foully slighted Ethiope maid! The Song. Priscilla Jane Thompson. CBWP-2

Oh! gentle sir, calm and secure. Love. Benjamin Clark. EBAP

Oh! give to me of the bright green leaves. I Am Fashion's Toy. Mary E. Tucker. CBWP-1

Oh God! my heart is thine. In the Valley. Priscilla Jane Thompson. CBWP-2

Oh, God of dust and rainbows, help us see. Langston Hughes. Fr. Two Somewhat Different Epigrams. CP-HughL; Klds

Oh! had I now an overcoat. Wish for an Overcoat. Alfred Islay Walden. AAP; AfAmPo

Oh, hear the stuffed gold eagle sing. (LL) On Lookout Mountain. Robert Hayden. CP-HaydR

Oh, how can I live in a torture so wild. Disappointment. Mary E. Tucker. CBWP-1

Oh how you used to walk. Just for a Time. Maya Angelou. CP-AngeM; SP-AngeM

Oh, I am hurt to death, my Love. One Life. Paul Laurence Dunbar. CP-DunbP

Oh, I am wild—wild! Sale of Souls. Adah Isaacs Menken. CBWP-1

Oh, I des received a letter f'om de sweetest little gal. A Love Letter. Paul Laurence Dunbar. CP-DunbP

Oh, I have n't got long to live, for we all. A Border Ballad. Paul Laurence Dunbar. CP-DunbP

Oh, I have tried to laugh the pain away. Futility. Claude McKay. SP-McKaC

Oh, I shall meet your friends, and chatter on. Nous n'irons plus au bois. Sterling A. Brown. CP-BrowS

Oh, ill-starred Ethiopia. Address to Ethiopia. Priscilla Jane Thompson. CBWP-2

Oh, I'm 10 Months Pregnant. Ntozake Shange. GT

Oh, I'm hitching my love for Jesus to my plow. Meditation over the Washtub. Marilyn Nelson. Fr. Thus Far by Faith. SP-NelsM

Oh Lawd have mussy now upon us. Blessing without Company. Unknown. BPo

Oh! liberty my native land. My Native Home. George Moses Horton. SP-HortG

Oh List to My Song! Clara Ann Thompson. CBWP-2

Oh, little Christ, why do you sigh. Christmas Eve in France. Jessie Redmond Fauset. BANP

Oh little fledgling out of the nest. Paul Laurence Dunbar. CP-DunbP

Oh, lonely Cross! (LL) Late Corner. Langston Hughes. CP-HughL; Klds

Oh, Lord! I lift my heart. A Prayer. Priscilla Jane Thompson. CBWP-2

Oh mother, mother, where is happiness? (LL) Appendix to the Anniad. Gwendolyn Brooks. BlSi; SP-BrooG

Oh Muse! I crave a favor. The Muse's Favor. Priscilla Jane Thompson. AAP; AfAmPo; CBWP-2

Oh, my God is in the whirlwind. Song of the Whirlwind. Fenton Johnson. NAAAL

Oh, my mother's moaning by the river. The Lonely Mother. Fenton Johnson. NAAAL

Oh, my soul had grown so weary. The Mother's Blessing. Frances Ellen Watkins Harper. CP-HarpF

Oh never on my youthful ear. My Mother's Voice. Mary E. Tucker. CBWP-1

Oh nimber, nimber Will-o! Chuck Will's Widow Song. Unknown. BPo

Oh, nobody knows da trubble ah see. Nobody Knows Da Trubble Ah See. African-American Oral Tradition. TtW

Oh, One was black of the wise men of the East. The Wise Men of the East. Claude McKay. SP-McKaC

Oh, one wide river to cross. (LL) Crossing. Sterling A. Brown. CP-BrowS; TtW

Oh, Poet of our Race. Poet of Our Race. Maggie Pogue Johnson. CBWP-4

Oh, pure and sportive little child. To a Little Colored Boy. Priscilla Jane Thompson. CBWP-2

Oh shit a riot! Jacques Wakefield. BlFi

Oh, silver tree! Jazzonia. Langston Hughes. AfAmPo; AmNP; BANP; CP-HughL; Klds

Oh! sing it in the light of freedom's morn. Albery Allson Whitman. AfAmPo; EBAP. *Fr.* "Upon the shells by Carribea's wave." *Fr.* Twasinta's Seminoles; Or Rape of Florida.

Oh sisters, kind and loving. To White Ribbons of Maine Who Gave to Me Their Blessed Gifts. Frances Ellen Watkins Harper. CP-HarpF

Oh something just now must be happening there! Home Thoughts. Claude McKay. SP-McKaC

Oh, summer has clothed the earth. In Summer. Paul Laurence Dunbar. CP-DunbP

Oh! surely for thee were the gates ajar. Rev. Samuel Weston. Mary Weston Fordham. CBWP-2

Oh! surely 'tis a theme sublime. Dedicated to the Right Rev'd D. A. Payne. Mary Weston Fordham. CBWP-2

Oh swings: beyond complete immortal now. (LL) Soledad. Robert Hayden. CP-HaydR; NAAAL

Oh! tell me not of fatherland. This Is a Fatherland to Me. Joseph Cephas Holly. AAP

Oh, that last long ride is a. Widow Woman. Langston Hughes. CP-HughL; SP-HughL

Oh, the blue blue bloom. Pansy. Mary Effie Lee Newsome. CDC

Oh the breeze is blowin' balmy. Till the Wind Gets Right. Paul Laurence Dunbar. CP-DunbP

Oh, the day has set me dreaming. Little Lucy Landman. Paul Laurence Dunbar. CP-DunbP

Oh the God-bus has a busted wheel. Harwood Alley Song. Bob Kaufman. SP-KaufB

Oh, the gorgeous leaves of autumn! Autumn Leaves. Clara Ann Thompson. CBWP-2

Oh, the little bird is rocking in the cradle of the wind. The Farm Child's Lullaby. Paul Laurence Dunbar. CP-DunbP

Oh, the poets may sing of their Lady Irenes. To Louise. Paul Laurence Dunbar. CP-DunbP

Oh, the tidal waves of our suffering. The Law. Albert E., Jr. Haynes. NBP

Oh they'll never cry and hunger any more. (LL) Incense of the Lucky Virgin. Robert Hayden. CP-HaydR

Oh, this is the tale the grandmas tell. The Ballad of the Brown Girl. Countee Cullen. CP-CullC

Oh, this little light of mine. This Little Light of Mine. *Unknown.* NAAAL

Oh to have you in May. In May. Paul Laurence Dunbar. CP-DunbP

Oh, to lick your love like tears. (LL) Black Ode. Maya Angelou. CP-AngeM; SP-AngeM

Oh, wash-woman, / Arms elbow-deep in white suds. A Song to a Negro Wash-woman. Langston Hughes. CP-HughL

Oh! waves in the sunlight gleaming. Sonnet to My First Born. Mary Weston Fordham. CBWP-2

Oh, we are given such a little while! (LL) Protest. Countee Cullen. CDC; CP-CullC

Oh, weep for Columbia! oh, weep for the time! The Patriot's Lament. Joseph Cephas Holly. AAP

Oh, what shall I do? I am wholly upset. The Disturber. Paul Laurence Dunbar. CP-DunbP

Oh, what sorrow! Mississippi. Langston Hughes. CP-HughL

Oh what sound is that, what sound is that. A Child's Nightmare. Bobb Hamilton. BrTr

Oh, when-a mah blood runs chilly and col, Ize got to go. When-a Mah Blood runs Chilly and Col. *African-American Oral Tradition.* TtW

Oh, when I come to die. Give Me Jesus. *Unknown.* BPo

Oh when I think of my long-suffering race. Enslaved. Claude McKay. AfAmPo; BALP; BPo; NAAAL; SP-McKaC

Oh, when this earthly tenement. "Ada." BlSi

Oh, Whence Comes the Gladness? Priscilla Jane Thompson. CBWP-2

Oh, where's the maid that I can love. One to Love. Alfred Islay Walden. AAP

Oh, who hath a balm that will impart. A Dialogue. Frances Ellen Watkins Harper. CP-HarpF

Oh, who is the Lord of the land of life. The Masters. Paul Laurence Dunbar. CP-DunbP

Oh, who would be sad tho' the sky be a-graying. Winter-Song. Paul Laurence Dunbar. CP-DunbP

Oh! Wilberforce, our star of hope. Golden Jubilee of Wilberforce. Mrs. Henry Linden. CBWP-4

Oh, will you wear red? I'll Wear Me a Cotton Dress. *Unknown.* BPo

Oh, wind of the spring-time, oh, free wind of May. Roses. Paul Laurence Dunbar. CP-DunbP

Oh wistful and heartrending earth, oh land. A Farewell to Morocco. Claude McKay. SP-McKaC

Oh Woman, Blessed Woman! Mrs. Henry Linden. CBWP-4

Oh—Yeah! Sharon Scott. JB

Oh you were quite the gypsy on that night. Telling Fortunes. Sterling A. Brown. CP-BrowS

Oh za ki tan ke parlay lot. Za Ki Tan Ke Parlay Lot. Audre Lorde. CP-LordA; SP-LordA

Ohhh break love with white things. Sacred Chant for the Return of Black Spirit and Power. Amiri Baraka. NBV

Okay. Sharon Scott. JB

Okay "Negroes." June Jordan. BPo

Ol' Doc' Hyar. James Edwin Campbell. AAP; AfAmPo; BANP; EBAP; TtW

Ol' time's gone, de new time's hyeah, De. Long Ago. Paul Laurence Dunbar. CP-DunbP

Ol' Tunes, The. Paul Laurence Dunbar. CP-DunbP

Old. Paul Laurence Dunbar. CP-DunbP

Old Age. Langston Hughes. CP-HughL

Old Age. Margaret Abigail Walker. CP-WalkM

Old and the New, The. Clara Ann Thompson. CBWP-2

Old Apple-Tree, The. Paul Laurence Dunbar. CP-DunbP

Old Black ladies. Weeksville Women. Elouise Loftin. PoBA

Old black man was stood on the block, The. Legend. Sterling A. Brown. CP-BrowS

Old black me! (LL) Parade. Langston Hughes. CP-HughL

Old Black Men. Georgia Douglas Johnson. CDC; PoBA

Old Black Men Say. James A. Emanuel. PoBA

Old Cabin, The. Paul Laurence Dunbar. CP-DunbP

Old Cods. *African-American Oral Tradition.* GetYo

Old Crib, The. Mary E. Tucker. CBWP-1

Old Days, The. Audre Lorde. CP-LordA

Old Dog Queenie / Was such a meanie. Langston Hughes. CP-HughL

Old Eddie's face, wrinkled with river lights. The Glory Trumpeter. Derek Walcott. GT

Old emotions like powdery tenements. City Home Detroit. Al Young. CP-YounA

Old farmer stopped me on the street one day, An. Ups on the Farm. *African-American Oral Tradition.* GetYo

Old Fashioned Cincinnati Blues, The. Al Young. CP-YounA

Old Folks Laugh. Maya Angelou. CP-AngeM

Old Freedman, The. Priscilla Jane Thompson. CBWP-2

Old Front Gate, The. Paul Laurence Dunbar. CP-DunbP

Old Gory, The. Gerald William Barrax. NBV

Old High School and the New, The. Paul Laurence Dunbar. CP-DunbP

Old Homestead, The. Paul Laurence Dunbar. CP-DunbP

Old Houses. Melvin B. Tolson. GT

Old King Cotton. Sterling A. Brown. CP-BrowS

Old Lem. Sterling A. Brown. BPo; CP-BrowS; FB; IDB; PoBA

Old Liberia Is Not the Place for Me. Joshua McCarter Simpson. AAP

Old Light. Al Young. CP-YounA

Old Love Butchered (Colorado Springs and Huachuca). Lance Jeffers. NBV

Old Maid's Soliloquy. Maggie Pogue Johnson. CBWP-4

Old Man Buzzard / Wid his bal' head. Sterling A. Brown. CP-BrowS

Old Man Know-All. *Unknown.* BPo

Old man / man black man. Tony Get the Boys. D. L. Graham. PoBA

Old man mumbling in his dotage, or crying child, unborn? (LL) For Malcolm X. Margaret Abigail Walker. BPo; CP-WalkM; NAAAL; PoBA

Old man planted and dug and tended, An. Disappointed. Paul Laurence Dunbar. CP-DunbP

Old-Marrieds, The. Gwendolyn Brooks. AmNP; PoBA

Old Mary. Gwendolyn Brooks. SP-BrooG

Old master always said. "No, Master, Never!" Joshua McCarter Simpson. AAP

Old Memory, An. Paul Laurence Dunbar. CP-DunbP

Old men and women, The. July. Sonia Sanchez. GT; SP-SancS

Old Molly Means was a hag and a witch. Molly Means. Margaret Abigail Walker. AmNP; BlSi; CP-WalkM; Klds

Old newspapers nobody's ever got to read again. (LL) Twenty-Year Marriage. Ai. GT

Old O.O. Blues, The. Al Young. CP-YounA

Old paths forget the bruised feet. They Are Not Missed. Jean Toomer. CP-ToomJ

Old Pettigrew. Melvin B. Tolson. GT

Old private charity. (LL) In Honor of David Anderson Brooks, My Father. Gwendolyn Brooks. SP-BrooG

Old Repair Man, The. Fenton Johnson. AmNP

Old Sac Village, The. Albery Allson Whitman. AAP Fr. Not a Man, and Yet a Man

Old Sailor. Langston Hughes. CP-HughL

Old Saint's Prayer, The. Priscilla Jane Thompson. CBWP-2

Old Section Boss, The. *Unknown.* BPo

Old Slave Woman, An. Joyce Sims Carrington. ShDr

Old Story, The. Paul Laurence Dunbar. CP-DunbP

Old, the cautious, the over-wise, The. Elderly Leaders. Langston Hughes. CP-HughL

Old time love withered, in seeing, off and on, An. All's Well. Amiri Baraka. SP-BaraA

Old Toyota, green as a frog, coughs and clanks, The. Talking in the Woods with Karl Amorelli. Etheridge Knight. SP-KnigE

Old Walt Whitman. Langston Hughes. CP-HughL; SP-HughL

Old Warrior Terror, The. Alice Walker. CP-WalkA

Old Witherington. Dudley Randall. NBV

Old Woman. Al Young. CP-YounA

Old woman across the way, The. The Whipping. Robert Hayden. CP-HaydR; IDB; PoBA; SSLK

Old woman in me walks patiently to the hospital, An. Revelation. Carole C. Gregory Clemmons. BlSi

Old Woman Remembers, An. Sterling A. Brown. CP-BrowS; PoBA

Old Words. Sonia Sanchez. SP-SancS

Old, worn harp that had been played, An. The Master-Player. Paul Laurence Dunbar. CP-DunbP

Old Yalluh Hammuh were a guy. Yalluh Hammuh. Margaret Abigail Walker. CP-WalkM

Old Year, The. Priscilla Jane Thompson. CBWP-2

Older, but no wiser than the defect of love. (LL) The New World. Amiri Baraka. SP-BaraA

Older than Mose / Will ever be. (LL) Mose is black and evil. Sterling A. Brown. CP-BrowS; Klds

Oldest joke / in the world, The. My Father's Telescope. Rita Dove. SP-DoveR

Ole Abe (God bless 'is ole soul!). Negro Soldier's Civil War Chant. *Unknown.* BPo

Ole Aunt Dinah, she's jes lak me. Jack and Dinah Want Freedom. *Unknown.* BPo; NAAAL

Ole King cotton, / Ole Man cotton. Old King Cotton. Sterling A. Brown. CP-BrowS

Ole Missus is a vile one. Southern Belle. Elma Stuckey. TtW

Ole Sheep Dey Know de Road, De. *Unknown.* BPo

Oliver Wendell Holmes. Joseph Seamon Cotter, Sr. EBAP

On a bright day, next week. Maya Angelou. CP-AngeM; SP-AngeM

On a Christmas Night. Langston Hughes. CP-HughL

On a Clean Book. Paul Laurence Dunbar. CP-DunbP

On a day when i would have believed. At Jonestown. Lucille Clifton. NAAAL

On a gnarled and naked tree. (LL) Song for a Dark Girl. Langston Hughes. CDC; CP-HughL; IDB; NAAAL; PoBA; SP-HughL

On a hill near Petersburg. James Hugo Johnston. Maggie Pogue Johnson. CBWP-4

On a New Year's Eve. June Jordan. SP-JordJ

On a Night of the Full Moon. Audre Lorde. CP-LordA; SP-LordA

On a Nook Called Fairyland. Henrietta Cordelia Ray. CBWP-3

On a Pallet of Straw. Langston Hughes. CP-HughL

On a quiet night. The Gathering. Charlie R. Braxton. CtF

On a Saturday night. (LL) Weekend Glory. Maya Angelou. CP-AngeM; SP-AngeM

On a snug evening I shall watch her fingers. Piano after War. Gwendolyn Brooks. AmNP; ESEAA; Klds; SP-BrooG

On a starry, wintry night. The Christ Child. Mary Weston Fordham. CBWP-2

On a straw-colored day. Dream. Solomon Edwards. NNP

On a summer's day as I sat by a stream. A Song. Paul Laurence Dunbar. CP-DunbP

On a verdant summer islet. Burial of a Fairy Queen. Mary E. Tucker. CBWP-1

On account of / You! (LL) Late last night I. Langston Hughes. CP-HughL; SP-HughL

On Aging. Maya Angelou. CP-AngeM; SP-AngeM

On an autumn day. Autumn God. Eugene B. Redmond. TtW

On an Old Deluded Soldier. George Moses Horton. SP-HortG

On Anne Spencer's table. Anne Spencer's Table. Langston Hughes. CP-HughL

On Apologies. Valerie Jean. SpiFl

On ballerina legs the dominant male commands the vista. Impala. Marilyn Nelson. SP-NelsM

On Becomin Successful. Ntozake Shange. TtW

On Becoming a Tiger. Lorna Goodison. GT

On Being Asked to Leave a Place of Honor for One of Comfort, Preferably in the Northern Suburbs. Alice Walker. CP-WalkA

On Being Brought from Africa to America. Phillis Wheatley. AfAmPo; BALP; CP-WheaP; CrDW; NAAAL; TtW

("May be refined, and join th' angelic train.") (LL) EBAP; Klds

On Being Head of the English Department. Pinkie Gordon Lane. BlSi; GT

On Broadway. Claude McKay. SP-McKaC

On Central Coast radio KTOM blasts. Watsonville after the Quake. Al Young. CP-YounA

On Death and the Resurrection. Margaret Abigail Walker. CP-WalkM

On Death's domain intent I fix my eyes. To a Gentleman and Lady on the Death of the Lady's Brother and Sister, and a Child of the Name Avis, Aged One Year. Phillis Wheatley. BlSi; CP-WheaP

On Declining Values. June Jordan. SP-JordJ

On Diverse Deviations. Maya Angelou. BlSi; CP-AngeM; SP-AngeM

On Extending the Olive Branch to My Own Self. Harriet Jacobs. SpiFl

On Friendship. Phillis Wheatley. CP-WheaP; EBAP

On Genessarett. Josephine D. Henderson Heard. CBWP-4

On Getting a Natural. Dudley Randall. FB; PoBA

On Hearing James W. Riley Read. Joseph Seamon Cotter, Sr. AAP; EBAP

On Hearing of the Intention of a Gentleman to Purchase the Poet's Freedom. George Moses Horton. AAP; EBAP; NAAAL

(Lines, On Hearing of the Intention of a Gentleman to Purchase the Poet's Freedom.) SP-HortG

On Hearing "The Girl with the Flaxen Hair." Nikki Giovanni. SP-GiovN

On her 36th birthday, Thomas had shown her. Wingfoot Lake. Rita Dove. SP-DoveR

On Imagination. Phillis Wheatley. BlSi; CP-WheaP; CrDW; NAAAL; TtW

("Cease then, my song, cease th' unequal lay.") (LL) EBAP

On jailhouse floor. (LL) Haiku: "Morning sun slants cell." Etheridge Knight. . ESEAA; TtW

On Liberty and Slavery. George Moses Horton. AAP; Klds; SP-HortG; TtW

(Liberty and Slavery.) AfAmPo

On Listening to the Spirituals. Lance Jeffers. PoBA; TtW

("When the master lived a king and I a starving hutted slave.") SSLK

On Lookout Mountain. Robert Hayden. CP-HaydR

On Messrs. Hussey and Coffin. Phillis Wheatley. CP-WheaP

On Midsummer's Eve. Audre Lorde. CP-LordA

On Moral Leadership as a Political Dilemma. June Jordan. SP-JordJ

On my back they've written history, Lord. Poem for Pearl's Dancers. Owen Dodson. TtW

On my desk is a small bottle. Jasmine. E. Ethelbert Miller. GT

On My Stand. Sharon Scott. JB

On My Way Out I passed You and the Varrazano Bridge. Audre Lorde. CP-LordA

On ochre walls in ice-formed caves shaggy Neanderthals marked their place in time. To My Son Parker, Asleep in the Next Room. Bob Kaufman. Klds; PoBA; SP-KaufB

On October the sixth it was a terrible night. Brock Hankton. *African-American Oral Tradition.* GetYo

On, on to the darkest continent. Dedicated to Dr. W. H. Sheppard. Maggie Pogue Johnson. CBWP-4

On Parting with a Friend. Mary Weston Fordham. CBWP-2

On Passing Two Negroes on a Dark Country Road Somewhere in Georgia. Conrad Kent Rivers. IDB; NNP

On Police Brutality. Margaret Abigail Walker. CP-WalkM

On Reaching Forty. Maya Angelou. CP-AngeM; SP-AngeM

On Recollection. Phillis Wheatley. CP-WheaP; EBAP

On Riots. Cy Leslie. NBP

On Seeing Diana Go Madddddddddd. Haki R. Madhubuti. BrTr

On Seeing the Black Male as #1 Sex Object in America. Etheridge Knight. SP-KnigE

On Seeing Two Brown Boys in a Catholic Church. Frank Horne. BANP; CDC; PoBA

On shining heights where Thought with stately tread. Emerson. Henrietta Cordelia Ray. CBWP-3

On Sight. Alice Walker. CP-WalkA

On smiling wealth, intemp'rance near began. The Intemperance Club. George Moses Horton. SP-HortG

On Stripping Bark from Myself. Alice Walker. CP-WalkA; NAAAL

On such a day as this I think. An April Day. Joseph Seamon Cotter, Sr. CDC

On Summer. George Moses Horton. AAP; SP-HortG

On summer afternoons I sit. La Vie C'est la Vie. Jessie Redmond Fauset. BANP; CDC

On sunny summer Sunday afternoons in Harlem. Passing. Langston Hughes. *Fr.* Montage of a Dream Deferred. CP-HughL

On the Anniversary Of Your Death. Karen L. Mitchell. GT

On the banks of her butterfly pond. Fishing among the Learned. Nikky Finney. SpiFl

On the Birth of a Black / Baby / Boy. Etheridge Knight. SP-KnigE

On the Birth of Bomani. Lucille Clifton. SP-ClifL

On the Birth of My Son, Malcolm Coltrane. Julius Lester. PoBA

On the bite of a kola nut. Africa I. Nikki Giovanni. SP-GiovN

On the bosom of his God. (LL) The Dying Fugitive. Frances Ellen Watkins Harper. CP-HarpF; TtW

On the Capture of General Lee. Phillis Wheatley. CP-WheaP

On the Concord River. Henrietta Cordelia Ray. CBWP-3

On the corner—116th and Lenox. Harlem Freeze Frame. Lebert Bethune. GT; PoBA

On the day that will always belong to you. Your Death. Rita Dove. Crnst

On the day when the Savoy. Projection. Langston Hughes. *Fr.* Montage of a Dream Deferred. CP-HughL

On the Death of a Young Gentleman. Phillis Wheatley. CP-WheaP; Crnst

On the Death of a Young Lady of Five Years of Age. Phillis Wheatley. CP-WheaP

On the Death of Allen's Son. Lucille Clifton. SP-ClifL

On the Death of Doctor Samuel Marshall. Phillis Wheatley. CP-WheaP

On the Death of Dr. Samuel Marshall. Phillis Wheatley. CP-WheaP

On the Death of Dr. Samuel Marshall, 1771. Phillis Wheatley. CP-WheaP

On the Death of General Wooster. Phillis Wheatley. CP-WheaP

On the Death of J.C. an Infant. Phillis Wheatley. CP-WheaP

On the Death of Lisa Lyman. Della Burt. BlSi

On the Death of Mr. Snider Murder'd by Richardson. Phillis Wheatley. CP-WheaP

On the Death of the Rev. Dr. Sewell, 1769. Phillis Wheatley. CP-WheaP

On the Death of the Rev. Mr. George Whitefield, 1770. Phillis Wheatley. EBAP

(Elegiac Poem on the Death of George Whitefield, An.) CP-WheaP

("Hail happy Saint on thy immortal throne!") CP-WheaP

(On the Death of the Rev. Mr. George Whitefield.) NAAAL

On the Death of the Rev'd Dr. Sewall, 1769. Phillis Wheatley. CP-WheaP

On the Death of W. C. Paul Laurence Dunbar. CP-DunbP

On the Death of William Edward Burghardt Du Bois by African Moonlight and Forgotten Shores. Conrad Kent Rivers. NBP; PoBA

On the Dedication of Dorothy Hall. Paul Laurence Dunbar. CP-DunbP

On the dusty earth-drum. Rain Music. Joseph Seamon Cotter, Sr. BANP; CDC; TtW

On the Edge. Audre Lorde. CP-LordA

On the Evening and the Morning. George Moses Horton. SP-HortG

On the Fine Arts Garden, Cleveland. Russell Atkins. PoBA

On the first day / I was told a lie. Pledge of Allegiance. Carl Hancock Rux. SpiFl

On the first day / malcolm. The Easter Bunny Blues or All I Want for Xmas Is the Loop. Ebon Dooley. PoBA

On the fourth of July in Sitka. On the Fourth of July in Sitka, 1982. Ishmael Reed. CP-ReedI

On the Fourth of July in Sitka, 1982. Ishmael Reed. CP-ReedI

On the Fugitive Slave Law. Elymas Payson Rogers. EBAP

"Law! What is law! The wise and sage." AAP

On the Ile de Gorée, M. Diop elegant. Double Take at Relais de L'Espadon. Thadious M. Davis. BlSi

On the last day of the year we have so much to be thankful for. The Last Day of the Year; or, New Year's Eve. Mrs. Henry Linden. CBWP-4

On the Loss of Energy. June Jordan. SP-JordJ

On the Morning St. Bernard. Glenn Joshua. CtF

On the morning you woke beside me—already thinking of going away. Mornings / of an impossible love. Alice Walker. CP-WalkA

On the Muse's huge, sun-spangled wings. (LL) Levitation with Baby. Marilyn Nelson. SP-NelsM

On the nights when the sky comes down. Sweet Honey in the Rock. E. Ethelbert Miller. TtW

On the outskirts of your tongue, tied still. (LL) Tongue-tied in Black and White. Michael S. Harper. ESEAA; SP-HarpM

On the Picture of a Child. Henrietta Cordelia Ray. CBWP-3

On the Pleasures of College Life. George Moses Horton. SP-HortG

On the Poetic Muse. George Moses Horton. SP-HortG

On the Projects Playground. Etheridge Knight. SP-KnigE

On the Pulse of Morning. Maya Angelou. CP-AngeM

On the radio a canary bewailed her luck. Lightnin' Blues. Rita Dove. SP-DoveR

On the rapids of the St. Lawrence. Henrietta Cordelia Ray. CBWP-3

On the Real World: Meditation #1. June Jordan. SP-JordJ

On the River. Paul Laurence Dunbar. CP-DunbP

On the Road. Paul Laurence Dunbar. CP-DunbP

On the Road. Claude McKay. SP-McKaC

On the road we met a blackman. Twenty-Six Ways of Looking at a Blackman. Raymond R. Patterson. ESEAA

On the Sea Wall. Paul Laurence Dunbar. CP-DunbP

On the shoals of Nowhere. Flotsam. Langston Hughes. CP-HughL

On the side of freedom stand? (LL) Slave Mother, The: "I have but four, the treasures of my soul." Frances Ellen Watkins Harper. CP-HarpF

On the side of God and changeless light. (LL) Nothing and Something. Frances Ellen Watkins Harper. CP-HarpF; EBAP

On the Spirit of Mildred Jordan. June Jordan. SP-JordJ

On the trunk of a haunted tree. (LL) The Haunted Oak. Paul Laurence Dunbar. AAP; AfAmPo; BANP; CP-DunbP; Klds; NAAAL

On the Truth of the Saviour. George Moses Horton. SP-HortG

On the Uptown Lexington Avenue Express: Martin Luther King Day 1995. Harris Duriel. SpiFl

On the wide veranda white. A Corn-Song. Paul Laurence Dunbar. CP-DunbP

On the Yard. Etheridge Knight. SP-KnigE

On their knees. (LL) Garden. Langston Hughes. CP-HughL; SP-HughL

On this bus to oblivion i bleed in the seat. Today I Am a Homicide in the North of the City. Wanda Coleman. NAAAL

On this day / the buffalo soldiers. Tyrone (1). Lucille Clifton. SP-ClifL

On Thursday's she buried her featherbed. Domino. Audre Lorde. CP-LordA

On Top of It All. Keith Gilyard. SpiFl

On top of two tall buildings. Gum. Jean Toomer. CP-ToomJ

On Trying to Imagine the Kiwi Pregnant. Clarence Major. GT

On Virtue. Phillis Wheatley. CP-WheaP; TtW

On Watching a Caterpillar Become a Butterfly. Clarence Major. NAAAL

On Watching a World Series Game. Sonia Sanchez. NBV

On Watching Politicians Perform at Martin Luther King's Funeral. Etheridge Knight. SP-KnigE

On Wednesday night. Wednesday Night Prayer Meeting. Jay Wright. PoBA

On what they hunger to become. (LL) Boat People. Yusef Komunyakaa. SP-KomuY

On Winter. George Moses Horton. SP-HortG

On Working White Liberals. Maya Angelou. CP-AngeM; SP-AngeM

On yardbird corners of embryonic hopes, drowned in a heroin tear. Bob Kaufman. SP-KaufB

On yonder oak, upon its lordliest height. Mistletoe. Mary E. Tucker. CBWP-1

On Youth and Age. Margaret Abigail Walker. CP-WalkM

On Youth and Age II. Margaret Abigail Walker. CP-WalkM

Once. Alice Walker. BlSi; CP-WalkA

"I/ never liked/ white folks." PoBA

"It is true--/ I've always loved." PoBA

Once a forest painted upon. Winter. Helen G. Quigless. BkSV

Once a Lady Told Me. Nikki Giovanni. SP-GiovN

Once a snowflake fell. Winter Poem. Nikki Giovanni. SP-GiovN

lnce a year marie laveau. Hoodoo Poem in Transient. Ishmael Reed. CP-ReedI

Once again simple. Alice Walker. CP-WalkA

Once and future dead, The. Lucille Clifton. SP-ClifL

Once I adopted. Madam and the Charity Child. Langston Hughes. CP-HughL; SP-HughL

Once I cried for new songs to sing. I Sing No New Songs. Frank Marshall Davis. PoBA

Once I lived the life of a millionaire. *African-American Oral Tradition.* GetYo

Once I saw large waves. At Sea. Jean Toomer. BALP; CP-ToomJ

Once i was chaste with. Sonia Sanchez. SP-SancS

Once I was good like the Virgin Mary and the Minister's wife. The Scarlet Woman. Fenton Johnson. BANP; EBAP; NAAAL; PoBA

Once I was immortal beside an ocean. The Maiden. Audre Lorde. CP-LordA; SP-LordA

Once in awhile. Poem on the Road; for Alice Walker. June Jordan. SP-JordJ

Once like a lady / In a silken dress. To the Three for Whom the Book. Countee Cullen. CP-CullC

Once Love grew bold and arrogant of air. Love's Chastening. Paul Laurence Dunbar. CP-DunbP

Once made a fairy rooster from. For My Sister Molly Who in the Fifties. Alice Walker. CP-WalkA; TtW

Once more I've begun the treatise; once more. Song: a Motion for History. Kenneth A. McClane. TtW

Once more, listening to the wind and rain. The Return. Arna Bontemps. CDC; GT; PoBA

Once more / The guns roar. Some Day. Langston Hughes. CP-HughL

Once on a Night in the Delta: A Report From Hell. Etheridge Knight. SP-KnigE

Once riding in Old Baltimore. Incident. Countee Cullen. BPo; CDC; CP-CullC; IDB; NAAAL; PoBA; SSLK

Once, the mighty waves of ocean. The Precious Pearl. Priscilla Jane Thompson. CBWP-2

Once the nation's chief was honored by the company of one. A Notable Dinner. Lizelia Augusta Jenkins Moorer. CBWP-3

Once they were sticks and stones. Names. Robert Hayden. CP-HaydR; GT

Once up u hurl a stone. Mike 65. Lennox Raphael. PoBA

Once Upon a Road. Jayne Cortez. SP-CortJ

Once upon a time, i a poet, transformed myself into a poem. Word Game. Wanda Coleman. TtW

Once upon a today and yesterday and nevermore there were 7 men. Fable. Etheridge Knight. SP-KnigE

Once when I walked into a room. Between Ourselves. Audre Lorde. CP-LordA

Once when my soul was newly shriven. The Light. Paul Laurence Dunbar. CP-DunbP

Once you were young. Parisian Beggar Woman. Langston Hughes. CP-HughL

One. Langston Hughes. CP-HughL; SP-HughL

One. Carolyn M. Rodgers. BPo

One beautiful morning in the month of May all was serene and / quiet. May. Mrs. Henry Linden. CBWP-4

One by one, the words. Reading Hölderlin on the Patio with the Aid of a Dictionary. Rita Dove. SP-DoveR

One cop enters a store. Treatment for Dance w/ Trick Ending. Ishmael Reed. CP-ReedI

One dark and dusty day. Stackolee. Unknown. NAAAL

One day Abba Jacob. Abba Jacob and Miracles. Marilyn Nelson. SP-NelsM

One day he became six eyes. Gangster Goes Legit. Ishmael Reed. CP-ReedI

One day I saw Chicago river move. Chicago. Margaret Abigail Walker. CP-WalkM; GT

One day I stopped by this friend of mine's house. Get In Out of the Rain. African-American Oral Tradition. GetYo

One day / Marilyn marched. Chic Freedom's Reflection. Alice Walker. CP-WalkA

One day she saw them coming into the garden. Rape Is Not a Poem. June Jordan. SP-JordJ

One day we lay beneath an apple tree. One Day We Played a Game. Countee Cullen. CP-CullC

One Day We Played a Game. Countee Cullen. CP-CullC

One day when me 'n' Dunbar wuz a-hoein' in de co'n. Me 'n' Dunbar. James David Corrothers. NAAAL

One day when the great Titanic was sinking away. Shine and the Titanic. Unknown. NAAAL

One day / You gonna walk in this house. Seduction. Nikki Giovanni. BrTr; SP-GiovN

One does such work as one will not. In the Matter of Two Men. James David Corrothers. BANP; TtW

One doubts, and one for pity's sake believes. (LL) A Thorn Forever in the Breast. Countee Cullen. CP-CullC

One Eyed Black Man in Nebraska. Sam Cornish. PoBA

One fatal mistake that is made today is gossip. Gossip. Mrs. Henry Linden. CBWP-4

One foot down, then hop! It's hot. Harlem Hopscotch. Maya Angelou. CP-AngeM; SP-AngeM

One for Charlie Mingus. Quincy Troupe. SpiFl

One for each foot. (LL) The Dozens. Audre Lorde. CP-LordA; SP-LordA

One Generation Passeth Away and Another Cometh. George Moses Horton. SP-HortG

One hand on her hip, one hand. Song of the Andoumboulou. Nathaniel Mackey. NAAAL

One hears and sees. Black Orpheus. Frederick, Jr. Bryant. BlFi

One horse you gave me, The. The Appaloosa. Michael S. Weaver. GT

One hundred and fifty million truth seekers. Holographs. Audre Lorde. CP-LordA

100,000 bees make a sturdy hive. Production. Audre Lorde. CP-LordA

125th Street. Langston Hughes. SP-HughL Fr. Montage of a Dream Deferred. CP-HughL

125th Street and Abomey. Audre Lorde. CP-LordA

One hundred years of headrags, bandages. Paul Laurence Dunbar: 1872-1906. Michael S. Harper. SP-HarpM

One innocent spring. Now Long Ago. Maya Angelou. CP-AngeM; SP-AngeM

One is an igloo. History as Bandages: Polka Dots and Moonbeams. Michael S. Harper. SP-HarpM

One / is never enough for me. Leanna's Poem. Lucille Clifton. SP-ClifL

One Life. Paul Laurence Dunbar. CP-DunbP

One Lives, One Dies: Both/And: A Choice of Colors. Michael S. Harper. SP-HarpM

One lovely summer afternoon when balmy breezes blew. To Clements' Ferry. Josephine D. Henderson Heard. CBWP-4

One Minus One Minus One. June Jordan. SP-JordJ

One More Round. Maya Angelou. CP-AngeM; SP-AngeM

One More "S" in the U.S.A. Langston Hughes. CP-HughL

One More Time. Alvin Aubert. TtW

One More Time. Amiri Baraka. SP-BaraA

One morning just before Christmas. The Lost Daughter. Marilyn Nelson. SP-NelsM

One morning there was a cloud couldn't be found. Hitler, You Lied to Me. African-American Oral Tradition. GetYo

One night as I awoke a little wee chintz spoke to me as I raised my head. The Chintz. African-American Oral Tradition. GetYo

One night in my room, still and beamless. The Phantom Kiss. Paul Laurence Dunbar. CP-DunbP

One / O-N-E / Stair / S-T-A-I-R. Sophie, Climbing the Stairs. Dolores Kendrick. ESEAA

One of our race's great lights has gone out to the world. Paul Laurence Dunbar. Mrs. Henry Linden. CBWP-4

One of our race's greatest needs in this country today. The Y. M. C. A. Mrs. Henry Linden. CBWP-4

One of the most distinguished members of his race. (LL) Mr. Z. M. Carl Holman. Klds

One of the signs of concussion. The Dangerous Carnival. Marilyn Nelson. SP-NelsM

One of those impossibly lonely. Still Lives. Al Young. CP-YounA

One ounce of truth benefits. Nikki Giovanni. SP-GiovN

One side tight in the case. From a Town in Minnesota. Michael S. Harper. SP-HarpM

One Sided Shoot-out. Don L. Lee. BPo; NBV; PoBA

One single word of heartfelt kindness. Kindness. Mary E. Tucker. CBWP-1

One Snapshot I Couldn't Take in France, The. Al Young. SpiFl

One spring the circus gave. A Hill of Beans. Rita Dove. SP-DoveR

One star that I loved ere the fields went brown. (LL) A Winter Twilight. Angelina Weld Grimké. CDC; NAAAL; PoBA; ShDr

One stormy April afternoon. I Fell Asleep on the Couch. Marilyn Nelson. Fr. I Dream the Book of Jonah. SP-NelsM

One tenth of the population. America's Young Black Joe! Langston Hughes. CP-HughL

One thing about me. Seven Women's Blessed Assurance. Maya Angelou. CP-AngeM

One thing you left with us, Jack Johnson. Strange Legacies. Sterling A. Brown. CP-BrowS; Klds; PoBA

One thousand saxophones infiltrate the city. Battle Report. Bob Kaufman. AmNP

One Time Henry Dreamed the Number. Doughtry Long. BPo; BrTr; PoBA

One to Love. Alfred Islay Walden. AAP

One, two, and three. Leaves. Countee Cullen. GT

One, two, three, / four tiny black wheels on a Dove Bar Cart. Washington Square Park and a Game of Chess. Christopher Stanard. SpiFl

One Volume Missing. Rita Dove. SP-DoveR

One wants a Teller in a time like this. Gwendolyn Brooks. SP-BrooG

One Way of Taking Leave. Sterling A. Brown. CP-BrowS

One-Way Ticket. Langston Hughes. CP-HughL; SP-HughL

One West Coast. Al Young. CP-YounA

One Who Got Away, The. Audre Lorde. CP-LordA

One who sings "chansons vulgaires." Young Singer. Langston Hughes. CP-HughL

One whose love will never end. Accompanying a Gift. Lizelia Augusta Jenkins Moorer. CBWP-3

One whose majestic presence ever here. In Memoriam Frederick Douglass. Henrietta Cordelia Ray. CBWP-3

One Within. Jean Toomer. CP-ToomJ

One Year After. Claude McKay. SP-McKaC

One Year Ago. David Llorens. BrTr

One Year Ago. Adah Isaacs Menken. CBWP-1

One Year to Life on the Grand Central Shuttle. Audre Lorde. CP-LordA

One's still in, a goose egg's. Sack 'A Woe: Gallstones as History. Michael S. Harper. SP-HarpM

Ones who live in the desert, The. Sonora Desert Poem. Lucille Clifton. SP-ClifL

Onion Bucket. Lorenzo Thomas. BlFi; GT; PoBA; TtW

Only a Blush. Mary E. Tucker. CBWP-1

Only a few will really understand. One Sided Shoot-out. Don L. Lee. BPo; NBV; PoBA

Only a little scrap of blue. A Little Child Shall Lead Them. Frances Ellen Watkins Harper. CP-HarpF

Only a word— a little word. Frances Ellen Watkins Harper. CP-HarpF

Only child was she of a rich pair, The. Albery Allson Whitman. *Fr.* Leelah Misled. EBAP

Only d clucks threw pennies. (LL) Catechism of d Neoamerican Hoodoo Church. Ishmael Reed. CP-ReedI; NBV

Only dumb guys fight. Prize Fighter. Langston Hughes. CP-HughL

Only heaven. (LL) Luck. Langston Hughes. CP-HughL; SP-HughL

Only hungers left, The. Sacrifice. Audre Lorde. CP-LordA; SP-LordA

Only / if we fail. (LL) No Reservations. Nikki Giovanni. BrTr; SP-GiovN

Only in This Way. Margaret Goss Burroughs. BlSi

Only just a prince. (LL) Let's Majeste. Maya Angelou. CP-AngeM; SP-AngeM

Only our hearts will argue hard. Roman Poem Number Thirteen. June Jordan. SP-JordJ

Only parts of the pain of living. Detroit 1958. Al Young. CP-YounA; ESEAA

Only quiet death. Threnody. Waring Cuney. AmNP; BANP

Only Race There Is, The. Al Young. CP-YounA

Only / railroad / guranteed / not to break down!, The. History-Wise #22. Amiri Baraka. SP-BaraA

Only the casket left, the jewel gone. Charles Sumner. Charlotte L. Forten Grimké. AAP

Only the deep well. I Break the Sky. Owen Dodson. PoBA

Only the infants / too young to know of tribes. At the Border of Constant Disaster. Jerry W., Jr. Ward. CtF

Only the Polished Skeleton. Countee Cullen. CP-CullC

Only the red-skins know what. Bitter Chocolate. Ishmael Reed. CP-ReedI

Only these black translucent wings. Murmur. Esther Iverem. GT

Only to keep / his little fear. After Kent State. Lucille Clifton. SP-ClifL

Only two mites, the widow said. The Widow's Mites. Frances Ellen Watkins Harper. CP-HarpF

Only Woman Blues. Langston Hughes. CP-HughL

"Onward Christian Soldiers!" Frank Marshall Davis. FB

Onward, onward, sons of freedom. Be Active. Frances Ellen Watkins Harper. CP-HarpF

Onward to her destination. Our Hero. Frances Ellen Watkins Harper. CP-HarpF

OoBlahDee / Ooolyacoo. Speech #38 (or Y We Say It This Way). Amiri Baraka. SP-BaraA

Oooo, moon you look so lovely. The Tutti Colori Quality of Light. Al Young. CP-YounA

Ooouu-oo-baby-I-love-you. (LL) Circling the Daughter. Etheridge Knight. SP-KnigE

Open Heart. Sekou Sundiata. SpiFl

Open Letter. Owen Dodson. BALP

Open Letter to All Black Poets, An. Samuel F. Reynolds. SpiFl

Open Letter to the South. Langston Hughes. CP-HughL

Open mouthed statues built with. Eclipse. Albert E., Jr. Haynes. BlFi

Open the drawer. / There are scissors there. For Mary, Fourth Month. Marilyn Nelson. SP-NelsM

Open your front door baby black dark come home for good. (LL) Blues for Franks Wooten; House of the Lifting of the Head. Tom Weatherly. GT; NBV

Opening Service, An. Clara Ann Thompson. CBWP-2

Opium-Eater, The. Mary E. Tucker. CBWP-1

Opportunity. Paul Laurence Dunbar. CP-DunbP

Oppression. Langston Hughes. CP-HughL

Opulent oracle—it's a terrible thing! It's a Terrible Thing! Everett Hoagland. BPo

Or bring men peace, or leave them satisfied. (LL) Whores. Margaret Abigail Walker. CP-WalkM

Or dead in the Mississippi mud. (LL) A Poem for Myself (Or Blues for a Mississippi Black Boy). Etheridge Knight. BkSV; SP-KnigE

Or does it explode? (LL) Harlem. Langston Hughes. CrDW; GT; NAAAL; PoBA; SP-HughL

Or having it, fulfill. (LL) Madrid. Jay Wright. ESEAA

Or / hoodoo ecology vs the judeo-. Al Capone in Alaska. Ishmael Reed. CP-ReedI

Or is really October in Houston? Houston in October. Al Young. CP-YounA

Or like the tender struggle of a fan. (LL) Flags. Gwendolyn Brooks. AmNP; SP-BrooG

Or silly / but always / white. (LL) Song for a Thin Sister. Audre Lorde. CP-LordA; SP-LordA

Or staring boy—and. (LL) Perseus. Robert Hayden. CP-HaydR

Or to his dances in old Tinbridge flat. (LL) When de Saints Go Ma'ching Home. Sterling A. Brown. AmNP; CP-BrowS

Orange Chiffon. Jayne Cortez. BlSi

Orator finished his eulogy, The. The Temple. Sterling A. Brown. CP-BrowS

Orchard at Night in Rain Light, The. Al Young. CP-YounA

Oregon. Bob Kaufman. GT

Orhan Vele, Turkish listener to Istanbul, I'm cool. Moon Over Matter. Al Young. CP-YounA

Oriental Ballerina, The. Rita Dove. NAAAL; SP-DoveR

Oriflamme. Jessie Redmond Fauset. BANP; BlSi; PoBA; ShDr

Original. / Ragged-round. / Rich-robust. Malcolm X. Gwendolyn Brooks. BALP; PoBA; TtW

Origins. Keorapetse W. Kgositsile. PoBA

Oriole sings in the greening grove, The. Summer in the South. Paul Laurence Dunbar. CP-DunbP; GT

Orisha. Jayne Cortez. BlSi

Orishas. Larry Neal. NBP

Orphan Girl, An. Mrs. Henry Linden. CBWP-4

Orphan, yes, An. But not. Fragment Reflection I. Doris Turner. JB

Osawatomie Brown / killed by pro-slavery. Reports: Kansas. Michael S. Harper. SP-HarpM

Oseola McCarty. Evelyn E. Shockley. CtF

Oshun's Table. Audre Lorde. CP-LordA

Ostriches and Grandmothers! Amiri Baraka. SP-BaraA

Othello Jones Dresses for Dinner. Ed Roberson. PoBA

Other acquainted years. On Reaching Forty. Maya Angelou. CP-AngeM; SP-AngeM

Other loves I have known. Proof. Bessie Calhoun Bird. BlSi

Other night I thought I heard a dog bark, The. Stackolee in Hell. *African-American Oral Tradition.* GetYo

Others may never feel tyrannic sway? (LL) Should you, my lord, while you pursue my song. Phillis Wheatley. BPo; Klds

Others might think it's like preaching to mules. Easter Sermon, 1866. Marilyn Nelson. *Fr.* Thus Far by Faith. SP-NelsM

Otter and quaking aspen. Naming the Stories. Audre Lorde. CP-LordA

Our anguish and our anodyne. (LL) From the corpse woodpiles, from the ashes. Robert Hayden. CP-HaydR

Our best singers. The Blues (in Two Parts). Val Ferdinand. NBV

Our birth and death are easy hours, like sleep. The Struggle Staggers Us. Margaret Abigail Walker. CP-WalkM

Our bodies made rain. Sonia Sanchez. SP-SancS

Our Club Work. Mrs. Henry Linden. CBWP-4

Our cup of joy was overfilled. A Dialogue. Lizelia Augusta Jenkins Moorer. CBWP-3

Our Days Are Numbered. Alicia Loy Johnson. BrTr

Our English Friends. Frances Ellen Watkins Harper. CP-HarpF

"Our Fadder, Which are in Heaben!" He Paid Me Seven. *Unknown.* BPo

Our family tree is in the sear. Joseph Cephas Holly. AAP

Our fancies are but joys all unexprest. A Fragment. Henrietta Cordelia Ray. CBWP-3

Our flesh that was a battle-ground. The Litany of the Dark People. Countee Cullen. CP-CullC

Our good knight, Ted, girds his broadsword on. The Knight. Paul Laurence Dunbar. CP-DunbP

Our Grandmothers. Maya Angelou. CP-AngeM

Our Growing Day. Jean Toomer. CP-ToomJ

Our hearts are filled with pride to-day. Welcome to Hon. Frederick Douglass. Josephine D. Henderson Heard. CBWP-4

Our hearts beat prouder for the blood we inherit. (LL) Memorial Wreath. Dudley Randall. IDB; NNP; PoBA

Our heliteam had mid-air blowout. Fixing Certificates: Dog Tags: Letters Home. Michael S. Harper. SP-HarpM

Our Hero. Frances Ellen Watkins Harper. CP-HarpF

Our hips, / they a poem to pulchritude. About Our Hips. Harriet Jacobs. SpiFl

Our Jake at three woke up one morning. Icarus Dream. Marilyn Nelson. *Fr.* The Plotinus Suite. SP-NelsM

Our kingdom was not of this world. Now the Time Is Ripe to Be. Jon Goncalves. BlFi

Our Land. Langston Hughes. CP-HughL

Our Lives. Sharon Scott. JB

Our Martyred Soldiers. Paul Laurence Dunbar. CP-DunbP

Our mothers, / when asked. Feminism. Carolyn M. Rodgers. TtW

Our mothers wrung hell and hardtack from row. American Sonnet (10). Wanda Coleman. NAAAL

Our moulting days are in the twilight stage. Garnishing the Aviary. Margaret Else Danner. *Fr.* Far from Africa: Four Poems. AmNP; BPo; NNP; PoBA

Our Natures Rise. Kalamu ya Salaam. *Fr.* New Orleans Haiku. SpiFl

Our Need. Margaret Abigail Walker. CP-WalkM

Our Noble Booker T. Washington. Mrs. Henry Linden. CBWP-4

Our own shadows disappear as the feet of thousands. Poem for South AFrican Women. June Jordan. SP-JordJ

Our park empty. Three O'Clock Love Song. Michael S. Harper. GT

Our Richard Allen in his early youth. Rt. Rev. Richard Allen. Josephine D. Henderson Heard. CBWP-4

Our roads are ridden. For Sammy Younge. Charlie Cobb. PoBA

Our speech slurs now. Nook. George Barlow. GT

Our Spirit Stands. Glenis Redmond Sherer. CtF

Our story didn't make the six o'clock news. Sand. Dominique Parker. SpiFl

Our summer's gone. My Life Has Turned to Blue. Maya Angelou. CP-AngeM; SP-AngeM

Our Task. Henrietta Cordelia Ray. CBWP-3

Our voices waved upwards into a tide / that wrapped itself around the island. Island within Island. Henry L. Dumas. GT

Our women we begin with you. Womenblack: We Begin with You. Haki R. Madhubuti. Crnst

Our / YOUR FRIEND CHARLIE pawnshop. Riot: 60's. Maya Angelou. CP-AngeM; SP-AngeM

Ours is the ancient story. For Daughters of Magdalen. Countee Cullen. CP-CullC

Out here, where any rambling bed—of sea-. The Reach. Carl Phillips. GT

Out in de night a sad bird moans. The Memory of Martha. Paul Laurence Dunbar. CP-DunbP

Out in the cold mid the dreary night. Frances Ellen Watkins Harper. CP-HarpF

Out in the Country of My Country (Peterborough, New Hampshire). June Jordan. SP-JordJ

Out in the Desert. Josephine D. Henderson Heard. CBWP-4

Out in the night thou art the sun. Star of Ethiopia. Lucian B. Watkins. BANP

Out in the sky the great dark clouds are massing. Ships That Pass in the Night. Paul Laurence Dunbar. BANP; CDC; CP-DunbP

Out in the street. (What Did I Do to Be So) Black and Blue? Thomas ("Fats") Waller, Andy Razaf *and* Harry Brooks. NAAAL

Out-of-Body Experience. Jenoyne Adams. CtF

Out of her womb of pain my mother spat me. Story Books on a Kitchen Table. Audre Lorde. CP-LordA; GT; SP-LordA

Out of love. No Regrets. Langston Hughes. CP-HughL; SP-HughL

Out of my flesh that hungers. On a Night of the Full Moon. Audre Lorde. CP-LordA; SP-LordA

Out of my heart, one day, I wrote a song. Misapprehension. Paul Laurence Dunbar. BPo; CP-DunbP

Out of my heart, one treach'rous winter's day. Love and Grief. Paul Laurence Dunbar. CP-DunbP

Out of my heart's long yearning. Birmingham, 1963. Margaret Abigail Walker. CP-WalkM

Out of Pocket. Kevin Powell. CtF

Out of silence. Koto Music/Singing. Al Young. CP-YounA

Out of the dark raw earth. Alabama. Julia Fields. PoBA

Out of the Deep. Clara Ann Thompson. CBWP-2

Out of the Depths. Derek Walcott. *Fr.* The Schooner *Flight.* ESEAA

Out of the depths of a heart of love. A Valentine. Priscilla Jane Thompson. CBWP-2

Out of the dust of dreams. Fairies. Langston Hughes. CP-HughL

Out of the Earth, this love. For Our Women. Larry Neal. BlFi

Out of the shadow, I am come in to you whole a black holy man. Study Peace. Amiri Baraka. PoBA

Out of the sunshine and out of the heat. The Dove. Paul Laurence Dunbar. CP-DunbP

Out of the tense awed darkness, my Frangepani comes. Rainy Season Love Song. Gladys May Casely Hayford. CDC; ShDr

Out of the Wind. Audre Lorde. CP-LordA

Out of Work. Langston Hughes. CP-HughL

Out to the Hard Road. Audre Lorde. CP-LordA

Out, upon the deep old ocean. On Genessarett. Josephine D. Henderson Heard. CBWP-4

Outcast, The. Josephine D. Henderson Heard. CBWP-4

Outcast. Claude McKay. AmNP; BALP; PoBA; SP-McKaC ("For the dim regions whence my father came.") NAAAL

Outcast. Alice Walker. NAAAL

Outcast from her home in Syria. Dedication Poem. Frances Ellen Watkins Harper. CP-HarpF

Outer space is / inconceivably / intimate. (LL) Anti-Father. Rita Dove. SP-DoveR

Outlines. Audre Lorde. CP-LordA

Outside. Audre Lorde. CP-LordA

Outside the rain upon the street. A Musical. Paul Laurence Dunbar. CP-DunbP

Over and over again. (LL) Love Poem. Audre Lorde. CP-LordA; SP-LordA

Over Manhattan Bridge. Brooklyn. Michael S. Weaver. SpiFl

Over my head. Freedom in the Air. *Unknown.* NAAAL

Over my shoulder, to the left. Waking Up in Santa Cruz at Sea. Al Young. CP-YounA

Over the earth, just as the legends prophesy. (LL) Tou Wan Speaks to Her Husband Liu Sheng. Rita Dove. ESEAA; SP-DoveR

Over the eye behind the moon's cloud. Raison d'Etre. Oliver Pitcher. AmNP; Klds; NNP

Over the foaming ocean. Poem, A: "Over the foaming ocean." Frances Ellen Watkins Harper. CP-HarpF

Over the free / cold / land. (LL) Harriet Tubman. Samuel Allen. Crnst; TtW

Over the hills and the valleys of dreaming. Paul Laurence Dunbar. CP-DunbP

Over the warts on the bumpy. Sadie's Playhouse. Margaret Else Danner. Klds; PoBA

Overheard / a brother saying. July 27. Norman Jordan. NBV

Overnights. Alice Walker. CP-WalkA

Owl In Daytime, The. Thylias Moss. GT

Owned her father all the fact'ries. The Pariah. James Edwin Campbell. AAP

Oxford is a legend. Margaret Abigail Walker. CP-WalkM

Oya. Audre Lorde. CP-LordA; SP-LordA

P

Pachuta, Mississippi/a /Memoir A Memoir. Al Young. CP-YounA

Paean. Jonathan Henderson Brooks. CDC

Pagan. Alice Walker. CP-WalkA

Pagan Isms, The. Claude McKay. BPo; SP-McKaC

Pagan Prayer. Countee Cullen. CP-CullC

Pages for a Friend. Ntozake Shange. IHS

Pain and labor of oppression gave the Western world its birth. The Pharaohs of Today. Lizelia Augusta Jenkins Moorer. CBWP-3

Pains of insecurity surround me. Back Again, Home. Haki R. Madhubuti. BALP; BPo; NAAAL

Pains with a Light Touch. Haki R. Madhubuti. BrTr

Paint. Langston Hughes. CP-HughL

Painted Lady, The. Margaret Else Danner. BPo

Painting Drunken Twilight. George Barlow. GT

Painting / (Frida Kahlo). Elizabeth Alexander. GT

Paintings with stiff. Primitives. Dudley Randall. BALP; BPo; BrTr; NBV

Pair in One. Langston Hughes. CP-HughL

Pair of soft, black eyes, A. A Home Greeting. Priscilla Jane Thompson. CBWP-2

Pale Ant. Ellease Southerland. GT

Pale Blue Casket, The. Oliver Pitcher. NNP; PoBA

Pale brown Moses went down to Egypt land. Benediction. Bob Kaufman. SP-KaufB

Pale, delightful lady. Pale Lady. Langston Hughes. CP-HughL

Pale Lady. Langston Hughes. CP-HughL

Pale morning light, dying in shadows. Picasso's Balcony. Bob Kaufman. SP-KaufB

Palm Drive Palo Alto. Al Young. CP-YounA

Palm Sunday. Lucille Clifton. SP-ClifL

Palm Sunday, 1866. Marilyn Nelson. *Fr.* Thus Far by Faith. SP-NelsM

Palm Wine Seller, The. Gladys May Casely Hayford. ShDr

Pamela. Rita Dove. SP-DoveR

Pansy. Mary Effie Lee Newsome. CDC

Panther. Sam Cornish. PoBA

Panther Man. James A. Emanuel. BPo; NBV

Papa called her Pearl when he came home. Taking in Wash. Rita Dove. SP-DoveR

Papa, don't you see my shoes? Barefoot Blues. Langston Hughes. CP-HughL

Paper is neither kind nor cruel. Paperweight. Audre Lorde. CP-LordA

Paperweight. Audre Lorde.
(After a First Book.) CP-LordA

Parable of the Moth. Marilyn Nelson. *Fr.* The Plotinus Suite. SP-NelsM

Parade. Langston Hughes. *Fr.* Montage of a Dream Deferred. CP-HughL

Paradox, The. Paul Laurence Dunbar. AAP; CP-DunbP; Klds; PoBA

Paradox. Angelina Weld Grimké. CDC

Parapoetics. Eugene B. Redmond. NBV; TtW

Parasitosis. Ronda M. Davis. JB

Pardners. Sterling A. Brown. CP-BrowS

Pardon Me. Oktavi. CtF

Pariah, The. James Edwin Campbell. AAP

Paris. Al Young. CP-YounA

Parish Doctor. Sterling A. Brown. CP-BrowS

Parisian Beggar Woman. Langston Hughes. CP-HughL

Park Bench. Langston Hughes. CP-HughL

Park Benching. Langston Hughes. CP-HughL

Parker's Mood. Clarence Beeks. NAAAL

Park's beautiful, The. On the Fine Arts Garden, Cleveland. Russell Atkins. PoBA

Parsley. Rita Dove. ESEAA; NAAAL; SP-DoveR; TtW

Part of my charm. Look for You Yesterday, Here You Come Today. Amiri Baraka. SP-BaraA; SSLK

Parted. Paul Laurence Dunbar. CP-DunbP

Parted. Clara Ann Thompson. CBWP-2

Particulars. Rita Dove. Crnst

Parting, The. Josephine D. Henderson Heard. CBWP-4

Parting. Audre Lorde. CP-LordA

Parting Hymn, A. Charlotte L. Forten Grimké. BlSi; NAAAL

Parting Kiss, The. Josephine D. Henderson Heard. CBWP-4

Parting Lovers, The. Mrs. Henry Linden. CBWP-4

Party, The. Paul Laurence Dunbar. AmNP; CP-DunbP

Party is on, The. Tequila Jazz. Bob Kaufman. SP-KaufB

Party Time. Audre Lorde. CP-LordA

Party was going at the Shady Nook, The. Hobo Ben. *African-American Oral Tradition.* GetYo

Partytime Monkey, *see also* Poolshooting Monkey *and* Signifying Monkey. *African-American Oral Tradition.* GetYo

Pass it on. (LL) Listen children / keep this in the place. Lucille Clifton. IHS; PoBA; SP-ClifL

Passage, The. Rita Dove. ESEAA

Passage, The, *from the German of* J. L. Uhland. Paul Laurence Dunbar. CP-DunbP

Passing. Langston Hughes. *Fr.* Montage of a Dream Deferred. CP-HughL

Passing Love. Langston Hughes. CP-HughL

Passing men in the street who are dead. Conclusion. Audre Lorde. CP-LordA; SP-LordA

Passing of the Old Year. Mary Weston Fordham. CBWP-2

Passing Time. Maya Angelou. CP-AngeM; SP-AngeM

Passion and Love. Paul Laurence Dunbar. CP-DunbP

Passions. Yusef Komunyakaa. SP-KomuY

Past, The. Mary Weston Fordham. CBWP-2

Past. Sonia Sanchez. SP-SancS
"Come into Black geography."
Earth Mother.
Woman.
Young/Black/Girl.

Past has been a mint, The. History. Langston Hughes. CP-HughL

Past my grave each night shall file,. (LL) When I Die. Fenton Johnson. CDC

Pastoral: "Annette came through the meadows." Henrietta Cordelia Ray. CBWP-3

Pastoral. Rita Dove. NAAAL

Pastoral. Langston Hughes. CP-HughL

Pastourelle. Donald Jeffrey Hayes. AmNP

Patchwork Quilt, A. Margaret Abigail Walker. CP-WalkM

Path, The. Paul Laurence Dunbar. CP-DunbP

Pathological Puzzle. Langston Hughes. CP-HughL

Pathway: From Son to Father. Lenard D. Moore. IHS

Pathways: From Mother to Mother. Audre Lorde. CP-LordA

Patience. Nikki Giovanni. SP-GiovN

Patience. . . patience. Frank Horne. BPo

Patient: Rockland County Sanitarium, The. Calvin C. Hernton. *See* Madhouse.

Patient, we pray and wait and weep and pray. The Sit-in. Darwin T. Turner. BALP

Patricia's Poem. June Jordan. SP-JordJ

Patriotic Ode on the Fourteenth Anniversary of the Persecution of Charlie Chaplin. Bob Kaufman. PoBA

Patriot's Lament, The. Joseph Cephas Holly. AAP

Patroness. Gerald William Barrax. Klds

Paul and Silas bound in jail. Keep Your Eyes on the Prize. *Unknown.* CrDW

Paul Laurence Dunbar. James David Corrothers. AfAmPo; BANP
("He came, a dark youth, singing in the dawn.") NAAAL

Paul Laurence Dunbar, *for Herbert Martin.* Robert Hayden. CP-HaydR; ESEAA; GT

Paul Laurence Dunbar. Mrs. Henry Linden. CBWP-4

Paul Laurence Dunbar: 1872-1906. Michael S. Harper. SP-HarpM

Paul Laurence Dunbar Chambers. Mr. P. C. Michael S. Harper. SP-HarpM

Paul Laurence Dunbar in the Tenderloin. Ishmael Reed. CP-Reed; ESEAA

Paul Robeson. Gwendolyn Brooks. BrTr; PoBA

Paul Vesey's Ledger. Samuel Allen. TtW
"As King grew cold on a Memphis slab."

Paula of the trembling brown cheeks and silent tears. For Paula Cooper (The 18 Year Old Who Waits on Death Row). Jackie Warren-Moore. SpiFl

Pauper's Grave, The. Benjamin Clark. EBAP

Pausing at the edge of the wood. Cassandra and Friend. Norman Henry, II Pritchard. GT

Pavlov. Naomi Long Madgett. BPo

Pay Day. Langston Hughes. *Fr.* Seven Moments of Love. CP-HughL

Pay Your Debts. Mrs. Henry Linden. CBWP-4

Paysagesque. Norman Henry, II Pritchard. GT

Peace. Frances Ellen Watkins Harper. CP-HarpF

Peace. Langston Hughes. BPo; CP-HughL

Peace Be Still. *Unknown.* NAAAL

Peace Be with You. Bob Kaufman. SP-KaufB

Peace Conference in an American Town. Langston Hughes. CP-HughL

Peace on Earth. Audre Lorde. CP-LordA

Peacock Poems: 1, The. Sherley Anne Williams. NAAAL

Peacock Room, The. Robert Hayden. CP-HaydR; FB

Pearl Harbor. *African-American Oral Tradition.* GetYo

Pearle's Poem. Primus St. John. GT

Pearls. Rita Dove. SP-DoveR

Peeps a maple-sugar child. (LL) Winter Sweetnes. Langston Hughes. CP-HughL

Peers. Jean Toomer. CP-ToomJ

Pen, The. Mary Weston Fordham. CBWP-2

Penitent Considers Another Coming of Mary, A. Gwendolyn Brooks. SP-BrooG

Penitential Cries of Jupiter Hammond, The. Gary Smith. GT

Pennsylvania Station in New York, The. Langston Hughes. CP-HughL; Klds
("Pennsylvania Station.") AmNP

Peonage System, The. Lizelia Augusta Jenkins Moorer. CBWP-3

People. Jean Toomer. CP-ToomJ; GT

People Burning, The. Amiri Baraka. SP-BaraA

People die from loneliness. One. Carolyn M. Rodgers. BPo

People have eaten fried fish. In Answer to Your Silly Question. Alice Walker. CP-WalkA

People know, The. A Little More about the Brothers and Sisters. Sharon Scott. JB

People of Letters. Al Young. CP-YounA

People of Unrest. Margaret Abigail Walker. CP-WalkM; GT

People protest in sprawling lightless ways. Gwendolyn Brooks. SP-BrooG

People say they have a hard time. For de Lawd. Lucille Clifton. PoBA; SP-ClifL

People who are going to be. Generations. Lucille Clifton. SP-ClifL

People who have no children can be hard. Gwendolyn Brooks. *Fr.* The Children of the Poor. Crnst, *sect.* 1, *pt.* 1–5; NAAAL; SP-BrooG, *sect.* 1, *pt.* 1–5.

People who have no children can be hard. The Children of the Poor. Gwendolyn Brooks. SP-BrooG, *sect.* I, *pt.* 1-5

People's Literary, De. Maggie Pogue Johnson. CBWP-4

Perception can force you to crawl. Looking a Mad Dog Dead in the Eyes. Yusef Komunyakaa. SP-KomuY

Perchance, the friend who cheered thy early years. Judge Not. Josephine D. Henderson Heard. CBWP-4

Perched at the railing of a Portuguese. Saudades: The Portuguese Blues. Al Young. CP-YounA

Percy / 68. Glenn Myles. NBP

Perfect Orchestra, The. Henrietta Cordelia Ray. CBWP-3

Perfection. Alice Walker. CP-WalkA

Performers, The. Robert Hayden. CP-HaydR

Perfume of your body dulls my sense, The. Flower of Love. Claude McKay. BALP; SP-McKaC

Perhaps. Lucille Clifton. SP-ClifL

Perhaps. Bob Kaufman. Klds

Perhaps a strange woman. Berlin Is Hard on Colored Girls. Audre Lorde. CP-LordA

Perhaps he left the newspaper stand that morning dazed, a few pennies lighter. Jack Johnson Does the Eagle Rock. Thylias Moss. ESEAA

Perhaps one morning the sky will be. Immani in Sunburst Summer: a Chant. Askia M. Toure. SpiFl

Perhaps these are not poetic / times / at all. (LL) For Saundra. Nikki Giovanni. BrTr; NAAAL; SP-GiovN; TtW

Perhaps / This is the way. Antigone I. Herbert Martin. PoBA

Perhaps what beans and potatoes. Customs and Culture? Ted Joans. TtW

Perhaps / You will recall / John Brown. (LL) October 16: The Raid. Langston Hughes. CP-HughL; PoBA; SP-HughL

Perhaps / You will remember / John Brown. October 16: The Raid. Langston Hughes. CP-HughL; PoBA; SP-HughL

Persephone Abducted. Rita Dove. NAAAL

Perseus. Robert Hayden. CP-HaydR

Personal. Langston Hughes. AmNP; CP-HughL; SP-HughL

Personal Jihad. Gaston Neal. BlFi

Personal Letter No. 2. Sonia Sanchez. SP-SancS

Personal Letter No. 3. Sonia Sanchez. ESEAA; SP-SancS; SSLK

Personality Sketch: Bill, A. Ronda M. Davis. JB

Perspectives. Dudley Randall. AmNP

Petals, the. (LL) Montmartre. Langston Hughes. CP-HughL; Klds

Petite Kid Everett. Ishmael Reed. CP-ReedI

Petulance is purple. Spectrum. Mari E. Evans. BPo

Petulant priests, greedy. Savior. Maya Angelou. CP-AngeM

Ph.D. Langston Hughes. CP-HughL

Phantom Kiss, The. Paul Laurence Dunbar. CP-DunbP

Phantom Light of All Our Day, The. Nathaniel Mackey. GT

Phantom Pains. Kelly Norman Ellis. SpiFl

Pharaohs of Today, The. Lizelia Augusta Jenkins Moorer. CBWP-3

Pharisees come bloom / water eddys the twilight air. Egyptian Book of the Dead. David Henderson. TtW

Pharoah sanders / had / finished. Blackmusic / a Beginning. Haki R. Madhubuti. BrTr

Phenomenal Woman. Maya Angelou. CP-AngeM; SP-AngeM

Philadelphia / a disguised southern city. Elegy (for MOVE and Philadelphia). Sonia Sanchez. Crnst; ESEAA; TtW

Philadelphia: Spring, 1985. Sonia Sanchez. ESEAA

Philis's Reply to the Answer in Our Last by the Gentleman in the Navy, see also To a Gentleman of the Navy by Phillis Wheatley and The Answer by Unknown. Phillis Wheatley. CP-WheaP

Phillis. Naomi Long Madgett. TtW

Philodendron. Helen Armstead Johnson. AmNP

Philosophical Perspective on Everyday Shit, A. Nadir Lasana Bomani. CtF

Philosophy. Paul Laurence Dunbar. BPo; CP-DunbP; NAAAL

Phoebe is the 9th satellite. Ishmael Reed. CP-ReedI

Phoenix. Carolyn M. Rodgers. JB

Phone duet over the radio, A. The Louisiana Weekly #4. David Henderson. PoBA

Photograph, The. Paul Laurence Dunbar. CP-DunbP

Photograph. Quandra Prettyman. PoBA

Photographs. Michael S. Harper. SP-HarpM

Photographs: A Vision of Massacre. Michael S. Harper. PoBA; SP-HarpM

Photographs of the Medusa. Marilyn Nelson. SP-NelsM

Photography. Nikki Giovanni. SP-GiovN

Phraseology. Jayne Cortez. BlSi

Phyllis, ah, Phyllis, my life is a gray day. Paul Laurence Dunbar. CP-DunbP

Physics of Loneliness, The. Al Young. CP-YounA

Piano after War. Gwendolyn Brooks. AmNP; ESEAA; Klds; SP-BrooG

Piano buttons, stitched on morning lights. Morning Joy. Bob Kaufman. SP-KaufB

Piano hums / again the clear, The. Effendi. Michael S. Harper. PoBA; SP-HarpM

Piano man, The. Haiku: "Piano man, The." Etheridge Knight. ESEAA; TtW

Picasso's Balcony. Bob Kaufman. SP-KaufB

Pick a Bale of Cotton. Unknown. NAAAL

Pickin Em Up and Layin Em Down. Maya Angelou. CP-AngeM; SP-AngeM

Picnic: the Liberated. M. Carl Holman. PoBA

Picture, A. Henrietta Cordelia Ray. CBWP-3

Picture is simply chile relleno, The. The Night before Michael Was Born. Al Young. CP-YounA

Picture of content should be complete, The. All Are Gay. Sterling A. Brown. CP-BrowS

Pictures on the television, The. Grandpa's Stories. Langston Hughes. CP-HughL

Pictures to the Wall. Langston Hughes. CP-HughL

Pidgin Moon. Al Young. CP-YounA

Pieced together, never broken, never end. (LL) In Hayden's Collage. Michael S. Harper. ESEAA; NAAAL

Pierrot. Langston Hughes. CP-HughL

Pierrot / Took his heart. Heart. Langston Hughes. CP-HughL

Pigalle: / A neon rose. Montmartre. Langston Hughes. CP-HughL; Klds

Piggy-back. Langston Hughes. CP-HughL

Pike Street Bus. Colleen J. McElroy. NAAAL

Pilgrimage and Staff, The. George Marion McClellan. Fr. The Legend of Tannhauser and Elizabeth. EBAP

Pimp, The, see also Pimping Sam and Wicked Nell. African-American Oral Tradition. GetYo

Pimping every day. (LL) Poppa Chicken. Margaret Abigail Walker. CP-WalkM; NAAAL

Pimping Sam, see also The Pimp and Wicked Nell. African-American Oral Tradition. GetYo

Pineapple is armored flower. Harryette Mullen. TtW

Ping Pong Joe. African-American Oral Tradition. GetYo

Pink Poem. Jackie Warren-Moore. SpiFl

Pioneer stands in front of the, The. Points of View. Ishmael Reed. CP-ReedI; TtW

Pioneers and the indians, The. Points of View. Ishmael Reed. CP-ReedI

Piping Down of God, The. Ishmael Reed. CP-ReedI

Pirouette. Audre Lorde. CP-LordA; NNP; SP-LordA

Piss / aint never smelled sweet. A Portrait of Johnny Doller. D. L. Graham. BlFi

Pisspot Pete, see also 'Flicted Arm Pete. African-American Oral Tradition. GetYo

Pit-vipers are asleep, The. Dead-Day: Malcolm, Feb. 21. Michael S. Harper. SP-HarpM

Pithos. Rita Dove. SP-DoveR

Pity all the frightened ones. Good Bluffers. Langston Hughes. CP-HughL

Pity for him who suffers from his waste. Suffer the Children. Audre Lorde. CP-LordA; PoBA

Pity the deep in love. Countee Cullen. CP-CullC

Pity this poor animal. Lucille Clifton. SP-ClifL

Place this bunch of mignonette. Dirge. Paul Laurence Dunbar. CP-DunbP

Place Where He Arose, The. George Barlow. GT

Place Where the Rainbow Ends, The. Paul Laurence Dunbar. CP-DunbP

Plague of Starlings, A. Robert Hayden. CP-HaydR; ESEAA

Plagued Journey, A. Maya Angelou. CP-AngeM; SP-AngeM

Plain Truth. Jayne Cortez. SP-CortJ

Plane: Earth, The. Sun-Ra. PoBA

Plane tilts in to Nashville, The. The Homecoming Singer. Jay Wright. PoBA

Planes flew low over the house, The. These Are Not Brushstrokes. Cyrus Cassells. GT

Planning the Perfect Evening. Rita Dove. Fr. A Suite for Augustus. GT; SP-DoveR

Plans. Helen Morgan Brooks. NNP

Plans. Michael S. Harper. SP-HarpM

Plans: 2. Michael S. Harper. SP-HarpM

Plant a fence post. Dark of the Moon. Sterling A. Brown. CP-BrowS

Plant de white-oak and de black-oak side by side. (LL) Sharecroppers. Sterling A. Brown. BrowS; Crnst

Plant your toes in the cool swamp mud. Flight. Langston Hughes. CP-HughL

Plantation Child's Lullaby, The. Paul Laurence Dunbar. CP-DunbP

Plantation Melody, A. Paul Laurence Dunbar. CP-DunbP

Plantation Portrait, A. Paul Laurence Dunbar. CP-DunbP

Plantation Proverbs. Joel Chandler Harris. CrDW

Plateau, The. Claude McKay. SP-McKaC

Play it once. Saturday Night. Langston Hughes. CP-HughL

Play me a game like Blind Man's dance. Bump d'Bump. Maya Angelou. CP-AngeM; SP-AngeM

Play that thing, / Jazz band! Jazz Band in a Parisian Cabaret. Langston Hughes. BANP; CP-HughL

Play the blues for me. Misery. Langston Hughes. CP-HughL; SP-HughL

Play the St. Louis Blues. Request for Requiems. Langston Hughes. CP-HughL

Play your guitar, boy. Blues on a Box. Langston Hughes. CP-HughL

Playboy of the dawn. Gone Boy. Langston Hughes. CP-HughL; SP-HughL

Played backwards on his grandson's eyes. (LL) Grandfather. Michael S. Harper. ESEAA; NAAAL; SP-HarpM

Players. E. Ethelbert Miller. SpiFl

Playing Solitaire, for Jessica. Thulani Davis. GT

Plea, A. Paul Laurence Dunbar. CP-DunbP

Plea. Bob Kaufman. SP-KaufB

Plea, The. Yusef Komunyakaa. SP-Komuÿ

Plea to My Sister, A. James Cunningham. JB

Please. Yusef Komunyakaa. SP-KomuY

Please be silent, now my country, while I fill the speaker's place. The Negro Schools. Lizelia Augusta Jenkins Moorer. CBWP-3

Please don't take this man o' mine. (LL) Gal's Cry for a Dying Lover. Langston Hughes. CP-HughL; NAAAL

Please forgive me, sir. When in Rome—Apologia. Yusef Komunyakaa. SP-KomuY

Please reach out yo' hand. (LL) Feet O' Jesus. Langston Hughes. CP-HughL; SP-HughL

Pleasures, The. Daniel Alexander Payne. EBAP

"Long hast thou slumber'd, O, my sounding lyre!" AAP

"Pledge me with wine," the maiden cried. The Fatal Pledge. Frances Ellen Watkins Harper. CP-HarpF

Pledge of Allegiance. Carl Hancock Rux. SpiFl

Plentiful light. Electricity of Blossoms. Lorenzo Thomas. GT

Plentiful sacrifice and believers in redemption. When the Saints Come Marching In. Audre Lorde. CP-LordA; SP-LordA

Plight, The. James W. Thompson. BPo

Plotinus Suite, The. Marilyn Nelson. SP-NelsM

  Behind a Descartes Bumpersticker.

  Enneads, I, vi.

  Hermitage Breakfast.

  Icarus Dream.

  Jesus Prayer, The.

  No Jazz.

  Parable of the Moth.

  Prayer of Singing Joy.

  Sneak Preview.

  To San Fransisco.

  True Magic, The.

  Union Apprehended.

Plowdens, Finns. Beginnings. Robert Hayden. CP-HaydR

Po' Boy Blues. Langston Hughes. BANP; CP-HughL; NAAAL

Po' los' boy, bebby, / Evahmo'. (LL) Southern Road. Sterling A. Brown. BALP; BANP; BPo; CP-BrowS; FB; PoBA; TtW

Pocadonia. Ishmael Reed. CP-ReedI

Poème d'Automne. Langston Hughes. CP-HughL

Poem. Calvin C. Hernton. GT

Poem: "Ah, I know what happiness is!" Blanche Taylor Dickinson. CDC

Poem: "Ah, / My black one." Langston Hughes. CP-HughL

Poem: "All the tom-toms of the jungles beat in my blood." Langston Hughes. CP-HughL

Poem: "I have considered / my reluctance." Nikki Giovanni. SP-GiovN

Poem: "I loved my friend." Langston Hughes. CP-HughL

Poem: "In the earnest path of duty." Charlotte Forten. BlSi

Poem: "Like a will-o'-the-wisp in the night." Nikki Giovanni. SP-GiovN

Poem: "Little brown boy." Helene Johnson. AmNP; BANP; CDC; NAAAL; PoBA; ShDr

Poem: "Look at me 8th / grade." Sonia Sanchez. PoBA; SP-SancS

Poem, A: "Over the foaming ocean." Frances Ellen Watkins Harper. CP-HarpF

Poem: "We drank Thunderbird all night." James T. Stewart. BlFi

Poem: "When young spring comes." Langston Hughes. CP-HughL

Poem: a Piece. James T. Stewart. BlFi

Poem about Intelligence for My Brothers and Sisters, A. June Jordan. SP-JordJ

Poem About My Rights. June Jordan. NAAAL; SP-JordJ

Poem about Police Violence. June Jordan. SP-JordJ

Poem about the Head of a Negro. June Jordan. TtW

Poem at the Midnight of My Life. June Jordan. SP-JordJ

Poem at Thirty. Sonia Sanchez. BPo; BlFi; BlSi; BrTr; NAAAL; PoBA; SP-SancS

Poem at Thirty-nine. Alice Walker. CP-WalkA

Poem Delivered Before Assembly of Colored People Held at Glide Memorial Church, Oct. 4, 1973 and Called to Protest Recent Events in the Sovereign Republic of Chile. Ishmael Reed. CP-ReedI

Poem For a Certain Lady on Her 33rd Birthday, The. Etheridge Knight. SP-KnigE

Poem for a Lady Whose Voice I Like. Nikki Giovanni. SP-GiovN

Poem . . . For a Lover. Mae V. Cowdery. ShDr

Poem for a Poet, A. Don L. Lee. PoBA

Poem for a Poet, A. Audre Lorde. CP-LordA

  (Poem for a Poet.) SP-LordA

Poem for a Poet. Audre Lorde. *See* A Poem for a Poet.

Poem for a Poet, A. Haki R. Madhubuti. BrTr

Poem for an Intellectual on the Way Up to Submit to His Lady. Langston Hughes. CP-HughL

Poem (For Anna Hedgeman and Alfreda Duster). Nikki Giovanni. SP-GiovN

Poem for Aretha. Nikki Giovanni. BPo; BrTr; PoBA; SP-GiovN

Poem for Benjamin Franklin. June Jordan. SP-JordJ

Poem for Black Boys. Nikki Giovanni. BPo; SP-GiovN

Poem for Black Hearts, A. Amiri Baraka. BrTr; IDB; NAAAL; PoBA

Poem for Black Hearts, A. LeRoi Jones *and* Imamu Amiri Baraka. SSLK

Poem for Black Relocation Centers, A. Etheridge Knight. *Fr.* Two Poems for Black Relocation Centers. BrTr; ESEAA; SP-KnigE

Poem (For BMC No. 1). Nikki Giovanni. BrTr; SP-GiovN

Poem (For BMC No. 2). Nikki Giovanni. SP-GiovN

Poem (For BMC No. 3). Nikki Giovanni. SP-GiovN

Poem for Buddy. June Jordan. SP-JordJ

Poem for Deep Thinkers, A. Amiri Baraka. SP-BaraA

Poem for Democrats, A. Amiri Baraka. SP-BaraA

Poem for Derrick Gilbert. June Jordan. CtF

Poem for Dorothy Dandridge, A. Al Young. CP-YounA

Poem for Dylan Thomas, A. Al Young. CP-YounA

Poem (for EMA). Nikki Giovanni. SP-GiovN

Poem for Etheridge. Sonia Sanchez. BPo

Poem for Flora. Nikki Giovanni. BPo; PoBA

  ("I want to be / like that.") (LL) SP-GiovN

Poem for Friends. Quincy Troupe. PoBA

Poem for Guatemala. June Jordan. NAAAL; SP-JordJ

Poem for Integration, A. Alvin Saxon. PoBA

Poem for Jan. June Jordan. SP-JordJ

Poem for Joy. June Jordan. SP-JordJ

Poem for July 4, 1994. Sonia Sanchez. SpiFl

Poem for Langston Hughes, A. Nikki Giovanni. SP-GiovN; SSLK

Poem for Langston Hughes, A. Lenard D. Moore. TtW

Poem for Lena Horne, A. Al Young. CP-YounA

Poem for Mark. June Jordan. SP-JordJ

Poem for My Family: Hazel Griffin and Victor Hernandez Cruz. June Jordan. BPo

Poem for My Father, A. Sonia Sanchez. BPo; BrTr; SP-SancS

Poem for My Sisters. Lucille Clifton. SP-ClifL

Poem for Myself (Or Blues for a Mississippi Black Boy), A. Etheridge Knight. BkSV; SP-KnigE

Poem for Nana. June Jordan. BlSi

Poem for Neutrals, A. Amiri Baraka. BPo; SP-BaraA

Poem (For Nina). Nikki Giovanni. SP-GiovN

Poem for Omar Khayyam (1050?-1123? A.D.). Al Young. CP-YounA

Poem (For PCH). Nikki Giovanni. SP-GiovN

Poem for Pearl's Dancers. Owen Dodson. TtW

Poem for Players, A. Al Young. CP-YounA

Poem for Positive Thinkers, A. Barbara Mahone. PoBA

Poem for Some Black Women. Carolyn M. Rodgers. BlSi

Poem for South African Women. June Jordan. SP-JordJ

Poem for Speculative Hipsters, A. Amiri Baraka. SP-BaraA

Poem for Sterling Brown, A. Sonia Sanchez. SP-SancS

Poem for the Birthday of Huey P. Newton. Sotère Torregian. NBV

Poem for the Liberation of Southern Africa. Etheridge Knight. SP-KnigE

Poem for Thel—the Very Tops of Trees. Joseph Major. NBP

Poem for Tracy (Chapman). Candice M. Jenkins. CtF

Poem for Two Daughters. Ishmael Reed. CP-ReedI

Poem for Willard Motley, A. Al Young. CP-YounA

Poem for Wille Best, A. Amiri Baraka. SP-BaraA

Poem for Women in Rage, A. Audre Lorde. CP-LordA; SP-LordA

Poem for Youth. Langston Hughes. CP-HughL

Poem Found Emptying Out My Pockets. Al Young. CP-YounA

Poem from Taped Testimony in the Tradition of Bernard Goetz. June Jordan. SP-JordJ

Poem from the Empire State. June Jordan. BPo

Poem in C. Jean Toomer. CP-ToomJ

Poem Instead of a Columbus Day Parade. June Jordan. SP-JordJ

Poem Looking for a Reader, A. Haki R. Madhubuti. BrTr

Poem No. 3. Sonia Sanchez. SP-SancS

Poem No. 4. Sonia Sanchez. SP-SancS

Poem No. 7. Sonia Sanchez. SP-SancS

Poem No. 8. Sonia Sanchez. SP-SancS

Poem No. 10. Sonia Sanchez. TtW

Poem (No Name No. 1). Nikki Giovanni. SP-GiovN

Poem (No Name No. 2). Nikki Giovanni. SP-GiovN

Poem (No Name No. 3). Nikki Giovanni. BrTr; SP-GiovN

Poem Number Two on Bell's Theorem. June Jordan. SP-JordJ

Poem of Angela Yvonne Davis. Nikki Giovanni. PoBA; SP-GiovN

Poem of Attrition, A. Etheridge Knight. GT; SP-KnigE; TtW

Poem of Friendship, A. Nikki Giovanni. IHS; SP-GiovN

Poem of Praise, A. Sonia Sanchez. SP-SancS

Poem of remembrance, a gift, a souvenir for you, A. (LL) A Ballad of Remembrance. Robert Hayden. AmNP; BPo; CP-HaydR; ESEAA; IDB; PoBA

Poem Off Center, A. Nikki Giovanni. SP-GiovN

Poem on. June Jordan. SP-JordJ

Poem on Bell's Theorem. June Jordan. SP-JordJ

Poem on My Fortieth Birthday to My Mother Who Died Young. Lucille Clifton. SP-ClifL

Poem on the Assassination of Robert F. Kennedy, A. Nikki Giovanni. SP-GiovN

Poem on the Death of Charles Eliot, Aged 12 Months, A. Phillis Wheatley. CP-WheaP

Poem on the Middle East "Peace Process", A. Etheridge Knight. SP-KnigE

Poem on the Road; for Alice Walker. June Jordan. SP-JordJ

Poem on the Second Consecutive Day of Rain. June Jordan. SP-JordJ

Poem # One. June Jordan. Fr. The Talking Back of Miss Valentine Jones. SP-JordJ

Poem Some People Will Have to Understand, A. Amiri Baraka. BPo; GT; SP-BaraA

Poem to a Dead Soldier. Langston Hughes. CP-HughL

Poem to a Nigger Cop. Bobb Hamilton. BlFi

Poem to Complement Other Poems, A. Haki R. Madhubuti. BPo; BrTr; NAAAL; NBV; TtW

Poem to Galway Kinnell, A. Etheridge Knight. SP-KnigE

Poem to the World. Bill Duke. CtF

Poem to Uncle Sam. Langston Hughes. CP-HughL

Poem Towards a Final Solution. June Jordan. SP-JordJ

Poem Welcoming Jonas Mekas to America, A. Amiri Baraka. SP-BaraA

Poem, we're going this way. Pike Street Bus. Colleen J. McElroy. NAAAL

Poem with Orange. Al Young. CP-YounA

Poem/Ditty-Bop. Carolyn M. Rodgers. JB

Poems. Julius Lester. Klds

  "Around the church."

  "As we got."

  "Man who tried to, The."

  "She should be."

  "Spring dawn."

  "With its fog-shroud the."

Poems about Playmates. Ronda M. Davis. JB

Poems are bullshit unless they are. Black Art. Amiri Baraka. BPo; BlFi; ESEAA; NAAAL; SP-BaraA

Poems are not places. Sterling Plumpp. GT

Poems: Birmingham 1962–1964. Julia Fields. PoBA

Poet, The. Lucille Clifton. SP-ClifL

Poet, The. Joseph Seamon Cotter, Sr. EBAP

Poet, The. Paul Laurence Dunbar. AAP; AfAmPo; BPo; CP-DunbP; CrDW; Klds; NAAAL

Poet. Donald Jeffrey Hayes. AmNP

Poet, The. Bob Kaufman. SP-KaufB

Poet and His Song, The. Paul Laurence Dunbar. CP-DunbP

Poet and the Baby, The. Paul Laurence Dunbar. CP-DunbP

Poet asks, and Phillis can't refuse, The. An Answer to the Rebus, by the Author of These Poems. Phillis Wheatley. CP-WheaP

Poet hath a realm within, and throne. Albery Allson Whitman. AAP; AfAmPo; EBAP Fr. Twasinta's Seminoles; Or Rape of Florida.

Poet is the dreamer, The. Loneliness. Al Young. CP-YounA; PoBA

Poet of Our Race. Maggie Pogue Johnson. CBWP-4

Poet of the serene and thoughtful lay! Wordsworth. Charlotte L. Forten Grimké. AAP; AfAmPo

Poet, poet, what is your task. Countee Cullen. CP-CullC

Poet Speaks, The. Georgia Douglas Johnson. AmNP

Poet the Dreamer, The. Norman Jordan. NBV

Poet to Bigot. Langston Hughes. CP-HughL

Poet to Patron. Langston Hughes. CP-HughL

Poet was busted by a topless judge, A. Sermonette. Ishmael Reed. CP-ReedI; PoBA

Poetry. Al Young. CP-YounA

Poetry is a trestle. Nikki Giovanni. SP-GiovN

Poetry is an applied science. Parapoetics. Eugene B. Redmond. NBV; TtW

Poetry is motion graceful. Nikki Giovanni. SP-GiovN

Poetry / like a bent ray. After Visiting Arl at the Hospital. Al Young. CP-YounA

Poetry Makes Rhythm in Philosophy. Ishmael Reed. CP-ReedI

Poetry should treat. Formula. Langston Hughes. CP-HughL

Poetry's a tree / forever at your door. Yes, the Secret Mind Whispers. Al Young. CP-YounA; PoBA; TtW

Poet's Feeble Petition, The. George Moses Horton. SP-HortG

Poet's Ideal, The. Henrietta Cordelia Ray. CBWP-3

Poet's Ministrants, The. Henrietta Cordelia Ray. CBWP-3

Poet's Shuffle, The. Calvin Forbes. GT

Point, The. Robert Hayden. CP-HaydR; ESEAA

Point is not to pacify the soul, The. Trying to Capture Rapture. June Jordan. SP-JordJ

Point of No Return. Mari E. Evans. NNP

Points of View. Ishmael Reed. CP-ReedI; TtW

Poison Light. Ishmael Reed. CP-ReedI

Polarity. Claude McKay. SP-McKaC

Policeman / is a pig, A. Definition for Blk/Children. Sonia Sanchez. PoBA

Political art, let it be, A. Short Speech to My Friends. Amiri Baraka. ESEAA; SP-BaraA

Political Poem. Amiri Baraka. SP-BaraA

Political Relations. Audre Lorde. CP-LordA

Politically erect, romanticizing about ancestral innocence. Curious White Boy. Cree Summer. CtF

Politics As History. Al Young. CP-YounA

Politics of Addiction, The. Audre Lorde. CP-LordA

Politics of Rich Painters, The. Amiri Baraka. SP-BaraA

Poll. Ed Roberson. PoBA

Polonius is still alive. To Be or Not to Be. Brian G. Gilmore. SpiFl

Pomade. Rita Dove. SP-DoveR

Pome. For Weird. Hearts. and All. Ahmed Legraham Alhamisi. BlFi

Ponce de León: A Morning Walk. Al Young. CP-YounA

Ponying up for / Appomattox! (LL) Chattanooga. Ishmael Reed. CP-ReedI; NAAAL

Pool, The. Paul Laurence Dunbar. CP-DunbP

Poolshooting Monkey, see also Partytime Monkey and Signifying Monkey. African-American Oral Tradition. GetYo

Poolshooting Monkey: "I don't know but I was told." African-American Oral Tradition. GetYo

Poolshooting Monkey: "It was in Speero's poolroom back in nineteen-ten." African-American Oral Tradition. GetYo

Poolshooting Monkey: "It was in Speero's poolroom in the year eighteen-ten." African-American Oral Tradition. GetYo

Poor bleeding Nanawawa is no more. (LL) Hunters mount menacing as they go, The. Albery Allson Whitman. AfAmPo

Poor bleeding Nanawawa is no more. (LL) Saville in Trouble. Albery Allson Whitman. AAP

Poor Form. June Jordan. SP-JordJ

Poor Girl. Maya Angelou. CP-AngeM; SP-AngeM

Poor Girl's Ruination. Langston Hughes. CP-HughL

Poor heart, unsatisfied! Shadow and Sunrise. Henrietta Cordelia Ray. CBWP-3

Poor Houses, The. Ed Roberson. GT

Poor, impious Soul! that fixes its high hopes. Aspiration. Adah Isaacs Menken. AAP; CBWP-1

Poor Lazarus. Unknown. NAAAL

Poor man went to the rich man's doors, The. Precedent. Paul Laurence Dunbar. CP-DunbP

Poor, poor fool! Ballad of the Fool. Langston Hughes. CP-HughL

Poor Rover. Langston Hughes. CP-HughL

Poor sam presents at. Anon. Poster. Ishmael Reed. CP-ReedI

Poor thing. She never hurt a soul. What beasts they are. (LL) Power. Audre Lorde. CP-LordA; TtW

Poor withered rose, she gave it me. Paul Laurence Dunbar. CP-DunbP

Pope Replies to the Ayatollah Khomeini, The. Ishmael Reed. CP-ReedI

Pope thinks, The. Addenda to the Papal Bull. June Jordan. SP-JordJ

Poplar Tree. Mae V. Cowdery. ShDr

Poplars are standing there still as death. Southern Mansion. Arna Bontemps. AmNP; BALP; BANP; FB; GT; IDB; Klds; NAAAL; PoBA

Poppa Chicken. Margaret Abigail Walker. CP-WalkM; NAAAL

Poppa Greer happened. Slim Lands a Job? Sterling A. Brown. CP-BrowS

Poppa Stoppa Speaks from His Grave. Larry Neal. TtW

Poppa was a sugah daddy. Poppa Chicken. Margaret Abigail Walker. CP-WalkM; NAAAL

Poppy Flower. Langston Hughes. CP-HughL

Pork chops. Lucille Clifton. SP-ClifL

Port Town. Langston Hughes. CP-HughL; SP-HughL

Porter. Langston Hughes. CP-HughL; SP-HughL

Porter. Marilyn Nelson. ESEAA; SP-NelsM

Portrait. George Leonard Allen. CDC

Portrait. Audre Lorde. CP-LordA

Portrait in Georgia. Jean Toomer. CP-ToomJ

Portrait of Johnny Doller, A. D. L. Graham. BlFi

Portrait of Malcolm X. Etheridge Knight. PoBA

Portrait of Mary. Etheridge Knight. SP-KnigE

Portraits of a Moment. Keith Gilyard. SpiFl

Portraiture. Anita Scott Coleman. ShDr

Positives. Jewel C. Latimore. PoBA

Positives for Sterling Plumpp. Don L. Lee. JB; PoBA

Possession. Paul Laurence Dunbar. CP-DunbP

Possibilities: Remembering Malcolm X. Haki R. Madhubuti. SpiFl

Possum. Paul Laurence Dunbar. CP-DunbP

Possum Trot. Paul Laurence Dunbar. CP-DunbP

Possum's a greasy critter, The. Roast Possum. Rita Dove. SP-DoveR

Post-Prandial Conversation. Marilyn Nelson. SP-NelsM

Postcard from Spain. Langston Hughes. CP-HughL

Pot was empty, The. Ballad of Roosevelt. Langston Hughes. CP-HughL

Potlicker Blues. Calvin Forbes. GT

Potted fern / in a Vine St apartment, A. 2 takes from Love in Los Angeles. Al Young. CP-YounA

Potter's Wheel, The, for Jane. Calvin Forbes. GT

Pour O pour that parting soul in song. Song of the Son. Jean Toomer. AmNP; CDC; CP-ToomJ; CrDW; Klds; PoBA; TtW

Pout is a thing with scales, A. Slaveship, German Model. Ishmael Reed. CP-ReedI

Poverty, remorseless spectre. Christmas Eve, South, 1865. Mary E. Tucker. CBWP-1

Powell; March 1991. Lucille Clifton. ESEAA

Power. Audre Lorde. CP-LordA; TtW

Power returns. We remember, The. III. Healing Song. Etheridge Knight. BkSV

Power to the People. Margaret Abigail Walker. CP-WalkM

Powers of Love, The. George Moses Horton. BALP

Practical Concerns. William J. Harris. PoBA

Practice makes perfect, the old folks said. Magic. Rita Dove. SP-DoveR

Practices brutality closing doors. Sixteen, Yeah. James A. Emanuel. BrTr

Practices / silence, the way of wind. As a Possible Lover. Amiri Baraka. SP-BaraA; TtW

Pragma's well-groomed and bland procurer is on long distance manufacturing heroes. The Ghost in Birmingham. Ishmael Reed. CP-ReedI

Praise of Creation. George Moses Horton. AAP; SP-HortG

Praise Song for Katherine Dunham: A Choreopoem. Chezia Thompson-Cager. CtF

Praising Dark Places. Yusef Komunyakaa. SP-KomuY

Pray, what can dreams avail. Dream Song II. Paul Laurence Dunbar. CP-DunbP

Pray why are you so bare, so bare. The Haunted Oak. Paul Laurence Dunbar. AAP; AfAmPo; BANP; CP-DunbP; Klds; NAAAL

Prayer. Lucille Clifton. NAAAL; SP-ClifL

Prayer, A. Mae V. Cowdery. ShDr

Prayer. Langston Hughes. See Litany: "Gather up / In the arms of your pity."

Prayer. Jean Toomer. CP-ToomJ; NAAAL

Prayer: "As I lie in bed." Joseph Seamon Cotter, Sr. BANP

Prayer: "Centaurian smoke blower / shyly smoking my breast." Shonda Buchanan. CtF

Prayer (I): "How we have strained at our dark works." Jean Toomer. CP-ToomJ

Prayer: "I ask you this: / Which way to go." Langston Hughes. CDC; CP-HughL; SP-HughL

Prayer: "I had thought of putting an / altar." Isabella Maria Brown. NNP

Prayer, A: "'Mid the discordant noises of the day I hear thee calling." Claude McKay. SP-McKaC

Prayer: "O Christ, who in Gethsemane." Henrietta Cordelia Ray. CBWP-3

Prayer, A: "O Lord, the hard-won miles." Paul Laurence Dunbar. CP-DunbP

Prayer, A: "Oh, Lord! I lift my heart." Priscilla Jane Thompson. CBWP-2

Prayer for a Winter Night. Langston Hughes. CP-HughL

Prayer Meeting. Langston Hughes. CP-HughL; SP-HughL

Prayer: Mt. Hood and Environs. Michael S. Harper. TtW

Prayer of Silence, The. Marilyn Nelson. SP-NelsM

Prayer of Singing Joy. Marilyn Nelson. Fr. The Plotinus Suite. SP-NelsM

Prayer to the White Man's God. Charles Anderson. BlFi

Praying in tongues. (LL) If i stand in my window. Lucille Clifton. BPo; SP-ClifL

Preacher, don't send me. Maya Angelou. CP-AngeM

Preacher: Ruminates Behind the Sermon, The. Gwendolyn Brooks. Fr. A Street in Bronzeville. BPo; BlSi; NAAAL; SP-BrooG

Precedent. Paul Laurence Dunbar. CP-DunbP

Precious Lord, take my hand. Take My Hand, Precious Lord. Unknown. NAAAL

Precious night-blooming cereus. Remembering Fannie Lou Hamer. Thadious M. Davis. BlSi

Precious Pearl, The. Priscilla Jane Thompson. CBWP-2

Preface to a Twenty Volume Suicide Note. Amiri Baraka. AmNP; CrDW; ESEAA; Klds; NAAAL; NNP; PoBA; SP-BaraA; TtW

Preference, A. Paul Laurence Dunbar. CP-DunbP

Preference. Langston Hughes. Fr. Montage of a Dream Deferred. CP-HughL

Preferred pain of the Western World, The. Hangover. Al Young. CP-YounA

Prejudice. Georgia Douglas Johnson. AmNP; PoBA; ShDr

Prejudice. Lizelia Augusta Jenkins Moorer. CBWP-3

Prelude: "Night and the hood." Conrad Kent Rivers. PoBA

Prelude. Al Young. CP-YounA

Prelude to a Parting. Maya Angelou. CP-AngeM; SP-AngeM

Prelude to Nothing. Sonia Sanchez. GT; SP-SancS

Prelude to Our Age. Langston Hughes. CP-HughL

Premonition. Paul Laurence Dunbar. CP-DunbP

Preparation. Paul Laurence Dunbar. CP-DunbP

Pres / spoke in a language. Amiri Baraka. SP-BaraA

Prescience. Maya Angelou. CP-AngeM; SP-AngeM

Presence of good, The. The Measure of Memory (The Navigator). Amiri Baraka. SP-BaraA

Present. Langston Hughes. CP-HughL

Present, Part Three. Sonia Sanchez. NAAAL; SP-SancS

Present Age, The. Frances Ellen Watkins Harper. AAP; CP-HarpF

Present is a gift, The. Fort Collins, Colorado. Al Young. CP-YounA

Preserving, The. Kevin Young. GT

President has thus disclosed, The. The Door of Hope. Lizelia Augusta Jenkins Moorer. CBWP-3

President Lincoln's Proclamation of Freedom. Frances Ellen Watkins Harper. CP-HarpF

President Roosevelt, you. Dear Mr. President. Langston Hughes. CP-HughL

Presidents, The. Lizelia Augusta Jenkins Moorer. CBWP-3

President's Four Freedoms, The. How about It, Dixie. Langston Hughes. CP-HughL

Press ahead, beloved children. Uncle Rube to the Young People. Clara Ann Thompson. CBWP-2

Press me to your bread-fruit chest. A Cultural Trip. Opal Palmer Adisa. GT

Pressed to the wall, dying, but—fighting back! (LL) If we must die—let it not be like hogs. Claude McKay. AmNP; BALP; BANP; BPo; CrDW; IDB; NAAAL; PoBA; SSLK

Pressures, The. Amiri Baraka. BPo

Prestidigitator 1, The. Al Young. CP-YounA; NBV

Prestidigitator 2, The. Al Young. CP-YounA; NBV

Pretty little black girl. Ballad for Phillis Wheatley. Margaret Abigail Walker. CP-WalkM

Pretty Pill. African-American Oral Tradition. GetYo

Pretty women wonder where my secret lies. Phenomenal Woman. Maya Angelou. CP-AngeM; SP-AngeM

Price of Disrespect, The. Lizelia Augusta Jenkins Moorer. CBWP-3

Price of / milk has, The. The Sacrifice. Norman Jordan. BlFi

Priests, the elders, and the scribes, The. Death and Resurrection. Priscilla Jane Thompson. CBWP-2

Primary Lesson: The Second Class Citizens. Sun-Ra. PoBA

Prime. Langston Hughes. CP-HughL; PoBA

Primer for the Nuclear Age. Rita Dove. SP-DoveR

Primitive, The. Don L. Lee. BPo

Primitives. Dudley Randall. BALP; BPo; BrTr; NBV

Prince New Year, welcome to thy throne. To the New Year. Priscilla Jane Thompson. CBWP-2

Princess / in darkness, A. (LL) For Each of You. Audre Lorde. CP-LordA; SP-LordA

Print is too small, distressing me, The. The Last Decision. Maya Angelou. CP-AngeM; SP-AngeM

Prism. Audre Lorde. CP-LordA

Prison-house in which I live, The. Renewal of Strength. Frances Ellen Watkins Harper. CP-HarpF

Prison house in which you dwell, The. To Bishop Payne. Frances Ellen Watkins Harper. CP-HarpF

Prisoner. Maya Angelou. CP-AngeM; SP-AngeM

Prisoners, The. Robert Hayden. CP-HaydR

Prisoners. Yusef Komunyakaa. SP-KomuY

Private Letter to Brazil, A. Gloria C. Oden. AmNP; ESEAA; GT; Klds; NNP

Privileged prisoners in a haunted land. (LL) Picnic: the Liberated. M. Carl Holman. PoBA

Prize Fighter. Langston Hughes. CP-HughL

Pro Patria—America, 1861. Adah Isaacs Menken. CBWP-1; EBAP

Probability and Birds in the Yard. Russell Atkins. FB
   ("Probability in the yard is this, The.") GT

Probably take you several hundred years / to get / out! (LL) Wise 1. Amiri Baraka. SP-BaraA

Problem here is that, The. Sherbet. Cornelius Eady. GT

Problem in Social Geometry—the Inverted Square! Ray Durem. NBP; PoBA

Problem of Identity, The. Al Young. CP-YounA

Problems. Langston Hughes. CP-HughL

Problems of Translation: Problems of Language. June Jordan. SP-JordJ

Process. Al Young. CP-YounA

Proclaim a fast, a solemn fast. Frances Ellen Watkins Harper. CP-HarpF

Proclamation / From Sleep, Arise. Carolyn M. Rodgers. JB

Prodigal's Return, The. Frances Ellen Watkins Harper. CP-HarpF

Product of our love, The. October, 1800: A Son in the Continuum. George Barlow. Fr. Gabriel. TtW

Production. Audre Lorde. CP-LordA

Profile on the Pillow, The. Dudley Randall. BPo; BrTr; PoBA

Progress, The. Gwendolyn Brooks. SP-BrooG

Progress Report. Audre Lorde. SP-LordA
   ("These days / when you do say hello I am never sure.") CP-LordA

Projection. Langston Hughes. Fr. Montage of a Dream Deferred. CP-HughL

Proletariat Speaks, The. Alice Moore Dunbar-Nelson. ShDr

Prologue: "Haunted by poems beginning with I." Audre Lorde. CP-LordA
   (Prologue.) ESEAA

Prologue to a Supposed Play. Joseph Seamon Cotter, Sr. EBAP

Promenade. Sam Cornish. BlFi

Prometheus stole from Heaven the sacred fire. Paul Laurence Dunbar. CP-DunbP

Promise, The. Toi Derricotte. GT

Promise, The. Paul Laurence Dunbar. CP-DunbP

Promise, The. Jewel C. Latimore. BlSi

Promise, The. Jean Toomer. CP-ToomJ

Promise of a thousand suns, The. Late-Winter Blues and Promises of Love. Houston A., Jr. Baker. TtW

Promised Land / Is always just ahead, The. Langston Hughes. CP-HughL

Promises. Rita Dove. SP-DoveR

Promises of Freedom. Unknown. BPo; CrDW; NAAAL

Prompt sadness of Schumann or Tchaikovsky, The. From Bowling Green. Al Young. CP-YounA; ESEAA

Proof. Bessie Calhoun Bird. BlSi

Proper evaluation of words and lettters. To the Peoples of Earth. Sun-Ra. BlFi

Proper myself, princess of properness. (LL) Hunchback Girl: She Thinks of Heaven. Gwendolyn Brooks. Klds

Prophet speaks, The. Saint Malcolm. Jewel C. Latimore. BPo

Prophets for a New Day. Margaret Abigail Walker. BPo; BrTr; NAAAL
   ("As the Word came to prophets of old.") CP-WalkM

Prophet's Warning or Shoot to Kill, The. Ebon Dooley. PoBA

Propositions. Marilyn Nelson. SP-NelsM

Prospect of the Future, The. Mrs. Henry Linden. CBWP-4

Protection of Movable Cultural Heritage. Yusef Komunyakaa. SP-KomuY

Protective Grigri, The. Ted Joans. PoBA

Protest. Countee Cullen. CDC; CP-CullC

Protest. Paul Laurence Dunbar. CP-DunbP

Proud banner of death. Tomorrow's Seed. Langston Hughes. CP-HughL

Proud Heart, The. Countee Cullen. CP-CullC

Proud, majestic Southern sun, The. The Husband's Return. Priscilla Jane Thompson. CBWP-2

Proud Nimrod first the bloody chase began. Henry Highland Garnet. CrDW

Prove It on Me Blues. Gertrude "Ma" Rainey. NAAAL

Proverbs. Marvin X. BrTr

Providence Journal V: Israel of Puerto Rico. Michael S. Weaver. SpiFl

Providence, Rhode Island. Al Young. CP-YounA

Proving. Georgia Douglas Johnson. CDC

Pruning, The. Adam David Miller. NBV

Psalm: "So many cars have driven past me." Marilyn Nelson. SP-NelsM

Psalm for Sonny Rollins. Walt Delegall. BlFi

"Psalm of Life" for thee is o'er, The. Longfellow. Henrietta Cordelia Ray. AAP; CBWP-3

Psychedelic Firemen. David Henderson. NBP

Psychophotos of Hampton. Michael S. Harper. SP-HarpM

Puck Goes to Court. Fenton Johnson. CDC

Pull at the rope! Lynching Song. Langston Hughes. CP-HughL

Pulled down over his eyes. (LL) Elegy for Thelonious. Yusef Komunyakaa. ESEAA; SP-KomuY

Pullin me in off the corner to wash my face an. Black Jam for Dr. Negro. Mari E. Evans. BPo; PoBA

Pullin' up to the stop pullin' up to the stop aw man god please. On the Morning St. Bernard. Glenn Joshua. CtF

Puppet Player, The. Angelina Weld Grimké. CDC

Pure in Heart Shall See God, The. Frances Ellen Watkins Harper. CP-HarpF

Pure nothing, in the middle of the day. (LL) Daystar. Rita Dove. NAAAL; SP-DoveR; TtW

Push Back the Catastrophes. Jayne Cortez. SP-CortJ

Pushed into the corner. Black Panther. Langston Hughes. CP-HughL

Pusher, The. Maya Angelou. CP-AngeM; SP-AngeM

Pussy ain't nothin' but a hairy split. African-American Oral Tradition. GetYo

Put 5 and 5 together. Addition: "Put 5 and 5 together." Langston Hughes. CP-HughL

Put away those insipid spoons. The Music That Hurts. Yusef Komunyakaa. SP-KomuY

Put on yo' red silk stockings. Red Silk Stockings. Langston Hughes. CP-HughL; NAAAL

Put one more s in the U.S.A. One More "S" in the U.S.A. Langston Hughes. CP-HughL

Put u red-eye in. Ron Welburn. NBV

Put yr cup on my tray. American Airlines Sutra. Ishmael Reed. CP-ReedI

Puttin' on Dog. Sterling A. Brown. CP-BrowS

Puttin' the Baby Away. Paul Laurence Dunbar. CP-DunbP

Puzzle faces in the dying elms. 'Mystery Boy' Looks for Kin in Nashville. Robert Hayden. CP-HaydR

Puzzled. Langston Hughes. SP-HughL
   (Harlem.) CP-HughL

Puzzlement. Langston Hughes. CP-HughL

Q

QPP, The. Alice Walker. CP-WalkA

Quadroon mermaids, Afro angels, black saints. A Ballad of Remembrance. Robert Hayden. AmNP; BPo; CP-HaydR; ESEAA; IDB; NAAAL; PoBA

Qualified to live / among your dead. (LL) Outcast. Alice Walker. CP-WalkA; NAAAL; TtW

Quality of Light, A. Yusef Komunyakaa. SP-KomuY

QUALITY OF NIGHT THAT YOU HATE MOST IS ITS BLACK, THE. Three Movements and a Coda. Amiri Baraka. NAAAL

Quarrel, The. Josephine D. Henderson Heard. CBWP-4

Quarter century ago, A. Wilberforce. Josephine D. Henderson Heard. CBWP-4

Quarter Moon Rise. Kalamu ya Salaam. Fr. New Orleans Haiku. SpiFl

Quarto Centennial, The. Josephine D. Henderson Heard. CBWP-4

Quatrain 2: "How strange that grass should sing." Gwendolyn B. Bennett. ShDr

Quatrains. Gwendolyn B. Bennett. CDC

Quavering cry. Screech-owl? A. Night, Death, Mississippi. Robert Hayden. CP-HaydR; Crnst

Quebec. Henrietta Cordelia Ray. CBWP-3

Queenie. Mary Weston Fordham. CBWP-2

Query. Ebon Dooley. PoBA

Quest. Naomi Long Madgett. BPo

Quest of the Ideal, The. Henrietta Cordelia Ray. CBWP-3

Questing. Anne Spencer. CDC

Question, A. Paul Laurence Dunbar. CP-DunbP

Question, The. Josephine D. Henderson Heard. CBWP-4

Question. Langston Hughes. *Fr.* Montage of a Dream Deferred. CP-HughL; SP-HughL

Question: "When the old junk man Death." Langston Hughes. CP-HughL

Question and Answer. Langston Hughes. BPo; CP-HughL

Question of Climate, A. Audre Lorde. CP-LordA

Question of *Essence*, A. Audre Lorde. CP-LordA

Questioning. Henrietta Cordelia Ray. CBWP-3

Quick Night / easy warmth. The World is Full of Remarkable Things. Amiri Baraka. BlFi; SSLK

Quiddity i cannot penetrate or name. (LL) [American Journal]. Robert Hayden. CP-HaydR

Quien sabe? Who really knows? (LL) Havana Dreams. Langston Hughes. CP-HughL; SP-HughL

Quiet afternoon, A. Compulsory Chapel. Alice Walker. CP-WalkA

Quiet fading out of life, The. Magnolia Flowers. Langston Hughes. CP-HughL; SP-HughL

Quiet has a hidden sound. William Stanley Braithwaite. NAAAL

Quiet Poem, A. Pinkie Gordon Lane. TtW

Quietly pacifist peaceful, The. The QPP. Alice Walker. CP-WalkA

Quietly the world lay sleeping. The Birth of Jesus. Josephine D. Henderson Heard. CBWP-4

Quilt, The. Mary Effie Lee Newsome. CDC

Quilting, The. Paul Laurence Dunbar. CP-DunbP

Quixote's Cervantes once died. (LL) Topsy: Part 2. Al Young. CP-YounA

Quoits. Mary Effie Lee Newsome. CDC

R

Rabbi, The. Robert Hayden. CP-HaydR

Raccoons have invaded the crawl space. In the Old Neighborhood. Rita Dove. SP-DoveR; SpiFl

Race Question, The. Naomi Long Madgett. BPo

Race Results, U.S.A., 1966. Sarah Webster Fabio. BrTr

Race to freedom and herself to fame, A. (LL) Harriet Beecher Stowe. Paul Laurence Dunbar. AAP; BPo; CP-DunbP; Klds

Racist Psychotherapy. Isaac J. Black. NBV

Radiator's hissing hot, The. Studio Up Over In Your Ear. Al Young. CP-YounA; GT

Radical, The. Waring Cuney. CDC

Radio. Cornelius Eady. ESEAA

Radio is teaching my goldfish Jujitsu, The. Heavy Water Blues. Bob Kaufman. NBV

Rag Man, The. Robert Hayden. CP-HaydR

Raga of the drum, the drum the drum the drum the drum, the heartbeat. Unanimity Has Been Achieved, Not a Dot Less for Its Accidentalness. Bob Kaufman. NAAAL

Rage. Alice Walker. CP-WalkA

Ragged Stocking, The. Frances Ellen Watkins Harper. CP-HarpF

Raid. Langston Hughes. CP-HughL

Railroad Avenue. Langston Hughes. CP-HughL; SP-HughL

Railroad Bill, a conjure man. Ishmael Reed. CP-ReedI; NAAAL

Railroad Bill, Railroad Bill. *Unknown.* NAAAL

Railroad Bill was free. (LL) Railroad Bill, a conjure man. Ishmael Reed. CP-ReedI; NAAAL

Railroad routes; / Indian territory. Plans. Michael S. Harper. SP-HarpM

Rain, falling, The. Evening. Helen G. Quigless. BkSV

Rain is / god's sperm falling. Nikki Giovanni. SP-GiovN

Rain Music. Joseph Seamon Cotter, Sr. BANP; CDC; TtW

Rain or shine each day. Till Death Do Us Part. Kalamu ya Salaam. *Fr.* New Orleans Haiku. SpiFl

Rain / rain drenches the city. Secret Messages. Tom Dent. TtW

Rain Rain on the Splintered Girl. Ishmael Reed. PoBA

Rain Song, The. Alex Rogers. BANP

Rain-Songs. Paul Laurence Dunbar. CP-DunbP

"Rain sounded just like that," he said, "on the roofs there," The. (LL) Nineteen. Elizabeth Alexander. GT

Rain streams down like harp-strings from the sky, The. Rain-Songs. Paul Laurence Dunbar. CP-DunbP

Rain tastes lovely, The. Sonia Sanchez. SP-SancS

Rainbow, The. Opal Palmer Adisa. GT

Rainbow, The. George Barlow. *Fr.* Gabriel. TtW

Raindrops / On the crumbling walls. Poem for Youth. Langston Hughes. CP-HughL

Rainy Season Love Song. Gladys May Casely Hayford. CDC; ShDr

Raise a Ruckus Tonight. *African-American Oral Tradition.* TtW

Raise a "Rucus" To-Night. *Unknown.* BPo

Raise a Song. Sterling A. Brown. CP-BrowS

Raising a Humid Flag. Thylias Moss. GT

Raising of Lazarus, The. Lucille Clifton. SP-ClifL

Raison d'Etre. Oliver Pitcher. AmNP; Klds; NNP

Rally Song. Mary Weston Fordham. CBWP-2

Rallying Cry, The. Frances Ellen Watkins Harper. CP-HarpF

Ran against walls. Jackie Robinson. Lucille Clifton. SP-ClifL

Randi Anderson's life story is sickening because. If Randi Could Write. Elaine Brown. CtF

Rank fennel and broom. Exodus. Mary Effie Lee Newsome. ShDr

Rap is no mystery. Christopher Stanard. SpiFl

Rape. Jayne Cortez. GT; SP-CortJ

Rape Is Not a Poem. June Jordan. SP-JordJ

Raphael. Henrietta Cordelia Ray. CBWP-3

Raphael. Priscilla Jane Thompson. CBWP-3

Rapping Along with Ronda Davis. James Cunningham. JB

Raptures of the Deep. Derek Walcott. *Fr.* The Schooner *Flight.* ESEAA

Rare medieval Spirit! brooding seer! Dante. Henrietta Cordelia Ray. CBWP-3

Rat-fink Baby. Brothers at the Bar. Naomi Long Madgett. NBV

Rather just / Stay here. (LL) Kid Sleepy. Langston Hughes. CP-HughL; SP-HughL

Ravel: Bolero. Al Young. SpiFl

Ray, almost a spinster, gave up. High and Haughty. Marilyn Nelson. SP-NelsM

Ray Charles at Mississippi State. Tom Dent. NBV

Ray Charles! His voice. Hanoi Hannah. Yusef Komunyakaa. SP-KomuY

Ray Charles is the black wind of Kilimanjaro. Blues Note. Bob Kaufman. PoBA

Ray teaches at the Boley Baptist School. Armed Men. Marilyn Nelson. SP-NelsM

Rayboy Blk and Bluz. Shirley Bradley LeFlore. SpiFl

Re-act for Action ("Re-act to Animals"). Don L. Lee. BPo; NBP

Re-creating the Scene. Yusef Komunyakaa. SP-KomuY

Reach, The. Carl Phillips. GT

Reach like you never reached before past Night's somber robes. Tauhid. Askia Muhammad Touré. PoBA

Reached no Alps: or, knows no Alps to reach. (LL) But can see better there, and laughing there. Gwendolyn Brooks. Klds

Reactionary Poet, The. Ishmael Reed. CP-ReedI; ESEAA; GT; TtW

Read the Bible, it will tell. The Bible. Lizelia Augusta Jenkins Moorer. CBWP-3

Read yr/exile / i had a mother too. A Poem for a Poet. Haki R. Madhubuti. BrTr; PoBA

Reader, listen ere we go. The Book's Creed. Joseph Seamon Cotter, Sr. AAP

Reading Hölderlin on the Patio with the Aid of a Dictionary. Rita Dove. SP-DoveR

Reading Nijinsky's Diary. Al Young. CP-YounA

Reading Walt Whitman. Calvin Forbes. ESEAA; NBV; PoBA

Real Life. Amiri Baraka. SP-BaraA

Real Mammy Song. Sterling A. Brown. CP-BrowS

Real People Loves One Another, The. Rob Penny. PoBA

Real Question, The. Paul Laurence Dunbar. CP-DunbP

Real slow, with sweet potatoes. (LL) Roast Possum. Rita Dove. SP-DoveR

Real Time. Al Young. CP-YounA

Realism. Al Young. CP-YounA

Realist, The. Carl H. Greene. NBV

Reapers. Jean Toomer. BPo; CDC; CP-ToomJ; GT; Klds; PoBA

Reason Dixie / Is so mean today, The. Total War. Langston Hughes. CP-HughL

Reason Why, The. George Clinton Rowe. AAP

Reason why i do it, The. The Making of Poems. Lucille Clifton. SP-ClifL

Reasons Why. Langston Hughes. CP-HughL

Reassurance. Alice Walker. CP-WalkA

Rebel, The. Mari E. Evans. AmNP; IDB; PoBA

Rebel. Elma Stuckey. TtW

Rebellion Suite. Askia Muhammad Touré. TtW

Rebellious. Living. The Nature of This Flower Is to Bloom. Alice Walker. CP-WalkA

Rebirth. Sonia Sanchez. SP-SancS

Rebolushinary X-mas. Carolyn M. Rodgers. JB

Rebus, A, see also An Answer to the Rebus by Phillis Wheatley. Unknown. CP-WheaP

Receiving the Stigmata. Rita Dove. NAAAL; SP-DoveR

Reception, The. June Jordan. SP-JordJ

Receptive, soft, and absolute. . . . . . . (LL) The Sundays of Satin-Legs Smith. Gwendolyn Brooks. NAAAL; SP-BrooG

Recessional. Georgia Douglas Johnson. CDC

Recitation. Ellease Southerland. GT

Recitation. Saul Stacey Williams. CtF

Reckoning, The. Naomi Long Madgett. Klds

Reckoning A.M. Thursday. Doris Turner. JB

Recollection. Donald D. Govan. NBP

Recollection. Phillis Wheatley. CP-WheaP

Recompensed? Henrietta Cordelia Ray. CBWP-3

Reconnaissance. Arna Bontemps. AmNP; BPo; Klds

Reconsideration of the Blackbird, A. Thylias Moss. ESEAA

Recovery. Maya Angelou. CP-AngeM; SP-AngeM

Recovery. Rita Dove. SP-DoveR

Recreation. Audre Lorde. CP-LordA

Recurrent Dream. Marilyn Nelson. SP-NelsM

Red carpet-ing, The. While Cecil Snores: Mom Drinks Cold Milk. James Cunningham. JB

Red Clay Blues. Langston Hughes. CP-HughL

Red Clay Blues. Richard Wright. TtW

Red, clear, / No color for fear. Blood, Sweat, and Fears. Marlon C. Williams. CtF

Red Cross. Langston Hughes. CP-HughL

Red Eye. Amiri Baraka. SP-BaraA

Red Flower, A. Claude McKay. SP-McKaC

Red is the Alabama road. Ballad of Ozie Powell. Langston Hughes. CP-HughL

Red Pepper Poet, The. Jayne Cortez. SP-CortJ

Red Roses. Langston Hughes. CP-HughL

Red Silk Stockings. Langston Hughes. CP-HughL; NAAAL

Red-tiled ships you see reflected, The. Five Vignettes. Jean Toomer. CP-ToomJ

Redemption. Pauli Murray. GT

Redemption's problem unto thee well solved. (LL) Milton. Henrietta Cordelia Ray. BlSi; CBWP-3; EBAP; TtW

Rediscovered Diary Entry. Al Young. CP-YounA

Refiner's Gold, The. Frances Ellen Watkins Harper. CP-HarpF

Refining Fire. Lizelia Augusta Jenkins Moorer. CBWP-3

Reflect an azure beam on me. (LL) Early Affection. George Moses Horton. AAP; AfAmPo; SP-HortG

Reflections. Carl Gardner. NNP; PoBA

Reflections After the June 12th March for Disarmament. Sonia Sanchez. ESEAA

Reflections from the Flash of a Meteor. George Moses Horton. SP-HortG

Reflections on a Lost Love. Haki R. Madhubuti. BrTr

Reflections on a Small Parade. Bob Kaufman. SP-KaufB

Reflections on Growing Older. Quincy Troupe. GT

Reflections, Written on Visiting the Grave of a Venerated Friend. Ann Plato. BlSi; EBAP

Refrain. Rita Dove. SP-DoveR

Refugee. Langston Hughes. CP-HughL

Refugee in America. Langston Hughes. See Words Like Freedom.

Refugee road, refugee road. Song of the Refugee Road. Langston Hughes. CP-HughL

Refusal. Maya Angelou. CP-AngeM; SP-AngeM

Refuse the meat of a female animal. Reins. Audre Lorde. CP-LordA

Reg wished me to go with him to the field. My Mother. Claude McKay. GT; NAAAL; SP-McKaC

Regenesis. Ron Welburn. NBP

Reggae or Not! Amiri Baraka. SP-BaraA

Reggie's Version. Al Young. CP-YounA

Rehabilitation & Treatment in the Prisons of America. Etheridge Knight. SP-KnigE

Reincarnation. Mae Jackson. PoBA

Reins. Audre Lorde. CP-LordA

Relativity. June Jordan. SP-JordJ

Release, The. Adah Isaacs Menken. CBWP-1

Release their light. (LL) Bahá'u'lláh in the Garden of Ridwan. Robert Hayden. CP-HaydR; PoBA

Release Time. Audre Lorde. CP-LordA; SP-LordA

Relevant Is Different Points on the Circle. Audre Lorde. CP-LordA; SP-LordA

Relief. Langston Hughes. Fr. Montage of a Dream Deferred. CP-HughL

Religion. Paul Laurence Dunbar. CP-DunbP

Religion of Sweet Jesus, The. "Onward Christian Soldiers!" Frank Marshall Davis. FB

Religious wars of Europe have been numbered with the past, The. The Peonage System. Lizelia Augusta Jenkins Moorer. CBWP-3

Reluctance. Paul Laurence Dunbar. CP-DunbP

Remember: / How on the reeking schooner. Raise a Song. Sterling A. Brown. CP-BrowS

Remember me? Alice Walker. CP-WalkA

Remember me baby in my best light. Poppa Stoppa Speaks from His Grave. Larry Neal. TtW

Remember Mexico. Michael S. Harper. ESEAA; SP-HarpM

Remember Not. Helene Johnson. BANP; NAAAL

Remember on our far-flung fronts. Fourth of July Thought. Langston Hughes. CP-HughL

Remember, poet, while gallivanting across the sky. Forget Me Not. Bob Kaufman. AmNP

Remember Times for Sandy. Carolyn M. Rodgers. JB

Remember / when the skin of your fingers healed. The Discoveries of Fire. Lucille Clifton. SP-ClifL

Remembrance. Langston Hughes. CP-HughL

Remembered. Paul Laurence Dunbar. CP-DunbP

Remembered, (for Virginia Louise Ferris). Sterling Plumpp. GT

Remembering. Maya Angelou. CP-AngeM; SP-AngeM

Remembering Fannie Lou Hamer. Thadious M. Davis. BlSi

Remembering Nat Turner. Sterling A. Brown. CP-BrowS; PoBA

Remembrance. Maya Angelou. CP-AngeM; SP-AngeM

Remnant Ghosts at Dawn. Oliver La Grone. FB; NBV

Remorse sits in my place. (LL) Conscience and Remorse. Paul Laurence Dunbar. CP-DunbP

Rencontre. Jessie Redmond Fauset. CDC

Renewal of Strength. Frances Ellen Watkins Harper. CP-HarpF

Rent Day Blues. Sterling A. Brown. CP-BrowS

Rent man knocked, The. Madam and the Rent Man. Langston Hughes. CP-HughL; SP-HughL

Rent-Party Shout. Langston Hughes. CP-HughL

Repeal of the Missouri Compromise Considered, The. Elymas Payson Rogers. EBAP

"Covetous Nebraskaites, The." AAP

Report. Frances Ellen Watkins Harper. CP-HarpF

Report from the Skull's Diorama. Yusef Komunyakaa. SP-KomuY

Report of the Reed Commission. Ishmael Reed. CP-ReedI

Report to the Mother. Etheridge Knight. SP-KnigE

Reports: Kansas. Michael S. Harper. SP-HarpM

Repose. Henrietta Cordelia Ray. CBWP-3

Representing the Universe. Alice Walker. CP-WalkA

Request. Maya Angelou. CP-AngeM; SP-AngeM

Request. Langston Hughes. Fr. Montage of a Dream Deferred. CP-HughL

Request for Requiems. Langston Hughes. CP-HughL

Request Number. G. N. Sprod. AAP

Requiem: "O, insatiable monster! Could'st thou not." Mary Weston Fordham. CBWP-2

Requiem: "She wears, my beloved, a rose upon her head." John Frederick Matheus. CDC

Requiescam. Countee Cullen. CP-CullC

Requiescat in Pace. Benjamin Clark. EBAP

"Rescue Work": Dues. Michael S. Harper. SP-HarpM

Resignation. Paul Laurence Dunbar. CP-DunbP

Resignation. Nikki Giovanni. SP-GiovN

Resist me / Make me strong. Saga of Resistance. Sun-Ra. BlFi

Resonance. George Barlow. ESEAA

Respect the season / and dance to the rattle. From an Almanac (2). Amiri Baraka. SP-BaraA

Respectfully Dedicated to Dr. Alexander Crummell on the Fiftieth Anniversary of His Pastorate. Frances Ellen Watkins Harper. CP-HarpF

Response. Paul Laurence Dunbar. CP-DunbP

Response. Bob Kaufman. Klds; SP-KaufB

Rest. (LL) Dedication. Alice Walker. CP-WalkA

Rest in Peace. Claude McKay. SP-McKaC

Rest thee aged pilgrim, now thy toils are o'er. Death of a Grandparent. Mrs. Jennette Bonneau. Mary Weston Fordham. CBWP-2

Resting. Josephine D. Henderson Heard. CBWP-4

Restoration. Audre Lorde. CP-LordA

Restrictive Covenants. Langston Hughes. CP-HughL

Results of a Lie Detector. Bob Kaufman. SP-KaufB

Resurgam. Adah Isaacs Menken. Fr. Infelicia. EBAP

Resurrection, The. Jonathan Henderson Brooks. AmNP; CDC; TtW

Resurrection. Frank Horne. PoBA

Resurrection of Jesus, The. Frances Ellen Watkins Harper. CP-HarpF

Retort. Paul Laurence Dunbar. CP-DunbP

Retreat from Moscow, The. George Moses Horton. SP-HortG

Retribution. Frances Ellen Watkins Harper. CP-HarpF

Retribution. Lizelia Augusta Jenkins Moorer. CBWP-3

Retrospect. Josephine D. Henderson Heard. CBWP-4

Retrospection. Paul Laurence Dunbar. CP-DunbP

Retrospection. Henrietta Cordelia Ray. CBWP-3

Return, The. Arna Bontemps. CDC; GT; PoBA

Return. Sterling A. Brown. BALP; CDC; CP-BrowS; Crnst

Return, The. Jessie Redmond Fauset. CDC

Return, The. Robert Hayden. CP-HaydR

Return. Jewel C. Latimore. BlSi

Return. Audre Lorde. SP-LordA

("You did not clock the falling of the leaves.") CP-LordA

Return is not a way of going forward. Roman Poem Number Nine. June Jordan. GT

Return of Julian the Apostate to Rome, The. Ishmael Reed. CP-ReedI

Return of the Native. Amiri Baraka. BPo

("Harlem is vicious.") SP-BaraA

Return to English Turn. Tom Dent. BkSV

Return to Sea. Langston Hughes. CP-HughL

Return to Temptation. Mary Weems. SpiFl

Returning me, returning me. (LL) The Train Runs Late to Harlem. Conrad Kent Rivers. IDB; PoBA

Returning Spring. Pauli Murray. GT

Reuben, Reuben. Michael S. Harper. SP-HarpM

Reunion, The. Frances Ellen Watkins Harper. CP-HarpF

Reunited. Henrietta Cordelia Ray. CBWP-3

Rev. Andrew Brown, over the Hill to Rest. Josephine D. Henderson Heard. CBWP-4

Rev. chickenwing / in his. Illusions. Kirk Hall. BlFi

Rev. Samuel Weston. Mary Weston Fordham. CBWP-2

Revel, The. Frances Ellen Watkins Harper. CP-HarpF

Revelation. Carole C. Gregory Clemmons. BlSi

Revelation. Blanche Taylor Dickinson. CDC

Revelation in Brick City. Amiri Baraka. CtF; SP-HortG

Revelations. Sterling A. Brown. CP-BrowS; Klds

Revenge. Mary E. Tucker. CBWP-1

Reverend Butler came by. Madam and the Minister. Langston Hughes. CP-HughL; SP-HughL

Reverie, A. Mary Weston Fordham. CBWP-2

Reverie. Henrietta Cordelia Ray. CBWP-3

Reverie on the Harlem River. Langston Hughes. CP-HughL; SP-HughL

Reverses. Maya Angelou. CP-AngeM; SP-AngeM

Review from Staten Island. Gloria C. Oden. GT; Klds; NNP; PoBA

Revolution. Brian G. Gilmore. SpiFl

Revolution. Langston Hughes. CP-HughL

Revolution! Richard W. Thomas. BlFi

Revolution Is One Form of Social Change. Audre Lorde. CP-LordA; SP-LordA

Revolution / Revolution / Brothers and sisters. Speech. CtF

Revolution Will Not Be Televised!, The. Gil Scott-Heron. Crnst; NAAAL

Revolutionary, The. Alvin Aubert. TtW

Revolutionary Dreams. Nikki Giovanni. SP-GiovN

Revolutionary Love. Amiri Baraka. CtF

Revolutionary Music. Nikki Giovanni. BrTr; SP-GiovN

Revolutionary Petunias. Alice Walker. BlSi; CP-WalkA

Revolutionary Screw, The. Haki R. Madhubuti. BrTr

Revolutionary War / gamed / sold / out. "There Was something I Wanted to Tell You." (33) Why? Amiri Baraka. SP-BaraA

Revolving doors compete with sales-day traffic. Shoplifter. Solomon Edwards. NNP

Rhapsody. William Stanley Braithwaite. AmNP; BALP; BANP; TtW

Rhetoric of Langston Hughes, The. Margaret Else Danner. BlSi; FB

Rhetorically Speaking. Nikkia Billingsley. CtF

Rhonda, Age 15 Emergency Room. Letta Simone-Nefertari Neely. CtF

Rhumba Negro. Lorenzo Thomas. TtW

Rhyme of the Antique Forest. Henrietta Cordelia Ray. CBWP-3

Rhymes are gems I run tracks like Ben Johnson/Dick Vitale said my style. Gems. Defari Herut. CtF

Rhythm and blues. The Blues Today. Mae Jackson. PoBA

Rhythm and Blues (I). Amiri Baraka. SP-BaraA

Rhythm it is we. Spirits Unchained. Keorapetse W. Kgositsile. PoBA

Rhythm of life, The. Lenox Avenue. Langston Hughes. CP-HughL

Ribbons and Lace. Elma Stuckey. TtW

Rich, flashy, puffy-faced. Cabaret. Sterling A. Brown. CP-BrowS; NAAAL

Rich with gifts on your return to Edinburgh. Made Connections. Michael S. Harper. SP-HarpM

Richard Hunt's "Arachne." Robert Hayden. CP-HaydR; FB

Richard penniman. Lucille Clifton. SP-ClifL

Richland County Lyric for Elizabeth Asleep, A. June Jordan. SP-JordJ

Riddle, The: "White men's children spread over the earth." Georgia Douglas Johnson. PoBA; TtW

Ride, The. Lucinda Roy. GT

Ride in, kind Saviour! Unknown. CrDW

Ride, Red, Ride. Langston Hughes. Fr. Ask Your Mama; 12 Moods for Jazz. CP-HughL

Ride the swing season. On Midsummer's Eve. Audre Lorde. CP-LordA

Riders to the Blood-Red Wrath. Gwendolyn Brooks. SP-BrooG

Riding Across John Lee's Finger, for Walter Lowe. Stanley Crouch. GT; PoBA

Riding the shadows of conquering air. (LL) The Night-Blooming Jasmine. Audre Lorde. CP-LordA

Riding to Town. Paul Laurence Dunbar. CP-DunbP

Right back on in. (LL) My Mama moved among the days. Lucille Clifton. BlSi; PoBA; SP-ClifL

Right name no / no NO. (LL) Blackie Thinks of His Brothers. Stanley Crouch. BlFi; GT

Right now two black people sit in a jury room. Affirmative Action Blues. Elizabeth Alexander. IHS

"RIGHT ON / MOTHERS / MOTHER." (LL) Grandson Is a Hoticeberg, A. Margaret Else Danner. BlSi; FB

Right On: White America. Sonia Sanchez. PoBA

Right or left forever, The. (LL) Division of an Estate. George Moses Horton. NAAAL; SP-HortG

Right to Die, The. Paul Laurence Dunbar. CP-DunbP

Right to Life, The: What Can the White Man Say to the Black Woman? Alice Walker. CP-WalkA

Right to make my dreams come true, The. Calling Dreams. Georgia Douglas Johnson. ShDr

Right up under our noses, roses. Intimacy. Al Young. CP-YounA

Right's Security. Paul Laurence Dunbar. CP-DunbP

Rilke's Third Elegy. Rainer Maria Rilke. SP-NelsM, tr. by Marilyn Nelson

Rilly, / im a brown man. Not No Socialism/Communism classical, but Some Power to the People Jazz. Daniel Gray-Kontar. SpiFl

Rime for the Christmas Baby. Anne Spencer. ShDr

Rimmed by spray and rainbowed by sunshine. (LL) Merl. Jean Toomer. CP-ToomJ; GT

Ring, The. Langston Hughes. CP-HughL

Ring, aye, ring the freedom bell. The Freedom Bell. Frances Ellen Watkins Harper. CP-HarpF

Ring. Damn you! (LL) The Telephone. Maya Angelou. CP-AngeM; SP-AngeM

Ring out, ye bells! Christmas Carol. Paul Laurence Dunbar. CP-DunbP

Ring the big bells. Contemporary Announcement. Maya Angelou. CP-AngeM; SP-AngeM

Ringo. African-American Oral Tradition. GetYo

Riot. Gwendolyn Brooks. BPo; NAAAL; NBV; PoBA

Riot. Gwendolyn Brooks. See The Rites for Cousin Vit.

Riot, A. Mrs. Henry Linden. CBWP-4

Riot Act, April 29, 1992. Ai. ESEAA

Riot: 60's. Maya Angelou. CP-AngeM; SP-AngeM

Riots and Rituals. Richard W. Thomas. PoBA

Rip-Off. Ronda M. Davis. BrTr

Ripley or not. A Street in Kaufman-ville. James Cunningham. JB

Rippling hospital sheets. Grandmother: Crossing Jordan. Melvin Dixon. ESEAA

Rise as the keys swung, ticking. (LL) Thomas at the Wheel. Rita Dove. SP-DoveR

Rise to one brimming golden, spilling cry! (LL) The Road. Helene Johnson. AmNP; BANP; BlSi; CDC; ShDr

Rise up! rise up! Oh Israel. Deliverance. Frances Ellen Watkins Harper. CP-HarpF

Rising, The. Jayne Cortez. NBV

Rising of the Storm, The. Paul Laurence Dunbar. CP-DunbP

Rising sun ... knowing ... a New Day ... is always ... / beginning, The. (LL) But Since You Finally Asked. Nikki Giovanni. CtF; SP-GiovN

Rising Waters. Langston Hughes. CP-HughL

Rite, The. Dudley Randall. BrTr

Rite of Passage. Audre Lorde. CP-LordA; PoBA

(Rites of Passage) SP-LordA

Rites for Cousin Vit, The. Gwendolyn Brooks. BPo; NAAAL; SP-BrooG

("'Forgive these nigguhs that know not what they do'.") (LL) SSLK

("John Cabot—out of Wilma, once a Wycliffe.") SSLK

(Riot.) SSLK

Rituals. Nikki Giovanni. SP-GiovN

Rivals, The. Paul Laurence Dunbar. CP-DunbP

Riven Quarry, The. Gloria C. Oden. GT; PoBA

River, The. Sam Cornish. PoBA

River is a decrepit old woman, the. Ethel M. Caution. ShDr

River jordan run red. Emmett Till. Wanda Coleman. NAAAL

River of Ruin, The. Paul Laurence Dunbar. CP-DunbP

River of tears is my story, A. A Song Waiting for Music. Raymond R. Patterson. TtW

River shines in the jungle's, A. Monsoon Season. Yusef Komunyakaa. SP-KomuY

River sleeps beneath the sky, The. Sunset. Paul Laurence Dunbar. CP-DunbP

River, why in ceaseless flow. Maiden and River. Mary Weston Fordham. CBWP-2

Riverbank Blues. Sterling A. Brown. CP-BrowS

Rizpah, the Daughter of Ai. Frances Ellen Watkins Harper. CP-HarpF

Roach / came struttin, A. John Raven. BPo

Road, The. Helene Johnson. AmNP; BANP; BlSi; CDC; ShDr

Road in Kentucky, A. Robert Hayden. CP-HaydR

Road / It takes you, The. Mongolian Sunset in Gobi Desert. Bob Kaufman. SP-KaufB

Road runs straight with no turning, the circle, The. Black People: This Is Our Destiny. Amiri Baraka. TtW

Road to Southampton is layered with days, The. Out to the Hard Road. Audre Lorde. CP-LordA

Road to the Bow, The. James David Corrothers. BANP

Road winds down through autumn hills, The. Tour 5. Robert Hayden. CP-HaydR

Roadway, A. Paul Laurence Dunbar. CP-DunbP

Roar, China! / Roar, old lion of the East! Langston Hughes. CP-HughL

Roar of the rushing train fearfully rocking. On the Road. Claude McKay. SP-McKaC

Roast Possum. Rita Dove. SP-DoveR

Robbie's Dance, The. Al Young. CP-YounA

Robert. Lucille Clifton. SP-ClifL

Robert G. Shaw. Henrietta Cordelia Ray. AAP; BlSi; CBWP-3

("In rev'rent love we guard thy memory.") (LL) AfAmPo; EBAP

("When War's red banners trailed along the sky.") AfAmPo

Robert Gould Shaw. Paul Laurence Dunbar. CP-DunbP; Klds

Robert Schumann, Or: Musical Genius Begins with Affliction. Rita Dove. SP-DoveR

Robert Whitmore. Frank Marshall Davis. BPo; Klds; PoBA; TtW

Roberta Lee. Sterling A. Brown. CP-BrowS

Robin Red Breast. Lula Lowe Weeden. CDC

Robin! Robin! call the Springtime. March. Henrietta Cordelia Ray. CBWP-3

Robin's Poem, A. Nikki Giovanni. AmNP; BrTr

Rock, A River, A Tree, A. On the Pulse of Morning. Maya Angelou. CP-AngeM

Rock, for ages, stern and high, A. Truth. Frances Ellen Watkins Harper. CP-HarpF

Rock Me, Baby. Ishmael Reed. CP-ReedI

Rock me to sleep, ye waves, and drift my boat. Eternity. George Marion McClellan. EBAP

Rock the boat to a fare-thee-well. Rites of Passage. Audre Lorde. SP-LordA

Rock Thrown into the Water Does Not Fear the Cold, A. Audre Lorde. CP-LordA

Rock, you are called, A. Peers. Jean Toomer. CP-ToomJ

Rocking her white feet. Sonia Sanchez. SP-SancS

Rocks and the firm roots of trees. Spirituals. Langston Hughes. CP-HughL; SP-HughL

Rocks Push. Yusef Komunyakaa. SP-KomuY

Rocks with silver spray were wet, The. (LL) At the Cascade. Henrietta Cordelia Ray. CBWP-3

Roland. Michael S. Harper. SP-HarpM

Roland Hayes Beaten (Georgia: 1942). Langston Hughes. *See* Warning.

Roland Navarro (1939-1961). Al Young. CP-YounA

Roll Jordan, roll. *Unknown.* CrDW; Crnst

Rolling, rolling. Jean Toomer. CP-ToomJ

Rolling Stone, The. Moss. Al Young. CP-YounA

Roman Poem Number Five. June Jordan. SP-JordJ

Roman Poem Number Six. June Jordan. SP-JordJ

Roman Poem Number Eight. June Jordan. SP-JordJ

Roman Poem Number Nine. June Jordan. GT

Roman Poem Number Thirteen. June Jordan. SP-JordJ

Roman Poem Number Fourteen. June Jordan. SP-JordJ

Romance. Claude McKay. SP-McKaC

Romance. Al Young. CP-YounA

Romance in Irony. June Jordan. SP-JordJ

Romance Without Finance. Al Young. CP-YounA

Rome is dying. Fenton Johnson. EBAP

Roofless houses, cartons of chalk. The Sahara Bus Trip. Rita Dove. SP-DoveR

Room, The. De Leon Harrison. PoBA

Room. Langston Hughes. CP-HughL

Room was a / red glow, The. We Dance Like Ella Riffs. Carolyn M. Rodgers. PoBA

Rooming houses are old women. Audre Lorde. CP-LordA; SP-LordA

Rooms are grotesque with furniture of snow. The Return. Robert Hayden. CP-HaydR

Roosevelt, Renaissance, Gem, Alhambra, The. Movies. Langston Hughes. *Fr.* Montage of a Dream Deferred. CP-HughL

Rooster crowed, the hen looked down, The. *African-American Oral Tradition.* GetYo

Roots. Lucille Clifton. SP-ClifL

Roots of your hair / what, The. Nappy Edges. Ntozake Shange. NAAAL

Rosabella—Purity of Heart. George Moses Horton. SP-HortG

Rose and gold and violet, The. The Afterglow. Henrietta Cordelia Ray. CBWP-3

Rose Bush, The. Nikki Giovanni. SP-GiovN

Rose of neon darkness. Chippy. Langston Hughes. CP-HughL

Rose Solitude. Jayne Cortez. SP-CortJ; TtW

Roses. Rita Dove. SP-DoveR

Roses. Paul Laurence Dunbar. CP-DunbP

Roses and Pearls. Paul Laurence Dunbar. CP-DunbP

Roses and Revolutions. Dudley Randall. BPo; BrTr; PoBA; TtW

Roses, roses, roses. June. Henrietta Cordelia Ray. CBWP-3

Rotation. Julian Bond. NNP

Rough Trade Slumlord Totem. Ishmael Reed. CP-ReedI

Roun' dat po' ol' cabin do'. (LL) The Old Cabin. Paul Laurence Dunbar. CP-DunbP

Round about Midnight. Bob Kaufman. SP-KaufB

Round about midnight / the clock's ugly stare. The Plea. Yusef Komunyakaa. SP-KomuY

Round Midnight. Clarence Major. NAAAL

Round Midnight, Place de Congo. Kalamu ya Salaam. *Fr.* New Orleans Haiku. SpiFl

Round the wide earth, from the red field your valour has won. The Conquerors. Paul Laurence Dunbar. CP-DunbP

Rover was in clover. Poor Rover. Langston Hughes. CP-HughL

Rt. Rev. Richard Allen. Josephine D. Henderson Heard. CBWP-4

Rubin. Charles Cooper. PoBA

Rubinstein Staccato Etude, The. Robert Nathaniel Dett. BANP

Ruby Brown. Langston Hughes. CP-HughL; SP-HughL

Rudolph Reed was oaken. The Ballad of Rudolph Reed. Gwendolyn Brooks. SP-BrooG

Ruined Gal, A. Langston Hughes. CP-HughL

RULE: It is important not to wear out the freshness and original taste of a person's. The Art of the Nickname. Dominique Parker. SpiFl

Ruminations of Luke Johnson. Sterling A. Brown. CP-BrowS

Rumors open up. The Morning Star. Primus St. John. PoBA

Run, Nigger, Run! *Unknown.* BPo

("Run, nigger, run; de patter-roller catch you.") NAAAL

Runagate Runagate. Robert Hayden. BALP; BPo; CP-HaydR; ESEAA; IDB; NAAAL; PoBA; SSLK; TtW

Runaway, The. Albery Allson Whitman. AAP *Fr.* Not a Man, and Yet a Man

Runaway Lil Bit Poem, A. June Jordan. SP-JordJ

Rundown at Ned's Bar B.Q., The. Al Young. CP-YounA

Running across to the lot. Lucille Clifton. SP-ClifL

Running after the sea. (LL) Sisters in Arms. Audre Lorde. CP-LordA

Running through the jungle with my dick in my hand. *African-American Oral Tradition.* GetYo

Runs falls rises stumbles on from darkness into darkness. Runagate Runagate. Robert Hayden. BALP; BPo; CP-HaydR; ESEAA; IDB; NAAAL; PoBA; SSLK; TtW

Rush hour. I board the train. The Time Leading Up To. Sekou Sundiata.
    Fr. Notes from the Defense of Colin Ferguson. SpiFl
Rushing headlong / into new silence. Smelling Wind. Audre Lorde. CP-
    LordA
Russian Cathedral. Claude McKay. See St. Isaac's Church, Petrograd.
Russia's Resentment. Lizelia Augusta Jenkins Moorer. CBWP-3
Ruth. Norman J. Loftis. SpiFl
Ruth. Colleen J. McElroy. BlSi
Ruth and Naomi. Frances Ellen Watkins Harper. CP-HarpF
Rye Bread. William Stanley Braithwaite. CDC; GT

S

S, C, M. Ted Wilson. BlFi
S M. Alice Walker. CP-WalkA
"S.P.W.": Journey of Consciousness. Michael S. Harper. SP-HarpM
S-sss-ss-sh! Langston Hughes. CP-HughL; SP-HughL
Sabbath Bells. Josephine D. Henderson Heard. CBWP-4
Sack 'A Woe: Gallstones as History. Michael S. Harper. SP-HarpM
Sacrament of Poverty, The, for Judy Maines. Marilyn Nelson. GT; SP-
    NelsM
Sacred Chant for the Return of Black Spirit and Power. Amiri Baraka.
    NBV
Sacred words?, The. (LL) Ka 'Ba. Amiri Baraka. BPo; CrDW; NBV
Sacrifice, The. Gerald William Barrax. Klds
Sacrifice, The. Norman Jordan. BlFi
Sacrifice. Audre Lorde. CP-LordA; SP-LordA
Sad. And it comes. Valèry as Dictator. Amiri Baraka. SP-BaraA
Sad Hour of Your Peace, The. Al Young. CP-YounA
Sad Moscow, thy fate do I see. The Retreat from Moscow. George Moses
    Horton. SP-HortG
Saddest day will have an eve, The. Hope. Clara Ann Thompson. CBWP-2
Sadie and Maud. Gwendolyn Brooks. Fr. A Street in Bronzeville. BPo;
    BlSi; ESEAA; NAAAL; SP-BrooG
Sadie Snuffs a Candle. Dolores Kendrick. ESEAA
Sadie's Playhouse. Margaret Else Danner. Klds; PoBA
Safari to Bwagamoyo / Safari to Bwagamoyo. Bwagamoyo. Lebert
    Bethune. BlFi; PoBA
Safari West. John A. Williams. NBP
Safe Subjects. Yusef Komunyakaa. SP-KomuY
Saga of Resistance. Sun-Ra. BlFi
Sahara. Audre Lorde. CP-LordA; TtW
Sahara Bus Trip, The. Rita Dove. SP-DoveR
Said / a hip / lip-ful. Leg-acy of a Blue Capricorn. James Cunningham.
    JB
Said, it's strange, strange things, how we young fakes can be. Strange,
    Strange Things. African-American Oral Tradition. GetYo
Said the lady, Can you do. Question: "Said the lady, Can you do."
    Langston Hughes. SP-HughL. Fr. Montage of a Dream Deferred. CP-
    HughL
Sailing Date. Langston Hughes. CP-HughL
Sailor. Langston Hughes. CP-HughL
Sailor in Africa, The. Rita Dove. SP-DoveR
Sailor Sings Back to the Casuarinas, The. Derek Walcott. Fr. The Schooner
    Flight. ESEAA
Sailors on Leave. Owen Dodson. AmNP
Sailor's Song, A. Paul Laurence Dunbar. CP-DunbP
Sails flashing to the wind like weapons. Middle Passage. Frederick
    Douglass. CrDW
Saint gets up, The. The Saint's Dream. Marilyn Nelson. Fr. The Life of a
    Saint. SP-NelsM
Saint has come back to town, The. The Saint Preaches. Marilyn Nelson.
    Fr. The Life of a Saint. SP-NelsM
St. Isaac's Church, Petrograd. Claude McKay. AmNP; Klds; NAAAL;
    PoBA; SP-McKaC
    (Russian Cathedral.) CDC
Saint Leaves His Father's House, The. Marilyn Nelson. Fr. The Life of a
    Saint. SP-NelsM
St. Louis Blues. Unknown. BkSV; Crnst
St. Louis / such a colored town / a whiskey. Nappy Edges (A Cross Country
    Sojourn). Ntozake Shange. BlSi
Saint Malcolm. Jewel C. Latimore. BPo
Saint Peter Relates an Incident of the Resurrection Day. James Weldon
    Johnson. Klds
Saint Preaches, The. Marilyn Nelson. Fr. The Life of a Saint. SP-NelsM
Saint's Dream, The. Marilyn Nelson. Fr. The Life of a Saint. SP-NelsM

Salavation comes by Christ alone. Jupiter Hammon. See Evening Thought,
    An [: Salvation by Christ with Penetential Cries].
Sale began—young girls were there, The. The Slave Auction. Frances Ellen
    Watkins Harper. BPo
Sale of Souls. Adah Isaacs Menken. CBWP-1
Sally: Twelfth Street. Naomi Long Madgett. NBV
Salt. George Barlow. GT
Salt. Lucille Clifton. SP-ClifL
Salt. Yusef Komunyakaa. SP-KomuY
Salt Bread and Broom. Moving In. Audre Lorde. CP-LordA
Salt Peanuts! Salt Peanuts! (LL) Rebellion Suite. Askia Muhammad Touré.
    TtW
Salt'peanuts! / De-dop! (LL) Children's Rhymes. Langston Hughes. BPo;
    SP-HughL
Salutamus. Sterling A. Brown. CDC; CP-BrowS
Salute. Oliver Pitcher. Klds; PoBA
Salute to Soviet Armies. Langston Hughes. CP-HughL
Salvation comes by Christ alone. Evening Thought, An [: Salvation by
    Christ with Penetential Cries]. Jupiter Hammon. CrDW
Sam Smiley. Sterling A. Brown. CP-BrowS; NAAAL
Sam Solomon said. Ballad of Sam Solomon. Langston Hughes. CP-HughL
Samantha Is My Negro Cat. William J. Harris. GT
Sambo's Mistakes: an Essay. Michael S. Harper. SP-HarpM
Same as from the start?, The. (LL) Common Dust. Georgia Douglas
    Johnson. AmNP; PoBA; ShDr
Same Death Over and Over or Lullabies Are for Children, The. Audre
    Lorde. CP-LordA
Same in Blues. Langston Hughes. Fr. Lenox Avenue Mural. AmNP; SP-
    HughL; SSLK Fr. Montage of a Dream Deferred. CP-HughL
    ("But I'm talking about / Harlem to you!") (LL) AmNP
Same old spark!, The. (LL) New Yorkers. Langston Hughes. CP-HughL
Sammy Lou of Rue. Revolutionary Petunias. Alice Walker. BlSi; CP-
    WalkA
San Francisco County Jail Cell B-6. Conyus. PoBA
Sand. Dominique Parker. SpiFl
Sand-Man, The. Paul Laurence Dunbar. CP-DunbP
Sand-man he's a jolly old fellow, The. Johnny Speaks. Paul Laurence
    Dunbar. CP-DunbP
Sand wet and cool, The. Dennis Brutus. GT
Sanders Bottom. Sterling Plumpp. TtW
Sandman walks abroad tonight, The. Mister Sandman. Langston Hughes.
    CP-HughL
Sandra. Demetrice A. Worley. SpiFl
Sandstone carriage, A. For Cal. James Cunningham. JB
Sandy Star and Willie Gee. William Stanley Braithwaite. BANP
Sang a maiden in a meadow. Reunited. Henrietta Cordelia Ray. CBWP-3
Sank through easeful. The Diver. Robert Hayden. BPo; CP-HaydR; Klds;
    NAAAL
Sankofa. Haile Gerima. CtF
Sarah was banged and. And the Devil Sent a Ford Pinto Which She Also
    Routed. Ishmael Reed. CP-ReedI
Sarajevo Moon. Al Young. CP-YounA
Sarajevo Moonlight. Al Young. CP-YounA
Saraswati. Bob Kaufman. SP-KaufB
Sassafras Memories. Edward S. Spriggs. BlFi
Sassafras Tea. Mary Effie Lee Newsome. ShDr
Sat a damsel on the hillside. The Messengers. Henrietta Cordelia Ray.   .
    CBWP-3
Sat in the sun. Virginia. Elouise Loftin. PoBA
Sat. Nite. Jamal. CtF
Sat singing spirituals to sons. (LL) Ghetto Lovesong—Migration. Carole C.
    Gregory Clemmons. NBP; PoBA
Satan has enough in hell. (LL) For a Mouthy Woman. Countee Cullen.
    CP-CullC; PoBA
Satan's Playground of Hell. African-American Oral Tradition. GetYo
Satchmo. Melvin Beaunearus Tolson. BPo; NAAAL
Sather Tower Mystery. Ishmael Reed. CP-ReedI
Satisfaction Coal Company, The. Rita Dove. SP-DoveR
Satori. Gayl Jones. BlSi
Satuday morning, Motown. Collection Day. Natasha Trethewey. SpiFl
Saturday, April 26, 1973. A Poem to Galway Kinnell. Etheridge Knight.
    SP-KnigE
Saturday Morning Pancakes. Paula White-Jackson. CtF
Saturday Night. Langston Hughes. CP-HughL
Saturday Night. I Can't Get Started. Ai. GT
Saturday's Child. Countee Cullen. CP-CullC; Klds; NAAAL; PoBA
Saudades: The Portuguese Blues. Al Young. CP-YounA

Sautéed, baked or fried. Everywhere You Eat. Kalamu ya Salaam. *Fr.*
New Orleans Haiku. SpiFl

Savage Dreamer, The. Timothy Thomas Fortune. EBAP

Save the Boys. Frances Ellen Watkins Harper. AAP; CP-HarpF

Saved. Adah Isaacs Menken. CBWP-1

Saved at Last. Frances Ellen Watkins Harper. CP-HarpF

Saved by Faith. Frances Ellen Watkins Harper. CP-HarpF

Saville in Trouble. Albery Allson Whitman. AAP *Fr.* Not a Man, and Yet
a Man

Savior. Maya Angelou. CP-AngeM

Saxon Legend of Language, The. Mary Weston Fordham. AAP; CBWP-2

Saxophone / Has a vulgar tone, The. Conservatory Student Struggles with
Higher Instrumentation. Langston Hughes. CP-HughL

Saxophone turned into a dolphin, The. Albert Ayler: Eulogy for a
Decomposed Saxophone Player. Stanley Crouch. PoBA

Say, a little fly flew past my door. The Fly. *African-American Oral
Tradition.* GetYo

Say a mass for my soul's repose, my brother. The Murdered Lover. Paul
Laurence Dunbar. CP-DunbP

Say, boys, you can all have all these whores that rob and steal. No Good
Whore and Crime Don't Pay. *African-American Oral Tradition.* GetYo

Say day lay day may fay come some bum'll. Bludoo Baby, Want Money,
and Alligator Got It to Give. Amiri Baraka. BlFi

Say deep down in the jungle in the coconut grove. Signifying Monkey: "Say
deep down in the jungle in the coconut grove." *African-American Oral
Tradition.* GetYo

Say / Did you see that magnificent blonde beast. Ski Trail. Samuel Allen.
FB

Say, don't feel so downhearted, old buddy. Don't Feel So Downhearted,
Buddy. *African-American Oral Tradition.* GetYo

Say, don't look so downhearted, buddy. Don't Look So Downhearted,
Buddy. *African-American Oral Tradition.* GetYo

Say, heav'nly muse, what king, or mighty God. Isaiah LXIII, 1–8. Phillis
Wheatley. CP-WheaP

Say Hello to John. Sherley Anne Williams. BlSi

Say Hey Homeboy. Charlie R. Braxton. TtW

Say, I beg your pardon, ladies and gentlemen, will you give me your
attention please? Limpty Lefty McCree. *African-American Oral
Tradition.* GetYo

Say, I was standin' on the corner of Forty-seventh and South Park. Corner
of 47th and South Park. *African-American Oral Tradition.* GetYo

Say, if you see my little girl in Denver, I know she gonna feel blue. If You
See My Little Girl in Denver. *African-American Oral Tradition.* GetYo

Say it again—we are / spared nothing. (LL) Landscape for the Disappeared.
Yusef Komunyakaa. SP-KomuY

Say, Mister! / Uh-huh? On the Projects Playground. Etheridge Knight.
SP-KnigE

Say, muse divine, can hostile scenes delight. To Captain H——D, of the
65th Regiment. Phillis Wheatley. CP-WheaP

Say not the age is hard and cold. The Present Age. Frances Ellen Watkins
Harper. AAP; CP-HarpF

Say, now boys, I got something to tell you, just to get it off my mind.
Dogass Pimp. *African-American Oral Tradition.* GetYo

Say, now, some a you boys is down on these women because they drink
wine. Winehead Girl. *African-American Oral Tradition.* GetYo

Say, now, there's little Willie Weeper. Willie the Weeper. *African-
American Oral Tradition.* GetYo

Say, old Joe the Grinder was coppin' a snooze. Joe the Grinder and G.I.
Joe. *African-American Oral Tradition.* GetYo

Say, she'll be in the courtroom on the day a your trial. No Good Whore.
African-American Oral Tradition. GetYo

Say skinny manysided tall on the ball. To Merle. Lucille Clifton. SP-ClifL

Say, there was a feeble old man and kid they call Dan. Feeble Old Man.
African-American Oral Tradition. GetYo

Say we we were pushed to name a time. Tune. Al Young. CP-YounA

Say, you subject to a fall and a trip to the Wall. Subject to a Fall: "Say,
you subject to a fall and a trip to the Wall." *African-American Oral
Tradition.* GetYo

Say, you talk about your big convention, here's one you won't forget.
Hoboes' Convention. *African-American Oral Tradition.* GetYo

Say, you told me a lie and it wasn't no need. You Told Me a Lie. *African-
American Oral Tradition.* GetYo

Say, you want you a bitch than can burglarize, rob, and steal. The Pimp.
African-American Oral Tradition. GetYo

Saying we cannot waste time / only ourselves. (LL) Movement Song.
Audre Lorde. CP-LordA; SP-LordA

Says-so is in a woe of shuddered. Irritable Song. Russell Atkins. AmNP

Scaling your words like crags I found. Mentor. Audre Lorde. CP-LordA;
SP-LordA

Scamp. Paul Laurence Dunbar. CP-DunbP

Scar. Audre Lorde. CP-LordA

Scared? / are responsible negros running. Concerning One Responsible
Negro with Too Much Power. Nikki Giovanni. BPo

Scarlet Woman, The. Fenton Johnson. BANP; PoBA
("Gin is better than all the water in Lethe.") (LL) EBAP; NAAAL

Scarred young lifer said, The. (LL) The Prisoners. Robert Hayden. CP-
HaydR

Scenario VI. Amiri Baraka. SP-BaraA

Scenery. Ted Joans. PoBA

Schad paced the length of his studio. Agosta the Winged Man and Rasha
the Black Dove. Rita Dove. SP-DoveR

School bus drove us home from high school, where, The. Sisters. Marilyn
Nelson. SP-NelsM

School Note. Audre Lorde. CP-LordA

Schooner *Flight*, The. Derek Walcott. ESEAA
   Adios, Carenage.
   After the Storm.
   Fight with the Crew.
   Flight Anchors in Castries Harbor, The.
   Flight, Passing Blanchisseuse, The.
   Maria Concepcion & the Book of Dreams.
   Out of the Depths.
   Raptures of the Deep.
   Sailor Sings Back to the Casuarinas, The.
   Shabine Encounters the Middle Passage.
   Shabine Leaves the Republic.

Schooners with their pale green lights, The. A Dream within a Song.
Henrietta Cordelia Ray. CBWP-3

Schwerner, Chaney, Goodman. Raymond R. Patterson. NBV

Scintilla. William Stanley Braithwaite. AmNP; BANP; CDC; TtW

'Sciplinin' Sister Brown. James Edwin Campbell. AAP; AfAmPo; EBAP

Scottsboro. Langston Hughes. CP-HughL

Scottsboro, Too, Is Worth Its Song. Countee Cullen. CP-CullC; PoBA; TtW

Scottsboro's just a little place. The Town of Scottsboro. Langston Hughes.
CP-HughL

Scotty Has His Say. Sterling A. Brown. CP-BrowS

Scrapbooks. Nikki Giovanni. SP-GiovN

Scraps of Time. Mrs. Henry Linden. CBWP-4

Scream, The. May Miller. TtW

Screaming through the streets. (LL) Malcolm. Lucille Clifton. NAAAL;
SP-ClifL

Screams in the birth of her fading away. (LL) The Lake in Central Park.
Jay Wright. ESEAA; GT

Screams / screams / malcolm / does not hear my screams. Interlude:
"Screams / screams / malcolm / does not hear my screams." Welton
Smith. *Fr.* Malcolm. BlFi

Scuba Diver Recovers the Body of a Drowned Child, The. Gerald William
Barrax. GT; NBV

Sculpted from the clay of Africa. First Man. Naomi Long Madgett. IHS

Sculptor musing sat one eve, A. The Sculptor's Vision. Henrietta Cordelia
Ray. CBWP-3

Sculptor's Vision, The. Henrietta Cordelia Ray. CBWP-3

Sea Cadences. Henrietta Cordelia Ray. AAP; CBWP-3

Sea Calm. Langston Hughes. CP-HughL; SP-HughL

Sea charm / The sea's own children. Langston Hughes. CP-HughL

Sea is a wilderness of waves, The. Long Trip. Langston Hughes. CP-
HughL; SP-HughL

Sea is deep, The. Exits. Langston Hughes. CP-HughL

Sea Level. Al Young. CP-YounA

Sea speaks to me of you, The. Paul Laurence Dunbar. CP-DunbP

Sea-Turtle and the Shark, The. Melvin Beaunearus Tolson. PoBA

Search. Langston Hughes. CP-HughL

Search thou my heart. Confessional. Paul Laurence Dunbar. CP-DunbP

Searching, The. Alice S. Cobb. BlSi

Seascape. Langston Hughes. CP-HughL; SP-HughL
("Coming home.") (LL) GT

Seashore through Dark Glasses (Atlantic City). Langston Hughes. CP-
HughL; SP-HughL

Seasoning. Audre Lorde. CP-LordA

Seattle's still behind me now, and yet. Leaving Home for Home. Al
Young. CP-YounA

Second class is the second grade, The. Primary Lesson: The Second Class
Citizens. Sun-Ra. PoBA

Second Coming, The. Carl Clark. JB

Second Generation: New York. Langston Hughes. CP-HughL

Second-hand sights, like crumpled. Newark, for Now (68). Carolyn M.
Rodgers. PoBA

Second man I love, The. Spring. Carole C. Gregory Clemmons. PoBA

2nd Rapp. Nikki Giovanni. BrTr

Second Sermon on the Warpland, The. Gwendolyn Brooks. BPo; PoBA

Second Spring. Audre Lorde. CP-LordA

Secondline Send Off. Kalamu ya Salaam. *Fr.* New Orleans Haiku. SpiFl

Secret. Gwendolyn B. Bennett. BlSi; CDC; ShDr

Secret, The. Paul Laurence Dunbar. CP-DunbP

Secret. Mary Jenness. ShDr

Secret Garden, The. Rita Dove. SP-DoveR

Secret Messages. Tom Dent. TtW

Secretary to the Spirits, A. Ishmael Reed. CP-ReedI

Secular. Natasha Trethewey. SpiFl

Secured by sooted windows. Through the Inner City to the Suburbs. Maya Angelou. CP-AngeM; SP-AngeM

Seducing the Saint. Marilyn Nelson. *Fr.* The Life of a Saint. SP-NelsM

Seduction. Nikki Giovanni. BrTr; SP-GiovN

Seduction. Jo Ann Hall-Evans. BlSi

See dis pictyah in my han'? The Photograph. Paul Laurence Dunbar. CP-DunbP

See how dark the night settles on my face. Nocturne. Naomi Long Madgett. BALP

See sad deluded love in years too late. On an Old Deluded Soldier. George Moses Horton. SP-HortG

See, see, moon, O see what you done done. Al Young. CP-YounA

See See Rider, see what you done done! Gertrude "Ma" Rainey. NAAAL

See that lady. Lady's Boogie. SP-HughL Langston Hughes. *Fr.* Montage of a Dream Deferred. CP-HughL

See the Heart. Jean Toomer. CP-ToomJ; IHS

See! the moon is smiling. Eliza in Uncle Tom's Cabin. Eloise Bibb. CBWP-4

See! There he stands; not brave, but with an air. Brothers. James Weldon Johnson. BANP; NAAAL

SEED OF MY DAY BEGINS, THE. Personal Jihad. Gaston Neal. BlFi

Seed of Nimrod, The. De Leon Harrison. PoBA

Seedling, The. Paul Laurence Dunbar. CP-DunbP

Seeds. Thurmond Snyder. NNP

Seeing dogwood trees in bloom. The Dogwood Trees. Robert Hayden. CP-HaydR

Seek to modernize. Heathen Technology & Media. Amiri Baraka. SP-BaraA

Seeker, The. Ahmos, II Zu-Bolton. TtW

Seeking Religion. Sterling A. Brown. CP-BrowS

Seems lak folks is mighty curus. Foolin' wid de Seasons. Paul Laurence Dunbar. CP-DunbP

Seems lak to me de stars don't shine so bright. Sence You Went Away. James Weldon Johnson. BALP; BANP; NAAAL

Seems like I heard. Sunnyland. Elmore James. NAAAL

Seems there was this Professor. Sather Tower Mystery. Ishmael Reed. CP-ReedI

Seen my lady home las' night. A Negro Love Song. Paul Laurence Dunbar. AAP; BANP; CP-DunbP; CrDW; NAAAL; SSLK; TtW

Seen you down at chu'ch las' night. Discovered. Paul Laurence Dunbar. CP-DunbP

Sees the man. The Carver. Lucille Clifton. SP-ClifL

Selassie at Geneva. Marcus B. Christian. TtW

Selectric II. Al Young. CP-YounA

Self. Norman Henry, II Pritchard. PoBA

Self Criticism. Countee Cullen. CP-CullC

Self Defense. Ai. ESEAA

Self-Doubt. Lance Jeffers. TtW

Self-Hatred of Don L. Lee, The. Haki R. Madhubuti. BPo; ESEAA

Self-Mastery. Henrietta Cordelia Ray. CBWP-3

Self-Portrait: Holding On. Al Young. CP-YounA

Self-Reliance. James M. Whitfield. NAAAL

Self World. Clarence Major. NBV

Selfless at this entrance to the universe. (LL) I sit in my room. Jean Toomer. CP-ToomJ; GT

Seminole, The. Benjamin Clark. EBAP

Sence You Went Away. James Weldon Johnson. BALP; BANP; NAAAL

Send for the pied paper and let him pipe the rats away. Final Call. Langston Hughes. CP-HughL

Send me no flowers, for they will die before they leave America. Junglegrave. S. E. Anderson. PoBA

Send me O' Allah as a. An Angels Prayer. Lefty Sims. BlFi

Send soldiers again to kill you, Garcia. Lines to Garcia Lorca. Amiri Baraka. NNP

Sending their negro / toms into the ghetto. The Wall. Haki R. Madhubuti. BrTr

Sense of Coolness, A, *for Stanley Crouch*. Quincy Troupe. GT; PoBA

Senses of Insecurity. Maya Angelou. CP-AngeM; SP-AngeM

Sensing death, / The buzzards gather. Dying Beast. Langston Hughes. CP-HughL

Sensuous / sloe eyed. Seduction. Jo Ann Hall-Evans. BlSi

Sent for You Yesterday. Jimmy Rushing. NAAAL

Sentience. Al Young. CP-YounA

Separation. Audre Lorde. SP-LordA

("Stars dwindle / and will not reward me, The.") CP-LordA

Sepia Fashion Show. Maya Angelou. BlSi; CP-AngeM; SP-AngeM

September. Henrietta Cordelia Ray. CBWP-3

September Night, A. George Marion McClellan. AAP; AfAmPo; EBAP

Sequelae. Audre Lorde. CP-LordA

Sequences. Sonia Sanchez. SP-SancS

Seravezza. Hoyt W. Fuller. PoBA

Serenade: "Sleep, love sleep." Mary Weston Fordham. CBWP-2

Series of small, on, A. Insignificant. Maya Angelou. CP-AngeM

Sermon in the Cotton Field. Marilyn Nelson. *Fr.* Thus Far by Faith. SP-NelsM

Sermon in the Ruined Garden. Marilyn Nelson. *Fr.* Thus Far by Faith. SP-NelsM

Sermon in the Woodlot. Marilyn Nelson. *Fr.* Thus Far by Faith. SP-NelsM

Sermon on the Warpland, The. Gwendolyn Brooks. BPo; PoBA

Sermonette. Ishmael Reed. CP-ReedI; PoBA

Servant met him at the outer gate, A. Albery Allson Whitman. *Fr.* Leelah Misled. EBAP

Served him right! How could he dare. The Dismissal of Tyng. Frances Ellen Watkins Harper. CP-HarpF

Service. Georgia Douglas Johnson. CDC

Serving Girl, The. Gladys May Casely Hayford. CDC; ShDr

Seth Bingham. William W. Cook. SpiFl

Setting / had no special theme, The. Slow Riff for Billy. James Cunningham. JB

Setting in the house with everything on my mind. In the House Blues. Bessie Smith. NAAAL

Setting in the wine-house. Wine-O. Langston Hughes. *Fr.* Montage of a Dream Deferred. CP-HughL

Setting / Slow Drag. Carolyn M. Rodgers. JB

Setting Sun, The. George Moses Horton. BALP

Seven Floating lead moons. Blue O'Clock. Bob Kaufman. SP-KaufB

7:47 a.m. Now's the Time. Al Young. CP-YounA

Seven holes in my heart where flames live. Vigil. Audre Lorde. CP-LordA

Seven ladies. Parade. Langston Hughes. *Fr.* Montage of a Dream Deferred. CP-HughL

Seven letters, / Seven songs. Ballad of the Seven Songs. Langston Hughes. CP-HughL

Seven Moments of Love. Langston Hughes. CP-HughL

  Bed Time.

  Daybreak.

  Letter.

  Pay Day.

  Sunday.

  Supper Time.

  Twilight Reverie.

7 + 7 + love =. Addition: "7 + 7 + love =." Langston Hughes. CP-HughL

Seven Wise Men, The. *African-American Oral Tradition*. GetYo

Seven Women's Blessed Assurance. Maya Angelou. CP-AngeM

Seven years without milk. Ethiopia. Audre Lorde. CP-LordA

1711. / Paramarimbo. Fugitive Slaves. Gale Jackson. SpiFl

17 luxury condominiums / electronically protected. The Politics of Addiction. Audre Lorde. CP-LordA

Seventh April. Al Young. CP-YounA

Seventh Sign, The. Audre Lorde. SP-LordA

(Seventh Sense, The.) CP-LordA

Seventh Son. Ed Roberson. PoBA

'70s, The. Lucille Clifton. SP-ClifL

Seventy-one years. Sonia Sanchez. SP-SancS

Sévignés, The. Anne Spencer. ShDr

Sewanee Hills of dear delight. The Hills of Sewanee. George Marion McClellan. BANP

Sewerplant Grows in Harlem or I'm a Stranger Here Myself When Does the Next Swan Leave, A. Audre Lorde. CP-LordA; SP-LordA

Sex fingers toes / in the marketplace. Dear John, Dear Coltrane. Michael S. Harper. NAAAL; SP-HarpM; TtW

Sexless, my brother flies. Song. Summer. Rita Dove. SP-DoveR

Sexual Privacy of Women on Welfare. Pinkie Gordon Lane. BlSi

Shabine Encounters the Middle Passage. Derek Walcott. *Fr.* The Schooner *Flight.* ESEAA

Shabine Leaves the Republic. Derek Walcott. *Fr.* The Schooner *Flight.* ESEAA

Shabine sang to you from the depths of the sea. (LL) After the Storm. Derek Walcott. ESEAA

Shadder in de valley. Noon. Paul Laurence Dunbar. CP-DunbP

Shade that was Elizabeth . . . immortal completeness! (LL) Life-long, Poor Browning. Anne Spencer. CDC

Shades of eve are quickly closing in, The. Night. Josephine D. Henderson Heard. CBWP-4

Shades of Pharoah Sanders Blues for My Baby. John O'Neal. NBV

Shades of Pigmeat. Langston Hughes. *Fr.* Ask Your Mama; 12 Moods for Jazz. CP-HughL

Shadow. Richard Bruce. CDC

Shadow and Sunrise. Henrietta Cordelia Ray. CBWP-3

Shadow faces. Chord. Langston Hughes. SP-HughL *Fr.* Montage of a Dream Deferred. CP-HughL

Shadow of an awful crime, The. The Lake City Tragedy. Frances Ellen Watkins Harper. CP-HarpF

Shadow people, projected on coffee-shop walls. Bagel Shop Jazz. Bob Kaufman. SP-KaufB

Shadows. Langston Hughes. CP-HughL

Shadows / Of too many nights of love, The. Soledad. Langston Hughes. CP-HughL

Shadows on the wall. Life Doesn't Frighten Me. Maya Angelou. CP-AngeM; SP-AngeM

Shadows, shadows, / Hug me round. Escape. Georgia Douglas Johnson. PoBA; ShDr; TtW

Shake your brown feet, honey. Song for a Banjo Dance. Langston Hughes. CP-HughL

Shaken by his bad press, the wolf. Foolology. Ishmael Reed. CP-ReedI

Shaker, Why Don't You Sing? Maya Angelou. CP-AngeM; SP-AngeM

Shakespeare. Henrietta Cordelia Ray. CBWP-3; EBAP

Shakespeare in Harlem. Langston Hughes. CP-HughL

Shakespeare Say. Rita Dove. SP-DoveR

Shall always share our admiration. (LL) Common Things. Paul Laurence Dunbar. CP-DunbP; GT

Shall bear thee up against their frown. (LL) To Cinque. James M. Whitfield. EBAP; TtW

Shall drink our tears. (LL) If You Come Softly. Audre Lorde. CP-LordA

Shall drink our tears. (LL) Memorial I. Audre Lorde. CP-LordA

Shall i die / shall i die. Life / Poem. Sonia Sanchez. BrTr

Shall I go all my bright days singing. Self Criticism. Countee Cullen. CP-CullC

Shall I make a record of your beauty? My Beloved. Langston Hughes. CP-HughL

Shall I tell you of my old, old dreams. Pictures to the Wall. Langston Hughes. CP-HughL

Shall not supplant our liberty! (LL) Though Tennyson, the poet king. James Madison Bell. AAP; AfAmPo

Shall the Good Go Down? Langston Hughes. CP-HughL

Shame on You. Langston Hughes. *Fr.* Montage of a Dream Deferred. CP-HughL

Shape the lips to an *o*, say *a*. Ö. Rita Dove. SP-DoveR

Share-Croppers. Langston Hughes. CP-HughL; SP-HughL

Sharecroppers. Sterling A. Brown. BrowS; Crnst

Sharers of a common country. Home, Sweet Home. Frances Ellen Watkins Harper. CP-HarpF

SHARK MONSTER Rockefeller. At the Colonial Y They Are Aesthetically and Culturally Deprived (Y's Later) (31). Amiri Baraka. SP-BaraA

Sharon Will Be No/Where on Nobody's Best-selling List. Sharon Scott. JB

She agitates / the quart developing tank. The Negatives. Michael S. Harper. SP-HarpM

She aint sold out yet & her tongue's still flapping. (LL) Not Her, She Aint No Gypsy. Al Young. CP-YounA

She asked me / the same thing. (LL) Strange beautiful woman, A. Marilyn Nelson. SP-NelsM

She came from the East a fair, young bride. Going East. Frances Ellen Watkins Harper. CP-HarpF

She came home blameless. (LL) The Mothering Blackness. Maya Angelou. CP-AngeM; SP-AngeM

She came home running. The Mothering Blackness. Maya Angelou. CP-AngeM; SP-AngeM

She came too late and lonely / to this place. (LL) The Singer Will Not Sing. Maya Angelou. CP-AngeM; SP-AngeM

She caught a butterfly. Patroness. Gerald William Barrax. Klds

She coaxes her fat in front of her. New Day. Naomi Long Madgett. BlSi

She coulda been somethin. Ho. Al Young. CP-YounA

She couldnot make him over. Sister Blues with Livewire Davis. Ahmos, II Zu-Bolton. TtW

She cried out for Mama, who did not. Persephone Abducted. Rita Dove. NAAAL

She cursed the circumstance. (LL) The Ballad of Sue Ellen Westerfield. Robert Hayden. CP-HaydR; ESEAA; Klds

She danced, near nude, to tom-tom beat. Zalka Peetruza. Ray Garfield Dandridge. BANP; PoBA

She decided it was all / right. (LL) Woman. Nikki Giovanni. SP-GiovN

She didn't know she was beautiful. On Getting a Natural. Dudley Randall. FB; PoBA

She didn't like to think in abstracts. Introspection. Nikki Giovanni. SP-GiovN

She discovered she felt better. Particulars. Rita Dove. Crnst

She does not know. No Images. Waring Cuney. AmNP; BANP; CDC; SSLK

She doesn't wear. Gwendolyn Brooks Elizabeth. Haki R. Madhubuti. ESEAA

She done put huh little hands. Conjured. Sterling A. Brown. CP-BrowS

She don't have no sense. (LL) Admonitions. Lucille Clifton. BPo; SP-ClifL

She draped naked buildings with daydreams. Doris. Angela Shannon. CtF

She draws fat birds. Why Tu Fu Does Not Speak of the Nubian. Colleen J. McElroy. TtW

She dreams the baby's so small she keeps. Motherhood. Rita Dove. NAAAL; SP-DoveR

She even thinks that up in heaven. For a Lady I Know. Countee Cullen. *Fr.* Four Epitaphs. AmNP; CDC; CP-CullC; IDB; PoBA; SSLK

She Gave Me a Rose. Paul Laurence Dunbar. CP-DunbP

She goes to different bars. There Is a Woman in This Town. Patricia Parker. BlSi

She grew up in bedeviled southern wilderness. The Ballad of Sue Ellen Westerfield. Robert Hayden. CP-HaydR; ESEAA; Klds

She Had Known Brothers. Sherley Anne Williams. GT

She has had to bear. (LL) The Whipping. Robert Hayden. CP-HaydR; IDB; PoBA; SSLK

She has not found herself a hard pillow. To Clarissa Scott Delany. Angelina Weld Grimké. AmNP; ShDr

She holds to the idea. Visit. Gerald William Barrax. GT

She Hugged Me and Kissed Me. *Unknown.* BPo

She, in dowdy dress and dumpy. Still Life: Lady with Birds. Quandra Prettyman. PoBA

She, / In the dark. Helen Keller. Langston Hughes. CP-HughL

She Insists on Me. Lucille Clifton. SP-ClifL

She Is Dreaming. Lucille Clifton. SP-ClifL

She is flat on her back. E. Ethelbert Miller. GT

She is glad to be home again. (LL) April Rape. Marilyn Nelson. SP-NelsM

She / Is like / A wrinkled apple. An Old Slave Woman. Joyce Sims Carrington. ShDr

She is lovely. Her eys are big almonds. Sub Shop Girl. Michael S. Weaver. SpiFl

She is not dead, but sleepeth. Mrs. Rebecca Weston. Mary Weston Fordham. CBWP-2

She jes' gits hold of us dataway. (LL) Ma Rainey. Sterling A. Brown. CP-BrowS; NAAAL; TtW

She kneads the kernels, grains. Kneading. Michael S. Harper. SP-HarpM

She kneeled before me begging. Confession. Donald Jeffrey Hayes. CDC

She knows / she knows. (LL) The Coming of Kali. Lucille Clifton. SP-ClifL

She knows / The end of the evening will come. Lady in Cabaret. Langston Hughes. CP-HughL

She lay, skin down on the moist dirt. Our Grandmothers. Maya Angelou. CP-AngeM

She leaned her head upon her hand. Vashti. Frances Ellen Watkins Harper. AAP; BlSi; CP-HarpF; EBAP; NAAAL; TtW

She leans across a golden table. Epitaph. Countee Cullen. CP-CullC

She lies down in a mess. About Enrique's Drawing. June Jordan. SP-JordJ

She lifts the two boys on. Oak. Michael S. Harper. SP-HarpM

She liked mornings the best—Thomas gone. Weathering Out. Rita Dove. SP-DoveR

She lived in sinful happiness. Girl. Langston Hughes. CP-HughL

She lived out a decent span of years. Departure. Langston Hughes. CP-HughL

She made the trip daily, though. Drapery Factory, Gulfport, Mississippi, 1956. Natasha Trethewey. SpiFl

She meditates on how rocks rise. The Thorn Merchant's Wife. Yusef Komunyakaa. SP-KomuY

She now retraces her steps once more. December Portrait. Kathleen Tankersley Young. ShDr

She of the Dancing Feet Sings. Countee Cullen. CP-CullC

She often wondered why people spoke. Turning (I Need a Better Title). Nikki Giovanni. SP-GiovN

She realized / she wasn't one. Life Cycles. Nikki Giovanni. SP-GiovN

She roamed the meadows long in hope. Recompensed? Henrietta Cordelia Ray. CBWP-3

She said she forgave me. Parted. Clara Ann Thompson. CBWP-2

She said the Jehovah Witness man. 3-31-70. Gayl Jones. BlSi

She said: "When I was with him." Alice Walker. CP-WalkA

She sang, and I listened the whole song thro'. Remembered. Paul Laurence Dunbar. CP-DunbP

She sang me the churchsong. Sunset Beach. Ahmos, II Zu-Bolton. TtW

She says Go fuck yourself. Translating Footsteps. Yusef Komunyakaa. SP-KomuY

She Sent Him Away. Clara Ann Thompson. CBWP-2

She shades the prints bathed. Utility Room. Michael S. Harper. SP-HarpM

She should be. Julius Lester. Fr. Poems. Klds

She Should Have Called 911. Pam Ward. CtF

She sits in the marketplace. Pearle's Poem. Primus St. John. GT

She sits there. Girl at the Window. Pinkie Gordon Lane. GT

She slid past. And She Was Bad. Marvin, Jr. Wyche. AmNP

She stands / In the quiet darkness. Troubled Woman. Langston Hughes. CP-HughL; SP-HughL

She stood at Jesus' feet. Mary at the Feet of Christ. Frances Ellen Watkins Harper. CP-HarpF

She stood hanging wash before sun. Ghetto Lovesong—Migration. Carole C. Gregory Clemmons. NBP; PoBA

She stood nakedly. After Her Man Had Left Her for the Sixth Time That Year / (An Uncommon Occurrence). Haki R. Madhubuti. GT

She stopped traffic. Tribal Marks. Saundra Sharp. SpiFl

She sweeps the kitchen floor of the river bed her husband saw fit. Pomade. Rita Dove. SP-DoveR

She talks too loud, her face. Aunt. Al Young. CP-YounA

She thought herself inspired. Blue Deep. Quo Vadis Gex-Breaux. TtW

She told her beads with downcast eyes. Paul Laurence Dunbar. CP-DunbP

She told the story, and the whole world wept. Harriet Beecher Stowe. Paul Laurence Dunbar. AAP; BPo; CP-DunbP; Klds

She tripped and fell against a star. Innocence. Anne Spencer. CDC; ShDr

She trips across the meadows. April. Henrietta Cordelia Ray. CBWP-3

She Understands Me. Lucille Clifton. SP-ClifL

She used to / pack poems. Emily Dickinson's Defunct. Marilyn Nelson. ESEAA; SP-NelsM

She waited on the 7th floor. Frank Albert and Viola Benzena Owens. Ntozake Shange. BlSi

She walked alone, as she did every morning. Spy. Rita Dove. SP-DoveR

She walked along the crowded street. Revelation. Blanche Taylor Dickinson. CDC

She walked nude beside them. Springtime. Norman Henry, II Pritchard. GT

She wanted a little room for thinking. Daystar. Rita Dove. NAAAL; SP-DoveR; Kids

She wanted pretty fine. Aunt Jessie. Wanda Coleman. GT

She wanted to be a blade. Woman. Nikki Giovanni. SP-GiovN

She wants to hear. Sunday Greens. Rita Dove. GT; SP-DoveR

She was afraid of men. Chicken-Licken. Maya Angelou. CP-AngeM; SP-AngeM

She was really neat, man. Jazzy Vanity. Richard W. Thomas. BlFi

She was the great baby sitter—tall dignified. Miss Jones. Wanda Coleman. IHS

She was young and beautiful. Ruby Brown. Langston Hughes. CP-HughL; SP-HughL

She wears, my beloved, a rose upon her head. Requiem. John Frederick Matheus. CDC

She went to buy a brand new hat. Colors. Countee Cullen. CP-CullC

She who dances in campfire flames. Amazon. Ojenke. CtF

She / Who searched for lovers. To a Little Lover-Lass, Dead. Langston Hughes. CP-HughL

She who was easy for any chance lover. Effie. Sterling A. Brown. BANP; CP-BrowS

She will know. (LL) The Scuba Diver Recovers the Body of a Drowned Child. Gerald William Barrax. GT; NBV

She winds her way down dark dingy avenues/alleys/mind. Shopping Bag Lady. Wanda Coleman. Crnst

She wished of him a lover's kiss and. Communication I. Maya Angelou. CP-AngeM; SP-AngeM

She / wore / her flossiest smile. Movie Queen. James P. Vaughn. NNP

She wrapped her soul in a lace of lies. Parted. Paul Laurence Dunbar. CP-DunbP

Shearing Time. Langston Hughes. CP-HughL

Shebba's sons slowly starve. Spirits Struggle. Christopher Stanard. CtF

She'd do it agin'! (LL) Ballad of the Girl Whose Name Is Mud. Langston Hughes. CP-HughL; SP-HughL

Shedding my years and. Sonia Sanchez. SP-SancS

Sheila. Bob Kaufman. SP-KaufB

Shepherd's Song at Christmas. Langston Hughes. CP-HughL

Sherbet. Cornelius Eady. GT

She's blacker / than the night which holds. Blues Alabama. Michael S. Harper. SP-HarpM

She's dreaming / of salt again. Nightmare. Rita Dove. SP-DoveR

She's Free! Frances Ellen Watkins Harper. BlSi

She's now yo' own. Salute yo' bride! (LL) Slave Marriage Ceremony Supplement. Unknown. BPo; CrDW

She's resting in the bosom of Jesus. (LL) Go Down Death. James Weldon Johnson. BkSV

Shet up dat noise, you chillen! Dar's some one at de do'. 'Sciplinin' Sister Brown. James Edwin Campbell. AAP; AfAmPo; EBAP

Shine and the Titanic. Unknown. NAAAL

Shine and the Titanic. Unknown. CrDW

(Sinking of the Titanic.) NAAAL

Shine down on that babe o' mine. (LL) Long Track Blues. Sterling A. Brown. CP-BrowS

Shine was in Sugar Ray's Bar drinking Seagrams Seven. (LL) Shine and the Titanic. Unknown. CrDW; NAAAL

Shine was up in Harlem damn near drunk. (LL) Dark Prophecy: I Sing of Shine. Etheridge Knight. BPo; Crnst; ESEAA; SP-KnigE

Shining Parlor, The. Anita Scott Coleman. ShDr

Shiny record albums scattered over. As You Leave Me. Etheridge Knight. BrTr; SP-KnigE

Ship is sailing, see! afar, A. The Dream. Francis A. Boyd. Fr. Columbiana. EBAP

Ship That Went Down, The. Adah Isaacs Menken. CBWP-1

Ships? / Sure I'll sail them. Call Letters: Mrs. V.B. Maya Angelou. CP-AngeM; SP-AngeM

Ships That Pass in the Night. Paul Laurence Dunbar. BANP; CDC; CP-DunbP

Shipwreck. Mary Weston Fordham. CBWP-2, tr. by Mary Ann Caws

Sho can't find no ease. (LL) Gypsy Man. Langston Hughes. CP-HughL; NAAAL

Shoot him while he run. (LL) Riot: 60's. Maya Angelou. CP-AngeM; SP-AngeM

Shooter in Jersey, black. Air Jordan, black, The. The Case through the Looking Glass. Sekou Sundiata. Fr. Notes from the Defense of Colin Ferguson. SpiFl

Shooting Back. Thomas Sayers Ellis. GT

Shoplifter. Solomon Edwards. NNP

Shopping Bag Lady. Wanda Coleman. Crnst

Shore is cabbage green and reeks, The. Early Morning on the Tel Aviv-Haifa Freeway. Rita Dove. SP-DoveR

Short magic / is a kiss. Magic. Sonia Sanchez. SP-SancS

Short Note to My Very Critical and Well-Beloved Friends and Comrades, A. June Jordan. SP-JordJ

Short Poem. Kenneth Carroll. SpiFl

Short Poem. Sonia Sanchez. SP-SancS

Short Speech to My Friends. Amiri Baraka. ESEAA; SP-BaraA

Shot me to the curb. Shot to the Curb. Derrick X. CtF

Shot through with silver gray light. The One Snapshot I Couldn't Take in France. Al Young. SpiFl

Shot to the Curb. Derrick X. CtF

Should blaze the path of thunder. (LL) Tableau. Countee Cullen. BANP; CP-CullC; Klds; NAAAL; PoBA

Should I sing a requiem, as the trap closes? Perhaps. Bob Kaufman. Klds

Should kill no one. (LL) Love is not concerned. Alice Walker. CP-WalkA

Should you, my lord, while you pursue my song. Phillis Wheatley. BPo; Klds

Shoulders sag. Junkie Monkey Reel. Maya Angelou. CP-AngeM; SP-AngeM

Shout. Langston Hughes. CP-HughL; SP-HughL

Show Fare, Please. Langston Hughes. Fr. Ask Your Mama; 12 Moods for Jazz. CP-HughL

Show Me Lord Show Me. Yusef Iman. BlFi

Showing that our ways agreed. For an Evolutionist and His Opponent. Countee Cullen. CP-CullC

Shredded sunset, The. Night Interpreted. Everett Hoagland. NBP

Shrine to What Should Be. Mari E. Evans. NNP

Shroud of Color, The. Countee Cullen. CP-CullC; NAAAL

Shy dawn tenderly. Sunrise on the River. Kalamu ya Salaam. *Fr.* New Orleans Haiku. SpiFl

Sic Vita. William Stanley Braithwaite. BANP; NAAAL

Sick / black grass will. For Cardinal Spellman Who Hated Voo Doo. Ishmael Reed. CP-ReedI

Sick Room. Langston Hughes. CP-HughL

Sick tightening. Brain damage movie, The. A Western Lady. Amiri Baraka. SP-BaraA

Sickle Pears. Owen Dodson. AmNP

Side by Side. Sterling A. Brown. CP-BrowS

Sifting the salt sea / air. (LL) African Images, Glimpses from a Tiger's Back. Alice Walker. CP-WalkA

Sight of the coffee was good for sore eyes, The. Upon Receipt of a Pound of Coffee in 1863. Mary E. Tucker. CBWP-1

Sighted a black tornado of. Comments. Peggy Susberry Kenner. JB

Sightseeing. Rita Dove. GT; SP-DoveR

Signal Gun, The. Mary E. Tucker. CBWP-1

Signals. Jewel C. Latimore. PoBA

Signifying Darkness, The. Owen Dodson. TtW

Signifying Monkey: "Back down in the jungle up under the stick." *African-American Oral Tradition.* GetYo

Signifying Monkey: "Deep down in the jungle in the coconut grove." *African-American Oral Tradition.* GetYo

Signifying Monkey: "Down in the jungle about treetop deep." *African-American Oral Tradition.* GetYo

Signifying Monkey: "It was early in the morning one bright summer day." *African-American Oral Tradition.* GetYo

Signifying Monkey: "Say deep down in the jungle in the coconut grove." *African-American Oral Tradition.* GetYo

Signifying Monkey: "There hadn't been no shift for quite a bit." *African-American Oral Tradition.* GetYo

Signifying Monkey, The. *Unknown.* CrDW; NAAAL

Signing the Pledge. Frances Ellen Watkins Harper. CP-HarpF

Signs. Audre Lorde. SP-LordA

("No one is left here to eat by my fire.") CP-LordA

Signs, The. Norman Henry, II Pritchard. NBV

Signs of Spring. Langston Hughes. CP-HughL

Signs of the Times. Paul Laurence Dunbar. CP-DunbP

Silence. Paul Laurence Dunbar. CP-DunbP

Silence. Langston Hughes. CP-HughL

Silence, and whirling worlds afar. Night. Paul Laurence Dunbar. CP-DunbP

Silence / between the floorboards. Neighbor. Bahiyyih Maroon. SpiFl

Silence slipping around like death, A. A Winter Twilight. Angelina Weld Grimké. CDC; NAAAL; PoBA; ShDr

Silent Night, The. Mrs. Henry Linden. CBWP-4

Silent One. Langston Hughes. CP-HughL

Silent Prophet, The. Norman Jordan. NBV

Silently / or LOUD. (LL) Black Art. Amiri Baraka. ESEAA; NAAAL; SP-BaraA

Silently without my window. Melancholia. Paul Laurence Dunbar. CP-DunbP

Silhouette. Langston Hughes. CP-HughL; SP-HughL

Silhouette / On the face of the moon. Shadow. Richard Bruce. CDC

Silly Animals. Langston Hughes. CP-HughL

Silvery Fountain. Mary E. Tucker. CBWP-1

Simon the Cyrenian Speaks. Countee Cullen. AmNP; BPo; CP-CullC

Simon's Countrymen. Frances Ellen Watkins Harper. CP-HarpF

Simon's Feast. Frances Ellen Watkins Harper. CP-HarpF

Simple, (For Langston Hughes). Naomi Long Madgett. FB; GT; PoBA

Simple dirt road, A. A Walk in the Daytime Is Just as Dangerous as a Walk in the Night. E. Ethelbert Miller. TtW

Simple silly terror, The. Doorknobs. Langston Hughes. CP-HughL

Simple Wisdom, The. Marilyn Nelson. SP-NelsM

Sin of Achar, The. Frances Ellen Watkins Harper. CP-HarpF

Since 1619. Margaret Abigail Walker. CP-WalkM

Since he had few intimate friends, and little. "Women of Color" Have Rarely Had the Opportunity to Write about Their Love Affairs. Alice Walker. CP-WalkA

Since I don't want to trip over your silence. Ghost. Audre Lorde. CP-LordA

Since I left the city's heat. At Loafing-Holt. Paul Laurence Dunbar. CP-DunbP

Since I left you, Anne. A Letter to Anne. Langston Hughes. CP-HughL

Since I was minutely hurt. Minutely Hurt. Countee Cullen. CP-CullC

Since men grow diffident at last. Youth Sings a Song of Rosebuds. Countee Cullen. BANP; CP-CullC

Since Naturally Black is Naturally Beautiful. Naturally. Audre Lorde. BlSi; CP-LordA

Since you wrote a poem. What Color Is Lonely. Carolyn M. Rodgers. BPo

Sing!/ Great dark oak. Lines to the Black Oak. Oliver La Grone. NBV

Sing a Song of Singapore. Al Young. CP-YounA

Sing Me a New Song. John Henrik Clarke. PoBA

Sing me a song of the Revolution. Song of the Revolution. Langston Hughes. CP-HughL

Sing of lusty foods. MAke You Go Oohhh! Kalamu ya Salaam. *Fr.* New Orleans Haiku. SpiFl

Singer, The. Gerald William Barrax. ESEAA

Singer, The. James Danner. BlFi

Singer Will Not Sing, The. Maya Angelou. CP-AngeM; SP-AngeM

Singers / singers like O-. Horn of Plenty. Langston Hughes. *Fr.* Ask Your Mama; 12 Moods for Jazz. CP-HughL

Singing black boatmen. Fog. Langston Hughes. CP-HughL

Singing Hallelujia. Fenton Johnson. NAAAL

Singing his name. Sweet Bread. Frank X. Walker. SpiFl

Singing in the Rain. Countee Cullen. CP-CullC

Singular prints filed along damp banks. The Biggest Fisherman. Bob Kaufman. SP-KaufB

Singular Yen, A. Al Young. CP-YounA

Singularly and in pairs the decade has been ripped by bullets. Lines. Herbert Martin. PoBA

Sinking of the *Titanic. Unknown. See* Shine and the Titanic.

Sinner. Langston Hughes. CP-HughL; SP-HughL

Sinner. Norman Jordan. BlFi

Sipping the new tea. Haiku: "Sipping the new tea." Lenard D. Moore. TtW

Sipping whiskey and gin. Analysands. Dudley Randall. BPo

Sir / I read of late. Four Questions Addressed to His Excellency, the Prime Minister. James P. Vaughn. AmNP

Sir, We Would See Jesus. Frances Ellen Watkins Harper. AAP; AfAmPo; CP-HarpF

Siren Bird, The. Henrietta Cordelia Ray. CBWP-3

Sister. Langston Hughes. *Fr.* Montage of a Dream Deferred. CP-HughL

Sister Blues with Livewire Davis. Ahmos, II Zu-Bolton. TtW

Sister Brother Don't You Stumble. Jon Goncalves. BlFi

Sister darling, ope the window, let the balmy air once more. The Dying Girl. Mary Weston Fordham. CBWP-2

Sister Johnson Marches. Langston Hughes. CP-HughL

Sister Johnson's Speech. Maggie Pogue Johnson. CBWP-4

Sister Lakin and Lally. Dorothy Perry Thompson. SpiFl

Sister Lou. Sterling A. Brown. AmNP; BkSV; CP-BrowS; PoBA

Sister, Morning Is a Time for Miracles. Audre Lorde. SP-LordA

("Core of the conversations we never had, A.") CP-LordA

Sister Outsider. Audre Lorde. CP-LordA

Sister Roll. Sabah As-Sabah. CtF

Sisters. Lucille Clifton. SP-ClifL

Sisters. Marilyn Nelson. SP-NelsM

Sisters!/ I love you. To Those of My Sisters Who Kept Their Naturals. Gwendolyn Brooks. TtW

Sisters in Arms. Audre Lorde. CP-LordA

Sit-in, The. Darwin T. Turner. BALP

Sit-Ins. Margaret Abigail Walker. CP-WalkM

"Sitr, cooks," the mistress whispers, in a rage. Albery Allson Whitman. *Fr.* Leelah Misled. EBAP

Sitting in the kitchen. Self-Portrait: Holding On. Al Young. CP-YounA

Situation. Langston Hughes. *Fr.* Montage of a Dream Deferred. CP-HughL

Six-Bits Blues. Langston Hughes. CP-HughL

Six long-headed jazzers play. (LL) Jazzonia. Langston Hughes. AfAmPo; AmNP; BANP; CP-HughL; Klds; NAAAL

6 : o' clock our passageway. Travois of the Nameless. Sotère Torregian. NBV

Six-pointed star, A. Peace on Earth. Audre Lorde. CP-LordA

Six Sunday. Hart Leroi Bibbs. NBP

Six Ten Sixty-Nine. Conyus. GT; PoBA

1686–1802 / Toll taker at Dunk's Ferry, Pennsylvania. Alice. Gale Jackson. SpiFl

Sixteen, Yeah. James A. Emanuel. BrTr

Sixth Street Corporate War. Ishmael Reed. CP-ReedI

Sixties brought a clash of arms, The. Emancipation Day. Lizelia Augusta Jenkins Moorer. CBWP-3

Sixties, / I told Black people, it would be all right, The. Clinton. Sterling Plumpp. BkSV

Sixties, / Youth says it can no longer be my friend, The. Clinton. Sterling Plumpp. BkSV

63rd and Broadway. Reuben Jackson. ESEAA

Skeptic, The. Clara Ann Thompson. CBWP-2

Sketch for an Aesthetic Project. Jay Wright. GT

Sketch of a Verying Evening Sky. John Boyd. EBAP

Sketches of Harlem. David Henderson. Klds; NNP

Sketching in the Transcendental. June Jordan. SP-JordJ

Ski Trail. Samuel Allen. FB

Skies o'ercast and fierce winds blow, The. December. Josephine D. Henderson Heard. CBWP-4

Skin back your teeth, damn you. Why Are They Happy People? Maya Angelou. CP-AngeM

Skin / of my poems, The. Genesis. Etheridge Knight. SP-KnigE

Skin quickens to noises, The. One Eyed Black Man in Nebraska. Sam Cornish. PoBA

Skin that is a closed curtain. Poll. Ed Roberson. PoBA

Skirt Dance. Ishmael Reed. CP-ReedI

Sky Diving. Nikki Giovanni. SP-GiovN

Sky Diving. Ishmael Reed. CP-ReedI; TtW

Sky hangs heavy tonight, The. Negro Woman. Lewis Alexander. CDC; PoBA

Sky, lazily disdaining to pursue, The. Georgia Dusk. Jean Toomer. AfAmPo; AmNP; BPo; CDC; CP-ToomJ; Klds; PoBA; TtW

Sky low down in distant West, The. To Mary. Mary E. Tucker. CBWP-1

Sky of brightest gray seems dark, The. Comparison. Paul Laurence Dunbar. CP-DunbP

Sky Picture. Henrietta Cordelia Ray. CBWP-3

Sky Pictures. Mary Effie Lee Newsome. CDC

Sky was a street map with stars for, The. Ode. Elizabeth Alexander. GT

Sky was blue, so blue, that day, The. For the Candle Light. Angelina Weld Grimké. BlSi; CDC; NAAAL

Skyline. Jean Toomer. CP-ToomJ

Skyline of New York does not excite me, The. Review from Staten Island. Gloria C. Oden. GT; Klds; NNP; PoBA

Skylines / Are marking me in today. Bessie Mayle. ShDr

Skymen coming down out the clouds land. A Poem for Deep Thinkers. Amiri Baraka. SP-BaraA

Slash of the wrist, A. Ways. Langston Hughes. CP-HughL

Slave, The. George Moses Horton. SP-HortG; TtW

Slave. Langston Hughes. CP-HughL

Slave and the Iron Lace, The. Margaret Else Danner. AmNP; BPo

Slave Auction, The. Frances Ellen Watkins Harper. BPo; CP-HarpF; EBAP; Klds

Slave Coffle. Maya Angelou. CP-AngeM; SP-AngeM

Slave is—what?, A. What Is a Slave? Benjamin Clark. EBAP

Slave Marriage Ceremony Supplement. *Unknown.* BPo; CrDW

Slave Mother, The: "Heard you that shriek? It rose." Frances Ellen Watkins Harper. CP-HarpF; CrDW; EBAP; NAAAL; TtW

Slave Mother, The: "I have but four, the treasures of my soul." Frances Ellen Watkins Harper. CP-HarpF

Slave Song. Langston Hughes. CP-HughL

Slave Song. *Unknown.* *See* Song: "We raise de wheat."

Slavery. George Moses Horton. EBAP; TtW

Slavery chain done broke at last, broke at last, broke at last. *Unknown.* BkSV

Slavery, thou peace-disturbing thief. George Moses Horton. SP-HortG

Slaves are said to have worked. St. Helena Island. Tom Dent. TtW

Slave's Complaint, The. George Moses Horton. AAP; CrDW; EBAP; SP-HortG

Slave's Critique of Practical Reason, The. Rita Dove. SP-DoveR

Slave's Reflections the Eve before His Sale, A. George Moses Horton. SP-HortG

Slaveship. Lucille Clifton. ESEAA

Slaveship, German Model. Ishmael Reed. CP-ReedI

Slay fowl and beast; pluck clean the vine. Cavalier. Richard Bruce. CDC

Sleek black boys in a cabaret. Harlem Night Club. Langston Hughes. CP-HughL

Sleep. Langston Hughes. CP-HughL

Sleep, Christian warrior, sleep. To Rev. Thaddeus Saltus. Mary Weston Fordham. CBWP-2

Sleep late with your dream. Owen Dodson. IDB; PoBA

Sleep, little one, sleep for me. Response. Bob Kaufman. Klds; SP-KaufB

Sleep, love sleep. Serenade. Mary Weston Fordham. CBWP-2

Sleeping / all alone. (LL) I'm not lonely. Nikki Giovanni. BrTr; SP-GiovN

Sleepless, I stare. The Broken Dark. Robert Hayden. CP-HaydR; GT

Sleepy Day at Half Moon Bay. Al Young. CP-YounA

Sleepy giant. Africa. Langston Hughes. CP-HughL; SP-HughL

Slender finger of light, A. Haiku 1. Etheridge Knight. SP-KnigE

Slender, shy, and sensitive young girl, The. For Gwen, 1969. Margaret Abigail Walker. CP-WalkM

Slices star bright ice. (LL) Haiku: "Under moon shadows." Etheridge Knight. ESEAA; TtW

Slick / silky / soul. JAZZ (a New Interpretation). Karen Williams. SpiFl

Slight Alterations. Bob Kaufman. SP-KaufB

Slim Greer. Sterling A. Brown. BALP; BANP; CP-BrowS; NAAAL

Slim Greer went to heaven. Slim in Hell. Sterling A. Brown. BPo; CP-BrowS; FB

Slim Hears "The Call." Sterling A. Brown. CP-BrowS

Slim in Atlanta. Sterling A. Brown. CP-BrowS

Slim in Hell ("Slim Greer went to heaven"). Sterling A. Brown. BPo; CP-BrowS; FB

Slim Lands a Job? Sterling A. Brown. CP-BrowS

Slim sentinels. Trees at Night. Helene Johnson. BlSi; ShDr

Slim / young fascist, A. On the Yard. Etheridge Knight. SP-KnigE

Slimy obscene creatures. insane. The Nigga Section. Welton Smith. *Fr.* Malcolm. BlFi

Sling along, sling along, sling along. Paul Laurence Dunbar. CP-DunbP

Slip / from my arm. (LL) Balboa, the Entertainer. Amiri Baraka. SP-BaraA

Slippery driftwood, icebreaking mudpacks. Early Loves. Bob Kaufman. SP-KaufB

Sliver. Langston Hughes. *Fr.* Montage of a Dream Deferred. CP-HughL

Sliver of Sermon. Langston Hughes. *Fr.* Montage of a Dream Deferred. CP-HughL

Slow de night's a-fallin'. Whip-Poor-Will and Katy-Did. Paul Laurence Dunbar. CP-DunbP

Slow moves the pageant of a climbing race. Slow Through the Dark. Paul Laurence Dunbar. CP-DunbP

Slow Riff for Billy. James Cunningham. JB

Slow-rolling beauty. The Mountains of California: Part 2. Al Young. CP-YounA

Slow, the chill that gravitates. Flu. Al Young. CP-YounA

Slow Through the Dark. Paul Laurence Dunbar. CP-DunbP

Slow wand'ring came the sightless seer and she. Antigone and Oedipus. Henrietta Cordelia Ray. AAP; BlSi; CBWP-3; EBAP

Slowly o'er his darkened features. The Dying Fugitive. Frances Ellen Watkins Harper. CP-HarpF; TtW

Slowly the night blooms, unfurling. Flowers of Darkness. Frank Marshall Davis. AmNP; IDB; PoBA

Sluggish, semi-stagnant / the water in Haitian gutters. Iron Flowers. Kalamu ya Salaam. TtW

Slum Dreams. Langston Hughes. CP-HughL

Slumbering Passion. Josephine D. Henderson Heard. CBWP-4

Slung basketballs at Jeffries. In the Projects. Michael S. Harper. SP-HarpM

Slurped / and waters moved. Lee-ers of Hew. James Cunningham. JB

Small / and glowing in this cold place. For My Jamaican Sister a Little Bit Lost on the Island of Manhattan. June Jordan. SP-JordJ

Small Bells of Benin, The. Margaret Else Danner. BrTr

Small Black World. Margaret Abigail Walker. CP-WalkM

Small Comment. Sonia Sanchez. NBP

("Nature of the beast is the, The.") SP-SancS

Small Memory. Langston Hughes. CP-HughL

Small Slaughter, A. Audre Lorde. CP-LordA

Small Town. Rita Dove. GT; SP-DoveR

Smash the Church. June Jordan. SP-JordJ

Smears re-bop / sound. (LL) Neon Signs. Langston Hughes. CP-HughL

Smell of Lebanon, The. Alice Walker. CP-WalkA

Smell of the sea in my nostrils, The. The Mystic Sea. Paul Laurence Dunbar. CP-DunbP

Smelling Wind. Audre Lorde. CP-LordA

Smelt Fishing. Robert Hayden. CP-HaydR

Smilax in our homes entwine, The. Christmas Eve. Lizelia Augusta Jenkins Moorer. CBWP-3

Smiley School, The. Ishmael Reed. CP-ReedI

Smiling Dawn, with diadem of dew, The. The Poet's Ministrants. Henrietta Cordelia Ray. CBWP-3

Smith at the organ is like an anvil being. The Sound of Afroamerican History Chapt II. S. E. Anderson. BlFi; PoBA

Smoke is my name for you. Michael S. Harper. SP-HarpM

Smoke seeping from my veins. Loss from. The Burning General. Amiri Baraka. SP-BaraA

Smooth smell of Manhattan taxis, The. Dance of the Infidels. Al Young. CP-YounA; ESEAA; NBV; PoBA

Smooths and burdens. Snow. Robert Hayden. CP-HaydR

Smothered Fires. Georgia Douglas Johnson. BlSi; ShDr

Smuggled Scotch for O'Hara, big government man. Raptures of the Deep. Derek Walcott. *Fr.* The Schooner *Flight.* ESEAA

Snail. Langston Hughes. CP-HughL; SP-HughL

Snail's Lesson, The. Priscilla Jane Thompson. CBWP-2

Snake. Langston Hughes. CP-HughL

Snake Eyes. Amiri Baraka. Klds; SP-BaraA

Snapping of the Bow, The. James David Corrothers. NAAAL

Snaps for Dinner, Snaps for Breakfast and Snaps for Supper. George Moses Horton. SP-HortG; TtW

Snapshots of the Cotton South. Frank Marshall Davis. PoBA

Sneak Preview. Marilyn Nelson. *Fr.* The Plotinus Suite. SP-NelsM

Sniffed, dilating my nostrils. Elvin's Blues. Michael S. Harper. BPo; SP-HarpM

Snob. Langston Hughes. CP-HughL

Snow. Robert Hayden. CP-HaydR

Snow Fairy, The. Claude McKay. SP-McKaC

Snow-Flakes, The. Priscilla Jane Thompson. CBWP-2

Snow hurries / the strawberries. Love in the Weather's Bells. Jay Wright. ESEAA

Snow in October. Alice Moore Dunbar-Nelson. BlSi; CDC; ShDr

Snow is weaving a soft, white, shroud, The. The Dying Year. Clara Ann Thompson. CBWP-2

Snow King, The. Rita Dove. SP-DoveR

Snow lies deep upon the ground, The. Christmas in the Heart. Paul Laurence Dunbar. CP-DunbP

Snow / nearly as soft, The. Poem on. June Jordan. SP-JordJ

Snow on fire, The. (LL) October— / its plangency, its glow. Robert Hayden. CP-HaydR; ESEAA

Snow Song. Henrietta Cordelia Ray. CBWP-3

Snow Storm, The. Mary Weston Fordham. CBWP-2

Snow White was nude at her wedding, she's so white. Lessons from a Mirror. Thylias Moss. ESEAA

Snow would be the easy. November for Beginners. Rita Dove. SP-DoveR

Snowdrop, The. Mary Weston Fordham. CBWP-2

Snowed. / They took. Some of Betty's Story Round 1850. Gale Jackson. SpiFl

Snowin'. Paul Laurence Dunbar. CP-DunbP

Snows of Kilimanjaro we planted, The. The War of the Heart. Marilyn Nelson. SP-NelsM

Snugly you rest, sweet globes. Grapes: Still-Life. Anne Spencer. ShDr

So? James P. Vaughn. AmNP

So Brooklyn has become a holy place. For Michael Angelo Thompson. June Jordan. SP-JordJ

So close / they come so close. Lucille Clifton. SP-ClifL

So dark and so dark in the briary light. (LL) A Road in Kentucky. Robert Hayden. CP-HaydR

So detached and cool she is. The Mask. Clarissa Scott Delany. CDC; ShDr; TtW

So does a man. (LL) Sister. Langston Hughes. CP-HughL

So easy to repair. (LL) Softened by Time's consummate plush. Emily Dickinson. CrDW

So he said: you ain't got no talent. Poem for a Lady Whose Voice I Like. Nikki Giovanni. SP-GiovN

So here come i. Palm Sunday. Lucille Clifton. SP-ClifL

So his wife and his daughters could qualify. Des Moines Iowa Rap. June Jordan. SP-JordJ

So hot so hot so hot so what. Song of the Law Abiding Citizen. June Jordan. SP-JordJ

So I can brush your back, I say! (LL) Mama and Daughter. Langston Hughes. CP-HughL; SP-HughL

So I don't dare remember in the morning. (LL) Blues at Dawn. Langston Hughes. SP-HughL

So is there life on you, moon? Al Young. CP-YounA

So Jonah Sang the Blues. Marilyn Nelson. *Fr.* I Dream the Book of Jonah. SP-NelsM

So long / is in the song. Langston Hughes. *Fr.* Montage of a Dream Deferred. CP-HughL

So long, / So far away. Afro-American Fragment. Langston Hughes. CP-HughL; Crnst; SP-HughL

So many cares to vex the day. Summer Magic. Leslie Pinckney Hill. BANP

So many cars have driven past me. Psalm: "So many cars have driven past me." Marilyn Nelson. SP-NelsM

So many elbows on the bandstand. In a Stream of Ink. Jayne Cortez. SP-CortJ

So Many Feathers. Jayne Cortez. BlSi; SP-CortJ

So many little flowers. New Flowers. Langston Hughes. CP-HughL

So many people lie in this alley. The Neighborhood House. Jay Wright. NBV

So much have I forgotten in ten years. Flame-Heart. Claude McKay. AfAmPo; AmNP; BALP; BANP; CDC; SP-McKaC

So my soul can sing. (LL) Feeling Fucked/Up Up. Etheridge Knight. GT; SP-KnigE

So now we have come. Malcolm's Blues. Michael S. Harper. SP-HarpM

So oft our hearts, belovèd lute. Dream and the Song. James David Corrothers. BANP

So quiet birds / start singing again. Ambush. Yusef Komunyakaa. SP-KomuY

So Quietly. Leslie Pinckney Hill. BANP; IDB; PoBA

So strange. Us: Colored. Langston Hughes. CP-HughL

So teach me to regard my day. Reflections from the Flash of a Meteor. George Moses Horton. SP-HortG

So / the body / of one black man. 4/30/92; for Rodney King. Lucille Clifton. ESEAA

So the King Sold the Farmer #39. Amiri Baraka. SP-BaraA

So the villa, having learned its many skills. Madrid. Jay Wright. ESEAA

So they change / themselves. (LL) Stations. Audre Lorde. CP-LordA

So they laid him down in a beautiful place. Medgar Evers, 1925-1963. Margaret Abigail Walker. CP-WalkM

So This Is Our Revolution. Sonia Sanchez. BrTr

So Tired Blues. Langston Hughes. CP-HughL

So tired! so weary. Catharine of Arragon. Eloise Bibb. CBWP-4

So we agrees! (LL) Madam and the Rent Man. Langston Hughes. CP-HughL; SP-HughL

So we, who've supped the self-same cup. After the Quarrel. Paul Laurence Dunbar. CDC; CP-DunbP

So we'd shine like dimes. (LL) Momma Sayings. Harryette Mullen. TtW

So We've Come at Last to Freud. Alice Walker. CP-WalkA

So what would you do? (LL) What? Langston Hughes. CP-HughL; SP-HughL

So who but the Lord / Can protect me? (LL) Who But the Lord? Langston Hughes. BPo; SP-HughL

So, you be'n to ole Kentucky. Answer to Dunbar's "After a Visit." Joseph Seamon Cotter, Sr. AAP; EBAP

So you say you're glad to see me, old pal. Hophead Willie. *African-American Oral Tradition.* GetYo

So you wanna kill white people. Something Easy for Ultra Black Nationalists. Kenneth Carroll. SpiFl

So youre playing / Macbeth in Singapore. Identities. Al Young. CP-YounA

So you's six foot under groun'. (LL) The Don't-Care Negro. Joseph Seamon Cotter, Sr. AAP; AfAmPo

So you've reached your thirty-eighth birthday. My Husband's Birthday. Josephine D. Henderson Heard. CBWP-4

So / zoom / your Special Spot. For a Brookline Lady I Love. Etheridge Knight. SP-KnigE

Soapship went a-rocking, A. The Voyage of Jimmy Poo. James A. Emanuel. AmNP; NNP

Social Glass, The. Lizelia Augusta Jenkins Moorer. CBWP-3

Social Life, The. Lizelia Augusta Jenkins Moorer. CBWP-3

Socialist Realism & Capitalist Realism. Realism. Al Young. CP-YounA

Socks and gloves / the medal of honor. Ode to Tenochtitlan. Michael S. Harper. SP-HarpM

Soft Black Eyes. Priscilla Jane Thompson. CBWP-2

Soft grey ghosts crawl up my sleeve. Remembering. Maya Angelou. CP-AngeM; SP-AngeM

Soft moon shimmers out. Quarter Moon Rise. Kalamu ya Salaam. *Fr.* New Orleans Haiku. SpiFl

Soft night comes back. The Bronze Buckaroo. Amiri Baraka. SP-BaraA

Soft songs, like birds, die in poison air. Apology for Apostasy? Etheridge Knight. SP-KnigE

Soft Targets, *for Black Girls.* Essex Hemphill. GT

Soft you day, be velvet soft. The Gamut. Maya Angelou. CP-AngeM; SP-AngeM

Softened by Time's consummate plush. Emily Dickinson. CrDW

Softly blow lightly. Nocturne. Donald Jeffrey Hayes. CDC

Softly now the day is dawning. The Signal Gun. Mary E. Tucker. CBWP-1

Soho Cinema. Audre Lorde. CP-LordA

Sojourner Truth: Black Sybil in Salem. Michael S. Harper. SP-HarpM

Sol took his nightcap off and gazed. After the Storm. Henrietta Cordelia Ray. CBWP-3

Solace. Clarissa Scott Delany. AmNP; CDC; PoBA

Solace. Josephine D. Henderson Heard. CBWP-4

Solace. Margaret Abigail Walker. CP-WalkM

Soldier Boy's Dream, The. Mary E. Tucker. CBWP-1

Soldier said to the general, The. Battle Ground. Langston Hughes. CP-HughL

Soldiers fuzz the city in khaki confusion. Habana. Julian Bond. NNP

Soldiers of the Dusk, The. Fenton Johnson. EBAP

Soledad. Robert Hayden. CP-HaydR; NAAAL

Soledad. Langston Hughes. CP-HughL

Solid citizens / Of the country club set, The. Undertow. Langston Hughes. CP-HughL

Solid—stolid / "There." Earth. Jean Toomer. CP-ToomJ

Solidarity. June Jordan. SP-JordJ

Soliloquy, The. Francis A. Boyd. *Fr.* Columbiana. EBAP

Soliloquy: Man Talking to a Mirror. Yusef Komunyakaa. SP-KomuY

Soliloquy of a Turkey. Paul Laurence Dunbar. BPo; CP-DunbP

Solitary Visions of a Kaufmanoid. James Cunningham. JB

Solomon. Lucille Clifton. SP-ClifL

Solomon Mahlangu, Freedom Fighter from Mamelodi. Jayne Cortez. SP-CortJ

Solstice. Audre Lorde. CP-LordA

Solutions to the Problem, / Of course, wait. (LL) Dinner Guest: Me. Langston Hughes. CP-HughL; SSLK

Some a you boys is speakin' about women, but I can tell you a thing or two. Pretty Pill. *African-American Oral Tradition.* GetYo

Some are coming on the passenger. They're Leaving Memphis in Droves. *Unknown.* CrDW

Some are teethed on a silver spoon. Saturday's Child. Countee Cullen. CP-CullC; Klds; NAAAL; PoBA

Some blues I've had. (LL) A Good Woman Feeling Bad. Maya Angelou. CP-AngeM; SP-AngeM

Some dawns / wait. (LL) Tomorrow may be. Langston Hughes. CP-HughL; SP-HughL

Some Day. Langston Hughes. CP-HughL

Some day, when trees have shed their leaves. After the Winter. Claude McKay. BANP; IDB; PoBA; SP-McKaC

Some Days / Out Walking Above. De Leon Harrison. PoBA

Some dichty folks / don't know the facts. Weekend Glory. Maya Angelou. CP-AngeM; SP-AngeM

Some dreams hang in the air. Lucille Clifton. SP-ClifL

Some folks say that Willie Green. Dolomite: "Some folks say that Willie Green." *African-American Oral Tradition.* GetYo

Some folks think. Freedom. Langston Hughes. CP-HughL

Some folks t'inks hit's right an' p'opah. Noddin' by de Fire. Paul Laurence Dunbar. CP-DunbP

Some for a little while do love, and some for long. Sonnet. Countee Cullen. CP-CullC

Some glowing in the common blood. / Some specialness within. (LL) Of Robert Frost. Gwendolyn Brooks. SP-BrooG

Some gold lies veiled behind each evening cloud. Hidden Essence. Henrietta Cordelia Ray. CBWP-3

Some Hands Are Lovelier. Mae V. Cowdery. ShDr

Some hated slavery. Kansas and America. Michael S. Harper. SP-HarpM

Some Jesus / has come on me. The Calling of the Disciples. Lucille Clifton. SP-ClifL

Some Kind of Crazy. Major L. Jackson. SpiFl

Some names there are that win the best applause. William Lloyd Garrison. Henrietta Cordelia Ray. CBWP-3

Some of Betty's Story Round 1850. Gale Jackson. SpiFl

Some of my best friends are white boys. Friends. Ray Durem. PoBA

Some of us know / porcelain, quiet. Intelligence Quotients. Dorothy Perry Thompson. SpiFl

Some of us / these days. Resurrection. Frank Horne. PoBA

Some old Mexico Lisbon set. Dream Take: 22. Al Young. CP-YounA

Some people despise me be-. June Jordan. SP-JordJ

Some people say. Granny Blak Poet (in Pastel). Arthur Pfister. BrTr

Some pimps wear summer hats. What? Langston Hughes. CP-HughL; SP-HughL

Some Recent Fiction. Al Young. CP-YounA

Some say he's from Georgia. John Henry. *Unknown.* CrDW

Some say that Chattanooga is the. Chattanooga. Ishmael Reed. CP-ReedI; NAAAL

Some say the radiance around the body. 11/10 Again. Lucille Clifton. GT

Some small island birthed. For a Lady of Pleasure Now Retired. Nikki Giovanni. BrTr; SP-GiovN

Some Spice for Jack Spicer. Al Young. CP-YounA

Some things are very dear to me. Gwendolyn B. Bennett. *Fr.* Sonnets. TtW

     (Sonnet—2) NAAAL

Some Things I Like about My Triple Bloods. Alice Walker. CP-WalkA

Some time, on the street. Revelation in Brick City. Amiri Baraka. CtF; SP-HortG

Some time turns inside out. Memorial III from a Phone Booth on Broadway. Audre Lorde. CP-LordA; SP-LordA

Some / times i dream bout. Last Poem I'm Gonna Write Bout Us. Sonia Sanchez. SP-SancS

Some / times / i / get / so / lone / ly. "5 Minutes, Mr. Salam." Kalamu ya Salaam. SpiFl

Some train has forgotten. (LL) Railroad Avenue. Langston Hughes. CP-HughL; SP-HughL

Some trees, standing in groves. Trees. Julia Fields. TtW

Some weep to find the Golden Pear. Colored Blues Singer. Countee Cullen. CP-CullC

Some women love / to wait. Stations. Audre Lorde. CP-LordA

Some/one / pleasereply soon. (LL) Blk/Rhetoric. Sonia Sanchez. Crnst; SP-SancS

Somebody almost walked off wid alla my stuff. Ntozake Shange. NAAAL

Somebody Call. Carolyn M. Rodgers. JB

Somebody come and carry me into a seven-day kiss. Alla Tha's All Right, But. June Jordan. SP-JordJ

Somebody coming in blackness. John. Lucille Clifton. SP-ClifL

Somebody, / Cut his hair. Young Poet. Myron O'Higgins. PoBA

Somebody muffed it? Somebody wanted to joke. (LL) A Sunset of the City. Gwendolyn Brooks. GT; SP-BrooG

Somehow began the / measured rise. (LL) The Diver. Robert Hayden. BPo; CP-HaydR; Klds

Someone is sitting in the red house. Small Town. Rita Dove. GT; SP-DoveR

Someone's Blood. Rita Dove. SP-DoveR

Somethin' Else and. Cannon Arrested. Michael S. Harper. SP-HarpM

Something about this boy. Joseph. Lucille Clifton. SP-ClifL

Something Easy for Ultra Black Nationalists. Kenneth Carroll. SpiFl

Something has passed between us more than blood. Kin. Naomi Long Madgett. TtW

Something Like a Sonnet for Phillis Miracle Wheatley. June Jordan. SP-JordJ

Something like the way. Look Good, Smell Good, Feel. Al Young. CP-YounA

Something Old, Something New. Carl H. Greene. NBV

Something to be Said for Silence. Nikki Giovanni. SP-GiovN

Something to Do. Frances Ellen Watkins Harper. CP-HarpF

Something uncertain moves. Again. Lenard D. Moore. GT

Sometime the world seems sad and lonely. Lonely World. Mrs. Henry Linden. CBWP-4

Sometimes. Maggie Pogue Johnson. CBWP-4

Sometimes a crumb falls. Luck. Langston Hughes. CP-HughL; SP-HughL

Sometimes / A night funeral. Dead in There. Langston Hughes. *Fr.* Montage of a Dream Deferred. CP-HughL

Sometimes a right white mountain. Sky Pictures. Mary Effie Lee Newsome. CDC

Sometimes at the beggining of a movie. A Little Poem About Jazz. Al Young. CP-YounA

Sometimes at the mouth of this river. A Poem for Willard Motley. Al Young. CP-YounA

Sometimes DeLiza. June Jordan. SP-JordJ

Sometimes DeLiza get so crazy she omit. A Runaway Lil Bit Poem. June Jordan. SP-JordJ

Sometimes he walked to occupy / his feet. Generations 2. Sam Cornish. GT

Sometimes he was cool like an eternal. Lester Young. Ted Joans. AmNP

Sometimes / I cool out. Spacin. Ronda M. Davis. JB

Sometimes I feel I have to express myself. Vice. Amiri Baraka. SP-BaraA

Sometimes I feel like a motherless child. Motherless Child. *African-American Oral Tradition.* TtW

Sometimes I feel like a motherless child. *Unknown.* BkSV; Crnst

Sometimes i feel like i just get in. Intellectualism. Nikki Giovanni. SP-GiovN

Sometimes / I feel like I will never stop. To Satch. Samuel Allen. AmNP; IDB; Klds; PoBA; TtW

Sometimes I feel so bad. Family Of. Alice Walker. CP-WalkA

Sometimes I get the feeling that I have been here before. Reincarnation. Mae Jackson. PoBA

Sometimes I Go to Camarillo and Sit in the Lounge. K. Curtis Lyle. NBV; PoBA

Sometimes I stare into an awning of spirit. Sometimes I Go to Camarillo and Sit in the Lounge. K. Curtis Lyle. NBV; PoBA

Sometimes I Wonder: / What to say to you now. Catch the Fire. Sonia Sanchez. CtF

Sometimes it seems as though some puppet player. The Puppet Player. Angelina Weld Grimké. CDC

Sometimes it's the flagrant accentuation. Jazz as Was. Al Young. CP-YounA; ESEAA

Sometimes it's the look of love. Big Sur. Al Young. CP-YounA

Sometimes it's the way the blues hits you. More Clues to the Blues. Al Young. CP-YounA

Sometimes / the poems. Sharon Scott. JB

Sometimes / the whoe world of women. She Is Dreaming. Lucille Clifton. SP-ClifL

Sometimes there's a wind in the Georgia dusk. Georgia Dusk. Langston Hughes. CP-HughL; Crnst; SP-HughL

Sometimes / when i wake up. Nikki Giovanni. SP-GiovN

Sometimes when I'm lonely. Hope: "Sometimes when I'm lonely." Langston Hughes. CP-HughL; SP-HughL

Sometimes, when you're called a bastard. When Something Happens. James A., Jr. Randall. BPo; SSLK

Sometimes with the waves. Al Young. CP-YounA

Sometimes you hear a question like "what is." Categories. Nikki Giovanni. SP-GiovN

Sometimes you love someone. Winter Leaves. Al Young. CP-YounA

Somewhere a white horse gallops with its mane. Elsewhere. Derek Walcott. Crnst

Somewhere in France a vacation album. Memento. Marilyn Nelson. SP-NelsM

Somewhere / in the light above the womb. My Grandfather Walks in the Woods. Marilyn Nelson. ESEAA; SP-NelsM

Somewhere it being yesterday. A Song of Mary. Lucille Clifton. SP-ClifL

Somewhere outside your window. A Sense of Coolness. Quincy Troupe. GT; PoBA

Somewhere there waits, waiting. Waiting. Bob Kaufman. SP-KaufB

Son, The. Rita Dove. SP-DoveR

Son. Al Young. CP-YounA

"Son, come tell me 'bout the meetin." The Old and the New. Clara Ann Thompson. CBWP-2

Son of Msippi. Henry L. Dumas. TtW

Son to Mother. Maya Angelou. CP-AngeM

Song. Cornelius Eady. ESEAA; GT

Song. Primus St. John. GT

Song: "Because I know deep in my own heart." Pauli Murray. BlSi

Song: "Bee hit sip some honey f'om de matermony vine, De." Paul Laurence Dunbar. CP-DunbP

Song: "Dressed up in my melancholy." M. Carl Holman. AmNP; Klds

Song: "I am weaving a song of waters." Gwendolyn B. Bennett. BlSi; ShDr

Song: "Lovely, dark, and lonely one." Langston Hughes. CP-HughL

Song: "My heart to thy heart." Paul Laurence Dunbar. CP-DunbP

Song, The: "My soul, lost in the music's mist." Paul Laurence Dunbar. CP-DunbP

Song: "O sweet, sad, singing river." Henrietta Cordelia Ray. CBWP-3

Song, The: "Oh, foully slighted Ethiope maid!" Priscilla Jane Thompson. CBWP-2

Song, A: "On a summer's day as I sat by a stream." Paul Laurence Dunbar. CP-DunbP

Song: "Sons of slaves and." Lucille Clifton. SP-ClifL

Song, A: "Thou art the soul of a summer's day." Paul Laurence Dunbar. AmNP; CP-DunbP

Song: "We raise de wheat." Unknown. BPo

(Slave Song.) CrDW

Song: "Wild trees have bought me." Audre Lorde. CP-LordA; SP-LordA

Song: "Wintah, summah, snow er shine." Paul Laurence Dunbar. CP-DunbP

Song: "World is full of colored, The." Alice Walker. CP-WalkA

Song: a Motion for History. Kenneth A. McClane. TtW

Song After Lynching. Langston Hughes. CP-HughL

Song for a Banjo Dance. Langston Hughes. CP-HughL

Song for a Dark Girl. Langston Hughes. CDC; CP-HughL; IDB; NAAAL; PoBA; SP-HughL

Song for a Thin Sister. Audre Lorde. CP-LordA; SP-LordA

Song for Billie Holiday. Langston Hughes. SP-HughL

("By sound that shimmers— / Where?") (LL) CP-HughL

Song for Many Movements, A. Audre Lorde. CP-LordA

Song for Ourselves. Langston Hughes. CP-HughL

Song for Soweto, A. June Jordan. SP-JordJ

Song for the Old Ones. Maya Angelou. CP-AngeM; SP-AngeM

Song for the unsung heroes who rose in the country's need, A. The Unsung Heroes. Paul Laurence Dunbar. BPo; CP-DunbP

Song: I Want a Witness. Michael S. Harper. SP-HarpM

Song in Spite of Myself. Countee Cullen. BALP; CP-CullC

Song in the Front Yard, A. Gwendolyn Brooks. Fr. A Street in Bronzeville. BPo; BlSi; ESEAA; IDB; NAAAL; PoBA; SP-BrooG

Song is a strong thing. (LL) Spirituals. Langston Hughes. CP-HughL; SP-HughL

Song is but a little thing, A. The Poet and His Song. Paul Laurence Dunbar. CP-DunbP

Song of Adoration. Langston Hughes. CP-HughL

Song of Devotion to the Forest, after the pygmies of the Ituri Forest. David Henderson. GT

Song of Fire, The. Rolland Snellings. BlFi

Song of Innocence. Julius E. Thompson. TtW

Song of Liberty and Parental Advice. George Moses Horton. SP-HortG

Song of Mary, A. Lucille Clifton. SP-ClifL

Song of Names and Faces, A. Audre Lorde. CP-LordA

Song of Praise, A. Countee Cullen. CP-CullC

Song of Praise. Countee Cullen. CP-CullC

Song of Sojourner Truth, A. June Jordan. SP-JordJ; TtW

Song of Sour Grapes, A. Countee Cullen. CP-CullC

Song of Spain. Langston Hughes. CP-HughL

Song of Summer. Paul Laurence Dunbar. CP-DunbP

Song of Thanks, A. Edward Smyth Jones. BANP

Song of the Andoumboulou. Nathaniel Mackey. NAAAL

Song of the Angels. Lizelia Augusta Jenkins Moorer. CBWP-3

Song of the Corn. James Edwin Campbell. AAP

Song of the Decanter. Alfred Gibbs Campbell. AAP

Song of the Law Abiding Citizen. June Jordan. SP-JordJ

Song of the Moon, A. Claude McKay. SP-McKaC

Song of the Moon. Priscilla Jane Thompson. CBWP-2

Song of the Refugee Road. Langston Hughes. CP-HughL

Song of the Revolution. Langston Hughes. CP-HughL

Song of the Smoke, The. William Edward Burghardt DuBois. NAAAL; PoBA; SSLK

Song of the Son. Jean Toomer. AmNP; CDC; CP-ToomJ; CrDW; Klds; PoBA; TtW

Song of the Whirlwind. Fenton Johnson. NAAAL

Song of Tom. Kirk Hall. BlFi

Song of Triumph. Sterling A. Brown. CP-BrowS

Song of Winnie. Gwendolyn Brooks. Fr. Winnie. ESEAA

Song Poem, The. Lenard D. Moore. SpiFl

Song skips around, The. Al Young. CP-YounA

Song. Summer. Rita Dove. SP-DoveR

Song to a Negro Wash-woman, A. Langston Hughes. CP-HughL

Song to Erin. Mary Weston Fordham. CBWP-2

Song to the Dark Virgin. Langston Hughes. CP-HughL

Song to the Runaway Slave. Unknown. BPo

Song Turning Back into Itself, The. Al Young. TtW

"Always it's either / a beginning."

Song Turning Back Into Itself 1. Al Young. CP-YounA

Song Waiting for Music, A. Raymond R. Patterson. TtW

Songbirds giggling all across California. Maya. Al Young. CP-YounA

Songless. Alice Walker. CP-WalkA

Songless Lark, The. Audre Lorde. CP-LordA

Songs. Paul Laurence Dunbar. CP-DunbP

Songs. Langston Hughes. CP-HughL

Songs for my Father. Yusef Komunyakaa. SP-KomuY

Songs for the Cisco Kid; or, Singing for the Face. K. Curtis Lyle. PoBA

Songs for the Cisco Kid; or, Singing: Song #2. K. Curtis Lyle. PoBA

Songs for the People. Frances Ellen Watkins Harper. AfAmPo; CP-HarpF; EBAP; TtW

("Let me make the songs for the people.") AAP; NAAAL

Songs that break. Gypsy Melodies. Langston Hughes. CP-HughL; SP-HughL

Sonia Told Them Women. Yona Harvey. CtF

Sonnet. Ed Roberson. GT

Sonnet: "Emblem of blasted hope and lost desire." Paul Laurence Dunbar. CP-DunbP

Sonnet: "He came in silvern armor, trimmed with black." Gwendolyn B. Bennett. AmNP; CDC; PoBA

Sonnet: "I had no thought of violets of late." Alice Moore Dunbar-Nelson. BANP; BlSi; CDC; PoBA

Sonnet: "I have not loved you in the noblest way." Countee Cullen. CP-CullC

Sonnet: "I know now how a man whose blood is hot." Countee Cullen. CP-CullC

Sonnet: "O thou who never harbored fear." Eloise Bibb. CBWP-4

Sonnet: "Some for a little while do love, and some for long." Countee Cullen. CP-CullC

Sonnet: "These are no wind-blown rumors, soft say-sos." Countee Cullen. CP-CullC

Sonnet: "What I am saying now was said before." Countee Cullen. CP-CullC

Sonnet: "Where are we to go when this is done?" Alfred A. Duckett. AmNP; PoBA

Sonnet—2: "Some things are very dear to me—." Gwendolyn B. Bennett. *See* "Some things are very dear to me."

Sonnet Dialogue. Countee Cullen. CP-CullC

Sonnet for A.B.T, A. June Jordan. SP-JordJ

Sonnet from the Stony Brook, A. June Jordan. SP-JordJ

Sonnet Sequence. Darwin T. Turner. BALP

Sonnet to a Negro in Harlem. Helene Johnson. AmNP; BANP; CDC; NAAAL; SSLK; ShDr

Sonnet to My First Born. Mary Weston Fordham. CBWP-2

Sonnet to Negro Soldiers. Joseph Seamon Cotter, Sr. PoBA

Sonnets. Gwendolyn B. Bennett. TtW
"He came in silvern armour, trimmed with black." AmNP; CDC; PoBA
"Some things are very dear to me."
(Sonnet—2) NAAAL

Sonora Desert Poem. Lucille Clifton. SP-ClifL

Sons of slaves and. Song: "Sons of slaves and." Lucille Clifton. SP-ClifL

Soon as the sun forsook the eastern main. An Hymn to the Evening. Phillis Wheatley. AfAmPo; CP-WheaP

Soon I will be done with the troubles of the world. *Unknown.* NAAAL

Soon one mawnin death come creepin in mah room. *African-American Oral Tradition.* TtW

Soon One Morning, I'll Fly Away. Kalamu ya Salaam. CtF

Sophie, Climbing the Stairs. Dolores Kendrick. ESEAA

Sorrow Home. Margaret Abigail Walker. CP-WalkM

Sorrow Is the Only Faithful One. Owen Dodson. AmNP; BALP

Sorrow Since Sitting Bull, A. George Barlow. ESEAA

Sorrow! Sorrow! / Sorrow! Sorrow! (LL) Night: Four Songs. Langston Hughes. CP-HughL; SP-HughL

SOS. Amiri Baraka. BPo; NAAAL; PoBA

Soul. Austin Black. NBP

Soul. D. L. Graham. Klds; PoBA

Soul, The. Frances Ellen Watkins Harper. CP-HarpF

Soul. Barbara Simmons. BlFi

Soul and fire of windsongs must not be neutral, The. Killing Memory. Haki R. Madhubuti. TtW

Soul and race / are private dominions. Here Where Coltrane Is. Michael S. Harper. ESEAA; NAAAL; PoBA; SP-HarpM

Soul dust with particles of. Music of the Other World. Ted Wilson. BlFi

Soul grows hunched, flinching away from pain, The. Propositions. Marilyn Nelson. SP-NelsM

Soul Incense. Henrietta Cordelia Ray. CBWP-3

Soul Make A Path Through Shouting, *for Elizabeth Eckford / Little Rock, Arkansas, 1957.* Cyrus Cassells. ESEAA

Soul Proprietorship. Ishmael Reed. CP-ReedI

Soul-Smiles. S. E. Anderson. BlFi

Soul that's fed on Nature is content, The. Nature's Uplifting. Henrietta Cordelia Ray. CBWP-3

Soulfolk, think a minute. To Soulfolk. Margaret Goss Burroughs. BlSi

Soul's Courts, The. Henrietta Cordelia Ray. CBWP-3

Sound like a great big crowd. (LL) Morning After. Langston Hughes. CP-HughL; SP-HughL

Sound of Afroamerican History Chapt I, The. S. E. Anderson. BlFi; PoBA

Sound of Afroamerican History Chapt II, The. S. E. Anderson. BlFi; PoBA

Sound Poem (I). Jean Toomer. CP-ToomJ

Sound Poem (II). Jean Toomer. CP-ToomJ

Sound variegated through beneath lit. Gyre's Galax. Norman Henry, II Pritchard. PoBA

Sounding down this world. (LL) We Dance Like Ella Riffs. Carolyn M. Rodgers. PoBA

Sounds / Like pearls. Maya Angelou. CP-AngeM; SP-AngeM

Sounds of driven, ruddered snow. (LL) The Drive In. Michael S. Harper. SP-HarpM

Sounds / Of the Harlem night, The. Summer Night. Langston Hughes. CP-HughL

South, The. Langston Hughes. CP-HughL; SP-HughL

South African Bloodstone. Quincy Troupe. Crnst

South Atlantic clouds rode low, The. Safari West. John A. Williams. NBP

South China Sea / drives in another herd, The. A Break from the Bush. Yusef Komunyakaa. SP-KomuY

South Street. Edward S. Silvera. CDC

South: The Name of Home. Alice Walker. CP-WalkA

Southeast Arkanasia. Maya Angelou. CP-AngeM; SP-AngeM

Southern Belle. Elma Stuckey. TtW

Southern Blues, The. *Unknown.* BkSV

Southern Cop. Sterling A. Brown. CP-BrowS

Southern gentle lady. Silhouette. Langston Hughes. CP-HughL; SP-HughL

Southern Mammy Sings. Langston Hughes. CP-HughL; SP-HughL

Southern Mansion. Arna Bontemps. AmNP; BALP; BANP; FB; GT; IDB; Klds; NAAAL; PoBA

Southern Negro Speaks. Langston Hughes. CP-HughL

Southern Press, The. Lizelia Augusta Jenkins Moorer. CBWP-3

Southern Pulpit, The. Lizelia Augusta Jenkins Moorer. CBWP-3

Southern Refugee, The. George Moses Horton. SP-HortG

Southern Road. Sterling A. Brown. BALP; BANP; BPo; FB; PoBA ("Evahmo'. . . .") (LL)
("Swing dat hammer—hunh.") CP-BrowS; TtW

Southern Road, The. Dudley Randall. BrTr; NNP; PoBA

Southern Roads/City Pavement. Virgia Brocks-Shedd. TtW

Southern Scene, A. Priscilla Jane Thompson. CBWP-2

Southern Song. Margaret Abigail Walker. CP-WalkM

Southern Work of Dr. and Mrs. L. M. Dunton. Lizelia Augusta Jenkins Moorer. CBWP-3

Souvenir. Naomi Long Madgett. NBV

Souvenirs. Dudley Randall. BPo; Klds

Soweto / when i hear your name. For the Brave Young Students in Soweto. Jayne Cortez. SP-CortJ

Sowing. Audre Lorde. CP-LordA; SP-LordA

Space in the lives of their friends, A. Ishmael Reed. *See* Beware: Do Not Read This Poem.

Spacin. Ronda M. Davis. JB

Spade Is Just a Spade, A. Walter Everette Hawkins. PoBA

Spanish Conversation. E. Ethelbert Miller. TtW

Spanish Needle, The. Claude McKay. SP-McKaC

Spanish sculptor named Cherino, A. Who Has Seen the Wind? Bob Kaufman. Klds; SP-KaufB

Sparkling eyes of diamond jet. To E.J.J. Ethel M. Caution. ShDr

Sparrow, The. Paul Laurence Dunbar. CP-DunbP

Sparrow's Fall, The. Frances Ellen Watkins Harper. CP-HarpF

Spatial depths of being survive. The Lost Dancer. Jean Toomer. BALP; CP-ToomJ; PoBA

Spawn of Slums, The. James W. Thompson. BPo

Speak earth and bless me with what is richest. Love Poem. Audre Lorde. CP-LordA; SP-LordA

Speak! fairy Moon, interpret this! (LL) The Dawn of Love. Henrietta Cordelia Ray. BlSi; CBWP-3; EBAP

Speak the truth to the people. Mari E. Evans. IHS; TtW

Speak to Her Tenderly. Mary E. Tucker. CBWP-1

Speaker must be brief. (LL) Lady Luncheon Club. Maya Angelou. CP-AngeM; SP-AngeM

Speakin' at de Cou't-House. Paul Laurence Dunbar. CP-DunbP

Speakin' o' Christmas. Paul Laurence Dunbar. CP-DunbP

Speaking of death / and decay. Exercises on Themes from Life. Alice Walker. CP-WalkA

Speaking of Food. Langston Hughes. CP-HughL

Speaking of Loss. Lucille Clifton. SP-ClifL

Spearo's Blues (or: Ode to a Grecian Yearn). Eugene B. Redmond. NBV

Special Bulletin. Langston Hughes. CP-HughL; PoBA

Special Section for the Niggas on the Lower Eastside or: Invert the Divisor and Multiply. Welton Smith. *Fr.* Malcolm. BlFi

Speckled frogs leap from my mouth. Fantasy and Conversation. Audre Lorde. CP-LordA; SP-LordA

Spectre is haunting america—the spectre of neo-hoodooism, A. Black Power Poem. Ishmael Reed. BPo; CP-ReedI

Spectrum. Mari E. Evans. BPo

Speculations on the Present through the Prism of the Past, *for Haruko.* June Jordan. GT

Speech. Sterling Plumpp. TtW

Speech #38 (or Y We Say It This Way). Amiri Baraka. SP-BaraA

Speech, or dark cities screaming. Johnie Scott. NBP

Speechless. Audre Lorde. CP-LordA

Spell number one / is the gingerbread brown. Hoodoo. DJ Renegade. CtF

Spellin'-Bee, The. Paul Laurence Dunbar. CP-DunbP

Sphinx. Robert Hayden. CP-HaydR; GT

Spice of Life, The. Kalamu ya Salaam. *Fr.* New Orleans Haiku. SpiFl

Spies are found wanting. They wanted. Are Their Blues Singers in Russia? Amiri Baraka. SP-BaraA

Spikes of lavender aster under Route 91. Every Traveler Has One Vermont Poem. Audre Lorde. CP-LordA

Spin him like a top! (LL) Homage to My Hips. Lucille Clifton. NAAAL; SP-ClifL

Spiral Death / The snake must be. Comment. Langston Hughes. CP-HughL

Spirit Flowers. Della Burt. BlSi

Spirit in the Dark. George Barlow. *Fr.* Gabriel. TtW

Spirit of the buffalo soldiers, The. Tyrone (2). Lucille Clifton. SP-ClifL

Spirit of the dead, rise up. Sankofa. Haile Gerima. CtF

Spirit, signals future light. (LL) Stars. Robert Hayden. CP-HaydR

Spirit Voice, or Liberty Call to the Disfranchised (State of New York), The. Charles Lewis Reason. AAP; EBAP

Spirit! What art thou erecting. The Poet's Ideal. Henrietta Cordelia Ray. CBWP-3

Spirits. Victor Hernandez Cruz. PoBA

Spirits of the abnormally born. October. Audre Lorde. CP-LordA; SP-LordA

Spirits Struggle. Christopher Stanard. CtF

Spirits Unchained. Keorapetse W. Kgositsile. PoBA

Spiritual. William W. Cook. SpiFl

Spiritual, A. Paul Laurence Dunbar. BPo; CP-DunbP

Spiritual Geography. Kalamu ya Salaam. *Fr.* New Orleans Haiku. SpiFl

Spirituals. Langston Hughes. CP-HughL; SP-HughL

Spirituals, The. Margaret Abigail Walker. CP-WalkM

Splat of bare feet on wet tile, The. Women's Locker Room. Marilyn Nelson. SP-NelsM

Split Standard. Hart Leroi Bibbs. BlFi

Splitting from Jack Delaney's, Sheridan Square. God Rest Ye Merry, Gentlemen. Derek Walcott. GT

Spoiled / the appetite? (LL) A Few Sirens. Alice Walker. CP-WalkA

Sport. Langston Hughes. CP-HughL

Sporting Beasley. Sterling A. Brown. CP-BrowS; Klds; NAAAL

Sporting people, The. Free Fantasia: Tiger Flowers. Robert Hayden. CP-HaydR; ESEAA

Spots on black skin. Blind Old Woman. Clarence Major. PoBA

Sprawled in the pigsty. For a Young Artist. Robert Hayden. CP-HaydR

Spray of pine-needles, A. Nullo. Jean Toomer. CP-ToomJ

Sprin' Fevah. Ray Garfield Dandridge. BANP

Spring. Carole C. Gregory Clemmons. PoBA

Spring. Pinkie Gordon Lane. GT

Spring. Helen G. Quigless. BkSV

Spring. Mary E. Tucker. CBWP-1

Spring 1937/ for Honoré Roussell. Alvin Aubert. TtW

Spring dawn. Julius Lester. *Fr.* Poems. Klds

Spring Fever. Paul Laurence Dunbar. CP-DunbP

Spring for Lovers. Langston Hughes. CP-HughL

Spring has no promise more than frost. The Promise. Jean Toomer. CP-ToomJ

Spring III. Audre Lorde. CP-LordA

Spring in New Hampshire. Claude McKay. BANP; BPo; CrDW; Klds; SP-McKaC

Spring is not so beautiful there, The. Water-Front Streets. Langston Hughes. CP-HughL; SP-HughL

Spring is the harshest. Spring III. Audre Lorde. CP-LordA

Spring moonrise. Haiku: "Spring moonrise." Lenard D. Moore. SpiFl

Spring People. Audre Lorde. CP-LordA; SP-LordA

Spring Reminiscence. Countee Cullen. CP-CullC

Spring Song. Lucille Clifton. SP-ClifL

Spring Song. Paul Laurence Dunbar. CP-DunbP

Spring Wooing, A. Paul Laurence Dunbar. CP-DunbP

Springtime. Norman Henry, II Pritchard. GT

Sprouting two small wings. (LL) Wingfoot Lake. Rita Dove. SP-DoveR

Sputin. Ishmael Reed. CP-ReedI

Spy. Rita Dove. SP-DoveR

Squared Circle, The. Carl Killebrew. BrTr

Squire sat alone beside the board, The. Little Fay's Thanksgiving. Henrietta Cordelia Ray. CBWP-3

Squirrels are skittering. Al Young. CP-YounA

St. Helena Island. Tom Dent. TtW

St. Julien's Eve. James Cunningham. JB

St. Louis Blues. William Christopher Handy. CrDW
("I hate to see de evenin' sun go down.") NAAAL

St. Louis Cemetery Crypt. Kalamu ya Salaam. *Fr.* New Orleans Haiku. SpiFl

St. Louis Out of Time. Audre Lorde. SP-LordA
("Dream / they are immortal.") (LL) CP-LordA
("If St. Louis / took its rhythms.") CP-LordA
(Visit to a City Out of Time.) CP-LordA

St. Louis Woman. Ishmael Reed. CP-ReedI

Stab incision below nipple. Debridement: Operation Harvest Moon: *On Repose*. Michael S. Harper. SP-HarpM

Staccato! Staccato! The Rubinstein Staccato Etude. Robert Nathaniel Dett. BANP

Stackalee. *Unknown, comp. by* Onah L. Spencer. CrDW

Stacked houses on either side, The. The Languages We Are. Frederick, Jr. Bryant. NBP

Stackolee. *Unknown.* NAAAL

Stackolee: "Back in forty-nine when times was hard." *African-American Oral Tradition.* GetYo

Stackolee: "I staggered in a place called the Bucket a Blood." *African-American Oral Tradition.* GetYo

Stackolee: "It was back in the time of nineteen hundred and two." *African-American Oral Tradition.* GetYo

Stackolee: "It was back in the year of forty-one when the times was hard." *African-American Oral Tradition.* GetYo

Stackolee: "This is supposed to be about two colored studs. It's truth. In New Orleans." *African-American Oral Tradition.* GetYo

Stackolee: "When I was young in my prime." *African-American Oral Tradition.* GetYo

Stackolee in Hell, *see also* Nineteen Thirty-Two. *African-American Oral Tradition.* GetYo

Stagnant, and green, and full of slimy things. (LL) October Journey. Margaret Abigail Walker. AmNP; CP-WalkM; GT; IDB; PoBA

Staircase, The. Samuel Allen. PoBA

Stairs mount to his eternity, The. The Staircase. Samuel Allen. PoBA

Stalingrad: 1942. Langston Hughes. CP-HughL

Stalking. Where Seed Falls. Essex Hemphill. GT

Stand and watch. / Maybe. (LL) Men. Maya Angelou. CP-AngeM; SP-AngeM

Stand by Me. *Unknown.* NAAAL

Standin' at de winder. Blue. Paul Laurence Dunbar. CP-DunbP

Standin' by de lonesome riverside. A Ruined Gal. Langston Hughes. CP-HughL

Standing in the doorway of Cuba's Spanish. The Flesh of the Young Men Is Burning. Lance Jeffers. BkSV

Stanzas for the First of August. James M. Whitfield. EBAP; TtW

Star-Fix. Marilyn Nelson. ESEAA; SP-NelsM

Star Journey. Naomi Long Madgett. BPo

Star of Ethiopia. Lucian B. Watkins. BANP

Star of peace the standard of the world, The. (LL) General Grant—the Hero of the War. George Moses Horton. AAP; SP-HortG

Star of the North! whose steadfast ray. The North Star. James M. Whitfield. TtW

Star Seeker. Langston Hughes. CP-HughL

Star Song. Henrietta Cordelia Ray. CBWP-3

Stardate Number 18628.190. Nikki Giovanni. SP-GiovN

Stare from your pillow into the sun. People of Unrest. Margaret Abigail Walker. CP-WalkM; GT

Staring into the fire. (LL) Poem at Thirty-nine. Alice Walker. CP-WalkA

Stark day corrodes the silver of the dream. Naomi Long Madgett. *Fr.* Trinity: a Dream Sequence. Klds

Starlight Scope Myopia. Yusef Komunyakaa. SP-KomuY

Starry Night, A. Paul Laurence Dunbar. CP-DunbP

Stars. Robert Hayden. CP-HaydR

Stars. Langston Hughes. CP-HughL; SP-HughL

Stars and Stripes. Mary Weston Fordham. CBWP-2

Stars dwindle / they will not reward me. Separation. Audre Lorde. SP-LordA

Stars from five wars, scars. At a VA Hospital in the Middle of the United States of America: An Act in a Play. Etheridge Knight. SP-KnigE

Stars in Alabama. Jessie Redmond Fauset. ShDr

Stars tied to the breath. The Brain to the Heart. Yusef Komunyakaa. SP-KomuY

Starter! / Her face is pale. Closing Time. Langston Hughes. CP-HughL

Starting All Over Again. Audre Lorde. CP-LordA

Starvation. Maya Angelou. CP-AngeM; SP-AngeM

State Street is lonely today. Aunt Jane Allen. Fenton Johnson. IDB; PoBA

State street was dead, wiped out. For Black People. Haki R. Madhubuti. BrTr

Statement. Langston Hughes. CP-HughL

Stations. Audre Lorde. CP-LordA

Statistic: The Witness. Rita Dove. NAAAL

Status Symbol. Mari E. Evans. IDB; NAAAL

Stay beautiful / but dont stay down underground too long. For Poets. Al Young. CP-YounA; PoBA

Stay, season of calm love and soulful snows! To Winter. Claude McKay. SP-McKaC

Staying overnight in a friend's house. Overnights. Alice Walker. CP-WalkA

Steal Away to Jesus. *Unknown.* BPo; CrDW; Crnst; NAAAL

Stealing from the night. Dancers. Langston Hughes. CP-HughL

Steel band had / entered the room, A. (LL) Poetry Makes Rhythm in Philosophy. Ishmael Reed. CP-ReedI

Steel doors—guillotine gates. The Prisoners. Robert Hayden. CP-HaydR

Steel Mills. Langston Hughes. CP-HughL

Stellar Nilotic (29). Amiri Baraka. SP-BaraA

Step me now a bridal measure. To Dan. Paul Laurence Dunbar. CP-DunbP

Step wid de banjo an' glide wid de fiddle. Christmas. Paul Laurence Dunbar. CP-DunbP

Stepfather: A Girl's Song. Yusef Komunyakaa. SP-KomuY

Stereo. Haki R. Madhubuti. AmNP; BrTr

Stern truth will never write, "By hands unknown." (LL) So Quietly. Leslie Pinckney Hill. BANP; IDB; PoBA

Stevedore. Leslie Morgan Collins. AmNP

Stick the finger inside. Black Mail. Alice Walker. CP-WalkA

Still and was a flower. (LL) Winter Poem. Nikki Giovanni. SP-GiovN

Still are there wonders of the dark and day. To Keep the Memory of Charlotte Forten Grimké. Angelina Weld Grimké. BlSi; ShDr

Still Do I Keep My Look, My Identity. . . . Gwendolyn Brooks. SP-BrooG

Still forever fare thee well! (LL) To Eliza. George Moses Horton. EBAP; SP-HortG; TtW

Still Here. Langston Hughes. BPo; CP-HughL; SP-HughL

Still I Rise. Maya Angelou. BlSi; CP-AngeM; NAAAL; SP-AngeM

Still, it is dear defiance now to carry. Flags. Gwendolyn Brooks. AmNP; SP-BrooG

Still / it was nice. Lucille Clifton. SP-ClifL

Still Life. Sharan Strange. GT

Still Life: Lady with Birds. Quandra Prettyman. PoBA

Still Life, Stealing Life / Caught Red-Handed. Kalamu ya Salaam. TtW

Still-Life with Woodstove. William W. Cook. SpiFl

Still Lives. Al Young. CP-YounA

Still visioning the stars! (LL) Oriflamme. Jessie Redmond Fauset. BANP; BlSi; PoBA; ShDr

Still Voice of Harlem, The. Conrad Kent Rivers. IDB; Klds; NNP; PoBA

Still you bring us with our hands bound. The Underground. Langston Hughes. CP-HughL

Stirring of a feathering cloud, The. Nature's Minor Chords. Henrietta Cordelia Ray. CBWP-3

Stirrup Cup, The. Paul Laurence Dunbar. CP-DunbP

Stirrups, leggings, a stainless. Love Medley: Patrice Cuchulain. Michael S. Harper. SP-HarpM

Stirs your blood. (LL) Danse Africaine. Langston Hughes. CP-HughL; NAAAL; SP-HughL

Stockpiling of frozen trees, The. Jayne Cortez. SP-CortJ

Stokely Malcolm Me. Langston Hughes. CP-HughL

Stomp of feet, A bevy of swift hands, A. (LL) Woman Me. Maya Angelou. BlSi; CP-AngeM; SP-AngeM

Stone / cold / daylight. Poem for Etheridge. Sonia Sanchez. BPo

Stonewall Jackson, 1886. Albery Allson Whitman. EBAP

Stony Lonesome. Langston Hughes. CP-HughL; SP-HughL

Stony lonesome reached out and grabbed me. Dannemora Contraband. Jackie Warren-Moore. SpiFl

Stood there then among. Stars. Robert Hayden. CP-HaydR

Stopped. Allen Polite. NNP

Stops. Lucille Clifton. SP-ClifL

Storm. Alice Walker. CP-WalkA

Storm and strife and stress. Death. Paul Laurence Dunbar. CP-DunbP

Storm-Beaten. Clara Ann Thompson. CBWP-2

Storm Ending. Jean Toomer. CP-ToomJ

Storm Figure. Derek Walcott. Crnst

Storm Poem, A. Lucille Clifton. SP-ClifL

Story Books on a Kitchen Table. Audre Lorde. CP-LordA; SP-LordA
   ("For the vanished mother / of a Black girl.") (LL) GT

Story goes: wide purple, The. Good Samaritan Hospital. Michael S. Harper. SP-HarpM

Story of Lovers Leap, The. Maggie Pogue Johnson. CBWP-4

Story of the Rebellion, A. Frances Ellen Watkins Harper. CP-HarpF

Story of the Zeros, The. Victor Hernandez Cruz. PoBA

Straight Talk from Plain Women. Sherley Anne Williams. GT

Straight, the swift, the debonair, The. Magnets. Countee Cullen. BALP; CP-CullC

Strange atoms unto ourselves. Lovelight. Georgia Douglas Johnson. AmNP

Strange beautiful woman, A. Marilyn Nelson. SP-NelsM

Strange but true is the story. The Sea-Turtle and the Shark. Melvin Beaunearus Tolson. PoBA *Fr.* Harlem Gallery. Klds

Strange / Distorted blades of grass. Garden. Langston Hughes. CP-HughL; SP-HughL

Strange Hurt. Langston Hughes. CP-HughL; GT; SP-HughL

Strange Legacies. Sterling A. Brown. Klds; PoBA
   ("Guess we'll give it one mo' try.") (LL) CP-BrowS

Strange, Strange Things. *African-American Oral Tradition.* GetYo

Strange summer sun shines round our globe of circumstance. Elegy: "Strange summer sun shines round our globe of circumstance." Margaret Abigail Walker. CP-WalkM

Strange / That in this nigger place. Esthete in Harlem. Langston Hughes. BANP; BPo; CP-HughL

Strangeness / And the stranger, The. Pair in One. Langston Hughes. CP-HughL

Stranger in Town. Langston Hughes. CP-HughL

Strangling women in the suburban bush. Das Kapital. Amiri Baraka. SP-BaraA

Strategies. Welton Smith. NBP; PoBA

Straw Hat. Rita Dove. SP-DoveR

Strawberry, The. Maggie Pogue Johnson. CBWP-4

Streaking (A Phenomenon Following the Sixties). Alice Walker. CP-WalkA

Stream, The. Lula Lowe Weeden. CDC

Street Called Crooked, The. Countee Cullen. CP-CullC

Street Car Gang. Sterling A. Brown. CP-BrowS

Street Demonstration. Margaret Abigail Walker. BPo; CP-WalkM

Street in Bronzeville, A. Gwendolyn Brooks. BPo; BlSi; SP-BrooG
   Hunchback Girl: She Thinks of Heaven. Klds
   Kitchenette Building. GT; NAAAL
   Mother, The. CrDW; Crnst; ESEAA; NAAAL; TtW
   Of De Witt Williams on His Way to Lincoln Cemetery. ESEAA
   Preacher: Ruminates Behind the Sermon, The. NAAAL
   Sadie and Maud. ESEAA; NAAAL
   Song in the Front Yard, A. ESEAA; IDB; NAAAL; PoBA
   Vacant Lot, The. NAAAL

Street in Kaufman-ville, A. James Cunningham. JB

Street Lamps in Early Spring. Gwendolyn B. Bennett. ShDr

Street light / On its lonely arm, The. Late Corner. Langston Hughes. CP-HughL; Klds

Street-Poisoned. Michael S. Harper. SP-HarpM

Street Song. Langston Hughes. *Fr.* Montage of a Dream Deferred. CP-HughL

Strength that bore her on for years, The. The Dying Queen. Frances Ellen Watkins Harper. CP-HarpF

Stretch cast out night's long,'d, The. Lakefront, Cleveland. Russell Atkins. GT

Stretching of the Belly, The. Etheridge Knight. SP-KnigE

String-chewing bass players. Mingus. Bob Kaufman. PoBA

Stroke, The. Rita Dove. SP-DoveR

Strokes the fern's / voluptuous braille. (LL) Fish in the Stone, The. Rita Dove. SP-DoveR

Strong demand, contend, prevail; the beggar is a fool!, The. (LL) The Suppliant. Georgia Douglas Johnson. BALP; CDC; PoBA; ShDr

Strong Men. Sterling A. Brown. BANP; BkSV; BPo; CP-BrowS; CrDW; FB; NAAAL; PoBA; TtW

Strong Men, Riding Horses / Lester after the Western. Gwendolyn Brooks. GT

Strong men. . . / Stronger. . . . (LL) Strong Men. Sterling A. Brown. BANP; BPo; BkSV; CrDW; FB; PoBA

Strong threads have bound your starry life. Angelic Eve. Jean Toomer. CP-ToomJ

Strong women / know the taste. Portrait. Audre Lorde. CP-LordA

Struggle-Road Dance. Ahmos, II Zu-Bolton. TtW

Struggle Staggers Us, The. Margaret Abigail Walker. CP-WalkM

Strung out on immortality's rag. (LL) Villon/Leadbelly. Yusef Komunyakaa. SP-KomuY; TtW

Strut and wiggle, / Shameless gal. To Midnight Nan at Leroy's. Langston Hughes. CP-HughL

Students / went out / of their way, The. Streaking (A Phenomenon Following the Sixties). Alice Walker. CP-WalkA

Studio Up Over In Your Ear. Al Young. CP-YounA; GT

Studs. Michael S. Harper. ESEAA

Study Peace. Amiri Baraka. PoBA

Studying the shadows of my face in this white place. A Sonnet from the Stony Brook. June Jordan. SP-JordJ

Sturdy I stand, books in my hand. Dark Youth of the U.S.A. Langston Hughes. CP-HughL

Suave big jigs in a conference room. The New Congo. Sterling A. Brown. CP-BrowS

Sub Shop Girl. Michael S. Weaver. SpiFl

Subject to a Fall: "Boys, you're subject to a fall and trip to the Walls." *African-American Oral Tradition.* GetYo

Subject to a Fall: "Say, you subject to a fall and a trip to the Wall." *African-American Oral Tradition.* GetYo

Submission. Clara Ann Thompson. CBWP-2

Submit, fight, run. Fugitive Paths. Michael S. Harper. SP-HarpM

Substitution. Anne Spencer. BlSi; CDC; ShDr

Subtle Art of Breathing, The. Asha Bandele. CtF

Subtlest strain a great musician weaves, The. Limitations. Henrietta Cordelia Ray. CBWP-3

Suburban Evening. Langston Hughes. CP-HughL

Subway, The. Conrad Kent Rivers. Klds

Subway Face. Langston Hughes. CP-HughL

Subway Rush Hour. Langston Hughes. *Fr.* Montage of a Dream Deferred. CP-HughL

Subway Wind. Claude McKay. SP-McKaC

Subway Witnesses, The. Lorenzo Thomas. GT; PoBA

Success, The. Amiri Baraka. SP-BaraA

Success. Langston Hughes. CP-HughL

Such are the liberal charms of college life. On the Pleasures of College Life. George Moses Horton. SP-HortG

Such are the little memories of you. To Theodore. George Marion McClellan. AAP

Such dissonance can e'er be sweet, and low. (LL) Incompleteness. Henrietta Cordelia Ray. CBWP-3

Suddenly / I touch upon wordlessness. The Curative Powers of Silence. Al Young. CP-YounA

Suddenly, the legs want a different sort of work. April. Cornelius Eady. ESEAA

Suddenly / when I hear airplanes overhead. Porter. Marilyn Nelson. ESEAA; SP-NelsM

Suffer the Children. Audre Lorde. CP-LordA; PoBA
("He is forever trapped.") SP-LordA

Suffering The Sea Change: All My Pretty Ones. Lucinda Roy. GT

Suffused in April twilight. Redemption. Pauli Murray. GT

Suga, come give sum rhythm to a mac who's all 'dat. In the Twilight. A. K. Toney. CtF

Sugar come / and sugar go. Winter Honey. June Jordan. SP-JordJ

Sugarfields. Barbara Mahone. PoBA

Suicide. Langston Hughes. CP-HughL

Suicide. Bob Kaufman. SP-KaufB

Suicide. Alice Walker. GT

Suicide. Al Young. CP-YounA

Suicide's Note. Langston Hughes. CDC; CP-HughL; SP-HughL

Suite for Augustus, A. Rita Dove. SP-DoveR
Planning the Perfect Evening. GT

Suite Repose. Carl Hancock Rux. SpiFl

Suitor, The. Paul Laurence Dunbar. CP-DunbP

Sukee River. Claude McKay. SP-McKaC

Sum, The. Paul Laurence Dunbar. CP-DunbP

Summah is de lovin' time. A Summer Night. Paul Laurence Dunbar. CP-DunbP

Summah night an' sighin' breeze. Lover's Lane. Paul Laurence Dunbar. BANP; CP-DunbP

Summah's nice, wif sun a-shinin'. Time to Tinker 'Roun'! Paul Laurence Dunbar. CP-DunbP

Summary. Sonia Sanchez. BPo; BlFi; BrTr; SP-SancS

Summer. Helen G. Quigless. BkSV

Summer. Al Young. CP-YounA

Summer brought fireflies in swarms. Childhood. Sharan Strange. GT

Summer comes / The ziczac hovers. Magalu. Helene Johnson. BlSi; CDC; PoBA; ShDr

Summer Evening (Calumet Avenue). Langston Hughes. CP-HughL; SP-HughL

Summer evening sun. Haiku: "Summer evening sun." Lenard D. Moore. TtW

Summer has sped a. Sonia Sanchez. SP-SancS

Summer in the South. Paul Laurence Dunbar. CP-DunbP; GT

Summer is / coming, The. The Cure All. Haki R. Madhubuti. BrTr

Summer Magic. Leslie Pinckney Hill. BANP

Summer matures. Brilliant Scorpion. Helene Johnson. *See* The Brilliant-bellied newt flashes.

Summer meant peeling: peaches. The Preserving. Kevin Young. GT

Summer Morn in New Hampshire. Claude McKay. SP-McKaC

Summer Night, A. Paul Laurence Dunbar. CP-DunbP

Summer Night. Langston Hughes. CP-HughL

Summer Oracle. Audre Lorde. BlSi; CP-LordA; PoBA; SP-LordA

Summer Pastoral, A. Paul Laurence Dunbar. CP-DunbP

Summer rains like my blood cries. From the Greenhouse. Audre Lorde. CP-LordA

Summer Words of a Sistuh Addict. Sonia Sanchez. BPo; BlSi; Crnst; NAAAL; SP-SancS

Summer's Night, A. Paul Laurence Dunbar. CP-DunbP

Summer's sun was beaming hot, The. Mother's Songs. Frank Barbour Coffin. AAP

Summertime and the Living. Robert Hayden. CP-HaydR; Klds; PoBA

Summertime / Is warm and bright. Year Round. Langston Hughes. CP-HughL

Sun and softness. Sun Song. Langston Hughes. CP-HughL; SP-HughL

Sun / bronzes your browns, The. Sweet Brown Rice and Red Bones. Lamont B. Steptoe. SpiFl

Sun came, Miss Brooks—, The. Etheridge Knight. BrTr; PoBA; SP-KnigE

Sun came up, The. The Decade That Screamed. Ishmael Reed. CP-ReedI

Sun came up, The. Rain Rain on the Splintered Girl. Ishmael Reed. PoBA

Sun, Creator of Suns. Bob Kaufman. SP-KaufB

Sun-god was reclining on a couch of rosy shells, The. Sunset Picture. Henrietta Cordelia Ray. CBWP-3

Sun has slipped his tether, The. Waiting. Paul Laurence Dunbar. CP-DunbP

Sun has sunk 'neath yonder distant hill, The. Belshazzar's Feast. Eloise Bibb. CBWP-4

Sun hath shed its kindly light, The. A Thanksgiving Poem. Paul Laurence Dunbar. CP-DunbP

Sun Heals, A. Jewel C. Latimore. JB

Sun hit shine an' de win' hit blow, De. Winter's Approach. Paul Laurence Dunbar. CP-DunbP

Sun House. Haki R. Madhubuti. ESEAA

Sun is folding, cars stall and rise, The. The New World. Amiri Baraka. SP-BaraA

Sun / Is gonna go down, The. Sunset in Dixie. Langston Hughes. CP-HughL

Sun is low, The. On the River. Paul Laurence Dunbar. CP-DunbP

Sun is shining in my backdoor, The. Myself When I Am Real. Al Young. CP-YounA; PoBA

Sun, / Like the red yolk of a rotten egg, The. Sunset—Coney Island. Langston Hughes. CP-HughL

Sun / make me whole again. Chorus. Audre Lorde. CP-LordA

Sun of Our Existence, The. Mrs. Henry Linden. CBWP-4

Sun Ra / Roi / Ho. The Myth Science of Our Time. Al Young. CP-YounA

Sun rises at midday, The. Unmeasured Tempo. Maya Angelou. CP-AngeM; SP-AngeM

Sun rose today, and, The. Birthday Poem. Etheridge Knight. SP-KnigE

Sun says she is there, The. The White Deer. Jay Wright. ESEAA

Sun shines bright, but sadly, The. Autumn. Priscilla Jane Thompson. CBWP-2

Sun shines so brightly on the hill. The Songless Lark. Audre Lorde. CP-LordA

Sun Song. Langston Hughes. CP-HughL; SP-HughL

Sun sought thy dim bed and brought forth light, The. Africa. Claude McKay. BALP; NAAAL; SP-McKaC

Sun went down in beauty, The. George Marion McClellan. AAP

Suncoming. Oliver La Grone. NBV

Sunday. Langston Hughes. *Fr.* Seven Moments of Love. CP-HughL

Sunday. Carl Phillips. GT

Sunday afternoon, / and couples walk the breakwater. Veracruz. Robert Hayden. *Fr.* An Inference of Mexico. AmNP; CP-HaydR

Sunday Afternoons. Herbert Asquith. NAAAL

Sunday by the Combination. Langston Hughes. *Fr.* Montage of a Dream Deferred. CP-HughL

Sunday Greens. Rita Dove. GT; SP-DoveR

Sunday Illumination. Al Young. CP-YounA

Sunday Meeting: *I b'lieve I'll go wid de ole man.* "Emperor": Shields Green: Fugitives. Michael S. Harper. SP-HarpM

Sunday Morning. Wayne Moreland. PoBA

Sunday morning and her mother's hands. Birmingham 1963. Raymond R. Patterson. PoBA; TtW

Sunday Morning Prophecy. Langston Hughes. SP-HughL
("And now / When the rumble of death.") CP-HughL

Sunday Night at Grandfather's. Rita Dove. SP-DoveR

Sunday Sonnet for My Mother's Mother, A. Al Young. CP-YounA

Sunday strollers along a sewage-choked Schuylkill. To Some Millions Who Survive Joseph E. Mander, Sr. Sarah E. Wright. PoBA

Sundays of Satin-Legs Smith, The. Gwendolyn Brooks. NAAAL; SP-BrooG

Sundays too my father got up early. Those Winter Sundays. Robert Hayden. CP-HaydR; ESEAA; IDB; PoBA; SSLK

Sunflower Sonnet Number One. June Jordan. TtW

Sunflower Sonnet Number Two. June Jordan. TtW

Sunflowers and Saturdays. Melba Joyce Boyd. BlSi

Sunny. Naomi Long Madgett. BrTr

Sunnyland. Elmore James. NAAAL

Sunrise. Henrietta Cordelia Ray. Fr. Idyl. CBWP-3; EBAP

Sunrise!! Rolland Snellings. BlFi

Sunrise on the River. Kalamu ya Salaam. Fr. New Orleans Haiku. SpiFl

Sun's a risin'. Hey! Hey! Langston Hughes. CP-HughL

Sun's a setting'. Hey! Langston Hughes. CP-HughL

Sun's accomplice, the tree. / Maurice. (LL) Dusting. Rita Dove. SP-DoveR

Sun's return is magical, The. Carnival. Primus St. John. GT

Sunset. Paul Laurence Dunbar. CP-DunbP

Sunset. Mary Weston Fordham. CBWP-2

Sunset. Henrietta Cordelia Ray. Fr. Idyl. CBWP-3; EBAP

Sunset Beach. Ahmos, II Zu-Bolton. CBWP-3

Sunset by the lake. Lake Murry. Pinkie Gordon Lane. GT

Sunset—Coney Island. Langston Hughes. CP-HughL

Sunset Horn. Myron O'Higgins. AmNP

Sunset in Dixie. Langston Hughes. CP-HughL

Sunset of the City, A. Gwendolyn Brooks. GT; SP-BrooG

Sunset Picture. Henrietta Cordelia Ray. CBWP-3

Sunshine after Cloud. Josephine D. Henderson Heard. CBWP-4

Sunshine and shadow play amid the trees. July. Henrietta Cordelia Ray. CBWP-3

Sunshine on der medders. A Warm Day in Winter. Paul Laurence Dunbar. CP-DunbP

Super-cool / ultrablack. But He Was Cool. Haki R. Madhubuti. BrTr; Crnst

Super-cool / ultrablack. But He Was Cool; or, He Even Stopped for Green Lights. Don L. Lee. AmNP; BPo; PoBA

Superstitions. Maggie Pogue Johnson. CBWP-4

Supper Time. Langston Hughes. Fr. Seven Moments of Love. CP-HughL

Suppliant, The. Georgia Douglas Johnson. BALP; CDC; PoBA; ShDr

Supplication. Joseph Seamon Cotter, Sr. BANP; CDC

Suppose. Paul Laurence Dunbar. CP-DunbP

Suppose they had cheated me out of my. Remember Times for Sandy. Carolyn M. Rodgers. JB

Suppose you were dreaming about your family. Benign Neglect / Mississippi, 1970. Primus St. John. PoBA

Supposing we could just go on and on as two. Sunflower Sonnet Number Two. June Jordan. TtW

Suppression. Jayne Cortez. NBV

Supremes done gone, The. Memorial. Sonia Sanchez. BlSi

Sure I know you! White Man. Langston Hughes. CP-HughL

Surely you stay my certain own, you stay. Love Note I: Surely. Gwendolyn Brooks. SP-BrooG

Surrender. Angelina Weld Grimké. CDC

Surrounded by scientists in a faculty. Homage to the New World. Michael S. Harper. ESEAA; SP-HarpM

Susannah, (Time of the Gingham Rooster, collage by Romare Bearden). Thulani Davis. GT

Suspension. Audre Lorde. CP-LordA; SP-LordA

Swallow for dear life. (LL) Yes, the Secret Mind Whispers. Al Young. CP-YounA; PoBA; TtW

Swallow the Lake. Clarence Major. ESEAA; GT; NAAAL; PoBA

Swamp, The. Derek Walcott. GT

Swamp Rat. Kiarri T-H Cheatwood. TtW

Swan, The—Vain Pleasures. George Moses Horton. BALP

Swans loom on the playground. Street-Poisoned. Michael S. Harper. SP-HarpM

Swaziland. Nikki Giovanni. SP-GiovN

Sweet and calm the breezes stealing. Sabbath Bells. Josephine D. Henderson Heard. CBWP-4

Sweet baked apple dappled cinnamon speckled sin of mine. Love Child—a Black Aesthetic. Everett Hoagland. BPo

Sweet beats of jazz impaled on slivers of wind. Walking Parker Home. Bob Kaufman. NAAAL; PoBA; SP-KaufB

Sweet Bread. Frank X. Walker. SpiFl

Sweet Brown Rice and Red Bones. Lamont B. Steptoe. SpiFl

Sweet children amid the apple boughs. On the Picture of a Child. Henrietta Cordelia Ray. CBWP-3

Sweet Dorothy, I know you're still. A Poem for Dorothy Dandridge. Al Young. CP-YounA

Sweet elfin music comes to me. A Dream of Elfland. Henrietta Cordelia Ray. CBWP-3

Sweet Ethel. Linda Piper. BlSi

Sweet girls, sweet girls. Listen Here Blues. Langston Hughes. CP-HughL

Sweet Honey in the Rock. E. Ethelbert Miller. TtW

Sweet Life! how lovely to be here. Winter in the Country. Claude McKay. SP-McKaC

Sweet Lovin' Rose, see also No Good Whore and Whores Are No Good. African-American Oral Tradition. GetYo

Sweet Mother! rare in gifts of tenderness! To My Mother. Henrietta Cordelia Ray. CBWP-3

Sweet nature, give me holy dreams. At Nature's Shrine. Henrietta Cordelia Ray. CBWP-3

Sweet on the house top falls the gentle shower. Meditation on a Cold, Dark and Rainy Night. George Moses Horton. SP-HortG

Sweet Sally took a cardboard box. The Ballad of the Light-Eyed Little Girl. Gwendolyn Brooks. SP-BrooG

Sweet silver trumpets / Jesus! (LL) When Sue Wears Red. Langston Hughes. CP-HughL; NAAAL; SP-HughL

Sweet Sixteen Lines. Al Young. CP-YounA

Sweet the perfume of an age bygone. To an Afro-American Maiden. Fenton Johnson. Crnst

Sweet timber land. Homing. Arna Bontemps. CDC

Sweet, winsome May, coy, pensive fay. May. Henrietta Cordelia Ray. CBWP-3

Sweet Words on Race. Langston Hughes. CP-HughL

Sweet words that take. Sweet Words on Race. Langston Hughes. CP-HughL

Sweeten 'Tatahs. James David Corrothers. EBAP

Sweetest of the flowers a-blooming. The Lily of the Valley. Paul Laurence Dunbar. CP-DunbP

Sweets you were glittering this morning. Dear Arl. Al Young. CP-YounA

Swift swallows sailing from the Spanish main. Homing Swallows. Claude McKay. SP-McKaC

Swift, Tiny and Fine. Ishmael Reed. CP-ReedI

Swing dat hammer—hunh—. Southern Road. Sterling A. Brown. BALP; BANP; BPo; FB; NAAAL; PoBA

Swing high, Iscariot. The Sacrifice. Gerald William Barrax. Klds

Swing low so I. Gospel. Rita Dove. SP-DoveR

Swing low, sweet chariot. Unknown. CrDW
("Coming for to carry me home.") (LL) NAAAL

Swing yo' lady roun' an' roun'. A Frolic. Paul Laurence Dunbar. CP-DunbP

Swinging horn softly confirming. His Horn. Bob Kaufman. SP-KaufB

Swinging through the trees with my dick in my hand. African-American Oral Tradition. GetYo

Sylvester's Dying Bed. Langston Hughes. CP-HughL; SP-HughL
("I work up this mornin'.") NAAAL

Symbols hang limply, The. Rhythm and Blues (I). Amiri Baraka. SP-BaraA

Sympathy. Paul Laurence Dunbar. AAP; AfAmPo; AmNP; CDC; CP-DunbP; CP-DunbP; CrDW; Crnst; GT; IDB; NAAAL; PoBA; SSLK; TtW

Sympathy. Lizelia Augusta Jenkins Moorer. CBWP-3

Symphony. Frank Horne. AmNP

Symphony Sid. Amiri Baraka. SP-BaraA

Syntax of the mind grips, The. Quincy Troupe. NBV; TtW

Syracuse Airport. Audre Lorde. CP-LordA

Syrophenician Woman, The. Frances Ellen Watkins Harper. CP-HarpF

T

T. B. Bees. African-American Oral Tradition. GetYo

T. C. Walter Bradford. BrTr

'T is better to sit here beside the sea. Silence. Paul Laurence Dunbar. CP-DunbP

'T is hard to judge if hatred's of one's race. Albery Allson Whitman. AfAmPo Fr. "Is manhood less because man's face is black." AAP Fr. Twasinta's Seminoles; Or Rape of Florida.

Tableau. Countee Cullen. BANP; CP-CullC; Klds; NAAAL; PoBA

Tadpoles are legless and never learn to curtsy. Pathways: From Mother to Mother. Audre Lorde. CP-LordA

Tag. Langston Hughes. SP-HughL Fr. Montage of a Dream Deferred. CP-HughL

Take a note and spin it around spin it around don't. The Geni in the Jar. Nikki Giovanni. SP-GiovN

Take in hand the cup of delusion. Drink On. Mary E. Tucker. CBWP-1

Take it not back! the priceless gift. Invocation to the Muse. Henrietta Cordelia Ray. CBWP-3

Take just / One star. (LL) Stars. Langston Hughes. CP-HughL; SP-HughL

Take me there. (LL) Island. Langston Hughes. CP-HughL; SP-HughL

Take me, Virginia. Forgive. Maya Angelou. CP-AngeM

Take My Hand, Precious Lord. Unknown. NAAAL

Take my share of Soul Food. High on the Hog. Julia Fields. TtW

Take my word for jewel in your open light. Audre Lorde. See Coal.

Take sackcloth of the darkest dye. Bible Defence of Slavery. Frances Ellen Watkins Harper. CP-HarpF

Take them out! June Jordan. SP-JordJ

Take this / black mother's anguish and wave. Zimbabwe. Sterling Plumpp. TtW

Take time as lubricant or. Continuing. Al Young. CP-YounA

Take Time Out. Maya Angelou. CP-AngeM; SP-AngeM

Take Tools Our Strength. Gerald L., Jr. Simmons. NBP

Taken from the. The Primitive. Don L. Lee. BPo

Taking in Wash. Rita Dove. SP-DoveR

Tale of Italy, A. Eloise Bibb. CBWP-4

Talk about Bosnia led to the Hutu and Tutsi, two. As Simple as That. Marilyn Nelson. SP-NelsM

Talk between the people and the soil. Clinton. Sterling Plumpp. BkSV

Talk is getting mean, The. (LL) Unidentified Flying Object. Robert Hayden. CP-HaydR

Talk scared him. Left alone, with me, The. This Is the Clearing I Once Spoke of. Amiri Baraka. SP-BaraA

Talk some shit, Richard. African-American Oral Tradition. GetYo

Talkin all that kinda truth. (LL) A Song of Sojourner Truth. June Jordan. SP-JordJ; TtW

Talking Back of Miss Valentine Jones, The. June Jordan. SP-JordJ Poem # One.

Talking in the Woods with Karl Amorelli. Etheridge Knight. SP-KnigE

Talking to a friend. (LL) Sister, Morning Is a Time for Miracles. Audre Lorde. CP-LordA; SP-LordA

Talking to My Grandmother Who Died Poor. Alice Walker. CP-WalkA

Talking to some people is like talking to a toilet. (LL) A Sewerplant Grows in Harlem or I'm a Stranger Here Myself When Does the Next Swan Leave. Audre Lorde. CP-LordA; SP-LordA

Tall man / Without clothes, A. Karamojongs. Alice Walker. CP-WalkA

Tall strips of carrion moonlight. Lost Window. Bob Kaufman. SP-KaufB

Tallest poet for his height. Arroyo. Tom Weatherly. PoBA

Tambourine. James Cunningham. JB

Tambourines! / Tambourines! Langston Hughes. CP-HughL; SP-HughL

Tambourines / To glory! (LL) Tambourines! / Tambourines! Langston Hughes. CP-HughL; SP-HughL

Tangled in sea weed minutes. The Baroness and the Black Musician. Larry Neal. BlFi

Tango. Ntozake Shange. GT

Tanka. Lenard D. Moore. CtF

Tanka (I–VIII). Lewis Alexander. CDC

Tanka: "After church meeting." Lenard D. Moore. SpiFl

Tanka: "Month of rain ends." Lenard D. Moore. SpiFl

Taped to the wall of my cell are 47 pictures: 47 black. The Idea of Ancestry. Etheridge Knight. BALP; BPo; BrTr; ESEAA; GT; NAAAL; PoBA; SP-KnigE; TtW

Tapestries. Colleen J. McElroy. NAAAL

Tapestry. Langston Hughes. CP-HughL

Tapping. Jayne Cortez. SP-CortJ

Tartar Wolf, A. Back to Africa. Ishmael Reed. CP-ReedI

Taste of soul's desire, The. (LL) God Give to Men. Arna Bontemps. BANP; BPo; CDC

Tattooed Man, The. Robert Hayden. CP-HaydR

Taught early that his mother's skin was the sign of error. Mr. Z. M. Carl Holman. Klds

Tauhid. Askia Muhammad Touré. PoBA

Tea Dancer Turns Thirty-Nine. Ishmael Reed. CP-ReedI

Teach me to sing. For My Brother. June Jordan. SP-JordJ

Teach Us to Number Our Days. Rita Dove. ESEAA; SP-DoveR

Teacher, The. Leslie Pinckney Hill. BANP

Teacher. Langston Hughes. CP-HughL

Teacher. Audre Lorde. CP-LordA; SP-LordA

Teacher, Jimmie's toe is bleedin'. Johnny's Pet Superstition. Clara Ann Thompson. CBWP-2

Teacher leaning hard on The, A. (LL) The Teacher. Leslie Pinckney Hill. BANP

Teacher was a bad man, The. Margaret Abigail Walker. CP-WalkM

Teaching. Al Young. CP-YounA

Tear another's tears bring forth, The. Sympathy. Paul Laurence Dunbar. CP-DunbP

Tears for the poet. Kamau Daáood. CtF

Tears have pressed white hair / to face. (LL) The Feral Pioneers. Ishmael Reed. CP-ReedI; PoBA

Tears, / hiding behind a doomed god. To Fanon. Keorapetse W. Kgositsile. BrTr

Tears of disillusion have always fallen from our black eye. Our Spirit Stands. Glenis Redmond Sherer. CtF

Tears that weep for shattered Sunday schools. The Song of Fire. Rolland Snellings. BlFi

Tears / The crystal rags. Maya Angelou. CP-AngeM; SP-AngeM

Ted, Ted? In the bay at the bottom of the wat. Real Life. Amiri Baraka. SP-BaraA

Tek a cool night, good an' cleah. Hunting Song. Paul Laurence Dunbar. CP-DunbP

Telegram to Alex/Bagel Shop, North Beach SF. Bob Kaufman. SP-KaufB

Telephone, The. Maya Angelou. CP-AngeM; SP-AngeM

Televised news turns. Maya Angelou. CP-AngeM

Television / radio sunday benevolent sunday. They Are Killing All the Young Men. David Henderson. PoBA

Television Speaks. Etheridge Knight. SP-KnigE

Tell all my mourners. Wake. Langston Hughes. CP-HughL; SP-HughL

Tell Her So. Mrs. Henry Linden. CBWP-4

Tell Me. Langston Hughes. Fr. Montage of a Dream Deferred. CP-HughL

"Tell me a story, father, please." The Natives of America. Ann Plato. BlSi

Tell me a story, Father, please do. Request Number. G. N. Sprod. AAP

Tell me about Soul. Soul. Barbara Simmons. BlFi

Tell me about the good things. How Long Has Trane Been Gone. Joe Corrie. NAAAL

Tell me again the Christmas story. The Christmas Story. Langston Hughes. CP-HughL

Tell me, dear beauty of the dusk. Jean Toomer. CP-ToomJ

Tell me, did the angels greet thee? To a Babe Smiling in Her Sleep. Frances Ellen Watkins Harper. CP-HarpF

Tell me, is it hard to wrap your tongue and fingers around a note. Kissing Keys. Karen Williams. CtF

Tell me is there anything lovelier. Greenness. Angelina Weld Grimké. CDC

Tell me, / Is there peace. Convent. Langston Hughes. CP-HughL

Tell me, Mama, can I get my show. Show Fare, Please. Langston Hughes. Fr. Ask Your Mama; 12 Moods for Jazz. CP-HughL

Tell me, mama, what is it that makes the mare go round? Money, Honey, Money. Margaret Abigail Walker. CP-WalkM

Tell me of thy heart's devotion. Whisper Words of Love to Me. Lizelia Augusta Jenkins Moorer. CBWP-3

Tell me, oh fate, is it decreed. James Ephriam McGirt. AAP

Tell me something / what you think would happen if. Poem about Police Violence. June Jordan. SP-JordJ

Tell me that the plutonium sludge. Jayne Cortez. SP-CortJ

Tell me, ye sad winds sighing. Timothy Thomas Fortune. EBAP

Tell them / them them loud and clear. I Will Not Let Them Take You. Opal Palmer Adisa. IHS

Tell your love where the roses blow. Diplomacy. Paul Laurence Dunbar. CP-DunbP

Telling. Alice Walker. CP-WalkA

Telling Fortunes. Sterling A. Brown. CP-BrowS

Telly Boob-Tube on the Idiot Box. Margaret Abigail Walker. CP-WalkM

Temple, The. Sterling A. Brown. CP-BrowS

Temples he built and palaces of air. The Dreamer. Paul Laurence Dunbar. CP-DunbP

Temptation. Paul Laurence Dunbar. CP-DunbP

Temptation. Elma Stuckey. TtW

$10,000: dead or alive won't catch her. Gen'l Tubman, as We Call Her. Michael S. Harper. SP-HarpM

Ten Years After Umbra. Tom Dent. TtW

Tenacious foliage; burgundy / rust, jaundice, sea-sick green. Nothing Lovely as a Tree. Frederick, Jr. Bryant. BlFi

Tenebris. Angelina Weld Grimké. CDC; NAAAL; PoBA; ShDr

Tennessee Hero, The. Frances Ellen Watkins Harper. CP-HarpF

Tennyson's Poems. Josephine D. Henderson Heard. CBWP-4

Tenth of May was a hell of a day, The. Titanic: "Tenth of May was a hell of a day, The." African-American Oral Tradition. GetYo

Tequila Jazz. Bob Kaufman. SP-KaufB

Terence MacSwiney. Anne Spencer. ShDr

Terror is more certain than all the rare desirable popular songs, A. Bob Kaufman. SP-KaufB

Test of Atlanta 1979, The. June Jordan. SP-JordJ

Testament. Lucille Clifton. SP-ClifL

Testament. Langston Hughes. CP-HughL

Testament of Loss. Gloria C. Oden. ESEAA

Testimonial. Langston Hughes. *Fr.* Montage of a Dream Deferred. CP-HughL

Testimony. Carolyn M. Rodgers. BPo

Tetuan. Claude McKay. SP-McKaC

Than passion's death! (LL) Dead Fires. Jessie Redmond Fauset. BANP

Than this stocking in my hand. (LL) The Ragged Stocking. Frances Ellen Watkins Harper. CP-HarpF

Thank God for Little Children. Frances Ellen Watkins Harper. CP-HarpF

Thank God that thou hast spoken. Lines to Charles Sumner. Frances Ellen Watkins Harper. CP-HarpF

Thank you for these tiny. Dusting. Marilyn Nelson. SP-NelsM

Thank You, Lord. Maya Angelou. SP-AngeM

Thanking him for spending. Abba Jacob and the Theologian. Marilyn Nelson. SP-NelsM

Thanks for the tree. Yusef Komunyakaa. SP-KomuY

Thanks to Jesse Jackson. Audre Lorde. CP-LordA

Thanksgibin' day am now at han'. Day befo' Thanksgibin', De. Maggie Pogue Johnson. CBWP-4

Thanksgiving. Lizelia Augusta Jenkins Moorer. CBWP-5

Thanksgiving Poem, A. Paul Laurence Dunbar. CP-DunbP

Thanksgiving Time. Langston Hughes. CP-HughL

That breathed the living breath of spring. (LL) The Resurrection. Jonathan Henderson Brooks. AmNP; CDC

That bright chimeric beast. Countee Cullen. AmNP; CP-CullC

That Christmas, unlike others. Gifts. Lenard D. Moore. SpiFl

That constant Susannah. Susannah. Thulani Davis. GT

"That cop was powerful mean." The Idiot. Dudley Randall. BPo

That Day. Nikki Giovanni. SP-GiovN

That doesn't mean / i / don't love. (LL) A Poem Looking for a Reader. Haki R. Madhubuti. BrTr

That early training. Lesson. Al Young. CP-YounA

That electrifies like poetry. (LL) Kiss. Al Young. CP-YounA; PoBA

That even then doesn't matter. (LL) Age. Nikki Giovanni. Crnst; SP-GiovN

That evening Sinda thought she heard the drums. The Dream. Robert Hayden. CP-HaydR; ESEAA; NBV

That Fame's immortal wreath has crowned his brow. (LL) In Memoriam Paul Laurence Dunbar. Henrietta Cordelia Ray. CBWP-3

That first birth. My Second Birth. Marilyn Nelson. SP-NelsM

That first night in the hotel bedroom. Touching/Not Touching: My Mother. Toi Derricotte. GT

That floats through many olden days. (LL) The Sculptor's Vision. Henrietta Cordelia Ray. CBWP-3

That flushes this wild fruit? (LL) Fruit of the Flower. Countee Cullen. CP-CullC

That force is lost. Snake Eyes. Amiri Baraka. Klds; SP-BaraA

That gaiety oh. Lear Is Gay. Robert Hayden. CP-HaydR

That Glove. Mary E. Tucker. CBWP-1

That grand and noble woman dear. Harriet Beecher Stowe's Works. Frank Barbour Coffin. AAP

That gypsy strain is. Head of a Woman. Al Young. CP-YounA

That he is human ... and living. Emperor Haile Selassie. Langston Hughes. CP-HughL

That Hill. Blanche Taylor Dickinson. CDC

That house has / a path of bad. Untitled II. Ishmael Reed. CP-ReedI

That Hypocrite. *Unknown.* BPo

That I have been looking. Subway Face. Langston Hughes. CP-HughL

That I must journey on. (LL) Supplication. Joseph Seamon Cotter, Sr. BANP; CDC

That Justice is a blind goddess. Justice. Langston Hughes. BPo; CP-HughL

That kid's my buddy. Buddy. Langston Hughes. *Fr.* Montage of a Dream Deferred. CP-HughL

That little Negro's married and got a kid. Sister. Langston Hughes. *Fr.* Montage of a Dream Deferred. CP-HughL

That little yaller gal. The New Cabaret Girl. Langston Hughes. CP-HughL

That lively organ, palpitant and red. The Proud Heart. Countee Cullen. CP-CullC

That living there I never could look up. (LL) The Glory Trumpeter. Derek Walcott. GT

That loves me too late. (LL) Song: "Wild trees have bought me." Audre Lorde. CP-LordA; SP-LordA

That man over there say. Ain't I a Woman? Sojourner Truth. BlSi

That mean old yesterday. Mean Old Yesterday. Langston Hughes. CP-HughL

That morning you found your lights on. Adagio. Gerald William Barrax. GT

That my heart is in the dough? (LL) Dinah Kneading Dough. Paul Laurence Dunbar. CP-DunbP; NAAAL

That my life was gone. (LL) Slave Coffle. Maya Angelou. CP-AngeM; SP-AngeM

That my meerschaum is colouring well. (LL) A Companion's Progress. Paul Laurence Dunbar. CP-DunbP; GT

That nearly swallowed you— / and me too. (LL) Belly Song. Etheridge Knight. BkSV

That never lifts its head / Again. (LL) Troubled Woman. Langston Hughes. CP-HughL; SP-HughL

That now devours / desire. (LL) Threatened by my rising need. Alice Walker. CP-WalkA

That Old Time Religion. Marvin E. Jackmon. BlFi

That Picture in the Paper. Sekou Sundiata. *Fr.* Notes from the Defense of Colin Ferguson. SpiFl

That same look. Leslie. Marvin, Jr. Wyche. AmNP

That she would grow again. (LL) For My Grandmother. Countee Cullen. CP-CullC; SSLK

That shy angle of his daughter's head. Variation on Gaining a Son. Rita Dove. SP-DoveR

That smokestack, for instance. Obedience. Rita Dove. SP-DoveR

That Stagoleee and an all-right lad. Bad-Man Stagolee. Margaret Abigail Walker. CP-WalkM

That summer in Culpeper, all there was to eat was white. Nineteen. Elizabeth Alexander. GT

That the dead, the dead are there! (LL) The Revel. Frances Ellen Watkins Harper. CP-HarpF

That they may not depart. (LL) To the First of August. Ann Plato. EBAP; TtW

That time my grandmother dragged me. The Weakness. Toi Derricotte. GT

That time / we all heard it. Paul Robeson. Gwendolyn Brooks. BrTr; PoBA

That Was Then. Kupenda Auset. CtF

That we die to learn it well. (LL) In Orangeburg My Brothers Did. Alfred B. Spellman. BPo; PoBA

That We Head Towards. Stephany Fuller. BPo

That what. Dream Thief. Nathaniel Mackey. GT

That which is inside me is screaming. Bloodbirth. Audre Lorde. CP-LordA; SP-LordA

That whiskey will cook the egg. Bar. Langston Hughes. SP-HughL *Fr.* Montage of a Dream Deferred. CP-HughL

That whole way to Delphi. Poor Form. June Jordan. SP-JordJ

That will someday dig his grave. (LL) Tunnels. Yusef Komunyakaa. SP-KomuY; TtW

That winter I stopped loving the President. A Suite for Augustus. Rita Dove. SP-DoveR

That without dust the rainbow would not be. (LL) Oh, God of dust and rainbows, help us see. Langston Hughes. CP-HughL; Klds

That woman stood to free the arms which hold the hands ... / which hold. (LL) Hands; For Mother's Day. Nikki Giovanni. IHS; SP-GiovN

That would be enough. (LL) What Would I Do White? June Jordan. SP-JordJ

That would not toil or spin. (LL) For Daughters of Magdalen. Countee Cullen. CP-CullC

That's all that I remember. (LL) Incident. Countee Cullen. BPo; CDC; CP-CullC; IDB; NAAAL; PoBA; SSLK

That's genius for you. (LL) A Poem about Intelligence for My Brothers and Sisters. June Jordan. SP-JordJ

That's Mexican for O youre too much! Malagueña Salerosa. Al Young. CP-YounA

That's not even it. Recitation. Ellease Southerland. GT

That's pretty much what they will do. (LL) A Poem for Players. Al Young. CP-YounA

That's right: keep on singing, "*Carry Me Back to Old Virginny.*" Carry Me Back to Old Virginny. Elma Ehrlich Levinger. ShDr

That's why societies usedta throw us away/ or sell us/ or. It's Not so Good to Be Born a Girl/ Sometimes. Ntozake Shange. SSLK

Thaw. Audre Lorde. CP-LordA

(The Recent Past). C. S. Giscombe. GT

Thee sacrosanct, Thee sweet, Thee crystalline. Firstly Inclined to Take What It Is Told. Gwendolyn Brooks. SP-BrooG

Theft. Esther Popel. ShDr

Their hair, pomaded, faces jaded. Sepia Fashion Show. Maya Angelou. BlSi; CP-AngeM; SP-AngeM

Their shimmering voices / singing. (LL) Confession. Lucille Clifton. TtW

Their shimmering voices / singing. (LL) In populated air. Lucille Clifton. SP-ClifL

Thelonious: An Intro. Al Young. CP-YounA

Thelonious. Reuben Jackson. ESEAA

Theme and Variation. Robert Hayden. CP-HaydR

Theme Brown Girl. Elton Hill-Abu Ishak. NBP

Theme for English B. Langston Hughes. Fr. Montage of a Dream Deferred. CP-HughL

Theme One: The Variations. August Wilson. PoBA

Then and Now. Paul Laurence Dunbar. CP-DunbP

Then and Now. Frances Ellen Watkins Harper. CP-HarpF

Then as now. (LL) Forgiveness. Alice Walker. CP-WalkA

Then be blessed with light, more light. (LL) Let the Light Enter! Frances Ellen Watkins Harper. CP-HarpF

Then call me traitor if you must. To Certain Critics. Countee Cullen. BPo; CP-CullC

Then Came Flowers. Rita Dove. SP-DoveR

Then, can I greedily consume / your presence. (LL) Remembrance. Maya Angelou. CP-AngeM; SP-AngeM

Then cease, my song, till fair Aurora rise. (LL) An Hymn to the Evening. Phillis Wheatley. AfAmPo; CP-WheaP

Then fled, O brethren, the wicked juba. The Ballad of Nat Turner. Robert Hayden. BALP; BPo; CP-HaydR

Then give us back our land. (LL) Zocalo. Michael S. Harper. NBV; SP-HarpM

Then Jonah Took Out His Guitar. Marilyn Nelson. Fr. I Dream the Book of Jonah. SP-NelsM

Then—like an atom bomb—it bursts apart. (LL) Lunch in a Jim Crow Car. Langston Hughes. SP-HughL

Then pain stalks in to plunder. (LL) In a time of secret wooing. Maya Angelou. CP-AngeM; SP-AngeM

Then rails to run. (LL) Prisoner. Maya Angelou. CP-AngeM; SP-AngeM

Then slowly opening. (LL) Courtship. Rita Dove. SP-DoveR

Then the golden hour. Length of Moon. Arna Bontemps. CDC

Then / You / Died. (LL) Fall Down. Calvin C. Hernton. PoBA

Theology. Paul Laurence Dunbar. CP-DunbP

Theory: Inconvenienced subject will return to hospital. The Family of Debridement. Michael S. Harper. SP-HarpM

Theory of Evil. Robert Hayden. CP-HaydR

Theory on Extinction or What Happened to the Dinosaurs? Kenneth Carroll. SpiFl

Ther' ain't no use in all this strife. An Easy-Goin' Feller. Paul Laurence Dunbar. CP-DunbP

Therapy. Audre Lorde. CP-LordA

There. Langston Hughes. CP-HughL

There ain't no pay beneath the sun. One More Round. Maya Angelou. CP-AngeM; SP-AngeM

There are afternoons in jazz. The Art of Benny Carter. Al Young. CP-YounA

There / are / Black men in the south. On Seeing the Black Male as #1 Sex Object in America. Etheridge Knight. SP-KnigE

There are brilliant heights of sorrow. Paul Laurence Dunbar. CP-DunbP

"There are dreams that need rest." Okay. Sharon Scott. JB

There are five people in this room. Representing the Universe. Alice Walker. CP-WalkA

There are flies / everywhere / i go. (LL) Alone. Nikki Giovanni. BrTr; SP-GiovN

There are just so many years. Turning Pro. Ishmael Reed. CP-ReedI

There are many and more. Many and More. Maya Angelou. CP-AngeM

There are no beaten paths to Glory's height. The Path. Paul Laurence Dunbar. CP-DunbP

There are / No clocks on the wall. End. Langston Hughes. CP-HughL; SP-HughL

There are no dry bones. The Bones of My Father. Etheridge Knight. SP-KnigE

There are no frogs in Soweto. Prism. Audre Lorde. CP-LordA

There are no hollows any more. Ironic: LL.D. William Stanley Braithwaite. BANP

There Are No Honest Poems about Dead Women. Audre Lorde. CP-LordA

There are no nightmares now. Only when memory settles. Seravezza. Hoyt W. Fuller. PoBA

There are no reservations. No Reservations. Nikki Giovanni. BrTr; SP-GiovN

There are no simple explanations. No Simple Explanations. Jayne Cortez. GT; SP-CortJ

There are no stars which fell on Alabama. Elements of Grammar. Calvin C. Hernton. NBP

There are no tigers. Alice Walker. CP-WalkA

There are old drunks among the tenements. The Griots Who Know Brer Fox. Colleen J. McElroy. NAAAL

There are so many diseases. Pathological Puzzle. Langston Hughes. CP-HughL

There are so many girls now in the street. Times Change and We Change with Them or We Seem to Have Lost Touch with Each Other. Audre Lorde. CP-LordA

There are so many roots to the tree of anger. Who Said It Was Simple. Audre Lorde. CP-LordA; SP-LordA

There are some nights when. Insomniac. Maya Angelou. CP-AngeM; SP-AngeM

There are some / secrets. July 31. Norman Jordan. PoBA

There are sounds / which shatter. Patience. Nikki Giovanni. SP-GiovN

There are teeth marks. The Thorn Merchant. Yusef Komunyakaa. SP-KomuY

There are the inactive ones who. Stalingrad: 1942. Langston Hughes. CP-HughL

There are things lovely and dangerous still. Of Nightsong and Flight. June Jordan. SP-JordJ

There are times that the. Sonia Sanchez. SP-SancS

There are two white captains. The Sailor in Africa. Rita Dove. SP-DoveR

There are words like Freedom. Words Like Freedom. Langston Hughes. BPo; CP-HughL; SP-HughL

There arent. Untitled Requiem for Tomorrow. Conyus. PoBA

There came a dove, an Easter dove. My Easter Dove. Henrietta Cordelia Ray. CBWP-3

There comes time I call my bonny. Clinton. Sterling Plumpp. BkSV

There had been quiet all that afternoon. In Emanuel's Nightmare: Another Coming of Christ. Gwendolyn Brooks. SP-BrooG

There hadn't been no shift for quite a bit. Signifying Monkey: "There hadn't been no shift for quite a bit." African-American Oral Tradition. GetYo

There he stands, see? Carl Wendell, Jr. Hines. Fr. Two Jazz Poems. Klds

There is a bitter river. The Bitter River. Langston Hughes. CP-HughL

There is a coarseness. Jungle Taste. Edward S. Silvera. CDC

There is a deep brooding. My Arkansas. Maya Angelou. BlSi; CP-AngeM; NAAAL; SP-AngeM

There is a dream in the land. Dream of Freedom. Langston Hughes. CP-HughL

There is a freedom too, a peculiar kind. Meanwhile, in Rwanda. Saundra Sharp. SpiFl

There is a gin mill on the avenue. Juice Joint: Northern City. Langston Hughes. CP-HughL

There Is a Girl Inside. Lucille Clifton. SP-ClifL

There is a heaven, for ever, day by day. Theology. Paul Laurence Dunbar. CP-DunbP

There is a hunger. Nikki Giovanni. SP-GiovN

There is a little lightning in his eyes. Of Robert Frost. Gwendolyn Brooks. SP-BrooG

There is a magic. Light Baggage. Alice Walker. CP-WalkA

There is a magic melting pot. The Melting Pot. Dudley Randall. BALP; BPo; NBV

There is a nation in my brawny scrotal sac. Lance Jeffers. NBV

There is a natty kind of mind. Unsuspecting. Jean Toomer. CP-ToomJ

There is a parrot imitating spring. Parsley. Rita Dove. ESEAA; NAAAL; SP-DoveR; TtW

There is a sadness to this world. Al Young. CP-YounA

There is a sphere, a secret sphere. The Inner Realm. Priscilla Jane Thompson. CBWP-2

There is a strange man attached to my backbone. Monkeyman. Audre Lorde. CP-LordA; SP-LordA

There is a tide in men's affairs. Modern Moses, or "My Policy" Man. James Madison Bell. AAP; EBAP

There is a timbre of voice. Echoes. Audre Lorde. CP-LordA

There is a tree by day. Tenebris. Angelina Weld Grimké. CDC; NAAAL; PoBA; ShDr

There is a way to enter a field. Receiving the Stigmata. Rita Dove. NAAAL; SP-DoveR

There Is a Woman in This Town. Patricia Parker. BlSi

There is always something. Adulthood II. Nikki Giovanni. Crnst; SP-GiovN; SP-GiovN

There is an ancient story. My Father's Story. Priscilla Jane Thompson. CBWP-2

There is an old story ... I learned in a church. Harvest. Nikki Giovanni. SP-GiovN

There is, at times, an evenin sky. George Boyer Vashon. *Fr.* Vincent Ogé. EBAP

There is enough. What We Know. Raymond R. Patterson. NBV

There is great peace to be earned. Malcolm's Messasge. Al Young. CP-YounA

There is music in me, the music of a peasant people. The Banjo Player. Fenton Johnson. BANP; Klds; TtW

There is no beauty / to the world I see. The World I See. Mari E. Evans. Klds

There is no chance that we will fall apart. Poem Number Two on Bell's Theorem. June Jordan. SP-JordJ

There is no door! (LL) End. Langston Hughes. CP-HughL; SP-HughL

There is no fall that wouldn't break itself. Afraid. Al Young. CP-YounA

There is no greater moon to contemplate. Carolina Moon. Al Young. CP-YounA

There is no memorial site. For Brother Malcolm. Edward S. Spriggs. BrTr

There / is / no moon tonight. The Keeping of a Promise. Etheridge Knight. SP-KnigE

There is no other hope. (LL) Tomorrow the heroes / will be named willie. their. Alfred B. Spellman. BlFi; PoBA

There is no radical the Negro's friend. The Negro's Friend. Claude McKay. SP-McKaC

There / Is no sweetness. For Salome. Langston Hughes. CP-HughL

There is no warning rattle at the door. A Plagued Journey. Maya Angelou. CP-AngeM; SP-AngeM

There is not much that he would ask for now. Coolwell Vignette. Sterling A. Brown. CP-BrowS

There is nothing ... that can be said ... that can frighten me. Her Cruising Car. Nikki Giovanni. SP-GiovN

There is so much misery in the world. How Thin a Blanket. Langston Hughes. CP-HughL

There is so much to write about. A Ballad of Negro History. Langston Hughes. CP-HughL

There is something / in me so cruel, so. The New Sheriff. Amiri Baraka. SP-BaraA

There is something strange about Africa. Africa. Margaret Abigail Walker. CP-WalkM

There is something / to be said for silence. Something to be Said for Silence. Nikki Giovanni. SP-GiovN

There is the woman. Radio. Cornelius Eady. ESEAA

There It Is. Jayne Cortez. SP-CortJ

There lived a dashing gentleman of worth. Albery Allson Whitman. *Fr.* Leelah Misled. EBAP

There once lived a whore around this town. Pisspot Pete. *African-American Oral Tradition.* GetYo

There shall be no more of you. (LL) The Still Voice of Harlem. Conrad Kent Rivers. IDB; Klds; NNP; PoBA

There shall be no more songs. Black Power. Alvin Saxon. PoBA

There stood the citadel—nothing left. The Ants of Argos. Rita Dove. SP-DoveR

There the black river, boundary to hell. The Southern Road. Dudley Randall. BrTr; NNP; PoBA

There they are. The Blackstone Rangers. Gwendolyn Brooks. ESEAA; PoBA

There they stand together, like Moses standing with Aaron. At the Lincoln Monument in Washington, August 28, 1963. Margaret Abigail Walker. CP-WalkM

There though where they. Degree Four. Nathaniel Mackey. ESEAA

There was a knock. Homecoming. Mawiyah Kai El-Jamah Bomani. CtF

There was a man / Whose name was Pete. The Tragedy of Pete. Joseph Seamon Cotter, Sr. CDC

There was a poor man living in the country. Ringo. *African-American Oral Tradition.* GetYo

There was a song. Gerald William Barrax. GT

There was a time. To My Daughter. Keorapetse W. Kgositsile. GT

There was a time when death was terror. New Fashions. George Moses Horton. SP-HortG

There was a time when in late afternoon. Adolescence. Claude McKay. SP-McKaC

There was an evil darkness way before. The Signifying Darkness. Owen Dodson. TtW

There was an old decan-/ ter. Song of the Decanter. Alfred Gibbs Campbell. AAP

There was an old Jim Crow by the name of Jim. Jim Crow's Last Stand. Langston Hughes. CP-HughL

There was fire & the people were yelling. running crazy. Urban Dream. Victor Hernandez Cruz. NBP; NBV

There was grief within our household. Jamie's Puzzle. Frances Ellen Watkins Harper. CP-HarpF

There was once seven wise men, they had knowledge fine. The Seven Wise Men. *African-American Oral Tradition.* GetYo

There was one among us who rose. Death of a Friend. Pauli Murray. PoBA

There was profusion in the gift. The Color Bane. George Marion McClellan. EBAP

"There Was something I Wanted to Tell You." (33) Why? Amiri Baraka. SP-BaraA

There was three whores settin' down in Boston. Three Whores Settin' Down in Boston. *African-American Oral Tradition.* GetYo

There wasn't any hot water for the teapot. For Dave: 1976. June Jordan. SP-JordJ

There wasn't any riot any more. (LL) An Old Woman Remembers. Sterling A. Brown. CP-BrowS

There were bizarre beginnings in old lands for the making. Dark Blood. Margaret Abigail Walker. CP-WalkM

There were fields where once we walked. Poem (For BMC No. 2). Nikki Giovanni. SP-GiovN

There were moons O there were moons. The New Mode of Production. Al Young. CP-YounA

There were palm trees. Alice Walker. CP-WalkA

There were signs of movement in Paris. (LL) Mama's Report. Michael S. Harper. SP-HarpM

There will be no Holyman crying out this year. Jitterbugging in the Streets. Calvin C. Hernton. BlFi; PoBA

Therefore, Adieu. Countee Cullen. CP-CullC

... Therefore I am? That's not it either. Behind a Descartes Bumpersticker. Marilyn Nelson. *Fr.* The Plotinus Suite. SP-NelsM

There'll be all the requisites. Invitation. Al Young. CP-YounA

There's a band of men who roam this land. Ballad of Badmen. Owen Dodson. FB

There's a fabulous story. The Place Where the Rainbow Ends. Paul Laurence Dunbar. CP-DunbP

There's a fresh light that follows a storm. After the Storm. Derek Walcott. *Fr.* The Schooner *Flight.* ESEAA

There's a life awaiting in California. (LL) It is Everywhere. Jean Toomer. CP-ToomJ; GT

There's a life awaiting on a rocky coast. It is Everywhere. Jean Toomer. CP-ToomJ; GT

There's a long-legged girl. Pickin Em Up and Layin Em Down. Maya Angelou. CP-AngeM; SP-AngeM

There's a magic man on Farish Street. Black Magic. Margaret Abigail Walker. CP-WalkM

There's a memory keeps a-runnin'. The Old Apple-Tree. Paul Laurence Dunbar. CP-DunbP

There's a mighty sound a-comin'. For Theodore Roosevelt. Paul Laurence Dunbar. CP-DunbP

There's a new skyline in Harlem. Hope for Harlem. Langston Hughes. CP-HughL

There's a new young moon. New Moon. Langston Hughes. CP-HughL

There's a ripple of fountains. The Land o' Used to Be. Paul Laurence Dunbar. CP-DunbP

There's a Sampson lying, sleeping in the land. The Black Sampson. Josephine D. Henderson Heard. CBWP-4

There's a serpent, namely, drinking. The Social Glass. Lizelia Augusta Jenkins Moorer. CBWP-3

There's a whale in my thigh. at. Ishmael Reed. CP-ReedI

There's a wonderful story. The Angel's Message. Clara Ann Thompson. CBWP-2

There's always weather, weather. Langston Hughes. CP-HughL

There's been an eagle on a nickel. Fact. Langston Hughes. *Fr.* Montage of a Dream Deferred. CP-HughL

There's hanging moss. Carolina Cabin. Langston Hughes. CP-HughL

There's History in My Hair. Karen Williams. SpiFl

"There's light ahead!" Hope ever cries. Hope Deferred. Clara Ann Thompson. CBWP-2

There's no such thing as a student. Teaching. Al Young. CP-YounA

There's no way you can know how it beginss. Moving, Merging, Fading, Standing Still. Al Young. CP-YounA

There's one, who never will her own forsake. Albery Allson Whitman. *Fr.* Leelah Misled. EBAP

There's some strange and queer tales that come through all jails. Eddie Ledoux: "There's some strange and queer tales that come through all jails." *African-American Oral Tradition.* GetYo

There's something disturbing. Worriation. Langston Hughes. CP-HughL

There's something or maybe even. Improvisation. Al Young. CP-YounA

There's the place where the rainbow ends. (LL) The Place Where the Rainbow Ends. Paul Laurence Dunbar. CP-DunbP

There's this womun I call. Sat. Nite. Jamal. CtF

These are no wind-blown rumors, soft say-sos. Sonnet. Countee Cullen. CP-CullC

These Are Not Brushstrokes. Cyrus Cassells. GT

These are songs if you have the / music. (LL) Three Movements and a Coda. Amiri Baraka. BlFi; NAAAL

These are the days of elfs and fays. The Discovery. Paul Laurence Dunbar. CP-DunbP

These autumn trees sit. Sonia Sanchez. SP-SancS

These Beasts and the Benin Bronze. Margaret Else Danner. Klds

These creatures of the languid Orient. Albery Allson Whitman. AAP

These daughters are bone. God's Mood. Lucille Clifton. SP-ClifL

These days I think of Belvie. Alice Walker. CP-WalkA

These days / when you do say hello I am never sure. Audre Lorde. See Progress Report.

These demonstrations of the one God. The Mountains of California: Part 1. Al Young. CP-YounA

These fell miasmic rings of mist, with ghoulish menace bound. Prejudice. Georgia Douglas Johnson. AmNP; PoBA; ShDr

These have no Christ to spit and stoop. Black Magdalens. Countee Cullen. BANP; CP-CullC

These hips are big hips. Homage to My Hips. Lucille Clifton. NAAAL; SP-ClifL

These know fear; for all their singing. Children of the Mississippi. Sterling A. Brown. BrowS; Crnst

These magnets draw my heart away. (LL) Magnets. Countee Cullen. BALP; CP-CullC

These men, / these proud black men. Tuskegee Airfield. Marilyn Nelson. ESEAA; GT; SP-NelsM

These men were kings, albeit they were black. Black Majesty. Countee Cullen. CP-CullC; PoBA

These men who do not die, but send to death. Not Sacco and Vanzetti. Countee Cullen. CP-CullC

These mornings of rain. Alice Walker. CP-WalkA

These mountains are my plan. "S.P.W.": Journey of Consciousness. Michael S. Harper. SP-HarpM

These new night / babies flying on ivory wings. Ivory Masks in Orbit. Keorapetse W. Kgositsile. BlFi; PoBA

These the dread days which the seers have foretold. The Death of Justice. Walter Everette Hawkins. PoBA

These truly are the Brave. The Negro Soldiers. Roscoe Conkling Jamison. BANP

These were our fields. Dust Bowl. Robert A. Davis. IDB

These words stained with red. Sonia Sanchez. SP-SancS

These Yet to Be United States. Maya Angelou. CP-AngeM

They ain't gonna never get. 2nd Rapp. Nikki Giovanni. BrTr

They always treat me mean. (LL) Cora. Langston Hughes. CP-HughL; SP-HughL

They and I are civilized. (LL) Heritage. Countee Cullen. AmNP; BANP; BPo; CP-CullC; CrDW; Crnst; NAAAL; PoBA; SSLK; TtW

They applaud at the periods and sigh. The Poet's Shuffle. Calvin Forbes. GT

They are all dying. Death as History. Jay Wright. ESEAA; PoBA

They are coming, coming slowly. Josephine D. Henderson Heard. AAP; AfAmPo; CBWP-4

They are going to some point true and unproven. (LL) Geometry. Rita Dove. SP-DoveR; TtW

They Are Killing All the Young Men. David Henderson. PoBA

They are made to stand side by side. The Poor Houses. Ed Roberson. GT

They are not for us any more: green fields where corn. Fanfare, Coda, and Finale. Margaret Abigail Walker. CP-WalkM

They Are Not Missed. Jean Toomer. CP-ToomJ

They Are the Same. Priscilla Jane Thompson. CBWP-2

They ask me to remember. Why Some People Be Mad at Me Sometimes. Lucille Clifton. ESEAA

They Ask Why. Maya Angelou. CP-AngeM

They brought in the brine-crusted drift-wood. Drift-Wood. Clara Ann Thompson. CBWP-2

They called us. The Charm. Rita Dove. SP-DoveR

They Came Again in 1970 in 1980. Jayne Cortez. SP-CortJ

They can shake their boodies but they can't shake you. (LL) The Blues Don't Change. Al Young. CP-YounA; GT

They Can't Do That. African-American Oral Tradition. GetYo

They carry on. / though sorrows completely. Floodtide. Askia Muhammad Touré. PoBA; TtW

They characterize / their lives, and I. Joseph to His Brothers. Amiri Baraka. SP-BaraA

They choke cities like snowstorms. Blonde White Women. Patricia Smith. GT

They clapped when we landed. Nikki Giovanni. SP-GiovN

They come into. Feeding the Lions. Norman Jordan. NBP; PoBA

They come on now! (LL) Early blue evening. Langston Hughes. CP-HughL

They come on now! (LL) Wonder. Langston Hughes. SP-HughL

They come to him for subscriptions. Parish Doctor. Sterling A. Brown. CP-BrowS

They come up here. My Brothers. Ishmael Reed. CP-ReedI

They could have stayed the iron hand of might. Selassie at Geneva. Marcus B. Christian. TtW

They / could tell / it was war. Speech. Sterling Plumpp. TtW

They crucified my Lord, an' He never said a mumbalin' word [or / And He never said a mumbaling word]. Crucifixion. Unknown. BPo

They deployed military troops. White Weekend. Quincy Troupe. NBP

They did not travel in an airplane. On a Pallet of Straw. Langston Hughes. CP-HughL

They done took Cordelia. Stony Lonesome. Langston Hughes. CP-HughL; SP-HughL

They don't hold grudges. First Monday Scottsboro Alabama. Tom Weatherly. PoBA

They dragged you from [the] homeland. Strong Men. Sterling A. Brown. BANP; BPo; CrDW; FB; PoBA

They dunked me in the creek. Baptism. Alice Walker. CP-WalkA

They eat beans mostly, this old yellow pair. The Bean Eaters. Gwendolyn Brooks. BlSi; Crnst; ESEAA; Klds; PoBA; SP-BrooG

They forced him into prison. Died of Starvation. Frances Ellen Watkins Harper. CP-HarpF

They gave me the wrong name, in the first place. Her Story. Naomi Long Madgett. PoBA

They get to Benvenuti's. There are booths. I Love Those Little Booths at Benvenuti's. Gwendolyn Brooks. SP-BrooG

They give to beauty here. Beauty. Langston Hughes. CP-HughL

They got pictures of V stamped on letter stamps. Conversation on V. Owen Dodson. Klds

They grew and charcoal bundle shakes itself. Brothers. Solomon Edwards. NNP

They had been there a month; the water had begun to tear them apart. A Negro Soldier's Viet Nam Diary. Herbert Martin. PoBA

They had begun to whisper. Move. Lucille Clifton. NAAAL

They had me laid out in a white. April Fools' Day. Yusef Komunyakaa. GT; SP-KomuY

They had never had one in the house before. Bronzeville Woman in a Red Hat. Gwendolyn Brooks. GT; SP-BrooG

They had supposed their formula was fixed. White Troops Had Their Orders but the Negroes Looked Like Men. Gwendolyn Brooks. SP-BrooG

They have breasts shaped. When I Look at Wilfredo Lam's Paintings. Jayne Cortez. SP-CortJ

They have dreamed as young men dream. Old Black Men. Georgia Douglas Johnson. CDC; PoBA

They have fenced in the dirt road. Burial. Alice Walker. CP-WalkA

They have not sown, and feed on bitter fruit. (LL) A Black Man Talks of Reaping. Arna Bontemps. AmNP; BANP; BPo; CDC; FB; IDB; Klds; NAAAL; PoBA; SSLK; TtW

They have put us on HOLD. Margaret Abigail Walker. CP-WalkM

They have sed. Hospital/Poem. Sonia Sanchez. BPo; PoBA

They have spent their. Old Folks Laugh. Maya Angelou. CP-AngeM

They heard the south wind sighing. The Crocuses. Frances Ellen Watkins Harper. BlSi; CP-HarpF

They howled 'til Pilate. Crucifixion. Waring Cuney. BANP

They in their cruel traps, and we in ours. Thoughts in a Zoo. Countee Cullen. CP-CullC

They keep coming at me. Stops. Lucille Clifton. SP-ClifL

They kept my race alive. (LL) Song for the Old Ones. Maya Angelou. CP-AngeM; SP-AngeM

They make love in his first langauge. Las Flores para una Niña Negra. Demetrice A. Worley. SpiFl

They may get better. A Lynching for Skip James. Rudy Bee Graham. BlFi

They Never Lose. Lorenzo Thomas. TtW

They now gonna make us shut up. Ease. The People Burning. Amiri Baraka. SP-BaraA

They please me not—these solemn songs. A Choice. Paul Laurence Dunbar. CP-DunbP

They please me so—these solemn lays. Answer to Dunbar's "A Choice." Joseph Seamon Cotter, Sr. EBAP

They put ma body in the ground. Judgment Day. Langston Hughes. CP-HughL; SP-HughL

They put my boy-friend. Madam and the Army. Langston Hughes. CP-HughL

They robed her for another groom. The Bride of Death. Frances Ellen Watkins Harper. CP-HarpF

They rode him to his grave. (LL) I once knew a man who had wild horses killed. Lucille Clifton. SP-ClifL; TtW

They rode north / funky and uneducated. Blackie Thinks of His Brothers. Stanley Crouch. BlFi; GT; PoBA

They said to my grandmother: "Please do not be bitter". Bitter Fruit of the Tree. Sterling A. Brown. CP-BrowS

They said, "Wait." Well, I waited. Alabama Centennial. Naomi Long Madgett. BALP; BPo

They say in nineteen hundred and forty-one. Pearl Harbor. *African-American Oral Tradition.* GetYo

They say / jab the pencils. Plain Truth. Jayne Cortez. SP-CortJ

They say she died. Young Bride. Langston Hughes. CP-HughL

They say "Son." Old Black Men Say. James A. Emanuel. PoBA

They say that black people. Patricia Smith. GT

They say that when they burned young Shelley's corpse. The Fishes and the Poet's Hands. Frank Yerby. AmNP

They say you are not for me. Forbidden Things. Alice Walker. CP-WalkA

They / say / you / went / abroad. Incidental Pieces to a Walk. James Cunningham. JB

They scorned her for her sinning. The Contrast. Frances Ellen Watkins Harper. CP-HarpF

They shall go down unto life's borderland. Sonnet to Negro Soldiers. Joseph Seamon Cotter, Sr. PoBA

They shall see Him in the crimson flush. The Pure in Heart Shall See God. Frances Ellen Watkins Harper. CP-HarpF

They shine like diamonds. (LL) Black Baby. Anita Scott Coleman. ShDr

They should have slept, would have. The Lynching. Thylias Moss. GT

They sit on edge. War Stories. Saundra Murray Nettles. IHS

They tell me that Casey Jones was a railroad man. Casey Jones. *African-American Oral Tradition.* GetYo

They tell me that Joe Turner's come and gone. Joe Turner. *Unknown.* CrDW

They think I lost. I think I won. (LL) Harlem Hopscotch. Maya Angelou. CP-AngeM; SP-AngeM

They think we're simple children. This Puzzles Me. Langston Hughes. CP-HughL

They told me to sit on the highest stool. Roland. Michael S. Harper. SP-HarpM

They told my cousin Rowena not to marry. Family Secrets. Toi Derricotte. SpiFl

They took away his seamless robe. Simon's Countrymen. Frances Ellen Watkins Harper. CP-HarpF

They took me out. Ku Klux. Langston Hughes. BPo; CP-HughL; SP-HughL

They tried to force Solomon Mahlangu. Solomon Mahlangu, Freedom Fighter from Mamelodi. Jayne Cortez. SP-CortJ

They Ugly / on purpose! Heathens. Amiri Baraka. SP-BaraA

They wait like darkness not becoming stars. The New Pietà: For the Mothers and Children of Detroit. June Jordan. PoBA

They watched her glide across the stage. A Dark Actress—Somewhere. Blanche Taylor Dickinson. ShDr

They went home and told their wives. Maya Angelou. CP-AngeM; SP-AngeM

They were crushed by a gigantic meteor. Theory on Extinction or What Happened to the Dinosaurs? Kenneth Carroll. SpiFl

They were like fish meal. Lead. Jayne Cortez. PoBA

They were moving gracefully. Bloodstorm. Kiarri T-H Cheatwood. TtW

They were women then. Women. Alice Walker. *Fr.* In These Dissenting Times. CP-WalkA; NAAAL; PoBA; TtW

They who feel death close as a breath. Alice Walker. CP-WalkA

They will blow from your mouth one morning. For the Mute. Lucille Clifton. SP-ClifL

They will let you have dope. Memo to Non-White People. Langston Hughes. CP-HughL

They will perhaps. Love Poem. Norman Henry, II Pritchard. GT

They will swoon no more his. Tea Dancer Turns Thirty-Nine. Ishmael Reed. CP-ReedI

They worshipped Joe. Joe Louis: "They worshipped Joe." SP-HughL Langston Hughes. *Fr.* Montage of a Dream Deferred. CP-HughL

They'd latch the screendoors. Sunday Afternoons. Herbert Asquith. NAAAL

They'd spend one night, or two or three, / But. (LL) They went home and told their wives. Maya Angelou. CP-AngeM; SP-AngeM

They'll turn and underrate thee. (LL) Frederick Douglass. Joseph Seamon Cotter, Sr. AAP; AfAmPo; EBAP

They're brooding in Rosedale. Brooding. Jayne Cortez. SP-CortJ

They're Leaving Memphis in Droves. *Unknown.* CrDW

They've killed you. Martyrdom. Richard W. Thomas. PoBA

Thick at the schoolgate are the ones. Soul Make A Path Through Shouting. Cyrus Cassells. GT

Thief. Alice Walker. CP-WalkA

Thief in me is running a / round in circles, The. Zapata & the Landlord. Alfred B. Spellman. NNP; PoBA

Thin legs balancing his atom of life, The. (LL) The Bird Frau. Rita Dove. SP-DoveR

Thin Water. Nadir Lasana Bomani. CtF

Thin wickedly intricate, The. Dark Area. Russell Atkins. FB; GT

Thine Eyes Shall See the King in His Beauty. Frances Ellen Watkins Harper. CP-HarpF

Thine Own. Josephine D. Henderson Heard. CBWP-4

Thine own reflection in Eternity! (LL) Aspiration. Adah Isaacs Menken. AAP; CBWP-1

Thine was a brain of nature's finest mould. Charles Sumner. Henrietta Cordelia Ray. CBWP-3

Thing about playing solitaire, The. Playing Solitaire. Thulani Davis. GT

Thing Itself, The. Alice Walker. CP-WalkA

Things begin again. Return. Jewel C. Latimore. BlSi

Things I Do Not Speak. M. Eliza Hamilton. CtF

Things I love I may not touch, The. Lines to Caste. Samuel Alfred Beadle. AAP

Things in motion / hv a tendency to. General Science. Ishmael Reed. CP-ReedI

Think about it. (LL) Poem for Aretha. Nikki Giovanni. BrTr; SP-GiovN

Think of Slavery. Y the Link Will Not Always Be "Missing" #40. Amiri Baraka. SP-BaraA

Think of sweet and chocolate. The Anniad. Gwendolyn Brooks. BlSi; SP-BrooG

Think you I am not fiend and savage too? To the White Fiends. Claude McKay. BANP; NAAAL; PoBA; SP-McKaC

Thinning hair / estee laundered. Poem (For Anna Hedgeman and Alfreda Duster). Nikki Giovanni. SP-GiovN

Third Degree. Langston Hughes. BPo; CP-HughL; SP-HughL

Third Sermon on the Warpland, The. Gwendolyn Brooks. BPo; NAAAL

Thirst. Claude McKay. SP-McKaC

Thirteens (Black), The. Maya Angelou. CP-AngeM; SP-AngeM

Thirteens (White), The. Maya Angelou. CP-AngeM; SP-AngeM

.38, The. Ted Joans. NNP

Thirty-eighth year, The. Lucille Clifton. SP-ClifL

35? I have been looking forward. The Author Reflects on His 35th Birthday. Ishmael Reed. CP-ReedI

This Age. Raymond R. Patterson. NBV

This ain't Torquemada. Dialect Quatrain. Marcus B. Christian. AmNP

This alone is what I wish for you: knowledge. Demeter's Prayer to Hades. Rita Dove. NAAAL

This ancient hag. Mexican Market Woman. Langston Hughes. CP-HughL; SP-HughL

This being a minimum security facility, it feels more like being on a reservation than in a touchable cage. Visiting Day. Al Young. CP-YounA

This birthday card. Poem for the Birthday of Huey P. Newton. Sotère Torregian. NBV

This bizness, of dancing, how. From an Almanac (3). Amiri Baraka. SP-BaraA

This Bridge Across. George Barlow. ESEAA

This Bridge Across. Christopher Gilbert. GT

This Child Is the Mother. Gloria C. Oden. BlSi

This cool night is strange. Nocturne. Gwendolyn B. Bennett. BANP; ShDr

This country might have. Right On: White America. Sonia Sanchez. PoBA

This Country's Needs ("This country needs more noble men"). Mrs. Henry Linden. CBWP-4

This crescent's arc is. Spiritual Geography. Kalamu ya Salaam. *Fr.* New Orleans Haiku. SpiFl

This day feels put together hastily. New Year's Day. Audre Lorde. SP-LordA

This Durgling was a dual personage. Delivered at the Knighting of Lord Durgling by Great Bruce-Jean. Jean Toomer. CP-ToomJ; GT

This far south such crippling. Aurora Borealis. Rita Dove. SP-DoveR

This first bright day has broken. Walking Our Boundaries. Audre Lorde. CP-LordA

This friend of mine. Confessional Poem. Marilyn Nelson. SP-NelsM

This garden too pleasant. Concert. Helen G. Quigless. NBP

This gold watch and chain. Ballad of the Pawnbroker. Langston Hughes. CP-HughL

This guy on t.v. The Electric Cop. Victor Hernandez Cruz. PoBA

This here's a tale of a sho-nuff man. Big John Henry. Margaret Abigail Walker. CP-WalkM

This Hour. Oliver La Grone. NNP

This house where Love a little while abode. Variations on a Theme. Countee Cullen. CP-CullC

This house will not stand forever. Future Promise. Audre Lorde. CP-LordA

This I have told you before. Rhumba Negro. Lorenzo Thomas. TtW

This is a big girl's pink poem. Pink Poem. Jackie Warren-Moore. SpiFl

This is a bridgeless blues. Two Fishing Villages. Ellease Southerland. GT

This Is a Fatherland to Me. Joseph Cephas Holly. AAP

This is a land in which you never were. To One Not There. Countee Cullen. CP-CullC

This is a quiet poem. A Quiet Poem. Pinkie Gordon Lane. TtW

This is a silence. Arabesque. Fred Johnson. PoBA

This is a simple poem. Scar. Audre Lorde. CP-LordA

This is a song for the genius child. Genius Child. Langston Hughes. CP-HughL; SP-HughL

This is a spirit poem. This Poem. Shirley Bradley LeFlore. SpiFl

This is a tale of a wanderer's trail. The Wanderer's Trail. African-American Oral Tradition. GetYo

This is a trip that strangers make. Roman Poem Number Five. June Jordan. SP-JordJ

This is a white. Imperial Thumbprint. Tom Weatherly. PoBA

This is about Shine O Shine. The captain was on his boat and he was. Titanic: "This is about Shine O Shine. The captain was on his boat and he was." African-American Oral Tradition. GetYo

This Is an African Worm. Margaret Else Danner. BPo; TtW

This is earthquake. Today. Langston Hughes. CP-HughL

This is for the kids who die. Kids Who Die. Langston Hughes. CP-HughL

This is how I came to be loved. Cables to Rage or I've Been Talking on This Street Corner a Hell of a Long Time. Audre Lorde. CP-LordA; SP-LordA

This Is It. Elma Stuckey. TtW

This is my black-eyed-susan school. These minds. Jackson State, May 15, 1970. Margaret Abigail Walker. CP-WalkM

This Is My Century. Margaret Abigail Walker. CP-WalkM

This is my country too. American Dialogue. Victor E. Blue. CtF

This is my last affair. (LL) Last Affair: Bessie's Blues Song. Michael S. Harper. ESEAA; SP-HarpM

This is my last cry. For Stephen Dixon. Zack Gilbert. PoBA

This is my page for English B. (LL) Theme for English B. Langston Hughes. BLAP; CP-HughL; SP-HughL; SSLK

This Is My Son's Song: "Ungie, Hi Ungie". Michael S. Harper. SP-HarpM

This is no mountain. The Gods Are Here. Jean Toomer. CP-ToomJ

This is not a dance. Large Room with Wood Floor. Clarence Major. GT

This is not a poem, nor. Houston A., Jr. Baker. TtW

This is not a poem ... this is hot chocolate. Stardate Number 18628.190. Nikki Giovanni. SP-GiovN

This is not a small voice. Sonia Sanchez. SpiFl

This Is Not for John Lennon. Nikki Giovanni. SP-GiovN

This is not Jordan River. Crossing. Sterling A. Brown. CP-BrowS; TtW

This is not to be acknowledged thru usual channels. Romance. Al Young. CP-YounA

This is not what I meant to keep. Souvenir. Naomi Long Madgett. NBV

This is really the story of a / sista. The House of Desire. Sherley Anne Williams. BlSi

This is supposed to be about two colored studs. It's truth. In New Orleans. Stackolee: "This is supposed to be about two colored studs. It's truth. In New Orleans." African-American Oral Tradition. GetYo

This is that dream i wake from. Powell; March 1991. Lucille Clifton. ESEAA

This is the camping ground. Struggle-Road Dance. Ahmos, II Zu-Bolton. TtW

This Is the Clearing I Once Spoke of. Amiri Baraka. SP-BaraA

This is the debt I pay. The Debt. Paul Laurence Dunbar. AmNP; BANP; CDC; CP-DunbP; Klds

This is the dream grown young. Lincoln University: 1954. Langston Hughes. CP-HughL

This is the morning. The Charge. Jay Wright. FB

This is the night. Harlem '67. Clarence Reed. BlFi

This is the Space Age. The Cosmic Age. Sun-Ra. BlFi

This is the stagnant hour. Drunken Lover. Owen Dodson. AmNP

This is the surest death. Mortality. Naomi Long Madgett. NNP; PoBA; TtW

This is the urgency: Live! The Second Sermon on the Warpland. Gwendolyn Brooks. BPo; PoBA

This is the way. The Squared Circle. Carl Killebrew. BrTr

This is the weather of change. Turning Thirty, I Contemplate Students Bicycling Home. Rita Dove. ESEAA

This is to-day, a golden summer's day. To an Ingrate. Paul Laurence Dunbar. CP-DunbP

This is to say that i am. Intro to My Final Book of Poems. Ahmos, II Zu-Bolton. TtW

This is to the women of Texas. African-American Oral Tradition. GetYo

This is where Jack Johnson. Boxing Day. Yusef Komunyakaa. SP-KomuY

This kiss / as soft as cotton. Mary. Lucille Clifton. SP-ClifL

This land is my block and my people. Song of Devotion to the Forest. David Henderson. GT

This land will not always be foreign. The Winds of Orisha. Audre Lorde. CP-LordA; NAAAL; SP-LordA

This land's salvation. (LL) My Blackness Is the Beauty of This Land. Lance Jeffers. BIFi; IHS; TtW

This Life. Rita Dove. GT; SP-DoveR

This life of mine is poor indeed. My Poverty and Wealth. Joseph Seamon Cotter, Sr. EBAP

This little girl left her parlor quite early, it was scarcely half-past nine. Through the Keyhole in the Door. African-American Oral Tradition. GetYo

This Little House Is Sugar. Winter Sweetnes. Langston Hughes. CP-HughL

This Little Light of Mine. Unknown. NAAAL

This little silent one. Silent One. Langston Hughes. CP-HughL

This love is a rich cry over. A Black Wedding Song. Gwendolyn Brooks. IHS

This lovely flower fell to seed. For My Grandmother. Countee Cullen. Fr. Four Epitaphs. AmNP; CDC; CP-CullC; PoBA; SSLK

This magic land of sun stars. It's India. Al Young. CP-YounA

This melodious / prison: crowds. Eastern European Eclogues. Rita Dove. SP-DoveR

This monkey dance? (LL) Junkie Monkey Reel. Maya Angelou. CP-AngeM; SP-AngeM

This morning I threw the windows. Jay Wright. NNP

This morning / this morning. Lucille Clifton. SP-ClifL

This morning, when he looked at me. Black All Day. Raymond R. Patterson. PoBA

This morning/ there is a woman giving a sermon/ Her voice trembles over the. On the Uptown Lexington Avenue Express: Martin Luther King Day 1995. Harris Duriel. SpiFl

This my time of minstrelsy, bright, sunny May. (LL) To the Mock-Bird. Mary Weston Fordham. CBWP-2

This nation has a faithful friend. The Nation's Friend. Alfred Islay Walden. AAP

This nigger too should be in history. Memo: For the Race Orators. Sterling A. Brown. CP-BrowS

This night was born for love, my Phaon. / Come. (LL) Brilliant-bellied newt flashes, The. Helene Johnson. BlSi; CDC; ShDr

This night's first star, hung. A Poem Welcoming Jonas Mekas to America. Amiri Baraka. SP-BaraA

This nutmeg stick of a boy in loose trousers! Notes from a Tunisian Journal. Rita Dove. SP-DoveR

This of that and the That of this, The. The Reckoning. Naomi Long Madgett. Klds

This one lie down on grass. The Astrologer Predicts at Mary's Birth. Lucille Clifton. SP-ClifL

This Poem. Ruth Forman. SpiFl

This Poem. Shirley Bradley LeFlore. SpiFl

This Poem for Black Women. Reginald Lockett. BlFi

This poem must be done to-day. The Lapse. Paul Laurence Dunbar. CP-DunbP

This Poetry Anthology I'm Reading. Ishmael Reed. CP-ReedI

This purple cloud of grief within my heart. Old Love Butchered (Colorado Springs and Huachuca). Lance Jeffers. NBV

This Puzzles Me. Langston Hughes. CP-HughL

This road is like a tomb. On Passing Two Negroes on a Dark Country Road Somewhere in Georgia. Conrad Kent Rivers. IDB; NNP

This ship is the ship of butchery and increase. Songs for the Cisco Kid; or, Singing: Song #2. K. Curtis Lyle. PoBA

This skinny little dude. Dude in Denver. Al Young. CP-YounA

This still mountain night is not still. Earth Screaming. Esther Iverem. GT

This street is like my grandma's patchwork quilt. A Patchwork Quilt. Margaret Abigail Walker. CP-WalkM

This Sun Is Hot. Unknown. BPo

This sunday morning breaks blue clear, in st paul de vence. In Jimmy's Garden. Quincy Troupe. GT

This, then, the river he had to swim. Thomas at the Wheel. Rita Dove. SP-DoveR

This time from the top. (LL) Don't say goodbye to the Porkpie Hat that rolled. Larry Neal. GT; TtW

This town of lost assholes, L. A. it's called. L. A. (Lost Assholes). Madd Vibe. CtF

This Urn Contains Earth from German Concentration Camps. Audre Lorde. CP-LordA

This verse is plain, that all may understand. Execution of Private Henry Anderson. George Moses Horton. SP-HortG

This vibrant, all-embracing, all-pervading. Psalm for Sonny Rollins. Walt Delegall. BlFi

This was not I repeat this was not a racial incident. Poem from Taped Testimony in the Tradition of Bernard Goetz. June Jordan. SP-JordJ

This whole pay check's just for me. Pay Day. Langston Hughes. Fr. Seven Moments of Love. CP-HughL

This will really try you. Mamma! Frank Horne. BPo

This Winter Day. Maya Angelou. CP-AngeM; SP-AngeM

This woman is Black. Need: A Chorale for Black Woman Voices. Audre Lorde. CP-LordA; SP-LordA

This woman vomiting her. Present. Sonia Sanchez. NAAAL; SP-SancS

This year, maybe, do you think I can graduate? Deferred. Langston Hughes. Fr. Montage of a Dream Deferred. CP-HughL

This year (so I hear). A Year without Seasons. Nance Williams. NNP

Thomas at the Wheel. Rita Dove. SP-DoveR

Thorn, The. Langston Hughes. CP-HughL

Thorn Forever in the Breast, A. Countee Cullen. CP-CullC

Thorn Merchant, The. Yusef Komunyakaa. SP-KomuY

Thorn Merchant's Mistress, The. Yusef Komunyakaa. SP-KomuY

Thorn Merchant's Right Hand Man, The. Yusef Komunyakaa. SP-KomuY

Thorn Merchant's Son, The. Yusef Komunyakaa. SP-KomuY

Thorn Merchant's Wife, The. Yusef Komunyakaa. SP-KomuY

Those Boys That Ran Together. Lucille Clifton. PoBA; SP-ClifL

Those days when it was all right. Letter to E. Franklin Frazier. Amiri Baraka. BPo; PoBA; SP-BaraA

Those five or six young guys. Blues. Derek Walcott. Crnst; GT

Those four black girls blown up. American History. Michael S. Harper. BPo; ESEAA; SP-HarpM

Those islands now are freedom's home. (LL) Stanzas for the First of August. James M. Whitfield. EBAP; TtW

Those mothers down there off the hill. Seventh Son. Ed Roberson. PoBA

Those things / which you so laughingly call. The Butterfly. Nikki Giovanni. SP-GiovN

Those who have ceased to love. See the Heart. Jean Toomer. CP-ToomJ; IHS

Those who say they knew you. Malcolm. Alice Walker. CP-WalkA

Those Winter Sundays. Robert Hayden. CP-HaydR; ESEAA; IDB; PoBA; SSLK

Thou arrant robber, Death! On the Death of W. C. Paul Laurence Dunbar. CP-DunbP

"Thou art a fool," said my head to my heart. Retort. Paul Laurence Dunbar. CP-DunbP

Thou art gone to thine island home. To My Wife. John Willis Menard. AAP

Thou art my lute, by thee I sing. Paul Laurence Dunbar. CP-DunbP

Thou art not dead, although the spoiler's hand. Africa. Lewis Alexander. CDC

Thou art not near me, but I see Thine eyes. I Love Thee. Josephine D. Henderson Heard. CBWP-4

Thou art the soul of a summer's day. A Song. Paul Laurence Dunbar. AmNP; CP-DunbP

Thou Lovest Me. Josephine D. Henderson Heard. CBWP-4

Thou mayst retire, but think of me. To a Departing Favorite. George Moses Horton. BALP

Thou monstrous gilt and rainbow-tinted thing. The New Organ. Josephine D. Henderson Heard. CBWP-4

Thou Pleiad of the lyric world. Adelina Patti. Adah Isaacs Menken. CBWP-1

Thou sweet-voiced stream that first gavest me drink. Sukee River. Claude McKay. SP-McKaC

Thou Venerene ascending to desire. To Gurdjieff Dying. Jean Toomer. CP-ToomJ

Though ain't no vision visited my cell. (LL) Sun came, Miss Brooks—, The. Etheridge Knight. BrTr; PoBA; SP-KnigE

Though I am not the first in English terms. To France. Countee Cullen. CP-CullC

Though I at the time, had no one. More Love to His Life. Alice Walker. CP-WalkA

Though i do wonder. Poem (for EMA). Nikki Giovanni. SP-GiovN

Though I go drunken. Faithful One. Langston Hughes. CP-HughL

Though I look like you. Hand Me Down Blues. Calvin Forbes. GT

Though I stand before these words. Bristol: Bicentenary Remembrances of Trade. Michael S. Harper. SP-HarpM

Though my stomach is still in Alabama pig / pens. (LL) King: April 4, 1968. Gerald William Barrax. ESEAA; GT

Though no blossoms cluster. Mrs. Mary Furman Weston Byrd. Mary Weston Fordham. CBWP-2

Though slavery's dead, yet there remains. James Madison Bell. See The Bondsman's gloomy night has passed.

Though slaves, a thousand come at her command. Albery Allson Whitman. Fr. Leelah Misled. EBAP

Though Tennyson, the poet king. James Madison Bell. AAP; AfAmPo

Though the cunning of the Indian and the Zulu's thirst for blood. Claflin's Alumni. Lizelia Augusta Jenkins Moorer. CBWP-3

Though the winds be dank. The Meadow Lark. Paul Laurence Dunbar. CP-DunbP

Though thou did'st hear the tempest from afar. To a Lady on Her Remarkable Preservation in an Hurricane in North-Carolina. Phillis Wheatley. CP-WheaP

Though with an angel's tongue. Rosabella—Purity of Heart. George Moses Horton. SP-HortG

Though you are a continent and two seasons away. Cape Coast Castle Revisited. Jo Ann Hall-Evans. BlSi

Thought at Walden, A. Henrietta Cordelia Ray. CBWP-3

Thought flashed 'cross a kindly mind, A. A Kindly Deed. Priscilla Jane Thompson. CBWP-2

Thought of Lake Ontario, A. Henrietta Cordelia Ray. CBWP-3

Thoughts. Maggie Pogue Johnson. CBWP-4

Thoughts from a Bottle. Carl Clark. JB

Thoughts in a Zoo. Countee Cullen. CP-CullC

Thoughts of death / Crowd over my happiness. Sterling A. Brown. CP-BrowS

Thoughts on the Works of Providence. Phillis Wheatley.
("Arise, my soul, on wings enraptur'd, rise.") CP-WheaP
(Thoughts on the Work of Providence.) EBAP

Thread / of meaning. Meaning light. The quick, A. The Dead Lady Canonized. Amiri Baraka. SP-BaraA

Threatened by abundance, the ranchers. Killing the Calves. Robert Hayden. CP-HaydR

Threatened by my rising need. Alice Walker. CP-WalkA

Threat'ning clouds of yesternight, The. While the Choir Sang. Priscilla Jane Thompson. CBWP-2

Three black boys. Panther. Sam Cornish. PoBA

Three Brown Girls Singing. M. Carl Holman. Klds

Three Days of Forest, a River, Free. Rita Dove. SP-DoveR

Three faces ... / mirrored in the muddy stream of living. For Andy Goodman—Michael Schwerner—and James Chaney. Margaret Abigail Walker. BPo; BrTr; CP-WalkM

Three grey boys tracked us to an old house. In One Battle. Amiri Baraka. BPo

Three hours have passed. English Lace. Cheryl Boyce Taylor. CtF

Three kings went down to the soul of the sea. James P. Vaughn. NNP

Three Men in a Tent. Marilyn Nelson. ESEAA

Three Modes of History and Culture. Amiri Baraka. ESEAA; SP-BaraA

Three Movements and a Coda. Amiri Baraka. BlFi; NAAAL

Three O'Clock Love Song. Michael S. Harper. GT

Three of us / in the bar. Jazz. Carolyn M. Rodgers. JB

Three of us went to the top of the city. Poem from the Empire State. June Jordan. BPo

Three students once tarried over the Rhine. From the German of Uhland. Ludwig Uhland, German. CDC, tr. by James Weldon Johnson

Three Whores Settin' Down in Boston. African-American Oral Tradition. GetYo

Three/Quarters Time. Nikki Giovanni. SP-GiovN

Threnody: "Let happy throats be mute." Donald Jeffrey Hayes. AmNP

Threnody: "Only quiet death." Waring Cuney. AmNP; BANP

Threnody for a Brown Girl. Countee Cullen. CP-CullC

Thrice hail! proud land, whose genius boasts a Clay! The Runaway. Albery Allson Whitman. AfAmPo Fr. Not a Man, and Yet a Man.
"I love Kentucky; tho' she merit scorn." AAP
(Runaway, The.) AAP

Thro' airy realms, he wings his instant flight. A Poem on the Death of Charles Eliot, Aged 12 Months. Phillis Wheatley. CP-WheaP

Thro' thickest glooms, look back, immortal Shade! On the Death of Doctor Samuel Marshall. Phillis Wheatley. CP-WheaP

Thro' thickest glooms, Look back, immortal Shade. On the Death of Dr. Samuel Marshall. Phillis Wheatley. CP-WheaP

Through a red prairie. Gwendolyn Brooks. See Bronzeville Mother Loiters in Mississippi. / Meanwhile, a Mississippi Mother Burns Bacon.

Through a red prairie. (LL) The Last Quatrain of the Ballad of Emmett Till. Gwendolyn Brooks. ESEAA; PoBA; SP-BrooG

Through a thicket of piney woods. The Boys of Summer. Kelly Norman Ellis. SpiFl

Through a two-way telescope of time. Aerolingual Poet of Prey. Eugene B. Redmond. SpiFl

Through Agony. Claude McKay. SP-McKaC

Through airy roads he wings his instant flight. A Funeral Poem on the Death of C.E., an Infant of Twelve Months. Phillis Wheatley. CP-WheaP

Through all the city's streets there poured a flood. The Gathering of the Grand Army. Charlotte L. Forten Grimké. AAP

Through congoed leaves of. Round Midnight, Place de Congo. Kalamu ya Salaam. Fr. New Orleans Haiku. SpiFl

Through deir dus'. (LL) Memphis Blues. Sterling A. Brown. CP-BrowS; NAAAL

Through pearly deeps of sky, cloud-mountains rose. Sky Picture. Henrietta Cordelia Ray. CBWP-3

Through random doors we wandered. Exits and Entrances. Naomi Long Madgett. BlSi; TtW

Through the dusky purple glimmer. Anita and Giovanni. Henrietta Cordelia Ray. CBWP-3

Through the Inner City to the Suburbs. Maya Angelou. CP-AngeM; SP-AngeM

Through the Keyhole in the Door. African-American Oral Tradition. GetYo

Through the long night the long trucks running the road. Sketching in the Transcendental. June Jordan. SP-JordJ

Through the long winter. And Fall Shall Sit in Judgment. Audre Lorde. NNP

Through the open porch window. Feeling Through. Alvin Aubert. BkSV

Through the pregnant universe rumbles life's terrific thunder. Exhortation: Summer, 1919. Claude McKay. CDC

Through the Varied Patterned Lace. Margaret Else Danner. Klds

Through the wide, grey loft window. A Village Life. Derek Walcott. GT

Through thickest glooms look bark, immortal shade. On the Death of Dr. Samuel Marshall, 1771. Phillis Wheatley. CP-WheaP

Through this suffering and the opened heart. Desire. Jean Toomer. CP-ToomJ

Through weathered wood dark. French Quarter Intimacies. Kalamu ya Salaam. Fr. New Orleans Haiku. SpiFl

Through you. (LL) To a Husband. Maya Angelou. CP-AngeM; SP-AngeM

Through you, I entered heaven and hell. Afterglow. Georgia Douglas Johnson. ShDr

Through your denials. (LL) Black Mother Woman. Audre Lorde. SP-LordA

Throughout our rambles much we find. The Woodman and the Money Hunter. George Moses Horton. SP-HortG

Throughout the afternoon I watched them there. The Snow Fairy. Claude McKay. SP-McKaC

Throughout the storm and party. Storm. Alice Walker. CP-WalkA

Thunder blossoms gorgeously above our heads. Storm Ending. Jean Toomer. CP-ToomJ

Thunder of the Rain God. A House in Taos. Langston Hughes. CDC; CP-HughL; NAAAL; SP-HughL

Thus ends my lay: Reluctantly I leave. Albery Allson Whitman. AAP Fr. Twasinta's Seminoles; Or Rape of Florida

Thus Far by Faith. Marilyn Nelson. SP-NelsM

Easter Sermon, 1866.

Good Friday Prayer.

Meditation over the Washtub.

Palm Sunday, 1866.

Sermon in the Cotton Field.

Sermon in the Ruined Garden.

Sermon in the Woodlot.

Thus man devotes his brother and destroys. Henry Highland Garnet. CrDW

Thus, San Augustine's church and prison joined. Albery Allson Whitman. AAP Fr. Twasinta's Seminoles; Or Rape of Florida

Thus she had lain. Africa. Maya Angelou. CP-AngeM; SP-AngeM

Thus, up to manhood he arose. His Manhood. George Clinton Rowe. AAP

Thwarted. Priscilla Jane Thompson. CBWP-2

Thy Gracious balm I need. (LL) A Prayer: "O Lord, the hard-won miles." Paul Laurence Dunbar. CP-DunbP

Thy life has touched the edges of my life. My Spirit's Complement. Henrietta Cordelia Ray. AAP; CBWP-3

Thy nearness our forgiving cure. (LL) The Broken Dark. Robert Hayden. CP-HaydR; GT

Thy spirit's wings unfolded in the light. (LL) Mignon. Henrietta Cordelia Ray. CBWP-3

Thy tones are silver melted into sound. To a Lady Playing the Harp. Paul Laurence Dunbar. CP-DunbP

Thy various works, imperial queen, we see. On Imagination. Phillis Wheatley. BlSi; CP-WheaP; CrDW; EBAP; NAAAL; TtW

Thy weary feet have pressed once more thy native soil. Welcome Home. Josephine D. Henderson Heard. CBWP-4

Tidal Friction ... Comments at Real Movie. Bob Kaufman. SP-KaufB

Tides of the mantra shore against your silence. Prayer of Singing Joy. Marilyn Nelson. Fr. The Plotinus Suite. SP-NelsM

Tidings! sad tidings for the daughter of Ai. Rizpah, the Daughter of Ai. Frances Ellen Watkins Harper. CP-HarpF

Tiger. Claude McKay. BPo; CrDW; SP-McKaC; TtW

Tiger in his strength his thirst must slake!, The. (LL) Tiger. Claude McKay. BPo; CrDW; SP-McKaC; TtW

Till comes the breath of Spring. (LL) The Snowdrop. Mary Weston Fordham. CBWP-2

Till Death Do Us Part. Kalamu ya Salaam. Fr. New Orleans Haiku. SpiFl

Till it drives you crazy, too. (LL) Evil. Langston Hughes. CP-HughL; SP-HughL

Till life divine re-animates his dust. (LL) On the Death of the Rev. Mr. George Whitefield, 1770. Phillis Wheatley. CP-WheaP; EBAP; NAAAL

Till the air is cured of its fever. (LL) Langston Hughes. Gwendolyn Brooks. SP-BrooG

Till the Sun Goes Down. Marvin X. BrTr

Till the Wind Gets Right. Paul Laurence Dunbar. CP-DunbP

Till they are incandescent. (LL) Her Lips Are Copper Wire. Jean Toomer. AfAmPo; CP-ToomJ; GT

Tim Murphy's gon' walkin' wid Maggie O'Neill. Circumstances Alter Cases. Paul Laurence Dunbar. CP-DunbP

Timber seasons better / if it is cut in the fourth quarter. Constuction. Audre Lorde. CP-LordA

Time collpases between the lips of strangers. Never to Dream of Spiders. Audre Lorde. CP-LordA

Time for Tyner: Folksong. Michael S. Harper. SP-HarpM

Time has brought about great changes. Scraps of Time. Mrs. Henry Linden. CBWP-4

Time I dropped your almost body down, The. The Lost Baby Poem. Lucille Clifton. BlSi; ESEAA; NAAAL; SP-ClifL

Time is a motor, you know. Tom Dent. TtW

Time is Berkeley. The Imitation Dance. Al Young. CP-YounA

"Time is unsportsmanlike with us," I said. Honey Mah Love. Sterling A. Brown. CP-BrowS

Time Leading Up To, The. Sekou Sundiata. Fr. Notes from the Defense of Colin Ferguson. SpiFl

Time of its life. (LL) Request. Maya Angelou. CP-AngeM; SP-AngeM

Time passed away, and Leelah downcast grew. Albery Allson Whitman. Fr. Leelah Misled. EBAP

Time Poem. Quentin Hill. NBP

Time-polished skulls of Yagan & Pemulwy. Protection of Movable Cultural Heritage. Yusef Komunyakaa. SP-KomuY

Time sitting on the throne of memory. October XXIX, 1795. William Stanley Braithwaite. CDC

Time to Die. Ray Garfield Dandridge. BANP; PoBA

Time to split now you & me. Lovesong of O. O. Gabugah. Al Young. CP-YounA

Time to Tinker 'Roun'! Paul Laurence Dunbar. CP-DunbP

Time to wipe away the slime. Now. Margaret Abigail Walker. CP-WalkM

Time with its narrow shores receded. Saved at Last. Frances Ellen Watkins Harper. CP-HarpF

Timepiece. Audre Lorde. CP-LordA

Times Change and We Change with Them or We Seem to Have Lost Touch with Each Other. Audre Lorde. CP-LordA

Times is mighty stirrin' 'mong de people up ouah way, De. How Lucy Backslid. Paul Laurence Dunbar. CP-DunbP

Times-Square-Shoeshine-Composition. Maya Angelou. CP-AngeM; SP-AngeM; TtW

Timid Lover. Countee Cullen. BANP

Timing. Audre Lorde. CP-LordA

Tin Roof Blues. Sterling A. Brown. NAAAL

("I'm going where de Southern crosses top de C. and O.") CP-BrowS

Tinkling treble. Dream Boogie: Variation. Langston Hughes. Fr. Montage of a Dream Deferred. CP-HughL

Tinsel Marie; the Coora Flower. Gwendolyn Brooks. Fr. Children Coming Home. ESEAA

Tiny Self-Portrait. Al Young. CP-YounA

Tip- / toe / in a badge. (LL) Chic Freedom's Reflection. Alice Walker. CP-WalkA

Tippler to His Bottle, The. George Moses Horton. SP-HortG

Tips / of her / fingers. (LL) Once. Alice Walker. BlSi; CP-WalkA

Tired. Langston Hughes. CP-HughL

Tired. Fenton Johnson. BANP; EBAP; IDB; Klds; NAAAL; PoBA; TtW

Tired cars go grumbling by, The. When Dawn Comes to the City. Claude McKay. SP-McKaC

Tired Man, The. Suliaman El-Hadi. SpiFl

Tired of waiting for me. Tongues in My Mouth. Demetrice A. Worley. SpiFl

TIRED. SICK AND TIRED. Burn, Baby, Burn. Marvin E. Jackmon. BlFi

Tired Worker, The. Claude McKay. BANP; BPo; SP-McKaC

Tireles Sculptor, The. Henrietta Cordelia Ray. CBWP-3

'Tis a noble gift to be brown, all brown. The Bronze Legacy. Mary Effie Lee Newsome. ShDr

'Tis a time for much rejoicing. Emancipation. Priscilla Jane Thompson. CBWP-2

'Tis an old deserted homestead. The Old Homestead. Paul Laurence Dunbar. CP-DunbP

'Tis bitter, yet 'tis sweet. Troubled with the Itch and Rubbing with Sulphur. George Moses Horton. AAP

'Tis but a phantom of the weary brain. Life for a Life. Mary E. Tucker. CBWP-1

'Tis done! the treach'rous deed is done. The Repeal of the Missouri Compromise Considered. Elymas Payson Rogers. EBAP

'Tis fine to play. A Boy's Summer Song. Paul Laurence Dunbar. CP-DunbP

'Tis Lent, the holy time of fast and prayer. The Easter Light. Clara Ann Thompson. CBWP-2

Tis of Thee. Henry L. Dumas. TtW

'Tis on October thirty-first. Hallowe'en. Lizelia Augusta Jenkins Moorer. CBWP-3

'Tis queer, it is, the ways o' men. The Ways o' Men. Angelina Weld Grimké. CDC

'Tis said but a name is friendship. Lines to Mrs. Isabel Peace. Mary Weston Fordham. CBWP-2

'Tis strange indeed to hear us plead. Joseph Seamon Cotter, Sr. See Dr. Booker T. Washington to the National Negro Business League.

'Tis strange indeed to hear us plead. Dr. Booker T. Washington to the National Negro Business League. Joseph Seamon Cotter, Sr. AAP

'Tis sweet to trace the setting sun. The Setting Sun. George Moses Horton. BALP

'Tis sweeter to forgive. (LL) Revenge. Mary E. Tucker. CBWP-1

"Tis the Octoroon ball! And the halls are alight!" Ballade des Belles Milatraisses. Rosalie Jonas. BlSi

'Tis the season when Nature awakes from her sleep. Easter; or, Spring-Time. Lizelia Augusta Jenkins Moorer. CBWP-3

'Tis well for thee my daughter. Lines to M.A.H. Frances Ellen Watkins Harper. CP-HarpF

'Tis wondrous strange in what things men find beauty. Beauty. Octavia Beatrice Wynbush. ShDr

Titanic: "All the old folks say the fourth a May was a hell of a day." African-American Oral Tradition. GetYo

Titanic: "Boys, you remember way back on the day of the eighth of May." African-American Oral Tradition. GetYo

Titanic: "Eighth a May was a hell of a day, The." African-American Oral Tradition. GetYo

Titanic: "I don't know, but my folks say." African-American Oral Tradition. GetYo

Titanic: "In the year of eighteen-twelve." African-American Oral Tradition. GetYo

Titanic: "It was sad indeed, it was sad in mind." African-American Oral Tradition. GetYo

Titanic: "Tenth of May was a hell of a day, The." African-American Oral Tradition. GetYo

Titanic: "This is about Shine O Shine. The captain was on his boat and he was." African-American Oral Tradition. GetYo

Titanic: "Twelfth of May was one hell of a day, The." African-American Oral Tradition. GetYo

(Title). Bob Bennett. BlFi

To ———: "Approaching night her mantle flings." James M. Whitfield. AAP

To ———: "Half in the dim light from the hall." William Stanley Braithwaite. BALP; PoBA

To a Babe Smiling in Her Sleep. Frances Ellen Watkins Harper. CP-HarpF

To a Brown Girl. Countee Cullen. CP-CullC

To a Captious Critic. Paul Laurence Dunbar. BPo; CP-DunbP; Klds

To a Certain Lady, in Her Garden. Sterling A. Brown. CDC; CP-BrowS

To a Clergyman on the Death of His Lady. Phillis Wheatley. CP-WheaP

To a Dark Dancer. Marjorie Marshall. ShDr

To a Dark Girl. Gwendolyn B. Bennett. BANP; BlSi; CDC; NAAAL; PoBA; ShDr

To a Dark Moses. Lucille Clifton. SP-ClifL

To a Daughter of Isaiah. Ishmael Reed. CP-ReedI

To a Dead Friend. Paul Laurence Dunbar. CP-DunbP

To a Dead Friend. Langston Hughes. CP-HughL

To a Deceased Friend. Priscilla Jane Thompson. CBWP-2

To a Departing Favorite. George Moses Horton. BALP

To a Freedom Fighter. Maya Angelou. CP-AngeM; SP-AngeM

To a Gentleman and Lady on the Death of the Lady's Brother and Sister, and a Child of the Name Avis, Aged One Year. Phillis Wheatley. BlSi; CP-WheaP

To a Gentleman of the Navy, see also The Answer by Unknown and Philis's Reply by Phillis Wheatley. Phillis Wheatley. CP-WheaP

To a Gentleman on his Voyage to Great-Britain for the Recovery of His Health. Phillis Wheatley. CP-WheaP

To a Girl Who Knew What Side Her Bread Was Buttered On. Audre Lorde. CP-LordA; SP-LordA

To a Gone Era. Irma McClaurin. BlSi

To a Husband. Maya Angelou. CP-AngeM; SP-AngeM

To a Lady and Her Children, on the Death of Her Son and Their Brother. Phillis Wheatley. CP-WheaP

To a Lady on Her Coming to North-America with Her Son, for the Recovery of Her Health. Phillis Wheatley. CP-WheaP

To a Lady on Her Remarkable Preservation in an Hurricane in North-Carolina. Phillis Wheatley. CP-WheaP

To a Lady on the Death of Her Husband. Phillis Wheatley. CP-WheaP

To a Lady on the Death of Three Relations. Phillis Wheatley. CP-WheaP

To a Lady Playing the Harp. Paul Laurence Dunbar. CP-DunbP

To a Little Colored Boy. Priscilla Jane Thompson. CBWP-2

To a Little Lover-Lass, Dead. Langston Hughes. CP-HughL

To a Loved One. Mary Weston Fordham. CBWP-2

To a Man. Maya Angelou. SP-AngeM
  ("My man is / Black Golden Amber.") CP-AngeM

To a Persistent Phantom. Frank Horne. AmNP; BANP; CDC

To a Poet and a Lady. Paul Laurence Dunbar. CP-DunbP

To a Poet I Knew. Jewel C. Latimore. PoBA

To a poor white poppy-flower. (LL) White Things. Anne Spencer. AfAmPo; Crnst

To a Publisher ... Cut-out. Amiri Baraka. SP-BaraA

To a Single Shadow without Pity. Sam Cornish. NBP; PoBA

To a Skull. Joshua Henry Jones. BANP

To a Suitor. Maya Angelou. CP-AngeM; SP-AngeM

To a Violet Found on All Saints' Day. Paul Laurence Dunbar. CP-DunbP

To a Weathercock. Raymond R. Patterson. TtW

To a Woman Poet That I Know. Pinkie Gordon Lane. TtW

To a Woman Who Wants Darkness and Time. Gerald William Barrax. PoBA

To a Young Girl Leaving the Hill Country. Arna Bontemps. GT; Klds
  ("Hills are wroth, The; the stones have scored you bitterly.") CDC

To a Young Wife. Georgia Douglas Johnson. ShDr

To Alice Dunbar. Paul Laurence Dunbar. CP-DunbP

To All Brothers. Sonia Sanchez. BPo; BrTr

To All Sisters. Sonia Sanchez. BlFi; PoBA

To all that blooming life that might have been. (LL) A January Dandelion. George Marion McClellan. AAP; AfAmPo; EBAP

To all the women. Touch Her. Anthony C. Lyons. CtF

To an Afro-American Maiden. Fenton Johnson. Crnst

To an Icicle. Blanche Taylor Dickinson. CDC; ShDr

To an Infant. Mary Weston Fordham. CBWP-2

To an Ingrate. Paul Laurence Dunbar. CP-DunbP

To an Old Black Woman, Homeless and Indistinct. Gwendolyn Brooks. ESEAA

To an Unknown Poet. Countee Cullen. CP-CullC

To Annie. Mary E. Tucker. CBWP-1

To Artina. Langston Hughes. SP-HughL
  (Artina.) CP-HughL

To avoid being laughed at during the day. (LL) Small Town. Rita Dove. GT; SP-DoveR

To be a Negro in a day like this. At the Closed Gate of Justice. James David Corrothers. AfAmPo; BANP; NAAAL; TtW

To be Alive. Heathen Bliss. Amiri Baraka. SP-BaraA

2 B BLK. Val Ferdinand. NBV

To be black Is / To be / Very-hot. (LL) But He Was Cool; or, He Even Stopped for Green Lights. Don L. Lee. AmNP; BPo; PoBA

To be dead, and never again behold my city! (LL) My City. James Weldon Johnson. BANP; CDC; IHS; NAAAL

To be forever young. Immortality. Frank Horne. BANP

To be in love. Gwendolyn Brooks. GT; SP-BrooG

To Be or Not to Be. Brian G. Gilmore. SpiFl

To Be Quicker. Don L. Lee. JB

To be so still that way. (LL) Sea Calm. Langston Hughes. CP-HughL; SP-HughL

To Be Somebody. Langston Hughes. CP-HughL; SP-HughL

To be stabbed on a lonely hill. (LL) Prophets for a New Day. Margaret Abigail Walker. BrTr; CP-WalkM; NAAAL

To be unraveling. (LL) The Rhetoric of Langston Hughes. Margaret Else Danner. BlSi; FB

To be up high. (LL) Get Up, Blues. James A. Emanuel. AmNP; PoBA

To Beat the Child Was Bad Enough. Maya Angelou. CP-AngeM; SP-AngeM

To Beauty. Langston Hughes. CP-HughL

To Bed. Rita Dove. SP-DoveR

To better the condition of humanity. Our Club Work. Mrs. Henry Linden. CBWP-4

To Bishop Payne. Frances Ellen Watkins Harper. CP-HarpF

To Bobby Seale. Lucille Clifton. PoBA; SP-ClifL

To Booker T. Washington. Paul Laurence Dunbar. CP-DunbP

To Captain H——D, of the 65th Regiment. Phillis Wheatley. CP-WheaP

To Captain Mulzac. Langston Hughes. CP-HughL

To care for others is the God in man. Albery Allson Whitman. Fr. Leelah Misled. EBAP

To cast the first hard stone. (LL) Black Magdalens. Countee Cullen. BANP; CP-CullC

To catch the spirit in its wayward flight. Self-Mastery. Henrietta Cordelia Ray. CBWP-3

To Certain "Brothers." Langston Hughes. CP-HughL

To Certain Critics. Countee Cullen. BPo; CP-CullC

To Certain Intellectuals. Langston Hughes. CP-HughL

To Certain Negro Leaders. Langston Hughes. CP-HughL

To "Chick." Frank Horne. Fr. Letters [or Notes] Found near a Suicide. AmNP; BPo; CDC; PoBA

To Children. Lawrence McGaugh. PoBA

To Cinque. James M. Whitfield. EBAP; TtW

To circle their wagons? (LL) Why Do So Few Blacks Study Creative Writing? Cornelius Eady. GT

To Clarissa Scott Delany. Angelina Weld Grimké. AmNP; ShDr

To clasp you now and feel your head close-pressed. Romance. Claude McKay. SP-McKaC

To Clements' Ferry. Josephine D. Henderson Heard. CBWP-4

To climb a hill that hungers for the sky. Fulfillment. Helene Johnson. CDC; ShDr

To conqueror me home. (LL) Love, Maybe. Audre Lorde. CP-LordA; SP-LordA

To cultivate in ev'ry noble mind. To the Rev. Dr. Thomas Amory on Reading Sermons on Daily Devotion, in Which That Duty Is Recommended and Assisted. Phillis Wheatley. CP-WheaP

To Dan. Paul Laurence Dunbar. CP-DunbP

To dance— / In the light of moon. Longings. Mae V. Cowdery. ShDr

To-day Is a King in Disguise. Frances Ellen Watkins Harper. CP-HarpF

To-day is a monarch in disguise. To-day Is a King in Disguise. Frances Ellen Watkins Harper. CP-HarpF

To dazzle your night! (LL) Nocturne Varial. Lewis Alexander. PoBA

To Desi as Joe as Smoky the Lover of 115th Street. Audre Lorde. CP-LordA

To die / And never know what killed you. Death in Africa. Langston Hughes. CP-HughL

To die at / thirty-nine. (LL) On Reaching Forty. Maya Angelou. CP-AngeM; SP-AngeM

To die before one / wakes / must be glad. Alice Walker. CP-WalkA

To Dinah Washington. Etheridge Knight. PoBA

To do celestial chores. (LL) For a Lady I Know. Countee Cullen. CP-CullC; IDB; SSLK

To Don Juan Baz. Mary E. Tucker. CBWP-1

To Dorothy Maynor. Langston Hughes. CP-HughL

To Dr. James Newton Matthews, Mason, Ill. Paul Laurence Dunbar. CP-DunbP

To dreamy languors and the violet mist. Dogwood Blossoms. George Marion McClellan. BANP

To drive us made. (LL) Madhouse. Calvin C. Hernton. IDB; NNP; PoBA

To E. H. K. Paul Laurence Dunbar. CP-DunbP

To E.J.J. Ethel M. Caution. ShDr

To Egypt. Gloria Davis. NBP

To Eliza. George Moses Horton. EBAP; SP-HortG; TtW

To Emerge from the Shadows. Sekou Sundiata. Fr. Notes from the Defense of Colin Ferguson. SpiFl

To Endymion. Countee Cullen. CP-CullC

To every man / His treehouse. The Treehouse. James A. Emanuel. AmNP; BPo; BrTr; NNP; PoBA

To face the dark alone. (LL) Return. Audre Lorde. CP-LordA; SP-LordA

To Fannie. Mary E. Tucker. CBWP-1

To Fanon. Keorapetse W. Kgositsile. BrTr

To Father. Mary E. Tucker. CBWP-1

To fling my arms wide. Dream Variations. Langston Hughes. AmNP; BALP; CDC; CP-HughL; IDB; NAAAL; PoBA; SP-HughL; SSLK

To float in the space between. (LL) The Idea of Ancestry. Etheridge Knight. BALP; BPo; BrTr; ESEAA; NAAAL; PoBA; SP-KnigE; TtW

To France. Countee Cullen. CP-CullC

To Free Nelson Mandela. June Jordan. SP-JordJ

To give us comfort through the lonely dark. (LL) Douglass. Paul Laurence Dunbar. AAP; CP-DunbP; NAAAL; TtW

To glorify the earth—and you—and me. (LL) Pennsylvania Station in New York, The. Langston Hughes. Klds

To go with me / to the darkness / where I go. (LL) Fantasy in Purple. Langston Hughes. BANP; CDC; CP-HughL; SP-HughL

To God the highest glory. Song of the Angels. Lizelia Augusta Jenkins Moorer. CBWP-3

To Gurdjieff Dying. Jean Toomer. CP-ToomJ

To Have Danced with Death. Yusef Komunyakaa. SP-KomuY

To hear ol' Jordan roll. (LL) Roll Jordan, roll. Unknown. CrDW; Crnst

To Hear the River. Kenneth A. McClane. TtW

To hear / to hear. To Hear the River. Kenneth A. McClane. TtW

To Hell with Whitey. Mario Van Peebles. CtF

To Her. Paul Laurence Dunbar. CP-DunbP

To herald in another year. January. Henrietta Cordelia Ray. CBWP-3

To him who in his absence from himself. Lance Jeffers. BkSV

To His Excellency General Washington. Phillis Wheatley. CP-WheaP; Klds; NAAAL; TtW

("Celestial choir! enthroned in realms of light.") EBAP

(To His Excellency George Washington.) EBAP

To His Honour the Lieutenant-Governor, on the Death of His Lady, March 24, 1773. Phillis Wheatley. CP-WheaP

To his two little girls. (LL) Star-Fix. Marilyn Nelson. ESEAA; SP-NelsM

To honey and bread old purity could love. (LL) My Dreams, My Works Must Wait Till after Hell. Gwendolyn Brooks. SP-BrooG; TtW

To J. Q. Paul Laurence Dunbar. CP-DunbP

To James. Frank Horne. Fr. Letters [or Notes] Found near a Suicide. AmNP; BPo; CDC; Klds; PoBA

To Joan. Lucille Clifton. SP-ClifL

To John Keats, Poet, at Springtime. Countee Cullen. AfAmPo; BANP; CDC; CP-CullC

(To John Keats, Poet, at Spring Time.) NAAAL

To Keep the Memory of Charlotte Forten Grimké. Angelina Weld Grimké. BlSi; ShDr

To Kelly Miller, Jr. Paul Laurence Dunbar. CP-DunbP

To know his / Place. (LL) Uncle Tom. Langston Hughes. CP-HughL; SP-HughL

To Know, in heart, in groin. Four Worthies: Souls of Black Folk. Michael S. Harper. SP-HarpM

To L. Julianne Perry. PoBA

To Laura. Henrietta Cordelia Ray. CBWP-3

To let my people go. (LL) Go down, Moses. Unknown. BPo; BkSV; CrDW; Crnst; NAAAL

To liberate my people from its yoke! (LL) Enslaved. Claude McKay. AfAmPo; NAAAL; SP-McKaC

To live and not to be thine own. Thine Own. Josephine D. Henderson Heard. CBWP-4

To look at a bunch of smashed statues. (LL) Sightseeing. Rita Dove. GT; SP-DoveR

To Louise. Paul Laurence Dunbar. CP-DunbP

To love a man wholly. Warning. Alice Walker. CP-WalkA

To love and live with them again! (LL) For Andy Goodman—Michael Schwerner—and James Chaney. Margaret Abigail Walker. BrTr; CP-WalkM

To Lovers of Earth: Fair Warning. Countee Cullen. CDC

To Mæcenas. Phillis Wheatley. CP-WheaP; NAAAL

To make a delta praise for the poets ah. (LL) For the Poets. Jayne Cortez. SP-CortJ

To make a Juju of my own. A Juju of My Own. Lebert Bethune. BlFi; PoBA

To make a poet black, and bid him sing! (LL) Yet Do I Marvel. Countee Cullen. AfAmPo; AmNP; BANP; BPo; CDC; CP-CullC; CrDW; Crnst; IDB; NAAAL; PoBA; SSLK

To make out the sound of my own background music. (LL) A Little More Traveling Music. Al Young. CP-YounA; NBV

To make the cotton yield. (LL) Share-Croppers. Langston Hughes. CP-HughL; SP-HughL

To make words sing. Langston Hughes. CP-HughL

To Marie, in Flight. Audre Lorde. CP-LordA

To Market. Marilyn Nelson. SP-NelsM

To Martha: a New Year. Audre Lorde. CP-LordA

To Mary. Mary E. Tucker. CBWP-1

To Mary Church Terrell. Paul Laurence Dunbar. CP-DunbP

To mate or man, or beast or bird. (LL) The Saxon Legend of Language. Mary Weston Fordham. AAP; CBWP-2

To me, like hauntings of a vagrant breath. To E. H. K. Paul Laurence Dunbar. CP-DunbP

To measure long journeys. (LL) Tour Guide: La Maison des Esclaves. Melvin Dixon. ESEAA

"To meet and then to part," and that is all. The Close of Day. Wesley Curtright. CDC

To Melody. George Leonard Allen. CDC

To Merle. Lucille Clifton. SP-ClifL

To Midnight Nan at Leroy's. Langston Hughes. CP-HughL

To Miss Mary Britton. Paul Laurence Dunbar. CP-DunbP

To Mr. and Mrs. —, on the Death of Their Infant Son. Phillis Wheatley. CP-WheaP

To Mr. and Mrs. W. F. Johnson on Their Twenty-Fifth Wedding Anniversary. Frances Ellen Watkins Harper. CP-HarpF

To Mrs. Harriet Beecher Stowe. Frances Ellen Watkins Harper. CP-HarpF

To Mrs. Leonard, on the Death of Her Husband. Phillis Wheatley. CP-WheaP

To Mother. Frank Horne. Fr. Letters [or Notes] Found near a Suicide. AmNP; CDC; BPo; PoBA

To Mother. Keorapetse W. Kgositsile. GT

To Mother and Steve. Mari E. Evans. BPo; PoBA

To mount the earth in my black people's time! (LL) Trellie. Lance Jeffers. FB; NBV; TtW

To Ms. Ann. Lucille Clifton. ESEAA; SP-ClifL

To muse on uncle Jim. (LL) Uncle Jim. Countee Cullen. BANP; CP-CullC; GT

To My Daughter. Keorapetse W. Kgositsile. GT

To My Daughter the Junkie on a Train. Audre Lorde. SP-LordA

("Curse their children because they became junk.") (LL) CP-LordA

To My Dead Brother. Clara Ann Thompson. CBWP-2

To My Father. Henrietta Cordelia Ray. AAP; BlSi; CBWP-3; EBAP; TtW

To my Friend, Jerina. Lucille Clifton. ESEAA

To My Mother. Mary Weston Fordham. CBWP-2

To My Mother. Henrietta Cordelia Ray. CBWP-3

To My Son Parker, Asleep in the Next Room. Bob Kaufman. Klds; PoBA; SP-KaufB; TtW

To My Wife. John Willis Menard. AAP

To O.E.A E. A. Claude McKay. BANP; BPo; GT; SP-McKaC

To One Coming North. Claude McKay. SP-McKaC

To One Not There. Countee Cullen. CP-CullC

To One Who Sleepeth. Mary E. Tucker. CBWP-1

To only the darker lamb? (LL) To Certain Critics. Countee Cullen. BPo; CP-CullC

To Our First Born or the Prophet Arrives. Ebon. BrTr

To Our Friends. Lucian B. Watkins. BANP

To Pfrimmer. Paul Laurence Dunbar. CP-DunbP

To Professor Byrd Prillerman. Maggie Pogue Johnson. CBWP-4

To prove we're still here. (LL) A Dance For Ma Rainey. Al Young. CP-YounA; NBP; NBV

To reassure her why. (LL) Epitaph: "She leans across a golden table." Countee Cullen. CP-CullC

To reconcile the pride and pain in me. (LL) Dark Blood. Margaret Abigail Walker. CP-WalkM

To rend me and redeem. (LL) Bone-Flower Elegy. Robert Hayden. CP-HaydR

To Rev. Thaddeus Saltus. Mary Weston Fordham. CBWP-2

To Richard Wright. Conrad Kent Rivers. AmNP; IDB; PoBA

To ride piggy-back. Slave. Langston Hughes. CP-HughL

To S. M., a Young African Painter, on Seeing His Works. Phillis Wheatley. BlSi; CP-WheaP; Crnst; EBAP; NAAAL

To Sallie, Walking. Sterling A. Brown. CP-BrowS; GT

To San Fransisco. Marilyn Nelson. Fr. The Plotinus Suite. SP-NelsM

To Satch. Samuel Allen. AmNP; Klds; PoBA; TtW

(American Gothic.) IDB

To scream for help through a horn. (LL) February in Sydney. Yusef Komunyakaa. ESEAA; NAAAL; SP-KomuY

To see herself tonight. (LL) A Brown Girl Dead. Countee Cullen. CP-CullC; GT; Klds

To See Ol' Booker T. Maggie Pogue Johnson. CBWP-4

To see those eyes. Philadelphia: Spring, 1985. Sonia Sanchez. ESEAA

To seek a new brown love. (LL) A Black Pierrot. Langston Hughes. CP-HughL; SP-HughL

To show the lab'ring bosom's deep intent. To S. M., a Young African Painter, on Seeing His Works. Phillis Wheatley. BlSi; CP-WheaP; Crnst; EBAP; NAAAL

To show thy little lamp: go forth, go forth! (LL) To the White Fiends. Claude McKay. NAAAL; SP-McKaC

To sing on the Georgia roads. (LL) Sun Song. Langston Hughes. CP-HughL; SP-HughL

To sit and dream, to sit and read. To You. Langston Hughes. CP-HughL

To Some Millions Who Survive Joseph E. Mander, Sr. Sarah E. Wright. PoBA

To Soulfolk. Margaret Goss Burroughs. BlSi

To stand for a while, and get warm. (LL) The Satisfaction Coal Company. Rita Dove. SP-DoveR

To steep my eyes in sleep. (LL) Night Rain. Countee Cullen. CP-CullC; GT

To Strike for Night. Lebert Bethune. NBP

To tell him so. (LL) Did This Happen to Your Mother? Did Your Sister Throw Up a Lot? Alice Walker. CP-WalkA

To tell the truth, each piece he read. On Hearing James W. Riley Read. Joseph Seamon Cotter, Sr. AAP; EBAP

To the child, / Music. (LL) Hymn: "I well remember / A time when." Alice Walker. CP-WalkA

To the Cleveland Union-Savers. Frances Ellen Watkins Harper. See To the Union Savers of Cleveland.

To the cold, dark grave they go. An Easter Ode. Paul Laurence Dunbar. CP-DunbP

To the Conference. Mrs. Henry Linden. CBWP-4

To the continuation of their creed / And their lives. (LL) "Negro" Hero. Gwendolyn Brooks. Klds; SP-BrooG

To the Czar of all the Russia's. The Vision of the Czar of Russia. Frances Ellen Watkins Harper. CP-HarpF

To the Dark Mercedes of "El Palacio de Amor." Langston Hughes. CP-HughL

To the Eagle. Mary Weston Fordham. CBWP-2

To the Eastern Shore. Paul Laurence Dunbar. CP-DunbP

To the First of August. Ann Plato. BlSi; TtW

("Brittania's isles proclaim.") EBAP

To the Girl Who Lives In a Tree. Audre Lorde. CP-LordA; SP-LordA

To the Hon. Commodore Hood on His Pardoning a Deserter. Phillis Wheatley. CP-WheaP

To the Hon'ble Thomas Hubbard, Esq.; on the Death of Mrs. Thankfull Leonard. Phillis Wheatley. CP-WheaP

To the honorable Senate and House. Belinda's Petition. Rita Dove. SP-DoveR

To the Honourable T.H. Esq.; on the Death of His Daughter. Phillis Wheatley. CP-WheaP

To the "J F K" Quintet. Al Fraser. BlFi

To the King's Most Excellent Majesty, 1768. Phillis Wheatley. CP-WheaP

To the King's Most Excellent Majesty on His Repealing the American Stamp Act. Phillis Wheatley. CP-WheaP

To the Little Front of San Lazaro on the Ocean Front, Havana. Langston Hughes. CP-HughL

To the Man in the Yellow Terry. Alice Walker. CP-WalkA

To the Memory of J. Horace Kimball. "Ada." BlSi

To the Memory of Mary Young. Paul Laurence Dunbar. CP-DunbP

To the Miami. Paul Laurence Dunbar. CP-DunbP

To the Mock-Bird. Mary Weston Fordham. CBWP-2

To the monkeys on Monkey Island. Monkey Island. Ishmael Reed. CP-ReedI

To the Muse. George Moses Horton. SP-HortG

To the New Annex to the Detroit County Jail. Richard W. Thomas. PoBA

To the New Year. Priscilla Jane Thompson. CBWP-2

To the Palmetto State, in the year seventy three. Southern Work of Dr. and Mrs. L. M. Dunton. Lizelia Augusta Jenkins Moorer. CBWP-3

To the Peoples of Earth. Sun-Ra. BlFi

To the Poet Who Happens to Be Black and the Black Poet Who Happens to Be a Woman. Audre Lorde. CP-LordA

To the Queen of the British Government. Mrs. Henry Linden. CBWP-4

To the Rev. Dr. Thomas Amory on Reading Sermons on Daily Devotion, in Which That Duty Is Recommended and Assisted. Phillis Wheatley. CP-WheaP

To the Rev. Mr. Pitkin, on the Death of His Lady. Phillis Wheatley. CP-WheaP

To the Right Hon. William Earl of Dartmouth, His Majesty's Secretary of State for North America, Etc. Etc. Etc. Phillis Wheatley. *See* To the Right Honourable William, Earl of Dartmouth, His Majesty's Principal Secretary of State for North-America, Etc.

To the Right Honourable William, Earl of Dartmouth, His Majesty's Principal Secretary of State for North-America, Etc. Phillis Wheatley. CrDW; NAAAL

(To the Right Hon. William Earl of Dartmouth, His Majesty's Secretary of State for North America, Etc. Etc. Etc.) CP-WheaP

To the Road. Paul Laurence Dunbar. CP-DunbP

To the scene of life now closes. The Close of Life. George Moses Horton. SP-HortG

To the screech and scrape of a corn-stalk fiddle. (LL) Corn-Stalk Fiddle, THe. Paul Laurence Dunbar. AAP; CP-DunbP

To the South. Paul Laurence Dunbar. CP-DunbP

To the state of West Virginia. The Story of Lovers Leap. Maggie Pogue Johnson. CBWP-4

To the Swimmer. Countee Cullen. CP-CullC

To / The territory of the non-memory. The Image Reach. Sun-Ra. BlFi

To the Three for Whom the Book. Countee Cullen. CP-CullC

To the Unborn and Waiting Children. Lucille Clifton. SP-ClifL

To the Union Savers of Cleveland. Frances Ellen Watkins Harper. AAP; AfAmPo

(To the Cleveland Union-Savers.) CP-HarpF

To the University of Cambridge, in New-England. Phillis Wheatley. BALP; EBAP; NAAAL; TtW

(To the University of Cambridge, Wrote in 1767.) CP-WheaP

("While an intrinsic ardor bids me write.") CP-WheaP

To the Wheel of Progress. Mrs. Henry Linden. CBWP-4

To the White Fiends. Claude McKay. BANP; NAAAL; PoBA; SP-McKaC

To the White People of America. Joshua McCarter Simpson. AAP; AfAmPo

To Thelma Who Worried Because I Couldn't Cook. Lucille Clifton. SP-ClifL

To them I'm just a crazy nigger. Newport Beach, 1979. Yusef Komunyakaa. SP-KomuY

To Theodore. George Marion McClellan. AAP

To those fair isles where crimson sunsets burn. Toussaint L'Ouverture. Henrietta Cordelia Ray. CBWP-3

To those fixed on white. People. Jean Toomer. CP-ToomJ; GT

To Those of My Sisters Who Kept Their Naturals. Gwendolyn Brooks. TtW

To Those Who Sing America. Frank Marshall Davis. FB

To Tommy who: / eats chocolate cookies and lamb chops. For Tommy. Nikki Giovanni. SP-GiovN

To Turn from Love. Sarah Webster Fabio. BlSi; TtW

To turn their hands against us. (LL) Vietnam Addenda. Audre Lorde. CP-LordA; SP-LordA

To Usward. Gwendolyn B. Bennett. BlSi; ShDr

To Vietnam. Charlie Cobb. PoBA

To W. L. G. on Reading His "Chosen Queen." Charlotte Forten. BlSi

To wait for that great gittin' up morning—Amem. (LL) Listen, Lord—[a Prayer]. James Weldon Johnson. BANP; BPo

To wander naked / In the cold. (LL) Strange Hurt. Langston Hughes. CP-HughL; SP-HughL

To wander through this living world. Remembrance. Langston Hughes. CP-HughL

To whistle and smile at the johns. (LL) As You Leave Me. Etheridge Knight. BrTr; SP-KnigE

To White Ribbons of Maine Who Gave to Me Their Blessed Gifts. Frances Ellen Watkins Harper. CP-HarpF

To Whittier. Josephine D. Henderson Heard. AAP; CBWP-4

To William Stanley Braithwaite. Georgia Douglas Johnson. BALP

To Winter. Claude McKay. SP-McKaC

To worship / At the altar of Beauty. To Beauty. Langston Hughes. CP-HughL

To write a blues song. Haiku: "To write a blues song." Etheridge Knight. ESEAA; TtW

To You. Frank Horne. *Fr.* Letters [*or* Notes] Found near a Suicide. AmNP; BPo; CDC; PoBA

To You. Langston Hughes. CP-HughL

To you / Who are the / Foam on the sea. Rising Waters. Langston Hughes. CP-HughL

To You/Who Almost Turned/Me On. Sonia Sanchez. SP-SancS

To Youth. Josephine D. Henderson Heard. CBWP-4

Toast. Frank Horne. BANP

Today. Langston Hughes. CP-HughL

Today. Gaston Neal. BlFi

Today. Margaret Abigail Walker. CP-WalkM; FB

Today as the news from Selma and Saigon. Monet's "Waterlilies." Robert Hayden. CP-HaydR; GT

Today at the edge of light. Clinton. Sterling Plumpp. BkSV

Today clouds come to visit. October Window. Al Young. CP-YounA

Today I Am a Homicide in the North of the City. Wanda Coleman. NAAAL

Today I am at home. A Few Sirens. Alice Walker. CP-WalkA

Today i am / tired of sabbaths. Sequences. Sonia Sanchez. SP-SancS

Today / I am 24. January 3, 1970. Mae Jackson. PoBA

Today I feel bearish. Untitled: "Today I feel bearish." Ishmael Reed. CP-ReedI

Today I go back to the sea. Return to Sea. Langston Hughes. CP-HughL

Today I heard my heart screeching like a subway train. Audre Lorde. *See* Hard Love Rock.

Today I learned the *coora* flower. Tinsel Marie; the Coora Flower. Gwendolyn Brooks. *Fr.* Children Coming Home. ESEAA

Today I saw a thing of arresting poignant beauty. Snow in October. Alice Moore Dunbar-Nelson. BlSi; CDC; ShDr

Today, I will see some empty spaces. Today: The Idea Market. Michael Nicholas. NBP

Today I'll give up living. (LL) The Last Decision. Maya Angelou. CP-AngeM; SP-AngeM

TODAY, is a black day for the Black man. Elegy for a Martyred Poet. El Rivera. CtF

Today Is Not Like They Said. Kirk Hall. NBV

Today Is Not the Day. Audre Lorde. CP-LordA

Today like yesterday. Monotony. Langston Hughes. CP-HughL

Today: The Idea Market. Michael Nicholas. NBP

Today the New York. Guilty, the New York Philharmonic Signs up a Whale. Ishmael Reed. CP-ReedI

Today Tutu Is Beating the Same Burru As Me. Lebert Bethune. GT

Today, you threaten to leave me. The Lie. Maya Angelou. CP-AngeM; SP-AngeM

Together, we looked down. Wedding Procession, from a Window. James A. Emanuel. Klds; NNP

"Toil! toil! toil!" The Wandering Jew. Eloise Bibb. CBWP-4

Toledo Slim. *African-American Oral Tradition.* GetYo

Tom Mooney! / Tom Mooney! Chant for Tom Mooney. Langston Hughes. CP-HughL

Tomcat born on railroad. Autobiography. Tom Weatherly. NBV

Tomorrow it returns to me. (LL) Changes. Maya Angelou. CP-AngeM; SP-AngeM

Tomorrow may be. Langston Hughes. *Fr.* Montage of a Dream Deferred. CP-HughL; SP-HughL

Tomorrow our landfall will be the Barbados. (LL) Shabine Encounters the Middle Passage. Derek Walcott. ESEAA

Tomorrow the heroes / will be named willie. their. Alfred B. Spellman. BlFi; PoBA

Tomorrow's Seed. Langston Hughes. CP-HughL

Tone of my life takes, The. Today. Gaston Neal. BlFi

Tone Poem. Amiri Baraka. SP-BaraA

Tones of the 60s vibrated, The. Donut Man. Adwin Brown. CtF

Tongue Is, The. Yusef Komunyakaa. SP-KomuY

Tongue-tied in Black and White. Michael S. Harper. ESEAA; SP-HarpM

Tongues in My Mouth. Demetrice A. Worley. SpiFl

Tonight, a beautiful redhead. The Undertaker's Daughter Feels Neglect. Thylias Moss. ESEAA

Tonight I feel the stars are out. Black String of Days. Yusef Komunyakaa. SP-KomuY

Tonight it is the wine (or not the wine). Excuse. Alice Walker. CP-WalkA

Tonight the waves march. Moonlight Night: Carmel. Langston Hughes. CP-HughL; GT; SP-HughL

Tonight we gonna have a ball. Bulldaggers' Hall. *African-American Oral Tradition.* GetYo

Tonight / when you spread your pallet. Accident. Maya Angelou. CP-AngeM; SP-AngeM

Tonight, within my heart! (LL) My Little Dreams. Georgia Douglas Johnson. BANP; BlSi; CDC; NAAAL

Tonite, thriller was. Beware: Do Not Read This Poem. Ishmael Reed. BPo; PoBA

Tonite, *thriller* was / abt an old woman, so vain she. Ishmael Reed. *See* Beware: Do Not Read This Poem.

TONTO IS DEAD, TONTO IS DEAD, TONTO IS DEAD. The Late Lamented Wind, Burned in Indignation. Bob Kaufman. SP-KaufB

Tony Get the Boys. D. L. Graham. PoBA

Too Blue. Langston Hughes. CP-HughL

Too Busy. Paul Laurence Dunbar. CP-DunbP

Too frail for combat, he stands [*or* stood]. Aircraft. Rita Dove. SP-DoveR

Too frail to soar—a feeble thing. The Sparrow's Fall. Frances Ellen Watkins Harper. CP-HarpF

Too green the springing April grass. Spring in New Hampshire. Claude McKay. BANP; BPo; CrDW; Klds; SP-McKaC

Too Many. Derrick I. M. Gilbert. CtF

Too many years. Down Where I Am. Langston Hughes. CP-HughL

Took us both in / Laughing. (LL) Fulfilment. Langston Hughes. CP-HughL; SP-HughL

Topsy: Part 2. Al Young. CP-YounA

Tore us down to the human. (LL) Blackbottom. Toi Derricotte. GT

Tormented. Claude McKay. SP-McKaC

Torn body, correspondent, A. Dichtung. Amiri Baraka. SP-BaraA

Torn in the sun. (LL) Echo. Audre Lorde. CP-LordA; SP-LordA

Torn Sky: Lesson #1, The. June Jordan. SP-JordJ

Tornados. Thylias Moss. GT

Torrent / of cobalt bullets, A. Lacrimas or There Is a Need to Scream. K. Curtis Lyle. NBV; PoBA

Torture. Alice Walker. CP-WalkA

Toss your gay heads. At April. Angelina Weld Grimké. BlSi; GT

Tossed on the stormy waves of time. "I Was a Stranger and Ye Took Me In." Mary E. Tucker. CBWP-1

Total Incandescence. Al Young. CP-YounA

Total War. Langston Hughes. CP-HughL

Tou Wan Speaks to Her Husband Liu Sheng. Rita Dove. ESEAA; SP-DoveR

Touch Her. Anthony C. Lyons. CtF

Touch / is what the eyes do, sometimes. From a Brother Dreaming in the Rye. James Cunningham. JB

Touch / making / me breathe. (LL) Black Magic. Sonia Sanchez. BrTr; SP-SancS

Touch me, touch me. Grass Fingers. Angelina Weld Grimké. CDC; ShDr; TtW

Touch-up Man. Yusef Komunyakaa. SP-KomuY

Touché. Jessie Redmond Fauset. BlSi; CDC; ShDr

Touching/Not Touching: My Mother. Toi Derricotte. GT

Tougaloo Blues. Kelly Norman Ellis. SpiFl

Tough guy / He fondles the public. Invasion. Ishmael Reed. CP-ReedI

Toughest gal I ever did see. Kissie Lee. Margaret Abigail Walker. BlSi; CP-WalkM

Tour 5. Robert Hayden. CP-HaydR

Tour Guide: La Maison des Esclaves. Melvin Dixon. ESEAA

Touring. Audre Lorde. CP-LordA

Toussaint L'Ouverture. Henrietta Cordelia Ray. CBWP-3

Toward lifting them above their crippling storm. (LL) The Elevator Man Adheres to Form. Margaret Else Danner. PoBA

Toward the laughter we no longer. To Mother. Keorapetse W. Kgositsile. GT

Towards a Walk in the Sun. Keorapetse W. Kgositsile. BlFi

Towards the songs' pretended sea. (LL) Legacy. Amiri Baraka. PoBA

Tower. Langston Hughes. CP-HughL

Towhomitmayconcern. Sonia Sanchez. TtW

Town of Scottsboro, The. Langston Hughes. CP-HughL

Toy Poem. Nikki Giovanni. BrTr

Tractor stuck between the strewn or, The. Poem on Bell's Theorem. June Jordan. SP-JordJ

Traditional Post-Modern Neo-HooDoo Afra-Centric Sister in a Purple Head Rag Mourning Death and Cooking. Michélle T. Clinton. SpiFl

Tragedy of Pete, The. Joseph Seamon Cotter, Sr. CDC

Train Runs Late to Harlem, The. Conrad Kent Rivers. IDB; PoBA

Trains in texas grass. (LL) In Texas Grass. Quincy Troupe. GT; NAAAL

Trains ran through the eleven, The. The Dance of the Elephants. Michael S. Harper. SP-HarpM

Trane / must have. The Silent Prophet. Norman Jordan. NBV

Trane, / Trane, / History Love Scream Oh. Am/trak. Amiri Baraka. SP-BaraA

Transcendental Blues Transcendental Blues. Yusef Rahman. BlFi

"Transcendental polygons are the forms of breasts." (LL) Delivered at the Knighting of Lord Durgling by Great Bruce-Jean. Jean Toomer. CP-ToomJ; GT

Transfer. Sterling A. Brown. CP-BrowS; TtW

Transformation. Lewis Alexander. CDC

Transition—S.M, The. Alfred Islay Walden. AAP

Translate this into higher math. The Physics of Loneliness. Al Young. CP-YounA

Translated furies ring. Brother Malcolm's Echo. Keorapetse W. Kgositsile. BrTr

Translating Footsteps. Yusef Komunyakaa. SP-KomuY

Translation. Anne Spencer. BANP

Transplanted southern girls. Phantom Pains. Kelly Norman Ellis. SpiFl

Transport or Slaves From Maryland to Mississippi, The. Rita Dove. SP-DoveR

Traveler, The. Maya Angelou. CP-AngeM; SP-AngeM

Traveling along. Return to English Turn. Tom Dent. BkSV

Traveling through Fog. Robert Hayden. CP-HaydR

Traveller take heed for journeys undertaken in the dark of the year. October Journey. Margaret Abigail Walker. AmNP; CP-WalkM; GT; IDB; PoBA

Travois of the Nameless. Sotère Torregian. NBV

Trays: a Portfolio. Michael S. Harper. SP-HarpM

Treacherous Breast. *African-American Oral Tradition.* GetYo

Treacherous sands had caught our boat, The. A Story of the Rebellion. Frances Ellen Watkins Harper. CP-HarpF

Tread not the earth where lies her youthful form. Mrs. E. Cohrs Brown. Mary Weston Fordham. CBWP-2

Treason? yes, make it treason, if ye will. Warning. Alfred Gibbs Campbell. AAP

Treat me nice, Miss Mandy Jane. A Plea. Paul Laurence Dunbar. CP-DunbP

Treatment for Dance w/ Trick Ending. Ishmael Reed. CP-ReedI

Tree Design, A. Arna Bontemps. CDC

Tree / is a tree, is, A. A Tree Is a Landscape: a Landscape Is a Point of View. Sarah Webster Fabio. TtW

Tree is more than a shadow, A. A Tree Design. Arna Bontemps. CDC

Tree of Knowledge, The. Lizelia Augusta Jenkins Moorer. CBWP-3

Tree Stillness. Karen L. Mitchell. GT

Treehouse, The. James A. Emanuel. AmNP; BPo; BrTr; NNP; PoBA

Trees. Julia Fields. TtW

Trees are laughing, The. Sonia Sanchez. SP-SancS

Trees are never felled ... in summer ... Not when the fruit. A Poem on the Assassination of Robert F. Kennedy. Nikki Giovanni. SP-GiovN

Trees at Night. Helene Johnson. BlSi; ShDr

Trees bend down along the stream, The. A Lazy Day. Paul Laurence Dunbar. CP-DunbP

Trees is bendin' in de sto'm, De. A Plantation Melody. Paul Laurence Dunbar. CP-DunbP

Treetalk and windsong are. Sugarfields. Barbara Mahone. PoBA

Trellie. Lance Jeffers. FB; NBV; TtW

Trembling November winds. Nocturnal Sounds. Kattie M. Cumbo. BlSi

Tremors of your network. These Yet to Be United States. Maya Angelou. CP-AngeM

Trials that the Saviour bore have paved the golden way, The. Benefits of Sorrow. Lizelia Augusta Jenkins Moorer. CBWP-3

Tribal Marks. Saundra Sharp. SpiFl

Tribe surnamed the Arradas, A. His Ancestry. George Clinton Rowe. AAP

Tribute. Eloise Bibb. CBWP-4

Tribute. Countee Cullen. CP-CullC

Tribute. Al Young. CP-YounA

Tribute to a Lost Steamer. Mary Weston Fordham. CBWP-2

Tribute to Capt. F. W. Dawson. Mary Weston Fordham. CBWP-2

Tribute to Robert Hayden. Margaret Abigail Walker. CP-WalkM

Tribute to the Bride and Groom, A. Priscilla Jane Thompson. CBWP-2

Trick / without anyone's, The. Geography of the Near Past. Al Young. CP-YounA

Tricked Again. Ridhiana. NBP

Trifle. Georgia Douglas Johnson. AmNP

Trinity: a Dream Sequence. Naomi Long Madgett. Klds

"Stark day corrodes the silver of the dream."

"You would not recognize yourself if I should tell you."

Trip, Dharma Trip, Sangha Trip, The. Bob Kaufman. SP-KaufB

Trip on the Staten Island Ferry, A. Audre Lorde. CP-LordA; SP-LordA

Trip: San Francisco. Langston Hughes. CP-HughL

Tripart. Gayl Jones. BlSi

Triple Benison, The. Henrietta Cordelia Ray. CBWP-3

Triple Overtime. Lucinda Roy. GT

Triviality, A. Waring Cuney. CDC

Trolley cars was rollin and the passengers all white, The. A Song of Sojourner Truth. June Jordan. SP-JordJ; TtW

Trollop Maiden, The. Audre Lorde. CP-LordA

Tropic green days, red. Height, Breadth, Depth. Kalamu ya Salaam. *Fr. New Orleans Haiku.* SpiFl

Tropics in New York, The. Claude McKay. AfAmPo; AmNP; CrDW; GT; PoBA

("Bananas ripe and green, and ginger-root.") Klds; SP-McKaC

Trouble in de Kitchen. Paul Laurence Dunbar. CP-DunbP

Trouble in mind, I'm blue. Richard M. Jones. NAAAL

Trouble / Mellows to a golden note. (LL) Trumpet Player. Langston Hughes. SP-HughL

Troubled Jesus. Waring Cuney. BANP

Troubled Water. Langston Hughes. CP-HughL

Troubled with the Itch and Rubbing with Sulphur. George Moses Horton. AfAmPo; AAP; SP-HortG

Troubled Woman. Langston Hughes. CP-HughL; SP-HughL

Troy. Wendy L. James. CtF

True American, The. Georgia Douglas Johnson. ShDr

True gut-funky blues to make her really dance, A. (LL) The Reception. June Jordan. SP-JordJ

True Import of Present Dialogue, Black vs. Negro. Nikki Giovanni. BPo; BrTr; Crnst; PoBA

True Love. Waring Cuney. CDC

True Magic, The. Marilyn Nelson. *Fr.* The Plotinus Suite. SP-NelsM

True nature first inspires the man. The Art of a Poet. George Moses Horton. EBAP; SP-HortG

True to our native land. (LL) Lift Ev're Voice and Sing. James Weldon Johnson. AfAmPo; CrDW; NAAAL; TtW

True to your might [*or* Truth to your mighty] winds on dusky shores. On the Death of William Edward Burghardt Du Bois by African Moonlight and Forgotten Shores. Conrad Kent Rivers. NBP; PoBA

True we are two grown men. Ed Roberson. GT

Trumpet Player. Langston Hughes. CP-HughL; SP-HughL

Trumpeter, The. George Barlow. *Fr.* Gabriel. TtW

Trunks clunk together behind me and Dora. To San Fransisco. Marilyn Nelson. *Fr.* The Plotinus Suite. SP-NelsM

Trunks of secret words / I CRY. (LL) When you come to me, unbidden. Maya Angelou. CP-AngeM; SP-AngeM

Trussy's Visit. Elliot B. Henderson. EBAP

Trust thrust first tinder kindling grown. Burnt Sienna. Norman Henry, II Pritchard. GT

Truth. Gwendolyn Brooks. SP-BrooG

Truth. Frances Ellen Watkins Harper. CP-HarpF

Truth. Josephine D. Henderson Heard. CBWP-4

Truth, The. Ted Joans. AmNP
   (Voice in the Crowd.) Klds

Truth. Claude McKay. BPo; SP-McKaC

Truth is, I envy them. Tornados. Thylias Moss. GT

Truth Suppressed, The. Lizelia Augusta Jenkins Moorer. CBWP-3

Try them and weigh me, whate'er be my due! (LL) Equipment. Paul Laurence Dunbar. CP-DunbP

Try to avoid inhaling the laden air. (LL) The Lovers of the Poor. Gwendolyn Brooks. ESEAA; NAAAL; SP-BrooG; SSLK

Trying to be white. (LL) The Way It Was. Lucille Clifton. SP-ClifL

Trying to become one with the god's. (LL) Carnival. Primus St. John. GT

Trying to Capture Rapture. June Jordan. SP-JordJ

Trying to make / Trouble. (LL) The Rebel. Mari E. Evans. AmNP; IDB; PoBA

Trying to see you. Therapy. Audre Lorde. CP-LordA

Tryst, The. Paul Laurence Dunbar. CP-DunbP

Tryst, The. Mary E. Tucker. CBWP-1

Tshew! Tshew The kid's got a toy man whose limbs. Woman Kills and Eats Own Infant. Marilyn Nelson. SP-NelsM

Tu / cson's of blackmens. Ron Welburn. NBV

Tu Do Street. Yusef Komunyakaa. SP-KomuY; TtW

Tuesdays all his kids would be out. No Trespassing. Al Young. CP-YounA

Tulips from Their Blood. Edwin Brooks. NBP

Tune. Al Young. CP-YounA

Tunnels. Yusef Komunyakaa. SP-KomuY; TtW

Turf Song. Sterling Plumpp. GT

Turk. Sam Cornish. BlFi

Turn Around Y36, The. Amiri Baraka. SP-BaraA

Turn Me to My Yellow Leaves. William Stanley Braithwaite. BANP; NAAAL

Turn my daughters, full of wo. Ruth and Naomi. Frances Ellen Watkins Harper. CP-HarpF

Turncoat, The. Priscilla Jane Thompson. CBWP-2

Turning (I Need a Better Title). Nikki Giovanni. SP-GiovN

Turning into my own. Lucille Clifton. SP-ClifL

Turning of the Babies in the Bed, The. Paul Laurence Dunbar. CP-DunbP

Turning Pro. Ishmael Reed. CP-ReedI

Turning Screw: In wave-guide. Rock Me, Baby. Ishmael Reed. CP-ReedI

Turning Thirty, I Contemplate Students Bicycling Home. Rita Dove. ESEAA

Turtle's Song, The. *Unknown.* BPo

Tuskegee. Leslie Pinckney Hill. BANP

Tuskegee Airfield, *for the Tuskegee Airmen.* Marilyn Nelson. ESEAA; GT; SP-NelsM

Tuskegee Song. Paul Laurence Dunbar. CP-DunbP

Tuskegee, thou pride of the swift growing South. Tuskegee Song. Paul Laurence Dunbar. CP-DunbP

Tuskegee, Tuskegee! Lance Jeffers. BkSV

Tutti Colori Quality of Light, The. Al Young. CP-YounA

'Twas a cloudless morn and the sun shone bright. The Cherokee. Mary Weston Fordham. CBWP-2

'Twas a fearful night—the tempest raved. Death of the Old Sea King. Frances Ellen Watkins Harper. CP-HarpF; EBAP

'Twas a night of dreadful horror. The Night of Death. Frances Ellen Watkins Harper. CP-HarpF

'Twas but a word, a careless word. The Careless Word. Frances Ellen Watkins Harper. CP-HarpF

'Twas eve, ah fatal eve! and no one near. Albery Allson Whitman. *Fr.* Leelah Misled. EBAP

'Twas eve, and far and near deep quiet reigned. Albery Allson Whitman. *Fr.* Leelah Misled. EBAP

'Twas eve, and there no parent's eye could see. Albery Allson Whitman. *Fr.* Leelah Misled. EBAP

'Twas eve in sunny Italy. A Tale of Italy. Eloise Bibb. CBWP-4

'Twas mercy brought me from my *Pagan* land. On Being Brought from Africa to America. Phillis Wheatley. AfAmPo; BALP; CP-WheaP; CrDW; EBAP; Klds; NAAAL; TtW

'Twas on a glorious summer eve. The Angel's Visit. Charlotte L. Forten Grimké. AAP

'Twas said by some, that Leelah was too fast. Albery Allson Whitman. *Fr.* Leelah Misled. EBAP

'Twas sunset's hour, the glorious day. The Exile's Reverie. Mary Weston Fordham. CBWP-2

'Twas the angel of death that to us downward flew. In Memoriam of E. B. Clark. Lizelia Augusta Jenkins Moorer. CBWP-3

'Twas the angel of Eden, to Adam he said. Dedication Day Poem. Lizelia Augusta Jenkins Moorer. CBWP-3

'Twas the apple that in Eden. The Unlucky Apple. Paul Laurence Dunbar. CP-DunbP

'Twas three an' thirty year ago. The Rivals. Paul Laurence Dunbar. CP-DunbP

'Twas when the Proclamation came. Bartow Black. Timothy Thomas Fortune. AAP

Twasinta's Seminoles; Or Rape of Florida. Albery Allson Whitman.
  Canto I
    "Come now, my love, the moon is on the take." AAP; AfAmPo
    "Poet hath a realm within, and throne, The." AAP; AfAmPo; EBAP
    "Upon the shells by Carribea's wave." AAP
    "Oh! sing it in the light of freedom's morn." AfAmPo; EBAP
  Canto II
    "Dark rose the walls, a church and prison joined." AAP
    "I never was a slave—a robber took." AAP; AdAmPo, *st.* VII *and* VIII only.
    "Is manhood less because man's face is black?" AAP
    "'T is hard to judge if hatred of one's race." AfAmPo
    "Thus, San Augustine's church and prison joined." AAP
  Canto IV
    "Hail! home of exiles and Seminoles!" AAP
    "Thus ends my lay: Reluctantly I leave." AAP
    "We leave theee with thy guests, thou sunny maid!" AAP

Twelfth of May was one hell of a day, The. Titanic: "Twelfth of May was one hell of a day, The." *African-American Oral Tradition.* GetYo

Twell de Night Is Pas'. Paul Laurence Dunbar. CP-DunbP

Twelve Gates. Lorenzo Thomas. BlFi

12 Gates to the City. Nikki Giovanni. PoBA

Twelve years to the day. Anniversary. Rita Dove. SP-DoveR

24th Avenue: City of Roses: Anesthesia: 2. Michael S. Harper. SP-HarpM

26th Person, The. Dolores Kendrick. GT

Twenty Grand (Saturday Night on the Block), The. Naomi Long Madgett. NBV

XXI. Essex Hemphill. NAAAL

XXII. Essex Hemphill. NAAAL

XXIV. Essex Hemphill. NAAAL

Twenty-one years of my life you have been. February 13, 1980. Lucille Clifton. SP-ClifL

Twenty-Six Ways of Looking at a Blackman. Raymond R. Patterson. ESEAA

Twenty-Two-Twenty told Automatic Jim to tell his fast-fucking sister Fanny. *African-American Oral Tradition.* GetYo

Twenty-Year Marriage. Ai. GT

Twilight. Paul Laurence Dunbar. CP-DunbP

Twilight—and you. El Beso. Angelina Weld Grimké. ShDr

Twilight glitters on the fragmented glass. Judeebug's Country. Joe Johnson. PoBA

Twilight Hour, The. Joshua McCarter Simpson. AAP

Twilight Musings. Mary Weston Fordham. CBWP-2

Twilight Reverie. Langston Hughes. *Fr.* Seven Moments of Love. CP-HughL

'Twill hope and fear, this condition's a war. Albery Allson Whitman. *Fr.* Leelah Misled. EBAP

Twin stars through my purpling pane. Dusk. Angelina Weld Grimké. CDC; ShDr

Twirls on the tips of a carnation. The Oriental Ballerina. Rita Dove. NAAAL; SP-DoveR

Twist the thread. Marilyn Nelson. SP-NelsM

Twisted and strange. Sailing Date. Langston Hughes. CP-HughL

Twister to Magnum. Citizen CB. Al Young. CP-YounA

Twitching in the cactus. Deathwatch. Michael S. Harper. NAAAL; PoBA; SP-HarpM

'Twixt a smile and a tear. Twilight. Paul Laurence Dunbar. CP-DunbP

Two A.M. Al Young. CP-YounA

Two-an'-Six. Claude McKay. BANP

2 and 2 are 4. Problems. Langston Hughes. CP-HughL

Two bad actors canonized by ballads. Villon/Leadbelly. Yusef Komunyakaa. SP-KomuY; TtW

Two days of listening to a police radio. Connections. Stephen Dobyns. SP-DoveR

Two Dedications. Gwendolyn Brooks. *See* The Chicago Picasso.

Two Dreams (for M. L. K.'s one). Clarence Franklin. BlFi

Two Egyptian Portrait Masks. Robert Hayden. CP-HaydR

Two Fishing Villages. Ellease Southerland. GT

Two-Gun Buster and Trigger Slim. Margaret Abigail Walker. CP-WalkM

Two-Gun Buster was a railroad han'. Two-Gun Buster and Trigger Slim. Margaret Abigail Walker. CP-WalkM

Two hours I've walked. Haiku. Etheridge Knight. SP-KnigE

Two Jazz Poems. Carl Wendell, Jr. Hines. Klds

  "There he stands, see?"

  "Yeah here am i / am standing."

Two Ladies Bidding Us "Good Morning." James P. Vaughn. NNP

2 lbs bananas. A Dance for Li Po. Al Young. CP-YounA

Two Lean Cats. Myron O'Higgins. PoBA

Two liddle niggers all dressed in white. Raise a "Rucus" To-Night. *Unknown.* BPo

Two little boots all rough an' wo'. Paul Laurence Dunbar. CP-DunbP

Two little children sit by my side. Mother's Treasures. Frances Ellen Watkins Harper. CP-HarpF

Two Mornings. Lawrence McGaugh. PoBA

Two Musicians, The. Henrietta Cordelia Ray. CBWP-3

Two or three things in the past. Dancer. Langston Hughes. *Fr.* Montage of a Dream Deferred. CP-HughL

2 Poems for Black Relocation Centers. Etheridge Knight. BrTr

Two Poems for Black Relocation Centers. Etheridge Knight. ESEAA

  "Dead. He died in Detroit, his beard." BrTr

  "Flukum couldn't stand the strain. Flukum." BrTr

  Poem for Black Relocation Centers, A.

Two Poems (from "Sketches from a Black-Nappy-Headed Poet"). Haki R. Madhubuti. BrTr

  "I ain't seen no poems stop a .38."

  "Last week / my mother died."

Two Poems, I. Robert J. Abrams. NNP

Two Poems, II. Robert J. Abrams. NNP

Two Points of View. Lucian B. Watkins. BANP

Two Questions. William Stanley Braithwaite. BALP

Two shining women. Angels. Lucille Clifton. SP-ClifL

Two Somewhat Different Epigrams. Langston Hughes. CP-HughL; Klds

  "I look with awe upon the human race."

  "Oh, God of dust and rainbows, help us see."

Two Songs. Paul Laurence Dunbar. CP-DunbP

Two strings, one pierced cry. Variation on Pain. Rita Dove. SP-DoveR

2 takes from *Love in Los Angeles.* Al Young. CP-YounA

Two things possess the power. Langston Hughes. CP-HughL

Two Thoughts of Death. Countee Cullen. CP-CullC

Two trees breathe. Some Hands Are Lovelier. Mae V. Cowdery. ShDr

Two undertaking parlors on this street. The House of Prayer. Margaret Abigail Walker. CP-WalkM

Two Who Crossed a Line (She Crosses). Countee Cullen. CP-CullC

Two Who Crossed a Line. Countee Cullen. CP-CullC

Two women in their twenties do a drunken. A Quality of Light. Yusef Komunyakaa. SP-KomuY

Two women on the lone wet strand. The Watchers. William Stanley Braithwaite. NAAAL

Two-year-old boy, A. This Is My Son's Song: *"Ungie, Hi Ungie".* Michael S. Harper. SP-HarpM

Tyrone (1). Lucille Clifton. SP-ClifL

Tyrone (2). Lucille Clifton. SP-ClifL

Tyrone (3). Lucille Clifton. SP-ClifL

Tyrone (4). Lucille Clifton. SP-ClifL

Tyrone married her this afternoon. The Wedding. June Jordan. SP-JordJ

Tyson's Corner. Primus St. John. PoBA

U

U bet u wer. To a Poet I Knew. Jewel C. Latimore. PoBA

U feel that way sometimes. Mixed Sketches. Don L. Lee. BPo

U feel that way sometimes. Mixed Sketches. Haki R. Madhubuti. BrTr

U.N.I.T.Y. Queen Latifah. Crnst

U Name This One. Carolyn M. Rodgers. BlSi; PoBA

U. S. 1946 King's X. Robert Frost. CrDW

U worry me whoever u are. Ishmael Reed. *See* Badman of the Guest Professor.

Ugliest little boy / that everyone ever saw. The Life of Lincoln West. Gwendolyn Brooks. BrTr; FB

Uh! I sho am tired. Broke. Langston Hughes. CP-HughL

Uhmmmmmm somebody's tellin me. Capitalism Is a Brutal Motherfucker. Tony Medina. CtF

Uhuru (freedom. now. swahili. east african lango). Ahmed Legraham Alhamisi. BlFi

Uhuru in the O.R. June Jordan. SP-JordJ

Ultimatum. Countee Cullen. CP-CullC

Ultimatum. Langston Hughes. SP-HughL *Fr.* Montage of a Dream Deferred. CP-HughL

Ultimatum: Kid to Kid. Langston Hughes. CP-HughL

Ulysses "Religion." Gwendolyn Brooks. TtW

Un-American Investigators. Langston Hughes. BPo; CP-HughL

Un Frère au Tombeau de Son Frère. Armand Lanusse. EBAP; TtW

Unable to sleep, or pray, I stand. Ice Storm. Robert Hayden. CP-HaydR; ESEAA

Unanimity Has Been Achieved, Not a Dot Less for Its Accidentalness. Bob Kaufman. NAAAL

Unasked and unheeded. (LL) Awaking in New York. Maya Angelou. CP-AngeM; SP-AngeM

Unc' Joe, *c'est drôle.* Uncle Joe. Sterling A. Brown. CP-BrowS

Uncle Bull-Boy. June Jordan. PoBA

Uncle Eph—Epicure. James Edwin Campbell. EBAP

Uncle Eph's Banjo Song. James Edwin Campbell. BANP

Uncle Ike's Holiday. Priscilla Jane Thompson. CBWP-2

Uncle Jacob often told us. Church Building. Frances Ellen Watkins Harper. CP-HarpF

Uncle Jim. Countee Cullen. BANP; CP-CullC; GT

Uncle Jimmie's Yarn. Priscilla Jane Thompson. CBWP-2

Uncle Joe. Sterling A. Brown. CP-BrowS

Uncle John, he makes me tired. A Confidence. Paul Laurence Dunbar. CP-DunbP

Uncle Ned an' de Mockin' Bird. Elliot B. Henderson. EBAP

Uncle Rube on the Race Problem. Clara Ann Thompson. CBWP-2

Uncle Rube to the Young People. Clara Ann Thompson. CBWP-2

Uncle Rube's Defense. Clara Ann Thompson. CBWP-2

Uncle Rufus. Melvin B. Tolson. TtW

Uncle Sam— / And old Jim Crow. Crow Goes, Too. Langston Hughes. CP-HughL

Uncle Sam / With old Jim Crow. Poem to Uncle Sam. Langston Hughes. CP-HughL

Uncle Tom. Langston Hughes. SP-HughL

  ("Within— / The beaten pride.") CP-HughL

Uncle Tom is a legend and a dream. Langston Hughes. CP-HughL

Uncle Tom, / When he was alive. Epitaph: "Uncle Tom, / When he was alive." Langston Hughes. CP-HughL

Under a burning tropic sun. The Color Sergeant. James Weldon Johnson. GT

Under a covering cloud / of my tears. (LL) And Don't Think I Won't Be Waiting. Audre Lorde. CP-LordA; SP-LordA

Under each man's eyelid. (LL) Camouflaging the Chimera. Yusef Komunyakaa. SP-KomuY

Under its cloak of lies. (LL) Summer Oracle. Audre Lorde. BlSi; CP-LordA; PoBA; SP-LordA

Under moon shadows. Haiku: "Under moon shadows." Etheridge Knight. ESEAA; TtW

Under my window. Letter in Winter. Raymond R. Patterson. PoBA

Under the Edge of February. Jayne Cortez. BlSi

Under the hemlocks Fancy came. On the Concord River. Henrietta Cordelia Ray. CBWP-3

Under the Oak Table. Colleen J. McElroy. GT

Under the Protestant gaze of society. Van/Dyke. Robert Farr. SpiFl

Under the urination of astronauts. Everything Is Wonderful. Jayne Cortez. SP-CortJ

Under the Viaduct, 1932. Rita Dove. SP-DoveR

Under the white man's menace, out of time. (LL) Outcast. Claude McKay. NAAAL; SP-McKaC

Under Weight Champion, The. Bob Kaufman. SP-KaufB

Underground, The. Langston Hughes. CP-HughL

Underneath the autumn sky. The Veteran. Paul Laurence Dunbar. CP-DunbP

Undertaker's Daughter Feels Neglect, The. Thylias Moss. ESEAA

Undertow. Langston Hughes. CP-HughL

Unemployment Monologue. June Jordan. SP-JordJ

Unequalled on the rack. (LL) A Kind of Love, Some Say. Maya Angelou. CP-AngeM; SP-AngeM

Unexpressed. Paul Laurence Dunbar. CP-DunbP

Unhelped, unhindered / On his own. (LL) Revelations. Sterling A. Brown. CP-BrowS; Klds

Unhistorical Events. Bob Kaufman. SP-KaufB

Unidentified Flying Object. Robert Hayden. CP-HaydR

Union. Langston Hughes. CP-HughL

Union Apprehended. Marilyn Nelson. Fr. The Plotinus Suite. SP-NelsM

Union of Parties, The. George Moses Horton. SP-HortG

Union of Two, The. Haki R. Madhubuti. SpiFl

Unite, ne'er more (rapt thought) to say "farewell!" (LL) On Parting with a Friend. Mary Weston Fordham. CBWP-2

Universality. Nikki Giovanni. SP-GiovN

Unlearned depths of me, The. (LL) Review from Staten Island. Gloria C. Oden. GT; Klds

Unless you remind me. Pavlov. Naomi Long Madgett. BPo

Unlucky Apple, The. Paul Laurence Dunbar. CP-DunbP

Unmeasured Tempo. Maya Angelou. CP-AngeM; SP-AngeM

Unnatural State of the Unicorn. Yusef Komunyakaa. SP-KomuY

Unraveling Ravel is no longer a secret. Ravel: Bolero. Al Young. SpiFl

Unrestricted / unrestrained / uncomprimising. Freedom Hair. Raymond Washington. NBV

Unromantic Awakening, An. Priscilla Jane Thompson. CBWP-2

Unsung Heroes, The. Paul Laurence Dunbar. BPo; CP-DunbP

Unsuspecting. Jean Toomer. CP-ToomJ

Until the crumpets and the christians. Jesus, The. Langston Hughes. CP-HughL

Until the storm passes over? (LL) Conversations in Crisis. Audre Lorde. CP-LordA; SP-LordA

Until They Have Stopped. Sarah E. Wright. PoBA

Untitle. Kuwasi Balagon. BlFi

Untitled I. Ishmael Reed. CP-ReedI

Untitled II. Ishmael Reed. CP-ReedI

Untitled III. Ishmael Reed. CP-ReedI

Untitled IV. Ishmael Reed. CP-ReedI

Untitled: "Alaska's rape." Ishmael Reed. CP-ReedI

Untitled: "I know of a man who treated his body like a dog." Ishmael Reed. CP-ReedI

Untitled: "Law isn't all." Ishmael Reed. CP-ReedI

Untitled: "Today I feel bearish." Ishmael Reed. CP-ReedI

Untitled: "When California is split in two." Ishmael Reed. CP-ReedI

Untitled Blues. Yusef Komunyakaa. ESEAA; GT; SP-KomuY

Untitled Requiem for Tomorrow. Conyus. PoBA

Unuttered Prayer. Josephine D. Henderson Heard. CBWP-4

Up-Beat. Langston Hughes. SP-HughL Fr. Montage of a Dream Deferred. CP-HughL

Up / from Msippi I grew. Son of Msippi. Henry L. Dumas. TtW

Up in the sky. Song of Tom. Kirk Hall. BlFi

Up in this warm, solid house of yours. East Boston. Al Young. CP-YounA

Up into the silent air / is to awaken. (LL) Loneliness. Al Young. CP-YounA; PoBA

Up Sister. Ruth Forman. IHS

Up the hillside beyond the road's. Glimpses. Christopher Gilbert. GT

Up the road. Apple Core. Clarence Major. GT

Up the shaken stairway. Poem about the Head of a Negro. June Jordan. TtW

Up to those heights where angels rest. The Perfect Orchestra. Henrietta Cordelia Ray. CBWP-3

Upon his dull ear fell the stern command. The Black Draftee from Dixie. Carrie Williams Clifford. BlSi

Upon Leaving the Parole Board Hearing. Conyus. GT; PoBA

Upon Meeting Don L. Lee, in a Dream. Rita Dove. SP-DoveR

Upon Receipt of a Pound of Coffee in 1863. Mary E. Tucker. CBWP-1

Upon the flood of praise! (LL) Praise of Creation. George Moses Horton. AAP; SP-HortG

Upon the future life we build. Timothy Thomas Fortune. AAP

Upon the grass. Noontide. Henrietta Cordelia Ray. Fr. Idyl. EBAP

Upon the seas of Crumbling Servitude. Mississippi Concerto. Rolland Snellings. BlFi

Upon the shells by Carribea's wave. Albery Allson Whitman. AAP Fr. Twasinta's Seminoles; Or Rape of Florida

"Oh! sing it in the light of freedom's moon." AfAmPo; EBAP

Upon thy purple may thy body bare. Flirtation. Claude McKay. SP-McKaC

Upon Your Leaving. Etheridge Knight. GT; SP-KnigE

Upper Marlboro. Kenneth Carroll. SpiFl

Upright abutment in the mouth, An. Making Love to Concrete. Audre Lorde. CP-LordA

Ups on the Farm. African-American Oral Tradition. GetYo

Upstairs on the third floor. Bottled [New York]. Helene Johnson. BlSi; CDC; PoBA; ShDr

Upstate. Derek Walcott. GT

Uptown on Lenox Avenue. Prime. Langston Hughes. CP-HughL; PoBA

Upward is this Actuality. Jean Toomer. CP-ToomJ

Ur ol' Hyar lib in ur house on de hill. Ol' Doc' Hyar. James Edwin Campbell. AAP; AfAmPo; BANP; EBAP; TtW

Uranne. Mary Weston Fordham. CBWP-2

Urban Dream. Victor Hernandez Cruz. NBP; NBV

Us. Julius Lester. PoBA

US and the USSR, The. Thanks to Jesse Jackson. Audre Lorde. CP-LordA

Us: Colored. Langston Hughes. CP-HughL

Us po' Black boys. Window Shopping. Lamont B. Steptoe. SpiFl

Use the muscle / in yr heart. (LL) Young Soul. Amiri Baraka. BPo

Used to be / the circus was for rich kids. Big Apple Circus. Audre Lorde. CP-LordA

Used to identify with my father first making me want to be a. The Problem of Identity. Al Young. CP-YounA

Using an old water-stained. The Thorn Merchant's Son. Yusef Komunyakaa. SP-KomuY

Usual is there, The. Landscape with Saxophonist. Thylias Moss. ESEAA

Usually at the helipad. Prisoners. Yusef Komunyakaa. SP-KomuY

Utility Room. Michael S. Harper. SP-HarpM

Utopia. Jewel C. Latimore. BPo

V

V. N. and C. I, The. Maggie Pogue Johnson. CBWP-4

Vacant Lot, The. Gwendolyn Brooks. Fr. A Street in Bronzeville. BPo; BlSi; NAAAL; SP-BrooG

Vacation. Rita Dove. SpiFl

Vachel Lindsay Fault, The. Ishmael Reed. CP-ReedI

Vagabonds. Langston Hughes. CP-HughL; SP-HughL

Vagrants. Paul Laurence Dunbar. CP-DunbP

Vague Opening. Jean Toomer. CP-ToomJ

Valentine, The. Mary Weston Fordham. CBWP-2

Valentine, A. Priscilla Jane Thompson. CBWP-2

Valentines. Henry L. Dumas. IHS

Valéry as Dictator. Amiri Baraka. SP-BaraA

Valley floors. A Collage for Richard Davis—Two Short Forms. De Leon Harrison. PoBA

Valse, The. Paul Laurence Dunbar. CP-DunbP

Vamp. Ishmael Reed. CP-ReedI

Vampire outlaw of the milky way. (LL) I Am a Cowboy in the Boat of Ra. Ishmael Reed. CP-ReedI; ESEAA; NAAAL; NBP; PoBA; TtW

Van Gogh would paint the landscape. In Hayden's Collage. Michael S. Harper. ESEAA; NAAAL

Van/Dyke. Robert Farr. SpiFl

Vari-Colored Song. Langston Hughes. CP-HughL

Variation on Gaining a Son. Rita Dove. SP-DoveR

Variation on Guilt. Rita Dove. SP-DoveR

Variation on Pain. Rita Dove. SP-DoveR

Variations on a Theme. Countee Cullen. CP-CullC

Variations on a theme by morning. Cocoa Morning. Bob Kaufman. AmNP; NBV; SP-KaufB

Various Protestations From Various People. Etheridge Knight. SP-KnigE

Vashti. Frances Ellen Watkins Harper. AAP; BlSi; EBAP

("But would not bow to shame.") (LL) CP-HarpF; NAAAL; TtW

Vaticide. Myron O'Higgins. IDB; PoBA

Vegetables are walking, The. (LL) Onion Bucket. Lorenzo Thomas. BlFi; GT; TtW

Veil of death hath fallen, The. To a Deceased Friend. Priscilla Jane Thompson. CBWP-2

Venereal moon / draws six women, The. Clark's Way Out West: Another Version. Michael S. Harper. SP-HarpM

Venetia. Adah Isaacs Menken. CBWP-1

Vengeance is Sweet. Paul Laurence Dunbar. CP-DunbP

Venus Hottentot. Elizabeth Alexander. ESEAA

Venus of Milo, The. Henrietta Cordelia Ray. CBWP-3

Venusburg, The. George Marion McClellan. Fr. The Legend of Tannhauser and Elizabeth. EBAP

Veracruz. Robert Hayden. Fr. An Inference of Mexico. AmNP; CP-HaydR

Veronica passes her cape between breath. For the Walking Dead. Yusef Komunyakaa. SP-KomuY

Verse, as a form, is artificial. Gatsby's Theory of Aesthetics. Amiri Baraka. SP-BaraA

Verse for Ronald Slapjack Who Publicly Declared, "I, Too, Am a Contra!" June Jordan. SP-JordJ

Verses to my Heart's-Sister. Henrietta Cordelia Ray. AAP; CBWP-3

(Verse to My Heart's-Sister.) AfAmPo

Very acme of my woe, The. Little Son. Georgia Douglas Johnson. CDC

Very due that being each one dwells. The Narrow Path. Norman Henry, II Pritchard. GT

Very fine conga of sweat, A. I See Chano Pozo. Jayne Cortez. SP-CortJ

Very friendly / prison, A. Tripart. Gayl Jones. BlSi

Very often when you are striving. The Would-be Critic. Mrs. Henry Linden. CBWP-4

Very proud / he barely asked directions. The Black Prince. Alice Walker. CP-WalkA

Very Simple Wish, A. Nikki Giovanni. SP-GiovN

Very soon the Yankee teachers. Learning to Read. Frances Ellen Watkins Harper. AAP; AfAmPo; BlSi; CP-HarpF; EBAP; NAAAL

Vestal Virgin, The. Eloise Bibb. CBWP-4

Veteran, The. Paul Laurence Dunbar. CP-DunbP

Vet's Rehabilitation. Ray Durem. PoBA

Vice. Amiri Baraka. SP-BaraA

Victor Garibaldi. Melvin B. Tolson. GT

Vietnam. Clarence Major. PoBA

Vietnam Addenda. Audre Lorde. SP-LordA

(Veit-Nam Addenda.) CP-LordA

Vietnam #4. Clarence Major. NBV; PoBA

Vietnam: I Need More Than This Crust of Salt. Lance Jeffers. BrTr

View from Rosehill Cemetery: Vicksburg. Alice Walker. CP-WalkA

View from the Corner. Samuel Allen. BrTr; SSLK

View of the Library of Congress from Paul Laurence Dunbar High School, for Doris Craig and Michael Olshausen. Thomas Sayers Ellis. GT

Vigil. Audre Lorde. CP-LordA

Village Blues. Michael S. Harper. SP-HarpM

Village Life, A, (for John Robertson). Derek Walcott. GT

Villages of high quality. Remember Mexico. Michael S. Harper. ESEAA; SP-HarpM

Villain shows his indiscretion. Curtain. Paul Laurence Dunbar. CP-DunbP

Villain skips, and all are happy. (LL) Curtain. Paul Laurence Dunbar. CP-DunbP

Villon/Leadbelly. Yusef Komunyakaa. SP-KomuY; TtW

Vincent Ogé. George Boyer Vashon. EBAP

"There is, at times, an evenin sky."

Viney, go put on de kittle, I got one o' mastah's chickens. (LL) Accountability. Paul Laurence Dunbar. CP-DunbP

Vineyard of My Beloved, The. Priscilla Jane Thompson. AAP; CBWP-2

Violent Space, The. Etheridge Knight. BPo; SP-KnigE

("But the air can not stand my singing long.") (LL) BrTr

Violet wash is streaked across the clouds, A. Dinosaur Spring. Marilyn Nelson. SP-NelsM

Virgin of the vestal flame. The Vestal Virgin. Eloise Bibb. CBWP-4

Virginia. Elouise Loftin. PoBA

Virginia Portrait. Sterling A. Brown. CP-BrowS; GT

Virginia Reel, A. Paul Laurence Dunbar. CP-DunbP

Vision, The. John Boyd. EBAP

Vision from the Ghetto. Raymond Washington. NBV

Vision of Eve, The. Henrietta Cordelia Ray. CBWP-3

Vision of Moonlight, A. Henrietta Cordelia Ray. CBWP-3

Vision of the Czar of Russia, The. Frances Ellen Watkins Harper. CP-HarpF

Visions ... Leaders. Clarence Franklin. BlFi

Visions of beauty, of light, and of love. Dreams of Beauty. Adah Isaacs Menken. CBWP-1

Visions of the Sea. Kiarri T-H Cheatwood. TtW

Visit. Gerald William Barrax. GT

Visit to a City Out of Time. Audre Lorde. See St. Louis Out of Time.

Visit to a Small College. Ishmael Reed. CP-ReedI

Visit to Gettysburg, A. Lucille Clifton. SP-ClifL

Visitation, The. Sun-Ra. BlFi

Visiting Day. Al Young. CP-YounA

Visiting hours are over. Open Heart. Sekou Sundiata. SpiFl

Visitor, The. Paul Laurence Dunbar. CP-DunbP

Visitors to the Black Belt. Langston Hughes. CP-HughL

Vive Noir! Mari E. Evans. NBV; PoBA

Vivid grass with visible delight, The. The Castaways. Claude McKay. SP-McKaC

Vivisection is up to date. Ape-Gods. Marilyn Nelson. SP-NelsM

Voice grows thicker. Drunkard. Langston Hughes. Fr. Montage of a Dream Deferred. CP-HughL

Voice in the Crowd. Ted Joans. See The Truth.

Voice of the Banjo, The. Paul Laurence Dunbar. CP-DunbP

Voice of the Negro, The. Lizelia Augusta Jenkins Moorer. CBWP-3

Voices crying in the wilderness. To Certain Negro Leaders. Langston Hughes. CP-HughL

Voices of the Rain. Henrietta Cordelia Ray. CBWP-3

Voodoo on the Un-Assing of Janis Joplin. Carolyn M. Rodgers. JB

Voodoo Queen, The. African-American Oral Tradition. GetYo

Vor cosma saga. Sound Poem (II). Jean Toomer. CP-ToomJ

Votaries know. A Poem for Integration. Alvin Saxon. PoBA

Voyage of Jimmy Poo, The. James A. Emanuel. AmNP; NNP

Voyage through death / to life upon these shores. (LL) Middle Passage. Robert Hayden. AmNP; BPo; CP-HaydR; IDB; NAAAL; PoBA

Voyager now, on a ship of night. Night Sung Sailor's Prayer. Bob Kaufman. SP-KaufB

Voyager, wanderer of the heart. Plea. Bob Kaufman. SP-KaufB

Vultures waft circles. Remnant Ghosts at Dawn. Oliver La Grone. FB; NBV

VW needs serious transmission work, The. January. Al Young. CP-YounA

W

W. H. Auden & Mantan Moreland. Al Young. CP-YounA

W. W. Amiri Baraka. NBP; PoBA

Wade in the water, children. God's A-Gonna Trouble the Water. Unknown. NAAAL

Wadin' in de Crick. Paul Laurence Dunbar. CP-DunbP

Wah-dah do, wah-dah-do. It Don't Mean a Thing (If It Ain't Got That Swing). Unknown. NAAAL

Wail of the Divorced. Mary E. Tucker. CBWP-1

Wait. Langston Hughes. CP-HughL

Waitin on Summer. Ruth Forman. SpiFl

Waiting. Paul Laurence Dunbar. CP-DunbP

Waiting. Bob Kaufman. SP-KaufB

Wake. Langston Hughes. CP-HughL; SP-HughL

Wake Cry. Waring Cuney. BANP

Wake not again the cannon's thundrous voice. Lines. Alfred Gibbs Campbell. AAP

Wake up Mister Morning. Telly Boob-Tube on the Idiot Box. Margaret Abigail Walker. CP-WalkM

Wake-up Niggers. Don L. Lee. PoBA

Waking Up in Santa Cruz at Sea. Al Young. CP-YounA

Walk. Frank Horne. BPo

Walk back eating peach seeds. Does the Secret Mind Whisper? Bob Kaufman. SP-KaufB

Walk in the Daytime Is Just as Dangerous as a Walk in the Night, A. E. Ethelbert Miller. TtW

Walk out into your country. Who Shall Die. James A., Jr. Randall. BPo; BrTr

"Walk right in, Brother Wilson—how you feelin' today?" The Rain Song. Alex Rogers. BANP

Walk this mile in silence. Pastourelle. Donald Jeffrey Hayes. AmNP

Walk Together Children. *Unknown*. BPo; NAAAL

Walk with de Mayor of Harlem. David Henderson. PoBA

Walk with the sun. Dream Song. Lewis Alexander. PoBA

Walker. Alice Walker. CP-WalkA

Walkers with the Dawn. Langston Hughes. CP-HughL

Walking backwards along shore. I Am Open. Michael Datcher. CtF

Walking down park. Nikki Giovanni. SP-GiovN

Walking east on 125th street. Ray Johnson. BlFi

Walking Hot Seasons. Bob Kaufman. SP-KaufB

Walking Our Boundaries. Audre Lorde. CP-LordA

Walking Parker Home. Bob Kaufman. NAAAL; PoBA; SP-KaufB

Walking through life's dusty highways. Lessons of the Street. Frances Ellen Watkins Harper. CP-HarpF

Wall, The. Gwendolyn Brooks. PoBA

Wall, The. Haki R. Madhubuti. BrTr

Walls. Langston Hughes. CP-HughL

Walls exploding with shabby tutus, The. (LL) The Oriental Ballerina. Rita Dove. NAAAL; SP-DoveR

Walls of Jericho, The. Blanche Taylor Dickinson. CDC

Wanderer's Return. Frances Ellen Watkins Harper. CP-HarpF

Wanderer's Trail, The, *see also* All You Tough Guys *and* My Reflection. *African-American Oral Tradition*. GetYo

Wandering in the dusk. Dusk. Langston Hughes. CP-HughL

Wandering Jew, The. Eloise Bibb. CBWP-4

Want. Mae V. Cowdery. ShDr

Want decides, let it be me. (LL) For My Unborn and Wretched Children. Alfred B. Spellman. PoBA

Want of You, The. Angelina Weld Grimké. ShDr

Want to trade me, do you, mistah? Oh, well, now, I reckon not. Dat Ol' Mare o' Mine. Paul Laurence Dunbar. CP-DunbP

Wanted more and cared less. (LL) Prescience. Maya Angelou. CP-AngeM; SP-AngeM

Wanting the shape of lips. (LL) The Scream. May Miller. TtW

Wants my son. White Lady. Lucille Clifton. ESEAA

War. Langston Hughes. CP-HughL

War and Memory. June Jordan. SP-JordJ

War Memoir: Jazz, Don't Listen to It at Your Own Risk. Bob Kaufman. ("And we feel / And live.") (LL) NAAAL
(O-JAZZ-O War Memoir: Jazz, Don't Listen To It At Your Own Risk.) SP-KaufB

War of the Heart, The. Marilyn Nelson. SP-NelsM

War over. Buffalo War. Lucille Clifton. SP-ClifL

War Poem. Amiri Baraka. SP-BaraA

War Stories. Saundra Murray Nettles. IHS

Warden is my shepherd, I shall always want, The. Convict's Prayer. *African-American Oral Tradition*. GetYo

Warden said to me the other day, The. Etheridge Knight. NBV; SP-KnigE

Wardrobe Master of Paradise, The. Ishmael Reed. CP-ReedI

Warm Day in Winter, A. Paul Laurence Dunbar. CP-DunbP

Warning. Alfred Gibbs Campbell. AAP

Warning. Langston Hughes. BPo; CP-HughL
(Roland Hayes Beaten (Georgia: 1942).) SP-HughL

Warning. Langston Hughes. *Fr.* Montage of a Dream Deferred. CP-HughL

Warning. Alice Walker. CP-WalkA

Warning: Augmented. Langston Hughes. SP-HughL *Fr.* Montage of a Dream Deferred. CP-HughL

Warriors Prancing, Women Dancing. Niema Rashidd. NBP

Warrior's Prayer, The. Paul Laurence Dunbar. CP-DunbP

Was born obedient. Robert. Lucille Clifton. SP-ClifL

Was heaven sent. (LL) Little Lyric (of Great Importance). Langston Hughes. CP-HughL; SP-HughL

Was it a blast to the balls dear brother. A Black Poet Leaps to His Death. Etheridge Knight. SP-KnigE

Was it really you all the time? Dream Sequence, Part 9. Naomi Long Madgett. BPo

Was it yesterday. Haiku: "Was it yesterday." Sonia Sanchez. SP-SancS

Was made for / men. (LL) To Bobby Seale. Lucille Clifton. SP-ClifL

Was slipped once more in place. (LL) The Mask. Clarissa Scott Delany. CDC; ShDr; TtW

Was taken and carried to Canada. (LL) Bar[']s Fight[, August 28, 1746]. Lucy Terry. BPo; BlSi; CrDW; EBAP; NAAAL

Was the only thing I had. (LL) Homecoming. Langston Hughes. CP-HughL; SP-HughL

Was you at de hall las' night. Leap Yeah Party, De. Maggie Pogue Johnson. CBWP-4

Was your / love. (LL) To Mother and Steve. Mari E. Evans. BPo; PoBA

Washer-Woman, The. Otto Leland Bohanan. BANP

Washerwoman, The. Mary Weston Fordham. CBWP-2

Washington Square Park and a Game of Chess. Christopher Stanard. SpiFl

WASP Woman Visits a Black Junkie in Prison, A. Etheridge Knight. NBV; SP-KnigE

Wasted flow of water hiding, A. Lonely Woman. Jayne Cortez. NBV

Wasting money & running to the store. Blues in December. Al Young. CP-YounA

Watch out fo the full moon of sonia. Towhomitmayconcern. Sonia Sanchez. TtW

Watch Out, Papa. Langston Hughes. CP-HughL

Watch tower once for pirates. To the Little Front of San Lazaro on the Ocean Front, Havana. Langston Hughes. CP-HughL

Watcher, The. Clara Ann Thompson. CBWP-2

Watchers, The. William Stanley Braithwaite. NAAAL

Water. Jean Toomer. CP-ToomJ

Water bubbles with night larvae. Swamp Rat. Kiarri T-H Cheatwood. TtW

Water Buffalo. Yusef Komunyakaa. SP-KomuY

Water-Front Streets. Langston Hughes. CP-HughL; SP-HughL

Water of Your Bath. Ahmasi. IHS

Waters I'm going to go walking beside, The. The New Mystic. Al Young. CP-YounA

Waters rippled, gleamed and fell, The. At the Cascade. Henrietta Cordelia Ray. CBWP-3

Watsonville after the Quake. Al Young. CP-YounA

Watts. Conrad Kent Rivers. PoBA

Watts. Alvin Saxon. PoBA

Wave of sorrow. Island. Langston Hughes. CP-HughL; SP-HughL

Waves know rocks by foam and recklessness, The. Merl. Jean Toomer. CP-ToomJ; GT

Waves of brooding. (LL) My Arkansas. Maya Angelou. BlSi; CP-AngeM; NAAAL; SP-AngeM

Waves the short two-by-four. Painting Drunken Twilight. George Barlow. GT

Waving to me across the years. (LL) Report from the Skull's Diorama. Yusef Komunyakaa. SP-KomuY

Way around usually ends up being the shortcut. (LL) From Bowling Green. Al Young. CP-YounA; ESEAA

Way down Souf whar de lillies grow. To See Ol' Booker T. Maggie Pogue Johnson. CBWP-4

Way Down South in Dixie. Song for a Dark Girl. Langston Hughes. CDC; CP-HughL; IDB; NAAAL; PoBA; SP-HughL

Way I Feel, The. Nikki Giovanni. SP-GiovN

Way I hear tell Aunt Jennie, The. Caledonia. Colleen J. McElroy. BlSi; NAAAL

Way It Is, The. Jon Goncalves. BlFi

Way It Was, The. Lucille Clifton. SP-ClifL

Way Out West. Amiri Baraka. PoBA; SP-BaraA

Way she played the piano, The. October 23, 1983. June Jordan. SP-JordJ

Way-Side Well, The. Joseph Seamon Cotter, Sr. CDC; TtW

Way the Cards Fall, The. Yusef Komunyakaa. GT; SP-KomuY

Way T'ings Come, De. Paul Laurence Dunbar. CP-DunbP

Ways. Langston Hughes. CP-HughL

Ways o' Men, The. Angelina Weld Grimké. CDC

Wayward Son, The. Mrs. Henry Linden. CBWP-4

Waz, adverse to thinking. No Bargains Today. Peggy Susberry Kenner. JB

We a BadddDDD PEOPLE. Sonia Sanchez. BrTr

We advance! (LL) Dark Symphony. Melvin Beaunearus Tolson. AmNP; BALP; NAAAL

We ain't got nobody. Evolutionary Poem No. 2. Etheridge Knight. SP-KnigE

We ain't got nowheres to run to. (LL) Warden said to me the other day, The. Etheridge Knight. NBV; SP-KnigE

We all start / as a speck. For Two Jameses. Nikki Giovanni. SP-GiovN

We alone can devalue gold. Alice Walker. CP-WalkA

We are all imprisoned *in the castle of our skins*. Poem (For Nina). Nikki Giovanni. SP-GiovN

We are bemoaned, befuddled, bespectacled. For Backwards Buppies. Karen Williams. SpiFl

We are breath of drop of rain. The Gods Wrote. Keorapetse W. Kgositsile. GT

We are children of the sun. Children of the Sun. Fenton Johnson. BANP

We are gatherers. Sonia Sanchez. SP-SancS

We Are Going to Be Here Now. Primus St. John. GT

We are going to do it. A Message All Black People Can Dig. Haki R. Madhubuti. BrTr

We are growing / through dream. (LL) Rites of Passage. Audre Lorde. CP-LordA; SP-LordA

We are not come to wage a strife. The Day-Breakers [or Daybreakers]. Arna Bontemps. AmNP; CDC; IDB; PoBA

We are not lovers. A Poem of Friendship. Nikki Giovanni. IHS; SP-GiovN

We Are Rising. George Clinton Rowe. AAP

We are rising, as a people. Frances Ellen Watkins Harper. CP-HarpF

We are sighing, for time is flying. Class Song of '91. Eloise Bibb. CBWP-4

We are singing for the face of cisco. Songs for the Cisco Kid; or, Singing for the Face. K. Curtis Lyle. PoBA

We are some of us. Wife. Lucille Clifton. SP-ClifL

We are the dead / ones the slow. Old Words. Sonia Sanchez. SP-SancS

We are the desperate. Vagabonds. Langston Hughes. CP-HughL; SP-HughL

We are the music ... we are the song. (LL) Three/Quarters Time. Nikki Giovanni. SP-GiovN

We are the ones we have been waiting for. (LL) Poem for South AFrican Women. June Jordan. SP-JordJ

We are the silent sex. Karma's Footsteps. Mariahadessa "Ekere" Tallie. CtF

We are the war-born. What are we to do? (LL) Sonnet: "Where are we to go when this is done?" Alfred A. Duckett. AmNP; PoBA

We are things of dry hours and the involuntary plan. Kitchenette Building. Gwendolyn Brooks. Fr. A Street in Bronzeville. BPo; BlSi; GT; NAAAL; SP-BrooG

We are two scars on a dead woman's belly. August the 12th. Lucille Clifton. SP-ClifL

We are unfair. We Own the Night. Amiri Baraka. CrDW; PoBA

We are with one another. No Smiles. Frank Lamont Phillips. AmNP

We arrived at my mother's island. Home. Audre Lorde. CP-LordA

We ask for peace. We, at the bound. Surrender. Angelina Weld Grimké. CDC

We Assume: On the Death of Our Son, Reuben Masai Harper. Michael S. Harper. GT; SP-HarpM

We assume / that in 28 hours. We Assume: On the Death of Our Son, Reuben Masai Harper. Michael S. Harper. GT; SP-HarpM

We be. gonna be. Sonia Sanchez. SP-SancS

We blk blues singers. For Walter Washington. Tom Dent. NBV

We buried him high on a windy hill. Death of an Old Seaman. Langston Hughes. CP-HughL

We can stand so much, then doan stan no mo'. (LL) Transfer. Sterling A. Brown. CP-BrowS; TtW

We cannot live / without our lives. (LL) Need: A Chorale for Black Woman Voices. Audre Lorde. CP-LordA; SP-LordA

We caught fireflies. Ruth. Norman J. Loftis. SpiFl

We climb the slopes of life with throbbing heart. Aspiration. Henrietta Cordelia Ray. CBWP-3

We come, but not to celebrate. For the Twenty-Fifth Anniversary of the "Old Folks' Home." Frances Ellen Watkins Harper. CP-HarpF

We could say / it was a saxophone flight. Imagination in Flight: an Improvisational Duet. Harriet Jacobs. SpiFl

We croon, "yeah." (LL) Nigger Song: An Odyssey. Rita Dove. SP-DoveR

We cross the vast divide. Willie Note 9/28/91. Quo Vadis Gex-Breaux. TtW

We cry among the skyscrapers. Afraid. Langston Hughes. CP-HughL

We dance in death's face. Funeraled Fare Well. Kalamu ya Salaam. Fr. New Orleans Haiku. SpiFl

We Dance Like Ella Riffs. Carolyn M. Rodgers. PoBA

We did our living in the kitchen. Still-Life with Woodstove. William W. Cook. SpiFl

We didn't think / nuthin. Poems about Playmates. Ronda M. Davis. JB

We die. The Detached. Maya Angelou. CP-AngeM; SP-AngeM

We do not care. Wisdom and War. Langston Hughes. CP-HughL

We dont drive so long distances are out. No More Doors Tonight. Al Young. CP-YounA

We drank Thunderbird all night. Poem: "We drank Thunderbird all night." James T. Stewart. BlFi

We entered silence / before the clock struck. Suspension. Audre Lorde. CP-LordA; SP-LordA

We exist living dead. The death of. Jacques Wakefield. BlFi

We fail, and white men call us faggots till the end of the earth. (LL) A Poem for Black Hearts. Amiri Baraka. BrTr; IDB; NAAAL; PoBA

We flame the river. Burning the Water Hyacinth. Audre Lorde. CP-LordA

We fly ahead into the past, good, we defeat progress. I Sigh a Marbled Sigh Ah, at Last. Bob Kaufman. SP-KaufB

We forget what is not possible. (LL) Beams. Audre Lorde. CP-LordA; ESEAA

We forgot to clear your grave, so we stood. On the Anniversary Of Your Death. Karen L. Mitchell. GT

We forgot to water the plantain shoots. Solstice. Audre Lorde. CP-LordA

We free singers be. Etheridge Knight. SP-KnigE

We gather where the weeping willow waves. Decoration Day. Josephine D. Henderson Heard. CBWP-4

We gave it life, mahogany hands. Black Spring. Michael S. Harper. SP-HarpM

We go back. Proclamation / From Sleep, Arise. Carolyn M. Rodgers. JB

"We gon have / mo room!" (LL) An Inconvenience. John Raven. BPo

We got crispy chicken. Menu. June Jordan. SP-JordJ

We got to the point of balloons all of us. Newport Jazz Festival: Saratoga Springs and Especially about George Benson and Everyone Who Was Listening. June Jordan. SP-JordJ

We greet thee now open this festal morn. Greeting. Henrietta Cordelia Ray. CBWP-3

We hacked them with broadswords. The Music of Broadswords. Michael S. Harper. SP-HarpM

We had a nice time together. I and I. Jayne Cortez. SP-CortJ

We had been school-mates,—she and I. Imogene. Eloise Bibb. CBWP-4

We had gathered for the love-feast on the time appointed. Who Is My Neighbor? Josephine D. Henderson Heard. CBWP-4

We had seen / our minds reach out. Ten Years After Umbra. Tom Dent. TtW

We have a beautiful / mother. Alice Walker. CP-WalkA

We Have a Map of the World. Alice Walker. CP-WalkA

We have always heard music. And Sometimes I Hear This Song in My Head. Harriet Jacobs. SpiFl

We have been believers in the black gods of an old land. Margaret Abigail Walker. CP-WalkM; PoBA; TtW

We have been seen. Kalamu ya Salaam. TtW

We have found you out. Arson and Cold Lace. Worth Long. NBP

We have grown a tree of knowledge, "Worthy Claflin" is the name. The Tree of Knowledge. Lizelia Augusta Jenkins Moorer. CBWP-3

We have no passions left to love the spring. Second Spring. Audre Lorde. CP-LordA

We have shored up so much. The Black Intellectual. Kenneth A. McClane. TtW

We have slept in. The Message on Cape Cod. Michael S. Weaver. GT

We have taken the best leaves. On the Birth of Bomani. Lucille Clifton. SP-ClifL

We have tomorrow. Youth. Langston Hughes. CP-HughL

We head for the source. (LL) Fishing the White Water. Audre Lorde. CP-LordA; GT

We is gathahed hyeah, my brothahs. An Ante-Bellum Sermon. Paul Laurence Dunbar. AAP; BALP; BPo; CP-DunbP; NAAAL; TtW

We knew how to order. Just the dash. Gay Chaps at the Bar. Gwendolyn Brooks. SP-BrooG

We knew, the coming day would see us parted. One Way of Taking Leave. Sterling A. Brown. CP-BrowS

We Know No More. Timothy Thomas Fortune. EBAP

We know where he is laid. (LL) The Death of Moses. Frances Ellen Watkins Harper. AAP

We know where he is laid. (LL) Moses: A Story of the Nile. Frances Ellen Watkins Harper. CP-HarpF

We lay red roses on his grave. Paul Laurence Dunbar. Robert Hayden. CP-HaydR; ESEAA; GT

We leave thee with thy guests, thou sunny maid! Albery Allson Whitman. AAP Fr. Twasinta's Seminoles; Or Rape of Florida

We leave thy courts to-day. Farewell to Allen University. Josephine D. Henderson Heard. CBWP-4

We lift the curtain of the past to-day. Lincoln. Henrietta Cordelia Ray. CBWP-3

We lift your weight from chair. Alice Braxton Johnson. Michael S. Harper. SP-HarpM

We, like shades that were first conjured up. And through the Caribbean Sea. Margaret Else Danner. BPo; TtW

We, limbed beings of the Earth. Words for a Hymn to the Sun. Jean Toomer. CP-ToomJ

We Live in a Cage. William J. Harris. GT; PoBA

We lived in language all our black selves. When the Wine Was Gone. Alvin Aubert. BkSV

We made it through the swamps. Tyrone (4). Lucille Clifton. SP-ClifL

We made strong poems for each other. Neighbors. Audre Lorde. CP-LordA; SP-LordA

We make up our faces. Make Up. Nikki Giovanni. SP-GiovN

We may sigh o'er the heavy burdens. The Burdens of All. Frances Ellen Watkins Harper. CP-HarpF

We Met. Mary E. Tucker. CBWP-1

We mourn to-day o'er our sister dead. Resting. Josephine D. Henderson Heard. CBWP-4

We move already thru a low-pitched heaven. Palm Drive Palo Alto. Al Young. CP-YounA

We move from one. The River. Sam Cornish. PoBA

We move thru rooms & down the middle of freeways. Dancing All Alone. Al Young. CP-YounA

We must kill our gods before they kill us. Black Trumpeter. Henry L. Dumas. PoBA

We must say it all, and as clearly. Each One, Pull One. Alice Walker. CP-WalkA

We never spent time in the mountains. Interlude: "We never spent time in the mountains." Welton Smith. PoBA *Fr. Malcolm.* BlFi

We open infant eyes. Dear Friends and Gentle Hearts. Countee Cullen. CP-CullC

We Own the Night. Amiri Baraka. PoBA

We packed our cuts. Lovely's Daughters: Visitors. Michael S. Harper. SP-HarpM

We passed their graves. Peace. Langston Hughes. BPo; CP-HughL

We prop him up. Good Joe. Yusef Komunyakaa. SP-KomuY

We Rainclouds. Marvin, Jr. Wyche. AmNP

We raise de wheat. Song. *Unknown.* BPo; CrDW; NAAAL

We reach for destinies beyond. Beyond What. Alice Walker. CP-WalkA

We real cool. We. Gwendolyn Brooks. CrDW; ESEAA; IDB; NAAAL; PoBA; SP-BrooG

We reconstruct lives in the intensive. Clan Meeting: Births and Nations: A Blood Song. Michael S. Harper. SP-HarpM

We ride down the coast hwy through the rain. The Great Santa Barbara Oil Disaster OR. Conyus. NBV

We rise up early and. Anna Speaks of the Childhood of Mary Her Daughter. Lucille Clifton. SP-ClifL

We run the dangercourse. We Walk the Way of the New World. Haki R. Madhubuti. BPo; ESEAA; PoBA; TtW

We run, / We run, / We cannot stand these shadows! Shadows. Langston Hughes. CP-HughL

We saw a bloody sunset over Courtland, once Jerusalem. Remembering Nat Turner. Sterling A. Brown. CP-BrowS; PoBA

We saw an Indian merchantman / Coming home. (LL) Seascape. Langston Hughes. CP-HughL; SP-HughL

We saw beyond our seeming. Maya Angelou. CP-AngeM; SP-AngeM

We say he is dead; ah, the word is too somber. Not Dead, but Sleeping. Clara Ann Thompson. CBWP-2

We search each other's shore for some crossing home. (LL) Bridge through My Windows. Audre Lorde. CP-LordA; SP-LordA

We search, yet find it not o'er widest lands. (LL) Lost Opportunities. Henrietta Cordelia Ray. CBWP-3

We shall not always plant while others reap. From the Dark Tower. Countee Cullen. AfAmPo; BALP; BANP; BPo; CDC; CP-CullC; CrDW; Crnst; IDB; Klds; PoBA; TtW

We shall overcome. *Unknown.* CrDW

We shall / we shall. (LL) The Near-Johannesburg Boy. Gwendolyn Brooks. ESEAA; TtW

We should cultivate our different tastes. Cultivation. Mrs. Henry Linden. CBWP-4

We should have a land of sun. Our Land. Langston Hughes. CP-HughL

We sit beside the Mississippi. Making Poems. Sekou Sundiata. SpiFl

We sit outside. Death of Dr. King. Sam Cornish. PoBA

We sit watching the afternoon summer smell ripely. James Powell on Imagination. Larry Neal. BPo

We six pile in, the engine churning ink. Nigger Song: An Odyssey. Rita Dove. SP-DoveR

We spoke / at all. (LL) The Night-Blooming Cereus. Robert Hayden. CP-HaydR; ESEAA; FB

We stand pinned / to the electric mural. Zocalo. Michael S. Harper. NBV; SP-HarpM

We stood there waiting. Nikki Giovanni. SP-GiovN

We strike camp on that portion of road completed. Corduroy Road. Rita Dove. SP-DoveR

We stumbled into. Sonia Sanchez. SP-SancS

We swallow the odors of Southern cities. A Georgia Song. Maya Angelou. CP-AngeM; SP-AngeM

We take place in what we believe. Elephant Rock. Primus St. John. PoBA

We talk of light things you and I in this. Sonia Sanchez. *See* Father and Daughter.

We talked all the time. YMCA #35. Amiri Baraka. SP-BaraA

We tend to fear old age. Age. Nikki Giovanni. Crnst; SP-GiovN

We think of lukewarm water, hope to get in it. (LL) Kitchenette Building. Gwendolyn Brooks. BPo; GT; NAAAL

We thought the grass. Photographs: A Vision of Massacre. Michael S. Harper. PoBA; SP-HarpM

We tied branches to our helmets. Camouflaging the Chimera. Yusef Komunyakaa. SP-KomuY

We, Too. Langston Hughes. CP-HughL

We touched land. Not That Far. May Miller. BlSi

We trace the pow'r of Death from tomb to tomb. To a Lady on the Death of Three Relations. Phillis Wheatley. CP-WheaP

We trekked into a far country. Translation. Anne Spencer. BANP

We turn aside from everything. Birthday Wishes to a Minister of the Gospel. Lizelia Augusta Jenkins Moorer. CBWP-3

We turn off. To Bed. Rita Dove. SP-DoveR

We used to gather at the high window. When Mahalia Sings. Quandra Prettyman. IDB; PoBA

We Waiting on You. Edward S. Spriggs. BlFi

We wake on the wrong side of the morning. The Wrong Side of the Morning. May Miller. TtW

We Walk the Way of the New World. Haki R. Madhubuti. BPo; ESEAA; PoBA; TtW

We walked and blinked at sunlight on the snow. Winter Sonnet. Linda Beatrice Brown. GT

We want to know what in the hell you'd say? (LL) Letter to the Academy. Langston Hughes. CP-HughL

We wear the mask that grins and lies. Paul Laurence Dunbar. AAP; AfAmPo; AmNP; CDC; CP-DunbP; CrDW; Crnst; IDB; NAAAL; PoBA; SSLK; TtW

We went there to confer. Detroit Conference of Unity and Art. Nikki Giovanni. SP-GiovN

We were alone and did your life. To Children. Lawrence McGaugh. PoBA

We were as tough as our glasses. Tyson's Corner. Primus St. John. PoBA

We were born in a poor time. Sister Outsider. Audre Lorde. CP-LordA

We were—clinging to our arboreal—rustled. The Jackal-Headed Cowboy. Ishmael Reed. CP-ReedI

We were entwined in red rings. Kin. Maya Angelou. CP-AngeM; SP-AngeM

We were forest people. A Bonding. Haki R. Madhubuti. CtF

We were here / *before*. Lord Haw Haw (as Pygmy) #37. Amiri Baraka. SP-BaraA

We were never meant to survive. (LL) A Litany for Survival. Audre Lorde. CP-LordA; NAAAL

We were not raised to look in. You Were Never Miss Brown to Me. Sherley Anne Williams. GT

We were raised on the lower eastside of detroit. First World. Haki R. Madhubuti. TtW

We were the breadlines. 1933. Margaret Abigail Walker. CP-WalkM

We were waiting at the station. The Parting Kiss. Josephine D. Henderson Heard. CBWP-4

We / Who have nothing to lose. Black Dancers. Langston Hughes. CP-HughL

We will not die for nothing. Revolution! Richard W. Thomas. BlFi

We will take you and kill you. Expendable. Langston Hughes. CP-HughL

We will wear. New Bones. Lucille Clifton. SP-ClifL

We wonder what the horoscope did show. Shakespeare. Henrietta Cordelia Ray. CBWP-3; EBAP

We worship revolution. (LL) When We'll Worship Jesus. Amiri Baraka. SP-BaraA

We would see Jesus; earth is grand. Sir, We Would See Jesus. Frances Ellen Watkins Harper. AAP; AfAmPo; CP-HarpF

Weakness, The. Toi Derricotte. GT

Weaknesses: / small good reading. Sambo's Mistakes: an Essay. Michael S. Harper. SP-HarpM

Wealth. Langston Hughes. CP-HughL

Wear it / Like a banner. Color. Langston Hughes. CP-HughL

Wearied, exhausted, dully sleeping. (LL) Spring in New Hampshire. Claude McKay. Klds; SP-McKaC

Weariness. Mary E. Tucker. CBWP-1

Wearing his equality like a too-small shoe. The Citizen. Vilma Howard. NNP

Wearing that same black dress. The Women You Are Accustomed To. Lucille Clifton. GT

Weary Blues, The. Langston Hughes. BALP; CP-HughL; NAAAL; SP-HughL

Weary was when coming on a stream. Asweley. Norman Henry, II Pritchard. PoBA

Weary, worn, and sorrow-laden. Storm-Beaten. Clara Ann Thompson. CBWP-2

Weathering Out. Rita Dove. SP-DoveR

("She liked mornings the best—Thomas gone.") ESEAA

Web, The. Robert Hayden. CP-HaydR

Wedding, The. June Jordan. SP-JordJ

Wedding in Hanover. Lorna Goodison. GT

Wedding Procession, from a Window. James A. Emanuel. Klds; NNP

Wednesday Night Prayer Meeting. Jay Wright. PoBA

Wednesdays at the bone orchard deliveries. Memo. Charles Lynch. PoBA

Weeds are in her face. Mission. Michael S. Harper. SP-HarpM

Week in Review, The. Sekou Sundiata. *Fr.* Notes from the Defense of Colin Ferguson. SpiFl

Weekend Equestrian, The. Michael S. Weaver. GT

Weekend Glory. Maya Angelou. CP-AngeM; SP-AngeM

Weekly I am murdering. Suicide. Al Young. CP-YounA

Week's gone since the memorial, A. The Wisdom of Signs. Michael S. Harper. SP-HarpM

Weeksville Women. Elouise Loftin. PoBA

Weep not, weep not. Go Down Death. James Weldon Johnson. AmNP; PoBA

Weep not, you who love her. Threnody for a Brown Girl. Countee Cullen. CP-CullC

Weep not, / You who loved her. Burial of the Young Love. Waring Cuney. BANP

WEEP weep weep / in B R O K E N bluebones. Transcendental Blues Transcendental Blues. Yusef Rahman. BlFi

Weeps out of western country something new. The Birth in a Narrow Room. Gwendolyn Brooks. BlSi

'Weh Down Souf. Daniel Webster Davis. BANP

Weird sister / the black witches know that. In Salem. Lucille Clifton. ESEAA; SP-ClifL

Welcome Address. Paul Laurence Dunbar. CP-DunbP

Welcome Back, Mr. Knight: Love of My Life. Etheridge Knight. SP-KnigE

Welcome children of the Spring. Dandelions. Frances Ellen Watkins Harper. CP-HarpF

Welcome for Etheridge, A. James Cunningham. JB

Welcome Home. Josephine D. Henderson Heard. CBWP-4

Welcome Peace! thou blest evangel. Peace. Frances Ellen Watkins Harper. CP-HarpF

Welcome, stranger! glad I greet thee. To Don Juan Baz. Mary E. Tucker. CBWP-1

Welcome to Hon. Frederick Douglass. Josephine D. Henderson Heard. CBWP-4

Well! And you? (LL) Heaven is / The place where. Langston Hughes. CP-HughL; SP-HughL

Well anyway even tho. Some Spice for Jack Spicer. Al Young. CP-YounA

Well, are you the lover or the loved? Are You the Lover or Loved? Al Young. CP-YounA

Well, gentlemen, / You flag wavers. To Those Who Sing America. Frank Marshall Davis. FB

We'll go our ways, the world is wide. (LL) After the Quarrel. Paul Laurence Dunbar. CDC; CP-DunbP

Well, God wakes me up from a nap on the couch. Jonah Begins His Story. Marilyn Nelson. *Fr.* I Dream the Book of Jonah. SP-NelsM

Well. / He was a poet. Alice Walker. CP-WalkA

Well here's to the fool that writes upon the shithouse walls. *African-American Oral Tradition.* GetYo

Well, I goes out in the desert. Now His Fingers Found the Melody. Marilyn Nelson. *Fr.* I Dream the Book of Jonah. SP-NelsM

Well i have almost come to the place where you fell. Poem on My Fortieth Birthday to My Mother Who Died Young. Lucille Clifton. SP-ClifL

Well, I know. Abe Lincoln. Langston Hughes. CP-HughL

Well I wanted to braid my hair. Poem # One. June Jordan. *Fr.* The Talking Back of Miss Valentine Jones. SP-JordJ

Well, I was at the dresser. Just How It Happened. Priscilla Jane Thompson. CBWP-2

Well, I was tryin to swim. Then Jonah Took Out His Guitar. Marilyn Nelson. *Fr.* I Dream the Book of Jonah. SP-NelsM

Well if I had a dog that could piss this stuff. *African-American Oral Tradition.* GetYo

Well it's six o'clock in Oakland. Oakland Blues. Ishmael Reed. CP-ReedI; NAAAL

Well! Johnnie thinks. *He has his nerve!.* The Fortunate Spill. Marilyn Nelson. SP-NelsM

Well Langston. A Message for Langston. "Kush." NBV

Well may I say my life has been. Miscellaneous Verses. Gustavus Vassa. EBAP

Well, old spy. Award. Ray Durem. BPo; IDB; NNP; PoBA

Well, one morning real early. The Reunion. Frances Ellen Watkins Harper. CP-HarpF

We'll run and never tire. Down in the Valley. *Unknown.* CrDW

Well, so youve gone & overdone it again. Herrick Hospital, Fifth Floor. Al Young. CP-YounA

Well, son de story of my life. The Favorite Slave's Story. Priscilla Jane Thompson. AAP; CBWP-2

Well, son, I'll tell you. Mother to Son. Langston Hughes. AfAmPo; AmNP; CDC; CP-HughL; Crnst; NAAAL; SP-HughL; TtW

We'll soon be free. *Unknown.* CrDW

Well, Teddy, I have found you. The Lost Teddy Bear. Maggie Pogue Johnson. CBWP-4

Well, that's Pretty Boy Emeritus. The Thorn Merchant's Right Hand Man. Yusef Komunyakaa. SP-KomuY

Well the cat started actin funny. Earthquake Blues. Ishmael Reed. CP-ReedI

Well, the las' time I saw my mother. Con/tin/u/way/shun Blues. Etheridge Knight. SP-KnigE

Well, the next thing I know. Now Jonah Began to Tune His Guitar. Marilyn Nelson. *Fr.* I Dream the Book of Jonah. SP-NelsM

Well, they rocked him with road-apples. Not a Movie. Langston Hughes. *Fr.* Montage of a Dream Deferred. CP-HughL

Well, things / be / pretty bad now, Mother. Report to the Mother. Etheridge Knight. SP-KnigE

"Well Uncle Ike! This beats me." Uncle Ike's Holiday. Priscilla Jane Thompson. CBWP-2

Well, we went down town a-shopping. The Christmas Rush. Clara Ann Thompson. CBWP-2

Well, well, you's cum at las'. People's Literary, De. Maggie Pogue Johnson. CBWP-4

We'll worship Jesus. When We'll Worship Jesus. Amiri Baraka. SP-BaraA

Welt. Georgia Douglas Johnson. BANP

Weltschmertz. Paul Laurence Dunbar. CP-DunbP

Weltschmerz. Frank Yerby. AmNP

W'en a feller's itchin' to be spanked. (LL) When a Feller's Itchin' to be Spanked. Paul Laurence Dunbar. BALP; CP-DunbP

W'en daih's chillun in de house. The Old Front Gate. Paul Laurence Dunbar. CP-DunbP

W'en de clouds is hangin' heavy in de sky. My Sweet Brown Gal. Paul Laurence Dunbar. CP-DunbP

W'en de colo'ed ban' comes ma'chin' down de street. The Colored Band. Paul Laurence Dunbar. CP-DunbP

W'en de evenin' shadders. The Boogah Man. Paul Laurence Dunbar. CP-DunbP

W'en de snow's a-fallin'. A Grievance. Paul Laurence Dunbar. CP-DunbP

W'en dey 'listed colo'ed sojers an' my 'Lias went to wah. (LL) When Dey 'Listed Colored Soldiers. Paul Laurence Dunbar. BPo; CP-DunbP

W'en I git up in de mo'nin' an' de clouds is big an' black. Fishing. Paul Laurence Dunbar. CP-DunbP

W'en I Gits Home. Paul Laurence Dunbar. CP-DunbP

W'en us fellers stomp around, makin' lots o' noise. When a Feller's Itchin' to be Spanked. Paul Laurence Dunbar. BALP; CP-DunbP

W'en you full o' worry. Advice. Paul Laurence Dunbar. CP-DunbP

Wendell Phillips. Henrietta Cordelia Ray. CBWP-3

Went down to the yards. Long Track Blues. Sterling A. Brown. CP-BrowS

Went out last night, had a great big fight. Prove It on Me Blues. Gertrude "Ma" Rainey. NAAAL

We're all in the telephone book. Langston Hughes. CP-HughL

We're Going to Miss Our Chance to go to Jail. (LL) Street Demonstration. Margaret Abigail Walker. BPo

We're hoping to be arrested. Street Demonstration. Margaret Abigail Walker. BPo; CP-WalkM

Were it not for your songs. (LL) Ardella. Langston Hughes. CP-HughL; SP-HughL

We're related—you and I. Brothers. SP-HughL Langston Hughes. *Fr.* Montage of a Dream Deferred. CP-HughL

Were you a leper bathed in wounds. Proving. Georgia Douglas Johnson. CDC

Were you dere when dey crucified my Lord? *African-American Oral Tradition.* TtW

Were you there when they crucified my Lord? [(were you there?)]. *Unknown.* BPo

("Were you there, when they crucified my Lord?") NAAAL

We's gathered here to tell our tales. The Big Gate. Elma Stuckey. TtW

We's invited down to brudder Browns. Krismas Dinnah. Maggie Pogue Johnson. CBWP-4

West Ridge Is Menthol-Cool, The. D. L. Graham. BlFi; PoBA

West Texas. Langston Hughes. CP-HughL; SP-HughL

Western Lady, A. Amiri Baraka. SP-BaraA

"Westward the course of empire takes its way." Welcome Address. Paul Laurence Dunbar. CP-DunbP

We've all been off some little while—some one place, some another. The Old High School and the New. Paul Laurence Dunbar. CP-DunbP

We've kept the faith. Our souls' high dreams. To Our Friends. Lucian B. Watkins. BANP

We've made a child. Audre Lorde. *See* And What About the Children.

We've room to build holy altars. Light in Darkness. Frances Ellen Watkins Harper. CP-HarpF

We've traveled long together. Verses to my Heart's-Sister. Henrietta Cordelia Ray. AAP; AfAmPo; CBWP-3

Wharf of singleness. Dock Song Crazy. Al Young. CP-YounA

What? Langston Hughes. CP-HughL; SP-HughL

What a cost to be pure! did e'er strike your mind. Refining Fire. Lizelia Augusta Jenkins Moorer. CBWP-3

What a grand time was the war! World War *II*. Langston Hughes. *Fr.* Montage of a Dream Deferred. CP-HughL

"What a waste of a beautiful girl!" Last Letter to the Western Civilization. D. T. Ogilvie. NBP

What about his feelings—. Beginning by Value. Christopher Gilbert. GT

What about that bad short you saw last week. Black People! Amiri Baraka. BPo

What am I ready to lose in this advancing summer? Seasoning. Audre Lorde. CP-LordA

What am I suppose to do. You Send Me: Bertha Franklin, December 11, 1964. E. Ethelbert Miller. SpiFl

What anger in my hard-won bones. Spring People. Audre Lorde. CP-LordA; SP-LordA

What are / influences? Betancourt. Amiri Baraka. SP-BaraA

What are the things that make life bright? To J. Q. Paul Laurence Dunbar. CP-DunbP

What are / these / words. Y's 18. Amiri Baraka. SP-BaraA

What art thou, Mignon, child of mystery? Mignon. Henrietta Cordelia Ray. CBWP-3

What boots it, Poet, that from realms above. The Poet. Joseph Seamon Cotter, Sr. EBAP

What can i say. Our Days Are Numbered. Alicia Loy Johnson. BrTr

What can purge my heart. Song for Billie Holiday. Langston Hughes. CP-HughL; SP-HughL

What can the white man say to the black woman? Right to Life, The: What Can the White Man Say to the Black Woman? Alice Walker. CP-WalkA

What can you do with a woman under thirty? Green Apples. Dudley Randall. FB

What cannot be committed to memory, this can save. Photograph. Quandra Prettyman. PoBA

What Cannot Be Kept. Reginald Shepherd. GT

What Color Is Lonely. Carolyn M. Rodgers. BPo

What connects me to this moon. Chemistry. Al Young. CP-YounA

What creeps in. At General Electric, Where They Eat Their/Young. Robert Farr. SpiFl

What desperate nightmare rapts me to this land. Legacy: My South. Dudley Randall. NNP; PoBA; TtW

What did he do except lie. Banneker. Rita Dove. ESEAA; SP-DoveR

(What Did I Do to Be So) Black and Blue? Thomas ("Fats") Waller, Andy Razaf *and* Harry Brooks. NAAAL

What Do I Care for Morning. Helene Johnson. CDC; ShDr

What do i know of. Sonia Sanchez. SP-SancS

What Do I Want from Men and Love? Lisa B. Thompson. CtF

What do the long years bring us. Retrospection. Henrietta Cordelia Ray. CBWP-3

What do we ask of ourselves? (LL) Astronauts. Robert Hayden. CP-HaydR; ESEAA

What do we want from each other. There Are No Honest Poems about Dead Women. Audre Lorde. CP-LordA

What do you do in a town where. July 1st, 1982. Ishmael Reed. CP-ReedI

What do you mean. But What Can You Teach My Daughter. Audre Lorde. CP-LordA

What do you mean / by Use? Of What Use Is Poetry? (Babalu Meets the Wolfman). Amiri Baraka. CtF

What does it matter? you ask. What Ovid Taught Me. Alice Walker. CP-WalkA

What does the cracker. Self. Norman Henry, II Pritchard. PoBA

What dost thou here, thou shining, sinless thing. A Butterfly in Church. George Marion McClellan. BANP

What dreams we have and how they fly. Dreams. Paul Laurence Dunbar. CP-DunbP

What / else / could they expect from me. Fighting My Homophobia. Gloria Wade-Gayles. IHS

What endures? Not the arranged. Still Life. Sharan Strange. GT

What face we had / what startling eyes. (LL) Spring People. Audre Lorde. CP-LordA; SP-LordA

What flag will fly for me. August 19th. Langston Hughes. CP-HughL

What goes up is bound to come down. The Under Weight Champion. Bob Kaufman. SP-KaufB

What happens to a dream deferred? Harlem: "What happens to a dream deferred?" Langston Hughes. *Fr.* Lenox Avenue Mural. AmNP; CrDW; GT; NAAAL; PoBA; SP-HughL; SSLK *Fr.* Montage of a Dream Deferred.

What happens to little cats? Little Cats. Langston Hughes. CP-HughL

What happens when the dog sits on a tiger. June Jordan. BPo

What hast thou ever done for me? The Tippler to His Bottle. George Moses Horton. SP-HortG

What have you got of your own. Al Young. CP-YounA

What hue lies in the slit of anger. Outlines. Audre Lorde. CP-LordA

What I am saying now was said before. Sonnet. Countee Cullen. CP-CullC

What i remember. Jonah. Lucille Clifton. SP-ClifL

What I remember about that day. The 1st. Lucille Clifton. SP-ClifL

What I Think. Langston Hughes. CP-HughL

What I thought was love. The Liar. Amiri Baraka. SP-BaraA

What if his glance is bold and free. To a Brown Girl. Countee Cullen. CP-CullC

What if the wind do howl without. Right's Security. Paul Laurence Dunbar. CP-DunbP

What is a blk poem & / or what is it. Food for Thought. Val Ferdinand. NBV

What Is a Slave? Benjamin Clark. EBAP

What is a troubadour? (LL) The Banjo Player. Fenton Johnson. BANP; TtW

What is Africa to me. Heritage. Countee Cullen. AmNP; BANP; BPo; CP-CullC; CrDW; Crnst; NAAAL; PoBA; SSLK; TtW

What is Africa to thee? The Africa Thing. Adam David Miller. NBV

What is ambition? 'tis unrest, defeat! Ambition. Henrietta Cordelia Ray. CBWP-3

What is Beautiful. Jay Wright. GT

What is failure? When the maiden. Failure. Henrietta Cordelia Ray. CBWP-3

What is it about. Sonia Sanchez. SP-SancS

What is nightfall. Prelude. Al Young. CP-YounA

What Is the Blues? Al Young. CP-YounA

What is the point. Songless. Alice Walker. CP-WalkA

What is there within this beggar lad. Beggar Boy. Langston Hughes. CP-HughL

What is this hip yearning smooching hot. Clinton. Sterling Plumpp. BkSV

What Is This in Reference To? or We Must Get Together Sometime Soon! June Jordan. SP-JordJ

What is this thing, this elusive conceit. All Singing in a Pie. Alvin Aubert. TtW

What Is Woman? Mrs. Henry Linden. CBWP-4

What isn't water in us must be bone. Suffering The Sea Change: All My Pretty Ones. Lucinda Roy. GT

What it does not invent. (LL) Teacher. Audre Lorde. CP-LordA; SP-LordA

What It Means to Be Beautiful. Audre Lorde. CP-LordA

What jungle tree have you slept under. Nude Young Dancer. Langston Hughes. CP-HughL

What kind of a people are we? (LL) The Test of Atlanta 1979. June Jordan. SP-JordJ

What kind of a person would kill Black children? The Test of Atlanta 1979. June Jordan. SP-JordJ

What marked the river's flow. "Stephany." NBV

What matters is the renewing and long running kinship. The Union of Two. Haki R. Madhubuti. SpiFl

What matters that I stormed and swore? For an Anarchist. Countee Cullen. CP-CullC

What means this host of advancing. The Advance of Education. Josephine D. Henderson Heard. CBWP-4

What means this vast assemblage here. Dedication Day. Maggie Pogue Johnson. CBWP-4

What more is there to say in a pome? Election Night Pome. Al Young. CP-YounA

What my child learns of the sea. Audre Lorde. CP-LordA; GT; NBP; PoBA; SP-LordA

What Need Have I for Memory? Georgia Douglas Johnson. CDC

What news from the bottle? Mosaic Harlem. Henry L. Dumas. BlFi

What now / what now dumb nigger damn near dead. Another Poem for Me (after Recovering from an O.D.). Etheridge Knight. SP-KnigE

What now / what now dumb nigger damn near dead. Elegy for Etheridge. Pinkie Gordon Lane. TtW

What Ovid Taught Me. Alice Walker. CP-WalkA

What right divine has mortal man received. The Slave. George Moses Horton. SP-HortG; TtW

What right has anyone to say. Poet to Patron. Langston Hughes. CP-HughL

What! Roses growing in a meadow. Wild Roses. Mary Effie Lee Newsome. CDC; ShDr

What sacrifice so great! A Mother's Love. Josephine D. Henderson Heard. CBWP-4

What says the wind to the waving trees? The Secret. Paul Laurence Dunbar. CP-DunbP

What seer is this. Ode on the Twentieth Century. Henrietta Cordelia Ray. CBWP-3

What shall I give my children? who are poor. Gwendolyn Brooks. *Fr.* The Children of the Poor. Crnst, *sect.* I, 1-5; NAAAL; SP-BrooG, *sect.* I, *pt.* 1-5.

What shall I leave my son. Testament. Langston Hughes. CP-HughL

What shall they grow for food? (LL) Blackstudies. Audre Lorde. CP-LordA; SP-LordA

What? So Soon! Langston Hughes. *Fr.* Montage of a Dream Deferred. CP-HughL

What song shall i sing you. A Poem for Sterling Brown. Sonia Sanchez. SP-SancS

What songs should rise, how constant, how divine! (LL) Thoughts on the Works of Providence. Phillis Wheatley. CP-WheaP; EBAP

What soul hath struck its need of melody. Incompleteness. Henrietta Cordelia Ray. CBWP-3

What spells racoon to me. Lucille Clifton. NAAAL

What star still choosing? (LL) Island Mary. Lucille Clifton. SP-ClifL

What sudden ill the world await. The Southern Refugee. George Moses Horton. SP-HortG

What summons do I hear? The Graduate Leaving College. George Moses Horton. SP-HortG

What the Finger Writes. Alice Walker. CP-WalkA

What the Mirror Said. Lucille Clifton. SP-ClifL

What the Women Told Me. E. Ethelbert Miller. GT

What THEY care / whatchu feel? (LL) Whitey, Baby. James A. Emanuel. BrTr; NBV

What they eats in Rome. (LL) When in Rome. Mari E. Evans. AmNP; ESEAA

What to do with a day. The Satisfaction Coal Company. Rita Dove. SP-DoveR

What Viet Nam means to me. The Long Reality. Haki R. Madhubuti. NAAAL

What was i doing anyway. On Extending the Olive Branch to My Own Self. Harriet Jacobs. SpiFl

What was Inez supposed to do for. Rape. Jayne Cortez. GT; SP-CortJ

What was it / that caught in our throats that day. The Greek Room. James W. Thompson. BPo

What we decided is. The Meeting After the Savior Gone. Lucille Clifton. SP-ClifL

What we do have / Is Good. (LL) So We've Come at Last to Freud. Alice Walker. CP-WalkA

What We Have Lost. Harris Duriel. SpiFl

What We Know. Raymond R. Patterson. NBV

What We Teach at Claflin. Lizelia Augusta Jenkins Moorer. CBWP-3

What we to-day prize and most fondly cherish. Instability. Henrietta Cordelia Ray. CBWP-3

What will we do. Poem for Nana. June Jordan. BlSi

What words / have smashed against. The New House. Maya Angelou. CP-AngeM

What would a little girl think ... boarding a big. Linkage. Nikki Giovanni. SP-GiovN

What Would I Do White? June Jordan. SP-JordJ

What year is this? Who can truthfully say? This Age. Raymond R. Patterson. NBV

What Yo' Gwine to [*or* t'] Do When Yo' [*or* de] Lamp Burn Down? *Unknown.* BPo

What you have / never really / had. (LL) As a Possible Lover. Amiri Baraka. SP-BaraA; TtW

What You Mean I Can't Irony? Ishmael Reed. CP-ReedI

What You Seize Is What You Git. Al Young. CP-YounA

WhatCHU care / what I feel. Whitey, Baby. James A. Emanuel. BrTr; NBV

What'd you get, black boy. Mr. Roosevelt Regrets. Pauli Murray. PoBA

Whatever Become of the Living. Al Young. CP-YounA

Whatever city or country road. Double Elegy. Michael S. Harper. ESEAA

Whatever i say. (LL) February 13, 1980. Lucille Clifton. SP-ClifL

Whatever your name, whatever. Antigone, This Is It. Ishmael Reed. CP-ReedI

Whatever you've given me, whiteface glass. I don't love you. Amiri Baraka. NAAAL

What's de Use ob Wukin in de Summer Time at All. Maggie Pogue Johnson. CBWP-4

What's Going On. Marvin Gaye. Crnst

What's in a name? What's in a name? Fame. Josephine D. Henderson Heard. CBWP-4

What's in this grave is worth your tear. For Myself. Countee Cullen. CP-CullC

What's Mo' Temptin' to de Palate? Maggie Pogue Johnson. CBWP-4

What's so fine as being a boy?/ Ha, Ha! (LL) A Boy's Summer Song. Paul Laurence Dunbar. CP-DunbP

What's the use o' folks a-frownin'. Paul Laurence Dunbar. CP-DunbP

Wheel, The. Robert Hayden. BPo; CP-HaydR

When a chile gets to be thirteen. Mystery. Langston Hughes. *Fr.* Montage of a Dream Deferred. CP-HughL

When a dark and fearful strife. An Appeal to the American People. Frances Ellen Watkins Harper. CP-HarpF

When a dream gets kicked around. (LL) Same in Blues. Langston Hughes. CP-HughL; SP-HughL; SSLK

When a Feller's Itchin' to be Spanked. Paul Laurence Dunbar. BALP; CP-DunbP

When-a Mah Blood runs Chilly and Col. *African-American Oral Tradition.* TtW

When a man starts out with nothing. Freedom's Plow. Langston Hughes. CP-HughL; SP-HughL

When a mask breaks in Benin. Wood Has No Mouth. Audre Lorde. CP-LordA

When a Negro comes in question you may watch the Southern press. The Southern Press. Lizelia Augusta Jenkins Moorer. CBWP-3

When A Woman Gets Blue. Norman Jordan. NBV

When a woman looks up at you with a twist about her eyes. The Made to Order Smile. Paul Laurence Dunbar. CP-DunbP; GT

When Adam dwelt in Eden's shades alone. The Cheerless Condition of Bachelorship. George Moses Horton. SP-HortG

When all is done, and my last word is said. Paul Laurence Dunbar. AAP; CP-DunbP

When all the cards are in. The Game of Game. Nikki Giovanni. BrTr

When all was quiet and serene, a storm broke out at the dead. A Riot. Mrs. Henry Linden. CBWP-4

When all your money's gone and you drain your last cup. Ain't It a Bitch? *African-American Oral Tradition.* GetYo

When and where did you first. Sexual Privacy of Women on Welfare. Pinkie Gordon Lane. BlSi

When Annie Mae Johnson condescends to take the air. Glory, Glory. Sterling A. Brown. BrTr

When are the children all happy and gay? Christmas Times. Maggie Pogue Johnson. CBWP-4

When August days are hot an' dry. In August. Paul Laurence Dunbar. CP-DunbP

When black boys fondle their guns on TV and. Let's Take All the Blame. Peter Harris. CtF

When Black People Are. Alfred B. Spellman. BPo; PoBA

When blue moons start to roll around. Real Time. Al Young. CP-YounA

When Brown Is Black. Keorapetse W. Kgositsile. BrTr

When California is split in two. Untitled: "When California is split in two." Ishmael Reed. CP-ReedI

When Daddy Cums from Wuk. Maggie Pogue Johnson. CBWP-4

When Dawn Comes to the City. Claude McKay. SP-McKaC

When dawn lights the sky. Lonely Nocturne. Langston Hughes. CP-HughL

When de Co'n Pone's Hot. Paul Laurence Dunbar. AAP; BANP; CP-DunbP; TtW

When de fiddle gits to singin' out a ol' Vahginny reel. Angelina. Paul Laurence Dunbar. CP-DunbP

When de Saints Go Ma'ching Home. Sterling A. Brown. AmNP; CP-BrowS

When de Sun Shines Hot. James Ephriam McGirt. AAP

When Dey 'Listed Colored Soldiers. Paul Laurence Dunbar. BPo; CP-DunbP

When e'er we enter life's open field. Ambition. Maggie Pogue Johnson. CBWP-4

When Egypt said, "Exterminate." Retribution. Lizelia Augusta Jenkins Moorer. CBWP-3

When Ella starts scatting. Duke Checks Out Ella as She Scats Like That. Michael War. CtF

When Evening bids the Sun to rest retire. On the Evening and the Morning. George Moses Horton. SP-HortG

When face to face we stand. Paradox. Angelina Weld Grimké. CDC

When faith in black candles. Number. Langston Hughes. CP-HughL

When first my bosom glowed with hope. Slavery. George Moses Horton. EBAP; TtW

When first of wise old Johnson taught. At Cheshire Cheese. Paul Laurence Dunbar. CP-DunbP

When first you sang a song to me. Your Songs. Gwendolyn B. Bennett. CDC

When first your glory shone upon my face. Commemoration. Claude McKay. BANP; SP-McKaC

When from the gates of Paradise fair Eve. The Vision of Eve. Henrietta Cordelia Ray. CBWP-3

When genial Spring first bears the mating thrush. Albery Allson Whitman. AAP

When Golda Meir. When Golda Meir Was in Africa. Alice Walker. CP-WalkA

When Golda Meir Was in Africa. Alice Walker. CP-WalkA

When great trees fall. Ailey, Baldwin, Floyd, Killens, and Mayfield. Maya Angelou. CP-AngeM; IHS

When hard luck overtakes you. Hard Luck. Langston Hughes. CP-HughL

When he came home. Poem No. 7. Sonia Sanchez. SP-SancS

When he, his heart had pledged, to full fifteen. Albery Allson Whitman. Fr. Leelah Misled. EBAP

When he the nation's heart had won. The Presidents. Lizelia Augusta Jenkins Moorer. CBWP-3

When Henry was a baby. Black Henry. Tejumola Ologboni. NBV

When Herbert Hoover was born. Herbert Hoover. African-American Oral Tradition. GetYo

When hit come ter de question er de female vote. Brother Baptis' on Woman Suffrage. Rosalie Jonas. BlSi

When I Am Dead. Owen Dodson. Klds

When I am dead, it will not be. Two Thoughts of Death. Countee Cullen. CP-CullC

When I am dead, withhold, I pray, your blooming legacy. Georgia Douglas Johnson. CDC

When I am gone. An Epitaph. Josephine D. Henderson Heard. AAP; CBWP-4

When I am obsolete. (LL) Dreams bite. Audre Lorde. CP-LordA; SP-LordA

When I ask what things they fear. Fears of the Eighth Grade. Toi Derricotte. GT

When I Awoke. Raymond R. Patterson. NBV; NNP; PoBA

When I Begin to Think When I Was a Young Man and in My Prime. African-American Oral Tradition. GetYo

When i blow open green bottles. Nighttrains. Jayne Cortez. SP-CortJ

When I come down to sleep death's endless night. My City. James Weldon Johnson. BANP; CDC; IHS; NAAAL

When I come in f'om de c'on-fiel' aftah wo'kin ha'd all day. At Candle-Lightin' Time. Paul Laurence Dunbar. CP-DunbP

When I Die. Fenton Johnson. CDC

When i die i hope no one who ever hurt me cries. Nikki Giovanni. SP-GiovN

When I / die / I'm sure. The Rebel. Mari E. Evans. AmNP; IDB; PoBA

When I do this sentence it'll be my last rap. Whores Are No Good and Crime Don't Pay. African-American Oral Tradition. GetYo

When i feel her jump up and dance. Homage to My Hair. Lucille Clifton. SP-ClifL

When I finally hear some woman say she. Memo. June Jordan. SP-JordJ

When I first saw you blooming the color was now. In Margaret's Garden. Audre Lorde. CP-LordA

When I gaze at the sun. A Moment Please. Samuel Allen. AmNP; IDB; PoBA; SSLK

When I get in Illinois. Can't You Line It? Unknown. NAAAL

When I get to be a composer. Daybreak in Alabama. Langston Hughes. CP-HughL; SP-HughL

When I get to heaven. Happy Day (or Independence Day). James Cunningham. JB

When I got up this mornin', I heah'd de ol' Southern whistle blow. The Southern Blues. Unknown. BkSV

When I grew up I went away to work. Whores. Margaret Abigail Walker. CP-WalkM

When I Heard Dat White Man Say. Zack Gilbert. PoBA

When I Know the Power of My Black Hand. Lance Jeffers. TtW

When I lay dis body down. (LL) I know moonlight, I know starlight. Unknown. BPo

When I lay dis body down. (LL) I know moon-rise, I know star-rise. Unknown. CrDW; NAAAL

When I Look at Wilfredo Lam's Paintings. Jayne Cortez. SP-CortJ

When i look at you. Sonia Sanchez. SP-SancS

When I move. Restrictive Covenants. Langston Hughes. CP-HughL

When i nap. Nikki Giovanni. SP-GiovN

When I no longer have your heart. Walker. Alice Walker. CP-WalkA

When I pat this floor. Tapping. Jayne Cortez. SP-CortJ

When i return home. Sonia Sanchez. SP-SancS

When I rolled three 7's. Situation. Langston Hughes. Fr. Montage of a Dream Deferred. CP-HughL

When I see a white man load a Black man's gun. (LL) On Working White Liberals. Maya Angelou. CP-AngeM; SP-AngeM

When I see the little Buddhist scouts. Reflections on a Small Parade. Bob Kaufman. SP-KaufB

When I see you bending over something rare. Ex-Slave. Margaret Abigail Walker. CP-WalkM

When i stepped off the plane i knew i was home. Rebirth. Sonia Sanchez. SP-SancS

When I studied my A-B-C's. The Kids in School with Me. Langston Hughes. CP-HughL

When I think about myself. Maya Angelou. CP-AngeM; SP-AngeM; TtW

When I think of the hosts of little ones. Mattinata. Mary Effie Lee Newsome. ShDr

When I walk the path this morning. The Homeplace. Lenard D. Moore. GT

When I was a boy desiring the title of man. George. Dudley Randall. BPo; Klds

When I was a child. King: April 4, 1968. Gerald William Barrax. ESEAA; GT

When I was a child I knew red miners. Childhood. Margaret Abigail Walker. CP-WalkM; Klds; PoBA

When I was a chile we used to play. Children's Rhymes. Langston Hughes. Fr. Montage of a Dream Deferred. BPo; CP-HughL; SP-HughL

When I was eight I listened to stories of love. Tapestries. Colleen J. McElroy. NAAAL

When I was five years old. Jamal; Nineteen Cows in a Slow Line Walking. Gwendolyn Brooks. Fr. Children Coming Home. ESEAA

When I was home de / Sunshine seemed like gold. Po' Boy Blues. Langston Hughes. BANP; CP-HughL; NAAAL

When i was six years old. Cuz' Mama Played Jazz. Daniel Gray-Kontar. SpiFl

When I was very very. Mama Knows. Sharon Scott. JB

When I was young I longed for Love. Vengeance is Sweet. Paul Laurence Dunbar. CP-DunbP

When I was young, I used to. Men. Maya Angelou. CP-AngeM; SP-AngeM

When I was young in my prime. Stackolee: "When I was young in my prime." African-American Oral Tradition. GetYo

When I watch my two boys, Walter and Robert, at play. I Am as Happy as a Queen on Her Throne. Mrs. Henry Linden. CBWP-4

When I watch you. Miss Rosie. Lucille Clifton. BlSi; ESEAA; PoBA; SP-ClifL

When I Would Die. Josephine D. Henderson Heard. CBWP-4

When in nineteen-thirty-seven, Etta Moten, sweet-heart. The Convert. Margaret Else Danner. BPo; BrTr

When in Rome. Mari E. Evans. AmNP

("Mattie dear / the box is full.") ESEAA

When in Rome—Apologia. Yusef Komunyakaa. SP-KomuY

When in the empty city a siren blasts through. Ear Training. Sekou Sundiata. SpiFl

When in the morning's misty hour. Forget Me Not. Ann Plato. EBAP

When Israel sate by Babel's stream and wept. The Lute of Afric's Tribe. Albery Allson Whitman. EBAP; TtW

When it is all over. Lost Moment. Hoyt W. Fuller. PoBA

When it is finally ours, this freedom, this liberty, this beautiful. Frederick Douglass. Robert Hayden. AmNP; CP-HaydR; ESEAA; IDB; Klds; NAAAL; PoBA; TtW

When it is past—the golden moment—gone! Lost Opportunities. Henrietta Cordelia Ray. CBWP-3

When it rain five days an' de skies turned dark as night. Backwater Blues. Unknown, sometimes at. to Bessie Smith. Crnst; NAAAL

When Jesus died at Calvary. Ballad of the Two Thieves. Langston Hughes. CP-HughL

When Jesus was leaving this sin-accursed land. Whoso Gives Freely, Shall Freely Receive! Josephine D. Henderson Heard. CBWP-4

When John Henry was a little babe [or fellow]. John Henry. *Unknown.* BPo

When John Henry was a little babe. *Unknown.* BPo

When John Henry was a little fellow. *Unknown. See* John Henry.

When June comes dancing on the death of May. A Memory of June. Claude McKay. SP-McKaC

When labor is light and the morning is fair. Riding to Town. Paul Laurence Dunbar. CP-DunbP

When Loneliness Is a Man. Yusef Komunyakaa. SP-KomuY

When love is a shimmering curtain. On Diverse Deviations. Maya Angelou. BlSi; CP-AngeM; SP-AngeM

When love leaps from my mouth. Legacy—Hers. Audre Lorde. CP-LordA

When lovers die they blossom. For Dancer. Ishmael Reed. CP-ReedI

When lovers / on the brink. Poem to the World. Bill Duke. CtF

When ma baby shouts in church. Lena Lovelace. Melvin B. Tolson. GT

When ma man looks at me. Ma Man. Langston Hughes. CP-HughL

When Ma Rainey / Comes to town. Ma Rainey. Sterling A. Brown. CP-BrowS; TtW

When Mahalia Sings. Quandra Prettyman. IDB; PoBA

When Malindy Sings. Paul Laurence Dunbar. AAP; CP-DunbP; NAAAL; PoBA

  ("G'way an' quit dat noise, Miss Lucy.") AfAmPo; Crnst

When Mark Deloach Ruled the World. Dominique Parker. SpiFl

When Mickey Mantle died. Players. E. Ethelbert Miller. SpiFl

When money clinks its story. (LL) Dr. Booker T. Washington to the National Negro Business League. Joseph Seamon Cotter, Sr. AAP; AfAmPo

When my dears die, the festival-colored brightness. Gwendolyn Brooks. *Fr.* The Children of the Poor.

When / my uncle willie saw. Carol Freeman. BlFi

When news came that your mother'd. Kin. Michael S. Harper. SP-HarpM; TtW

When night comes down upon the Chesapeake. Night on the Chesapeake. Paul Laurence Dunbar. CP-DunbP

When night moved through the air. A Poem for Dylan Thomas. Al Young. CP-YounA

When Ol' Sis' Judy Pray. James Edwin Campbell. AAP; BANP

When on life's ocean first I spread my sail. On Hearing of the Intention of a Gentleman to Purchase the Poet's Freedom. George Moses Horton. AAP; EBAP; NAAAL; SP-HortG

When on the earth had settled moral night. The Divine Mission. Alfred Gibbs Campbell. AAP

When Phyllis sighs and from her eyes. Response. Paul Laurence Dunbar. CP-DunbP

When pimps out of loneliness cry. Sliver of Sermon. Langston Hughes. *Fr.* Montage of a Dream Deferred. CP-HughL

When relatives came from out of town. Blackbottom. Toi Derricotte. GT

When Sam'l Sings. Paul Laurence Dunbar. CP-DunbP

When Science, trembling in the lengthened shade. Hymn to the Nation. Albery Allson Whitman. EBAP

When she and i. Gas Station Attendant. Brian G. Gilmore. SpiFl

When She Spoke of God. Lance Jeffers. BrTr

When she was little. Poem for Flora. Nikki Giovanni. BPo; PoBA; SP-GiovN

When she worked in their kitchens. (LL) Ruby Brown. Langston Hughes. CP-HughL; SP-HughL

When Slavery Seems Sweet. Ed Bullins. NBP

When sleep comes down to seal the weary eyes. (LL) Ere sleep comes down to soothe the weary eyes. Paul Laurence Dunbar. BALP; BANP; CDC; CP-DunbP; NAAAL

When smiling Summer's charms are past. On Winter. George Moses Horton. SP-HortG

When Something Happens. James A., Jr. Randall. BPo; SSLK

When spring / And life / Are new. (LL) In time of silver rain. Langston Hughes. CP-HughL; SP-HughL

When storms arise. Hymn. Paul Laurence Dunbar. CP-DunbP

When Sue Wears Red. Langston Hughes. CP-HughL; NAAAL; SP-HughL

When summer time has come, and all. In Summer Time. Paul Laurence Dunbar. CP-DunbP

When Susanna Jones wears red. When Sue Wears Red. Langston Hughes. CP-HughL; NAAAL; SP-HughL

When the African Arts. At Home in Dakar. Margaret Else Danner. BlSi; FB

When the Armies Passed. Langston Hughes. CP-HughL

When the autumn's breezes. Mr. Edward Fordham. Mary Weston Fordham. CBWP-2

When the bees are humming in the honeysuckle vine. Love's Seasons. Paul Laurence Dunbar. CP-DunbP

When the boys came home, everything stopped. The Bird Frau. Rita Dove. SP-DoveR

When the cold comes. Where? When? Which? Langston Hughes. BPo; CP-HughL; Klds

When the corn's all cut and the bright stalks shine. Corn-Stalk Fiddle, The. Paul Laurence Dunbar. AAP; CP-DunbP

When the fiat of the most High. Ocean. John Boyd. EBAP

When the Green Lies over the Earth. Angelina Weld Grimké. CDC; NAAAL

When the heavens with stars are gleaming. For Who? Mary Weston Fordham. CBWP-2

When the last man living. The Last Man Living. Langston Hughes. CP-HughL

When the lips. Sleep. Langston Hughes. CP-HughL

When the man is busy. Revolution Is One Form of Social Change. Audre Lorde. CP-LordA; SP-LordA

When the master lived a king and I a starving hutted slave beneath the lash, and. On Listening to the Spirituals. Lance Jeffers. PoBA; TtW

When the night winds whistle through the trees and blow the crisp brown leaves a-crackling down. Thanksgiving Time. Langston Hughes. CP-HughL

When the old junk man Death. Question: "When the old junk man Death." Langston Hughes. CP-HughL

When the Old Man Smokes. Paul Laurence Dunbar. CP-DunbP

When the people knew you. Lonely Particular. Alice Walker. CP-WalkA

When the revolution comes. Abiodun Oyewole. CtF

When the rooster jumps up on the windowsill. Cuba, 1962. Ai. ESEAA

When the Sabbath was declining, just at twilight's mystic hour. In Memoriam. Susan Eugenia Bennett. Mary Weston Fordham. CBWP-2

When the Saints Come Marching In. Audre Lorde. CP-LordA; SP-LordA

When the shoe strings break. The Blues. Langston Hughes. CP-HughL

When the stars self were young over Castries. The *Flight* Anchors in Castries Harbor. Derek Walcott. *Fr.* The Schooner *Flight.* ESEAA

When the storms of life are raging. Stand by Me. *Unknown.* NAAAL

When the / sun. August 2. Norman Jordan. PoBA

When the sun leaves dusk. And Pass. Jean Toomer. CP-ToomJ

When the verdict / was read. After the Verdict. Tony Medina. SpiFl

When the white folks get through. Office Building: Evening. Langston Hughes. CP-HughL

When the Wine Was Gone. Alvin Aubert. BkSV

When the world ends. The Dance. Cornelius Eady. GT

When their brains got. Heathens in Evolution. Amiri Baraka. SP-BaraA

When they hear. Children's Children. Sterling A. Brown. CP-BrowS

When they rode up at first dark and called his name. Sharecroppers. Sterling A. Brown. BrowS; Crnst

When they shot Malcolm Little down. At That Moment. Raymond R. Patterson. BrTr; PoBA; TtW

When / they speak of my death. Notes for a Poem from the Middle Passage of Years. Lamont B. Steptoe. SpiFl

When they torture your mother. Torture. Alice Walker. CP-WalkA

When this ancient, wallpapered melody. The Day a Dancer Learned to Sing of Dreamless Escapades. L. Goodwin. BlFi

When three, he fished these lakes. Fishermen. James A. Emanuel. BrTr

When through the winding cobbled streets of time. The Noonday April Sun. George Love. IDB; NNP

When Tiger left his native yard. The Fate of an Innocent Dog. George Moses Horton. SP-HortG

When time has rocked the present age to sleep. To William Stanley Braithwaite. Georgia Douglas Johnson. BALP

When to sweet music my lady is dancing. The Valse. Paul Laurence Dunbar. CP-DunbP

When war's red banner trailed along the sky. Robert G. Shaw. Henrietta Cordelia Ray. AAP; BlSi; CBWP-3; EBAP

When we count out our gold at the end of the day. Service. Georgia Douglas Johnson. CDC

When we crossed the railed road. Mr. Tut's House A Recollection. Julia Fields. BkSV

When we hear the eye open there, in that place. Bob Kaufman. SP-KaufB

When we met. The Awakening. Alice Walker. CP-WalkA

When we speak to each other our voices are a little gruff. (LL) Beverly Hills, Chicago. Gwendolyn Brooks. ESEAA; SP-BrooG

When We'll Worship Jesus. Amiri Baraka. SP-BaraA

When we're apart. (LL) Greyday. Maya Angelou. CP-AngeM; SP-AngeM

When white people speak of being uptight. The Dancer. Al Young. CP-YounA; PoBA

When winter covering all the ground. When Winter Darkening All Around. Paul Laurence Dunbar. CP-DunbP

When Winter Darkening All Around. Paul Laurence Dunbar. CP-DunbP

When Winter's royal robes of white. A Parting Hymn. Charlotte L. Forten Grimké. BlSi; NAAAL

When woods are odorous at eve. Wood Carols. Henrietta Cordelia Ray. CBWP-3

When words fail. (LL) Strategies. Welton Smith. NBP; PoBA

When you and I were young, the days. Retrospection. Paul Laurence Dunbar. CP-DunbP

When you appeared it was as if. Happenstance. Rita Dove. SP-DoveR

When you are called on to perform a duty. Do Your Best. Mrs. Henry Linden. CBWP-4

When you can no longer / eat. Attentiveness. Alice Walker. CP-WalkA

When you come out of that. Jalapeña Gypsies. Jay Wright. NBV

When you come to me, unbidden. Maya Angelou. CP-AngeM; SP-AngeM

When you discovered. A Dance Lesson. A. Van Jordan. SpiFl

When you do say hello I am never sure. Progress Report. Audre Lorde. SP-LordA

When you enter. Al Fitnah Muhajir. Nazzam Al-Sudan. NBP

When You Have Forgotten Sunday: The Love Story. Gwendolyn Brooks. BPo

("And when you have forgotten the bright bedclothes on a.") NAAAL

When you left I ran. Sonia Sanchez. SP-SancS

When you lie again. To a Woman Poet That I Know. Pinkie Gordon Lane. TtW

When You Read This Poem. Pinkie Gordon Lane. BlSi

When you remember me, my child. Mississippi Winter II. Alice Walker. CP-WalkA

When you see me sitting quietly. On Aging. Maya Angelou. CP-AngeM; SP-AngeM

When you see them. Take Time Out. Maya Angelou. CP-AngeM; SP-AngeM

When you show me. Colors for Mama. Barbara Mahone. PoBA

When you thrill with joy. Watch Out, Papa. Langston Hughes. CP-HughL

When you turn the corner. Final Curve. Langston Hughes. CP-HughL; SP-HughL

When you were. For Angela. Zack Gilbert. PoBA

When you were here in wonderful Detroit. Goodbye David Tamunoemi West. Margaret Else Danner. BPo

When young spring comes. Poem: "When young spring comes." Langston Hughes. CP-HughL

When your brave eyes are stopped with dust. Against That Day. Sterling A. Brown. CP-BrowS

When your eyes gaze seaward. Golden Moonrise. William Stanley Braithwaite. PoBA

When your heels fit together and your head feel queer. Drinkin'. *African-American Oral Tradition*. GetYo

Whenever I do not create. Beast. Alice Walker. CP-WalkA

Whenever we're left alone in the room she performs. Gloria's Clues. Yusef Komunyakaa. SP-KomuY

When's the last time you. Bitch. Ishmael Reed. CP-ReedI

Where are my people? To Egypt. Gloria Davis. NBP

Where are the warriors, the young men? Earth. Askia Muhammad Touré. BrTr

Where are the warriors, the young men? Earth. Rolland Snellings. BlFi

Where are we to go when this is done? Sonnet. Alfred A. Duckett. AmNP; PoBA

Where are your heroes, my little black ones. Poem for Black Boys. Nikki Giovanni. BPo; SP-GiovN

Where contemplation finds her sacred spring. To a Clergyman on the Death of His Lady. Phillis Wheatley. CP-WheaP

Where Contemplation finds her sacred Spring. To the Rev. Mr. Pitkin, on the Death of His Lady. Phillis Wheatley. CP-WheaP

Where Dave went. (LL) Ballad of the Fortune Teller. Langston Hughes. CP-HughL; SP-HughL

Where death. There. Langston Hughes. CP-HughL

"Where did I come from, Mother, and why?" Christmas Lullaby for a New-Born Child. Yvonne Gregory. AmNP

Where did they go. The Writers. Mari E. Evans. TtW

Where Do School Days End? Josephine D. Henderson Heard. CBWP-4

Where does heart rest, breath originate. Soon One Morning, I'll Fly Away. Kalamu ya Salaam. CtF

Where / from / here. 2 B LK. Val Ferdinand. NBV

Where have the people gone. From Spain to Alabama. Langston Hughes. CP-HughL

Where Have You Gone? Mari E. Evans. BPo; NNP; TtW

Where he stood and where. Jew. James A., Jr. Randall. BPo

Where I go the lily blooms. The Ethiopian's Song. Fenton Johnson. Crnst

Where I grew up, I used to see. The Rabbi. Robert Hayden. CP-HaydR

Where I was born, make my eternal bed. (LL) I love Kentucky; tho' she merit scorn. Albery Allson Whitman. AfAmPo *Fr.* Not a Man, and Yet a Man

Where in the new fruit. A Morning Poem for Michael. Al Young. CP-YounA

Where is that sugar, Hammond. Early Evening Quarrel. Langston Hughes. CP-HughL; SP-HughL

Where Is the Guilt. May Miller. TtW

Where is the Jim Crow section. Merry-Go-Round. Langston Hughes. CP-HughL; SP-HughL

Where is the promise of my years. Infelix. Adah Isaacs Menken. AAP; CBWP-1

Where is the star of Bethlehem? Christmas 1959 Et Cetera. Gerald William Barrax. Klds

Where it all began. (LL) Revolution Is One Form of Social Change. Audre Lorde. SP-LordA

Where light is. To a Woman Who Wants Darkness and Time. Gerald William Barrax. PoBA

Where, like the prophet, thou shalt find thy God. (LL) To the Right Honourable William, Earl of Dartmouth, His Majesty's Principal Secretary of State for North-America, Etc. Phillis Wheatley. CP-WheaP; CrDW; NAAAL

Where Martin Luther King could have lived and preached non-violence. (LL) The Funeral of Martin Luther King, Jr. Nikki Giovanni. AmNP; BPo

Where most surely comes a day. Day. Langston Hughes. CP-HughL

Where my grandmother lived. Number Four. Doughtry Long. PoBA

Where now shall I begin this Spacious Feild. Atheism. Phillis Wheatley. CP-WheaP

Where Seed Falls. Essex Hemphill. GT

Where Service Is Needed. Langston Hughes. CP-HughL

Where shall I lead the flocks to-day? Where the Flocks Shall Be Led. Adah Isaacs Menken. CBWP-1

Where shall we meet, who knows, who knows? (LL) A Song: "Thou art the soul of a summer's day." Paul Laurence Dunbar. AmNP; CP-DunbP

Where the Danube and Sava Rivers Meet. Al Young. CP-YounA

Where the Flocks Shall Be Led. Adah Isaacs Menken. CBWP-1

Where the fruit, vegetables, woodpile, lie. (LL) The Families Album. Michael S. Harper. SP-HarpM

Where the good God sits to spangle through. (LL) Lady, Lady, I saw your face. Anne Spencer. BlSi; NAAAL; PoBA; ShDr

Where the Heart Is. Ntozake Shange. GT

Where the string. O-Jazz-O. Bob Kaufman. SP-KaufB

Where the sunsets bleed. (LL) Georgia Dusk. Langston Hughes. CP-HughL; Crnst; SP-HughL

Where the wheel turned the water / gently shirred. Rita Dove. *See* The Event.

Where We Belong, A Duet. Maya Angelou. CP-AngeM; SP-AngeM

Where we were other for an hour or two? (LL) Double Feature. Robert Hayden. CP-HaydR

Where When Was. Reginald Shepherd. GT

Where? When? Which? Langston Hughes. BPo; CP-HughL; Klds

Where your skin / is your passport. (LL) Untitled Blues. Yusef Komunyakaa. GT; SP-KomuY

Wherefore this busy labor without rest? Tuskegee. Leslie Pinckney Hill. BANP

Wherein are words sublime or noble? What. Karenge Ya Marenge. Countee Cullen. CP-CullC; TtW

Wherein to play your violin with grace. (LL) First fight. Then fiddle. Ply the slipping string. Gwendolyn Brooks. Crnst; SP-BrooG; TtW

Whi / te boys gone. Val Ferdinand. NBV

Whi-te reaction to it won't, The. (LL) Poem (No Name No. 3). Nikki Giovanni. BrTr; SP-GiovN

Which knows no pain. (LL) Solace. Clarissa Scott Delany. AmNP; CDC; PoBA; ShDr

Which, lit his inmost-self, and spurned all mean control. (LL) Upon the shells by Carribea's wave. Albery Allson Whitman. AAP *Fr.* Twasinta's Seminoles; Or Rape of Florida

Which me will survive / all these liberations. (LL) Who Said It Was Simple. Audre Lorde. CP-LordA; SP-LordA

Which out of sight and sound is passing, passing? (LL) Ships That Pass in the Night. Paul Laurence Dunbar. BANP; CDC; CP-DunbP

Which reminds of another knock-on-wood. Minor Miracle. Marilyn Nelson. SP-NelsM

Whichway. Ron Welburn. NBV

While an intrinsic ardor prompts to write. To the University of Cambridge, in New-England. Phillis Wheatley. BALP; CP-WheaP; EBAP; NAAAL; TtW

While Byron's fame through endless time will reign! (LL) Byron's Oak at Newstead Abbey. Timothy Thomas Fortune. AAP; EBAP

While Cecil Snores: Mom Drinks Cold Milk. James Cunningham. JB

While deep you mourn beneath the cypress-shade. To the Honourable T.H. Esq.; on the Death of His Daughter. Phillis Wheatley. CP-WheaP

While driving north, lost. I Was Looking for the University. Clarence Major. GT

While hireling scribblers prostitute their pen. An Ode on the Birthday of Pompey Stockbridge. Phillis Wheatley. EBAP

While i was in the middle of the night. Easter Sunday. Lucille Clifton. SP-ClifL

While it breaks, breaks, breaks on the sheltering bars. (LL) Heart of a Woman, The. Georgia Douglas Johnson. BlSi; CDC; NAAAL; ShDr; TtW

While love is unfashionable. Alice Walker. CP-WalkA

While others chant the gay *Elysian* scenes. To a Gentleman on his Voyage to Great-Britain for the Recovery of His Health. Phillis Wheatley. CP-WheaP

While playing short coin in the Golden West. *African-American Oral Tradition*. GetYo

While Poets Are Watching. Colleen J. McElroy. TtW

While raging tempests shake the shore. Ode to Neptune. Phillis Wheatley. CP-WheaP

While sittin' and thinking in deep meditation. Wicked Nell: "While sittin' and thinking in deep meditation." *African-American Oral Tradition*. GetYo

While sittin' down in deep meditation, little girl, lookin' at you. Wicked Nell: "While sittin' down in deep meditation, little girl, lookin' at you." *African-American Oral Tradition*. GetYo

While sittin' here chattin' with you. Pimping Sam. *African-American Oral Tradition*. GetYo

While sitting in my room kind Miss. Dedicated to a Young Lady Representing the Indian Race at Howard University. Alfred Islay Walden. AAP

While smoking her cigarette down to the very end. (LL) The Great Palaces of Versailles. Rita Dove. ESEAA

While some "rap" over this turmoil. The Rhetoric of Langston Hughes. Margaret Else Danner. BlSi; FB

While the Choir Sang. Priscilla Jane Thompson. CBWP-2

While thus you mourn beneath the Cypress shade. To the Hon'ble Thomas Hubbard, Esq.; on the Death of Mrs. Thankfull Leonard. Phillis Wheatley. CP-WheaP

While young moons rage and wander in the sky. (LL) Father and Daughter. Sonia Sanchez. GT; SP-SancS

Whilst tracing thy visage, I sink in emotion. Love. George Moses Horton. SP-HortG

Whip it to a jelly! Rent-Party Shout. Langston Hughes. CP-HughL

Whip-Poor-Will and Katy-Did. Paul Laurence Dunbar. CP-DunbP

Whipping, The. Robert Hayden. CP-HaydR; IDB; PoBA; SSLK

Whipping, The. Samuel F. Reynolds. SpiFl

Whisper it, / "Oh Hayden." And, Yes, Those Spiritual Matters. Christopher Gilbert. ESEAA

Whisper of yellow globes. Her Lips Are Copper Wire. Jean Toomer. AfAmPo; CP-ToomJ; GT

Whisper Words of Love to Me. Lizelia Augusta Jenkins Moorer. CBWP-3

Whispers / Of springtime. Fragments. Langston Hughes. CP-HughL

White america / comfortable and disillusioned. Black and White. Umar Abd Rahim Hasson. BrTr

White Arrow. Jean Toomer. CP-ToomJ

White / as / snow. (LL) Angels wings is white as snow, The. Langston Hughes. CP-HughL; SP-HughL

White Blues: the Master's Song. George Barlow. *Fr.* Gabriel. TtW

White Boy, The. Lucille Clifton. SP-ClifL

White City, The. Claude McKay. BPo; CrDW; SP-McKaC

White coats / White aprons. Interne at Provident. Langston Hughes. CP-HughL; SP-HughL

White Days. Reginald Shepherd. GT

White Deer, The. Jay Wright. ESEAA

"White folks is white," says Uncle Jim. Uncle Jim. Countee Cullen. BANP; CP-CullC; GT

White folks, / You better get some new jive. Get Up off That Old Jive. Langston Hughes. CP-HughL

White Friend Flies in from the Coast, A. Michael S. Harper. SP-HarpM

White Hope. Ishmael Reed. CP-ReedI

White House, The. Claude McKay. AmNP; Crnst; NAAAL; PoBA; SP-McKaC; TtW

White is right. Argument: "White is right." Langston Hughes. SP-HughL *Fr.* Montage of a Dream Deferred. CP-HughL

White Lady. Lucille Clifton. ESEAA

White Lady has asked me to dance, The. Fourth Dance Poem. Gerald William Barrax. PoBA

White Man. Langston Hughes. CP-HughL

White man is, The. 12 Gates to the City. Nikki Giovanni. PoBA

White man is a tiger at my throat, The. Tiger. Claude McKay. BPo; CrDW; SP-McKaC; TtW

White man tells me he told a white woman, A. En Passant. June Jordan. SP-JordJ

White men's children spread over the earth. Riddle, The: "White men's children spread over the earth." Georgia Douglas Johnson. PoBA; TtW

White Ones, The. Langston Hughes. CP-HughL

White People. David Henderson. PoBA

White poets call the past. (LL) Driving through New England. Lucille Clifton. ESEAA; SP-ClifL

White Powder! Victor Hernandez Cruz. BlFi

White southern businessman needed, The. New Windows. Claudia Rankine. GT

White substitute teacher, A. View of the Library of Congress from Paul Laurence Dunbar High School. Thomas Sayers Ellis. GT

White Things. Anne Spencer. AfAmPo; Crnst; ShDr

White Troops Had Their Orders but the Negroes Looked Like Men. Gwendolyn Brooks. SP-BrooG

White Weekend. Quincy Troupe. NBP

White Witch, The. James Weldon Johnson. AfAmPo; BANP; CDC; TtW

White woman have you heard. Montgomery. Sam Cornish. PoBA

White workers of the South. Open Letter to the South. Langston Hughes. CP-HughL

White yuppies in santa monica go through their attics. History as Trash. Michélle T. Clinton. SpiFl

Whites alone upon the jury in a number of the states. Injustice of the Courts. Lizelia Augusta Jenkins Moorer. CBWP-3

Whites had taught him how to rip, The. Sam Smiley. Sterling A. Brown. CP-BrowS; NAAAL

Whitey, Baby. James A. Emanuel. BrTr; NBV

Whitey drops Napalm on the Yellow man. To Hell with Whitey. Mario Van Peebles. CtF

Whittier. Paul Laurence Dunbar. CP-DunbP

Who am I? The Big-Timer. Langston Hughes. CP-HughL

Who am I to love. Footnote to a Pretentious Book. Amiri Baraka. SP-BaraA

Who are they to be in their skin. The Subway Witnesses. Lorenzo Thomas. GT; PoBA

Who are we, S.S. The Poem For a Certain Lady on Her 33rd Birthday. Etheridge Knight. SP-KnigE

Who are we to love. A Footnote to a Gray Bird's Pause. James Cunningham. JB

Who are we? Who. Towards a Walk in the Sun. Keorapetse W. Kgositsile. BlFi

Who are you? Napoleon or something? Back to Back: 3rd Eye. Ishmael Reed. CP-ReedI

Who are you / that your name comes. To Desi as Joe as Smoky the Lover of 115th Street. Audre Lorde. CP-LordA

Who are you/ iden. Sonia Sanchez. SP-SancS

Who But the Lord? Langston Hughes. BPo; CP-HughL; SP-HughL

Who Can Be Born Black. Mari E. Evans. TtW

Who can forget the attitude of mothering? Rita Dove. NAAAL

Who can hold up the intellect and say. Oliver Wendell Holmes. Joseph Seamon Cotter, Sr. EBAP

Who cannot / Weep. (LL) Vagabonds. Langston Hughes. CP-HughL; SP-HughL

Who cares / About the hurt in your heart? Hurt. Langston Hughes. CP-HughL

Who collects the pain. "Stephany." NBV *Fr.* Moving Deep. BrTr

Who dat knockin' at de do'? Encouragement. Paul Laurence Dunbar. CP-DunbP

Who fought for Uncle Sam! (LL) The Colored Soldiers. Paul Laurence Dunbar. AAP; CP-DunbP; NAAAL

Who fought their way from night to day and struggled up to God. (LL) The Unsung Heroes. Paul Laurence Dunbar. BPo; CP-DunbP

Who got used to making it through murdered sons. (LL) For de Lawd. Lucille Clifton. PoBA

Who has ever stopped to think of the divinity of Lamont Cranston? In Memory of Radio. Amiri Baraka. NAAAL; SP-BaraA

Who has not been. Alice Walker. CP-WalkA

Who Has Seen the Wind? Bob Kaufman. Klds; SP-KaufB

Who hath not sent out ships to sea? The Ship That Went Down. Adah Isaacs Menken. CBWP-1

Who have to buy in white men's stores next week. (LL) Chopin. Marilyn Nelson. SP-NelsM

Who I break my head against. First Claims Poem. Victor Hernandez Cruz. NBV

Who is a white / woman / and. For Mary Ellen McAnally. Etheridge Knight. SP-KnigE

Who is black. (LL) Kali / queen of fertility. Lucille Clifton. NAAAL; SP-ClifL

Who is director of this movie. Hallucinogenic Halleluuuu. Al Young. CP-YounA

Who Is My Brother? Pinkie Gordon Lane. BlSi

Who Is My Neighbor? Josephine D. Henderson Heard. CBWP-4

Who is not a stranger still. "Stephany." BPo *Fr.* Moving Deep. BrTr

Who Is That a-Walking in the Corn? Fenton Johnson. TtW

Who is that running away. C. C. Rider. Lucille Clifton. GT

Who knows where you go. The Odds. Al Young. CP-YounA

Who knows why we talk of death. The Drowning of the Facts of a Life. Michael S. Harper. ESEAA

Who leads hither what he finds? Words to Drive out the White Growth in the Eyes. Everett Hoagland. BrTr

Who lies with his milk-white maiden. Song of Praise. Countee Cullen. CP-CullC

Who likes to glitter. Complicity. Jayne Cortez. SP-CortJ

Who Look at Me. June Jordan. SP-JordJ

Who of us is not mad. Reading Nijinsky's Diary. Al Young. CP-YounA

Who Said It Was Simple. Audre Lorde. CP-LordA; SP-LordA

Who says my hea't ain't true to you? Protest. Paul Laurence Dunbar. CP-DunbP

Who says that the Earth is blind? Living Earth. Jean Toomer. CP-ToomJ

Who Shall Die. James A., Jr. Randall. BPo; BrTr

Who take today and jerk it out of joint. Young Africans. Gwendolyn Brooks. BrTr

Who taught thee conflict with the pow'rs of night. On the Death of a Young Gentleman. Phillis Wheatley. CP-WheaP; Crnst

Who was a man. (LL) Malcolm X. Gwendolyn Brooks. BALP; NAAAL; PoBA; TtW

Who was it who held me on her knee? Mother. Josephine D. Henderson Heard. CBWP-4

Who will know Bessie now of those who loved her. Bessie. Sterling A. Brown. CP-BrowS

Who would have thought she'd end that way? (LL) Mourning Poem for the Queen of Sunday. Robert Hayden. CP-HaydR; NAAAL; PoBA

Who would not sing in May. (LL) The Crazy Woman. Gwendolyn Brooks. SP-BrooG

Who would paint a people. Who Look at Me. June Jordan. SP-JordJ

Who would / who could. Now Ain't That Love? Carolyn M. Rodgers. BPo; BrTr

Who you gonna put in it? Air Raid over Harlem. Langston Hughes. CP-HughL

Whoever it was who brought the first wood and coal. Banking Coal. Jean Toomer. CP-ToomJ

Whole Two Weeks After the Million Man March; and Still, if You Asked Me about It, This Is All I Could Say about It, A. Richard Rykard. SpiFl

Who'll Be a Witness for My Lord? *Unknown.* CrDW

Whom can I confess to? In the Interest of Black Salvation. Haki R. Madhubuti. BrTr

Whores. Margaret Abigail Walker. CP-WalkM

Whores Are No Good and Crime Don't Pay, *see also* No Good Whore *and* Sweet Lovin' Rose. *African-American Oral Tradition.* GetYo

Who's gonna make all. Blk/Rhetoric. Sonia Sanchez. Crnst; SP-SancS

Whose broken window is a cry of art. Boy Breaking Glass. Gwendolyn Brooks. ESEAA

Whose children are these? Gerald William Barrax. TtW

Whose life connects / The migratory sea. One Within. Jean Toomer. CP-ToomJ

Whose little lady is you, chile. Possession. Paul Laurence Dunbar. CP-DunbP

Whose name should be you. (LL) Sowing. Audre Lorde. CP-LordA; SP-LordA

Whose wife / I am. (LL) And What About the Children. Audre Lorde. CP-LordA; PoBA; SP-LordA

Whoso Gives Freely, Shall Freely Receive! Josephine D. Henderson Heard. CBWP-4

Whuh folks, whuh folks, don' wuk muh brown too hahd! Scotty Has His Say. Sterling A. Brown. CP-BrowS

Whut dat you whisperin' keepin' f'om me? The News. Paul Laurence Dunbar. CP-DunbP

Whut do i keer ef de white-folks do 'buse us! Uncle Rube's Defense. Clara Ann Thompson. CBWP-2

Whut time 'd dat clock strike? At Night. Paul Laurence Dunbar. CP-DunbP

Whut you say, dah? huh, uh! chile. A Cabin Tale. Paul Laurence Dunbar. CP-DunbP; NAAAL

Why? Melba Joyce Boyd. BlSi

Why a Hush Should Not Be Rushed. Al Young. CP-YounA

Why Adam Sinned. Alex Rogers. BANP

Why am I not as they? (LL) Lineage. Margaret Abigail Walker. BlSi; CP-WalkM; Klds; PoBA; TtW

Why anyone bothered. (LL) And Was Not Improved. Lerone, Jr. Bennett. PoBA

Why are candles brightly burning. The Christmas Tree. Lizelia Augusta Jenkins Moorer. CBWP-3

Why are our ancestors. Ancestors. Dudley Randall. BPo

Why Are They Happy People? Maya Angelou. CP-AngeM

Why cherish thus the senseless thing? That Glove. Mary E. Tucker. CBWP-1

Why deck with flow'rs these humble mounds? Memorial Day. Paul Laurence Dunbar. CP-DunbP

Why did the sun his beams conceal. The Crucifixion. Mary Weston Fordham. CBWP-2

Why did you stay away. The Way the Cards Fall. Yusef Komunyakaa. GT; SP-KomuY

Why do men smile when I speak. Is It Because I Am Black? Joseph Seamon Cotter, Sr. BANP; NNP; TtW

Why do people sit in darkness as regards the Negro race? The Truth Suppressed. Lizelia Augusta Jenkins Moorer. CBWP-3

Why do poets / Like to die. More Letters Found near a Suicide. Frank Horne. BANP

Why Do So Few Blacks Study Creative Writing? Cornelius Eady. GT

Why do they walk so tragical. Harlem Street Walkers. Sterling A. Brown. CP-BrowS

Why do you want me to slap you. Mojo Queen of the Feathery Plumes. Ishmael Reed. CP-ReedI

Why don't we rock the casket here in the moonlight? The Pale Blue Casket. Oliver Pitcher. NNP; PoBA

Why dont you go on and integrate a. On Becomin Successful. Ntozake Shange. TtW

Why fades a dream? Paul Laurence Dunbar. CP-DunbP

Why have crowds as magnets drawn. Why We Meet. Lizelia Augusta Jenkins Moorer. CBWP-3

Why I Like Movies. Patricia Jones. BlSi

Why I Must Make Language. Angela Jackson. TtW

Why I Often Allude to Osiris. Ishmael Reed. CP-ReedI; GT

Why I Turned Vegetarian. Rita Dove. SP-DoveR

Why i would bring a wagon into battle. Willie B (2). Lucille Clifton. SP-ClifL

Why in all the many races of the country where we live. Why Negroes Don't Unite. Lizelia Augusta Jenkins Moorer. CBWP-3

Why Is It? Lizelia Augusta Jenkins Moorer. CBWP-3

Why must i string my hate. Sonia Sanchez. SP-SancS

Why Negroes Don't Unite. Lizelia Augusta Jenkins Moorer. CBWP-3

Why should I be eaten by love. James A., Jr. Randall. BPo

Why should it be *my* dream / deferred / overlong? (LL) Tell Me. Langston Hughes. CP-HughL

Why should it be *my* loneliness. Tell Me. Langston Hughes. *Fr.* Montage of a Dream Deferred. CP-HughL

Why Should the American Negro Be Proud? Maggie Pogue Johnson. CBWP-4

Why Some People Be Mad at Me Sometimes. Lucille Clifton. ESEAA

Why stand aghast. He Hath Need of Rest. Josephine D. Henderson Heard. CBWP-4

Why stirs, with sad alarm, the heart. Farewell Song. Paul Laurence Dunbar. CP-DunbP

Why this girl has no fear. Carmen. Victor Hernandez Cruz. PoBA

Why this preoccupation, soul, with Death. Sonnet Dialogue. Countee Cullen. CP-CullC

Why Tu Fu Does Not Speak of the Nubian. Colleen J. McElroy. TtW

Why was I born if this ends all. My Song. James Ephriam McGirt. AAP

Why was it that the thunder voice of Fate. Robert Gould Shaw. Paul Laurence Dunbar. CP-DunbP; Klds

Why We Meet. Lizelia Augusta Jenkins Moorer. CBWP-3

Why would anybody build a monument to civil war? Grand Army Plaza. June Jordan. SP-JordJ

Why Would I Want. William J. Harris. PoBA

Why Write ABOUT. Bob Kaufman. SP-KaufB

Wicked Nell: "While sittin' and thinking in deep meditation." *African-American Oral Tradition.* GetYo

Wicked Nell: "While sittin' down in deep meditation, little girl, lookin' at you." *African-American Oral Tradition.* GetYo

Wicked stepmother bursts into her husband's, The. No Worst. Marilyn Nelson. SP-NelsM

Wide River. Langston Hughes. CP-HughL

Widow Woman. Langston Hughes. CP-HughL; SP-HughL

Widow's Mites, The. Frances Ellen Watkins Harper. CP-HarpF

Wife. Lucille Clifton. SP-ClifL

Wife-Woman, The. Anne Spencer. BANP; NAAAL

Wig. Kirk Hall. BlFi

Wilberforce. Josephine D. Henderson Heard. CBWP-4

Wild-eared, / singing. (LL) Sunday Greens. Rita Dove. GT; SP-DoveR

Wild Goat, The. Claude McKay. CDC; SP-McKaC

Wild May. Claude McKay. SP-McKaC

Wild Negro Bill. *Unknown.* BPo; NAAAL

Wild Pansies. Marilyn Nelson. SP-NelsM

Wild poppy-flower, A. Poppy Flower. Langston Hughes. CP-HughL

Wild rice grows along the banks. One Lives, One Dies: Both/And: A Choice of Colors. Michael S. Harper. SP-HarpM

Wild Roses. Mary Effie Lee Newsome. CDC; ShDr

Wild trees have bought me. Song. Audre Lorde. CP-LordA; SP-LordA

Wild winds flowed from out God's hand, The. It Shall Not Come Nigh Thee. Frances Ellen Watkins Harper. CP-HarpF

Wilderness of water, A. (LL) Long Trip. Langston Hughes. CP-HughL; SP-HughL

Will. Alice Walker. CP-WalkA

Will and the Swan, The. George Barlow. *Fr.* Gabriel. TtW

Will be the days. The '70s. Lucille Clifton. SP-ClifL

Will find its symbol, the woman thinks. (LL) History. Rita Dove. NAAAL

Will have the blues. (LL) The Backlash Blues. Langston Hughes. CP-HughL

Will I have some mo' dat pie? Reluctance. Paul Laurence Dunbar. CP-DunbP

Will it be like this, Charlie. A Black Stick with a Ball of Cotton for a Head and a Running Machine for a Mouth. Calvin C. Hernton. BlFi

Will live, the sinking soul to cheer! (LL) There is, at times, an evenin sky. George Boyer Vashon. EBAP

Will not change / all that. (LL) Summary. Sonia Sanchez. BlFi; BrTr; SP-SancS

Will not contain you. (LL) Did John's Music Kill Him? Alfred B. Spellman. NAAAL

Will not die politely / either. (LL) A Birthday Memorial to Seventh Street. Audre Lorde. CP-LordA; SP-LordA

Will press the life-drops from the heart. (LL) The Slave Auction. Frances Ellen Watkins Harper. BPo; CP-HarpF; EBAP; Klds

Will surely get you down. (LL) Blue Monday. Langston Hughes. CP-HughL; SP-HughL

Will the machinegunners please step forward? (LL) A Poem Some People Will Have to Understand. Amiri Baraka. GT; SP-BaraA

Will V-Day Be Me-Day Too? Langston Hughes. CP-HughL

Will you leave the hills of Scotland? Highland Mary. Mary Weston Fordham. CBWP-2

Wille B (3). Lucille Clifton. SP-ClifL

William Carlos Williams. Cornelius Eady. GT

William Lloyd Garrison. Joseph Seamon Cotter, Sr. AAP

William Lloyd Garrison. Henrietta Cordelia Ray. CBWP-3

Willie B (1). Lucille Clifton. SP-ClifL

Willie B (2). Lucille Clifton. SP-ClifL

Willie B (4). Lucille Clifton. SP-ClifL

Willie Note 9/28/91. Quo Vadis Gex-Breaux. TtW

Willie the Weeper. *African-American Oral Tradition.* GetYo

Willie was a man without fame. Maya Angelou. CP-AngeM; SP-AngeM

Willy is a silly boy. The Lament of a Vanquished Beau. Langston Hughes. CP-HughL

Wilmington Delaware. Nikki Giovanni. BrTr

Wilmington is a funni negro. Wilmington Delaware. Nikki Giovanni. BrTr

Win' a-blowin' gentle so de san' lay low. A Florida Night. Paul Laurence Dunbar. CP-DunbP

Win' is blowin' wahmah, De. A Christmas Folksong. Paul Laurence Dunbar. CP-DunbP

Win' is hollahin' "Daih you,"De. A Little Christmas Basket. Paul Laurence Dunbar. CP-DunbP

Wind and the Sea, The. Paul Laurence Dunbar. CP-DunbP

Wind / blade cutting in, The. Impressions / of Chicago; For Howlin' Wolf. Quincy Troupe. NAAAL; NBV

Wind Bloweth Where It Listeth, The. Countee Cullen. CP-CullC; GT

Wind blows, The. Mae V. Cowdery. ShDr

Wind is eating, The. A Storm Poem. Lucille Clifton. SP-ClifL

Wind is in the cane. Come along. Jean Toomer. *Fr.* Carma. Klds

Wind is out in its rage tonight, The. The Fisher Child's Lullaby. Paul Laurence Dunbar. CP-DunbP

Wind is ruffling the tawny pelt, A. A Far Cry from Africa. Derek Walcott. ESEAA

Wind led me here, The. Wind Thoughts. Pinkie Gordon Lane. GT

Wind, rain, / cracks in the sky. History Is Thunder and Rain. George Barlow. *Fr.* Gabriel. TtW

Wind Thoughts. Pinkie Gordon Lane. GT

Wind told the little leaves to hurry, The. The Chase. Paul Laurence Dunbar. CP-DunbP

Window Shopping. Lamont B. Steptoe. SpiFl

Windows of America, The. Prayer: Mt. Hood and Environs. Michael S. Harper. TtW

Winds of Orisha, The. Audre Lorde. CP-LordA; NAAAL; SP-LordA

Wine-maiden / Of the jazz-tuned night. Midnight Dancer. Langston Hughes. CP-HughL; SP-HughL

Wine-O. Langston Hughes. *Fr.* Montage of a Dream Deferred. CP-HughL

Winehead Girl. *African-American Oral Tradition.* GetYo

Winged Abyss. Nathaniel Mackey. ESEAA

Winged women was saying. Mary's Dream. Lucille Clifton. SP-ClifL

Wingfoot Lake, Independence Day, 1964. Rita Dove. SP-DoveR

Winin' boy, / if you were mine. Jelly Roll Morton. Sybil Klein. TtW

Winnie. Gwendolyn Brooks. ESEAA
Song of Winnie.

Winnie Mandela We Love You. Alice Walker. CP-WalkA

Wintah Styles, De. Maggie Pogue Johnson. CBWP-4

Wintah, summah, snow er shine. Song. Paul Laurence Dunbar. CP-DunbP

Wintah time hit comin'. The Plantation Child's Lullaby. Paul Laurence Dunbar. CP-DunbP

Winter. Nikki Giovanni. SP-GiovN

Winter. Helen G. Quigless. BkSV

Winter alleys are warm. Daddy's Friends. Esther Iverem. GT

Winter birds, The. Migration. Pinkie Gordon Lane. BlSi

Winter days are drawin' nigh, De. Winter is Coming. Waverly Turner Carmichael. BANP

Winter Honey. June Jordan. SP-JordJ

Winter in the Country. Claude McKay. SP-McKaC

Winter is Coming. Waverly Turner Carmichael. BANP

Winter is settling on the place; the sedge. Virginia Portrait. Sterling A. Brown. CP-BrowS; GT

Winter Leaves. Al Young. CP-YounA

Winter Moon. Langston Hughes. CP-HughL; SP-HughL

Winter Night, A. Priscilla Jane Thompson. CBWP-2

Winter Poem. Nikki Giovanni. SP-GiovN

Winter-Song. Paul Laurence Dunbar. CP-DunbP

Winter Sonnet. Linda Beatrice Brown. GT

Winter stillness. Haiku: "Winter stillness." Lenard D. Moore. TtW

Winter Sweetnes. Langston Hughes. CP-HughL

Winter Twilight, A. Angelina Weld Grimké. CDC; NAAAL; PoBA; ShDr

Winter's Approach. Paul Laurence Dunbar. CP-DunbP

Winter's Day, A. Paul Laurence Dunbar. CP-DunbP

Wipes / her nose / on the draperies. Spills drinks. Crow Jane in High Society. Amiri Baraka. SP-BaraA

Wisdom. Langston Hughes. CP-HughL

Wisdom. Frank Yerby. AmNP

Wisdom and War. Langston Hughes. CP-HughL

Wisdom Cometh with the Years. Countee Cullen. CP-CullC; Klds

Wisdom of Signs, The. Michael S. Harper. SP-HarpM

Wise, The. Countee Cullen. CP-CullC; Crnst

Wise 1. Amiri Baraka. SP-BaraA

Wise 2. Amiri Baraka. SP-BaraA

Wise 4. Amiri Baraka. SP-BaraA

Wise and queer tales float through all the jails. Eddie Ledoux: "Wise and queer tales float through all the jails." *African-American Oral Tradition.* GetYo

Wise / as west coast waters. Sonia Told Them Women. Yona Harvey. CtF

Wise guys / tell me, The. Kid Stuff. Frank Horne. AmNP; Klds; PoBA

Wise: Having the Ability to Perceive and Adopt the Best Means for Accomplishing an End. Lucille Clifton. SP-ClifL

Wise Men. Langston Hughes. CP-HughL

Wise Men of the East, The. Claude McKay. SP-McKaC

Wish for an Overcoat. Alfred Islay Walden. AAP; AfAmPo

Wishbone. Frank X. Walker. SpiFl

Wishes. Georgia Douglas Johnson. ShDr

Wishes for Sons. Lucille Clifton. NAAAL

Witch Doctor. Robert Hayden. AmNP; CP-HaydR

Witch doctor / come uptown. We Waiting on You. Edward S. Spriggs. BlFi

With a Gasoline can. (LL) The Beginning of a Long Poem on Why I Burned the City. Lawrence Benford. NBP

With All Deliberate Speed. Don L. Lee. JB

With angry brow and stately tread. The Earthquake of 1886. Josephine D. Henderson Heard. CBWP-4

With bits of toiletry from the ten cent store. (LL) The Proletariat Speaks. Alice Moore Dunbar-Nelson. ShDr

With bleeding back, from tyrant's lash. The Fugitive. Priscilla Jane Thompson. CBWP-2

With blusings / Disappear. (LL) Sounds / Like pearls. Maya Angelou. CP-AngeM; SP-AngeM

With bruise of lash or stone. (LL) Simon the Cyrenian Speaks. Countee Cullen. AmNP; BPo; CP-CullC

With cotton to the doorstep. The Young Ones. Sterling A. Brown. CP-BrowS

With Dad gone, Mom and I worked. Adolescence—III. Rita Dove. SP-DoveR

With gold unfading, WASHINGTON! be thine. (LL) To His Excellency General Washington. Phillis Wheatley. CP-WheaP; EBAP; Klds; NAAAL; TtW

With gypsies and sailors. Farewell, A: "With gypsies and sailors." Langston Hughes. CP-HughL

With hands all reddened and sore. The Washerwoman. Mary Weston Fordham. CBWP-2

With hands behind him clasped, that father walked. Albery Allson Whitman. *Fr. Leelah Misled.* EBAP

With her buskins tipped with dew. May's Invocation after a Tardy Spring. Henrietta Cordelia Ray. CBWP-3

With her confessionals. (LL) A Poem for My Father. Sonia Sanchez. BrTr; SP-SancS

With her shiny black-patent sandals. Juneteenth. Marilyn Nelson. SP-NelsM

With his corn and wine. (LL) Alaska. Mary Weston Fordham. CBWP-2

With its fog-shroud the. Julius Lester. *Fr.* Poems. Klds

With only itself to love. (LL) Elvin's Blues. Michael S. Harper. SP-HarpM

With our own / open eyes. (LL) Poem for Buddy. June Jordan. SP-JordJ

With perilous stairs / Between. (LL) The Treehouse. James A. Emanuel. AmNP; BPo; BrTr; NNP; PoBA

With pigment and space and leftover light. (LL) How the Rainbow Works. Al Young. CP-YounA; ESEAA

With pinched cheeks hollow and wan. The Outcast. Josephine D. Henderson Heard. CBWP-4

With proud and tilted chin! (LL) Haven. Donald Jeffrey Hayes. AmNP

With sombre mien, the Evening Grey. Farewell to Arcady. Paul Laurence Dunbar. CP-DunbP

With songs of Liberty! (LL) On Liberty and Slavery. George Moses Horton. AAP; AfAmPo; Klds; SP-HortG; TtW

With stones, then drive away. (LL) Paul Laurence Dunbar. Robert Hayden. CP-HaydR; ESEAA; GT

With subtle poise he grips his tray. Atlantic City Waiter. Countee Cullen. CP-CullC

With the ante / raised. (LL) On Watching Politicians Perform at Martin Luther King's Funeral. Etheridge Knight. SP-KnigE

With the clothes on your back. (LL) Studio Up Over In Your Ear. Al Young. CP-YounA; GT

With the damn wonder of it. (LL) There Is a Girl Inside. Lucille Clifton. SP-ClifL

With the door closed. (LL) Hanging Fire. Audre Lorde. CP-LordA

With the drought. (LL) Juliet. Langston Hughes. CP-HughL; SP-HughL

With the Lark. Paul Laurence Dunbar. CP-DunbP

With the last whippoorwill call of evening. Birmingham. Margaret Abigail Walker. CP-WalkM; PoBA

With the storm moved on the next town. Centipede. Rita Dove. SP-DoveR

With their money they bought ignorance. Killers. Alice Walker. CP-WalkA

With their throb and yearn, their sad. Exeunt the Viols. Rita Dove. SP-DoveR

With thy rugged, ice-girt shore. Alaska. Mary Weston Fordham. CBWP-2

With time / and space. The Poet the Dreamer. Norman Jordan. NBV

With two white roses on her breasts. A Brown Girl Dead. Countee Cullen. CP-CullC; GT; Klds

With what a gentle sound. September. Henrietta Cordelia Ray. CBWP-3

With what panache, he said. The Lions. Robert Hayden. CP-HaydR

With what thou gavest me, O Master. Equipment. Paul Laurence Dunbar. CP-DunbP

With which to cool my husband's dinner. (LL) Paperweight. Audre Lorde. CP-LordA

With you I learned my part in nature. In My Grandmother's Living Room. Karen Williams. SpiFl

Within a dark and cheerless hut. The Old Saint's Prayer. Priscilla Jane Thompson. CBWP-2

Within a London garret high. The Garret. Paul Laurence Dunbar. CP-DunbP

Within a native hut, ere stirred the dawn. Nativity. Gladys May Casely Hayford. CDC

Within an avalanche of glory hallelujah skybreaks. Avalanche. Quincy Troupe. SpiFl

Within my casement came one night. The Dawn of Love. Henrietta Cordelia Ray. BlSi; CBWP-3; EBAP

Within— / The beaten pride. Uncle Tom. Langston Hughes. SP-HughL

Within the shadow of the moon you danced. To a Dark Dancer. Marjorie Marshall. ShDr

Within the soul's courts is a temple fair. The Soul's Courts. Henrietta Cordelia Ray. CBWP-3

Within the Veil. Michelle Cliff. NAAAL

Within this black hive to-night. Beehive. Jean Toomer. CP-ToomJ; GT; IDB; PoBA

Within this grave lie. Epitaph: "Within this grave lie." Langston Hughes. CP-HughL

Within us ever stirs. Can we repine? (LL) Aspiration. Henrietta Cordelia Ray. CBWP-3

Within, without, the vassal heart--its reasoning who know? (LL) Recessional. Georgia Douglas Johnson. CDC

Without a doubt / rome did the whi. The Black Christ. Haki R. Madhubuti. TtW

Without Benefit of Declaration. Langston Hughes. AmNP; CP-HughL

Without Commercials. Alice Walker. CP-WalkA

Without expectation / there is no end. Summer Oracle. Audre Lorde. BlSi; CP-LordA; PoBA; SP-LordA

Without knowing a page / Of it / Themselves. (LL) Women. Alice Walker. TtW

Without my melancholia I am lonely. After the Shrink. Alice Walker. CP-WalkA

Without my own. (LL) All the World Moved. June Jordan. GT; NBP; PoBA

Without my watch and you. (LL) Could be Hastings Street. Langston Hughes. CP-HughL; SP-HughL

Without Name. Pauli Murray. AmNP; PoBA

Woke up crying the blues. A Day in the Life of a Poet. Quincy Troupe. NBV

Woman. Nikki Giovanni. SP-GiovN

Woman. Elouise Loftin. PoBA

Woman. Audre Lorde. CP-LordA

Woman. Sonia Sanchez. *Fr.* Past. SP-SancS

Woman begins to weep, A. (LL) Afterimages. Audre Lorde. CP-LordA; SP-LordA

Woman, I Got the Blues. Yusef Komunyakaa. SP-KomuY

Woman Is Not a Potted Plant, A. Alice Walker. CP-WalkA

Woman Kills and Eats Own Infant. Marilyn Nelson. SP-NelsM

Woman like me is free! (LL) Widow Woman. Langston Hughes. CP-HughL; SP-HughL

Woman Me. Maya Angelou. BlSi; CP-AngeM; SP-AngeM

Woman Poem. Nikki Giovanni. BlSi; SP-GiovN

Woman power / is / Black power. NOW. Audre Lorde. CP-LordA; SP-LordA

Woman precedes me up the long rope, A. Climbing. Lucille Clifton. GT

Woman. rocking her. Sonia Sanchez. SP-SancS

Woman Speaks, A. Audre Lorde. CP-LordA

Woman standing in the doorway, A. Evening Song. Langston Hughes. *Fr.* Montage of a Dream Deferred. CP-HughL

Woman Thing, The. Audre Lorde. BlSi; CP-LordA; SP-LordA
 ("Hunters are back, The.") GT

Woman when we met on the solstice. Meet. Audre Lorde. CP-LordA

Woman Who Died in Line, The. Saundra Sharp. SpiFl

Woman who lives at 830 Broadway, The. Soho Cinema. Audre Lorde. CP-LordA

Woman who loves, A. Lucille Clifton. NAAAL

Woman who made, A. Sonia Sanchez. SP-SancS

Woman. whose color. Sonia Sanchez. SP-SancS

Woman with a burning flame, A. Smothered Fires. Georgia Douglas Johnson. BlSi; ShDr

Woman with Flower. Naomi Long Madgett. AmNP; FB; GT

Woman Work. Maya Angelou. CP-AngeM; SP-AngeM

Woman/Dirge for Wasted Children, A. Audre Lorde. CP-LordA

Woman's sense is not her education, A. They Never Lose. Lorenzo Thomas. TtW

Woman's sho' a cur'ous critter. The Turning of the Babies in the Bed. Paul Laurence Dunbar. CP-DunbP

Woman's Song, A. Colleen J. McElroy. BlSi

Woman's Work. Frances Ellen Watkins Harper. CP-HarpF

Woman's worth to the world can never be told. Oh Woman, Blessed Woman! Mrs. Henry Linden. CBWP-4

Women. Alice Walker. *Fr.* In These Dissenting Times. CP-WalkA; NAAAL; PoBA; TtW

Women at the Crossroad / (May Elegba Forever Guard the Right Doors). Opal Palmer Adisa. GT

Women gather, The. Nikki Giovanni. SP-GiovN

"Women of Color" Have Rarely Had the Opportunity to Write about Their Love Affairs. Alice Walker. CP-WalkA

Women of Dan Dance with Swords in Their Hands to Mark the Time When They Were Warriors, The. Audre Lorde. CP-LordA

Women of Nigeria. Night in Nigeria. Ellease Southerland. GT

Women on Trains. Audre Lorde. CP-LordA

Women were making clay bowls, The. What the Women Told Me. E. Ethelbert Miller. GT

Women / who build nations. The Seventh Sign. Audre Lorde. CP-LordA; SP-LordA

Women win hands down. (LL) To the Girl Who Lives In a Tree. Audre Lorde. CP-LordA; SP-LordA

Women You Are Accustomed To, The. Lucille Clifton. GT

Womenblack: We Begin with You. Haki R. Madhubuti. Crnst

Women's Locker Room. Marilyn Nelson. SP-NelsM

Wonder. Maya Angelou. CP-AngeM; SP-AngeM

Wonder. Langston Hughes. SP-HughL

Wonder / And pain. Juliet. Langston Hughes. CP-HughL; SP-HughL

WONDER BAR. Neon Signs. Langston Hughes. *Fr.* Montage of a Dream Deferred. CP-HughL

Wonder what they'd tell me. (LL) Alabama Poem. Nikki Giovanni. BkSV; SP-GiovN

Wonder Woman, The. Nikki Giovanni. SP-GiovN

Wonderful time—the War, A. Green Memory. Langston Hughes. *Fr.* Montage of a Dream Deferred. CP-HughL

Wood Carols. Henrietta Cordelia Ray. CBWP-3

Wood Has No Mouth. Audre Lorde. CP-LordA

Woodman and the Money Hunter, The. George Moses Horton. SP-HortG

Wooing, The. Paul Laurence Dunbar. CP-DunbP

Wooing, A. Langston Hughes. CP-HughL

Word Game. Wanda Coleman. TtW

Word is writ that he who runs may read, The. Booker T. Washington. Paul Laurence Dunbar. CP-DunbP

Word Poem (Perhaps Worth Considering). Nikki Giovanni. PoBA ("As things be/come.") SP-GiovN

Word *Son* that she gave to each of the seed of Ethiopia? (LL) Aunt Jane Allen. Fenton Johnson. IDB; PoBA

Word to the violent has never been sufficient, A. "Word to the Wise Is Enough, A." Raymond R. Patterson. NBV

"Word to the Wise Is Enough, A." Raymond R. Patterson. NBV

WORD, Was, Is, Will, BE, The. Genesis 11. Etheridge Knight. SP-KnigE

Words. Helen Morgan Brooks. NNP

Words are but leaves to the tree of mind. Samuel Alfred Beadle. AAP

Words for a Hymn to the Sun. Jean Toomer. CP-ToomJ

Words for the Hour. Frances Ellen Watkins Harper. CP-HarpF

Words in the Mourning Time. Robert Hayden. CP-HaydR

Words Like Freedom. Langston Hughes. BPo; CP-HughL (Refugee in America.) SP-HughL

Words to Drive out the White Growth in the Eyes. Everett Hoagland. BrTr

Words! Words! Jessie Redmond Fauset. CDC

Wordsworth. Charlotte L. Forten Grimké. AAP; AfAmPo

Work. Yusef Komunyakaa. SP-KomuY

Work? / I don't have to work. Necessity. Langston Hughes. *Fr.* Montage of a Dream Deferred. CP-HughL

Work out. Ten laps. Heartbeats. Melvin Dixon. ESEAA

Work-week's end and there's enough. Secular. Natasha Trethewey. SpiFl

Worker, The. Richard W. Thomas. BlFi; PoBA

Workers Rose on May Day or Postscript to Karl Marx, The. Audre Lorde. CP-LordA; SP-LordA

Worker's Song. Maya Angelou. CP-AngeM

Workin' Man. Langston Hughes. CP-HughL

Working and Waiting. Adah Isaacs Menken. CBWP-1

Working night shift. Soliloquy: Man Talking to a Mirror. Yusef Komunyakaa. SP-KomuY

Working the strawberry fields. (LL) How I See Things. Yusef Komunyakaa. ESEAA; SP-KomuY

World I See, The. Mari E. Evans. Klds

World Is a Mighty Ogre, The. Fenton Johnson. AmNP

World is a snob, and the man who wins, The. For the Man Who Fails. Paul Laurence Dunbar. CP-DunbP

World is full of colored, The. Song. Alice Walker. CP-WalkA

World is Full of Remarkable Things, The. Amiri Baraka. BlFi; SSLK

World Is Not a Pleasant Place to Be, The. Nikki Giovanni. SP-GiovN

World is suddenly emptied of a certain, The. Milestones: September 28, 1991. Askia M. Toure. CtF

World shall echo with our Lincoln's name, The. (LL) Lincoln. Henrietta Cordelia Ray. CBWP-3

World War *II*. Langston Hughes. *Fr.* Montage of a Dream Deferred. CP-HughL

World was fading from his view, The. Give My Love to the World. Frances Ellen Watkins Harper. CP-HarpF

World-wide dusk. Black Seed. Langston Hughes. CP-HughL

World with all of its thought and action, The. God's Electric Power. Mrs. Henry Linden. CBWP-4

World would have run out of / bones, The. (LL) Poem for Two Daughters. Ishmael Reed. CP-ReedI

Worn like a hand-me-down. Growing into My Name. Harriet Jacobs. SpiFl

Worn Out. Paul Laurence Dunbar. CP-DunbP; NAAAL

Worriation. Langston Hughes. CP-HughL

Worst is not knowing if I do take somebody's, The. Fragments from a Parable. June Jordan. SP-JordJ

Worth of all it so despised, The. (LL) Only the Polished Skeleton. Countee Cullen. CP-CullC

Would-be Critic, The. Mrs. Henry Linden. CBWP-4

Would I for all that were. Sun-Ra. BlFi

Would I might mend the fabric of my youth. Welt. Georgia Douglas Johnson. BANP

Would it please you if I strung my tears. The Race Question. Naomi Long Madgett. BPo

Would that i could i'd write a poem. Missions and Magnolias. Nayo-Barbara Watkins. TtW

Would / That I were a jewel. Song to the Dark Virgin. Langston Hughes. CP-HughL

Would you? (LL) Relief. Langston Hughes. CP-HughL

Would you please return. Sonia Sanchez. SP-SancS

Would You Wear My Eyes? Bob Kaufman. GT; SP-KaufB; TtW

Wouldnt think / t look at m. Panther Man. James A. Emanuel. BPo; NBV

Wraith, The. Paul Laurence Dunbar. CP-DunbP

Wrapped in their cool immunity. (LL) The Wise. Countee Cullen. CP-CullC; Crnst

Wreath of Holly, A. Joseph Cephas Holly. AAP

Wren dropped down on my window sill, A. A Little Wren. Priscilla Jane Thompson. CBWP-2

Wretched of the earth, The. I Arrive In Madrid. Al Young. CP-YounA; GT

Wrinkles on the brown face, The. The Militance of a Photograph in the Passbook of a Bantu under Detention. Michael S. Harper. TtW

Write hung things, mad mess. Why Write ABOUT. Bob Kaufman. SP-KaufB

Write to thine eyes? Why, my poor pen. To Fannie. Mary E. Tucker. CBWP-1

Writers, The. Mari E. Evans. TtW

Written in Bracing, Gray L.A. Rainlight. Al Young. SpiFl

Written upon my face. (LL) A Poem for Women in Rage. Audre Lorde. CP-LordA; SP-LordA

Wrong Color. Christopher Stanard. SpiFl

Wrong Side of the Morning, The. May Miller. TtW

Wrongs we bear shall be redressed, The. (LL) America, it is to thee. James M. Whitfield. EBAP; NAAAL

Wrongs we bear shall be redressed, The. (LL) From America. James M. Whitfield. BPo

X

Xeroxed on brainmatter. The Tongue Is. Yusef Komunyakaa. SP-KomuY

Y

Y. M. C. A, The. Mrs. Henry Linden. CBWP-4

Y the Link Will Not Always Be "Missing" #40. Amiri Baraka. SP-BaraA

Y'all listen to me. Self Defense. Ai. ESEAA

Yall / out there. A Chant for Young/Brothas and Sistuhs. Sonia Sanchez. BPo

Yalluh Hammuh. Margaret Abigail Walker. CP-WalkM

Yardbird's Skull. Owen Dodson. AmNP; IDB; PoBA

Ye are builders little builders. The Little Builders. Frances Ellen Watkins Harper. CP-HarpF

Ye Bards of England. Albery Allson Whitman. EBAP

Ye blind, ye deaf, ye mute! Ho, here's healing! Lines for a Hospital. Countee Cullen. CP-CullC

Ye martial pow'rs, and all ye tuneful nine. Goliath of Gath. Phillis Wheatley. BALP; CP-WheaP

Ye who read in musty volumes. The Old Sac Village. Albery Allson Whitman. AAP

Yea, I have put thee from me utterly. Dictum. Countee Cullen. CP-CullC

Y-e-a-h! (LL) Dream Boogie. Langston Hughes. NAAAL; SSLK

Yeah here am i / am standing. Carl Wendell, Jr. Hines. Fr. Two Jazz Poems. Klds

Yeah, I been to juvee, what about it? Rhonda, Age 15 Emergency Room. Letta Simone-Nefertari Neely. CtF

Yeah if i were a poet i'd kid / nap you. (LL) Kidnap Poem. Nikki Giovanni. SP-GiovN

Yeah JAZZ IS MY RELIGION. (LL) JAZZ is my religion. Ted Joans. TtW

Yeah. / my man. / got no place else. To You/Who Almost Turned/Me On. Sonia Sanchez. SP-SancS

"Yeah" she said "my man's gone too." Conversation. Nikki Giovanni. SP-GiovN

Yeah. / they hang you up. To All Brothers. Sonia Sanchez. BPo; BrTr

Yeah. / you can really. Rebolushinary X-mas. Carolyn M. Rodgers. JB

Year after year the artist wrought. The Lost Bells. Frances Ellen Watkins Harper. CP-HarpF

Year burns an icon, The. 1984. Yusef Komunyakaa. SP-KomuY

Year I was born was a nodal year, The. On Youth and Age. Margaret Abigail Walker. CP-WalkM

Year of the Child, The. Robert Hayden. CP-HaydR

Year Round. Langston Hughes. CP-HughL

Year was 1914, The. St. Louis Woman. Ishmael Reed. CP-ReedI

Year without Seasons, A. Nance Williams. NNP

Years / Fall like dry leaves, The. New Year. Langston Hughes. CP-HughL

Years later / I fall back in. The Robbie's Dance. Al Young. CP-YounA

Years of manhood had not tinged, The. Charley du Bignon. Mary E. Tucker. CBWP-1

Years pass on, and overhead, The. His Prime. George Clinton Rowe. AAP

Yeh. / Billie. For Our Lady. Sonia Sanchez. NAAAL

Yellow. De Leon Harrison. PoBA

Yellow Bird, The. James W. Thompson. PoBA

Yellow Dog Blues. William Christopher Handy. NAAAL

Yellow ears are crammed in Mr. Cromartie's bin. Master and Man. Sterling A. Brown. CP-BrowS

Yellow scarf runs through his fingers, A. Courtship, Diligence. Rita Dove. SP-DoveR

Yellow/brown woman. I Am Becoming My Mother. Lorna Goodison. GT

Yes Baby: / "Unrest in the Philippines." Poem Instead of a Columbus Day Parade. June Jordan. SP-JordJ

Yes Bees ! JA ZZ : (The "Say what?") IS IS JA LIVES. Amiri Baraka. SpiFl

Yes, brother your word had come. Hearing James Brown at the Café des Nattes. Richard A. Long. AmNP

Yes brothers you invented jazz. Tribute. Al Young. CP-YounA

Yes! Ethiopia yet shall stretch. Ethiopia. Frances Ellen Watkins Harper. CP-HarpF; NAAAL

Yes, girl, he was fine. All night he'd groan I love you. Beauty Shoppe. Marilyn Nelson. SP-NelsM

Yes I'm glad. The Leadbelly Song. Al Young. CP-YounA

Yes, it'll be me. (LL) Note on Commercial Theatre. Langston Hughes. CP-HughL; SP-HughL; SSLK

Yes, May and I are friends. After Church. Samuel Alfred Beadle. AAP

Yes, my darling, when life's shadows. In Memoriam. Alphonse Campbell Fordham. Mary Weston Fordham. AAP; CBWP-2

Yes, my ha't 's ez ha'd ez stone. A Coquette Conquered. Paul Laurence Dunbar. CP-DunbP

Yes, sir! (LL) Porter. Langston Hughes. CP-HughL

Yes! strike again that sounding string. James M. Whitfield. NAAAL

Yes, the Secret Mind Whispers. Al Young. CP-YounA; PoBA; TtW

Yes the simplicity of my life. Dancing. Al Young. CP-YounA

Yes! there I shall be blest! (LL) Slavery. George Moses Horton. EBAP; TtW

Yes these are ours ... the spirituals. The Spirituals. Margaret Abigail Walker. CP-WalkM

Yes, theyll let you play. A Poem for Players. Al Young. CP-YounA

Yes we did! (LL) Martin's Blues. Michael S. Harper. PoBA

Yes, yes, dear love! I am dead! Resurgam. Adah Isaacs Menken. Fr. Infelicia. EBAP

Yes, yes / it's time. My Spring Thing. Everett Hoagland. BPo

Yesterday. Mary Weems. SpiFl

Yesterday and Today. Langston Hughes. CP-HughL

Yesterday and Tomorrow. Paul Laurence Dunbar. CP-DunbP

Yesterday, / I heard a blind man. God's Trombone. Sarah Webster Fabio. TtW

Yesterday I held your hand. Yesterday and Tomorrow. Paul Laurence Dunbar. CP-DunbP

Yesterday, I was sitting in the corner of my glass bubble with my feet. Moment 9/The Woman. John W. Love, Jr. CtF

Yesterday in new york city. After Hearing a Radio Announcement: a Comment on Some Conditions. Quincy Troupe. Crnst

Yesterday / out the window. Learning to Dance. Rudy Bee Graham. BlFi

Yesterday was Doomsday. Judgement Day: For Big Red the Darwinian Doge. R.I.P. Kent Foreman. BrTr

Yet count this quest the holiest of thy days. (LL) The Quest of the Ideal. Henrietta Cordelia Ray. CBWP-3

Yet Do I Marvel. Countee Cullen. AfAmPo; AmNP; BANP; BPo; CDC; CP-CullC; CrDW; Crnst; IDB; NAAAL; PoBA; SSLK

Yet gives no sweet / release. (LL) The Pusher. Maya Angelou. CP-AngeM; SP-AngeM

YMCA #35. Amiri Baraka. SP-BaraA

Yo Yo / I want to dedicate this song to. Biological Didn't Bother. Shaquille, O'Neal. CtF

You ain't part Indian. Wake-up Niggers. Don L. Lee. PoBA

"You almost home boy. Go on cross that sea!" (LL) My Father's Geography. Michael S. Weaver. GT

You and I Are Disappearing. Yusef Komunyakaa. SP-KomuY

You Are a Part of Me. Frank Yerby. AmNP

You are a Sunrise. Etheridge Knight. SP-KnigE

You are all these people. To a Single Shadow without Pity. Sam Cornish. NBP; PoBA

You Are Alms. James W. Thompson. PoBA

You are amble and. Sonia Sanchez. SP-SancS

You are but these to me: a freckled face. Sonnet Sequence. Darwin T. Turner. BALP

You are disdainful and magnificent—. Sonnet to a Negro in Harlem. Helene Johnson. AmNP; BANP; CDC; NAAAL; SSLK; ShDr

You Are Here. Carl Phillips. GT

You are instantly enfolded. "Stephany." Fr. Moving Deep. BrTr

You are like a warm dark dusk. Young Negro Girl. Langston Hughes. CP-HughL

You are, my dear, my sweet black bear! (LL) Planning the Perfect Evening. Rita Dove. GT

You are no friend of mine. To Certain Intellectuals. Langston Hughes. CP-HughL

You are not to trouble yourself. For Joanne in Poland. Al Young. CP-YounA

You are oversized, you are overrated, you are overblown. Tis of Thee. Henry L. Dumas. TtW

You are sad. It is the same with me. (LL) Nocturne at Bethesda. Arna Bontemps. AmNP; BALP; BANP; CDC; NAAAL; TtW

You Are the Brave. In Time of Crisis. Raymond R. Patterson. IDB; NBP; PoBA

You are the lice. Special Section for the Niggas on the Lower Eastside or: Invert the Divisor and Multiply. Welton Smith. Fr. Malcolm. BlFi

You are the one. To a Dark Moses. Lucille Clifton. SP-ClifL

You Are There. Nikki Giovanni. SP-GiovN

You are too splendid for this city street. (LL) Sonnet to a Negro in Harlem. Helene Johnson. AmNP; BANP; CDC; NAAAL; SSLK; ShDr

You are with me Oregon. Oregon. Bob Kaufman. GT

You ask why I am sad to-day. Weltschmertz. Paul Laurence Dunbar. CP-DunbP

You asked, I came. The Evil That Men Do. Queen Latifah. NAAAL

You be tellin' me You Be Black. An Open Letter to All Black Poets. Samuel F. Reynolds. SpiFl

You bet it would've made a tender movie! Sweet Sixteen Lines. Al Young. CP-YounA

You / beyond the door. (LL) Arrival. Maya Angelou. CP-AngeM; SP-AngeM

You bid me hold my peace. Worn Out. Paul Laurence Dunbar. CP-DunbP; NAAAL

You black out the sun. Ed Roberson. PoBA

You bothered, / father. (LL) Grape Sherbet. Rita Dove. SP-DoveR

You cain't never tell. The Ballad of Joe. Sterling A. Brown. CP-BrowS

You came / to be / in the Month of Malcolm. Circling the Daughter. Etheridge Knight. SP-KnigE

You Came, Too. Nikki Giovanni. SP-GiovN

You came with a cello in one hand. The Left-Handed Cellist. Rita Dove. SP-DoveR

You can actually hear it in his voice. Leadbelly. Cornelius Eady. ESEAA

You can call me Herbie Jr. or Ashamah. Unemployment Monologue. June Jordan. SP-JordJ

You can catch the wind. Free Man. Langston Hughes. CP-HughL

You can sigh o'er the sad-eyed Armenian. An Appeal to My Countrywomen. Frances Ellen Watkins Harper. BlSi; CP-HarpF; NAAAL

You can talk about. Visitors to the Black Belt. Langston Hughes. CP-HughL

You cannot love me. Do You Know Me? Nayo-Barbara Watkins. TtW

You can't sleep here. Drama for Winter Night (Fifth Avenue). Langston Hughes. CP-HughL

You come to me. Quincy Troupe. NBV

You could never catch her. Alice Flips the Script. Ta-Nehisi Coates. CtF

You could stop the factory whistles blowing. If You Would. Langston Hughes. *Fr.* Ask Your Mama; 12 Moods for Jazz. CP-HughL

You danced a magnetic dance. So Many Feathers. Jayne Cortez. BlSi; SP-CortJ

You declare you seem me dimly. Equality. Maya Angelou. CP-AngeM

You delight, / So it would seem. Note to All Nazis Fascists and Klansmen. Langston Hughes. CP-HughL

You did arrive, smiling, / but too late. (LL) Unmeasured Tempo. Maya Angelou. CP-AngeM; SP-AngeM

You did not clock the turning of the leaves. Return. Audre Lorde. SP-LordA

You did not know we loved you. (LL) We Assume: On the Death of Our Son, Reuben Masai Harper. Michael S. Harper. GT; SP-HarpM

You didn't send for them. They Came Again in 1970 in 1980. Jayne Cortez. SP-CortJ

You dig instant revolution: against. Down Wind against the Highest Peaks. Clarence Major. NBP

You do not know how beautiful you are. Ode to a Beautiful Woman. Carl Clark. JB

You do not know the. Sonia Sanchez. SP-SancS

You don't know or maybe you do. Dear Mama. Wanda Coleman. Crnst

You Don't Know What Love Is. Al Young. CP-YounA

You dragged me into your love pond. Pocadonia. Ishmael Reed. CP-ReedI

You drink a bitter draught. To a Freedom Fighter. Maya Angelou. CP-AngeM; SP-AngeM

You figure out why! (LL) Madam and the Charity Child. Langston Hughes. CP-HughL; SP-HughL

You . . . flowing through selves / Toward you. (LL) Now That I Am Forever with Child. Audre Lorde. IHS; NAAAL; PoBA; SP-LordA

You get right down into the physical world. Drawing. Al Young. CP-YounA

You get the blues in twos. Memo #43. Etheridge Knight. SP-KnigE

You goes to hell? (LL) Madam and the Number Writer. Langston Hughes. CP-HughL; SP-HughL

You got a Miss Ann's scrubbing. (LL) Sepia Fashion Show. Maya Angelou. BlSi; SP-AngeM

You got to take me / Like I am. (LL) Me and the Mule. Langston Hughes. IDB; SP-HughL

You gotta watch / out for the "Ol Liver." (LL) Welcome Back, Mr. Knight: Love of My Life. Etheridge Knight. SP-KnigE

You have been good to me, I give you this. Idolatry. Arna Bontemps. AmNP

You have broken the path of the dragonfly. Pearls. Rita Dove. SP-DoveR

You have forgotten me well. (LL) When You Have Forgotten Sunday: The Love Story. Gwendolyn Brooks. BPo; NAAAL

You have no word for soldiers to enjoy. Looking. Gwendolyn Brooks. SP-BrooG

You have not heard my love's dark throat. A Song of Praise. Countee Cullen. CP-CullC

You have pierced me so. Sonia Sanchez. SP-SancS

You have stamped your hour. Sonia Sanchez. SP-SancS

You have / two hands equally lean and clean. It's About You: on the Beach. June Jordan. SP-JordJ

You intend no doubt. Gift. Alice Walker. CP-WalkA

You judge a woman. XXI. Essex Hemphill. NAAAL

You jump right out of your skin. The Moon Up Close in Winter by the Telescope. Al Young. CP-YounA

You keep me waiting in a truck. Twenty-Year Marriage. Ai. GT

You keep saying you were always there. Poem No. 10. Sonia Sanchez. TtW

You kin talk about yer anthems. The Ol' Tunes. Paul Laurence Dunbar. CP-DunbP

You kin talk erbout yo' 'lasses an' yo' steamin' buckwheat cakes. Uncle Eph—Epicure. James Edwin Campbell. EBAP

You know, dear, that this vicious world. Mrs. Myrick's Lecture. Mary E. Tucker. CBWP-1

You know Heather Bell, she lives around the corner. Heather Bell. Bob Kaufman. SP-KaufB

You know / I sure would like to write a blues. Jayne Cortez. SP-CortJ

You know my trouble: story. Round Midnight. Clarence Major. NAAAL

You know you've come back home again. American Time. Al Young. CP-YounA

You Langston, / you black man who is waiting. A Poem for Langston Hughes. Lenard D. Moore. TtW

You laugh, and I must hide the wound. The Negro Laughs Back. Mary Jenness. ShDr

You laugh / Because I'm poor and black and funny. The Black Crown. Langston Hughes. CP-HughL

You let down, from arched. Family Affairs. Maya Angelou. CP-AngeM; SP-AngeM

You lie now in many coffins. For Malcolm: After Mecca. Gerald William Barrax. PoBA

You load, focus, aim. Shooting Back. Thomas Sayers Ellis. GT

You look at me with children. Johann. Alice Walker. CP-WalkA

You lucky to be a spider. 403 Blues. Langston Hughes. CP-HughL

You Made It Rain. Ruby C. Saunders. BlSi

You May Go But This Will Bring You Back. *Unknown.* NAAAL

You may leave and go to Hali-ma-fack. You May Go But This Will Bring You Back. *Unknown.* NAAAL

You may speak of a grave in a distant land. A Reverie. Mary Weston Fordham. CBWP-2

You may write me down in history. Still I Rise. Maya Angelou. BlSi; CP-AngeM; NAAAL; SP-AngeM

You must remember structures beyond cotton plants. If Blood is Black Then Spirit Neglects My Unborn Son. Conrad Kent Rivers. BrTr; PoBA

You must thank / yo dookey don't stank. What You Seize Is What You Git. Al Young. CP-YounA

You name your buildings after. Visit to a Small College. Ishmael Reed. CP-ReedI

You named those lies clustered. Blasphemy. Yusef Komunyakaa. SP-KomuY

You need the untranslatable ice to watch. Appendix to the Anniad. Gwendolyn Brooks. BlSi; SP-BrooG

You, no doubt, have heard the story told of Charleston by the sea? The Crum Appointment. Lizelia Augusta Jenkins Moorer. CBWP-3

You no doubt will be surprised at finding. Letter to Madame Lindé from Justine, Her Creole Servant. Sybil Klein. TtW

You ought not to ask. The Jesus Prayer. Marilyn Nelson. *Fr.* The Plotinus Suite. SP-NelsM

You ought to know! (LL) Bar. Langston Hughes. CP-HughL; SP-HughL

You press down hard enough. (LL) The Evening News. Audre Lorde. CP-LordA; NAAAL; SP-LordA

You probably could put their names to them. "As When Emotion Too Far Exceeds Its Cause." Gloria C. Oden. AmNP; Klds

You read with Auden. In Memorium: Robert Hayden. Norman J. Loftis. SpiFl

You / Refuse to see. Out. Riots and Rituals. Richard W. Thomas. PoBA

You said it. / You got that right. Verse for Ronald Slapjack Who Publicly Declared, "I, Too, Am a Contra!" June Jordan. SP-JordJ

You said that your people. To Richard Wright. Conrad Kent Rivers. AmNP; IDB; PoBA

You sang a race from wood and stone to Christ. (LL) O Black and unknown bards of long ago. James Weldon Johnson. AfAmPo; AmNP; BANP; BPo; CrDW; NAAAL; PoBA; TtW

You say I O.K.ed. Madam and the Phone Bill. Langston Hughes. SP-HughL

"You say that you believe in Democracy for everybody." Everybody but Me. Margaret Goss Burroughs. BlSi; FB

You say yes and I say yes. Point of No Return. Mari E. Evans. NNP

You see boy. Universality. Nikki Giovanni. SP-GiovN

You see, my whole life. Woman Poem. Nikki Giovanni. BlSi; SP-GiovN

You see them on the low hills of the Barbados. The Sailor Sings Back to the Casuarinas. Derek Walcott. *Fr.* The Schooner *Flight.* ESEAA

You Send Me: Bertha Franklin, December 11, 1964. E. Ethelbert Miller. SpiFl

You should a been with me in the year of twenty-three. Freaks' Ball. *African-American Oral Tradition.* GetYo

You should hammer on him to clean. Son. Al Young. CP-YounA

You should have, Jean, stopped them. One More Time. Alvin Aubert. TtW

You sicken me with lies. To Certain "Brothers." Langston Hughes. CP-HughL

You sing, and the gift of State's applause. To a Poet and a Lady. Paul Laurence Dunbar. CP-DunbP

You sit in the back. A Sorrow Since Sitting Bull. George Barlow. ESEAA

You sit, puckered and dry. 24th Avenue: City of Roses: Anesthesia: 2. Michael S. Harper. SP-HarpM

You sit there, sissified. Die Black Pervert. Reginald Lockett. BlFi

You So Woman. Ruth Forman. SpiFl

You stand waist-high in snakes. Alice. Michael S. Harper. SP-HarpM

You start here—Cozumel—it's an island, some people. You Are Here. Carl Phillips. GT

You take trips to contain the mystery. (LL) One West Coast. Al Young. CP-YounA

You talk like. Comment on Curb. Langston Hughes. *Fr.* Lenox Avenue Mural. AmNP; SP-HughL *Fr.* Montage of a Dream Deferred. CP-HughL

You tell me they only do to us. My Brother. James Danner. BlFi

You think about the first thing you ever stole, or lied about, or killed. (LL) Visiting Day. Al Young. CP-YounA

You think you / need me. Masquerade. Carolyn M. Rodgers. BlSi

You Told Me a Lie. *African-American Oral Tradition.* GetYo

You too if you work hard enough. Ponce de León: A Morning Walk. Al Young. CP-YounA

You too listless to examine. Lines to Our Elders. Countee Cullen. CDC

You touch when you run? (LL) Demand. Langston Hughes. CP-HughL; SP-HughL

You turn on your pillow. It Is God that Moves in Your Heart. Al Young. CP-YounA

You used to say, "June?" 1977: Poem for Mrs. Fannie Lou Hamer. June Jordan. SP-JordJ

You wake in Córdoba. Don José Gorostiza Encounters El Cordobés. Jay Wright. ESEAA

You walk downstairs. Roman Poem Number Six. June Jordan. SP-JordJ

You walked the length of Italy. Catherine of Siena. Rita Dove. SP-DoveR

You want help. you are sorry you are born with ears. (LL) John Coltrane: An Impartial Review. Alfred B. Spellman. NNP; PoBA

You want to integrate me into your anonymity. Black Narcissus. Gerald William Barrax. Klds; PoBA

You want to know. Stellar Nilotic (29). Amiri Baraka. SP-BaraA

You were a sophist. Advice. Gwendolyn B. Bennett. BlSi; CDC

You were gone. Nikki Giovanni. SP-GiovN

You were half-right, I did lie. On Apologies. Valerie Jean. SpiFl

You Were Never Miss Brown to Me. Sherley Anne Williams. GT

You were our first brave ones to defy their dissonance of hate. Sit-Ins. Margaret Abigail Walker. CP-WalkM

You weren't even a. To L. Julianne Perry. PoBA

You will be alone at last. For the Mad. Lucille Clifton. SP-ClifL

You will bloom. Conversation with My Grandson, Waiting to Be Conceived. Lucille Clifton. SP-ClifL

You will enter morning. For the Blind. Lucille Clifton. SP-ClifL

You will not be able to stay home, brother. The Revolution Will Not Be Televised! Gil Scott-Heron. Crnst; NAAAL

You will of course remember the night. Sing a Song of Singapore. Al Young. CP-YounA

You wished for a love-letter, Doctor. A Love-letter. Mary E. Tucker. CBWP-1

You / with your bullshit niggerish ways. Black Judgements. Nikki Giovanni. BrTr

You wore blue peddle pushers and polka dot tops. Girl. Kelly Norman Ellis. SpiFl

You worry me whoever you are. Badman of the Guest Professor. Ishmael Reed. BPo; SSLK

You would know why. (LL) Words Like Freedom. Langston Hughes. BPo; CP-HughL; SP-HughL

You would not bend. For Kinte. Oliver La Grone. FB

You would not recognize yourself if I should tell you. Naomi Long Madgett. *Fr.* Trinity: a Dream Sequence. Klds

You would not take the job. (LL) S M. Alice Walker. CP-WalkA

You would see beings. (LL) People. Jean Toomer. CP-ToomJ; GT

You would think that night could lift. Testament of Loss. Gloria C. Oden. ESEAA

You wound my soul with a thousand spears. Nonette. Langston Hughes. CP-HughL

You, you, there you go again. Moonlessness. Al Young. CP-YounA

You'll always be my friend. More Girl Than Boy. Yusef Komunyakaa. SP-KomuY

You'll be wonderin' whut's de reason. Expectation. Paul Laurence Dunbar. CP-DunbP

You'll go far in this world. (LL) Tuskegee Airfield. Marilyn Nelson. ESEAA; GT; SP-NelsM

You'll never miss the water till your well runs dry. Joe Turner Blues. William Christopher Handy. CrDW

You'll never sleep tonight. Insomnia. Cornelius Eady. ESEAA

Young Africans. Gwendolyn Brooks. BrTr

Young body, light, A. To Beat the Child Was Bad Enough. Maya Angelou. CP-AngeM; SP-AngeM

Young Bride. Langston Hughes. CP-HughL

Young Gal's Blues. Langston Hughes. CP-HughL; SP-HughL

Young Heroes. Gwendolyn Brooks. BPo; NAAAL

Young Negro Girl. Langston Hughes. CP-HughL

Young Negro poet / came from 'way down South. Calvin C. Hernton. AmNP; Klds

Young niggers / die old. Dedication to the Final Confrontation. Lloyd M., Jr. Corbin. PoBA

Young Ones, The. Sterling A. Brown. CP-BrowS

Young Ones, Flip Side, The. James A. Emanuel. Klds

Young Poet. Myron O'Higgins. PoBA

Young Prostitute. Langston Hughes. CP-HughL

Young queen Nature, ever sweet and fair, The. Nature and Art. Paul Laurence Dunbar. CP-DunbP

Young Sailor. Langston Hughes. CP-HughL; SP-HughL

Young Singer. Langston Hughes. CP-HughL

Young Soul. Amiri Baraka. BPo

Young Training. Lawrence McGaugh. PoBA

Young visitor / wearing an Angels cap, A. Abba Jacob at Bat. Marilyn Nelson. SP-NelsM

Young Womanhood. Sonia Sanchez. TtW

Young/Black/Girl. Sonia Sanchez. *Fr.* Past. SP-SancS

Youngest sister / works a dangerous ground, The. The One Who Got Away. Audre Lorde. CP-LordA

Your Basic Black Poet. Al Young. CP-YounA

Your beauty is a thunder. Black Ode. Maya Angelou. CP-AngeM; SP-AngeM

Your body is a dark wine. Hunger. Kathleen Tankersley Young. ShDr

Your body was a sacred cell always. Memorial. Claude McKay. SP-McKaC

Your canoe stops. Continuous Visit. Michael S. Harper. SP-HarpM

Your Death. Rita Dove. Crnst

Your door is shut against my tightened face. The White House. Claude McKay. AmNP; Crnst; NAAAL; PoBA; SP-McKaC; TtW

Your every day is a pilgrimage. To an Old Black Woman, Homeless and Indistinct. Gwendolyn Brooks. ESEAA

Your eyes are blinding me / Genevieve. (LL) Memorial II. Audre Lorde. CP-LordA; SP-LordA

Your eyes are mirth. Tom Weatherly. NBV

Your eyes are widely open flowers. Mysteries. Alice Walker. CP-WalkA

Your Eyes Have Their Silence. Gerald William Barrax. PoBA

Your force is greater than your use of it. White Arrow. Jean Toomer. CP-ToomJ

Your hair is Celebration in the world! (LL) To Those of My Sisters Who Kept Their Naturals. Gwendolyn Brooks. TtW

Your Hands. Angelina Weld Grimké. CDC; PoBA

Your hands easy. Remembrance. Maya Angelou. CP-AngeM; SP-AngeM

Your insomniac sorrow settles. Alba. Al Young. CP-YounA

Your land is crowned with regal men. Our English Friends. Frances Ellen Watkins Harper. CP-HarpF

Your lashes leave me naked in the square. Barren. Audre Lorde. CP-LordA; SP-LordA

Your lips are like a southern lily red. A Red Flower. Claude McKay. SP-McKaC

Your lips were so laughing. Langston Blues. Dudley Randall. FB

Your love to me was like an unread book. Bright Bindings. Countee Cullen. CP-CullC

Your / mind nigger. (LL) A Poem to Compliment Other Poems. Haki R. Madhubuti. BPo; BrTr; NAAAL; NBV; TtW

Your Momma kissed the chauffeur. The Thirteens (White). Maya Angelou. SP-AngeM

Your Momma took to shouting. The Thirteens (Black). Maya Angelou. CP-AngeM; SP-AngeM

Your morning peace still drums. Clinton. Sterling Plumpp. BkSV

Your name in hers, and in mine. (LL) Alice. Michael S. Harper. SP-HarpM

Your name is the Wheel of Progress—a pleasant name indeed. To the Wheel of Progress. Mrs. Henry Linden. CBWP-4

Your name scrawled on a bit of paper moves me. What the Finger Writes. Alice Walker. CP-WalkA

Your people first. a quiet strength. Black Manhood: Toward a Definition. Haki R. Madhubuti. Crnst

Your presence like a benison to me. To Her. Paul Laurence Dunbar. CP-DunbP

Your scent is in the room. Jasmine. Claude McKay. GT; SP-McKaC

Your skin like dawn. Passing Time. Maya Angelou. CP-AngeM; SP-AngeM

Your smile, delicate. Woman Me. Maya Angelou. BlSi; CP-AngeM; SP-AngeM

Your son baby / Respectably as ever, / Joe. (LL) Letter. Langston Hughes. SP-HughL

Your Songs. Gwendolyn B. Bennett. CDC

Your soul shines. Alice Walker. CP-WalkA

Your spoken words are roses fine and sweet. Roses and Pearls. Paul Laurence Dunbar. CP-DunbP

Your Subjects hope. To the King's Most Excellent Majesty on His Repealing the American Stamp Act. Phillis Wheatley. CP-WheaP

Your subjects hope, dread Sire. To the King's Most Excellent Majesty, 1768. Phillis Wheatley. CP-WheaP

Your Tears Feel Good on the Hood of My Car. K. Curtis Lyle. CtF

Your tune is a tempest of heat. July. Daniel Gray-Kontar. SpiFl

Your upset / or mine? (LL) Bible Study. Gloria C. Oden. ESEAA; GT

Your vividness grants color where. To Sallie, Walking. Sterling A. Brown. CP-BrowS; GT

Your voice at times a fist. To a Husband. Maya Angelou. CP-AngeM; SP-AngeM

Your voice is the color of a robin's breast. To O.E.A E. A. Claude McKay. BANP; BPo; GT; SP-McKaC

Your wife's forty-five. Gift Horse. Yusef Komunyakaa. GT

Your words dropped into my heart like pebbles into a pool. Absence. Claude McKay. CDC; SP-McKaC

Your world is as big as you make it. Georgia Douglas Johnson. AmNP; ShDr

Your world is unimportant to me. The Invisible Man. Conrad Kent Rivers. Klds

You're all that I can call my own. (LL) Woman Work. Maya Angelou. CP-AngeM; SP-AngeM

You're bigger than the / Barrel. (LL) Jacket Notes. Ishmael Reed. CP-ReedI

You're in there. (LL) Zeppelin factory, The. Rita Dove. SP-DoveR

You're Nothing but a Spanish Colored Kid. Felipe Luciano. PoBA

Yours is the face, my dear. (LL) When the Green Lies over the Earth. Angelina Weld Grimké. NAAAL

Youth. Langston Hughes. CP-HughL

Youth. Georgia Douglas Johnson. BANP; NAAAL

Youth in Heaven. Frances Ellen Watkins Harper. CP-HarpF

Youth Sings a Song of Rosebuds. Countee Cullen. BANP; CP-CullC

Youth went faring up and down, A. The Wooing. Paul Laurence Dunbar. CP-DunbP

Youth, with proud heart, pure and strong, A. The After-Glow of Pain. Clara Ann Thompson. CBWP-2

You've been asking me that question. Blue Clay. Ellease Southerland. GT

You've done taken my blues and gone—. Langston Hughes. *See* Note on Commercial Theatre.

You've got another love. Poor Girl. Maya Angelou. CP-AngeM; SP-AngeM

You've heard no doubt of Irish bulls. Lines to Miles O'Reiley. Frances Ellen Watkins Harper. CP-HarpF

You've just got to dig sly. Revolutionary Music. Nikki Giovanni. BrTr; SP-GiovN

You've taken my blues and gone. Note on Commercial Theatre. Langston Hughes. CP-HughL; SP-HughL

Yr shit / as rightly / burning! (LL) Am/trak. Amiri Baraka. SP-BaraA

Y's 18. Amiri Baraka. SP-BaraA

Yuh Lookin Good. Carolyn M. Rodgers. BPo

Your number's coming out! Blues in Stereo. Langston Hughes. *Fr.* Ask Your Mama; 12 Moods for Jazz. CP-HughL

Z

Za Ki Tan Ke Parlay Lot. Audre Lorde. CP-LordA; SP-LordA

Zalka Peetruza. Ray Garfield Dandridge. BANP; PoBA

Zapata & the Landlord. Alfred B. Spellman. NNP; PoBA

Zebra Goes Wild Where the Sidewalk Ends, The. Henry L. Dumas. GT

Zella Wheeler! did I evah? The Interrupted Reproof. Priscilla Jane Thompson. CBWP-2

Zeppelin factory, The. Rita Dove. SP-DoveR

Zero / zero / zero / the museum of modern art. The Story of the Zeros. Victor Hernandez Cruz. PoBA

Zeus over Redeye. Robert Hayden. CP-HaydR

Zimbabwe. Sterling Plumpp. TtW

Zinnias. Robert Hayden. CP-HaydR

Zocalo. Michael S. Harper. NBV; SP-HarpM

Zones of warmth around his heart, The. Sandy Star and Willie Gee. William Stanley Braithwaite. BANP

Zorro Man, A. Maya Angelou. CP-AngeM; SP-AngeM

AUTHOR INDEX

Pseudonymous names are enclosed in quotation marks.

A

Abrams, Robert J.
Two Poems, I.
Two Poems, II.
"Ada" (Sarah L. Forten) (1814–1898?)
Lines: "From fair Jamaica's fertile plains."
Lines Suggested on Reading "An Appeal to Christian Women of the South," by A. E. Grimke.
Oh, when this earthly tenement.
To the Memory of J. Horace Kimball.
Adams, Jenoyne
Out-of-Body Experience.
Adisa, Opal Palmer
Cultural Trip, A.
Discover Me.
I Will Not Let Them Take You.
Rainbow, The.
Women at the Crossroad / (May Elegba Forever Guard the Right Doors).
African-American Oral Tradition
Ain't It a Bitch?
All you tough guys that thinks you're wise.
Alphabet, The.
And here's to the duck that swim the pond.
And may your life become unlivable, boy.
Annabelle Jones, a noble kid.
Annabelle Jones from Shrevesport City.
Bend your back when I say "Go."
Boothill McCoy.
Brock Hankton.
Bulldaggers' Hall.
Casey Jones.
Chintz, The.
Cocaine Nell.
Cocaine Shorty.
Cock is a crickly creature.
Convict's Prayer.
Corner of 47th and South Park.
Dance of the Freaks: "It was a cool and mystic rain."
Dance of the Freaks: "It was cold and mist and rain in old Spokane."
Derringer Youngblood, the jet-black nigger.
Do, Lawd.
Dogass Pimp.
Dolomite: "Some folks say that Willie Green."
Dolomite first originated in San Antone.
Don't Feel So Downhearted, Buddy.
Don't Look So Downhearted, Buddy.
Down and Out.
Drinkin'.
Eddie Ledoux: "Wise and queer tales float through all the jails."
Eddie Ledoux: "There's some strange and queer tales that come through all jails."
Feeble Old Man.
Feeble Old Man and a Kid Named Dan.
'Flicted Arm Pete: "It was way down in this little town that they call Louisville."
Fly, The.
Ford, The.
Forty-nine Ford and a tank full of gas.
Freaks' Ball.
Get In Out of the Rain.
Girl told me, A.

He-frog told the she-frog, The.
Herbert Hoover.
Here's to the lady with the little red shoes.
Here's to you, Mag, you dirty hag.
Herman from the Shark-Tooth Shore.
Hickory wood is the best of wood.
Hitler, You Lied to Me.
Hobo Ben.
Hoboes' Convention.
Hophead Willie.
Hustlin' Dan.
I got a job down in Florida for Croft.
I used to be a cowboy.
I used to could diddle all night long.
I was sittin' in the jail to do a stretch of time.
I woke up this morning with a hard on.
If You See My Little Girl in Denver.
Jesse James.
Joe the Grinder and G.I. Joe.
JUba dis and JUba dat an.
Juber up and Juber down.
Junkies' Ball.
Junkies' Heaven.
Knockin' down chairs and slammin' doors.
L.A. Street.
Lady Liberty.
Lame and the Whore, The.
Life of a Junkie.
Life's a funny old proposition.
Limpty Lefty McCree.
Little Girl in the Gambler's Nest.
Little Old Wicked Nell.
Marie.
Mary, don you weep an Marthie don you moan.
Mary had a little lamb for which she cared no particle.
Miss Lookingood.
Mistah Rabbit, Mistah Rabbit, yo tale's mighty white.
Motherfuck a woman lay flat on her back.
Motherless Child.
My Reflection.
My uncle had a old gray horse.
My Uncle Sam was a good old man.
Nineteen Thirty-Two.
No Good Whore.
No Good Whore and Crime Don't Pay.
Nobody Knows Da Trubble Ah See.
Old Cods.
Once I lived the life of a millionaire.
Partytime Monkey.
Pearl Harbor.
Pimp, The.
Pimping Sam.
Ping Pong Joe.
Pisspot Pete.
Poolshooting Monkey: "It was in Speero's poolroom back in nineteen-ten."
Poolshooting Monkey: "It was in Speero's poolroom in the year eighteen-ten."
Poolshooting Monkey: "I don't know but I was told."
Pretty Pill.
Pussy ain't nothin' but a hairy split.
Raise a Ruckus Tonight.
Ringo.
Rooster crowed, the hen looked down, The.

Running through the jungle with my dick in my hand.
Satan's Playground of Hell.
Seven Wise Men, The.
Signifying Monkey: "Back down in the jungle up under the stick."
Signifying Monkey: "Deep down in the jungle in the coconut grove."
Signifying Monkey: "Down in the jungle about treetop deep."
Signifying Monkey: "It was early in the morning one bright summer day."
Signifying Monkey: "Say deep down in the jungle in the coconut grove."
Signifying Monkey: "There hadn't been no shift for quite a bit."
Soon one mawnin death come creepin in mah room.
Stackolee: "Back in forty-nine when times was hard."
Stackolee: "I staggered in a place called the Bucket a Blood."
Stackolee: "It was back in the time of nineteen hundred and two."
Stackolee: "It was back in the year of forty-one when the times was hard."
Stackolee: "This is supposed to be about two colored studs. It's truth. In New Orleans."
Stackolee: "When I was young in my prime."
Stackolee in Hell.
Strange, Strange Things.
Subject to a Fall: "Boys, you're subject to a fall and trip to the Walls."
Subject to a Fall: "Say, you subject to a fall and a trip to the Wall."
Sweet Lovin' Rose.
Swinging through the trees with my dick in my hand.
T. B. Bees.
Talk some shit, Richard.
They Can't Do That.
This is to the women of Texas.
Three Whores Settin' Down in Boston.
Through the Keyhole in the Door.
Titanic: "All the old folks say the fourth a May was a hell of a day."
Titanic: "Boys, you remember way back on the day of the eighth of May."
Titanic: "Eighth a May was a hell of a day, The."
Titanic: "I don't know, but my folks say."
Titanic: "In the year of eighteen-twelve."
Titanic: "It was sad indeed, it was sad in mind."
Titanic: "Tenth of May was a hell of a day, The."
Titanic: "This is about Shine O Shine. The captain was on his boat and he was."
Titanic: "Twelfth of May was one hell of a day, The."
Toledo Slim.
Treacherous Breast.
Twenty-Two-Twenty told Automatic Jim to tell his fast-fucking sister Fanny.
Ups on the Farm.
Voodoo Queen, The.
Wanderer's Trail, The.
Well here's to the fool that writes upon the shithouse walls.

Well if I had a dog that could piss this stuff.
Were you dere when dey crucified my Lord?
When-a Mah Blood Runs Chilly and Col.
When I Begin to Think When I Was a
  Young Man and in My Prime.
While playing short coin in the Golden West.
Whores Are No Good and Crime Don't Pay.
Wicked Nell: "While sittin' and thinking in
  deep meditation."
Wicked Nell: "While sittin' down in deep
  meditation, little girl, lookin' at you."
Willie the Weeper.
Winehead Girl.
You Told Me a Lie.

Ahmasi
Water of Your Bath.

"Ai" (Florence Anthony) (b. 1947)
Before You Leave.
Country Midwife: A Day, The.
Cuba, 1962.
Endangered Species.
I Can't Get Started.
Kid, The.
More.
Riot Act, April 29, 1992.
Self Defense.
Twenty-Year Marriage.

Al-Sudan, Nazzam (b. 1944)
Al Fitnah Muhajir.

Alba, Nanina (1917–68)
Be Daedalus.
For Malcolm X.

Alexander, Elizabeth (b. 1962)
Affirmative Action Blues.
Boston Year.
Farewell to You.
Narrative: Ali.
Nineteen.
Ode: "Sky was a street map with stars for,
  The."
Painting / (Frida Kahlo).
Venus Hottentot.

Alexander, Kwame
Just Us.

Alexander, Lewis (1900–1945)
Africa.
Dark Brother, The.
Day and Night.
Dream Song.
Enchantment.
Japanese Hokku.
Negro Woman.
Nocturne Varial.
Tanka (I–VIII).
Transformation.

Alexander, Margaret Walker. *See* **Walker,
Margaret Abigail**

Alhamisi, Ahmed Legraham
Pome. For Weird. Hearts. and All.
Uhuru (freedom. now. swahili. east african
  lango).

Allah, Fareedah. *See* **Saunders, Ruby C.**

Allen, George Leonard (b. 1905)
Portrait.
To Melody.

Allen, J. Mord (*fl.* 1906)
Devil and Sis' Viney, The.

Allen, Samuel ("Paul Vesey") (b. 1917)
About Poetry and South Africa.
Benin Bronze.
Dylan, Who Is Dead.
Harriet Tubman.
If the Stars Should Fall.
Love Song.
Moment Please, A.
My Friend.
Nat Turner.
Paul Vesey's Ledger, *sels.*
Ski Trail.
Staircase, The.
To Satch.
View from the Corner.

Anderson, Charles
Finger Pop'in.
Prayer to the White Man's God.

Anderson, S. E. (b. 1943)
Junglegrave.
New Dance, A.
Soul-Smiles.
Sound of Afroamerican History Chapt I, The.
Sound of Afroamerican History Chapt II,
  The.

Angelou, Maya (b. 1928)
Accident.
Africa.
After.
Ailey, Baldwin, Floyd, Killens, and Mayfield.
Ain't That Bad.
Alone.
America.
Amoebaean for Daddy.
Arrival.
Artful Pose.
Avec Merci, Mother.
Awaking in New York.
Black Ode.
Born That Way.
Brief Innocence.
Bump d'Bump.
Caged Bird.
California Prodigal.
Call Letters: Mrs. V.B.
Calling of Names, The.
Changes.
Changing.
Chicken-Licken.
Child Dead in Old Seas.
Coleridge Jackson had nothing.
Come, and Be My Baby.
Communication I.
Communication II.
Conceit, A.
Contemporary Announcement.
Country Lover.
Couple, The.
Detached, The.
Elegy: "I lay down in my grave."
Equality.
Faces and more remember.
Family Affairs.
Fightin' was natural.
For Us, Who Dare Not Dare.
Forgive.
Gamut, The.
Georgia Song, A.
Glory falls around us.
Good Woman Feeling Bad, A.
Greyday.
Harlem Hopscotch.
Health-Food Diner, The.
Here's to Adhering.
How I Can Lie to You.
Human Family.
I almost remember.
Impeccable Conception.
In a time of secret wooing.
In my Missouri.
In Retrospect.
Insignificant.
Insomniac.
Is Love.
John J.
Junkie Monkey Reel.
Just for a Time.
Just like Job.
Kin.
Kind of Love, Some Say, A.
Known to Eve and Me.
Lady Luncheon Club.
Last Decision, The.
Late October.
Lesson, The.
Let's Majeste.
Letter to an Aspiring Junkie.
Lie, The.
Life Doesn't Frighten Me.
Little Girl Speakings.
London.
Lord, in My Heart.
Loss of love and youth, The.
Love Letter.
Man Bigot.

Many and More.
Martial Choreograph.
Me and My Work.
Memory, The.
Men.
Miss Scarlet, Mr. Rhett and Other Latter-Day
  Saints.
Momma Welfare Roll.
Mothering Blackness, The.
Mourning Grace.
My Arkansas.
My guilt is "slavery's chains," too long.
My Life Has Turned to Blue.
New House, The.
No Loser, No Weeper.
No No No No.
Nothing Much.
Now Long Ago.
Old Folks Laugh.
On a bright day, next week.
On Aging.
On Diverse Deviations.
On Reaching Forty.
On the Pulse of Morning.
On Working White Liberals.
One More Round.
Our Grandmothers.
Passing Time.
Phenomenal Woman.
Pickin Em Up and Layin Em Down.
Plagued Journey, A.
Poor Girl.
Preacher, don't send me.
Prelude to a Parting.
Prescience.
Prisoner.
Pusher, The.
Recovery.
Refusal.
Remembering.
Remembrance.
Request.
Reverses.
Riot: 60's.
Savior.
Senses of Insecurity.
Sepia Fashion Show.
Seven Women's Blessed Assurance.
Shaker, Why Don't You Sing?
Singer Will Not Sing, The.
Slave Coffle.
Son to Mother.
Song for the Old Ones.
Sounds / Like pearls.
Southeast Arkansasia.
Starvation.
Still I Rise.
Take Time Out.
Tears / The crystal rags.
Telephone, The.
Televised news turns.
Thank You, Lord.
These Yet to Be United States.
They Ask Why.
They went home and told their wives.
Thirteens (Black), The.
Thirteens (White), The.
This Winter Day.
Through the Inner City to the Suburbs.
Times-Square-Shoeshine-Composition.
To a Freedom Fighter.
To a Husband.
To a Man.
To a Suitor.
To Beat the Child Was Bad Enough.
Traveler, The.
Unmeasured Tempo.
We saw beyond our seeming.
Weekend Glory.
When I think about myself.
When you come to me, unbidden.
Where We Belong, A Duet.
Why Are They Happy People?
Willie was a man without fame.
Woman Me.
Woman Work.
Wonder.

Worker's Song.
Zorro Man, A.
Anthony, Florence. *See* **"Ai"**
As-Sabah, Sabah
Love.
Sister Roll.
Asim, Jabari
Mumble the Magic Words.
Asquith, Herbert (1881–1947)
Banking Potatoes.
Birds on a Powerline.
Sunday Afternoons.
Atkins, Russell (b. 1926)
At War.
Dark Area.
Editorial Poem on an Incident of Effects Far-
reaching.
Irritable Song.
It's Here In The.
Lakefront, Cleveland.
Lisbon.
Narrative.
New Storefront.
Night and a Distant Church.
On the Fine Arts Garden, Cleveland.
Probability and Birds in the Yard.
Aubert, Alvin (b. 1930)
All Singing in a Pie.
Baptism.
Feeling Through.
For Mark James Robert Essex d. 1973.
Nat Turner in the Clearing.
One More Time.
Revolutionary, The.
Spring 1937/ for Honoré Roussell.
When the Wine Was Gone.
Auset, Kupenda (Joette Harland Watts)
That Was Then.
Austin, Louie. *See* **Hunter, Albert** *and* **Louie
Austin**
Ayers, Vivian
Instantaneous ("Instantaneously!")

B

Baker, Houston A., Jr. (b. 1943)
Late-Winter Blues and Promises of Love.
No matter where you travel.
This is not a poem, nor.
Balagon, Kuwasi
Children of the Cosmos.
Untitle.
Bandele, Asha
Subtle Art of Breathing, The.
Baraka, Amiri (LeRoi Jones) (b. 1934)
Agony. An. As Now.
All's Well.
Am/trak.
American Ecstasy.
Are Their Blues Singers in Russia?
As a Possible Lover.
At the Colonial Y They Are Aesthetically
and Culturally Deprived (Y's Later) (31).
Audubon, Drafted.
Babylon Revisited.
Balboa, the Entertainer.
Beautiful Black Women.
Betancourt.
Black Art.
Black Bourgeoisie.
Black Dada Nihilismus.
Black People!
Black People: This Is Our Destiny.
Bludoo Baby, Want Money, and Alligator
Got It to Give.
Bridge, The.
Bronze Buckaroo, The.
Bumi.
Burning General, The.
Christ Was Never in Europe!
Civil Rights Bill #666.
Clay.
Cold Term.
Contract. (For the Destruction and Rebuilding
of Paterson), A.

Crow Jane in High Society.
Crow Jane the Crook.
Crow Jane's Manner.
Das Kapital.
Dead Lady Canonized, The.
Death Is Not as Natural as You Fags Seem
to Think.
Devil Worship.
Dichtung.
Duke's World / is the explanation.
Duncan Spoke of a Process.
Election Day.
End of Man Is His Beauty, The.
Epistrophe.
Footnote to a Pretentious Book.
For Crow Jane (Mama Death).
For Hettie.
From an Almanac.
From an Almanac (2).
From an Almanac (3).
Gatsby's Theory of Aesthetics.
Green Lantern's Solo.
Guerilla Handbook, A.
Heathen Bliss.
Heathen Technology & Media.
Heathens.
Heathens in Evolution.
Heathens Think Fascism Is Civilization.
History on Wheels.
History-Wise #22.
Horatio Alger Uses Scag.
Hymn to Lanie Poo, *sels.*
I don't love you.
If into Love the Image Burdens.
In Memory of Radio.
In One Battle.
In the Tradition.
Insidious Dr. Fu Man Chu, The.
Invention of Comics, The.
JA   ZZ   :   (The "Say what?")   IS
     IS   JA   LIVES.
Joseph to His Brothers.
Ka 'Ba.
Legacy.
Leroy.
Letter to E. Franklin Frazier.
Liar, The.
Lines to Garcia Lorca.
Look for You Yesterday, Here You Come
Today.
Lord Haw Haw (as Pygmy) #37.
Measure of Memory (The Navigator), The.
New Reality Is Better Than a New Movie,
A!
New Sheriff, The.
New World, The.
1929: Y you ask? (26).
Notes for a Speech.
Numbers, Letters.
Of What Use Is Poetry? (Babalu Meets the
Wolfman).
One More Time.
Ostriches and Grandmothers!
People Burning, The.
Poem for Black Hearts, A.
Poem for Deep Thinkers, A.
Poem for Democrats, A.
Poem for Half White College Students.
Poem for Neutrals, A.
Poem for Speculative Hipsters, A.
Poem for Wille Best, A.
Poem Some People Will Have to Understand,
A.
Poem Welcoming Jonas Mekas to America,
A.
Political Poem.
Politics of Rich Painters, The.
Pres / spoke in a language.
Pressures, The.
Real Life.
Red Eye.
Reggae or Not!
Return of the Native.
Revelation in Brick City.
Revolutionary Love.
Rhythm and Blues (I).

Sacred Chant for the Return of Black Spirit
and Power.
Scenario VI.
Short Speech to My Friends.
Snake Eyes.
So the King Sold the Farmer #39.
SOS.
Speech #38 (or Y We Say It This Way).
Stellar Nilotic (29).
Study Peace.
Success, The.
Symphony Sid.
"There Was Something I Wanted to Tell
You." (33) Why?
This Is the Clearing I Once Spoke of.
Three Modes of History and Culture.
Three Movements and a Coda.
To a Publisher ... Cut-out.
Tone Poem.
Turn Around Y36, The.
Valéry as Dictator.
Vice.
W. W.
War Poem.
Way Out West.
We Own the Night.
Western Lady, A.
When We'll Worship Jesus.
Wise 2.
Wise 4.
World is Full of Remarkable Things, The.
Y the Link Will Not Always Be "Missing"
#40.
YMCA #35.
Young Soul.
Y's 18.
Barlow, George (b. 1948)
Dream of the Ring: the Great Jack Johnson,
A.
Gabriel, *sels.*
In My Father's House.
Nook.
Painting Drunken Twilight.
Place Where He Arose, The.
Resonance.
Salt.
Sorrow Since Sitting Bull, A.
This Bridge Across.
Barrax, Gerald William (b. 1933)
Adagio.
Black Narcissus.
Christmas 1959 Et Cetera.
Death of a Squirrel in McKinley Park, The.
Domestic Tranquility.
Efficiency Apartment.
For a Black Poet.
For Malcolm: After Mecca.
Fourth Dance Poem.
Greenhouse.
In the Restaurant.
King: April 4, 1968.
Last Letter.
Patroness.
Sacrifice, The.
Scuba Diver Recovers the Body of a
Drowned Child, The.
Singer, The.
There was a song.
To a Woman Who Wants Darkness and
Time.
Visit.
Whose children are these?
Your Eyes Have Their Silence.
Baudelaire, Charles (1821–67)
Cat, The.
Cats.
Death to the Poor.
Beadle, Samuel Alfred (1857–1932)
After Church.
Lines: "How I love country you have heard."
Lines to Caste.
Words are but leaves to the tree of mind.
Beeks, Clarence ("King Pleasure")
Parker's Mood.
Bell, James Madison (1826–1902)
Modern Moses, or "My Policy" Man.

Benford, Lawrence (b. 1946)
Beginning of a Long Poem on Why I Burned the City, The.

Benjamin, Robert Charles O'Hara (1855–1900)
Colored Heroes, Hark the Bugle.
Farmer's Soliloquy, The.

Bennett, Bob
It is time for action.
(Title).

Bennett, Gwendolyn B. (1902–81)
Advice.
Fantasy.
Hatred.
Heritage.
Lines Written at the Grave of Alexander [or Alexandre] Dumas.
Nocturne: "This cool night is strange."
Quatrain 2: "How strange that grass should sing."
Quatrains.
Secret.
Song: "I am weaving a song of waters."
Sonnet: "He came in silvern armor, trimmed with black."
Sonnet—2: "Some things are very dear to me—."
Sonnets, *sels.*
Street Lamps in Early Spring.
To a Dark Girl.
To Usward.
Your Songs.

Bennett, Lerone, Jr. (b. 1928)
And Was Not Improved.
Blues and Bitterness.

Bethune, Lebert (b. 1937)
Blue Tanganyika.
Bwagamoyo.
For Singing In Good Mood.
Harlem Freeze Frame.
Juju of My Own, A.
To Strike for Night.
Today Tutu Is Beating the Same Burru As Me.

Bibb, Eloise (Eloise Bibb Thompson) (1878–1927)
After Reading Bryant's Lines to a Waterfowl.
Anne Boleyn.
Belshazzer's Feast.
Capt. Smith and Pocahontas.
Catharine of Arragon.
Charmion's Lament.
Class Song of '91.
Destiny.
Early spring's sweet blush, The.
Eliza in Uncle Tom's Cabin.
Expulsion of Hagar, The.
Gerarda.
Hermit, The.
Imogene.
In Memoriam Frederick Douglass.
In Memory of Arthur Clement Williams.
Judith.
Leona, dear, twelve months ago.
Lines to Mrs. M. C. Turner.
Lines to the Hon. George L. Knox.
Ode to the Sun.
Offering, An.
Sonnet: "O thou who never harbored fear."
Tale of Italy, A.
Tribute.
Vestal Virgin, The.
Wandering Jew, The.

Bibbs, Hart Leroi (b. 1930)
Dirge for J. A. Rogers.
Liberalissimo.
Six Sunday.
Split Standard.

Billingsley, Nikkia
Rhetorically Speaking.

Bird, Bessie Calhoun (b. 1906)
Proof.

Black, Austin (b. 1929)
Soul.

Black, Isaac J.
Racist Psychotherapy.

Blount, Sonny. *See* "Sun Ra"

Blue, Victor E.
American Dialogue.

Bohanan, Otto Leland
Dawn's Awake, The!
Washer-Woman, The.

Bomani, Mawiyah Kai El-Jamah
Homecoming.

Bomani, Nadir Lasana
Philosophical Perspective on Everyday Shit, A.
Thin Water.

Bond, Julian (b. 1940)
Bishop of Atlanta: Ray Charles, The.
Habana.
Rotation.

Bontemps, Arna (1902–73)
Black Man Talks of Reaping, A.
Blight.
Close Your Eyes!
Day-Breakers [or Daybreakers], The.
Gethsemane.
God Give to Men.
Golgotha Is a Mountain.
Homing.
Idolatry.
Lancelot.
Length of Moon.
Miracles.
My Heart has Known its Winter.
Nocturne at Bethesda.
Nocturne of the Wharves.
Reconnaissance.
Return, The.
Southern Mansion.
To a Young Girl Leaving the Hill Country.
Tree Design, A.

Boyd, Francis A. *(fl. 1870)*
Columbiana, *sels.*

Boyd, John *(fl. 1834)*
Ocean.
Sketch of a Verying Evening Sky.
Vision, The.

Boyd, Melba Joyce (b. 1950)
Beer Drops.
Sunflowers and Saturdays.
Why?

Bradford, Walter
T.C.

Braithwaite, William Stanley (1878–1962)
City Garden, A.
Del Cascar, Del Cascar.
Golden Moonrise.
House of Falling Leaves, The.
Hymn for the Slain in Battle.
If I Could Touch.
In a Grave-Yard.
Ironic: LL.D.
October XXIX, 1795.
Quiet has a hidden sound.
Rhapsody.
Rye Bread.
Sandy Star and Willie Gee.
Scintilla.
Sic Vita.
To ———: "Half in the dim light from the hall."
Turn Me to My Yellow Leaves.
Two Questions.
Watchers, The.

Brathwaite, Edward Kamau (b. 1930)
Blues.
New Year Letter.

Brawley, Benjamin (1882–1939)
Chaucer.
My Hero.

Braxton, Charlie R. (b. 1961)
Gathering, The.
Jazzy St. Walk.
Say Hey Homeboy.

Brocks-Shedd, Virgia (b. 1943)
Southern Roads/City Pavement.

Brooks, Edwin (b. 1929)
Tulips from Their Blood.

Brooks, Gwendolyn (b. 1917)
Anniad, The.
Appendix to the Anniad.
Aspect of Love, Alive in the Ice and Fire, An.
Ballad of Rudolph Reed, The.
Bean Eaters, The.
Birth in a Narrow Room, The.
Black Wedding Song, A.
Blackstone Rangers, The.
Boy Breaking Glass.
Boy died in my alley, The.
Bronzeville Man with a Belt in the Back.
Bronzeville Mother Loiters in Mississippi. / Meanwhile, a Mississippi Mother Burns Bacon.
Bronzeville Woman in a Red Hat.
Chicago *Defender* Sends a Man to Little Rock, The.
Children Coming Home, *sels.*
Children of the Poor, The, *sels.*
Crazy Woman, The.
Egg Boiler, The.
Empty woman took toys! The.
Estimable Mable.
Firstly Inclined to Take What It Is Told.
Flags.
Gay Chaps at the Bar.
God Works in a Mysterious Way.
In Emanuel's Nightmare: Another Coming of Christ.
In Honor of David Anderson Brooks, My Father.
Jessie Mitchell's Mother.
Kojo "I Am a Black."
Langston Hughes.
Last Quatrain of the Ballad of Emmett Till, The.
Life of Lincoln West, The.
Looking.
Love Note I: Surely.
Lovely Love, A.
Lovers of the Poor, The.
Malcolm X.
Man of the Middle Class, A.
Martin Luther King, Jr.
Maxie Allen always taught her.
Medgar Evers.
Mentors.
Merle "Uncle Seagram."
Mrs. Small went to the kitchen for her pocketbook.
My Dreams, My Works Must Wait Till after Hell.
My little 'bout-town gal has gone.
Near-Johannesburg Boy, The.
"Negro" Hero.
Of Robert Frost.
Old-Marrieds, The.
Old Mary.
Paul Robeson.
Penitent Considers Another Coming of Mary, A.
Piano after War.
Progress, The.
Riders to the Blood-Red Wrath.
Riot.
Second Sermon on the Warpland, The.
Sermon on the Warpland, The.
Still Do I Keep My Look, My Identity.
Street in Bronzeville, A, *sels.*
Strong Men, Riding Horses / Lester after the Western.
Sundays of Satin-Legs Smith, The.
Sunset of the City, A.
Third Sermon on the Warpland, The.
To an Old Black Woman, Homeless and Indistinct.
To be in love.
To Those of My Sisters Who Kept Their Naturals.
We real cool. We.
When You Have Forgotten Sunday: The Love Story.
White Troops Had Their Orders but the Negroes Looked Like Men.
Womanhood, The, *sels.*

Young Africans.
Young Heroes.
Brooks, Harry. *See* **Waller, Thomas ("Fats"), Andy Razaf,** *and* **Harry Brooks**
Brooks, Helen Morgan
Plans.
Words.
Brooks, Jonathan Henderson (1904–45)
Last Quarter Moon of the Dying Year, The.
Paean.
Resurrection, The.
Brown, Adwin
Donut Man.
Brown, Elaine (b. 1943)
If Randi Could Write.
Brown, Isabella Maria (b. 1917)
Prayer: "I had thought of putting an / altar."
Brown, Kysha N.
Brown Girl Blues.
Brown, Linda Beatrice
Green arbor that I once knew, A.
Winter Sonnet.
Brown, Sterling Allen (1901–89)
After Winter.
Against That Day.
All Are Gay.
April in Coolwell.
Arkansas Chant.
Bad, Bad Man, A.
Ballad of Joe, The.
Bessie.
Bitter Fruit of the Tree.
Break of Day.
Cabaret.
Call Boy.
Call for Barnum.
Challenge.
Checkers.
Children of the Mississippi.
Children's Children.
Chillen Get Shoes.
Choices.
Cloteel: / Rampart Street knows you now: the golden.
Colloquy.
Conjured.
Convict.
Coolwell Vignette.
Crispus Attacks McKoy.
Crossing.
Dark of the Moon.
Effie.
Elder Mistletoe.
Episode.
Foreclosure.
Frankie and Johnny.
Funeral.
Georgie Grimes, with a red suitcase.
Glory, Glory.
Harlem Happiness.
Harlem Street Walkers.
He Was a Man.
Honey Mah Love.
Idyll.
Isaiah to Mandy.
Johnny Thomas.
Kentucky Blues.
Last Ride of Wild Bill.
Law for George, The.
Legend.
Let us suppose him differently placed.
Long Gone.
Long Track Blues.
Louisiana Pastoral.
Ma Rainey.
Master and Man.
Maumee Ruth.
Mecca.
Memo: For the Race Orators.
Memories of Salem.
Memphis Blues.
Mill Mountain.
Mr. Danny.
Mister Samuel and Sam.
Mose is black and evil.
Negro Improvement League.

New Congo, The.
New St. Louis Blues.
New steps / O my Lawd.
No More Worlds to Conquer.
Nous n'irons plus au bois.
Odyssey of Big Boy.
Old King Cotton.
Old Lem.
Old Man Buzzard / Wid his bal' head.
Old Woman Remembers, An.
One Way of Taking Leave.
Pardners.
Parish Doctor.
Puttin' on Dog.
Raise a Song.
Real Mammy Song.
Remembering Nat Turner.
Rent Day Blues.
Return.
Revelations.
Riverbank Blues.
Roberta Lee.
Ruminations of Luke Johnson.
Salutamus.
Sam Smiley.
Scotty Has His Say.
Seeking Religion.
Sharecroppers.
Side by Side.
Sister Lou.
Slim Greer.
Slim Hears "The Call".
Slim in Atlanta.
Slim in Hell ("Slim Greer went to heaven").
Slim Lands a Job?
Song of Triumph.
Southern Cop.
Southern Road.
Sporting Beasley.
Strange Legacies.
Street Car Gang.
Strong Men.
Telling Fortunes.
Temple, The.
Thoughts of death / Crowd over my happiness.
Tin Roof Blues.
To a Certain Lady, in Her Garden.
To Sallie, Walking.
Transfer.
Uncle Joe.
Virginia Portrait.
When de Saints Go Ma'ching Home.
Young Ones, The.
Browne, William
Harlem Sounds: Hallelujah Corner.
Bruce, Richard (b. 1906)
Cavalier.
Shadow.
Brutus, Dennis (b. 1924)
Off to Philadelphia in the morning.
Sand wet and cool, The.
Bryant, Frederick, Jr. (b. 1942)
Black Orpheus.
Cathexis.
Languages We Are, The.
Nothing Lovely as a Tree.
Buchanan, Shonda
Prayer: "Centaurian smoke blower / shyly smoking my breast."
Bullins, Ed (b. 1935)
When Slavery Seems Sweet.
Burnette, Beverly Fields
Artichoke Pickle Passion: Sonnet.
Burroughs, Margaret Goss (b. 1917)
Black Pride.
Everybody but Me.
Only in This Way.
To Soulfolk.
Burt, Della (b. 1944)
Little Girl's Dream World, A.
On the Death of Lisa Lyman.
Spirit Flowers.
Byrnes, Lillian
Chalk-Dust.
Nordic.

C

Calderón, Paul
It's hard being / folded/licked.
Campbell, Alfred Gibbs (b. 1826?)
Cry "Infidel!"
Divine Mission, The.
Lines: "Wake not again the cannon's thundrous voice."
Song of the Decanter.
Warning.
Campbell, James Edwin (1867–96)
Compensation.
De Cunjah Man.
Mobile-Buck.
Mors et Vita.
Negro Serenade.
Ol' Doc' Hyar.
Pariah, The.
'Sciplinin' Sister Brown.
Song of the Corn.
Uncle Eph—Epicure.
Uncle Eph's Banjo Song.
When Ol' Sis' Judy Pray.
Cannon, Noah Calwell (1796?–1850)
Ark, The.
Carmichael, Waverly Turner
Keep Me, Jesus, Keep Me ("Keep me 'neath Thy mighty wing").
Winter is Coming.
Carr, Leroy (1905–1935)
How Long Blues.
Carrington, Joyce Sims
Old Slave Woman, An.
Carroll, Kenneth (b. 1959)
Domino Theory (Or Snoop Dogg Rules the World), The.
Short Poem.
Something Easy for Ultra Black Nationalists.
Theory on Extinction or What Happened to the Dinosaurs?
Upper Marlboro.
Cassells, Cyrus (b. 1957)
Courtesy, A Trenchant Grace, A.
Soul Make A Path Through Shouting.
These Are Not Brushstrokes.
Cater, Catharine (b. 1917)
Here and Now.
Caution, Ethel M.
Last night I danced on the rim of the moon.
River is a decrepit old woman, the.
To E.J.J.
Chandler, Len (b. 1935)
I Would Be a Painter Most of All.
Cheatwood, Kiarri T-H
Bloodstorm.
Swamp Rat.
Visions of the Sea.
Christian, Marcus B. (b. 1900)
Craftsman, The.
Dialect Quatrain.
Go Down, Moses!
McDonogh Day in New Orleans.
Selassie at Geneva.
Clark, Benjamin (fl. 1835–67)
Do they miss me at home.
Emigrant, The.
Love.
No Enemies.
Pauper's Grave, The.
Requiescat in Pace.
Seminole, The.
What Is a Slave?
Clark, Carl (b. 1932)
Allegory in Black.
Conundrum.
No More.
Ode to a Beautiful Woman.
Second Coming, The.
Thoughts from a Bottle.
Clarke, John Henrik (b. 1915)
Determination.
Sing Me a New Song.
Clemmons, Carole C. Gregory (b. 1945)
Freedom Song for the Black Woman, A.
Ghetto Lovesong—Migration.

Greater Friendship Baptist Church, The.
I'm Just a Stranger Here, Heaven Is My
　Home.
Love from My Father.
Love Letter.
Revelation.
Spring.

Cliff, Michelle (b. 1946)
Within the Veil.

Clifford, Carrie Williams (1882–1958)
Black Draftee from Dixie, The.

Clifton, Lucille (b. 1936)
Adam and Eve.
Admonitions.
Adupe.
Africa.
After Kent State.
Angels.
Anna Speaks of the Childhood of Mary Her
　Daughter.
Apology (to the Panthers).
4/30/92; for Rodney King.
Astrologer Predicts at Mary's Birth, The.
At Jonestown.
At last we killed the roaches.
Atlantic is a sea of bones.
August the 12th.
Aunt Agnes Hatcher Tells.
Being property once myself.
Bodies broken on, The.
Breaklight.
Buffalo War.
C. C. Rider.
Cain.
Ca'line's Prayer.
Calling of the Disciples, The.
Calming Kali.
Carver, The.
Climbing.
Come home from the movies.
Coming of Kali, The.
Confession.
Conversation with My Grandson, Waiting to
　Be Conceived.
Cutting Greens.
Daddy.
Daniel.
Discoveries of Fire, The.
Driving through New England.
Earth.
Easter Sunday.
Eldridge.
11/10 Again.
Explanations.
1st, The.
Flowers.
For de Lawd.
For her hiding place.
For the Bird Who Flew against Our Window
　One Morning and Broke His Natural Neck.
For the Blind.
For the Lame.
For the Mad.
For the Mute.
Forgiving My Father.
Friends Come.
Generations.
God Send Easter.
God waits for the wandering world.
God's Mood.
Good Friday.
Good Times.
Harriet / if i be you.
Her Love Poem.
Holy Night.
Homage to My Hair.
Homage to My Hips.
How He Is Coming Then.
I am high on the man called crazy.
I Am Not Done Yet.
I am running into a new year.
I. At Nagasaki.
I once knew a man who had wild horses
　killed.
I was born in a hotel.
I was born with twelve fingers.
I went to the valley.

If He Ask You Was I Laughing.
If i stand in my window.
If mama / could see.
If Something Should Happen.
In populated air.
In Salem.
In the Evenings.
In the Inner City.
In this garden.
Incandescence / formless form.
Island Mary.
Jackie Robinson.
Job easy / is the pride.
John.
Jonah.
Joseph.
Kali / queen of fertility.
Kind of Man He Is, The.
Lane Is the Pretty One.
Last Note to My Girls.
Lately / everybody i meet.
Later i'll say / i spent my life.
Leanna's Poem.
Lesson of the Falling Leaves, The.
Let There Be New Flowering.
Light / on my mother's tongue.
Light that came to lucille clifton, The.
Listen children / keep this in the place.
Lost Baby Poem, The.
Love rejected / hurts so much more.
Lucy and Her Girls.
Lucy one-eye.
Making of Poems, The.
Malcolm.
Mary.
Mary　mary astonished by God.
Mary's Dream.
Meeting After the Savior Gone, The.
Miss Rosie.
Monticello.
More than once.
Moses.
Mother, i am mad.
Move.
My boys beauty is.
My daddy's fingers move among the
　couplers.
My Friends.
My Mama moved among the days.
My Poem.
Mystery that surely is present, The.
New Bones.
New Year.
News, The.
Now my first wife never did come out of her
　room.
On the Birth of Bomani.
On the Death of Allen's Son.
Once and future dead, The.
Palm Sunday.
Perhaps.
Pity this poor animal.
Poem for My Sisters.
Poem on My Fortieth Birthday to My Mother
　Who Died Young.
Poet, The.
Pork chops.
Powell; March 1991.
Prayer.
Raising of Lazarus, The.
Richard penniman.
Robert.
Roots.
Running across to the lot.
Salt.
'70s, The.
She Insists on Me.
She Is Dreaming.
She Understands Me.
Sisters.
Slaveship.
So close / they come so close.
Solomon.
Some dreams hang in the air.
Song: "Sons of slaves and."
Song of Mary, A.
Sonora Desert Poem.

Speaking of Loss.
Spring Song.
Still / it was nice.
Stops.
Storm Poem, A.
Testament.
There Is a Girl Inside.
Thirty-eighth year, The.
This morning / this morning.
Those Boys That Ran Together.
To a Dark Moses.
To Bobby Seale.
To Joan.
To Merle.
To Ms. Ann.
To my Friend, Jerina.
To the Unborn and Waiting Children.
To Thelma Who Worried Because I Couldn't
　Cook.
Turning into my own.
Tyrone (1).
Tyrone (2).
Tyrone (3).
Tyrone (4).
Visit to Gettysburg, A.
Way It Was, The.
What spells racoon to me.
What the Mirror Said.
White Boy, The.
White Lady.
Why Some People Be Mad at Me
　Sometimes.
Wife.
Willie B (1).
Willie B (2).
Willie B (3).
Willie B (4).
Wise: Having the Ability to Perceive and
　Adopt the Best Means for Accomplishing
　an End.
Wishes for Sons.
Woman who loves, A.
Women You Are Accustomed To, The.

Clinton, Michélle T. (b. 1954)
History as Trash.
Traditional Post-Modern Neo-HooDoo Afra-
　Centric Sister in a Purple Head Rag
　Mourning Death and Cooking.

Coates, Ta-Nehisi
Alice Flips the Script.

Cobb, Alice S. (b. 1942)
Angela Davis.
Searching, The.

Cobb, Charlie (b. 1944)
Containing Communism.
For Sammy Younge.
Nation.
To Vietnam.

Coffin, Frank Barbour (1870?–1951)
Ajax' Conclusion.
Harriet Beecher Stowe's Works.
Mother's Songs.

Coleman, Anita Scott (b. 1906)
Black Baby.
Black Faces.
Negro laughter.
Portraiture.
Shining Parlor, The.

Coleman, Wanda (b. 1946)
American Sonnet (10).
At the Record Hop.
Aunt Jessie.
Be Quiet, Go Away.
Bedtime Story.
Breast Examination.
Cousin Mary.
Dear Mama.
Doing Battle with the Wolf.
Emmett Till.
In This Waking.
Las Turistas Negras Grande.
Mastectomy.
Miss Jones.
Shopping Bag Lady.
Today I Am a Homicide in the North of the
　City.
Word Game.

Collins, Leslie Morgan (b. 1919)
Stevedore.

Conyus (b. 1942)
Confession to Malcolm.
Day in the Life of . . . , A.
Great Santa Barbara Oil Disaster OR, The.
He's Doing Natural Life.
I rode with Geronimo.
San Francisco County Jail Cell B-6.
Six Ten Sixty-Nine.
Untitled Requiem for Tomorrow.
Upon Leaving the Parole Board Hearing.

Cook, Mike (b. 1939)
Bootie Black and the Seven Giants.

Cook, William W.
Seth Bingham.
Spiritual.
Still-Life with Woodstove.

Cooper, Charles (b. 1948)
Dreams.
Rubin.

Corbin, Lloyd M., Jr. (Djangatolum) (b. 1949)
Ali.
Dedication to the Final Confrontation.

Cornish, Sam (b. 1935)
Black Man, A.
Death of Dr. King.
Frederick Douglass.
Generations 1.
Generations 2.
His Fingers Seem to Sing.
Montgomery.
One Eyed Black Man in Nebraska.
Panther.
Promenade.
River, The.
To a Single Shadow without Pity.
Turk.

Corrie, Joe (b. 1894)
How Long Has Trane Been Gone.

Corrothers, James David (1869–1917)
At the Closed Gate of Justice.
De Black Cat Crossed His Luck.
Der Rabbit's Foot.
Dream and the Song.
In the Matter of Two Men.
Indignation Dinner, An.
Me 'n' Dunbar.
Negro Singer, The.
Paul Laurence Dunbar.
Road to the Bow, The.
Snapping of the Bow, The.
Sweeten 'Tatahs.

Cortez, Jayne (b. 1936)
Acceptance Speech.
Blood Suckers.
Bowery Street.
Brooding.
Complicity.
Consultation.
Do you think this is a sad day.
Everything Is Wonderful.
Expenditures; Economic Love Song 1.
Feathers.
Firespitters / spitting across the desert.
Flame.
For Real.
For the Brave Young Students in Soweto.
For the Poets.
Give Me the Red on the Black of the Bullet.
Grinding Vibrato.
I Am New York City.
I and I.
I See Chano Pozo.
If the drum is a woman.
I'm A Worker.
In a Stream of Ink.
In the Morning.
Initiation.
It's nothing / this tragedy in our arms.
Jazz Fan Looks Back.
Lead.
Lonely Woman.
Lynch Fragment 2.
Nighttrains.
No Simple Explanations.

Once Upon a Road.
Orange Chiffon.
Orisha.
Phraseology.
Plain Truth.
Push Back the Catastrophes.
Rape.
Red Pepper Poet, The.
Rising, The.
Rose Solitude.
So Many Feathers.
Solomon Mahlangu, Freedom Fighter from
    Mamelodi.
Stockpiling of frozen trees, The.
Suppression.
Tapping.
Tell me that the plutonium sludge.
There It Is.
They Came Again in 1970 in 1980.
Under the Edge of February.
When I Look at Wilfredo Lam's Paintings.
You know / I sure would like to write a
    blues.

Cotter, Joseph Seamon, Sr. (1861–1949)
Algernon Charles Swinburne.
And What Shall You Say?
Answer to Dunbar's "A Choice."
Answer to Dunbar's "After a Visit."
April Day, An.
Band of Gideon roam the sky, The.
Book's Creed, The.
Contradiction.
Deserter, The.
Don't-Care Negro, The.
Dr. Booker T. Washington to the National
    Negro Business League.
Emerson.
Frederick Douglass.
Is It Because I Am Black?
Let none ignobly halt because.
My Poverty and Wealth.
Ned's Psalm of Life for the Negro.
Oliver Wendell Holmes.
On Hearing James W. Riley Read.
Poet, The.
Prayer: "As I lie in bed."
Prologue to a Supposed Play.
Rain Music.
Sonnet to Negro Soldiers.
Supplication.
Tragedy of Pete, The.
Way-Side Well, The.
William Lloyd Garrison.

Cowdery, Mae V. (b. 1910)
After the Japanese.
Brown Aesthete Speaks, A.
Dusk.
Exultation.
Farewell: "No more / The feel of your hand."
God / Is kind.
Having had you once.
Heritage.
I Sit and Wait for Beauty.
If I must know sorrow.
Insatiate.
Interlude.
Lines to a Sophisticate.
Longings.
Of Earth.
Poem . . . for a Lover.
Poplar Tree.
Prayer, A.
Some Hands Are Lovelier.
Want.
Wind blows, The.

Crouch, Stanley (b. 1945)
Albert Ayler: Eulogy for a Decomposed
    Saxophone Player.
BLACKIE Speaks on Campus: a Valentine
    for Vachel Lindsay.
Blackie Thinks of His Brothers.
Chops Are Flyin.
Like a Blessing.
No New Music.
Riding Across John Lee's Finger.

Cruz, Victor Hernandez (b. 1949)
Carmen.

Electric Cop, The.
Energy.
First Claims Poem.
O. K. / you scat taking.
Spirits.
Story of the Zeros, The.
Urban Dream.
White Powder!

Cullen, Countee (1903–46)
Advice to a Beauty.
After a Visit.
Any Human to Another.
Apostrophe to the Land.
At a Parting.
At the Wailing Wall in Jerusalem.
Atlantic City Waiter.
Ballad of the Brown Girl, The.
Black Christ, The.
Black Magdalens.
Black Majesty.
Bright Bindings.
Brown Boy to Brown Girl.
Brown Girl Dead, A.
Christus Natus Est.
Colored Blues Singer.
Colors.
Cor cordium is written there.
Counter Mood.
Dear Friends and Gentle Hearts.
Dictum.
Epilogue: "Lily, being white not red, The."
Epitaph: "She leans across a golden table."
Foolish Heart, The.
For a Mouthy Woman.
For a Pessimist.
For a Poet.
For an Anarchist.
For an Atheist.
For an Evolutionist and His Opponent.
For Daughters of Magdalen.
For Helen Keller.
For Joseph Conrad.
For Myself.
Four Epitaphs, *sels.*
From the Dark Tower.
Fruit of the Flower.
Ghosts.
Harsh World that lashest me each day.
Heritage.
Hunger.
I have a rendezvous with Life.
If You Should Go.
In Spite of Death.
Incident.
Judas Iscariot.
Karenge Ya Marenge.
La Belle, La Douce, La Grande.
Lament: "Now let all lovely things embark."
Leaves.
Life's Rendezvous.
Lines for a Hospital.
Lines to My Father.
Lines to Our Elders.
Litany of the Dark People, The.
Little Sonnet to Little Friends.
Love Tree, The.
Love's Way.
Magnets.
Medusa.
Minutely Hurt.
Mood.
More Than a Fool's Song.
Negro Mother's Lullaby, A.
Night Rain.
Not Sacco and Vanzetti.
Nothing endures, / Not even love.
One Day We Played a Game.
Only the Polished Skeleton.
Pagan Prayer.
Pity the deep in love.
Poet, poet, what is your task.
Protest.
Proud Heart, The.
Requiescam.
Saturday's Child.
Scottsboro, Too, Is Worth Its Song.
Self Criticism.

She of the Dancing Feet Sings.
Shroud of Color, The.
Simon the Cyrenian Speaks.
Singing in the Rain.
Song in Spite of Myself.
Song of Praise, A.
Song of Sour Grapes, A.
Sonnet Dialogue.
Sonnet: "I have not loved you in the noblest
    way."
Sonnet: "I know now how a man whose
    blood is hot."
Sonnet: "Some for a little while do love, and
    some for long."
Sonnet: "These are no wind-blown rumors,
    soft say-sos."
Sonnet: "What I am saying now was said
    before."
Spring Reminiscence.
Street Called Crooked, The.
Tableau.
That bright chimeric beast.
Therefore, Adieu.
Thorn Forever in the Breast, A.
Thoughts in a Zoo.
Threnody for a Brown Girl.
Timid Lover.
To a Brown Girl.
To an Unknown Poet.
To Certain Critics.
To Endymion.
To France.
To John Keats, Poet, at Springtime.
To Lovers of Earth: Fair Warning.
To One Not There.
To the Swimmer.
To the Three for Whom the Book.
Tribute.
Two Thoughts of Death.
Two Who Crossed a Line (She Crosses).
Two Who Crossed a Line.
Ultimatum.
Uncle Jim.
Variations on a Theme.
Wind Bloweth Where It Listeth, The.
Wisdom Cometh with the Years.
Wise, The.
Yet Do I Marvel.
Youth Sings a Song of Rosebuds.
Translations, Coauthored Poems, etc.:
    Cat, The.
    Cats.
    Death to the Poor.

Cumbo, Kattie M. (b. 1938)
Black Sister.
Ceremony.
Domestics.
I'm a Dreamer.
Morning after . . . Love, The.
Nocturnal Sounds.

Cuney, Waring (1906–76)
Burial of the Young Love.
Conception.
Crucifixion.
Death Bed, The.
Dust, / Through which.
Finis.
I Think I See Him There.
No Images.
Radical, The.
Threnody: "Only quiet death."
Triviality, A.
Troubled Jesus.
True Love.
Wake Cry.

Cunningham, James ("Olumo") (b. 1936)
City Rises, The.
Covenant, The.
Footnote to a Gray Bird's Pause, A.
For Cal.
From a Brother Dreaming in the Rye.
Happy Day (or Independence Day).
High-cool/2.
Incidental Pieces to a Walk.
Lee-ers of Hew.
Leg-acy of a Blue Capricorn.
Plea to My Sister, A.

Rapping Along with Ronda Davis.
Slow Riff for Billy.
Solitary Visions of a Kaufmanoid.
St. Julien's Eve.
Street in Kaufman-ville, A.
Tambourine.
Welcome for Etheridge, A.
While Cecil Snores: Mom Drinks Cold Milk.
Curtright [*or* Curtwright], Wesley (b. 1910)
Close of Day, The.

D

D, Chuck
But Can You Kill the Nigga in You?
"D-Knowledge." *See* **Gilbert, Derrick I. M.**
Daáood, Kamau
Tears for the poet.
Dandridge, Ray Garfield (1882–1930)
Drum Majah, De.
'Ittle Touzle Head.
Sprin' Fevah.
Time to Die.
Zalka Peetruza.
Danner, James
My Brother.
Singer, The.
Danner Margaret (b. 1915)
And through the Caribbean Sea.
At Home in Dakar.
Best Loved of Africa.
Convert, The.
Elevator Man Adheres to Form, The.
Etta Moten's Attic.
Goodbye David Tamunoemi West.
Grandson Is a Hoticeberg, A.
I'll walk the tightrope that's been stretched
    for me.
Painted Lady, The.
Rhetoric of Langston Hughes, The.
Sadie's Playhouse.
Slave and the Iron Lace, The.
Small Bells of Benin, The.
These Beasts and the Benin Bronze.
This Is an African Worm.
Through the Varied Patterned Lace.
Datcher, Michael (b.1962)
I Am Open.
Davis, Daniel Webster (1862–1913)
Aunt Chloe's Lullaby.
Hog Meat.
I Can Trust.
Linin' ub De Hymns, De.
Miss Liza's Banjer.
My Childhood's Happy Days.
Negro Meets to Pray, The.
Nigger's Got to Go, De.
'Weh Down Souf.
Davis, Frank Marshall (b. 1905)
Arthur Ridgewood, M.D.
Dancing Gal.
Duke Ellington.
Flowers of Darkness.
Four Glimpses of Night.
Giles Johnson, Ph.D.
I Sing No New Songs.
Little and Big.
Onward Christian Soldiers!
Robert Whitmore.
Snapshots of the Cotton South.
To Those Who Sing America.
Davis, Gloria
To Egypt.
Davis, Robert A. (b. 1917)
Dust Bowl.
Davis Ronda M. (b. 1940)
Invitation (To the Night and All Other
    Things Dark).
Parasitosis.
Personality Sketch: Bill, A.
Poems about Playmates.
Rip-Off.
Spacin.

Davis, Thadious M. (b. 1944)
Asante Sana, Te Te.
Double Take at Relais de L'Espadon.
Honeysuckle Was the Saddest Odor of All, I
    Think.
It's All the Same.
Remembering Fannie Lou Hamer.
Davis, Thulani
Boppin' is Safer than Grindin'.
Playing Solitaire.
Susannah.
Desbrosses, Nelson
Le Retour au Village aux Perles.
Delany, Clarissa Scott (1901–27)
Interim.
Joy shakes me like the wind that lifts a sail.
Mask, The.
Solace.
Delegall, Walt
Elegy for a Lady.
Psalm for Sonny Rollins.
Dent, Tom (b. 1932)
Come Visit My Garden.
Dream Orpheum Balcony.
For Lil Louis.
For Walter Washington.
Love.
Nightdreams (Black).
Ray Charles at Mississippi State.
Return to English Turn.
Secret Messages.
St. Helena Island.
Ten Years After Umbra.
Time is a motor, you know.
Derricotte, Toi (b. 1941)
Black Boys Play the Classics.
Blackbottom.
Christmas Eve: My Mother Dressing.
Family Secrets.
Fears of the Eighth Grade.
From a Letter: About Snow.
1994 Inventory.
Promise, The.
Touching/Not Touching: My Mother.
Weakness, The.
Dett, Robert Nathaniel (1882–1943)
Rubinstein Staccato Etude, The.
Dickey, Ralph
Father.
Leaving Eden.
Mulatto Lullaby.
Dickinson, Blanche Taylor (b. 1942)
Dark Actress—Somewhere, A.
Four Walls.
Poem: "Ah, I know what happiness is!"
Revelation.
That Hill.
To an Icicle.
Walls of Jericho, The.
Dickinson, Emily (1830–86)
Softened by Time's consummate plush.
Dixon, Melvin
Grandmother: Crossing Jordan.
Heartbeats.
Tour Guide: La Maison des Esclaves.
Dixon, Ruth G.
Epitome.
Djangatolum. See Corbin, Lloyd M., Jr.
Dobyns, Stephen (b. 1941)
Connections.
Dodson, Owen (1914–83)
Ballad of Badmen.
Circle One.
Confession Stone, The.
Conversation on V.
Drunken Lover.
Hymn Written after Jeremiah Preached to Me
    in a Dream.
I Break the Sky.
Job's Ancient Lament.
Mary Passed This Morning.
Morning Duke Ellington Praised the Lord and
    Six Little Black Davids Tapped Danced
    Unto, The.
Open Letter.

Poem for Pearl's Dancers.
Sailors on Leave.
Sickle Pears.
Signifying Darkness, The.
Sorrow Is the Only Faithful One.
When I Am Dead.
Yardbird's Skull.

Dooley, Ebon (b. 1942)
Easter Bunny Blues or All I Want for Xmas
   Is the Loop, The.
Prophet's Warning or Shoot to Kill, The.
Query.

Douglass, Frederick (c.1817–1895)
Middle Passage.

Dove, Rita (b. 1952)
Abduction, The.
Adolescence—I.
Adolescence—II.
Adolescence—III.
After Reading *Mickey in the Night Kitchen*
   for the Third Time Before Bed.
Agosta the Winged Man and Rasha the Black
   Dove.
Aircraft.
Anniversary.
Anti-Father.
Ants of Argos, The.
At the German Writers Conference in
   Munich.
Aurora Borealis.
Banneker.
Beauty and the Beast.
Belinda's Petition.
Bird Frau, The.
Boast, The.
Boccaccio: The Plague Years.
Canary.
Catherine of Alexandria.
Catherine of Siena.
Centipede.
Champagne.
Charm, The.
Cholera.
Company.
Compendium.
Copper Beech, The.
Corduroy Road.
Courtship.
Courtship, Diligence.
David Walker (1785–1830).
Daystar.
Definition in the Face of Unnamed Fury.
Delft.
Dusting.
Early Morning on the Tel Aviv–Haifa
   Freeway.
Eastern European Eclogues.
Event, The.
Exeunt the Viols.
Father out Walking on the Lawn, A.
Fiammetta Breaks Her Peace.
First Kiss.
Fish in the Stone, The.
Five Elephants.
Flash Cards.
Flirtation.
For Kazuko.
Geometry.
Gospel.
Grape Sherbet.
Great Palaces of Versailles, The.
Great Uncle Beefheart.
Happenstance.
Headdress.
Hill Has Something to Say, The.
Hill of Beans, A.
His Shirt.
House on Bishop Street, The.
House Slave, The.
Ike.
In the Bulrush.
In the Old Neighborhood.
Jiving.
Kadava Kumbis Devise a Way to Marry for
   Love, The.
Kentucky, 1833.
Left-Handed Cellist, The.

Lightnin' Blues.
Lines Muttered in Sleep.
Magic.
Motherhood.
Musician Talks about "Process," The.
My Father's Telescope.
Nestor's Bathtub.
Nexus.
Nigger Song: An Odyssey.
Night Watch.
Nightmare.
Notes from a Tunisian Journal.
Nothing Down.
November for Beginners.
Ö.
Obedience.
One Volume Missing.
Oriental Ballerina, The.
Pamela.
Parsley.
Particulars.
Passage, The.
Pastoral.
Pearls.
Pithos.
Pomade.
Primer for the Nuclear Age.
Promises.
Reading Hölderlin on the Patio with the Aid
   of a Dictionary.
Receiving the Stigmata.
Recovery.
Refrain.
Roast Possum.
Roses.
Sahara Bus Trip, The.
Sailor in Africa, The.
Satisfaction Coal Company, The.
Secret Garden, The.
Shakespeare Say.
Sightseeing.
Slave's Critique of Practical Reason, The.
Small Town.
Snow King, The.
Someone's Blood.
Son, The.
Song. Summer.
Spy.
Straw Hat.
Stroke, The.
Sunday Greens.
Sunday Night at Grandfather's.
Taking in Wash.
Teach Us to Number Our Days.
Then Came Flowers.
This Life.
Thomas at the Wheel.
Three Days of Forest, a River, Free.
To Bed.
Tou Wan Speaks to Her Husband Liu Sheng.
Transport or Slaves From Maryland to
   Mississippi, The.
Turning Thirty, I Contemplate Students
   Bicycling Home.
Under the Viaduct, 1932.
Upon Meeting Don L. Lee, in a Dream.
Vacation.
Variation on Gaining a Son.
Variation on Guilt.
Variation on Pain.
Weathering Out.
Why I Turned Vegetarian.
Wingfoot Lake.
Your Death.
Zeppelin factory, The.

**DuBois, William Edward Burghardt (1868–
1963)**
Litany of [*or* at] Atlanta, A.
Song of the Smoke, The.

Duckett, Alfred A. (b. 1918)
Sonnet: "Where are we to go when this is
   done?"

Duke, Bill
Poem to the World.

Dumas Henry L. (1935–68)
Afro-American.
America.
Black Star Line.
Black Trumpeter.
Buffalo.
Cuttin Down to Size.
Island within Island.
Knees of a Natural Man.
Knock on Wood.
Mosaic Harlem.
Son of Msippi.
Tis of Thee.
Valentines.
Zebra Goes Wild Where the Sidewalk Ends,
   The.

Dunbar-Nelson, Alice Moore (1875–1935)
April is on the way!
I sit and sew—a useless task it seems.
Music! Lilting, soft and languorous.
Proletariat Speaks, The.
Snow in October.
Sonnet: "I had no thought of violets of late."

Dunbar, Paul Laurence (1872–1906)
Absence.
Accountability.
Advice.
After a Visit.
After Many Days.
After the Quarrel.
After While.
Alexander Crummel—Dead.
Alice.
Anchored.
Angelina.
Ante-Bellum Sermon, An.
Appreciation.
At Candle-Lightin' Time.
At Cheshire Cheese.
At Loafing-Holt.
At Night.
At Sunset Time.
At the Tavern.
Awakening, The.
Back-Log Song, A.
Ballad: "I know my love is true."
Ballade: "By Mystic's banks I held my
   dream."
Banjo Song, A.
Barrier, The.
Behind the Arras.
Bein' Back Home.
Beyond the years the answer lies.
Black Samson of Brandywine.
Blue.
Bohemian, The.
Boogah Man, The.
Booker T. Washington.
Border Ballad, A.
Boy's Summer Song, A.
Breaking the Charm.
Bridal Measure, A.
By rugged ways and thro' the night.
By the stream I dream in calm delight, and
   watch as in a glass.
Cabin Tale, A.
Capture, The.
Career, A.
Change, The.
Change has come, and Helen sleeps, The.
Changing Time.
Chappie, A.
Charity.
Chase, The.
Choice, A.
Chrismus Is A-Comin'.
Chrismus on the Plantation.
Christmas.
Christmas Carol: "Ring out, ye bells!"
Christmas Folksong, A.
Christmas in the Heart.
"Chronic Kicker," The.
Circumstances Alter Cases.
Colored Band, The.
Colored Soldiers, The.
Columbian Ode.
Come and Kiss Me Sweet and Twenty.

Common Things.
Communion.
Companion's Progress, A.
Comparison.
Compensation.
Comrade.
Concert, The.
Confessional.
Confidence, A.
Confirmation.
Conquerors, The.
Conscience and Remorse.
Content.
Coquette Conquered, A.
Corn-Song, A.
Corn-Stalk Fiddle, The.
Crisis, The.
Critters' Dance, De.
Crumb, a crumb, and a little seed, A.
Curiosity.
Curtain.
Dance, The.
Dat Ol' Mare o' Mine.
Dawn.
Day.
Deacon Jones' Grievance.
Dead.
Death.
Death of the First Born, The.
Death Song[, A].
Debt, The.
Delinquent, The.
Dely.
Deserted Plantation, The.
Despair.
Differences.
Dilettante: A Modern Type, The.
Dinah Kneading Dough.
Diplomacy.
Dirge for a Soldier.
Dirge: "Place this bunch of mignonette."
Disappointed.
Discovered.
Discovery, The.
Distinction.
Disturber, The.
Douglass.
Dove, The.
Dream Song I.
Dream Song II.
Dreamer, The.
Dreamin' Town.
Dreams.
Drizzle.
Drowsy Day, A.
Easter Ode, An.
Easy-Goin' Feller, An.
Emancipation.
Encouraged.
Encouragement.
End of the Chapter, The.
Equipment.
Ere sleep comes down to soothe the weary
  eyes.
Evening.
Expectation.
Faith.
Farewell Song.
Farewell to Arcady.
Farm Child's Lullaby, The.
Fisher Child's Lullaby, The.
Fishing.
Florida Night, A.
Foolin' wid de Seasons.
For the Man Who Fails.
For Theodore Roosevelt.
Forest Greeting, The.
Forever.
Fount of Tears, The.
Frederick Douglass.
Frolic, A.
From the Porch at Runnymede.
Fulfilment.
Garret, The.
God Reigns.
Goin' Back.
Goin' Home.

Golden Day, A.
Good-Night.
Gourd, The.
Grievance, A.
Growin' Gray.
Harriet Beecher Stowe.
Haunted Oak, The.
He had his dream, and all through life.
Her Thought and His.
Home Longings.
Hope.
How Lucy Backslid.
How shall I woo thee to win thee, mine
  own?
Howdy, Honey, Howdy!
Hunting Song.
Hymn, A: "Lead gently, Lord, and slow."
Hymn: "O li'l lamb out in de col'."
Hymn: "When storms arise."
If I could but forget.
If life were but a dream, my love.
In a English Garden.
In August.
In May.
In Summer.
In Summer Time.
In the Morning.
In the tents of Akbar.
Inspiration.
Invitation to Love.
Ione.
Itching Heels.
Jack Frost at Bedtime.
James Whitcomb Riley.
Jealous.
Jilted.
Joggin' Erlong.
John Boyle O'Reilly.
Johnny Speaks.
Just whistle a bit, if the day be dark.
Justice.
Keep A-Pluggin' Away.
Keep a Song Up on de Way.
Kidnaped.
King is Dead, The.
Knight, The.
Lager Beer.
Land o' Used to Be, The.
Lapse, The.
Lawyers' Ways, The.
Lazy Day, A.
Lesson, The.
Letter, A.
Life.
Life's Tragedy.
Light, The.
Light was on the golden sands, The.
Li'l' Gal.
Lily of the Valley, The.
Limitations.
Lincoln.
Little brown baby wif spa'klin' eyes.
Little Christmas Basket, A.
Little Lucy Landman.
Liza May.
Lonesome.
Long Ago.
'Long To'ds Night.
Longing.
Looking-Glass, The.
Lost Dream, A.
Love.
Love and Grief.
Love Despoiled.
Love is a star that lights the night.
Love is the light of the world, my dear.
Love Letter, A.
Love Song, A: "Ah, love, my love is like a
  cry in the night."
Love-Song: "If Death should claim me for
  her own to-day."
Lover and the Moon, The.
Lover's Lane.
Love's Apotheosis.
Love's Castle.
Love's Chastening.
Love's Draft.

Love's Humility.
Love's Phases.
Love's Pictures.
Love's Seasons.
Lullaby: "Bedtime's come fu' little boys."
Lullaby: "Kiver up yo' haid, my little lady."
Lyric, A: "My lady love lives far away."
Made to Order Smile, The.
Madrigal, A: "Dream days of fond delight
  and hours."
Mare Rubrum.
Master-Player, The.
Masters, The.
Matter of Locality, A.
Meadow Lark, The.
Melancholia.
Memorial Day.
Memory of Martha, The.
Merry Autumn.
Misapprehension.
Misty Day, A.
Monk's Walk, The.
Morning.
Morning Song of Love.
Mortality.
Murdered Lover, The.
Musical, A.
My Best Girl.
My Corn-Cob Pipe.
My dear love died last night.
My Lady of Castle Grand.
My Little March Girl.
My Love Irene.
My Sort o' Man.
My Sweet Brown Gal.
Mystery, The.
Mystic Sea, The.
Nature and Art.
Negro Love Song, A.
News, The.
Night.
Night, dim night, and it rains, my love, it
  rains.
Night of Love.
Night on the Chesapeake.
Noddin' by de Fire.
Noon.
Nora: a Serenade.
Not they who soar, but they who plod.
Nutting Song.
October is the treasurer of the year.
Ode for Memorial Day.
Ode to Ethiopia.
Oh little fledgling out of the nest.
Ol' Tunes, The.
Old.
Old Apple-Tree, The.
Old Cabin, The.
Old Front Gate, The.
Old High School and the New, The.
Old Homestead, The.
Old Memory, An.
Old Story, The.
On a Clean Book.
On the Death of W.C.
On the Dedication of Dorothy Hall.
On the River.
On the Road.
On the Sea Wall.
One Life.
Opportunity.
Our Martyred Soldiers.
Over the hills and the valleys of dreaming.
Paradox, The.
Parted.
Party, The.
Passage, The.
Passion and Love.
Path, The.
Phantom Kiss, The.
Philosophy.
Photograph, The.
Phyllis, ah, Phyllis, my life is a gray day.
Place Where the Rainbow Ends, The.
Plantation Child's Lullaby, The.
Plantation Melody, A.
Plantation Portrait, A.

Plea, A.
Poet, The.
Poet and His Song, The.
Poet and the Baby, The.
Pool, The.
Poor withered rose, she gave it me.
Possession.
Possum.
Possum Trot.
Prayer, A: "O Lord, the hard-won miles."
Precedent.
Preference, A.
Premonition.
Preparation.
Prometheus stole from Heaven the sacred fire.
Promise.
Protest.
Puttin' the Baby Away.
Question, A.
Quilting, The.
Rain-Songs.
Real Question, The.
Religion.
Reluctance.
Remembered.
Resignation.
Response.
Retort.
Retrospection.
Riding to Town.
Right to Die, The.
Right's Security.
Rising of the Storm, The.
Rivals, The.
River of Ruin, The.
Roadway, A.
Robert Gould Shaw.
Roses.
Roses and Pearls.
Sailor's Song, A.
Sand-Man, The.
Scamp.
Sea speaks to me of you, The.
Secret, The.
Seedling, The.
She Gave Me a Rose.
She told her beads with downcast eyes.
Ships That Pass in the Night.
Signs of the Times.
Silence.
Sling along, sling along, sling along.
Slow Through the Dark.
Snowin'.
Soliloquy of a Turkey.
Song: "Bee hit sip some honey f'om de matermony vine, De."
Song: "My heart to thy heart."
Song, The: "My soul, lost in the music's mist."
Song, A: "On a summer's day as I sat by a stream."
Song, A: "Thou art the soul of a summer's day."
Song: "Wintah, summah, snow er shine."
Song of Summer.
Songs.
Sonnet: "Emblem of blasted hope and lost desire."
Sparrow, The.
Speakin' at de Cou't-House.
Speakin' o' Christmas.
Spellin'-Bee, The.
Spiritual, A.
Spring Fever.
Spring Song.
Spring Wooing, A.
Starry Night, A.
Stirrup Cup, The.
Suitor, The.
Sum, The.
Summer in the South.
Summer Night, A.
Summer Pastoral, A.
Summer's Night, A.
Sunset.
Suppose.

Sympathy.
Temptation.
Thanksgiving Poem, A.
Then and Now.
Theology.
There are brilliant heights of sorrow.
Thou art my lute, by thee I sing.
Till the Wind Gets Right.
Time to Tinker 'Roun'!
To a Captious Critic.
To a Dead Friend.
To a Lady Playing the Harp.
To a Poet and a Lady.
To a Violet Found on All Saints' Day.
To Alice Dunbar.
To an Ingrate.
To Booker T. Washington.
To Dan.
To Dr. James Newton Matthews, Mason, Ill.
To E.H.K.
To Her.
To J.Q.
To Kelly Miller, Jr.
To Louise.
To Mary Church Terrell.
To Miss Mary Britton.
To Pfrimmer.
To the Eastern Shore.
To the Memory of Mary Young.
To the Miami.
To the Road.
To the South.
Too Busy.
Trouble in de Kitchen.
Tryst, The.
Turning of the Babies in the Bed, The.
Tuskegee Song.
Twell de Night Is Pas'.
Twilight.
Two little boots all rough an' wo'.
Two Songs.
Unexpressed.
Unlucky Apple, The.
Unsung Heroes, The.
Vagrants.
Valse, The.
Vengeance is Sweet.
Veteran, The.
Virginia Reel, A.
Visitor, The.
Voice of the Banjo, The.
Wadin' in de Crick.
Waiting.
Warm Day in Winter, A.
Warrior's Prayer, The.
Way T'ings Come, De.
We wear the mask that grins and lies.
Welcome Address.
Weltschmertz.
W'en I Gits Home.
What's the use o' folks a-frownin'.
When a Feller's Itchin' to be Spanked.
When all is done, and my last word is said.
When de Co'n Pone's Hot.
When Dey 'Listed Colored Soldiers.
When Malindy Sings.
When Sam'l Sings.
When the Old Man Smokes.
When Winter Darkening All Around.
Whip-Poor-Will and Katy-Did.
Whittier.
Why fades a dream?
Wind and the Sea, The.
Winter-Song.
Winter's Approach.
Winter's Day, A.
With the Lark.
Wooing, The.
Worn Out.
Wraith, The.
Yesterday and Tomorrow.

Durem, Ray (1915–63)
Award.
Friends.
I Know I'm Not Sufficiently Obscure.

Problem in Social Geometry—the Inverted Square!
Vet's Rehabilitation.

E

Eady, Cornelius (b. 1954)
April.
Crows in a Strong Wind.
Dance, The.
Insomnia.
Leadbelly.
Muddy Waters & the Chicago Blues.
Radio.
Sherbet.
Song.
Why Do So Few Blacks Study Creative Writing?
William Carlos Williams.
Ebon
To Our First Born or the Prophet Arrives.
Eckels, Jon
Hell, Mary / Bell Jones.
Edwards, Harry (b. 1942)
How to Change the U.S.A.
Edwards, Solomon (b. 1932)
Brothers.
Dream.
Shoplifter.
"Ekere." *See* **Tallie, Mariahadessa**
El-Hadi, Suliaman (1936–95)
Drama, The.
Tired Man, The.
Ellis, Kelly Norman
Boys of Summer, The.
Girl.
Phantom Pains.
Tougaloo Blues.
Ellis, Thomas Sayers
Kiss in the Dark, A.
Shooting Back.
View of the Library of Congress from Paul Laurence Dunbar High School.
Emanuel, James A.
Black Man, 13th Floor.
Church Burning: Mississippi.
Emmett Till.
Fishermen.
For "Mr. Dudley," a Black Spy.
Freedom Rider: Washout.
Get Up, Blues.
Negritude.
Negro, The.
Nightmare.
Old Black Men Say.
Panther Man.
Sixteen, Yeah.
Treehouse, The.
Voyage of Jimmy Poo, The.
Wedding Procession, from a Window.
Whitey, Baby.
Young Ones, Flip Side, The.
Evans, Mari E. (b. 1923)
And the Old Women Gathered.
Black Jam for Dr. Negro.
Daufuskie.
Emancipation of George-Hector (a Colored Turtle), The.
How Will You Call Me, Brother.
I Am a Black Woman.
If there be sorrow.
Into Blackness Softly.
Marrow of My Bone.
Point of No Return.
Rebel, The.
Shrine to What Should Be.
Speak the truth to the people.
Spectrum.
Status Symbol.
To Mother and Steve.
Vive Noir!
When in Rome.
Where Have You Gone?
Who Can Be Born Black.
World I See, The.
Writers, The.

F

Fabio, Sarah Webster (1928–79)
All Day We've Longed for Night.
Back into the Garden.
Black Man's Feast.
Evil Is No Black Thing.
God's Trombone.
Hurt of It All, The.
I would be for you rain.
Of Puddles, Worms, Slimy Things.
Race Results, U.S.A., 1966.
To Turn from Love.
Tree Is a Landscape: a Landscape Is a Point of View, A.

Farr, Robert (b. 1958)
At General Electric, Where They Eat Their/ Young.
Van/Dyke.

Fauset, Jessie Redmond (1888–1961)
Christmas Eve in France.
Dead Fires.
Fragment: "Breath of life imbued those few dim days, The."
La Vie C'est la Vie.
Noblesse Oblige.
Oblivion.
Oriflamme.
Rencontre.
Return, The.
Stars in Alabama.
Touché.
Words! Words!

Felton, B.
Ghetto Waif.

Ferdinand, Val
Blues (in Two Parts), The.
Food for Thought.
2 B BLK.
Whi / te boys gone.

Fernandez, Renaldo
Legacy of a Brother.

Fields, Julia (b. 1938)
Alabama.
Black Students.
Citizen.
High on the Hog.
I Heard a Young Man Saying.
Jolly fat widows, The.
Madness One Monday Evening.
Mr. Tut's House A Recollection.
No Time for Poetry.
Trees.

Finney, Nikky (b. 1957)
Fishing among the Learned.
Lobengula: Having a Son at 38.

Fletcher, Bob (b. 1938)
Love Dirge to the Whitehouse, A.

Forbes, Calvin (b. 1945)
Blue Monday.
Dark Mirror.
Europe / Is endowed with the first move.
Hand Me Down Blues.
Home.
Lullaby for Ann-Lucian.
My Father's House.
Poet's Shuffle, The.
Potlicker Blues.
Potter's Wheel, The.
Reading Walt Whitman.

Fordham, Mary Weston (fl. c.1897)
Alaska.
Atlanta Exposition Ode.
Bells of St. Michael.
By the Rivers of Babylon.
Cherokee, The.
Chicago Exposition Ode.
Christ Child, The.
Coming Woman, The.
Creation.
Crucifixion, The.
Death of a Grandparent. Mrs. Jennette Bonneau.
Dedicated to the Right Rev'd D. A. Payne.
Dying Girl, The.

Exile's Reverie, The.
For Who?
Grafted Bud, The.
Highland Mary.
In Memoriam. Alphonse Campbell Fordham.
In Memoriam. Susan Eugenia Bennett.
June.
Lines to———.
Lines to Florence.
Lines to Mrs. Isabel Peace.
Magnolia.
Maiden and River.
Marriage.
Mother's Recall.
Mr. Edward Fordham.
Mrs. E. Cohrs Brown.
Mrs. Louise B. Weston.
Mrs. Mary Furman Weston Byrd.
Mrs. Rebecca Weston.
Nativity, The.
Nestle-down Cottage.
October.
Ode to Peace.
On Parting with a Friend.
Passing of the Old Year.
Past, The.
Pen, The.
Queenie.
Rally Song.
Requiem: "O, insatiable monster! Could'st thou not."
Rev. Samuel Weston.
Reverie, A.
Saxon Legend of Language, The.
Serenade: "Sleep, love sleep."
Shipwreck.
Snow Storm, The.
Snowdrop, The.
Song to Erin.
Sonnet to My First Born.
Stars and Stripes.
Sunset.
To a Loved One.
To an Infant.
To My Mother.
To Rev. Thaddeus Saltus.
To the Eagle.
To the Mock-Bird.
Tribute to a Lost Steamer.
Tribute to Capt. F. W. Dawson.
Twilight Musings.
Uranne.
Valentine, The.
Washerwoman, The.

Foreman, Kent
Judgement Day: For Big Red the Darwinian Doge. R.I.P.

Forman, Ruth (b. 1968)
Green Boots n Lil Honeys.
This Poem.
Up Sister.
Waitin on Summer.
You So Woman.

Forten, Charlotte (1839–1914)
Parting Hymn, A.
Poem: "In the earnest path of duty."
To W.L.G. on Reading His "Chosen Queen."

Forten, Sarah L. *See* "Ada"

Fortune, Timothy Thomas (1856–1928)
Bartow Black.
Byron's Oak at Newstead Abbey.
Dreams of Life, *sels.*
Edgar Allan Poe.
Every Man a King.
Savage Dreamer, The.
Tell me, ye sad winds sighing.
We Know No More.

Franklin, Clarence
Death of Days and Nights of Life.
Two Dreams (for M.L.K.'s one).
Visions . . . Leaders.

Fraser, Al
To the "JFK" Quintet.

Freeman, Carol [or Carole] (b. 1941)
Christmas Morning I.
I saw them lynch festus whiteside and.

When / my uncle willie saw.

Fuller, Hoyt W. (b. 1928)
Lost Moment.
Seravezza.

Fuller, Stephany (b. 1947)
In the Silence.
Let Me Be Held When the Longing Comes.
My Love When This Is Past.
That We Head Towards.
Who is not a stranger still.

G

Gardner, Carl (b. 1931)
Dead Man Dragged from the Sea, The.
Reflections.

Garnet, Henry Highland (1817–82)
Bound on a voyage of awful length.
Down let the shrine of Moloch sink.
Hear ye not how, from all high points of Time.
Proud Nimrod first the bloody chase began.
Thus man devotes his brother and destroys.

Gaye, Marvin
What's Going On.

Gee, Lethonia
Black Music Man.
By glistening, dancing seas.

Gerima, Haile
Sankofa.

Gex-Breaux, Quo Vadis
Blue Deep.
Willie Note 9/28/91.

Gilbert, Christopher (b. 1950)
African Sculpture.
And, Yes, Those Spiritual Matters.
Beginning by Value.
Directions, The.
Glimpses.
Kite-Flying.
Now.
This Bridge Across.

Gilbert, Derrick I. M. ("D-Knowledge")
Fire in the Drum, The.
Miracle.
Too Many.

Gilbert, Zack (b. 1925)
For Angela.
For Stephen Dixon.
My Own Hallelujahs.
When I Heard Dat White Man Say.

Gilmore, Brian G. (b. 1962)
Coming to the Net.
Gas Station Attendant.
Hazing.
Revolution.
To Be or Not to Be.

Gilyard, Keith (b. 1952)
Daughter, That Picture of You.
Letter.
On Top of It All.
Portraits of a Moment.

Giovanni, Nikki (b. 1943)
Adulthood.
Adulthood II.
Africa.
Africa I.
Africa II.
Age.
Alabama Poem.
All i gotta do.
Alone.
And sometimes i sit.
Atrocities.
Autumn Prison.
Balances.
Beautiful Black Men.
Beep Beep Poem, The.
Being and Nothingness.
Black Judgements.
Black Power.
Black Separatism.
Boxes.
But Since You Finally Asked.

Butterfly, The.
Cancers are a serious condition.
Categories.
Certain Peace, A.
Charles White.
Charting the Night Winds.
Choices.
Communication.
Concerning One Responsible Negro with Too Much Power.
Conversation.
Cotton Candy on a Rainy Day.
Crutches.
December of My Springs, The.
Detroit Conference of Unity and Art.
Dreams.
Drums ... Pa-Rum ... the rat-tat-tat ... of drums, The.
Each Sunday.
Eagles are a majestic species ... living in the thin searing air.
Ego Tripping.
Ever want to crawl.
For a Lady of Pleasure Now Retired.
For an Intellectual Audience.
For Saundra.
For Theresa.
For Tommy.
For Two Jameses.
Forced Retirement.
Funeral of Martin Luther King, Jr, The.
Game of Game, The.
Geni in the Jar, The.
Great Pax Whitie, The.
Gus.
Habits.
Hampton, Virginia.
Hands; For Mother's Day.
Harvest.
Her Cruising Car.
Housecleaning.
How do you write a poem.
I am she ... making rainbows.
I remember learning you jump.
I want to sing.
I wrote a good omelet ... and ate a hot poem.
I'm not lonely.
I'm not lonely / sleeping all alone.
Intellectualism.
Introspection.
Journey, A.
Just a New York Poem.
Kidnap Poem.
Knoxville, Tennessee.
Legacies.
Life Cycles.
Life I Led, The.
Linkage.
Lorraine Hansberry: an Emotional View.
Love: Is a Human Condition.
Luxury.
Make Up.
Master Charge Blues.
Mirrors.
Moon shines down, The.
Mothers.
Mother's Habits.
My House.
My Poem.
My Tower.
New Yorkers, The.
Night.
Nikki-Rosa.
No Reservations.
On Hearing "The Girl with the Flaxen Hair."
Once a Lady Told Me.
One ounce of truth benefits.
Patience.
Photography.
Poem: "I have considered / my reluctance."
Poem: "Like a will-o'-the-wisp in the night."
Poem for a Lady Whose Voice I Like.
Poem (For Anna Hedgeman and Alfreda Duster).
Poem for Aretha.
Poem for Black Boys.
Poem (For BMC No. 1).

Poem (For BMC No. 2).
Poem (For BMC No. 3).
Poem (for EMA).
Poem for Flora.
Poem for Langston Hughes, A.
Poem (For Nina).
Poem (For PCH).
Poem (No Name No. 1).
Poem (No Name No. 2).
Poem (No Name No. 3).
Poem of Angela Yvonne Davis.
Poem of Friendship, A.
Poem Off Center, A.
Poem on the Assassination of Robert F. Kennedy, A.
Poetry is a trestle.
Poetry is motion graceful.
Rain is / god's sperm falling.
Resignation.
Revolutionary Dreams.
Revolutionary Music.
Rituals.
Robin's Poem, A.
Rose Bush, The.
Scrapbooks.
2nd Rapp.
Seduction.
Sky Diving.
Something to be Said for Silence.
Sometimes / when i wake up.
Stardate Number 18628.190.
Swaziland.
That Day.
There is a hunger.
They clapped when we landed.
This Is Not for John Lennon.
Three/Quarters Time.
Toy Poem.
True Import of Present Dialogue, Black vs. Negro.
Turning (I Need a Better Title).
12 Gates to the City.
Universality.
Very Simple Wish, A.
Walking down park.
Way I Feel, The.
We stood there waiting.
When i die i hope no one who ever hurt me cries.
When i nap.
Wilmington Delaware.
Winter.
Winter Poem.
Woman.
Woman Poem.
Women gather, The.
Wonder Woman, The.
Word Poem (Perhaps Worth Considering).
World Is Not a Pleasant Place to Be, The.
You Are There.
You Came, Too.
You were gone.

Giscombe, C. S. (b. 1950)
  (1980).
  (1978, Remembering 1962).
  (1962 At the Edge of Town).
  (Recent Past, The).
Goncalves, Jon
  Now the Time Is Ripe to Be.
  Sister Brother Don't You Stumble.
  Way It Is, The.
Goodison, Lorna (b. 1947)
  I Am Becoming My Mother.
  Jamaica 1980.
  Kenscoff.
  On Becoming a Tiger.
  Wedding in Hanover.
Goodwin, L.
  Day a Dancer Learned to Sing of Dreamless Escapades, The.
Gordon, Charles F. (b. 1943)
  Long Night Home, The.
Govan, Donald D. (b. 1945)
  Recollection.
Graham, D. L. (1944–70)
  Clown, The.
  Portrait of Johnny Doller, A.

  Soul.
  Tony Get the Boys.
  West Ridge Is Menthol-Cool, The.
Graham, Rudy Bee (b. 1947)
  Learning to Dance.
  Lynching for Skip James, A.
Grandmaster Flash and the Furious Five
  Message, The.
Grant, Richard E. (b. 1949)
  Broken Heart, Broken Machine.
Gray-Kontar, Daniel (b. 1971)
  Cuz' Mama Played Jazz.
  July.
  Not No Socialism/Communism Classical, but Some Power to the People Jazz.
Greene, Carl H. (b. 1945)
  Excuse, The.
  Realist, The.
  Something Old, Something New.
Gregory, Yvonne (b. 1919)
  Christmas Lullaby for a New-Born Child.
Griffin, Eddie
  Mind of a Madman kills.
Grimké, Angelina Weld (1880–1958)
  At April.
  At the Spring Dawn.
  Black Finger, The.
  Butterflies, white butterflies, in the sunshine.
  Dawn.
  Dusk.
  El Beso.
  Eyes of My Regret, The.
  For the Candle Light.
  Grass Fingers.
  Greenness.
  Hushed by the Hands of Sleep.
  I weep / Not as the young do noisily.
  Little grey dreams.
  Mona Lisa, A.
  Paradox.
  Puppet Player, The.
  Surrender.
  Tenebris.
  To Clarissa Scott Delany.
  To Keep the Memory of Charlotte Forten Grimké.
  Want of You, The.
  Ways o' Men, The.
  When the Green Lies over the Earth.
  Winter Twilight, A.
  Your Hands.
Grimké, Charlotte L. Forten (1837–1914)
  Angel's Visit, The.
  Charles Sumner.
  Gathering of the Grand Army, The.
  Parting Hymn, A.
  Wordsworth.

H

Hall-Evans, Jo Ann (b. 1934)
  Cape Coast Castle Revisted.
  Seduction.
Hall, Kirk (b. 1944)
  Blackgoldblueswoman.
  Illusions.
  Impressions.
  Song of Tom.
  Today Is Not Like They Said.
  Wig.
Hamilton, Bobb (b. 1928)
  Brother Harlem Bedford Watts Tells Mr. Charlie Where Its At.
  Child's Nightmare, A.
  Poem to a Nigger Cop.
Hamilton, M. Eliza
  Things I Do Not Speak.
Hammon, Jupiter (1720?–1806?)
  Evening Thought, An [: Salvation by Christ with Penentential Cries].
Hand, Q. R.
  And I can Remember still your first lies America.
  I wonder.

Handy, William Christopher (1873–1958)
Beale Street Blues.
Joe Turner Blues.
St. Louis Blues.
Yellow Dog Blues.

Harper, Frances Ellen Watkins (1825–1911)
Advice to the Girls.
Appeal to My Countrywomen, An.
Appeal to the American People, An.
Artist, The.
Aunt Chloe.
Aunt Chloe's Politics.
Be Active.
Behold the lilies of the field.
Bible Defence of Slavery.
Blessed Hope, The.
Bride of Death, The.
Building, The.
Burdens of All, The.
Burial of Moses, The.
Burial of Srah.
Bury Me in a Free Land.
Careless Word, The.
Change, The.
Christmas Carol, A.
Christ's Entry into Jerusalem.
Church Building.
Contrast, The.
Crocuses, The.
Dandelions.
Days of my childhood I woo you not back.
Death of the Old Sea King.
Death of Zombi.
Dedication Poem.
Deliverance.
Dialogue, A.
Died of Starvation.
Dismissal of Tyng, The.
"Do Not Cheer, Men Are Dying," Said Capt.
    Phillips, in the Spanish-American War.
Double Standard, A.
Drunkard's Child, The.
Dying Bondman, The.
Dying Child to Her Blind Father, The.
Dying Christian, The.
Dying Fugitive, The.
Dying Mother, The.
Dying Queen, The.
Eliza Harris.
Ethiopia.
Eva's Farewell.
Fairer Hope, a Brighter Morn, A.
Fatal Pledge, The.
Fifteenth Amendment.
Fishers of Men.
For the Twenty-Fifth Anniversary of the "Old
    Folks' Home."
Free Labor.
Freedom Bell, The.
Fugitive's Wife, The.
Give My Love to the World.
Go work in my vineyard, said the Lord.
God Bless Our Native Land.
Going East.
Gone to God.
Grain of Sand, A.
He "Had Not Where to Lay His Head."
Hermit's Sacrifice, The.
His Name.
Home, Sweet Home.
How Are the Mighty Fallen!
I thirst, but earth cannot allay.
In Commemoration of the Centennial of the
    A.M.E. Church.
It Shall Not Come Nigh Thee.
Jamie's Puzzle.
Jesus.
Jewish Grandfather's Story, The.
John and Jacob—a Dialogue on Woman's
    Rights.
Lake City Tragedy, The.
Learning to Read.
Lessons of the Street.
Let the Light Enter!
"Let there be light," a joyous thrill.
Light in Darkness.
Lines: "At the Portals of the Future."

Lines to Charles Sumner.
Lines to Hon. Thaddeus Stevens.
Lines to M.A.H.
Lines to Miles O'Reiley.
Little Builders, The.
Little Child Shall Lead Them, A.
Little Bells, The.
Lost Bells, The.
Maceo dead! a thrill of sorrow.
Martyr of Alabama, The.
Mary at the Feet of Christ.
Mission of the Flowers, The.
Moses: A Story of the Nile, *sels.*
Mother's Blessing, The.
Mother's Heroism, A.
Mother's Treasures.
My mother's kiss, my mother's kiss.
Night of Death, The.
Nothing and Something.
Obituary for J. Edwards Barnes.
Only a word— a little word.
Our English Friends.
Our Hero.
Out in the cold mid the dreary night.
Peace.
Poem, A: "Over the foaming ocean."
Present Age, The.
President Lincoln's Proclamation of Freedom.
Proclaim a fast, a solemn fast.
Prodigal's Return, The.
Pure in Heart Shall See God, The.
Ragged Stocking, The.
Rallying Cry, The.
Refiner's Gold, The.
Renewal of Strength.
Report.
Respectfully Dedicated to Dr. Alexander
    Crummell on the Fiftieth Anniversary of
    His Pastorate.
Resurrection of Jesus, The.
Retribution.
Reunion, The.
Revel, The.
Rizpah, the Daughter of Ai.
Ruth and Naomi.
Save the Boys.
Saved at Last.
Saved by Faith.
She's Free!
Signing the Pledge.
Simon's Countrymen.
Simon's Feast.
Sin of Achar, The.
Sir, We Would See Jesus.
Slave Auction, The.
Slave Mother, The: "Heard you that shriek?
    It rose."
Slave Mother, The: "I have but four, the
    treasures of my soul."
Something to Do.
Songs for the People.
Soul, The.
Sparrow's Fall, The.
Story of the Rebellion, A.
Syrophenician Woman, The.
Tennessee Hero, The.
Thank God for Little Children.
Then and Now.
Thine Eyes Shall See the King in His
    Beauty.
To a Babe Smiling in Her Sleep.
To Bishop Payne.
To-day Is a King in Disguise.
To Mr. and Mrs. W. F. Johnson on Their
    Twenty-Fifth Wedding Anniversary.
To Mrs. Harriet Beecher Stowe.
To the Union Savers of Cleveland.
To White Ribbons of Maine Who Gave to
    Me Their Blessed Gifts.
Truth.
Vashti.
Vision of the Czar of Russia, The.
Wanderer's Return.
We are rising, as a people.
Widow's Mites, The.
Woman's Work.
Words for the Hour.
Youth in Heaven.

Harper, Michael S. (b. 1938)
Afterword: a Film.
Alice.
Alice Braxton Johnson.
Allegheny Shadows.
America Calls!
American History.
At the Cemetery.
Barricades hammered into place.
Battle of Saratoga (Springs) Revisited, The.
Biafra Blues.
"Bird Lives": Charles Parker.
Black Angel, The.
Black Spring.
Blackjack.
Blue Ruth: America.
Blues Alabama.
Borning Room, The.
Breaded Meat, Breaded Hands.
Br'er Sterling and the Rocker.
Bristol: Bicentenary Remembrances of Trade.
Brother John.
Buck.
Called.
Cannon Arrested.
Caves.
Christian's Box Seat: So What!
Clan Meeting: Births and Nations: A Blood
    Song.
Clark's Way Out West: Another Version.
Come Back Blues.
Conferences with the Unknown.
Continuous Visit.
Corktown.
Corrected Review.
Crossing Lake Michigan.
Dance of the Elephants, The.
Dark Way Home: Survivors, The.
Dead-Day: Malcolm, Feb. 21.
Dead Oaks.
Dear John, Dear Coltrane.
Deathwatch.
Debridement.
Debridement: Operation Harvest Moon: *On
    Repose.*
Dining from a Treed Condition, an Historical
    Survey.
Double Elegy.
Dreams: American.
Drive In, The.
Drowning of the Facts of a Life, The.
Effendi.
Elvin's Blues.
"Emperor": Shields Green: Fugitives.
Eve (Rachel).
Families Album, The.
Family of Debridement, The.
Fireplace, The.
Fixing Certificates: Dog Tags: Letters Home.
For Bud.
Forty Days Looking Backwards: Notes from
    a Surveyor.
Founding Fathers in Philadelphia, The.
Four Worthies: Souls of Black Folk.
From a Town in Minnesota.
Fugitive Paths.
Gains.
Gen'l Tubman, as We Call Her.
Ghost of Soul-making, The.
Goin' to the Territory.
Good Samaritan Hospital.
Grandfather.
Guerrilla-Cong, The.
Healing Song.
Heartblow: Messages.
Here Where Coltrane Is.
Herring run / in the silver morning.
High Modes: Vision as Ritual: Confirmation.
History as Apple Tree.
History as Bandages: Polka Dots and
    Moonbeams.
History as Cap'n Brown.
Homage to the New World.
Ice-Fishing House, The.
In Hayden's Collage.
In the Projects.
Jim Daniels: Hamilton Massacre: Parable.

Kansas and America.
Kin.
Kneading.
Landfill.
Last Affair: Bessie's Blues Song.
Lathe: Shirl's Tree.
"League of Gileadites": Messages.
Loon.
Love Medley: Patrice Cuchulain.
Lovely's Daughters: Visitors.
Made Connections.
Madimba.
Makin' Jump Shots.
Malcolm's Blues.
Mama's Report.
Manual for the Patriotic Volunteer.
Martin's Blues.
Meaning of Protest, The.
Militance of a Photograph in the Passbook of
    a Bantu under Detention, The.
Mission.
Molasses and the Three Witches.
Mother Speaks: The Algiers Motel Incident,
    Detroit, A.
Mr. P.C.
Music of Broadswords, The.
Negatives, The.
New Season.
Newletter from My Mother.
Night of Frost, The.
Nightmare Begins Responsibility.
No. 24.
Oak.
Ode to Tenochtitlan.
One Lives, One Dies: Both/And: A Choice of
    Colors.
Paul Laurence Dunbar: 1872-1906.
Photographs.
Photographs: A Vision of Massacre.
Plans.
Plans: 2.
Prayer: Mt. Hood and Environs.
Psychophotos of Hampton.
Remember Mexico.
Reports: Kansas.
"Rescue Work": Dues.
Reuben, Reuben.
Roland.
"S.P.W.": Journey of Consciousness.
Sack 'A Woe: Gallstones as History.
Sambo's Mistakes: an Essay.
Smoke is my name for you.
Sojourner Truth: Black Sybil in Salem.
Song: I Want a Witness.
Street-Poisoned.
Studs.
This Is My Son's Song: "Ungie, Hi Ungie."
Three O'Clock Love Song.
Time for Tyner: Folksong.
Tongue-tied in Black and White.
Trays: a Portfolio.
24th Avenue: City of Roses: Anesthesia: 2.
Utility Room.
Village Blues.
We Assume: On the Death of Our Son,
    Reuben Masai Harper.
White Friend Flies in from the Coast, A.
Wisdom of Signs, The.
Zocalo.

Harris, Duriel E. (b. 1969)
But There Are Miles.
For My Father.
Landscapes.
On the Uptown Lexington Avenue Express:
    Martin Luther King Day 1995.
What We Have Lost.

Harris, Joel Chandler (1848–1908)
Uncle Remus and His Friends.

Harris, Peter (b. 1955)
Be Somebody Fragrant.
Let's Take All the Blame.

Harris, William J. (b. 1942)
Daddy Poem, A.
For Bill Hawkins, a Black Militant.
Grandfather Poem, A.
My baby / loves flowers.
Practical Concerns.

Samantha Is My Negro Cat.
We Live in a Cage.
Why Would I Want.

Harrison, De Leon (b. 1941)
Collage for Richard Davis—Two Short
    Forms, A.
Room, The.
Seed of Nimrod, The.
Some Days / Out Walking Above.
Yellow.

Harvey, Yona
Sonia Told Them Women.

Hasson, Umar Abd Rahim (Tony Rutherford)
Black and White.

Hawkins, Walter Everette (b. 1886)
Death of Justice, The.
Spade Is Just a Spade, A.

Hayden, Robert Earl (1913–80)
American Journal.
Approximations.
As my blood was drawn.
Astronauts.
Aunt Jemima of the Ocean Waves.
Bahá'u'lláh in the Garden of Ridwan.
Ballad of Nat Turner, The.
Ballad of Remembrance, A.
Ballad of Sue Ellen Westerfield, The.
Belsen, Day of Liberation.
Bone-Flower Elegy.
Broken Dark, The.
Burly fading one beside the engine, The.
Butterfly Piece.
Crispus Attucks.
"Dance the Orange."
Dawnbreaker.
Diver, The.
Dogwood Trees, The.
Double Feature.
Dream, The.
El-Hajj Malik El-Shabazz.
Electrical Storm.
Elegies for Paradise Valley.
For a Young Artist.
Frederick Douglass.
Free Fantasia: Tiger Flowers.
From the corpse woodpiles, from the ashes.
Full Moon.
Gulls.
Homage to Paul Robeson.
Homage to the Empress of the Blues.
Ice Storm.
In the Mourning Time.
Incense of the Lucky Virgin.
Islands, The.
John Brown.
Killing the Calves.
Kodachromes of the Island.
Lear Is Gay.
Letter.
Letter from Phillis Wheatley, A.
Lions, The.
Locus.
Middle Passage.
Mirages, The.
Monet's "Waterlilies."
Moose Wallow, The.
Mourning Poem for the Queen of Sunday.
'Mystery Boy' Looks for Kin in Nashville.
Names.
Night-Blooming Cereus, The.
Night, Death, Mississippi.
O Daedalus, Fly Away Home.
October— / its plangency, its glow.
On Lookout Mountain.
Paul Laurence Dunbar.
Peacock Room, The.
Performers, The.
Perseus.
Plague of Starlings, A.
Point, The.
Prisoners, The.
Rabbi, The.
Rag Man, The.
Return, The.
Richard Hunt's "Arachne."
Road in Kentucky, A.
Runagate Runagate.

Smelt Fishing.
Snow.
Snow Lamp, The, *sels.*
Soledad.
Sphinx.
Summertime and the Living.
Tattooed Man, The.
Theme and Variation.
Theory of Evil.
Those Winter Sundays.
Tour 5.
Traveling through Fog.
Two Egyptian Portrait Masks.
Unidentified Flying Object.
Web, The.
Wheel, The.
Whipping, The.
Witch Doctor.
Year of the Child, The.
Zeus over Redeye.
Zinnias.

Hayes, Donald Jeffrey (b. 1904)
After all and after all.
Alien.
Appoggiatura.
Auf Wiedersehen.
Benediction.
Confession.
Haven.
Inscription: "He wrote upon his heart."
Night like purple flakes of snow.
Nocturne: "Softly blow lightly."
Pastourelle.
Poet.
Threnody: "Let happy throats be mute."

**Hayford, Gladys May Casely (Aquah Laluah)
(1904–50)**
Baby Cobina.
Lullaby: "Close your sleepy eyes, or the pale
    moonlight will steal you."
Nativity.
Palm Wine Seller, The.
Rainy Season Love Song.
Serving Girl, The.

Haynes, Albert E., Jr.
Eclipse.
Law, The.

Heard, Josephine D. Henderson (b. 1861)
Admiration.
Advance of Education, The.
Assurance.
Bereft.
Birth of Jesus, The.
Birth of Time, The.
Bishop James A. Shorter.
Black Sampson, The.
City by the Sea, The.
Day after Conference, The.
December.
Deception.
Decoration Day.
Do You Think?
Doxology.
Earthquake of 1886, The.
Easter Morn.
Epitaph, An: "When I am gone."
Eternity.
Fame.
Farewell to Allen University.
Forgetfulness!
General Robert Smalls.
Happy Heart, A.
He Comes Not To-night.
He Hath Need of Rest.
Heart-Hungry.
Hope Thou in God.
Hope! Thou vain, delusive maiden.
I Love Thee.
I Will Look Up.
In Memory of James M. Rathel.
Judge Not.
Love Letters.
Matin Hymn.
Message to a Loved One Dead, A.
Morn.
Mother.
Mother's Love, A.

Music.
My Canary.
My Grace Is Sufficient.
My Husband's Birthday.
My Mocking Bird.
National Cemetery, Beaufort, South Carolina, The.
New Organ, The.
Night.
On Genessarett.
Out in the Desert.
Outcast, The.
Parting, The.
Parting Kiss, The.
Quarrel, The.
Quarto Centennial, The.
Question, The.
Resting.
Retrospect.
Rev. Andrew Brown, over the Hill to Rest.
Rt. Rev. Richard Allen.
Sabbath Bells.
Slumbering Passion.
Solace.
Sunshine after Cloud.
Tennyson's Poems.
They are coming, coming slowly.
Thine Own.
Thou Lovest Me.
To Clements' Ferry.
To Whittier.
To Youth.
Truth.
Unuttered Prayer.
Welcome Home.
Welcome to Hon. Frederick Douglass.
When I Would Die.
Where Do School Days End?
Who Is My Neighbor?
Whoso Gives Freely, Shall Freely Receive!
Wilberforce.

Hemphill, Essex (1957–95)
Family Jewels.
Homocide.
Soft Targets.
XXI.
Where Seed Falls.

Henderson, David (b. 1943)
Alvin Cash/Keep on Dancin'.
Boston Road Blues.
Burgundy Street.
Do Nothing Till You Hear from Me.
Downtown-Boy Uptown.
Egyptian Book of the Dead.
Horizon Blues.
Keep on Pushing.
Louisiana Weekly #4, The.
Neon Diaspora.
Psychedelic Firemen.
Sketches of Harlem.
Song of Devotion to the Forest.
They Are Killing All the Young Men.
Walk with de Mayor of Harlem.
White People.

Henderson, Elliot Blaine (1877–1944)
Git on Board, Chillun.
Good Bye, Honey—Good Bye.
Trussy's Visit.
Uncle Ned an' de Mockin' Bird.

Henderson-Holmes, Safiya (b. 1952)
"C" ing in Colors: Blue.
"C" ing in Colors: Red.

Hernton, Calvin C. (b. 1932)
Black Stick with a Ball of Cotton for a Head and a Running Machine for a Mouth, A.
D Blues.
Distant Drum, The.
Elements of Grammar.
Fall Down.
Jitterbugging in the Streets.
Long Blues, The.
Madhouse.
Medicine Man.
Poem.
Young Negro poet / came from 'way down South.

Herut, Defari
Gems.

Hill, Leslie Pinckney (1880–1960)
Christmas at Melrose.
So Quietly.
Summer Magic.
Teacher, The.
Tuskegee.

Hill, Quentin (b. 1950)
Time Poem.

Hines, Carl Wendell, Jr. (b. 1940)
Two Jazz Poems, *sels.*

Hoagland, Everett (b. 1942)
Anti-Semanticist, The.
Big Zeb Johnson.
Georgia—It's the Gospel Truth.
Gorée ten miles offshore beckons.
It's a Terrible Thing!
Love Child—a Black Aesthetic.
My Spring Thing.
Night Interpreted.
Words to Drive out the White Growth in the Eyes.

Holiday, Billie (1915–1959)
Fine and Mellow.

Holloway, John Wesley (b. 1865)
Black Mammies.
Calling the Doctor.
Corn Song, The.
Miss Melerlee.

Holloway, Lucy Ariel Williams (b. 1905)
Northboun'.

Holly, Joseph Cephas (1825–55)
Our family tree is in the sear.
Patriot's Lament, The.
This Is a Fatherland to Me.
Wreath of Holly, A.

Holman, M. Carl (b. 1919)
And on This Shore.
Letter across Doubt and Distance.
Mr. Z.
Notes for a Movie Script.
Picnic: the Liberated.
Song: "Dressed up in my melancholy."
Three Brown Girls Singing.

Horne, Frank (b. 1899)
Immortality.
Kid Stuff.
Letters Found near a Suicide, *sels.*
Mamma!
More Letters Found near a Suicide.
Nigger.
On Seeing Two Brown Boys in a Catholic Church.
Patience . . . patience.
Resurrection.
Symphony.
To a Persistent Phantom.
Toast.
Walk.

Horton, George Moses (1797?–1883?)
Acrostics.
Art of a Poet, The.
Cheerless Condition of Bachelorship, The.
Close of Life, The.
Connubial Felicity.
Creditor to His Proud Debtor, The.
Death of an Old Carriage Horse.
Division of an Estate.
Early Affection.
Excited from Reading the Obedience of Nature to her Lord in the Vessel on the Sea.
Execution of Private Henry Anderson.
Eye of Love, The.
Farewell to Frances.
Fate of an Innocent Dog, The.
Fearful Traveller in the Haunted Castle, The.
For the Fair Miss M. M. McLean.
General Grant—the Hero of the War.
George Moses Horton, Myself.
Graduate Leaving College, The.
Gratitude.
Heavenly Love.
Horse Stolen from the Camp, The.
Imploring to Be Resigned at Death.

Intemperance Club, The.
Jefferson in a Tight Place.
Liberty.
Lincoln Is Dead.
Lines to My—.
Love.
Lover's Farewell, The.
Man, a Torch.
Meditation on a Cold, Dark and Rainy Night.
My Native Home.
New Fashions.
Obstruction of Genius, The.
On an Old Deluded Soldier.
On Hearing of the Intention of a Gentleman to Purchase the Poet's Freedom.
On Liberty and Slavery.
On Summer.
On the Evening and the Morning.
On the Pleasures of College Life.
On the Poetic Muse.
On the Truth of the Saviour.
On Winter.
One Generation Passeth Away and Another Cometh.
Poet's Feeble Petition, The.
Powers of Love, The.
Praise of Creation.
Reflections from the Flash of a Meteor.
Retreat from Moscow, The.
Rosabella—Purity of Heart.
Setting Sun, The.
Slave, The.
Slavery.
Slavery, thou peace-disturbing thief.
Slave's Complaint, The.
Slave's Reflections the Eve before His Sale, A.
Snaps for Dinner, Snaps for Breakfast and Snaps for Supper.
Song of Liberty and Parental Advice.
Southern Refugee, The.
Swan—Vain Pleasures, The.
Tippler to His Bottle, The.
To a Departing Favorite.
To Eliza.
To the Muse.
Troubled with the Itch and Rubbing with Sulphur.
Union of Parties, The.
Woodman and the Money Hunter, The.

Houston, Virginia A.
Class Room.
Ecstasy.

Howard, Vilma
Citizen, The.

Hughes, Langston (1902–67)
Abe Lincoln.
Acceptance.
Addition: "Put 5 and 5 together."
Addition: "7 + 7 + love =."
Advertisement for the Waldorf-Astoria.
Advice.
Afraid.
Africa.
Afro-American Fragment.
After Many Springs.
Air Raid: Barcelona.
Air Raid over Harlem.
Alabama Earth.
Always the Same.
America.
American Heartbreak.
America's Young Black Joe!
Angels wings is white as snow, The.
Angola Question Mark.
Anne Spencer's Table.
Announcement.
April Rain Song.
Ardella.
Argument: "Now lookahere, gal."
Argument: "White is right."
As Befits a Man.
As I Grew Older.
Ask Your Mama: 12 Moods for Jazz, *sels.*
Aspiration.
August 19th.
Aunt Sue's Stories.

Autumn Note.
Autumn Thought.
Azikiwe in Jail.
Baby.
Backlash Blues, The.
Bad Luck Card.
Bad Man.
Bad Morning.
Ballad of Booker T.
Ballad of Gin Mary.
Ballad of Harry Moore.
Ballad of Little Sallie.
Ballad of Margie Polite.
Ballad of Mary's Son.
Ballad of Negro History, A.
Ballad of Ozie Powell.
Ballad of Roosevelt.
Ballad of Sam Solomon.
Ballad of the Black Sheep.
Ballad of the Fool.
Ballad of the Fortune Teller.
Ballad of the Girl Whose Name Is Mud.
Ballad of the Gypsy.
Ballad of the Killer Boy.
Ballad of the Landlord.
Ballad of the Man Who's Gone.
Ballad of the Miser.
Ballad of the Pawnbroker.
Ballad of the Seven Songs.
Ballad of the Sinner.
Ballad of the Two Thieves.
Ballad of Walter White.
Ballads of Lenin.
Bar.
Barefoot Blues.
Battle Ground.
Be-Bop Boys.
Beale Street.
Beale Street Love.
Beaumont to Detroit: 1943.
Beauty.
Beggar Boy.
Being Old.
Bells Toll Kindly, The.
Better in the quiet night.
Bible Belt.
Big Buddy, Big Buddy.
Big Sur.
Big-Timer, The.
Birmingham Sunday.
Birth.
Bitter River, The.
Black Crown, The.
Black Dancers.
Black Gal.
Black Man Speaks, The.
Black Maria.
Black Panther.
Black Pierrot, A.
Black Seed.
Black Workers.
Blacklash Blues.
Blind.
Blue Bayou.
Blue Monday.
Blues, The.
Blues at Dawn.
Blues Fantasy.
Blues on a Box.
Boarding House.
Bombings in Dixie.
Bonds for All.
Bonds: In Memoriam.
Boogie: 1 A.M.
Border Line.
Bound No'th Blues.
Bouquet.
Brand New Clothes.
Brass Spittoons.
Breath of a Rose.
Brief Encounter.
Broadcast on Ethiopia.
Broadcast to the West Indies.
Broke.
Brotherly Love.
Brothers.
Buddy.

Burden.
Cabaret.
Cabaret Girl Dies on Welfare Island.
Café: 3 A.M.
Call of Ethiopia.
Call to Creation.
Caribbean Sunset.
Carol of the Brown King.
Carolina Cabin.
Casual.
Casualty.
Cat and the Saxophone (2 a.m.), The.
Catch.
Change.
Chant for May Day.
Chant for Tom Mooney.
Chicago Blues.
Children's Rhymes.
Chippy.
Chord.
Christ in Alabama.
Christian Country, A.
Christmas Eve: Nearing Midnight in New
   York.
Christmas Story, The.
Circles spin round.
City.
Closing Time.
College Formal: Renaissance Casino.
Color.
Colored Soldier, The.
Columbia, / My dear girl.
Comment.
Comment on War.
Communion.
Communiqué.
Conservatory Student Struggles with Higher
   Instrumentation.
Consider me, / A colored boy.
Consumptive, The.
Convent.
Cora.
Corner Meeting.
Could Be Hastings Street.
Country.
Crap Game.
Croon.
Cross.
Crossing.
Crow Goes, Too.
Crowing Hen Blues.
Crowns and Garlands.
Cubes.
Cultural Exchange.
Curious.
Dancer.
Dancers.
Danse Africaine.
Dare.
Dark Youth of the U.S.A.
Day.
Daybreak in Alabama.
Dead in There.
Dear Lovely Death.
Dear Mr. President.
Death in Africa.
Death in Harlem.
Death in Yorkville.
Death of an Old Seaman.
Death of Do Dirty: A Rounder's Song.
Deceased.
Declaration.
Deferred.
Delinquent.
Demand.
Democracy will not come.
Demonstration.
Departure.
Desert.
Desire to us.
Dime.
Dimout in Harlem.
Dinner Guest: Me.
Disillusion.
Dive.
Dixie Man to Uncle Sam.
Dixie South Africa.

Do You Reckon?
Doorknobs.
Dove, The.
Down and Out.
Down Where I Am.
Draftees.
Drama for Winter Night (Fifth Avenue).
Dream.
Dream Boogie.
Dream Boogie: Variation.
Dream Dust.
Dream Keeper, The.
Dream of Freedom.
Dream Variations.
Dreamer.
Dreams.
Dressed Up.
Drum.
Drums.
Drunkard.
Dusk.
Dustbowl.
Dying Beast.
Early Evening Quarrel.
Earth Song.
Easy Boogie.
Elderly Leaders.
Elevator Boy.
Emperor Haile Selassie.
Empty House.
Encounter.
End.
Enemy.
English, The.
Ennui.
Envoy to Africa.
Epitaph: "Uncle Tom, / When he was alive."
Epitaph: "Within this grave lie."
Esthete in Harlem.
Evenin' Air Blues.
Evening Song.
Evil.
Evil Morning.
Evil Woman.
Exits.
Expendable.
Explain It, Please.
Fact.
Fairies.
Faithful One.
Fantasy in Purple.
Farewell, A: "With gypsies and sailors."
Fascination.
Feet O' Jesus.
50–50.
Final Call.
Final Curve.
Fire-Caught.
Fire, / Fire, Lord!
Fired.
First of May.
Flatted Fifths.
Flight.
Florida Road Workers.
Flotsam.
Fog.
For an Indian Screen.
For Dead Mimes.
For Russell and Rowena Jelliffe.
For Salome.
Formula.
Fortune Teller Blues.
403 Blues.
Fourth of July Thought.
Fragments.
Frederick Douglass: 1817-1895.
Free Man.
Freedom: "Some folks think."
Freedom Seeker.
Freedom Train.
Freedom will not come.
Freedom's Plow.
Friendly in a Friendly Way.
From Selma.
From Spain to Alabama.
Frosting.
Fulfilment.

Funeral.
Gal's Cry for a Dying Lover.
Gangsters.
Garden.
Garment.
Gauge.
Genius Child.
Georgia Dusk.
Get Up off That Old Jive.
Ghandhi Is Fasting.
Ghosts of 1619.
Girl.
Give Us Our Peace.
Go *slow*, they say.
God.
God to Hungry Child.
Gods.
Gone Boy.
Good Bluffers.
Good-morning, Revolution.
Good Morning, Stalingrad.
Goodbye Christ.
Governor Fires Dean.
Graduation.
Grandpa's Stories.
Grant Park.
Grave Yard.
Green Memory.
Grief.
Grocery Store.
Gypsy Man.
Gypsy Melodies.
Hard Daddy.
Hard Luck.
Harlem Dance Hall.
Harlem Night.
Harlem Night Club.
Harlem Night Song.
Harlem Sweeties.
Havana Dreams.
Heart.
Heart of Harlem, The.
Heaven is / The place where.
Helen Keller.
Hero—International Brigade.
Hey!
Hey! Hey!
Hey-Hey Blues.
High to Low.
History.
Homecoming.
Homesick Blues.
Honey babe, / You braid your hair too tight.
Hope: "He rose up on his dying bed."
Hope: "Sometimes when I'm lonely."
Hope for Harlem.
House in Taos, A.
House in the World.
How about It, Dixie.
How Thin a Blanket.
Hurt.
I dream a world where man.
I Thought It Was Tangiers I Wanted.
I too, sing America.
If-ing.
Imagine! / They are afraid of you.
Impasse.
In a Troubled Key.
In Explanation of Our Times.
In the mist of the moon I saw you.
In time of silver rain.
Interne at Provident.
Irish Wake.
Island.
It Gives Me Pause.
Jaime.
Jam Session.
Jazz Band in a Parisian Cabaret.
Jazz Girl.
Jazzonia.
Jester, The.
Jesus, The.
Jim Crow's Last Stand.
Jitney.
Joe Louis.
Joe Louis is a man.
Johannesburg Mines.

Joy.
Judge William Hastie.
Judgment Day.
Juice Joint: Northern City.
Juke Box Love Song.
Juliet.
Junior Addict.
Just an Ordinary Guy.
Justice.
Kid in the Park.
Kid Sleepy.
Kids in School with Me, The.
Kids Who Die.
Ku Klux.
Labor Storm.
Lady in Cabaret.
Lady's Boogie.
Lament for Dark Peoples.
Lament of a Vanquished Beau, The.
Lament over Love.
Last Call.
Last Feast of Belshazzar, The.
Last Man Living, The.
Last Prince of the East.
Late Corner.
Late last night I.
Laughers.
Lenin walks around the world.
Lenox Avenue.
Lenox Avenue Mural, *sels.*
Let America Be American Again.
Letter from Spain.
Letter to Anne, A.
Letter to the Academy.
Liars.
Life Is Fine.
Likewise.
Lincoln Monument: Washington.
Lincoln Theatre.
Lincoln University: 1954.
Listen Here Blues.
Litany: "Gather up / In the arms of your pity."
Little Cats.
Little Green Tree.
Little Lyric (of Great Importance).
Little Old Letter.
Little Song.
Little Song on Housing.
Live and Let Live.
Lonely Nocturne.
Lonesome Corner.
Lonesome Place.
Long Song for Antonia.
Long Trip.
Long View: Negro.
Love Again Blues.
Love is a wild wonder.
Love Song for Lucinda.
Lover's Return.
Low to High.
Luck.
Lullaby: "My little dark baby."
Lumumba's Grave ("Lumumba was black.")
Lunch in a Jim Crow Car.
Lynching Song.
Ma Lord ain't no stuck-up man.
Ma Man.
Madam and Her Madam.
Madam and Her Might-Have-Been.
Madam and the Army.
Madam and the Census Man.
Madam and the Charity Child.
Madam and the Crime Wave.
Madam and the Fortune Teller.
Madam and the Insurance Man.
Madam and the Minister.
Madam and the Movies.
Madam and the Newsboy.
Madam and the Number Writer.
Madam and the Phone Bill.
Madam and the Rent Man.
Madam and the Wrong Visitor.
Madam's Calling Cards.
Madam's Christmas (or Merry Christmas Everybody).
Madam's Past History.

Magnolia Flowers.
Mama and Daughter.
Mammy.
Man.
Man into Men.
March Moon.
Maybe.
Mazie Dies Alone in the City Hospital.
Me and My Song.
Me and the Mule.
Mean Old Yesterday.
Mellow.
Memo to Non-White People.
Merry Christmas, China.
Merry-Go-Round.
Message to the President.
Metropolitan Museum.
Mexican Market Woman.
Midnight Chippie's Lament.
Midnight Dancer.
Midnight Raffle.
Midwinter Blues.
Migrant.
Migration.
Militant.
Minnie Sings Her Blues.
Minstrel Man.
Misery.
Miss Blues'es Child.
Mississippi.
Mississippi Levee.
Mister Sandman.
Mitchell Case, The.
Moan.
Monotony.
Monroe's Blues.
Montage of a Dream Deferred, *sels.*
Montmartre.
Moonlight in Valencia: Civil War.
Moonlight Night: Carmel.
Morning After.
Mother in Wartime.
Mother to Son.
Motherland.
Motto.
Movies.
Mulatto.
My Beloved.
My Loves.
My People.
Mystery.
NAACP.
Natcha, offering love.
Naughty child / Who ventured to go cut flowers, The.
Necessity.
Negro.
Negro Dancers.
Negro Ghetto.
Negro Mother, The.
Negro Servant.
Negro Speaks of Rivers, The.
Neighbor.
Neon Signs.
New Cabaret Girl, The.
New Flowers.
New Moon.
New Song, A.
New Year.
New Yorkers.
Night: Four Songs.
Night funeral / In Harlem.
Night Song.
Nightmare Boogie.
No Regrets.
Nocturne for the Drums.
Nonette.
Northern Liberal.
Not a Movie.
Not Else—But.
Not Often.
Not What Was.
Note in Music.
Note on Commercial Theatre.
Note to All Nazis Fascists and Klansmen.
Nude Young Dancer.
Number.

Numbered.
Numbers.
October 16: The Raid.
Office Building: Evening.
Official Notice.
Old Age.
Old Dog Queenie / Was such a meanie.
Old Sailor.
Old Walt Whitman.
On a Christmas Night.
On a Pallet of Straw.
One.
125th Street.
One More "S" in the U.S.A.
One-Way Ticket.
Only Woman Blues.
Open Letter to the South.
Oppression.
Our Land.
Out of Work.
Paint.
Pair in One.
Pale Lady.
Parade.
Parisian Beggar Woman.
Park Bench.
Park Benching.
Passing.
Passing Love.
Pastoral.
Pathological Puzzle.
Peace.
Peace Conference in an American Town.
Pennsylvania Station in New York, The.
Personal.
Ph.D.
Pictures to the Wall.
Pierrot.
Piggy-back.
Po' Boy Blues.
Poème d'Automne.
Poem: "Ah, / My black one."
Poem: "All the tom-toms of the jungles beat
    in my blood."
Poem: "I loved my friend."
Poem: "When young spring comes."
Poem for an Intellectual on the Way Up to
    Submit to His Lady.
Poem for Youth.
Poem to a Dead Soldier.
Poem to Uncle Sam.
Poet to Bigot.
Poet to Patron.
Poor Girl's Ruination.
Poor Rover.
Poppy Flower.
Port Town.
Porter.
Postcard from Spain.
Prayer for a Winter Night.
Prayer: "I ask you this: / Which way to go."
Prayer Meeting.
Preference.
Prelude to Our Age.
Present.
Prime.
Prize Fighter.
Problems.
Projection.
Promised Land / Is always just ahead, The.
Puzzled.
Puzzlement.
Question: "Said the Lady, Can you do."
Question: "When the old junk man Death."
Question and Answer.
Raid.
Railroad Avenue.
Reasons Why.
Red Clay Blues.
Red Cross.
Red Roses.
Red Silk Stockings.
Refugee.
Relief.
Remembrance.
Rent-Party Shout.
Request.

Request for Requiems.
Restrictive Covenants.
Return to Sea.
Reverie on the Harlem River.
Revolution.
Ring, The.
Rising Waters.
Roar, China! / Roar, old lion of the East!
Room.
Ruby Brown.
Ruined Gal, A.
S-sss-ss-sh!
Sailing Date.
Sailor.
Salute to Soviet Armies.
Saturday Night.
Scottsboro.
Sea Calm.
Sea charm / The sea's own children.
Search.
Seascape.
Seashore through Dark Glasses (Atlantic
    City).
Second Generation: New York.
Seven Moments of Love, sels.
Shadows.
Shakespeare in Harlem.
Shall the Good Go Down?
Shame on You.
Share-Croppers.
Shearing Time.
Shepherd's Song at Christmas.
Shout.
Sick Room.
Signs of Spring.
Silence.
Silent One.
Silhouette.
Silly Animals.
Sinner.
Sister.
Sister Johnson Marches.
Situation.
Six-Bits Blues.
Slave.
Slave Song.
Sleep.
Sliver.
Sliver of Sermon.
Slum Dreams.
Small Memory.
Snail.
Snake.
Snob.
So long / is in the song.
So Tired Blues.
Soledad.
Some Day.
Song: "Lovely, dark, and lonely one."
Song After Lynching.
Song for a Banjo Dance.
Song for a Dark Girl.
Song for Billie Holiday.
Song for Ourselves.
Song of Adoration.
Song of Spain.
Song of the Refugee Road.
Song of the Revolution.
Song to a Negro Wash-woman, A.
Song to the Dark Virgin.
Songs.
South, The.
Southern Mammy Sings.
Southern Negro Speaks.
Speaking of Food.
Special Bulletin.
Spirituals.
Sport.
Spring for Lovers.
Stalingrad: 1942.
Star Seeker.
Stars.
Statement.
Steel Mills.
Still Here.
Stokely Malcolm Me.
Stony Lonesome.

Strange Hurt.
Stranger in Town.
Street Song.
Suburban Evening.
Subway Face.
Subway Rush Hour.
Success.
Suicide.
Suicide's Note.
Summer Evening (Calumet Avenue).
Summer Night.
Sun Song.
Sunday by the Combination.
Sunday Morning Prophecy.
Sunset—Coney Island.
Sunset in Dixie.
Sweet Words on Race.
Sylvester's Dying Bed.
Tag.
Tambourines! / Tambourines!
Tapestry.
Teacher.
Tell Me.
Testament.
Testimonial.
Thanksgiving Time.
Theme for English B.
There.
There's always weather, weather.
Third Degree.
This Puzzles Me.
Thorn, The.
Tired.
To a Dead Friend.
To a Little Lover-Lass, Dead.
To Artina.
To Be Somebody.
To Beauty.
To Captain Mulzac.
To Certain "Brothers."
To Certain Intellectuals.
To Certain Negro Leaders.
To Dorothy Maynor.
To make words sing.
To Midnight Nan at Leroy's.
To the Dark Mercedes of "El Palacio de
    Amor."
To the Little Front of San Lazaro on the
    Ocean Front, Havana.
To You.
Today.
Tomorrow may be.
Tomorrow's Seed.
Too Blue.
Total War.
Tower.
Town of Scottsboro, The.
Trip: San Francisco.
Troubled Water.
Troubled Woman.
Trumpet Player.
Twilight Reverie.
Two Somewhat Different Epigrams, sels.
Two things possess the power.
Ultimatum.
Ultimatum: Kid to Kid.
Un-American Investigators.
Uncle Tom.
Uncle Tom is a legend and a dream.
Underground, The.
Undertow.
Union.
Up-Beat.
Us: Colored.
Vagabonds.
Vari-Colored Song.
Visitors to the Black Belt.
Wait.
Wake.
Walkers with the Dawn.
Walls.
War.
Warning.
Warning: Augmented.
Watch Out, Papa.
Water-Front Streets.
Ways.

We, Too.
Wealth.
Weary Blues, The.
We're all in the telephone book.
West Texas.
What?
What I Think.
What? So Soon!
When Sue Wears Red.
When the Armies Passed.
Where Service Is Needed.
Where? When? Which?
White Man.
White Ones, The.
Who But the Lord?
Wide River.
Widow Woman.
Will V-Day Be Me-Day Too?
Wine-O.
Winter Moon.
Winter Sweetnes.
Wisdom.
Wisdom and War.
Wise Men.
Without Benefit of Declaration.
Wonder.
Wooing, A.
Words Like Freedom.
Workin' Man.
World War II.
Worriation.
Year Round.
Yesterday and Today.
Young Bride.
Young Gal's Blues.
Young Negro Girl.
Young Prostitute.
Young Sailor.
Young Singer.
Youth.

Hunter, Albert (1897–1984) *and* **Louie Austin (1897–1972)**
Down-Hearted Blues.

Hurston, Zora Neale
Faith hasn't got no eyes, but she long-legged.

I

Iman, Yusef
Love Your Enemy.
Show Me Lord Show Me.

Ishak, Elton Hill-Abu (b. 1950)
Theme Brown Girl.

Iverem, Esther
Daddy's Friends.
Earth Screaming.
Keeper.
Murmur.

J

Jackmon, Marvin E. *See* "X, Marvin"

Jackson, Angela (b. 1951)
Beginning for New Beginnings, A.
Why I Must Make Language.

Jackson, Gale (b. 1958)
Alice.
Fugitive Slaves.
Some of Betty's Story Round 1850.

Jackson, Mae (b. 1946)
Blues Today, The.
For Some Poets.
I Remember ("I remember / January, / 1968.")
January 3, 1970.
Reincarnation.

Jackson, Major L. (b. 1968)
Blunts.
Don Pullen at the Zanzibar Blue Jazz Cafe, 1994.
Some Kind of Crazy.

Jackson, Michael (b. 1940)
Man in the Mirror.

Jackson, Reuben (b. 1956)
After the Dance.
For Duke Ellington.
Jamal's Lamentation.
Lady's Way.
Lonely Affair, A.
1973.
63rd and Broadway.
Thelonious.

Jacobs, Harriet (b. 1951)
About Our Hips.
And Sometimes I Hear This Song in My Head.
Goree.
Growing into My Name.
Imagination in Flight: an Improvisational Duet.
On Extending the Olive Branch to My Own Self.

Jamal
Sat. Nite.

James, Elmore (1918–1963)
Sunnyland.

James, Wendy L.
Troy.

Jamison, Roscoe Conkling (1888–1918)
Negro Soldiers, The.

Jean, Valerie (b. 1953)
Lesson on Braces.
On Apologies.

Jeffers, Honorée F.
I Was Looking at Miles.

Jeffers, Lance (1919–85)
Black Soul of the Land.
But I Know That Unseen Anger Runs a Raft.
Flesh of the Young Men Is Burning, The.
Grief Streams Down My Chest.
How High the Moon.
I do not know the power of my hand.
Love Pictures You as Black and Long-faced.
Man with a Furnace in His Hand.
My Blackness Is the Beauty of This Land.
O Africa, where I baked my bread.
Old Love Butchered (Colorado Springs and Huachuca).
On Listening to the Spirituals.
Self-Doubt.
There is a nation in my brawny scrotal sac.
To him who in his absence from himself.
Trellie.
Tuskegee, Tuskegee!
Vietnam: I Need More Than This Crust of Salt.
When I Know the Power of My Black Hand.
When She Spoke of God.

Jenkins, Candice M.
Poem for Tracy (Chapman).

Jenness, Mary
Negro Laughs Back, The.
Secret.

Joans, Ted (b. 1928)
Customs and Culture?
It is time for the United States to spend money on education so that every American would be hipper, *thus no war!*
Its Curtains.
JAZZ is my religion.
Lester Young.
My Ace of Spades.
Protective Grigri, The.
Scenery.
.38, The.
Truth, The.

Johnson, Alicia Loy (b. 1944)
Black Lotus.
Our Days Are Numbered.

Johnson, Charles Bertram (b. 1880)
Little Cabin, A.
Negro Poets.

Johnson, Don Allen ("Mustafa") (b. 1942)
O White Mistress.

Johnson, Fenton (1886–1958)
Aunt Jane Allen.
Banjo Player, The.
Children of the Sun.
Counting.
Daily Grind, The.
Ethiopia.
Ethiopian's Song, The.
Lonely Mother, The.
Long de cool o' night w'en day am daid.
Marathon Runner, The.
Minister, The.
My God in Heaven said to me.
Negro Peddler's Song, A.
New Day, The.
Old Repair Man, The.
Puck Goes to Court.
Rome is dying.
Scarlet Woman, The.
Singing Hallelujia.
Soldiers of the Dusk, The.
Song of the Whirlwind.
Tired.
To an Afro-American Maiden.
When I Die.
Who Is That a-Walking in the Corn?
World Is a Mighty Ogre, The.

Johnson, Fred (b. 1940)
Arabesque.
Fire, Hair, Meat and Bone.

Johnson, Georgia Douglas (1886–1966)
Afterglow.
Armageddon.
Black Woman.
Calling Dreams.
Common Dust.
Conquest.
Credo.
Dreams of the Dreamer, The.
Escape.
Heart of a Woman, The.
Hope.
I Want to Die While You Love Me.
Lethe.
Little Son.
Lost Illusions.
Lovelight.
Motherhood.
My Little Dreams.
Old Black Men.
Poet Speaks, The.
Prejudice.
Proving.
Recessional.
Riddle, The: "White men's children spread over the earth."
Service.
Smothered Fires.
Suppliant, The.
To a Young Wife.
To William Stanley Braithwaite.
Trifle.
True American, The.
Welt.
What Need Have I for Memory?
When I am dead, withhold, I pray, your blooming legacy.
Wishes.
Your World ("Your world is as big as you make it.")
Youth.

Johnson, Helen Armstead (b. 1920)
Affirmation.
Philodendron.

Johnson, Helene (1907–95)
Bottled [New York].
Brilliant-bellied newt flashes, The.
Fulfillment.
Invocation: "Let me be buried in the rain."
Magalu.
My Race.
Poem: "Little brown boy."
Remember Not.
Road, The.
Sonnet to a Negro in Harlem.
Trees at Night.
What Do I Care for Morning.

Johnson, James Weldon (1871–1938)
Before a Painting.
Brothers.
Color Sergeant, The.

Fifty Years.
Girl of fifteen.
Glory of the Day Was in Her Face, The.
Go Down Death.
Lift Ev're Voice and Sing.
Listen, Lord—[a Prayer].
My City.
O Black and unknown bards of long ago.
Saint Peter Relates an Incident of the
    Resurrection Day.
Since You Went Away.
White Witch, The.

Johnson, Joe (b. 1940)
If I Ride This Train.
Judeebug's Country.

Johnson, Maggie Pogue (b. 1949)
Ambition.
As We Sow We Shall Reap.
Christmas Times.
Dat Mule ob Brudder Wright's.
Day befo' Thanksgibin', De.
Dedicated to Dr. W. H. Sheppard.
Dedication Day.
Dream, A.
I Wish I Was a Grown Up Man.
James Hugo Johnston.
Krismas Dinnah.
Leap Yeah Party, De.
Lost Teddy Bear, The.
Meal Time.
Men Folks ob Today, De.
Negro Has a Chance, The.
Old Maid's Soliloquy.
People's Literary, De.
Poet of Our Race.
Sister Johnson's Speech.
Sometimes.
Story of Lovers Leap, The.
Strawberry, The.
Superstitions.
Thoughts.
To Professor Byrd Prillerman.
To See Ol' Booker T.
V. N. and C. I, The.
What's de Use ob Wukin in de Summer
    Time at All.
What's Mo' Temptin' to de Palate?
When Daddy Cums from Wuk.
Why Should the American Negro Be Proud?
Wintah Styles, De.

Johnson, Ray
Walking east on 125th street.

Johnson, Robert (c.1898–1937)
Hellhound on My Trail.

Jonas, Rosalie (1861?–1953)
Ballade des Belles Milatraisses.
Brother Baptis' on Woman Suffrage.
Crowded Out.

Jones, Edward Smyth (b. 1881)
Song of Thanks, A.

Jones, Gayl (b. 1949)
Many Die Here.
Satori.
Tripart.

Jones, Howard (1892–1980)
Fall To.

Jones, Ira B.
Image of Myself 3.

Jones, Joshua Henry (1856–1932)
To a Skull.

Jones, LeRoi. *See* **Baraka, Amiri**

Jones, Patricia (b. 1951)
I Done Got So Thirsty That My Mouth
    Waters at the Thought of Rain.
Why I Like Movies.

Jones, Richard M. (c. 1889–1945)
Trouble in mind, I'm blue.

Jordan, A. Van (b. 1965)
Dance Lesson, A.
If I Write a Poem.
My Father's Retirement.

Jordan, June (b. 1936)
About Enrique's Drawing.
About Long Distances on Saturday.
Addenda to the Papal Bull.

Aftermath.
Ah, Momma, / Did the house ever know.
All the World Moved.
Alla Tha's All Right, But.
Always Lei of Ginger Blossoms for the First
    Lady of Hawai'i: Queen Lili'uokalani, An.
Another Poem about the Man.
Apologies to All the People in Lebanon.
At some moment the confidence snaps.
Calling on All Silent Minorities.
Cameo No. II.
Case in Point.
Current Events.
Dance: Nicaragua.
DeLiza and the TV News.
DeLiza Come to London Town; a Birthday
    Poem for Mark.
Deliza Questioning Perplexities.
Des Moines Iowa Rap.
Don't Estimate!
Double Standard Lifestyle Studies: #1.
En Passant.
Famine.
Female and the Silence of a Man, The.
Financial Planning.
First Poem from Nicaragua Libre:
    Teotcacinte.
For Dave: 1976.
For Ethelbert.
For Michael Angelo Thompson.
For My Brother.
For My Jamaican Sister a Little Bit Lost on
    the Island of Manhattan.
Fragments from a Parable.
Free Flight.
From Nicaragua Libre: Photograph of
    Managua.
From Sea to Shining Sea.
Gettin Down to Get over.
Ghazal at Full Moon.
Grand Army Plaza.
Home: January 29, 1984.
I Must Become a Menace to My Enemies.
If You Saw a Negro Lady.
In Memoriam: Martin Luther King, Jr.
In Paris.
Intifada.
It's About You: on the Beach.
Juice of a Lemon on the Trail of a Little
    Yellow.
Last Poem on Bell's Theorem.
Letter to My Friend the Poet Ntozake
    Shange.
Letter to the Local Police.
Madison Experience, The.
Memo.
Menu.
Meta-Rhetoric.
Morning on the mountains where the mist,
    The.
Moving Towards Home.
My Sadness Sits around Me.
New Pietà: For the Mothers and Children of
    Detroit, The.
Newport Jazz Festival: Saratoga Springs and
    Especially about George Benson and
    Everyone Who Was Listening.
Nightline: September 20, 1982.
1977: Poem for Mrs. Fannie Lou Hamer.
No Poem Because Time Is Not a Name.
Nobody Riding the Roads Today.
October 23, 1983.
Of Nightsong and Flight.
Okay "Negroes."
On a New Year's Eve.
On Declining Values.
On Moral Leadership as a Political Dilemma.
On the Loss of Energy.
On the Real World: Meditation #1.
On the Spirit of Mildred Jordan.
One Minus One Minus One.
Out in the Country of My Country
    (Peterborough, New Hampshire).
Patricia's Poem.
Poem about Intelligence for My Brothers and
    Sisters, A.
Poem About My Rights.

Poem about Police Violence.
Poem about the Head of a Negro.
Poem at the Midnight of My Life.
Poem for Benjamin Franklin.
Poem for Buddy.
Poem for Derrick Gilbert.
Poem for Guatemala.
Poem for Jan.
Poem for Joy.
Poem for Mark.
Poem for My Family: Hazel Griffin and
    Victor Hernandez Cruz.
Poem for Nana.
Poem for South AFrican Women.
Poem from Taped Testimony in the Tradition
    of Bernard Goetz.
Poem from the Empire State.
Poem Instead of a Columbus Day Parade.
Poem Number Two on Bell's Theorem.
Poem on.
Poem on Bell's Theorem.
Poem on the Road; for Alice Walker.
Poem on the Second Consecutive Day of
    Rain.
Poem Towards a Final Solution.
Poor Form.
Problems of Translation: Problems of
    Language.
Rape Is Not a Poem.
Reception, The.
Relativity.
Richland County Lyric for Elizabeth Asleep,
    A.
Roman Poem Number Five.
Roman Poem Number Six.
Roman Poem Number Eight.
Roman Poem Number Nine.
Roman Poem Number Thirteen.
Roman Poem Number Fourteen.
Romance in Irony.
Runaway Lil Bit Poem, A.
Short Note to My Very Critical and Well-
    Beloved Friends and Comrades, A.
Sketching in the Transcendental.
Smash the Church.
Solidarity.
Some people despise me be-.
Something Like a Sonnet for Phillis Miracle
    Wheatley.
Sometimes DeLiza.
Song for Soweto, A.
Song of Sojourner Truth, A.
Song of the Law Abiding Citizen.
Sonnet for A.B.T, A.
Sonnet from the Stony Brook, A.
Speculations on the Present through the Prism
    of the Past.
Sunflower Sonnet Number One.
Sunflower Sonnet Number Two.
Take them out!
Talking Back of Miss Valentine Jones, The,
    sels.
Test of Atlanta 1979, The.
To Free Nelson Mandela.
Torn Sky: Lesson #1, The.
Trying to Capture Rapture.
Uhuru in the O.R.
Uncle Bull-Boy.
Unemployment Monologue.
Verse for Ronald Slapjack Who Publicly
    Declared, "I, Too, Am a Contra!"
Wedding, The.
What happens when the dog sits on a tiger.
What Is This in Reference To? or We Must
    Get Together Sometime Soon!
What Would I Do White?
Who Look at Me.
Winter Honey.

Jordan, Norman (b. 1938)
August 2.
Be You.
Black Warrior.
Feeding the Lions.
I have seen them trying.
July 31.
July 27.
Poet the Dreamer, The.

Sacrifice, The.
Silent Prophet, The.
Sinner.
When A Woman Gets Blue.
Joshua, Glenn
On the Morning St. Bernard.

K

Kalunda-rae
Hoochie Route.
Kaufman, Bob (b. 1925)
Abomunist Manifesto.
African Dream.
Afterwards, They Shall Dance.
Alien winds sweeping the highway.
All those ships that never sailed.
Ancient Rain, The.
Bagel Shop Jazz.
Battle Report.
Believe, Believe.
Benediction.
Biggest Fisherman, The.
Bird with Painted Wings.
Blue O'Clock.
Blue Slanted into Blueness.
Blues Note.
Buddhist experience, A.
But as love.
Carl Chessman Interviews the P.T.A. in His
    Swank Gas Chamber Before Leaving on
    His Annual Inspection of Capital, Tour of
    Northern California Death Universities,
    Happy.
Cat Is Sleeping on a Poem, The.
Cincophrenicpoet.
Cocoa Morning.
Come let us journey to.
Countess Erica Blaise: Chorus.
Crootey Songo.
Cross Winds.
Does the Secret Mind Whisper?
Drunk Time.
Early Loves.
Enormous Gas Bill at the Dwarf Factory. A
    Horror Movie to be Shot with Eyes, The.
Falling.
Forget Me Not.
Geneology.
Grandfather Was Queer, Too.
Harwood Alley Song.
Hawk Lawler: Chorus.
Heather Bell.
Heavy Water Blues.
His Horn.
I Have Folded My Sorrows.
I Sigh a Marbled Sigh Ah, at Last.
I, Too, Know What I Am Not.
I wish that whoever it is inside of me.
Inside Connie.
J'Accuse.
Jail Poems.
Jazz Chick.
Late Lamented Wind, Burned in Indignation,
    The.
Lost Window.
"Michelangelo" the Elder.
Mind for All Its Reasoning, The.
Mingus.
Mongolian Sunset in Gobi Desert.
Morning Joy.
My mysteries created for me.
Night Sung Sailor's Prayer.
Night that Lorca Comes, The.
No More Jazz at Alcatraz.
O-Jazz-O.
On yardbird corners of embryonic hopes,
    drowned in a heroin tear.
Oregon.
Patriotic Ode on the Fourteenth Anniversary
    of the Persecution of Charlie Chaplin.
Peace Be with You.
Perhaps.
Picasso's Balcony.
Plea.
Poet, The.

Reflections on a Small Parade.
Response.
Results of a Lie Detector.
Round about Midnight.
Saraswati.
Sheila.
Slight Alterations.
Suicide.
Sun, Creator of Suns.
Telegram to Alex/Bagel Shop, North Beach
    SF.
Tequila Jazz.
Terror is more certain than all the rare
    desirable popular songs, A.
Tidal Friction . . . Comments at Real Movie.
To My Son Parker, Asleep in the Next
    Room.
Trip, Dharma Trip, Sangha Trip, The.
Unanimity Has Been Achieved, Not a Dot
    Less for Its Accidentalness.
Under Weight Champion, The.
Unhistorical Events.
Waiting.
Walking Hot Seasons.
Walking Parker Home.
War Memoir: Jazz, Don't Listen to It at
    Your Own Risk.
When we hear the eye open there, in that
    place.
Who Has Seen the Wind?
Why Write ABOUT.
Would You Wear My Eyes?
Kendrick, Dolores (b. 1927)
Jenny in Love.
Jenny in Sleep.
Sadie Snuffs a Candle.
Sophie, Climbing the Stairs.
Kenner, Peggy Susberry (b. 1937)
Black Taffy.
Comments.
Image in the Mirror.
No Bargains Today.
Kgositsile, Keorapetse W. (b. 1938)
Awakening, The.
Brother Malcolm's Echo.
Elegy for David Diop.
For Eusi, Ayi Kwei and Gwen Brooks.
Gods Wrote, The.
Ivory Masks in Orbit.
Mandela's Sermon.
My Name Is Afrika.
Origins.
Spirits Unchained.
To Fanon.
To Mother.
To My Daughter.
Towards a Walk in the Sun.
When Brown Is Black.
Killebrew, Carl
Squared Circle, The.
"King Pleasure." *See* **Beeks, Clarence**
Klein, Sybil
Cofaire?
Fragments from the Diary of Amelie Patiné,
    Quadroon Mistress of Monsieur Jacques
    R-------.
Jelly Roll Morton.
Letter to Madame Lindé from Justine, Her
    Creole Servant.
Knight, Etheridge (1933–91)
And Tell Me Poet, Can Love Exist in
    Slavery?
Another Poem for Me (after Recovering from
    an O.D.).
Apology for Apostasy?
As You Leave Me.
At a VA Hospital in the Middle of the
    United States of America: An Act in a
    Play.
Belly Song.
Birthday Poem.
Black Poet Leaps to His Death, A.
Bones of My Father, The.
Boston 5:00 A.M.—10/74.
Cell Song.
Circling the Daughter.
Con/tin/u/way/shun Blues.

Cop-Out Session.
Crazy pigeon strutting outside my cell.
Dark Prophecy: I Sing of Shine.
Eat Helen B Happy (a Found Poem).
Evolutionary Poem No. 1.
Evolutionary Poem No. 2.
Fable: "Once upon a today and yesterday and
    nevermore there were 7 men."
Feeling Fucked/Up Up.
For a Brookline Lady I Love.
For Black Poets Who Think of Suicide.
For Freckle-Faced Gerald.
For Langston Hughes.
For Malcolm, a Year After.
For Mary Ellen McAnally.
Genesis.
Genesis 11.
Green Grass and Yellow Balloons.
Haiku, *sels.*
Haiku: "Bare pecan tree, A."
Haiku: "Eastern guard tower."
Haiku: "Falling snow flakes, The."
Haiku: "In the August grass."
Haiku: "Making jazz swing in."
Haiku: "Morning sun slants cell."
Haiku: "Piano man, The."
Haiku: "To write a blues song."
Haiku: "Under moon shadows."
Haiku 1: "Slender finger of light, A."
Hard Rock Returns to Prison from the
    Hospital for the Criminal Insane.
He sees through stone.
I And Your Eyes.
Idea of Ancestry, The.
Ilu, the Talking Drum.
It was a funky deal.
Keeping of a Promise, The.
Last Words By "Slick."
Love Poem, A: "I do not expect the spirit of
    Penelope."
Memo #2.
Memo #5.
Memo #9.
Memo #32.
Memo #43.
My life, the quality of which.
My Uncle is My Honor and a Guest in My
    House.
No moon floods the memory of that night.
On Seeing the Black Male as #1 Sex Object
    in America.
On the Birth of a Black / Baby / Boy.
On the Projects Playground.
On the Yard.
On Watching Politicians Perform at Martin
    Luther King's Funeral.
Once on a Night in the Delta: A Report
    From Hell.
Poem For a Certain Lady on Her 33rd
    Birthday, The.
Poem for Myself (Or Blues for a Mississippi
    Black Boy), A.
Poem for the Liberation of Southern Africa.
Poem of Attrition, A.
Poem on the Middle East "Peace Process",
    A.
Poem to Galway Kinnell, A.
Portrait of Malcolm X.
Portrait of Mary.
Rehabilitation & Treatment in the Prisons of
    America.
Report to the Mother.
Stretching of the Belly, The.
Sun came, Miss Brooks—, The.
Talking in the Woods with Karl Amorelli.
Television Speaks.
To Dinah Washington.
Two Poems for Black Relocation Centers,
    sels.
Upon Your Leaving.
Various Protestations From Various People.
Violent Space, The.
Warden said to me the other day, The.
WASP Woman Visits a Black Junkie in
    Prison, A.
We free singers be.

Weeksville Women.
Woman.
Loftis, Norman J. (b. 1943)
Big John.
Brief Encounter.
Delirium.
Fights After School.
In Memorium: Robert Hayden.
Ruth.
Lomax, Pearl Cleage (b. 1948)
Glimpse.
Long, Doughtry ("Doc Long")
Ginger Bread Mama.
Negro Dreams.
Number Four.
One Time Henry Dreamed the Number.
Long, Richard A. (1927–1974?)
Hearing James Brown at the Café des Nattes.
Juan de Pareja: Painted by Velazquez.
Long, Worth (b. 1936)
Arson and Cold Lace.
Lorde, Audre (1934–92)
About Religion.
Afterimages.
Afterlove.
All Hallows Eve.
American Cancer Society Or There Is More
    Than One Way to Skin a Coon.
And Don't Think I Won't Be Waiting.
And Fall Shall Sit in Judgment.
And What About the Children.
Anniversary.
Art of Response, The.
Artisan.
As I Grew Up Again.
At First I Thought You Were Talking about.
Ballad for Ashes.
Ballad from Childhood.
Barren.
Bazaar.
Beams.
Bees, The.
Berlin Is Hard on Colored Girls.
Between Ourselves.
Beverly's Poem.
Bicentennial Poem #21,000,000.
Big Apple Circus.
Birthday Memorial to Seventh Street, A.
Black Mother Woman.
Black unicorn is greedy, The.
Blackstudies.
Bloodbirth.
Bridge through My Windows.
Brother Alvin.
Brown Menace or Poem to the Survival of
    Roaches, The.
Building.
Burning the Water Hyacinth.
But What Can You Teach My Daughter.
Cables To Rage Or I've Been Talking On
    This Street Corner.
Call.
Chain.
Change.
Change of Season.
Child Shall Lead, A.
Chorus.
Coal.
Conclusion.
Coniagui women / wear their flesh like war,
    The.
Constuction.
Contact Lenses.
Conversations in Crisis.
Coping.
Dahomey.
Day they eulogized Mahalia, The.
Dear Joe.
Dear Toni Instead of a Letter of
    Congratulation.
Death Dance for a Poet.
Depreciation.
Diaspora.
Digging.
Do You Remember Laura.
Domino.
Dozens, The.

Dream/Songs from the Moon of Beulah
    Land.
Dreams bite.
East Berlin.
Echo.
Echoes.
Electric Slide Boogie, The.
Equal Opportunity.
Equinox.
Ethiopia.
Eulogy: "Girl in my sister's house, A."
Eulogy for Alvin Frost.
Even.
Evening News, The.
Every Traveler Has One Vermont Poem.
Fallen, The.
Family Resemblance, A.
Fantasy and Conversation.
Father Son and Holy Ghost.
Father the year has fallen.
Father, the Year Is Fallen.
Fishing the White Water.
Florida.
Fog Report.
For Assata.
For Craig.
For Each of You.
For Jose and Regina.
For Judith.
For My Singing Sister.
For the King and Queen of Summer.
For the Record.
From Inside an Empty Purse.
From the Cave.
From the Greenhouse.
From the House of Yemanjá.
Future Promise.
Gemini.
Generation.
Generation II.
Generation III.
Ghost.
Girlfriend.
Good Mirrors are Not Cheap.
Hanging Fire.
Hard Love Rock.
Hard Love Rock #II.
Harriet there was always somebody calling us
    crazy.
Holographs.
Home.
Horse casts a shoe, The.
Hugo I.
I Die for All Mysterious Things.
If You Come Softly.
In Margaret's Garden.
Inheritance—His.
Jessehelms.
Journeystones.
Judith's Fancy.
Keyfoods.
Kitchen Linoleum.
Learning to Write.
Legacy—Hers.
Letter for Jan.
Lightly.
Litany for Survival, A.
Love, Maybe.
Love Poem.
Lover's Song, A.
Lunar Eclipse.
Maiden, The.
Making It.
Making Love to Concrete.
Martha this is a catalog of days.
Mawu.
Meet.
Meeting of Minds, A.
Memorial I.
Memorial II.
Memorial III from a Phone Booth on
    Broadway.
Memorial IV.
Mentor.
Monkeyman.
Movement Song.
Moving In.

Moving Out Or the End of Cooperative
    Living.
My Fifth Trip to Washington Ended in
    Northeast Delaware.
Naming the Stories.
Naturally.
Need: A Chorale for Black Woman Voices.
Neighbors.
Never Take Fire for a Woman.
Never to Dream of Spiders.
New Year's Day.
New York City 1970.
Night-Blooming Jasmine, The.
Nightstone.
NOW.
Now That I Am Forever with Child.
Oaxaca.
October.
Old Days, The.
On a Night of the Full Moon.
On Midsummer's Eve.
On My Way Out I passed You and the
    Varrazano Bridge.
On the Edge.
125th Street and Abomey.
One Who Got Away, The.
One Year to Life on the Grand Central
    Shuttle.
Oshun's Table.
Out of the Wind.
Out to the Hard Road.
Outlines.
Outside.
Oya.
Paperweight.
Parting.
Party Time.
Pathways: From Mother to Mother.
Peace on Earth.
Pirouette.
Poem for a Poet, A.
Poem for Women in Rage, A.
Political Relations.
Politics of Addiction, The.
Portrait.
Power.
Prism.
Production.
Progress Report.
Question of Climate, A.
Question of *Essence*, A.
Recreation.
Reins.
Release Time.
Relevant Is Different Points on the Circle.
Restoration.
Return.
Revolution Is One Form of Social Change.
Rite of Passage.
Rites of Passage.
Rock Thrown into the Water Does Not Fear
    the Cold, A.
Rooming houses are old women.
Sacrifice.
Sahara.
Same Death Over and Over or Lullabies Are
    for Children, The.
Scar.
School Note.
Seasoning.
Second Spring.
Separation.
Sequelae.
Seventh Sign, The.
Sewerplant Grows in Harlem or I'm a
    Stranger Here Myself When Does the Next
    Swan Leave, A.
Signs.
Sister, Morning Is a Time for Miracles.
Sister Outsider.
Sisters in Arms.
Small Slaughter, A.
Smelling Wind.
Soho Cinema.
Solstice.
Song for a Thin Sister.
Song for Many Movements, A.

Song of Names and Faces, A.
Song: "Wild trees have bought me."
Songless Lark, The.
Sowing.
Speechless.
Spring III.
Spring People.
St. Louis Out of Time.
Starting All Over Again.
Stations.
Story Books on a Kitchen Table, *sels.*
Suffer the Children.
Summer Oracle.
Suspension.
Syracuse Airport.
Teacher.
Thanks to Jesse Jackson.
Thaw.
Therapy.
There Are No Honest Poems about Dead
　Women.
This Urn Contains Earth from German
　Concentration Camps.
Timepiece.
Times Change and We Change with Them or
　We Seem to Have Lost Touch with Each
　Other.
Timing.
To a Girl Who Knew What Side Her Bread
　Was Buttered On.
To Desi as Joe as Smoky the Lover of 115th
　Street.
To Marie, in Flight.
To Martha: a New Year.
To My Daughter the Junkie on a Train.
To the Girl Who Lives In a Tree.
To the Poet Who Happens to Be Black and
　the Black Poet Who Happens to Be a
　Woman.
Today Is Not the Day.
Touring.
Trip on the Staten Island Ferry, A.
Trollop Maiden, The.
Vietnam Addenda.
Vigil.
Walking Our Boundaries.
What It Means to Be Beautiful.
What my child learns of the sea.
When the Saints Come Marching In.
Who Said It Was Simple.
Winds of Orisha, The.
Woman.
Woman Speaks, A.
Woman Thing, The.
Woman/Dirge for Wasted Children, A.
Women of Dan Dance with Swords in Their
　Hands to Mark the Time When They Were
　Warriors, The.
Women on Trains.
Wood Has No Mouth.
Workers Rose on May Day or Postscript to
　Karl Marx, The.
Za Ki Tan Ke Parlay Lot.

Love, George (d. 1924?)
　Noonday April Sun, The.
Love, John W., Jr.
　Mocha Regions.
Luciano, Felipe
　You're Nothing but a Spanish Colored Kid.
Lyle, K. Curtis (b.1944)
　Lacrimas or There Is a Need to Scream.
　Sometimes I Go to Camarillo and Sit in the
　　Lounge.
　Songs for the Cisco Kid; or, Singing for the
　　Face.
　Songs for the Cisco Kid; or, Singing: Song
　　#2.
　Your Tears Feel Good on the Hood of My
　　Car.
Lynch, Charles (b. 1943)
　If We Cannot Live People as People.
　Memo.
Lyons, Anthony C.
　Touch Her.

"Lyte, M. C." *See* **Moorer, Lana**

M

Mack, L. V. (b. 1947)
　Biafra.
　Death Songs.
Mackey, Nathaniel (b. 1947)
　Degree Four.
　Dream Thief.
　Falso Brilhante.
　Phantom Light of All Our Day, The.
　Song of the Andoumboulou.
　Winged Abyss.
**Madgett, Naomi Long (Naomi Long
　Witherspoon) (b. 1923)**
　Alabama Centennial.
　Black Woman.
　Brothers at the Bar.
　Deacon Morgan.
　Dream Sequence, Part 9.
　Exits and Entrances.
　First Man.
　Her Story.
　Homage.
　Kin.
　Midway.
　Mortality.
　New Day.
　Nocturne.
　Nomen.
　Offspring.
　Pavlov.
　Phillis.
　Quest.
　Race Question, The.
　Reckoning, The.
　Sally: Twelfth Street.
　Simple.
　Souvenir.
　Star Journey.
　Sunny.
　Trinity: a Dream Sequence, *sels.*
　Twenty Grand (Saturday Night on the Block),
　　The.
　Woman with Flower.
Madhubuti, Haki R. (Don. L. Lee) (b. 1942)
　After Her Man Had Left Her for the Sixth
　　Time That Year / (An Uncommon
　　Occurrence).
　Afterword: For Gwen Brooks, An.
　America calling.
　Assassination.
　Awareness.
　Back Again, Home.
　Big Momma.
　Black Christ, The.
　Black Manhood: Toward a Definition.
　Blackmusic / a Beginning.
　Blackwoman.
　Bonding, A.
　But He Was Cool.
　Change Is Not Always Progress.
　Change-up.
　Communication in Whi-te.
　Cure All, The.
　Death Dance, The.
　Don't Cry, Scream.
　Education.
　First World.
　For Black People.
　Gwendolyn Brooks Elizabeth.
　In a Period of Growth.
　In the Interest of Black Salvation.
　Killing Memory.
　Loneliness, A.
　Long Reality, The.
　Magnificent Tomorrows.
　Malcolm Spoke / Who Listened?
　Message All Black People Can Dig, A.
　Mixed Sketches.
　Move Un-noticed to Be Noticed: a
　　Nationhood Poem.
　New Integrationist, The.
　Mwilu / or Poem for the Living.
　On Seeing Diana Go Maddddddddd.

Pains with a Light Touch.
Poem for a Poet, A.
Poem Looking for a Reader, A.
Poem to Complement Other Poems, A.
Poet: What Ever Happened to Luther?
Positives for Sterling Plumpp.
Possibilities: Remembering Malcolm X.
Primitive, The.
Re-act for Action.
Reflections on a Lost Love.
Revolutionary Screw, The.
Self-Hatred of Don L. Lee, The.
Stereo.
Sun House.
To Be Quicker.
Two Poems (from "Sketches from a Black
　Nappy-Headed Poet"), *sels.*
Union of Two, The.
Wake-up Niggers.
Wall, The.
We Walk the Way of the New World.
With All Deliberate Speed.
Womenblack: We Begin with You.
Mahone, Barbara (b. 1944)
　Colors for Mama.
　Poem for Positive Thinkers, A.
　Sugarfields.
Major, Clarence (b. 1936)
　Apple Core.
　Blind Old Woman.
　Celebrated Return.
　Cotton Club, The.
　Design, The.
　Down Wind against the Highest Peaks.
　Giant Red Woman.
　I Was Looking for the University.
　In the Interest of Personal Appearance.
　Large Room with Wood Floor.
　On Trying to Imagine the Kiwi Pregnant.
　On Watching a Caterpillar Become a
　　Butterfly.
　Round Midnight.
　Self World.
　Swallow the Lake.
　Vietnam.
　Vietnam #4.
Major, Joseph (b. 1948)
　Poem for Thel—the Very Tops of Trees.
Margetson, George Reginald (b. 1877)
　Fledgling Bard and the Poetry Society, The.
Marie, Sonja
　Dream Fix.
Maroon, Bahiyyih (1968–92)
　Fire Keeper.
　Neighbor.
　Nude Woman Spotted in Cappuccino Cup as
　　Advertising Dollar Co-Opts Another Life.
Marshall, Marjorie
　Autumn.
　Desire.
　Night's Protégé.
　Nostalgia.
　To a Dark Dancer.
Martin, Herbert (b. 1933)
　Antigone I.
　Antigone VI.
　Lines: "Singularly and in pairs the decade
　　has been ripped by bullets."
　Negro Soldier's Viet Nam Diary, A.
Mason, Keith Antar
　Friday night / the bullet ripped.
Matheus, John Frederick (1887–1983)
　Requiem: "She wears, my beloved, a rose
　　upon her head."
Matthews, Dorothea
　Lynching, The.
Mayle, Bessie
　Night is like an avalanche.
　Skylines / Are marking me in today.
McCall, James Edward (b. 1880)
　New Negro, The.
McClane, Kenneth A.
　Black Intellectual, The.
　Jazz.
　Song: a Motion for History.

To Hear the River.
McClaurin, Irma (b. 1945)
I, Woman.
Mask, The.
To a Gone Era.
McClellan, George Marion (b. 1860)
April of Alabama, The.
Butterfly in Church, A.
Color Bane, The.
Daybreak.
Dogwood Blossoms.
Eternity.
Feet of Judas, The.
Hills of Sewanee, The.
Hydromel and Rue.
In the Heart of a Rose.
January Dandelion, A.
Legend of Tannhauser and Elizabeth, The, *sels.*
Lines to Mount Glen.
Love is a flame that burns with sacred fire.
September Night, A.
Sun went down in beauty, The.
To Theodore.
McElroy, Colleen J. (b. 1935)
Caledonia.
Cutting a Road from Manaus to Belém.
Ghost-Who-Walks, The.
Griots Who Know Brer Fox, The.
Horoscope.
In My Mother's Room.
Learning to Swim at Forty-Five.
Looking for a Country under Its Original Name.
Pike Street Bus.
Ruth.
Tapestries.
Under the Oak Table.
While Poets Are Watching.
Why Tu Fu Does Not Speak of the Nubian.
Woman's Song, A.
McGaugh, Lawrence (b. 1940)
To Children.
Two Mornings.
Young Training.
McGirt, James Ephriam (1874–1930)
Born like the pines to sing.
Century Prayer, The.
Memory of Lincoln and the Yankees.
My Song.
Nothing to Do.
Tell me, oh fate, is it decreed.
When de Sun Shines Hot.
McKay, Claude (1889–1948)
Absence.
Adolescence.
Africa.
After the Winter.
Alfonso, Dressing to Wait at Table.
America.
Baptism.
Barcelona.
Barrier, The.
Castaways, The.
City's Love, The.
Commemoration.
Courage.
Dawn in New York.
December, 1919.
Desolate.
Easter Flower, The.
Enslaved.
Exhortation: Summer, 1919.
Farewell to Morocco, A.
Flame-Heart.
Flirtation.
Flower of Love.
French Leave.
Futility.
Harlem Dancer, The.
Harlem Shadows.
Heritage.
Home Thoughts.
Homing Swallows.
I Know My Soul.
I shall return again. I shall return.
If we must die—let it not be like hogs.

In Bondage.
Jasmine.
Like a strong tree that in the virgin earth.
Look Within.
Lynching, The.
Memorial.
Memory of June, A.
Morning Joy.
Moscow for many loving her was dead.
My House.
My Mother.
Negro's Friend, The.
Negro's Tragedy, The.
North and South.
O word I love to sing! thou art too tender.
On Broadway.
On the Road.
One Year After.
Outcast.
Pagan Isms, The.
Plateau, The.
Polarity.
Prayer, A: "'Mid the discordant noises of the day I hear thee calling."
Red Flower, A.
Rest in Peace.
Romance.
St. Isaac's Church, Petrograd.
Snow Fairy, The.
Song of the Moon, A.
Spanish Needle, The.
Spring in New Hampshire.
Subway Wind.
Sukee River.
Summer Morn in New Hampshire.
Tetuan.
Thirst.
Through Agony.
Tiger.
Tired Worker, The.
To O.E.A.
To One Coming North.
To the White Fiends.
To Winter.
Tormented.
Tropics in New York, The.
Truth.
Two-an'-Six.
When Dawn Comes to the City.
White City, The.
White House, The.
Wild Goat, The.
Wild May.
Winter in the Country.
Wise Men of the East, The.
Medina, Tony (b. 1966)
After the Verdict.
Big House Revisited, The.
Capitalism Is a Brutal Motherfucker.
Menard, John Willis (1838–93)
Good-bye! Off for Kansas.
Negro's Lament, A.
To My Wife.
Menken, Adah Isaacs (1839?–1868)
Adelina Patti.
Answer Me.
Aspiration.
Autograph on the Soul, The.
Battle of the Stars.
Dreams of Beauty.
Drifts That Bar My Door.
Dying.
Fragment: "Cold chain of life presseth heavily on me tonight, The."
Genius is power.
Hear, O Israel! and plead my cause against the ungodly nation.
Hemlock in the Furrows.
In Vain.
Infelicia, *sels.*
Infelix.
Into the Depths.
Judith.
Karazah to Karl.
Memory, A.
Miserimus.
"My heritage!" It is to live within.

Myself.
One Year Ago.
Pro Patria—America, 1861.
Release, The.
Resurgam.
Sale of Souls.
Saved.
Ship That Went Down, The.
Venetia.
Where the Flocks Shall Be Led.
Working and Waiting.
Miller, Adam David (b. 1922)
Africa Thing, The.
Crack in the Wall Holds Flowers.
Hungry Black Child, The.
Mulch.
Pruning, The.
Miller, E. Ethelbert (b. 1950)
Boys of Summer, The.
Grenada.
Jasmine.
Mississippi.
Moses.
Mountain Wife.
My Father's Girlfriend.
Night Before the First Day of School, The.
Players.
She is flat on her back.
Spanish Conversation.
Sweet Honey in the Rock.
Walk in the Daytime Is Just as Dangerous as a Walk in the Night, A.
What the Women Told Me.
You Send Me: Bertha Franklin, December 11, 1964.
Miller, May (b. 1918)
Calvary Way.
Gift from Kenya.
Not That Far.
Scream, The.
Where Is the Guilt.
Wrong Side of the Morning, The.
Mitchell, Karen L. (b. 1955)
Monster, The.
Night Rain.
On the Anniversary Of Your Death.
Tree Stillness.
Mkalimoto, Ernie
Energy for a New Thang.
Moore, Lenard D. (b. 1958)
Again.
Eternal Landscape, The.
From the Field.
Gifts.
Haiku: "Black woman, A."
Haiku: "Cloudless summer day."
Haiku: "Family reunion."
Haiku: "Sipping the new tea."
Haiku: "Spring moonrise."
Haiku: "Summer evening sun."
Haiku: "Winter stillness."
Homeplace, The.
Indian Girl.
Message to Etheridge Knight.
Pathway: From Son to Father.
Poem for Langston Hughes, A.
Song Poem, The.
Tanka: "After church meeting."
Tanka: "Month of rain ends."
Moore, Lynn G.
Haiku: "Morning fog / my daughter dropped off at camp."
Moore, Maiisha L.
Haiku: "Dark rock-road, The."
Moore, William H. A.
Dusk Song.
It Was Not Fate.
Moorer, Lana ("M. C. Lyte")
Everyday I need my shit done in a special way.
Moorer, Lizelia Augusta Jenkins
Accompanying a Gift ("From thy patient, who while here.")
Accompanying a Gift ("One whose love will never end.")
Africa.

Benefits of Sorrow.
Bible, The.
Birthday Wishes to a Husband.
Birthday Wishes to a Minister of the Gospel.
Birthday Wishes to a Physician.
Christmas Eve.
Christmas Tree, The.
Circle, The.
Claflin's Alumni.
Crum Appointment, The.
Dedication Day Poem.
Dialogue, A.
Door of Hope, The.
Duty, or Truth at Work.
Easter; or, Spring-Time.
Emancipation Day.
Eutawville Lynching, The.
Hallowe'en.
Immortality.
In Memoriam of E. B. Clark.
Injustice of the Courts.
Jim Crow Cars.
Legal Mouse, A.
Lela's Charms.
Lines to a Graduate.
Loyalty to the Flag.
Lynching.
Misunderstood.
Mountain Tops.
Must Be Freed.
Negro Ballot, The.
Negro Heroines.
Negro Schools, The.
Notable Dinner, A.
Peonage System, The.
Pharaohs of Today, The.
Prejudice.
Presidents, The.
Price of Disrespect, The.
Refining Fire.
Retribution.
Russia's Resentment.
Social Glass, The.
Social Life, The.
Song of the Angels.
Southern Press, The.
Southern Pulpit, The.
Southern Work of Dr. and Mrs. L. M. Dunton.
Sympathy.
Thanksgiving.
Tree of Knowledge, The.
Truth Suppressed, The.
Voice of the Negro, The.
What We Teach at Claflin.
Whisper Words of Love to Me.
Why Is It?
Why Negroes Don't Unite.
Why We Meet.
Moreland, Wayne (b. 1948)
Sunday Morning.
Morganfield, McKinley. See **Waters, Muddy**
Mosley, Joseph M., Jr.
Black Church on Sunday.
Moss, Thylias (b. 1954)
Anointing, An.
Fisher Street.
Jack Johnson Does the Eagle Rock.
Landscape with Saxophonist.
Lessons from a Mirror.
Lynching, The.
Owl In Daytime, The.
Raising a Humid Flag.
Reconsideration of the Blackbird, A.
Tornados.
Undertaker's Daughter Feels Neglect, The.
Mullen, Harryette
Bête Noire.
Floorwax Mother.
Momma Sayings.
Pineapple is armored flower.
Murphy, Merilene M.
Fat Grass and Slow Rain.
Murray, Pauli (b. 1910)
Conquest.
Dark Testament.
Death of a Friend.

For Mack C. Parker.
Harlem Riot, 1943.
Inquietude.
Mr. Roosevelt Regrets.
Redemption.
Returning Spring.
Song: "Because I know deep in my own heart."
Without Name.
"Mustafa." See **Johnson, Don Allen**
Myles, Glenn (b. 1933)
Percy / 68.

N

"Nayo." See **Watkins, Nayo-Barbara**
Neal, Gaston
Personal Jihad.
Today.
Neal, Larry (b. 1937)
Baroness and the Black Musician, The.
Don't say goodbye to the Porkpie Hat that rolled.
For Our Women.
Harlem Gallery: From the Inside.
James Powell on Imagination.
Lady's Days.
Malcolm X—an Autobiography.
Middle Passage and After, The.
Morning Raga for Malcolm.
Narrative of Black Magicians, The.
Orishas.
Poppa Stoppa Speaks from His Grave.
Neely, Letta Simone-Nefertari
Rhonda, Age 15 Emergency Room.
Nelson, Marilyn (b. 1946)
Abba Jacob and Miracles.
Abba Jacob and St. Francis.
Abba Jacob and the Angel.
Abba Jacob and the Businessman.
Abba Jacob and the Theologian.
Abba Jacob at Bat.
Abba Jacob Gets Down.
Abba Jacob in the Well.
Abba Jacob's Aside on Hell.
Abba Jacob's Seven Devils.
Aches and Pains.
Ape-Gods.
April Rape.
Armed Men.
As Simple as That.
At Prayer.
Aunt Annie's Prayer.
Balance.
Bali Hai Calls Mama.
Ballad of Aunt Geneva, The.
Beauty Shoppe.
Blessing the Boats.
Boys in the Park.
Canticle for Abba Jacob, A.
Century Quilt, The.
Chopin.
Chosen.
Churchgoing.
Clown Nose.
Confessional Poem.
Cover Photograph.
Dangerous Carnival, The.
Daughters, 1900.
Dinosaur Spring.
Diverne's House.
Diverne's Waltz.
Don't Throw Out Wine Bottles.
Dream's Wisdom, The.
Dusting.
Emily Dickinson's Defunct.
Epithalamium and Shivaree.
Fish and Floor-Dust Bouquet.
For Mary, Fourth Month.
Fortunate Spill, The.
Freeman Field.
Fruit of Faith, The.
High and Haughty.
House on Moscow Street, The.
How I Discovered Poetry.

Hurrah, Hurrah.
I am you again.
I Decide Not to Have Children.
I Dream the Book of Jonah, sels.
I imagine driving across country.
I Knew That.
I Send Mama Home.
Impala.
Is She Okay?
It's All in Your Head.
Juneteenth.
La Peste.
Laughter as the Highest Form of Contemplation.
Leaving the Hospice.
Letter to a Benedictine Monk.
Levitation with Baby.
Life of a Saint, The, sels.
Light under the Door.
Like Father, Like Son.
Lonely Eagles.
Lost Daughter, The.
Lovesong.
Mama I remember.
Mama's Murders.
Mama's Promise.
Marriage Nightmare, The.
May Your Love Convert Lucifer.
Memento.
Men in the Kitchen.
Minor Miracle.
My Grandfather Walks in the Woods.
My Second Birth.
No No, Bad Daddy.
No Worst.
Photographs of the Medusa.
Plotinus Suite, The, sels.
Porter.
Post-Prandial Conversation.
Prayer of Silence, The.
Propositions.
Psalm: "So many cars have driven past me."
Recurrent Dream.
Sacrament of Poverty, The.
Simple Wisdom, The.
Sisters.
Star-Fix.
Strange beautiful woman, A.
Three Men in a Tent.
Thus Far by Faith, sels.
To Market.
Tuskegee Airfield.
Twist the thread.
War of the Heart, The.
Wild Pansies.
Woman Kills and Eats Own Infant.
Women's Locker Room.
Nettles, Saundra Murray
War Stories.
Newsome, Mary Effie Lee (1885–1979)
Baker's boy delivers loaves, The.
Bird in the Cage, The.
Bronze Legacy, The.
Exodus.
Mattinata.
Memory.
Morning Light.
Pansy.
Quilt, The.
Quoits.
Sassafras Tea.
Sky Pictures.
Wild Roses.
Nicholas, Michael (b. 1941)
Today: The Idea Market.
Nixon, Art
Ju-Ju Man.
Nuriddin, Jalaluddin Mansur (b. 1944)
Children of the Future.
Nurigan, V. Kali
I'm raising CHILDREN.

O

Odaro
Alafia.

Oden, Gloria C. (b. 1923)
"As When Emotion Too Far Exceeds Its Cause."
Bible Study.
Carousel, The.
Man White, Brown Girl and All That Jazz.
Map, The.
Private Letter to Brazil, A.
Review from Staten Island.
Riven Quarry, The.
Testament of Loss.
This Child Is the Mother.

Ogilvie, D. T.
Last Letter to the Western Civilization.

O'Higgins, Myron (b. 1918)
Sunset Horn.
Two Lean Cats.
Vaticide.
Young Poet.

"Ojenke" (Alvin Saxon)
Amazon.
Black Power.
Poem for Integration.
Watts.

Oktavi
Pardon Me.

Ologboni, Tejumola ("Rockie D. Taylor") (b. 1945)
Black Henry.
Changed Mind (or the Day I Woke Up).
I Wonta Thank Ya.

"Olumo." See Cunningham, James

O'Neal, John
Shades of Pharoah Sanders Blues for My Baby.

O'Neal, Shaquille
Biological Didn't Bother.

Oyewole, Abiodun
Future Shock.
When the revolution comes.

P

Parker, Dominique
Art of the Nickname, The.
Foxfire.
Sand.
When Mark Deloach Ruled the World.

Parker, Patricia (b. 1944)
From the Cavities of Bones.
I Followed a Path.
There Is a Woman in This Town.

Patterson, Charles (b. 1935)
Listen.

Patterson, Raymond R. (b. 1929)
At That Moment.
Birmingham 1963.
Black All Day.
Black Power.
In Time of Crisis.
I've Got a Home in That Rock.
Letter in Winter.
Night-Piece.
Schwerner, Chaney, Goodman.
Song Waiting for Music, A.
This Age.
To a Weathercock.
Twenty-Six Ways of Looking at a Blackman.
What We Know.
When I Awoke.
"Word to the Wise Is Enough, A."

Payne, Daniel Alexander (1811–93)
May I not love the beauteous flow'rs.
Mournful Lute or the Preceptor's Farewell, The.
Pleasures, The, sels.

Penny, Rob (b. 1940)
And We Conquered.
Be Cool, Baby.
I Remember How She Sang.
Real People Loves One Another, The.

Perry, Julianne (b. 1952)
No Dawns.
To L.

Pfister, Arthur
Granny Blak Poet (in Pastel).

Phillips, Carl (b. 1959)
Reach, The.
Sunday.
You Are Here.

Phillips, Frank Lamont (b. 1923)
Genealogy.
Maryuma.
No Smiles.

Piper, Linda (b. 1949)
Missionaries in the Jungle.
Sweet Ethel.

Pitcher, Oliver (b. 1923)
Pale Blue Casket, The.
Raison d'Etre.
Salute.

Plato, Ann (fl. 1841)
Advice to Young Ladies.
Forget Me Not.
Natives of America, The.
Reflections, Written on Visiting the Grave of a Venerated Friend.
To the First of August.

Plumpp, Sterling (b. 1940)
Another mule kicking.
Beyond the Nigger.
Black Ethics.
Half Black, Half Blacker.
I Told Jesus.
Living Truth, The.
Mississippi Griot.
Poems are not places.
Remembered.
Sanders Bottom.
Speech.
Turf Song.
Zimbabwe.

"Poet X." See Williams, Marlon C.

Poetri
Don't hate me cause my skin is smooth like fine lustrous fiber forming a tuft.

Polite, Allen
Am Driven Mad.
Stopped.

Pompili [or Pompilj], Vittoria Aganoor (1855–1910)
October.

Poole, Tom (b. 1938)
I wonder why.

Popel, Esther
Night comes walking out our way.
Theft.

Powell, Kevin
Out of Pocket.

Preston, Rohan B.
Lovesong to My Father.

Prettyman, Quandra (b. 1933)
Mood, The.
Photograph.
Still Life: Lady with Birds.
When Mahalia Sings.

Priestley, Eric
Eye and eye.

Prince, Lucy Terry (Lucy Terry) (1730–1821)
Bar[']s Fight[, August 28, 1746].

Pritchard, Norman Henry, II
Aswelay.
Burnt Sienna.
Cassandra and Friend.
Cloak, The.
Gyre's Galax.
Landscape with Nymphs and Satyrs.
Love Poem.
Metagnomy.
Narrow Path, The.
Paysagesque.
Self.
Signs, The.
Springtime.

Public Enemy (fl. 1986)
Don't believe the hype.
Fight the Power.

Pushkin, Aleksandr Sergeyevich (1799–1851)
I Loved You Once.

Q

Queen Latifah
Evil That Men Do, The.
U.N.I.T.Y.

Quigless, Helen G. (b. 1944)
Concert.
Evening.
Moving.

R

Rahman, Yusef
Transcendental Blues Transcendental Blues.

Rainey, Gertrude ("Ma") (1886–1939)
Prove It on Me Blues.
See See Rider, see what you done done!

Randall, Dudley (b. 1914)
Abu / 's a stone black revolutionary.
Analysands.
Ancestors.
Ballad of Birmingham.
Black Poet, White Critic.
Blackberry Sweet.
Booker T. and W. E. B.
Coral Atoll.
Different Image, A.
George.
Green Apples.
Hail, Dionysos.
Idiot, The.
Intellectuals, The.
Langston Blues.
Legacy: My South.
Melting Pot, The.
Memorial Wreath.
Old Witherington.
On Getting a Natural.
Perspectives.
Primitives.
Profile on the Pillow, The.
Rite, The.
Roses and Revolutions.
Southern Road, The.
Souvenirs.

Randall, James A., Jr. (b. 1938)
Don't Ask Me Who I Am.
Execution.
Jew.
When Something Happens.
Who Shall Die.
Why should I be eaten by love.

Rankine, Claudia
Eden.
Man. His Bowl. His Raspberries, The.
New Windows.

Raphael, Lennox (b. 1940)
Infants of Summer.
Mike 65.

Rashidd, Amir (b. 1943)
Eclipse.

Rashidd, Niema
Warriors Prancing, Women Dancing.

Raven, John (b. 1936)
Assailant.
Inconvenience, An.
Roach / came struttin, A.

Ray, Henrietta Cordelia (1861?–1916)
After the Storm.
Afterglow, The.
Ambition.
Among the Berkshire Hills.
Anita and Giovanni.
Antigone and Oedipus.
April.
Aspiration.
At Christmas-Tide.
At Nature's Shrine.
At Sunset.
At the Cascade.
August.
Awakening.
Beethoven.
Boat Song.

Broken Heart.
Charity.
Charles Sumner.
Chateaux en Espagne.
Cloud Fantasy.
Cloud Song.
Coming of Spring, The.
Compensation.
Cuckoo Song.
Dante.
Dawn of Love, The.
Dawn's Carol.
December.
Dream of Elfland, A.
Dream within a Song, A.
Easter Carol.
Echo Reverie.
Echo's Complaint.
Emerson.
Enchanted Shell, The.
Evening Prayer.
Fading Skiff, The.
Failure.
Fancy and Imagination.
February.
Fisherman's Story, The.
Fragment, A: "Our fancies are but joys all
    unexprest."
Full Vision.
God's Ways, Not Our Ways.
Greeting.
Hermit and the Soul, The.
Hidden Essence.
Hour's Glory, The.
Hymn to the Thousand Islands.
Ideal, An.
Idyl, *sels.*
Idyl of Spring, An.
In Memoriam Frederick Douglass.
In Memoriam Paul Laurence Dunbar.
Incompleteness.
Instability.
Invocation to the Muse.
January.
July.
June.
Life.
Life's Boundary.
Limitations.
Lincoln.
Lines Written on a Farewell View of the
    Franconia Mountains at Twilight.
Listening Nydia.
Little Fay's Thanksgiving.
Longfellow.
Lost Opportunities.
Love's Vista.
Maid of Ehrenthal, The.
March.
May.
May's Invocation after a Tardy Spring.
Messengers, The.
Mignon.
Mildred's Doves.
Milton.
Mist Maiden, The.
Musidora's Vision.
My Easter Dove.
My Spirit's Complement.
Nature's Minor Chords.
Nature's Uplifting.
Niobe.
November.
O Restless Heart, Be Still!
Ocean Musing, An.
October.
Ode on the Twentieth Century.
On a Nook Called Fairyland.
On the Concord River.
On the Picture of a Child.
On the rapids of the St. Lawrence.
Our Task.
Pastoral: "Annette came through the
    meadows."
Perfect Orchestra, The.
Picture, A.
Poet's Ideal, The.

Poet's Ministrants, The.
Prayer: "O Christ, who in Gethsemane."
Quebec.
Quest of the Ideal, The.
Questioning.
Raphael.
Recompensed?
Repose.
Retrospection.
Reunited.
Reverie.
Rhyme of the Antique Forest.
Robert G. Shaw.
Sculptor's Vision, The.
Sea Cadences.
Self-Mastery.
September.
Shadow and Sunrise.
Shakespeare.
Siren Bird, The.
Sky Picture.
Snow Song.
Song: "O sweet, sad, singing river."
Soul Incense.
Soul's Courts, The.
Star Song.
Sunset Picture.
Thought at Walden, A.
Thought of Lake Ontario, A.
Tireles Sculptor, The.
To Laura.
To My Father.
To My Mother.
Toussaint L'Ouverture.
Triple Benison, The.
Two Musicians, The.
Venus of Milo, The.
Verses to my Heart's-Sister.
Vision of Eve, The.
Vision of Moonlight, A.
Voices of the Rain.
Wendell Phillips.
William Lloyd Garrison.
Wood Carols.

Razaf, Andy. *See* **Waller, Thomas ("Fats"),**
    Andy Razaf, *and* **Harry Brooks**

Reason, Charles Lewis (1818–93)
    Spirit Voice, The; or Liberty Call to the
      Disfranchised (State of New York).

Redmond, Eugene B. (b. 1937)
    Aerolingual Poet of Prey.
    Autumn God.
    Cane-Brake-Blues.
    Definition of Nature.
    Gods in Vietnam.
    Gwensways.
    His Eminence Plays the Soular System.
    Milestone: The Birth of an Ancestor.
    Parapoetics.
    Spearo's Blues (or: Ode to a Grecian Yearn).

Reed, Clarence
    Harlem '67.
    In a Harlem Store Front Church.
    Invaders, The.
    My Brother and Me.

Reed, Ishmael (b. 1938)
    Al Capone in Alaska.
    American Airlines Sutra.
    And the Devil Sent a Ford Pinto Which She
      Also Routed.
    Anon. Poster.
    Antigone, This Is It.
    Atlantic Monthly, December 1970, The.
    Author Reflects on His 35th Birthday, The.
    Back to Africa.
    Back to Back: 3rd Eye.
    Badman of the Guest Professor.
    Ballad of Charlie James, The.
    Betty's Ball Blues.
    Beware: Do Not Read This Poem.
    Bitch.
    Bitter Chocolate.
    Black Cock, The.
    Black Power Poem.
    But Nobody Was There.
    Catechism of d Neoamerican Hoodoo Church.
    Chattanooga.

Columbia.
Crocodiles.
Cuckoo is a funny bird, A.
Datsun's Death.
Decade That Screamed, The.
Dialog outside the Lakeside Grocery.
Dragon's Blood.
Dress Rehearsal Paranoia #2.
Dualism in Ralph Ellison's Invisible Man.
Earthquake Blues.
El Paso Monologue.
Epistolary Monologue.
Feral Pioneers, The.
.05.
Foolology.
For Cardinal Spellman Who Hated Voo Doo.
For Dancer.
From the Files of Agent 22.
Gangster Goes Legit.
Gangster's Death, The.
General Science.
Ghost in Birmingham, The.
Grizzly.
Guilty, the New York Philharmonic Signs up
    a Whale.
Haitians.
Home Sweet Earth.
Hoodoo Poem in Transient.
I Am a Cowboy in the Boat of Ra.
I am not the walrus.
Ice Age.
If My Enemy Is a Clown, a Natural Born
    Clown.
I'm running for the office of love.
Inaugural Day, 1981.
Inside Track, The.
Instructions to a Princess.
Introducing a New Loa.
Invasion.
Jackal-Headed Cowboy, The.
Jacket Notes.
Judas.
July 1st, 1982.
Kali's Galaxy.
Kardek Method, The.
Katskills Kiss Romance Goodbye, The.
Lake Bud.
Last Week in 30, The.
Life is a screwball comedy.
Loup Garou Means Change Into.
Man or Butterfly.
Martine's Keen Eyes.
Middle Class Blues, The.
Mojo Queen of the Feathery Plumes.
Monkey Island.
Monsters from the Ozarks.
Mossy.
My Brothers.
My Thing abt Cats.
Mystery 1st Lady.
Neo-HooDoo Aesthetic, The.
Neo-HooDoo Manifesto.
Nov 22, 1988.
Oakland Blues.
Off d Pig.
On the Fourth of July in Sitka, 1982.
Paul Laurence Dunbar in the Tenderloin.
Petite Kid Everett.
Phoebe is the 9th satellite.
Piping Down of God, The.
Pocadonia.
Poem Delivered Before Assembly of Colored
    People Held at Glide Memorial Church,
    Oct. 4, 1973 and Called to Protest Recent
    Events in the Sovereign Republic of Chile.
Poem for Two Daughters.
Poetry Makes Rhythm in Philosophy.
Points of View.
Poison Light.
Pope Replies to the Ayatollah Khomeini,
    The.
Railroad Bill, a conjure man.
Rain Rain on the Splintered Girl.
Reactionary Poet, The.
Report of the Reed Commission.
Return of Julian the Apostate to Rome, The.
Rock Me, Baby.

Rough Trade Slumlord Totem.
Sather Tower Mystery.
Secretary to the Spirits, A.
Sermonette.
Sixth Street Corporate War.
Skirt Dance.
Sky Diving.
Slaveship, German Model.
Smiley School, The.
Soul Proprietorship.
Sputin.
St. Louis Woman.
Swift, Tiny and Fine.
Tea Dancer Turns Thirty-Nine.
There's a whale in my thigh. at.
This Poetry Anthology I'm Reading.
To a Daughter of Isaiah.
Treatment for Dance w/ Trick Ending.
Turning Pro.
Untitled: "Alaska's rape."
Untitled: "I know of a man who treated his
    body like a dog."
Untitled: "Law isn't all."
Untitled: "Today I feel bearish."
Untitled: "When California is split in two."
Untitled I.
Untitled II.
Untitled III.
Untitled IV.
Vachel Lindsay Fault, The.
Vamp.
Visit to a Small College.
Wardrobe Master of Paradise, The.
What You Mean I Can't Irony?
White Hope.
Why I Often Allude to Osiris.

Reese, S. Carolyn
Letter from a Wife.

Renegade, DJ
Haiku: "Jazz is / the way brown sugar."
Hoodoo.

Reynolds, Samuel F. (b. 1967)
Moon/Light Quarter/Back Sack.
Open Letter to All Black Poets, An.
Whipping, The.

Rice, Albert (b. 1903)
Black Madonna, The.

Ridhiana
Tricked Again.

Rilke, Rainer Maria (1875–1926)
Rilke's Third Elegy.

Rivera, El
Elegy for a Martyred Poet.

Rivers, Conrad Kent (1933–68)
Death of a Negro Poet, The.
Four Sheets to the Wind and a One-Way
    Ticket to France.
If Blood is Black Then Spirit Neglects My
    Unborn Son.
In Defense of Black Poets.
Invisible Man, The.
Mourning Letter from Paris, A.
On Passing Two Negroes on a Dark Country
    Road Somewhere in Georgia.
On the Death of William Edward Burghardt
    Du Bois by African Moonlight and
    Forgotten Shores.
Prelude: "Night and the hood."
Still Voice of Harlem, The.
Subway, The.
To Richard Wright.
Train Runs Late to Harlem, The.
Watts.

Roberson, Ed (b. 1939)
Blue Horses.
Eclipse.
Four Lines of a Black Love Letter Between
    Teachers.
If the Black Frog Will Not Ring.
Mayday.
Othello Jones Dresses for Dinner.
Poll.
Poor Houses, The.
Seventh Son.
Sonnet.
True we are two grown men.

Rodgers, Carolyn M. (b. 1942)
And When the Revloution Came.
And While We Are Waiting.
Breakthrough.
Brief Synopsis, A.
Feminism.
For H. W. Fuller.
For Sistuhs Wearin' Straight Hair.
How I Got Ovah.
"In This House, There Shall Be No Idols."
It Is Deep.
Jazz.
Jesus Was Crucified or: It Must Be Deep.
Look at My Face, a Collage.
Masquerade.
Me, in Kulu Se and Karma.
Missing Beat.
Newark, for Now (68).
Now Ain't That Love?
One.
Phoenix.
Poem for Some Black Women.
Poem/Ditty-Bop.
Proclamation / From Sleep, Arise.
Rebolushinary X-mas.
Remember Times for Sandy.
Setting / Slow Drag.
Somebody Call.
Testimony.
U Name This One.
Voodoo on the Un-Assing of Janis Joplin.
We Dance Like Ella Riffs.
What Color Is Lonely.
Yuh Lookin Good.

Rogers, Alex (1876–1930)
Rain Song, The.
Why Adam Sinned.

Rogers, Elymas Payson (1815–61)
On the Fugitve Slave Law, sels.
Poem on the Fugitive Slave Law, A.

"Roland Poet X" (Roland Hayes Porter, Jr.)
Divided States of America, The.

Rowe, George Clinton (1853–1903)
God Speed.
Mrs. Francis Ellen Harper.
Reason Why, The.
We Are Rising.

Roy, Lucinda
Bread Man, The.
Ride, The.
Suffering The Sea Change: All My Pretty
    Ones.
Triple Overtime.

Rushing, Jimmy (1903–1972)
Good Morning, Blues.
Sent for You Yesterday.

**Rutherford, Tony. See Hasson, Umar Abd
Rahim**

Rux, Carl Hancock (b. 1967)
Pledge of Allegiance.
Suite Repose.

Rykard, Richard (b. 1964)
Whole Two Weeks After the Million Man
    March; and Still, if You Asked Me about
    It, This Is All I Could Say about It, A.

S

St. John, Primus (b. 1939)
Benign Neglect / Mississippi, 1970.
Carnival.
Elephant Rock.
Lynching and Burning.
Morning Star, The.
Ocean of the Streams of Story.
Pearle's Poem.
Song.
Tyson's Corner.
We Are Going to Be Here Now.

Salaam, Kalamu ya (b. 1947)
Always Know.
Bush Mama.
Danny Barker/Danny Banjo.
"5 Minutes, Mr. Salam."

I Just Heard John Buffington Died.
I live in the mouth of history.
Iron Flowers.
New Orleans Haiku, sels.
Soon One Morning, I'll Fly Away.
Still Life, Stealing Life / Caught Red-
    Handed.
We have been seen.

Sanchez, Sonia (b. 1935)
And the joy. feeling.
Answer to Yo / Question.
Arabs / ain't got no, The.
At the center of.
Autumn. a bonfire.
Away from you these.
Baby. you are sweet.
Ballad for Stirling Street, A.
Bear the rhythm of.
Before i travel.
Black Magic.
Blk/Rhetoric.
Blues.
Catch the Fire.
Cause we are carving.
Chant for Young/Brothas and Sistuhs, A.
Definition for Blk/Children.
Depression.
Don't go. if you go.
Earth eyes. breathing me.
Elegy: "Philadelphia / a disguised southern
    city."
Elegy (for MOVE and Philadelphia).
Familiarize your.
Father and Daughter.
For Our Lady.
Haiku: "Did ya ever cry."
Haiku: "I am now in the."
Haiku: "I saw you today."
Haiku: "If i had known, if."
Haiku: "O i am so sad, i."
Haiku: "O i was wide and."
Haiku: "Was it yesterday."
His voice used to sing.
Homecoming.
Hospital/Poem.
How can you comfort.
I am on top of.
I am settling down.
I guess. this is what.
I have looked into.
I have walked a long time.
I kneel down like a.
I lean back and feel.
I listen for yo.
I paraplegic.
I wish it were mid.
I'm in the middle.
Indianapolis/Summer/1969/Poem.
July.
Just the two of us.
Just you. just me. must.
Kwa Mama Zetu Waliotuzaa.
Last Poem I'm Gonna Write Bout Us.
Let me be your flute.
Let us begin the real work.
Liberation / Poem.
Life / Poem.
Like bigger thomas.
Listenen to Big Black at S. F. State.
Love Poem Written for Sterling Brown, A.
Love. you are. you are.
Magic.
Malcolm.
Man, i am trying.
Memorial.
Missing you is like.
Morning snow falling.
My body waiting.
Needed/Poem/ for My Salvation, A.
Never may my thirst.
Nigger.
Night pumping like an.
Now Poem. For Us.
Old Words.
On Watching a World Series Game.
Once i was chaste with.
Our bodies made rain.

Past, *sels.*
Personal Letter No. 2.
Personal Letter No. 3.
Philadelphia: Spring, 1985.
Poem at Thirty.
Poem for Etheridge.
Poem for July 4, 1994.
Poem for My Father, A.
Poem for Sterling Brown, A.
Poem: "Look at me 8th / grade."
Poem No. 3.
Poem No. 4.
Poem No. 7.
Poem No. 8.
Poem No. 10.
Poem of Praise, A.
Prelude to Nothing.
Present.
Rain tastes lovely, The.
Rebirth.
Reflections After the June 12th March for
    Disarmament.
Right On: White America.
Rocking her white feet.
Sequences.
Seventy-one years.
Shedding my years and.
Short Poem.
Small Comment.
So This Is Our Revolution.
Summary.
Summer has sped a.
Summer Words of [*or* for] a Sistuh [*or*
    Sister] Addict.
There are times that the.
These autumn trees sit.
These words stained with red.
This is not a small voice.
To All Brothers.
To All Sisters.
To You/Who Almost Turned/Me On.
Towhomitmayconcern.
Trees are laughing, The.
We a BadddDDD PEOPLE.
We are gatherers.
We be. gonna be.
We stumbled into.
What do i know of.
What is it about.
When i look at you.
When i return home.
When you left i ran.
Who are you/ iden.
Why must i string my hate.
Woman. rocking her.
Woman who made, A.
Woman. whose color.
Would you please return.
You are amble and.
You do not know the.
You have pierced me so.
You have stamped your hour.
Young Womanhood.

Saunders, Ruby C. (Fareedah Allah)
Cinderella.
Funky Football.
Generation Gap, The.
Hush Honey.
Lawd, Dese Colored Chillum.
You Made It Rain.

Saxon, Alvin. *See* "Ojenke"

Scott-Heron, Gil (b. 1949)
Revolution Will Not Be Televised!, The.

Scott, Johnie (b. 1946)
American Dream, The.

Scott, Sharon (b. 1951)
Between Me and Anyone Who Can
    Understand.
Come On Home.
Discovering.
Fisk is / a / negroid / institution.
For Both of Us at Fisk.
Just Taking Note.
Little More about the Brothers and Sisters, A.
Mama Knows.
Oh—Yeah!
Okay.

On My Stand.
Our Lives.
Sharon Will Be No/Where on Nobody's Best-
    selling List.
Sometimes / the poems.

Séjour, Victor (1817–74)
Le Retour de Napoléon.

Shackleford, Theodore Henry (1888–1923)
Big Bell in Zion, The.

Shange, Ntozake (b. 1948)
Ancestral Messengers/Composition 13.
Bocas: A Daughter's Geography.
Dream of Pairing.
Elegance in the extreme.
Frank Albert and Viola Benzena Owens.
Inquiry.
It's Not so Good to be Born a Girl/
    Sometimes.
Lizard Series, The.
Nappy Edges (A Cross Country Sojourn).
Oh, I'm 10 Months Pregnant.
On Becomin Successful.
Pages for a Friend.
Somebody almost walked off wid alla my
    stuff.
Tango.
Where the Heart Is.

Shannon, Angela
Doris.

Sharp, Saundra
Finding His Fist.
Good Nights.
In the Tradition of Bobbitt.
Meanwhile, in Rwanda.
Tribal Marks.
Woman Who Died in Line, The.

Shepard, Ollie (1897–1984)
It's a Low Down Dirty Shame.

Shepherd, Reginald (b. 1963)
Lucky One, The.
What Cannot Be Kept.
Where When Was.
White Days.

Sherer, Glenis Redmond
Our Spirit Stands.

Shockley, Evelyn E.
Oseola McCarty.

Silvera, Edward S. (1906–37)
Jungle Taste.
South Street.

Simmons, Barbara
Soul.

Simmons, Gerald L., Jr. (b. 1936)
Take Tools Our Strength.

Simmons, Herbert A. (b. 1930)
Ascendancy.

Simpson, Joshua McCarter (1820–76)
Away to Canada.
First of August in Jamaica, The.
"No, Master, Never!"
Old Liberia Is Not the Place for Me.
To the White People of America.
Twilight Hour, The.

Sims, Lefty
Angels Prayer, An.

Sinclair, John (*fl.* c.1818)
Breakthrough.

Smith, Bessie (1895–1937)
Backwater Blues.
In the House Blues.

Smith, Gary
Penitential Cries of Jupiter Hammond, The.

Smith, Lucy (1869–1939)
Face of Poverty.

Smith, Patricia (b. 1955)
Annie Pearl Smith Discovers Moonlight.
Asking for a Heart Attack.
Biting Back.
Blonde White Women.
Building Nicole's Mama.
Dylan, Two Days.
They say that black people.

Smith, Welton
Beast Section, The.
Interlude.

Malcolm.
Malcolm, *sels.*
Nigga Section, The.
Strategies.

Snellings, Rolland
Earth.
Mississippi Concerto.
Song of Fire, The.
Sunrise!!

Snyder, Thurmond
Beale Street, Memphis.
Beast with Chrome Teeth, The.
Seeds.

Southerland, Ellease
Blue Clay.
Night in Nigeria.
Pale Ant.
Recitation.
Two Fishing Villages.

Speech
Revolution / Revolution / Brothers and
    sisters.

Spellman, Alfred B. (b. 1934)
Beautiful Day #9, The.
Did John's Music Kill Him?
For My Unborn and Wretched Children.
Friends i am   like you   tied.
I Looked and Saw History Caught.
In Orangeburg My Brothers Did.
John Coltrane: An Impartial Review.
Tomorrow the heroes / will be named willie.
    their.
When Black People Are.
Zapata & the Landlord.

Spencer, Anne (1882–1975)
At the Carnival.
Before the Feast of Shushan.
Black man o' mine.
Creed.
Dunbar.
For Jim, Easter Eve.
God never planted a garden.
Grapes: Still-Life.
I Have a Friend.
Innocence.
Lady, Lady, I saw your face.
Letter to My Sister.
Life-long, Poor Browning.
Lines to a Nasturtium.
Neighbors.
Questing.
Rime for the Christmas Baby.
Sévignés, The.
Substitution.
Terence MacSwiney.
Translation.
White Things.
Wife-Woman, The.

Spriggs, Edward S. (b. 1934)
Every Harlem Face IS AFROMANISM
    Surviving.
For Brother Malcolm.
For the Truth (Because It Is Necessary).
My Beige Mom.
Sassafras Memories.
We Waiting on You.

Sprod, G. N.
Request Number.

Stanard, Christopher (b. 1967)
Baseball.
Rap is no mystery.
Spirits Struggle.
Washington Square Park and a Game of
    Chess.
Wrong Color.

"Stephany"
I have spent my life.
It is again.
Moving deep.
Moving Deep, *sels.*
What marked the river's flow.
Who collects the pain.

Steptoe, Lamont B. (b. 1949)
Mississippi Blues.
Notes for a Poem from the Middle Passage
    of Years.

Sweet Brown Rice and Red Bones.
Window Shopping.

Stewart, James T.
Announcement.
Poem: "We drank Thunderbird all night."
Poem: a Piece.

Strange, Sharan (b. 1959)
Childhood.
Offering.
Still Life.

Stuckey, Elma
Big Gate, The.
Defense.
Let them come / As they usually do by
    night.
Long Cotton Row.
Rebel.
Ribbons and Lace.
Southern Belle.
Temptation.
This Is It.

Summer, Cree
Curious White Boy.

"Sun-Ra" (Sonny Blount)
Cosmic Age, The.
Image Reach, The.
Nothing Is.
Of the Cosmic-Blueprints.
Plane: Earth, The.
Primary Lesson: The Second Class Citizens.
Saga of Resistance.
To the Peoples of Earth.
Visitation, The.
Would I for all that were.

Sundiata, Sekou (fl. c.1990–1995)
Ear Training.
Making Poems.
Notes from the Defense of Colin Ferguson,
    sels.
Open Heart.

T

Tallie, Mariahadessa ("Ekere")
Karma's Footsteps.

Taylor, Cheryl Boyce
English Lace.

"Taylor, Rockie D." See Ologboni, Tejumola

Terry, Lucy. See Prince, Lucy Terry

Thierry, Camille
Adieu.

Thomas, Lorenzo (b. 1944)
Electricity of Blossoms.
Historiography.
Inauguration.
My Office.
Onion Bucket.
Rhumba Negro.
Subway Witnesses, The.
They Never Lose.
Twelve Gates.

Thomas, Margaret L.
Locust Trees.

Thomas, Richard W. (b. 1939)
Amen.
Index to a Black Catharsis.
Jazzy Vanity.
Life after Death.
Martyrdom.
Revolution!
Riots and Rituals.
To the New Annex to the Detroit County
    Jail.
Worker, The.

Thompson-Cager, Chezia
Praise Song for Katherine Dunham: A
    Choreopoem.

Thompson, Clara Ann (b. 1887?)
After-Glow of Pain, The.
Angel's Message, The.
Autumn Day, An.
Autumn Leaves.
Christmas Rush, The.
Church Bells.

Doubt crept into a heart one day, A.
Drift-Wood.
Dying Year, The.
Easter Bonnet, The.
Easter Light, The.
Empty Tomb, The.
His Answer.
Hope.
Hope Deferred.
If Thou Shouldst Return.
I'll Follow Thee.
Johnny's Pet Superstition.
Lullaby: "Hush ye, hush ye! honey, darlin'."
Memorial Day.
Mrs. Johnson Objects.
Not Dead, but Sleeping.
Oh List to My Song!
Old and the New, The.
Opening Service, An.
Out of the Deep.
Parted.
She Sent Him Away.
Skeptic, The.
Storm-Beaten.
Submission.
To My Dead Brother.
Uncle Rube on the Race Problem.
Uncle Rube to the Young People.
Uncle Rube's Defense.
Watcher, The.

Thompson, Dorothy Perry (b. 1944)
Blues at 1.
Dancing in Menopause.
Intelligence Quotients.
Laurel Street, 1950.
Sister Lakin and Lally.

Thompson, Eloise Bibb. See Bibb, Eloise

Thompson, James W. (b. 1936)
Constant Labor, A.
Greek Room, The.
Plight, The.
Spawn of Slums, The.
Yellow Bird, The.
You Are Alms.

Thompson, Julius E. (b. 1946)
Devil's Music in Hell, The.
In my mind's eye.
Song of Innocence.

Thompson, Larry (b. 1950)
Black Is Best.

Thompson, Lisa B.
What Do I Want from Men and Love?

Thompson, Priscilla Jane (b. 1882)
Address to Ethiopia.
Adieu, Adieu, Forever.
Adown the heights of Ages.
After the Quarrel.
Afternoon Gossip, An.
Alberta, lovely little dame.
Athelstane.
Autumn ("List to the sad wind, drearily
    moaning.")
Autumn ("Sun shines bright, but sadly,
    The.")
Christmas Ghost, A.
Common Occurrence, A.
Consumptive, The.
David and Goliath.
Death and Resurrection.
Domestic Storm, A.
Emancipation.
Evelyn.
Examination, The.
Favorite Slave's Story, The.
Freedom at McNealy's.
Fugitive, The.
Glimpses of Infancy.
Happy Pair, A.
Home Greeting, A.
Husband's Return, The.
Hymn: "Lord, within thy fold I be."
In the Valley.
Inner Realm, The.
Insulted.
Interrupted Reproof, The.
Just How It Happened.
Kindly Deed, A.

King's Favorites, The.
Knight of My Maiden Love.
Lines on a Dead Girl.
Lines to an Old School-House.
Lines to Emma.
Little Wren, A.
Muse's Favor, The.
My Father's Story.
Oh, Whence Comes the Gladness?
Old Freedman, The.
Old Saint's Prayer, The.
Old Year, The.
Prayer, A: "Oh, Lord! I lift my heart."
Precious Pearl, The.
Raphael.
Snail's Lesson, The.
Snow-Flakes, The.
Soft Black Eyes.
Song of the Moon.
Song, The: "Oh, foully slighted Ethiope
    maid!"
Southern Scene, A.
They Are the Same.
Thwarted.
To a Deceased Friend.
To a Little Colored Boy.
To the New Year.
Tribute to the Bride and Groom, A.
Turncoat, The.
Uncle Ike's Holiday.
Uncle Jimmie's Yarn.
Unromantic Awakening, An.
Valentine, A.
Vineyard of My Beloved, The.
While the Choir Sang.
Winter Night, A.

T'Kalla
Nuns in the Basement of God.

Tolson, Melvin B.
African China.
Dark Symphony.
Festus Conrad.
Harlem.
Harlem Gallery, sels.
Lena Lovelace.
Madame Alpha Devine she made a million.
Note, The.
Old Houses.
Old Pettigrew.
Uncle Rufus.
Victor Garibaldi.

Tolson, Melvin Beaunearus (1898–1966)
African China.
Black boy / let me get up from the white
    man's table of fifty sounds.
Dark Symphony.
Ex-Judge at the Bar, An.
Legend of Versailles, A.
Satchmo.

Toney, A. K.
In the Twilight.

Toomer, Jean (1894–1967)
Air.
And Pass.
Angelic Eve.
As the Eagle Soars.
At Sea.
Banking Coal.
Be with Me.
Beehive.
Carma, sels.
Chase, The.
Cloud.
Conversion.
Cotton Song.
Delivered at the Knighting of Lord Durgling
    by Great Bruce-Jean.
Desire.
Earth.
Evening Song.
Face.
Fire.
Five Vignettes.
Georgia Dusk.
Gods Are Here, The.
Gum.
Harvest Song.

Her Lips Are Copper Wire.
Honey of Being.
I See Her Lovely There.
I sit in my room.
Imprint for Rio Grande.
It is Everywhere.
Karintha, *sels.*
Living Earth.
Lost Dancer, The.
Men.
Mended.
Merl.
Motion and Rest.
Not for me—and may nothing enhance.
November Cotton Flower.
Nullo.
One Within.
Our Growing Day.
Peers.
People.
Poem in C.
Portrait in Georgia.
Prayer: "My body is opaque to the soul."
Prayer (I): "How we have strained at our dark works."
Promise, The.
Reapers.
Rolling, rolling.
See the Heart.
Skyline.
Song of the Son.
Sound Poem (I).
Sound Poem (II).
Storm Ending.
Tell me, dear beauty of the dusk.
They Are Not Missed.
To Gurdjieff Dying.
Unsuspecting.
Upward is this Actuality.
Vague Opening.
Water.
White Arrow.
Words for a Hymn to the Sun.

Torregian, Sotère (b. 1941)
Newark Public Library Reading Room, The.
Poem for the Birthday of Huey P. Newton.
Travois of the Nameless.

Toure, Askia M. (b. 1958)
Azuri.
Immani in Sunburst Summer: a Chant.
Milestones: September 28, 1991.
O Mystic Light! A Mystic Sage Returns to Realms of Eternity.

Touré, Askia Muhammad (b. 1938)
Earth.
Floodtide.
JuJu.
Rebellion Suite.
Tauhid.

Tretheway, Quincy
And Syllables Grow Wings There.

Trethewey, Natasha (b. 1966)
Collection Day.
Domestic Work, 1937.
Drapery Factory, Gulfport, Mississippi, 1956.
Hot Comb.
Naolo Beauty Academy, New Orleans, Louisiana, 1943.
Secular.

Troupe, Quincy (b. 1943)
After Hearing a Radio Announcement: a Comment on Some Conditions.
Avalanche.
Collage.
Conversation Overheard.
Day in the Life of a Poet, A.
Dirge: "It is the endless dance of the dead."
For Malcolm Who Walks in the Eyes of Our Children.
Impressions / of Chicago; For Howlin' Wolf.
In Jimmy's Garden.
In Memoriam; for James Baldwin (1924–1987).
In Texas Grass.
It is not who or what.
My poems have holes sewn into them.
One for Charlie Mingus.

Poem for Friends.
Reflections on Growing Older.
Sense of Coolness, A.
South African Bloodstone.
Syntax of the mind grips, The.
White Weekend.
You come to me.

Truth, Sojourner (1797–1883)
Ain't I a Woman?

Tucker, Mary E. (b. 1838?)
Adieu.
All Alone.
Apple Dumplings.
Arria to Poetus.
Autumn Thoughts.
Beautiful Sea, The.
Beautiful, The! what is not perfect here below.
Blight of Love, The.
Burial of a Fairy Queen.
Charley du Bignon.
Child Life.
Christmas Eve, South, 1865.
Christmas, South, 1866.
Crazed.
Crushed Flower, The.
"Did You Call Me, Father?"
Disappointment.
Drink On.
Drunkard's Wife, The.
Evanishings.
Family Portraits.
Father's Love, The.
First Grey Hair, The.
Found—Who Lost?
Gone, with all her sparkling beauty.
Heart's Ease.
Hope.
Hugging the Shore.
Humming-Bird, The.
I Am Fashion's Toy.
I am Weary, Mother.
I Smile, but Oh! My Heart Is Breaking.
"I Was a Stranger and Ye Took Me In."
Kindness.
Kiss? A. Pray tell me, what is in a kiss.
Knitting.
Life.
Life for a Life.
Lift Me Higher.
Light in Darkness.
Lines on the Death of the Rev. S. K. Talmage.
Lines to an Old Dress.
Little Bell.
Love-letter, A.
Mail Has Come, The.
Mine.
Mistletoe.
Mother's Lament, The.
Mrs. Myrick's Lecture.
My Mother's Voice.
Mysteries of Life.
No Letter.
Old Crib, The.
Only a Blush.
Opium-Eater, The.
Revenge.
Signal Gun, The.
Silvery Fountain.
Soldier Boy's Dream, The.
Speak to Her Tenderly.
Spring.
That Glove.
To Annie.
To Don Juan Baz.
To Fannie.
To Father.
To Mary.
To One Who Sleepeth.
Tryst, The.
Upon Receipt of a Pound of Coffee in 1863.
Wail of the Divorced.
We Met.
Weariness.

Turner, Darwin T. (b. 1931)
Death is not a dream; death lives.

Guest Lecturer.
Love.
Night Slivers.
Sit-in, The.
Sonnet Sequence.

Turner, Doris (b. 1930)
Fragment Reflection I.
Reckoning A.M. Thursday.

U

Uhland, Ludwig (Johann Ludwig Uhland) (1787–1862)
From the German of Uhland.

V

Valcour, B.
Malvina, A.

Van Peebles, Mario
To Hell with Whitey.

Vashon, George Boyer (1824–78)
Vincent Ogé, *sels.*

Vassa, Gustavus
Miscellaneous Verses.

Vaughn, James P. (b. 1929)
Four Questions Addressed to His Excellency, the Prime Minister.
Movie Queen.
So?
Three kings went down to the soul of the sea.
Two Ladies Bidding Us "Good Morning."

"Vesey, Paul." *See* **Allen, Samuel**

"Vibe, Madd"
L.A. (Lost Assholes).

W

Wade-Gayles, Gloria (b. 1940)
Fighting My Homophobia.
For a Friend Who Considers Suicide.

Wakefield, Jacques
Days Prior to.
Oh shit a riot!
We exist living dead. The death of.

Walcott, Derek (b. 1930)
Blues.
Elsewhere.
Eulogy to W. H. Auden.
Far Cry from Africa, A.
Fist, The ("Fist clenched round my heart, The.")
Glory Trumpeter, The.
God Rest Ye Merry, Gentlemen.
Schooner *Flight*, The, *sels.*
Storm Figure.
Swamp, The.
Upstate.
Village Life, A.

Walden, Alfred Islay (1847–84)
Dedicated to a Young Lady Representing the Indian Race at Howard University.
Introductory to Second Edition.
Nation's Friend, The.
One to Love.
Transition—S.M, The.
Wish for an Overcoat.

Walker, Alice (b. 1944)
Abduction of Saints, The.
African Images, Glimpses from a Tiger's Back.
After the Shrink.
Armah: October 12, 1990.
At first I did not fight it.
Attentiveness.
Awakening, The.
Ballad of the Brown Girl.
Baptism.
Beast.
Beyond What.
Black Mail.

Black Prince, The.
Burial.
Chic Freedom's Reflection.
Clutter-up People.
Compulsory Chapel.
Confession.
Dedication.
Democratic Order, The: Such Things in Twenty Years I Understood.
Diamonds on Liz's bosom, The.
Did This Happen to Your Mother? Did Your Sister Throw Up a Lot?
Each One, Pull One.
Eagle Rock.
Early Losses: a Requiem.
Ending.
Enemy, The.
Even as I hold you.
Every morning I exercise.
Excuse.
Exercises on Themes from Life.
Expect nothing. Live frugally.
Facing the Way.
Family Of.
Few Sirens, A.
First, they said we were savages.
For My Sister Molly Who in the Fifties.
Forbidden Things.
Forgive me if my praises.
Forgiveness.
Gift.
Girl Who Died #1, The.
Girl Who Died #2, The.
Good Night, Willie Lee, I'll See You in the Morning.
Gray.
Having eaten two pillows.
He said come.
He said: I want you to be happy.
How Poems Are Made: A Discredited View.
Hymn: "I well remember / A time when."
I said to Poetry: "I'm finished."
If there was any justice.
If "those people" like you.
I'm really very fond of you.
In Answer to Your Silly Question.
In Uganda an early king chose.
Instant of Our Parting, The.
J, My Good Friend (Another Foolish Innocent).
Janie Crawford.
January 10, 1973.
Johann.
Judge Every One with Perfect Calm.
Karamojongs.
Killers.
Kiss, The.
Last time, The.
Light Baggage.
Listen, / I never dreamed.
Lonely Particular.
Lost My Voice? Of Course.
Love is not concerned.
Malcolm.
Medicine.
Mississippi Winter I.
Mississippi Winter II.
Mississippi Winter III.
Mississippi Winter IV.
Moody.
More Love to His Life.
Mornings / of an impossible love.
My daughter is coming!
My Heart Has Reopened to You.
My husband says.
Mysteries.
Natural Star.
Nature of This Flower Is to Bloom, The.
Ndebele.
Never Offer Your Heart to Someone Who Eats Hearts.
New Face.
1971.
No Fixed Place.
No One Can Watch the Wasichu.
Nothing is right.
Now that the book is finished.

Old Warrior Terror, The.
On Being Asked to Leave a Place of Honor for One of Comfort, Preferably in the Northern Suburbs.
On Sight.
On Stripping Bark from Myself.
Once again simple.
Outcast.
Overnights.
Pagan.
Perfection.
Poem at Thirty-nine.
QPP, The.
Rage.
Reassurance.
Remember me?
Representing the Universe.
Revolutionary Petunias.
Right to Life: What Can the White Man Say to the Black Woman?, The.
S M.
She said: "When I was with him."
Smell of Lebanon, The.
So We've Come at Last to Freud.
Some Things I Like about My Triple Bloods.
Song: "World is full of colored, The."
Songless.
South: The Name of Home.
Storm.
Streaking (A Phenomenon Following the Sixties).
Suicide.
Talking to My Grandmother Who Died Poor.
Telling.
There are no tigers.
There were palm trees.
These days I think of Belvie.
These mornings of rain.
They who feel death close as a breath.
Thief.
Thing Itself, The.
Threatened by my rising need.
To die before one / wakes / must be glad.
To the Man in the Yellow Terry.
Torture.
View from Rosehill Cemetery: Vicksburg.
Walker.
Warning.
We alone can devalue gold.
We have a beautiful / mother.
We Have a Map of the World.
Well. / He was a poet.
What Ovid Taught Me.
What the Finger Writes.
When Golda Meir Was in Africa.
While love is unfashionable.
Who has not been.
Will.
Winnie Mandela We Love You.
Without Commercials.
Woman Is Not a Potted Plant, A.
"Women of Color" Have Rarely Had the Opportunity to Write about Their Love Affairs.
Your soul shines.

Walker, Frank X. (b. 1961)
Crooked Afro.
Sweet Bread.
Wishbone.

Walker, Margaret Abigail (b. 1915)
Africa.
African Village, The.
Amos, 1963.
Amos (Postscript, 1968).
At the Lincoln Monument in Washington, August 28, 1963.
Bad-Man Stagolee.
Ballad for Phillis Wheatley.
Ballad of the Free, The.
Ballad of the Hoppy-Toad.
Big John Henry.
Birmingham.
Birmingham, 1963.
Black Magic.
Black Paramour.
Chicago.
Childhood.

Crystal Palace used to be, The.
Dark Blood.
Dear are the names that charmed me in my youth.
Delta.
Dies Irae.
Disillusion for Flower Children of Long Ago.
Elegy: "Strange summer sun shines round our globe of circumstance."
Epitaph for My Father.
Ex-Slave.
Fanfare, Coda, and Finale.
Five Black Men.
For Andy Goodman—Michael Schwerner— and James Chaney.
For Gwen, 1969.
For Malcolm X.
For Mary McLeod Bethune.
For my people everywhere singing their slave songs repeatedly.
For Owen Dodson, 1983.
For Paul Laurence Dunbar.
Giants of My Century.
Girl Held without Bail.
Gus, the lineman / Route forty-nine.
Harriet Tubman.
Hosea.
House of Prayer, The.
How many silent centuries sleep in my sultry veins?
I hear a rumbling underground.
I want to write.
Inflation blues is what we got.
Iowa Farmer.
Isaiah was a man of the court.
Jackson, Mississippi.
Jackson State, May 15, 1970.
Jeremiah, prophet of Jerusalem.
Joel, that young prophet-son of Pethuel!
Kissie Lee.
Labyrinth of Life, The.
Lineage.
Litany from the Dark People, A.
Litany of Black History for Black People, A.
Long John Nelson and Sweetie Pie.
Love Song for Alex, 1979.
Medgar Evers, 1925-1963.
Memory.
Micah was a young man of the people.
Molly Means.
Money, Honey, Money.
Monologue.
My Mississippi Spring.
My Truth and My Flame.
1933.
Now.
October Journey.
Ode on the Occasion of the Inauguration of the Sixth President of Jackson State College.
Old Age.
On Death and the Resurrection.
On Police Brutality.
On Youth and Age.
On Youth and Age II.
Our Need.
Oxford is a legend.
Patchwork Quilt, A.
People of Unrest.
Poppa Chicken.
Power to the People.
Prophets for a New Day.
Since 1619.
Sit-Ins.
Small Black World.
Solace.
Sorrow Home.
Southern Song.
Spirituals, The.
Street Demonstration.
Struggle Staggers Us, The.
Teacher was a bad man, The.
Telly Boob-Tube on the Idiot Box.
They have put us on HOLD.
This Is My Century.
Today.
Tribute to Robert Hayden.

Two-Gun Buster and Trigger Slim.
We have been believers in the black gods of an old land.
Whores.
Yalluh Hammuh.

Waller, Thomas ("Fats"), Andy Razaf, *and* Harry Brooks
(What Did I Do to Be So) Black and Blue?

Walter, Roni
Familee reunion tyme iz a special tyme.

Walton, Eda Lou (b. 1896)
Kiss Requested, A.

Wangara, Malaika Ayo
From a Bus.

War, Michael
Duke Checks Out Ella as She Scats Like That.

Ward, Jerry W., Jr. (b. 1943)
At the Border of Constant Disaster.
Don't Be Fourteen (In Mississippi).
Jazz to Jackson to John.

Ward, Pam
She Should Have Called 911.

Warner, Malcolm-Jamal
My Woman.

Warren-Moore, Jackie (b. 1950)
All-Night Issue, The.
Dannemora Contraband.
For Etheridge Knight.
For Paula Cooper (The 18 Year Old Who Waits on Death Row).
Pink Poem.

Washington, Raymond
Freedom Hair.
Moon Bound.
Vision from the Ghetto.

Waters, Muddy (McKinley Morganfield) (1915–1983)
Hoochie Coochie.

Watkins, Lucian B. (b. 1879)
Star of Ethiopia.
To Our Friends.
Two Points of View.

Watkins, Nayo-Barbara ("Nayo")
Bedtime Story.
Black Woman Throws a Tantrum.
Do You Know Me?
Easy way out.
First time I was sweet sixteen.
Hard Times A' Coming.
I watched little black boys.
Missions and Magnolias.
Near Miss.

Watts, Joette Harland. See Auset, Kupenda

Weatherly, Tom (b. 1942)
Arroyo.
Autobiography.
Blues for Franks Wooten.
Canto 7: First Thesis.
First Monday Scottsboro Alabama.
Imperial Thumbprint.
Mud Water Shango.
Your eyes are mirth.

Weaver, Michael S.
Appaloosa, The.
Borders.
Brooklyn.
Easy Living.
Luxembourg Garden.
Message on Cape Cod, The.
My Father's Geography.
Providence Journal V: Israel of Puerto Rico.
Sub Shop Girl.
Weekend Equestrian, The.

Weeden, Lula Lowe (b. 1918)
Dance.
Have You Seen It.
Little Dandelion, The.
Me Alone.
Robin Red Breast.
Stream, The.

Weems, Mary (b. 1954)
B.B. Blues.
Dime after Dime.
Funk.

Return to Temptation.
Yesterday.

Welburn, Ron (b. 1944)
And universals / are not that world.
Avoidances.
Black is beautiful.
Cecil County.
Condition Blue/ Dress.
Eulogy for Populations.
First Essay on the Art of the U. S.
It is overdue time.
Lyrics shimmy like.
Put u red-eye in.
Regenesis.
Tu / cson's of blackmens.
Whichway.

Wheatley, Phillis (1753–84)
Address to the Atheist, By P. Wheatley at the Age of 14 Years—1767.
Address to the Deist—1767, An.
America.
Anniversary Poem Entitled the Progress of Liberty, An, *sels.*
Answer to the *Rebus*, by the Author of These Poems, An.
Atheism.
Deism.
Elegy on Leaving —, An.
Elegy, Sacred to the Memory of That Great Divine, the Reverend and Learned Dr. Samuel Cooper, Who Departed This Life December 29, 1783, Ætatis 59, An.
Elegy, to Miss Mary Moorhead, An.
Farewell to America.
Funeral Poem on the Death of C.E., an Infant of Twelve Months, A.
Goliath of Gath.
Hymn to Humanity, An.
Hymn to the Evening, An.
Hymn to the Morning, An.
Isaiah LXIII, 1–8.
Moses: a Story of the Nile, *sels.*
Niobe in Distress for Her Children Slain by Apollo, from Ovid's Metamorphoses, Book VI, and from a View of the Painting of Mr. Richard Wilson.
Ode of Verses on the Death of George Whitefield, An.
Ode on the Birthday of Pompey Stockbridge, An.
Ode to Neptune.
On Being Brought from Africa to America.
On Friendship.
On Imagination.
On Messrs. Hussey and Coffin.
On Recollection.
On the Capture of General Lee.
On the Death of a Young Gentleman.
On the Death of a Young Lady of Five Years of Age.
On the Death of Doctor Samuel Marshall.
On the Death of Dr. Samuel Marshall.
On the Death of Dr. Samuel Marshall, 1771.
On the Death of General Wooster.
On the Death of J.C. an Infant.
On the Death of Mr. Snider Murder'd by Richardson.
On the Death of the Rev. Dr. Sewell, 1769.
On the Death of the Rev. Mr. George Whitefield, 1770.
On the Death of the Rev'd Dr. Sewall, 1769.
On Virtue.
Philis's Reply to the Answer in Our Last by the Gentleman in the Navy.
Poem Entitled the Day and the War, A, *sels.*
Poem on the Death of Charles Eliot, Aged 12 Months, A.
Recollection.
Thoughts on the Works of Providence.
To a Clergyman on the Death of His Lady.
To a Gentleman and Lady on the Death of the Lady's Brother and Sister, and a Child of the Name Avis, Aged One Year.
To a Gentleman of the Navy.
To a Gentleman on his Voyage to Great-Britain for the Recovery of His Health.

To a Lady and Her Children, on the Death of Her Son and Their Brother.
To a Lady on Her Coming to North-America with Her Son, for the Recovery of Her Health.
To a Lady on Her Remarkable Preservation in an Hurricane in North-Carolina.
To a Lady on the Death of Her Husband.
To a Lady on the Death of Three Relations.
To Captain H——D, of the 65th Regiment.
To His Excellency General Washington.
To His Honour the Lieutenant-Governor, on the Death of His Lady, March 24, 1773.
To Mæcenas.
To Mr. and Mrs. —, on the Death of Their Infant Son.
To Mrs. Leonard, on the Death of Her Husband.
To S. M., a Young African Painter, on Seeing His Works.
To the Hon. Commodore Hood on His Pardoning a Deserter.
To the Hon'ble Thomas Hubbard, Esq.; on the Death of Mrs. Thankfull Leonard.
To the Honourable T.H. Esq.; on the Death of His Daughter.
To the King's Most Excellent Majesty, 1768.
To the King's Most Excellent Majesty on His Repealing the American Stamp Act.
To the Rev. Dr. Thomas Amory on Reading Sermons on Daily Devotion, in Which That Duty Is Recommended and Assisted.
To the Rev. Mr. Pitkin, on the Death of His Lady.
To the Right Honourable William, Earl of Dartmouth, His Majesty's Principal Secretary of State for North-America, Etc.
To the University of Cambridge, in New-England.

Wheeler, Charles Enoch (b. 1909)
Adjuration.

White-Jackson, Paula
Saturday Morning Pancakes.

White, Joseph Blanco (1775–1841)
Black Is a Soul.

Whitfield, James Monroe (1823–78)
From America.
How long, oh gracious God! how long.
Misanthropist, The.
North Star, The.
Self-Reliance.
Stanzas for the First of August.
To ——: "Approaching night her mantle flings."
To Cinque.
Yes! strike again that sounding string.

Whitman, Albery Allson (1851–1901)
Custer's Last Ride.
Hymn to the Nation.
Leelah Misled, *sels.*
Lute of Afric's Tribe, The.
Not a Man, and Yet a Man, *sels.*
Stonewall Jackson, 1886.
Twasinta's Seminoles; Or Rape of Florida, *sels.*
Ye Bards of England.

Williams, Clarence (1893–1965)
Gulf Coast Blues.

Williams, Crystal A.
In Search of Aunt Jemima.

Williams, Edward W. (1863–91)
At Harper's Ferry Just before the Attack.

Williams, John A. (b. 1925)
Safari West.

Williams, Karen (b. 1962)
For Backwards Buppies.
In My Grandmother's Living Room.
JAZZ (a New Interpretation).
Kissing Keys.
Little Black Girls, The Original Eve (Spreadin' More Beautiful Brown Around).
Ntarama (Rwanda) Chronicles.
There's History in My Hair.

Williams, Lana C.
Flying High.

Williams, Marlon C. ("Poet X;")
　Blood, Sweat, and Fears.
Williams, Nance
　For Lover Man, and All the Other Young
　　Men Who Failed to Return from World
　　War II.
　Year without Seasons, A.
Williams, Niama Leslie JoAnn (b. 1962)
　Afrocentricity.
　Companion Pieces.
　For the Dancer.
　Meaning of the Smell of Sweat, The.
　Merging.
Williams, Saul Stacey
　Recitation.
Williams, Sherley Anne (b. 1944)
　Driving Wheel.
　Empress Brand Trim: Ruby Reminisces, The.
　House of Desire, The.
　I Want Aretha to Set This to Music.
　Letters from a New England Negro.
　Peacock Poems: 1, The.
　Say Hello to John.
　She Had Known Brothers.
　Straight Talk from Plain Women.
　You Were Never Miss Brown to Me.
Wilson, A(e)rin
　Grenudita.
Wilson, August (b. 1945)
　Theme One: The Variations.
Wilson, Ted
　Count Basie's place.
　Music of the Other World.
　S, C, M.
Witherspoon, Naomi Long. *See* **Madgett, Naomi
Long**
Wonder, Stevie
　Living for the City.
Worley, Demetrice A. (b. 1960)
　Dancing in the Dark.
　Las Flores para una Niña Negra.
　Sandra.
　Tongues in My Mouth.
Wright, Bruce McM. (b. 1918)
　African Affair, The.
Wright, Jay (b. 1935)
　Albuquerque Graveyard, The.
　Altars and Sacrifice.
　Appearance of a Lost Goddess, The.
　Benjamin Banneker Helps to Build a City.
　Charge, The.
　Compassion's Bird.
　Cutting Greens.
　Dead, The.
　Death as History.
　Desire's Persistence.
　Don José Gorostiza Encounters El Cordobés.
　End of Ethnic Dream, The.
　Frightened Lover's Sleep, The.
　Homecoming Singer, The.
　Invention of a Garden, The.
　Invitation to Madison County, An.
　Jalapeña Gypsies.
　Journey to the Place of Ghosts.
　Lake in Central Park, The.
　Love in the Weather's Bells.
　Madrid.
　Meta-A and the A of Absolutes.
　Neighborhood House, The.
　Sketch for an Aesthetic Project.
　This morning I threw the windows.
　Wednesday Night Prayer Meeting.
　What is Beautiful.
　White Deer, The.
Wright, Richard (1808–60)
　Between the World and Me.
　I Have Seen Black Hands.
　Red Clay Blues.
Wright, Sarah E. (b. 1927)
　To Some Millions Who Survive Joseph E.
　　Mander, Sr.
　Until They Have Stopped.
Wyche, Marvin, Jr. (b. 1951)
　And She Was Bad.
　Five Sense.

Leslie.
　We Rainclouds.
Wynbush, Octavia Beatrice
　Beauty.

X

"X, Derrick" (Goldie Williams)
　Shot to the Curb.
"X, Marvin" (Marvin E. Jackmon)
　Burn, Baby, Burn.
　Proverbs.
　Till the Sun Goes Down.
　That Old Time Religion.

Y

Yerby, Frank (b. 1916)
　Calm after Storm.
　Fishes and the Poet's Hands, The.
　Weltschmerz.
　Wisdom.
　You Are a Part of Me.
Young, Al (b. 1939)
　Absent from the United States.
　Afraid.
　After Visiting Arl at the Hospital.
　Afternoon After, The.
　Alba.
　American Glamour.
　American Time.
　Any Inner City Blues.
　April Blue.
　Arabia it's so fine so hot.
　Are You the Lover or Loved?
　Ars Poetica.
　Art of Benny Carter, The.
　Aunt.
　Available Light.
　Backtracking.
　Bear Gulch Road.
　Beauty of Milwaukee cold with rain, The.
　Belgrade moon, where are you.
　Berkeley Pome.
　Big ocean-waving, woman-pulling moon.
　Big Sur.
　Billie.
　Birthday Poem.
　Bitter Spring Again, The.
　Black Queen for More Than a Day.
　Blue Monday.
　Blues Don't Change, The.
　Blues in December.
　Boogie With O.O. Gabugah.
　Brand New Morning Love Song, A.
　By Heart.
　California Peninsula: El Camino Real.
　Carolina Moon.
　Chemistry.
　Citizen CB.
　City Home Detroit.
　Coastal Moon.
　Conjugal Visits.
　Continuing.
　Curative Powers of Silence, The.
　Dance for Aging Hipsters, A.
　Dance for Li Po, A.
　Dance For Ma Rainey, A.
　Dance for Militant Dilettantes, A.
　Dance of the Infidels.
　Dancer, The.
　Dancing.
　Dancing All Alone.
　Dancing Day to Day.
　Dancing in the Laundromat [or] Dust: an
　　Ordinary Song.
　Dancing in the Street.
　Dancing Naked.
　Dancing Pierrot.
　Dancing Together.
　Day Kennedy Died.
　Dear Arl.
　Dear Old Stockholm.
　Dear Ravi Shankar.

Demerol.
　Detroit 1958.
　Dexter Gordon at Keystone Korner.
　Dock Song Crazy.
　Drawing.
　Dream Take: 22.
　Dreamjot: 1962.
　Dreams of Paradise.
　Dude in Denver.
　East Boston.
　Election Night Pome.
　Elegy: "Good morning! / Good morning!"
　Erosong.
　Eternity.
　Everywhere.
　Falling Asleep in a Darkening Room.
　Fifty-Fifty.
　Flirt.
　Flu.
　Foggy Morning.
　For Arl in Her Sixth Month.
　For Janet Kafka, Dead at 30.
　For Joanne in Poland.
　For Kenneth & Miriam Patchen.
　For Poets.
　Fort Collins, Colorado.
　Friday the 12th.
　From Bowling Green.
　Fun City Samba.
　Geography of the Near Past.
　Going Back Home.
　Green Is a Feeling, Not a Color.
　Grizzly Peak.
　Groupie.
　H_2O.
　Hallucinogenic Halleluuuu.
　Hangover.
　Hawk Revsited, The.
　Head of a Woman.
　Here in violet light.
　Herrick Hospital, Fifth Floor.
　Ho.
　Hoboken Broken Down: A Hasty
　　Recollection.
　Hot House.
　Houston in October.
　How Stars Start.
　How the Rainbow Works.
　I Arrive In Madrid.
　Ian.
　Identities.
　Imitation Dance, The.
　Improvisation.
　In a twinkling, the green.
　In Marin Again.
　In the tender woodland.
　Indiana Gig, The.
　Intimacy.
　Invitation.
　It Is God that Moves in Your Heart.
　It's India.
　Jackie McLean: Alto Saxophone.
　James Cotton Band at Keystone, The.
　January.
　Jazz as Was.
　John Coltrane Dance, The.
　Jolt.
　Joy/Spring.
　Jungle Strut.
　Kicking.
　Kiss.
　Koto Music/Singing.
　Leadbelly Song, The.
　Leaving Home for Home.
　Leaving Rochester.
　Leaving Syracuse.
　Lemons, Lemons.
　Lesson.
　Lester Leaps In.
　Life at the Back of the Plane.
　Lightning, Divine Lightning.
　Little More Traveling Music, A.
　Little Poem About Jazz, A.
　Loneliness.
　Lonesome in the Country.
　Look Good, Smell Good, Feel.
　Lovesong of O. O. Gabugah.

Madness.
Madrid 1963: Some Changes.
Making Love After Hours.
Malagueña Salerosa.
Malcolm's Messasge.
Manhattan March, The 1970s.
Maya.
Mexico City Lover.
Michael At Sixteen Months.
Mid-Life Crises: A Critical Review.
Midnight Special Revisited, The.
Moon, How Do I Measure Up?
Moon of no return, never the same.
Moon Over Matter.
Moon, the Whole Moon, and Nothing but the Moon, The.
Moon Up Close in Winter by the Telescope, The.
Moon Watching by Lake Chapala.
Moonlessness.
More Clues to the Blues.
Morning Poem for Michael, A.
Moss.
Mountains of California: Part 1, The.
Mountains of California: Part 2, The.
Move Continuing, The.
Moving, Merging, Fading, Standing Still.
My Spanish Heart.
Myself When I Am Real.
Myth Science of Our Time, The.
New Autumn, New York.
New Mode of Production, The.
New Moon Over Grove Street.
New Mystic, The.
New Orleans Intermissiom.
Night before Michael Was Born, The.
No More Doors Tonight.
No Strings Attached.
No Trespassing.
Not Her, She Aint No Gypsy.
Now's the Time.
O!
October Variations, The.
October Window.
Old Fashioned Cincinnati Blues, The.
Old Light.
Old O.O. Blues, The.
Old Woman.
One Snapshot I Couldn't Take in France, The.
One West Coast.
Only Race There Is, The.
Orchard at Night in Rain Light, The.
Pachuta, Mississippi/a /Memoir A Memoir.
Palm Drive Palo Alto.

Paris.
People of Letters.
Physics of Loneliness, The.
Pidgin Moon.
Poem for Dorothy Dandridge, A.
Poem for Dylan Thomas, A.
Poem for Lena Horne, A.
Poem for Omar Khayyam (1050?-1123? A.D.).
Poem for Players, A.
Poem for Willard Motley, A.
Poem Found Emptying Out My Pockets.
Poem with Orange.
Poetry.
Politics As History.
Ponce de León: A Morning Walk.
Prelude.
Prestidigitator 1, The.
Prestidigitator 2, The.
Problem of Identity, The.
Process.
Providence, Rhode Island.
Ravel: Bolero.
Reading Nijinsky's Diary.
Real Time.
Realism.
Rediscovered Diary Entry.
Reggie's Version.
Robbie's Dance, The.
Roland Navarro (1939-1961).
Romance.
Romance Without Finance.
Rundown at Ned's Bar B.Q, The.
Sad Hour of Your Peace, The.
Sarajevo Moon.
Sarajevo Moonlight.
Saudades: The Portuguese Blues.
Sea Level.
See, see, moon, O see what you done done.
Selectric II.
Self-Portrait: Holding On.
Sentience.
Seventh April.
Sing a Song of Singapore.
Singular Yen, A.
Sleepy Day at Half Moon Bay.
So is there life on you, moon?
Some Recent Fiction.
Some Spice for Jack Spicer.
Sometimes with the waves.
Son.
Song Turning Back Into Itself, *sels.*
Squirrels are skittering.
Still Lives.
Studio Up Over In Your Ear.
Suicide.

Summer.
Sunday Illumination.
Sunday Sonnet for My Mother's Mother, A.
Sweet Sixteen Lines.
Teaching.
Thelonious: An Intro.
There is a sadness to this world.
Tiny Self-Portrait.
Topsy: Part 2.
Total Incandescence.
Tribute.
Tune.
Tutti Colori Quality of Light, The.
Two A.M.
2 takes from *Love in Los Angeles.*
Visiting Day.
W. H. Auden & Mantan Moreland.
Waking Up in Santa Cruz at Sea.
Watsonville after the Quake.
What have you got of your own.
What Is the Blues?
What You Seize Is What You Git.
Whatever Become of the Living.
Where the Danube and Sava Rivers Meet.
Why a Hush Should Not Be Rushed.
Winter Leaves.
Written in Bracing, Gray L.A. Rainlight.
Yes, the Secret Mind Whispers.
You Don't Know What Love Is.
Your Basic Black Poet.

Young, Kathleen Tankersley
All Things Insensible.
December Portrait.
Hunger.

Young, Kevin (b. 1970)
Casting.
Escape Artist, The.
Field Trip.
Preserving, The.

Yusef, Imam
Love Your Enemy.

Z

Zu-Bolton, Ahmos, II (b. 1935)
Ain't No Spring Chicken.
By the 5th Generation Louisiana, After Slavery.
Governor of the Ollie Street, The.
Intro to My Final Book of Poems.
Seeker, The.
Sister Blues with Livewire Davis.
Struggle-Road Dance.
Sunset Beach.

SUBJECT INDEX

*Poems under each subject are listed alphabetically by author. Subjects range from specific (for example, persons) to general (for example, **Faith**).*

Some subject headings show cross-references to related subjects. Some subjects, such as **Love**, *are so broad that they appear here only to refer the user to related subjects.*

A

Abandonment
Bomani, M. Homecoming.
Clifton, L. Speaking of Loss.
Dove, R. Adolescence—III.
Giovanni. Forced Retirement.
Harper, F. Contrast, The.
Hayden, R. Incense of the Lucky Virgin.
Hughes, L. Mama and Daughter.
  Midwinter Blues.
Jordan, J. Gettin Down to Get over.
  Poem on Bell's Theorem.
Knight, E. Keeping of a Promise, The.
Lorde. And Don't Think I Won't Be Waiting.
Madhubuti. After Her Man Had Left Her for the Sixth Time That Year / (An Uncommon Occurrence).
Nelson, M. Beauty Shoppe.
O'Neal, S. Biological Didn't Bother.
Unknown. Easy rider, see what you done done, Lawd, Lawd.

Abolitionists
Cullen, C. Negro Mother's Lullaby, A.
Dove, R. David Walker (1785–1830).
Dunbar, P. Douglass.
Forten. To W. L. G. on Reading His "Chosen Queen."
Harper, F. Bible Defence of Slavery.
  Bury Me in a Free Land.
  Give My Love to the World.
  Lines to Charles Sumner.
  Lines to Hon. Thaddeus Stevens.
  Then and Now.
Harper, M. History as Cap'n Brown.
Hayden, R. Runagate Runagate.
Hughes, L. Ballad of the Seven Songs.
Jordan, J. Last Poem on Bell's Theorem.
Reason. Spirit Voice; or Liberty Call to the Disfranchised (State of New York), The.
Whitman, A. Lute of Afric's Tribe, The.
Williams, E. At Harper's Ferry Just before the Attack.

Abortion
Ai. Country Midwife: A Day, The.
Atkins. Lakefront, Cleveland.
Brooks, G. Mother, The.
Clifton, L. Lost Baby Poem, The.
Lorde. Woman/Dirge for Wasted Children, A.
Walker, A. Ballad of the Brown Girl.

Absence
Angelou. After.
Brown, S. Long Track Blues.
Dunbar, P. Absence.
  Waiting.
Giovanni. World Is Not a Pleasant Place to Be, The.
Hughes, L. Letter to Anne, A.
  Shakespeare in Harlem.
  So *long* / is in the song.
  Yesterday and Today.
Jordan, J. Relativity.
  Sonnet for A.B.T., A.
Kaufman, B. Sheila.
McKay, C. Absence.
  Harlem Dancer, The.
Oden. Private Letter to Brazil, A.

Sanchez, S. Missing you is like.
Thomas, R. Jazzy Vanity.
Young, A. Absent from the United States.
  Moonlessness.
  Moving, Merging, Fading, Standing Still.
  Odds, The.
See also **Isolation; Loneliness; Separation**

Academia
Worley, D. Dancing in the Dark.

Acceptance
Angelou. John J.
Braithwaite. Rhapsody.
Derricotte. Promise, The.
Giovanni. Choices.
  For Theresa.
  Poetry is motion graceful.
Hughes, L. Motto.

Accidents
Atkins. It's Here In The.
Davis, R. M. Poems about Playmates.
Knight, E. Poem of Attrition, A.
Komunyakaa. April Fools' Day.
Lorde. Martha this is a catalog of days.
McElroy, C. Ruth.
Thomas, R. Worker, The.
Young, A. Roland Navarro (1939-1961).

Achilles
Cullen, C. Sonnet: "I have not loved you in the noblest way."

Acrobatics and Acrobats
Hughes, L. Aspiration.
See also **Circus; Tightropes and Tightrope Walkers**

Acting and Actors
Baraka. Poem for Wille Best, A.
  Scenario VI.
Dickinson, B. Dark Actress—Somewhere, A.
Jordan, J. Deliza Questioning Perplexities.
Reed, I. Poison Light.
Young, A. Poem for Dorothy Dandridge, A.
See also **Motion Pictures; Show Business; Theater and Theaters**

Adam and Eve
Angelou. Couple, The.
Clifton, L. Adam and Eve.
Cullen, C. One Day We Played a Game.
Horton, G. Cheerless Condition of Bachelorship, The.
Kaufman, B. Geneology.
See also **Eden; Eve**

Adderley, Julian ("Cannonball")
Harper, M. Cannon Arrested.

Admiration
Angelou. Just for a Time.
Brown, S. Coolwell Vignette.
Coleman, W. Miss Jones.
Cotter, Sr. On Hearing James W. Riley Read.
Cullen, C. To John Keats, Poet, at Springtime.
Gilyard. Letter.
Giovanni. Poem (for EMA).
Joshua. On the Morning St. Bernard.
Knight, E. For Mary Ellen McAnally.
  You are a Sunrise.
Lorde. Dear Toni Instead of a Letter of Congratulation.
  For Craig.

Hard Love Rock.
Mentor.
Poem for a Poet, A.
Political Relations.
To a Girl Who Knew What Side Her Bread Was Buttered On.
McKay, C. America.
Randall, D. George.
Williams, Karen. In My Grandmother's Living Room.
Young, A. Bear Gulch Road.
  Brand New Morning Love Song, A.
  Dear Arl.
  Election Night Pome.
  Groupie.
  Moon, the Whole Moon, and Nothing but the Moon, The.
  Mountains of California: Part 1, The.
  Poem for Lena Horne, A.
  Whatever Become of the Living.

Adolescence
Angelou. Born That Way.
Barlow, G. Resonance.
Clifton, L. There Is a Girl Inside.
Coates. Alice Flips the Script.
Cornish, S. Turk.
Dove, R. Adolescence—I.
  Adolescence—II.
Ellis, K. Girl.
Emanuel, J. Sixteen, Yeah.
Hughes, L. Delinquent.
Jackson, M. L. Blunts.
Jean, V. Lesson on Braces.
Kaufman, B. Heather Bell.
Komunyakaa. Child's Play.
  Thorn Merchant's Son, The.
Lorde. Hanging Fire.
Penny, R. I Remember How She Sang.
Rodgers, C. Brief Synopsis, A.
Sanchez, S. Poem: "Look at me 8th / grade."
  Prelude to Nothing.
See also **Boys; Childhood and Children; Girls; Teenagers**

Adoption and the Adopted
Hughes, L. Madam and the Charity Child.

Adultery and Adulterers
Angelou. They went home and told their wives.
Hughes, L. Sister.
Komunyakaa. Boy Wearing a Dead Man's Clothes.
Shepard, O. It's a Low Down Dirty Shame.
Unknown. Frankie and Johnny were lovers.
See also **Infidelity**

Adventure and Adventurers
Brooks, G. Old Mary.
Brown, S. Odyssey of Big Boy.

Advertising
Hall, K. Wig.
Hughes, L. Neon Signs.
Lorde. American Cancer Society Or There Is More Than One Way to Skin a Coon.
Reed, I. Atlantic Monthly, December 1970, The.

Advice
African-American Oral Tradition. All you tough guys that thinks you're wise.

Don't Feel So Downhearted, Buddy.
Don't Look So Downhearted, Buddy.
Feeble Old Man.
Feeble Old Man and a Kid Named Dan.
Limpty Lefty McCree.
My Reflection.
Subject to a Fall: "Boys, you're subject to a
  fall and trip to the Walls."
Subject to a Fall: "Say, you subject to a fall
  and a trip to the Wall."
Wanderer's Trail, The.
Brown, S. Law for George, The.
  Pardners.
Clifton, L. To my Friend, Jerina.
Grimké, A. At April.
Harper, F. Lines to M.A.H.
Hughes, L. Advice.
  Ballad of the Sinner.
  Black Seed.
  Get Up off That Old Jive.
  Go *slow*, they say.
  Listen Here Blues.
  Mother to Son.
  Prayer: "I ask you this: / Which way to go."
  Snob.
  Warning.
  Warning: Augmented.
  Watch Out, Papa.
Joans. *It is time* for the United States to spend
  money on education so that every American
  would be hipper, *thus no war!*
Lorde. For Each of You.
  For My Singing Sister.
Mullen, H. Floorwax Mother.
Plato. Advice to Young Ladies.
Redmond. Parapoetics.
Wade-Gayles. For a Friend Who Considers
  Suicide.
Wheatley, P. To the University of Cambridge,
  in New-England.
Young, A. O!

Affection
Bennett, G. Sonnet—2: "Some things are very
  dear to me—."
Bontemps. Idolatry.
Brown, S. Louisiana Pastoral.
  Parish Doctor.
Clifton, L. Woman who loves, A.
Cullen, C. To One Not There.
Dunbar, P. Negro Love Song, A.
Giovanni. How do you write a poem.
  I remember learning you jump.
  Moon shines down, The.
  Poem of Friendship, A.
  Winter Poem.
Holiday. Fine and Mellow.
Horton, G. Early Affection.
  Lover's Farewell, The.
Hughes, L. Fascination.
  Gal's Cry for a Dying Lover.
  Gypsy Man.
  My Loves.
  Night funeral / In Harlem.
  Reasons Why.
Johnson, G. I Want to Die While You Love
  Me.
Johnson, H. Remember Not.
Jordan, J. Roman Poem Number Thirteen.
  Sonnet for A.B.T., A.
Kaufman, B. Response.
Lorde. Dozens, The.
  Poem for a Poet, A.
  Progress Report.
Madhubuti. Bonding, A.
Penny, R. Real People Loves One Another,
  The.
Ray, H. Verses to my Heart's-Sister.
Rushing. Sent for You Yesterday.
Spencer, A. Black man o' mine.
  White Things.
  Wife-Woman, The.
Stephany. You are instantly enfolded.
Toomer. Evening Song.
Turner, D. Love.
Walker, A. Love is not concerned.
Young, A. Only Race There Is, The.

Affliction
Giovanni. Forced Retirement.
Africa
Ahmasi. Water of Your Bath.
Alexander, L. Africa.
Angelou. Africa.
  For Us, Who Dare Not Dare.
  To a Husband.
Asim. Mumble the Magic Words.
Baraka. Ka 'Ba.
  New Reality Is Better Than a New Movie, A!
  Notes for a Speech.
Bennett, G. Heritage.
Bethune, L. Blue Tanganyika.
  Bwagamoyo.
Bontemps. Nocturne at Bethesda.
  Nocturne of the Wharves.
Cheatwood. Bloodstorm.
Clifton, L. Africa.
  Driving through New England.
Crouch, S. Riding Across John Lee's Finger.
Cullen, C. Brown Boy to Brown Girl.
  Heritage.
Cumbo. Ceremony.
Danner, M. Etta Moten's Attic.
Dumas, H. Afro-American.
Dunbar, P. Ode to Ethiopia.
Gerima. Sankofa.
Giovanni. Africa.
  Africa I.
  Africa II.
  Night.
  Swaziland.
  They clapped when we landed.
Harper, F. Ethiopia.
Haynes, A. Eclipse.
Hernton. Medicine Man.
Hughes, L. Africa.
  Afro-American Fragment.
  Call of Ethiopia.
  Danse Africaine.
  Death in Africa.
  Drums.
  Envoy to Africa.
  Me and My Song.
  Motherland.
  Negro.
  We, Too.
Jeffers, L. Flesh of the Young Men Is
  Burning, The.
  O Africa, where I baked my bread.
Johnson, F. Ethiopia.
Jordan, N. Black Warrior.
Kaufman, B. African Dream.
Knight, E. Idea of Ancestry, The.
Komunyakaa. Back Then.
La Grone. Africland.
  Suncoming.
Lane, P. Girl at the Window.
Long, D. Number Four.
Lorde. Coniagui women / wear their flesh like
  war, The.
  Dahomey.
  Generation III.
  125th Street and Abomey.
  Thanks to Jesse Jackson.
  Women of Dan Dance with Swords in Their
  Hands to Mark the Time When They Were
  Warriors, The.
Madgett. First Man.
Madhubuti. Change Is Not Always Progress.
  Poem for a Poet, A.
  Union of Two, The.
McElroy, C. Cutting a Road from Manaus to
  Belém.
McKay, C. Africa.
Miller, A. Africa Thing, The.
Moorer. Africa.
Reed, I. Sermonette.
  Why I Often Allude to Osiris.
Salaam. Spiritual Geography.
Sanchez, S. I have looked into.
Shange. Bocas: A Daughter's Geography.
Simpson, J. Old Liberia Is Not the Place for
  Me.
Southerland. Pale Ant.
Steptoe. Mississippi Blues.

Thompson, J. Song of Innocence.
Toomer. Conversion.
Unknown. Answer, The.
Walcott. Far Cry from Africa, A.
Walker, A. African Images, Glimpses from a
  Tiger's Back.
  Karamojongs.
  There are no tigers.
  There were palm trees.
Walker, M. Africa.
  African Village, The.
  For my people everywhere singing their slave
  songs repeatedly.
Weaver, M. My Father's Geography.
Wheatley, P. Philis's Reply to the Answer in
  Our Last by the Gentleman in the Navy.
Whitman, A. Lute of Afric's Tribe, The.
Wright, B. African Affair, The.

African Americans
Ai. Endangered Species.
  Riot Act, April 29, 1992.
  Self Defense.
Alexander, E. Affirmative Action Blues.
  Boston Year.
  Ode.
Alhamisi. Uhuru (freedom. now. swahili. east
  african lango).
Allen, S. Moment Please, A.
  View from the Corner.
Anderson, S. Sound of Afroamerican History
  Chapt I, The.
  Sound of Afroamerican History Chapt II, The.
Angelou. Ain't That Bad.
  Amoebaean for Daddy.
  Black Ode.
  Calling of Names, The.
  Family Affairs.
  On Working White Liberals.
  Passing Time.
  Sepia Fashion Show.
  Son to Mother.
  Song for the Old Ones.
  Still I Rise.
  Thank You, Lord.
  Through the Inner City to the Suburbs.
  To a Husband.
  To a Suitor.
  Why Are They Happy People?
As-Sabah. Sister Roll.
Baker, H. This is not a poem, nor.
Baraka. Beautiful Black Women.
  Black Art.
  Black Dada Nihilismus.
  Clay.
  Election Day.
  History-Wise #22.
  I don't love you.
  In the Tradition.
  Ka 'Ba.
  Leroy.
  Notes for a Speech.
  Poem for Black Hearts, A.
  Poem Some People Will Have to Understand,
  A.
  Return of the Native.
  Revelation in Brick City.
  Short Speech to My Friends.
  SOS.
  Three Movements and a Coda.
  W. W.
Barlow, G. Painting Drunken Twilight.
  Place Where He Arose, The.
Barrax. For a Black Poet.
Bennett, Bob. (Title).
Bennett, G. Heritage.
  Song: "I am weaving a song of waters."
  Sonnet—2: "Some things are very dear to
  me—."
  To a Dark Girl.
  To Usward.
Bethune, L. Harlem Freeze Frame.
Black, I. Racist Psychotherapy.
Bontemps. Black Man Talks of Reaping, A.
  God Give to Men.
Brooks, G. Ballad of Rudolph Reed, The.
  Kojo "I Am a Black."
  Third Sermon on the Warpland, The.

To Those of My Sisters Who Kept Their
  Naturals.
We real cool. We.
Young Heroes.
Brown, S. All Are Gay.
Bad, Bad Man, A.
Ballad of Joe, The.
Break of Day.
Call for Barnum.
Children's Children.
Crispus Attacks McKoy.
He Was a Man.
Kentucky Blues.
Law for George, The.
Legend.
Negro Improvement League.
New Congo, The.
No More Worlds to Conquer.
Odyssey of Big Boy.
Old Woman Remembers, An.
Real Mammy Song.
Roberta Lee.
Ruminations of Luke Johnson.
Scotty Has His Say.
Slim in Atlanta.
Slim Lands a Job?
Southern Cop.
Sporting Beasley.
Strong Men.
To Sallie, Walking.
Burroughs, M. Black Pride.
Only in This Way.
To Soulfolk.
Cassells. Soul Make A Path Through
  Shouting.
Cheatwood. Visions of the Sea.
Clark, Benjamin. Emigrant, The.
Clark, C. Allegory in Black.
Clemmons. Freedom Song for the Black
  Woman, A.
Cliff. Within the Veil.
Clifton, L. Admonitions.
4/30/92; for Rodney King.
Ca'line's Prayer.
Come home from the movies.
For de Lawd.
Good Times.
In Salem.
Kind of Man He Is, The.
Later i'll say / i spent my life.
Light / on my mother's tongue.
Listen children / keep this in the place.
Richard penniman.
Robert.
So close / they come so close.
Still / it was nice.
Thirty-eighth year, The.
Those Boys That Ran Together.
Tyrone (1).
Way It Was, The.
Clinton. History as Trash.
Traditional Post-Modern Neo-HooDoo Afra-
  Centric Sister in a Purple Head Rag
  Mourning Death and Cooking.
Coleman, A. Black Baby.
Coleman, W. American Sonnet (10).
Emmett Till.
Conyus. Confession to Malcolm.
Corrie. How Long Has Trane Been Gone.
Corrothers. At the Closed Gate of Justice.
Indignation Dinner, An.
Cortez. Give Me the Red on the Black of the
  Bullet.
Cotter, Sr. Is It Because I Am Black?
Ned's Psalm of Life for the Negro.
Crouch, S. BLACKIE Speaks on Campus: a
  Valentine for Vachel Lindsay.
Blackie Thinks of His Brothers.
Cullen, C. Black Christ, The.
Black Majesty.
Brown Girl Dead, A.
Colored Blues Singer.
From the Dark Tower.
Heritage.
Litany of the Dark People, The.
Pagan Prayer.
Shroud of Color, The.

Song of Praise, A.
Yet Do I Marvel.
Cumbo. Black Sister.
Cuney. No Images.
Chuck D. But Can You Kill the Nigga in
  You?
Danner, J. My Brother.
Danner, M. And through the Caribbean Sea.
At Home in Dakar.
Grandson Is a Hoticeberg, A.
This Is an African Worm.
Davis, R. M. Rip-Off.
Dent. Secret Messages.
Derricotte. Blackbottom.
Dove, R. Wingfoot Lake.
DuBois, W. Song of the Smoke, The.
Dumas, H. Afro-American.
Black Star Line.
Zebra Goes Wild Where the Sidewalk Ends,
  The.
Dunbar, P. Black Samson of Brandywine.
Colored Band, The.
Colored Soldiers, The.
Negro Love Song, A.
Unsung Heroes, The.
We wear the mask that grins and lies.
When Dey 'Listed Colored Soldiers.
Eady. Why Do So Few Blacks Study Creative
  Writing?
Ebon. To Our First Born or the Prophet
  Arrives.
Emanuel, J. Negro, The.
Old Black Men Say.
Whitey, Baby.
Evans, M. How Will You Call Me, Brother.
I Am a Black Woman.
Speak the truth to the people.
Status Symbol.
Vive Noir!
Who Can Be Born Black.
Fabio. God's Trombone.
Hurt of It All, The.
Race Results, U.S.A., 1966.
Fauset. Touché.
Ferdinand. Food for Thought.
Fordham. Atlanta Exposition Ode.
Forman, R. Green Boots n Lil Honeys.
Garnet. Thus man devotes his brother and
  destroys.
Gerima. Sankofa.
Gilbert, D. Fire in the Drum, The.
Miracle.
Gilmore, B. To Be or Not to Be.
Giovanni. Adulthood.
Africa II.
Beautiful Black Men.
But Since You Finally Asked.
Ego Tripping.
Geni in the Jar, The.
Linkage.
Lorraine Hansberry: an Emotional View.
Nikki-Rosa.
On Hearing "The Girl with the Flaxen Hair."
Poem for Flora.
Stardate Number 18628.190.
They clapped when we landed.
Woman Poem.
Giscombe. (1980).
(1962 At the Edge of Town).
Grandmaster Flash and the Furious
  Five. Message, The.
Gray-Kontar. Cuz' Mama Played Jazz.
Not No Socialism/Communism classical, but
  Some Power to the People Jazz.
Grimké, A. Black Finger, The.
Hamilton, B. Brother Harlem Bedford Watts
  Tells Mr. Charlie Where ITs At.
Poem to a Nigger Cop.
Hand. I wonder.
Handy, W. Beale Street Blues.
Harper, F. She's Free!
Simon's Countrymen.
We are rising, as a people.
Harper, M. Afterword: a Film.
Barricades hammered into place.
Black Spring.
Brother John.

Debridement.
Effendi.
Four Worthies: Souls of Black Folk.
Grandfather.
Herring run / in the silver morning.
High Modes: Vision as Ritual: Confirmation.
History as Apple Tree.
Song: I Want a Witness.
White Friend Flies in from the Coast, A.
Harris, P. Let's Take All the Blame.
Harris, W. Daddy Poem, A.
Hayden, R. Aunt Jemima of the Ocean
  Waves.
Frederick Douglass.
Hemphill. Family Jewels.
XXI.
Henderson, D. Neon Diaspora.
Hernton. Jitterbugging in the Streets.
Holman, M. Mr. Z.
Hughes, L. Afraid.
America.
America's Young Black Joe!
Aunt Sue's Stories.
Ballad of Margie Polite.
Ballad of Sam Solomon.
Ballad of Walter White.
Be-Bop Boys.
Beaumont to Detroit: 1943.
Brothers.
Carol of the Brown King.
Colored Soldier, The.
Consider me, / A colored boy.
Cross.
Crowns and Garlands.
Dark Youth of the U.S.A.
Dinner Guest: Me.
Dream Boogie.
Dream Variations.
Flatted Fifths.
Freedom Train.
Freedom's Plow.
Gal's Cry for a Dying Lover.
Ghosts of 1619.
Graduation.
Grant Park.
High to Low.
I too, sing America.
Juice Joint: Northern City.
Low to High.
Madam and the Newsboy.
Me and the Mule.
Merry-Go-Round.
Message to the President.
Migrant.
Migration.
My People.
Negro.
Negro Ghetto.
Negro Mother, The.
Negro Servant.
Negro Speaks of Rivers, The.
Neighbor.
Nightmare Boogie.
One-Way Ticket.
Parade.
Porter.
Postcard from Spain.
Prayer Meeting.
Prelude to Our Age.
Red Silk Stockings.
Ruby Brown.
Seashore through Dark Glasses (Atlantic City)
Shame on You.
Share-Croppers.
Song to a Negro Wash-woman, A.
South, The.
Southern Negro Speaks.
Stars.
Sun Song.
Theme for English B.
This Puzzles Me.
Trumpet Player.
Uncle Tom.
Us: Colored.
Weary Blues, The.
What? So Soon!
When Sue Wears Red.

Where Service Is Needed.
Will V-Day Be Me-Day Too?
Iman.   Love Your Enemy.
Iverem.   Daddy's Friends.
Jackson, G.   Fugitive Slaves.
Some of Betty's Story Round 1850.
Jackson, R.   After the Dance.
Jamal's Lamentation.
Jeffers, L.   My Blackness Is the Beauty of
This Land.
O Africa, where I baked my bread.
When I Know the Power of My Black Hand.
Johnson, C.   Negro Poets.
Johnson, F.   Ethiopia.
Soldiers of the Dusk, The.
Tired.
To an Afro-American Maiden.
Johnson, H.   Bottled [New York].
Sonnet to a Negro in Harlem.
Johnson, J.   Brothers.
Fifty Years.
Lift Ev're Voice and Sing.
O Black and unknown bards of long ago.
Jonas, R.   Ballade des Belles Milatraisses.
Brother Baptis' on Woman Suffrage.
Jones, G.   Tripart.
Jones, L. et al.   Poem for Black Hearts, A.
Jordan, A.   If I Write a Poem.
Jordan, J.   For Michael Angelo Thompson.
Gettin Down to Get over.
If You Saw a Negro Lady.
Last Poem on Bell's Theorem.
Poem about Intelligence for My Brothers and
Sisters, A.
Who Look at Me.
Jordan, N.   Be You.
Kaufman, B.   Hawk Lawler: Chorus.
I, Too, Know What I Am Not.
Oregon.
Kenner.   Image in the Mirror.
Knight, E.   Another Poem for Me (after
Recovering from an O.D.).
Black Poet Leaps to His Death, A.
Bones of My Father, The.
Con/tin/u/way/shun Blues.
Fable: "Once upon a today and yesterday and
nevermore there were 7 men."
For Black Poets Who Think of Suicide.
Haiku: "Two hours I've walked."
Hard Rock Returns to Prison from the
Hospital for the Criminal Insane.
Idea of Ancestry, The.
Memo #32.
My life, the quality of which.
On Seeing the Black Male as #1 Sex Object
in America.
Once on a Night in the Delta: A Report From
Hell.
Various Protestations From Various People.
Warden said to me the other day, The.
Komunyakaa.   Addendum.
Blues Chant Hoodoo Revival.
Gift Horse.
How I See Things.
"Kush."   Message for Langston, A.
Latifah.   U.N.I.T.Y.
Lee, D.   Awareness.
Poem to Complement Other Poems, A.
Stereo.
Loftin.   Weeksville Women.
Loftis.   Big John.
Lorde.   About Religion.
American Cancer Society Or There Is More
Than One Way to Skin a Coon.
Between Ourselves.
Call.
Coal.
Eulogy for Alvin Frost.
Florida.
For the Record.
Generation II.
Monkeyman.
Naturally.
Need: A Chorale for Black Woman Voices.
Song for Many Movements, A.
To the Poet Who Happens to Be Black and

the Black Poet Who Happens to Be a
Woman.
Madgett.   Black Woman.
Midway.
Madhubuti.   America calling.
Big Momma.
Blackmusic / a Beginning.
Blackwoman.
But He Was Cool.
First World.
For Black People.
Gwendolyn Brooks Elizabeth.
Malcolm Spoke / Who Listened?
Message All Black People Can Dig, A.
Mixed Sketches.
Move Un-noticed to Be Noticed: a Nationhood
Poem.
Poem for a Poet, A.
Poem to Compliment Other Poems, A.
Poet: What Ever Happened to Luther?
Revolutionary Screw, The.
Stereo.
Wall, The.
We Walk the Way of the New World.
McCall, J.   New Negro, The.
McClane.   Black Intellectual, The.
Song: a Motion for History.
To Hear the River.
McClaurin.   I, Woman.
Mask, The.
To a Gone Era.
McElroy, C.   Ghost-Who-Walks, The.
Griots Who Know Brer Fox, The.
Tapestries.
Under the Oak Table.
While Poets Are Watching.
Why Tu Fu Does Not Speak of the Nubian.
Woman's Song, A.
McKay, C.   Harlem Dancer, The.
If we must die—let it not be like hogs.
In Bondage.
Negro's Friend, The.
Negro's Tragedy, The.
One Year After.
To the White Fiends.
White House, The.
Medina, T.   Big House Revisited, The.
Capitalism Is a Brutal Motherfucker.
Moss, T.   Raising a Humid Flag.
Murray, P.   Dark Testament.
Neal, L.   Don't say goodbye to the Porkpie
Hat that rolled.
For Our Women.
Harlem Gallery: From the Inside.
Narrative of Black Magicians, The.
Nelson, M.   Armed Men.
Balance.
Ballad of Aunt Geneva, The.
Chopin.
Diverne's Waltz.
Star-Fix.
Three Men in a Tent.
Tuskegee Airfield.
Nixon.   Ju-Ju Man.
Oden.   Man White, Brown Girl and All That
Jazz.
Oyewole.   Future Shock.
Parker, Dominique.   Sand.
Patterson, R.   Black Power.
Twenty-Six Ways of Looking at a Blackman.
What We Know.
Pfister.   Granny Blak Poet (in Pastel).
Powell, K.   Out of Pocket.
Public Enemy.   Don't believe the hype.
Fight the Power.
Queen Latifah.   Evil That Men Do, The.
Randall, D.   Abu / 's a stone black
revolutionary.
Blackberry Sweet.
Booker T. and W. E. B.
Different Image, A.
Melting Pot, The.
Roses and Revolutions.
Randall, J.   Execution.
Reed, I.   Bitter Chocolate.
Chattanooga.
Jacket Notes.

My Brothers.
Railroad Bill, a conjure man.
Smiley School, The.
Rivers, C.   In Defense of Black Poets.
Rodgers, C.   For Sistuhs Wearin' Straight Hair.
It Is Deep.
Jesus Was Crucified or: It Must Be Deep.
Poem for Some Black Women.
Rykard.   Whole Two Weeks After the Million
Man March; and Still, if You Asked Me
about It, This Is All I Could Say about It, A.
Salaam.   Bush Mama.
We have been seen.
Sanchez, S.   Ballad for Stirling Street, A.
Blk/Rhetoric.
Elegy: "Philadelphia / a disguised southern
city."
Haiku: "Did ya ever cry."
Homecoming.
Let us begin the real work.
Life / Poem.
Like bigger thomas.
Memorial.
Poem at Thirty.
Poem for Sterling Brown, A.
Poem: "Look at me 8th / grade."
Present.
Rebirth.
Reflections After the June 12th March for
Disarmament.
To All Brothers.
We a BadddDDD PEOPLE.
Young Womanhood.
Saunders, R.   Generation Gap, The.
Hush Honey.
Lawd, Dese Colored Chillum.
Scott-Heron.   Revolution Will Not Be
Televised!, The.
Scott, W.   For Both of Us at Fisk.
Shange.   Nappy Edges.
Nappy Edges (A Cross Country Sojourn).
Somebody almost walked off wid alla my
stuff.
Shannon, A.   Doris.
Sharp, S.   Tribal Marks.
Sherer.   Our Spirit Stands.
Smith, P.   Blonde White Women.
Building Nicole's Mama.
They say that black people.
Snellings.   Mississippi Concerto.
Speech.   Revolution / Revolution / Brothers
and sisters.
Spellman.   Did John's Music Kill Him?
When Black People Are.
Spriggs.   Every Harlem Face Is
AFROMANISM Surviving.
Stanard.   Baseball.
Steptoe.   Window Shopping.
Thomas, L.   Rhumba Negro.
Thomas, R.   Amen.
Thompson, C.   Mrs. Johnson Objects.
Thompson, J.   In my mind's eye.
Thompson, L.   Black Is Best.
Thompson, P.   Muse's Favor, The.
Tolson, M.   Dark Symphony.
Ex-Judge at the Bar, An.
Harlem.
Toure, A.   Immani in Sunburst Summer: a
Chant.
Touré, A.   JuJu.
Troupe.   In Texas Grass.
Unknown.   Me and My Captain.
Shine and the Titanic.
Song: "We raise de wheat."
Walcott.   Swamp, The.
Walker, M.   African Village, The.
Delta.
Five Black Men.
For my people everywhere singing their slave
songs repeatedly.
I want to write.
Litany from the Dark People, A.
Patchwork Quilt, A.
Poppa Chicken.
They have put us on HOLD.
We have been believers in the black gods of
an old land.

Waller, T. *et al.* (What Did I Do to Be So) Black and Blue?
Washington. Freedom Hair.
Watkins, N. Bedtime Story.
Do You Know Me?
Weatherly. Mud Water Shango.
Weaver, M. Easy Living.
Luxembourg Garden.
Welburn. Black is beautiful.
Wheatley, P. On Being Brought from Africa to America.
Whitman, A. 'T is hard to judge if hatred of one's race.
Williams, Karen. For Backwards Buppies.
Williams, Niama. Afrocentricity.
Williams, S. I Want Aretha to Set This to Music.
Letters from a New England Negro.
Peacock Poems: 1, The.
Straight Talk from Plain Women.
You Were Never Miss Brown to Me.
Wonder. Living for the City.
Worley, D. Dancing in the Dark.
Wright, J. Albuquerque Graveyard, The.
End of Ethnic Dream, The.
Wright, R. Between the World and Me.
I Have Seen Black Hands.
Wyche. We Rainclouds.
Young, A. Birthday Poem.
Boogie With O.O. Gabugah.
Dance for Militant Dilettantes, A.
Identities.
Old O.O. Blues, The.
Poem for Players, A.
Some Recent Fiction.
What You Seize Is What You Git.
Your Basic Black Poet.
Zu-Bolton. Sunset Beach.

Afterlife
Cullen, C. Poet, poet, what is your task.
Harper, F. Dying Child to Her Blind Father, The.
Dying Christian, The.
Eva's Farewell.
Obituary for J. Edwards Barnes.
Youth in Heaven.
Nelson, M. Cover Photograph.
Reed, I. Wardrobe Master of Paradise, The.
Toomer. Upward is this Actuality.
Walker, M. On Death and the Resurrection.
Wheatley, P. On the Death of a Young Lady of Five Years of Age.
To a Clergyman on the Death of His Lady.
To a Lady and Her Children, on the Death of Her Son and Their Brother.
To the Rev. Mr. Pitkin, on the Death of His Lady.

Afternoon
Young, A. Afternoon After, The.

Aggression
Young, A. Are You the Lover or Loved?
Dance for Militant Dilettantes, A.

Aging
African-American Oral Tradition. I used to could diddle all night long.
Angelou. Loss of love and youth, The.
On Aging.
On Reaching Forty.
Unmeasured Tempo.
Baraka. Way Out West.
Bontemps. To a Young Girl Leaving the Hill Country.
Braithwaite. Turn Me to My Yellow Leaves.
Brooks, G. Old Mary.
Sunset of the City, A.
Brown, S. Against That Day.
Clifton, L. Climbing.
More than once.
There Is a Girl Inside.
Thirty-eighth year, The.
Derricotte. Touching/Not Touching: My Mother.
Dunbar, P. At Sunset Time.
Lost Dream, A.
Vengeance is Sweet.
Emanuel, J. Fishermen.
Giovanni. Adulthood.

Adulthood II.
Age.
Life I Led, The.
One ounce of truth benefits.
Turning (I Need a Better Title).
You were gone.
Harper, M. Lovely's Daughters: Visitors.
Hayden, R. Lear Is Gay.
Horton, G. Connubial Felicity.
On Winter.
Hughes, L. Change.
Little Green Tree.
Watch Out, Papa.
Young Gal's Blues.
Johnson, J. Girl of fifteen.
Jones, L. *et al.* Look for You Yesterday, Here You Come Today.
Knight, E. Poem For a Certain Lady on Her 33rd Birthday, The.
Loftin. Weeksville Women.
Lorde. As I Grew Up Again.
Beams.
Generation II.
Memorial II.
Timing.
Madhubuti. Big Momma.
McKay, C. Adolescence.
Nelson, M. It's All in Your Head.
Reed, I. Turning Pro.
Roberson. True we are two grown men.
Sanchez, S. July.
Personal Letter No. 3.
Stuckey. Ribbons and Lace.
Toomer. Delivered at the Knighting of Lord Durgling by Great Bruce-Jean.
Troupe. Reflections on Growing Older.
Walker, A. Mississippi Winter III.
Young, A. Morning Poem for Michael, A.
Move Continuing, The.
Real Time.
See also **Middle Age**

Agnew, Spiro Theodore
Reed, I. Monsters from the Ozarks.
Agnosticism and Agnostics. *See* **Doubt**
AIDS (acquired immune deficiency syndrome)
Dixon, M. Heartbeats.
Nelson, M. Sacrament of Poverty, The.
Air
Oden. "As When Emotion Too Far Exceeds Its Cause."
Sanchez, S. Haiku: "Was it yesterday."
Toomer. Air.
Air Travel
Dove, R. Vacation.
Reed, I. American Airlines Sutra.
See also **Airports**
Air Warfare
Jordan, J. Moving Towards Home.
Nelson, M. Lonely Eagles.
Three Men in a Tent.
Redmond. Gods in Vietnam.
See also **Bombs and Bombing**
Airplanes
Nelson, M. Porter.
Rankine. New Windows.
Young, A. American Glamour.
Life at the Back of the Plane.
Airports
Wright, J. Invitation to Madison County, An.
See also **Air Travel**
Alabama (state)
Fauset. Stars in Alabama.
Fields, J. Alabama.
Mr. Tut's House A Recollection.
Hughes, L. Alabama Earth.
Ballad of Ozie Powell.
Birmingham Sunday.
Croon.
Daybreak in Alabama.
From Spain to Alabama.
Lorde. Domino.
McClellan. April of Alabama, The.
Patterson, R. Birmingham 1963.
Tolson, M. Uncle Rufus.
Alaska (state)
Fordham. Alaska.

Reed, I. Ice Age.
Points of View.
Untitled: "Alaska's rape."
Alcoholism and Alcoholics
Brown, S. Kentucky Blues.
Maumee Ruth.
Harper, F. Fatal Pledge, The.
Ragged Stocking, The.
Signing the Pledge.
Woman's Work.
Hughes, L. Ballad of Gin Mary.
Drunkard.
Wine-O.
Reed, C. My Brother and Me.
Walker, F. Crooked Afro.
Young, A. Old Woman.
See also **Drunkards**
Ali, Muhammad
Alexander, E. Narrative: Ali.
Alienation
Angelou. Chicken-Licken.
Detached, The.
Faces and more remember.
Baraka. Invention of Comics, The.
Brooks, G. Bronzeville Man with a Belt in the Back.
Forbes, C. Blue Monday.
Hayden, R. Soledad.
Herndon. Poem.
Lee, D. Back Again, Home.
Lorde. Dozens, The.
Madhubuti. Back Again, Home.
McKay, C. Outcast.
Reed, I. Dualism in Ralph Ellison's Invisible Man.
Poem for Two Daughters.
Sanchez, S. Poem of Praise, A.
Scott, W. Between Me and Anyone Who Can Understand.
Sharp, S. Tribal Marks.
Young, A. Ian.
See also **Blacks**
Aliens
Nuriddin. Children of the Future.
All Souls' Day
Atkins. Lisbon.
Allen, Richard
Heard, J. Rt. Rev. Richard Allen.
Alligators. *See* **Crocodiles**
Alphabet Poems
African-American Oral Tradition. Alphabet, The.
Toomer. Poem in C.
Ambition
Clifton, L. Climbing.
Cornish, S. Generations 2.
Fortune. We Know No More.
Horton, G. Division of an Estate.
George Moses Horton, Myself.
Hughes, L. Down Where I Am.
Johnson, M. Ambition.
Mitchell, K. Monster, The.
Ray, H. Ambition.
Rowe, G. We Are Rising.
Thomas, L. They Never Lose.
Ambivalence
Hughes, L. Nonette.
Ambulances
Moore, L. Tanka: "Month of rain ends."
America
Ai. More.
Anderson, C. Finger Pop'in.
Angelou. America.
Balagon. Children of the Cosmos.
Untitle.
Baraka. People Burning, The.
Revelation in Brick City.
Success, The.
"There Was something I Wanted to Tell You." (33) Why?
Three Modes of History and Culture.
Brown, S. Raise a Song.
Clark, Benjamin. Emigrant, The.
Cortez. Once Upon a Road.
Crouch, S. BLACKIE Speaks on Campus: a Valentine for Vachel Lindsay.

Cruz, V. O. K. / you scat taking.
Daáood. Tears for the poet.
Dumas, H. Afro-American.
America.
Tis of Thee.
Zebra Goes Wild Where the Sidewalk Ends, The.
Eckels. Hell, Mary / Bell Jones.
Giovanni. This Is Not for John Lennon.
Hamilton, B. Brother Harlem Bedford Watts Tells Mr. Charlie Where ITs At.
Hand. And I can Remember still your first lies America.
Harper, M. American History.
Prayer: Mt. Hood and Environs.
Hasson. Black and White.
Hayden, R. &[;American Journal&];.
Hughes, L. America.
Freedom's Plow.
I too, sing America.
Kids in School with Me, The.
Let America Be American Again.
Iman. Love Your Enemy.
Jackmon. Burn, Baby, Burn.
Jeffers, L. My Blackness Is the Beauty of This Land.
Johnson, F. To an Afro-American Maiden.
Johnson, G. True American, The.
Kaufman, B. Ancient Rain, The.
Benediction.
Enormous Gas Bill at the Dwarf Factory. A Horror Movie to be Shot with Eyes, The.
Heavy Water Blues.
On yardbird corners of embryonic hopes, drowned in a heroin tear.
Tidal Friction .. Comments at Real Movie.
Kgositsile. Awakening, The.
Lorde. Vietnam Addenda.
Madhubuti. For Black People.
Killing Memory.
McKay, C. America.
Tiger.
Menken. Pro Patria—America, 1861.
Neal, L. Narrative of Black Magicians, The.
Oktavi. Pardon Me.
Ologboni. Changed Mind (or the Day I Woke Up).
Plato. Natives of America, The.
Public Enemy. Fight the Power.
Randall, D. Melting Pot, The.
Randall, J. Who Shall Die.
Reed, I. American Airlines Sutra.
Back to Back: 3rd Eye.
Black Power Poem.
Feral Pioneers, The.
Jackal-Headed Cowboy, The.
Katskills Kiss Romance Goodbye, The.
Untitled: "Alaska's rape."
Roland Poet X. Divided States of America, The.
St. John, P. We Are Going to Be Here Now.
Sanchez, S. Poem for July 4, 1994.
Right On: White America.
Scott-Heron. Revolution Will Not Be Televised!, The.
Spellman. Tomorrow the heroes / will be named willie. their.
Summer. Curious White Boy.
Toomer. It is Everywhere.
Walcott. Blues.
Glory Trumpeter, The.
Upstate.
Weaver, M. My Father's Geography.
Welburn. First Essay on the Art of the U. S.
Wheatley, P. Farewell to America.
To a Lady on Her Coming to North-America with Her Son, for the Recovery of Her Health.
Whitman, A. Hymn to the Nation.
Young, A. American Time.

See also **United States**

American Revolution
Dunbar, P. Black Samson of Brandywine.
Wheatley, P. America.
On the Capture of General Lee.
On the Death of General Wooster.

On the Death of Mr. Snider Murder'd by Richardson.
Whitman, A. Hymn to the Nation.
Americans
Hayden, R. American Journal.
Hughes, L. Let America Be American Again.
Madam's Calling Cards.
Johnson, G. True American, The.
Knight, E. Idea of Ancestry, The.
Walker, M. For my people everywhere singing their slave songs repeatedly.
Watkins, N. Missions and Magnolias.
Amon Ra
Reed, I. I Am a Cowboy in the Boat of Ra.
Anarchism and Anarchists
Cullen, C. For an Anarchist.
Ancestry and Ancestors
Angelou. Family Affairs.
Aubert, A. Baptism.
Barlow, G. Sorrow Since Sitting Bull, A.
This Bridge Across.
Bennett, G. Heritage.
Brooks, G. Sundays of Satin-Legs Smith, The.
Brown, S. Children's Children.
Clifton, L. In populated air.
Roots.
Clinton. History as Trash.
Cortez. I See Chano Pozo.
Cullen, C. Heritage.
Dixon, M. Tour Guide: La Maison des Esclaves.
Dumas, H. Black Star Line.
Gilbert, C. This Bridge Across.
Giovanni. Hands; For Mother's Day.
Harper, M. Continuous Visit.
Made Connections.
Roland.
Hughes, L. Afraid.
Negro Speaks of Rivers, The.
Not Often.
Jeffers, L. Flesh of the Young Men Is Burning, The.
Trellie.
Jordan, J. Poem about the Head of a Negro.
Kaufman, B. African Dream.
Geneology.
Knight, E. Bones of My Father, The.
Idea of Ancestry, The.
Komunyakaa. Salt.
Lorde. Dahomey.
Home.
Oshun's Table.
McKay, C. Heritage.
Neal, L. Narrative of Black Magicians, The.
Nelson, M. Men in the Kitchen.
Phillips, F. Genealogy.
Randall, D. Ancestors.
Redmond. Milestone: The Birth of an Ancestor.
Salaam. Funeraled Fare Well.
Sanchez, S. How can you comfort.
Present.
Sherer. Our Spirit Stands.
Stewart, James T. Poem: a Piece.
Troupe. Sense of Coolness, A.
Walker, M. Dark Blood.
How many silent centuries sleep in my sultry veins?
Lineage.
Worley, D. Tongues in My Mouth.
Angels
Angelou. Arrival.
Bontemps. Nocturne at Bethesda.
Clifton, L. Confession.
Cotter, Sr. Band of Gideon roam the sky, The.
Dunbar, P. Jack Frost at Bedtime.
Harper, F. Light in Darkness.
Harper, M. Black Angel, The.
Hughes, L. Angels wings is white as snow, The.
Mackey, N. Song of the Andoumboulou.
Winged Abyss.
Nelson, M. Abba Jacob and the Angel.
Toomer. Angelic Eve.
Unknown. My Way's Cloudy.
Anger
Allen, S. Moment Please, A.

Angelou. Son to Mother.
Baraka. Black Dada Nihilismus.
Contract. (For The Destruction and Rebuilding of Paterson), A.
Brown, S. Crispus Attacks McKoy.
Episode.
Cortez. Acceptance Speech.
Lynch Fragment 2.
Plain Truth.
Derricotte. Promise, The.
Giovanni. Black Power.
Poem (For BMC No. 3).
Harper, M. Corktown.
Hughes, L. Evil Morning.
Iverem. Daddy's Friends.
Jeffers, L. But I Know That Unseen Anger Runs a Raft.
My Blackness Is the Beauty of This Land.
Vietnam: I Need More Than This Crust of Salt.
Jordan, J. Female and the Silence of a Man, The.
For My Brother.
Poem About My Rights.
Knight, E. Apology for Apostasy?
Lorde. Sequelae.
Nelson, M. April Rape.
Good Friday Prayer.
Like Father, Like Son.
Sanchez, S. Summer Words of [*or* for] a Sistuh [*or* Sister] Addict.
When you left i ran.
Walker, M. Ex-Slave.
See also **Quarrels**
Angola
Hughes, L. Angola Question Mark.
Animals
Baraka. Footnote to a Pretentious Book.
Clifton, L. What spells racoon to me.
Cullen, C. Thoughts in a Zoo.
Dunbar, P. Critters' Dance, De.
See also **Death of Animals**
Anniversaries
Harper, F. To Mr. and Mrs. W. F. Johnson on Their Twenty-Fifth Wedding Anniversary.
Lorde. Anniversary.
Antarctica
Jordan, J. Torn Sky: Lesson #1, The.
Anticipation
Angelou. They Ask Why.
Brown, S. Convict.
Dunbar, P. Expectation.
Waiting.
When de Co'n Pone's Hot.
Giovanni. Hampton, Virginia.
Patience.
Winter.
Harper, F. Sir, We Would See Jesus.
Hayden, R. Night-Blooming Cereus, The.
Hughes, L. Red Roses.
Jordan, J. Of Nightsong and Flight.
Relativity.
Lorde. Father the year has fallen.
Memorial III from a Phone Booth on Broadway.
Rooming houses are old women.
Suspension.
Madhubuti. Poem Looking for a Reader, A.
McKay, C. Absence.
Nelson, M. Daughters, 1900.
Reed, I. But Nobody Was There.
Sanchez, S. My body waiting.
Young, A. Night before Michael Was Born, The.
Antigone
Ray, H. Antigone and Oedipus.
Reed, I. Antigone, This Is It.
Anti-Semitism
Hughes, L. Un-American Investigators.
Anxiety
Baraka. Three Modes of History and Culture.
Davis, F. Arthur Ridgewood, M.D.
Gilyard. Daughter, That Picture of You.
Giovanni. Boxes.
Introspection.
Life Cycles.

Graham, D. Portrait of Johnny Doller, A.
Hayden, R. Ice Storm.
Lorde. Hanging Fire.
  Litany for Survival, A.
  Memorial III from a Phone Booth on Broadway.
Miller, E. Walk in the Daytime Is Just as Dangerous as a Walk in the Night, A.
Nelson, M. It's All in Your Head.
Thomas, L. Onion Bucket.
Wright, J. Frightened Lover's Sleep, The.

Apartheid
Brooks, G. Near-Johannesburg Boy, The.
Cortez. Solomon Mahlangu, Freedom Fighter from Mamelodi.
Hughes, L. Dixie South Africa.
  Where? When? Which?
Komunyakaa. Blasphemy.
Lorde. Sisters in Arms.

See also **Oppression; Segregation**

Apartments
Hughes, L. Madam and the Rent Man.
Lorde. Moving Out Or the End of Cooperative Living.
Sanchez, S. Personal Letter No. 2.

Apes
Danner, M. Best Loved of Africa.
Nelson, M. Ape-Gods.

Apocalypse
Foreman. Judgement Day: For Big Red the Darwinian Doge. R.I.P.
Unknown. Steal Away to Jesus.

See also **End of the World; Judgment Day**

Apollinaire, Guillaume
Kaufman, B. Unhistorical Events.

Apollo
Wheatley, P. Niobe in Distress for Her Children Slain by Apollo, from Ovid's Metamorphoses, Book VI, and from a View of the Painting of Mr. Richard Wilson.

Apoplexy. *See* **Strokes**

Apostles
Clifton, L. Calling of the Disciples, The.

Apple Trees and Apples
Dunbar, P. Old Apple-Tree, The.
  Unlucky Apple, The.
Harper, M. At the Cemetery.
  History as Apple Tree.
Major, C. Apple Core.

Approval
Young, A. Moon, How Do I Measure Up?

April
Dunbar-Nelson. April is on the way!
Grimké, A. At April.
Hughes, L. April Rain Song.
Ray, H. April.

Arab-Israeli Wars
Jordan, J. Intifada.
  Moving Towards Home.

Arabia
Young, A. Arabia it's so fine so hot.

Arachne
Hayden, R. Richard Hunt's "Arachne."

Arcadia
Dunbar, P. Ballade: "By Mystic's banks I held my dream."
  Farewell to Arcady.

Aristocracy
Baraka. Politics of Rich Painters, The.

Arkansas (state)
Angelou. My Arkansas.
Brown, S. Slim Lands a Job?

Armstrong, Louis
Tolson, M. Satchmo.

Army Life
African-American Oral Tradition. Joe the Grinder and G.I. Joe.
Nelson, M. Beauty Shoppe.
  Freeman Field.
  Lonely Eagles.
  Star-Fix.
  Three Men in a Tent.

See also **Soldiers**

Art and Artists
Baraka. Black Art.
  New World, The.
  Politics of Rich Painters, The.
Brooks, G. Egg Boiler, The.
Daáood. Tears for the poet.
Danner, M. Convert, The.
  Etta Moten's Attic.
  These Beasts and the Benin Bronze.
Dunbar, P. Nature and Art.
Giovanni. Charles White.
  Charting the Night Winds.
Harper, F. Artist, The.
  Lost Bells, The.
Hughes, L. Metropolitan Museum.
  Paint.
Johnson, J. Before a Painting.
Jordan, J. Poem about the Head of a Negro.
Kaufman, B. Believe, Believe.
  Bird with Painted Wings.
  Carl Chessman Interviews the P.T.A. in His Swank Gas Chamber Before Leaving on His Annual Inspection of Capital, Tour of Northern California Death Universities, Happy.
  Countess Erica Blaise: Chorus.
  I Sigh a Marbled Sigh Ah, at Last.
  "Michelangelo" the Elder.
  To My Son Parker, Asleep in the Next Room.
  Waiting.
Kgositsile. Mandela's Sermon.
Komunyakaa. Blasphemy.
Loftis. Delirium.
Lorde. Jessehelms.
Madhubuti. Wall, The.
Neal, L. Baroness and the Black Musician, The.
Randall, D. Primitives.
  Rite, The.
Reed, I. Catechism of d Neoamerican Hoodoo Church.
  Martine's Keen Eyes.
Sanchez, S. You are amble and.
Thompson-Cager. Praise Song for Katherine Dunham: A Choreopoem.
Walker, A. Songless.
Welburn. First Essay on the Art of the U. S.
Wheatley, P. Hymn to Humanity, An.

Arthurian Legend
Bontemps. Lancelot.

Artichokes
Burnette. Artichoke Pickle Passion: Sonnet.

Ashe, Arthur
Gilmore, B. Coming to the Net.

Asia
Lorde. Thanks to Jesse Jackson.

Asphodels
Hughes, L. Metropolitan Museum.

Aspirations
Dove, R. Magic.
Horton, G. George Moses Horton, Myself.
Hughes, L. America.
  Aspiration.
  Deferred.
  Negro Mother, The.
  Stars.
  To Be Somebody.
Lorde. Seventh Sign, The.
Salaam. I live in the mouth of history.
Trethewey. Domestic Work, 1937.
Wheatley, P. On Virtue.

Assassinations and Assassins
Barrax. For Malcolm: After Mecca.
King: April 4, 1968.
Emanuel, J. Panther Man.
Giovanni. Adulthood.
Knight, E. It was a funky deal.
Lawrence, J. For Malcolm.
Lee, D. Assassination.
Lorde. Equinox.
Madhubuti. Assassination.
Patterson, R. At That Moment.
Reed, I. Nov 22, 1988.
Young, A. Day Kennedy Died.

Astrology and Astrologers
Clifton, L. Astrologer Predicts at Mary's Birth, The.
McElroy, C. Horoscope.

Astronomy and Astronomers. *See* **Stars**

Astronauts
Hayden, R. Astronauts.

Atheism
Cullen, C. For an Atheist.
Hughes, L. Goodbye Christ.
Wheatley, P. Address to the Atheist, By P. Wheatley at the Age of 14 Years—1767. Atheism.

Athletics and Athletes
Williams, Marlon. Blood, Sweat, and Fears.

See also **Games; Listings for specific sports**

Atlanta, Georgia
Brown, S. All Are Gay.
  Old Woman Remembers, An.
  Slim in Atlanta.
  Transfer.
DuBois, W. Litany of [or at] Atlanta, A.
Fordham. Atlanta Exposition Ode.
Toure, A. Immani in Sunburst Summer: a Chant.

Atlantic Ocean
Clifton, L. Atlantic is a sea of bones.

Atomic Bomb
Frost, R. U. S. 1946 King's X.
Hughes, L. Lunch in a Jim Crow Car.

See also **Hiroshima, Japan; Nagasaki, Japan; Nuclear War**

Attucks, Crispus
Hayden, R. Crispus Attucks.

Auden, Wystan Hugh
Loftis. In Memorium: Robert Hayden.
Walcott. Eulogy to W. H. Auden.
Young, A. W. H. Auden & Mantan Moreland.

August
Dunbar, P. In August.
Knight, E. Haiku: "In the August grass."
Ray, H. August.

Aunt Jemima
Hayden, R. Aunt Jemima of the Ocean Waves.

Aunts
Dunbar, P. Appreciation.
Hughes, L. Aunt Sue's Stories.
Tolson, M. Old Houses.
Young, A. Aunt.

Automobile Accidents
Harper, M. Roland.
Lorde. Do You Remember Laura.
  Poem for a Poet, A.

Automobiles
African-American Oral Tradition. Ford, The.
Atkins. New Storefront.
Barrax. Adagio.
Eady. Song.
Forman, R. Green Boots n Lil Honeys.
Gilbert, C. Now.
Gilmore, B. Gas Station Attendant.
Jackson, M. L. Some Kind of Crazy.
Moore, Maiisha. Haiku: "Dark rock-road, The."
Reed, I. Datsun's Death.
Slaveship, German Model.

See also **Driving and Drivers**

Autumn
Alexander, M. October Journey.
Angelou. Late October.
Braithwaite. Turn Me to My Yellow Leaves.
Brooks, G. Sunset of the City, A.
Dunbar, P. Merry Autumn.
  Signs of the Times.
Hughes, L. Autumn Note.
  Autumn Thought.
  Poème d'Automne.
  Thanksgiving Time.
Linden, M. Fall Is Here, The.
Lorde. Return.
  What my child learns of the sea.
Marshall, M. Autumn.
Moore, L. Haiku: "Black woman, A."

Redmond. Autumn God.
Sanchez, S. Autumn. a bonfire.
These autumn trees sit.
Thompson, C. Autumn Day, An.
Autumn Leaves.
Thompson, P. Autumn ("List to the sad wind, drearily moaning").
Autumn ("Sun shines bright, but sadly, The").
Tucker, M. Autumn Thoughts.
Young, A. New Autumn, New York.
October Variations, The.

See also **Leaves**

Aviation and Aviators. *See* **Air Travel**

Axes
African-American Oral Tradition. Bend your back when I say "Go."

Azikiwe, Benjamin Nnamdi
Hughes, L. Azikiwe in Jail.

B

Babies
Adisa. Rainbow, The.
African-American Oral Tradition. Forty-nine Ford and a tank full of gas.
Get In Out of the Rain.
Bennett, G. Secret.
Brown, S. Seeking Religion.
Clifton, L. On the Birth of Bomani.
Davis, D. Aunt Chloe's Lullaby.
Dove, R. Pastoral.
Dunbar, P. Little brown baby wif spa'klin' eyes.
Poet and the Baby, The.
Puttin' the Baby Away.
Turning of the Babies in the Bed, The.
Two little boots all rough an' wo'.
Freeman, C. When / my uncle willie saw.
Harper, F. To a Babe Smiling in Her Sleep.
Harper, M. Clan Meeting: Births and Nations: A Blood Song.
Hughes, L. Lullaby: "My little dark baby."
Lorde. Now That I Am Forever with Child.
Moore, L. Haiku: "Black woman, A."
Nelson, M. Wild Pansies.
Smith, P. Dylan, Two Days.
Young, A. Michael At Sixteen Months.

See also **Infant Death**

Baboons
African-American Oral Tradition. Poolshooting Monkey: "It was in Speero's poolroom back in nineteen-ten."
Poolshooting Monkey: "I don't know but I was told."

Bachelors
Horton, G. Cheerless Condition of Bachelorship, The.

Backs
Lorde. Monkeyman.

Baker, Josephine
Cortez. So Many Feathers.

Baldness
Henderson-Holmes. "C" ing in Colors: Red.

Baldwin, James
Troupe. In Jimmy's Garden.
In Memoriam; for James Baldwin (1924–1987).

Balloons
Knight, E. Green Grass and Yellow Balloons.

Baltimore, Maryland
Cullen, C. Incident.
Weaver, M. Weekend Equestrian, The.

Bamboo
Sanchez, S. We are gatherers.

Bands
Dunbar, P. Colored Band, The.
Hughes, L. Harlem Dance Hall.

Banjos
Brown, S. Honey Mah Love.
Davis, D. Miss Liza's Banjer.
Dunbar, P. Banjo Song, A.
Voice of the Banjo, The.
Hughes, L. Song for a Banjo Dance.

Johnson, F. Banjo Player, The.

Banking and Bankers
Hughes, L. To the Little Front of San Lazaro on the Ocean Front, Havana.

Baptism
Aubert, A. Baptism.
Walker, A. Baptism.

Barcelona, Spain
Hughes, L. Air Raid: Barcelona.
McKay, C. Barcelona.

Bards
Johnson, J. O Black and unknown bards of long ago.

Barns
Moore, L. Haiku: "Winter stillness."
Pritchard, N. Paysagesque.

Bars and Bartenders
African-American Oral Tradition. Stackolee: "This is supposed to be about two colored studs. It's truth. In New Orleans."
Stackolee: "Back in forty-nine when times was hard."
Stackolooee: "I staggered in a place called the Bucket a Blood."
Stackolee: "It was back in the time of nineteen hundred and two."
Stackolee: "It was back in the year of forty-one when the times was hard."
Stackolee: "When I was young in my prime."
Hughes, L. Bar.
Tolson, M. Ex-Judge at the Bar, An.
Young, A. Topsy: Part 2.

Baseball
Allen, S. To Satch.
Clifton, L. Jackie Robinson.
Harper, M. No. 24.
Miller, E. Boys of Summer, The.
Players.
Nelson, M. Abba Jacob at Bat.
Reed, I. Turning Pro.
Stanard. Baseball.
Zu-Bolton. Intro to My Final Book of Poems.

Basketball
Harper, M. Makin' Jump Shots.

Baths and Bathing
Ahmasi. Water of Your Bath.
Davis, T. Susannah.
Emanuel, J. Voyage of Jimmy Poo, The.
Lorde. From the Cave.
Mackey, N. Dream Thief.
Nelson, M. Women's Locker Room.

Battlefields
Murray, P. Redemption.
Wheatley, P. Goliath of Gath.

Bayous
Salaam. Spiritual Geography.

Beaches
Brutus. Sand wet and cool, The.
Mitchell, K. Tree Stillness.
Toomer. Merl.
Young, A. Sad Hour of Your Peace, The.

See also **Shores**

Beads
Dunbar, P. She told her beads with downcast eyes.

Beards
Dove, R. This Life.
Farr. Van/Dyke.

Bears
African-American Oral Tradition. Poolshooting Monkey: "It was in Speero's poolroom in the year eighteen-ten."
Dunbar, P. Cabin Tale, A.
Reed, I. Grizzly.
Points of View.
Untitled: "Today I feel bearish."
Roberson. Sonnet.

Beatings
Angelou. Kind of Love, Some Say, A.
Knight, E. Hard Rock Returns to Prison from the Hospital for the Criminal Insane.
Unknown. No more auction block for me.

Beatniks
Durem. Problem in Social Geometry—the Inverted Square!

Kaufman, B. Bagel Shop Jazz.
Heather Bell.

Beaufort, South Carolina
Heard, J. National Cemetery, Beaufort, South Carolina, The.

Beauty
Angelou. Black Ode.
Phenomenal Woman.
Baraka. Cold Term.
Duncan Spoke of a Process.
Ostriches and Grandmothers!
Return of the Native.
Braithwaite. Sic Vita.
Brooks, J. Last Quarter Moon of the Dying Year, The.
Brown, S. Glory, Glory.
To Sallie, Walking.
Christian. Craftsman, The.
Clifton, L. Lane Is the Pretty One.
My boys beauty is.
Cullen, C. Advice to a Beauty.
Bright Bindings.
Life's Rendezvous.
Medusa.
Song of Praise, A.
To John Keats, Poet, at Springtime.
Cuney. No Images.
Desbrosses. Le Retour au Village aux Perles.
Derricotte. Christmas Eve: My Mother Dressing.
Dunbar-Nelson. Proletariat Speaks, The.
Dunbar, P. Alice.
Love's Pictures.
Song, A: "On a summer's day as I sat by a stream."
Fields, J. Alabama.
Forman, R. You So Woman.
Franklin, C. Death of Days and Nights of Life.
Giovanni. Beautiful Black Men.
Poem for Flora.
Grimké, A. Mona Lisa, A.
Harris, W. Daddy Poem, A.
Harvey, Y. Sonia Told Them Women.
Hemphill. Soft Targets.
Hoagland, E. Anti-Semanticist, The.
Horton, G. Acrostics.
For the Fair Miss M. M. McLean.
Love.
Hughes, L. Beauty.
Call to Creation.
Fascination.
Harlem Sweeties.
I too, sing America.
In the mist of the moon I saw you.
Jazzonia.
My Beloved.
My People.
Poem: "Ah, / My black one."
To Beauty.
To the Dark Mercedes of "El Palacio de Amor."
When Sue Wears Red.
Wooing, A.
Jeffers, L. My Blackness Is the Beauty of This Land.
Trellie.
Johnson, H. Poem: "Little brown boy."
Jordan, J. It's About You: on the Beach.
On Declining Values.
Poem # One.
Jordan, N. July 31.
Lorde. Lover's Song, A.
Naturally.
Madgett. Black Woman.
Madhubuti. Poem Looking for a Reader, A.
McKay, C. O word I love to sing! thou art too tender.
Red Flower, A.
To O.E.A. E. A.
Nelson, M. Strange beautiful woman, A.
Women's Locker Room.
Roberson. Eclipse.
St. John, P. Pearle's Poem.
Sanchez, S. "Look at me 8th / grade."
Smith, P. Blonde White Women.
Thompson, D. Sister Lakin and Lally.

Tolson, M. Madame Alpha Devine she made a million.
Toney. In the Twilight.
Toomer. I See Her Lovely There.
 November Cotton Flower.
 Tell me, dear beauty of the dusk.
Trethewey. Hot Comb.
Wheatley, P. To S. M., a Young African Painter, on Seeing His Works.
Williams, S. Straight Talk from Plain Women.
Wright, J. What is Beautiful.
Young, A. Dance For Ma Rainey, A.

Bedrooms
Komunyakaa. Between Days.
Lane, P. Midnight Song.

Beds
African-American Oral Tradition. Chintz, The.
Coleman, W. Bedtime Story.
Hughes, L. Sick Room.
Lorde. Change.
Madhubuti. Loneliness, A.
Walker, A. Overnights.
Warren-Moore. All-Night Issue, The.

Beech Trees and Beechnuts
Dove, R. Copper Beech, The.

Beer
Dunbar, P. Lager Beer.

Bees and Beekeeping
Aubert, A. One More Time.
Lorde. Bees, The.
 Production.
Toomer. Beehive.

Beethoven, Ludwig van
Ray, H. Beethoven.

Beetles
Dove, R. Roses.

Begging and Beggars
Harper, F. Lessons of the Street.
Hughes, L. Beggar Boy.
Jordan, J. On Declining Values.
Lorde. Ballad for Ashes.
Major, C. Blind Old Woman.
Unknown. Mamie's Blues.
See also **Homeless, The**

Bells
Danner, M. Small Bells of Benin, The.
Fordham. Bells of St. Michael.
Harper, F. Freedom Bell, The.
 Lost Bells, The.
Heard, J. Sabbath Bells.
Hughes, L. Bells Toll Kindly, The.
Linden, M. Church Bells, The.
Thompson, C. Church Bells.

Belshazzar
Bibb. Belshazzar's Feast.
Hughes, L. Last Feast of Belshazzar, The.

Benches
Harper, M. For Bud.

Bennett, Susan Eugenia
Fordham. In Memoriam. Susan Eugenia Bennett.

Berkshire Hills, Massachusetts
Ray, H. Among the Berkshire Hills.

Berlin, Germany
Christian. Go Down, Moses!
Lorde. Berlin Is Hard on Colored Girls.
 East Berlin.
 Peace on Earth.
 Restoration.

Berryman, John
Harper, M. Tongue-tied in Black and White.

Bethune, Mary McLeod
Walker, M. For Mary McLeod Bethune.

Betrayal
African-American Oral Tradition. Eddie Ledoux: "There's some strange and queer tales that come through all jails."
 Eddie Ledoux: "Wise and queer tales float through all the jails."
 My Reflection.
 Wanderer's Trail, The.
Angelou. Communication I.
Baraka. Are Their Blues Singers in Russia?
 Burning General, The.

Cullen, C. Judas Iscariot.
Chuck D. But Can You Kill the Nigga in You?
Evans, M. Writers, The.
Hall, K. Illusions.
Hand. And I can Remember still your first lies America.
Harper, F. Sin of Achar, The.
 To the Union Savers of Cleveland.
Hughes, L. Could be Hastings Street.
Klein, S. Fragments from the Diary of Amelie Patiné, Quadroon Mistress of Monsieur Jacques R-------.
Lockett. Die Black Pervert.
Lorde. Conversations in Crisis.
McClellan. Feet of Judas, The.
Medina, T. Big House Revisited, The.
Reed, I. Cuckoo is a funny bird, A.
 Judas.
Unknown. Frankie and Johnny were lovers.

Bible
Giovanni. Great Pax Whitie, The.
 Poem for Flora.
Harper, F. Bible Defence of Slavery.
Jordan, N. Sinner.
Knight, E. Genesis 11.
Madhubuti. Black Christ, The.
Moorer. Bible, The.
 Mountain Tops.
Oden. Bible Study.

Birds
Asquith. Birds on a Powerline.
Atkins. Probability and Birds in the Yard.
Conyus. Day in the Life of. . . , A.
Dove, R. In the Old Neighborhood.
Dunbar, P. Crumb, a crumb, and a little seed, A.
 Oh little fledgling out of the nest.
 Preparation.
 Sympathy.
 Two Songs.
Gilbert, C. African Sculpture.
Hughes, L. Worriation.
Johnson, G. Heart of a Woman, The.
Komunyakaa. Birds on a Powerline.
Linden, M. Bird Song, The.
Lorde. Ballad from Childhood.
 Trip on the Staten Island Ferry, A.
Mackey, N. Winged Abyss.
Major, C. Apple Core.
 On Trying to Imagine the Kiwi Pregnant.
Newsome. Bird in the Cage, The.
Oden. "As When Emotion Too Far Exceeds Its Cause."
Prettyman. Still Life: Lady with Birds.
Toomer. Motion and Rest.
Wright, J. Invention of a Garden, The.
See also **Listings for specific birds**

Birmingham, Alabama
Giscombe. (1962 At the Edge of Town).
 (The Recent Past).
Hughes, L. Birmingham Sunday.
Patterson, R. Birmingham 1963.
Randall, D. Ballad of Birmingham.
Reed, I. Ghost in Birmingham, The.
Walker, M. Birmingham.
 Birmingham, 1963.

Birth
Ai. Country Midwife: A Day, The.
Brooks, G. Birth in a Narrow Room, The.
Brown, S. Young Ones, The.
Clifton, L. On the Birth of Bomani.
Dove, R. Variation on Guilt.
Ebon. To Our First Born or the Prophet Arrives.
Evans, M. Who Can Be Born Black.
Harper, M. Deathwatch.
 Love Medley: Patrice Cuchulain.
Hughes, L. Birth.
 S-sss-ss-sh!
Knight, E. On the Birth of a Black / Baby / Boy.
 Stretching of the Belly, The.
Lorde. And What About the Children.
 Now That I Am Forever with Child.
Miller, E. Jasmine.
Nelson, M. Chosen.

My Second Birth.
 Wild Pansies.
Sanchez, S. Present.
 Rebirth.
 Woman who made, A.
Shange. Oh, I'm 10 Months Pregnant.
Williams, Karen. Little Black Girls, The Original Eve (Spreadin' More Beautiful Brown Around).
Williams, S. Say Hello to John.
Wright, J. Lake in Central Park, The.

Birth Control
Miller, E. She is flat on her back.

Birthdays
Angelou. On Reaching Forty.
Clifton, L. August the 12th.
Heard, J. My Husband's Birthday.
Jordan, J. If You Saw a Negro Lady.
Knight, E. Birthday Poem.
Komunyakaa. Gift Horse.
Lorde. Birthday Memorial to Seventh Street, A.
 Ethiopia.
Moorer. Birthday Wishes to a Husband.
 Birthday Wishes to a Minister of the Gospel.
 Birthday Wishes to a Physician.
Reed, I. Author Reflects on His 35th Birthday, The.
 Last Week in 30, The.
Torregian. Poem for the Birthday of Huey P. Newton.
Zu-Bolton. Sunset Beach.

Birthplaces
Harper, M. Borning Room, The.
Hughes, L. New Yorkers.

Bitterness
Baraka. If into Love the Image Burdens.
Brooks, G. Piano after War.
Brown, S. Bitter Fruit of the Tree.
Dove, R. Definition in the Face of Unnamed Fury.
Dunbar, P. Then and Now.
Giovanni. Poem (No Name No. 2).
 When i die i hope no one who ever hurt me cries.
Lorde. American Cancer Society Or There Is More Than One Way to Skin a Coon.
 And Don't Think I Won't Be Waiting.
 Cables To Rage Or I've Been Talking On This Street Corner.
 Conversations in Crisis.
 Dozens, The.
 New York City 1970.
 Spring People.
 Who Said It Was Simple.
Walker, M. Dear are the names that charmed me in my youth.
 Fanfare, Coda, and Finale.

Black (color)
Fabio. Evil Is No Black Thing.
Madhubuti. Poem Looking for a Reader, A.
Salaam. Spiritual Geography.
Sanchez, S. Haiku: "Was it yesterday."
Thompson, L. Black Is Best.
Welburn. Black is beautiful.

Black Panthers
Giovanni. Black Power.
Hughes, L. Black Panther.

Black Power
Angelou. No No No No.
 Pusher, The.
Baraka. In the Tradition.
 Ka 'Ba.
 Sacred Chant for the Return of Black Spirit and Power.
Barrax. For a Black Poet.
Clifton, L. Apology (to the Panthers).
 For her hiding place.
 Malcolm.
 To Bobby Seale.
 Tyrone (2).
 Tyrone (4).
DuBois, W. Song of the Smoke, The.
Evans, M. Vive Noir!
Ferdinand. 2 B BLK.
Gilmore, B. Revolution.

Giovanni. Black Power.
Black Separatism.
Detroit Conference of Unity and Art.
My Poem.
No Reservations.
Poem (No Name No. 2).
Poem (No Name No. 3).
Poem of Angela Yvonne Davis.
2nd Rapp.
Harper, M. High Modes: Vision as Ritual: Confirmation.
Madimba.
Meaning of Protest, The.
Song: I Want a Witness.
Hasson. Black and White.
Haynes, A. Eclipse.
Hoagland, E. Anti-Semanticist, The.
Hughes, L. I too, sing America.
Jackmon. That Old Time Religion.
Jeffers, L. I do not know the power of my hand.
My Blackness Is the Beauty of This Land.
Kgositsile. Awakening, The.
When Brown Is Black.
Knight, E. Dark Prophecy: I Sing of Shine.
Lawrence, J. For Malcolm.
Lee, D. Poem to Complement Other Poems, A.
Lorde. NOW.
Madhubuti. Death Dance, The.
Stereo.
Ologboni. Black Henry.
Reed, I. Badman of the Guest Professor.
Sanchez, S. Blk/Rhetoric.
Liberation / Poem.
Malcolm.
Poem: "Look at me 8th / grade."
Tolson, M. Dark Symphony.

Blackberries
Aubert, A. All Singing in a Pie.

Blackbirds
Moss, T. Reconsideration of the Blackbird, A.

Blacks
Adisa. I Will Not Let Them Take You.
African-American Oral Tradition. Titanic: "All the old folks say the fourth a May was a hell of a day."
Titanic: "Boys, you remember way back on the day of the eighth of May."
Titanic: "Eighth a May was a hell of a day, The."
Titanic: "I don't know, but my folks say."
Titanic: "In the year of eighteen-twelve."
Titanic: "It was sad indeed, it was sad in mind."
Titanic: "Tenth of May was a hell of a day, The."
Titanic: "This is about Shine O Shine. The captain was on his boat and he was."
Titanic: "Twelfth of May was one hell of a day, The."
Ups on the Farm.
Alexander, E. Venus Hottentot.
Alexander, K. Just Us.
Allen, S. Benin Bronze.
Moment Please, A.
Anderson, S. Soul-Smiles.
Angelou. Televised news turns.
Baker, H. No matter where you travel.
Baraka. Black Art.
Black Bourgeoisie.
Black People: This Is Our Destiny.
Ka 'Ba.
Notes for a Speech.
Poem for Black Hearts, A.
Reggae or Not!
Speech #38 (or Y We Say It This Way).
Wise 2.
Y's 18.
Barrax. Black Narcissus.
Bibbs. Split Standard.
Bontemps. God Give to Men.
Brooks, G. Black Wedding Song, A.
Kojo "I Am a Black."
Life of Lincoln West, The.
Young Africans.
Brown, S. Strong Men.

Bryant, F. Nothing Lovely as a Tree.
Carroll, K. Something Easy for Ultra Black Nationalists.
Upper Marlboro.
Clifton, L. Listen children / keep this in the place.
Coleman, W. Dear Mama.
Cortez. I and I.
Cullen, C. From the Dark Tower.
Yet Do I Marvel.
Danner, M. Convert, The.
Davis, F. Giles Johnson, Ph.D.
Derricotte. Black Boys Play the Classics.
Family Secrets.
DuBois, W. Song of the Smoke, The.
Dunbar, P. We wear the mask that grins and lies.
Emanuel, J. Negritude.
Negro, The.
Evans, M. Speak the truth to the people.
Who Can Be Born Black.
Farr. At General Electric, Where They Eat Their/Young.
Forman, R. Up Sister.
Franklin, C. Death of Days and Nights of Life.
Two Dreams (for M. L. K.'s one).
Gerima. Sankofa.
Giovanni. Beautiful Black Men.
Black Judgements.
Detroit Conference of Unity and Art.
Ego Tripping.
For an Intellectual Audience.
Geni in the Jar, The.
Great Pax Whitie, The.
Nikki-Rosa.
Poem (For Anna Hedgeman and Alfreda Duster).
Poem for Black Boys.
Poem (For Nina).
Poem Off Center, A.
Toy Poem.
True Import of Present Dialogue, Black vs. Negro.
Universality.
Very Simple Wish, A.
Wilmington Delaware.
Henderson, D. Neon Diaspora.
Henderson-Holmes. "C" ing in Colors: Red.
Hernton. Medicine Man.
Holman, M. Mr. Z.
Hughes, L. Always the Same.
Angola Question Mark.
Ballad of Negro History, A.
Black Crown, The.
Black Dancers.
Black Gal.
Black Seed.
Black Workers.
Broadcast to the West Indies.
Call of Ethiopia.
Carol of the Brown King.
Cross.
Dream Variations.
Emperor Haile Selassie.
First of May.
House in the World.
How about It, Dixie.
Imagine! / They are afraid of you.
Justice.
Letter from Spain.
Man into Men.
Me and My Song.
Memo to Non-White People.
Negro.
Negro Speaks of Rivers, The.
Neighbor.
New Song, A.
Nocturne for the Drums.
Poem: "Ah, / My black one."
Prelude to Our Age.
Question and Answer.
Red Cross.
To Certain Intellectuals.
We, Too.
Worriation.
Young Negro Girl.

Jean, V. On Apologies.
Jeffers, L. My Blackness Is the Beauty of This Land.
Johnson, F. Ethiopian's Song, The.
Tired.
Johnson, J. Saint Peter Relates an Incident of the Resurrection Day.
Jordan, J. For My Brother.
1977: Poem for Mrs. Fannie Lou Hamer.
Poem about Intelligence for My Brothers and Sisters, A.
Poem about the Head of a Negro.
Sometimes DeLiza.
Unemployment Monologue.
Knight, E. Dark Prophecy: I Sing of Shine.
For Black Poets Who Think of Suicide.
For Freckle-Faced Gerald.
Lockett. This Poem for Black Women.
Loftin. Weeksville Women.
Lorde. Beams.
Berlin Is Hard on Colored Girls.
Between Ourselves.
Coal.
East Berlin.
For the Record.
Naturally.
Question of *Essence*, A.
Woman Speaks, A.
Madhubuti. Awareness.
Black Manhood: Toward a Definition.
But He Was Cool.
In a Period of Growth.
Magnificent Tomorrows.
Malcolm Spoke / Who Listened?
New Integrationist, The.
Poem Looking for a Reader, A.
Self-Hatred of Don L. Lee, The.
Womenblack: We Begin with You.
McKay, C. Enslaved.
If we must die—let it not be like hogs.
Wise Men of the East, The.
Moss, T. Lessons from a Mirror.
Nayo. Hard Times A' Coming.
Neal, G. Today.
Neal, L. Don't say goodbye to the Porkpie Hat that rolled.
Patterson, R. Twenty-Six Ways of Looking at a Blackman.
Plumpp. Half Black, Half Blacker.
Zimbabwe.
Quigless. Moving.
Randall, D. Roses and Revolutions.
Reed, I. Guilty, the New York Philharmonic Signs up a Whale.
Haitians.
Reynolds, S. Open Letter to All Black Poets, An.
Rivers, C. Invisible Man, The.
Salaam. I live in the mouth of history.
Soon One Morning, I'll Fly Away.
Sanchez. Catch the Fire.
This is not a small voice.
To All Sisters.
We be. gonna be.
Woman who made, A.
Snellings. Sunrise!!
Spencer, A. Black man o' mine.
White Things.
Spriggs. Every Harlem Face Is AFROMANISM Surviving.
Sun-Ra. Visitation, The.
Thomas, R. Amen.
Tolson, M. African China.
Madame Alpha Devine she made a million.
Toomer. Song of the Son.
Toure, A. Azuri.
Walker, M. Black Paramour.
Fanfare, Coda, and Finale.
Litany of Black History for Black People, A.
My Truth and My Flame.
Small Black World.
This Is My Century.
Ward, Jr., J. Don't Be Fourteen (In Mississippi).
Watkins, N. Missions and Magnolias.
WEEMS. Funk.

Wheatley, P.   On Being Brought from Africa to America.
Williams, Karen.   In My Grandmother's Living Room.
  Little Black Girls, The Original Eve (Spreadin' More Beautiful Brown Around).
  There's History in My Hair.
Wright, J.   Benjamin Banneker Helps to Build a City.
Wright, R.   Between the World and Me.
X, M.   Till the Sun Goes Down.
See also **African Americans**

Blake, William
Kaufman, B.   Suicide.

Blessings
Lorde.   Relevant Is Different Points on the Circle.

Blindness
Clifton, L.   For the Blind.
Harper, F.   Dying Child to Her Blind Father, The.
Hughes, L.   Blind.

Blizzards. See Storms

Blood
Ai.   Country Midwife: A Day, The.
Harper, M.   Breaded Meat, Breaded Hands.
Hughes, L.   Georgia Dusk.
  Negro Speaks of Rivers, The.
Iverem.   Keeper.
Lorde.   Need: A Chorale for Black Woman Voices.
  Separation.
Reed, I.   Vachel Lindsay Fault, The.
Sanchez, S.   You have pierced me so.
Thomas, L.   Subway Witnesses, The.
Walker, A.   Suicide.

Blue (color)
Jacobs, H.   Goree.
Stanard.   Wrong Color.
Toure, A.   Azuri.
Young, A.   Pidgin Moon.

Blueberries
Moore, L.   Indian Girl.

Blues (mood)
Angelou.   Good Woman Feeling Bad, A.
  My Life Has Turned to Blue.
Beeks.   Parker's Mood.
Brown, Kysha.   Brown Girl Blues.
Brown, S.   Tin Roof Blues.
Derricotte.   Blackbottom.
Dunbar, P.   Blue.
Emanuel, J.   Get Up, Blues.
Fabio.   Hurt of It All, The.
Handy, W.   Joe Turner Blues.
  St. Louis Blues.
Hernton.   Long Blues, The.
Hughes, L.   Blues, The.
  Bound No'th Blues.
  Evenin' Air Blues.
  403 Blues.
  Hard Daddy.
  Hard Luck.
  Hey!
  Hey! Hey!
  Hey-Hey Blues.
  Homesick Blues.
  Love Again Blues.
  Misery.
  Miss Blues'es Child.
  Monroe's Blues.
  New Cabaret Girl, The.
  Out of Work.
  Red Clay Blues.
  So Tired Blues.
  Too Blue.
  Weary Blues, The.
Jordan, N.   When A Woman Gets Blue.
Knight, E.   Con/tin/u/way/shun Blues.
  Memo #43.
  Poem for Myself (Or Blues for a Mississippi Black Boy), A.
Komunyakaa.   Annabelle.
  Translating Footsteps.
  Woman, I Got the Blues.
Nelson, M.   I Fell Asleep on the Couch.
  So Jonah Sang the Blues.

Rahman.   Transcendental Blues Transcendental Blues.
Randall, D.   Langston Blues.
Redmond.   Cane-Brake-Blues.
Sanchez, S.   Blues.
Thomas, L.   Onion Bucket.
Unknown.   Backwater Blues.
  Hard Times Blues.
  Southern Blues, The.
Waller, T. *et al.*   (What Did I Do to Be So) Black and Blue?
Young, A.   Any Inner City Blues.
  Blue Monday.
  Blues Don't Change, The.
  James Cotton Band at Keytstone, The.
  More Clues to the Blues.
  See, see, moon, O see what you done done.
  What Is the Blues?
Zu-Bolton.   Sister Blues with Livewire Davis.
See also **Depression (psychological); Melancholy**

Blues (music)
Anderson, S.   Sound of Afroamerican History Chapt I, The.
Baraka.   In the Tradition.
  Legacy.
Brathwaite, E.   Blues.
Brown, S.   New St. Louis Blues.
Carr, L.   How Long Blues.
Corrie.   How Long Has Trane Been Gone.
Cortez.   You know / I sure would like to write a blues.
Cullen, C.   Colored Blues Singer.
Dent.   For Walter Washington.
Dove, R.   Shakespeare Say.
Eady.   Muddy Waters & the Chicago Blues.
Emanuel, J.   Get Up, Blues.
Ferdinand.   Blues (in Two Parts), The.
Graham, D.   Soul.
Handy, W.   St. Louis Blues.
Harper, M.   Blues Alabama.
  For Bud.
Hayden, R.   Homage to the Empress of the Blues.
Haynes, A.   Eclipse.
Hernton.   D Blues.
Hughes, L.   Blues Fantasy.
  Blues on a Box.
  Brass Spittoons.
  Love Again Blues.
  Minnie Sings Her Blues.
  Misery.
  Monroe's Blues.
  Note on Commercial Theatre.
  Po' Boy Blues.
  Song for Billie Holiday.
  To Midnight Nan at Leroy's.
  Weary Blues, The.
Hunter, A. *et al.*   Down-Hearted Blues.
Jackson, M.   Blues Today, The.
Johnson, R.   Hellhound on My Trail.
Jones, R.   Trouble in mind, I'm blue.
Kaufman, B.   Blues Note.
Knight, E.   Haiku: "To write a blues song."
  To Dinah Washington.
Komunyakaa.   Addendum.
  Villon/Leadbelly.
McClaurin.   Mask, The.
Moore, L.   Haiku: "Spring moonrise."
Neal, L.   Don't say goodbye to the Porkpie Hat that rolled.
Penny, R.   I Remember How She Sang.
Plumpp.   Mississippi Griot.
  Remembered.
Rahman.   Transcendental Blues Transcendental Blues.
Rushing.   Good Morning, Blues.
Salaam.   Spiritual Geography.
Sanchez, S.   For Our Lady.
  Liberation / Poem.
Smith, B.   Backwater Blues.
  In the House Blues.
Walcott.   Blues.
Weatherly, T.   Blues for Franks Wooten.
Williams, C.   Gulf Coast Blues.
Young, A.   Blues Don't Change, The.
  Old Fashioned Cincinnati Blues, The.
  Old O.O. Blues, The.

Zu-Bolton.   Struggle-Road Dance.

Boarding Houses
Hughes, L.   Boarding House.

Boasting
African-American Oral Tradition.   Cocaine Shorty.
  Hustlin' Dan.
  Pimp, The.
  Pimping Sam.
  Swinging through the trees with my dick in my hand.
  Three Whores Settin' Down in Boston.
  Wicked Nell: "While sittin' and thinking in deep meditation."
  Wicked Nell: "While sittin' down in deep meditation, little girl, lookin' at you."
Angelou.   Little Girl Speakings.
Dunbar, P.   Career, A.
Forman, R.   This Poem.

Boats and Boating
Dunbar, P.   On the River.
  Passage, The.
Harper, F.   Our Hero.
Komunyakaa.   Boat People.
Nelson, M.   Blessing the Boats.
See also **Ferry Boats; Ships and Shipbuilding**

Bodies
Ahmasi.   Water of Your Bath.
Baraka.   Crow Jane's Manner.
Brooks, G.   Still Do I Keep My Look, My Identity.
Clifton, L.   11/10 Again.
  Homage to My Hips.
  Lost Baby Poem, The.
Grimké, A.   Black Finger, The.
Harper, M.   Debridement: Operation Harvest Moon: On Repose.
  Studs.
Hoagland, E.   Georgia—It's the Gospel Truth.
Hughes, L.   Red Silk Stockings.
Jordan, J.   It's About You: on the Beach.
Kaufman, B.   Does the Secret Mind Whisper?
  Would You Wear My Eyes?
Madhubuti.   Reflections on a Lost Love.
McKay, C.   Flirtation.
Nayo.   Near Miss.
Nelson, M.   Confessional Poem.
Reed, I.   Untitled: "I know of a man who treated his body like a dog."
Sanchez, S.   Black Magic.
  My body waiting.
  Our bodies made rain.
Toomer.   Portrait in Georgia.
  Prayer.
Unknown.   I know moon-rise, I know star-rise.
Wright, J.   What is Beautiful.
Young, A.   Flu.
  Green Is a Feeling, Not a Color.
  Tiny Self-Portrait.
See also **Nudity and Nudists**

Bohemian Life
Baraka.   New World, The.
Durem.   Problem in Social Geometry—the Inverted Square!

Boleyn, Anne
Bibb.   Anne Boleyn.

Bombs and Bombing
Horne, F.   Kid Stuff.
Hughes, L.   Air Raid: Barcelona.
  Ballad of Harry Moore.
  Bombings in Dixie.
  Moonlight in Valencia: Civil War.
  Song of Spain.
Randall, D.   Ballad of Birmingham.
Sanchez, S.   Elegy: "Philadelphia / a disguised southern city."
See also **Air Warfare**

Bones
Clifton, L.   Atlantic is a sea of bones.
Hughes, L.   Poor Rover.
Lorde.   Ethiopia.
Roy, L.   Suffering The Sea Change: All My Pretty Ones.

Bonneau, Jennette
Fordham.   Death of a Grandparent. Mrs. Jennette Bonneau.

Books
Dove, R.   One Volume Missing.
Dunbar, P.   On a Clean Book.
   Sonnet: "Emblem of blasted hope and lost desire."
Rowe, G.   God Speed.
Walden.   Introductory to Second Edition.
Bootlegging and Bootleggers
Brown, S.   No More Worlds to Conquer.
Boots
Dunbar, P.   Two little boots all rough an' wo'.
Boredom
Baraka.   Epistrophe.
   Look for You Yesterday, Here You Come Today.
Giovanni.   Categories.
   Forced Retirement.
Hughes, L.   Monotony.
Lorde.   Beverly's Poem.
Reed, I.   Untitled III.
Bores
Dunbar, P.   To a Captious Critic.
Boston, Massachusetts
Brown, S.   Crispus Attacks McKoy.
Young, A.   East Boston.
Bourgeoisie
Angelou.   Sepia Fashion Show.
Baraka.   Black Bourgeoisie.
   Christ Was Never in Europe!
   Civil Rights Bill #666.
   Heathens.
   Heathens Think Fascism Is Civilization.
Brooks, G.   Man of the Middle Class, A.
Brown, S.   New Congo, The.
Clinton.   History as Trash.
Kaufman, B.   Why Write ABOUT.
Madhubuti.   Malcolm Spoke / Who Listened?
   Pains with a Light Touch.
Reed, I.   Middle Class Blues, The.
Bowery, The, New York City
Cortez.   Bowery Street.
Boxing and Boxers
Angelou.   Fightin' was natural.
Barlow, G.   Dream of the Ring: the Great Jack Johnson, A.
Harper, M.   Buck.
Hayden, R.   Free Fantasia: Tiger Flowers.
Hughes, L.   Joe Louis.
   Prize Fighter.
Killebrew.   Squared Circle, The.
Komunyakaa.   Boxing Day.
Reed, I.   Petite Kid Everett.
   White Hope.
Boy Scouts
Kaufman, B.   Reflections on a Small Parade.
Boys
Baraka.   Crow Jane's Manner.
Clifton, L.   Those Boys That Ran Together.
Cornish, S.   Generations 1.
Dunbar, P.   Boy's Summer Song, A.
Giovanni.   Universality.
Hughes, L.   Tag.
Lorde.   Bees, The.
See also **Adolescence; Childhood and Children**
Brahms, Johannes
Derricotte.   Black Boys Play the Classics.
Braithwaite, William Stanley
Johnson, G.   To William Stanley Braithwaite.
Brazil
Oden.   Private Letter to Brazil, A.
Bread
Brooks, G.   My Dreams, My Works Must Wait Till after Hell.
Dunbar, P.   Dinah Kneading Dough.
Harper, M.   Kneading.
Roy, L.   Bread Man, The.
Breakfast
Rankine.   Man. His Bowl. His Raspberries, The.
Sanchez, S.   His voice used to sing.
Breasts
Coleman, W.   Breast Examination.
Jordan, J.   Poem on.
Breath
Sanchez, S.   Would you please return.

Brides
Harper, F.   Bride of Death, The.
Hughes, L.   Young Bride.
Unknown.   Slave Marriage Ceremony Supplement.
See also **Weddings**
Bridges
Baraka.   Bridge, The.
Hughes, L.   Trip: San Francisco.
Lorde.   On My Way Out I passed You and the Varrazano Bridge.
Plumpp.   Poems are not places.
Bristol, England
Harper, M.   Bristol: Bicentenary Remembrances of Trade.
British Empire
Hughes, L.   Azikiwe in Jail.
   Explain It, Please.
   Ghandhi Is Fasting.
Walcott.   Far Cry from Africa, A.
See also **Colonialism**
Broadway, New York City
Hughes, L.   Note on Commercial Theatre.
McKay, C.   On Broadway.
Bronx, The, New York City
Henderson, D.   Boston Road Blues.
Lorde.   Big Apple Circus.
Brooklyn, New York City
Jordan, J.   For Michael Angelo Thompson.
Weaver, M.   Brooklyn.
Brooks and Streams
Dunbar, P.   Wadin' in de Crick.
Weeden, L.   Stream, The.
See also **Rivers**
Brooks, Gwendolyn Elizabeth
Madhubuti.   Gwendolyn Brooks.
Redmond.   Gwensways.
Sanchez, S.   Woman. whose color.
Brotherhood
Baraka.   Return of the Native.
Clifton, L.   Carver, The.
   Listen children / keep this in the place.
Hayden, R.   In the Mourning Time.
Hughes, L.   Give Us Our Peace.
   I dream a world where man.
   Projection.
Murray, P.   Dark Testament.
Nayo.   Hard Times A' Coming.
Young, A.   W. H. Auden & Mantan Moreland.
Brothers
Angelou.   Kin.
Clifton, L.   August the 12th.
Dove, R.   Song. Summer.
Dunbar, P.   Ione.
Forbes, C.   Hand Me Down Blues.
Harper, M.   Drowning of the Facts of a Life, The.
Lanusse.   Un Frère Au Tombeau de Son Frère.
Lorde.   For Craig.
Nelson, M.   I imagine driving across country.
Reed, C.   My Brother and Me.
Thompson, C.   To My Dead Brother.
Walker, F.   Crooked Afro.
Brown (color)
Grimké, A.   At April.
Brown, Andrew
Heard, J.   Rev. Andrew Brown, over the Hill to Rest.
Brown, James
Giovanni.   Revolutionary Music.
Brown, John
Atkins.   Narrative.
Cullen, C.   Negro Mother's Lullaby, A.
Harper, M.   Allegheny Shadows.
   Dreams: American.
   Forty Days Looking Backwards: Notes from a Surveyor.
   History as Cap'n Brown.
   Plans.
   Plans: 2.
   Reports: Kansas.
   "S.P.W.": Journey of Consciousness.
Hayden, R.   John Brown.
Hughes, L.   October 16: The Raid.

Walker, M.   Ballad of the Free, The.
Brown, Mrs. E. Cohrs
Fordham.   Mrs. E. Cohrs Brown.
Brown, Sterling A.
Harper, M.   Br'er Sterling and the Rocker.
Sanchez, S.   Love Poem Written for Sterling Brown, A.
   Poem for Sterling Brown, A.
Browning, Robert
Spencer, A.   Life-long, Poor Browning.
Buddhism and Buddhists
Kaufman, B.   Buddhist experience, A.
   Reflections on a Small Parade.
   Saraswati.
   Unanimity Has Been Achieved, Not a Dot Less for Its Accidentalness.
Toomer.   To Gurdjieff Dying.
See also **Zen Buddhism**
Buffaloes
Kaufman, B.   Enormous Gas Bill at the Dwarf Factory. A Horror Movie to be Shot with Eyes, The.
Komunyakaa.   Water Buffalo.
Bugles and Buglers
LeFlore.   Rayboy Blk and Bluz.
Buildings and Builders
Dove, R.   Corduroy Road.
Harper, F.   Building, The.
   Church Building.
   Little Builders, The.
Komunyakaa.   Instructions for Building Straw Huts.
Lorde.   Building.
   Constuction.
   Workers Rose on May Day or Postscript to Karl Marx, The.
Nelson, M.   Abba Jacob in the Well.
Oden.   Review from Staten Island.
Reed, I.   Dragon's Blood.
Bullets
Cortez.   Give Me the Red on the Black of the Bullet.
Dove, R.   Teach Us to Number Our Days.
Hughes, L.   Death in Yorkville.
   Too Blue.
Bullying and Bullies
Angelou.   Thirteens (Black), The.
   Thirteens (White), The.
Parker, Dominique.   When Mark Deloach Ruled the World.
Zu-Bolton.   Governor of the Ollie Street, The.
Bureaucracy and Bureaucrats
Kaufman, B.   Believe, Believe.
Burial
Brown, S.   Maumee Ruth.
Dodson, O.   When I Am Dead.
Ellis, K.   Boys of Summer, The.
Giovanni.   Women gather, The.
Harper, F.   Burial of Srah.
   Bury Me in a Free Land.
Harper, M.   Family of Debridement, The.
Hughes, L.   Death of an Old Seaman.
   Girl.
Knight, E.   Last Words By "Slick."
Mitchell, K.   On the Anniversary Of Your Death.
Southerland.   Blue Clay.
Troupe.   After Hearing a Radio Announcement: a Comment on Some Conditions.
See also **Cemeteries; Funerals; Grief; Mourning and Mourners; Tombs**
Buses
Joshua.   On the Morning St. Bernard.
McElroy, C.   Pike Street Bus.
Business and Businesspeople
Farr.   At General Electric, Where They Eat Their/Young.
Hughes, L.   Madam's Past History.
Nelson, M.   Abba Jacob and the Businessman.
Tolson, M.   Madame Alpha Devine she made a million.
See also **Merchants**
Butchering and Butchers
Hughes, L.   Joy.

Butter
Sanchez, S. I am settling down.
Butterflies
Barrax. Patroness.
Grimké, A. Butterflies, white butterflies, in the sunshine.
Hayden, R. Butterfly Piece.
Major, C. On Watching a Caterpillar Become a Butterfly.
Buzzards
Brown, S. Old Man Buzzard / Wid his bal' head.
Hughes, L. Dying Beast.
Byrd, Donald
Gray-Kontar. Cuz' Mama Played Jazz.
Byrd, Mary Furman Weston
Fordham. Mrs. Mary Furman Weston Byrd.
Byron, George Gordon Noel Byron, 6th Baron
Fortune. Byron's Oak at Newstead Abbey.
Whitman, A. Ye Bards of England.

C

Cafés
Kaufman, B. Bagel Shop Jazz.
California (state)
Angelou. California Prodigal.
Hughes, L. City.
  Trip: San Francisco.
Kaufman, B. Alien winds sweeping the highway.
  Carl Chessman Interviews the P.T.A. in His Swank Gas Chamber Before Leaving on His Annual Inspection of Capital, Tour of Northern California Death Universities, Happy.
  Mongolian Sunset in Gobi Desert.
Reed, I. Oakland Blues.
  Untitled: "When California is split in two."
Young, A. California Peninsula: El Camino Real.
  One West Coast.
Calm
Clifton, L. Calming Kali.
Hayden, R. Islands, The.
Hughes, L. Sea Calm.
Toomer. Mended.
Calvary
Bontemps. Golgotha Is a Mountain.
Hughes, L. Ballad of the Two Thieves.
See also **Cross, The; Crucifixion, The**
Cambridge, Massachusetts
Alexander, E. Boston Year.
See also **Harvard University**
Cameras. *See* **Photography and Photographers**
Campaigns, Political. *See* **Voting and Voters**
Camping
Young, A. No More Doors Tonight.
Zu-Bolton. Struggle-Road Dance.
Canaan
Brown, S. Crossing.
Canada
Simpson, J. Away to Canada.
Canaries
Heard, J. My Canary.
Cancer (disease)
Giovanni. Cancers are a serious condition.
Henderson-Holmes. "C" ing in Colors: Blue.
  "C" ing in Colors: Red.
Lorde. American Cancer Society Or There Is More Than One Way to Skin a Coon.
Candles
Dunbar, P. At Candle-Lightin' Time.
Cannibalism and Cannibals
Goodison. Jamaica 1980.
Harper, M. Battle of Saratoga (Springs) Revisited, The.
Canning
Young, K. Preserving, The.
Cape Cod, Massachusetts
Knight, E. Television Speaks.
Weaver, M. Message on Cape Cod, The.

Capital Punishment
African-American Oral Tradition. Eddie Ledoux: "There's some strange and queer tales that come through all jails."
  Eddie Ledoux: "Wise and queer tales float through all the jails."
  Treacherous Breast.
See also **Executions and Executioners**
Capitalism
Angelou. Times-Square-Shoeshine-Composition.
Dunbar-Nelson. Proletariat Speaks, The.
Hughes, L. Black Workers.
  Labor Storm.
  White Man.
Knight, E. Memo #9.
McElroy, C. Cutting a Road from Manaus to Belém.
Medina, T. Capitalism Is a Brutal Motherfucker.
Reed, I. El Paso Monologue.
  Jackal-Headed Cowboy, The.
  Sixth Street Corporate War.
Salaam. Still Life, Stealing Life / Caught Red-Handed.
See also **Banking and Bankers**
Captivity
Barrax. Patroness.
Dunbar, P. Sympathy.
Wheatley, P. On the Capture of General Lee.
Card Games
African-American Oral Tradition. Poolshooting Monkey: "I don't know but I was told."
  Poolshooting Monkey: "It was in Speero's poolroom back in nineteen-ten."
  Poolshooting Monkey: "It was in Speero's poolroom in the year eighteen-ten."
Davis, T. Playing Solitaire.
Dove, R. Sailor in Africa, The.
Caribbean Sea
Barrax. Scuba Diver Recovers the Body of a Drowned Child, The.
See also **West Indies**
Caring
Angelou. Me and My Work.
Hughes, L. How Thin a Blanket.
Carmichael, Stokely
Hughes, L. Stokely Malcolm Me.
Carnivals
St. John, P. Carnival.
Spencer, A. At the Carnival.
Carpe Diem
Angelou. Come, And Be My Baby.
  Weekend Glory.
Brown, S. Call Boy.
  Old Man Buzzard / Wid his bal' head.
Cullen, C. I have a rendezvous with Life.
Hughes, L. Big-Timer, The.
  Bouquet.
  Harlem Night Club.
  Lady in Cabaret.
  Numbered.
  Saturday Night.
  Young Sailor.
Young, A. Sunday Illumination.
Carpentry and Carpenters
Komunyakaa. Apprenticeship.
Castration
African-American Oral Tradition. Titanic: "Tenth of May was a hell of a day, The."
Hayden, R. Night, Death, Mississippi.
Sharp, S. In the Tradition of Bobbitt.
Cathedrals
Fields, J. Citizen.
Johnson, J. Before a Painting.
Catherine of Siena, Saint
Dove, R. Catherine of Siena.
Catholicism and Catholics
Lorde. Release Time.
Reed, I. Pope Replies to the Ayatollah Khomeini, The.
See also **Papacy**
Cats
Atkins. Probability and Birds in the Yard.

Baudelaire. Cat, The.
  Cats.
Edwards, S. Brothers.
Harris, W. Samantha Is My Negro Cat.
Hughes, L. Little Cats.
  Silly Animals.
  Worriation.
Lorde. Domino.
Madgett. Homage.
Reed, I. Mossy.
  My Thing abt Cats.
Caution
Cullen, C. Advice to a Beauty.
  To a Brown Girl.
Holman, M. Mr. Z.
Hughes, L. Elderly Leaders.
Lorde. New Year's Day.
Reed, I. From the Files of Agent 22.
Cavalry
Brooks, G. Riders to the Blood-Red Wrath.
Cellars
Lorde. Depreciation.
Cemeteries
Braithwaite. In a Grave-Yard.
Fordham. Magnolia.
Harper, M. At the Cemetery.
Heard, J. National Cemetery, Beaufort, South Carolina, The.
Hughes, L. Boarding House.
  Grave Yard.
Moore, L. Again.
Salaam. St. Louis Cemetery Crypt.
Wright, J. Albuquerque Graveyard, The.
See also **Burial; Tombs**
Centipedes
Dove, R. Centipede.
Central Intelligence Agency
Reed, I. Gangster's Death, The.
Central Park, New York City
Hughes, L. Dive.
Wright, J. Lake in Central Park, The.
Cereus, Night-blooming
Hayden, R. Night-Blooming Cereus, The.
Certainty
Cullen, C. Brown Boy to Brown Girl.
Giovanni. How do you write a poem.
Cézanne, Paul
Strange. Still Life.
Chance
Young, A. Now's the Time.
See also **Fate**
Change
Angelou. Changes.
  In Retrospect.
  To a Man.
Baraka. Liar, The.
Brooks, G. Young Africans.
Clifton, L. I am running into a new year.
Clinton. Traditional Post-Modern Neo-HooDoo Afra-Centric Sister in a Purple Head Rag Mourning Death and Cooking.
Dove, R. Jiving.
  Ö.
  Straw Hat.
  Sunday Greens.
  Wingfoot Lake.
Dunbar, P. Change has come, and Helen sleeps, The.
Gilbert, D. Fire in the Drum, The.
Giovanni. Adulthood.
  Charting the Night Winds.
  Cotton Candy on a Rainy Day.
Hayden, R. Full Moon.
  Theme and Variation.
Horton, G. New Fashions.
Hughes, L. Dear lovely Death.
Jackson, M. Man in the Mirror.
Jordan, J. Roman Poem Number Nine.
Komunyakaa. Way the Cards Fall, The.
Lee, D. Change-up.
  Poem to Complement Other Poems, A.
Lorde. Stations.
Madhubuti. Poem to Complement Other Poems, A.
Miller, A. Pruning, The.

Oyewole. When the revolution comes.
Reed, I. Loup Garou Means Change Into.
St. John, P. Carnival.
Sanchez, S. Bear the rhythm of.
Walker, M. Crystal Palace used to be, The.
 For my people everywhere singing their slave
 songs repeatedly.
 On Youth and Age.
Young, A. California Peninsula: El Camino
 Real.
 Imitation Dance, The.
 Leadbelly Song, The.
 Madrid 1963: Some Changes.
 Odds, The.
 Tune.
See also **Transience**

Chaos
Baraka. Three Modes of History and Culture.
Reed, I. Decade That Screamed, The.
St. John, P. Carnival.

Chaplin, Charlie
Kaufman, B. Patriotic Ode on the Fourteenth
 Anniversary of the Persecution of Charlie
 Chaplin.

Charity
Brooks, G. Lovers of the Poor, The.
Harper, F. Dedication Poem.
 To Mr. and Mrs. W. F. Johnson on Their
 Twenty-Fifth Wedding Anniversary.
Pritchard, N. Cloak, The.
Ray, H. Charity.
 Triple Benison, The.

Charles, Ray
Bond, J. Bishop of Atlanta: Ray Charles, The.
Dent. Ray Charles at Mississippi State.
Kaufman, B. Blues Note.

Charleston, South Carolina
Derricotte. 1994 Inventory.
Heard, J. New Organ, The.

Charm
Desbrosses. Le Retour au Village aux Perles.

Chastity
Sanchez, S. Once i was chaste with.
Wheatley, P. On Virtue.

Chaucer, Geoffrey
Brawley. Chaucer.
Whitman, A. Ye Bards of England.

Chemical Warfare
Cortez. Stockpiling of frozen trees, The.

Chemistry and Chemists
Young, A. Chemistry.

Chesapeake Bay
Dunbar, P. Night on the Chesapeake.
 To the Eastern Shore.

Chess
Stanard. Washington Square Park and a Game
 of Chess.

Chicago, Illinois
African-American Oral Tradition. Corner of
 47th and South Park.
Alexander, M. Chicago.
Brooks, G. Lovers of the Poor, The.
Ellis, K. Phantom Pains.
Fordham. Chicago Exposition Ode.
Duriel. Landscapes.
Hughes, L. Chicago Blues.
 Grant Park.
 Migrant.
 Poor Girl's Ruination.
Loftis. Big John.
Rodgers, C. U Name This One.
Troupe. Impressions / of Chicago; For
 Howlin' Wolf.
Unknown. Goin' to Chicago Blues.
Walker, M. Chicago.
 For Gwen, 1969.

Chickens
Jordan, J. Menu.
Rankine. Eden.
Shange. Ancestral Messengers/Composition 13.
See also **Hens; Roosters**

Child Abuse
Angelou. Coleridge Jackson had nothing.
 To Beat the Child Was Bad Enough.

Bomani, N. Thin Water.
Hayden, R. Whipping, The.
Jordan, J. Poem for Jan.
Komunyakaa. Stepfather: A Girl's Song.
Lorde. Chain.
 Party Time.
Nelson, M. Like Father, Like Son.
 Marriage Nightmare, The.
 No Worst.

Childhood and Children
Angelou. Born That Way.
 Elegy: "I lay down in my grave."
 John J.
 Kin.
 Little Girl Speakings.
 Televised news turns.
Asquith. Sunday Afternoons.
Baraka. From an Almanac (3).
Barlow, G. Painting Drunken Twilight.
Barrax. Efficiency Apartment.
 Scuba Diver Recovers the Body of a Drowned
 Child, The.
 Visit.
 Whose children are these?
Boyd, M. Why?
Braithwaite. City Garden, A.
Brocks-Shedd. Southern Roads/City Pavement.
Brooks, G. Bronzeville Woman in a Red Hat.
 Life of Lincoln West, The.
Brown, S. Chillen Get Shoes.
 Conjured.
Burnette. Artichoke Pickle Passion: Sonnet.
Campbell, J. De Cunjah Man.
Clifton, L. Admonitions.
 C. C. Rider.
 Listen children / keep this in the place.
 My boys beauty is.
 Willie B (1).
 Willie B (2).
Cullen, C. Incident.
 Saturday's Child.
Davis, D. My Childhood's Happy Days.
Dent. Nightdreams (Black).
Derricotte. Fears of the Eighth Grade.
Dickey. Father.
 Mulatto Lullaby.
Dickinson, E. Softened by Time's consummate
 plush.
Dove, R. Flash Cards.
Dumas, H. Knock on Wood.
Dunbar, P. Boy's Summer Song, A.
 Charity.
 Little brown baby wif spa'klin' eyes.
 Liza May.
 Lullaby: "Bedtime's come fu' little boys."
 Scamp.
 Wadin' in de Crick.
 When a Feller's Itchin' to be Spanked.
Gilmore, B. Revolution.
Giovanni. Eagles are a majestic species ...
 living in the thin searing air.
 For Tommy.
 Her Cruising Car.
 Legacies.
 My Tower.
 Nikki-Rosa.
 Poem for Black Boys.
 Poem for Flora.
 Rose Bush, The.
Graham, D. Clown, The.
Harper, F. Aunt Chloe.
 Days of my childhood I woo you not back.
 Little Builders, The.
 Mother's Treasures.
 Out in the cold mid the dreary night.
 Slave Mother, The: "I have but four, the
 treasures of my soul."
 Thank God for Little Children.
Harper, M. Herring run / in the silver
 morning.
 No. 24.
 One Lives, One Dies: Both/And: A Choice of
 Colors.
 This Is My Son's Song: *"Ungie, Hi Ungie".*
Duriel. What We Have Lost.
Hayden, R. Rabbi, The.
 Those Winter Sundays.

Whipping, The.
 Year of the Child, The.
Hoagland, E. Big Zeb Johnson.
Horne, F. Mamma!
Hughes, L. Children's Rhymes.
 Genius Child.
 Kid in the Park.
 Naughty child / Who ventured to go cut
 flowers, The.
 To Be Somebody.
 Ultimatum: Kid to Kid.
 Winter Sweetnes.
Jean, V. On Apologies.
Johnson, G. Riddle, The: "White men's
 children spread over the earth."
Johnson, H. Poem: "Little brown boy."
Johnson, J. Judeebug's Country.
Jones, I. Image of Myself 3.
Jordan, A. If I Write a Poem.
Jordan, J. Juice of a Lemon on the Trail of a
 Little Yellow.
 Smash the Church.
 Test of Atlanta 1979, The.
Knight, E. Green Grass and Yellow Balloons.
 On the Projects Playground.
 Poem of Attrition, A.
Komunyakaa. Gloria's Clues.
 Good Memory, A.
 Salt.
Loftis. Ruth.
Lorde. And What About the Children.
 As I Grew Up Again.
 Ballad from Childhood.
 Blackstudies.
 Bloodbirth.
 Brother Alvin.
 Chain.
 Child Shall Lead, A.
 Conclusion.
 Digging.
 Equinox.
 For Jose and Regina.
 Generation.
 Harriet there was always somebody calling us
 crazy.
 Inheritance—His.
 Release Time.
 Relevant Is Different Points on the Circle.
 Rites of Passage.
 Sacrifice.
 School Note.
 Seventh Sign, The.
 Signs.
 Song for a Thin Sister.
 Suffer the Children.
 Teacher.
 To My Daughter the Junkie on a Train.
 What It Means to Be Beautiful.
 What my child learns of the sea.
 Woman Thing, The.
Mackey, N. Phantom Light of All Our Day,
 The.
Madgett. Offspring.
 Sunny.
McKay, C. Flame-Heart.
 Homing Swallows.
 Spanish Needle, The.
 Sukee River.
Mullen, H. Momma Sayings.
Nelson, M. Boys in the Park.
 I am you again.
 Levitation with Baby.
 Light under the Door.
 Lost Daughter, The.
 Mama's Promise.
 Sacrament of Poverty, The.
Nurigan. I'm raising CHILDREN.
Parker, Dominique. When Mark Deloach
 Ruled the World.
Ray, H. On the Picture of a Child.
Reed, C. Invaders, The.
Reed, I. Poem for Two Daughters.
Roy, L. Suffering The Sea Change: All My
 Pretty Ones.
Sanchez, S. Cause we are carving.
 Let us begin the real work.

Poem at Thirty.
We stumbled into.
Smith, P. Biting Back.
Spencer, A. Rime for the Christmas Baby.
Spriggs. Sassafras Memories.
Strange. Childhood.
Thompson, C. Mrs. Johnson Objects.
Tucker, M. Old Crib, The.
Unknown. Walk Together Children.
Walker, A. Enemy, The.
Walker, M. Childhood.
On Youth and Age II.
Ward, J. At the Border of Constant Disaster.
WEEMS. Yesterday.
Williams, Karen. There's History in My Hair.
Williams, S. Peacock Poems: 1, The.

See also **Adolescence; Boys; Girls**

Chile
Reed, I. Poem Delivered Before Assembly of
Colored People Held at Glide Memorial
Church, Oct. 4, 1973 and Called to Protest
Recent Events in the Sovereign Republic of
Chile.

Chimney Sweepers
African-American Oral Tradition. Willie the
Weeper.

China
Braithwaite. Del Cascar, Del Cascar.
Hughes, L. Roar, China! / Roar, old lion of
the East!

Chinese, The
Tolson, M. African China.

Choices
Lorde. Spring III.
Timepiece.

Cholera
Dove, R. Cholera.

Christenings. See Baptism

Christianity and Christians
Angelou. Lord, in My Heart.
Savior.
Bradford, Walter. T. C.
Cullen, C. Heritage.
Mood.
Sonnet: "I know now how a man whose blood
is hot."
Dunbar, P. Light, The.
Religion.
Harper, F. Be Active.
Bible Defence of Slavery.
Deliverance.
Dying Christian, The.
Fairer Hope, a Brighter Morn, A.
His Name.
Martyr of Alabama, The.
Poem, A: "Over the foaming ocean."
Rallying Cry, The.
Words for the Hour.
Harper, M. Christian's Box Seat: So What!
Kaufman, B. Hawk Lawler: Chorus.
Komunyakaa. Quality of Light, A.
McKay, C. Wise Men of the East, The.
Nelson, M. Churchgoing.
Plato. Advice to Young Ladies.
Reed, I. Al Capone in Alaska.
Simpson, J. To the White People of America.
Wheatley, P. Address to the Deist—1767, An.
Deism.
On Being Brought from Africa to America.
To Captain H——D, of the 65th Regiment.

Christmas
Barrax. Christmas 1959 Et Cetera.
Corrothers. Indignation Dinner, An.
Cullen, C. Christus Natus Est.
Dunbar, P. Back-Log Song, A.
Chrismus Is A-Comin'.
Christmas.
Christmas Carol: "Ring out, ye bells!"
Christmas Folksong, A.
Christmas in the Heart.
Little Christmas Basket, A.
Speakin' o' Christmas.
Fordham. Nativity, The.
Freeman, C. Christmas Morning I.
Gregory. Christmas Lullaby for a New-Born
Child.

Harper, F. Christmas Carol, A.
Ragged Stocking, The.
Heard, J. Birth of Jesus, The.
Horne, F. Kid Stuff.
Hughes, L. Carol of the Brown King.
Christmas Story, The.
Merry Christmas, China.
On a Christmas Night.
On a Pallet of Straw.
Shepherd's Song at Christmas.
Johnson, M. Christmas Times.
Krismas Dinnah.
Lorde. Peace on Earth.
Moore, L. Gifts.
Moorer. Christmas Eve.
Nelson, M. Prayer of Silence, The.
Ray, H. At Christmas-Tide.
Thompson, C. Christmas Rush, The.
Tucker, M. Christmas, South, 1866.

See also **Nativity, The**

Christmas Cards
Hughes, L. Madam's Christmas (or Merry
Christmas Everybody).

Christmas Eve
African-American Oral Tradition. Junkies'
Heaven.
Dunbar, P. Chrismus on the Plantation.
Hughes, L. Christmas Eve: Nearing Midnight
in New York.
Thompson, P. Christmas Ghost, A.
Tucker, M. Christmas Eve, South, 1865.

Christmas Trees
Moorer. Christmas Tree, The.

Churches
Brown, S. New steps / O my Lawd.
Side by Side.
Campbell, J. 'Sciplinin' Sister Brown.
Clemmons. Greater Friendship Baptist Church,
The.
Giovanni. Knoxville, Tennessee.
Harper, F. Church Building.
In Commemoration of the Centennial of the
A.M.E. Church.
Hayden, R. Those Winter Sundays.
Horne, F. On Seeing Two Brown Boys in a
Catholic Church.
Hughes, L. Bible Belt.
Jordan, J. Smash the Church.
Lorde. About Religion.
McKay, C. St. Isaac's Church, Petrograd.
Moore, L. Tanka: "After church meeting."
Nelson, M. Palm Sunday, 1866.
Reed, C. In a Harlem Store Front Church.
Reed, I. Neo-HooDoo Manifesto.
Thompson, C. Opening Service, An.
Tolson, M. Lena Lovelace.
Wright, J. Wednesday Night Prayer Meeting.

See also **Religion; Worship and Worshipers**

Cicadas
Eady. Dance, The.

Cigarettes
Jordan, N. Sacrifice, The.
Lorde. American Cancer Society Or There Is
More Than One Way to Skin a Coon.

See also **Smoking and Smokers**

Cinema. See Motion Pictures

Circus
Alexander, E. Venus Hottentot.
Dove, R. Hill of Beans, A.
Jordan, J. What happens when the dog sits on
a tiger.
Komunyakaa. Dog Act, The.
Lorde. Big Apple Circus.
Reed, I. Grizzly.

Cities
Angelou. Through the Inner City to the
Suburbs.
Baraka. Poem for Democrats, A.
Braithwaite. City Garden, A.
Brown, S. Bessie.
Clifton, L. In the Inner City.
Tyrone (1).
Cruz, V. Urban Dream.
Cumbo. Nocturnal Sounds.
Cunningham, J. City Rises, The.

Dove, R. Spy.
Straw Hat.
Under the Viaduct, 1932.
Fields, J. Citizen.
Hughes, L. City.
From Selma.
Juice Joint: Northern City.
Summer Evening (Calumet Avenue).
Iverem. Earth Screaming.
Jordan, J. Speculations on the Present through
the Prism of the Past.
Kaufman, B. Battle Report.
J'Accuse.
Lane, P. Wind Thoughts.
Lorde. Making Love to Concrete.
McKay, C. White City, The.
Plumpp. Another mule kicking.
Redmond. Definition of Nature.
Reed, I. Man or Butterfly.
Toomer. Gum.
Walker, M. Memory.
Wright, J. Benjamin Banneker Helps to Build
a City.

See also **Towns; Villages**

Citizenship
Jordan, J. Song of the Law Abiding Citizen.

Civil Rights Movement, United States
Baraka. Civil Rights Bill #666.
History on Wheels.
Barrax. Black Narcissus.
Brooks, G. Bronzeville Mother Loiters in
Mississippi. / Meanwhile, a Mississippi
Mother Burns Bacon.
Carroll, K. Theory on Extinction or What
Happened to the Dinosaurs?
Ellis, K. Boys of Summer, The.
Emanuel, J. Freedom Rider: Washout.
Fabio. Race Results, U.S.A., 1966.
Goncalves. Way It Is, The.
Hughes, L. Ballad of Harry Moore.
Bitter River, The.
Brotherly Love.
Demonstration.
Dinner Guest: Me.
Ghosts of 1619.
Lincoln University: 1954.
NAACP.
Northern Liberal.
Southern Negro Speaks.
To Certain Negro Leaders.
Undertow.
Lorde. Rites of Passage.
Patterson, R. Birmingham 1963.
Randall, D. Ballad of Birmingham.
Southern Road, The.
Reed, I. Ghost in Birmingham, The.
Walker, M. For Andy Goodman—Michael
Schwerner—and James Chaney.
Sit-Ins.

See also **Integration**

Civil War, Nigeria
Harper, M. Biafra Blues.

Civil War, Spain
Hughes, L. Air Raid: Barcelona.
Hero—International Brigade.
Letter from Spain.
Moonlight in Valencia: Civil War.
Postcard from Spain.
Tomorrow's Seed.

See also **Spain**

Civil War, United States
Clifton, L. Visit to Gettysburg, A.
Dunbar, P. Colored Soldiers, The.
News, The.
Robert Gould Shaw.
Unsung Heroes, The.
When Dey 'Listed Colored Soldiers.
Fordham. Atlanta Exposition Ode.
Harper, F. Appeal to the American People,
An.
Deliverance, The.
Home, Sweet Home.
Lines to Miles O'Reiley.
Words for the Hour.
Harper, M. Psychophotos of Hampton.
Hayden, R. Dream, The.

Horton, G. General Grant—the Hero of the War.
Jefferson in a Tight Place.
Hughes, L. Ballad of the Seven Songs.
Jordan, J. Grand Army Plaza.
Menken. Pro Patria—America, 1861.
Randall, D. Memorial Wreath.
Ray, H. Robert G. Shaw.
Reed, I. Chattanooga.
Unknown. Negro Soldier's Civil War Chant.
Walker, M. Oxford is a legend.
Whitman, A. Hail dawning Peace! Speed on thy glorious rise!
Williams, E. At Harper's Ferry Just before the Attack.

Civilization
Allen, S. Benin Bronze.
Baraka. Heathens Think Fascism Is Civilization.
Clifton, L. Pity this poor animal.
Cullen, C. Heritage.
Harris, W. We Live in a Cage.
Hughes, L. Fog.
Lament for Dark Peoples.
Letter to the Academy.
Liars.
Poem: "All the tom-toms of the jungles beat in my blood."
Iverem. Earth Screaming.
Johnson, F. Tired.
Sanchez, S. How can you comfort.
Shange. Ancestral Messengers/Composition 13.

Classicism
Derricotte. Black Boys Play the Classics.
Hughes, L. Letter to the Academy.
Wheatley, P. To Mæcenas.

Cleanliness
Dove, R. Great Palaces of Versailles, The.
Hughes, L. Brand New Clothes.
Tolson, M. Old Houses.
Trethewey. Domestic Work, 1937.

Clergy
African-American Oral Tradition. Junkies' Ball.
Angelou. Preacher, don't send me.
Brown, S. Elder Mistletoe.
Memories of Salem.
Seeking Religion.
Slim Hears "The Call."
Harper, F. Poem, A: "Over the foaming ocean."
Respectfully Dedicated to Dr. Alexander Crummell on the Fiftieth Anniversary of His Pastorate.
To Bishop Payne.
Harper, M. Village Blues.
Hughes, L. Madam and the Minister.
Sunday Morning Prophecy.
Johnson, F. Minister, The.
Moorer. Birthday Wishes to a Minister of the Gospel.
Wheatley, P. Elegy, Sacred to the Memory of That Great Divine, the Reverend and Learned Dr. Samuel Cooper, Who Departed This Life December 29, 1783, Ætatis 59, An.
See also **Monks; Preaching and Preachers; Rabbis; Religious Life**

Clerks
Weaver, M. Sub Shop Girl.
See also **Office Workers**

Cleveland, Ohio
Atkins. Lakefront, Cleveland.
Harper, F. To the Union Savers of Cleveland.

Clocks
Hughes, L. Bells Toll Kindly, The.
See also **Watches**

Clothing
Brown, S. Sporting Beasley.
Derricotte. Christmas Eve: My Mother Dressing.
Dunbar, P. Bohemian, The.
Giovanni. Poem (For Anna Hedgeman and Alfreda Duster).
Hughes, L. Brand New Clothes.
Dressed Up.
Garment.

What?
When Sue Wears Red.
Johnson, M. Wintah Styles, De.
Jordan, J. Last Poem on Bell's Theorem.
On the Real World: Meditation #1.
Sometimes DeLiza.
Komunyakaa. Boy Wearing a Dead Man's Clothes.
Madhubuti. But He Was Cool.
Steptoe. Window Shopping.
Tucker, M. Lines to an Old Dress.
Walden. Wish for an Overcoat.
See also **Fashion; Jewelry**

Clouds
Atkins. Dark Area.
Hughes, L. Garment.
Newsome. Sky Pictures.
Ray, H. Cloud Song.
Sundiata. Making Poems.

Clowns
Hughes, L. Black Crown, The.
For Dead Mimes.
See also **Circus**

Clumsiness
Dunbar, P. My Best Girl.

Coal Mining and Coal Miners
Lorde. Coal.
Toomer. Banking Coal.
See also **Mining and Miners**

Cocaine
Ai. Self Defense.
Brown, S. Maumee Ruth.
Clifton, L. White Lady.
Harper, M. Elvin's Blues.

Cockroaches
Clifton, L. At last we killed the roaches.
Lorde. Kitchen Linoleum.
Raven. Roach / came struttin, A.

Coffee
Tucker, M. Upon Receipt of a Pound of Coffee in 1863.

Coins
Hughes, L. Fact.
Tomorrow may be.
Weems. Dime after Dime.

Cold
Brown, S. Convict.
Dunbar, P. Misty Day, A.
Giovanni. Hampton, Virginia.
Harper, F. Out in the cold mid the dreary night.
Horton, G. On Winter.
Hughes, L. Prayer for a Winter Night.
Walden. Wish for an Overcoat.

Colleges and Universities
Harper, M. Barricades hammered into place.
Hill, L. Tuskegee.
Horton, G. On the Pleasures of College Life.
Moorer. Claflin's Alumni.
Dedication Day Poem.
What We Teach at Claflin.
Nelson, M. Letter to a Benedictine Monk.
Reed, I. Visit to a Small College.
Scott, W. Fisk is / a / negroid / institution.
Wheatley, P. To the University of Cambridge, in New-England.
See also **Education; School and Schools; Students; Teaching and Teachers**

Colonialism
Cortez. They Came Again in 1970 in 1980.
Dunbar, P. Conquerors, The.
Ferdinand. Whi / te boys gone.
Reed, I. Inaugural Day, 1981.
Points of View.
Simpson, J. Old Liberia Is Not the Place for Me.
Unknown. Rebus, A.
Walcott. Far Cry from Africa, A.
Wheatley, P. America.
Answer to the *Rebus*, by the Author of These Poems, An.
See also **British Empire**

Colorado (state)
Komunyakaa. Fever.

Colors
Brown, S. Choices.
Cullen, C. Colors.
Gray-Kontar. Not No Socialism/Communism Classical, but Some Power to the People Jazz.
Hughes, L. Color.
Little Song.
Madhubuti. Poem Looking for a Reader, A.
Salaam. Height, Breadth, Depth.
New Orleans Rainbow.
Sanchez, S. At the center of.
Stanard. Wrong Color.
Steptoe. Sweet Brown Rice and Red Bones.
Toomer. People.
Wilson, Ted. S. C. M.
Young, A. How the Rainbow Works.

Colosseum, Rome
Harper, F. Hermit's Sacrifice, The.

Coltrane, John
Baker, H. No matter where you travel.
Baraka. Am/trak.
Wise 4.
Graham, D. Soul.
Harper, M. Brother John.
Dear John, Dear Coltrane.
Here Where Coltrane Is.
Homage to the New World.
Ode to Tenochtitlan.
Jordan, N. Silent Prophet, The.
Kaufman, B. Buddhist experience, A.
Madhubuti. Don't Cry, Scream.
McClane. Jazz.
Nixon. Ju-Ju Man.
Spellman. Did John's Music Kill Him?
John Coltrane: An Impartial Review.
Touré, A. JuJu.
Young, A. John Coltrane Dance, The.

Colts. *See* **Horses**

Columbia University
Hughes, L. Theme for English B.

Columbus, Christopher
Dunbar, P. Columbian Ode.

Combs
Trethewey. Hot Comb.
Williams, Karen. There's History in My Hair.

Comedians
Reed, I. Life is a screwball comedy.

Comfort
Baraka. Political Poem.
Cullen, C. To France.
Sanchez, S. How can you comfort.
Walker, A. Facing the Way.

Commencement Day
Horton, G. Graduate Leaving College, The.

Communication
Angelou. Communication I.
Communication II.
Clifton, L. To Merle.
Giovanni. Legacies.
Poem of Friendship, A.
Hughes, L. Silence.
Jordan, J. About Long Distances on Saturday.
For Dave: 1976.
What Is This in Reference To? or We Must Get Together Sometime Soon!
Lorde. At First I Thought You Were Talking about.
Bridge through My Windows.
From Inside an Empty Purse.
Sewerplant Grows in Harlem or I'm a Stranger Here Myself When Does the Next Swan Leave, A.
Plumpp. Speech.
Young, A. After Visiting Arl at the Hospital.
By Heart.
Lightning, Divine Lightning.
Moving, Merging, Fading, Standing Still.

Communism
Dove, R. Eastern European Eclogues.
Hughes, L. Goodbye Christ.
Last Prince of the East.
Lenin walks around the world.
One More "S" in the U.S.A.
Salute to Soviet Armies.

When the Armies Passed.
White Man.
Worley, D. Las Flores para una Niña Negra.

Commuting and Commuters
Lorde. One Year to Life on the Grand Central
Shuttle.
See also **Suburbs and Suburban Life**

Companionship and Companions
Angelou. Alone.
Conceit, A.
Baraka. Revolutionary Love.
Cullen, C. Ghosts.
Dunbar, P. To Her.
Hayden, R. Dogwood Trees, The.
Hughes, L. Minnie Sings Her Blues.
Lorde. Memorial I.
To the Girl Who Lives In a Tree.
McKay, C. Wild Goat, The.
Thompson, D. Sister Lakin and Lally.
Walcott. Village Life, A.
Walker, A. Forgive me if my praises.
Gift.
Young, A. Making Love After Hours.
Mexico City Lover.
No Trespassing.
See also **Friendship**

Compassion
Angelou. I almost remember.
Cullen, C. Magnets.
Emanuel, J. Whitey, Baby.
McKay, C. Courage.
Salaam. Bush Mama.
Toomer. See the Heart.
Wright, J. Compassion's Bird.

Competition
Sanchez, S. Small Comment.
Williams, Marlon. Blood, Sweat, and Fears.
Young, A. Roland Navarro (1939-1961).
See also **Rivalry**

Complacency
Braxton, C. Gathering, The.
Clark, Benjamin. No Enemies.
Cotter, Sr. Contradiction.
Jordan, J. Song of the Law Abiding Citizen.
Komunyakaa. Fog Galleon.
Lorde. Art of Response, The.
Timing.
Sanchez, S. So This Is Our Revolution.
Van Peebles. To Hell with Whitey.
Wakefield, J. We exist living dead. The death
of.

Concentration Camps
Hayden, R. Belsen, Day of Liberation.
Henderson, D. Alvin Cash/Keep on Dancin'.
Lorde. This Urn Contains Earth from German
Concentration Camps.

Concerts
Dunbar, P. Concert, The.

Confederacy
Brown, S. Song of Triumph.
Horton, G. Jefferson in a Tight Place.
See also **Civil War, United States**

Confessions
Brooks, G. Strong Men, Riding Horses /
Lester after the Western.
Derricotte. Weakness, The.
Hughes, L. Third Degree.
Madhubuti. In the Interest of Black Salvation.
Walker, A. Confession.

Confidence
Giovanni. Poem for a Lady Whose Voice I
Like.

Conflict
Coleman, W. Doing Battle with the Wolf.
Graham, D. Clown, The.
Harris, P. Let's Take All the Blame.
Hughes, L. Troubled Water.
Johnson, F. To an Afro-American Maiden.
Jordan, J. Meta-Rhetoric.
Lorde. Conversations in Crisis.
Dream/Songs from the Moon of Beulah Land.
Love, Maybe.
Madhubuti. For Black People.
McKay, C. America.
Polarity.

Ward, P. She Should Have Called 911.
Warner, M. My Woman.
Young, A. Belgrade moon, where are you.

Conformity
Brooks, G. To Those of My Sisters Who Kept
Their Naturals.
Cortez. Plain Truth.
Giovanni. Toy Poem.

Confusion
Baraka. Vice.
Giovanni. I wrote a good omelet ... and ate a
hot poem.
Hughes, L. Circles spin round.
Knight, E. Various Protestations From Various
People.
Lorde. Bloodbirth.
New Year's Day.
October.
Pirouette.
Therapy.
Nelson, M. Bali Hai Calls Mama.
Don't Throw Out Wine Bottles.
Spellman. Friends i am like you tied.
Toomer. I sit in my room.
Williams, Karen. For Backwards Buppies.

Congo River
Angelou. For Us, Who Dare Not Dare.
Bethune, L. For Singing In Good Mood.
Kgositsile. Gods Wrote, The.

Conrad, Joseph
Cullen, C. For Joseph Conrad.

Conscience
Dunbar, P. Conscience and Remorse.
Harriet Beecher Stowe.
Hughes, L. Call to Creation.
Summer. Curious White Boy.
Walcott. Elsewhere.

Conscientious Objectors. *See* **Pacifism and
Pacifists**

Consciousness
Sun-Ra. Would I for all that were.
Walcott. Elsewhere.

Conscription, Military
Hughes, L. Draftees.
Madam and the Army.
Tag

Consolation
Dove, R. Five Elephants.
Giovanni. Women gather, The.
Young, A. Elegy: "Good morning! / Good
morning!"
For Joanne in Poland.
Grizzly Peak.

Conspiracy
Cortez. Brooding.
Komunyakaa. Fragging.
Nuriddin. Children of the Future.

Constellations. *See* **Sky**

Consumerism
Baraka. Look for You Yesterday, Here You
Come Today.

Contempt
Cortez. Acceptance Speech.
Once Upon a Road.
Cullen, C. Song of Sour Grapes, A.

Contentment
Bontemps. God Give to Men.
Brown, S. Odyssey of Big Boy.
Cullen, C. To France.
Dunbar, P. Content.
Foolin' wid de Seasons.
Limitations.
Giovanni. Once a Lady Told Me.
Jackson, M. L. Some Kind of Crazy.
Johnson, F. Ethiopian's Song, The.
Nelson, M. High and Haughty.
Walker, M. Iowa Farmer.
Young, A. Ars Poetica.
Dance for Li Po, A.
Look Good, Smell Good, Feel.
Romance.
Sunday Illumination.
See also **Happiness**

Continuity
Harper, M. High Modes: Vision as Ritual:
Confirmation.

Young, A. Black Queen for More Than a
Day.
Green Is a Feeling, Not a Color.
How Stars Start.

Convalescence
Lorde. Martha this is a catalog of days.

Conventionality
Thomas, L. Electricity of Blossoms.

Convents
Hughes, L. Convent.
See also **Nuns**

Conversation
Baraka. This is the Clearing I Once Spoke of.
Coleman, W. Be Quiet, Go Away.
Dunbar, P. Drizzle.
Jackson, M. L. Blunts.
Jordan, J. Patricia's Poem.
Lorde. Building.
Conversations in Crisis.
Fantasy and Conversation.
Suspension.
Oden. Bible Study.
Reed, I. Untitled III.
What You Mean I Can't Irony?
Troupe. Conversation Overheard.
Young, A. Dancer, The.

Conversion
Hayden, R. El-Hajj Malik El-Shabazz.
Toomer. Conversion.
Wheatley, P. On Being Brought from Africa
to America.

Cooking and Cooks
Brooks, G. Egg Boiler, The.
Clifton, L. Cutting Greens.
Dunbar, P. Capture, The.
Curiosity.
Forbes, C. Potlicker Blues.
Harper, M. Breaded Meat, Breaded Hands.
Hughes, L. Frosting.
Lorde. From the House of Yemanjá.
Moore, L. Tanka: "After church meeting."
Nelson, M. Bali Hai Calls Mama.
Men in the Kitchen.
Reed, I. Neo-HooDoo Aesthetic, The.
Salaam. Everywhere You Eat.
Strange. Offering.
Wright, J. Cutting Greens.

Coral
Randall, D. Coral Atoll.

Cormorants
Clifton, L. To the Unborn and Waiting
Children.

Corn
African-American Oral Tradition. Juber up and
Juber down.
Campbell, J. Song of the Corn.
Dunbar, P. Corn-Stalk Fiddle, The.

Corpses
Southerland. Blue Clay.

Corruption
Baraka. Dichtung.
Election Day.
Heathen Technology & Media.
New Reality Is Better Than a New Movie, A!
Real Life.
Red Eye.
Success, The.
Three Modes of History and Culture.
Western Lady, A.
YMCA #35.
Carroll, K. Domino Theory (Or Snoop Dogg
Rules the World), The.
Cortez. Blood Suckers.
Complicity.
They Came Again in 1970 in 1980.
Cruz, V. O. K. / you scat taking.
Dumas, H. Tis of Thee.
Dunbar, P. Poet, The.
Franklin, C. Visions ... Leaders.
Giovanni. This Is Not for John Lennon.
Harper, F. Aunt Chloe's Politics.
Harper, M. Music of Broadswords, The.
Hemphill. Family Jewels.
Jordan, J. Juice of a Lemon on the Trail of a
Little Yellow.

Jackson, G.   Some of Betty's Story Round 1850.
Jeffers, L.   On Listening to the Spirituals.
  To him who in his absence from himself.
Lane, P.   On Being Head of the English Department.
Lorde.   School Note.
McKay, C.   Homing Swallows.
Reynolds, S.   Whipping, The.
Sanchez, S.   These autumn trees sit.
Shange.   It's Not so Good to be Born a Girl/ Sometimes.

Cruelty to Animals
Derricotte.   From a Letter: About Snow.
Dunbar, P.   Forest Greeting, The.

Crum, William
Moorer.   Crum Appointment, The.

Cuba
Ai.   Cuba, 1962.
Hughes, L.   To the Little Front of San Lazaro on the Ocean Front, Havana.
Jeffers, L.   Flesh of the Young Men Is Burning, The.
Miller, E.   Grenada.

Cuckoos
Ray, H.   Cuckoo Song.

Culture
Angelou.   Ain't That Bad.
Baker, H.   No matter where you travel.
Calderón.   It's hard being / folded/licked.
Joans.   Customs and Culture?
Madhubuti.   But He Was Cool.
Weaver, M.   Brooklyn.
WEEMS.   Funk.
Welburn.   Eulogy for Populations.
Williams, Niama.   Afrocentricity.
Young, A.   American Time.

Cups
Knight, E.   Haiku: "In the August grass."

Curiosity
Hughes, L.   Curious.
Komunyakaa.   Praising Dark Places.
Lorde.   Ballad from Childhood.

Curses
African-American Oral Tradition.   And may your life become unlivable, boy.
  Here's to you, Mag, you dirty hag.
  You Told Me a Lie.
Hernton.   Medicine Man.
Reed, I.   Black Cock, The.
  For Cardinal Spellman Who Hated Voo Doo.

Custer, George Armstrong
Whitman, A.   Custer's Last Ride.

Custom
Hughes, L.   English, The.

Cuvier, Georges Léopold Chrétien Frédéric Dagobert, Baron
Alexander, E.   Venus Hottentot.

Cuyahoga Falls, Ohio
Jordan, A.   If I Write a Poem.

Cynicism and Cynics
Dunbar, P.   Vengeance is Sweet.

Czechoslovakia
Hughes, L.   Song for Ourselves.
Walker, A.   Kiss, The.

D

Daedalus
Alba.   Be Daedalus.
Hayden, R.   O Daedalus, Fly Away Home.

Daffodils
McKay, C.   Castaways, The.

Damnation and the Damned
Hughes, L.   Fire, / Fire, Lord!

Dancing and Dancers
Ai.   More.
Alexander, E.   Ode.
Baraka.   From an Almanac (2).
  From an Almanac (3).
Barlow, G.   Nook.
Brown, S.   Scotty Has His Say.
Campbell, J.   Mobile-Buck.
'Sciplinin' Sister Brown.

Cortez.   So Many Feathers.
  Tapping.
Crouch, S.   Riding Across John Lee's Finger.
Cullen, C.   She of the Dancing Feet Sings.
Dandridge, R.   Zalka Peetruza.
Davis, T.   Boppin' is Safer than Grindin'.
Dunbar, P.   Angelina.
  Critters' Dance, De.
  Dance, The.
  Frolic, A.
  Valse, The.
  Virginia Reel, A.
Gilbert, C.   Directions, The.
Giovanni.   Swaziland.
  Three/Quarters Time.
Graham, R.   Learning to Dance.
Henderson, D.   Alvin Cash/Keep on Dancin'.
Hughes, L.   College Formal: Renaissance Casino.
  Dancer.
  Dancers.
  Danse Africaine.
  Dream Boogie.
  Dream Variations.
  Midnight Dancer.
  Negro Dancers.
  Nude Young Dancer.
  Song for a Banjo Dance.
  Sunday by the Combination.
Johnson, H.   Bottled [New York].
Jordan, A.   Dance Lesson, A.
Jordan, J.   About Enrique's Drawing.
Kendrick, D.   Jenny in Love.
Lorde.   Electric Slide Boogie, The.
  Scar.
  Wood Has No Mouth.
Major, C.   Large Room with Wood Floor.
Marshall, M.   To a Dark Dancer.
McKay, C.   Harlem Dancer, The.
Moss, T.   Tornados.
Nelson, M.   Confessional Poem.
  Diverne's Waltz.
Reed, I.   Black Cock, The.
  Tea Dancer Turns Thirty-Nine.
Rodgers, C.   We Dance Like Ella Riffs.
Salaam.   All Nite Long.
Shange.   Dream of Pairing.
Smith, P.   They say that black people.
Thompson-Cager.   Praise Song for Katherine Dunham: A Choreopoem.
Thompson, D.   Dancing in Menopause.
Toomer.   Lost Dancer, The.
Weeden, L.   Dance.
Young, A.   Ravel: Bolero.

Dandelions
Harper, F.   Dandelions.
McClellan.   January Dandelion, A.
McKay, C.   Castaways, The.
Weeden, L.   Little Dandelion, The.

Daniel
Hughes, L.   Last Feast of Belshazzar, The.
Unknown.   Didn't my Lord Deliver Daniel.

Dante Alighieri
Ray, H.   Dante.

Danube
Young, A.   Where the Danube and Sava Rivers Meet.

Darkness
Barrax.   Greenhouse.
Cullen, C.   From the Dark Tower.
Davis, F.   Flowers of Darkness.
Dunbar, P.   Love is the light of the world, my dear.
  Slow Through the Dark.
Ellis, T.   Shooting Back.
Hemphill.   Where Seed Falls.
Hughes, L.   Dare.
  Dimout in Harlem.
  Dive
  Moonlight Night: Carmel.
  Night Song.
  Walkers with the Dawn.
Komunyakaa.   Cage Walker, The.
  Praising Dark Places.
Lane, P.   Lake Murry.
Toomer.   And Pass.
Whitfield.   Misanthropist, The.

Darwin, Charles. *See* Evolution

Dating
Angelou.   Country Lover.
Dunbar, P.   Lover's Lane.
  Negro Love Song, A.
Jordan, J.   Patricia's Poem.

Daughters
Baraka.   Preface to a Twenty Volume Suicide Note.
Brooks, G.   Jessie Mitchell's Mother.
  Maxie Allen always taught her.
Clifton, L.   Admonitions.
  Anna Speaks of the Childhood of Mary Her Daughter.
  If He Ask You Was I Laughing.
  If mama / could see.
  Last Note to My Girls.
  Lucy and Her Girls.
Coleman, W.   Cousin Mary.
Dove, R.   After Reading *Mickey in the Night Kitchen* for the Third Time Before Bed.
  Variation on Guilt.
Gilyard.   Daughter, That Picture of You.
Goodison.   I Am Becoming My Mother.
Hamilton, M.   Things I Do Not Speak.
Harper, F.   Lines to M.A.H.
  Rizpah, the Daughter of Ai.
Harper, M.   Crossing Lake Michigan.
  Eve (Rachel).
  Mission.
Hughes, L.   Mama and Daughter.
  Sylvester's Dying Bed.
Kgositsile.   To My Daughter.
Knight, E.   Circling the Daughter.
Lorde.   But What Can You Teach My Daughter.
  Dear Toni Instead of a Letter of Congratulation.
  Progress Report.
Madgett.   Offspring.
McElroy, C.   In My Mother's Room.
Moore, Lynn.   Haiku: "Morning fog / my daughter dropped off at camp."
Moss, T.   Undertaker's Daughter Feels Neglect, The.
Mullen, H.   Momma Sayings.
Nelson, M.   Daughters, 1900.
Reed, I.   Poem for Two Daughters.
Rodgers, C.   It Is Deep.
Walker, A.   Forgiveness.
  My daughter is coming!
  Poem at Thirty-nine.
WEEMS.   Dime after Dime.
Wheatley, P.   To the Hon'ble Thomas Hubbard, Esq.; on the Death of Mrs. Thankful Leonard.
  To the Honourable T.H. Esq.; on the Death of His Daughter.

David (Bible)
Thompson, P.   David and Goliath.
Wheatley, P.   Goliath of Gath.

Davis, Angela
Cobb, A.   Angela Davis.
Giovanni.   Poem of Angela Yvonne Davis.
Jordan, J.   Solidarity.

Davis, Miles
Brathwaite, E.   Blues.
Harper, M.   Brother John.
Jeffers, H.   I Was Looking at Miles.
Komunyakaa.   Boxing Day.
Redmond.   Milestone: The Birth of an Ancestor.
Sundiata.   Open Heart.
Toure, A.   Milestones: September 28, 1991.
Troupe.   Collage.

Dawn
Angelou.   Brief Innocence.
Clifton, L.   Breaklight.
Dunbar, P.   Dawn.
Fortune.   Tell me, ye sad winds sighing.
Grimké, A.   Dawn.
Hughes, L.   Black Maria.
  Daybreak in Alabama.
  Lonely Nocturne.
Lane, P.   Spring.
McKay, C.   Dawn in New York.
  Morning Joy.

Summer Morn in New Hampshire.
When Dawn Comes to the City.
Ray, H. Dawn's Carol.
Salaam. Sunrise on the River.
Toomer. Merl.
See also **Morning**
Dawson, F. W.
Fordham. Tribute to Capt. F. W. Dawson.
Day
Angelou. Plagued Journey, A.
Dunbar, P. Day.
Drowsy Day, A.
Warm Day in Winter, A.
Salaam. Height, Breadth, Depth.
Sanchez, S. When i return home.
Daydreams
Dunbar, P. By the stream I dream in calm
delight, and watch as in a glass.
McKay, C. Home Thoughts.
Thompson, Lisa. What Do I Want from Men
and Love?
Young, A. Afternoon After, The.
Loneliness.
See also **Dreams and Dreaming**
Death and the Dead
"Ada." Oh, when this earthly tenement.
African-American Oral Tradition. Do, Lawd.
Junkies' Ball.
Pisspot Pete.
Raise a Ruckus Tonight.
Soon one mawnin death come creepin in mah
room.
When-a Mah Blood runs Chilly and Col.
Ai. Cuba, 1962.
Allen, S. Staircase, The.
Angelou. Ailey, Baldwin, Floyd, Killens, and
Mayfield.
Elegy: "I lay down in my grave."
Gamut, The.
Lesson, The.
Mourning Grace.
Atkins. Narrative.
Aubert, A. For Mark James Robert Essex d.
1973.
Bandele. Subtle Art of Breathing, The.
Baraka. Clay.
Dead Lady Canonized, The.
For Crow Jane (Mama Death).
Guerilla Handbook, A.
Invention of Comics, The.
Barlow, G. This Bridge Across.
Barrax. Last Letter.
Scuba Diver Recovers the Body of a Drowned
Child, The.
Baudelaire. Death to the Poor.
Bennett, G. Sonnet: "He came in silvern
armor, trimmed with black."
Bethune, L. For Singing In Good Mood.
Harlem Freeze Frame.
Bibbs. Dirge for J. A. Rogers.
Braithwaite. In a Grave-Yard.
Scintilla.
Brooks, G. Boy died in my alley, The.
In Honor of David Anderson Brooks, My
Father.
Last Quatrain of the Ballad of Emmett Till,
The.
Medgar Evers.
Mentors.
Of De Witt Williams on His Way to Lincoln
Cemetery, Southeast Corner.
We real cool. We.
White Troops Had Their Orders but the
Negroes Looked Like Men.
Brown, S. Challenge.
Conjured.
Dark of the Moon.
Effie.
Funeral.
Maumee Ruth.
Odyssey of Big Boy.
Puttin' on Dog.
Sister Lou.
Thoughts of death / Crowd over my happiness.
Virginia Portrait.
Burt, D. On the Death of Lisa Lyman.
Campbell, J. Mors et Vita.

Cassells. Courtesy, A Trenchant Grace, A.
Clifton, L. After Kent State.
At Jonestown.
Bodies broken on, The.
Buffalo War.
Cain.
Daddy.
News, The.
Once and future dead, The.
Poem on My Fortieth Birthday to My Mother
Who Died Young.
Raising of Lazarus, The.
Running across to the lot.
Coleman, W. Today I Am a Homicide in the
North of the City.
Cornish, S. Death of Dr. King.
Cortez. Give Me the Red on the Black of the
Bullet.
I and I.
Cotter, Sr. Let none ignobly halt because.
Cullen, C. Brown Girl Dead, A.
Epilogue: "Lily, being white not red, The."
Foolish Heart, The.
For an Anarchist.
For an Evolutionist and His Opponent.
In Spite of Death.
Only the Polished Skeleton.
Poet, poet, what is your task.
Protest.
Proud Heart, The.
Requiescam.
Sonnet Dialogue.
Threnody for a Brown Girl.
Two Thoughts of Death.
Wise, The.
Cuney. Death Bed, The.
Threnody: "Only quiet death."
Triviality, A.
Danner, J. Singer, The.
Delegall. Elegy for a Lady.
Dixon, M. Grandmother: Crossing Jordan.
Dodson, O. When I Am Dead.
Dove, R. Company.
Event, The.
Oriental Ballerina, The.
Teach Us to Number Our Days.
Thomas at the Wheel.
Tou Wan Speaks to Her Husband Liu Sheng.
Your Death.
Zeppelin factory, The.
Dunbar, P. Alexander Crummel—Dead.
Behind the Arras.
Border Ballad, A.
"Chronic Kicker," The.
Communion.
Compensation.
Dead.
Death.
Death of the First Born, The.
Death Song[, A].
Dirge: "Place this bunch of mignonette."
Frederick Douglass.
Goin' Home.
In the tents of Akbar.
Love-Song: "If Death should claim me for her
own to-day."
Masters, The.
My dear love died last night.
News, The.
On the Death of W. C.
Paradox, The.
Premonition.
Puttin' the Baby Away.
Remembered.
Right to Die, The.
To a Dead Friend.
To Alice Dunbar.
To the Memory of Mary Young.
Two little boots all rough an' wo'.
W'en I Gits Home.
When all is done, and my last word is said.
Ellis, K. Boys of Summer, The.
Evans, M. Rebel, The.
Fauset. Oblivion.
Fernandez, R. Legacy of a Brother.
Fordham. Dying Girl, The.
Magnolia.

On Parting with a Friend.
To My Mother.
Twilight Musings.
Gerima. Sankofa.
Gilbert, D. Too Many.
Giovanni. One ounce of truth benefits.
When i die i hope no one who ever hurt me
cries.
Women gather, The.
Graham, R. Lynching for Skip James, A.
Grimké, A. Grass Fingers.
Grimké. Charles Sumner.
Hamilton, M. Things I Do Not Speak.
Harper, F. Artist, The.
Bride of Death, The.
Church Building.
Death of the Old Sea King.
Death of Zombi.
Died of Starvation.
Dying Bondman, The.
Dying Christian, The.
Dying Fugitive, The.
Dying Mother, The.
Dying Queen, The.
Eva's Farewell.
Fatal Pledge, The.
Give My Love to the World.
Going East.
Gone to God.
Jamie's Puzzle.
Lessons of the Street.
Let the Light Enter!
Maceo dead! a thrill of sorrow.
Night of Death, The.
Obituary for J. Edwards Barnes.
Revel, The.
Youth in Heaven.
Harper, M. Alice Braxton Johnson.
Biafra Blues.
Christian's Box Seat: So What!
Dead-Day: Malcolm, Feb. 21.
Dead Oaks.
Family of Debridement, The.
Mother Speaks: The Algiers Motel Incident,
Detroit, A.
Nightmare Begins Responsibility.
Ode to Tenochtitlan.
Reuben, Reuben.
We Assume: On the Death of Our Son,
Reuben Masai Harper.
Wisdom of Signs, The.
Hayden, R. Approximations.
Broken Dark, The.
Burly fading one beside the engine, The.
Mourning Poem for the Queen of Sunday.
Paul Laurence Dunbar.
Heard, J. Message to a Loved One Dead, A.
Resting.
Hernton. Black Stick with a Ball of Cotton for
a Head and a Running Machine for a Mouth,
A.
Fall Down.
Horton, G. Close of Life, The.
Division of an Estate.
Execution of Private Henry Anderson.
Imploring to Be Resigned at Death.
Lincoln Is Dead.
Man, a Torch.
One Generation Passeth Away and Another
Cometh.
Reflections from the Flash of a Meteor.
Hughes, L. As Befits a Man.
Bells Toll Kindly, The.
Cabaret Girl Dies on Welfare Island.
Casual.
Cross.
Dear lovely Death.
Death in Africa.
Deceased.
Departure.
Drum.
Dying Beast.
Epitaph: "Within this grave lie."
Fantasy in Purple.
For Dead Mimes.
Gal's Cry for a Dying Lover.
Judgment Day.

Mammy.
Mazie Dies Alone in the City Hospital.
Note in Music.
Pair in One.
Peace.
Question: "When the old junk man Death."
Slave.
Small Memory.
Song for a Dark Girl.
Stony Lonesome.
Sylvester's Dying Bed.
Teacher.
There.
To a Little Lover-Lass, Dead.
Tower.
Two things possess the power.
Wake.
War.
Widow Woman.
World War II.
Young Bride.
Young Gal's Blues.
Jackson, G. Some of Betty's Story Round 1850.
Johnson, F. My God in Heaven said to me.
Song of the Whirlwind.
Johnson, G. I Want to Die While You Love Me.
When I am dead, withhold, I pray, your blooming legacy.
Johnson, J. Color Sergeant, The.
Glory of the Day Was in Her Face, The.
Go Down Death.
Jordan, J. Aftermath.
First Poem from Nicaragua Libre: *Teotcacinte*.
Out in the Country of My Country (Peterborough, New Hampshire).
Kaufman, B. Ancient Rain, The.
Late Lamented Wind, Burned in Indignation, The.
Plea.
Terror is more certain than all the rare desirable popular songs, A.
Kgositsile. Elegy for David Diop.
Knight, E. Dead. He died in Detroit, his beard.
Last Words By "Slick."
Poem of Attrition, A.
Sun came, Miss Brooks—, The.
Komunyakaa. April Fools' Day.
Between Days.
Birds on a Powerline.
Boy Wearing a Dead Man's Clothes.
Chair Gallows.
Changes: or, Reveries at a Window Overlooking a Country Road, with Two Women Talking Blues in the Kitchen.
In the Background of Silence.
Jonestown: More Eyes for *Jadwiga's Dream*.
Landscape for the Disappeared.
1938.
Songs for my Father.
You and I Are Disappearing.
Lane, P. Elegy for Etheridge.
Lanusse. Un Frère Au Tombeau de Son Frère.
Llorens. One Year Ago.
Loftis. In Memoriam: Robert Hayden.
Lorde. Anniversary.
Day they eulogized Mahalia, The.
Dear Joe.
Equinox.
Eulogy for Alvin Frost.
Father Son and Holy Ghost.
Fog Report.
Hanging Fire.
Holographs.
If You Come Softly.
Kitchen Linoleum.
Legacy—Hers.
Martha this is a catalog of days.
Mawu.
Memorial I.
Memorial II.
Memorial IV.
Night-Blooming Jasmine, The.
Poem for a Poet, A.
Speechless.

Suffer the Children.
Today Is Not the Day.
Vigil.
Madgett. Mortality.
Major, C. Swallow the Lake.
Mason, K. Friday night / the bullet ripped.
McKay, C. December, 1919.
If we must die—let it not be like hogs.
My Mother.
Rest in Peace.
Menken. Dying.
Resurgam.
Miller, E. Players.
Miller, M. Wrong Side of the Morning, The.
Mitchell, K. On the Anniversary Of Your Death.
Moorer. In Memoriam of E. B. Clark.
Moss, T. Fisher Street.
Neal, L. Poppa Stoppa Speaks from His Grave.
Nelson, M. Leaving the Hospice.
Mama I remember.
Mama's Murders.
Twist the thread.
Oden. Review from Staten Island.
Parker, Dominique. Foxfire.
Pitcher. Pale Blue Casket, The.
Plato. Reflections, Written on Visiting the Grave of a Venerated Friend.
Randall, D. Old Witherington.
Redmond. Milestone: The Birth of an Ancestor.
Reed, I. For Dancer.
I am not the walrus.
Oakland Blues.
Salaam. Funeraled Fare Well.
I Just Heard John Buffington Died.
Secondline Send Off.
Sanchez, S. Blues.
Kwa Mama Zetu Waliotuzaa.
Life / Poem.
Malcolm.
Philadelphia: Spring, 1985.
Sejour. Le Retour de Napoléon.
Sharp, S. Woman Who Died in Line, The.
Smith, P. Building Nicole's Mama.
Spellman. Did John's Music Kill Him?
Spencer, A. Dunbar.
Steptoe. Notes for a Poem from the Middle Passage of Years.
Stuckey. Ribbons and Lace.
Temptation.
Thomas, R. Revolution!
Worker, The.
Thompson, C. Not Dead, but Sleeping.
To My Dead Brother.
Thompson, P. Afternoon Gossip, An.
Consumptive, The.
Lines on a Dead Girl.
Song, The: "Oh, foully slighted Ethiope maid!"
To a Deceased Friend.
Tolson, M. Festus Conrad.
Old Pettigrew.
Toomer. Be with Me.
They Are Not Missed.
To Gurdjieff Dying.
Upward is this Actuality.
Toure, A. Milestones: September 28, 1991.
Troupe. After Hearing a Radio Announcement: a Comment on Some Conditions.
Day in the Life of a Poet, A.
In Memoriam; for James Baldwin (1924–1987).
Syntax of the mind grips, The.
Tucker, M. "Did You Call Me, Father?"
Gone, with all her sparkling beauty.
Lift Me Higher.
Turner, D. Death is not a dream; death lives.
Uhland. From the German of Uhland.
Unknown. I know moon-rise, I know star-rise.
I Thank God I'm Free at Las'.
No more auction block for me.
Soon I will be done with the troubles of the world.
Steal Away to Jesus.
Swing low, sweet chariot.

Wakefield, J. We exist living dead. The death of.
Walcott. Village Life, A.
Walker, A. Burial.
Girl Who Died #1, The.
Girl Who Died #2, The.
Good Night, Willie Lee, I'll See You in the Morning.
To die before one / wakes / must be glad.
Walker, M. Big John Henry.
Birmingham.
Black Magic.
Elegy: "Strange summer sun shines round our globe of circumstance."
For Owen Dodson, 1983.
Gus, the lineman / Route forty-nine.
On Death and the Resurrection.
Our Need.
Weems. Return to Temptation.
Welburn. Eulogy for Populations.
Wheatley, P. Elegy, Sacred to the Memory of That Great Divine, the Reverend and Learned Dr. Samuel Cooper, Who Departed This Life December 29, 1783, Ætatis 59, An.
Elegy, to Miss Mary Moorhead, An.
Ode of Verses on the Death of George Whitefield, An.
On the Death of a Young Gentleman.
On the Death of Doctor Samuel Marshall.
On the Death of Dr. Samuel Marshall.
On the Death of Dr. Samuel Marshall, 1771.
On the Death of the Rev. Dr. Sewall, 1769.
On the Death of the Rev. Mr. George Whitefield, 1770.
On the Death of the Rev'd Dr. Sewall, 1769.
Thoughts on the Works of Providence.
To a Clergyman on the Death of His Lady.
To a Gentleman and Lady on the Death of the Lady's Brother and Sister, and a Child of the Name Avis, Aged One Year.
To a Lady on the Death of Her Husband.
To a Lady on the Death of Three Relations.
To His Honour the Lieutenant-Governor, on the Death of His Lady, March 24, 1773.
To Mrs. Leonard, on the Death of Her Husband.
To the Hon'ble Thomas Hubbard, Esq.; on the Death of Mrs. Thankfull Leonard.
To the Honourable T.H. Esq.; on the Death of His Daughter.
To the Rev. Mr. Pitkin, on the Death of His Lady.
Whitman, A. I love Kentucky; tho' she merit scorn.
Wright, J. Death as History.
Don José Gorostiza Encounters El Cordobés.
Journey to the Place of Ghosts.
Young, A. W. H. Auden & Mantan Moreland.
Why a Hush Should Not Be Rushed.
Young, K. Escape Artist, The.

See also **War Dead**

Death in Childhood
Angelou. Child Dead in Old Seas.
To Beat the Child Was Bad Enough.
Brown, E. If Randi Could Write.
Clark, Benjamin. Requiescat in Pace.
Clifton, L. On the Death of Allen's Son.
Dunbar, P. Death of the First Born, The.
Fordham. In Memoriam. Alphonse Campbell Fordham.
Queenie.
To an Infant.
Harper, F. Drunkard's Child, The.
Dying Child to Her Blind Father, The.
Mother's Heroism, A.
Harper, M. Mother Speaks: The Algiers Motel Incident, Detroit, A.
Nightmare Begins Responsibility.
Reuben, Reuben.
Heard, J. Solace.
Jordan, J. Test of Atlanta 1979, The.
Lorde. Brother Alvin.
Rites of Passage.
Same Death Over and Over or Lullabies Are for Children, The.
Moorer. Russia's Resentment.
Nelson, M. Mama's Promise.

Randall, D. Ballad of Birmingham.
Reed, I. Oakland Blues.
Sharp, S. Meanwhile, in Rwanda.
Thompson, D. Laurel Street, 1950.
Wheatley, P. Funeral Poem on the Death of
  C.E., an Infant of Twelve Months, A.
On the Death of a Young Lady of Five Years
  of Age.
To a Lady and Her Children, on the Death of
  Her Son and Their Brother.

Death of Animals
African-American Oral Tradition. JUba dis
  and JUba dat an.
Mary had a little lamb for which she cared no
  particle.
Barrax. Death of a Squirrel in McKinley Park,
  The.
King: April 4, 1968.
Patroness.
Clifton, L. For the Bird Who Flew against
  Our Window One Morning and Broke His
  Natural Neck.
I once knew a man who had wild horses
  killed.
Harper, F. Sparrow's Fall, The.
Harper, M. Called.
Drive In, The.
Hayden, R. Gulls.
Killing the Calves.
Plague of Starlings, A.
Horton, G. Death of an Old Carriage Horse.
Fate of an Innocent Dog, The.
Lorde. Domino.
Rock Thrown into the Water Does Not Fear
  the Cold, A.
Madhubuti. On Seeing Diana Go
  Maddddddddd.

Debauchery
Komunyakaa. 1938.

Debt
African-American Oral Tradition. Life's a
  funny old proposition.
Ups on the Farm.
Dunbar, P. Debt, The.
Horton, G. Creditor to His Proud Debtor, The.
Hughes, L. Little Lyric (of Great Importance).
Madam and the Phone Bill.
Jordan, J. Financial Planning.

Decadence
El-Hadi. Drama, The.

Decay
Cullen, C. Apostrophe to the Land.
Harper, F. How Are the Mighty Fallen!
Horton, G. Connubial Felicity.
Johnson, F. Rome is dying.
Komunyakaa. In the Background of Silence.
Reed, I. From the Files of Agent 22.
Untitled: "I know of a man who treated his
  body like a dog."

December
Giovanni. December of My Springs, The.
Heard, J. December.
Ray, H. December.

Deception
African-American Oral Tradition. Herman
  from the Shark-Tooth Shore.
Marie.
Poolshooting Monkey: "I don't know but I
  was told."
Poolshooting Monkey: "It was in Speero's
  poolroom back in nineteen-ten."
Poolshooting Monkey: "It was in Speero's
  poolroom in the year eighteen-ten."
Signifying Monkey: "Back down in the jungle
  up under the stick."
Signifying Monkey: "Deep down in the jungle
  in the coconut grove."
Signifying Monkey: "Down in the jungle about
  treetop deep."
Signifying Monkey: "It was early in the
  morning one bright summer day."
Signifying Monkey: "Say deep down in the
  jungle in the coconut grove."
Signifying Monkey: "There hadn't been no
  shift for quite a bit."
Angelou. How I Can Lie to You.

Baraka. From an Almanac.
Cotter, Sr. Prologue to a Supposed Play.
Davis, T. Playing Solitaire.
Dunbar, P. Ballad: "I know my love is true."
Made to Order Smile, The.
Parted.
We wear the mask that grins and lies.
Hamilton, B. Brother Harlem Bedford Watts
  Tells Mr. Charlie Where ITs At.
Horton, G. On an Old Deluded Soldier.
To Eliza.
Komunyakaa. Touch-up Man.
Loftis. Brief Encounter.
Lorde. Chorus.
Love, Maybe.
Making It.
McElroy, C. Horoscope.
Neely. Rhonda, Age 15 Emergency Room.
Nelson, M. Impala.
Thomas, L. They Never Lose.
Unknown. Me and My Captain.
Signifying Monkey, The.
Walker, M. Yalluh Hammuh.

Decisions
Angelou. Last Decision, The.
Davis, F. Arthur Ridgewood, M.D.
Emanuel, J. Fishermen.
Hughes, L. Prayer: "I ask you this: / Which
  way to go."
Kaufman, B. Perhaps.

See also **Free Will**

Decorum
Hughes, L. English, The.

Deer
Conyus. Upon Leaving the Parole Board
  Hearing.
Wright, J. White Deer, The.

See also **Hunting and Hunters**

Defeat
Hughes, L. Total War.

Degas, Edgar
Kaufman, B. Bird with Painted Wings.

Dehumanization
Angelou. Junkie Monkey Reel.
Rivers, C. Subway, The.

See also **Bureaucracy and Bureaucrats**

Deism
Wheatley, P. Address to the Deist—1767, An.
Deism.

Dejection. *See* **Melancholy**

Delaware (state)
Giovanni. Wilmington Delaware.

Delight
Young, A. Morning Poem for Michael, A.

Deliverance
Harper, F. Deliverance.
Lorde. Call.
Unknown. Didn't my Lord Deliver Daniel.
Go down, Moses.

Democracy
Evans, M. Speak the truth to the people.
Hughes, L. Beaumont to Detroit: 1943.
Black Man Speaks, The.
Democracy will not come.
We're all in the telephone book.

Demons
Clifton, L. Her Love Poem.
Horton, G. Troubled with the Itch and
  Rubbing with Sulphur.
Lorde. Blackstudies.
Sims, L. Angels Prayer, An.

See also **Monsters; Satan**

Denial
Angelou. No No No No.
Remembering.
We saw beyond our seeming.

Dentistry and Dentists
Jean, V. Lesson on Braces.

Department Stores
Derricotte. Weakness, The.

Depression (psychological)
Hayden, R. Ice Storm.
Hughes, L. Neighbor.

See also **Blues (mood); Melancholy**

Deserts
Clifton, L. Sonora Desert Poem.
Dove, R. Sahara Bus Trip, The.
Forbes, C. Dark Mirror.
Hughes, L. Desert.
Komunyakaa. Man Who Carries the Desert
  Around Inside Himself: For Wally, The.
Lorde. Sahara.
Walker, A. On Sight.

Desire
Ahmasi. Water of Your Bath.
Angelou. Black Ode.
Here's to Adhering.
On Diverse Deviations.
Prescience.
Zorro Man, A.
Brooks, G. Ballad of Chocolate Mabbie, The.
Buchanan, S. Prayer: "Centaurian smoke
  blower / shyly smoking my breast."
Clifton, L. Leanna's Poem.
My Friends.
Cullen, C. Timid Lover.
Daáood. Tears for the poet.
Dove, R. Happenstance.
His Shirt.
Secret Garden, The.
Sunday Greens.
Dunbar, P. Change, The.
If I could but forget.
In a English Garden.
Night, dim night, and it rains, my love, it
  rains.
Retort.
Emanuel, J. Treehouse, The.
Giovanni. Balances.
Beautiful Black Men.
Ever want to crawl.
I want to sing.
Poem: "Like a will-o'-the-wisp in the night."
Poem of Friendship, A.
That Day.
There is a hunger.
Grimké, A. El Beso.
Mona Lisa, A.
Want of You, The.
Harris, P. Be Somebody Fragrant.
Horton, G. Acrostics.
Houston, V. Ecstasy.
Hughes, L. Advice.
Desire to us.
Spring for Lovers.
Jamal. Sat. Nite.
James, Wendy. Troy.
Jordan, J. Alla Tha's All Right, But.
No Poem Because Time Is Not a Name.
Joshua. On the Morning St. Bernard.
Kgositsile. Ivory Masks in Orbit.
Knight, E. On Seeing the Black Male as #1
  Sex Object in America.
Komunyakaa. Apprenticeship.
Beg Song.
Blue Light Lounge Sutra for the Performance
  Poets at Harold Park Hotel.
Epilogue to the Opera of Dead on Arrival.
For You, Sweetheart, I'll Sell Plutonium
  Reactors.
Heart's Graveyard Shift, The.
Rocks Push.
Safe Subjects.
Thorn Merchant's Mistress, The.
When in Rome—Apologia.
Woman, I Got the Blues.
Work.
Lorde. Burning the Water Hyacinth.
Conversations in Crisis.
Echoes.
Political Relations.
Trollop Maiden, The.
What It Means to Be Beautiful.
McKay, C. Flirtation.
Harlem Dancer, The.
On Broadway.
Romance.
Thirst.
Nelson, M. Balance.
Confessional Poem.

Randall, D.　Hail, Dionysos.
Reed, I.　Kali's Galaxy.
Renegade.　Hoodoo.
Rilke.　Rilke's Third Elegy.
Sanchez, S.　I kneel down like a.
Toomer.　Her Lips Are Copper Wire.
　I See Her Lovely There.
Walker, M.　Teacher was a bad man, The.
Wright, J.　Desire's Persistence.
Young, A.　Black Queen for More Than a
　Day.
Young, K.　All Things Insensible.
　Hunger.
See also **Erotic Love**

Desolation
Bontemps.　Blight.
Cullen, C.　Black Magdalens.
Jordan, N.　When A Woman Gets Blue.
Knight, E.　Feeling Fucked/Up Up.

Despair
African-American Oral Tradition.　Motherless
　Child.
Baraka.　Measure of Memory (The Navigator),
　The.
　Poem Some People Will Have to Understand,
　A.
　Preface to a Twenty Volume Suicide Note.
　Rhythm and Blues (I).
Clifton, L.　White Boy, The.
Cullen, C.　At a Parting.
　Therefore, Adieu.
Delany.　Interim.
Dickinson, E.　Softened by Time's consummate
　plush.
Dove, R.　Aurora Borealis.
Dunbar, P.　Blue.
　Despair.
　One Life.
　River of Ruin, The.
　Ships That Pass in the Night.
　There are brilliant heights of sorrow.
　Worn Out.
　Wraith, The.
Emanuel, J.　Whitey, Baby.
Fabio.　Hurt of It All, The.
Giovanni.　Forced Retirement.
　Sometimes / when i wake up.
Grandmaster Flash *and* the Furious
　Five.　Message, The.
Griffin, E.　Mind of a Madman kills.
Hall, K.　Wig.
Harper, F.　Contrast, The.
Horton, G.　Slave's Complaint, The.
Jordan, J.　Poor Form.
　Roman Poem Number Thirteen.
Knight, E.　As You Leave Me.
　Report to the Mother.
Komunyakaa.　Charmed.
　Dog Act, The.
　Plea, The.
　Soliloquy: Man Talking to a Mirror.
　When Loneliness Is a Man.
Lorde.　Generation.
　Za Ki Tan Ke Parlay Lot.
McClellan.　January Dandelion, A.
McKay, C.　Desolate.
　Futility.
Nelson, M.　And Jonah Began to Stroke a
　Tentative Rhythm.
Stewart, James T.　Poem: "We drank
　Thunderbird all night."
Unknown.　Sometimes i feel like a motherless
　child.
Walker, M.　Disillusion for Flower Children of
　Long Ago.
Whitfield.　Misanthropist, The.
Young, A.　Herrick Hospital, Fifth Floor.
　January.

Destruction
Baraka.　Poem Some People Will Have to
　Understand, A.
Brooks, G.　Boy Breaking Glass.
Brown, S.　Memphis Blues.
Cortez.　Expenditures; Economic Love Song 1.
Giovanni.　Word Poem (Perhaps Worth
　Considering).
Harper, F.　Night of Death, The.

Horton, G.　Retreat from Moscow, The.
Jordan, J.　Poem Towards a Final Solution.
　Take them out!
LeFlore.　Dream/eaters on the edge.
Lorde.　Bees, The.
Nelson, M.　Diverne's House.
Randall, D.　Primitives.
Sanchez, S.　Elegy (for MOVE and
　Philadelphia).
Thomas, L.　Onion Bucket.
Young, A.　Old Woman.
　Watsonville after the Quake.

Detectives
Hughes, L.　Café: 3 A.M.

Determination
African-American Oral Tradition.　Titanic: "All
　the old folks say the fourth a May was a hell
　of a day."
Titanic: "Boys, you remember way back on
　the day of the eighth of May."
Titanic: "Eighth a May was a hell of a day,
　The."
Titanic: "I don't know, but my folks say."
Titanic: "In the year of eighteen-twelve."
Titanic: "It was sad indeed, it was sad in
　mind."
Titanic: "Tenth of May was a hell of a day,
　The."
Titanic: "This is about Shine O Shine. The
　captain was on his boat and he was."
Titanic: "Twelfth of May was one hell of a
　day, The."
Angelou.　Call Letters: Mrs. V.B.
　Still I Rise.
Giovanni.　No Reservations.
Horton, G.　Love.
Hughes, L.　Song: "Lovely, dark, and lonely
　one."
Knight, E.　Dark Prophecy: I Sing of Shine.

Detroit, Michigan
Hughes, L.　Poor Girl's Ruination.
Madhubuti.　First World.
Young, A.　City Home Detroit.

Devil, The. *See* **Satan**

Diabetes
Hoagland, E.　Big Zeb Johnson.

Diana (mythology)
Cullen, C.　To Endymion.

Diaries
Lorde.　Martha this is a catalog of days.

Dickinson, Emily
Nelson, M.　Emily Dickinson's Defunct.

Dinosaurs
Carroll, K.　Theory on Extinction or What
　Happened to the Dinosaurs?
Nelson, M.　Dinosaur Spring.

Dionysus
Randall, D.　Hail, Dionysos.

Diplomacy and Diplomats
Christian.　Selassie at Geneva.
Hughes, L.　Envoy to Africa.
Lorde.　Political Relations.

Disappointment
Angelou.　Shaker, Why Don't You Sing?
Brown, S.　Dark of the Moon.
Clifton, L.　Thirty-eighth year, The.
Dove, R.　Lightnin' Blues.
Lorde.　My Fifth Trip to Washington Ended in
　Northeast Delaware.
　Sewerplant Grows in Harlem or I'm a Stranger
　Here Myself When Does the Next Swan
　Leave, A.
Menken.　"My heritage!" It is to live within.

Disasters
Clifton, L.　If Something Should Happen.
Reed, I.　Earthquake Blues.

Discipline
Gilmore, B.　Revolution.
Mullen, H.　Momma Sayings.
Neal, G.　Personal Jihad.
Nelson, M.　Clown Nose.

Discontent
Byrnes.　Chalk-Dust.
Dunbar-Nelson.　Proletariat Speaks, The.
Giovanni.　Alone.
　Balances.

Being and Nothingness.
　December of My Springs, The.
Houston, V.　Class Room.
Murray, P.　Inquietude.
Toomer.　I sit in my room.
Walker, M.　Memory.

Discovery
Giovanni.　Poem (For BMC No. 1).
Jordan, J.　Fragments from a Parable.
Lorde.　Ballad from Childhood.
Young, A.　No Strings Attached.

Disdain
Lorde.　Suffer the Children.
Nelson, M.　Balance.

Disease
Hayden, R.　As my blood was drawn.
Hughes, L.　Pathological Puzzle.

Disgrace
Nelson, M.　Is She Okay?

Dishonesty
African-American Oral Tradition.　Herman
　from the Shark-Tooth Shore.
Baraka.　Measure of Memory (The Navigator),
　The.
Dove, R.　Compendium.
Giovanni.　Make Up.
Nelson, M.　Chopin.
　Is She Okay?

Disillusion
Angelou.　Accident.
Cullen, C.　Bright Bindings.
　La Belle, La Douce, La Grande.
Giovanni.　Adulthood.
　Categories.
　We stood there waiting.
Kgositsile.　Mandela's Sermon.
McClellan.　January Dandelion, A.
Roland Poet X.　Divided States of America,
　The.
Walker, M.　Disillusion for Flower Children of
　Long Ago.
Whitfield.　Misanthropist, The.
Wright, J.　End of Ethnic Dream, The.
Young, A.　Providence, Rhode Island.

Disorder
Baraka.　Bridge, The.
　End of Man Is His Beauty, The.
Hughes, L.　Bad Morning.
Lorde.　Syracuse Airport.
Nelson, M.　Bali Hai Calls Mama.
Young, A.　Son.

Distrust
Clifton, L.　Kind of Man He Is, The.
Hughes, L.　Madam and Her Might-Have-Been.
Lorde.　Family Resemblance, A.
Reed, I.　Author Reflects on His 35th Birthday,
　The.

Diversity
Angelou.　Human Family.
Dunbar, P.　Accountability.
Hughes, L.　Mystery.
Salaam.　Height, Breadth, Depth.

Dives (Bible)
Harper, F.　Save the Boys.

Diving and Divers
Hayden, R.　Diver, The.
Knight, E.　Poem of Attrition, A.

Divining and Diviners
Hughes, L.　Gal's Cry for a Dying Lover.

Divorce
Dunbar, P.　Chappie, A.
Reed, I.　Grizzly.
Tucker, M.　Wail of the Divorced.
Williams, Niama.　Companion Pieces.

Doctors, Medical. *See* **Physicians**

Dogs
African-American Oral Tradition.　Well if I
　had a dog that could piss this stuff.
Derricotte.　From a Letter: About Snow.
Gilbert, C.　Glimpses.
Giscombe.　(1978, Remembering 1962).
Harper, M.　Called.
Horton, G.　Fate of an Innocent Dog, The.
Hughes, L.　Old Dog Queenie / Was such a
　meanie.

Dolls

Poor Rover.
Silly Animals.
Warning.
Warning: Augmented.
Jordan, J.   Richland County Lyric for Elizabeth Asleep, A.
Komunyakaa.   Dog Act, The.
Madhubuti.   On Seeing Diana Go Maddddddddd.
Reed, I.   Bitch.
Untitled: "I know of a man who treated his body like a dog."
Thompson, P.   Unromantic Awakening, An.

See also **Listings for specific dogs**

Dolls

Freeman, C.   Christmas Morning I.
Hemphill.   Soft Targets.
Komunyakaa.   Nazi Doll, The.

Dominican Republic

Dove, R.   Parsley.

Doors

Hughes, L.   Doorknobs.
Mackey, N.   Dream Thief.
McKay, C.   White House, The.
Reed, I.   Why I Often Allude to Osiris.
Sanchez, S.   When you left i ran.

Doubt

Bontemps.   Miracles.
Brooks, G.   Love Note I: Surely.
Clifton, L.   Confession.
Hughes, L.   Convent.
Jordan, J.   At some moment the confidence snaps.
McKay, C.   Pagan Isms, The.
Public Enemy.   Don't believe the hype.
Thompson, C.   Doubt crept into a heart one day, A.
Skeptic, The.

Douglass, Frederick

Bibb.   In Memoriam Frederick Douglass.
Brown, S.   Memo: For the Race Orators.
Cornish, S.   Frederick Douglass.
Cotter, Sr.   Frederick Douglass.
Dunbar, P.   Douglass.
Frederick Douglass.
Hayden, R.   Frederick Douglass.
Heard, J.   Welcome to Hon. Frederick Douglass.
Hughes, L.   Frederick Douglass: 1817-1895.
Johnson, F.   Ethiopia.
Jordan, J.   Last Poem on Bell's Theorem.
Ray, H.   In Memoriam Frederick Douglass.
Walker, M.   Five Black Men.

Doves

Dunbar, P.   Dove, The.
Hughes, L.   Dove, The.
Miller, E.   What the Women Told Me.
Ray, H.   My Easter Dove.
Young, A.   Sentience.

Drawing

Jordan, J.   About Enrique's Drawing.
Young, A.   Drawing.

Dreams and Dreaming

African-American Oral Tradition.   Willie the Weeper.
Angelou.   To a Freedom Fighter.
Baraka.   New World, The.
Brooks, G.   Kitchenette Building.
My Dreams, My Works Must Wait Till after Hell.
Clifton, L.   Anna Speaks of the Childhood of Mary Her Daughter.
Mary's Dream.
Powell; March 1991.
Some dreams hang in the air.
Corrothers.   Snapping of the Bow, The.
Cullen, C.   For a Poet.
Hunger.
Cumbo.   I'm a Dreamer.
Dove, R.   Oriental Ballerina, The.
This Life.
Upon Meeting Don L. Lee, in a Dream.
Dunbar, P.   Dream Song I.
Dream Song II.
Dreamer, The.
Dreamin' Town.

Dreams.
Ere sleep comes down to soothe the weary eyes.
He had his dream, and all through life.
If life were but a dream, my love.
Lost Dream, A.
Over the hills and the valleys of dreaming.
Pool, The.
Why fades a dream?
Franklin, C.   Two Dreams (for M. L. K.'s one).
Gilbert, C.   Kite-Flying.
Giovanni.   Dreams.
I am she .. making rainbows.
I'm not lonely.
I'm not lonely / sleeping all alone.
Revolutionary Dreams.
Sky Diving.
When i nap.
Wonder Woman, The.
Word Poem (Perhaps Worth Considering).
Giscombe.   (1980).
(The Recent Past).
Goodwin.   Day a Dancer Learned to Sing of Dreamless Escapades, The.
Grimké, A.   Little grey dreams.
Harper, M.   Negatives, The.
Hayden, R.   Bone-Flower Elegy.
Horton, G.   Meditation on a Cold, Dark and Rainy Night.
Hughes, L.   Beale Street.
Dream.
Dream Boogie.
Dream Dust.
Dream Keeper, The.
Dream of Freedom.
Dream Variations.
Dreamer.
Dreams.
Havana Dreams.
Little Song.
Mister Sandman.
Morning After.
Oppression.
Pictures to the Wall.
Slum Dreams.
To You.
Water-Front Streets.
Johnson, G.   Calling Dreams.
My Little Dreams.
Johnson, M.   Dream, A.
Kaufman, B.   African Dream.
Komunyakaa.   April Fools' Day.
Dreambook Bestiary.
Lane, P.   Girl at the Window.
Lorde.   Barren.
Change.
Dreams bite.
From the Greenhouse.
Meeting of Minds, A.
Never Take Fire for a Woman.
Never to Dream of Spiders.
Nightstone.
Rites of Passage.
Song: "Wild trees have bought me."
Sowing.
St. Louis Out of Time.
Mackey, N.   Winged Abyss.
Major, C.   Round Midnight.
Marie.   Dream Fix.
Mitchell, K.   Monster, The.
Nelson, M.   Century Quilt, The.
Dream's Wisdom, The.
I Fell Asleep on the Couch.
I Woke Up and Wrote About It.
Marriage Nightmare, The.
Recurrent Dream.
Saint's Dream, The.
So Jonah Sang the Blues.
Priestley.   Eye and eye.
Randall, J.   Who Shall Die.
Reed, I.   Off d Pig.
Salaam.   Round Midnight, Place de Congo.
Sanchez, S.   Blues.
Shange.   Dream of Pairing.
Toomer.   Evening Song.
White Arrow.

Whitfield.   To ———: "Approaching night her mantle flings."
Wright, J.   Compassion's Bird.
End of Ethnic Dream, The.
Young, A.   Curative Powers of Silence, The.
Dream Take: 22.
Dreamjot: 1962.
Falling Asleep in a Darkening Room.
It Is God that Moves in Your Heart.
Joy/Spring.
2 takes from *Love in Los Angeles*.

See also **Nightmares**

Drinks and Drinking

African-American Oral Tradition.   Cocaine Nell.
Drinkin'.
Strange, Strange Things.
Well if I had a dog that could piss this stuff.
When I Begin to Think When I Was a Young Man and in My Prime.
Ai.   I Can't Get Started.
Baraka.   Crow Jane in High Society.
Boyd, M.   Beer Drops.
Brooks, G.   We real cool. We.
Cornish, S.   His Fingers Seem to Sing.
Dumas, H.   Knees of a Natural Man.
Dunbar, P.   At the Tavern.
Preference, A.
Stirrup Cup, The.
Forbes, C.   Potter's Wheel, The.
Horton, G.   Intemperance Club, The.
Hughes, L.   Cat and the Saxophone (2 a.m.), The.
Deceased.
Flatted Fifths.
Hey-Hey Blues.
Jazz Girl.
Neighbor.
Raid.
Sport.
Jamal.   Sat. Nite.
Johnson, F.   Tired.
Jordan, J.   Runaway Lil Bit Poem, A.
Kaufman, B.   Drunk Time.
Madgett.   Sally: Twelfth Street.
Moorer.   Circle, The.
Social Glass, The.
Nelson, M.   Diverne's Waltz.
Epithalamium and Shivaree.
Randall, D.   Old Witherington.
Reed, I.   Loup Garou Means Change Into.
Middle Class Blues, The.
Salaam.   All Nite Long.
Toomer.   Beehive.
Walcott.   God Rest Ye Merry, Gentlemen.
Wright, J.   Journey to the Place of Ghosts.
Young, A.   I Arrive In Madrid.

See also **Alcoholism and Alcoholics; Drunkards**

Driving and Drivers

Dove, R.   Nigger Song: An Odyssey.
Giovanni.   Beep Beep Poem, The.
Nelson, M.   Fish and Floor-Dust Bouquet.
I imagine driving across country.
Psalm: "So many cars have driven past me."
Reed, I.   Datsun's Death.
Young, A.   Palm Drive Palo Alto.

See also **Automobiles**

Drought

Davis, R.   Dust Bowl.
Hughes, L.   Dustbowl.
Toomer.   November Cotton Flower.
Touré, A.   Floodtide.

Drowning

Barrax.   Scuba Diver Recovers the Body of a Drowned Child, The.
Gardner, C.   Dead Man Dragged from the Sea, The.
Hughes, L.   Naughty child / Who ventured to go cut flowers, The.

Drowsiness

Dunbar, P.   Drowsy Day, A.
Young, A.   American Glamour.

Drug Addiction

African-American Oral Tradition.   Junkies' Ball.
Junkies' Heaven.

Life of a Junkie.
Ping Pong Joe.
Ai. Self Defense.
Angelou. Junkie Monkey Reel.
Letter to an Aspiring Junkie.
Pusher, The.
Bandele. Subtle Art of Breathing, The.
Baraka. Babylon Revisited.
Brown, E. If Randi Could Write.
Clifton, L. Cain.
White Lady.
Cruz, V. White Powder!
Harper, M. Elvin's Blues.
Street-Poisoned.
Hughes, L. Junior Addict.
Knight, E. Another Poem for Me (after
Recovering from an O.D.).
Idea of Ancestry, The.
Welcome Back, Mr. Knight: Love of My Life.
Komunyakaa. Thorn Merchant's Wife, The.
Lorde. To My Daughter the Junkie on a Train.
Mackey, N. Falso Brilhante.
Reed, C. My Brother and Me.
Sanchez, S. Homecoming.
So This Is Our Revolution.
Summer Words of [or for] a Sistuh [or Sister]
Addict.
Thomas, L. Historiography.
Troupe. Syntax of the mind grips, The.
Tucker, M. Opium-Eater, The.
Worley, D. Sandra.
Young, A. Ho.

Drugs
Angelou. Pusher, The.
Jordan, N. Sinner.
Knight, E. Feeling Fucked/Up Up.
Idea of Ancestry, The.
Komunyakaa. Plea, The.
Lorde. For My Singing Sister.
Walker, M. On Youth and Age II.
Young, A. Demerol.
Hallucinogenic Halleluuuu.
Lovesong of O. O. Gabugah.
Moss.

Drums
Bethune, L. For Singing In Good Mood.
Cortez. If the drum is a woman.
Tapping.
Giovanni. Drums ... Pa-Rum ... the rat-tat-tat
... of drums, The.
Herrnton. Distant Drum, The.
Hughes, L. Danse Africaine.
Drums.
Jaime.
Knight, E. Ilu, the Talking Drum.
Komunyakaa. Back Then.
Plumpp. Speech.
Smith, P. They say that black people.
Young, K. Escape Artist, The.

Drunkards
African-American Oral Tradition. Drinkin'.
Knockin' down chairs and slammin' doors.
Baraka. Poem Welcoming Jonas Mekas to
America, A.
Brooks, G. Merle "Uncle Seagram."
Clifton, L. Lately / everybody i meet.
Danner, M. Sadie's Playhouse.
Dunbar, P. Delinquent, The.
Lager Beer.
Harper, F. Drunkard's Child, The.
Horton, G. Tippler to His Bottle, The.
Hughes, L. Ballad of the Sinner.
Crowing Hen Blues.
Drunkard.
Knight, E. Haiku: "Morning sun slants cell."
Komunyakaa. Soliloquy: Man Talking to a
Mirror.
Randall, D. Old Witherington.
Reed, I. Datsun's Death.
Tucker, M. Drunkard's Wife, The.

See also **Alcoholism and Alcoholics**

Du Bois, William Edward Burghardt
Latimer. For William Edward Burghardt Du
Bois on His Eightieth Birthday.
Randall, D. Booker T. and W. E. B.
Rivers, C. On the Death of William Edward

Burghardt Du Bois by African Moonlight and
Forgotten Shores.
Walker, A. "Women of Color" Have Rarely
Had the Opportunity to Write about Their
Love Affairs.
Walker, M. Five Black Men.
Giants of My Century.

Ducks
African-American Oral Tradition. And here's
to the duck that swim the pond.
Dunbar, P. Capture, The.

Dunbar, Paul Laurence
Corrothers. Paul Laurence Dunbar.
Harper, M. Paul Laurence Dunbar: 1872-1906.
Hayden, R. Paul Laurence Dunbar.
Linden. Paul Laurence Dunbar.
Ray, H. In Memoriam Paul Laurence Dunbar.
Reed, I. Paul Laurence Dunbar in the
Tenderloin.
Spencer, A. Dunbar.
Walker, M. For Paul Laurence Dunbar.

Dust
Johnson, G. Common Dust.
Nelson, M. Dusting.

Duty
Allen, S. View from the Corner.
Harper, F. Be Active.
Something to Do.
Horton, G. George Moses Horton, Myself.
Reflections from the Flash of a Meteor.
Hughes, L. Joe Louis is a man.
Just an Ordinary Guy.
Song to a Negro Wash-woman, A.
Jordan, A. My Father's Retirement.
Moorer. Duty, or Truth at Work.

E

Eagles
Fordham. To the Eagle.
Giovanni. Eagles are a majestic species ..
living in the thin searing air.
Hughes, L. Fact.

Ears
Sharp, S. Finding His Fist.

Earth
Allen, S. Moment Please, A.
Baraka. Audubon, Drafted.
Clifton, L. Earth.
Cowdery. Of Earth.
Dodson, O. When I Am Dead.
Iverem. Earth Screaming.
Johnson, F. Ethiopian's Song, The.
Lorde. Dreams bite.
Sowing.
Murray, P. Conquest.
Reed, I. Home Sweet Earth.
Reynolds, S. Moon/Light Quarter/Back Sack.
St. John, P. Lynching and Burning.
Sanchez, S. Earth eyes. breathing me.
Toomer. Earth.
Living Earth.
Touré, A. Earth.
Walcott. Elsewhere.
Walker, A. We have a beautiful / mother.

Earthquakes
Heard, J. Earthquake of 1886, The.
Miller, A. Crack in the Wall Holds Flowers.
Reed, I. Dress Rehearsal Paranoia #2.
Earthquake Blues.
Sharp, S. Good Nights.
Young, A. Watsonville after the Quake.

Easter
Brooks, J. Resurrection, The.
Clifton, L. Easter Sunday.
God Send Easter.
Dunbar, P. Easter Ode, An.
Heard, J. Easter Morn.
McKay, C. Easter Flower, The.
Moorer. Easter; or, Spring-Time.
Nelson, M. Juneteenth.
Ray, H. Easter Carol.
Thompson, C. Easter Light, The.

See also **Resurrection, The**

Eating
Barrax. In the Restaurant.

Brooks, G. Bean Eaters, The.
Campbell, J. Uncle Eph—Epicure.
Dunbar, P. Possum.
Giovanni. Just a New York Poem.
Harper, M. Fireplace, The.
Horton, G. Snaps for Dinner, Snaps for
Breakfast and Snaps for Supper.
Knight, E. Eat Helen B Happy (a Found
Poem).
Lorde. Oshun's Table.
Moore, L. Tanka.
Nelson, M. Hermitage Breakfast.
Salaam. Everywhere You Eat.

See also **Cooking and Cooks; Food**

Echo Lake, New Hampshire
Ray, H. Echo Reverie.

Echo (mythology)
Ray, H. Echo's Complaint.

Echoes
Lorde. Echoes.

Eclipses
Lorde. Lunar Eclipse.
Roberson. Eclipse.

Ecstasy
Dove, R. Catherine of Alexandria.
McClellan. In the Heart of a Rose.
Nelson, M. Lovesong.
Sanchez, S. Poem No. 3.

Eden
Dunbar, P. Unlucky Apple, The.
Goodison. Jamaica 1980.

See also **Adam and Eve**

Education
Baraka. Poem for Half White College
Students.
Poem for Neutrals, A.
Davis, F. Giles Johnson, Ph.D.
Dove, R. Flash Cards.
Finney, N. Fishing among the Learned.
Forten. Poem: "In the earnest path of duty."
Heard, J. Advance of Education, The.
Horton, G. On the Pleasures of College Life.
Hughes, L. Ballad of Booker T.
Lincoln University: 1954.
Lorde. Learning to Write.
Randall, D. Booker T. and W. E. B.
Thomas, L. They Never Lose.

See also **Colleges and Universities; Scholarship
and Scholars; School and Schools;
Students; Teaching and Teachers**

Eggs
Brooks, G. Egg Boiler, The.
Hughes, L. Bar.

Egotism and Egotists
Giovanni. Ego Tripping.
Waters, M. Hoochie Coochie.

Egypt
Angelou. For Us, Who Dare Not Dare.
McKay, C. Africa.
Reed, I. I Am a Cowboy in the Boat of Ra.
Why I Often Allude to Osiris.
Unknown. Go down, Moses.

Einstein, Albert
Jordan, J. Poem about Intelligence for My
Brothers and Sisters, A.
Walker, M. Giants of My Century.

Electricity
Thomas, L. Electricity of Blossoms.

Elephants
African-American Oral Tradition. Signifying
Monkey: "Back down in the jungle up under
the stick."
Signifying Monkey: "Deep down in the jungle
in the coconut grove."
Signifying Monkey: "Down in the jungle about
treetop deep."
Signifying Monkey: "It was early in the
morning one bright summer day."
Signifying Monkey: "Say deep down in the
jungle in the coconut grove."
Signifying Monkey: "There hadn't been no
shift for quite a bit."
Unknown. Signifying Monkey, The.

Elevators
Hughes, L. Elevator Boy.

Ellington, Edward Kennedy (Duke)
Baraka. Duke's World / is the explanation.
Cortez. Rose Solitude.
Davis, F. Duke Ellington.
Dodson, O. Morning Duke Ellington Praised the Lord and Six Little Black Davids Tapped Danced Unto, The.
Jackson, R. For Duke Ellington.
Major, C. Cotton Club, The.
War. Duke Checks Out Ella as She Scats Like That.

Ellison, Ralph Waldo
Reed, I. Dualism in Ralph Ellison's Invisible Man.
Rivers, C. Invisible Man, The.

Elopement
Derricotte. Family Secrets.

Elves
Dunbar, P. Discovery, The.
Ray, H. Dream of Elfland, A.
See also **Fairies**

Emancipation (1863–65)
Dunbar, P. Deserted Plantation, The.
Emancipation.
To the South.
Harper, F. Deliverance, The.
Fifteenth Amendment.
President Lincoln's Proclamation of Freedom.
Reunion, The.
Heard, J. General Robert Smalls.
Hughes, L. Long View: Negro.
Moorer. Emancipation Day.
Nelson, M. Juneteenth.
Thompson, P. Emancipation.
Freedom at McNealy's.
Hymn: "Lord, within thy fold I be."
Unknown. No more auction block for me.
Slavery chain done broke at last, broke at last, broke at last.

Emerson, Ralph Waldo
Cotter, Sr. Emerson.
Ray, H. Emerson.

Emptiness
Angelou. After.
Cullen, C. After a Visit.
Hunger.
Knight, E. Cell Song.

Enchantment
Young, A. Billie.
Erosong.

End of the World
Angelou. On a bright day, next week.
Derricotte. Fears of the Eighth Grade.
Eady. Dance, The.
Nuriddin. Children of the Future.
Patterson, R. When I Awoke.
See also **Apocalypse; Judgment Day**

Endurance
African-American Oral Tradition. Nobody Knows Da Trubble Ah See.
Allen, S. To Satch.
Angelou. On Aging.
Why Are They Happy People?
Willie was a man without fame.
Baraka. Bridge, The.
Joseph to His Brothers.
To a Publisher ... Cut-out.
Brooks, G. My Dreams, My Works Must Wait Till after Hell.
Brown, S. Memphis Blues.
Salutamus.
Strange Legacies.
Cortez. It's nothing / this tragedy in our arms.
Cullen, C. From the Dark Tower.
Harsh World that lashest me each day.
Evans, M. I Am a Black Woman.
Fortune. Savage Dreamer, The.
Giovanni. But Since You Finally Asked.
Hands; For Mother's Day.
Introspection.
Journey, A.
Mothers.
Harper, F. Ruth and Naomi.
Harper, M. Corrected Review.
Horton, G. Early Affection.

Lines to My—.
Rosabella—Purity of Heart.
Hughes, L. Flotsam.
Freedom: "Some folks think."
Still Here.
Jeffers, L. Black Soul of the Land.
But I Know That Unseen Anger Runs a Raft.
Jordan, J. Gettin Down to Get over.
Grand Army Plaza.
Trying to Capture Rapture.
Kaufman, B. Grandfather Was Queer, Too.
Knight, E. Love Poem, A: "I do not expect the spirit of Penelope."
Lorde. Lover's Song, A.
Nightstone.
Party Time.
Rooming houses are old women.
Sahara.
Walking Our Boundaries.
Madhubuti. Big Momma.
Mixed Sketches.
McKay, C. Like a strong tree that in the virgin earth.
Neal, L. For Our Women.
Nelson, M. Cover Photograph.
Dinosaur Spring.
House on Moscow Street, The.
Sermon in the Woodlot.
Patterson, R. Song Waiting for Music, A.
Plato. Forget Me Not.
Randall, D. Profile on the Pillow, The.
Ray, H. Verses to my Heart's-Sister.
Rodgers, C. How I Got Ovah.
Sanchez, S. Catch the Fire.
I have walked a long time.
We be. gonna be.
Sherer. Our Spirit Stands.
Stanard. Spirits Struggle.
Stephany. Because I have wandered long through my own darkness.
Strange. Still Life.
Toomer. Banking Coal.
Touré, A. Earth.
Walker, M. Litany from the Dark People, A.
Litany of Black History for Black People, A.
Solace.
Struggle Staggers Us, The.
Young, A. Thelonious: An Intro.

Endymion
Cullen, C. To Endymion.

Enemies
Barrax. In the Restaurant.
Clark, Benjamin. No Enemies.
Hughes, L. Enemy.
War.
Iman. Love Your Enemy.
Reed, I. Vamp.

Energy
Walker, M. Power to the People.
Young, A. Jolt.

England
Angelou. London.
Hughes, L. Crow Goes, Too.
Seascape.
Jordan, J. DeLiza Come to London Town; a Birthday Poem for Mark.
Poem for Mark.
Plato. To the First of August.
Unknown. Rebus, A.
Walcott. Far Cry from Africa, A.
Wheatley, P. America.
Answer to the *Rebus*, by the Author of These Poems, An.
Farewell to America.
Ode to Neptune.
Philis's Reply to the Answer in Our Last by the Gentleman in the Navy.
To a Gentleman on his Voyage to Great-Britain for the Recovery of His Health.
To Captain H——D, of the 65th Regiment.
Whitman, A. Ye Bards of England.

English, The
Dunbar, P. Letter, A.
Harper, F. Our English Friends.
Hughes, L. English, The.
Envoy to Africa.
Jesus, The.

Reed, I. Epistolary Monologue.

Envy
Brown, S. Break of Day.
Chillen Get Shoes.
Nelson, M. Women's Locker Room.
See also **Jealousy**

Equality
Adisa. Women at the Crossroad / (May Elegba Forever Guard the Right Doors).
Angelou. Equality.
Brown, S. Mister Samuel and Sam.
Side by Side.
Eady. Why Do So Few Blacks Study Creative Writing?
Fortune. Every Man a King.
Harper, F. John and Jacob—a Dialogue on Woman's Rights.
Horton, G. Slavery, thou peace-disturbing thief.
Hughes, L. Democracy will not come.
Envoy to Africa.
Question: "When the old junk man Death."
We're all in the telephone book.
Jordan, J. What Would I Do White?
Lorde. Equal Opportunity.
Patterson, R. Song Waiting for Music, A.
Sanchez, S. Poem for July 4, 1994.
Wheatley, P. On Being Brought from Africa to America.
Whitman, A. Free schools, free press, free speech and equal laws.
See also **Social Class**

Erie, Lake
Weems. Dime after Dime.

Erotic Love
Ai. Twenty-Year Marriage.
Angelou. Remembrance.
Shaker, Why Don't You Sing?
Zorro Man, A.
Baraka. Betancourt.
World is Full of Remarkable Things, The.
Carroll, K. Short Poem.
Cortez. Feathers.
Cowdery. Farewell: "No more / The feel of your hand."
Insatiate.
Some Hands Are Lovelier.
Cullen, C. At a Parting.
Bright Bindings.
Brown Boy to Brown Girl.
If You Should Go.
Love Tree, The.
Love's Way.
One Day We Played a Game.
Pity the deep in love.
Song of Praise, A.
Sonnet: "I have not loved you in the noblest way."
Street Called Crooked, The.
To a Brown Girl.
Variations on a Theme.
Wind Bloweth Where It Listeth, The.
Cunningham, J. Rapping Along with Ronda Davis.
Datcher. I Am Open.
Dove, R. For Kazuko.
Duke. Poem to the World.
Dunbar, P. Negro Love Song, A.
Gilyard. Portraits of a Moment.
Giovanni. Butterfly, The.
I want to sing.
I wrote a good omelet ... and ate a hot poem.
Poem: "Like a will-o'-the-wisp in the night."
Rain is / god's sperm falling.
That Day.
Turning (I Need a Better Title).
Way I Feel, The.
Graham, R. Learning to Dance.
Grimké, A. El Beso.
Hughes, L. Fired.
Poem: "When young spring comes."
Johnson, G. I Want to Die While You Love Me.
Jordan, J. For Dave: 1976.
Grand Army Plaza.
On a New Year's Eve.

Poem for Mark.
Roman Poem Number Fourteen.
Kaufman, B.   Early Loves.
Klein, S.   Fragments from the Diary of Amelie
  Patiné, Quadroon Mistress of Monsieur
  Jacques R-------.
Lorde.   Bridge through My Windows.
Echo.
Horse casts a shoe, The.
Letter for Jan.
Love Poem.
Making It.
Meet.
On a Night of the Full Moon.
Progress Report.
Recreation.
Scar.
Sequelae.
Lyle.   Your Tears Feel Good on the Hood of
  My Car.
Lyons, Anthony.   Touch Her.
McKay, C.   Commemoration.
Flower of Love.
Memorial.
Memory of June, A.
Romance.
Miller, E.   Moses.
Nayo.   Near Miss.
Nelson, M.   Ballad of Aunt Geneva, The.
Epithalamium and Shivaree.
Randall, D.   Blackberry Sweet.
Profile on the Pillow, The.
Rodgers, C.   Now Ain't That Love?
Salaam.   Our Natures Rise.
Sanchez, S.   Baby. you are sweet.
Magic.
Man, i am trying.
Rain tastes lovely, The.
To You/Who Almost Turned/Me On.
Young Womanhood.
Steptoe.   Sweet Brown Rice and Red Bones.
Stewart, James T.   Poem: "We drank
  Thunderbird all night."
Thompson, Lisa.   What Do I Want from Men
  and Love?
Troupe.   You come to me.
Unknown.   Easy rider, see what you done
  done, Lawd, Lawd.
Walker, A.   I'm really very fond of you.
Smell of Lebanon, The.
Walker, F.   Sweet Bread.
Warren-Moore.   Pink Poem.
Williams, Niama.   Merging.
Young, A.   In Marin Again.

See also **Desire; Sex**

Escapes
African-American Oral Tradition.   Convict's
  Prayer.
Ai.   Kid, The.
Allen, S.   Harriet Tubman.
Baraka.   Stellar Nilotic (29).
Brown, S.   Transfer.
Cheatwood.   Swamp Rat.
Clark, Benjamin.   Do they miss me at home.
Dove, R.   Pamela.
Three Days of Forest, a River, Free.
Giovanni.   Kidnap Poem.
2nd Rapp.
Graham, D.   West Ridge Is Menthol-Cool, The.
Harper, F.   Dying Fugitive, The.
Eliza Harris.
Fugitive's Wife, The.
Slave Mother, The: "I have but four, the
  treasures of my soul."
Harper, M.   Allegheny Shadows.
Dance of the Elephants, The.
Dreams: American.
Fugitive Paths.
Manual for the Patriotic Volunteer.
Hayden, R.   Runagate Runagate.
Jackson, G.   Fugitive Slaves.
Kendrick, D.   Sadie Snuffs a Candle.
Komunyakaa.   Boat People.
Lorde.   Diaspora.
Reed, I.   And the Devil Sent a Ford Pinto
  Which She Also Routed.
Simpson, J.   Away to Canada.

Toomer.   Beehive.
Wheatley, P.   On Messrs. Hussey and Coffin.
Young, K.   Escape Artist, The.
Eskimos
Reed, I.   Al Capone in Alaska.
Esther, Book of (Bible)
Harper, F.   Vashti.
Spencer, A.   Before the Feast of Shushan.
Estrangement
Adams, Jenoyne.   Out-of-Body Experience.
Auset.   That Was Then.
Brown, Kysha.   Brown Girl Blues.
Dunbar, P.   Parted.
Song, A: "Thou art the soul of a summer's
  day."
Giovanni.   Crutches.
There is a hunger.
Horton, G.   Connubial Felicity.
Hughes, L.   Declaration.
Only Woman Blues.
Seven Moments of Love.
Lorde.   Dozens, The.
From the Greenhouse.
Separation.
Sequelae.
Song of Names and Faces, A.
Songless Lark, The.
McKay, C.   Commemoration.
Futility.
Memorial.
Reed, I.   Pocadonia.
Stephany.   My love when this is past.
Walker, F.   Wishbone.
Young, A.   Dance of the Infidels.
Dancing in the Street.
East Boston.
Eternity
Dunbar, P.   Forever.
Harper, M.   Corrected Review.
Heard, J.   Eternity.
Henderson, D.   Egyptian Book of the Dead.
Horton, G.   Lines to My—.
Hughes, L.   Question: "When the old junk man
  Death."
Tower.
Lockett.   Death of the Moonshine Supermen.
Toomer.   As the Eagle Soars.
Walker, M.   Elegy: "Strange summer sun
  shines round our globe of circumstance."
Young, A.   Blues Don't Change, The.
  H_2O.
See also **Immortality**
Ethiopia
Dunbar, P.   Ode to Ethiopia.
Harper, F.   Ethiopia.
Hughes, L.   Broadcast on Ethiopia.
Johnson, F.   Ethiopia.
Lorde.   Ethiopia.
Watkins, L.   Star of Ethiopia.
Etiquette
Nelson, M.   Daughters, 1900.
Eucharist
Hughes, L.   Communion.
See also **Last Supper**
Europe
Dove, R.   Eastern European Eclogues.
Lorde.   Thanks to Jesse Jackson.
Evangelism and Evangelists
Harper, F.   Fishers of Men.
Hayden, R.   Witch Doctor.
Oden.   This Child Is the Mother.
Eve
Angelou.   Known to Eve and Me.
Harper, M.   Eve (Rachel).
Ray, H.   Vision of Eve, The.
Toomer.   Angelic Eve.
See also **Adam and Eve**
Evening
Dove, R.   Reading Hölderlin on the Patio with
  the Aid of a Dictionary.
Hughes, L.   Wonder.
Quigless.   Evening.
Toomer.   Georgia Dusk.
See also **Night; Twilight**
Evers, Medgar
Brooks, G.   Medgar Evers.

Walker, M.   Medgar Evers, 1925-1963.
Micah was a young man of the people.
Evictions
Clifton, L.   1st, The.
Evil
Baraka.   Red Eye.
Corrothers.   De Black Cat Crossed His Luck.
El-Hadi.   Drama, The.
Fabio.   Evil Is No Black Thing.
Harper, F.   Bible Defence of Slavery.
Hayden, R.   As my blood was drawn.
Theory of Evil.
Hoagland, E.   Words to Drive out the White
  Growth in the Eyes.
Hughes, L.   Bad Man.
Evil.
Tired.
Jackson, M. L.   Don Pullen at the Zanzibar
  Blue Jazz Cafe, 1994.
Jordan, J.   Roman Poem Number Six.
Nelson, M.   As Simple as That.
Impala.
La Peste.
Photographs of the Medusa.
Propositions.
Woman Kills and Eats Own Infant.
Reed, I.   Antigone, This Is It.
Simpson, J.   To the White People of America.
Sims, L.   Angels Prayer, An.
Walcott.   God Rest Ye Merry, Gentlemen.
Evolution
Cullen, C.   For an Evolutionist and His
  Opponent.
Executions and Executioners
Cullen, C.   Not Sacco and Vanzetti.
Harper, F.   Rizpah, the Daughter of Ai.
Horton, G.   Execution of Private Henry
  Anderson.
Hughes, L.   August 19th.
Lorde.   Death Dance for a Poet.
Rivera, E.   Elegy for a Martyred Poet.
Unknown.   Frankie and Johnny were lovers.
See also **Capital Punishment; Hanging**
Exercise
Walker, A.   Every morning I exercise.
Exhilaration
Lorde.   NOW.
Exile
Baraka.   Notes for a Speech.
Fordham.   Exile's Reverie, The.
Harper, F.   Vashti.
Horton, G.   Southern Refugee, The.
Madhubuti.   Poem for a Poet, A.
McKay, C.   Outcast.
Ray, H.   Antigone and Oedipus.
Toomer.   Imprint for Rio Grande.
Walker, A.   Outcast.
Existentialism and Existentialists
Baraka.   Black Dada Nihilismus.
Exodus
Dunbar, P.   Ante-Bellum Sermon, An.
Harper, F.   Deliverance.
Unknown.   Go down, Moses.
Experience
Angelou.   Wonder.
Giovanni.   Alabama Poem.
Horton, G.   Art of a Poet, The.
Hughes, L.   Esthete in Harlem.
Toomer.   As the Eagle Soars.
Honey of Being.
Young, A.   For Poets.
Leadbelly Song, The.
Poem for Omar Khayyam (1050?-1123? A.D.).
Poetry.
Prestidigitator 1, The.
W. H. Auden & Mantan Moreland.
Exploring and Explorers
Nelson, M.   Star-Fix.
Explosions
Jordan, J.   First Poem from Nicaragua Libre:
  Teotcacinte.
Komunyakaa.   Fragging.
Exterminating and Exterminators
Lorde.   Vietnam Addenda.

Extinction
Carroll, K. Theory on Extinction or What Happened to the Dinosaurs?
Extrasensory Perception
Komunyakaa. Beg Song.
Young, A. Process.
Eyes
Barrax. Your Eyes Have Their Silence.
Bontemps. "Close Your Eyes!"
Grimké, A. Mona Lisa, A.
Horton, G. Early Affection.
Hughes, L. Ardella.
Soledad.
Kaufman, B. Would You Wear My Eyes?
Knight, E. He sees through stone.
I And Your Eyes.
Lorde. Contact Lenses.
Sanchez, S. And the joy. feeling.
Earth eyes. breathing me.
Seventy-one years.
Thompson, P. Soft Black Eyes.

F

Faces
Hughes, L. Chord.
125th Street.
Komunyakaa. Facing It.
Lorde. From the House of Yemanjá.
Toomer. Face.
Factories
Alexander, M. Chicago.
Shepherd, R. What Cannot Be Kept.
Failure
Braxton, C. Gathering, The.
Clifton, L. Making of Poems, The.
Dunbar, P. For the Man Who Fails.
Harris, P. Let's Take All the Blame.
Hughes, L. Dancer.
Knight, E. Report to the Mother.
Ray, H. Failure.
Fairies
Dunbar, P. Discovery, The.
Hughes, L. After Many Springs.
Fairies.
Ray, H. On a Nook Called Fairyland.
See also **Elves**
Fairs
Young, A. People of Letters.
Faith
Angelou. Just like Job.
Brooks, G. Firstly Inclined to Take What It Is Told.
Brown, S. Rent Day Blues.
Young Ones, The.
Clifton, L. Confession.
Cullen, C. Counter Mood.
Lines to My Father.
Sonnet: "These are no wind-blown rumors, soft say-sos."
Davis, D. I Can Trust.
Dunbar, P. After Many Days.
After While.
By rugged ways and thro' the night.
Faith.
Mare Rubrum.
Resignation.
Slow Through the Dark.
Gilbert, C. Directions, The.
Giovanni. Poem: "I have considered / my reluctance."
Harper, F. Dying Christian, The.
Jamie's Puzzle.
Saved by Faith.
Syrophenician Woman, The.
Harper, M. Four Worthies: Souls of Black Folk.
Hoagland, E. Georgia—It's the Gospel Truth.
Horton, G. On the Truth of the Saviour.
Rosabella—Purity of Heart.
Hurston. Faith hasn't got no eyes, but she long-legged.
Jeffers, L. When She Spoke of God.
Johnson, F. Song of the Whirlwind.
Jordan, J. Roman Poem Number Fourteen.

Kaufman, B. Alien winds sweeping the highway.
Believe, Believe.
Komunyakaa. Instructions for Building Straw Huts.
Lorde. Call.
To Martha: a New Year.
McKay, C. Pagan Isms, The.
Truth.
Nelson, M. Easter Sermon, 1866.
Fruit of Faith, The.
Sermon in the Ruined Garden.
War of the Heart, The.
Payne, D. Mournful Lute or the Preceptor's Farewell, The.
Ray, H. Triple Benison, The.
Smith, P. Annie Pearl Smith Discovers Moonlight.
Thomas, L. Electricity of Blossoms.
Unknown. Sometimes I feel like a motherless child.
Walker, M. Solace.
We have been believers in the black gods of an old land.
Wheatley, P. Address to the Atheist, By P. Wheatley at the Age of 14 Years—1767.
Atheism.
See also **Religion**
Faith Healers
Komunyakaa. Faith Healer.
See also **Miracles**
Falling
Davis, T. Boppin' is Safer than Grindin'.
Giovanni. Crutches.
Sky Diving.
Komunyakaa. Falling.
Lorde. Ballad for Ashes.
Reed, I. Sky Diving.
Fame
Heard, J. Fame.
Hughes, L. Crowns and Garlands.
Joe Louis.
Thomas, L. Twelve Gates.
Unknown. Rebus, A.
Wheatley, P. Answer to the *Rebus*, by the Author of These Poems, An.
See also **Greatness**
Family
Alexander, K. Just Us.
Angelou. Coleridge Jackson had nothing.
Baker, H. This is not a poem, nor.
Clifton, L. Aunt Agnes Hatcher Tells.
Conversation with My Grandson, Waiting to Be Conceived.
I was born with twelve fingers.
If He Ask You Was I Laughing.
Light / on my mother's tongue.
Sisters.
Coleman, W. Dear Mama.
El-Hadi. Drama, The.
Giovanni. Mothers.
Harper, F. Ruth and Naomi.
Harper, M. Alice Braxton Johnson.
Families Album, The.
Kin.
Kneading.
Holly. Our family tree is in the sear.
Jordan, J. Female and the Silence of a Man, The.
Knight, E. My Uncle is My Honor and a Guest in My House.
Komunyakaa. Salt.
Madgett. Kin.
Madhubuti. Union of Two, The.
Marie. Dream Fix.
Maroon. Neighbor.
Miller, E. My Father's Girlfriend.
Moore, L. Haiku: "Family reunion."
Nelson, M. Porter.
Plumpp. Sanders Bottom.
Walcott. Glory Trumpeter, The.
Walker, A. Dedication.
Walker, M. Love Song for Alex, 1979.
Walter, R. Familee reunion tyme iz a special tyme.
Family Life
Barrax. Domestic Tranquility.

Clifton, L. Good Times.
Dove, R. Daystar.
Taking in Wash.
Dunbar, P. At Candle-Lightin' Time.
'Long To'ds Night.
Giovanni. Nikki-Rosa.
Harper, M. Trays: a Portfolio.
Hayden, R. Those Winter Sundays.
Hughes, L. Piggy-back.
Jordan, J. Fragments from a Parable.
Knight, E. Idea of Ancestry, The.
Komunyakaa. Songs for my Father.
Madgett. Sunny.
McElroy, C. Looking for a Country under Its Original Name.
Moore, L. Tanka.
Nelson, M. Bali Hai Calls Mama.
Chopin.
Light under the Door.
Marriage Nightmare, The.
War of the Heart, The.
White-Jackson. Saturday Morning Pancakes.
Williams, Niama. Companion Pieces.
Young, A. Elegy: "Good morning! / Good morning!"
Famine
Jordan, J. Famine.
Lorde. Ethiopia.
Walker, A. Few Sirens, A.
Fanon, Frantz Omar
Kgositsile. To Fanon.
Fantasies
Barlow, G. Dream of the Ring: the Great Jack Johnson, A.
Dove, R. Adolescence—III.
Hughes, L. Flatted Fifths.
Old Sailor.
Spring for Lovers.
Reed, I. Poetry Makes Rhythm in Philosophy.
Rivers, C. Subway, The.
Steptoe. Window Shopping.
Sun-Ra. Image Reach, The.
Thompson, D. Dancing in Menopause.
Walker, A. She said: "When I was with him."
Weems. B.B. Blues.
Young, A. Brand New Morning Love Song, A.
Farewell
Alexander, E. Farewell to You.
Baraka. Audubon, Drafted.
Dunbar, P. My Love Irene.
Henderson, E. B. Good Bye, Honey—Good Bye.
Horton, G. Farewell to Frances.
Lover's Farewell, The.
Knight, E. Cell Song.
Lorde. Dream/Songs from the Moon of Beulah Land.
McKay, C. Farewell to Morocco, A.
Thierry. Adieu.
Walker, A. Good Night, Willie Lee, I'll See You in the Morning.
Wheatley, P. Elegy on Leaving —, An.
Farewell to America.
Farming and Farmers
African-American Oral Tradition. Juber up and Juber down.
Ups on the Farm.
Alexander, M. Iowa Farmer.
Angelou. Southeast Arkanasia.
Benjamin, R. Farmer's Soliloquy, The.
Bontemps. Black Man Talks of Reaping, A.
Brown, S. After Winter.
Foreclosure.
Master and Man.
Dove, R. Small Town.
Dunbar, P. Disappointed.
Gilbert, C. Glimpses.
Harper, M. Dark Way Home: Survivors, The.
Sack 'A Woe: Gallstones as History.
Hughes, L. Dustbowl.
Jordan, J. Poem on Bell's Theorem.
Lorde. Every Traveler Has One Vermont Poem.
Oaxaca.
Nelson, M. High and Haughty.
Plumpp. Sanders Bottom.

Reed, I. White Hope.
Toomer. Reapers.
Touré, A. Floodtide.
Walker, M. Iowa Farmer.
Farmworkers
Brown, S. Master and Man.
Fascism and Fascists
Cullen, C. Apostrophe to the Land.
Hughes, L. Beaumont to Detroit: 1943.
  Good Morning, Stalingrad.
  Note to All Nazis Fascists and Klansmen.
  Salute to Soviet Armies.
  Underground, The.
Reed, I. Why I Often Allude to Osiris.
Fashion
Barlow, G. Place Where He Arose, The.
Brown, S. Sporting Beasley.
Madhubuti. But He Was Cool.
Steptoe. Window Shopping.
See also **Clothing; Jewelry**
Fate
Beadle. Lines to Caste.
Bethune, L. Juju of My Own, A.
Bibb. Destiny.
Braithwaite. House of Falling Leaves, The.
Clifton, L. I Am Not Done Yet.
  Kali / queen of fertility.
  She Insists on Me.
  Thirty-eighth year, The.
Cortez. Flame.
Cullen, C. Judas Iscariot.
  Ultimatum.
Dunbar, P. Crisis, The.
  Robert Gould Shaw.
Forbes, C. Hand Me Down Blues.
Hughes, L. Bad Luck Card.
  Beggar Boy.
  Subway Face.
McGirt. Tell me, oh fate, is it decreed.
Thomas, L. Twelve Gates.
Toomer. I See Her Lovely There.
See also **Chance; Fortune; Luck**
Fathers
African-American Oral Tradition. Derringer
  Youngblood, the jet-black nigger.
Angelou. Amoebaean for Daddy.
Barrax. Efficiency Apartment.
  Visit.
Boyd, M. Sunflowers and Saturdays.
Brown, S. Dark of the Moon.
Clemmons. Love from My Father.
Clifton, L. Daddy.
  Forgiving My Father.
  I went to the valley.
  My daddy's fingers move among the couplers.
Coleman, W. Cousin Mary.
Cullen, C. Lines to My Father.
Dickey. Father.
Dove, R. Anti-Father.
  Father out Walking on the Lawn, A.
  Grape Sherbet.
  My Father's Telescope.
  Taking in Wash.
Dumas, H. Zebra Goes Wild Where the
  Sidewalk Ends, The.
Dunbar, P. Little brown baby wif spa'klin'
  eyes.
Gilmore, B. Hazing.
  Revolution.
Gilyard. Daughter, That Picture of You.
Giovanni. Gus.
Harper, M. Smoke is my name for you.
  Duriel. For My Father.
  What We Have Lost.
Harris, W. Daddy Poem, A.
Hayden, R. Those Winter Sundays.
Hughes, L. Sylvester's Dying Bed.
Jordan, A. My Father's Retirement.
Kgositsile. To My Daughter.
Komunyakaa. Moonshine.
  Songs for my Father.
Lorde. Father Son and Holy Ghost.
  Inheritance—His.
  Love Poem.
Miller, E. Jasmine.
  My Father's Girlfriend.
  Night Before the First Day of School, The.

Moore, L. Gifts.
  Pathway: From Son to Father.
Moore, Maiisha. Haiku: "Dark rock-road,
  The."
Moss, T. Lynching, The.
Murphy, M. Fat Grass and Slow Rain.
Nelson, M. Daughters, 1900.
  Recurrent Dream.
  Star-Fix.
Newsome. Quoits.
O'Neal, S. Biological Didn't Bother.
Preston, R. Lovesong to My Father.
Ray, H. To My Father.
Sanchez, S. Father and Daughter.
  I have looked into.
  Poem for My Father, A.
Stewart, James T. Poem: a Piece.
Thomas, R. Worker, The.
Tucker, M. To Father.
Walker, A. Forgive me if my praises.
  Good Night, Willie Lee, I'll See You in the
    Morning.
  Poem at Thirty-nine.
Walker, M. Epitaph for My Father.
Weaver, M. My Father's Geography.
WEEMS. Dime after Dime.
Wheatley, P. Elegy, to Miss Mary Moorhead,
  An.
White-Jackson. Saturday Morning Pancakes.
Young, K. Field Trip.
Fauns
Hughes, L. Young Singer.
Fear
Angelou. Chicken-Licken.
  Life Doesn't Frighten Me.
Baraka. Contract. (For The Destruction and
  Rebuilding of Paterson), A.
  Liar, The.
Brown, S. Children of the Mississippi.
  Seeking Religion.
Clifton, L. After Kent State.
  Breaklight.
  Holy Night.
  In Salem.
  Pity this poor animal.
  Powell; March 1991.
Derricotte. Fears of the Eighth Grade.
  From a Letter: About Snow.
Dove, R. Centipede.
  Motherhood.
  Nightmare.
Dunbar, P. Boogah Man, The.
  Lullaby: "Kiver up yo' haid, my little lady."
Forbes, C. My Father's House.
Giovanni. Sometimes / when i wake up.
Hayden, R. Soledad.
Horton, G. Fearful Traveller in the Haunted
  Castle, The.
  Imploring to Be Resigned at Death.
Hughes, L. Afraid.
  Departure.
  Good Bluffers.
  Imagine! / They are afraid of you.
  Poem: "All the tom-toms of the jungles beat
    in my blood."
  Ring, The.
  Situation.
  Suburban Evening.
  Sweet Words on Race.
  Tag.
Jordan, J. Poor Form.
Kaufman, B. Terror is more certain than all
  the rare desirable popular songs, A.
Knight, E. Love Poem, A: "I do not expect
  the spirit of Penelope."
Komunyakaa. Black String of Days.
  Thorn Merchant, The.
Loftis. Fights After School.
Lorde. Blackstudies.
  Diaspora.
  Eulogy.
  Generation II.
  Litany for Survival, A.
McKay, C. Baptism.
Nelson, M. April Rape.
  Dangerous Carnival, The.
  Mama's Promise.

Parker, Dominique. When Mark Deloach
  Ruled the World.
Shange. Where the Heart Is.
Toomer. Five Vignettes.
Walcott. God Rest Ye Merry, Gentlemen.
Walker, A. Old Warrior Terror, The.
  Threatened by my rising need.
Wheatley, P. On Messrs. Hussey and Coffin.
Young, A. Afraid.
Feasts and Feasting
Corrothers. Indignation Dinner, An.
Dunbar, P. Back-Log Song, A.
February
Ray, H. February.
Federal Bureau of Investigation
Durem. Award.
Feet
Hughes, L. Feet O' Jesus.
Major, C. Large Room with Wood Floor.
Sanchez, S. Rocking her white feet.
Feminism and Feminists
Parker, P. There Is a Woman in This Town.
Rodgers, C. Feminism.
Truth. Ain't I a Woman?
Ferry Boats
Jackson, G. Alice.
Lorde. Trip on the Staten Island Ferry, A.
Fever
Hoagland, E. Words to Drive out the White
  Growth in the Eyes.
Fiddles and Fiddlers
Dunbar, P. Itching Heels.
  My Sweet Brown Gal.
  Temptation.
Fidelity
Cullen, C. Street Called Crooked, The.
Hughes, L. Better in the quiet night.
  Cat and the Saxophone (2 a.m.), The.
  Faithful One.
  Pierrot.
Jordan, J. Double Standard Lifestyle Studies:
  #1.
O'Neal. Shades of Pharoah Sanders Blues for
  My Baby.
Sanchez, S. I guess. this is what.
Warner, M. My Woman.
Fields and Pastures
Conyus. Day in the Life of. . . , A.
Pritchard, N. Paysagesque.
Ray, H. Pastoral: "Annette came through the
  meadows."
Fig Trees and Figs
Dove, R. This Life.
Fights
African-American Oral Tradition. I got a job
  down in Florida for Croft.
  Running through the jungle with my dick in
    my hand.
  Signifying Monkey: "Back down in the jungle
    up under the stick."
  Signifying Monkey: "Deep down in the jungle
    in the coconut grove."
  Signifying Monkey: "Down in the jungle about
    treetop deep."
  Signifying Monkey: "It was early in the
    morning one bright summer day."
  Signifying Monkey: "Say deep down in the
    jungle in the coconut grove."
  Signifying Monkey: "There hadn't been no
    shift for quite a bit."
Angelou. Fightin' was natural.
Dunbar, P. Rivals, The.
  Trouble in de Kitchen.
  Warrior's Prayer, The.
Giovanni. Poem (For BMC No. 3).
Graham, D. Clown, The.
Hughes, L. Evil Woman.
  Ultimatum: Kid to Kid.
Jean, V. On Apologies.
Komunyakaa. Thorn Merchant's Right Hand
  Man, The.
Loftis. Fights After School.
McKay, C. If we must die—let it not be like
  hogs.
Nelson, M. Sisters.

Walker, M.   Two-Gun Buster and Trigger
  Slim.

Filipinos. *See* **Philippines, The, and Filipinos**

Fingers
Clifton, L.   I was born with twelve fingers.
  My daddy's fingers move among the couplers.
Grimké, A.   Black Finger, The.

Fire and Fires
Clifton, L.   Discoveries of Fire, The.
  Move.
Dunbar, P.   Back-Log Song, A.
  Noddin' by de Fire.
Harper, M.   Fireplace, The.
  Landfill.
Hemphill.   Soft Targets.
Hughes, L.   Fire-Caught.
  Fire, / Fire, Lord!
Komunyakaa.   How I See Things.
  You and I Are Disappearing.
Lorde.   Day they eulogized Mahalia, The.
  Summer Oracle.
Moss, T.   Lynching, The.
Roy, L.   Ride, The.
Sanchez, S.   Elegy (for MOVE and
  Philadelphia).
  Philadelphia: Spring, 1985.
Toomer.   Banking Coal.
  Fire.
Wright, R.   Between the World and Me.
Zu-Bolton.   Struggle-Road Dance.

Fireflies
Strange.   Childhood.

Fish
Dove, R.   Fish in the Stone, The.
Dumas, H.   Knees of a Natural Man.
Kaufman, B.   Biggest Fisherman, The.
Nelson, M.   Fish and Floor-Dust Bouquet.
See also **Listings for specific fish**

Fishing and Fishermen
Barrax.   Visit.
Dunbar, P.   Fishing.
  Lazy Day, A.
  Till the Wind Gets Right.
Emanuel, J.   Fishermen.
Finney, N.   Fishing among the Learned.
Harper, F.   Fishers of Men.
Harper, M.   Ice-Fishing House, The.
Hayden, R.   Smelt Fishing.
Hughes, L.   Catch.
Kaufman, B.   Biggest Fisherman, The.
Lorde.   Fishing the White Water.
Ray, H.   Fisherman's Story, The.
St. John, P.   Song.
Young, K.   Casting.
See also **Clams and Clamming; Listings for
  specific fish**

Fitzgerald, Ella
War.   Duke Checks Out Ella as She Scats Like
  That.

Flags
Thomas, L.   Subway Witnesses, The.

Flags, United States
Baraka.   Western Lady, A.
Fordham.   Stars and Stripes.

Flies
African-American Oral Tradition.   Fly, The.

Flight
Angelou.   Recovery.
Hughes, L.   Declaration.
Toomer.   Motion and Rest.

Flirtation
Cullen, C.   Timid Lover.
Dove, R.   Flirtation.
Jordan, J.   Reception, The.
  Roman Poem Number Eight.
Young, A.   Flirt.

Flood, The
Brown, S.   Children of the Mississippi.

Floods
Brown, S.   Children of the Mississippi.
  Foreclosure.
Dunbar, P.   Right's Security.
Hayden, R.   Burly fading one beside the
  engine, The.
Hughes, L.   Mississippi Levee.

Jordan, J.   Poem for Buddy.
Knight, E.   Poem to Galway Kinnell, A.
Unknown.   Backwater Blues.

Florida (state)
Clark, Benjamin.   Seminole, The.
Cortez.   Blood Suckers.
Dunbar, P.   Florida Night, A.
  To the Miami.
Hughes, L.   Ballad of Harry Moore.
  Florida Road Workers.
Lorde.   Florida.

Flowers
Clifton, L.   Flowers.
Crouch, S.   Chops Are Flyin.
Dove, R.   In the Old Neighborhood.
  Then Came Flowers.
Dunbar, P.   Seedling, The.
Goodison.   Kenscoff.
Hayden, R.   Night-Blooming Cereus, The.
Hughes, L.   Autumn Thought.
  New Flowers.
  Red Roses.
  Spring for Lovers.
Jackson, R.   Lady's Way.
Jordan, J.   Poem on the Second Consecutive
  Day of Rain.
Lorde.   Night-Blooming Jasmine, The.
Madgett.   Woman with Flower.
Sanchez, S.   Haiku: "I saw you today."
Shepherd, R.   White Days.
Walker, A.   Enemy, The.
Young, A.   For Kenneth & Miriam Patchen.
  Realism.

Flutes
Hughes, L.   Beggar Boy.
Sanchez, S.   Let me be your flute.

Flying Saucers
Hayden, R.   Unidentified Flying Object.

Fog
Hayden, R.   Traveling through Fog.
Hughes, L.   Fog.
See also **Mist**

Food
Angelou.   Health-Food Diner, The.
Brown, S.   After Winter.
Campbell, J.   Uncle Eph—Epicure.
Davis, D.   Hog Meat.
Dunbar, P.   Curiosity.
  When de Co'n Pone's Hot.
Evans, M.   When in Rome.
Fields, J.   High on the Hog.
Jordan, J.   Free Flight.
Long, D.   Number Four.
McKay, C.   Tropics in New York, The.
Phillips, C.   Sunday.
Salaam.   Makes You Go Oohhh!
Young, A.   Night before Michael Was Born,
  The.
See also **Cooking and Cooks; Eating**

Food Poisoning
Young, A.   Rundown at Ned's Bar B.Q, The.

Fools
Baraka.   Poem for Speculative Hipsters, A.
Hughes, L.   Ballad of the Fool.
Nelson, M.   Abba Jacob and the Businessman.
  Blessing the Boats.
Reed, I.   Foolology.
See also **Jesters**

Football
Saunders, R.   Funky Football.

Fordham, Alphonse Campbell
Fordham.   In Memoriam. Alphonse Campbell
  Fordham.

Fordham, Edward
Fordham.   Mr. Edward Fordham.

Forests
Dunbar, P.   Forest Greeting, The.
Harper, M.   New Season.
Henderson, D.   Song of Devotion to the Forest.
Jordan, J.   Richland County Lyric for Elizabeth
  Asleep, A.
  Take them out!
Nelson, M.   My Grandfather Walks in the
  Woods.

Pritchard, N.   Cassandra and Friend.
  Landscape with Nymphs and Satyrs.
  Narrow Path, The.
Ray, H.   Wood Carols.
Toomer.   Nullo.
See also **Woods**

Forgetfulness
Clifton, L.   For the Lame.
Nelson, M.   Post-Prandial Conversation.

Forgiveness
Angelou.   Forgive.
Baraka.   Dead Lady Canonized, The.
Barrax.   Whose children are these?
Clifton, L.   I am running into a new year.
Corrothers.   At the Closed Gate of Justice.
Dunbar, P.   How Lucy Backslid.
Harper, F.   Mary at the Feet of Christ.
  Simon's Feast.
Horton, G.   Union of Parties, The.
Kaufman, B.   Benediction.
Komunyakaa.   Please.
Lorde.   Making Love to Concrete.
McKay, C.   Polarity.
Nelson, M.   Abba Jacob and St. Francis.
  Mama's Murders.

Fortune
Harper, F.   Light in Darkness.
Hughes, L.   Chicago Blues.
See also **Fate; Luck**

Fortunetelling and Fortunetellers
Brown, S.   Telling Fortunes.
Hughes, L.   Ballad of the Fortune Teller.
  Ballad of the Gypsy.
  Fortune Teller Blues.
  Madam and the Fortune Teller.

Fossils
Dove, R.   Fish in the Stone, The.

Fountains
Dunbar, P.   Fount of Tears, The.

Fourth of July
Hughes, L.   Fourth of July Thought.
Reed, I.   On the Fourth of July in Sitka, 1982.
Sanchez, S.   Poem for July 4, 1994.
Sharp, S.   Good Nights.
Young, A.   Summer.
Zu-Bolton.   Sunset Beach.

France
Clifton, L.   Women You Are Accustomed To,
  The.
Cullen, C.   La Belle, La Douce, La Grande.
  To France.
Dove, R.   Great Palaces of Versailles, The.
Hughes, L.   Cubes.
Rivers, C.   Four Sheets to the Wind and a
  One-Way Ticket to France.
Sejour.   Le Retour de Napoléon.
Shepherd, R.   Lucky One, The.
Weaver, M.   Luxembourg Garden.
  My Father's Geography.

Francis of Assisi, Saint
Young, A.   Berkeley Pome.

Franconia Mountains
Ray, H.   Lines Written on a Farewell View of
  the Franconia Mountains at Twilight.

Frankenstein
Barlow, G.   Painting Drunken Twilight.

Franklin, Aretha
Giovanni.   Poem for Aretha.
  Revolutionary Music.
  2nd Rapp.
Smith, P.   Asking for a Heart Attack.

Franklin, Benjamin
Jordan, J.   Poem for Benjamin Franklin.

Free Will
Cullen, C.   Ultimatum.

Freedom
"Ada."   Lines.
African-American Oral Tradition.   Raise a
  Ruckus Tonight.
Ai.   Twenty-Year Marriage.
Angelou.   Caged Bird.
  Equality.
  To a Freedom Fighter.
Billingsley.   Rhetorically Speaking.

Brooks, G. Independent Man, The.
Clifton, L. Being property once myself.
To Bobby Seale.
Crouch, S. Like a Blessing.
Cullen, C. Karenge Ya Marenge.
Wind Bloweth Where It Listeth, The.
Dodson, O. Conversation on V.
Dove, R. Geometry.
Pamela.
Three Days of Forest, a River, Free.
Transport or Slaves From Maryland to Mississippi, The.
Dunbar, P. Ante-Bellum Sermon, An.
Awakening, The.
Emancipation.
Sympathy.
Evans, M. Speak the truth to the people.
Fortune. Every Man a King.
Giovanni. Africa.
Beep Beep Poem, The.
Black Separatism.
Funeral of Martin Luther King, Jr, The.
Harper, F. Appeal to the American People, An.
Bury Me in a Free Land.
Dying Bondman, The.
Eliza Harris.
Ethiopia.
Free Labor.
Freedom Bell, The.
Little Builders, The.
President Lincoln's Proclamation of Freedom.
Slave Mother, The: "I have but four, the treasures of my soul."
Then and Now.
Words for the Hour.
Harper, M. Madimba.
Hayden, R. Frederick Douglass.
Runagate Runagate.
Heard, J. They are coming, coming slowly.
Holly. Wreath of Holly, A.
Horton, G. Gratitude.
Heavenly Love.
Liberty.
My Native Home.
On Hearing of the Intention of a Gentleman to Purchase the Poet's Freedom.
On Liberty and Slavery.
Poet's Feeble Petition, The.
Slavery.
Hughes, L. Ballad of the Seven Songs.
Black Crown, The.
Call of Ethiopia.
Call to Creation.
Democracy will not come.
Dream Boogie.
Dream of Freedom.
Dream Variations.
Dusk.
Free Man.
Freedom: "Some folks think."
Freedom Train.
Freedom will not come.
Freedom's Plow.
Frosting.
How about It, Dixie.
Jam Session.
Let America Be American Again.
Message to the President.
Refugee.
Slave Song.
To Captain Mulzac.
Tomorrow's Seed.
Uncle Tom is a legend and a dream.
What I Think.
Words Like Freedom.
Jeffers, L. How High the Moon.
When I Know the Power of My Black Hand.
Joans. My Ace of Spades.
Johnson, J. Fifty Years.
Lift Ev're Voice and Sing.
Jordan, J. Current Events.
I Must Become a Menace to My Enemies.
Runaway Lil Bit Poem, A.
Smash the Church.
Kaufman, B. Carl Chessman Interviews the P.T.A. in His Swank Gas Chamber Before

Leaving on His Annual Inspection of Capital, Tour of Northern California Death Universities, Happy.
Night that Lorca Comes, The.
Slight Alterations.
To My Son Parker, Asleep in the Next Room.
Knight, E. Various Protestations From Various People.
We free singers be.
Madgett. Midway.
McClane. Jazz.
McKay, C. Enslaved.
In Bondage.
Menken. Pro Patria—America, 1861.
Murray, P. Dark Testament.
Neal, G. Today.
Nelson, M. Meditation over the Washtub.
Newsome. Bird in the Cage, The.
Patterson, R. Black Power.
Plato. To the First of August.
Ray, H. To My Father.
Reason. Spirit Voice, The; or Liberty Call to the Disfranchised (State of New York).
Reed, I. Catechism of d Neoamerican Hoodoo Church.
Railroad Bill, a conjure man.
Sanchez, S. Never may my thirst.
Sharp, S. Meanwhile, in Rwanda.
Woman Who Died in Line, The.
Simpson, J. Away to Canada.
First of August in Jamaica, The.
"No, Master, Never!"
Twilight Hour, The.
Thomas, R. Index to a Black Catharsis.
Thompson, J. In my mind's eye.
Thompson, P. Emancipation.
Fugitive, The.
Prayer, A: "Oh, Lord! I lift my heart."
Tolson, M. Festus Conrad.
Unknown. Freedom in the Air.
Go down, Moses.
I Thank God I'm Free at Las'.
Keep Your Eyes on the Prize.
No more auction block for me.
O Freedom! / O Freedom!
Promises of Freedom.
Slavery chain done broke at last, broke at last, broke at last.
Swing low, sweet chariot.
We'll soon be free.
Vashon. Vincent Ogé.
Walker, M. At the Lincoln Monument in Washington, August 28, 1963.
For my people everywhere singing their slave songs repeatedly.
Washington. Freedom Hair.
Wheatley, P. To the Right Honourable William, Earl of Dartmouth, His Majesty's Principal Secretary of State for North-America, Etc.
Whitfield. Stanzas for the First of August.
Whitman, A. Free schools, free press, free speech and equal laws.
Wright, J. Wednesday Night Prayer Meeting.
Young, A. Now's the Time.
October Window.
Zu-Bolton. Struggle-Road Dance.

Freedom Train
Hughes, L. Freedom Train.

Freud, Sigmund
Walker, A. So We've Come at Last to Freud.
Walker, M. Giants of My Century.

Friendship
Angelou. Many and More.
Clifton, L. Angels.
Friends Come.
Sisters.
Corrothers. Me 'n' Dunbar.
Cortez. I and I.
Cullen, C. Dear Friends and Gentle Hearts.
Little Sonnet to Little Friends.
Tableau.
Dunbar, P. After the Quarrel.
Comrade.
Silence.
To a Dead Friend.
To Dr. James Newton Matthews, Mason, Ill.

Durem. Friends.
Giovanni. Her Cruising Car.
Poem (for EMA).
Poem of Friendship, A.
You Came, Too.
Hayden, R. Letter.
Henderson, E. B. Trussy's Visit.
Horton, G. Farewell to Frances.
Hughes, L. Death of Do Dirty: A Rounder's Song.
Poem: "I loved my friend."
Jordan, J. Grand Army Plaza.
Short Note to My Very Critical and Well-Beloved Friends and Comrades, A.
Komunyakaa. More Girl Than Boy.
Lorde. Dear Toni Instead of a Letter of Congratulation.
For Judith.
Sister, Morning Is a Time for Miracles.
McKay, C. Rest in Peace.
Moss, T. Anointing, An.
Reed, I. Judas.
Smith, W. Interlude.
Spencer, A. Creed.
I Have a Friend.
Walcott. Village Life, A.
Walker, A. These days I think of Belvie.
Wheatley, P. On Friendship.
To a Gentleman of the Navy.
Young, A. Roland Navarro (1939-1961).
See also **Companionship and Companions**

Frogs
African-American Oral Tradition. He-frog told the she-frog, The.
Lorde. Prism.

Frost
Harper, M. Night of Frost, The.

Frost, Robert
Brooks, G. Of Robert Frost.

Fruit Trees and Fruit
Adisa. Discover Me.
McKay, C. Flame-Heart.
Tropics in New York, The.
Mullen, H. Pineapple is armored flower.
Nelson, M. Fruit of Faith, The.
Rankine. Man. His Bowl. His Raspberries, The.
Strange. Still Life.

Fulfillment
Angelou. Unmeasured Tempo.
Bontemps. God Give to Men.
Clifton, L. Turning into my own.
Cullen, C. From the Dark Tower.
Giovanni. Choices.
Communication.
Luxury.
My Tower.
Toomer. Honey of Being.
Young, A. Erosong.
What Is the Blues?

Fun
Hughes, L. Advice.
Poor Rover.
See also **Play**

Funerals
African-American Oral Tradition. Brock Hankton.
Bulddaggers' Hall.
'Flicted Arm Pete: "It was way down in this little town that they call Louisville."
Barlow, G. Salt.
Brown, S. Funeral.
Cullen, C. Brown Girl Dead, A.
Dove, R. Tou Wan Speaks to Her Husband Liu Sheng.
Evans, M. Rebel, The.
Gilbert, C. Too Many.
Henderson, D. Do Nothing Till You Hear from Me.
Hughes, L. As Befits a Man.
Ballad of the Man Who's Gone.
Dead in There.
Funeral.
Night funeral / In Harlem.
Request for Requiems.
Komunyakaa. April Fools' Day.

Mitchell, K.   On the Anniversary Of Your
    Death.
Salaam.   Funeraled Fare Well.
Walker, A.   Burial.
See also **Burial; Cemeteries; Grief; Mourning**
    and Mourners; Tombs
Future
Baraka.   Letter to E. Franklin Frazier.
    Valéry as Dictator.
Barlow, G.   Sorrow Since Sitting Bull, A.
Clifton, L.   Mystery that surely is present, The.
    New Year.
    '70s, The.
Dodson, O.   Poem for Pearl's Dancers.
Dunbar, P.   Beyond the years the answer lies.
    To Kelly Miller, Jr.
Giovanni.   December of My Springs, The.
    You Are There.
Holman, M.   Three Brown Girls Singing.
Hughes, L.   History.
    Promised Land / Is always just ahead, The.
    Sunset in Dixie.
Kaufman, B.   When we hear the eye open
    there, in that place.
Lorde.   Fishing the White Water.
    When the Saints Come Marching In.
Madhubuti.   Killing Memory.
    Union of Two, The.
McKay, C.   After the Winter.
    America.
Miller, M.   Wrong Side of the Morning, The.
Neal, G.   Today.
Oyewole.   When the revolution comes.
Salaam.   I live in the mouth of history.
Stephany.   My love when this is past.
Toomer.   It is Everywhere.

G

Gambling and Gamblers
African-American Oral Tradition.   Little Girl in
    the Gambler's Nest.
    While playing short coin in the Golden West.
Hughes, L.   Crap Game.
    Madam and the Insurance Man.
    Madam and the Number Writer.
    Number.
    Numbers.
    Situation.
Long, D.   One Time Henry Dreamed the
    Number.
Young, A.   Studio Up Over In Your Ear.
Games
Bond, J.   Rotation.
Gilbert, C.   This Bridge Across.
Giovanni.   Game of Game, The.
    Poem for Black Boys.
Harper, M.   Makin' Jump Shots.
Komunyakaa.   Child's Play.
    Gloria's Clues.
Roy, L.   Triple Overtime.
See also **Card Games**
Gandhi, Mohandas Karamchand
Cullen, C.   Karenge Ya Marenge.
Hughes, L.   Ghandhi Is Fasting.
O'Higgins, M.   Vaticide.
Gangs and Gangsters
Brooks, G.   Blackstone Rangers, The.
Brown, S.   Last Ride of Wild Bill.
Hughes, L.   Gangsters.
Garbage and Garbage Men
Harper, M.   Landfill.
Gardens and Gardening
Brown, S.   To a Certain Lady, in Her Garden.
Dunbar, P.   In a English Garden.
Hughes, L.   Black Seed.
    Garden.
Lorde.   Walking Our Boundaries.
Miller, A.   Mulch.
    Pruning, The.
Southerland.   Night in Nigeria.
Spencer, A.   For Jim, Easter Eve.
Wright, J.   Invention of a Garden, The.
Garrison, William Lloyd
Ray, H.   William Lloyd Garrison.

Garvey, Marcus Moziah
Brown, S.   Temple, The.
Neal, L.   Malcolm X—an Autobiography.
Walker, M.   Five Black Men.
Gasoline Stations
Gilmore, B.   Gas Station Attendant.
Gates
Bontemps.   "Close Your Eyes!"
Dunbar, P.   Old Front Gate, The.
Gauguin, Paul
Danner, M.   Etta Moten's Attic.
Geese
Nelson, M.   Bali Hai Calls Mama.
Generals
Hughes, L.   Battle Ground.
Wheatley, P.   On the Capture of General Lee.
    On the Death of General Wooster.
Generosity
African-American Oral Tradition.   Winehead
    Girl.
Angelou.   Many and More.
Harper, F.   For the Twenty-Fifth Anniversary
    of the "Old Folks' Home."
    Widow's Mites, The.
Hughes, L.   Departure.
    Honey babe, / You braid your hair too tight.
    Preference.
Nelson, M.   High and Haughty.
Sanchez, S.   This is not a small voice.
Spencer, A.   Creed.
Genius
Cotter, Sr.   On Hearing James W. Riley Read.
Horton, G.   Obstruction of Genius, The.
Hughes, L.   Genius Child.
Jordan, J.   Poem about Intelligence for My
    Brothers and Sisters, A.
Menken.   Genius is power.
    "My heritage!" It is to live within.
Geography and Geographers
Sharp, S.   Good Nights.
Geometry
Dove, R.   Geometry.
George III, King of England
Wheatley, P.   To the King's Most Excellent
    Majesty, 1768.
    To the King's Most Excellent Majesty on His
    Repealing the American Stamp Act.
Georgia (state)
Angelou.   Georgia Song, A.
Brown, S.   Slim in Atlanta.
Davis, F.   Robert Whitmore.
Evans, M.   Daufuskie.
Hughes, L.   Georgia Dusk.
    Governor Fires Dean.
    Red Clay Blues.
    Sun Song.
Toomer.   Georgia Dusk.
    Portrait in Georgia.
Wright, R.   Red Clay Blues.
Germans, The
Dove, R.   At the German Writers Conference
    in Munich.
Geronimo
Harper, M.   Conferences with the Unknown.
Gethsemane
Hayden, R.   Full Moon.
Hughes, L.   Ballad of Mary's Son.
Gettysburg, Battle of (1863)
Clifton, L.   Visit to Gettysburg, A.
Ghettos
Dumas, H.   Mosaic Harlem.
Felton.   Ghetto Waif.
Harper, M.   In the Projects.
Hughes, L.   Question and Answer.
    Visitors to the Black Belt.
Lorde.   New York City 1970.
    Same Death Over and Over or Lullabies Are
    for Children, The.
Madhubuti.   Cure All, The.
    For Black People.
Powell, K.   Out of Pocket.
Rodgers, C.   U Name This One.
Salaam.   Bush Mama.
Sanchez, S.   Ballad for Stirling Street, A.

Ghosts
Baraka.   So the King Sold the Farmer #39.
Bontemps.   Southern Mansion.
Brooks, G.   Mentors.
Cullen, C.   Ghosts.
    Two Who Croseed a Line (She Crosses).
Dunbar, P.   Wraith, The.
Gilbert, C.   This Bridge Across.
Giovanni.   Once a Lady Told Me.
Harper, M.   Ghost of Soul-making, The.
Horton, G.   Fearful Traveller in the Haunted
    Castle, The.
Jordan, J.   Out in the Country of My Country
    (Peterborough, New Hampshire).
Nelson, M.   House on Moscow Street, The.
    Recurrent Dream.
Reed, I.   General Science.
    Kardek Method, The.
    Loup Garou Means Change Into.
Walker, M.   Molly Means.
Weaver, M.   Appaloosa, The.
Giants
Major, C.   Giant Red Woman.
Gifts and Giving
Dunbar, P.   She Gave Me a Rose.
Freeman, C.   Christmas Morning I.
Harper, F.   Dedication Poem.
Hughes, L.   Present.
Komunyakaa.   Gift Horse.
Madhubuti.   Bonding, A.
Moore, L.   Gifts.
Moorer.   Accompanying a Gift ("From thy
    patient, who while here")..
    Accompanying a Gift ("One whose love will
    never end")..
Reed, I.   Mossy.
Shockley.   Oseola McCarty.
Walker, A.   Gift.
Young, A.   Reggie's Version.
Girls
Angelou.   Little Girl Speakings.
Bontemps.   To a Young Girl Leaving the Hill
    Country.
Cassells.   Soul Make A Path Through
    Shouting.
Clifton, L.   This morning / this morning.
Dunbar, P.   My Little March Girl.
Ellis, K.   Girl.
Duriel.   What We Have Lost.
Holman, M.   Three Brown Girls Singing.
Hughes, L.   Delinquent.
    Listen Here Blues.
    Poor Girl's Ruination.
    Young Negro Girl.
Johnson, J.   Girl of fifteen.
Jordan, A.   Dance Lesson, A.
Madgett.   Sunny.
Moss, T.   Anointing, An.
Randall, D.   Blackberry Sweet.
Weatherly.   Mud Water Shango.
Williams, Karen.   Little Black Girls, The
    Original Eve (Spreadin' More Beautiful
    Brown Around).
See also **Adolescence; Childhood and Children**
Glaciers
Reed, I.   Ice Age.
Glory
Angelou.   Glory falls around us.
Gloves
Tucker, M.   That Glove.
See also **Mittens**
Gluttony and Gluttons
Campbell, J.   Uncle Eph—Epicure.
Jordan, J.   Famine.
McKay, C.   On the Road.
Goats
Shange.   Ancestral Messengers/Composition 13.
God
"Ada."   Lines.
African-American Oral Tradition.   Do, Lawd.
Allen, S.   To Satch.
Anderson, C.   Prayer to the White Man's God.
Angelou.   Arrival.
    Just like Job.
    Thank You, Lord.

Baraka.   Are Their Blues Singers in Russia?
  Black People: This Is Our Destiny.
  Lord Haw Haw (as Pygmy) #37.
  People Burning, The.
Baudelaire.   Death to the Poor.
Bontemps.   Golgotha Is a Mountain.
  Miracles.
  Nocturne at Bethesda.
Boyd, J.   Vision, The.
Braithwaite.   Rye Bread.
Brooks, G.   God Works in a Mysterious Way.
  Maxie Allen always taught her.
  Preacher: Ruminates behind the Sermon, The.
Brown, S.   Sister Lou.
Clifton, L.   Confession.
  God waits for the wandering world.
  God's Mood.
  Incandescence / formless form.
  Kali / queen of fertility.
  Mary   mary astonished by God.
  Prayer.
  Testament.
  To a Dark Moses.
Cotter, Sr.   Answer to Dunbar's "A Choice."
  Band of Gideon roam the sky, The.
  Rain Music.
Cowdery.   God / Is kind.
Cullen, C.   Dictum.
  Epitaph: "She leans across a golden table."
  For a Mouthy Woman.
  For an Atheist.
  Shroud of Color, The.
  Sonnet: "These are no wind-blown rumors,
    soft say-sos."
  To the Three for Whom the Book.
  Yet Do I Marvel.
Danner, M.   Through the Varied Patterned
    Lace.
Davis, D.   I Can Trust.
Dodson, O.   Hymn Written after Jeremiah
    Preached to Me in a Dream.
Dunbar, P.   Compensation.
  Equipment.
  God Reigns.
  Hymn, A: "Lead gently, Lord, and slow."
  Hymn: "When storms arise."
  Night.
  Not they who soar, but they who plod.
  Plantation Melody, A.
  Possession.
  Resignation.
  Spiritual, A.
  To the Memory of Mary Young.
  Too Busy.
Fields, J.   Jolly fat widows, The.
Garnet.   Hear ye not how, from all high points
    of Time.
Giovanni.   Poem for a Lady Whose Voice I
    Like.
  Poem for Flora.
Grimké.   Parting Hymn, A.
Harper, F.   Behold the lilies of the field.
  Dandelions.
  Ethiopia.
  Go work in my vineyard, said the Lord.
  Gone to God.
  Grain of Sand, A.
  How Are the Mighty Fallen!
  "Let there be light," a joyous thrill.
  Maceo dead! a thrill of sorrow.
  Moses: A Story of the Nile.
  Mother's Blessing, The.
  Present Age, The.
  Pure in Heart Shall See God, The.
  Rallying Cry, The.
  Refiner's Gold, The.
  Retribution.
  Thine Eyes Shall See the King in His Beauty.
  We are rising, as a people.
Hayden, R.   Ice Storm.
Heard, J.   Hope Thou in God.
  I Will Look Up.
Henderson, E. B.   Git on Board, Chillun.
Horton, G.   Praise of Creation.
Hughes, L.   Acceptance.
  Christian Country, A.
  God.

God to Hungry Child.
  High to Low.
  Last Call.
  Pennsylvania Station in New York, The.
  Personal.
  Tambourines! / Tambourines!
Iman.   Show Me Lord Show Me.
Jackson, M. L.   Blunts.
Johnson, F.   My God in Heaven said to me.
  Old Repair Man, The.
  Singing Hallelujia.
  Song of the Whirlwind.
Johnson, J.   Go Down Death.
  Lift Ev're Voice and Sing.
Kaufman, B.   I wish that whoever it is inside
    of me.
  My mysteries created for me.
  Waiting.
Komunyakaa.   Faith Healer.
Linden, M.   God's Electric Power.
Lorde.   When the Saints Come Marching In.
McKay, C.   Pagan Isms, The.
  Truth.
Neal, G.   Personal Jihad.
Nelson, M.   And Jonah Began to Stroke a
    Tentative Rhythm.
  Aunt Annie's Prayer.
  Canticle for Abba Jacob, A.
  Epithalamium and Shivaree.
  I Knew That.
  Jonah Begins His Story.
  Lovesong.
  Seducing the Saint.
  Simple Wisdom, The.
Oden.   Bible Study.
Payne, D.   May I not love the beauteous
    flow'rs.
  Mournful Lute or the Preceptor's Farewell,
    The.
Phillips, C.   Sunday.
Ray, H.   God's Ways, Not Our Ways.
Reed, I.   Piping Down of God, The.
Rodgers, C.   It Is Deep.
  Testimony.
Smith, G.   Penitential Cries of Jupiter
    Hammond, The.
Southerland.   Pale Ant.
Spencer, A.   Creed.
  God never planted a garden.
  Strange.   Offering.
  Stuckey.   Long Cotton Row.
Thompson, P.   In the Valley.
Toomer.   Chase, The.
  Cloud.
  Mended.
  Not for me—and may nothing enhance.
  One Within.
  Prayer (I): "How we have strained at our dark
    works."
  Promise, The.
  They Are Not Missed.
  To Gurdjieff Dying.
  Vague Opening.
Tucker, M.   Mysteries of Life.
Unknown.   Been in the Storm So Long.
  Didn't my Lord Deliver Daniel.
  Freedom in the Air.
  God.
  God's A-Gonna Trouble the Water.
  I'm a-rollin', I'm a-rollin', I'm a-rollin',
    through an unfriendly world.
  Peace Be Still.
  Slave Marriage Ceremony Supplement.
  Soon I will be done with the troubles of the
    world.
  Stand by Me.
  Steal Away to Jesus.
  Take My Hand, Precious Lord.
  This Little Light of Mine.
  We'll soon be free.
  Who'll Be a Witness for My Lord?
Walker, M.   Dies Irae.
Wheatley, P.   Address to the Atheist, By P.
    Wheatley at the Age of 14 Years—1767.
  Atheism.
  Elegy, to Miss Mary Moorhead, An.
  On Being Brought from Africa to America.

On Imagination.
  On the Death of a Young Gentleman.
  Thoughts on the Works of Providence.
  To the Rev. Dr. Thomas Amory on Reading
    Sermons on Daily Devotion, in Which That
    Duty Is Recommended and Assisted.
Whitfield.   Self-Reliance.
Wright, J.   Meta-A and the A of Absolutes.
Young, A.   By Heart.
  I Arrive In Madrid.
  Kicking.
  Myself When I Am Real.
Gods and Goddesses
  Baraka.   YMCA #35.
  Clifton, L.   Coming of Kali, The.
    Kali / queen of fertility.
  Hughes, L.   Gods.
  Jeffers, L.   When She Spoke of God.
  Kgositsile.   Mandela's Sermon.
  Komunyakaa.   Lost Wax.
  Lorde.   Call.
    October.
    Oya.
    When the Saints Come Marching In.
    Wood Has No Mouth.
  Reed, I.   I Am a Cowboy in the Boat of Ra.
    Off d Pig.
    Why I Often Allude to Osiris.
  Spencer, A.   Letter to My Sister.
  Toomer.   Conversion.
    Gods Are Here, The.
  Walker, M.   On Death and the Resurrection.
    This Is My Century.
  Wright, J.   Appearance of a Lost Goddess,
    The.
    Benjamin Banneker Helps to Build a City.
God's Protection
  Harper, F.   It Shall Not Come Nigh Thee.
    Night of Death, The.
    Sparrow's Fall, The.
  Nelson, M.   How His Fingers Found the
    Melody.
  Wheatley, P.   Isaiah LXIII, 1–8.
    To a Lady on Her Remarkable Preservation in
    an Hurricane in North-Carolina.
Gold
  Dunbar, P.   Real Question, The.
  Lorde.   Family Resemblance, A.
Golden Rule, The
  Angelou.   Lord, in My Heart.
  Hughes, L.   Motto.
Goliath
  Thompson, P.   David and Goliath.
  Wheatley, P.   Goliath of Gath.
Good
  Dunbar, P.   God Reigns.
  Hughes, L.   Abe Lincoln.
    Poem: "Ah, / My black one."
    Shall the Good Go Down?
    Wealth.
  Wheatley, P.   On Virtue.
  Wright, J.   Meta-A and the A of Absolutes.
Good Friday
  Clifton, L.   Good Friday.
Gorillas
  Danner, M.   Best Loved of Africa.
Gospel Music
  Dove, R.   Gospel.
  Evans, M.   And the Old Women Gathered.
  Lorde.   About Religion.
  Miller, E.   Sweet Honey in the Rock.
  Smith, P.   Asking for a Heart Attack.
Gossip and Gossips
  Dunbar, P.   Circumstances Alter Cases.
    Protest.
  Harper, F.   Careless Word, The.
  Hughes, L.   Argument: "Now lookahere, gal."
    Joe Louis.
  Komunyakaa.   Changes: or, Reveries at a
    Window Overlooking a Country Road, with
    Two Women Talking Blues in the Kitchen.
  Linden, M.   Gossip.
Government
  Lorde.   Revolution Is One Form of Social
    Change.
  Madhubuti.   Cure All, The.

Grace
Bontemps. God Give to Men.
Brown, S. To Sallie, Walking.
Clifton, L. Lesson of the Falling Leaves, The.
    My daddy's fingers move among the couplers.
Cullen, C. Atlantic City Waiter.
Giovanni. Life I Led, The.
Harper, F. Refiner's Gold, The.
Kaufman, B. Jazz Chick.
McKay, C. White House, The.
Shange. Elegance in the extreme.
Wheatley, P. To the Rev. Dr. Thomas Amory
    on Reading Sermons on Daily Devotion, in
    Which That Duty Is Recommended and
    Assisted.
Williams, Niama. For the Dancer.

Graffiti
African-American Oral Tradition. Well here's
    to the fool that writes upon the shithouse
    walls.
Lorde. To Desi as Joe as Smoky the Lover of
    115th Street.
Madhubuti. Wall, The.

Grandchildren
Clifton, L. Conversation with My Grandson,
    Waiting to Be Conceived.
Giovanni. Legacies.
Sanchez, S. Father and Daughter.

Grandfathers
Dove, R. Musician Talks about "Process",
    The.
    Roast Possum.
    Sunday Night at Grandfather's.
Harper, M. Grandfather.
Harris, W. Grandfather Poem, A.
Hughes, L. Grandpa's Stories.
Kaufman, B. Grandfather Was Queer, Too.
Loftis. Big John.
Nelson, M. My Grandfather Walks in the
    Woods.

Grandmothers
Angelou. Our Grandmothers.
Davis, T. It's All the Same.
Derricotte. Weakness, The.
Dixon, M. Grandmother: Crossing Jordan.
Dunbar, P. Opportunity.
Finney, N. Fishing among the Learned.
Giovanni. Legacies.
Hughes, L. Dime.
Iverem. Murmur.
Jordan, J. Sunflower Sonnet Number One.
Komunyakaa. Little Man around the House.
Long, D. Number Four.
Moore, L. Tanka: "After church meeting."
    Tanka.
Southerland. Pale Ant.
Trethewey. Drapery Factory, Gulfport,
    Mississippi, 1956.
Walker, A. Medicine.
Walker, M. Lineage.
Williams, Karen. In My Grandmother's Living
    Room.
Young, A. Sunday Sonnet for My Mother's
    Mother, A.

Grandparents
Ellis, K. Tougaloo Blues.

Grant, Ulysses Simpson
Horton, G. General Grant—the Hero of the
    War.

Grapes
Spencer, A. Grapes: Still-Life.

Grass
Grimké, A. Grass Fingers.
Knight, E. Haiku: "In the August grass."
Madhubuti. Loneliness, A.

Gratitude
Angelou. Thank You, Lord.
Braithwaite. Rhapsody.
Cotter, Sr. My Poverty and Wealth.
Dunbar, P. To an Ingrate.
Gex-Breaux. Willie Note 9/28/91.
Giovanni. For Theresa.
    For Tommy.
    Poem (For Anna Hedgeman and Alfreda
    Duster).
Horton, G. Gratitude.

Hughes, L. Honey babe, / You braid your hair
    too tight.
Jordan, J. Poem at the Midnight of My Life.
Komunyakaa. Thanks for the tree.
Nelson, M. Aches and Pains.
    Aunt Annie's Prayer.
    Dusting.
Payne, D. May I not love the beauteous
    flow'rs.
Reed, I. Home Sweet Earth.
Toomer. Words for a Hymn to the Sun.
Wheatley, P. To the King's Most Excellent
    Majesty, 1768.
    To the King's Most Excellent Majesty on His
    Repealing the American Stamp Act.
Young, A. It's India.
    Two A.M.

Graves
Clark, Benjamin. Pauper's Grave, The.
Ellis, K. Tougaloo Blues.
Giovanni. Funeral of Martin Luther King, Jr,
    The.
Harper, F. Burial of Moses, The.
    Bury Me in a Free Land.
Harper, M. Alice.
Hayden, R. Paul Laurence Dunbar.
Hughes, L. Epitaph: "Within this grave lie."
Johnson, H. Invocation: "Let me be buried in
    the rain."
Kgositsile. Mandela's Sermon.
Lanusse. Un Frère Au Tombeau de Son Frère.
Lorde. Father Son and Holy Ghost.
Plato. Reflections, Written on Visiting the
    Grave of a Venerated Friend.
Salaam. St. Louis Cemetery Crypt.
Trethewey. Collection Day.
Troupe. After Hearing a Radio Announcement:
    a Comment on Some Conditions.
Walker, M. Medgar Evers, 1925-1963.
Wright, J. Albuquerque Graveyard, The.

See also **Burial**

Great Depression
Dove, R. Hill of Beans, A.
Hughes, L. Ballad of Roosevelt.
    Madam's Past History.
    Relief.
Walker, M. Monologue.
    1933.

Great Lakes
Jordan, J. Madison Experience, The.

Greatness
Harper, F. How Are the Mighty Fallen!
Walker, M. Epitaph for My Father.
    Giants of My Century.

See also **Fame**

Greece
Dove, R. Ants of Argos, The.
    Nestor's Bathtub.
    Pithos.

Greed
Coleman, W. Aunt Jessie.
Cortez. Complicity.
    Expenditures; Economic Love Song 1.
Chuck D. But Can You Kill the Nigga in
    You?
Dunbar, P. For the Man Who Fails.
Horton, G. Woodman and the Money Hunter,
    The.
Hughes, L. Ballad of the Miser.
    Elderly Leaders.
    Union.
Jordan, J. Poem on the Second Consecutive
    Day of Rain.
Komunyakaa. For You, Sweetheart, I'll Sell
    Plutonium Reactors.
Lorde. Suffer the Children.
McElroy, C. Cutting a Road from Manaus to
    Belém.
Reed, I. Sixth Street Corporate War.
Wakefield, J. Oh shit a riot!

Green (color)
Young, A. Green Is a Feeling, Not a Color.

Grenada
Miller, E. Grenada.
Reed, I. Invasion.

Grief
Ai. Cuba, 1962.
Brown, S. Virginia Portrait.
Clifton, L. For de Lawd.
Delany. Interim.
Dodson, O. Sorrow Is the Only Faithful One.
Dunbar, P. Change has come, and Helen
    sleeps, The.
    In the tents of Akbar.
    Love and Grief.
    Love's Chastening.
    Phyllis, ah, Phyllis, my life is a gray day.
    Sea speaks to me of you, The.
    Yesterday and Tomorrow.
Evans, M. Where Have You Gone?
Giovanni. Poem on the Assassination of
    Robert F. Kennedy, A.
    Women gather, The.
Graham, D. Portrait of Johnny Doller, A.
Graham, R. Lynching for Skip James, A.
Harper, F. Rizpah, the Daughter of Ai.
Harper, M. Homage to the New World.
    Wisdom of Signs, The.
Heard, J. Bereft.
Hemphill. Homicide.
Horton, G. Lover's Farewell, The.
    To Eliza.
Hughes, L. Grief.
    Monroe's Blues.
    Widow Woman.
Johnson, J. Glory of the Day Was in Her
    Face, The.
Jordan, J. In Memoriam: Martin Luther King,
    Jr.
Knight, E. As You Leave Me.
Komunyakaa. Jonestown: More Eyes for
    Jadwiga's Dream.
Lanusse. Un Frère au Tombeau de Son Frère.
Lorde. Anniversary.
    Girlfriend.
    Holographs.
    Memorial I.
    Parting.
    Suffer the Children.
Madhubuti. On Seeing Diana Go
    Madddddddd.
McKay, C. December, 1919.
Nelson, M. Sacrament of Poverty, The.
Oden. Carousel, The.
Patterson, R. To a Weathercock.
Ray, H. Antigone and Oedipus.
Reed, I. Oakland Blues.
Rivers, C. If Blood is Black Then Spirit
    Neglects My Unborn Son.
"Stephany." Who collects the pain.
Walker, A. At first I did not fight it.
Walker, M. For Owen Dodson, 1983.
Wheatley, P. On the Death of a Young
    Gentleman.
    To Mr. and Mrs. —, on the Death of Their
    Infant Son.
Young, A. Day Kennedy Died.
    Dreams of Paradise.

See also **Funerals; Mourning and Mourners;
    Sorrow**

Growth
Dunbar, P. Old Front Gate, The.
    Song: "My heart to thy heart."
Giovanni. Rose Bush, The.
    Woman.
Harper, F. In Commemoration of the
    Centennial of the A.M.E. Church.
Hughes, L. For Russell and Rowena Jelliffe.
Lorde. Dear Toni Instead of a Letter of
    Congratulation.
Major, C. Giant Red Woman.
Oden. Review from Staten Island.
Toomer. Our Growing Day.
Young, A. Dancing Naked.
    Winter Leaves.

Guatemala
Jordan, J. Poem for Guatemala.

Guests
Bontemps. Southern Mansion.
Nelson, M. Abba Jacob's Seven Devils.

See also **Hospitality**

Guilt
Angelou. My guilt is "slavery's chains," too long.
Dunbar, P. Debt, The.
Giovanni. For Theresa.
Hughes, L. Dinner Guest: Me.
Kaufman, B. Results of a Lie Detector.
Nelson, M. Mama's Murders.

Gulls
Hayden, R. Gulls.

Guns
African-American Oral Tradition. Boothill McCoy.
Derringer Youngblood, the jet-black nigger.
Partytime Monkey.
Signifying Monkey: "There hadn't been no shift for quite a bit."
Ai. Kid, The.
Giovanni. This Is Not for John Lennon.
Harper, M. Corktown.
From a Town in Minnesota.
Homage to the New World.
Joans. .38, The.
Mason, K. Friday night / the bullet ripped.
Reed, I. Gangster Goes Legit.
Kardek Method, The.
Young, K. Casting.

Gypsies
Hughes, L. Fortune Teller Blues.
Pompili [*or* Pompilj]. October.
Wright, J. Jalapeña Gypsies.

H

Habits
Ai. I Can't Get Started.
Dove, R. Particulars.
Giovanni. Habits.
I remember learning you jump.
Life Cycles.
Young, A. Kicking.

Hades
Salaam. Secondline Send Off.

Hagar
Bibb. Expulsion of Hagar, The.

Haiku (form)
Knight, E. Haiku: "Making jazz swing in."

Haile Selassie
Hughes, L. Emperor Haile Selassie.

Hair
Clifton, L. Homage to My Hair.
Dove, R. Nightmare.
Henderson-Holmes. "C" ing in Colors: Red.
Lorde. Naturally.
Question of *Essence*, A.
Moss, T. Raising a Humid Flag.
Tornados.
Randall, D. On Getting a Natural.
Sanchez, S. Woman. rocking her.
Tolson, M. Madame Alpha Devine she made a million.
Toomer. Face.
Portrait in Georgia.
Trethewey. Naolo Beauty Academy, New Orleans, Louisiana, 1943.
Tucker, M. First Grey Hair, The.
Washington. Freedom Hair.
Williams, Karen. There's History in My Hair.

Hairdressers
Trethewey. Naolo Beauty Academy, New Orleans, Louisiana, 1943.

Haiti
Cullen, C. Black Majesty.
Reed, I. Gangster's Death, The.
Haitians.
Salaam. Iron Flowers.

Haley, Alex
La Grone. For Kinte.

Halloween
Lorde. All Hallows Eve.
Moorer. Hallowe'en.

Hamer, Fannie Lou
Davis, T. Remembering Fannie Lou Hamer.

Duriel. On the Uptown Lexington Avenue Express: Martin Luther King Day 1995.

Hamlet
Gilmore, B. To Be or Not to Be.

Hammers and Hammering
Brown, S. Southern Road.

Handicaps and the Handicapped
Angelou. Willie was a man without fame.
Clifton, L. For the Lame.
My Friends.

Hands
Brooks, G. Medgar Evers.
Brown, S. Conjured.
Ellis, K. Phantom Pains.
Giovanni. Butterfly, The.
Hands; For Mother's Day.
Grimké, A. Your Hands.
Jeffers, L. I do not know the power of my hand.
Loftis. In Memoriam: Robert Hayden.
Lorde. Pirouette.
St. John, P. Ocean of the Streams of Story.
Sanchez, S. My body waiting.
Wright, R. I Have Seen Black Hands.

Hanging
Angelou. No No No No.
We saw beyond our seeming.
Barrax. Sacrifice, The.
Brown, S. Frankie and Johnny.
Johnny Thomas.

See also **Executions and Executioners; Lynching**

Hangovers
Young, A. Hangover.

Hanukkah
Lorde. Peace on Earth.

Happiness
Brown, S. Honey Mah Love.
Clifton, L. Good Times.
Cullen, C. One Day We Played a Game.
Spring Reminiscence.
Delany. Joy shakes me like the wind that lifts a sail.
Dove, R. Pearls.
Dunbar, P. Love Letter, A.
Hayden, R. Islands, The.
Heard, J. Happy Heart, A.
Hughes, L. Dream Boogie.
I Thought It Was Tangiers I Wanted.
World War II.
Knight, E. Eat Helen B Happy (a Found Poem).
Madhubuti. Pains with a Light Touch.
Nelson, M. Abba Jacob's Aside on Hell.
Preston, R. Lovesong to My Father.
Sun-Ra. Would I for all that were.
Walker, A. Mississippi Winter II.
Young, A. In Marin Again.
Madness.
O!

See also **Contentment**

Harlem, New York City
Angelou. Harlem Hopscotch.
Baraka. Return of the Native.
Bethune, J. Harlem Freeze Frame.
Brown, S. Harlem Happiness.
Harlem Street Walkers.
Mecca.
Roberta Lee.
Browne, W. Harlem Sounds: Hallelujah Corner.
Cortez. Under the Edge of February.
Dent. Nightdreams (Black).
Dumas, H. Mosaic Harlem.
Henderson, D. Do Nothing Till You Hear from Me.
Keep on Pushing.
Sketches of Harlem.
Walk with de Mayor of Harlem.
Hernton. Jitterbugging in the Streets.
Young Negro poet / came from 'way down South.
Hughes, L. Air Raid over Harlem.
Ballad of Margie Polite.
Broadcast to the West Indies.
College Formal: Renaissance Casino.
Dimout in Harlem.

Disillusion.
Dive.
Esthete in Harlem.
Harlem Night.
Harlem Night Song.
Harlem Sweeties.
Heart of Harlem, The.
Hope for Harlem.
Jazzonia.
Juke Box Love Song.
Lenox Avenue.
Likewise.
Montage of a Dream Deferred.
Neighbor.
Night funeral / In Harlem.
Not a Movie.
Passing.
Prime.
Projection.
Puzzled.
Subway Face.
Summer Night.
Theme for English B.
Weary Blues, The.
Young Prostitute.
Young Singer.
Johnson, H. Sonnet to a Negro in Harlem.
Johnson, Ray. Walking east on 125th street.
McElroy, C. While Poets Are Watching.
McKay, C. Harlem Dancer, The.
Harlem Shadows.
Neal, L. Harlem Gallery: From the Inside.
Patterson, R. At That Moment.
Reed, C. Harlem '67.
Invaders, The.
Rivers, C. Still Voice of Harlem, The.
Train Runs Late to Harlem, The.
Tolson, M. African China.
Harlem.
Tolson, M. African China.

Harper's Ferry, West Virginia
Atkins. Narrative.
Harper, M. Gen'l Tubman, as We Call Her.
Plans: 2.
Williams, E. At Harper's Ferry Just before the Attack.

Harps and Harpists
Dunbar, P. Master-Player, The.
To a Lady Playing the Harp.

Harvard University
Wheatley, P. To the University of Cambridge, in New-England.

Harvest
Horton, G. On Summer.
Toomer. Reapers.

Hate
Angelou. Artful Pose.
Faces and more remember.
Baraka. Agony, An. As Now.
Poem Some People Will Have to Understand, A.
Bennett, G. Hatred.
Blue. American Dialogue.
Brown, S. Episode.
Cullen, C. Apostrophe to the Land.
Black Christ, The.
Dunbar, P. To an Ingrate.
Evans, M. World I See, The.
Hughes, L. Georgia Dusk.
Jordan, J. Poem for Derrick Gilbert.
Some people despise me be-.
McKay, C. America.
Enslaved.
O word I love to sing! thou art too tender.
White City, The.
White House, The.
Poetri. Don't hate me cause my skin is smooth like fine lustrous fiber forming a tuft.
Sanchez, S. Why must i string my hate.
Walker, A. First, they said we were savages.
January 10, 1973.
Watkins, N. Easy way out.
Zu-Bolton. By the 5th Generation Louisiana, After Slavery.
Seeker, The.

Hats
Dove, R. Headdress.

Hughes, L. When the Armies Passed.
Neal, L. Don't say goodbye to the Porkpie Hat that rolled.
Nelson, M. Abba Jacob at Bat.
Thompson, C. Easter Bonnet, The.
Unknown. Stackalee.

Haunted Houses
Bontemps. Southern Mansion.

Havana, Cuba
Bond, J. Habana.
Komunyakaa. Boxing Day.

Hawaii
Jordan, J. Always Lei of Ginger Blossoms for the First Lady of Hawai'i: Queen Lili'uokalani, An.

Hawks
Brown, S. Idyll.
Young, A. Sentience.

Hayden, Robert
Gilbert, C. And, Yes, Those Spiritual Matters.
Harper, M. Healing Song.
Loftis. In Memoriam: Robert Hayden.
Reed, I. Swift, Tiny and Fine.
Walker, M. Tribute to Robert Hayden.

Heads
Sanchez, S. When you left i ran.
Young, A. Head of a Woman.

Hearts
Angelou. Greyday.
Cotter, Sr. Way-Side Well, The.
Cullen, C. Foolish Heart, The.
Proud Heart, The.
Davis, T. Playing Solitaire.
Dumas, H. Valentines.
Giovanni. Cancers are a serious condition.
Photography.
Poetry is a trestle.
Hughes, L. Heart.
Johnson, G. Heart of a Woman, The.
Jordan, J. Uhuru in the O.R.
Sundiata. Open Heart.
Toomer. Honey of Being.
See the Heart.
Walcott. Fist, The ("Fist clenched round my heart, The").
Walker, A. Never Offer Your Heart to Someone Who Eats Hearts.

Heat
Dunbar, P. Summer Pastoral, A.
Giovanni. Ever want to crawl.
Knoxville, Tennessee.
Loftin. Weeksville Women.
Oden. Riven Quarry, The.
Sanchez, S. I lean back and feel.
Toomer. Fire.
Young, A. Hot House.

Heaven
African-American Oral Tradition. Junkies' Ball.
Angelou. Arrival.
Preacher, don't send me.
Boyd, J. Vision, The.
Brooks, G. Hunchback Girl: She Thinks of Heaven.
Brown, S. Isaiah to Mandy.
Sister Lou.
Slim in Hell ("Slim Greer went to heaven").
Sporting Beasley.
When de Saints Go Ma'ching Home.
Cullen, C. She of the Dancing Feet Sings.
Dunbar, P. Path, The.
Theology.
W'en I Gits Home.
Harper, F. Thine Eyes Shall See the King in His Beauty.
Youth in Heaven.
Horton, G. Heavenly Love.
Praise of Creation.
Rosabella—Purity of Heart.
Hughes, L. Ballad of the Two Thieves.
Heaven is / The place where.
Madam and the Number Writer.
Prayer for a Winter Night.
Johnson, F. My God in Heaven said to me.
Singing Hallelujia.
Nelson, M. *Enneads*, I, vi.

Phillips, C. Sunday.
Salaam. Secondline Send Off.
Smith, P. Annie Pearl Smith Discovers Moonlight.
Unknown. City Called Heaven.
I got a home in dat Rock.
Roll Jordan, roll.
Sometimes I feel like a motherless child.
Swing low, sweet chariot.
Walk Together Children.
Wheatley, P. Elegy, Sacred to the Memory of That Great Divine, the Reverend and Learned Dr. Samuel Cooper, Who Departed This Life December 29, 1783, Ætatis 59, An.
Elegy, to Miss Mary Moorhead, An.
Funeral Poem on the Death of C.E., an Infant of Twelve Months, A.
On the Death of J.C. an Infant.
Poem on the Death of Charles Eliot, Aged 12 Months, A.
To His Honour the Lieutenant-Governor, on the Death of His Lady, March 24, 1773.
To Mr. and Mrs. —, on the Death of Their Infant Son.
To the Hon'ble Thomas Hubbard, Esq.; on the Death of Mrs. Thankfull Leonard.
To the Honourable T.H. Esq.; on the Death of His Daughter.
Young, A. Not Her, She Aint No Gypsy.
Palm Drive Palo Alto.
Written in Bracing, Gray L.A. Rainlight.

Hedonism
Weaver, M. Providence Journal V: Israel of Puerto Rico.

Hell
African-American Oral Tradition. Lame and the Whore, The.
Satan's Playground of Hell.
Stackolee in Hell.
Titanic: "Twelfth of May was one hell of a day, The."
Baraka. Heathens in Evolution.
I don't love you.
Brown, S. Last Ride of Wild Bill.
Slim in Hell ("Slim Greer went to heaven").
Dunbar, P. Theology.
Harper, F. Save the Boys.
Hughes, L. Madam and the Number Writer.
Nelson, M. Abba Jacob Gets Down.
Abba Jacob's Aside on Hell.
Unknown. Dere's no hidin' place down dere.
Stackolee.

Help
African-American Oral Tradition. Ain't It a Bitch?
Harper, F. Our English Friends.
Holman, M. Song: "Dressed up in my melancholy."
Hughes, L. Down and Out.
To You.
Lorde. To My Daughter the Junkie on a Train.

Hemingway, Ernest
Walcott. Swamp, The.

Hens
African-American Oral Tradition. Rooster crowed, the hen looked down, The.
See also **Chickens**

Hermits
Bibb. Hermit, The.
Harper, F. Hermit's Sacrifice, The.
Nelson, M. War of the Heart, The.
Ray, H. Hermit and the Soul, The.

Hero and Leander
Oden. Private Letter to Brazil, A.

Heroes and Heroines
Brooks, G. "Negro" Hero.
Brown, S. Crispus Attacks McKoy.
Davis, F. Little and Big.
Dunbar, P. Lincoln.
Giovanni. Mirrors.
Poem for Black Boys.
Harper, F. Mother's Heroism, A.
Our Hero.
Harper, M. No. 24.
Hughes, L. Final Call.
Nelson, M. Hurrah, Hurrah.

Reed, I. Ghost in Birmingham, The.
Whitman, A. Oh! sing it in the light of freedom's morn.

Hiking and Hikers
Young, A. Bear Gulch Road.
Sunday Illumination.

Hills and Mountains
Bontemps. Golgotha Is a Mountain.
To a Young Girl Leaving the Hill Country.
Hughes, L. Big Sur.
Porter.
Komunyakaa. Boat People.
Sanchez, S. Missing you is like.
See also **Mountain Climbing**

Hippies
Angelou. Take Time Out.

Hips
Clifton, L. Homage to My Hips.
Jacobs, H. About Our Hips.

Hiroshima, Japan
Kaufman, B. Plea.

History and Historians
Anderson, S. Sound of Afroamerican History Chapt I, The.
Angelou. Family Affairs.
Baraka. Poem for Half White College Students.
Poem for Neutrals, A.
"There Was something I Wanted to Tell You." (33) Why?
Three Modes of History and Culture.
Tone Poem.
Bontemps. Golgotha Is a Mountain.
Brown, S. Memo: For the Race Orators.
Remembering Nat Turner.
Clinton. Traditional Post-Modern Neo-HooDoo Afra-Centric Sister in a Purple Head Rag Mourning Death and Cooking.
Conyus. I rode with Geronimo.
Evans, M. Status Symbol.
Giovanni. Ego Tripping.
Harvest.
Harper, F. How Are the Mighty Fallen!
Jewish Grandfather's Story, The.
Harper, M. American History.
Blue Ruth: America.
Dining from a Treed Condition, an Historical Survey.
Effendi.
Goin' to the Territory.
History as Apple Tree.
Zocalo.
Hughes, L. Ballad of Negro History, A.
Prelude to Our Age.
Jordan, J. DeLiza and the TV News.
Roman Poem Number Five.
Kaufman, B. Ancient Rain, The.
Geneology.
To My Son Parker, Asleep in the Next Room.
Knight, E. And Tell Me Poet, Can Love Exist in Slavery?
Lorde. Outlines.
Plumpp. Living Truth, The.
Turf Song.
Reed, I. Dualism in Ralph Ellison's Invisible Man.
Salaam. French Quarter Intimacies.
Sanchez, S. How can you comfort.
Sun-Ra. Of the Cosmic-Blueprints.
Walker, M. Litany of Black History for Black People, A.
On Youth and Age.
Wright, J. Death as History.
Young, A. Politics As History.

Hitchhiking and Hitchhikers
Knight, E. Talking in the Woods with Karl Amorelli.

Hitler, Adolf
African-American Oral Tradition. Hitler, You Lied to Me.
Hughes, L. Governor Fires Dean.
Just an Ordinary Guy.
Poem to Uncle Sam.
Total War.

"Holiday, Billie" (Eleanora Fagan McKay)
Delegall. Elegy for a Lady.

Dove, R. Canary.
Hughes, L. Song for Billie Holiday.
Jackson, R. 63rd and Broadway.
Kaufman, B. Afterwards, They Shall Dance.
Madhubuti. Don't Cry, Scream.
Sanchez, S. Old Words.
Thompson, J. Devil's Music in Hell, The.

Holidays
Harper, M. Studs.
Reed, I. On the Fourth of July in Sitka, 1982.

See also **Listings for specific holidays**

Holmes, Oliver Wendell
Cotter, Sr. Oliver Wendell Holmes.

Holocaust
Hayden, R. From the corpse woodpiles, from the ashes.
Lorde. This Urn Contains Earth from German Concentration Camps.

Home
Bethune, L. Bwagamoyo.
Brooks, G. Ballad of Rudolph Reed, The.
Clifton, L. In the Inner City.
Dove, R. Dusting.
Dunbar, P. Hope.
Possum Trot.
Forbes, C. Home.
Harper, F. Home, Sweet Home.
Hayden, R. O Daedalus, Fly Away Home.
Heard, J. Welcome Home.
Horton, G. Southern Refugee, The.
Hughes, L. Carolina Cabin.
Croon.
Kid in the Park.
Po' Boy Blues.
Jordan, J. 1977: Poem for Mrs. Fannie Lou Hamer.
Roman Poem Number Six.
Song for Soweto, A.
Lorde. Home.
Moving In.
McElroy, C. While Poets Are Watching.
McKay, C. Spanish Needle, The.
To Winter.
Nelson, M. House on Moscow Street, The.
Patterson, R. I've Got a Home in That Rock.
Rodgers, C. For Sistuhs Wearin' Straight Hair.
Sanchez, S. I lean back and feel.
I paraplegic.
When i return home.
Unknown. Deep river, my home is over Jordan.
Steal Away to Jesus.
Walker, A. On Being Asked to Leave a Place of Honor for One of Comfort, Preferably in the Northern Suburbs.
Walker, M. Jackson, Mississippi.
Watkins, N. Black Woman Throws a Tantrum.
Whitman, A. I love Kentucky; tho' she merit scorn.
Young, A. Dancing Day to Day.
Going Back Home.
Indiana Gig, The.

See also **Houses**

Homecoming
Angelou. Mothering Blackness, The.
Dove, R. Son, The.
Dunbar, P. Bein' Back Home.
Goin' Back.
Ellis, K. Tougaloo Blues.
Giovanni. Africa I.
Harper, F. Going East.
Wanderer's Return.
Harper, M. Come Back Blues.
Hughes, L. Return to Sea.
Knight, E. Poem for Myself (Or Blues for a Mississippi Black Boy), A.
Welcome Back, Mr. Knight: Love of My Life.
Komunyakaa. At the Screen Door.
Birds on a Powerline.
More Girl Than Boy.
Way the Cards Fall, The.
Lorde. Pirouette.
Nelson, M. April Rape.
I Send Mama Home.
Salaam. Funeraled Fare Well.
Sanchez, S. Rebirth.

Smith, P. Dylan, Two Days.
Williams, Niama. For the Dancer.

Homeless, The
Baraka. Legacy.
Brooks, G. To an Old Black Woman, Homeless and Indistinct.
Clifton, L. Miss Rosie.
Coleman, W. Shopping Bag Lady.
Giovanni. New Yorkers, The.
Harper, F. He "Had Not Where to Lay His Head."
Hughes, L. Drama for Winter Night (Fifth Avenue).
Park Bench.
Vagabonds.
Jordan, J. On Declining Values.
Lorde. Politics of Addiction, The.
McKay, C. Castaways, The.

See also **Begging and Beggars**

Homesickness
African-American Oral Tradition. Motherless Child.
Dunbar, P. Home Longings.
Letter, A.
To the Eastern Shore.
Horton, G. My Native Home.
Hughes, L. Evenin' Air Blues.
Homesick Blues.
McKay, C. Home Thoughts.
I shall return again. I shall return.
Outcast.
To One Coming North.
Tropics in New York, The.
When Dawn Comes to the City.
Wright, R. Red Clay Blues.

Homophobia
Dumas, H. Cuttin Down to Size.
Hughes, L. Café: 3 A.M.
Jordan, A. Dance Lesson, A.
Jordan, J. From Sea to Shining Sea.
Lorde. Poem for Women in Rage, A.
Wade-Gayles. Fighting My Homophobia.

Homosexuality and Homosexuals
African-American Oral Tradition. Marie.
Voodoo Queen, The.
Baraka. Burning General, The.
Hemphill. Homicide.
Where Seed Falls.
Hughes, L. Café: 3 A.M.
Jordan, J. Meta-Rhetoric.
Poem for Buddy.
Klein, S. Letter to Madame Lindé from Justine, Her Creole Servant.
Knight, E. For Freckle-Faced Gerald.
Lorde. Meet.
Outlines.
Rainey. Prove It on Me Blues.
Wade-Gayles. Fighting My Homophobia.
Williams, S. She Had Known Brothers.

Honduras
Lorde. To the Girl Who Lives In a Tree.

Honesty
Dunbar, P. My Sort o' Man.
Harper, F. Report.
Jordan, J. On Moral Leadership as a Political Dilemma.
Lorde. Question of Climate, A.

Honey
Brooks, G. My Dreams, My Works Must Wait Till after Hell.
Toomer. Beehive.

Honor
Hughes, L. Shame on You.
Today.
McKay, C. If we must die—let it not be like hogs.
Young, A. Dancing Naked.

Hoover, Herbert Clark
African-American Oral Tradition. Herbert Hoover.

Hope
Angelou. Glory falls around us.
No No No No.
On the Pulse of Morning.
Plagued Journey, A.

Starvation.
Televised news turns.
Baker, H. Late-Winter Blues and Promises of Love.
Baraka. Three Modes of History and Culture.
Brown, S. After Winter.
Salutamus.
Clifton, L. '70s, The.
Spring Song.
Cullen, C. Brown Boy to Brown Girl.
From the Dark Tower.
Dent. Ten Years After Umbra.
Dove, R. Fiammetta Breaks Her Peace.
First Kiss.
Dunbar, P. Disappointed.
Fordham. Atlanta Exposition Ode.
Gilbert, D. Miracle.
Giovanni. Life I Led, The.
Harper, F. Aunt Chloe.
Blessed Hope, The.
Heard, J. Hope! Thou vain, delusive maiden.
Horton, G. On Liberty and Slavery.
Slave's Complaint, The.
Slave's Reflections the Eve before His Sale, A.
Hughes, L. Hope: "Sometimes when I'm lonely."
Hope.
Prayer Meeting.
Slave Song.
Some Day.
Jackson, A. Beginning for New Beginnings, A.
Jeffers, L. I do not know the power of my hand.
Johnson, G. Armageddon.
Johnson, J. Lift Ev're Voice and Sing.
Knight, E. Green Grass and Yellow Balloons.
Komunyakaa. Gerry's Jazz.
Lorde. Afterlove.
On My Way Out I Passed You and the Varrazano Bridge.
Out of the Wind.
McKay, C. America.
Menken. Aspiration.
Moorer. Door of Hope, The.
Murray, P. Dark Testament.
Ray, H. Aspiration.
Triple Benison, The.
Rivers, C. Still Voice of Harlem, The.
Thompson, C. Hope.
Hope Deferred.
Tucker, M. Hope.
Walker, M. For my people everywhere singing their slave songs repeatedly.
People of Unrest.
Wheatley, P. On the Death of Dr. Samuel Marshall.
On the Death of Dr. Samuel Marshall, 1771.
Williams, Niama. Meaning of the Smell of Sweat, The.
Young, A. Dreams of Paradise.
For Kenneth & Miriam Patchen.
Poem Found Emptying Out My Pockets.
Problem of Identity, The.
Seventh April.
Zu-Bolton. By the 5th Generation Louisiana, After Slavery.

See also **Optimism**

Horseback Riding
Weaver, M. Weekend Equestrian, The.

Horses
African-American Oral Tradition. My uncle had a old gray horse.
Ai. Before You Leave.
Clifton, L. C. C. Rider.
Dunbar, P. Dat Ol' Mare o' Mine.
Horton, G. Death of an Old Carriage Horse.
Horse Stolen from the Camp, The.
Lorde. Horse casts a shoe, The.
Moore, L. Eternal Landscape, The.
Roberson. Blue Horses.
Roy, L. Ride, The.
Weaver, M. Appaloosa, The.

See also **Colts**

Hospitality
Cotter, Sr. Answer to Dunbar's "After a
Visit."
See also **Guests**

Hospitals
Cullen, C. Lines for a Hospital.
Harper, M. Clan Meeting: Births and Nations:
A Blood Song.
One Lives, One Dies: Both/And: A Choice of
Colors.
Hayden, R. Broken Dark, The.
Hernton. Madhouse.
Knight, E. At a VA Hospital in the Middle of
the United States of America: An Act in a
Play.
Parker, Dominique. Foxfire.
Randall, D. George.
Young, A. Herrick Hospital, Fifth Floor.
See also **Physicians; Surgery**

Hotels
Emanuel, J. Black Man, 13th Floor.
Hughes, L. Advertisement for the Waldorf-
Astoria.
See also **Motels**

Housekeeping
Dove, R. Dusting.
Pomade.
Giovanni. Housecleaning.
My House.
See also **Housewives**

Houses
Angelou. New House, The.
Cornish, S. Promenade.
Dove, R. House on Bishop Street, The.
Dunbar, P. Old Homestead, The.
Forbes, C. My Father's House.
Giovanni. My House.
Harper, F. Building, The.
To Bishop Payne.
Harper, M. Families Album, The.
Hughes, L. Curious.
Empty House.
House in the World.
Little Song on Housing.
Winter Sweetnes.
Iverem. Murmur.
Jordan, J. Financial Planning.
Home: January 29, 1984.
Lorde. Constuction.
Future Promise.
Rooming houses are old women.
McKay, C. White House, The.
Nelson, M. Diverne's House.
House on Moscow Street, The.
Roberson. Poor Houses, The.
Sanchez, S. When you left i ran.
Shange. Where the Heart Is.
Toomer. Gods Are Here, The.
See also **Home**

Housewives
Dove, R. Daystar.
Young, A. California Peninsula: El Camino
Real.
See also **Housekeeping**

Hughes, Langston
Allen, S. About Poetry and South Africa.
Brooks, G. Langston Hughes.
Danner, M. Rhetoric of Langston Hughes,
The.
Forbes, C. Reading Walt Whitman.
Giovanni. Poem for Langston Hughes, A.
Henderson, D. Do Nothing Till You Hear
from Me.
Knight, E. For Langston Hughes.
Madgett. Simple.
McClane. To Hear the River.
Moore, L. Poem for Langston Hughes, A.
Randall, D. Langston Blues.

Human Folly
Fortune. We Know No More.

Humankind
Angelou. Human Family.
Baraka. Balboa, the Entertainer.
Brooks, G. Riders to the Blood-Red Wrath.

Clifton, L. Pity this poor animal.
Danner, M. Through the Varied Patterned
Lace.
Dunbar, P. Slow Through the Dark.
Horton, G. Man, a Torch.
Praise of Creation.
Hughes, L. Comment.
Jeffers, L. To him who in his absence from
himself.
Johnson, G. Common Dust.
Kaufman, B. Geneology.
To My Son Parker, Asleep in the Next Room.
Komunyakaa. Audacity of the Lower Gods.
Madgett. First Man.
McKay, C. St. Isaac's Church, Petrograd.
Reed, I. Bitch.
Monkey Island.
Sanchez, S. Small Comment.
Toomer. As the Eagle Soars.
Living Earth.
Men.
One Within.
Our Growing Day.
Peers.
See also **Modern Man**

Humility
Angelou. Avec Merci, Mother.
Cotter, Sr. Contradiction.
Cullen, C. Any Human to Another.
Heritage.
Dunbar, P. Love's Humility.
Giovanni. Age.
Hughes, L. Joy.
Just an Ordinary Guy.
Negro Ghetto.
Wisdom.
Komunyakaa. Unnatural State of the Unicorn.
McClellan. Feet of Judas, The.
Nelson, M. Sacrament of Poverty, The.

Hummingbirds
Tucker, M. Humming-Bird, The.

Hungary
Reed, I. Dualism in Ralph Ellison's Invisible
Man.

Hunger
Angelou. Starvation.
Televised news turns.
Asquith. Banking Potatoes.
Harper, F. Died of Starvation.
Lorde. Litany for Survival, A.
Woman Thing, The.
Miller, A. Hungry Black Child, The.
Toomer. Harvest Song.
Walker, A. Few Sirens, A.

Hunting and Hunters
Dobyns. Connections.
Dunbar, P. Forest Greeting, The.
Hunting Song.
Garnet. Proud Nimrod first the bloody chase
began.
Harper, M. Drive In, The.
From a Town in Minnesota.
Lorde. Woman Thing, The.
Reed, I. Al Capone in Alaska.
Crocodiles.
Mojo Queen of the Feathery Plumes.
Wright, J. White Deer, The.
Young, A. Prelude.
See also **Deer**

Hurricanes
Wheatley, P. To a Lady on Her Remarkable
Preservation in an Hurricane in North-
Carolina.
See also **Storms**

Hurston, Zora Neale
Reed, I. Back to Back: 3rd Eye.

Husbands
Angelou. To a Husband.
Brooks, G. Bronzeville Mother Loiters in
Mississippi. / Meanwhile, a Mississippi
Mother Burns Bacon.
Brown, S. Bad, Bad Man, A.
Clifton, L. Daddy.
Dove, R. Recovery.
Harper, F. Advice to the Girls.
Heard, J. My Husband's Birthday.

Hughes, L. Madam and Her Might-Have-Been.
Present.
Kendrick, D. Sadie Snuffs a Candle.
Thompson, P. Husband's Return, The.
See also **Marriage**

Hymns
Johnson, J. O Black and unknown bards of
long ago.

Hypocrisy and Hypocrites
Baraka. Green Lantern's Solo.
Cotter, Sr. Poet, The.
Dunbar, P. Religion.
Giovanni. Black Judgements.
Hall, K. Impressions.
Harper, F. Double Standard, A.
Hughes, L. American Heartbreak.
Battle Ground.
Bible Belt.
Dixie Man to Uncle Sam.
Do You Reckon?
Explain It, Please.
Get Up off That Old Jive.
Merry Christmas, China.
Northern Liberal.
Song After Lynching.
To Certain "Brothers."
To Certain Negro Leaders.
Knight, E. Memo #9.
On Watching Politicians Perform at Martin
Luther King's Funeral.
Lorde. Vietnam Addenda.
Spriggs. For the Truth.
For the Truth (Because It Is Necessary).

I

Ice
Harper, M. Drive In, The.
Hayden, R. Ice Storm.

Ice Cream
Stanard. Washington Square Park and a Game
of Chess.

Icicles
Dickinson, B. To an Icicle.
Roberson. Poor Houses, The.

Idealism and Idealists
Angelou. Glory falls around us.
Hughes, L. As I Grew Older.
Dark Youth of the U.S.A.
Hero—International Brigade.
Jaime.
Our Land.
Some Day.
Teacher.
Union.
Sanchez, S. Poem for July 4, 1994.

Identity Crisis
Baraka. Agony, An. As Now.
Calderón. It's hard being / folded/licked.
Hayden, R. Names.
Hughes, L. Theme for English B.
Kaufman, B. Cincophrenicpoet.
I, Too, Know What I Am Not.
Kgositsile. Towards a Walk in the Sun.
Madgett. Exits and Entrances.
Miller, E. Spanish Conversation.
Randall, J. Execution.
Reed, I. Black Power Poem.
Off d Pig.
St. John, P. We Are Going to Be Here Now.
Sanchez, S. Poem No. 4.
Young, A. Hoboken Broken Down: A Hasty
Recollection.
Problem of Identity, The.

Idleness
Baraka. Look for You Yesterday, Here You
Come Today.
Gex-Breaux. Blue Deep.
Giovanni. Being and Nothingness.
Harper, F. Nothing and Something.
Jordan, J. What Would I Do White?
McKay, C. North and South.

Ignorance
Angelou. Bump d'Bump.
Baraka. Heathen Bliss.

Derricotte. Blackbottom.
Hughes, L. Man.
Johnson, F. Banjo Player, The.
Komunyakaa. Salt.
Lorde. Sewerplant Grows in Harlem or I'm a Stranger Here Myself When Does the Next Swan Leave, A.
Young, A. Intimacy.
Malcolm's Messsage.
Now's the Time.

Illegitimacy
Hughes, L. Mulatto.
S-sss-ss-sh!

Illinois (state)
Brooks, G. Lovers of the Poor, The.

Illness
Coleman, W. Aunt Jessie.
Dixon, M. Heartbeats.
Harper, F. Saved by Faith.
Harper, M. Sack 'A Woe: Gallstones as History.
This Is My Son's Song: *"Ungie, Hi Ungie"*.
Hayden, R. Broken Dark, The.
Hughes, L. Madam and the Wrong Visitor.
Sick Room.
Sunset—Coney Island.
McKay, C. Wild May.
Reed, I. I am not the walrus.
Walker, A. Medicine.
Wheatley, P. To a Gentleman on his Voyage to Great-Britain for the Recovery of His Health.
Young, A. Flu.

Illusion
Cullen, C. Only the Polished Skeleton.
Dunbar, P. We wear the mask that grins and lies.
Johnson, G. Lost Illusions.

Imagination
Baraka. Green Lantern's Solo.
Brooks, G. Anniad, The.
Lovers of the Poor, The.
Clifton, L. Her Love Poem.
Dove, R. Banneker.
Geometry.
Dunbar, P. By the stream I dream in calm delight, and watch as in a glass.
Hughes, L. In the mist of the moon I saw you.
Pastoral.
Komunyakaa. Rocks Push.
Lorde. Summer Oracle.
Nelson, M. I imagine driving across country.
Woman Kills and Eats Own Infant.
Ray, H. Fancy and Imagination.
Sun-Ra. Image Reach, The.
Wheatley, P. On Imagination.

Immigration and Immigrants
Brown, S. Raise a Song.
Hughes, L. Second Generation: New York.
Shange. Lizard Series, The.

Immortality
"Ada." Oh, when this earthly tenement.
Angelou. Wonder.
Hughes, L. Judgment Day.
Kgositsile. Elegy for David Diop.
Lorde. Maiden, The.
Moorer. Immortality.
Wheatley, P. Elegy, to Miss Mary Moorhead, An.
On the Death of Dr. Samuel Marshall.
On the Death of Dr. Samuel Marshall, 1771.
On the Death of General Wooster.
On the Death of J.C. an Infant.
On the Death of the Rev. Dr. Sewell, 1769.
On the Death of the Rev. Mr. George Whitefield, 1770.
Poem on the Death of Charles Eliot, Aged 12 Months, A.
To a Gentleman and Lady on the Death of the Lady's Brother and Sister, and a Child of the Name Avis, Aged One Year.
To a Lady and her Children, on the Death of Her Son and Their Brother.
To a Lady on the Death of Her Husband.
To a Lady on the Death of Three Relations.

To Mr. and Mrs. —, on the Death of Their Infant Son.
To Mrs. Leonard, on the Death of Her Husband.
See also **Eternity**

Imperialism
Angelou. Africa.
London.
Conyus. Day in the Life of ..., A.
Harper, F. How Are the Mighty Fallen!
Hughes, L. Columbia, / My dear girl.
Cubes.
Explain It, Please.
Lament for Dark Peoples.
Last Prince of the East.
Roar, China! / Roar, old lion of the East!
To the Little Fort of San Lazaro on the Ocean Front, Havana.
What I Think.
Plato. Natives of America, The.
Spellman. Tomorrow the heroes / will be named willie. their.

Impotence
African-American Oral Tradition. Dogass Pimp.

Incest
Lorde. Chain.

Inconstancy
Davis, F. Arthur Ridgewood, M.D.

Independence
Brooks, G. Independent Man, The.
Dunbar, P. Easy-Goin' Feller, An.
Young, A. Dance For Ma Rainey, A.

India
Cullen, C. Karenge Ya Marenge.
Hughes, L. Ghandhi Is Fasting.
Jordan, J. Ghazal at Full Moon.
Young, A. It's India.

Indiana (state)
Young, A. Indiana Gig, The.

Indians, American
Barlow, G. Sorrow Since Sitting Bull, A.
Clark, Benjamin. Seminole, The.
Coleman, W. Las Turistas Negras Grande.
Harper, M. America Calls!
Clark's Way Out West: Another Version.
Dining from a Treed Condition, an Historical Survey.
History as Apple Tree.
History as Bandages: Polka Dots and Moonbeams.
Ice-Fishing House, The.
Prayer: Mt. Hood and Environs.
Psychophotos of Hampton.
Jordan, J. Ghazal at Full Moon.
Poem for Derrick Gilbert.
Poem for Joy.
Plato. Natives of America, The.
Reed, I. Points of View.
Smiley School, The.
Terry, L. Bar['Js Fight[, August 28, 1746].
Toomer. Imprint for Rio Grande.

Indifference
Baraka. Preface to a Twenty Volume Suicide Note.
Hughes, L. Ballad of the Fool.
Hurt.
Impasse.

Individualism and Individualists
Dunbar, P. Bohemian, The.
Path, The.
Harper, F. Mission of the Flowers, The.
Jordan, N. Be You.
Madgett. Offspring.
Walker, A. Light Baggage.
On Stripping Bark from Myself.
Outcast.
See also **Egotism and Egotists**

Indulgences
Young, A. Hangover.
Madness.

Industrialization
Dunbar, P. Ballade: "By Mystic's banks I held my dream."
Giovanni. Walking down park.

Komunyakaa. Fog Galleon.
Madhubuti. Change Is Not Always Progress.
Stuckey. Defense.

Ineptitude
Davis, F. Giles Johnson, Ph.D.
Hughes, L. Communiqué.

Infant Death
Dunbar, P. Two little boots all rough an' wo'.
Giovanni. Robin's Poem, A.
Harper, M. Deathwatch.
Reuben, Reuben.
We Assume: On the Death of Our Son, Reuben Masai Harper.
Nelson, M. I Decide Not to Have Children.
Mama I remember.
Mama's Murders.
Wheatley, P. On the Death of J.C. an Infant.
Poem on the Death of Charles Eliot, Aged 12 Months, A.
To Mr. and Mrs. —, on the Death of Their Infant Son.
See also **Death in Childhood**

Infanticide
Brown, S. Sam Smiley.

Infatuation
Angelou. Senses of Insecurity.
Brooks, G. Flags.
Brown, S. Conjured.
Desbrosses. Le Retour au Village aux Perles.
Hughes, L. Love Again Blues.
Only Woman Blues.
Sanchez, S. Love. you are. you are.
Valcour. Malvina, A.
Weaver, M. Sub Shop Girl.

Infidelity
African-American Oral Tradition. Don't Feel So Downhearted, Buddy.
Don't Look So Downhearted, Buddy.
No Good Whore.
No Good Whore and Crime Don't Pay.
Pretty Pill.
Strange, Strange Things.
Sweet Lovin' Rose.
Toledo Slim.
Whores Are No Good and Crime Don't Pay.
Alexander, E. Nineteen.
Angelou. Pickin Em Up and Layin Em Down.
Poor Girl.
They went home and told their wives.
Brooks, G. My little 'bout-town gal has gone.
Brown, S. Funeral.
Dove, R. Definition in the Face of Unnamed Fury.
Handy, W. St. Louis Blues.
Yellow Dog Blues.
Hayden, R. Burly fading one beside the engine, The.
Hughes, L. Announcement.
Black Gal.
Gypsy Man.
In a Troubled Key.
Pierrot.
Rent-Party Shout.
Ultimatum.
Hunter, A. *et al.* Down-Hearted Blues.
McElroy, C. Caledonia.
Horoscope.
Rainey. See See Rider, see what you done done!
Unknown. Frankie and Johnny were lovers.
Walker, A. My husband says.
Walker, M. Long John Nelson and Sweetie Pie.
Williams, C. Gulf Coast Blues.
See also **Adultery and Adulterers**

Infinity
Young, A. Singular Yen, A.

Inflation
Hughes, L. Grandpa's Stories.
Walker, M. Inflation blues is what we got.

Ingratitude
Boyd, J. Ocean.
Hayden, R. Those Winter Sundays.

Inheritance
Angelou. My guilt is "slavery's chains," too long.

Injuries

Horton, G. Division of an Estate.
Lorde. What my child learns of the sea.

Injuries
Baraka. American Ecstasy.
Harper, M. Continuous Visit.
History as Bandages: Polka Dots and
Moonbeams.
Nelson, M. Dangerous Carnival, The.

Injustice
African-American Oral Tradition. They Can't
Do That.
Aubert, A. For Mark James Robert Essex d.
1973.
Bontemps. Black Man Talks of Reaping, A.
Brown, S. Ballad of Joe, The.
Bitter Fruit of the Tree.
Old Lem.
Street Car Gang.
Clifton, L. 4/30/92; for Rodney King.
I. At Nagasaki.
Conyus. I rode with Geronimo.
Cortez. Everything Is Wonderful.
Give Me the Red on the Black of the Bullet.
If the drum is a woman.
There It Is.
Cullen, C. Scottsboro, Too, Is Worth Its Song.
Dunbar, P. Haunted Oak, The.
Harper, F. Lines: "At the Portals of the
Future."
Proclaim a fast, a solemn fast.
Slave Auction, The.
Harper, M. Christian's Box Seat: So What!
Militance of a Photograph in the Passbook of
a Bantu under Detention, The.
Mother Speaks: The Algiers Motel Incident,
Detroit, A.
Heard, J. They are coming, coming slowly.
Horton, G. On Liberty and Slavery.
Slave, The.
Slavery, thou peace-disturbing thief.
Hughes, L. Christ in Alabama.
Gangsters.
Scottsboro.
Town of Scottsboro, The.
Jeffers, L. Man with a Furnace in His Hand.
Johnson, F. Ethiopia.
Komunyakaa. Epilogue to the Opera of Dead
on Arrival.
Lorde. Power.
Revolution Is One Form of Social Change.
Vietnam Addenda.
McKay, C. Negro's Friend, The.
Moorer. Injustice of the Courts.
Sanchez, S. Old Words.
Steptoe. Notes for a Poem from the Middle
Passage of Years.
Thompson, P. Muse's Favor, The.
Unknown. Song: "We raise de wheat."
Walker, M. On Police Brutality.
Whitfield. How long, oh gracious God! how
long.
Whitman, A. Lute of Afric's Tribe, The.
See also **Protest, Social**

Innocence
Angelou. Martial Choreograph.
Son to Mother.
Atkins. New Storefront.
Brown, S. Bessie.
Cullen, C. Dear Friends and Gentle Hearts.
Horton, G. Fate of an Innocent Dog, The.
Hughes, L. Disillusion.
Johnson, F. Banjo Player, The.
Jordan, A. If I Write a Poem.
Jordan, J. All the World Moved.
Juice of a Lemon on the Trail of a Little
Yellow.
Knight, E. Circling the Daughter.
Loftis. Ruth.
McKay, C. Flame-Heart.
Sanchez, S. Once i was chaste with.
Toomer. Angelic Eve.
Walcott. Blues.
Young, A. Michael At Sixteen Months.
Sweet Sixteen Lines.

Insects
African-American Oral Tradition. Chintz, The.
Brooks, G. Birth in a Narrow Room, The.

Clifton, L. At last we killed the roaches.
Komunyakaa. Dreambook Bestiary.
Lorde. Brown Menace or Poem to the
Survival of Roaches, The.
Nelson, M. Abba Jacob and St. Francis.
Wright, J. Invention of a Garden, The.

Insomnia and Insomniacs
Angelou. Insomniac.
Eady. Insomnia.
Giovanni. Introspection.
Hayden, R. Broken Dark, The.
Ice Storm.
Hughes, L. Summer Night.
Kaufman, B. I wish that whoever it is inside
of me.
Sanchez, S. Summary.

Inspiration
Angelou. Impeccable Conception.
Brooks, G. Martin Luther King, Jr.
Dunbar, P. Inspiration.
Harper, F. Songs for the People.
Horton, G. On the Poetic Muse.
To the Muse.
Nelson, M. How I Discovered Poetry.
Wheatley, P. Hymn to Humanity, An.
To S. M., a Young African Painter, on Seeing
His Works.
Young, A. By Heart.
Dear Ravi Shankar.
Dexter Gordon at Keystone Korner.
Jungle Strut.
Poem for Dylan Thomas, A.
Prestidigitator 2, The.
Whatever Become of the Living.

Installment Buying
Trethewey. Collection Day.

Instinct
Baraka. Footnote to a Pretentious Book.

Insults
African-American Oral Tradition. Hobo Ben.
Hustlin' Dan.
Partytime Monkey.
Pimp, The.
Pimping Sam.
Wicked Nell: "While sittin' and thinking in
deep meditation."
Wicked Nell: "While sittin' down in deep
meditation, little girl, lookin' at you."
Clifton, L. What spells racoon to me.
Hughes, L. Sliver.

Integration
Hughes, L. Jim Crow's Last Stand.
Kids in School with Me, The.
Lincoln University: 1954.
Mitchell Case, The.
Peace Conference in an American Town.
To Captain Mulzac.
Where Service Is Needed.
Shange. On Becomin Successful.
See also **Civil Rights Movement, United States**

Integrity
Brown, S. Coolwell Vignette.
Sharecroppers.
Madhubuti. Possibilities: Remembering
Malcolm X.

Intellect and Intellectuals
Alhamisi. Pome. For Weird. Hearts. and All.
Baraka. Green Lantern's Solo.
Poem for Deep Thinkers, A.
Poem for Speculative Hipsters, A.
Political Poem.
Giovanni. For an Intellectual Audience.
Intellectualism.
Hughes, L. To Certain Intellectuals.
Jordan, J. Poem about Intelligence for My
Brothers and Sisters, A.
Kaufman, B. Saraswati.
Tidal Friction ... Comments at Real Movie.
Madhubuti. Death Dance, The.
Reed, I. Untitled IV.
Wright, J. End of Ethnic Dream, The.
See also **Mind; Reason; Thought**

Interracial Love and Marriage
African-American Oral Tradition. Joe the
Grinder and G.I. Joe.

Brown, S. Frankie and Johnny.
Slim Greer.
Cullen, C. Ballad of the Brown Girl, The.
Eady. Sherbet.
Holman, M. Mr. Z.
Hughes, L. Black Gal.
Cross.
Do You Reckon?
Flight.
Little Song.
Red Silk Stockings.
Sanchez, S. To You/Who Almost Turned/Me
On.
Tolson, M. African China.
Walker, A. Ballad of the Brown Girl.
Johann.

Introspection
Angelou. I almost remember.
Clifton, L. Turning into my own.
Cornish, S. Turk.
Dunbar, P. Ere sleep comes down to soothe
the weary eyes.
Hughes, L. Border Line.
Helen Keller.
Young, A. Dancing All Alone.

Invocation
Cortez. I See Chano Pozo.

Iowa (state)
Alexander, M. Iowa Farmer.
Walker, M. Iowa Farmer.

Iran and Iranians
Jordan, J. Current Events.
Reed, I. Pope Replies to the Ayatollah
Khomeini, The.

Ireland
Fordham. Song to Erin.
Hughes, L. Seascape.
See also **Listings for specific counties**

Irish, The
Dunbar, P. John Boyle O'Reilly.

Iron. See Steel

Irony
Jordan, J. Uhuru in the O.R.
Young, A. Poem for Willard Motley, A.
Sad Hour of Your Peace, The.

Isaiah
Wheatley, P. Isaiah LXIII, 1–8.

Islam
Giovanni. Harvest.
Jordan, J. Intifada.

Islam and Muslims
Hayden, R. El-Hajj Malik El-Shabazz.
Jordan, J. Intifada.
McKay, C. Farewell to Morocco, A.
Neal, L. Malcolm X—an Autobiography.
Morning Raga for Malcolm.
Saunders, R. Hush Honey.
Sims, L. Angels Prayer, An.

Islands
Dent. St. Helena Island.
Dumas, H. Island within Island.
Hughes, L. Island.
Jordan, J. Always Lei of Ginger Blossoms for
the First Lady of Hawai'i: Queen
Lili'uokalani, An.
McKay, C. After the Winter.
When Dawn Comes to the City.
Phillips, C. You Are Here.
Weaver, M. Easy Living.

Isolation
Kaufman, B. Heavy Water Blues.
Night that Lorca Comes, The.
See also **Absence**

Israel
Dove, R. Early Morning on the Tel Aviv-
Haifa Freeway.
Harper, F. Deliverance.
Jewish Grandfather's Story, The.
Moses: A Story of the Nile.
Jordan, J. Intifada.
Knight, E. Poem on the Middle East "Peace
Process", A.
Unknown. Go down, Moses.
See also **Palestine**

Italians, The
Jordan, J. Roman Poem Number Six.

Italy
Jordan, J. Roman Poem Number Five.
Young, A. Here in violet light.
So is there life on you, moon?
Tutti Colori Quality of Light, The.

Itching
Horton, G. Troubled with the Itch and
Rubbing with Sulphur.

J

Jack the Ripper
Komunyakaa. Light on the Subject.

Jackson, Mahalia
Lorde. Day they eulogized Mahalia, The.
Prettyman. When Mahalia Sings.

Jackson, Thomas Jonathan ("Stonewall")
Whitman, A. Stonewall Jackson, 1886.

Jamaica, West Indies
Goodison. Jamaica 1980.
Jordan, J. Roman Poem Number Six.
McKay, C. Home Thoughts.
I shall return again. I shall return.
North and South.
Tropics in New York, The.
Two-an'-Six.
Wheatley, P. To a Lady on Her Coming to
North-America with Her Son, for the
Recovery of Her Health.
See also **West Indies**

James, Jesse
African-American Oral Tradition. Jesse James.

January
Ray, H. January.
Young, A. January.

Japanese, The
African-American Oral Tradition. Joe the
Grinder and G.I. Joe.

Jasmine
Lorde. Night-Blooming Jasmine, The.
McKay, C. Jasmine.

Jazz
Anderson, S. Sound of Afroamerican History
Chapt II, The.
Baraka. Am/trak.
In the Tradition.
Pres / spoke in a language.
Speech #38 (or Y We Say It This Way).
Barlow, G. In My Father's House.
Barrax. Singer, The.
Braxton, C. Jazzy St. Walk.
Brooks, G. Third Sermon on the Warpland,
The.
We real cool. We.
Brown, S. Cabaret.
Ma Rainey.
New St. Louis Blues.
Corrie. How Long Has Trane Been Gone.
Cortez. Jazz Fan Looks Back.
Rose Solitude.
Tapping.
Delegall. Psalm for Sonny Rollins.
Dove, R. Canary.
Eady. William Carlos Williams.
Gilyard. On Top of It All.
Giovanni. Geni in the Jar, The.
Graham, D. Soul.
Harper, M. Brother John.
Dear John, Dear Coltrane.
For Bud.
Mr. P. C.
Reuben, Reuben.
Time for Tyner: Folksong.
Hayden, R. Soledad.
Henderson, D. Egyptian Book of the Dead.
Hughes, L. Be-Bop Boys.
Cabaret.
Communiqué.
Drums.
Harlem Night Club.
Jam Session.
Jazz Band in a Parisian Cabaret.
Jazz Girl.
Jazzonia.

Nocturne for the Drums.
Song for Billie Holiday.
Young Singer.
Jackson, M. L. Don Pullen at the Zanzibar
Blue Jazz Cafe, 1994.
Jacobs, H. Imagination in Flight: an
Improvisational Duet.
Jeffers, L. How High the Moon.
Joans. JAZZ is my religion.
Lester Young.
Kaufman, B. Bagel Shop Jazz.
Battle Report.
His Horn.
Jazz Chick.
Mingus.
Morning Joy.
No More Jazz at Alcatraz.
O-Jazz-O.
Round about Midnight.
Tequila Jazz.
Walking Parker Home.
War Memoir: Jazz, Don't Listen to It at Your
Own Risk.
Klein, S. Jelly Roll Morton.
Knight, E. Haiku: "Making jazz swing in."
Komunyakaa. Changes: or, Reveries at a
Window Overlooking a Country Road, with
Two Women Talking Blues in the Kitchen.
Copacetic Mingus.
Elegy for Thelonious.
February in Sydney.
Gerry's Jazz.
Plea, The.
Madhubuti. Blackmusic / a Beginning.
Don't Cry, Scream.
McClane. Jazz.
Song: a Motion for History.
Neal, L. Don't say goodbye to the Porkpie
Hat that rolled.
Nixon. Ju-Ju Man.
Redmond. His Eminence Plays the Soular
System.
Reed, I. Lake Bud.
Poetry Makes Rhythm in Philosophy.
Soul Proprietorship.
Renegade. Haiku: "Jazz is / the way brown
sugar."
Rodgers, C. We Dance Like Ella Riffs.
Rux. Suite Repose.
Salaam. I Just Heard John Buffington Died.
Spellman. Did John's Music Kill Him?
John Coltrane: An Impartial Review.
Thomas, L. Historiography.
Tolson, M. Satchmo.
Touré, A. Rebellion Suite.
Troupe. Collage.
One for Charlie Mingus.
Unknown. It Don't Mean a Thing (If It Ain't
Got That Swing).
Ward, Jr., J. Jazz to Jackson to John.
Williams, Karen. JAZZ (a New Interpretation).
Wilson, Ted. Music of the Other World.
Young, A. Art of Benny Carter, The.
Dance of the Infidels.
Jackie McLean: Alto Saxophone.
Jazz as Was.
Lester Leaps In.
Little Poem About Jazz, A.
Thelonious: An Intro.

Jealousy
Brown, S. Chillen Get Shoes.
Cowdery. Insatiate.
Dunbar, P. Jealous.
Hughes, L. Lament of a Vanquished Beau,
The.
Rent-Party Shout.
Jordan, J. About Long Distances on Saturday.
Reception, The.
Kaufman, B. J'Accuse.
Komunyakaa. After Summer Fell Apart.
McKay, C. Tormented.
Nelson, M. Women's Locker Room.
Reed, I. Betty's Ball Blues.
Unknown. Frankie and Johnny were lovers.
See also **Envy**

Jefferson, Thomas
Clifton, L. Monticello.

Jeremiah (Bible)
Dodson, O. Hymn Written after Jeremiah
Preached to Me in a Dream.

Jerusalem
Cullen, C. At the Wailing Wall in Jerusalem.

Jesters
Hughes, L. Jester, The.
Shakespeare in Harlem.
See also **Fools**

Jesus Christ
African-American Oral Tradition. Nobody
Knows Da Trubble Ah See.
Anderson, C. Prayer to the White Man's God.
Angelou. Savior.
Baraka. When We'll Worship Jesus.
Boyd, J. Vision, The.
Braxton, C. Gathering, The.
Brooks, G. In Emanuel's Nightmare: Another
Coming of Christ.
Brooks, J. Resurrection, The.
Brown, S. Temple, The.
Clark, C. Second Coming, The.
Clifton, L. Calling of the Disciples, The.
Easter Sunday.
God Send Easter.
How He Is Coming Then.
Spring Song.
Cullen, C. Black Christ, The.
Christus Natus Est.
Judas Iscariot.
Fordham. Christ Child, The.
Nativity, The.
Hamilton, B. Child's Nightmare, A.
Hammon. Evening Thought, An [: Salvation
by Christ with Penetential Cries].
Harper, F. Blessed Hope, The.
Burdens of All, The.
Christmas Carol, A.
Fishers of Men.
He "Had Not Where to Lay His Head."
His Name.
Jesus.
Let the Light Enter!
Lines to M.A.H.
Mary at the Feet of Christ.
Resurrection of Jesus, The.
Saved by Faith.
Simon's Feast.
Sir, We Would See Jesus.
Syrophenician Woman, The.
Thank God for Little Children.
Hayden, R. Full Moon.
Heard, J. Birth of Jesus, The.
Horton, G. Heavenly Love.
On the Truth of the Saviour.
Hughes, L. Ballad of Mary's Son.
Ballad of the Two Thieves.
Carol of the Brown King.
Christ in Alabama.
Christmas Story, The.
Encounter.
Feet O' Jesus.
Goodbye Christ.
Judgment Day.
Ma Lord ain't no stuck-up man.
On a Christmas Night.
On a Pallet of Straw.
Pastoral.
Shepherd's Song at Christmas.
Shout.
Hurston. Faith hasn't got no eyes, but she
long-legged.
Johnson, J. Go Down Death.
Jordan, J. All the World Moved.
Madhubuti. Black Christ, The.
McClellan. Feet of Judas, The.
Miller, M. Calvary Way.
Moorer. Benefits of Sorrow.
Sympathy.
Nelson, M. As Simple as That.
I Knew That.
Meditation over the Washtub.
O'Higgins, M. Young Poet.
Plumpp. I Told Jesus.
Ray, H. Prayer: "O Christ, who in
Gethsemane."
Thompson, C. Empty Tomb, The.

Thompson, P. Death and Resurrection.
Toomer. Georgia Dusk.
  Gum.
  Promise, The.
  Song of the Son.
  Upward is this Actuality.
Unknown. Down in the Valley.
  Give Me Jesus.
  Ride in, kind Saviour!
  Steal Away to Jesus.
  Were you there when they crucified my Lord?
    [(were you there?)].
Vassa. Miscellaneous Verses.
Walcott. God Rest Ye Merry, Gentlemen.
Walker, A. Abduction of Saints, The.
  J, My Good Friend (Another Foolish
    Innocent).
Wheatley, P. Hymn to Humanity, An.
  On the Death of the Rev. Dr. Sewell, 1769.
  To the University of Cambridge, in New-
    England.

Jewelry
Harper, M. Studs.
Sanchez, S. I kneel down like a.
See also **Fashion; Rings**

Joan of Arc
Clifton, L. To Joan.

Job (Bible)
Angelou. Just like Job.
Clifton, L. Job easy / is the pride.
Nelson, M. I Knew That.

Johannesburg, South Africa
Hughes, L. Johannesburg Mines.
Sharp, S. Meanwhile, in Rwanda.

"John Henry" (folk hero)
Unknown. John Henry.

John the Baptist, Saint
Clifton, L. John.
Hughes, L. For Salome.

Johnson Andrew
Bell, J. Modern Moses, or "My Policy" Man.

Johnson, Samuel
Dunbar, P. Then and Now.

Johnston, James Hugo
Johnson, M. James Hugo Johnston.

Jonah (Bible)
Clifton, L. Jonah.

Joseph, Saint
Clifton, L. Holy Night.
  Joseph.

Joshua (Bible)
Harper, F. Sin of Achar, The.
Unknown. Joshua fit de battle of Jericho [*or*
  ob Jerico].

Journalism and Journalists
Moorer. Southern Press, The.
Sharp, S. Meanwhile, in Rwanda.
See also **Magazines; Newspapers**

Joy
Braithwaite. Sic Vita.
Clifton, L. My Poem.
  Palm Sunday.
  To Joan.
Delany. Joy shakes me like the wind that lifts
  a sail.
Dunbar, P. Lesson, The.
  Little brown baby wif spa'klin' eyes.
  Old Cabin, The.
  To J. Q.
  When de Co'n Pone's Hot.
Evans, M. Who Can Be Born Black.
Giovanni. Just a New York Poem.
  My House.
  Rain is / god's sperm falling.
  Way I Feel, The.
Harper, F. Change, The.
  Mother's Treasures.
  Thank God for Little Children.
Hughes, L. Earth Song.
  Gypsy Melodies.
  Harlem Night Club.
  Joy.
  Midnight Dancer.
Lorde. Meet.
McKay, C. City's Love, The.

Murphy, M. Fat Grass and Slow Rain.
Nelson, M. Juneteenth.
Phillips, C. Reach, The.
Ray, H. Shadow and Sunrise.
Sanchez, S. And the joy. feeling.
Tolson, M. Victor Garibaldi.
Young, A. Joy/Spring.
  Maya.

Judaism and Jews
Bibb. Wandering Jew, The.
Harper, F. Deliverance.
  Jewish Grandfather's Story, The.
Hayden, R. Rabbi, The.
Hughes, L. America.
  Likewise.
  Un-American Investigators.

Judas Iscariot
Barrax. Sacrifice, The.
Cullen, C. Judas Iscariot.
McClellan. Feet of Judas, The.
Reed, I. Judas.

Judges
African-American Oral Tradition. Ain't It a
  Bitch?
  No Good Whore.
  Stackolee: "Back in forty-nine when times was
    hard."
  Stackoloee: "I staggered in a place called the
    Bucket a Blood."
  Stackolee: "It was back in the time of nineteen
    hundred and two."
  Stackolee: "It was back in the year of forty-
    one when the times was hard."
  Stackolee: "This is supposed to be about two
    colored studs. It's truth. In New Orleans."
Dunbar, P. To Mary Church Terrell.
Gilyard. Letter.
Hughes, L. Brief Encounter.
  Judge William Hastie.

Judgment
Gaye. What's Going On.
Giovanni. Game of Game, The.
  Women gather, The.
Harper, F. Retribution.
Jordan, J. At some moment the confidence
  snaps.
Kaufman, B. Carl Chessman Interviews the
  P.T.A. in His Swank Gas Chamber Before
  Leaving on His Annual Inspection of Capital,
  Tour of Northern California Death
  Universities, Happy.
Lorde. Father Son and Holy Ghost.
Simpson, J. To the White People of America.
Walker, A. Judge Every One with Perfect
  Calm.
Walker, M. Dies Irae.
Warren-Moore. For Etheridge Knight.
  For Paula Cooper (The 18 Year Old Who
  Waits on Death Row).

Judgment Day
Johnson, J. Saint Peter Relates an Incident of
  the Resurrection Day.
Unknown. I know moon-rise, I know star-rise.
See also **Apocalypse**

Judith (Apocrypha)
Bibb. Judith.
Menken. Judith.

July
Gray-Kontar. July.
Ray, H. July.
Sanchez, S. July.

Jumping
African-American Oral Tradition. My Uncle
  Sam was a good old man.

June
Fordham. June.
McKay, C. Memory of June, A.
Ray, H. June.

Jungles
Bethune, L. Blue Tanganyika.
Hughes, L. Poem: "All the tom-toms of the
  jungles beat in my blood."

Justice
Brown, S. When de Saints Go Ma'ching
  Home.
Cortez. If the drum is a woman.

Cotter, Sr. Band of Gideon roam the sky, The.
Dunbar, P. Justice.
  To Miss Mary Britton.
Harper, F. Words for the Hour.
Hawkins, W. Death of Justice, The.
Hughes, L. Dream of Freedom.
  Final Call.
  Freedom Train.
  Freedom's Plow.
  How about It, Dixie.
  Justice.
  What I Think.
  Who But the Lord?
Jackson, M. Man in the Mirror.
Komunyakaa. Light on the Subject.
Linden, M. All We Ask Is Justice.
Nelson, M. I Knew That.
Walker, M. Amos, 1963.
  Amos (Postscript, 1968).

Justice, David
Stanard. Baseball.

Justification
Giovanni. Poem: "I have considered / my
  reluctance."

Juvenile Delinquency
Brooks, G. We real cool. We.
Brown, S. Johnny Thomas.

K

Kahlo, Frida
Alexander, E. Painting / (Frida Kahlo).

Kansas (state)
Harper, M. Forty Days Looking Backwards:
  Notes from a Surveyor.
  Jim Daniels: Hamilton Massacre: Parable.
  Manual for the Patriotic Volunteer.
  Music of Broadswords, The.

Kansas City, Kansas and Missouri
Beeks. Parker's Mood.

Katharine of Aragón, Queen of England
Bibb. Catharine of Arragon.

Katydids
Dunbar, P. Whip-Poor-Will and Katy-Did.

Keats, John
Braithwaite. October XXIX, 1795.
Brown, L. Green arbor that I once knew, A.
Cullen, C. To John Keats, Poet, at Springtime.
Hughes, L. Metropolitan Museum.

Keller, Helen
Cullen, C. For Helen Keller.
Hughes, L. Helen Keller.

Kennedy, John Fitzgerald
Fraser, A. To the "J F K" Quintet.
Reed, I. Nov 22, 1988.
Young, A. Day Kennedy Died.

Kennedy, Robert Francis
Giovanni. Poem on the Assassination of
  Robert F. Kennedy, A.

Kent State University, Ohio
Clifton, L. After Kent State.

Kentucky (state)
Brown, S. Kentucky Blues.
Cotter, Sr. Answer to Dunbar's "After a
  Visit."
Dunbar, P. After a Visit.
Whitman, A. I love Kentucky; tho' she merit
  scorn.
  Thrice hail! proud land, whose genius boasts a
  Clay!

Keys
Forbes, C. Home.
Hernton. Fall Down.

Kidnapping and Kidnappers
Dove, R. Abduction, The.
Giovanni. Kidnap Poem.
Jordan, J. DeLiza and the TV News.
Reed, I. Beware: Do Not Read This Poem.

Killing and Killers
Barrax. King: April 4, 1968.
Brown, S. Sam Smiley.
Carroll, K. Something Easy for Ultra Black
  Nationalists.

Coleman, W. Emmett Till.
Giovanni. True Import of Present Dialogue,
  Black vs. Negro.
Hayden, R. Killing the Calves.
Hughes, L. Brief Encounter.
  Comment.
  Death in Harlem.
  Death in Yorkville.
  Death of Do Dirty: A Rounder's Song.
  Expendable.
  Wisdom and War.
Unknown. Poor Lazarus.

Kindness
Brooks, G. Young Africans.
Cullen, C. Tribute.
Dunbar, P. My Sort o' Man.
  Plea, A.
Jordan, J. If You Saw a Negro Lady.
Reed, I. Untitled: "Law isn't all."
Stanard. Baseball.
Thompson, P. Kindly Deed, A.
Tucker, M. Kindness.

King, B. B.
Weems. B.B. Blues.

King, Martin Luther, Jr
Barrax. King: April 4, 1968.
Brooks, G. Martin Luther King, Jr.
Cornish, S. Death of Dr. King.
Giovanni. Drums ... Pa-Rum ... the rat-tat-tat
  ... of drums, The.
  Funeral of Martin Luther King, Jr, The.
Harper, M. Crossing Lake Michigan.
  Martin's Blues.
  Studs.
Jordan, J. In Memoriam: Martin Luther King,
  Jr.
Komunyakaa. Report from the Skull's
  Diorama.
Lee, D. Assassination.
Lorde. Rites of Passage.
Madhubuti. Assassination.
Nelson, M. Boys in the Park.
Troupe. Day in the Life of a Poet, A.
  White Weekend.
Walker, A. Abduction of Saints, The.
  Killers.
Walker, M. Five Black Men.

Kings
Cullen, C. Black Majesty.
DuBois, W. Song of the Smoke, The.
Harper, F. To-day Is a King in Disguise.
Walker, A. In Uganda an early king chose.
See also **Royalty; Listings for specific kings**

Kisses
Braithwaite. Scintilla.
Dove, R. Adolescence—I.
Dunbar, P. Breaking the Charm.
  Come and Kiss Me Sweet and Twenty.
  Her Thought and His.
  Negro Love Song, A.
  Phantom Kiss, The.
Harper, F. My mother's kiss, my mother's
  kiss.
Hughes, L. Suicide's Note.
Jordan, J. Alla Tha's All Right, But.
Nelson, M. Canticle for Abba Jacob, A.
Sanchez, S. Magic.
Toomer. Her Lips Are Copper Wire.
Tucker, M. Kiss? A. Pray tell me, what is in
  a kiss.
Walker, A. Kiss, The.
Walton, E. Kiss Requested, A.
Williams, Niama. Merging.
Young, A. Curative Powers of Silence, The.
  Kiss.

Kissinger, Henry
Baraka. Horatio Alger Uses Scag.

Kitchens
Brooks, G. Mrs. Small went to the kitchen for
  her pocketbook.
Cook, W. Still-Life with Woodstove.
Davis, T. Boppin' is Safer than Grindin'.
Dove, R. Sunday Greens.
Dunbar, P. Trouble in de Kitchen.
Salaam. Everywhere You Eat

Kites (toys)
Gilbert, C. Kite-Flying.

Thompson, D. Laurel Street, 1950.

Knight, Etheridge
Lane, P. Elegy for Etheridge.
Moore, L. Message to Etheridge Knight.
Sanchez, S. Hospital/Poem.

Knighthood and Knights
Dunbar, P. Knight, The.

Knights of Pythias
Linden, M. For the Good of the Pythian
  Order.

Knitting and Knitters
Nelson, M. Twist the thread.
Tucker, M. Knitting.

Knives
Knight, E. Haiku: "Under moon shadows."
Lorde. On the Edge.
  Poem for Women in Rage, A.
Sharp, S. In the Tradition of Bobbitt.

Knowledge
Aubert, A. Nat Turner in the Clearing.
Baraka. New World, The.
Clifton, L. Adam and Eve.
Dove, R. Particulars.
Hughes, L. Acceptance.
Jordan, J. For Ethelbert.
Lorde. But What Can You Teach My
  Daughter.
  Second Spring.
Nelson, M. Simple Wisdom, The.
Rux. Pledge of Allegiance.
Salaam. Always Know.

Knox, George L.
Bibb. Lines to the Hon. George L. Knox.

Knoxville, Tennessee
Giovanni. Knoxville, Tennessee.

Ku Klux Klan
Hayden, R. Night, Death, Mississippi.
Hughes, L. Ballad of Sam Solomon.
  Ku Klux.
  Note to All Nazis Fascists and Klansmen.
  Special Bulletin.
Johnson, J. Saint Peter Relates an Incident of
  the Resurrection Day.
St. John, P. Lynching and Burning.
Spellman. When Black People Are.

L

Labor and Laborers
African-American Oral Tradition. I got a job
  down in Florida for Croft.
Angelou. Me and My Work.
  One More Round.
  Worker's Song.
Baraka. Poem Some People Will Have to
  Understand, A.
Brown, S. Break of Day.
  Call Boy.
  Colloquy.
  Mose is black and evil.
  Odyssey of Big Boy.
  Southern Road.
  Street Car Gang.
Collins, L. Stevedore.
Conyus. Six Ten Sixty-Nine.
DuBois, W. Song of the Smoke, The.
Dunbar, P. Equipment.
  Not they who soar, but they who plod.
Harper, F. Free Labor.
Hayden, R. Those Winter Sundays.
Horton, G. Song of Liberty and Parental
  Advice.
Hughes, L. Ballads of Lenin.
  Brass Spittoons.
  Chant for May Day.
  Chant for Tom Mooney.
  Florida Road Workers.
  Good-morning, Revolution.
  Goodbye Christ.
  Labor Storm.
  Office Building: Evening.
  Open Letter to the South.
  Sister Johnson Marches.
  Song of Spain.
  Steel Mills.

Johnson, M. What's de Use ob Wukin in de
  Summer Time at All.
Jordan, A. My Father's Retirement.
Jordan, J. If You Saw a Negro Lady.
Lorde. Song for Many Movements, A.
Madhubuti. America calling.
McKay, C. Tired Worker, The.
Moore, L. From the Field.
Nelson, M. Abba Jacob in the Well.
Randall, D. George.
Rivers, C. Train Runs Late to Harlem, The.
Rodgers, C. It Is Deep.
Shange. Tango.
Thomas, R. Worker, The.
Toomer. Reapers.
Trethewey. Drapery Factory, Gulfport,
  Mississippi, 1956.
Unknown. Can't You Line It?
  Go Down, Old Hannah.
  John Henry.
  Pick a Bale of Cotton.
  This Sun Is Hot.
  When John Henry was a little babe.
Young, A. New Mode of Production, The.

Labor Unions
Hughes, L. Open Letter to the South.
See also **Strikes and Strikers**

Lakes and Ponds
Dunbar, P. Matter of Locality, A.
Harper, M. Crossing Lake Michigan.
Lane, P. Lake Murry.
Major, C. Swallow the Lake.
Pritchard, N. Paysagesque.
Reed, I. Hoodoo Poem in Transient.
  Lake Bud.
Wright, J. Lake in Central Park, The.

Lambs
African-American Oral Tradition. Mary had a
  little lamb for which she cared no particle.
Dunbar, P. Hymn: "O li'l lamb out in de
  col'."
Roberson. Blue Horses.
See also **Sheep**

Lament (form)
Hughes, L. Ruined Gal, A.
See also **Lament in Title, First Line, and Last
  Line Index**

Lancelot du Lac
Bontemps. Lancelot.

Landlords and Landladies
Angelou. Contemporary Announcement.
Hughes, L. Ballad of the Landlord.
  Madam and the Rent Man.
  Red Clay Blues.
Joans. Scenery.
Reed, I. Rough Trade Slumlord Totem.

Landscape
Young, A. Old Light.

Language
Aubert, A. When the Wine Was Gone.
Baraka. Death Is Not as Natural as You Fags
  Seem to Think.
  Measure of Memory (The Navigator), The.
  Wise 2.
Clifton, L. For the Mute.
Cortez. Phraseology.
Crouch, S. Blackie Thinks of His Brothers.
Eady. Sherbet.
Fordham. Saxon Legend of Language, The.
Giovanni. Charting the Night Winds.
  Communication.
  Poem for Langston Hughes, A.
Jackson, A. Why I Must Make Language.
Jordan, J. Fragments from a Parable.
Lorde. Coal.
  Thaw.
Miller, E. Spanish Conversation.
Plumpp. Turf Song.
Reed, I. Untitled III.
Sanchez, S. Nigger.
Sun-Ra. To the Peoples of Earth.
Thomas, L. Electricity of Blossoms.
Troupe. My poems have holes sewn into
  them.
Walcott. Far Cry from Africa, A.

Warren-Moore. For Etheridge Knight.
  For Paula Cooper (The 18 Year Old Who
  Waits on Death Row).
Weaver, M. Luxembourg Garden.
Worley, D. Las Flores para una Niña Negra.
  Tongues in My Mouth.
See also **Speech; Words**
Lanterns
Brown, S. Long Track Blues.
Larks
Dunbar, P. With the Lark.
See also **Meadowlarks**
Last Supper
Hughes, L. Ballad of Mary's Son.
Latin America and Latin Americans
Cortez. Everything Is Wonderful.
Laughter
Angelou. Old Folks Laugh.
Dunbar, P. We wear the mask that grins and
  lies.
Hughes, L. Homesick Blues.
  Laughers.
  Railroad Avenue.
Johnson, G. I Want to Die While You Love
  Me.
Lorde. Restoration.
Nelson, M. Laughter as the Highest Form of
  Contemplation.
Sanchez, S. Autumn. a bonfire.
  Let me be your flute.
  Trees are laughing, The.
  Woman. whose color.
Unknown. Me and My Captain.
Laundry and Laundering
Barrax. Domestic Tranquility.
Bohanan. Washer-Woman, The.
Fordham. Washerwoman, The.
Moss, T. Fisher Street.
Rankine. Eden.
Shockley. Oseola McCarty.
Young, A. Dancing in the Laundromat [or]
  Dust: an Ordinary Song.
Law and Lawyers
African-American Oral Tradition. No Good
  Whore.
  They Can't Do That.
Dunbar, P. Lawyers' Ways, The.
Jordan, J. Letter to the Local Police.
  Song of the Law Abiding Citizen.
Medina, T. After the Verdict.
Moorer. Injustice of the Courts.
  Legal Mouse, A.
Reed, I. Untitled: "Law isn't all."
Tolson, M. Ex-Judge at the Bar, An.
Lazarus (Bible)
Clifton, L. Raising of Lazarus, The.
Laziness
Cotter, Sr. Don't-Care Negro, The.
Dunbar, P. In the Morning.
Hughes, L. Kid Sleepy.
  Madam and the Army.
McGirt. Nothing to Do.
  When de Sun Shines Hot.
Leadbelly (Huddie Ledbetter)
Eady. Leadbelly.
Komunyakaa. Villon/Leadbelly.
Leadership
Franklin, C. Visions ... Leaders.
Gilbert, D. Fire in the Drum, The.
Giovanni. Drums ... Pa-Rum ... the rat-tat-tat
  ... of drums, The.
Hughes, L. Ballad of Walter White.
Reed, I. Soul Proprietorship.
Walker, M. Five Black Men.
Zu-Bolton. Governor of the Ollie Street, The.
Leap Year
Johnson, M. Leap Yeah Party, De.
Learning
Dove, R. Flash Cards.
Giovanni. All i gotta do.
Kendrick, D. Sophie, Climbing the Stairs.
Lorde. As I Grew Up Again.
  Black Mother Woman.
  For Judith.
  Legacy—Hers.
  On Midsummer's Eve.

Plato. Advice to Young Ladies.
Wheatley, P. Elegy, Sacred to the Memory of
  That Great Divine, the Reverend and Learned
  Dr. Samuel Cooper, Who Departed This Life
  December 29, 1783, Ætatis 59, An.
Young, A. Teaching.
Leaves
Clifton, L. Lesson of the Falling Leaves, The.
Cullen, C. Leaves.
Dunbar, P. Chase, The.
Harper, M. New Season.
Hughes, L. New Year.
Pritchard, N. Landscape with Nymphs and
  Satyrs.
Redmond. Autumn God.
Thompson, C. Autumn Leaves.
See also **Autumn**
Lebanon and Lebanese
Jordan, J. Apologies to All the People in
  Lebanon.
  Moving Towards Home.
Leda
Jordan, J. Female and the Silence of a Man,
  The.
Legs
Durem. Vet's Rehabilitation.
Eady. April.
Hughes, L. Red Silk Stockings.
Sanchez, S. Man, i am trying.
Leisure
Dove, R. One Volume Missing.
Dunbar, P. Lazy Day, A.
Lemons
Young, A. Lemons, Lemons.
Lenin, Vladimir Ilyich
Hughes, L. Ballads of Lenin.
  Lenin walks around the world.
McKay, C. Moscow for many loving her was
  dead.
Lennon, John
Giovanni. This Is Not for John Lennon.
Letters
Dunbar, P. Love Letter, A.
Gilyard. Letter.
Hayden, R. Letter.
Heard, J. Love Letters.
Hughes, L. Little Old Letter.
  Personal.
Lorde. Learning to Write.
  Martha this is a catalog of days.
  Trip on the Staten Island Ferry, A.
Madhubuti. Poem Looking for a Reader, A.
Shange. Pages for a Friend.
Spencer, A. Rime for the Christmas Baby.
Tucker, M. Love-letter, A.
Walker, A. Suicide.
  What the Finger Writes.
Williams, S. Letters from a New England
  Negro.
See also **Mail and Mailmen**
Liberalism and Liberals
Angelou. On Working White Liberals.
Bibbs. Liberalissimo.
Hughes, L. Northern Liberal.
Jackson, R. Lonely Affair, A.
Reed, I. Sather Tower Mystery.
Libraries and Librarians
Ellis, T. View of the Library of Congress
  from Paul Laurence Dunbar High School.
Lies and Lying
African-American Oral Tradition. Hitler, You
  Lied to Me.
Signifying Monkey: "Back down in the jungle
  up under the stick."
Signifying Monkey: "Deep down in the jungle
  in the coconut grove."
Signifying Monkey: "Down in the jungle about
  treetop deep."
Signifying Monkey: "It was early in the
  morning one bright summer day."
Signifying Monkey: "Say deep down in the
  jungle in the coconut grove."
Signifying Monkey: "There hadn't been no
  shift for quite a bit."
You Told Me a Lie.

Angelou. How I Can Lie to You.
Brown, S. Uncle Joe.
Cullen, C. To an Unknown Poet.
Dove, R. Boast, The.
Dunbar, P. We wear the mask that grins and
  lies.
Giovanni. Introspection.
Hand. And I can Remember still your first
  lies America.
Hughes, L. Black Panther.
  Comment on War.
  Liars.
Jordan, J. Apologies to All the People in
  Lebanon.
Lorde. From Inside an Empty Purse.
Major, C. In the Interest of Personal
  Appearance.
Rux. Pledge of Allegiance.
Life
African-American Oral Tradition. Life's a
  funny old proposition.
Angelou. Call Letters: Mrs. V.B.
  Is Love.
  Lesson, The.
  Life Doesn't Frighten Me.
  Nothing Much.
  Old Folks Laugh.
Braithwaite. Sic Vita.
  Turn Me to My Yellow Leaves.
Brooks, G. Kitchenette Building.
  Sadie and Maud.
Brown, S. Odyssey of Big Boy.
Campbell, J. Mors et Vita.
Clifton, L. Cutting Greens.
  New Bones.
  Sonora Desert Poem.
Coleman, W. Doing Battle with the Wolf.
Cotter, Sr. Let none ignobly halt because.
Cullen, C. Life's Rendezvous.
  More Than a Fool's Song.
  Protest.
  Self Criticism.
Dove, R. Charm, The.
  Fish in the Stone, The.
  Ike.
  This Life.
Dunbar, P. By rugged ways and thro' the
  night.
  Common Things.
  If life were but a dream, my love.
  Life.
  Long Ago.
  Passage, The.
  Sum, The.
Giovanni. Journey, A.
  Life I Led, The.
  Poem Off Center, A.
Harper, F. Let the Light Enter!
  To-day Is a King in Disguise.
Hayden, R. Whipping, The.
Hughes, L. Advice.
  Ballad of the Pawnbroker.
  Border Line.
  Consider me, / A colored boy.
  Doorknobs.
  Dreams.
  Esthete in Harlem.
  Lenox Avenue.
  Life Is Fine.
  Monotony.
  Mother to Son.
  Motto.
  Note in Music.
  Pair in One.
  Ph.D.
  Search.
  Song: "Lovely, dark, and lonely one."
  Still Here.
Jordan, J. Poem at the Midnight of My Life.
Kaufman, B. Grandfather Was Queer, Too.
  Heavy Water Blues.
  Night Sung Sailor's Prayer.
Knight, E. My life, the quality of which.
Komunyakaa. Corrigenda.
  Unnatural State of the Unicorn.
Madhubuti. Poet: What Ever Happened to
  Luther?

McClellan. Hydromel and Rue.
Menken. Infelix.
Nelson, M. Abba Jacob and Miracles.
  Abba Jacob at Bat.
  It's All in Your Head.
Pitcher. Pale Blue Casket, The.
Ray, H. Life.
  Life's Boundary.
Reed, I. Life is a screwball comedy.
St. John, P. Carnival.
Salaam. Spice of Life, The.
  Til Death Do Us Part.
Sanchez, S. Don't go. if you go.
  Morning snow falling.
  Poem of Praise, A.
  What is it about.
Sun-Ra. Nothing Is.
Toomer. As the Eagle Soars.
  Desire.
  It is Everywhere.
  Living Earth.
Troupe. Conversation Overheard.
Tucker, M. Life.
  Mysteries of Life.
Unknown. I been rebuked and I been scorned.
  I'm a-rollin', I'm a-rollin', I'm a-rollin',
    through an unfriendly world.
Walden. Transition—S.M, The.
Walker, M. Labyrinth of Life, The.
Wright, J. Cutting Greens.
  Death as History.
Young, A. Afraid.
  Alba.
  Birthday Poem.
  Bitter Spring Again, The.
  Blues in December.
  Citizen CB.
  Continuing.
  Dancing.
  Dancing Day to Day.
  Dancing in the Street.
  Detroit 1958.
  Elegy: "Good morning! / Good morning!"
  Everywhere.
  From Bowling Green.
  How Stars Start.
  How the Rainbow Works.
  Intimacy.
  Invitation.
  Little More Traveling Music, A.
  Malcolm's Message.
  Morning Poem for Michael, A.
  Myself When I Am Real.
  New Mystic, The.
  Now's the Time.
  Poem with Orange.
  Rediscovered Diary Entry.
  Some Spice for Jack Spicer.
  Song Turning Back Into Itself 1.
  There is a sadness to this world.
  Tribute.

Light
Clifton, L. Holy Night.
  Incandescence / formless form.
  Mother, i am mad.
  Testament.
Crouch, S. Like a Blessing.
Dunbar, P. Light, The.
  Light was on the golden sands, The.
Harper, F. Let the Light Enter!
  "Let there be light," a joyous thrill.
Hayden, R. Full Moon.
Hughes, L. Dare.
  Late Corner.
  Shadows.
  Wonder.
Knight, E. Haiku 1: "Slender finger of light,
  A."
Komunyakaa. Praising Dark Places.
Moore, L. Homeplace, The.
Nelson, M. Sneak Preview.
Thomas, L. Electricity of Blossoms.
Toomer. Cloud.
  Prayer (I): "How we have strained at our dark
    works."
Unknown. This Little Light of Mine.
Young, A. Hot House.

Lemons, Lemons.
Moon Up Close in Winter by the Telescope,
  The.
New Moon Over Grove Street.
Sea Level.
Tutti Colori Quality of Light, The.
Written in Bracing, Gray L.A. Rainlight.

Lightning
Young, A. Lightning, Divine Lightning.

Lilies
McKay, C. Easter Flower, The.

Lilies of the Valley
Dunbar, P. Lily of the Valley, The.

Lincoln, Abraham
Dunbar, P. Lincoln.
Harper, F. President Lincoln's Proclamation of
  Freedom.
Horton, G. Lincoln Is Dead.
Hughes, L. Abe Lincoln.
  Lincoln Monument: Washington.
  Lincoln Theatre.
McClellan. Daybreak.
McGirt. Memory of Lincoln and the Yankees.
Ray, H. Lincoln.
Walker, M. At the Lincoln Monument in
  Washington, August 28, 1963.

Lions
African-American Oral Tradition. Partytime
  Monkey.
  Signifying Monkey: "Back down in the jungle
    up under the stick."
  Signifying Monkey: "Deep down in the jungle
    in the coconut grove."
  Signifying Monkey: "Down in the jungle about
    treetop deep."
  Signifying Monkey: "It was early in the
    morning one bright summer day."
  Signifying Monkey: "Say deep down in the
    jungle in the coconut grove."
  Signifying Monkey: "There hadn't been no
    shift for quite a bit."
Unknown. Signifying Monkey, The.

Lips
Lorde. Pirouette.
McKay, C. Red Flower, A.
Sanchez, S. Baby. you are sweet.
Toomer. Evening Song.
  Her Lips Are Copper Wire.

Lisbon, Portugal
Atkins. Lisbon.

Listening and Listeners
Hughes, L. Lady's Boogie.
Madhubuti. In the Interest of Black Salvation.
Nelson, M. Memento.
Young, A. You Don't Know What Love Is.

Literature
Baraka. Of What Use Is Poetry? (Babalu
  Meets the Wolfman).
Reed, I. Badman of the Guest Professor.
  This Poetry Anthology I'm Reading.
See also **Writing and Writers**

Little Bighorn, Battle of (1876)
Whitman, A. Custer's Last Ride.

Lizards
Bethune, L. Today Tutu Is Beating the Same
  Burru As Me.

Locomotives
Angelou. Worker's Song.
See also **Trains**

Locusts
McKay, C. Homing Swallows.

London, England
Angelou. London.

Loneliness
Angelou. Greyday.
  Traveler, The.
Baraka. As a Possible Lover.
Brooks, G. Empty woman took toys! The.
  Preacher: Ruminates behind the Sermon, The.
  Sunset of the City, A.
Brown, S. Revelations.
Clifton, L. More than once.
Cortez. Lonely Woman.
Dove, R. Catherine of Siena.

Duke, B. Poem to the World.
Dunbar, P. Lonesome.
  Memory of Martha, The.
  My Lady of Castle Grand.
Giovanni. Alone.
  Balances.
  Cotton Candy on a Rainy Day.
  For a Lady of Pleasure Now Retired.
  Habits.
  I'm not lonely.
  Master Charge Blues.
  Night.
  Poem (For BMC No. 2).
  World Is Not a Pleasant Place to Be, The.
Hughes, L. Desert.
  Dressed Up.
  Empty House.
  50–50.
  God.
  Hope: "Sometimes when I'm lonely."
  Kid in the Park.
  Little Song.
  Lonesome Corner.
  Miss Blues'es Child.
  One.
  Poem: "I loved my friend."
  Seven Moments of Love.
  Stony Lonesome.
  Stranger in Town.
Jordan, J. One Minus One Minus One.
  Romance in Irony.
Jordan, N. When A Woman Gets Blue.
Knight, E. Poem to Galway Kinnell, A.
Komunyakaa. Thorn Merchant's Wife, The.
  When Loneliness Is a Man.
Linden, M. Lonely World.
Lorde. Keyfoods.
  Sister Outsider.
Madhubuti. In the Interest of Black Salvation.
McElroy, C. In My Mother's Room.
McKay, C. On Broadway.
Nelson, M. No Jazz.
Randall, D. Old Witherington.
Rodgers, C. One.
  Poem for Some Black Women.
  What Color Is Lonely.
Salaam. "5 Minutes, Mr. Salam."
Sanchez, S. Away from you these.
  Summary.
Unknown. Hard Times Blues.
Walker, A. He said: I want you to be happy.
Wright, J. Lake in Central Park, The.
Young, A. Dance for Aging Hipsters, A.
  Hallucinogenic Halleluuuu.
  Loneliness.
  Making Love After Hours.
  Physics of Loneliness, The.
  Rediscovered Diary Entry.
  Topsy: Part 2.
See also **Absence; Isolation; Separation**

Longfellow, Henry Wadsworth
Ray, H. Longfellow.

Longing
Angelou. Savior.
Baraka. To a Publisher .. Cut-out.
Brooks, G. To be in love.
Brown, S. Long Track Blues.
Clifton, L. Climbing.
Cowdery. Longings.
Cullen, C. Lament: "Now let all lovely things
  embark."
  To the Swimmer.
Dove, R. Boccaccio: The Plague Years.
Dunbar, P. Longing.
Giovanni. And sometimes i sit.
  Cotton Candy on a Rainy Day.
  Crutches.
  December of My Springs, The.
  Sky Diving.
  World Is Not a Pleasant Place to Be, The.
  You Came, Too.
Grimké, A. When the Green Lies over the
  Earth.
Harper, F. I thirst, but earth cannot allay.
Duriel. But There Are Miles.
Hayden, R. Ballad of Sue Ellen Westerfield,
  The.

Hughes, L. Afro-American Fragment.
Letter to Anne, A.
To Midnight Nan at Leroy's.
Wide River.
Yesterday and Today.
Jordan, J. Poem for Derrick Gilbert.
Poem # One.
Relativity.
Romance in Irony.
Sonnet for A.B.T., A.
Knight, E. I And Your Eyes.
Lorde. Between Ourselves.
Change of Season.
Echo.
From the House of Yemanjá.
Memorial II.
Sowing.
There Are No Honest Poems about Dead
Women.
To Martha: a New Year.
To the Girl Who Lives In a Tree.
Vigil.
Marie. Dream Fix.
McKay, C. Absence.
I shall return again. I shall return.
Summer Morn in New Hampshire.
Nelson, M. Behind a Descartes Bumpersticker.
Parable of the Moth.
Oden. Private Letter to Brazil, A.
Randall, D. Souvenirs.
Ray, H. Dawn of Love, The.
Sanchez, S. Last Poem I'm Gonna Write Bout
Us.
Sequences.
Stephany. Who is not a stranger still.
Turner, D. Love.
Walker, A. Will.
Young, A. Maya.
Zu-Bolton. Sister Blues with Livewire Davis.

Lookout Mountain, Battle of (1863)
Hayden, R. On Lookout Mountain.

Loons
Harper, M. Loon.

Los Angeles, California
African-American Oral Tradition. L.A. Street.
Rivers, C. Watts.
Vibe. L. A. (Lost Assholes).

Loss
Angelou. Loss of love and youth, The.
No Loser, No Weeper.
Prelude to a Parting.
Baraka. American Ecstasy.
Crow Jane the Crook.
This Is the Clearing I Once Spoke of.
Brooks, G. Appendix to the Anniad.
Brown, Adwin. Donut Man.
Clifton, L. Earth.
Poem for My Sisters.
So close / they come so close.
Speaking of Loss.
To Ms. Ann.
Cowdery. Farewell: "No more / The feel of
your hand."
Cullen, C. Lament: "Now let all lovely things
embark."
Sonnet: "I know now how a man whose blood
is hot."
Therefore, Adieu.
Threnody for a Brown Girl.
Variations on a Theme.
Wind Bloweth Where It Listeth, The.
Dove, R. Exeunt the Viols.
Dunbar, P. Golden Day, A.
Ione.
Jilted.
Wraith, The.
Yesterday and Tomorrow.
Evans, M. Where Have You Gone?
Giovanni. I'm not lonely.
Master Charge Blues.
Poem on the Assassination of Robert F.
Kennedy, A.
Rose Bush, The.
Turning (I Need a Better Title).
You were gone.
Graham, D. Portrait of Johnny Doller, A.
Handy, W. Joe Turner Blues.

Harper, F. Aunt Chloe.
Light in Darkness.
Harper, M. Alice Braxton Johnson.
Conferences with the Unknown.
Drowning of the Facts of a Life, The.
Ode to Tenochtitlan.
Hayden, R. Road in Kentucky, A.
Horton, G. Close of Life, The.
Horse Stolen from the Camp, The.
To Eliza.
Hughes, L. Cora.
Homecoming.
Lament over Love.
Pictures to the Wall.
Young Gal's Blues.
Jordan, J. On a New Year's Eve.
Kaufman, B. Cross Winds.
Early Loves.
Falling.
Klein, S. Fragments from the Diary of Amelie
Patiné, Quadroon Mistress of Monsieur
Jacques R-------.
Knight, E. Feeling Fucked/Up Up.
No moon floods the memory of that night.
Komunyakaa. After Summer Fell Apart.
Annabelle.
When Loneliness Is a Man.
Lorde. Eulogy for Alvin Frost.
Gemini.
Ghost.
Girlfriend.
Harriet there was always somebody calling us
crazy.
Lunar Eclipse.
Mawu.
Scar.
Seasoning.
Separation.
Sister, Morning Is a Time for Miracles.
Songless Lark, The.
Suffer the Children.
McKay, C. Adolescence.
Desolate.
Outcast.
Nelson, M. Letter to a Benedictine Monk.
Oden. Testament of Loss.
Reed, I. But Nobody Was There.
Reese, S. Letter from a Wife.
Sanchez, S. Father and Daughter.
Smith, P. Building Nicole's Mama.
Snellings. Earth.
Sundiata. Open Heart.
Taylor, Cheryl. English Lace.
Walker, A. Walker.
WEEMS. Dime after Dime.
Wright, J. Frightened Lover's Sleep, The.
Young, A. Afraid.

Louis, Joe (Joseph Louis Barrow)
Hughes, L. Joe Louis is a man.

Louisiana (state)
Brown, S. Let us suppose him differently
placed.
Louisiana Pastoral.
Uncle Joe.
Dent. Return to English Turn.
Komunyakaa. Landscape for the Disappeared.

Lowell, Amy
Cullen, C. Epitaph: "She leans across a golden
table."

Loyalty
Brown, S. Sharecroppers.
Clifton, L. Listen children / keep this in the
place.
Harper, F. Ruth and Naomi.
Hughes, L. Big Buddy, Big Buddy.

Luck
Angelou. On Aging.
Corrothers. De Black Cat Crossed His Luck.
Der Rabbit's Foot.
Dunbar, P. Way T'ings Come, De.
Hughes, L. Bad Luck Card.
403 Blues.
Hard Luck.
Luck.
Reed, I. Untitled II.
Young, A. Friday the 12th.

See also **Chance; Fate; Fortune**

Lullabies
Bennett, G. Secret.
Davis, D. Aunt Chloe's Lullaby.
Kaufman, B. Response.

See also **Cradle Song in Title, First Line, and
Last Line Index**

Lumbering and Lumbermen
Brown, S. Coolwell Vignette.

Lumumba, Patrice
Hughes, L. Lumumba's Grave ("Lumumba
was black").

Lunch
Hughes, L. Lunch in a Jim Crow Car.

Lust
Adams, Jenoyne. Out-of-Body Experience.
Baraka. Death Is Not as Natural as You Fags
Seem to Think.
New Sheriff, The.
New World, The.
Clifton, L. There Is a Girl Inside.
Emanuel, J. Sixteen, Yeah.
Johnson, J. White Witch, The.
Jordan, J. Double Standard Lifestyle Studies:
#1.
Roman Poem Number Eight.
Sunflower Sonnet Number One.
Kaufman, B. Does the Secret Mind Whisper?
Round about Midnight.
Komunyakaa. For the Walking Dead.
Gloria's Clues.
Le Xuan, Beautiful Spring.
Thorn Merchant's Son, The.
Lorde. Hard Love Rock #II.
Madhubuti. Reflections on a Lost Love.
Nelson, M. Balance.
Diverne's Waltz.
Marriage Nightmare, The.
No Jazz.
Rodgers, C. Now Ain't That Love?
Sanchez, S. Poem for My Father, A.
To All Brothers.
Shange. Lizard Series, The.
Stuckey. Southern Belle.
Toney. In the Twilight.
Walker, A. She said: "When I was with him."
Young, A. Flirt.

See also **Desire; Erotic Love; Sex**

Lutes
Dunbar, P. Thou art my lute, by thee I sing.

Lutheranism
Nelson, M. Churchgoing.

Lynching
Brown, S. Bad, Bad Man, A.
Call for Barnum.
Frankie and Johnny.
He Was a Man.
Sam Smiley.
Dunbar-Nelson. April is on the way!
Durem. I Know I'm Not Sufficiently Obscure.
Emanuel, J. Emmett Till.
Evans, M. I Am a Black Woman.
Freeman, C. I saw them lynch festus whiteside
and.
Harper, F. Lake City Tragedy, The.
Hayden, R. Night, Death, Mississippi.
Hill, L. So Quietly.
Hughes, L. Blue Bayou.
Flight.
Lynching Song.
Silhouette.
Song for a Dark Girl.
Southern Mammy Sings.
Jeffers, L. Tuskegee, Tuskegee!
Lorde. Afterimages.
Matthews, D. Lynching, The.
McKay, C. Lynching, The.
Moorer. Eutawville Lynching, The.
Lynching.
Retribution.
Moss, T. Lynching, The.
St. John, P. Lynching and Burning.
Stuckey. Let them come / As they usually do
by night.
Toomer. Portrait in Georgia.

Wright, R.   Between the World and Me.
See also **Hanging**

M

Machines
Komunyakaa.   1984.
Unknown.   John Henry.
When John Henry was a little babe.

Madness
Baraka.   Betancourt.
Das Kapital.
Preface to a Twenty Volume Suicide Note.
Snake Eyes.
Clifton, L.   For the Mad.
I am high on the man called crazy.
Perhaps.
Dove, R.   Great Uncle Beefheart.
Griffin, E.   Mind of a Madman kills.
Harper, M.   Dreams: American.
Kaufman, B.   Inside Connie.
Under Weight Champion, The.
Would You Wear My Eyes?
Knight, E.   Dead. He died in Detroit, his
beard.
Komunyakaa.   Beast & Burden: Seven
Improvisations, The.
Beg Song.
Cage Walker, The.
Looking a Mad Dog Dead in the Eyes.
1938.
Reed, I.   Inside Track, The.
Invasion.
Petite Kid Everett.
Report of the Reed Commission.
This Poetry Anthology I'm Reading.
Sanchez, S.   I paraplegic.
Shange.   Elegance in the extreme.
Toomer.   Delivered at the Knighting of Lord
Durgling by Great Bruce-Jean.
Tucker, M.   Crazed.
Weaver, M.   Appaloosa, The.
Young, A.   Madness.
Reading Nijinsky's Diary.
See also **Mental Illness**

Madrid, Spain
Wright, J.   Madrid.
Young, A.   I Arrive In Madrid.
Madrid 1963: Some Changes.

Magazines
Reed, I.   Atlantic Monthly, December 1970,
The.
See also **Journalism and Journalists**

Magi
Hughes, L.   Carol of the Brown King.
On a Pallet of Straw.
McKay, C.   Wise Men of the East, The.

Magic
Baraka.   Ka 'Ba.
Brown, S.   Conjured.
Lorde.   Death Dance for a Poet.
Fantasy and Conversation.
Neighbors.
Summer Oracle.
Reed, I.   Black Cock, The.
Sermonette.
Sanchez, S.   Black Magic.
Magic.
Unknown.   Another Man Done Gone.
You May Go But This Will Bring You Back.

Magnolias
Hughes, L.   Magnolia Flowers.

Mail and Mailmen
Tucker, M.   Mail Has Come, The.
See also **Letters**

Maine (state)
Toomer.   Merl.

Malaysia
Hughes, L.   Last Prince of the East.

Malcolm X (Malcolm Little)
Alba.   For Malcolm X.
Baraka.   Poem for Black Hearts, A.
Barrax.   For Malcolm: After Mecca.
Brooks, G.   Malcolm X.

Clifton, L.   Malcolm.
Conyus.   Confession to Malcolm.
Foreman.   Judgement Day: For Big Red the
Darwinian Doge. R.I.P.
Giovanni.   Atrocities.
Harper, M.   Dead-Day: Malcolm, Feb. 21.
Malcolm's Blues.
Hayden, R.   El-Hajj Malik El-Shabazz.
Henderson, D.   They Are Killing All the
Young Men.
Hughes, L.   Stokely Malcolm Me.
Jackmon.   That Old Time Religion.
Jackson, M.   I Remember ("I remember /
January, / 1968").
Joans.   My Ace of Spades.
Jones, L. *et al.*   Poem for Black Hearts, A.
Kgositsile.   Awakening, The.
Brother Malcolm's Echo.
When Brown Is Black.
Knight, E.   For Malcolm, a Year After.
It was a funky deal.
Portrait of Malcolm X.
Sun came, Miss Brooks—, The.
Lawrence, J.   For Malcolm.
Llorens.   One Year Ago.
Madhubuti.   Malcolm Spoke / Who Listened?
Possibilities: Remembering Malcolm X.
Neal, L.   Malcolm X—an Autobiography.
Morning Raga for Malcolm.
Patterson, R.   At That Moment.
Plumpp.   Half Black, Half Blacker.
Rivers, C.   If Blood is Black Then Spirit
Neglects My Unborn Son.
Sanchez, S.   Malcolm.
Spriggs.   For Brother Malcolm.
Troupe.   For Malcolm Who Walks in the Eyes
of Our Children.
Walker, A.   Abduction of Saints, The.
Malcolm.
Walker, M.   Five Black Men.
For Malcolm X.
Young, A.   Malcolm's Message.

Mandela, Nelson
Jordan, J.   To Free Nelson Mandela.
Lorde.   Evening News, The.
Sharp, S.   Finding His Fist.
Watkins, N.   Missions and Magnolias.

**Mandela, Winnie (Nomzano Zaniewe
Winnifred)**
Watkins, N.   Missions and Magnolias.

Mangoes
Adisa.   Cultural Trip, A.
Bethune, L.   Today Tutu Is Beating the Same
Burru As Me.
Nelson, M.   Canticle for Abba Jacob, A.

Mankind. *See* **Humankind**

Mantle, Mickey
Miller, E.   Players.

Maps
Oden.   Map, The.
Private Letter to Brazil, A.

March
Dunbar, P.   My Little March Girl.
Ray, H.   March.

Marching and Marches
Rykard.   Whole Two Weeks After the Million
Man March; and Still, if You Asked Me
about It, This Is All I Could Say about It, A.
See also **Parades**

Marijuana
African-American Oral Tradition.   Cocaine
Nell.
Life of a Junkie.
Strange, Strange Things.
Coleman, W.   In This Waking.
Gilmore, B.   Hazing.
Hughes, L.   Gauge.
Jackson, M. L.   Blunts.
Knight, E.   As You Leave Me.

Markets
Dumas, H.   Knees of a Natural Man.
Forbes, C.   Potlicker Blues.
Goodison.   Kenscoff.
Hughes, L.   Grocery Store.
Lorde.   Keyfoods.
Signs.

St. John, P.   Pearle's Poem.

Marriage
African-American Oral Tradition.   Don't Feel
So Downhearted, Buddy.
Don't Look So Downhearted, Buddy.
Ai.   Twenty-Year Marriage.
Brooks, G.   Bronzeville Mother Loiters in
Mississippi. / Meanwhile, a Mississippi
Mother Burns Bacon.
Old-Marrieds, The.
To be in love.
Cassells.   These Are Not Brushstrokes.
Clifton, L.   Now my first wife never did come
out of her room.
Wife.
Cullen, C.   Wind Bloweth Where It Listeth,
The.
Derricotte.   Promise, The.
Dove, R.   Beauty and the Beast.
Kadava Kumbis Devise a Way to Marry for
Love, The.
Promises.
Refrain.
Dunbar, P.   Bridal Measure, A.
Encouragement.
Emanuel, J.   Wedding Procession, from a
Window.
Fordham.   Marriage.
Harper, M.   Elvin's Blues.
Horton, G.   Cheerless Condition of
Bachelorship, The.
Connubial Felicity.
Hughes, L.   Ballad of Little Sallie.
Broke.
Jackson, R.   Jamal's Lamentation.
Lanusse.   Le Carnaval.
Linden, M.   Marriage Vow.
Madhubuti.   Pains with a Light Touch.
Union of Two, The.
McElroy, C.   Caledonia.
McKay, C.   Wild Goat, The.
Nelson, M.   Bali Hai Calls Mama.
Oden.   Man White, Brown Girl and All That
Jazz.
St. John, P.   Ocean of the Streams of Story.
Unknown.   Slave Marriage Ceremony
Supplement.
Walker, F.   Wishbone.
Walker, M.   Long John Nelson and Sweetie
Pie.
Young, A.   Two A.M.
See also **Husbands; Weddings; Wives**

Marshes
Dove, R.   Delft.

Martial Arts
Angelou.   Love Letter.

Martyrs
Harper, F.   Artist, The.
Hughes, L.   Kids Who Die.
Lawrence, J.   For Malcolm.
Rivera, E.   Elegy for a Martyred Poet.
Walker, A.   They who feel death close as a
breath.
Walker, M.   For Andy Goodman—Michael
Schwerner—and James Chaney.
Wheatley, P.   On the Death of Mr. Snider
Murder'd by Richardson.

Marx, Karl
Hughes, L.   White Man.
Lorde.   Workers Rose on May Day or
Postscript to Karl Marx, The.
Walker, M.   Giants of My Century.

Mary, Blessed Virgin
Angelou.   Avec Merci, Mother.
Brooks, G.   Penitent Considers Another
Coming of Mary, A.
Clifton, L.   Anna Speaks of the Childhood of
Mary Her Daughter.
Astrologer Predicts at Mary's Birth, The.
Holy Night.
Island Mary.
Mary.
Mary   mary astonished by God.
Mary's Dream.
Song of Mary, A.
Hughes, L.   Christmas Story, The.

Steptoe. Sweet Brown Rice and Red Bones.
Stewart, James T. Poem: "We drank Thunderbird all night."
Thompson, D. Laurel Street, 1950.
Walcott. Glory Trumpeter, The.
Village Life, A.
Walker, M. Birmingham.
Dear are the names that charmed me in my youth.
Weaver, M. Easy Living.
Wheatley, P. On Recollection.
Recollection.
Wright, J. Albuquerque Graveyard, The.
End of Ethnic Dream, The.
Young, A. City Home Detroit.
Dancing Together.
East Boston.
Fort Collins, Colorado.
Hawk Revsited, The.
Hoboken Broken Down: A Hasty Recollection.
Houston in October.
Lesson.
Not Her, She Aint No Gypsy.
Old Light.
Poem for Willard Motley, A.
Young, K. Preserving, The.
Zu-Bolton. Ain't No Spring Chicken.

Memphis, Tennessee
Brown, S. Memphis Blues.
Handy, W. Beale Street Blues.
Hughes, L. Gypsy Man.
Knight, E. Memo #43.
Snyder, T. Beale Street, Memphis.

Men
Ai. Before You Leave.
Angelou. In my Missouri.
Man Bigot.
Men.
Son to Mother.
To a Man.
Baraka. Tone Poem.
Barlow, G. Place Where He Arose, The.
Brooks, G. Independent Man, The.
Strong Men, Riding Horses / Lester after the Western.
Clifton, L. Running across to the lot.
Wishes for Sons.
Crouch, S. Chops Are Flyin.
Gilbert, C. Beginning by Value.
Giovanni. Beautiful Black Men.
Gus.
Handy, W. St. Louis Blues.
Holiday. Fine and Mellow.
Hughes, L. Addition: "Put 5 and 5 together."
Bad Man.
Gypsy Man.
Iverem. Daddy's Friends.
Jordan, J. Deliza Questioning Perplexities.
Memo.
Knight, E. On Seeing the Black Male as #1 Sex Object in America.
Komunyakaa. Beast & Burden: Seven Improvisations, The.
Moonshine.
Rocks Push.
Lorde. Hard Love Rock #II.
Seventh Sign, The.
Touring.
Madgett. Black Woman.
Madhubuti. Black Manhood: Toward a Definition.
McKay, C. St. Isaac's Church, Petrograd.
Queen Latifah. Evil That Men Do, The.
Rainey. See See Rider, see what you done done!
Randall, D. George.
Roberson. Eclipse.
True we are two grown men.
Rykard. Whole Two Weeks After the Million Man March; and Still, if You Asked Me about It, This Is All I Could Say about It, A.
Sanchez, S. Poem of Praise, A.
Prelude to Nothing.
To All Sisters.
Sharp, S. In the Tradition of Bobbitt.
Troupe. Reflections on Growing Older.

Unknown. Railroad Bill, Railroad Bill.
Stackolee.
Walker, A. Did This Happen to Your Mother? Did Your Sister Throw Up a Lot?
Waters, M. Hoochie Coochie.
Williams, S. She Had Known Brothers.

Menopause
Cook, W. Seth Bingham.

Menstruation
Coleman, W. Doing Battle with the Wolf.
Dove, R. After Reading *Mickey in the Night Kitchen* for the Third Time Before Bed.
Lorde. To Marie, in Flight.
Trethewey. Drapery Factory, Gulfport, Mississippi, 1956.

Mental Illness
Herton. Madhouse.
Hughes, L. Neighbor.
Knight, E. Hard Rock Returns to Prison from the Hospital for the Criminal Insane.
Sanchez, S. Prelude to Nothing.
Williams, Niama. Meaning of the Smell of Sweat, The.

See also **Madness**

Mercenaries
Hughes, L. Poet to Patron.

Merchants
Hughes, L. Likewise.
Mexican Market Woman.

See also **Business and Businesspeople**

Mercy
"Ada." Lines.
Angelou. On a bright day, next week.
Harper, F. Behold the lilies of the field.
Maceo dead! a thrill of sorrow.
Mother's Blessing, The.
Hughes, L. Feet O' Jesus.
Litany: "Gather up / In the arms of your pity."
Johnson, F. Singing Hallelujia.
Stanard. Spirits Struggle.
Wheatley, P. On Being Brought from Africa to America.

Mermaids and Mermen
Fields, J. Madness One Monday Evening.
Hughes, L. Catch.

Merry-Go-Rounds
Hughes, L. Merry-Go-Round.
Oden. Carousel, The.

Messiah
Brooks, G. In Emanuel's Nightmare: Another Coming of Christ.

Metaphor
Williams, S. S. Recitation.

See also **Symbols**

Mexico
Coleman, W. Las Turistas Negras Grande.
Dove, R. Night Watch.
Harper, M. Remember Mexico.
Reed, I. El Paso Monologue.
Shange. Lizard Series, The.
Young, A. Absent from the United States.
Going Back Home.
Moon Watching by Lake Chapala.

Mexico City
Young, A. Malagueña Salerosa.
Mexico City Lover.
Ponce de León: A Morning Walk.

Mice
Hughes, L. Silly Animals.
Moorer. Legal Mouse, A.

Microbes
Giovanni. Love: Is a Human Condition.

Middle Age
Clifton, L. Thirty-eighth year, The.
Thompson, D. Dancing in Menopause.
Laurel Street, 1950.
Tucker, M. First Grey Hair, The.
Young, A. Fifty-Fifty.
Mid-Life Crises: A Critical Review.

See also **Aging**

Middle Passage
Harper, F. Death of the Old Sea King.
Harper, M. Bristol: Bicentenary Remembrances of Trade.

See also **Slavery**

Midnight
Fields, J. No Time for Poetry.
Hughes, L. Jam Session.
Lenox Avenue.
Kaufman, B. Round about Midnight.
Komunyakaa. Boat People.
Lane, P. Midnight Song.
Sanchez, S. I wish it were mid.

Migration
Brown, S. Bessie.
Hughes, L. Migration.
New Yorkers.
Lane, P. Migration.
Weaver, M. Brooklyn.

Militarism
Cortez. Expenditures; Economic Love Song 1.
Stockpiling of frozen trees, The.
Stuckey. Defense.

Mills and Millers
Hughes, L. Steel Mills.

Milton, John
Ray, H. Milton.

Milwaukee, Wisconsin
Young, A. Beauty of Milwaukee cold with rain, The.

Mind
Reed, I. There's a whale in my thigh. at.

See also **Intellect and Intellectuals; Reason; Thought**

Mingus, Charles
Troupe. One for Charlie Mingus.

Mining and Miners
Allen, S. About Poetry and South Africa.
Dunbar, P. Gourd, The.
Hughes, L. Johannesburg Mines.
Walker, M. Childhood.

See also **Coal Mining and Coal Miners**

Minstrels
Mullen, H. Bête Noire.

Miracles
Bontemps. Miracles.
Gilbert, D. Miracle.
Lorde. Martha this is a catalog of days.
Nelson, M. Abba Jacob and Miracles.
Epithalamium and Shivaree.
Smith, G. Penitential Cries of Jupiter Hammond, The.

See also **Faith Healers**

Mirages
Hayden, R. Mirages, The.

Mirrors
Dunbar, P. Looking-Glass, The.
Giovanni. Mirrors.
Hemphill. Family Jewels.
Lorde. Good Mirrors are Not Cheap.
Memorial II.
Nelson, M. Strange beautiful woman, A.
Reed, I. Beware: Do Not Read This Poem.
Troupe. Sense of Coolness, A.

Misanthropy
Whitfield. Misanthropist, The.

Misfortune
Angelou. Memory, The.
Brown, S. Pardners.
Salutamus.
Strange Legacies.
Corrothers. De Black Cat Crossed His Luck.
Hughes, L. Juliet.
Lorde. Out of the Wind.
Reed, I. Untitled II.

Misogyny
African-American Oral Tradition. Cocaine Nell.
Hickory wood is the best of wood.
Hobo Ben.
Life of a Junkie.
Motherfuck a woman lay flat on her back.
Treacherous Breast.
Lorde. Need: A Chorale for Black Woman Voices.

Missionaries
Johnson, H. Magalu.
Linden, M. Missionary, The.

Moorer. Africa.

Mississippi (state)
Angelou. In my Missouri.
Brooks, G. Bronzeville Mother Loiters in
   Mississippi. / Meanwhile, a Mississippi
   Mother Burns Bacon.
Crouch, S. No New Music.
Dumas, H. Son of Msippi.
Ellis, K. Phantom Pains.
Emanuel, J. Church Burning: Mississippi.
Hayden, R. Night, Death, Mississippi.
Hughes, L. Mississippi.
Knight, E. Once on a Night in the Delta: A
   Report From Hell.
Poem for Myself (Or Blues for a Mississippi
   Black Boy), A.
Miller, E. Mississippi.
Plumpp. Mississippi Griot.
Walker, M. Delta.
Jackson, Mississippi.
My Mississippi Spring.
Ode on the Occasion of the Inauguration of
   the Sixth President of Jackson State College.
Wonder. Living for the City.
Wright, J. Invitation to Madison County, An.
Young, A. Birthday Poem.

Mississippi River
Brown, S. Children of the Mississippi.
Crossing.
Riverbank Blues.
Dove, R. Someone's Blood.
Hayden, R. Night, Death, Mississippi.
Hughes, L. Mississippi Levee.
Lorde. St. Louis Out of Time.
Steptoe. Mississippi Blues.
Sundiata. Making Poems.

Missouri (state)
Angelou. In my Missouri.
Knight, E. Poem to Galway Kinnell, A.

Missouri River
Brown, S. Foreclosure.

Mist
Dunbar, P. Misty Day, A.
See also **Fog**

Mistletoe
Tucker, M. Mistletoe.

Mistresses
Angelou. They went home and told their
   wives.
Komunyakaa. Thorn Merchant's Mistress, The.
Lorde. Barren.
Nelson, M. Ballad of Aunt Geneva, The.
Saint Preaches, The.

Misunderstanding
Gaye. What's Going On.
Hughes, L. Maybe.
Present.
Troubled Water.
Lorde. Black unicorn is greedy, The.
Fallen, The.
Hard Love Rock #II.
Sister, Morning Is a Time for Miracles.
Reed, I. If My Enemy Is a Clown, a Natural
   Born Clown.

Mittens
Hughes, L. Winter Sweetnes.
See also **Gloves**

Mobility
Jordan, J. Roman Poem Number Nine.

Mockingbirds
Fordham. To the Mock-Bird.
Hayden, R. Mourning Poem for the Queen of
   Sunday.
Heard, J. My Mocking Bird.
Henderson, E. B. Uncle Ned an' de Mockin'
   Bird.

Moderation
Cullen, C. Song in Spite of Myself.

Modern Man
Balagon. Children of the Cosmos.
Baraka. Bronze Buckaroo, The.
End of Man Is His Beauty, The.
Green Lantern's Solo.
Poem for Democrats, A.
Political Poem.
Three Movements and a Coda.

Cruz, V. O. K. / you scat taking.
Dumas, H. Tis of Thee.
Forbes, C. Blue Monday.
Foreman. Judgement Day: For Big Red the
   Darwinian Doge. R.I.P.
Harper, M. Prayer: Mt. Hood and Environs.
Harris, P. Let's Take All the Blame.
Hughes, L. In Explanation of Our Times.
Jordan, J. Famine.
From Sea to Shining Sea.
Menu.
On the Loss of Energy.
What Is This in Reference To? or We Must
   Get Together Sometime Soon!
Kaufman, B. Benediction.
Heavy Water Blues.
On yardbird corners of embryonic hopes,
   drowned in a heroin tear.
Tidal Friction ... Comments at Real Movie.
Komunyakaa. 1984.
Lorde. Lightly.
Soho Cinema.
Solstice.
Madhubuti. Change Is Not Always Progress.
Killing Memory.
Randall, D. Primitives.
Reed, I. Decade That Screamed, The.
Jackal-Headed Cowboy, The.
Katskills Kiss Romance Goodbye, The.
Report of the Reed Commission.
Walker, M. On Youth and Age II.
Young, A. Myth Science of Our Time, The.
See also **Humankind**

Modesty
Harper, F. Report.

Moloch
Garnet. Down let the shrine of Moloch sink.

Monarchy
Wheatley, P. To the King's Most Excellent
   Majesty, 1768.
To the King's Most Excellent Majesty on His
   Repealing the American Stamp Act.

Monasteries
Nelson, M. Clown Nose.
Fish and Floor-Dust Bouquet.
See also **Monks**

Monday
Fields, J. Madness One Monday Evening.
Hughes, L. Blue Monday.

Monet, Claude
Hayden, R. Monet's "Waterlilies."
Kaufman, B. Bird with Painted Wings.

Money
African-American Oral Tradition. Down and
   Out.
If You See My Little Girl in Denver.
Lady Liberty.
Once I lived the life of a millionaire.
Baraka. Bludoo Baby, Want Money, and
   Alligator Got It to Give.
Brooks, G. Maxie Allen always taught her.
Brown, S. New Congo, The.
Rent Day Blues.
Street Car Gang.
Dumas, H. America.
Dunbar, P. Real Question, The.
Horton, G. Creditor to His Proud Debtor, The.
Woodman and the Money Hunter, The.
Hughes, L. Ballad of the Miser.
Dancer.
50–50.
Green Memory.
If-ing.
Little Lyric (of Great Importance).
Paint.
Request.
What?
Wooing, A.
Johnson, F. Minister, The.
Jordan, J. Financial Planning.
Young, A. Romance Without Finance.

Monk, Thelonius Sphere
Baraka. Wise 4.
Jackson, R. 63rd and Broadway.
Thelonious.
Komunyakaa. Elegy for Thelonious.

Salaam. Always Know.
Touré, A. Rebellion Suite.

Monkeys
African-American Oral Tradition. Partytime
   Monkey.
Poolshooting Monkey: "I don't know but I
   was told."
Poolshooting Monkey: "It was in Speero's
   poolroom back in nineteen-ten."
Poolshooting Monkey: "It was in Speero's
   poolroom in the year eighteen-ten."
Signifying Monkey: "Back down in the jungle
   up under the stick."
Signifying Monkey: "Deep down in the jungle
   in the coconut grove."
Signifying Monkey: "Down in the jungle about
   treetop deep."
Signifying Monkey: "It was early in the
   morning one bright summer day."
Signifying Monkey: "Say deep down in the
   jungle in the coconut grove."
Signifying Monkey: "There hadn't been no
   shift for quite a bit."
Lorde. For the King and Queen of Summer.
Monkeyman.
Reed, I. Monkey Island.
Unknown. Signifying Monkey, The.

Monks
Dunbar, P. Monk's Walk, The.
Nelson, M. Letter to a Benedictine Monk.
See also **Clergy; Monasteries**

Monotony
Baraka. All's Well.
Horton, G. Snaps for Dinner, Snaps for
   Breakfast and Snaps for Supper.

Monsters
Cullen, C. To the Three for Whom the Book.
Dunbar, P. Boogah Man, The.
Hughes, L. Genius Child.
Mitchell, K. Monster, The.
See also **Demons**

Monuments
Hughes, L. Lincoln Monument: Washington.
Komunyakaa. Facing It.

Moods
Dunbar, P. Response.
Walker, A. Moody.

Moon
Braithwaite. Golden Moonrise.
Brooks, J. Last Quarter Moon of the Dying
   Year, The.
Dunbar, P. Lover and the Moon, The.
Giovanni. Moon shines down, The.
Hayden, R. Full Moon.
Hughes, L. Change.
In the mist of the moon I saw you.
Lullaby: "My little dark baby."
March Moon.
Moonlight Night: Carmel.
New Moon.
Winter Moon.
Knight, E. Haiku: "Under moon shadows."
Lorde. Gemini.
Maiden, The.
McKay, C. Plateau, The.
Song of the Moon, A.
Moore, L. Haiku: "Spring moonrise."
Popel. Theft.
Ray, H. Dawn of Love, The.
Vision of Moonlight, The.
Rushing. Sent for You Yesterday.
Salaam. Quarter Moon Rise.
Sanchez, S. What do i know of.
When i look at you.
Saunders, R. You Made It Rain.
Toomer. Beehive.
Washington. Moon Bound.
Young, A. Big ocean-waving, woman-pulling
   moon.
Carolina Moon.
Coastal Moon.
Dancing Pierrot.
Here in violet light.
Moon, How Do I Measure Up?
Moon of no return, never the same.
Moon Over Matter.

Moon, the Whole Moon, and Nothing but the Moon, The.
Moon Up Close in Winter by the Telescope, The.
Moon Watching by Lake Chapala.
Moonlessness.
Orchard at Night in Rain Light, The.
Pidgin Moon.
Sarajevo Moon.
Sarajevo Moonlight.
See, see, moon, O see what you done done.
Sing a Song of Singapore.
So is there life on you, moon?
Tutti Colori Quality of Light, The.
Waking Up in Santa Cruz at Sea.

Moors (people)
McKay, C. Tetuan.

Moose
Hayden, R. Moose Wallow, The.

Morning
Angelou. On the Pulse of Morning.
Baraka. Way Out West.
Cortez. In the Morning.
Dunbar, P. Barrier, The.
In the Morning.
Morning.
Morning Song of Love.
Fields, J. No Time for Poetry.
Heard, J. Matin Hymn.
Morn.
Horton, G. On the Evening and the Morning.
Hughes, L. Bad Morning.
Blues at Dawn.
Montmartre.
Johnson, H. What Do I Care for Morning.
Jordan, J. Morning on the mountains where the mist, The.
Kaufman, B. Cocoa Morning.
Knight, E. Boston 5:00 A.M.—10/74.
Haiku: "Morning sun slants cell."
Newsome. Mattinata.
Southerland. Recitation.
Young, A. Waking Up in Santa Cruz at Sea.
See also **Dawn**

Morocco
McKay, C. Farewell to Morocco, A.
Tetuan.

Mortality
Cullen, C. Epitaph: "She leans across a golden table."
Leaves.
Nothing endures, / Not even love.
Sonnet: "These are no wind-blown rumors, soft say-sos."
Dunbar, P. Mortality.
Hughes, L. Numbered.
Madgett. Mortality.
Unknown. Steal Away to Jesus.
What Yo' Gwine to [or t'] Do When Yo' [or de] Lamp Burn Down?
Young, A. Mountains of California: Part 2, The.

Moscow, Russia
Horton, G. Retreat from Moscow, The.
McKay, C. Moscow for many loving her was dead.

Moses
African-American Oral Tradition. Mary, don you weep an Marthie don you moan.
Allen, S. Harriet Tubman.
Bell, J. Modern Moses, or "My Policy" Man.
Clifton, L. Moses.
To a Dark Moses.
Harper, F. Burial of Moses, The.
Deliverance.
Moses: A Story of the Nile.
Unknown. Go down, Moses.

Mothers
Adisa. I Will Not Let Them Take You.
Angelou. Mothering Blackness, The.
Bennett, G. Secret.
Brooks, G. Jessie Mitchell's Mother.
Maxie Allen always taught her.
Mrs. Small went to the kitchen for her pocketbook.
Brown, S. Funeral.

Maumee Ruth.
Virginia Portrait.
Clemmons. Revelation.
Clifton, L. Admonitions.
Atlantic is a sea of bones.
If mama / could see.
In the Evenings.
Mary mary astonished by God.
Mother, i am mad.
My Mama moved among the days.
Poem on My Fortieth Birthday to My Mother Who Died Young.
Song of Mary, A.
Thirty-eighth year, The.
To the Unborn and Waiting Children.
Coleman, W. American Sonnet (10).
Dear Mama.
Cullen, C. Brown Girl Dead, A.
Tribute.
Derricotte. Christmas Eve: My Mother Dressing.
Touching/Not Touching: My Mother.
Dickey. Mulatto Lullaby.
Dove, R. After Reading *Mickey in the Night Kitchen* for the Third Time Before Bed.
Bird Frau, The.
Motherhood.
Pastoral.
Dumas, H. Afro-American.
Dunbar, P. Appreciation.
Scamp.
Turning of the Babies in the Bed, The.
Finney, N. Lobengula: Having a Son at 38.
Fordham. Mother's Recall.
To My Mother.
Giovanni. Hands; For Mother's Day.
Mothers.
Mother's Habits.
Goodison. I Am Becoming My Mother.
Govan. Recollection.
Gray-Kontar. Cuz' Mama Played Jazz.
Grimké. Angel's Visit, The.
Hamilton, M. Things I Do Not Speak.
Harper, F. Dying Mother, The.
Eliza Harris.
Mother's Heroism, A.
My mother's kiss, my mother's kiss.
Slave Mother, The: "Heard you that shriek? It rose."
Slave Mother, The: "I have but four, the treasures of my soul."
Harper, M. Kneading.
Mama's Report.
Hayden, R. Whipping, The.
Heard, J. Mother.
Hughes, L. Baby.
Mama and Daughter.
Mother in Wartime.
Mother to Son.
Negro Mother, The.
Iverem. Murmur.
Jackson, R. 1973.
Johnson, F. Lonely Mother, The.
Johnson, G. Motherhood.
Jordan, J. Ah, Momma, / Did the house ever know.
On the Spirit of Mildred Jordan.
Kgositsile. To Mother.
Knight, E. Report to the Mother.
Stretching of the Belly, The.
Lorde. Bazaar.
Black Mother Woman.
Coniagui women / wear their flesh like war, The.
Dear Toni Instead of a Letter of Congratulation.
From the House of Yemanjá.
Hanging Fire.
Home.
Now That I Am Forever with Child.
Pathways: From Mother to Mother.
To the Girl Who Lives In a Tree.
What my child learns of the sea.
Madgett. Offspring.
McElroy, C. In My Mother's Room.
Ruth.

McKay, C. December, 1919.
My Mother.
Miller, E. My Father's Girlfriend.
Moore, L. Haiku: "Black woman, A."
Mullen, H. Floorwax Mother.
Momma Sayings.
Nelson, M. Bali Hai Calls Mama.
Dream's Wisdom, The.
I Send Mama Home.
Levitation with Baby.
Lost Daughter, The.
Mama I remember.
Mama's Promise.
My Second Birth.
Nurigan. I'm raising CHILDREN.
Ray, H. To My Mother.
Rilke. Rilke's Third Elegy.
Rodgers, C. It Is Deep.
St. John, P. Pearle's Poem.
Sanchez, S. Summer Words of [or for] a Sistuh [or Sister] Addict.
Smith, P. Biting Back.
Spriggs. My Beige Mom.
Thompson, D. Laurel Street, 1950.
Trethewey. Hot Comb.
Tucker, M. My Mother's Voice.
Wheatley, P. Niobe in Distress for Her Children Slain by Apollo, from Ovid's Metamorphoses, Book VI, and from a View of the Painting of Mr. Richard Wilson.
Worley, D. Sandra.
Young, A. Moving, Merging, Fading, Standing Still.

Moths
Hughes, L. Fire-Caught.
Nelson, M. Parable of the Moth.

Motion
Reed, I. General Science.
Toomer. Earth.

Motion Pictures
Hayden, R. Double Feature.
Hughes, L. Lincoln Theatre.
Madam and the Movies.
Movies.
Jones, P. Why I Like Movies.
Reed, I. Poison Light.
Worley, D. Las Flores para una Niña Negra.
See also **Show Business**

Motorcycles and Motorcycling
Jordan, J. Speculations on the Present through the Prism of the Past.
Walker, A. Kiss, The.

Mountains
Bontemps. Golgotha Is a Mountain.
Hughes, L. Love Song for Lucinda.
Jordan, J. Morning on the mountains where the mist, The.
McClellan. Lines to Mount Glen.
Toomer. I sit in my room.
Young, A. Mountains of California: Part 1, The.
See also **Hills and Mountains**

Mourning and Mourners
Angelou. Mourning Grace.
Cornish, S. Death of Dr. King.
Dunbar, P. Easter Ode, An.
Weltschmertz.
Harper, M. Drowning of the Facts of a Life, The.
Hayden, R. Approximations.
Mourning Poem for the Queen of Sunday.
Hughes, L. To a Dead Friend.
Wake.
Johnson, J. Go Down Death.
Troupe. Day in the Life of a Poet, A.
Walker, A. Natural Star.
See also **Funerals**

Mouths
Toomer. Her Lips Are Copper Wire.

Movies. *See* **Motion Pictures**

Moving and Movers
Hughes, L. Moving.
Lorde. Moving In.
Moving Out Or the End of Cooperative Living.
Toomer. Reapers.

Mowing and Mowers
Komunyakaa. Work.
Toomer. Reapers.
Mozart, Wolfgang Amadeus
Lorde. Chorus.
Mud
Brown, S. Riverbank Blues.
Knight, E. Poem for Myself (Or Blues for a Mississippi Black Boy), A.
Weatherly. Mud Water Shango.
Mules
Hughes, L. Me and the Mule.
Plumpp. Another mule kicking.
Mummies
Sanchez, S. Love Poem Written for Sterling Brown, A.
Murder and Murderers
African-American Oral Tradition. Boothill McCoy.
Brock Hankton.
Derringer Youngblood, the jet-black nigger.
Dolomite: "Some folks say that Willie Green."
Dolomite first originated in San Antone.
Eddie Ledoux: "There's some strange and queer tales that come through all jails."
Eddie Ledoux: "Wise and queer tales float through all the jails."
Jesse James.
Lame and the Whore, The.
Nineteen Thirty-Two.
Pretty Pill.
Stackolee: "Back in forty-nine when times was hard."
Stackoloee: "I staggered in a place called the Bucket a Blood."
Stackolee: "It was back in the time of nineteen hundred and two."
Stackolee: "It was back in the year of forty-one when the times was hard."
Stackolee: "This is supposed to be about two colored studs. It's truth. In New Orleans."
Stackolee: "When I was young in my prime."
Stackolee in Hell.
Toledo Slim.
Ai. Kid, The.
Blue. American Dialogue.
Brooks, G. Bronzeville Mother Loiters in Mississippi. / Meanwhile, a Mississippi Mother Burns Bacon.
Brown, S. Break of Day.
Georgie Grimes, with a red suitcase.
Puttin' on Dog.
Sharecroppers.
Southern Cop.
Cortez. Rape.
Dodson, O. Signifying Darkness, The.
Dumas, H. Cuttin Down to Size.
Dunbar, P. Murdered Lover, The.
Emanuel, J. Panther Man.
Goncalves. Way It Is, The.
Harper, F. Martyr of Alabama, The.
Harper, M. Fireplace, The.
History as Cap'n Brown.
Hughes, L. Rent-Party Shout.
Joans. Scenery.
.38, The.
Jordan, J. For Michael Angelo Thompson.
Moving Towards Home.
Poem about Police Violence.
Test of Atlanta 1979, The.
To Free Nelson Mandela.
Kaufman, B. War Memoir: Jazz, Don't Listen to It at Your Own Risk.
Lee, D. Assassination.
Lorde. Need: A Chorale for Black Woman Voices.
Power.
Same Death Over and Over or Lullabies Are for Children, The.
Mason, K. Friday night / the bullet ripped.
Miller, E. You Send Me: Bertha Franklin, December 11, 1964.
Nelson, M. As Simple as That.
Photographs of the Medusa.
Pitcher. Salute.
Rainey. See See Rider, see what you done done!

Reed, I. Ballad of Charlie James, The.
Betty's Ball Blues.
Unknown. Frankie and Johnny were lovers.
Stackalee.
Walker, A. Family Of.
Killers.
1971.
Revolutionary Petunias.
Walker, M. For Andy Goodman—Michael Schwerner—and James Chaney.
Ward, P. She Should Have Called 911.
Wheatley, P. Niobe in Distress for Her Children Slain by Apollo, from Ovid's Metamorphoses, Book VI, and from a View of the Painting of Mr. Richard Wilson.
Wright, R. Between the World and Me.
Muses
Cullen, C. After a Visit.
Horton, G. On Hearing of the Intention of a Gentleman to Purchase the Poet's Freedom.
On the Poetic Muse.
To the Muse.
Hughes, L. Formula.
Nelson, M. Levitation with Baby.
Ray, H. Invocation to the Muse.
Thompson, P. Muse's Favor, The.
Walcott. Upstate.
Wheatley, P. Hymn to Humanity, An.
On Recollection.
Philis's Reply to the Answer in Our Last by the Gentleman in the Navy.
Recollection.
To Mæcenas.
Whitman, A. Poet hath a realm within, and throne, The.
Museums
Fields, J. Mr. Tut's House A Recollection.
Gilbert, C. African Sculpture.
Hughes, L. Metropolitan Museum.
Reed, I. Return of Julian the Apostate to Rome, The.
Music and Musicians
Alexander, E. Farewell to You.
Allen, G. To Melody.
Allen, S. To Satch.
Anderson, S. Sound of Afroamerican History Chapt II, The.
Atkins. Dark Area.
Baraka. Am/trak.
In the Tradition.
Reggae or Not!
Rhythm and Blues (I).
Symphony Sid.
Barlow, G. In My Father's House.
Resonance.
Barrax. Singer, The.
Braithwaite. To ———: "Half in the dim light from the hall."
Braxton, C. Jazzy St. Walk.
Say Hey Homeboy.
Brooks, G. Piano after War.
Third Sermon on the Warpland, The.
Brown, S. Ma Rainey.
Mose is black and evil.
Slim Greer.
When de Saints Go Ma'ching Home.
Browne, W. Harlem Sounds: Hallelujah Corner.
Campbell, J. 'Sciplinin' Sister Brown.
Cornish, S. His Fingers Seem to Sing.
Cortez. I See Chano Pozo.
Crouch, S. No New Music.
Cullen, C. Night Rain.
Singing in the Rain.
Davis, D. Miss Liza's Banjer.
Delegall. Psalm for Sonny Rollins.
Dent. For Lil Louis.
Ray Charles at Mississippi State.
Secret Messages.
Derricotte. Black Boys Play the Classics.
Blackbottom.
Dett. Rubinstein Staccato Etude, The.
Dove, R. Canary.
Definition in the Face of Unnamed Fury.
Event, The.
Jiving.
Left-Handed Cellist, The.

Musician Talks about "Process", The.
Robert Schumann, Or: Musical Genius Begins with Affliction.
Shakespeare Say.
Variation on Pain.
Dunbar-Nelson. Music! Lilting, soft and languorous.
Dunbar, P. Concert, The.
Corn-Stalk Fiddle, The.
Master-Player, The.
Musical, A.
Ol' Tunes, The.
Question, A.
Thou art my lute, by thee I sing.
To a Lady Playing the Harp.
Valse, The.
Virginia Reel, A.
Voice of the Banjo, The.
When Malindy Sings.
Emanuel, J. Get Up, Blues.
Sixteen, Yeah.
Evans, M. I Am a Black Woman.
Fabio. Hurt of It All, The.
Ferdinand. Blues (in Two Parts), The.
Gee. Black Music Man.
Giovanni. Geni in the Jar, The.
Revolutionary Music.
Three/Quarters Time.
Goodwin. Day a Dancer Learned to Sing of Dreamless Escapades, The.
Graham, D. Soul.
Graham, R. Learning to Dance.
Gray-Kontar. Cuz' Mama Played Jazz.
Harper, F. Songs for the People.
Harper, M. Dear John, Dear Coltrane.
Elvin's Blues.
For Bud.
Here Where Coltrane Is.
Mr. P. C.
Time for Tyner: Folksong.
Heard, J. Music.
Henderson, D. Boston Road Blues.
Egyptian Book of the Dead.
Neon Diaspora.
Hughes, L. Be-Bop Boys.
Boogie: 1 A.M.
Conservatory Student Struggles with Higher Instrumentation.
Daybreak in Alabama.
Dream Boogie: Variation.
Easy Boogie.
Imploring Mecca.
Juice Joint: Northern City.
Juke Box Love Song.
Ma Man.
Note in Music.
Note on Commercial Theatre.
Request for Requiems.
Trumpet Player.
Weary Blues, The.
When Sue Wears Red.
Jackson, R. Lady's Way.
Jacobs, H. And Sometimes I Hear This Song in My Head.
Jeffers, L. How High the Moon.
On Listening to the Spirituals.
Jenkins, C. Poem for Tracy (Chapman).
Johnson, F. Banjo Player, The.
Jordan, J. Newport Jazz Festival: Saratoga Springs and Especially about George Benson and Everyone Who Was Listening.
October 23, 1983.
Kaufman, B. Battle Report.
Blues Note.
Cocoa Morning.
His Horn.
Late Lamented Wind, Burned in Indignation, The.
Unanimity Has Been Achieved, Not a Dot Less for Its Accidentalness.
Kgositsile. Spirits Unchained.
Klein, S. Jelly Roll Morton.
Knight, E. As You Leave Me.
Haiku: "Piano man, The."
Komunyakaa. Copacetic Mingus.
Elegy for Thelonious.
Euphony.

February in Sydney.
More Girl Than Boy.
Lane, P. Lyric: I Am Looking at Music.
Madhubuti. Blackmusic / a Beginning.
Don't Cry, Scream.
Sun House.
McClane. Song: a Motion for History.
Moss, T. Landscape with Saxophonist.
Neal, L. Baroness and the Black Musician, The.
Don't say goodbye to the Porkpie Hat that rolled.
Harlem Gallery: From the Inside.
Nelson, M. Abba Jacob and the Angel.
Fortunate Spill, The.
It's All in Your Head.
Payne, D. May I not love the beauteous flow'rs.
Rahman. Transcendental Blues Transcendental Blues.
Randall, D. Langston Blues.
Ray, H. Perfect Orchestra, The.
Two Musicians, The.
Redmond. His Eminence Plays the Soular System.
Reed, I. Anon. Poster.
Home Sweet Earth.
Lake Bud.
Neo-HooDoo Manifesto.
Soul Proprietorship.
St. Louis Woman.
To a Daughter of Isaiah.
Rodgers, C. We Dance Like Ella Riffs.
Rux. Suite Repose.
Salaam. Always Know.
Danny Barker/Danny Banjo.
Secondline Send Off.
Sanchez, S. Old Words.
Shepherd, R. Lucky One, The.
Spellman. Did John's Music Kill Him?
John Coltrane: An Impartial Review.
Thomas, L. Historiography.
Onion Bucket.
Toure, A. O Mystic Light! A Mystic Sage Returns to Realms of Eternity.
Touré, A. Rebellion Suite.
Troupe. Avalanche.
Collage.
Impressions / of Chicago; For Howlin' Wolf.
Unknown. It Don't Mean a Thing (If It Ain't Got That Swing).
Walker, A. Hymn: "I well remember / A time when."
Weems. Return to Temptation.
Whitfield. Yes! strike again that sounding string.
Williams, Karen. Kissing Keys.
Williams, L. Flying High.
Wilson, Ted. Music of the Other World.
S, C, M.
Wright, J. End of Ethnic Dream, The.
What is Beautiful.
Young, A. Billie.
By Heart.
Dance of the Infidels.
Dexter Gordon at Keystone Korner.
From Bowling Green.
Jackie McLean: Alto Saxophone.
Jazz as Was.
Lester Leaps In.
Little More Traveling Music, A.
Moss.
No Trespassing.
Poem for Dylan Thomas, A.
Ravel: Bolero.
Selectric II.
Studio Up Over In Your Ear.
Thelonious: An Intro.
Tune.
See also Blues (music)
Music Festivals
Whitman, A. Lute of Afric's Tribe, The.
Mutiny
Whitfield. To Cinque.
Mystery
Angelou. Phenomenal Woman.
Brooks, G. God Works in a Mysterious Way.

Clifton, L. Mystery that surely is present, The.
Cullen, C. Yet Do I Marvel.
Dove, R. Particulars.
Hughes, L. Consider me, / A colored boy.
Johnson, F. Who Is That a-Walking in the Corn?
Kaufman, B. My mysteries created for me.
Lorde. Progress Report.
Nelson, M. Don't Throw Out Wine Bottles.
Young, A. Still Lives.
Mysticism
Young, A. New Mystic, The.
Mythology
Cullen, C. To the Three for Whom the Book.
Dunbar, P. Black Samson of Brandywine.
Toure, A. O Mystic Light! A Mystic Sage Returns to Realms of Eternity.
Wheatley, P. To Mæcenas.

N

Nagasaki, Japan
Clifton, L. I. At Nagasaki.
See also Atomic Bomb; Hiroshima, Japan; Nuclear War
Nakedness
Hughes, L. March Moon.
Names
Angelou. Calling of Names, The.
Brooks, G. Kojo "I Am a Black."
Brown, S. Elder Mistletoe.
Clifton, L. Light / on my mother's tongue.
Crouch, S. Riding Across John Lee's Finger.
Freeman, C. When / my uncle willie saw.
Giovanni. True Import of Present Dialogue, Black vs. Negro.
Harper, F. His Name.
Hayden, R. 'Mystery Boy' Looks for Kin in Nashville.
Names.
Hughes, L. In Explanation of Our Times.
Madam and the Census Man.
Poem for an Intellectual on the Way Up to Submit to His Lady.
We're all in the telephone book.
Jackson, R. Jamal's Lamentation.
Komunyakaa. Audacity of the Lower Gods.
Madgett. Nomen.
Madhubuti. In a Period of Growth.
Miller, E. Mississippi.
Mullen, H. Momma Sayings.
Parker, Dominique. Art of the Nickname, The.
Sanchez, S. Bear the rhythm of.
Spencer, A. Terence MacSwiney.
Spriggs. My Beige Mom.
Williams, S. You Were Never Miss Brown to Me.
Nantucket, Massachusetts
Wheatley, P. On Messrs. Hussey and Coffin.
Napoleon I
SEJOUR. Le Retour de Napoléon.
Napoleonic Wars
Horton, G. Retreat from Moscow, The.
Narcissism and Narcissists
Giovanni. Love: Is a Human Condition.
Sanchez, S. To You/Who Almost Turned/Me On.
Nationalism
Hughes, L. Azikiwe in Jail.
Lorde. Bicentennial Poem #21,000,000.
Seventh Sign, The.
Native Americans. See Indians, American
Nativity, The
Clifton, L. Holy Night.
Harper, F. Christmas Carol, A.
Nativity, The
Fordham. Cherokee, The.
Harper, M. History as Apple Tree.
Jordan, J. Poem for Guatemala.
Poem for Nana.
Moore, L. Indian Girl.
Plato. Natives of America, The.
Terry, L. Bar[']s Fight[, August 28, 1746].

Walden. Dedicated to a Young Lady Representing the Indian Race at Howard University.
See also Christmas
Naturalists
Harper, M. Oak.
Nature
Baraka. Guerilla Handbook, A.
Bennett, G. Sonnet—2: "Some things are very dear to me—."
Bontemps. Reconnaissance.
Braithwaite. City Garden, A.
Brown, S. Idyll.
Return.
Clifton, L. Being property once myself.
Earth.
Cullen, C. Singing in the Rain.
Dove, R. Fish in the Stone, The.
Dunbar, P. From the Porch at Runnymede.
Lapse, The.
Nature and Art.
Secret, The.
Giovanni. Charting the Night Winds.
Harper, F. Behold the lilies of the field.
Dandelions.
Hayden, R. Point, The.
Horton, G. On Summer.
On Winter.
Woodman and the Money Hunter, The.
Hughes, L. Fulfilment.
House in Taos, A.
My Loves.
To a Dead Friend.
Jordan, J. Aftermath.
Kaufman, B. Waiting.
Komunyakaa. Audacity of the Lower Gods.
Lorde. Echo.
Love Poem.
Naming the Stories.
October.
Return.
McClellan. April of Alabama, The.
Murray, P. Returning Spring.
Newsome. Memory.
Oden. Review from Staten Island.
Ojenke. Amazon.
Ray, H. At Nature's Shrine.
Instability.
Nature's Minor Chords.
Nature's Uplifting.
Redmond. Definition of Nature.
Roberson. Blue Horses.
St. John, P. Carnival.
Toomer. I sit in my room.
It is Everywhere.
Living Earth.
Mended.
One Within.
Rolling, rolling.
Whitman, A. I never was a slasve—a robber took.
Williams, S. S. Recitation.
Wyche. We Rainclouds.
Young, A. Big ocean-waving, woman-pulling moon.
Big Sur.
For Poets.
Mountains of California: Part 2, The.
No More Doors Tonight.
October Window.
Navy Life
Dove, R. Passage, The.
Nazis
Christian. Go Down, Moses!
Hughes, L. Note to All Nazis Fascists and Klansmen.
Komunyakaa. Nazi Doll, The.
Nebraska (state)
Kaufman, B. Enormous Gas Bill at the Dwarf Factory. A Horror Movie to be Shot with Eyes, The.
Need
Baraka. Balboa, the Entertainer.
Clifton, L. Salt.
To Thelma Who Worried Because I Couldn't Cook.

Cortez. For the Poets.
Komunyakaa. Black String of Days.
Lorde. Memorial III from a Phone Booth on Broadway.
On the Edge.
Toomer. See the Heart.
Walker, A. Did This Happen to Your Mother? Did Your Sister Throw Up a Lot? Threatened by my rising need.
Walker, M. Our Need.
Struggle Staggers Us, The.
Young, A. Backtracking.
Dance of the Infidels.

See also **Poverty**

Neglect
Brooks, G. Boy died in my alley, The.
Dunbar, P. Poet, The.
Hughes, L. Beauty.
Christian Country, A.
Delinquent.
How Thin a Blanket.
Lorde. And Don't Think I Won't Be Waiting.
Thompson, D. Sister Lakin and Lally.

Negro Spirituals
Johnson, J. O Black and unknown bards of long ago.

Neighbors
Dove, R. House on Bishop Street, The.
Dunbar, P. Differences.
Hughes, L. Little Song on Housing.
Peace Conference in an American Town.
Lorde. Cables To Rage Or I've Been Talking On This Street Corner.
Judith's Fancy.
Moving Out Or the End of Cooperative Living.
Maroon. Neighbor.
Spencer, A. Neighbors.
Young, A. Dancing Day to Day.
Studio Up Over In Your Ear.

Neruda, Pablo
Reed, I. Poem Delivered Before Assembly of Colored People Held at Glide Memorial Church, Oct. 4, 1973 and Called to Protest Recent Events in the Sovereign Republic of Chile.

New England
Braithwaite. House of Falling Leaves, The.
Clifton, L. Driving through New England.
Harper, M. History as Apple Tree.
Wheatley, P. Farewell to America.
Williams, S. Letters from a New England Negro.

New Hampshire (state)
Jordan, J. Out in the Country of My Country (Peterborough, New Hampshire).
Sometimes DeLiza.
McKay, C. Spring in New Hampshire.

New Jersey (state)
Baraka. Contract. (For The Destruction and Rebuilding of Paterson), A.
Jackson, R. 63rd and Broadway.
Young, A. Hoboken Broken Down: A Hasty Recollection.

New Mexico (state)
Toomer. Imprint for Rio Grande.
Rolling, rolling.

New Orleans, Louisiana
African-American Oral Tradition. Stackolee: "This is supposed to be about two colored studs. It's truth. In New Orleans."
Brown, S. Cloteel: / Rampart Street knows you now: the golden.
Parish Doctor.
Dent. For Lil Louis.
Secret Messages.
Henderson, D. Burgundy Street.
Hughes, L. Beale Street Love.
Jonas, R. Ballade des Belles Milatraisses.
Klein, S. Cofaire?
Salaam. Danny Barker/Danny Banjo.
I Just Heard John Buffington Died.
New Orleans Haiku.
Steptoe. Mississippi Blues.
Young, A. New Orleans Intermissiom.

New Year
Brathwaite, E. New Year Letter.
Clifton, L. I am running into a new year.
Fordham. Passing of the Old Year.
Linden, M. Last Day of the Year; or, New Year's Eve, The.
New Year's Morning; or, the First Day of the Year.
Lorde. Electric Slide Boogie, The.
New Year's Day.
To Martha: a New Year.
Thompson, P. Old Year, The.
To the New Year.
Tolson, M. Festus Conrad.

New York City
Angelou. Awaking in New York.
Times-Square-Shoeshine-Composition.
Baraka. Epistrophe.
Way Out West.
Brown, S. Negro Improvement League.
Brutus. Off to Philadelphia in the morning.
Cortez. Do you think this is a sad day.
I Am New York City.
Giovanni. Just a New York Poem.
Moon shines down, The.
New Yorkers, The.
Night.
Poem: "I have considered / my reluctance."
Walking down park.
Duriel. On the Uptown Lexington Avenue Express: Martin Luther King Day 1995.
Hernton. Black Stick with a Ball of Cotton for a Head and a Running Machine for a Mouth, A.
Hughes, L. Christmas Eve: Nearing Midnight in New York.
Grant Park.
New Yorkers.
Pennsylvania Station in New York, The.
Projection.
Second Generation: New York.
Jackson, R. 63rd and Broadway.
Johnson, H. Bottled [New York].
Johnson, J. My City.
Jordan, J. For My Jamaican Sister a Little Bit Lost on the Island of Manhattan.
Lorde. Birthday Memorial to Seventh Street, A.
New York City 1970.
Soho Cinema.
To Desi as Joe as Smoky the Lover of 115th Street.
McKay, C. City's Love, The.
Dawn in New York.
Song of the Moon, A.
Subway Wind.
When Dawn Comes to the City.
White City, The.
Oden. Private Letter to Brazil, A.
Review from Staten Island.
Reed, I. Martine's Keen Eyes.
Toomer. Skyline.
Walcott. Blues.
God Rest Ye Merry, Gentlemen.
Village Life, A.
Weaver, M. Providence Journal V: Israel of Puerto Rico.
Wonder. Living for the City.
Young, A. Dance of the Infidels.
Fun City Samba.
Little Poem About Jazz, A.

See also **Bowery, The, New York City; Broadway, New York City; Bronx, The, New York City; Brooklyn, New York City; Central Park, New York City; Harlem, New York City; Queens, New York City; Washington Square, New York City**

New York (state)
Harper, M. Grandfather.
Walcott. Upstate.
Young, A. Leaving Syracuse.

Newark, New Jersey
Rodgers, C. Newark, for Now (68).

News
Angelou. Televised news turns.
Gilbert, D. Miracle.
Lorde. Party Time.

Newspapers
Hughes, L. Madam and the Newsboy.
Lorde. Syracuse Airport.
Timing.
Moorer. Southern Press, The.
Moss, T. Jack Johnson Does the Eagle Rock.

See also **Journalism and Journalists**

Nicaragua
Jordan, J. Dance: Nicaragua.
From Nicaragua Libre: Photograph of Managua.
Verse for Ronald Slapjack Who Publicly Declared, "I, Too, Am a Contra!"
Walker, A. Songless.

Nigeria
Allen, S. Benin Bronze.
Cortez. Firespitters / spitting across the desert.
Danner, M. These Beasts and the Benin Bronze.
Hughes, L. Azikiwe in Jail.
Southerland. Blue Clay.
Night in Nigeria.
Williams, J. Safari West.

See also **Civil War, Nigeria**

Night
Baraka. Three Movements and a Coda.
Bennett, G. Nocturne: "This cool night is strange."
Street Lamps in Early Spring.
Brown, S. Mill Mountain.
Caution. Last night I danced on the rim of the moon.
Cullen, C. Night Rain.
Cumbo. Nocturnal Sounds.
Davis, F. Flowers of Darkness.
Four Glimpses of Night.
Delany. Interim.
Dove, R. Nigger Song: An Odyssey.
Night Watch.
To Bed.
Dunbar, P. At Candle-Lightin' Time.
Barrier, The.
Evening.
'Long To'ds Night.
Night.
Night, dim night, and it rains, my love, it rains.
Night of Love.
Summer Night, A.
Twell de Night Is Pas'.
With the Lark.
Giovanni. Night.
Grimké, A. El Beso.
For the Candle Light.
Hayden, R. O Daedalus, Fly Away Home.
Hayes, D. Night like purple flakes of snow.
Heard, J. Night.
Horton, G. Fearful Traveller in the Haunted Castle, The.
On the Evening and the Morning.
Hughes, L. Ardella.
Chord.
Gone Boy.
Harlem Night Song.
Midnight Raffle.
Montmartre.
My People.
Night: Four Songs.
Raid.
Street Song.
Suburban Evening.
Summer Night.
Johnson, F. Long de cool o' night w'en day am daid.
Jones, L. et al. World Is Full of Remarkable Things, The.
Jordan, J. Free Flight.
Of Nightsong and Flight.
Kaufman, B. Lost Window.
Night Sung Sailor's Prayer.
Knight, E. Haiku: "Under moon shadows."
Haiku: "Piano man, The."
Komunyakaa. Starlight Scope Myopia.
Lane, P. Nocturne: "Listening for the sound."
Quiet Poem, A.
Linden, M. Silent Night, The.

Lorde. Gemini.
  Naming the Stories.
Mayle. Night is like an avalanche.
McClellan. September Night, A.
Patterson, R. Night-Piece.
Popel. Night comes walking out our way.
Salaam. All Nite Long.
  Our Natures Rise.
  Quarter Moon Rise.
Sanchez, S. Night pumping like an.
  Poem at Thirty.
Sharp, S. Good Nights.
Thompson, P. Winter Night, A.
Walcott. God Rest Ye Merry, Gentlemen.
Wheatley, P. Hymn to the Evening, An.
Young, A. New Mode of Production, The.
  New Moon Over Grove Street.
See also **Evening; Twilight**

Nightclubs
Hughes, L. Closing Time.
  Death in Harlem.
  Jam Session.
  Jazz Band in a Parisian Cabaret.
  Jazzonia.
  Lady in Cabaret.
  Montmartre.
  Neon Signs.
  New Cabaret Girl, The.
  Sport.
Major, C. Cotton Club, The.
Walker, M. Crystal Palace used to be, The.
Wilson, Ted. Count Basie's place.

Nightmares
Dove, R. Nightmare.
Harper, M. Nightmare Begins Responsibility.
Lorde. Conclusion.
  Eulogy.
  On the Edge.
  One Who Got Away, The.
See also **Dreams and Dreaming**

Nihilism
Baraka. Black Dada Nihilismus.
Hughes, L. Teacher.
See also **Nothingness**

1960s
Alhamisi. Uhuru (freedom. now. swahili. east african lango).
Anderson, C. Finger Pop'in.
Angelou. Riot: 60's.
Giovanni. Atrocities.
  Being and Nothingness.
Komunyakaa. How I See Things.
Lorde. Equinox.
Reed, I. Gangster's Death, The.
Walker, M. Disillusion for Flower Children of Long Ago.

Niobe
Ray, H. Niobe.
Wheatley, P. Niobe in Distress for Her Children Slain by Apollo, from Ovid's Metamorphoses, Book VI, and from a View of the Painting of Mr. Richard Wilson.

Nixon, Richard Milhous
Reed, I. Inside Track, The.

Noises
Dunbar, P. When Malindy Sings.
Sundiata. Ear Training.

Noon
Dunbar, P. Noon.

North Carolina (state)
Harper, F. Lake City Tragedy, The.
Lorde. Poem for a Poet, A.

North, The, United States
Crouch, S. Blackie Thinks of His Brothers.
Hughes, L. Evenin' Air Blues.
  Northern Liberal.
  Vari-Colored Song.
Young, A. Leaving Home for Home.

Nostalgia
Angelou. Just for a Time.
  London.
Dunbar, P. Land o' Used to Be, The.
  Old High School and the New, The.
  Old Memory, An.
Harper, F. Days of my childhood I woo you not back.

Hughes, L. Po' Boy Blues.
Lewis, Mendi. I remember 1983.
Reed, I. Reactionary Poet, The.
Weems. Yesterday.
Young, A. Afternoon After, The.
  Dance for Aging Hipsters, A.
  Dancing Together.
  Foggy Morning.
  For Janet Kafka, Dead at 30.
  Malagueña Salerosa.
  My Spanish Heart.
  Old Fashioned Cincinnati Blues, The.
  Romance.

Nothingness
Clifton, L. I. At Nagasaki.
Hernton. Madhouse.
Hughes, L. End.
  To a Little Lover-Lass, Dead.
Sun-Ra. Nothing Is.
See also **Nihilism**

November
Brown, S. Convict.
Dunbar, P. Nutting Song.
Ray, H. November.
Toomer. November Cotton Flower.

Nuclear Energy
Jordan, J. Poem Towards a Final Solution.
Sanchez, S. Reflections After the June 12th March for Disarmament.

Nuclear War
Clifton, L. I. At Nagasaki.
Cortez. Tell me that the plutonium sludge.
Walker, A. We Have a Map of the World.
See also **Atomic Bomb; Hiroshima, Japan; Nagasaki, Japan**

Nudity and Nudists
Clifton, L. If i stand in my window.
Komunyakaa. Work.
Pritchard, N. Springtime.
Walker, A. Streaking (A Phenomenon Following the Sixties).

Numbers
Hughes, L. Madam and the Number Writer.
  Number.

Nuns
T'Kalla. Nuns in the Basement of God.
See also **Convents**

Nursery Rhymes
Kaufman, B. Under Weight Champion, The.

Nurses
Hughes, L. Where Service Is Needed.
Moorer. Negro Heroines.

Nursing Homes
Harper, F. Dedication Poem.
  For the Twenty-Fifth Anniversary of the "Old Folks' Home."

Nymphs
Hughes, L. Young Singer.
Pritchard, N. Landscape with Nymphs and Satyrs.

O

Oak Trees
Harper, M. Dead Oaks.
  Oak.
La Grone. Lines to the Black Oak.
Roberson. Sonnet.

Obituaries
Holman, M. Mr. Z.

Oblivion
Brooks, G. When You Have Forgotten Sunday: The Love Story.
Hughes, L. Blues at Dawn.
  Shame on You.

Obscenity
Lorde. Jessehelms.

Obscurity
Durem. I Know I'm Not Sufficiently Obscure.
Toomer. Cloud.

Obsessions
Dunbar, P. Disturber, The.
Giovanni. Seduction.

Lorde. Fog Report.

Occupations
African-American Oral Tradition. Seven Wise Men, The.

Ocean
Mackey, N. Phantom Light of All Our Day, The.
See also **Sea**

October
Alexander, M. October Journey.
Angelou. Late October.
Dunbar, P. October is the treasurer of the year.
Fordham. October.
Hayden, R. October— / its plangency, its glow.
Linden, M. October Is Here.
Ray, H. October.
Walker, M. October Journey.
Young, A. Houston in October.
  October Variations, The.

Oedipus
Ray, H. Antigone and Oedipus.

Office Workers
Lee, D. Back Again, Home.
Madhubuti. Back Again, Home.
Thomas, L. My Office.
See also **Clerks**

Ohio (state)
Angelou. In my Missouri.
Harper, F. To the Union Savers of Cleveland.

Ohio River
Harper, F. Slave Mother, The: "I have but four, the treasures of my soul."

Oil
Sanchez, S. / arabs / ain't got no, The.

Old Age
African-American Oral Tradition. Old Cods.
  When I Begin to Think When I Was a Young Man and in My Prime.
Angelou. Last Decision, The.
  Old Folks Laugh.
  On Aging.
Bontemps. To a Young Girl Leaving the Hill Country.
Brooks, G. Bean Eaters, The.
  To an Old Black Woman, Homeless and Indistinct.
Brown, S. Honey Mah Love.
Campbell, J. Ol' Doc' Hyar.
Cheatwood. Bloodstorm.
Clifton, L. Island Mary.
  Miss Rosie.
Cullen, C. To France.
Dunbar, P. Goin' Back.
  Growin' Gray.
  Old.
  Old Story, The.
  Parted.
  When the Old Man Smokes.
Giovanni. Age.
  Alabama Poem.
  Conversation.
  For a Lady of Pleasure Now Retired.
  Once a Lady Told Me.
  Poem (For Anna Hedgeman and Alfreda Duster).
  You Are There.
Harper, F. Dedication Poem.
  For the Twenty-Fifth Anniversary of the "Old Folks' Home."
  My mother's kiss, my mother's kiss.
  Renewal of Strength.
  To Bishop Payne.
Harper, M. 24th Avenue: City of Roses: Anesthesia: 2.
Duriel. For My Father.
Horton, G. Close of Life, The.
Hughes, L. Being Old.
  Elderly Leaders.
  Old Age.
  Old Sailor.
  Parisian Beggar Woman.
Jeffers, L. Black Soul of the Land.
Johnson, G. Old Black Men.
Komunyakaa. Good Joe.

Linden, M. Life's Golden Sunset.
Prospect of the Future, The.
Loftin. Weeksville Women.
Lorde. Return.
Rooming houses are old women.
Madgett. New Day.
Nelson, M. Aches and Pains.
Ballad of Aunt Geneva, The.
Parker, P. I Followed a Path.
Pfister. Granny Blak Poet (in Pastel).
Randall, D. George.
Rite, The.
Sanchez, S. July.
Seventy-one years.
Woman. rocking her.
Thompson, P. Old Freedman, The.
Walcott. Glory Trumpeter, The.
Walker, A. Medicine.
Walker, M. Old Age.
Zu-Bolton. Ain't No Spring Chicken.
See also **Retirement and Retirees**

Omar Khayyám
Young, A. Poem for Omar Khayyam (1050?-1123? A.D.).

Onions
Goodison. I Am Becoming My Mother.

Ontario, Lake
Ray, H. Thought of Lake Ontario, A.

Opium
African-American Oral Tradition. Pretty Pill.
Willie the Weeper.
Tucker, M. Evanishings.
Opium-Eater, The.

Opossums
Dunbar, P. Possum.

Opportunity
Nelson, M. Levitation with Baby.

Oppression
Angelou. No No No No.
To a Freedom Fighter.
We saw beyond our seeming.
Baraka. Burning General, The.
Death Is Not as Natural as You Fags Seem to Think.
1929: Y you ask? (26).
Reggae or Not!
Revelation in Brick City.
Rhythm and Blues (I).
When We'll Worship Jesus.
Wise 2.
Bennett, Bob. It is time for action.
Campbell, A. Cry "Infidel!"
Clarke, J. Determination.
Clifton, L. Bodies broken on, The.
Stops.
Corrothers. Snapping of the Bow, The.
Crouch, S. BLACKIE Speaks on Campus: a Valentine for Vachel Lindsay.
Cullen, C. From the Dark Tower.
Danner, M. This Is an African Worm.
Dent. Return to English Turn.
Dove, R. Parsley.
El-Hadi. Tired Man, The.
Garnet. Thus man devotes his brother and destroys.
Giovanni. Africa II.
Each Sunday.
Poem of Angela Yvonne Davis.
Toy Poem.
Graham, D. West Ridge Is Menthol-Cool, The.
Harper, F. Dismissal of Tyng, The.
Ethiopia.
Harper, M. America Calls!
Heard, J. They are coming, coming slowly.
Hughes, L. Dream Boogie.
Freedom: "Some folks think."
I too, sing America.
Memo to Non-White People.
Negro.
Oppression.
Johnson, G. Heart of a Woman, The.
Jordan, J. Calling on All Silent Minorities.
For Michael Angelo Thompson.
From Sea to Shining Sea.
Intifada.
Poem About My Rights.

Poem for Benjamin Franklin.
Poem Towards a Final Solution.
Rape Is Not a Poem.
Song for Soweto, A.
Komunyakaa. Protection of Movable Cultural Heritage.
Lorde. Black unicorn is greedy, The.
Meeting of Minds, A.
Revolution Is One Form of Social Change.
Sisters in Arms.
Madhubuti. Death Dance, The.
Killing Memory.
McClane. Black Intellectual, The.
McKay, C. Africa.
In Bondage.
Medina, T. Capitalism Is a Brutal Motherfucker.
Menard. Negro's Lament, The.
Miller, M. Scream, The.
Moss, T. Lessons from a Mirror.
Nelson, M. Chopin.
Randall, D. Roses and Revolutions.
Randall, J. Who Shall Die.
Reed, I. Catechism of d Neoamerican Hoodoo Church.
Rivera, E. Elegy for a Martyred Poet.
Sanchez, S. On Watching a World Series Game.
Young Womanhood.
Snellings. Song of Fire, The.
T'Kalla. Nuns in the Basement of God.
Tolson, M. Dark Symphony.
Unknown. Go Down, Old Hannah.
Van Peebles. To Hell with Whitey.
Vibe. L. A. (Lost Assholes).
Walcott. Elsewhere.
Walker, A. Ndebele.
Walker, M. For my people everywhere singing their slave songs repeatedly.
I hear a rumbling underground.
Micah was a young man of the people.
Money, Honey, Money.
Prophets for a New Day.
Since 1619.
Spirituals, The.
They have put us on HOLD.
We have been believers in the black gods of an old land.
Washington. Moon Bound.
Watkins, N. Bedtime Story.
Whitfield. How long, oh gracious God! how long.
Wright, R. I Have Seen Black Hands.
Young, A. Dude in Denver.
Old O.O. Blues, The.
Poem for Players, A.
Some Recent Fiction.
What You Seize Is What You Git.
See also **Apartheid**

Optimism
Dunbar, P. Keep A-Pluggin' Away.
Hughes, L. Friendly in a Friendly Way.
See also **Hope**

Orange Trees and Oranges
Young, A. Poem with Orange.

Oratory
Brown, S. Memo: For the Race Orators.

Order
Jordan, J. From Sea to Shining Sea.

Oregon (state)
Kaufman, B. Oregon.

Organs and Organists
Heard, J. New Organ, The.

Orioles
Dunbar, P. Summer in the South.

Orphans
Harper, F. To Mr. and Mrs. W. F. Johnson on Their Twenty-Fifth Wedding Anniversary.
Linden, M. Orphan Girl, An.
Wheatley, P. On the Death of Dr. Samuel Marshall.
On the Death of Dr. Samuel Marshall, 1771.

Owls
Moss, T. Owl In Daytime, The.

P

Pacifism and Pacifists
Sinclair, J. Breakthrough.
Walker, A. QPP, The.

Paganism and Pagans
Cullen, C. Pagan Prayer.
Wheatley, P. Address to the Atheist, By P. Wheatley at the Age of 14 Years—1767.
Atheism.

Paige, Leroy (Satchel)
Allen, S. To Satch.

Pain
Angelou. Kind of Love, Some Say, A.
Baraka. Agony, An. As Now.
Clifton, L. She Understands Me.
Cullen, C. Protest.
Saturday's Child.
Song in Spite of Myself.
Sonnet: "I know now how a man whose blood is hot."
Sonnet: "What I am saying now was said before."
Dove, R. Variation on Pain.
Dunbar, P. Itching Heels.
Giovanni. There is a hunger.
Graham, D. Soul.
Hayden, R. Road in Kentucky, A.
Whipping, The.
Horton, G. Troubled with the Itch and Rubbing with Sulphur.
Hughes, L. Dream Boogie: Variation.
Soledad.
Walls.
Jordan, J. Sonnet from the Stony Brook, A.
Kaufman, B. Blue O'Clock.
Komunyakaa. Touch-up Man.
Lorde. At First I Thought You Were Talking about.
Bloodbirth.
Ghost.
Hard Love Rock.
Out to the Hard Road.
McClellan. Love is a flame that burns with sacred fire.
Nelson, M. My Second Birth.
Nettles. War Stories.
Roy, L. Triple Overtime.
Sanchez, S. Rain tastes lovely, The.
There are times that the.
To All Sisters.
Why must i string my hate.
You do not know the.
Stephany. Who collects the pain.
Thompson, C. After-Glow of Pain, The.
Walcott. Fist, The ("Fist clenched round my heart, The").
Walker, A. Excuse.
Young, A. Detroit 1958.
See also **Suffering**

Painting and Painters
Alexander, E. Painting / (Frida Kahlo).
Baraka. Politics of Rich Painters, The.
Cassells. These Are Not Brushstrokes.
Cortez. When I Look at Wilfredo Lam's Paintings.
Danner, M. Sadie's Playhouse.
Dove, R. Agosta the Winged Man and Rasha the Black Dove.
Harper, M. Zocalo.
Johnson, J. Before a Painting.
McElroy, C. Why Tu Fu Does Not Speak of the Nubian.
Wheatley, P. To S. M., a Young African Painter, on Seeing His Works.
See also **Portraits**

Palestine
Jordan, J. Moving Towards Home.
See also **Israel**

Palm Sunday
Clifton, L. Palm Sunday.
Harper, F. Christ's Entry into Jerusalem.

Palm Trees
Cuney. No Images.

Pan (god)
Horton, G. On the Evening and the Morning.

Pancakes
White-Jackson. Saturday Morning Pancakes.
Pansies
Newsome. Pansy.
Papacy
Jordan, J. Addenda to the Papal Bull.
See also **Catholicism and Catholics**
Parachuting and Parachutists. *See* **Skydiving and Skydivers**
Parades
Hughes, L. Parade.
Kaufman, B. Reflections on a Small Parade.
See also **Marching and Marchers**
Paradise
Reed, I. Wardrobe Master of Paradise, The.
Paradoxes
Cullen, C. More Than a Fool's Song.
Hughes, L. Not Else—But.
Songs.
Paranoia
Baraka. Das Kapital.
Nelson, M. April Rape.
It's All in Your Head.
Pardons and Pardoners
Wheatley, P. To the Hon. Commodore Hood on His Pardoning a Deserter.
Parenthood
Dove, R. Daystar.
Lorde. And What About the Children.
What my child learns of the sea.
Madgett. Offspring.
Parents
Cullen, C. Fruit of the Flower.
Dunbar, P. Dilettante, The: A Modern Type.
Ellis, T. Kiss in the Dark, A.
Jordan, J. One Minus One Minus One.
Lorde. Outside.
Nurigan. I'm raising CHILDREN.
Walker, F. Wishbone.
Young, A. Son.
Paris, France
Hughes, L. Montmartre.
Jordan, J. In Paris.
Rivers, C. Four Sheets to the Wind and a One-Way Ticket to France.
Mourning Letter from Paris, A.
Young, A. Dance of the Infidels.
One Snapshot I Couldn't Take in France, The. Paris.
Parker, Charlie
Brathwaite, E. Blues.
Dodson, O. Yardbird's Skull.
Harper, M. "Bird Lives" : Charles Parker.
Brother John.
Kaufman, B. Walking Parker Home.
Neal, L. Don't say goodbye to the Porkpie Hat that rolled.
Malcolm X—an Autobiography.
Reed, I. Haitians.
Poetry Makes Rhythm in Philosophy.
Thomas, L. Historiography.
Parks
Atkins. On the Fine Arts Garden, Cleveland.
Hughes, L. Kid in the Park.
Oden. Carousel, The.
Redmond. Definition of Nature.
Parrots
Dove, R. Parsley.
Parties
African-American Oral Tradition. Bulldaggers' Hall.
Dance of the Freaks: "It was a cool and mystic rain."
Dance of the Freaks: "It was cold and mist and rain in old Spokane."
'Flicted Arm Pete: "It was way down in this little town that they call Louisville."
Freaks' Ball.
Partytime Monkey.
Raise a Ruckus Tonight.
Twenty-Two-Twenty told Automatic Jim to tell his fast-fucking sister Fanny.
Alexander, E. Ode.
Baraka. Crow Jane in High Society.
Vice.

Dunbar, P. Party, The.
Eady. Song.
Harper, F. Revel, The.
Hernton. Poem.
Jordan, J. Reception, The.
Kaufman, B. Tequila Jazz.
Reed, I. Hoodoo Poem in Transient.
Untitled III.
What You Mean I Can't Irony?
Parting
Angelou. Gamut, The.
Lie, The.
Prelude to a Parting.
Baraka. Audubon, Drafted.
Brown, Kysha. Brown Girl Blues.
Brown, S. Elder Mistletoe.
One Way of Taking Leave.
Cullen, C. At a Parting.
If You Should Go.
Two Who Croseed a Line (She Crosses).
Two Who Crossed a Line.
Dove, R. Then Came Flowers.
Thomas at the Wheel.
Dunbar, P. Farewell Song.
My Love Irene.
Parted.
Premonition.
Evans, M. Where Have You Gone?
Harper, F. Fugitive's Wife, The.
Slave Auction, The.
Hayden, R. Ballad of Sue Ellen Westerfield, The.
Road in Kentucky, A.
Heard, J. Parting, The.
Parting Kiss, The.
Henderson, E. B. Good Bye, Honey—Good Bye.
Horton, G. Farewell to Frances.
Lover's Farewell, The.
Hughes, L. Farewell, A: "With gypsies and sailors."
Request.
Jordan, J. About Long Distances on Saturday.
Knight, E. As You Leave Me.
Komunyakaa. Translating Footsteps.
Lorde. Dream/Songs from the Moon of Beulah Land.
Movement Song.
One Who Got Away, The.
Parting.
To the Girl Who Lives In a Tree.
McKay, C. Snow Fairy, The.
Menard. Good-bye! Off for Kansas.
Moore, Lynn. Haiku: "Morning fog / my daughter dropped off at camp."
Randall, D. Souvenirs.
Sanchez, S. Don't go. if you go.
Thompson, P. Adown the heights of Ages.
Tucker, M. Adieu.
Unknown. Another Man Done Gone.
They're Leaving Memphis in Droves.
You May Go But This Will Bring You Back.
Walker, A. Even as I hold you.
He said: I want you to be happy.
Instant of Our Parting, The.
Mornings / of an impossible love.
Passion
Baraka. Footnote to a Pretentious Book.
Baudelaire. Cats.
Brooks, G. Flags.
To be in love.
Campbell, J. Ol' Doc' Hyar.
Pariah, The.
Caution. Last night I danced on the rim of the moon.
Clifton, L. Salt.
Cortez. Feathers.
Cullen, C. Love's Way.
Nothing endures, / Not even love.
One Day We Played a Game.
Pity the deep in love.
Song in Spite of Myself.
Sonnet: "I have not loved you in the noblest way."
Sonnet: "Some for a little while do love, and some for long."
Datcher. I Am Open.

Dunbar, P. Passion and Love.
Fabio. To Turn from Love.
Giovanni. Charles White.
Resignation.
Harper, F. Artist, The.
Heard, J. Slumbering Passion.
Horton, G. For the Fair Miss M. M. McLean.
Lines to My—.
Jeffers, H. I Was Looking at Miles.
Jeffers, L. Man with a Furnace in His Hand.
Jordan, J. No Poem Because Time Is Not a Name.
Sunflower Sonnet Number One.
Trying to Capture Rapture.
Kaufman, B. "Michelangelo" the Elder.
Knight, E. Belly Song.
Lorde. Never Take Fire for a Woman.
McClellan. Love is a flame that burns with sacred fire.
McKay, C. Barcelona.
Flower of Love.
Memorial.
O word I love to sing! thou art too tender.
One Year After.
Prayer, A: "'Mid the discordant noises of the day I hear thee calling."
To O.E.A E. A.
Tormented.
Menken. "My heritage!" It is to live within.
Nelson, M. Ballad of Aunt Geneva, The.
Salaam. Spice of Life, The.
Sanchez. Catch the Fire.
Stephany. Because I have wandered long through my own darkness.
Toomer. Desire.
Walker, M. Joel, that young prophet-son of Pethuel!
Love Song for Alex, 1979.
Williams, Karen. Kissing Keys.
X, M. Till the Sun Goes Down.
Young, A. Dreamjot: 1962.
Jolt.
Mexico City Lover.
Romance Without Finance.
Passivity
Cullen, C. Requiescam.
Young, A. Are You the Lover or Loved?
Robbie's Dance, The.
Past
Ai. Twenty-Year Marriage.
Angelou. New House, The.
Reverses.
Still I Rise.
Zorro Man, A.
Baker, H. Late-Winter Blues and Promises of Love.
This is not a poem, nor.
Baraka. In Memory of Radio.
Letter to E. Franklin Frazier.
Bontemps. Return, The.
Southern Mansion.
Cheatwood. Bloodstorm.
Clifton, L. Aunt Agnes Hatcher Tells.
Generations.
I am running into a new year.
I was born with twelve fingers.
Light / on my mother's tongue.
News, The.
Roots.
Cullen, C. Litany of the Dark People, The.
Danner, M. Small Bells of Benin, The.
Dunbar, P. Long Ago.
Ol' Tunes, The.
Passage, The.
Gex-Breaux. Blue Deep.
Giovanni. Poem (For BMC No. 2).
Scrapbooks.
Swaziland.
Walking down park.
Harper, M. Black Angel, The.
Corrected Review.
Families Album, The.
From a Town in Minnesota.
Good Samaritan Hospital.
Kin.
Hayden, R. Locus.

'Mystery Boy' Looks for Kin in Nashville.
Return, The.
Hoagland, E. Gorée ten miles offshore beckons.
Horton, G. New Fashions.
Hughes, L. Georgia Dusk.
Grandpa's Stories.
History.
Mean Old Yesterday.
Watch Out, Papa.
Yesterday and Today.
Johnson, F. To an Afro-American Maiden.
Jordan, J. Roman Poem Number Five.
Kaufman, B. Early Loves.
Falling.
I Sigh a Marbled Sigh Ah, at Last.
Walking Hot Seasons.
Komunyakaa. Addendum.
Blues Chant Hoodoo Revival.
Salt.
Lorde. Change.
Even.
Inheritance—His.
Moving In.
Old Days, The.
Paperweight.
Song of Names and Faces, A.
Women on Trains.
McElroy, C. Ghost-Who-Walks, The.
Under the Oak Table.
McKay, C. Heritage.
Neal, L. Narrative of Black Magicians, The.
Nelson, M. Dinosaur Spring.
Randall, D. Legacy: My South.
Primitives.
Rankine. Eden.
Reed, I. Reactionary Poet, The.
Tea Dancer Turns Thirty-Nine.
Walcott. Storm Figure.
Walker, M. Black Paramour.
Dark Blood.
Delta.
How many silent centuries sleep in my sultry veins?
Ode on the Occasion of the Inauguration of the Sixth President of Jackson State College.
Sorrow Home.
Young, A. Fort Collins, Colorado.
Geography of the Near Past.
Young, K. Field Trip.

Paths
Moore, L. Homeplace, The.
Pritchard, N. Narrow Path, The.

Patience
Clifton, L. God waits for the wandering world.
Harriet / if i be you.
Sonora Desert Poem.
Corrothers. At the Closed Gate of Justice.
Cullen, C. From the Dark Tower.
Two Thoughts of Death.
Dunbar, P. Plantation Melody, A.
Fields, J. Jolly fat widows, The.
Giovanni. All i gotta do.
Patience.
Horne, F. Patience. . . patience.
Hughes, L. Earth Song.
Song: "Lovely, dark, and lonely one."
Lorde. Father, the Year Is Fallen.
Thompson, C. His Answer.
Walker, F. Sweet Bread.

Patriarchy
Jordan, J. Some people despise me be-.

Patriotism and Patriots
Harper, F. God Bless Our Native Land.
Harper, M. Debridement.
Holly. This Is a Fatherland to Me.
Hughes, L. Bonds for All.
Bonds: In Memoriam.
Fourth of July Thought.
Mother in Wartime.
Speaking of Food.
Moorer. Loyalty to the Flag.
Wheatley, P. On the Death of General Wooster.

Patrons
Kaufman, B. Countess Erica Blaise: Chorus.

Neal, L. Baroness and the Black Musician, The.
Wheatley, P. To Mæcenas.

Pawnbrokers and Pawnshops
Hughes, L. Ballad of the Pawnbroker.

Payne, D. A.
Fordham. Dedicated to the Right Rev'd D. A. Payne.

Peace
Angelou. Georgia Song, A.
Baraka. Three Modes of History and Culture.
Cheatwood. Visions of the Sea.
Clifton, L. Let There Be New Flowering.
Cortez. Push Back the Catastrophes.
Tell me that the plutonium sludge.
Cullen, C. Apostrophe to the Land.
Wise, The.
Dunbar, P. At Loafing-Holt.
Ere sleep comes down to soothe the weary eyes.
From the Porch at Runnymede.
Fordham. Ode to Peace.
Gex-Breaux. Willie Note 9/28/91.
Giovanni. Certain Peace, A.
My Tower.
Harper, F. Home, Sweet Home.
Lost Bells, The.
Peace.
Songs for the People.
Vision of the Czar of Russia, The.
Horne, F. Kid Stuff.
Hughes, L. Carolina Cabin.
Convent.
Give Us Our Peace.
I dream a world where man.
Projection.
To Dorothy Maynor.
Jordan, J. Addenda to the Papal Bull.
Kaufman, B. Peace Be with You.
Knight, E. Apology for Apostasy?
Poem on the Middle East "Peace Process", A.
McKay, C. Adolescence.
Rest in Peace.
Neal, L. Morning Raga for Malcolm.
Nelson, M. At Prayer.
Icarus Dream.
Randall, D. Roses and Revolutions.
Reed, I. Back to Africa.
Sanchez, S. Reflections After the June 12th March for Disarmament.
Southerland. Two Fishing Villages.
Stuckey. Temptation.
Tolson, M. Legend of Versailles, A.
Toomer. Motion and Rest.
Unknown. Deep river, my home is over Jordan.
Soon I will be done with the troubles of the world.
Watkins, N. Missions and Magnolias.
Whitman, A. Hail dawning Peace! Speed on thy glorious rise!
Young, A. Available Light.
Dancing.
Dreams of Paradise.
In the tender woodland.

Peace, Isabel
Fordham. Lines to Mrs. Isabel Peace.

Pearls
Dunbar, P. Roses and Pearls.
Lorde. Bridge through My Windows.
Thompson, P. Precious Pearl, The.

Peasants
Reed, I. Sputin.

Peddling and Peddlers
Johnson, F. Negro Peddler's Song, A.

Pentecost
Harper, F. Resurrection of Jesus, The.

Perception
Brooks, G. To be in love.
Cullen, C. For Helen Keller.
Jordan, J. Who Look at Me.
Kaufman, B. Cat Is Sleeping on a Poem, The.
Mind for All Its Reasoning, The.
Slight Alterations.
Komunyakaa. Looking a Mad Dog Dead in the Eyes.

Toomer. Five Vignettes.
Troupe. It is not who or what.
Young, A. Drawing.
How the Rainbow Works.
Process.
Still Lives.

Perfection
Jordan, J. Sunflower Sonnet Number Two.
Randall, D. Coral Atoll.
Walker, A. Perfection.

Perfumes
Harris, P. Be Somebody Fragrant.

Perplexity
Eady. Sherbet.

Persecution
Baraka. People Burning, The.
Hayden, R. From the corpse woodpiles, from the ashes.
Jordan, J. Poem for Buddy.

Perseus
Hayden, R. Perseus.

Perseverance
Allen, S. Harriet Tubman.
Cullen, C. From the Dark Tower.
Thorn Forever in the Breast, A.
Danner, M. I'll walk the tightrope that's been stretched for me.
Dunbar, P. Joggin' Erlong.
Forman, R. Up Sister.
Hernton. Distant Drum, The.
Young Negro poet / came from 'way down South.
Hughes, L. Dusk.
Evil.
Mother to Son.
Stalingrad: 1942.
Madhubuti. First World.
Sanchez, S. Poem No. 10.
Walker, M. Gus, the lineman / Route forty-nine.
Whitfield. Self-Reliance.
Young, A. Dance For Ma Rainey, A.

Persians. *See* **Iran and Iranians**

Pessimism
Cotter, Sr. Don't-Care Negro, The.
Cullen, C. For a Pessimist.
Dunbar, P. What's the use o' folks a-frownin'.
Hughes, L. Day.
Lorde. Conclusion.

Peter, Saint
Brown, S. Slim in Hell ("Slim Greer went to heaven").
Johnson, J. Saint Peter Relates an Incident of the Resurrection Day.

Pets
Reed, I. Dialog outside the Lakeside Grocery.

Philadelphia, Pennsylvania
Brutus. Off to Philadelphia in the morning.
Dove, R. Musician Talks about "Process", The.
Sanchez, S. Elegy: "Philadelphia / a disguised southern city."
Elegy (for MOVE and Philadelphia).
Philadelphia: Spring, 1985.
Poem for July 4, 1994.
Summer has sped a.
Silvera. South Street.

Philippines, The, and Filipinos
Jordan, J. Poem Instead of a Columbus Day Parade.

Phillips, Wendell
Ray, H. Wendell Phillips.

Philosophy and Philosophers
Baraka. Balboa, the Entertainer.

Phoenix
Cullen, C. That bright chimeric beast.

Photography and Photographers
Cassells. Courtesy, A Trenchant Grace, A.
Clinton. History as Trash.
Dunbar, P. Photograph, The.
Ellis, T. Shooting Back.
Giovanni. Scrapbooks.
Harper, M. Negatives, The.
Photographs.
Smoke is my name for you.

Three O'Clock Love Song.
Trays: a Portfolio.
Utility Room.
Lorde. For Assata.
Madgett. Sunny.
Nelson, M. Memento.
True Magic, The.
Prettyman. Photograph.
Salaam. Iron Flowers.
Shepherd, R. What Cannot Be Kept.
Sundiata. Making Poems.
Tucker, M. Family Portraits.

Physicians
Brown, S. Parish Doctor.
Campbell, J. Ol' Doc' Hyar.
Davis, F. Arthur Ridgewood, M.D.
Dunbar, P. To Dan.
Hughes, L. Interne at Provident.
Moorer. Birthday Wishes to a Physician.
See also **Hospitals; Medicine; Surgery**

Physics and Physicists
Jordan, J. Poem about Intelligence for My
  Brothers and Sisters, A.

Pianos
Jordan, J. October 23, 1983.

Picasso, Pablo
Cassells. These Are Not Brushstrokes.
Hughes, L. Cubes.
Dove, The.
Kaufman, B. Bird with Painted Wings.

Picnics and Barbecues
Holman, M. Picnic: the Liberated.
Lorde. This Urn Contains Earth from German
  Concentration Camps.
Toomer. Georgia Dusk.

Pies
Dunbar, P. Reluctance.

Piety
Harper, F. Jesus.

Pigeons
Knight, E. Crazy pigeon strutting outside my
  cell.

Pigs
McKay, C. If we must die—let it not be like
  hogs.

Pilgrimages and Pilgrims
Unknown. City Called Heaven.

Pilots
Hughes, L. Judge William Hastie.
Nelson, M. Freeman Field.
Lonely Eagles.
Porter.
Star-Fix.
Tuskegee Airfield.
See also **Air Travel; Air Warfare; Airplanes**

Pine Trees
Toomer. Nullo.

Pioneers
Reed, I. Points of View.
Sanchez, S. Right On: White America.

Piracy and Pirates
Hughes, L. To the Little Front of San Lazaro
  on the Ocean Front, Havana.
Komunyakaa. Boat People.

Pittsburgh, Pennsylvania
Steptoe. Window Shopping.

Pity
Giovanni. Poem Off Center, A.
Harper, F. Appeal to My Countrywomen, An.
Horton, G. Poet's Feeble Petition, The.
Hughes, L. Good Bluffers.
Lover's Return.

Plague
Dove, R. Fiammetta Breaks Her Peace.
Harper, F. Moses: A Story of the Nile.
Toomer. November Cotton Flower.

Plants
Harper, F. Truth.
Madgett. Woman with Flower.
McKay, C. Flame-Heart.
Spanish Needle, The.
Phillips, C. Reach, The.
Young, A. Look Good, Smell Good, Feel.

See also **Listings for specific plants**
Play
Angelou. Harlem Hopscotch.
Emanuel, J. Voyage of Jimmy Poo, The.
Hughes, L. Little Song.
Piggy-back.
Young, A. Squirrels are skittering.
See also **Fun; Games**

Playmates
Sanchez, S. We stumbled into.

Pleasure
Giovanni. Butterfly, The.
Hughes, L. Dancers.
Old Walt Whitman.
To Beauty.
Lorde. Sacrifice.

Plum Trees and Plums
Hughes, L. Love Song for Lucinda.
Toomer. Song of the Son.

Plumbing and Plumbers
Lorde. Depreciation.

Pocahontas
Bibb. Capt. Smith and Pocahontas.

Poe, Edgar Allan
Fortune. Edgar Allan Poe.
Kaufman, B. Afterwards, They Shall Dance.

Poetics
Baraka. Balboa, the Entertainer.
Black Art.
Gatsby's Theory of Aesthetics.
Bibb. After Reading Bryant's Lines to a
  Waterfowl.
Cullen, C. After a Visit.
Poet, poet, what is your task.
Sonnet: "What I am saying now was said
  before."
That bright chimeric beast.
To an Unknown Poet.
Yet Do I Marvel.
Dunbar, P. To E. H. K.
Forman, R. This Poem.
Giovanni. Poem for Langston Hughes, A.
Poetry is motion graceful.
Harris, W. Grandfather Poem, A.
Hughes, L. Formula.
Knight, E. And Tell Me Poet, Can Love Exist
  in Slavery?
Genesis.
Haiku: "Eastern guard tower."
McElroy, C. Pike Street Bus.
Wheatley, P. To Mæcenas.

Police Stations and Police
African-American Oral Tradition. Dolomite
  first originated in San Antone.
Junkies' Heaven.
Limpty Lefty McCree.
Stackolee: "When I was young in my prime."
Ai. Endangered Species.
Alexander, E. Affirmative Action Blues.
Brooks, G. Boy died in my alley, The.
"Negro" Hero.
Brown, S. Ballad of Joe, The.
Last Ride of Wild Bill.
Southern Cop.
Clifton, L. Powell; March 1991.
Cortez. Give Me the Red on the Black of the
  Bullet.
Rape.
Dumas, H. Knock on Wood.
Durem. Award.
Hamilton, B. Poem to a Nigger Cop.
Hughes, L. Ballad of Margie Polite.
Third Degree.
Who But the Lord?
Jordan, J. Poem about Police Violence.
Poem from Taped Testimony in the Tradition
  of Bernard Goetz.
Komunyakaa. Cage Walker, The.
Parker, Dominique. Sand.
Randall, D. Idiot, The.
Reed, I. Ballad of Charlie James, The.
Treatment for Dance w/ Trick Ending.
Sanchez, S. Definition for Blk/Children.
Philadelphia: Spring, 1985.
Unknown. Railroad Bill, Railroad Bill.
Walker, M. On Police Brutality.

Politics and Politicians
Ai. Self Defense.
Allen, S. View from the Corner.
Baraka. Clay.
Election Day.
Real Life.
Cortez. I and I.
Dunbar, P. Speakin' at de Cou't-House.
Giovanni. Poem: "I have considered / my
  reluctance."
Seduction.
Harper, F. Aunt Chloe's Politics.
Horton, G. Union of Parties, The.
Hughes, L. Corner Meeting.
Un-American Investigators.
Jordan, J. On Moral Leadership as a Political
  Dilemma.
Poem About My Rights.
Poem Instead of a Columbus Day Parade.
Poem Towards a Final Solution.
Knight, E. On Watching Politicians Perform at
  Martin Luther King's Funeral.
Lorde. Jessehelms.
Sisters in Arms.
Reed, I. Sather Tower Mystery.
Tolson, M. Legend of Versailles, A.
Young, A. Politics As History.

Pollution
Harper, M. Come Back Blues.
Jordan, J. Torn Sky: Lesson #1, The.
Nuriddin. Children of the Future.
Reed, I. El Paso Monologue.
Lake Bud.

Pompeii, Italy
Jordan, J. Roman Poem Number Five.
Ray, H. Listening Nydia.

Pool (game)
African-American Oral Tradition. Poolshooting
  Monkey: "I don't know but I was told."
Poolshooting Monkey: "It was in Speero's
  poolroom back in nineteen-ten."
Poolshooting Monkey: "It was in Speero's
  poolroom in the year eighteen-ten."
Bond, J. Rotation.
Brooks, G. We real cool. We.
Brown, S. Puttin' on Dog.

Poppies
Hughes, L. Poppy Flower.

Pornography
Nelson, M. No Jazz.

Portraits
African-American Oral Tradition. Jesse James.
Coleman, A. Portraiture.
Hughes, L. Not Often.
See also **Painting and Painters**

Portugal
Young, A. Saudades: The Portuguese Blues.

Posterity
Brown, S. Memo: For the Race Orators.
Hughes, L. Promised Land / Is always just
  ahead, The.
Tomorrow's Seed.
Rivers, C. Still Voice of Harlem, The.
Toomer. Song of the Son.
Young, A. Fifty-Fifty.

Potatoes
Asquith. Banking Potatoes.
Corrothers. Sweeten 'Tatahs.

Pottery and Potters
Forbes, C. Potter's Wheel, The.
Komunyakaa. Back Then.
Miller, E. What the Women Told Me.

Poverty
African-American Oral Tradition. Ain't It a
  Bitch?
Ai. Riot Act, April 29, 1992.
Angelou. Bump d'Bump.
Preacher, don't send me.
Baraka. Das Kapital.
Short Speech to My Friends.
Baudelaire. Death to the Poor.
Brooks, G. Bean Eaters, The.
Lovers of the Poor, The.
My Dreams, My Works Must Wait Till after
  Hell.

To an Old Black Woman, Homeless and
  Indistinct.
Brown, E. If Randi Could Write.
Brown, S. All Are Gay.
  Arkansas Chant.
  Episode.
  Mister Samuel and Sam.
  Rent Day Blues.
  Side by Side.
Cassells. Courtesy, A Trenchant Grace, A.
Clark, Benjamin. Pauper's Grave, The.
Clifton, L. Forgiving My Father.
  Good Times.
  In the Inner City.
  Job easy / is the pride.
  Wise: Having the Ability to Perceive and
    Adopt the Best Means for Accomplishing an
    End.
Coleman, W. Aunt Jessie.
  Dear Mama.
Cornish, S. Promenade.
Cortez. I'm A Worker.
Cotter, Sr. My Poverty and Wealth.
Crouch, S. No New Music.
Cullen, C. Saturday's Child.
Dent. Ten Years After Umbra.
Dunbar-Nelson. Proletariat Speaks, The.
Dunbar, P. Common Things.
  Companion's Progress, A.
  Precedent.
Eckels. Hell, Mary / Bell Jones.
Fabio. Of Puddles, Worms, Slimy Things.
Fields, J. High on the Hog.
Freeman, C. Christmas Morning I.
Giovanni. New Yorkers, The.
  Nikki-Rosa.
  On Hearing "The Girl with the Flaxen Hair."
Harper, F. Dedication Poem.
Harper, M. Allegheny Shadows.
  In the Projects.
Hernton. Black Stick with a Ball of Cotton for
  a Head and a Running Machine for a Mouth,
  A.
Hoagland, E. Big Zeb Johnson.
Hughes, L. Advertisement for the Waldorf-
  Astoria.
  Ballad of Roosevelt.
  Ballad of the Man Who's Gone.
  Barefoot Blues.
  Broke.
  Consider me, / A colored boy.
  Cross.
  Dime.
  Down and Out.
  Ennui.
  First of May.
  God to Hungry Child.
  Grant Park.
  Madam and the Charity Child.
  Madam and the Rent Man.
  Necessity.
  Park Bench.
  Prayer for a Winter Night.
  Puzzlement.
  Slum Dreams.
  Success.
  Visitors to the Black Belt.
  Workin' Man.
Johnson, F. Scarlet Woman, The.
Jordan, J. DeLiza Come to London Town; a
  Birthday Poem for Mark.
Jordan, N. I have seen them trying.
Knight, E. Dead. He died in Detroit, his
  beard.
  Report to the Mother.
Long, D. One Time Henry Dreamed the
  Number.
Lorde. New York City 1970.
  Politics of Addiction, The.
  Rooming houses are old women.
Madgett. Simple.
Miller, E. Mountain Wife.
Nayo. Hard Times A' Coming.
Nelson, M. Sacrament of Poverty, The.
Reed, I. Feral Pioneers, The.
Roberson. Poor Houses, The.
Smith, L. Face of Poverty.

Toomer. Harvest Song.
Tucker, M. Christmas Eve, South, 1865.
Unknown. Wish for an Overcoat.
Walden. Wish for an Overcoat.
Walker, A. Facing the Way.
  Talking to My Grandmother Who Died Poor.
Walker, M. Childhood.
  Inflation blues is what we got.
  Monologue.
  1933.
  Today.
Wonder. Living for the City.
Wright, J. Invitation to Madison County, An.
Young, A. January.
See also Need

Power
Adisa. Women at the Crossroad / (May
  Elegba Forever Guard the Right Doors).
Angelou. Love Letter.
  These Yet to Be United States.
Baraka. Election Day.
  Short Speech to My Friends.
Danner, J. My Brother.
Harper, F. How Are the Mighty Fallen!
Harper, M. Song: I Want a Witness.
Hayden, R. Wheel, The.
Hughes, L. Gangsters.
  Poet to Bigot.
  This Puzzles Me.
  Two things possess the power.
Jeffers, L. When I Know the Power of My
  Black Hand.
Komunyakaa. Good Joe.
Madhubuti. I ain't seen no poems stop a .38.
Ojenke. Amazon.
Reed, I. Invasion.
Tolson, M. Dark Symphony.
Walker, M. For my people everywhere singing
  their slave songs repeatedly.
  Power to the People.

Prayer
Angelou. Thank You, Lord.
Baraka. Preface to a Twenty Volume Suicide
  Note.
Barrax. In the Restaurant.
Campbell, J. When Ol' Sis' Judy Pray.
Clifton, L. Prayer.
  Slaveship.
Cowdery. Prayer, A.
Cullen, C. Pagan Prayer.
Cuney. Death Bed, The.
Dunbar, P. Crisis, The.
Garnet. Down let the shrine of Moloch sink.
Hayden, R. Incense of the Lucky Virgin.
Heard, J. Unuttered Prayer.
Hughes, L. Gal's Cry for a Dying Lover.
  Imploring Mecca.
  Last Call.
  Moan.
  Prayer: "I ask you this: / Which way to go."
  Prayer Meeting.
  Sinner.
Hunter, A. et al. Down-Hearted Blues.
Iman. Show Me Lord Show Me.
Komunyakaa. Birds on a Powerline.
Lorde. All Hallows Eve.
  October.
  Release Time.
Mackey, N. Falso Brilhante.
McGirt. Century Prayer, The.
McKay, C. St. Isaac's Church, Petrograd.
Nelson, M. At Prayer.
  Aunt Annie's Prayer.
  Canticle for Abba Jacob, A.
  Good Friday Prayer.
  May Your Love Convert Lucifer.
  Prayer of Silence, The.
  Prayer of Singing Joy.
Ray, H. Evening Prayer.
  Prayer: "O Christ, who in Gethsemane."
Reed, I. Off d Pig.
Sanchez, S. You do not know the.
Stuckey. This Is It.
Thompson, C. Out of the Deep.
Thompson, P. Old Saint's Prayer, The.
Unknown. Been in the Storm So Long.
  I been rebuked and I been scorned.

I'm a-rollin', I'm a-rollin', I'm a-rollin',
  through an unfriendly world.
Preaching and Preachers
Allen, J. M. Devil and Sis' Viney, The.
Brown, S. Checkers.
  Foreclosure.
Duriel. On the Uptown Lexington Avenue
  Express: Martin Luther King Day 1995.
Moorer. Southern Pulpit, The.
Nelson, M. Easter Sermon, 1866.
  Sermon in the Cotton Field.
Tolson, M. Old Pettigrew.
Zu-Bolton. Governor of the Ollie Street, The.
See also Clergy
Predators
Brown, S. Idyll.
Hughes, L. Worriation.
Komunyakaa. Charmed.
Pregnancy
African-American Oral Tradition. Forty-nine
  Ford and a tank full of gas.
As-Sabah. Love.
Baraka. For Hettie.
Dove, R. Weathering Out.
Giovanni. Robin's Poem, A.
Hughes, L. What? So Soon!
Lorde. Now That I Am Forever with Child.
  Reins.
Major, C. On Trying to Imagine the Kiwi
  Pregnant.
Nelson, M. For Mary, Fourth Month.
Shange. Oh, I'm 10 Months Pregnant.
Young, A. For Arl in Her Sixth Month.
  Night before Michael Was Born, The.
Prejudice
Baraka. Agony. As Now, An.
Cassells. Soul Make A Path Through
  Shouting.
Derricotte. Weakness, The.
Dunbar, P. To Miss Mary Britton.
Eady. Sherbet.
Jenness. Secret.
Moorer. Prejudice.
Reed, I. Jacket Notes.
Saunders, R. Lawd, Dese Colored Chillum.
See also Racial Prejudice
Presence
Young, A. Available Light.
  Blues Don't Change, The.
  Kicking.
  Orchard at Night in Rain Light, The.
  Total Incandescence.
  Yes, the Secret Mind Whispers.
Presidency, The, United States
Hughes, L. Message to the President.
Moorer. Presidents, The.
Pretension
Baraka. Politics of Rich Painters, The.
Brown, S. Mecca.
Horton, G. Creditor to His Proud Debtor, The.
Hughes, L. Good Bluffers.
  Warning: Augmented.
Pride
Angelou. Phenomenal Woman.
  Seven Women's Blessed Assurance.
Bennett, G. To a Dark Girl.
Brooks, G. To Those of My Sisters Who Kept
  Their Naturals.
Brown, S. Sporting Beasley.
  To Sallie, Walking.
Clifton, L. Listen children / keep this in the
  place.
  Richard penniman.
Cullen, C. Advice to a Beauty.
  To an Unknown Poet.
Danner, M. Convert, The.
Davis, F. Robert Whitmore.
Dove, R. Sunday Greens.
Emanuel, J. Old Black Men Say.
Evans, M. Who Can Be Born Black.
Fabio. God's Trombone.
Freeman, C. When / my uncle willie saw.
Giovanni. But Since You Finally Asked.
  Poem (For Nina).
  Stardate Number 18628.190.

Harper, F. Nothing and Something.
Vashti.
Hughes, L. America's Young Black Joe!
Ballad of the Girl Whose Name Is Mud.
Color.
Hope for Harlem.
Madam and the Census Man.
Jeffers, L. My Blackness Is the Beauty of This Land.
Lorde. Naturally.
Outside.
Woman Speaks, A.
Madhubuti. Awareness.
Death Dance, The.
In a Period of Growth.
New Integrationist, The.
Wall, The.
McKay, C. If we must die—let it not be like hogs.
Miller, M. Where Is the Guilt.
Plumpp. Black Ethics.
Sanchez, S. Needed/Poem/ for My Salvation, A.
We a BadddDDD PEOPLE.
Young Womanhood.
Snellings. Mississippi Concerto.

Prillerman, Byrd
Johnson, M. Sister Johnson's Speech.
To Professor Byrd Prillerman.

Printing and Printers
Hughes, L. Madam's Calling Cards.

Prisons and Prisoners
African-American Oral Tradition. All you tough guys that thinks you're wise.
Convict's Prayer.
Don't Feel So Downhearted, Buddy.
Don't Look So Downhearted, Buddy.
Eddie Ledoux: "There's some strange and queer tales that come through all jails."
Eddie Ledoux: "Wise and queer tales float through all jails."
Feeble Old Man.
Feeble Old Man and a Kid Named Dan.
I was sittin' in the jail to do a stretch of time.
Limpty Lefty McCree.
Little Girl in the Gambler's Nest.
My Reflection.
No Good Whore.
No Good Whore and Crime Don't Pay.
Satan's Playground of Hell.
Strange, Strange Things.
Subject to a Fall: "Boys, you're subject to a fall and trip to the Walls."
Subject to a Fall: "Say, you subject to a fall and a trip to the Wall."
Sweet Lovin' Rose.
They Can't Do That.
Toledo Slim.
Voodoo Queen, The.
Wanderer's Trail, The.
While playing short coin in the Golden West.
Whores Are No Good and Crime Don't Pay.
Winehead Girl.
Angelou. Prisoner.
Brown, S. Convict.
Johnny Thomas.
Puttin' on Dog.
Southern Road.
Clifton, L. To Bobby Seale.
Conyus. Great Santa Barbara Oil Disaster OR, The.
Upon Leaving the Parole Board Hearing.
Cullen, C. Thoughts in a Zoo.
Dunbar, P. Garret, The.
Sympathy.
Gilyard. Letter.
Giovanni. For Two Jameses.
Harper, F. Died of Starvation.
Harris, W. We Live in a Cage.
Hayden, R. Prisoners, The.
Henderson, D. Alvin Cash/Keep on Dancin'.
Hernton. Fall Down.
Hughes, L. Ballad of Gin Mary.
Ballad of the Killer Boy.
Chant for Tom Mooney.
Freedom Seeker.
Johnson, G. Heart of a Woman, The.

Kaufman, B. Jail Poems.
Knight, E. Cell Song.
Crazy pigeon strutting outside my cell.
Fable: "Once upon a today and yesterday and nevermore there were 7 men."
For Freckle-Faced Gerald.
Haiku: "Eastern guard tower."
Haiku: "Morning sun slants cell."
Hard Rock Returns to Prison from the Hospital for the Criminal Insane.
He sees through stone.
Idea of Ancestry, The.
Rehabilitation & Treatment in the Prisons of America.
Warden said to me the other day, The.
WASP Woman Visits a Black Junkie in Prison, A.
Komunyakaa. Prisoners.
Lorde. For Assata.
Maroon. Fire Keeper.
Tucker, M. Soldier Boy's Dream, The.
Unknown. Poor Lazarus.
Walker, F. Crooked Afro.
Walker, M. Girl Held without Bail.
Warren-Moore. Dannemora Contraband.
Young, A. Conjugal Visits.
Visiting Day.

Privacy
Ellis, T. Kiss in the Dark, A.
Harris, W. We Live in a Cage.
Hughes, L. Room.
Lane, P. Sexual Privacy of Women on Welfare.
See also **Solitude**

Procrastination
Dunbar, P. Lapse, The.

Prodigal Son
Harper, F. Prodigal's Return, The.
Hughes, L. Ballad of the Black Sheep.

Prodigality
Brown, S. Checkers.
Dark of the Moon.
Foreclosure.

Progress
Baraka. Valèry as Dictator.
Cotter, Sr. Dr. Booker T. Washington to the National Negro Business League.
Gilbert, D. Fire in the Drum, The.
Harper, F. We are rising, as a people.
Jackson, A. Beginning for New Beginnings, A.
Kaufman, B. I Sigh a Marbled Sigh Ah, at Last.
Linden, M. To the Wheel of Progress.
Lorde. Rites of Passage.
Oyewole. Future Shock.
Salaam. Still Life, Stealing Life / Caught Red-Handed.

Prometheus
Dunbar, P. Prometheus stole from Heaven the sacred fire.

Promises
Angelou. Preacher, don't send me.
Brown, S. Chillen Get Shoes.
Hughes, L. Promised Land / Is always just ahead, The.
Johnson, H. Remember Not.
Lanusse. Le Carnaval.
Lorde. Gemini.
Sanchez, S. I guess. this is what.

Pronunciation
Dove, R. Parsley.

Propaganda
Cortez. Solomon Mahlangu, Freedom Fighter from Mameledi.
There It Is.
Hughes, L. Shall the Good Go Down?

Property
Young, A. What have you got your own.

Prophecy and Prophets
Bradford, Walter. T. C.
Clifton, L. Explanations.
I am high on the man called crazy.
John.
Cortez. Consultation.

Harper, F. Burial of Moses, The.
Syrophenician Woman, The.
Hernton. Jitterbugging in the Streets.
Joans. My Ace of Spades.
Kaufman, B. Poet, The.
Lorde. Equinox.
Nelson, M. Now Jonah Began to Tune His Guitar.
Reed, I. There's a whale in my thigh. at.
Walker, M. Amos, 1963.
Amos (Postscript, 1968).
Hosea.
Isaiah was a man of the court.
Jeremiah, prophet of Jerusalem.
Joel, that young prophet-son of Pethuel!
Micah was a young man of the people.
Prophets for a New Day.

Prostitution and Prostitutes
African-American Oral Tradition. And here's to the duck that swim the pond.
Cocaine Nell.
Corner of 47th and South Park.
Dogass Pimp.
Hobo Ben.
Hustlin' Dan.
Lame and the Whore, The.
Little Girl in the Gambler's Nest.
Little Old Wicked Nell.
Pimp, The.
Pimping Sam.
Ping Pong Joe.
Pretty Pill.
Satan's Playground of Hell.
Strange, Strange Things.
Three Whores Settin' Down in Boston.
While playing short coin in the Golden West.
Wicked Nell: "While sittin' and thinking in deep meditation."
Wicked Nell: "While sittin' down in deep meditation, little girl, lookin' at you."
Winehead Girl.
Angelou. Born That Way.
Baraka. Bludoo Baby, Want Money, and Alligator Got It to Give.
Crow Jane the Crook.
Brown, S. Harlem Street Walkers.
Cullen, C. Black Magdalens.
Hughes, L. Chippy.
Evening Song.
Midnight Chippie's Lament.
Natcha, offering love.
Red Silk Stockings.
Ruby Brown.
Sliver of Sermon.
Workin' Man.
Young Prostitute.
Johnson, F. Scarlet Woman, The.
Kalunda-rae. Hoochie Route.
Knight, E. As You Leave Me.
Violent Space, The.
Komunyakaa. Tu Do Street.
Lorde. Touring.
McKay, C. Harlem Shadows.
Piper, L. Sweet Ethel.
Sanchez, S. Indianapolis/Summer/1969/Poem.
Walker, M. House of Prayer, The.
Poppa Chicken.
Whores.
Young, A. Ho.

Prostitution and Prostitutes Magdalene
Cullen, C. For Daughters of Magdalen.

Protest, Social
Angelou. Take Time Out.
Brooks, G. Lovers of the Poor, The.
Clark, C. No More.
Cornish, S. Montgomery.
Cortez. For the Brave Young Students in Soweto.
Cullen, C. Scottsboro, Too, Is Worth Its Song.
Henderson-Holmes. "C" ing in Colors: Blue.
Hughes, L. Demonstration.
Ghandhi Is Fasting.
Ghosts of 1619.
Kids Who Die.
Un-American Investigators.
Jeffers, L. Vietnam: I Need More Than This Crust of Salt.

Jordan, J. Poem for South African Women.
Kenner. Comments.
Komunyakaa. How I See Things.
Levinger. Carry Me Back to Old Virginny.
Lorde. Art of Response, The.
   Revolution Is One Form of Social Change.
   Workers Rose on May Day or Postscript to
    Karl Marx, The.
Madgett. Alabama Centennial.
McKay, C. If we must die—let it not be like
   hogs.
Moorer. Jim Crow Cars.
Randall, D. Ballad of Birmingham.
Reed, I. Sather Tower Mystery.
   Untitled I.
Rykard. Whole Two Weeks After the Million
   Man March; and Still, if You Asked Me
   about It, This Is All I Could Say about It, A.
Scott, W. Just Taking Note.
Spencer, A. White Things.
Turner, D. Sit-in, The.
Unknown. Ain't Gonna Let Nobody Turn Me
   Round.
   We shall overcome.
Walker, A. Chic Freedom's Reflection.
Walker, M. For my people everywhere singing
   their slave songs repeatedly.
   Girl Held without Bail.
   Street Demonstration.
Wright, S. Until They Have Stopped.
See also **Civil Rights Movement, United States;**
   Injustice

Providence
African-American Oral Tradition. When-a Mah
   Blood runs Chilly and Col.
Angelou. Just like Job.
Horton, G. Excited from Reading the
   Obedience of Nature to her Lord in the
   Vessel on the Sea.
   On Hearing of the Intention of a Gentleman to
   Purchase the Poet's Freedom.
McKay, C. Prayer, A: "'Mid the discordant
   noises of the day I hear thee calling."
Nelson, M. Canticle for Abba Jacob, A.
   Psalm: "So many cars have driven past me."
Payne, D. Mournful Lute or the Preceptor's
   Farewell, The.
Wheatley, P. Thoughts on the Works of
   Providence.

Providence, Rhode Island
Weaver, M. Providence Journal V: Israel of
   Puerto Rico.
Young, A. Providence, Rhode Island.

Psychiatry and Psychiatrists
Walker, A. After the Shrink.
See also **Mental Illness**

Psychoanalysis and Psychoanalysts
Randall, D. Analysands.

Psychological Testing
Nelson, M. Ape-Gods.

Puberty
Lorde. Generation II.

Puerto Ricans
Luciano. You're Nothing but a Spanish
   Colored Kid.

Puerto Rico
Weaver, M. Providence Journal V: Israel of
   Puerto Rico.

Punishment
Gilmore, B. Hazing.
Hayden, R. Whipping, The.
Hughes, L. It Gives Me Pause.
Young, A. Lesson.

Purity
Sanchez, S. Haiku: "I am now in the."
Young, A. Art of Benny Carter, The.

Pursuit
Unknown. Run, Nigger, Run!
Young, A. Backtracking.

Pyramids
Giovanni. Ego Tripping.

Q

Quarrels
Dunbar, P. After the Quarrel.

Fauset. Words! Words!
Heard, J. Quarrel, The.
Hughes, L. Early Evening Quarrel.
Thompson, P. After the Quarrel.
   Domestic Storm, A.
See also **Anger**

Quebec (city), Canada
Ray, H. Quebec.
Unknown. Rebus, A.
Wheatley, P. Answer to the *Rebus*, by the
   Author of These Poems, An.

Queens
Harper, F. Dying Queen, The.
See also **Royalty**

Queens, New York City
Parker, Dominique. When Mark Deloach
   Ruled the World.
Wright, J. Invitation to Madison County, An.

Questions
Dunbar, P. Mystery, The.
Hughes, L. Cross.
   Go *slow*, they say.
   Prayer: "I ask you this: / Which way to go."
   Shakespeare in Harlem.
Kaufman, B. Perhaps.
Lorde. Progress Report.
Sanchez, S. What is it about.
Welburn. Whichway.

Quests
Brown, S. Crossing.
Horne, F. Kid Stuff.
Hughes, L. Farewell, A: "With gypsies and
   sailors."
   Old Walt Whitman.
   Pennsylvania Station in New York, The.
   Search.
   Star Seeker.
   To a Little Lover-Lass, Dead.
Nelson, M. Saint Leaves His Father's House,
   The.
Toomer. They Are Not Missed.

Quilts and Quilting
Dunbar, P. Quilting, The.
Nelson, M. Century Quilt, The.
Newsome. Quilt, The.
Walker, M. Patchwork Quilt, A.

R

Rabbis
Hayden, R. Rabbi, The.

Rabbits
African-American Oral Tradition. Mistah
   Rabbit, Mistah Rabbit, yo tale's mighty
   white.
Dunbar, P. Winter's Approach.
Moore, L. Again.

Race
Brooks, G. To Those of My Sisters Who Kept
   Their Naturals.
Danner, J. My Brother.
Dumas, H. Tis of Thee.
Evans, M. Writers, The.
Fields, J. High on the Hog.
Hall, K. Illusions.
   Song of Tom.
Hamilton, B. Brother Harlem Bedford Watts
   Tells Mr. Charlie Where ITs At.
Hand. I wonder.
Hughes, L. Abe Lincoln.
   Blind.
   Color.
   Man into Men.
   Sweet Words on Race.
   War.
Johnson, G. Riddle, The: "White men's
   children spread over the earth."
Klein, S. Cofaire?
Lockett. Die Black Pervert.
Lorde. Black unicorn is greedy, The.
   Judith's Fancy.
   Need: A Chorale for Black Woman Voices.
   Outlines.
   Outside.

Sequelae.
Song for a Thin Sister.
Thanks to Jesse Jackson.
Madhubuti. Black Christ, The.
   Malcolm Spoke / Who Listened?
Moss, T. Lessons from a Mirror.
Mullen, H. Bête Noire.
Shange. On Becomin Successful.
Thomas, L. Rhumba Negro.
Tolson, M. Uncle Rufus.
Watkins, N. Black Woman Throws a Tantrum.

Racial Prejudice
African-American Oral Tradition. Ups on the
   Farm.
Alhamisi. Pome. For Weird. Hearts. and All.
Allen, S. Moment Please, A.
Angelou. Bump d'Bump.
   Coleridge Jackson had nothing.
   Man Bigot.
   No No No No.
Baraka. Poem for Wille Best, A.
Bibbs. Liberalissimo.
Brooks, G. Ballad of Rudolph Reed, The.
   Bronzeville Woman in a Red Hat.
   Near-Johannesburg Boy, The.
   Riot.
Brown, S. Choices.
   Colloquy.
   Crispus Attacks McKoy.
   Law for George, The.
   Let us suppose him differently placed.
   Old Lem.
   Sam Smiley.
   Slim Greer.
   Southern Cop.
   When de Saints Go Ma'ching Home.
Burroughs, M. Everybody but Me.
Clifton, L. Bodies broken on, The.
   Love rejected / hurts so much more.
Cobb, A. Searching, The.
Coleman, W. Emmett Till.
Cornish, S. Montgomery.
Corrothers. At the Closed Gate of Justice.
   In the Matter of Two Men.
   Indignation Dinner, An.
Cullen, C. Colors.
   Incident.
   Tableau.
   Uncle Jim.
Danner, M. These Beasts and the Benin
   Bronze.
Davis, F. Robert Whitmore.
Davis, R. M. Parasitosis.
Derricotte. Family Secrets.
Dodson, O. Signifying Darkness, The.
Dumas, H. Cuttin Down to Size.
   Mosaic Harlem.
Emanuel, J. Negro, The.
   Old Black Men Say.
   Whitey, Baby.
Giovanni. Categories.
   Harvest.
   Wilmington Delaware.
Harper, M. American History.
   Goin' to the Territory.
   Grandfather.
Harris, W. Daddy Poem, A.
Hemphill. Family Jewels.
Holman, M. Mr. Z.
Horne, F. On Seeing Two Brown Boys in a
   Catholic Church.
Hughes, L. Backlash Blues, The.
   Birmingham Sunday.
   Black Crown, The.
   Blacklash Blues.
   Children's Rhymes.
   Colored Soldier, The.
   Cross.
   Dream Boogie.
   I too, sing America.
   Merry-Go-Round.
   This Puzzles Me.
   Ultimatum: Kid to Kid.
   Where? When? Which?
Jackmon. Burn, Baby, Burn.
Johnson, G. Prejudice.
Johnson, J. White Witch, The.

Jones, G. Tripart.
Jordan, J. En Passant.
Poem About My Rights.
Poem about Police Violence.
Song of Sojourner Truth, A.
Unemployment Monologue.
What Would I Do White?
Lee, D. Stereo.
With All Deliberate Speed.
Lorde. Judith's Fancy.
Poem for Women in Rage, A.
Power.
Revolution Is One Form of Social Change.
Sisters in Arms.
Madhubuti. Death Dance, The.
First World.
For Black People.
Move Un-noticed to Be Noticed: a Nationhood
Poem.
Stereo.
Major, C. Vietnam #4.
McClellan. Color Bane, The.
McKay, C. Barrier, The.
Enslaved.
Look Within.
Negro's Friend, The.
Outcast.
Tiger.
White House, The.
Miller, E. Boys of Summer, The.
Nelson, M. Freeman Field.
Palm Sunday, 1866.
Quigless. Moving.
Randall, D. Black Poet, White Critic.
Melting Pot, The.
Randall, J. Execution.
Reed, I. Guilty, the New York Philharmonic
Signs up a Whale.
Poison Light.
Spellman. Friends i am   like you   tied.
Stanard. Wrong Color.
Sun-Ra. Visitation, The.
Toomer. People.
Trethewey. Drapery Factory, Gulfport,
Mississippi, 1956.
Unknown. Learn to Count.
Walcott. Blues.
Walker, A. First, they said we were savages.
January 10, 1973.
Right to Life, The: What Can the White Man
Say to the Black Woman?
South: The Name of Home.
Walker, M. Monologue.
Waller, T. *et al.* (What Did I Do to Be So)
Black and Blue?
Ward, Jr., J. Don't Be Fourteen (In
Mississippi).
Wilson, A. Grenudita.
Young, A. Dance for Militant Dilettantes, A.
Poem for Players, A.
Your Basic Black Poet.

See also **Apartheid; Prejudice**

Racism and Racists
Ai. Endangered Species.
Self Defense.
Alexander, E. Boston Year.
Venus Hottentot.
Allen, S. Moment Please, A.
Anderson, C. Finger Pop'in.
Angelou. Miss Scarlet, Mr. Rhett and other
Latter-Day Saints.
No No No No.
Baker, H. Late-Winter Blues and Promises of
Love.
Baraka. At the Colonial Y They Are
Aesthetically and Culturally Deprived (Y's
Later) (31).
Christ Was Never in Europe!
Contract. (For The Destruction and Rebuilding
of Paterson), A.
History on Wheels.
New Reality Is Better Than a New Movie, A!
1929: Y you ask? (26).
One More Time.
People Burning, The.
Y's 18.
Black, I. Racist Psychotherapy.

Blue. American Dialogue.
Bomani, N. Philosophical Perspective on
Everyday Shit, A.
Brooks, G. Ballad of Rudolph Reed, The.
Bronzeville Mother Loiters in Mississippi. /
Meanwhile, a Mississippi Mother Burns
Bacon.
Bronzeville Woman in a Red Hat.
Chicago *Defender* Sends a Man to Little Rock,
The.
"Negro" Hero.
White Troops Had Their Orders but the
Negroes Looked Like Men.
Brown, S. Bitter Fruit of the Tree.
Call for Barnum.
Mr. Danny.
Old Woman Remembers, An.
Roberta Lee.
Slim in Atlanta.
Strong Men.
Brutus. Off to Philadelphia in the morning.
Bryant, F. Cathexis.
Campbell, J. Pariah, The.
Carroll, K. Domino Theory (Or Snoop Dogg
Rules the World), The.
Something Easy for Ultra Black Nationalists.
Upper Marlboro.
Christian. Go Down, Moses!
Clifton, L. After Kent State.
Powell; March 1991.
Willie B (4).
Coffin, F. Ajax' Conclusion.
Coleman, W. Dear Mama.
Cornish, S. His Fingers Seem to Sing.
Corrothers. In the Matter of Two Men.
Cortez. Give Me the Red on the Black of the
Bullet.
Rape.
There It Is.
Cotter, Sr. Is It Because I Am Black?
Cullen, C. Ballad of the Brown Girl, The.
Black Christ, The.
From the Dark Tower.
Incident.
Tableau.
Uncle Jim.
Davis, D. Nigger's Got to Go, De.
Davis, F. Giles Johnson, Ph.D.
Dove, R. Great Palaces of Versailles, The.
Dumas, H. Afro-American.
Dunbar, P. Harriet Beecher Stowe.
Eady. Sherbet.
Song.
William Carlos Williams.
Eckels, Mary / Bell Jones.
Forbes, C. Poet's Shuffle, The.
Fortune. Bartow Black.
Freeman, C. I saw them lynch festus whiteside
and.
Gerima. Sankofa.
Gilyard. Letter.
Giovanni. Black Power.
Great Pax Whitie, The.
Universality.
Graham, D. West Ridge Is Menthol-Cool, The.
Gray-Kontar. Not No Socialism/Communism
classical, but Some Power to the People Jazz.
Harper, F. Fairer Hope, a Brighter Morn, A.
Lines to Miles O'Reiley.
Martyr of Alabama, The.
Simon's Countrymen.
Harper, M. American History.
Debridement.
Grandfather.
Meaning of Protest, The.
Nightmare Begins Responsibility.
Duriel. On the Uptown Lexington Avenue
Express: Martin Luther King Day 1995.
Harris, W. Daddy Poem, A.
Hasson. Black and White.
Hayden, R. American Journal.
Frederick Douglass.
From the corpse woodpiles, from the ashes.
Monet's "Waterlilies."
'Mystery Boy' Looks for Kin in Nashville.
Heard, J. Black Sampson, The.
Hemphill. Family Jewels.

Hernton. Jitterbugging in the Streets.
Hill, L. Tuskegee.
Holman, M. Mr. Z.
Hughes, L. Angola Question Mark.
Argument.
As I Grew Older.
Ballad of Ozie Powell.
Ballad of Sam Solomon.
Ballad of the Landlord.
Ballad of Walter White.
Beaumont to Detroit: 1943.
Birmingham Sunday.
Blue Bayou.
Broadcast to the West Indies.
Children's Rhymes.
Christ in Alabama.
Cross.
Death in Yorkville.
Dream Boogie: Variation.
Flight.
Freedom Train.
Gods.
Good Morning, Stalingrad.
I too, sing America.
Imagine! / They are afraid of you.
In Explanation of Our Times.
Ku Klux.
Lament for Dark Peoples.
Lincoln Monument: Washington.
Lunch in a Jim Crow Car.
Lynching Song.
Memo to Non-White People.
Migration.
Movies.
Mulatto.
Not a Movie.
Note on Commercial Theatre.
Parade.
Porter.
Puzzled.
Red Cross.
Scottsboro.
Song After Lynching.
Song for a Dark Girl.
Song of Adoration.
Southern Mammy Sings.
Tell Me.
Theme for English B.
Ultimatum: Kid to Kid.
Uncle Tom is a legend and a dream.
Us: Colored.
Vari-Colored Song.
West Texas.
White Man.
White Ones, The.
Iman. Love Your Enemy.
Iverem. Keeper.
Jackson, R. Lonely Affair, A.
Jeffers, H. I Was Looking at Miles.
Jeffers, L. My Blackness Is the Beauty of
This Land.
Johnson, J. Color Sergeant, The.
Saint Peter Relates an Incident of the
Resurrection Day.
Jordan, A. If I Write a Poem.
Jordan, J. From Sea to Shining Sea.
1977: Poem for Mrs. Fannie Lou Hamer.
Poem for Buddy.
Poem from Taped Testimony in the Tradition
of Bernard Goetz.
Solidarity.
Test of Atlanta 1979, The.
Uhuru in the O.R.
Who Look at Me.
Kaufman, B. Benediction.
Knight, E. Fable: "Once upon a today and
yesterday and nevermore there were 7 men."
For Freckle-Faced Gerald.
Hard Rock Returns to Prison from the
Hospital for the Criminal Insane.
Once on a Night in the Delta: A Report From
Hell.
Rehabilitation & Treatment in the Prisons of
America.
Komunyakaa. Back Then.
February in Sydney.

How I See Things.
Newport Beach, 1979.
Lawrence, J. For Malcolm.
Lorde. Afterimages.
American Cancer Society Or There Is More
Than One Way to Skin a Coon.
Diaspora.
East Berlin.
Every Traveler Has One Vermont Poem.
For the Record.
Revolution Is One Form of Social Change.
Suffer the Children.
Who Said It Was Simple.
Madgett. Race Question, The.
Madhubuti. Don't Cry, Scream.
McElroy, C. Ghost-Who-Walks, The.
McKay, C. Lynching, The.
Tiger.
To the White Fiends.
White House, The.
Medina, T. After the Verdict.
Big House Revisited, The.
Capitalism Is a Brutal Motherfucker.
Miller, E. Walk in the Daytime Is Just as
Dangerous as a Walk in the Night, A.
Moss, T. Reconsideration of the Blackbird, A.
Nelson, M. Armed Men.
Ballad of Aunt Geneva, The.
Boys in the Park.
Diverne's Waltz.
Hurrah, Hurrah.
Minor Miracle.
Tuskegee Airfield.
Ologboni. Changed Mind (or the Day I Woke
Up).
Patterson, R. Song Waiting for Music, A.
Pitcher. Salute.
Plumpp. Mississippi Griot.
Poetri. Don't hate me cause my skin is
smooth like fine lustrous fiber forming a tuft.
Public Enemy. Fight the Power.
Randall, D. Idiot, The.
Melting Pot, The.
Randall, J. When Something Happens.
Who Shall Die.
Rankine. New Windows.
Reed, I. Ballad of Charlie James, The.
Bitter Chocolate.
Jacket Notes.
My Brothers.
Railroad Bill, a conjure man.
Rivers, C. If Blood is Black Then Spirit
Neglects My Unborn Son.
Invisible Man, The.
Roland Poet X. Divided States of America,
The.
Salaam. I live in the mouth of history.
Sanchez, S. Malcolm.
Poem for July 4, 1994.
Right On: White America.
Smith, P. Blonde White Women.
Spellman. When Black People Are.
Spencer, A. White Things.
Steptoe. Window Shopping.
Summer. Curious White Boy.
Thompson, C. Uncle Rube on the Race
Problem.
Uncle Rube to the Young People.
Toomer. People.
Van Peebles. To Hell with Whitey.
Walcott. Blues.
Glory Trumpeter, The.
Walker, A. Thing Itself, The.
Walker, M. Birmingham, 1963.
For my people everywhere singing their slave
songs repeatedly.
Now.
Since 1619.
Sorrow Home.
Washington. Moon Bound.
Weaver, M. Borders.
Whitman, A. 'T is hard to judge if hatred of
one's race.
Williams, C. A. In Search of Aunt Jemima.
Wonder. Living for the City.
Wright, R. Between the World and Me.
Young, A. Midnight Special Revisited, The.

Young, K. Field Trip.
See also **Apartheid; Racial Prejudice;
Segregation**
Radio
Baraka. In Memory of Radio.
SOS.
Barlow, G. Resonance.
Eady. Radio.
Komunyakaa. Hanoi Hannah.
Railroads
African-American Oral Tradition. Casey Jones.
Brown, S. Break of Day.
Call Boy.
Long Track Blues.
Side by Side.
Southern Road.
Carr, L. How Long Blues.
Conyus. Six Ten Sixty-Nine.
Hughes, L. Homesick Blues.
Mitchell Case, The.
James, E. Sunnyland.
Jones, R. Trouble in mind, I'm blue.
Komunyakaa. False Leads.
Reed, I. Railroad Bill, a conjure man.
Troupe. In Texas Grass.
Unknown. Can't You Line It?
John Henry.
Old Section Boss, The.
Railroad Bill, Railroad Bill.
When John Henry was a little babe.
Walker, M. Two-Gun Buster and Trigger
Slim.
See also **Locomotives; Trains**
Railway Stations
Hughes, L. Pennsylvania Station in New York,
The.
Railway Travel
Handy, W. Yellow Dog Blues.
Harper, M. Dance of the Elephants, The.
Lorde. Women on Trains.
McKay, C. On the Road.
Rain
Bontemps. Return, The.
Brown, S. April in Coolwell.
Convict.
Cotter, Sr. Rain Music.
Cullen, C. Night Rain.
Singing in the Rain.
Dunbar, P. Drizzle.
Rain-Songs.
Time to Tinker 'Roun'!
Fabio. I would be for you rain.
Giovanni. Rain is / god's sperm falling.
Horton, G. Meditation on a Cold, Dark and
Rainy Night.
Hughes, L. April Rain Song.
In time of silver rain.
Strange Hurt.
Johnson, H. Invocation: "Let me be buried in
the rain."
Jordan, J. Poem for Buddy.
Poem on the Second Consecutive Day of Rain.
Kaufman, B. Ancient Rain, The.
Kgositsile. Gods Wrote, The.
Lorde. Coping.
Fallen, The.
My Fifth Trip to Washington Ended in
Northeast Delaware.
Mitchell, K. Night Rain.
Moore, L. Tanka: "Month of rain ends."
Ray, H. Voices of the Rain.
Rogers, A. Rain Song, The.
Sanchez, S. Haiku: "O i was wide and."
Just the two of us.
Shepherd, R. Where When Was.
Young, A. Beauty of Milwaukee cold with
rain, The.
Rainbows
Dunbar, P. Place Where the Rainbow Ends,
The.
Salaam. New Orleans Rainbow.
Rainey, Gertrude ("Ma")
Brown, S. Ma Rainey.
Young, A. Dance For Ma Rainey, A.
Rap Music
Carroll, K. Domino Theory (Or Snoop Dogg
Rules the World), The.

Herut. Gems.
Lewis, Mendi. I remember 1983.
Stanard. Rap is no mystery.
T'Kalla. Nuns in the Basement of God.
Rape
African-American Oral Tradition. Lame and
the Whore, The.
Stackolee in Hell.
Cortez. Rape.
Jordan, J. Case in Point.
Female and the Silence of a Man, The.
Poem About My Rights.
Poem from Taped Testimony in the Tradition
of Bernard Goetz.
Poem on the Road; for Alice Walker.
Rape Is Not a Poem.
Komunyakaa. Re-creating the Scene.
Neely. Rhonda, Age 15 Emergency Room.
Nelson, M. April Rape.
Chosen.
Shange. It's Not so Good to be Born a Girl/
Sometimes.
Sharp, S. In the Tradition of Bobbitt.
Walker, A. Thing Itself, The.
Raphael Santi
Ray, H. Raphael.
Rastafarianism and Rastafarians
Stanard. Washington Square Park and a Game
of Chess.
Rathel, James M.
Heard, J. In Memory of James M. Rathel.
Rats
Atkins. Probability and Birds in the Yard.
Cook, W. Still-Life with Woodstove.
Raven. Assailant.
Toomer. Reapers.
Reading and Readers
Cotter, Sr. Book's Creed, The.
Dove, R. Reading Hölderlin on the Patio with
the Aid of a Dictionary.
Dunbar, P. End of the Chapter, The.
Forbes, C. Poet's Shuffle, The.
Reading Walt Whitman.
Harper, F. Learning to Read.
Jordan, J. From Nicaragua Libre: Photograph
of Managua.
Kendrick, D. Sophie, Climbing the Stairs.
Madhubuti. Poem Looking for a Reader, A.
Poet: What Ever Happened to Luther?
Nelson, M. Chopin.
How I Discovered Poetry.
Reed, I. Badman of the Guest Professor.
Reagan, Ronald Wilson
Jordan, J. Verse for Ronald Slapjack Who
Publicly Declared, "I, Too, Am a Contra!"
Reed, I. Inaugural Day, 1981.
Reality
Baraka. Poem for Deep Thinkers, A.
Y's 18.
Brutus. Sand wet and cool, The.
Clifton, L. Friends Come.
Dove, R. Anti-Father.
Young, A. Singular Yen, A.
Reaping and Reapers
Bontemps. Black Man Talks of Reaping, A.
Harper, F. Go work in my vineyard, said the
Lord.
Toomer. Harvest Song.
Reapers.
Reason
Baraka. Burning General, The.
Dove, R. Geometry.
Harper, F. Advice to the Girls.
Kaufman, B. Cat Is Sleeping on a Poem, The.
Wheatley, P. Ode on the Birthday of Pompey
Stockbridge, An.
See also **Intellect and Intellectuals; Mind;
Thought**
Rebellions and Rebels
Baraka. Wise 4.
Cortez. Solomon Mahlangu, Freedom Fighter
from Mamelodi.
Dunbar, P. Conquerors, The.
Farr. At General Electric, Where They Eat
Their/Young.

Hughes, L. In Explanation of Our Times.
Thorn, The.
Jordan, J. Problems of Translation: Problems of Language.
Verse for Ronald Slapjack Who Publicly Declared, "I, Too, Am a Contra!"
Lorde. Relevant Is Different Points on the Circle.
Nelson, M. Ballad of Aunt Geneva, The.
Reed, I. Badman of the Guest Professor.
I Am a Cowboy in the Boat of Ra.
Introducing a New Loa.
Return of Julian the Apostate to Rome, The.
Reynolds, S. Whipping, The.
Stuckey. Rebel.
Walker, A. Outcast.
Rage.
Walker, M. Ballad of the Free, The.
I hear a rumbling underground.
Since 1619.
Whitfield. To Cinque.
See also **Revolution and Revolutionaries**

Rebirth
Ai. More.
Bontemps. My Heart has Known its Winter.
Clifton, L. There Is a Girl Inside.
Giovanni. For Two Jameses.
Grimké, A. At April.
Hayden, R. El-Hajj Malik El-Shabazz.
Hughes, L. Girl.
In time of silver rain.
McKay, C. Baptism.
Salaam. Soon One Morning, I'll Fly Away.
Toomer. Be with Me.
Promise, The.
Vague Opening.
White Arrow.
See also **Regeneration; Renewal**

Rebuilding
Giovanni. Very Simple Wish, A.

Recognition
Young, A. Sleepy Day at Half Moon Bay.

Reconciliation
Gaye. What's Going On.
Heard, J. Sunshine after Cloud.
Hughes, L. Brotherly Love.

Reconstruction, United States
Baraka. At the Colonial Y They Are Aesthetically and Culturally Deprived (Y's Later) (31).
Bell, J. Modern Moses, or "My Policy" Man.
Dunbar, P. To the South.
Harper, F. Appeal to the American People, An.
Learning to Read.

Record Players
African-American Oral Tradition. Junkies' Heaven.
Barlow, G. Resonance.
Gray-Kontar. Cuz' Mama Played Jazz.
Trethewey. Secular.

Red (color)
Hughes, L. When Sue Wears Red.
Sanchez, S. Haiku: "I am now in the."

Redding, Otis
Sanchez, S. Night pumping like an.

Redemption
Murray, P. Redemption.
Unknown. What Yo' Gwine to [*or* t'] Do When Yo' [*or* de] Lamp Burn Down?
Vassa. Miscellaneous Verses.

Reflections
Clifton, L. What the Mirror Said.
Knight, E. Belly Song.
Lorde. Birthday Memorial to Seventh Street, A.
Moss, T. Lessons from a Mirror.
Reed, I. Beware: Do Not Read This Poem.
Young, A. Fun City Samba.
Move Continuing, The.
Some Spice for Jack Spicer.

Refugees
Hughes, L. Song of the Refugee Road.
Komunyakaa. Boat People.

Regeneration
Clifton, L. To my Friend, Jerina.

See also **Rebirth; Renewal**

Regret
Angelou. Refusal.
Clifton, L. Lane Is the Pretty One.
Cullen, C. Song of Sour Grapes, A.
Dunbar, P. Debt, The.
Life's Tragedy.
Old Memory, An.
Giovanni. Charles White.
Walking down park.
Grimké, A. Eyes of My Regret, The.
Hayden, R. Ballad of Sue Ellen Westerfield, The.
Horton, G. On an Old Deluded Soldier.
Hughes, L. Cross.
Reverie on the Harlem River.
Kaufman, B. Walking Hot Seasons.
Knight, E. Sun came, Miss Brooks—, The.

Reincarnation
Clifton, L. Once and future dead, The.

Rejection
African-American Oral Tradition. Dogass Pimp.
Ping Pong Joe.
Angelou. Prescience.
Refusal.
Brooks, G. Life of Lincoln West, The.
Clifton, L. Love rejected / hurts so much more.
Coleman, W. In This Waking.
Dove, R. Aircraft.
Dunbar, P. Jilted.
Gex-Breaux. Blue Deep.
Hughes, L. Ballad of the Gypsy.
Black Pierrot, A.
Croon.
Fortune Teller Blues.
Late last night I.
Lonesome Place.
Long Song for Antonia.
Migration.
Suicide.
Lorde. Dozens, The.
Small Slaughter, A.
Reed, I. .05.
X, D. Shot to the Curb.

Relatives
Lorde. And What About the Children.
Young, A. 2 takes from *Love in Los Angeles.*

Relativity
Cullen, C. Sonnet: "Some for a little while do love, and some for long."
Dunbar, P. Comparison.

Religion
Atkins. Lisbon.
Braithwaite. Rye Bread.
Brown, S. Seeking Religion.
Campbell, A. Divine Mission, The.
Clifton, L. At Jonestown.
Davis, F. "Onward Christian Soldiers!"
Dove, R. Receiving the Stigmata.
Dunbar, P. Faith.
How Lucy Backslid.
Possession.
Spiritual, A.
Temptation.
Harper, F. Dialogue, A.
Present Age, The.
Hayden, R. Those Winter Sundays.
Hughes, L. Mystery.
Song for a Dark Girl.
Johnson, F. Minister, The.
Kaufman, B. Oregon.
Lorde. Release Time.
When the Saints Come Marching In.
Winds of Orisha, The.
Moorer. Southern Pulpit, The.
Nelson, M. Churchgoing.
Plato. Advice to Young Ladies.
Prettyman. When Mahalia Sings.
Reed, C. In a Harlem Store Front Church.
Reed, I. I Am a Cowboy in the Boat of Ra.
Rodgers, C. And When the Revl2ution Came.
Touré, A. JuJu.
Unknown. My army cross over.
Wright, J. Sketch for an Aesthetic Project.
Wednesday Night Prayer Meeting.

See also **Faith; Worship and Worshipers**

Religious Life
Brooks, G. Firstly Inclined to Take What It Is Told.
Giovanni. Each Sunday.
Harper, F. Deliverance.
Nelson, M. Abba Jacob and the Businessman.
Blessing the Boats.
Clown Nose.
Toomer. Not for me—and may nothing enhance.

See also **Clergy**

Remorse
Grimké, A. El Beso.
Jordan, J. For Ethelbert.
Smash the Church.
Lorde. Separation.
Nelson, M. Minor Miracle.

Renewal
Angelou. Africa.
Recovery.
Request.
Brooks, G. Young Africans.
Clifton, L. Let There Be New Flowering.
Light that came to lucille clifton, The.
New Bones.
There Is a Girl Inside.
Dodson, O. Circle One.
Dove, R. Turning Thirty, I Contemplate Students Bicycling Home.
Fabio. I would be for you rain.
Giovanni. Autumn Prison.
Harper, F. Change, The.
Crocuses, The.
Only a word— a little word.
Ragged Stocking, The.
Refiner's Gold, The.
Renewal of Strength.
Signing the Pledge.
Harper, M. New Season.
Hughes, L. Africa.
Black Maria.
Pastoral.
Question and Answer.
To You.
Jackson, A. Beginning for New Beginnings, A.
Kaufman, B. All those ships that never sailed.
Trip, Dharma Trip, Sangha Trip, The.
Kgositsile. Ivory Masks in Orbit.
Lorde. Afterlove.
Restoration.
Solstice.
Madhubuti. We Walk the Way of the New World.
McKay, C. Easter Flower, The.
Morning Joy.
Through Agony.
Miller, M. Wrong Side of the Morning, The.
Nelson, M. Leaving the Hospice.
Reed, I. Last Week in 30, The.
Snellings. Sunrise!!
Walker, A. These mornings of rain.
Walker, M. Labyrinth of Life, The.
My Mississippi Spring.
Young, A. April Blue.
James Cotton Band at Keytstone, The.

See also **Rebirth; Regeneration**

Repentance
Angelou. Thank You, Lord.
Brown, S. Colloquy.

Repression
Cullen, C. Timid Lover.

Reproach
Cullen, C. For an Atheist.
Jean, V. On Apologies.

Reputation
African-American Oral Tradition. Hustlin' Dan.
Hughes, L. Mean Old Yesterday.
Red Cross.

Rescues
Harper, F. Out in the cold mid the dreary night.
Harper, M. "League of Gileadites": Messages.
"Rescue Work": Dues.

Hughes, L.　Final Call.

Resistance
Angelou.　Our Grandmothers.
Clifton, L.　Tyrone (2).
Cortez.　Push Back the Catastrophes.
　There It Is.
Cullen, C.　In Spite of Death.
Hughes, L.　Underground, The.
Jean, V.　Lesson on Braces.
Jordan, J.　I Must Become a Menace to My
　Enemies.
　1977: Poem for Mrs. Fannie Lou Hamer.
Jordan, N.　Black Warrior.
Lorde.　Spring People.
　Summer Oracle.
Madgett.　Exits and Entrances.
McKay, C.　If we must die—let it not be like
　hogs.
　Tiger.
Patterson, R.　Song Waiting for Music, A.
Plumpp.　Zimbabwe.
Powell, K.　Out of Pocket.
Salaam.　Bush Mama.
Shannon, A.　Doris.
Sims, L.　Angels Prayer, An.
Snellings.　Mississippi Concerto.
Spencer, A.　Letter to My Sister.
Sun Ra.　Saga of Resistance.
Tolson, M.　Uncle Rufus.
Ward, J.　At the Border of Constant Disaster.
Whitman, A.　'T is hard to judge if hatred of
　one's race.
Young, A.　Geography of the Near Past.

Resorts
Hughes, L.　Seashore through Dark Glasses
　(Atlantic City).

Respectability
Moorer.　Everyday I need my shit done in a
　special way.

Responsibility
Angelou.　On Working White Liberals.
Clifton, L.　Come home from the movies.
　Generations.
　If mama / could see.
Giovanni.　Adulthood II.
　December of My Springs, The.
　Gus.
Horton, G.　Song of Liberty and Parental
　Advice.
Jordan, J.　Poem at the Midnight of My Life.
O'Neal, S.　Biological Didn't Bother.

Rest
Bontemps.　"Close Your Eyes!"
Dunbar, P.　Noddin' by de Fire.
Johnson, F.　Long de cool o' night w'en day
　am daid.
McKay, C.　French Leave.
　Through Agony.
Toomer.　Motion and Rest.
Young, A.　No Trespassing.

Restaurants
Brown, S.　Slim Lands a Job?

Restlessness
Alexander, M.　Memory.
　People of Unrest.
Lane, P.　Spring.
Young, A.　I Arrive In Madrid.

Resurrection, The
Brooks, J.　Resurrection, The.
Clifton, L.　Raising of Lazarus, The.
Harper, F.　Resurrection of Jesus, The.
Thompson, C.　Empty Tomb, The.
Unknown.　Steal Away to Jesus.

See also **Easter**

Retirement and Retirees
Dove, R.　Satisfaction Coal Company, The.
Jordan, A.　My Father's Retirement.
Reed, I.　White Hope.

See also **Old Age**

Retribution
Harper, M.　Sambo's Mistakes: an Essay.

Reunions
Bomani, M.　Homecoming.
Cullen, C.　Two Who Crossed a Line.
Harper, F.　Reunion, The.

Hughes, L.　Lover's Return.
Lorde.　Meet.
Moore, L.　Haiku: "Family reunion."
Reed, I.　Anon. Poster.
Walter, R.　Familee reunion tyme iz a special
　tyme.

Revenge
Baraka.　Poem for Black Hearts, A.
Brown, S.　Ballad of Joe, The.
Cheatwood.　Swamp Rat.
Harper, F.　Ethiopia.
　Retribution.
Jordan, J.　Poem about Police Violence.
Komunyakaa.　Fragging.
Loftis.　Brief Encounter.
McKay, C.　Enslaved.
　To the White Fiends.
Reed, I.　Rough Trade Slumlord Totem.
　Sermonette.
Sanchez, S.　Towhomitmayconcern.
Tucker, M.　Revenge.
Walker, M.　Kissie Lee.

Revivalism and Revivalists
See **Evangelism and Evangelists**

Revolution and Revolutionaries
Alhamisi.　Uhuru (freedom. now. swahili. east
　african lango).
Aubert, A.　Revolutionary, The.
Balagon.　Children of the Cosmos.
　Untitle.
Baraka.　In the Tradition.
　New Reality Is Better Than a New Movie, A!
　Poem for Deep Thinkers, A.
　Reggae or Not!
　Revolutionary Love.
　Short Speech to My Friends.
　"There Was something I Wanted to Tell You."
　(33) Why?
　When We'll Worship Jesus.
Barrax.　For a Black Poet.
Bennett, Bob.　It is time for action.
Brown, Adwin.　Donut Man.
Brown, S.　Old Woman Remembers, An.
Coates.　Alice Flips the Script.
Cortez.　No Simple Explanations.
Franklin, C.　Two Dreams (for M. L. K.'s
　one).
Giovanni.　Black Judgements.
　Categories.
　Detroit Conference of Unity and Art.
　For Saundra.
　My Poem.
　No Reservations.
　Poem (No Name No. 3).
　Revolutionary Dreams.
　Revolutionary Music.
　Seduction.
　We stood there waiting.
　When i die i hope no one who ever hurt me
　cries.
Gray-Kontar.　July.
Harper, M.　Song: I Want a Witness.
Hughes, L.　Advertisement for the Waldorf-
　Astoria.
　Air Raid over Harlem.
　Always the Same.
　Chant for May Day.
　Good-morning, Revolution.
　Letter to the Academy.
　Militant.
　New Song, A.
　Revolution.
　Roar, China! / Roar, old lion of the East!
　Song of the Revolution.
　Tired.
　Wait.
　Warning.
Jackson, R.　Lonely Affair, A.
Jeffers, L.　Flesh of the Young Men Is
　Burning, The.
　When I Know the Power of My Black Hand.
Johnson, A.　Our Days Are Numbered.
Jordan, J.　On the Loss of Energy.
　Poem for Guatemala.
Kaufman, B.　Hawk Lawler: Chorus.
Kgositsile.　To Fanon.
　When Brown Is Black.

Knight, E.　On the Yard.
Lorde.　Building.
　NOW.
　On My Way Out I passed You and the
　Varrazano Bridge.
　Sisters in Arms.
Madhubuti.　For Black People.
　Malcolm Spoke / Who Listened?
　Message All Black People Can Dig, A.
　Revolutionary Screw, The.
　We Walk the Way of the New World.
Maroon.　Fire Keeper.
McKay, C.　Exhortation: Summer, 1919.
Medina, T.　Capitalism Is a Brutal
　Motherfucker.
Oyewole.　When the revolution comes.
Randall, D.　Abu / 's a stone black
　revolutionary.
　Roses and Revolutions.
Randall, J.　Who Shall Die.
Reed, I.　Jackal-Headed Cowboy, The.
　Reactionary Poet, The.
Rodgers, C.　And When the Revloution Came.
　U Name This One.
Salaam.　Still Life, Stealing Life / Caught Red-
　Handed.
Sanchez, S.　Indianapolis/Summer/1969/Poem.
　So This Is Our Revolution.
Scott-Heron.　Revolution Will Not Be
　Televised!, The.
Speech.　Revolution / Revolution / Brothers
　and sisters.
Spriggs.　For the Truth (Because It Is
　Necessary).
　We Waiting on You.
Thomas, R.　Index to a Black Catharsis.
　Revolution!
Walker, A.　Facing the Way.
　Lost My Voice? Of Course.
　Well. / He was a poet.
Walker, M.　For my people everywhere singing
　their slave songs repeatedly.
Watkins, N.　Bedtime Story.
Welburn.　First Essay on the Art of the U. S.
Wright, R.　I Have Seen Black Hands.
Young, A.　Myth Science of Our Time, The.

See also **Rebellion and Rebels**

Rewards
Hughes, L.　Ballad of the Two Thieves.

Rhythm
Bennett, Bob.　(Title).
Jordan, J.　About Enrique's Drawing.
Knight, E.　Ilu, the Talking Drum.
Reed, I.　Poetry Makes Rhythm in Philosophy.
Sanchez, S.　Bear the rhythm of.
Wilson, Ted.　S, C, M.

Rice
Strange.　Offering.

Riddles
Hayden, R.　Sphinx.
Nelson, M.　Laughter as the Highest Form of
　Contemplation.
Unknown.　Rebus, A.
Wheatley, P.　Answer to the *Rebus*, by the
　Author of These Poems, An.

Righteousness
Baraka.　Success, The.
Clark, Benjamin.　No Enemies.
Jackson, M.　Man in the Mirror.
Jordan, J.　I Must Become a Menace to My
　Enemies.
Payne, D.　Mournful Lute or the Preceptor's
　Farewell, The.

Riley, James Whitcomb
Dunbar, P.　James Whitcomb Riley.

Rilke, Rainer Maria
Goodison.　On Becoming a Tiger.

Rimbaud, Arthur
Kaufman, B.　Blue Slanted into Blueness.
　Harwood Alley Song.

Riots and Rioters
Ai.　Riot Act, April 29, 1992.
Alexander, E.　Affirmative Action Blues.
Anderson, S.　New Dance, A.
Angelou.　Riot: 60's.
Brooks, G.　Riot.

Brown, S. Old Woman Remembers, An.
Cortez. Nighttrains.
Cruz, V. Urban Dream.
DuBois, W. Litany of [or at] Atlanta, A.
Harper, M. Molasses and the Three Witches.
Henderson, D. Keep on Pushing.
Kgositsile. Brother Malcolm's Echo.
Leslie, C. On Riots.
Linden, M. Riot, A.
Murray, P. Harlem Riot, 1943.
  Mr. Roosevelt Regrets.
Reed, I. Decade That Screamed, The.
  Untitled I.
Wakefield, J. Days Prior to.
  Oh shit a riot!
Walker, M. Jackson State, May 15, 1970.

Rituals
Barrax. Domestic Tranquility.
Fields, J. Citizen.
Giovanni. Rituals.
Kaufman, B. African Dream.
Knight, E. He sees through stone.
Komunyakaa. Faith Healer.
Lorde. Coniagui women / wear their flesh like
  war, The.
  Women of Dan Dance with Swords in Their
  Hands to Mark the Time When They Were
  Warriors, The.
Moore, L. Eternal Landscape, The.
Plumpp. Remembered.

Rivalry
Corrothers. Me 'n' Dunbar.
See also **Competition**

Rivers
Brown, S. Riverbank Blues.
Caution. River is a decrepit old woman, the.
Dove, R. Event, The.
  In the Bulrush.
Dunbar, P. On the River.
Fordham. Maiden and River.
Giovanni. Poem (No Name No. 1).
Goodison. Wedding in Hanover.
Hughes, L. Dream Variations.
  Life Is Fine.
  Negro Speaks of Rivers, The.
  Reverie on the Harlem River.
  Suicide's Note.
  Wide River.
McKay, C. Sukee River.
Murray, P. Conquest.
Salam. Sunrise on the River.
Southerland. Night in Nigeria.
See also **Brooks and Streams; Listings for
  specific rivers**

Roads
Dove, R. Corduroy Road.
  Early Morning on the Tel Aviv-Haifa
  Freeway.
Dunbar, P. On the Road.
  Riding to Town.
  Roadway, A.
  To the Road.
Hughes, L. Bound No'th Blues.
  Florida Road Workers.
Johnson, H. Road, The.
Kaufman, B. Alien winds sweeping the
  highway.
  Mongolian Sunset in Gobi Desert.
See also **Streets**

Robeson, Paul
Brooks, G. Paul Robeson.
Hayden, R. Homage to Paul Robeson.

Robinson, Jackie
Clifton, L. Jackie Robinson.
  Tyrone (3).
  Wille B (3).
Harper, M. Blackjack.
Knight, E. Belly Song.
Miller, E. Boys of Summer, The.

Rockets
Brathwaite, E. New Year Letter.
See also **Space and Space Travel**

Romanticism and Romantics
Hughes, L. Madam and the Movies.

Rome, Italy
Johnson, F. Rome is dying.

Jordan, J. Roman Poem Number Five.
Reed, I. Return of Julian the Apostate to
  Rome, The.

Romeo and Juliet
Hughes, L. Juliet.

Roosevelt, Franklin Delano
Hughes, L. Ballad of Roosevelt.
  Dear Mr. President.
  How about It, Dixie.

Roosevelt, Theodore
Dunbar, P. For Theodore Roosevelt.

Roosters
African-American Oral Tradition. Rooster
  crowed, the hen looked down, The.
See also **Chickens**

Rope
Clifton, L. Climbing.
Komunyakaa. How I See Things.

Roses
Dunbar, P. Fulfilment.
  Poor withered rose, she gave it me.
  Promise.
  Roses.
  Roses and Pearls.
  She Gave Me a Rose.
  Summer in the South.
Hughes, L. Breath of a Rose.
  Not What Was.
  Rememberance.
Jordan, J. Letter to the Local Police.
McClellan. In the Heart of a Rose.
Moore, L. Haiku: "Sipping the new tea."
Newsome. Wild Roses.
Randall, D. Roses and Revolutions.

Rousseau, Henri
Kaufman, B. Bird with Painted Wings.

Royalty
Angelou. Let's Majeste.
Harper, F. Vashti.
Kaufman, B. Countess Erica Blaise: Chorus.
Reed, I. Epistolary Monologue.
See also **Kings; Queens**

Ruins
Dove, R. Ants of Argos, The.
  Nestor's Bathtub.
  Sightseeing.

Rumor. *See* **Gossip and Gossips**

Running and Runners
Hughes, L. Shadows.

Russia
Harper, F. Vision of the Czar of Russia, The.
Hughes, L. Good Morning, Stalingrad.
  Salute to Soviet Armies.
  Stalingrad: 1942.
McKay, C. St. Isaac's Church, Petrograd.
Reed, I. El Paso Monologue.

Russian Revolution
Reed, I. Sputin.

Russians, The
Reed, I. Sputin.

Rwanda
Sharp, S. Meanwhile, in Rwanda.
Williams, Karen. Ntarama (Rwanda)
  Chronicles.

S

Sabbath. *See* **Saturday; Sunday**
Sacco-Vanzetti Case
Cullen, C. Not Sacco and Vanzetti.
Sacrifices
Angelou. Many and More.
Clifton, L. She Insists on Me.
Hughes, L. Speaking of Food.
Jordan, J. Sunflower Sonnet Number Two.
Jordan, N. Sacrifice, The.
Randall, D. Rite, The.
Sanchez, S. Life / Poem.
Shockley. Oseola McCarty.
Sadism and Sadists
Brown, S. Frankie and Johnny.
Sadness
Baraka. Invention of Comics, The.
Cortez. Lonely Woman.

Hughes, L. Cabaret Girl Dies on Welfare
  Island.
  Late last night I.
  Mazie Dies Alone in the City Hospital.
  Miss Blues'es Child.
James, E. Sunnyland.
Kaufman, B. Picasso's Balcony.
Komunyakaa. Epilogue to the Opera of Dead
  on Arrival.
Ray, H. Broken Heart.
  Shadow and Sunrise.
Sanchez, S. Haiku: "O i am so sad, i."
Walker, A. S. M.
Young, A. Detroit 1958.
  There is a sadness to this world.

Sailing and Sailors
Angelou. Martial Choreograph.
Bontemps. Nocturne of the Wharves.
Dunbar, P. Sailor's Song, A.
Horton, G. Excited from Reading the
  Obedience of Nature to her Lord in the
  Vessel on the Sea.
Hughes, L. Death of an Old Seaman.
  Long Trip.
  Old Sailor.
  Port Town.
  Sailing Date.
  Sailor.
  Seascape.
  To Captain Mulzac.
  Young Sailor.
Lorde. Starting All Over Again.
Ray, H. Boat Song.
Tucker, M. Hugging the Shore.
See also **Seafaring and Seafarers**

Saint Lawrence (river), Canada
Ray, H. On the rapids of the St. Lawrence.

St. Louis, Missouri
Lorde. St. Louis Out of Time.
Reed, I. St. Louis Woman.

Saints
Derricotte. Weakness, The.
Dove, R. Catherine of Alexandria.
Hughes, L. Wealth.
Nelson, M. Abba Jacob's Seven Devils.
Walker, A. Abduction of Saints, The.

Salt
Barlow, G. Salt.
Dove, R. Nightmare.
Phillips, C. Reach, The.

Saltus, Thaddeus
Fordham. To Rev. Thaddeus Saltus.

Salvation
African-American Oral Tradition. Soon one
  mawnin death come creepin in mah room.
Bontemps. Nocturne at Bethesda.
Clifton, L. Meeting After the Savior Gone,
  The.
  White Boy, The.
Cullen, C. Shroud of Color, The.
Giovanni. Poem (For BMC No. 1).
Hammon. Evening Thought, An [: Salvation
  by Christ with Penetential Cries].
Harper, F. Fishers of Men.
  I thirst, but earth cannot allay.
  Prodigal's Return, The.
  Save the Boys.
  Saved at Last.
Henderson, E. B. Git on Board, Chillun.
Hughes, L. Encounter.
Johnson, F. Who Is That a-Walking in the
  Corn?
Lorde. Timepiece.
Toomer. To Gurdjieff Dying.
Wheatley, P. Isaiah LXIII, 1–8.
  On the Death of the Rev. Dr. Sewell, 1769.
  To the University of Cambridge, in New-
  England.

Samson
Clemmons. Love Letter.

San Francisco, California
African-American Oral Tradition. Little Old
  Wicked Nell.
  Toledo Slim.
Harper, M. Three O'Clock Love Song.

Hughes, L. City.
  Trip: San Francisco.
Reed, I. Dress Rehearsal Paranoia #2.
Young, A. Berkeley Pome.
Sanctuaries
Cowdery. Interlude.
Sand
Harper, F. Grain of Sand, A.
Lorde. Sahara.
Santa Barbara, California
Conyus. Great Santa Barbara Oil Disaster OR, The.
Sappho
Johnson, H. Brilliant-bellied newt flashes, The.
Sarah (Bible)
Harper, F. Burial of Srah.
Sarajevo, Yugoslavia
Young, A. Moon Over Matter.
  Sarajevo Moon.
  Sarajevo Moonlight.
Saratoga, New York
Harper, M. Dining from a Treed Condition, an Historical Survey.
  Founding Fathers in Philadelphia, The.
Satan
African-American Oral Tradition. Casey Jones.
  Herbert Hoover.
  Lame and the Whore, The.
  Stackolee in Hell.
Allen, J. M. Devil and Sis' Viney, The.
Angelou. Known to Eve and Me.
Baraka. Devil Worship.
Brown, S. Arkansas Chant.
  Slim in Hell ("Slim Greer went to heaven").
Cullen, C. Dictum.
  For a Mouthy Woman.
Nelson, M. May Your Love Convert Lucifer.
Salaam. "5 Minutes, Mr. Salam."
Tolson, M. Old Pettigrew.
See also **Demons**
Satiric Verse
Brown, S. Real Mammy Song.
Saturday
Hughes, L. Saturday Night.
Thompson, D. Blues at 1.
Trethewey. Collection Day.
See also **Sabbath**
Scheherazade
St. John, P. Ocean of the Streams of Story.
Scholarship and Scholars
Baudelaire. Cats.
Davis, F. Giles Johnson, Ph.D.
Hughes, L. Ph.D.
  Wise Men.
School and Schools
Brooks, G. We real cool. We.
Byrnes. Chalk-Dust.
Cassells. Soul Make A Path Through Shouting.
Dove, R. Flash Cards.
Dunbar, P. Old High School and the New, The.
  Wadin' in de Crick.
Harper, F. Learning to Read.
Holman, M. Three Brown Girls Singing.
Houston, V. Class Room.
Hughes, L. Graduation.
  Kids in School with Me, The.
Jean, V. On Apologies.
Lane, P. On Being Head of the English Department.
Loftis. Fights After School.
Lorde. Bees, The.
  Hanging Fire.
  Release Time.
  School Note.
Major, C. I Was Looking for the University.
Miller, E. Night Before the First Day of School, The.
Moorer. Negro Schools, The.
  Tree of Knowledge, The.
Nelson, M. How I Discovered Poetry.
Reed, I. Smiley School, The.
Thompson, P. Examination, The.
  Lines to an Old School-House.

See also **Colleges and Universities; Education; Students; Teaching and Teachers**
Science and Scientists
Alexander, E. Venus Hottentot.
Nelson, M. Ape-Gods.
Scorn
Lorde. Poem for Women in Rage, A.
Unknown. I been rebuked and I been scorned.
Scotland
Fordham. Highland Mary.
Scottsboro Case
Cullen, C. Scottsboro, Too, Is Worth Its Song.
Hughes, L. August 19th.
  Scottsboro.
  Town of Scottsboro, The.
Screams
Bryant, F. Black Orpheus.
Jordan, J. On the Real World: Meditation #1.
Miller, M. Scream, The.
Sanchez, S. You do not know the.
Sharp, S. Finding His Fist.
Sculpture and Sculptors
Danner, M. Convert, The.
Gilbert, C. African Sculpture.
Kaufman, B. Who Has Seen the Wind?
Ray, H. Sculptor's Vision, The.
  Tireles Sculptor, The.
Sea
Atkins. Lakefront, Cleveland.
Baraka. Betancourt.
Barrax. There was a song.
Boyd, J. Ocean.
Braithwaite. House of Falling Leaves, The.
  Watchers, The.
Cheatwood. Visions of the Sea.
Clifton, L. Lost Baby Poem, The.
Cullen, C. For Joseph Conrad.
Dove, R. Fish in the Stone, The.
Dunbar, P. Fisher Child's Lullaby, The.
  Mystic Sea, The.
  On the Sea Wall.
  Sea speaks to me of you, The.
  Wind and the Sea, The.
Forbes, C. Dark Mirror.
  Home.
Hughes, L. Feet O' Jesus.
  Return to Sea.
  Rising Waters.
  Sea Calm.
  Sea charm / The sea's own children.
Komunyakaa. Break from the Bush, A.
  Newport Beach, 1979.
Lorde. Maiden, The.
  What my child learns of the sea.
Mackey, N. Dream Thief.
  Phantom Light of All Our Day, The.
McClellan. Eternity.
Pritchard, N. Burnt Sienna.
St. John, P. Song.
Toomer. At Sea.
  Merl.
Tucker, M. Beautiful Sea, The.
Wheatley, P. On Messrs. Hussey and Coffin.
Young, A. Sometimes with the waves.
See also **Ocean; Sailing and Sailors**
Seafaring and Seafarers
Bontemps. Nocturne of the Wharves.
Harper, F. Death of the Old Sea King.
  Story of the Rebellion, A.
Hughes, L. Long Trip.
  Seascape.
Toomer. At Sea.
See also **Sailing and Sailors**
Seamstresses. *See* **Sewing**
Seasons
Angelou. In Retrospect.
  My Life Has Turned to Blue.
Cullen, C. Leaves.
Delany. Solace.
Dunbar, P. Foolin' wid de Seasons.
  Love's Seasons.
  Roses.
Hughes, L. Year Round.
Kaufman, B. Sun, Creator of Suns.
Lorde. Change of Season.
  Father the year has fallen.

Pirouette.
  Return.
  Second Spring.
  Songless Lark, The.
  Spring III.
  What my child learns of the sea.
McKay, C. Flame-Heart.
  To One Coming North.
Nelson, M. Twist the thread.
Sanchez, S. Missing you is like.
Wright, J. Love in the Weather's Bells.
Seclusion
Hayden, R. Soledad.
Reed, I. Instructions to a Princess.
Secrecy and Secrets
Angelou. In a time of secret wooing.
Clifton, L. Listen children / keep this in the place.
Dove, R. Adolescence—I.
Dunbar, P. We wear the mask that grins and lies.
Harper, F. Tennessee Hero, The.
Hughes, L. Personal.
Knight, E. He sees through stone.
Lorde. As I Grew Up Again.
  Out to the Hard Road.
McKay, C. Red Flower, A.
Reed, I. Dragon's Blood.
  Instructions to a Princess.
Welburn. Eulogy for Populations.
Security
Clifton, L. To my Friend, Jerina.
Cullen, C. For a Poet.
Dunbar, P. Farm Child's Lullaby, The.
Lorde. Woman.
Walker, M. Iowa Farmer.
Seduction
Carroll, K. Short Poem.
Giovanni. Seduction.
Hall-Evans. Seduction.
Lorde. On a Night of the Full Moon.
Seeds
Campbell, J. Mors et Vita.
Dunbar, P. Seedling, The.
Hughes, L. For Russell and Rowena Jelliffe.
Lorde. Coping.
Segregation
Clifton, L. Still / it was nice.
Hughes, L. Bible Belt.
  Bitter River, The.
  Black Man Speaks, The.
  Crow Goes, Too.
  Dear Mr. President.
  Dixie Man to Uncle Sam.
  Dixie South Africa.
  Get Up off That Old Jive.
  Go *slow*, they say.
  Governor Fires Dean.
  How about It, Dixie.
  Jim Crow's Last Stand.
  Judge William Hastie.
  Little Song on Housing.
  Lunch in a Jim Crow Car.
  Merry-Go-Round.
  Message to the President.
  Mitchell Case, The.
  Poem to Uncle Sam.
  Restrictive Covenants.
  Southern Negro Speaks.
  Total War.
  Where Service Is Needed.
  Where? When? Which?
  Will V-Day Be Me-Day Too?
Nelson, M. Freeman Field.
Sun-Ra. Visitation, The.
See also **Apartheid**
Self
Alexander, E. Painting / (Frida Kahlo).
Angelou. Reverses.
Baraka. Agony, An. As Now.
Balboa, the Entertainer.
  Bridge, The.
  Liar, The.
  Poem Some People Will Have to Understand, A.
  Symphony Sid.

Bethune, L. Juju of My Own, A.
Brooks, G. My Dreams, My Works Must Wait
 Till after Hell.
 Sundays of Satin-Legs Smith, The.
Clifton, L. Good Friday.
 I Am Not Done Yet.
 I am running into a new year.
 I was born in a hotel.
 If i stand in my window.
 If mama / could see.
 In this garden.
 Lucy and Her Girls.
 Lucy one-eye.
 My Poem.
 New Year.
 Poet, The.
 To my Friend, Jerina.
 Turning into my own.
 Why Some People Be Mad at Me Sometimes.
Cortez. Do you think this is a sad day.
 I Am New York City.
 Lynch Fragment 2.
Cullen, C. For Myself.
Dickey. Leaving Eden.
Dunbar, P. Advice.
 Vagrants.
Giovanni. Poem (For Nina).
Hamilton, M. Things I Do Not Speak.
Hayden, R. Names.
Horton, G. Fearful Traveller in the Haunted
 Castle, The.
 George Moses Horton, Myself.
Hughes, L. Big-Timer, The.
 Cross.
 Epitaph: "Within this grave lie."
 Final Curve.
 There.
Jacobs, H. On Extending the Olive Branch to
 My Own Self.
Jordan, J. Fragments from a Parable.
 Poem # One.
 Short Note to My Very Critical and Well-
 Beloved Friends and Comrades, A.
Kaufman, B. Blue Slanted into Blueness.
 Grandfather Was Queer, Too.
 Would You Wear My Eyes?
Knight, E. Belly Song.
 Cop-Out Session.
 Report to the Mother.
 Welcome Back, Mr. Knight: Love of My Life.
Lorde. Bicentennial Poem #21,000,000.
 Good Mirrors are Not Cheap.
 Memorial II.
 Solstice.
 Therapy.
Menken. Infelix.
 Myself.
Nelson, M. *Enneads*, I, vi.
 Icarus Dream.
 Sneak Preview.
 Strange beautiful woman, A.
 Union Apprehended.
Ray, H. Self-Mastery.
Reed, I. Man or Butterfly.
Rilke. Rilke's Third Elegy.
Roy, L. Ride, The.
St. John, P. Carnival.
Sanchez, S. Like bigger thomas.
 Present.
 Towhomitmayconcern.
Shange. On Becomin Successful.
Stephany. You are instantly enfolded.
Toomer. Delivered at the Knighting of Lord
 Durgling by Great Bruce-Jean.
 I sit in my room.
Williams, S. S. Recitation.
Young, A. Self-Portrait: Holding On.
 Seventh April.
 Tiny Self-Portrait.
 What have you got of your own.

Self-Deceit
Baraka. Black Bourgeoisie.
Bibbs. Split Standard.
Lorde. Between Ourselves.
 Monkeyman.

Self-Doubt
Baraka. Insidious Dr. Fu Man Chu, The.
 Poem Welcoming Jonas Mekas to America, A.
Brown, Adwin. Donut Man.
Clifton, L. Light that came to lucille clifton,
 The.
 To Thelma Who Worried Because I Couldn't
 Cook.
 Way It Was, The.
Cullen, C. Self Criticism.
Giovanni. Intellectualism.
Jeffers, L. Self-Doubt.
Toomer. Prayer.
X, D. Shot to the Curb.

Self-Knowledge
Angelou. When I think about myself.
Brooks, G. Strong Men, Riding Horses /
 Lester after the Western.
 To Those of My Sisters Who Kept Their
 Naturals.
Clifton, L. Turning into my own.
Derricotte. Blackbottom.
Giovanni. Turning (I Need a Better Title).
Harper, M. Blue Ruth: America.
Hughes, L. Man into Men.
 Me and the Mule.
Jordan, J. Poem About My Rights.
Lorde. Bloodbirth.
 But What Can You Teach My Daughter.
 For Each of You.
Madhubuti. Self-Hatred of Don L. Lee, The.
McKay, C. I Know My Soul.
Moorer. Everyday I need my shit done in a
 special way.
Reed, I. Foolology.
Sanchez, S. Needed/Poem/ for My Salvation,
 A.
Toomer. Prayer.
X, M. Proverbs.
Young, A. Dancing.
 Dancing All Alone.
 Fifty-Fifty.

Self-Reliance
Baraka. Duncan Spoke of a Process.
Carroll, K. Something Easy for Ultra Black
 Nationalists.
Clifton, L. Later i'll say / i spent my life.
 Meeting After the Savior Gone, The.
Chuck D. But Can You Kill the Nigga in
 You?
Dove, R. Canary.
Giovanni. Poem for a Lady Whose Voice I
 Like.
Horton, G. Song of Liberty and Parental
 Advice.
Hughes, L. Black Crown, The.
 Black Dancers.
 Down Where I Am.
 Impasse.
Jordan, N. Be You.
Knight, E. Evolutionary Poem No. 1.
 Evolutionary Poem No. 2.
Lorde. Stations.
Madhubuti. Move Un-noticed to Be Noticed: a
 Nationhood Poem.
 Poem to Compliment Other Poems, A.
Thomas, M. Amen.

Self-Restraint
Angelou. Lie, The.
McKay, C. White House, The.

Self-Righteousness
Baraka. New World, The.
 Numbers, Letters.
Giovanni. When i die i hope no one who ever
 hurt me cries.

Selfishness
Dunbar, P. Career, A.
Giovanni. Poem (For PCH).

Senegal
Davis, T. Double Take at Relais de
 L'Espadon.
Dixon, M. Tour Guide: La Maison des
 Esclaves.
Hughes, L. Cubes.

Senses
Angelou. Senses of Insecurity.
Baraka. Symphony Sid.

Bryant, F. Black Orpheus.
Eady. April.
Kaufman, B. When we hear the eye open
 there, in that place.
Troupe. It is not who or what.

Sensitivity
Baraka. Gatsby's Theory of Aesthetics.
Clifton, L. Perhaps.
Jordan, J. Rape Is Not a Poem.

Sensuality
Baudelaire. Cat, The.

Separation
Angelou. My Life Has Turned to Blue.
Baraka. Agony, An. As Now.
Cullen, C. Dictum.
 Therefore, Adieu.
 To One Not There.
Dove, R. Someone's Blood.
Dunbar, P. Comrade.
 Lyric, A: "My lady love lives far away."
Emanuel, J. Fishermen.
Evans, M. Where Have You Gone?
Giovanni. Certain Peace, A.
 Housecleaning.
 Something to be Said for Silence.
Hayes, D. Auf Wiedersehen.
Horton, G. Division of an Estate.
Hughes, L. Afro-American Fragment.
 Autumn Note.
 Better in the quiet night.
 Dream.
 Shakespeare in Harlem.
 So long / is in the song.
James, E. Sunnyland.
Johnson, J. Sence You Went Away.
Jordan, J. Double Standard Lifestyle Studies:
 #1.
 Poem for Derrick Gilbert.
Knight, E. For a Brookline Lady I Love.
 Memo #5.
 Upon Your Leaving.
Komunyakaa. Tu Do Street.
Lorde. Memorial III from a Phone Booth on
 Broadway.
 125th Street and Abomey.
 Smelling Wind.
McKay, C. Summer Morn in New Hampshire.
 Through Agony.
Nelson, M. Star-Fix.
Sanchez, S. Poem No. 10.
Thompson, P. Adown the heights of Ages.
Unknown. Southern Blues, The.
Walker, A. Walker.
Young, A. Only Race There Is, The.
 What Is the Blues?

See also **Absence; Isolation; Loneliness**

September
McClellan. September Night, A.
Ray, H. September.

Sequoia Trees
Kaufman, B. Mongolian Sunset in Gobi
 Desert.

Serenity
Brown, S. To Sallie, Walking.
Harper, F. Grain of Sand, A.
Hayden, R. Monet's "Waterlilies."
Horton, G. On the Poetic Muse.
Jordan, J. In Paris.
Kaufman, B. Cocoa Morning.
Lane, P. Quiet Poem, A.
Nelson, M. Jesus Prayer, The.

Sermons
Hughes, L. Sunday Morning Prophecy.
Wheatley, P. To the Rev. Dr. Thomas Amory
 on Reading Sermons on Daily Devotion, in
 Which That Duty Is Recommended and
 Assisted.

Servants
Angelou. When I think about myself.
Brooks, G. Bronzeville Woman in a Red Hat.
Brown, S. Law for George, The.
 Ruminations of Luke Johnson.
 Scotty Has His Say.
Cumbo. Domestics.
Cuney. No Images.
Evans, M. When in Rome.

Hughes, L. Madam and Her Madam.
  Madam's Past History.
  Porter.
  Ruby Brown.
  Song to a Negro Wash-woman, A.
Klein, S. Letter to Madame Lindé from
  Justine, Her Creole Servant.
Trethewey. Domestic Work, 1937.
Williams, S. Letters from a New England
  Negro.

Sewing
Dunbar-Nelson. I sit and sew—a useless task
  it seems.
Dunbar, P. Quilting, The.

Sex
Adisa. Discover Me.
African-American Oral Tradition. Bulddaggers'
  Hall.
Casey Jones.
Cocaine Shorty.
Cock is a crickly creature.
Corner of 47th and South Park.
Dance of the Freaks: "It was a cool and
  mystic rain."
Dance of the Freaks: "It was cold and mist
  and rain in old Spokane."
Dogass Pimp.
Dolomite: "Some folks say that Willie Green."
'Flicted Arm Pete: "It was way down in this
  little town that they call Louisville."
Forty-nine Ford and a tank full of gas.
Freaks' Ball.
Girl told me, A.
He-frog told the she-frog, The.
Herbert Hoover.
Here's to the lady with the little red shoes.
I used to could diddle all night long.
I woke up this morning with a hard on.
Knockin' down chairs and slammin' doors.
L.A. Street.
Life of a Junkie.
Little Old Wicked Nell.
Miss Lookingood.
My Uncle Sam was a good old man.
Old Cods.
Pisspot Pete.
Pussy ain't nothin' but a hairy split.
Rooster crowed, the hen looked down, The.
Running through the jungle with my dick in
  my hand.
Seven Wise Men, The.
Stackolee: "It was back in the time of nineteen
  hundred and two."
Stackolee: "This is supposed to be about two
  colored studs. It's truth. In New Orleans."
Swinging through the trees with my dick in
  my hand.
Three Whores Settin' Down in Boston.
Through the Keyhole in the Door.
Twenty-Two-Twenty told Automatic Jim to
  tell his fast-fucking sister Fanny.
Ai. Before You Leave.
Angelou. Remembrance.
  Zorro Man, A.
Asquith. Sunday Afternoons.
Baraka. All's Well.
Barrax. Adagio.
Billingsley. Rhetorically Speaking.
Coleman, W. At the Record Hop.
  Breast Examination.
  Mastectomy.
Cornish, S. Generations 1.
Cortez. Suppression.
Dove, R. Adolescence—II.
Dunbar, P. Confirmation.
Ellis, T. Kiss in the Dark, A.
Giovanni. Autumn Prison.
  Something to be Said for Silence.
Handy, W. Yellow Dog Blues.
Harper, M. Elvin's Blues.
Duriel. What We Have Lost.
Hemphill. Where Seed Falls.
Hoagland, E. Georgia—It's the Gospel Truth.
Hughes, L. Listen Here Blues.
  Nude Young Dancer.
Jamal. Sat. Nite.

Johnson, G. I Want to Die While You Love
  Me.
Jordan, J. Addenda to the Papal Bull.
  For Dave: 1976.
  Poem at the Midnight of My Life.
Kalunda-rae. Hoochie Route.
Kaufman, B. Does the Secret Mind Whisper?
Komunyakaa. Apprenticeship.
Loftis. Brief Encounter.
Lorde. Echoes.
Lyle. Your Tears Feel Good on the Hood of
  My Car.
Major, C. On Trying to Imagine the Kiwi
  Pregnant.
McKay, C. Wild May.
Miller, E. She is flat on her back.
Nelson, M. No Jazz.
Parker, Dominique. Foxfire.
Reed, I. Betty's Ball Blues.
  Kali's Galaxy.
  Mojo Queen of the Feathery Plumes.
  Skirt Dance.
  To a Daughter of Isaiah.
Sanchez, S. Haiku: "O i was wide and."
  I am on top of.
  I'm in the middle.
  Poem for My Father, A.
  Prelude to Nothing.
  Short Poem.
Smith, P. Dylan, Two Days.
Stephany. Who is not a stranger still.
Tolson, M. Lena Lovelace.
Walker, A. She said: "When I was with him."
Waters, M. Hoochie Coochie.
Weatherly, T. Blues for Franks Wooten.
Weaver, M. Message on Cape Cod, The.
Young, A. Conjugal Visits.
See also **Erotic Love; Lust**

Sexism
Baraka. Dead Lady Canonized, The.
Giovanni. Woman Poem.
Harper, F. Double Standard, A.
Jordan, J. Case in Point.
  From Sea to Shining Sea.
  Memo.
  Poem About My Rights.
  Poem on the Road; for Alice Walker.
  Some people despise me be-.
Latifah. U.N.I.T.Y.
Lorde. Equal Opportunity.
  Revolution Is One Form of Social Change.
  Who Said It Was Simple.
Mullen, H. Floorwax Mother.
Shange. It's Not so Good to be Born a Girl/
  Sometimes.
Tallie. Karma's Footsteps.

Sexual Abuse
As-Sabah. Love.
Brooks, G. Merle "Uncle Seagram."
Clifton, L. To my Friend, Jerina.
Lorde. Chain.
Miller, E. Mountain Wife.
Neely. Rhonda, Age 15 Emergency Room.
Nelson, M. No No, Bad Daddy.
  No Worst.
Reed, I. And the Devil Sent a Ford Pinto
  Which She Also Routed.

Sexual Exploitation
Baraka. For Crow Jane (Mama Death).
Maroon. Nude Woman Spotted in Cappuccino
  Cup as Advertising Dollar Co-Opts Another
  Life.
Sanchez, S. Poem No. 7.

Sexuality
African-American Oral Tradition. Annabelle
  Jones, a noble kid.
  Annabelle Jones from Shrevesport City.
Angelou. Seven Women's Blessed Assurance.
Clifton, L. Mary.
Dove, R. After Reading *Mickey in the Night
  Kitchen* for the Third Time Before Bed.
Giovanni. Seduction.
Komunyakaa. Thorn Merchant's Mistress, The.
Lorde. Meet.
McElroy, C. In My Mother's Room.

Shadows
Alexander, L. Nocturne Varial.

Angelou. Life Doesn't Frighten Me.
Atkins. Dark Area.
Cuney. Death Bed, The.
Grimké, A. Tenebris.
Hayden, R. Broken Dark, The.
Hughes, L. Shadows.
Johnson, G. Escape.
Jordan, J. Sonnet from the Stony Brook, A.
Knight, E. Haiku: "Bare pecan tree, A."
  Haiku: "Under moon shadows."
Madhubuti. After Her Man Had Left Her for
  the Sixth Time That Year / (An Uncommon
  Occurrence).
Moore, L. Haiku: "Summer evening sun."
Sanchez, S. When i return home.
Troupe. Sense of Coolness, A.

Shakespeare, William
Cullen, C. *Cor cordium* is written there.
Ray, H. Shakespeare.
Whitman, A. Ye Bards of England.

Shame
Angelou. Amoebaean for Daddy.
  Memory, The.
Hughes, L. I too, sing America.
Lorde. Kitchen Linoleum.
Miller, M. Where Is the Guilt.
Shepard, O. It's a Low Down Dirty Shame.

Sharecroppers
Brown, S. Old King Cotton.
  Sharecroppers.
  Young Ones, The.
Hughes, L. Share-Croppers.

Shaw, Robert Gould
Brawley. My Hero.
Dunbar, P. Robert Gould Shaw.
Ray, H. Robert G. Shaw.

Sheep
Hughes, L. Shearing Time.
See also **Lambs**

Sheepshearing and Sheepshearers
Hughes, L. Shearing Time.

Sheets
Sanchez, S. Away from you these.
Warren-Moore. All-Night Issue, The.

Shelley, Percy Bysshe
Cullen, C. *Cor cordium* is written there.
Yerby. Fishes and the Poet's Hands, The.

Shells
Ray, H. Enchanted Shell, The.
See also **Snails**

Shepherds and Shepherdesses
Hughes, L. Shepherd's Song at Christmas.

Sheppard, W. H.
Johnson, M. Dedicated to Dr. W. H.
  Sheppard.

Ships and Shipbuilding
Bontemps. Nocturne of the Wharves.
Clifton, L. Slaveship.
Dunbar, P. Ships That Pass in the Night.
Harper, M. Bristol: Bicentenary
  Remembrances of Trade.
Hughes, L. *Jesus, The.*
  Return to Sea.
Komunyakaa. Fog Galleon.
Lorde. Fishing the White Water.
See also **Boats and Boating**

Shipwrecks
Fordham. Shipwreck.
  Tribute to a Lost Steamer.
Hayden, R. Diver, The.
Knight, E. Dark Prophecy: I Sing of Shine.
Menken. Ship That Went Down, The.

Shoes and Shoemakers
Hughes, L. Bad Morning.
  Barefoot Blues.
Weaver, M. Sub Shop Girl.

Shopping and Shops
Atkins. New Storefront.
Derricotte. 1994 Inventory.
Giovanni. Master Charge Blues.
Thompson, C. Christmas Rush, The.
Tolson, M. African China.

Shores
Hayden, R. Point, The.
Hughes, L. Moonlight Night: Carmel.

Kaufman, B. Picasso's Balcony.
Lorde. Bridge through My Windows.
McKay, C. North and South.
Plateau, The.
Toomer. Merl.
Young, A. Big Sur.
See also **Beaches**

Shorter, James A.
Heard, J. Bishop James A. Shorter.

Show Business
Giovanni. Poem for Aretha.
Komunyakaa. Communique.
Young, A. Ian.
See also **Acting and Actors; Motion Pictures; Theater and Theaters**

Sierra Nevada Mountains
Reed, I. Phoebe is the 9th satellite.

Sight
Brown, S. Glory, Glory.
Giovanni. Photography.
Komunyakaa. When in Rome—Apologia.
Young, A. How the Rainbow Works.

Silence
Angelou. On Aging.
Baraka. As a Possible Lover.
Braithwaite. Quiet has a hidden sound.
Dunbar, P. Silence.
Gilmore, B. Gas Station Attendant.
Giovanni. Something to be Said for Silence.
Hayes, D. Pastourelle.
Hughes, L. Silence.
Silent One.
Jordan, J. Case in Point.
Komunyakaa. Music That Hurts, The.
Lane, P. Wind Thoughts.
Lorde. If You Come Softly.
Suspension.
Moore, L. Eternal Landscape, The.
Nelson, M. At Prayer.
Jesus Prayer, The.
Prayer of Singing Joy.
Pritchard, N. Cloak, The.
Rux. Suite Repose.
Sanchez, S. Familiarize your.
Sharp, S. Finding His Fist.
Southerland. Recitation.
Thomas, L. Onion Bucket.
Warren-Moore. All-Night Issue, The.
Young, A. Curative Powers of Silence, The.
Koto Music/Singing.

Silk
Shange. Elegance in the extreme.

Silver
Dunbar, P. Real Question, The.

Simon of Cyrene
Cullen, C. Simon the Cyrenian Speaks.
Harper, F. Simon's Countrymen.

Simplicity
Young, A. Real Time.

Sin
Cotter, Sr. Contradiction.
Cullen, C. For Daughters of Magdalen.
Dunbar, P. Distinction.
How Lucy Backslid.
Harper, F. Contrast, The.
Double Standard, A.
Nothing and Something.
Save the Boys.
Hughes, L. Angels wings is white as snow, The.
It Gives Me Pause.
Madam and the Minister.
Sinner.
Saunders, R. Cinderella.
Walker, A. Compulsory Chapel.
Mississippi Winter II.

Singing and Singers
Angelou. Shaker, Why Don't You Sing?
Singer Will Not Sing, The.
Barrax. Singer, The.
Brooks, G. Paul Robeson.
Coffin, F. Mother's Songs.
Cullen, C. Colored Blues Singer.
Danner, J. Singer, The.
Davis, D. Linin' ub De Hymns, De.

Dove, R. Canary.
Dunbar, P. Banjo Song, A.
Deacon Jones' Grievance.
Lesson, The.
Question, A.
Sympathy.
When Malindy Sings.
When Sam'l Sings.
With the Lark.
Evans, M. And the Old Women Gathered.
Fields, J. Alabama.
Giovanni. Dreams.
Geni in the Jar, The.
Harper, M. Blues Alabama.
Hayes, D. Threnody: "Let happy throats be mute."
Henderson, D. Song of Devotion to the Forest.
Hughes, L. Harlem Night Song.
I too, sing America.
Song for Billie Holiday.
To Dorothy Maynor.
Weary Blues, The.
Jackson, R. Lady's Way.
Jenkins, C. Poem for Tracy (Chapman).
Johnson, J. Lift Ev'ry Voice and Sing.
O Black and unknown bards of long ago.
Jordan, J. For My Brother.
Newport Jazz Festival: Saratoga Springs and Especially about George Benson and Everyone Who Was Listening.
Kgositsile. Ivory Masks in Orbit.
Lorde. Day they eulogized Mahalia, The.
For My Singing Sister.
Madhubuti. On Seeing Diana Go Madddddddddd.
McGirt. Born like the pines to sing.
My Song.
McKay, C. Alfonso, Dressing to Wait at Table.
Neal, L. Lady's Days.
Penny, R. I Remember How She Sang.
Reed, C. In a Harlem Store Front Church.
Reed, I. I'm running for the office of love.
Thompson, D. Blues at 1.
Toomer. Georgia Dusk.
Walker, M. Since 1619.
Spirituals, The.
Young, A. Dance For Ma Rainey, A.
Jungle Strut.
Poem for Lena Horne, A.

Sisters
Angelou. Kin.
Bandele. Subtle Art of Breathing, The.
Clifton, L. Lane Is the Pretty One.
Leanna's Poem.
Sisters.
To Ms. Ann.
Jordan, J. For My Jamaican Sister a Little Bit Lost on the Island of Manhattan.
Knight, E. Violent Space, The.
Lorde. Bridge through My Windows.
Family Resemblance, A.
Harriet there was always somebody calling us crazy.
In Margaret's Garden.
Never Take Fire for a Woman.
One Who Got Away, The.
Sister Outsider.
Nelson, M. I Decide Not to Have Children.
I imagine driving across country.
Ray, H. Verses to my Heart's-Sister.
Walker, A. For My Sister Molly Who in the Fifties.
Telling.

Skating and Skaters
Harper, M. Mission.
Reed, I. Columbia.

Skin
Angelou. Passing Time.
Lorde. Hanging Fire.
Thomas, L. Subway Witnesses, The.
Toomer. People.
Wilson, A. Grenudita.

Skulls
Dodson, O. Yardbird's Skull.
Jones, J. To a Skull.

Sky
Boyd, J. Sketch of a Verying Evening Sky.
Dove, R. Teach Us to Number Our Days.
Gilbert, C. Directions, The.
Grimké, A. For the Candle Light.
Henderson, D. Horizon Blues.
Kaufman, B. Blue O'Clock.
Lost Window.
Ray, H. Sky Picture.
Young, A. Grizzly Peak.

Skydiving and Skydivers
Reed, I. Sky Diving.

Skylarks. See Larks

Skyscrapers
Hughes, L. Hope for Harlem.
Toomer. Skyline.

Slaughterhouses
Alexander, M. Chicago.

Slavery
"Ada." Lines: "From fair Jamaica's fertile plains."
Allen, S. Harriet Tubman.
Angelou. Africa.
Forgive.
My guilt is "slavery's chains," too long.
One More Round.
Our Grandmothers.
Slave Coffle.
Song for the Old Ones.
Southeast Arkanasia.
Asim. Mumble the Magic Words.
Baraka. At the Colonial Y They Are Aesthetically and Culturally Deprived (Y's Later) (31).
Contract. (For The Destruction and Rebuilding of Paterson), A.
So the King Sold the Farmer #39.
Stellar Nilotic (29).
Turn Around Y36, The.
Y the Link Will Not Always Be "Missing" #40.
Y's 18.
Barrax. Greenhouse.
Bennett, G. To a Dark Girl.
Bethune, L. Bwagamoyo.
Bontemps. Southern Mansion.
Brown, S. Bitter Fruit of the Tree.
Legend.
Raise a Song.
Strong Men.
Campbell, A. Lines: "Wake not again the cannon's thundrous voice."
Carrington, J. Old Slave Woman, An.
Cheatwood. Bloodstorm.
Swamp Rat.
Clark, Benjamin. Do they miss me at home.
Emigrant, The.
What Is a Slave?
Clifton, L. Bodies broken on, The.
I went to the valley.
Monticello.
Slaveship.
Song: "Sons of slaves and."
Corrothers. In the Matter of Two Men.
Crouch, S. Chops Are Flyin.
Cullen, C. Negro Mother's Lullaby, A.
Dent. Return to English Turn.
St. Helena Island.
Derricotte. 1994 Inventory.
Dixon, M. Tour Guide: La Maison des Esclaves.
Dodson, O. Poem for Pearl's Dancers.
Douglass, F. Middle Passage.
Dove, R. Abduction, The.
Adolescence—I.
Belinda's Petition.
House Slave, The.
Kentucky, 1833.
Pamela.
Slave's Critique of Practical Reason, The.
Transport or Slaves From Maryland to Mississippi, The.
Dunbar, P. Ante-Bellum Sermon, An.
Corn-Song, A.
Deserted Plantation, The.
News, The.
Old Cabin, The.

Parted.
Sympathy.
To the South.
Harper, F. Aunt Chloe.
Bible Defence of Slavery.
Bury Me in a Free Land.
Death of Zombi.
Deliverance, The.
Dismissal of Tyng, The.
Dying Bondman, The.
Dying Fugitive, The.
Eliza Harris.
Fairer Hope, a Brighter Morn, A.
Free Labor.
Freedom Bell, The.
Fugitive's Wife, The.
Lines: "At the Portals of the Future."
Our English Friends.
President Lincoln's Proclamation of Freedom.
She's Free!
Slave Auction, The.
Slave Mother, The: "Heard you that shriek? It rose."
Slave Mother, The: "I have but four, the treasures of my soul."
Tennessee Hero, The.
Then and Now.
To the Union Savers of Cleveland.
Harper, M. America Calls!
American History.
Battle of Saratoga (Springs) Revisited, The.
Bristol: Bicentenary Remembrances of Trade.
Dining from a Treed Condition, an Historical Survey.
Effendi.
"Emperor": Shields Green: Fugitives.
Forty Days Looking Backwards: Notes from a Surveyor.
Founding Fathers in Philadelphia, The.
Fugitive Paths.
Good Samaritan Hospital.
History as Cap'n Brown.
Jim Daniels: Hamilton Massacre: Parable.
Kansas and America.
"League of Gileadites": Messages.
Makin' Jump Shots.
Manual for the Patriotic Volunteer.
Plans.
Plans: 2.
Psychophotos of Hampton.
Reports: Kansas.
"Rescue Work": Dues.
"S.P.W.": Journey of Consciousness.
Sambo's Mistakes: an Essay.
Sojourner Truth: Black Sybil in Salem.
Hayden, R. Ballad of Nat Turner, The.
Frederick Douglass.
Middle Passage.
Runagate Runagate.
Haynes, A. Eclipse.
Hoagland, E. Gorée ten miles offshore beckons.
Holly. Patriot's Lament, The.
Horton, G. Division of an Estate.
Obstruction of Genius, The.
On Hearing of the Intention of a Gentleman to Purchase the Poet's Freedom.
On Liberty and Slavery.
Poet's Feeble Petition, The.
Slave, The.
Slavery.
Slavery, thou peace-disturbing thief.
Slave's Complaint, The.
Slave's Reflections the Eve before His Sale, A.
Hughes, L. American Heartbreak.
Aunt Sue's Stories.
Drums.
Ghosts of 1619.
Jesus, The.
New Song, A.
Slave.
Slave Song.
Uncle Tom is a legend and a dream.
Iman. Love Your Enemy.
Jackson, G. Alice.
Fugitive Slaves.

Jeffers, L. On Listening to the Spirituals.
Trellie.
Johnson, F. Ethiopia.
Johnson, J. Brothers.
Jordan, J. DeLiza and the TV News.
Speculations on the Present through the Prism of the Past.
Kendrick, D. Sadie Snuffs a Candle.
Sophie, Climbing the Stairs.
Kgositsile. To Mother.
Knight, E. And Tell Me Poet, Can Love Exist in Slavery?
Komunyakaa. Back Then.
Lost Wax.
Lee, D. Primitive, The.
Lorde. Between Ourselves.
Song for Many Movements, A.
Madhubuti. Long Reality, The.
McElroy, C. Woman's Song, A.
McKay, C. Enslaved.
In Bondage.
Moorer. Emancipation Day.
Must Be Freed.
Peonage System, The.
Murray, P. Dark Testament.
Neal, L. Narrative of Black Magicians, The.
Nelson, M. Chosen.
Diverne's House.
I Knew That.
Sermon in the Woodlot.
To Market.
Oyewole. Future Shock.
Patterson, R. Black Power.
Plato. To the First of August.
Plumpp. Remembered.
Turf Song.
Randall, D. Southern Road, The.
Ray, H. To My Father.
Reason. Spirit Voice, The; or Liberty Call to the Disfranchised (State of New York).
Reed, I. Slaveship, German Model.
Reynolds, S. Whipping, The.
Sanchez, S. Reflections After the June 12th March for Disarmament.
Shannon, A. Doris.
Simpson, J. Away to Canada.
To the White People of America.
Smith, G. Penitential Cries of Jupiter Hammond, The.
Spencer, A. Sévignés, The.
Stuckey. Big Gate, The.
Rebel.
Ribbons and Lace.
Southern Belle.
This Is It.
Sun Ra. Of the Cosmic-Blueprints.
Thompson, P. Address to Ethiopia.
Favorite Slave's Story, The.
Fugitive, The.
Husband's Return, The.
Prayer, A: "Oh, Lord! I lift my heart."
Tolson, M. Dark Symphony.
Toomer. Song of the Son.
Unknown. Go down, Moses.
Jack and Dinah Want Freedom.
Many Thousand Gone.
Me and My Captain.
No more auction block for me.
Pick a Bale of Cotton.
Promises of Freedom.
Run, Nigger, Run!
Slavery chain done broke at last, broke at last, broke at last.
Song to the Runaway Slave.
Song: "We raise de wheat."
Steal Away to Jesus.
Wild Negro Bill.
Walker, A. Early Losses: a Requiem.
Right to Life, The: What Can the White Man Say to the Black Woman?
Walker, M. At the Lincoln Monument in Washington, August 28, 1963.
Ex-Slave.
Ode on the Occasion of the Inauguration of the Sixth President of Jackson State College.
Since 1619.
Wheatley, P. On Being Brought from Africa

to America.
To the Right Honourable William, Earl of Dartmouth, His Majesty's Principal Secretary of State for North-America, Etc.
Whitfield. From America.
How long, oh gracious God! how long.
North Star, The.
Stanzas for the First of August.
To Cinque.
Whitman, A. I never was a slave—a robber took.
Lute of Afric's Tribe, The.
Oh! sing it in the light of freedom's morn.
Thrice hail! proud land, whose genius boasts a Clay!
Williams, J. Safari West.
Williams, S. Letters from a New England Negro.
Wright, J. Sketch for an Aesthetic Project.
See also **Middle Passage**
Sleep
Brown, S. Mill Mountain.
Clifton, L. Women You Are Accustomed To, The.
Cullen, C. Night Rain.
Derricotte. Touching/Not Touching: My Mother.
Dove, R. Lines Muttered in Sleep.
Dunbar, P. At Night.
Ere sleep comes down to soothe the weary eyes.
Farm Child's Lullaby, The.
Fisher Child's Lullaby, The.
Good-Night.
Johnny Speaks.
Lullaby: "Bedtime's come fu' little boys."
Lullaby: "Kiver up yo' haid, my little lady."
Sand-Man, The.
Forbes, C. Dark Mirror.
Giovanni. When i nap.
Harper, F. To a Babe Smiling in Her Sleep.
Horton, G. Meditation on a Cold, Dark and Rainy Night.
Hughes, L. Ardella.
Fired.
Fulfilment.
Mister Sandman.
Morning After.
Sleep.
Weary Blues, The.
Jordan, J. Home: January 29, 1984.
Kaufman, B. Response.
Kendrick, D. Jenny in Sleep.
Lorde. Dreams bite.
From the Greenhouse.
McClellan. Eternity.
Moore, L. Again.
Reed, I. Katskills Kiss Romance Goodbye, The.
Sanchez, S. Poem at Thirty.
When i return home.
Toomer. Evening Song.
Warren-Moore. All-Night Issue, The.
Wright, J. Frightened Lover's Sleep, The.
Young, A. Falling Asleep in a Darkening Room.
It Is God That Moves in Your Heart.
Sleeping Beauty
Angelou. Let's Majeste.
Knight, E. Portrait of Mary.
Slums
Brooks, G. Lovers of the Poor, The.
Dove, R. Teach Us to Number Our Days.
Hayden, R. Summertime and the Living.
Joans. Scenery.
Johnson, J. Judeebug's Country.
Jordan, N. Feeding the Lions.
Latimore. Childhood.
Patterson, R. Letter in Winter.
Thomas, R. To the New Annex to the Detroit County Jail.
Turner, D. Reckoning A.M. Thursday.
Wright, J. Neighborhood House, The.
Smalls, Robert
Heard, J. General Robert Smalls.
Smells
African-American Oral Tradition. Mary had a

little lamb for which she cared no particle.
Pussy ain't nothin' but a hairy split.
This is to the women of Texas.
Giovanni. When i nap.
Harris, P. Be Somebody Fragrant.
Hayes, D. Alien.
Hughes, L. Rememberance.
McKay, C. Jasmine.
Moore, L. Haiku: "Sipping the new tea."
Salaam. Our Natures Rise.
Sanchez, S. I listen for yo.
There are times that the.

Smiles
Angelou. Changing.
I almost remember.
Barlow, G. Nook.
Dunbar, P. Made to Order Smile, The.
Philosophy.
Response.
We wear the mask that grins and lies.
Harper, F. To a Babe Smiling in Her Sleep.
Hughes, L. Me and the Mule.
Nelson, M. Hermitage Breakfast.
Sanchez, S. And the joy. feeling.
What do i know of.
When i look at you.
Warren-Moore. Dannemora Contraband.

Smith, Bessie
Harper, M. Last Affair: Bessie's Blues Song.
Hayden, R. Homage to the Empress of the
Blues.

Smith, John (1580–1631)
Bibb. Capt. Smith and Pocahontas.

Smoke
DuBois, W. Song of the Smoke, The.

Smoking and Smokers
Angelou. Health-Food Diner, The.
Dunbar, P. Companion's Progress, A.
My Corn-Cob Pipe.
When the Old Man Smokes.
Young, A. Life at the Back of the Plane.
See also **Cigarettes**

Snails
Hughes, L. Snail.
Lorde. Rock Thrown into the Water Does Not
Fear the Cold, A.
Thompson, P. Snail's Lesson, The.
See also **Shells**

Snakes
Angelou. Known to Eve and Me.
Bethune, L. Today Tutu Is Beating the Same
Burru As Me.
Dumas, H. Island within Island.
Harper, M. Alice.
Hughes, L. Snake.
Lorde. Call.
See also **Listings for specific snakes**

Snobbery and Snobs
Dunbar, P. Jealous.
Hughes, L. High to Low.
Low to High.
Snob.
To Certain Intellectuals.
Young, A. One Snapshot I Couldn't Take in
France, The.
See also **Social Class**

Snoring
Hughes, L. Morning After.

Snow
Brown, L. Winter Sonnet.
Dunbar-Nelson. Snow in October.
Dunbar, P. Grievance, A.
Snowin'.
Fordham. Snow Storm, The.
Snowdrop, The.
Giovanni. Winter Poem.
Hayden, R. Snow.
Hughes, L. Angels wings is white as snow,
The.
Winter Sweetnes.
Jordan, J. Poem on.
Knight, E. Haiku: "Falling snow flakes, The."
Lorde. Woman Thing, The.
McKay, C. Snow Fairy, The.
Ray, H. Snow Song.

Reed, I. Phoebe is the 9th satellite.
Sanchez, S. Morning snow falling.
Thompson, P. Snow-Flakes, The.
See also **Snowflakes**

Snow White
Moss, T. Lessons from a Mirror.

Snowdrops
Fordham. Snowdrop, The.

Snowflakes
Knight, E. Haiku: "Falling snow flakes, The."
See also **Snow**

Social Class
Angelou. Amoebaean for Daddy.
Bump d'Bump.
Sepia Fashion Show.
Baraka. Crow Jane in High Society.
History on Wheels.
YMCA #35.
Brooks, G. Lovers of the Poor, The.
Brown, S. Chillen Get Shoes.
Master and Man.
Negro Improvement League.
New Congo, The.
No More Worlds to Conquer.
Clifton, L. In the Inner City.
Way it was, The.
Cook, W. Still-Life with Woodstove.
Cullen, C. Saturday's Child.
Fortune. Savage Dreamer, The.
Giovanni. On Hearing "The Girl with the
Flaxen Hair."
Hughes, L. Graduation.
Low to High.
Office Building: Evening.
Poem for an Intellectual on the Way Up to
Submit to His Lady.
Knight, E. WASP Woman Visits a Black
Junkie in Prison, A.
Thompson, D. Intelligence Quotients.
See also **Snobbery and Snobs**

Social Work and Social Workers
Jordan, N. Feeding the Lions.

Socialism
Baraka. Reggae or Not!
Hughes, L. Black Workers.
Komunyakaa. Protection of Movable Cultural
Heritage.
Young, A. Moon Over Matter.

Solace
Harris, W. Samantha Is My Negro Cat.
Wheatley, P. On the Death of a Young
Gentleman.

Soldiers
Baraka. War Poem.
Beadle. Lines: "How I love country you have
heard."
Brooks, G. Gay Chaps at the Bar.
Looking.
Brown, S. Sam Smiley.
Dunbar, P. Black Samson of Brandywine.
Colored Soldiers, The.
Dirge for a Soldier.
Our Martyred Soldiers.
Veteran, The.
When Dey 'Listed Colored Soldiers.
Evans, M. I Am a Black Woman.
Grimké. Gathering of the Grand Army, The.
Harper, F. Home, Sweet Home.
Harper, M. Guerrilla-Cong, The.
Hayden, R. Dream, The.
Hughes, L. Ballad of Margie Polite.
Battle Ground.
Colored Soldier, The.
Dear Mr. President.
Hero—International Brigade.
Joe Louis is a man.
Just an Ordinary Guy.
When the Armies Passed.
Johnson, F. Soldiers of the Dusk, The.
Komunyakaa. Break from the Bush, A.
Le Xuan, Beautiful Spring.
To Have Danced with Death.
Miller, E. What the Women Told Me.
Tucker, M. Soldier Boy's Dream, The.
Wheatley, P. To Captain H——D, of the 65th
Regiment.

Young, A. Some Recent Fiction.
Suicide.
See also **Army Life; Veterans; War**

Solipsism
Hughes, L. Last Man Living, The.

Solitude
Brown, S. Revelations.
Cortez. Consultation.
Dove, R. Daystar.
Weathering Out.
Dunbar, P. Career, A.
Lost Dream, A.
Giovanni. Alone.
Certain Peace, A.
Hayden, R. Road in Kentucky, A.
Hughes, L. Crossing.
Lonely Nocturne.
Room.
Johnson, G. Escape.
Komunyakaa. Heart's Graveyard Shift, The.
Man Who Carries the Desert Around Inside
Himself: For Wally, The.
Lorde. Hanging Fire.
Madhubuti. Loneliness, A.
Nelson, M. Icarus Dream.
Sanchez, S. Haiku: "I am now in the."
Personal Letter No. 2.
Toomer. And Pass.
Walker, A. Outcast.
These mornings of rain.
Wright, J. Lake in Central Park, The.
Young, A. Mid-Life Crises: A Critical
Review.
Saudades: The Portuguese Blues.
Still Lives.

Somnambulism and Somnambulists
Sanchez, S. Poem at Thirty.

Songs
Barrax. There was a song.
Brown, S. Children's Children.
Dark of the Moon.
Honey Mah Love.
Dunbar, P. Compensation.
Corn-Song, A.
Joggin' Erlong.
Just whistle a bit, if the day be dark.
Keep a Song Up on de Way.
Ol' Tunes, The.
Poet and His Song, The.
Prometheus stole from Heaven the sacred fire.
Remembered.
Songs.
Gregory. Christmas Lullaby for a New-Born
Child.
Harper, F. Songs for the People.
Hughes, L. Ardella.
Bouquet.
Burden.
Gypsy Melodies.
Me and My Song.
Sliver.
Songs.
To make words sing.
Johnson, J. Lift Ev're Voice and Sing.
Moore, L. Song Poem, The.
Nelson, M. Saint Preaches, The.
Sanchez, S. For Our Lady.
We are gatherers.
Toomer. Cotton Song.
Song of the Son.
Walker, M. For my people everywhere singing
their slave songs repeatedly.
Weaver, M. Sub Shop Girl.
Young, A. Dock Song Crazy.
Malagueña Salerosa.

Sonnets
Dunbar, P. Poet and the Baby, The.

Sons
Clifton, L. Admonitions.
On the Death of Allen's Son.
Coleman, A. Black Baby.
Cullen, C. Fruit of the Flower.
Dickey. Mulatto Lullaby.
Finney, N. Lobengula: Having a Son at 38.
Fordham. Sonnet to My First Born.
Harper, M. Mama's Report.
Nightmare Begins Responsibility.

Roland.
  We Assume: On the Death of Our Son,
    Reuben Masai Harper.
Hughes, L. Mother in Wartime.
  Official Notice.
  Silent One.
Komunyakaa. Little Man around the House.
Linden, M. Wayward Son, The.
Lorde. As I Grew Up Again.
  Child Shall Lead, A.
  For Craig.
  Starting All Over Again.
Young, A. Foggy Morning.
  Son.

Sorrow
Alexander, M. People of Unrest.
Baraka. If into Love the Image Burdens.
Bontemps. Nocturne at Bethesda.
Braithwaite. House of Falling Leaves, The.
Brown, Kysha. Brown Girl Blues.
Cullen, C. Any Human to Another.
  Lament: "Now let all lovely things embark."
  Love Tree, The.
  Pagan Prayer.
  Saturday's Child.
  Two Who Croseed a Line (She Crosses).
  Variations on a Theme.
Dodson, O. Sorrow Is the Only Faithful One.
Dunbar, P. Song, The: "My soul, lost in the
    music's mist."
  We wear the mask that grins and lies.
El-Hadi. Tired Man, The.
Evans, M. If there be sorrow.
Horton, G. On an Old Deluded Soldier.
Hughes, L. Island.
  Motherland.
  Troubled Woman.
  Walls.
Johnson, G. Escape.
Komunyakaa. Translating Footsteps.
Lorde. If You Come Softly.
  In Margaret's Garden.
  New Year's Day.
Nelson, M. Beauty Shoppe.
Toomer. Face.
Young, A. Alba.

See also **Funerals; Grief; Mourning and
  Mourners**

Soul
Angelou. Ailey, Baldwin, Floyd, Killens, and
    Mayfield.
  Willie was a man without fame.
Baraka. Agony, An. As Now.
  Dichtung.
  From an Almanac (3).
  Invention of Comics, The.
Bethune, L. Juju of My Own, A.
Braithwaite. Rye Bread.
Clifton, L. To the Unborn and Waiting
    Children.
Cowdery. Wind blows, The.
Cullen, C. For an Evolutionist and His
    Opponent.
  Sonnet Dialogue.
Dunbar, P. Ere sleep comes down to soothe
    the weary eyes.
  Light was on the golden sands, The.
  Vagrants.
Fabio. Of Puddles, Worms, Slimy Things.
Gee. Black Music Man.
Giovanni. Very Simple Wish, A.
Harper, F. Soul, The.
Horton, G. For the Fair Miss M. M. McLean.
Hughes, L. Negro Speaks of Rivers, The.
  To Artina.
Jordan, J. Sketching in the Transcendental.
Kgositsile. Brother Malcolm's Echo.
McKay, C. Desolate.
  I Know My Soul.
  To the White Fiends.
Nelson, M. Propositions.
  Sneak Preview.
Ray, H. Soul's Courts, The.
Salaam. "5 Minutes, Mr. Salam."
Sanchez, S. Poem No. 4.
Simmons, B. Soul.
Smith, P. Asking for a Heart Attack.

Toomer. Chase, The.
  Living Earth.
  Our Growing Day.
  Peers.
  Prayer.
  Promise, The.
  Song of the Son.
  They Are Not Missed.
Unknown. I know moon-rise, I know star-rise.
  This Little Light of Mine.
Wheatley, P. On Being Brought from Africa
    to America.
Whitfield. Yes! strike again that sounding
    string.
Wright, J. Journey to the Place of Ghosts.
Young, A. Leaving Rochester.

Sound
Angelou. Sounds / Like pearls.
Clifton, L. Explanations.
Cumbo. Nocturnal Sounds.
Giovanni. Patience.
Hughes, L. Burden.
Sanchez, S. I listen for yo.
  Poem No. 3.
Sundiata. Ear Training.
Troupe. Avalanche.
Young, A. John Coltrane Dance, The.
  Koto Music/Singing.

Soup
Angelou. This Winter Day.
Sanchez, S. Autumn. a bonfire.

South Africa
Allen, S. About Poetry and South Africa.
Brooks, G. Near-Johannesburg Boy, The.
Harper, M. Founding Fathers in Philadelphia,
    The.
  Militance of a Photograph in the Passbook of
    a Bantu under Detention, The.
Hughes, L. Dixie South Africa.
Jordan, J. Poem About My Rights.
  Poem for South African Women.
  To Free Nelson Mandela.
Knight, E. Poem for the Liberation of
    Southern Africa.
  Television Speaks.
Lorde. Evening News, The.
  Holographs.
  Party Time.
  Prism.
  Sisters in Arms.
Madhubuti. Killing Memory.
Troupe. South African Bloodstone.

See also **Johannesburg, South Africa; Soweto,
  South Africa**

South America
Jordan, J. Problems of Translation: Problems
    of Language.

See also **Listings for specific South American
  countries**

South Carolina (state)
Moorer. Crum Appointment, The.

South, The, United States
Angelou. Georgia Song, A.
  Miss Scarlet, Mr. Rhett and other Latter-Day
    Saints.
  Southeast Arkanasia.
Bontemps. Southern Mansion.
Brocks-Shedd. Southern Roads/City Pavement.
Brown, S. Children's Children.
  Last Ride of Wild Bill.
  Let us suppose him differently placed.
  Roberta Lee.
Corrothers. Sweeten 'Tatahs.
Crouch, S. Blackie Thinks of His Brothers.
Davis, F. Snapshots of the Cotton South.
Dove, R. Nothing Down.
Dunbar, P. Chrismus on the Plantation.
  Plantation Child's Lullaby, The.
Ellis, K. Phantom Pains.
Giscombe. (1978, Remembering 1962).
  (The Recent Past).
Harper, F. Appeal to My Countrywomen, An.
Duriel. Landscapes.
Hayden, R. Runagate Runagate.
  Tour 5.
Hernton. Young Negro poet / came from 'way
    down South.

Hill, L. Tuskegee.
Horton, G. Southern Refugee, The.
Hughes, L. Bitter River, The.
  Bombings in Dixie.
  Dixie Man to Uncle Sam.
  Dixie South Africa.
  Not a Movie.
  One-Way Ticket.
  Silhouette.
  South, The.
  Sunset in Dixie.
  Total War.
  Vari-Colored Song.
Jeffers, L. Tuskegee, Tuskegee!
Lorde. Afterimages.
McClellan. September Night, A.
Randall, D. Legacy: My South.
  Southern Road, The.
Sanchez, S. Father and Daughter.
Toomer. Georgia Dusk.
  Portrait in Georgia.
Walker, A. Hymn: "I well remember / A time
    when."
  South: The Name of Home.
Walker, M. Childhood.
  Jeremiah, prophet of Jerusalem.
  Sorrow Home.
  Southern Song.
Weaver, M. Borders.
  Easy Living.
Wright, J. Invitation to Madison County, An.
Young, A. Sunday Sonnet for My Mother's
    Mother, A.

Soweto, South Africa
Cortez. For the Brave Young Students in
    Soweto.
Jordan, J. Song for Soweto, A.
Sharp, S. Woman Who Died in Line, The.

Space and Space Travel
Barrax. Christmas 1959 Et Cetera.
Jordan, J. Don't Estimate!
Reed, I. Introducing a New Loa.
Smith, P. Annie Pearl Smith Discovers
    Moonlight.
Sun-Ra. Cosmic Age, The.
  Would I for all that were.

See also **Rockers**

Spain
Hughes, L. From Spain to Alabama.
  Song of Spain.
Wright, J. Madrid.
Young, A. My Spanish Heart.
  Ravel: Bolero.
  Topsy: Part 2.

See also **Civil War, Spain**

Spanish-American War
Harper, F. "Do Not Cheer, Men Are Dying,"
    Said Capt. Phillips, in the Spanish-American
    War.
  Proclaim a fast, a solemn fast.

Spankings
Dunbar, P. When a Feller's Itchin' to Be
    Spanked.
Hayden, R. Whipping, The.

Sparrows
Dunbar, P. Sparrow, The.
Harper, F. Sparrow's Fall, The.

Speech
Barlow, G. Nook.
Clifton, L. For the Mute.
Cotter, Sr. Is It Because I Am Black?

See also **Language Screams; Talk; Voices**

Spelling Bees
Dunbar, P. Spellin'-Bee, The.

Sphinx
Hayden, R. Sphinx.

Spider Webs
Hayden, R. Web, The.

Spiders
Hughes, L. 403 Blues.
Reed, I. Back to Africa.

Spiritualism and Spiritualists
Lorde. October.
  Oya.
  Signs.
  Winds of Orisha, The.

Reed, I.   Secretary to the Spirits, A.

Spirituals
Hughes, L.   Note on Commercial Theatre.
   Spirituals.
   Tambourines! / Tambourines!
Johnson, J.   O Black and unknown bards of
   long ago.
Unknown.   Go down, Moses.
   I Thank God I'm Free at Las'.

Spittoons
Hughes, L.   Brass Spittoons.

Spring
Bennett, G.   Street Lamps in Early Spring.
Bibb.   Early spring's sweet blush, The.
Bontemps.   My Heart has Known its Winter.
Brown, S.   After Winter.
Clifton, L.   Spring Song.
Conyus.   Upon Leaving the Parole Board
   Hearing.
Cullen, C.   Spring Reminiscence.
   To John Keats, Poet, at Springtime.
Dandridge, R.   Sprin' Fevah.
Dove, R.   Turning Thirty, I Contemplate
   Students Bicycling Home.
Duke, B.   Poem to the World.
Dunbar, P.   Come and Kiss Me Sweet and
   Twenty.
   Little Lucy Landman.
   Song: "Bee hit sip some honey f'om de
   matermony vine, De."
   Spring Fever.
   Spring Song.
   Spring Wooing, A.
   When Winter Darkening All Around.
Grimké, A.   At April.
   At the Spring Dawn.
   When the Green Lies over the Earth.
Grimké.   Parting Hymn, A.
Harper, F.   Crocuses, The.
Hughes, L.   After Many Springs.
   April Rain Song.
   Earth Song.
   Poem: "When young spring comes."
   Red Roses.
   Signs of Spring.
   Year Round.
Lane, P.   Spring.
Lorde.   Spring People.
McKay, C.   Spring in New Hampshire.
Moore, L.   Haiku: "Spring moonrise."
Moorer.   Easter; or, Spring-Time.
Murray, P.   Returning Spring.
Pritchard, N.   Springtime.
Ray, H.   Coming of Spring, The.
   Idyl of Spring, An.
Shepherd, R.   Where When Was.
   White Days.
Toomer.   Promise, The.
Tucker, M.   Spring.
Walker, M.   My Mississippi Spring.

Springfield, Ohio
Linden, M.   Riot, A.

Spying and Spies
Baraka.   Are Their Blues Singers in Russia?

Squirrels
Barrax.   Death of a Squirrel in McKinley Park,
   The.
Dove, R.   Musician Talks about "Process",
   The.
Gilbert, C.   Glimpses.
Young, A.   Squirrels are skittering.

Sri Lanka
Lorde.   For the King and Queen of Summer.

Stairs
Brown, S.   New steps / O my Lawd.
Hughes, L.   Mother to Son.

Starlings
Hayden, R.   Plague of Starlings, A.

Stars
Allen, S.   If the Stars Should Fall.
   To Satch.
Baraka.   Ostriches and Grandmothers!
   Poem Welcoming Jonas Mekas to America, A.
   Stellar Nilotic (29).
Cullen, C.   To Endymion.

Dunbar, P.   Love is a star that lights the night.
   Starry Night, A.
Hughes, L.   Love Song for Lucinda.
   Lullaby: "My little dark baby."
   Slave Song.
   Star Seeker.
   Stars.
Johnson, F.   Counting.
Johnson, J.   Sence You Went Away.
Jordan, J.   Don't Estimate!
Lockett.   Death of the Moonshine Supermen.
Lorde.   Separation.
Ray, H.   Star Song.
Whitfield.   North Star, The.
Young, A.   How Stars Start.

Statues
Hughes, L.   Lincoln Theatre.
Lorde.   Sacrifice.
Ray, H.   Venus of Milo, The.

Steak
Moore, L.   Haiku: "Family reunion."

Steel
Conyus.   Six Ten Sixty-Nine.
Hughes, L.   Steel Mills.

Stepfathers and Stepmothers
Bomani, N.   Thin Water.
Komunyakaa.   Stepfather: A Girl's Song.

Stevens, Thaddeus
Bell, J.   Modern Moses, or "My Policy" Man.
Harper, F.   Lines to Hon. Thaddeus Stevens.

Stockholm, Sweden
Young, A.   Dear Old Stockholm.

Stonecutting and Stonecutters
Fields, J.   Mr. Tut's House A Recollection.

Stones and Rocks
Dove, R.   Fish in the Stone, The.
Harper, F.   Truth.
Knight, E.   He sees through stone.
Lorde.   Parting.
Patterson, R.   I've Got a Home in That Rock.
Pritchard, N.   Cassandra and Friend.
   Narrow Path, The.
Toomer.   Peers.

Storms
Aubert, A.   Spring 1937/ for Honoré Roussell.
Bontemps.   Reconnaissance.
Boyd, J.   Ocean.
Braithwaite.   Watchers, The.
Dunbar, P.   Changing Time.
   Right's Security.
   Rising of the Storm, The.
Fordham.   Snow Storm, The.
Harper, F.   Death of the Old Sea King.
   Night of Death, The.
   Story of the Rebellion, A.
Hayden, R.   Electrical Storm.
Horton, G.   Excited from Reading the
   Obedience of Nature to her Lord in the
   Vessel on the Sea.
Lorde.   Hugo I.
   Oaxaca.
   Suspension.
Mitchell, K.   Tree Stillness.
Smith, B.   Backwater Blues.
Toomer.   Storm Ending.
Unknown.   Backwater Blues.
   Been in the Storm So Long.
   Peace Be Still.
   Stand by Me.
Walcott.   Storm Figure.
Wheatley, P.   On Messrs. Hussey and Coffin.
See also **Blizzards; Hurricanes**

Storytelling and Storytellers
Angelou.   When I think about myself.
Brown, S.   Uncle Joe.
Dove, R.   Roast Possum.
Dunbar, P.   Cabin Tale, A.
   Harriet Beecher Stowe.
Giovanni.   Africa.
Giscombe.   (1978, Remembering 1962).
Hughes, L.   Aunt Sue's Stories.
   Grandpa's Stories.
Komunyakaa.   Blues Chant Hoodoo Revival.
   Moonshine.
Lorde.   Naming the Stories.
   Teacher.

Madhubuti.   Union of Two, The.
McElroy, C.   Griots Who Know Brer Fox,
   The.
   Tapestries.
   Under the Oak Table.
Reed, I.   Railroad Bill, a conjure man.
St. John, P.   We Are Going to Be Here Now.
Sprod.   Request Number.
Stuckey.   Big Gate, The.

Stowe, Harriet Beecher
Dunbar, P.   Harriet Beecher Stowe.
Harper, F.   To Mrs. Harriet Beecher Stowe.
Ray, H.   Greeting.
See also **Uncle Tom's Cabin**

Strangers
Clifton, L.   C. C. Rider.
Hughes, L.   Stranger in Town.
Nelson, M.   True Magic, The.
Sanchez, S.   Haiku: "If i had known, if."
Shange.   Elegance in the extreme.
Stephany.   Who is not a stranger still.
Wright, J.   Invitation to Madison County, An.
Young, A.   Manhattan March, The 1970s.
   Sing a Song of Singapore.

Strawberries
Johnson, M.   Strawberry, The.

Street Performers
Brown, S.   Mose is black and evil.
Moore, L.   Haiku: "Cloudless summer day."

Streetcars
Brown, S.   Transfer.

Streets
Angelou.   Letter to an Aspiring Junkie.
Harris, W.   Samantha Is My Negro Cat.
Hughes, L.   Dive.
   Lonesome Corner.
Kaufman, B.   Harwood Alley Song.
Moss, T.   Fisher Street.
Salaam.   French Quarter Intimacies.
Sanchez, S.   Ballad for Stirling Street, A.
Walker, M.   Black Magic.
   Patchwork Quilt, A.
   Small Black World.
See also **Roads**

Strength
Brooks, G.   Strong Men, Riding Horses /
   Lester after the Western.
Brown, S.   Strong Men.
Clifton, L.   Daniel.
   Eldridge.
Cullen, C.   Minutely Hurt.
   To the Swimmer.
Dunbar, P.   Warrior's Prayer, The.
Evans, M.   I Am a Black Woman.
Gilbert, C.   Beginning by Value.
Hughes, L.   Helen Keller.
Jeffers, L.   Black Soul of the Land.
Jordan, J.   On the Spirit of Mildred Jordan.
Lorde.   October.
   125th Street and Abomey.
   Portrait.
McKay, C.   Like a strong tree that in the
   virgin earth.
Plumpp.   Black Ethics.
Randall, D.   George.
Sanchez, S.   Familiarize your.
   Just you. just me. must.
Snellings.   Earth.
Spriggs.   For Brother Malcolm.
   My Beige Mom.
Sun-Ra.   Saga of Resistance.
Unknown.   Freedom in the Air.
   Take My Hand, Precious Lord.
Walker, M.   Big John Henry.
   Lineage.
   My Truth and My Flame.
Whitfield.   Self-Reliance.

Strikes and Strikers
Clifton, L.   Pork chops.
Hughes, L.   Labor Storm.
Troupe.   After Hearing a Radio Announcement:
   a Comment on Some Conditions.
See also **Labor Unions**

Strokes
Dove, R.   Recovery.
   Stroke, The.

Students
Angelou. Communication II.
Coates. Alice Flips the Script.
Dove, R. Flash Cards.
Giovanni. Alabama Poem.
Horton, G. Graduate Leaving College, The.
On the Pleasures of College Life.
Hughes, L. Theme for English B.
Lorde. Workers Rose on May Day or
Postscript to Karl Marx, The.
Nelson, M. Letter to a Benedictine Monk.
Wheatley, P. To the University of Cambridge,
in New-England.
Young, A. Teaching.
See also **Colleges and Universities; Education;
Scholarship and Scholars; School and
Schools; Teaching and Teachers**
Stuttering and Stutterers
Sanchez, S. Haiku: "O i am so sad, i."
Submission
Angelou. Song for the Old Ones.
Emanuel, J. Negro, The.
Hall, K. Illusions.
Song of Tom.
Lockett. Die Black Pervert.
Murray, P. Conquest.
Suburbs and Suburban Life
Angelou. Through the Inner City to the
Suburbs.
Brooks, G. Lovers of the Poor, The.
Derricotte. Blackbottom.
Hughes, L. Undertow.
Subways
Baraka. Clay.
Duriel. On the Uptown Lexington Avenue
Express: Martin Luther King Day 1995.
Hughes, L. Midnight Raffle.
Subway Face.
Subway Rush Hour.
Jordan, J. All the World Moved.
Lorde. One Year to Life on the Grand Central
Shuttle.
McKay, C. Subway Wind.
Rivers, C. Subway, The.
Walcott. Village Life, A.
Success
Davis, F. Robert Whitmore.
Hughes, L. America's Young Black Joe!
Imploring Mecca.
Reed, I. Sixth Street Corporate War.
Turning Pro.
Tolson, M. Madame Alpha Devine she made a
million.
Young, A. Poem for Dorothy Dandridge, A.
Suffering
African-American Oral Tradition. Nobody
Knows Da Trubble Ah See.
Alexander, M. Memory.
Angelou. These Yet to Be United States.
Baraka. History-Wise #22.
Poem for Half White College Students.
Poem for Neutrals, A.
Wise 4.
Bontemps. My Heart has Known its Winter.
Brooks, G. My Dreams, My Works Must Wait
Till after Hell.
Clifton, L. Job easy / is the pride.
Prayer.
She Understands Me.
Crouch, S. BLACKIE Speaks on Campus: a
Valentine for Vachel Lindsay.
Cullen, C. From the Dark Tower.
Harsh World that lashest me each day.
Magnets.
Shroud of Color, The.
Thorn Forever in the Breast, A.
Daáood. Tears for the poet.
Delany. Mask, The.
Dent. Ten Years After Umbra.
Dunbar, P. Prayer, A: "O Lord, the hard-won
miles."
We wear the mask that grins and lies.
Evans, M. I Am a Black Woman.
Gilbert, D. Fire in the Drum, The.
Too Many.
Giovanni. Photography.
Woman Poem.

Harper, F. Appeal to My Countrywomen, An.
Burdens of All, The.
Christ's Entry into Jerusalem.
"Do Not Cheer, Men Are Dying," Said Capt.
Phillips, in the Spanish-American War.
Gone to God.
Slave Auction, The.
Woman's Work.
Harper, M. Kin.
Hayden, R. Soledad.
Horton, G. Death of an Old Carriage Horse.
On Liberty and Slavery.
Hughes, L. Angola Question Mark.
Call to Creation.
Christ in Alabama.
High to Low.
History.
How Thin a Blanket.
Hurt.
Minstrel Man.
Mississippi.
Strange Hurt.
Jordan, J. In Memoriam: Martin Luther King,
Jr.
Kaufman, B. Would You Wear My Eyes?
Lane, P. Midnight Song.
To a Woman Poet That I Know.
Lorde. Coping.
For the Record.
Pathways: From Mother to Mother.
Small Slaughter, A.
There Are No Honest Poems about Dead
Women.
Woman/Dirge for Wasted Children, A.
McKay, C. Negro's Tragedy, The.
Plumpp. Sanders Bottom.
Randall, D. Roses and Revolutions.
Redmond. Cane-Brake-Blues.
Taylor, Cheryl. English Lace.
Toomer. Desire.
Trethewey. Hot Comb.
Vassa. Miscellaneous Verses.
Walker, A. At first I did not fight it.
Diamonds on Liz's bosom, The.
Walker, M. Fanfare, Coda, and Finale.
Litany from the Dark People, A.
Old Age.
Today.
Wright, R. I Have Seen Black Hands.
See also **Pain**
Sugar
Jordan, J. Winter Honey.
Sugar Cane
Ai. Cuba, 1962.
Suicide
Angelou. Chicken-Licken.
Bandele. Subtle Art of Breathing, The.
Barrax. Sacrifice, The.
Cullen, C. Ballad of the Brown Girl, The.
Mood.
Dunbar, P. Right to Die, The.
Hughes, L. Bad Luck Card.
Exits.
Lament over Love.
Lonesome Place.
Reverie on the Harlem River.
Ruined Gal, A.
Suicide.
Suicide's Note.
Too Blue.
Ways.
Jones, R. Trouble in mind, I'm blue.
Jordan, J. Des Moines Iowa Rap.
Jordan, N. Sinner.
Kaufman, B. Suicide.
Knight, E. Black Poet Leaps to His Death, A.
For Black Poets Who Think of Suicide.
Komunyakaa. Corrigenda.
Lorde. Between Ourselves.
Miller, E. Mississippi.
Nelson, M. April Rape.
Reed, I. July 1st, 1982.
Wade-Gayles. For a Friend Who Considers
Suicide.
Walker, A. Suicide.
Summer
Alexander, E. Nineteen.

Baraka. Ostriches and Grandmothers!
Braithwaite. Quiet has a hidden sound.
Cornish, S. Generations 1.
Dunbar, P. Boy's Summer Song, A.
In Summer.
In Summer Time.
Lover's Lane.
Song of Summer.
Song, A: "On a summer's day as I sat by a
stream."
Summer in the South.
Summer Night, A.
Summer Pastoral, A.
Summer's Night, A.
Two Songs.
Forman, R. Waitin on Summer.
Gilbert, C. Now.
Giovanni. Knoxville, Tennessee.
Gray-Kontar. July.
Hayden, R. Summertime and the Living.
Hill, L. Summer Magic.
Horton, G. On Summer.
Hughes, L. Poem: "When young spring
comes."
Johnson, H. Brilliant-bellied newt flashes, The.
Lorde. On Midsummer's Eve.
Seasoning.
Madhubuti. Cure All, The.
McGirt. When de Sun Shines Hot.
Moore, L. Haiku: "Cloudless summer day."
Haiku: "Summer evening sun."
Indian Girl.
Tanka: "After church meeting."
Sanchez, S. Rebirth.
Summer has sped a.
Strange. Childhood.
Young, A. Summer.
Young, K. Preserving, The.
Sumner, Charles
Bell, J. Modern Moses, or "My Policy" Man.
Harper, F. Lines to Charles Sumner.
Ray, H. Charles Sumner.
Sun
Alexander, M. People of Unrest.
Bibb. Ode to the Sun.
Bontemps. To a Young Girl Leaving the Hill
Country.
Brooks, G. Boy Breaking Glass.
Henderson, D. Horizon Blues.
Hughes, L. Sun Song.
Kaufman, B. Sun, Creator of Suns.
Knight, E. Haiku: "In the August grass."
McClellan. Sun went down in beauty, The.
Nelson, M. Parable of the Moth.
Roy, L. Bread Man, The.
Toomer. Words for a Hymn to the Sun.
Toure, A. O Mystic Light! A Mystic Sage
Returns to Realms of Eternity.
Unknown. Go Down, Old Hannah.
Walker, M. People of Unrest.
Sun Ra (Sonny Blount)
Toure, A. O Mystic Light! A Mystic Sage
Returns to Realms of Eternity.
Sunday
Brooks, G. Sundays of Satin-Legs Smith, The.
Dove, R. Kentucky, 1833.
Hayden, R. Mourning Poem for the Queen of
Sunday.
Those Winter Sundays.
Heard, J. Sabbath Bells.
Trethewey. Domestic Work, 1937.
Troupe. In Jimmy's Garden.
See also **Sabbath**
Sunrise
Angelou. Plagued Journey, A.
Hughes, L. Hey! Hey!
Kgositsile. Ivory Masks in Orbit.
La Grone. Suncoming.
Wheatley, P. Hymn to the Morning, An.
Sunset
Dunbar, P. Sunset.
Fordham. Sunset.
Horton, G. Setting Sun, The.
Hughes, L. Caribbean Sunset.
Hey!
Sunset—Coney Island.
Sunset in Dixie.

Lane, P. Lake Murry.
Ray, H. Afterglow, The.
  At Sunset.
  Sunset Picture.
Sanchez, S. I have looked into.
Toomer. And Pass.
Young, A. Where the Danube and Sava Rivers
  Meet.

Superiority
Sanchez, S. Small Comment.

Superstition
Dove, R. Cholera.
Hughes, L. Gods.
  Number.
Johnson, M. Superstitions.
Lorde. Reins.
Thompson, C. Johnny's Pet Superstition.

Surgery
Gilyard. Daughter, That Picture of You.
Harper, M. Deathwatch.
  Debridement: Operation Harvest Moon: *On
  Repose.*
Knight, E. Hard Rock Returns to Prison from
  the Hospital for the Criminal Insane.
See also **Hospitals; Medicine; Physicians**

Surprise
African-American Oral Tradition. Ain't It a
  Bitch?
Bethune, L. Blue Tanganyika.
Madhubuti. Reflections on a Lost Love.

Surrealism and Surrealists
Kaufman, B. Abomunist Manifesto.

Survival
African-American Oral Tradition. Titanic: "All
  the old folks say the fourth a May was a hell
  of a day."
Titanic: "Boys, you remember way back on
  the day of the eighth of May."
Titanic: "Eighth a May was a hell of a day,
  The."
Titanic: "I don't know, but my folks say."
Titanic: "In the year of eighteen-twelve."
Titanic: "It was sad indeed, it was sad in
  mind."
Titanic: "Tenth of May was a hell of a day,
  The."
Titanic: "This is about Shine O Shine. The
  captain was on his boat and he was."
Titanic: "Twelfth of May was one hell of a
  day, The."
Angelou. Alone.
  Song for the Old Ones.
Barrax. Greenhouse.
Bethune, L. Harlem Freeze Frame.
Cliff. Within the Veil.
Clifton, L. My Mama moved among the days.
  This morning / this morning.
Coleman, W. Doing Battle with the Wolf.
Cullen, C. Harsh World that lashest me each
  day.
  Only the Polished Skeleton.
Dove, R. Zeppelin factory, The.
Graham, D. Soul.
Knight, E. Dark Prophecy: I Sing of Shine.
Lorde. Artisan.
  Brown Menace or Poem to the Survival of
  Roaches, The.
  Litany for Survival, A.
  Martha this is a catalog of days.
  Naming the Stories.
Madgett. Homage.
Nelson, M. La Peste.
Reed, C. My Brother and Me.
Salaam. We have been seen.
Sanchez, S. Small Comment.
Spriggs. Every Harlem Face Is
  AFROMANISM Surviving.
Stanard. Spirits Struggle.
Walden. Wish for an Overcoat.
Young, K. Casting.
Zu-Bolton. Struggle-Road Dance.

Swallows
McKay, C. Homing Swallows.

Swamps
Komunyakaa. Landscape for the Disappeared.
Walcott. Swamp, The.

Swans
Horton, G. Swan, The—Vain Pleasures.

Swimming and Swimmers
African-American Oral Tradition. Titanic: "All
  the old folks say the fourth a May was a hell
  of a day."
Titanic: "Boys, you remember way back on
  the day of the eighth of May."
Titanic: "Eighth a May was a hell of a day,
  The."
Titanic: "I don't know, but my folks say."
Titanic: "In the year of eighteen-twelve."
Titanic: "It was sad indeed, it was sad in
  mind."
Titanic: "Tenth of May was a hell of a day,
  The."
Titanic: "This is about Shine O Shine. The
  captain was on his boat and he was."
Titanic: "Twelfth of May was one hell of a
  day, The."
Cullen, C. To the Swimmer.
Knight, E. Dark Prophecy: I Sing of Shine.
Lorde. Question of Climate, A.
McElroy, C. Learning to Swim at Forty-Five.
Mitchell, K. Night Rain.
Young, A. Sleepy Day at Half Moon Bay.

Swinburne, Algernon Charles
Cotter, Sr. Algernon Charles Swinburne.

Symbiosis
Finney, N. Lobengula: Having a Son at 38.

Symbols
Dodson, O. Conversation on V.
Dove, R. Five Elephants.
Farr. Van/Dyke.
Hughes, L. Emperor Haile Selassie.
See also **Metaphor**

Sympathy
Angelou. Poor Girl.
  To a Freedom Fighter.
Cullen, C. Magnets.
Dove, R. Variation on Gaining a Son.
Dunbar, P. Passion and Love.
  Sympathy.
Moorer. Sympathy.
Warren-Moore. For Etheridge Knight.
  For Paula Cooper (The 18 Year Old Who
  Waits on Death Row).

T

Talk
African-American Oral Tradition. Talk some
  shit, Richard.
Angelou. Thirteens (Black), The.
  Thirteens (White), The.
Brown, S. Nous n'irons plus au bois.
Joans. Truth, The.
See also **Speech**

Talmage, S. K.
Tucker, M. Lines on the Death of the Rev. S.
  K. Talmage.

Taos, New Mexico
Hughes, L. House in Taos, A.

Tapestries
Hughes, L. Tapestry.

Taste
Salaam. Makes You go Oohhh!
Sanchez, S. I am settling down.

Tattoos (skin markings)
Hayden, R. Tattooed Man, The.
Sanchez, S. You have stamped your hour.

Taverns
Dunbar, P. At the Tavern.
Hughes, L. Juice Joint: Northern City.

Taxes
Wheatley, P. America.

Taxis
Hemphill. Family Jewels.
Hughes, L. Jitney.
Knight, E. Memo #2.

Tea
Moore, L. Haiku: "Sipping the new tea."
Newsome. Sassafras Tea.

Teaching and Teachers
Angelou. Communication II.
Finney, N. Fishing among the Learned.
Gilbert, C. And, Yes, Those Spiritual Matters.
Harper, F. Learning to Read.
Hill, L. Teacher, The.
Hughes, L. Governor Fires Dean.
Lee, D. Education.
Lorde. Teacher.
McElroy, C. Learning to Swim at Forty-Five.
Nelson, M. Bali Hai Calls Mama.
Payne, D. Mournful Lute or the Preceptor's
  Farewell, The.
Sanchez, S. Let us begin the real work.
See also **Colleges and Universities; Education;
  Scholarhip and Scholars; School and
  Schools; Students**

Tears
Angelou. Avec Merci, Mother.
  Tears / The crystal rags.
Bennett, G. Sonnet—2: "Some things are very
  dear to me—."
Braithwaite. Del Cascar, Del Cascar.
Brown, S. Chillen Get Shoes.
Dove, R. Particulars.
Dunbar, P. Fount of Tears, The.
Grimké, A. I weep / Not as the young do
  noisily.
Harper, F. Slave Auction, The.
Johnson, J. Sence You Went Away.
Sanchez, S. Depression.
  Haiku: "Did ya ever cry."
Stephany. Who collects the pain.
Unknown. Me and My Captain.
Walker, A. S. M.

Technology and Technologists
Kaufman, B. Heavy Water Blues.

Teenagers
Brooks, G. We real cool. We.
Dove, R. Adolescence—I.
  Adolescence—II.
  Adolescence—III.
Hughes, L. Junior Addict.
Johnson, J. Girl of fifteen.
Smith, P. Biting Back.
See also **Adolescence; Boys; Childhood and
  Children; Girls**

Telephones and Telephoning
Angelou. Telephone, The.
Giovanni. Poem (For BMC No. 3).
Hughes, L. Madam and the Phone Bill.
Jordan, J. What Is This in Reference To? or
  We Must Get Together Sometime Soon!
Lorde. Memorial III from a Phone Booth on
  Broadway.
Toomer. Her Lips Are Copper Wire.

Television
Ai. Riot Act, April 29, 1992.
Angelou. Televised news turns.
Baraka. In the Tradition.
Cruz, V. Electric Cop, The.
Jordan, J. Nightline: September 20, 1982.
Knight, E. Television Speaks.
Lorde. Lightly.
Nelson, M. Sermon in the Cotton Field.
Scott-Heron. Revolution Will Not Be
  Televised!, The.
Walker, M. Telly Boob-Tube on the Idiot
  Box.

Temperance
Harper, F. Little Child Shall Lead Them, A.
  To White Ribbons of Maine Who Gave to Me
  Their Blessed Gifts.
  Woman's Work.
Horton, G. Intemperance Club, The.
  Song of Liberty and Parental Advice.

Temptation
Allen, J. M. Devil and Sis' Viney, The.
Cullen, C. Street Called Crooked, The.
Brooks, G. Song in the Front Yard, The.
Dunbar, P. After Many Days.
  Reluctance.
  Temptation.
Harper, F. Dialogue, A.
  Fatal Pledge, The.
  Wanderer's Return.

Hayden, R. Diver, The.
Lorde. Generation.
 Monkeyman.
 To a Girl Who Knew What Side Her Bread
  Was Buttered On.
McElroy, C. Cutting a Road from Manaus to
  Belém.
McKay, C. Wild Goat, The.
Nelson, M. Sermon in the Cotton Field.
Sanchez, S. To All Brothers.
Stuckey. Temptation.

Tennessee (state)
Giovanni. Knoxville, Tennessee.
McClellan. Hills of Sewanee, The.
Reed, I. Chattanooga.

Tennis
Gilmore, B. Coming to the Net.

Tennyson, Alfred Tennyson, 1st Baron
Heard, J. Tennyson's Poems.

Texas (state)
African-American Oral Tradition. This is to
  the women of Texas.
Hughes, L. West Texas.
Troupe. In Texas Grass.
Young, A. Midnight Special Revisited, The.

Thanksgiving
Angelou. Thank You, Lord.
Dunbar, P. Thanksgiving Poem, A.
Harper, F. Dandelions.
Hughes, L. Thanksgiving Time.
Moorer. Thanksgiving.
Williams, Niama. Companion Pieces.
See also **Gratitude**

Thanksgiving Day
Dunbar, P. Signs of the Times.
Johnson, M. Day befo' Thanksgibin', De.
 Story of Lovers Leap, The.

Theater and Theaters
Baraka. Scenario VI.
Cotter, Sr. Prologue to a Supposed Play.
Dent. Dream Orpheum Balcony.
Dunbar, P. Curtain.
Hughes, L. Lincoln Theatre.
 Note on Commercial Theatre.
Young, A. Identities.
See also **Acting and Actors; Motion Pictures
 Show Business**

Theology
Horton, G. On the Pleasures of College Life.
Nelson, M. Abba Jacob and the Theologian.

Thieves
Bontemps. Black Man Talks of Reaping, A.
Corrothers. Indignation Dinner, An.
Horton, G. Horse Stolen from the Camp, The.
Hughes, L. Ballad of the Fortune Teller.
 Ballad of the Two Thieves.
Kaufman, B. Results of a Lie Detector.
Shange. Somebody almost walked off wid alla
  my stuff.
Young, A. Dude in Denver.
See also **Crime and Criminals**

Thinness
Lorde. Song for a Thin Sister.

Thirst
McKay, C. Thirst.
Sanchez, S. Never may my thirst.
See also **Hunger**

Thomas, Dylan
Kaufman, B. Afterwards, They Shall Dance.
Young, A. Poem for Dylan Thomas, A.

Thomson, James (1700-1748)
Whitman, A. Ye Bards of England.

Thoreau, Henry David
Ray, H. Thought at Walden, A.

Thought
Baraka. From an Almanac.
 Political Poem.
Dove, R. Your Death.
Dunbar, P. Unexpressed.
Giovanni. And sometimes i sit.
 Poem (For PCH).
Jones, L. *et al.* Look for You Yesterday, Here
  You Come Today.
Kaufman, B. Inside Connie.
 Mind for All Its Reasoning, The.

When we hear the eye open there, in that
  place.
Komunyakaa. Music That Hurts, The.
Lee, D. Awareness.
Madhubuti. Awareness.
Reed, I. Untitled IV.
Toomer. People.
 Unsuspecting.
Young, A. After Visiting Arl at the Hospital.
See also **Intellect and Intellectuals; Mind;
 Reason; Wisdom**

Thunder
Toomer. Storm Ending.

Tigers
Goodison. On Becoming a Tiger.
Hughes, L. For an Indian Screen.
Walker, A. There are no tigers.

Tightropes and Tightrope Walkers
Danner, M. I'll walk the tightrope that's been
  stretched for me.
See also **Acrobatics and Acrobats**

Till, Emmett
Alexander, E. Narrative: Ali.
Brooks, G. Last Quatrain of the Ballad of
  Emmett Till, The.
Emanuel, J. Emmett Till.
Lorde. Afterimages.
Pitcher. Salute.
Plumpp. Mississippi Griot.

Time
Allen, S. Moment Please, A.
Angelou. In a time of secret wooing.
 Unmeasured Tempo.
Baraka. Ostriches and Grandmothers!
 Poem for Half White College Students.
 Poem for Neutrals, A.
Bontemps. Nocturne at Bethesda.
 To a Young Girl Leaving the Hill Country.
Braithwaite. Quiet has a hidden sound.
Brooks, G. Old Mary.
Brown, L. Green arbor that I once knew, A.
Brown, S. Challenge.
 Honey Mah Love.
Dent. Time is a motor, you know.
Dove, R. Hill Has Something to Say, The.
Dunbar, P. King is Dead, The.
 Love Despoiled.
 Time to Tinker 'Roun'!
Harper, F. How Are the Mighty Fallen!
 To-day Is a King in Disguise.
Heard, J. Birth of Time, The.
Horton, G. New Fashions.
 One Generation Passeth Away and Another
  Cometh.
Hughes, L. Lincoln Monument: Washington.
 Long View: Negro.
 Negro Speaks of Rivers, The.
 Number.
Johnson, H. Remember Not.
Kaufman, B. Falling.
 Harwood Alley Song.
 Picasso's Balcony.
 Results of a Lie Detector.
Knight, E. He sees through stone.
 Poem For a Certain Lady on Her 33rd
  Birthday, The.
Komunyakaa. Brain to the Heart, The.
 Way the Cards Fall, The.
Linden, M. Scraps of Time.
Lorde. Future Promise.
 Generation.
 Seasoning.
Mackey, N. Winged Abyss.
Nelson, M. Dinosaur Spring.
 House on Moscow Street, The.
Pritchard, N. Cloak, The.
Sanchez, S. I have walked a long time.
Sundiata. Ear Training.
Thompson, P. Adown the heights of Ages.
Walker, M. This Is My Century.
Young, A. California Peninsula: El Camino
  Real.
 Continuing.
 Eternity.
 Fort Collins, Colorado.
 Hot House.

Imitation Dance, The.
 Poem for Omar Khayyam (1050?-1123? A.D.).
 Why a Hush Should Not Be Rushed.

Titanic (ship)
African-American Oral Tradition. Titanic: "All
  the old folks say the fourth a May was a hell
  of a day."
Titanic: "Boys, you remember way back on
  the day of the eighth of May."
Titanic: "Eighth a May was a hell of a day,
  The."
Titanic: "I don't know, but my folks say."
Titanic: "In the year of eighteen-twelve."
Titanic: "It was sad indeed, it was sad in
  mind."
Titanic: "Tenth of May was a hell of a day,
  The."
Titanic: "This is about Shine O Shine. The
  captain was on his boat and he was."
Titanic: "Twelfth of May was one hell of a
  day, The."
Knight, E. Dark Prophecy: I Sing of Shine.
Moss, T. Jack Johnson Does the Eagle Rock.
Unknown. Shine and the *Titanic.*

Tobacco
African-American Oral Tradition. Juber up and
  Juber down.
Moore, L. From the Field.

Tojo, Hideki
African-American Oral Tradition. Hitler, You
  Lied to Me.
 Pearl Harbor.

Tolerance
Cortez. It's nothing / this tragedy in our arms.
Dunbar, P. Accountability.
Hughes, L. Live and Let Live.
 Poor Girl's Ruination.
 White Ones, The.
Joans. Customs and Culture?
Poetri. Don't hate me cause my skin is
  smooth like fine lustrous fiber forming a tuft.

Tombs
African-American Oral Tradition. Herman
  from the Shark-Tooth Shore.
Lanusse. Un Frère au Tombeau de Son Frère.
Moore, L. Haiku: "Summer evening sun."
See also **Burial; Cemeteries; Funerals**

Tongues
Dove, R. Adolescence—II.
Komunyakaa. Tongue Is, The.
Lorde. Echoes.
Salaam. Makes you go Oohhh!
Warren-Moore. Pink Poem.

Tools
Reed, I. Rock Me, Baby.

Tornadoes
Moss, T. Tornados.

Torture
Harper, F. Tennessee Hero, The.
Jordan, J. Poem for Jan.
Lorde. Barren.
Oden. Riven Quarry, The.
Walker, A. Torture.

Touch
Lyons, Anthony. Touch Her.
Renegade. Hoodoo.
Sanchez, S. And the joy. feeling.
 There are times that the.

Tourism and Tourists
Adisa. Cultural Trip, A.
Dove, R. Sightseeing.
Hoagland, E. Gorée ten miles offshore
  beckons.
Phillips, C. You Are Here.
Weaver, M. Message on Cape Cod, The.

Toussaint L'Ouverture, François Dominique
Goodison. Kenscoff.
Ray, H. Toussaint L'Ouverture.
Walker, M. Ballad of the Free, The.

Towns
Dove, R. Small Town.
Dunbar, P. Possum Trot.
See also **Cities; Villages**

Toys
Johnson, M. Lost Teddy Bear, The.

Tradition
Baraka. In the Tradition.
Bibbs. Dirge for J. A. Rogers.
Lorde. Generation.
Madhubuti. Union of Two, The.

Traffic
Brown, S. Glory, Glory.
Young, A. Beauty of Milwaukee cold with rain, The.

Trains
Alexander, E. Farewell to You.
Angelou. Insignificant.
Baraka. History-Wise #22.
Brown, S. Call Boy.
 Long Track Blues.
 Sister Lou.
Cortez. Nighttrains.
Dent. Dream Orpheum Balcony.
Dunbar, P. Ballade: "By Mystic's banks I held my dream."
Hayden, R. Runagate Runagate.
Hughes, L. Freedom Train.
 Homesick Blues.
 Lunch in a Jim Crow Car.
 Pennsylvania Station in New York, The.
 Porter.
Jordan, J. Song of Sojourner Truth, A.
Moorer. Jim Crow Cars.
Randall, D. Southern Road, The.
Roberson. True we are two grown men.
Unknown. Railroad Bill, Railroad Bill.
 Southern Blues, The.
See also **Locomotives; Railroads**

Trakl, Georg
Lorde. And Don't Think I Won't Be Waiting.
 Need: A Chorale for Black Woman Voices.
 St. Louis Out of Time.

Transformation
Clifton, L. Poem for My Sisters.
 Turning into my own.
Cullen, C. Protest.
 That bright chimeric beast.
Goodison. On Becoming a Tiger.
Harper, F. Christ's Entry into Jerusalem.
Hughes, L. Dear lovely Death.
Llorens. One Year Ago.
Madhubuti. We Walk the Way of the New World.
McKay, C. Baptism.
Randall, D. Hail, Dionysos.
Toomer. Chase, The.

Transience
Dobyns. Connections.
Hayden, R. Theme and Variation.
Hughes, L. Passing Love.
Toomer. At Sea.
See also **Change**

Trapezes and Trapeze Artists
Hughes, L. Aspiration.

Traveling and Travelers
Alexander, M. October Journey.
Allen, S. Harriet Tubman.
Angelou. Traveler, The.
Beeks. Parker's Mood.
Bontemps. Nocturne of the Wharves.
Brown, S. Tin Roof Blues.
Cortez. Once Upon a Road.
Crouch, S. Blackie Thinks of His Brothers.
Dove, R. Sahara Bus Trip, The.
Dunbar, P. Keep a Song Up on de Way.
Giovanni. They clapped when we landed.
Hayden, R. Tour 5.
Hughes, L. Bound No'th Blues.
 I Thought It Was Tangiers I Wanted.
Jordan, J. Letter to My Friend the Poet Ntozake Shange.
 Poem on the Road; for Alice Walker.
 Roman Poem Number Nine.
Kaufman, B. Grandfather Was Queer, Too.
Komunyakaa. Annabelle.
Lorde. For the King and Queen of Summer.
 My Fifth Trip to Washington Ended in Northeast Delaware.
 Touring.
Madhubuti. Poet: What Ever Happened to Luther?

Miller, M. Not That Far.
Nelson, M. To San Francisco.
Sanchez, S. Before i travel.
Toomer. It is Everywhere.
 Rolling, rolling.
Walker, M. October Journey.
Weaver, M. My Father's Geography.
Wheatley, P. Farewell to America.
 Ode to Neptune.
 To a Lady on Her Coming to North-America with Her Son, for the Recovery of Her Health.
Wright, J. Sketch for an Aesthetic Project.
Young, A. Leaving Home for Home.
 Leaving Rochester.
 Leaving Syracuse.

Treason and Traitors
Campbell, A. Warning.
Cullen, C. La Belle, La Douce, La Grande.
Harper, F. Sin of Achar, The.

Treasures
Harper, F. Ragged Stocking, The.

Trees
Adisa. Rainbow, The.
African-American Oral Tradition. Bend your back when I say "Go."
Angelou. Ailey, Baldwin, Floyd, Killens, and Mayfield.
Barrax. There was a song.
Bontemps. Blight.
 Tree Design, A.
Brooks, G. Birth in a Narrow Room, The.
Brown, L. Green arbor that I once knew, A.
Bryant, F. Nothing Lovely as a Tree.
Coleman, A. Portraiture.
Cowdery. Poplar Tree.
Cullen, C. Love Tree, The.
Dove, R. Dusting.
Dunbar, P. Haunted Oak, The.
Fabio. Tree Is a Landscape: a Landscape Is a Point of View, A.
Fields, J. Trees.
Giovanni. Alabama Poem.
Grimké, A. Tenebris.
Harper, F. In Commemoration of the Centennial of the A.M.E. Church.
Hughes, L. For Russell and Rowena Jelliffe.
 Little Green Tree.
Johnson, H. Trees at Night.
Knight, E. Haiku: "Bare pecan tree, A."
Komunyakaa. Thanks for the tree.
La Grone. Lines to the Black Oak.
Lorde. Ballad from Childhood.
 Song: "Wild trees have bought me."
 Speechless.
Moore, L. From the Field.
Nelson, M. Now His Fingers Found the Melody.
Salaam. Found Midnight, Place de Congo..
Sanchez, S. These autumn trees sit.
 Trees are laughing, The.
Shepherd, R. What Cannot Be Kept.
Thomas, M. Locust Trees.
See also **Listings for specific trees**

Troubadours
Johnson, F. Banjo Player, The.

Trucks and Truckers
Barrax. Death of a Squirrel in McKinley Park, The.
Jordan, J. Sketching in the Transcendental.

Trujillo Molina, Rafael Leonidas
Dove, R. Parsley.

Trumpets
Jeffers, L. How High the Moon.

Trust
Angelou. Sounds / Like pearls.
Brown, S. Parish Doctor.
Davis, D. I Can Trust.
Giovanni. You Are There.
Madgett. Homage.
Oden. "As When Emotion Too Far Exceeds Its Cause."
Priestley. Eye and eye.
Pritchard, N. Burnt Sienna.
Toomer. Be with Me.
Warner, M. My Woman.

Truth
Angelou. Accident.
Clifton, L. Light that came to lucille clifton, The.
Cotter, Sr. Prologue to a Supposed Play.
Cullen, C. To Certain Critics.
Evans, M. Speak the truth to the people.
Giovanni. Linkage.
 One ounce of truth benefits.
Harper, F. Truth.
Harper, M. Alice.
Heard, J. Truth.
Hughes, L. Comment on War.
 Theme for English B.
Joans. Truth, The.
Johnson, G. Lost Illusions.
Kaufman, B. Poet, The.
Komunyakaa. Safe Subjects.
Lorde. Song: "Wild trees have bought me."
 Summer Oracle.
McKay, C. Romance.
 Truth.
Moorer. Duty, or Truth at Work.
 Truth Suppressed, The.
Rodgers, C. Feminism.
Rux. Pledge of Allegiance.
Walker, A. Confession.
Wheatley, P. Address to the Atheist, By P. Wheatley at the Age of 14 Years—1767.
 Atheism.
Young, A. Dancing Naked.
 Reading Nijinsky's Diary.

Truth, Sojourner
Fauset. Oriflamme.
Harper, M. Sojourner Truth: Black Sybil in Salem.
Jordan, J. Song of Sojourner Truth, A.
Truth. Ain't I a Woman?

Tuberculosis
African-American Oral Tradition. T. B. Bees.
Hughes, L. Consumptive, The.
Thompson, P. Consumptive, The.

Tubman, Harriet
Allen, S. Harriet Tubman.
Brown, S. Memo: For the Race Orators.
Harper, M. Gen'l Tubman, as We Call Her.
Hayden, R. Runagate Runagate.
Jacobs, H. Growing into My Name.
Walker, H. Harriet Tubman.

Turkeys
Dunbar, P. Soliloquy of a Turkey.

Turner, Mrs. Bishop
Heard, J. Resting.

Turner, Nat
Allen, S. Nat Turner.
Aubert, A. Nat Turner in the Clearing.
Brown, S. Remembering Nat Turner.
Hayden, R. Ballad of Nat Turner, The.
Walker, M. Ballad of the Free, The.

Turtles
Unknown. Turtle's Song, The.

Tuskegee Institute
Dunbar, P. Tuskegee Song.
Hill, L. Tuskegee.
Hughes, L. Ballad of Booker T.

Twilight
Dunbar, P. Twilight.
Grimké, A. Dusk.
 Winter Twilight, A.
Hughes, L. Dusk.
 Georgia Dusk.
 Railroad Avenue.
Komunyakaa. Boat People.
Pritchard, N. Burnt Sienna.
Toomer. Georgia Dusk.
 Tell me, dear beauty of the dusk.
See also **Evening; Night**

Tyranny
Fortune. Every Man a King.
Hughes, L. Dixie Man to Uncle Sam.
 Last Prince of the East.
Johnson, F. Rome is dying.
Reed, I. Poem Delivered Before Assembly of Colored People Held at Glide Memorial Church, Oct. 4, 1973 and Called to Protest

Recent Events in the Sovereign Republic of Chile.
Walcott. Elsewhere.

U

Uganda
Walker, A. In Uganda an early king chose.
Ugliness
Brooks, G. Life of Lincoln West, The.
Evans, M. World I See, The.
Moss, T. Owl In Daytime, The.
Uncertainty
Davis, F. Arthur Ridgewood, M.D.
Giovanni. Poem (For PCH).
Hall, K. Impressions.
Hayden, R. Traveling through Fog.
Uncle Tom's Cabin
Bibb. Eliza in Uncle Tom's Cabin.
Harper, F. She's Free!
Hughes, L. Epitaph: "Uncle Tom, / When he was alive."
Uncle Tom.
Uncle Tom is a legend and a dream.
See also **Stowe, Harriet Beecher**
Uncles
Barlow, G. Salt.
Brooks, G. Merle "Uncle Seagram."
Brown, S. Uncle Joe.
Cullen, C. Uncle Jim.
Dove, R. Great Uncle Beefheart.
Harper, M. Gains.
Hayden, R. Burly fading one beside the engine, The.
Knight, E. My Uncle is My Honor and a Guest in My House.
Walker, F. Crooked Afro.
Underground Railroad
Allen, S. Harriet Tubman.
Hayden, R. Runagate Runagate.
Undertakers
Moss, T. Owl In Daytime, The.
Undertaker's Daughter Feels Neglect, The.
Troupe. After Hearing a Radio Announcement: a Comment on Some Conditions.
Unemployment
Angelou. Contemporary Announcement.
Brown, S. Episode.
Hughes, L. Broke.
Fired.
Junior Addict.
Out of Work.
Park Benching.
Jordan, J. Des Moines Iowa Rap.
Unemployment Monologue.
Unicorns
Cullen, C. That bright chimeric beast.
Randall, D. Black Poet, White Critic.
United States
Angelou. Request.
These Yet to Be United States.
Baraka. Das Kapital.
I don't love you.
Carroll, K. Domino Theory (Or Snoop Dogg Rules the World), The.
Evans, M. Status Symbol.
Harper, F. God Bless Our Native Land.
Then and Now.
Harper, M. Goin' to the Territory.
Horton, G. Union of Parties, The.
Hughes, L. Columbia, / My dear girl.
Crow Goes, Too.
I too, sing America.
One More "S" in the U.S.A.
Poem to Uncle Sam.
Jeffers, L. My Blackness Is the Beauty of This Land.
Joans. *It is time* for the United States to spend money on education so that every American would be hipper, *thus no war!*
Kaufman, B. To My Son Parker, Asleep in the Next Room.
La Grone. My America.
Lewis, A. America Bleeds.

Lorde. Thanks to Jesse Jackson.
McKay, C. America.
Nelson, M. Hurrah, Hurrah.
Randall, D. Melting Pot, The.
See also **America; North, The, United States; South, The, United States**
Unity
Angelou. Human Family.
Baraka. Black People: This Is Our Destiny.
Clifton, L. Cutting Greens.
Cullen, C. Tableau.
Danner, M. Through the Varied Patterned Lace.
Davis, R. M. Rip-Off.
Gilmore, B. Coming to the Net.
Harper, F. Burdens of All, The.
Home, Sweet Home.
Present Age, The.
To White Ribbons of Maine Who Gave to Me Their Blessed Gifts.
Horton, G. Union of Parties, The.
Hughes, L. Letter to the Academy.
Open Letter to the South.
We, Too.
Jacobs, H. On Extending the Olive Branch to My Own Self.
Jordan, J. Calling on All Silent Minorities.
Poem Number Two on Bell's Theorem.
Lorde. Hard Love Rock #II.
Madhubuti. Message All Black People Can Dig, A.
McKay, C. If we must die—let it not be like hogs.
Nelson, M. Union Apprehended.
Parker, P. There Is a Woman in This Town.
Sanchez, S. We a BadddDDD PEOPLE.
Toomer. Desire.
Men.
One Within.
Williams, Niama. Merging.
Wright, J. Cutting Greens.
Young, A. Chemistry.
In a twinkling, the green.
Manhattan March, The 1970s.
Seventh April.
Song Turning Back Into Itself 1.
Universe
Young, A. Improvisation.
Process.
Urns
Cullen, C. Uncle Jim.

V

Vacation
Knight, E. For a Brookline Lady I Love.
Vagabonds
African-American Oral Tradition. Hobo Ben.
Hoboes' Convention.
Hayden, R. Rag Man, The.
Komunyakaa. False Leads.
Valentine's Day
Dumas, H. Valentines.
Thompson, P. Valentine, A.
Value
Angelou. Nothing Much.
Baraka. Of What Use Is Poetry? (Babalu Meets the Wolfman).
Hughes, L. Addition: "7 + 7 + love =."
Ballad of the Pawnbroker.
Rodgers, C. Feminism.
Walker, A. We alone can devalue gold.
Vampires
Reed, I. Vamp.
Van Doren, Mark
Hayden, R. Ballad of Remembrance, A.
Van Gogh, Vincent
Harper, M. In Hayden's Collage.
Walker, A. If there was any justice.
Vanity
Brown, S. Memories of Salem.
Hughes, L. Being Old.
Rodgers, C. Feminism.

Vashti
Harper, F. Vashti.
Spencer, A. Before the Feast of Shushan.
Vaudeville
Brown, S. Real Mammy Song.
Vegetables
Clifton, L. Cutting Greens.
Dove, R. Sunday Greens.
Forbes, C. Potlicker Blues.
McKay, C. Tropics in New York, The.
Thomas, L. Onion Bucket.
Wright, J. Cutting Greens.
Vegetarians
Angelou. Health-Food Diner, The.
Dove, R. Why I Turned Vegetarian.
Velázquez, Diego Rodríguez de Silva y
Long, R. Juan de Pareja: Painted by Velazquez.
Venereal Disease
African-American Oral Tradition. And here's to the duck that swim the pond.
I used to be a cowboy.
Vengeance
Brown, S. Georgie Grimes, with a red suitcase.
When de Saints Go Ma'ching Home.
Cortez. Rape.
Dunbar, P. Vengeance is Sweet.
Hughes, L. Enemy.
Hard Daddy.
Red Clay Blues.
Snellings. Song of Fire, The.
Vermont (state)
Lorde. Every Traveler Has One Vermont Poem.
Reed, I. Phoebe is the 9th satellite.
Veterans
Dunbar, P. Veteran, The.
Knight, E. At a VA Hospital in the Middle of the United States of America: An Act in a Play.
Komunyakaa. Fever.
Jungle Surrender.
Report from the Skull's Diorama.
See also **Soldiers**
Victoria, Queen of England
Linden, M. To the Queen of the British Government.
Victory
Dodson, O. Conversation on V.
Unknown. Joshua fit de battle of Jericho [or ob Jerico].
Vietnam
Alexander, E. Nineteen.
Anderson, S. Junglegrave.
Bennett, Bob. It is time for action.
Cobb, C. "Containing Communism."
Evans, M. I Am a Black Woman.
Fernandez, R. Legacy of a Brother.
Giovanni. Atrocities.
Harper, M. Caves.
Fixing Certificates: Dog Tags: Letters Home.
Mama's Report.
White Friend Flies in from the Coast, A.
Hayden, R. In the Mourning Time.
Jeffers, L. Vietnam: I Need More Than This Crust of Salt.
Kgositsile. Elegy for David Diop.
Knight, E. Flukum couldn't stand the strain.
Flukum.
Komunyakaa. Boat People.
Break from the Bush, A.
Camouflaging the Chimera.
Communique.
Facing It.
Hanoi Hannah.
Jungle Surrender.
Missing in Action.
Monsoon Season.
Please.
Prisoners.
Report from the Skull's Diorama.
Starlight Scope Myopia.
Thanks for the tree.
Tu Do Street.

Tunnels.
Water Buffalo.
Lorde. Vietnam Addenda.
Lynch, C. Memo.
Madhubuti. Long Reality, The.
Major, C. Vietnam.
Vietnam #4.
Martin, H. Negro Soldier's Viet Nam Diary, A.
Redmond. Gods in Vietnam.
Reed, I. Gangster's Death, The.
July 1st, 1982.
Spellman. Beautiful Day #9, The.
Tomorrow the heroes / will be named willie. their.
Walker, M. Jackson State, May 15, 1970.
Zu-Bolton. Seeker, The.

Vietnam War
Moore, L. Gifts.
Tanka: "Month of rain ends."

Vigilantes
Jordan, J. Poem from Taped Testimony in the Tradition of Bernard Goetz.

Villages
Dove, R. Sightseeing.
Harper, M. Village Blues.
Southerland. Two Fishing Villages.
Young, A. Leaving Rochester.
See also **Cities; Towns**

Villon, François
Komunyakaa. Villon/Leadbelly.

Violence
African-American Oral Tradition. Dolomite: "Some folks say that Willie Green."
Dolomite first originated in San Antone.
Lame and the Whore, The.
Ai. Endangered Species.
Angelou. Coleridge Jackson had nothing.
Baraka. Poem Some People Will Have to Understand, A.
Barrax. King: April 4, 1968.
Clifton, L. 4/30/92; for Rodney King.
Dickey. Father.
Dumas, H. Knock on Wood.
Grandmaster Flash and the Furious Five. Message, The.
Hayden, R. American Journal.
Locus.
Hughes, L. Bad Man.
Beale Street Love.
Birmingham Sunday.
Bombings in Dixie.
Evil Woman.
Georgia Dusk.
Ku Klux.
Third Degree.
Joans. .38, The.
Jordan, J. Female and the Silence of a Man, The.
I Must Become a Menace to My Enemies.
Kaufman, B. Geneology.
Komunyakaa. Songs for my Father.
Lorde. For the Record.
McKay, C. To the White Fiends.
Nelson, M. Like Father, Like Son.
Unknown. Railroad Bill, Railroad Bill.
Stackolee.
Walcott. Blues.
Walker, M. On Police Brutality.
Poppa Chicken.
Williams, Karen. Ntarama (Rwanda) Chronicles.

Violets
Dunbar-Nelson. Sonnet: "I had no thought of violets of late."
Dunbar, P. To a Violet Found on All Saints' Day.

Virginia (state)
Angelou. Forgive.
Brown, S. Virginia Portrait.
Clifton, L. I went to the valley.
Eady. Sherbet.
Spencer, A. Life-long, Poor Browning.

Virginity and Virgins
Baraka. New Sheriff, The.
Goodison. Wedding in Hanover.

Greene, C. Something Old, Something New.

Virtue
Boyd, J. Sketch of a Verying Evening Sky.
Cullen, C. Tribute.
Harper, F. Pure in Heart Shall See God, The.
Rallying Cry, The.
Madhubuti. Black Manhood: Toward a Definition.
Nelson, M. Abba Jacob and the Theologian.
Boys in the Park.
Wheatley, P. Ode on the Birthday of Pompey Stockbridge, An.
On Virtue.
To a Gentleman of the Navy.
To the Rev. Dr. Thomas Amory on Reading Sermons on Daily Devotion, in Which That Duty Is Recommended and Assisted.

Viruses
Reed, I. I am not the walrus.

Vision
Baraka. Epistrophe.
Clifton, L. 11/10 Again.
Giovanni. Lorraine Hansberry: an Emotional View.
Hughes, L. Island.
Jordan, J. Who Look at Me.
Loftis. Delirium.
Lorde. Contact Lenses.
Therapy.
Toomer. People.
Young, A. Sea Level.

Visiting and Visitors
Dunbar, P. Opportunity.
Visitor, The.
Harper, F. Simon's Feast.
Harper, M. Lovely's Daughters: Visitors.
Henderson, E. B. Trussy's Visit.
Reed, I. Visit to a Small College.
Young, A. Dance for Li Po, A.
New Orleans Intermissiom.
One West Coast.
Visiting Day.

Vitality
Cullen, C. Counter Mood.
Epilogue: "Lily, being white not red, The."
Life's Rendezvous.
Hughes, L. Demand.
Young, A. Foggy Morning.

Voices
Clifton, L. Friends Come.
To Joan.
Dunbar, P. Musical, A.
Johnson, J. Lift Ev'ry Voice and Sing.
Lorde. Echoes.
Lover's Song, A.
Night-Blooming Jasmine, The.
McKay, C. To O.E.A E. A.
Renegade. Hoodoo.
Salaam. French Quarter Intimacies.
Sanchez, S. His voice used to sing.
This is not a small voice.
Southerland. Recitation.
Troupe. Avalanche.
See also **Screams; Talk**

Volcanoes
Ray, H. Listening Nydia.

Voodoo
African-American Oral Tradition. JUba dis and JUba dat an.
Campbell, J. De Cunjah Man.
Nelson, M. Women's Locker Room.
Reed, I. Black Cock, The.
Catechism of d Neoamerican Hoodoo Church.
For Cardinal Spellman Who Hated Voo Doo.
Neo-HooDoo Aesthetic, The.
Neo-HooDoo Manifesto.
Railroad Bill, a conjure man.
Sermonette.
Walker, M. Black Magic.

Voting and Voters
Hughes, L. Ballad of Sam Solomon.
Ghosts of 1619.
Not a Movie.
Moorer. Negro Ballot, The.
Roberson. Poll.
Sharp, S. Woman Who Died in Line, The.

See also **Woman Suffrage**

Voyages
Garnet. Bound on a voyage of awful length.
Wheatley, P. Ode to Neptune.
To a Gentleman on his Voyage to Great-Britain for the Recovery of His Health.

Voyeurism and Voyeurs
African-American Oral Tradition. Through the Keyhole in the Door.
Dove, R. Small Town.

Vulnerability
Lorde. Even.
Young, A. Mid-Life Crises: A Critical Review.

W

Wailing Wall, The
Cullen, C. At the Wailing Wall in Jerusalem.

Waiters and Waitresses
Cullen, C. Atlantic City Waiter.
Eady. Sherbet.
McKay, C. Alfonso, Dressing to Wait at Table.

Waiting Rooms
Dove, R. Vacation.

Wakes
Hughes, L. Irish Wake.

Waking
Angelou. Awaking in New York.
Brown, S. Call Boy.
Giovanni. Sometimes / when i wake up.
Harper, F. Dying Queen, The.
Kaufman, B. Morning Joy.
Mackey, N. Phantom Light of All Our Day, The.
Toomer. Angelic Eve.
White Arrow.
Wakefield, J. We exist living dead. The death of.

Walking and Walkers
Bethune, L. Harlem Freeze Frame.
Bontemps. "Close Your Eyes!"
Brown, L. Winter Sonnet.
Cornish, S. Generations 2.
Dunbar, P. Spring Wooing, A.
Harper, M. Night of Frost, The.
Hughes, L. Harlem Night Song.
Walkers with the Dawn.
Johnson, Ray. Walking east on 125th street.
Jordan, J. Poem About My Rights.
Knight, E. Green Grass and Yellow Balloons.
Miller, E. Walk in the Daytime Is Just as Dangerous as a Walk in the Night, A.
Plumpp. Poems are not places.
Unknown. Walk Together Children.
Young, A. New Autumn, New York.
New Moon Over Grove Street.
Ponce de León: A Morning Walk.

Walls
Hughes, L. Mellow.
Walls.
Plumpp. Another mule kicking.

Wanderlust
Baraka. Legacy.
Brown, S. Long Gone.
Harper, F. Wanderer's Return.
Hughes, L. Bound No'th Blues.
Lorde. Smelling Wind.
Trollop Maiden, The.
McKay, C. One Year After.
Wild Goat, The.
Payne, D. Mournful Lute or the Preceptor's Farewell, The.
Young, A. City Home Detroit.

War
Ai. I Can't Get Started.
Baraka. Three Movements and a Coda.
War Poem.
Brooks, G. Looking.
Progress, The.
White Troops Had Their Orders but the Negroes Looked Like Men.
Brown, S. Sam Smiley.

Clifton, L.   Buffalo War.
  Generations.
  Powell; March 1991.
  Willie B (2).
Cortez.   Rape.
Dunbar-Nelson.   I sit and sew—a useless task
  it seems.
Greene, C.   Excuse, The.
Grimké.   Gathering of the Grand Army, The.
Harper, F.   "Do Not Cheer, Men Are Dying,"
  Said Capt. Phillips, in the Spanish-American
  War.
Harper, M.   Guerrilla-Cong, The.
Hayden, R.   Monet's "Waterlilies."
Hughes, L.   Bonds for All.
  Broadcast on Ethiopia.
  Comment on War.
  Fourth of July Thought.
  Green Memory.
  Mother in Wartime.
  Relief.
  Some Day.
  Speaking of Food.
  War.
  Without Benefit of Declaration.
Johnson, J.   Color Sergeant, The.
Jordan, J.   Another Poem about the Man.
  First Poem from Nicaragua Libre: Teotcacinte.
Kaufman, B.   Peace Be with You.
Komunyakaa.   Ambush.
  Camouflaging the Chimera.
  For the Walking Dead.
  Re-creating the Scene.
  Starlight Scope Myopia.
  You and I Are Disappearing.
Lorde.   For Jose and Regina.
  Starting All Over Again.
  Vietnam Addenda.
Mackey, N.   Phantom Light of All Our Day,
  The.
O'Higgins, M.   Sunset Horn.
Rowe, G.   Reason Why, The.
Southerland.   Two Fishing Villages.
Terry, L.   Bar[']s Fight[, August 28, 1746].
Walden.   Nation's Friend, The.
Walker, A.   Enemy, The.
Walker, M.   Today.
Young, A.   Suicide.
See also Soldiers; Listings for specific wars and
  battles
War Casualties
Dove, R.   Bird Frau, The.
Hughes, L.   Casualty.
Knight, E.   At a VA Hospital in the Middle of
  the United States of America: An Act in a
  Play.
Komunyakaa.   At the Screen Door.
See also Soldiers
War Dead
Brooks, G.   Appendix to the Anniad.
  Piano after War.
Dunbar, P.   Memorial Day.
  Our Martyred Soldiers.
  Robert Gould Shaw.
  Unsung Heroes, The.
Graham, R.   Lynching for Skip James, A.
Harper, M.   Photographs: A Vision of
  Massacre.
Heard, J.   Decoration Day.
  National Cemetery, Beaufort, South Carolina,
  The.
Holman, M.   Notes for a Movie Script.
Hughes, L.   Bonds: In Memoriam.
  Hero—International Brigade.
  Official Notice.
  Poem to a Dead Soldier.
Knight, E.   Flukum couldn't stand the strain.
  Flukum.
Komunyakaa.   Break from the Bush, A.
  Facing It.
  Missing in Action.
  To Have Danced with Death.
  You and I Are Disappearing.
Lynch, C.   Memo.
Nelson, M.   Lonely Eagles.
Randall, D.   Memorial Wreath.
Terry, L.   Bar[']s Fight[, August 28, 1746].

Wheatley, P.   On the Death of General
  Wooster.
See also Soldiers
Warning
African-American Oral Tradition.   Girl told me,
  A.
Dove, R.   Primer for the Nuclear Age.
Hughes, L.   Day.
  Evil Morning.
  In a Troubled Key.
Lorde.   For Each of You.
  From the Cave.
Weaver, M.   Providence Journal V: Israel of
  Puerto Rico.
Washington, Booker Taliaferro
Cotter, Sr.   Dr. Booker T. Washington to the
  National Negro Business League.
Dunbar, P.   Booker T. Washington.
  To Booker T. Washington.
Hughes, L.   Alabama Earth.
  Ballad of Booker T.
Johnson, M.   To See Ol' Booker T.
Linden, M.   Our Noble Booker T. Washington.
Moorer.   Notable Dinner, A.
Randall, D.   Booker T. and W. E. B.
Washington, D.C.
Dove, R.   Banneker.
Hemphill.   Family Jewels.
Iverem.   Keeper.
Washington, George
Jordan, J.   Cameo No. II.
Wheatley, P.   On the Capture of General Lee.
  To His Excellency General Washington.
Washington Square, New York City
Stanard.   Washington Square Park and a Game
  of Chess.
Watches
Harper, M.   Roland.
Hughes, L.   Could be Hastings Street.
See also Clocks
Water
Ahmasi.   Water of Your Bath.
Dunbar, P.   Gourd, The.
  Pool, The.
Jordan, J.   October 23, 1983.
Lorde.   Fishing the White Water.
McKay, C.   Thirst.
Mitchell, K.   Night Rain.
  Tree Stillness.
Roy, L.   Suffering The Sea Change: All My
  Pretty Ones.
Toomer.   Water.
Unknown.   God's A-Gonna Trouble the Water.
Wright, J.   Appearance of a Lost Goddess,
  The.
  Journey to the Place of Ghosts.
  Lake in Central Park, The.
Young, A.   H₂O.
Waterfalls
Ray, H.   At the Cascade.
Watermelons
Sanchez, S.   Baby. you are sweet.
Watts, Los Angeles, California
Kgositsile.   Elegy for David Diop.
Rivers, C.   Watts.
Waves
Hughes, L.   Moonlight Night: Carmel.
Young, A.   Sometimes with the waves.
Wealth
African-American Oral Tradition.   Down and
  Out.
  Herman from the Shark-Tooth Shore.
  Hophead Willie.
  Hustlin' Dan.
  Once I lived the life of a millionaire.
  Willie the Weeper.
Baraka.   Politics of Rich Painters, The.
Brown, S.   Mister Samuel and Sam.
Cotter, Sr.   Dr. Booker T. Washington to the
  National Negro Business League.
  My Poverty and Wealth.
Dunbar, P.   Common Things.
  Place Where the Rainbow Ends, The.
  Precedent.
Fields, J.   High on the Hog.

Giovanni.   Luxury.
Harper, F.   Going East.
  Soul, The.
Herndon.   Poem.
Hughes, L.   Advertisement for the Waldorf-
  Astoria.
  Cross.
  Park Bench.
  Puzzlement.
  Rising Waters.
  Success.
Jordan, J.   What Would I Do White?
Knight, E.   Dark Prophecy: I Sing of Shine.
Lorde.   Beverly's Poem.
McClellan.   Color Bane, The.
Reed, I.   .05.
Thomas, L.   They Never Lose.
Walker, M.   Money, Honey, Money.
Weapons
Cortez.   Stockpiling of frozen trees, The.
Hayden, R.   Zeus over Redeye.
Komunyakaa.   Starlight Scope Myopia.
Weariness
Cullen, C.   Mood.
Dunbar, P.   Goin' Home.
Giovanni.   Harvest.
  Poem for Aretha.
Grimké, A.   Butterflies, white butterflies, in the
  sunshine.
Harper, F.   Mother's Blessing, The.
Hughes, L.   So Tired Blues.
  Weary Blues, The.
Johnson, F.   Tired.
Jordan, J.   Aftermath.
Lorde.   Electric Slide Boogie, The.
McKay, C.   French Leave.
  Spring in New Hampshire.
  Through Agony.
  Tired Worker, The.
Reese, S.   Letter from a Wife.
Sanchez, S.   Sequences.
Stuckey.   Long Cotton Row.
  This Is It.
Toomer.   Harvest Song.
Tucker, M.   I am Weary, Mother.
  Weariness.
Weather
Dove, R.   Turning Thirty, I Contemplate
  Students Bicycling Home.
Hughes, L.   Strange Hurt.
  There's always weather, weather.
Weathervanes
Patterson, R.   To a Weathercock.
Weddings
Adisa.   Rainbow, The.
Brooks, G.   Black Wedding Song, A.
Dove, R.   In the Old Neighborhood.
  Variation on Gaining a Son.
Dunbar, P.   To Dan.
Emanuel, J.   Wedding Procession, from a
  Window.
Giovanni.   Rituals.
Goodison.   Wedding in Hanover.
Jordan, J.   Wedding, The.
Thompson, P.   Tribute to the Bride and
  Groom, A.
See also Marriage
Weekends
Angelou.   Weekend Glory.
Trethewey.   Secular.
Welcome
Angelou.   Arrival.
Dunbar, P.   Invitation to Love.
Harper, F.   Poem, A: "Over the foaming
  ocean."
Henderson, E. B.   Trussy's Visit.
Welfare
Angelou.   Momma Welfare Roll.
Jordan, N.   Feeding the Lions.
Lane, P.   Sexual Privacy of Women on
  Welfare.
Wells
Cotter, Sr.   Way-Side Well, The.
Werewolves
Sanchez, S.   When i look at you.

West Indies
Clark, Benjamin. Emigrant, The.
Hughes, L. Broadcast to the West Indies.
  Caribbean Sunset.
Lorde. Za Ki Tan Ke Parlay Lot.
Whitfield. Stanzas for the First of August.
See also **Caribbean Sea; Jamaica, West Indies**
West, The, United States
African-American Oral Tradition. Boothill
  McCoy.
Brooks, G. Strong Men, Riding Horses /
  Lester after the Western.
Dunbar, P. Welcome Address.
Harper, M. Clark's Way Out West: Another
  Version.
  Conferences with the Unknown.
Jordan, J. Poem for Joy.
West Virginia (state)
Atkins. Narrative.
Weston, Louise B.
Fordham. Mrs. Louise B. Weston.
Weston, Rebecca
Fordham. Mrs. Rebecca Weston.
Weston, Samuel
Fordham. Rev. Samuel Weston.
Whales and Whaling
Reed, I. Al Capone in Alaska.
Wharves
Bontemps. Nocturne of the Wharves.
Wheat
Alexander, M. Iowa Farmer.
Wheatley, Phillis
Giovanni. Linkage.
Hayden, R. Letter from Phillis Wheatley, A.
Jordan, J. Something Like a Sonnet for Phillis
  Miracle Wheatley.
Madgett. Phillis.
Unknown. Answer, The.
Walker, M. Ballad for Phillis Wheatley.
Whippoorwills
Dunbar, P. Whip-Poor-Will and Katy-Did.
Whiskey
Hughes, L. Bar.
Whistling and Whistlers
Dunbar, P. Breaking the Charm.
  Just whistle a bit, if the day be dark.
White (color)
Hughes, L. Angels wings is white as snow,
  The.
Moss, T. Lessons from a Mirror.
Whitefield, George
Wheatley, P. Ode of Verses on the Death of
  George Whitefield, An.
  On the Death of the Rev. Mr. George
  Whitefield, 1770.
  On the Death of the Rev'd Dr. Sewall, 1769.
  Thoughts on the Works of Providence.
Whites
African-American Oral Tradition. Corner of
  47th and South Park.
Titanic: "All the old folks say the fourth a
  May was a hell of a day."
Titanic: "Boys, you remember way back on
  the day of the eighth of May."
Titanic: "Eighth a May was a hell of a day,
  The."
Titanic: "I don't know, but my folks say."
Titanic: "In the year of eighteen-twelve."
Titanic: "It was sad indeed, it was sad in
  mind."
Titanic: "Tenth of May was a hell of a day,
  The."
Titanic: "This is about Shine O Shine. The
  captain was on his boat and he was."
Titanic: "Twelfth of May was one hell of a
  day, The."
Ups on the Farm.
Alhamisi. Pome. For Weird. Hearts. and All.
Anderson, C. Prayer to the White Man's God.
Anderson, S. Sound of Afroamerican History
  Chapt I, The.
Baraka. Clay.
Corrothers. In the Matter of Two Men.
Dove, R. Great Palaces of Versailles, The.
Hamilton, B. Brother Harlem Bedford Watts
  Tells Mr. Charlie Where ITs At.

Hughes, L. Ballad of Walter White.
  Dinner Guest: Me.
  Do You Reckon?
  Get Up off That Old Jive.
  Imagine! / They are afraid of you.
  Song of Adoration.
  Worriation.
Jackmon. Burn, Baby, Burn.
Jordan, N. Black Warrior.
Knight, E. Dark Prophecy: I Sing of Shine.
Lorde. Chorus.
Madhubuti. Malcolm Spoke / Who Listened?
McKay, C. Tiger.
Spellman. Beautiful Day #9, The.
Whitman, Walt
Forbes, C. Reading Walt Whitman.
Hughes, L. Old Walt Whitman.
Whittier, John Greenleaf
Dunbar, P. Whittier.
Harper, F. Give My Love to the World.
  Words for the Hour.
Heard, J. To Whittier.
Widows and Widowers
Fields, J. Jolly fat widows, The.
Harper, F. Widow's Mites, The.
Hughes, L. Widow Woman.
Komunyakaa. Facing It.
Wheatley, P. On the Death of Doctor Samuel
  Marshall.
  On the Death of Dr. Samuel Marshall.
  On the Death of Dr. Samuel Marshall, 1771.
  To a Clergyman on the Death of His Lady.
  To a Lady on the Death of Her Husband.
  To His Honour the Lieutenant-Governor, on
  the Death of His Lady, March 24, 1773.
  To Mrs. Leonard, on the Death of Her
  Husband.
  To the Rev. Mr. Pitkin, on the Death of His
  Lady.
Wigs
Hemphill. Homocide.
Wilberforce University
Heard, J. Wilberforce.
Linden, M. Golden Jubilee of Wilberforce.
  To the Conference.
Wilderness
Cook, W. Spiritual.
Lorde. Song: "Wild trees have bought me."
Williams, Arthur Clement
Bibb. In Memory of Arthur Clement Williams.
Williams, William Carlos
Eady. William Carlos Williams.
Wills
Hughes, L. Testament.
Wilson, John. *See* **"North, Christopher"**
Wind
Dunbar, P. Chase, The.
  Plantation Child's Lullaby, The.
  Till the Wind Gets Right.
  Wind and the Sea, The.
Fortune. Tell me, ye sad winds sighing.
Kaufman, B. Cross Winds.
  Who Has Seen the Wind?
Kgositsile. Gods Wrote, The.
Lane, P. Wind Thoughts.
Lorde. Blackstudies.
  Bloodbirth.
  Hugo I.
Moore, L. Homeplace, The.
Patterson, R. To a Weathercock.
Salaam. Our Natures Rise.
Window Washing and Window Washers
Hayden, R. Performers, The.
Windows
Baraka. Epistrophe.
Brooks, G. Boy Breaking Glass.
Lane, P. Girl at the Window.
Madhubuti. After Her Man Had Left Her for
  the Sixth Time That Year / (An Uncommon
  Occurrence).
Rankine. New Windows.
Shange. Tango.
Young, A. October Window.
Wine
Campbell, A. Song of the Decanter.
Dove, R. Champagne.

Nelson, M. Epithalamium and Shivaree.
Reed, I. Vachel Lindsay Fault, The.
Wings
Dove, R. Wingfoot Lake.
Hughes, L. Angels wings is white as snow,
  The.
  Freedom Seeker.
Oden. "As When Emotion Too Far Exceeds
  Its Cause."
Winter
Angelou. This Winter Day.
Brown, L. Winter Sonnet.
Brown, S. Virginia Portrait.
Dove, R. November for Beginners.
  Snow King, The.
Dunbar, P. Jack Frost at Bedtime.
  Plantation Child's Lullaby, The.
  Warm Day in Winter, A.
  When Winter Darkening All Around.
  Winter-Song.
  Winter's Approach.
  Winter's Day, A.
Giovanni. Hampton, Virginia.
  Winter.
Grimké, A. Winter Twilight, A.
Grimké. Parting Hymn, A.
Harper, M. Drive In, The.
Hayden, R. Those Winter Sundays.
Horton, G. On Winter.
Hughes, L. Midwinter Blues.
  Prayer for a Winter Night.
  Where? When? Which?
  Winter Moon.
  Winter Sweetnes.
Jordan, J. Winter Honey.
Lanusse. Le Carnaval.
Lorde. Cables To Rage Or I've Been Talking
  On This Street Corner.
  Father the year has fallen.
  Father, the Year Is Fallen.
  Teacher.
  Woman Thing, The.
McKay, C. After the Winter.
  To Winter.
  Winter in the Country.
Moore, L. Haiku: "Winter stillness."
Roberson. Blue Horses.
"Stephany." What marked the river's flow.
Thompson, P. Winter Night, A.
Walcott. Village Life, A.
Wright, J. Desire's Persistence.
Young, A. Ars Poetica.
Wisconsin (state)
Jordan, J. Madison Experience, The.
Wisdom
Baraka. Insidious Dr. Fu Man Chu, The.
Clifton, L. I was born in a hotel.
  Solomon.
  Wise: Having the Ability to Perceive and
  Adopt the Best Means for Accomplishing an
  End.
Cullen, C. Threnody for a Brown Girl.
  Wisdom Cometh with the Years.
  Wise, The.
Dunbar, P. At Cheshire Cheese.
Giovanni. Alabama Poem.
  Conversation.
Harper, F. I thirst, but earth cannot allay.
  Lessons of the Street.
Harvey, Y. Sonia Told Them Women.
Hughes, L. Acceptance.
  Being Old.
  Wisdom.
Kaufman, B. Trip, Dharma Trip, Sangha Trip,
  The.
Lorde. Child Shall Lead, A.
  Hugo I.
  Song: "Wild trees have bought me."
Nelson, M. Aches and Pains.
  Simple Wisdom, The.
Stuckey. Ribbons and Lace.
Sun-Ra. To the Peoples of Earth.
Tolson, M. African China.
Walker, M. Our Need.
Wheatley, P. Thoughts on the Works of
  Providence.
Williams, L. Flying High.

See also **Mind; Reason; Thought**

Wishes

African-American Oral Tradition. Cock is a crickly creature.

Brooks, G. Black Wedding Song, A.

Clifton, L. Wishes for Sons.

Cook, W. Spiritual.

Hughes, L. Disillusion.

If-ing.

Little Lyric (of Great Importance).

Song to the Dark Virgin.

Johnson, G. Wishes.

Lorde. All Hallows Eve.

Sanchez, S. I wish it were mid.

Toomer. Beehive.

WEEMS. Dime after Dime.

Wit

Angelou. Changing.

Witchcraft and Witches

Brown, S. Memories of Salem.

Clifton, L. In Salem.

Johnson, J. White Witch, The.

Lorde. Neighbors.

Thaw.

Reed, I. Black Cock, The.

Walker, M. Ballad of the Hoppy-Toad.

Molly Means.

Wives

African-American Oral Tradition. Jesse James.

Baraka. For Hettie.

Brooks, G. Bronzeville Mother Loiters in Mississippi. / Meanwhile, a Mississippi Mother Burns Bacon.

Clifton, L. Now my first wife never did come out of her room.

Wife.

Dove, R. Daystar.

Dunbar, P. To a Poet and a Lady.

To Alice Dunbar.

Harper, F. Report.

Harper, M. Kin.

Johnson, G. To a Young Wife.

Kendrick, D. Sadie Snuffs a Candle.

Knight, E. Portrait of Mary.

Komunyakaa. Thorn Merchant's Wife, The.

Lorde. Evening News, The.

Menard. To My Wife.

Walden. One to Love.

Walker, A. In Uganda an early king chose.

See also **Marriage**

Woman Suffrage

Harper, F. John and Jacob—a Dialogue on Woman's Rights.

Jonas, R. Brother Baptis' on Woman Suffrage.

See also **Voting and Voters**

Women

Adisa. Discover Me.

African-American Oral Tradition. Here's to the lady with the little red shoes.

Motherfuck a woman lay flat on her back.

This is to the women of Texas.

Alexander, L. Negro Woman.

Anderson, S. Soul-Smiles.

Angelou. Family Affairs.

Lady Luncheon Club.

Man Bigot.

Momma Welfare Roll.

Phenomenal Woman.

Seven Women's Blessed Assurance.

Woman Me.

Woman Work.

As-Sabah. Sister Roll.

Baraka. Beautiful Black Women.

Revolutionary Love.

Baudelaire. Cat, The.

Bennett, Bob. (Title).

Bennett, G. To a Dark Girl.

Bohanan. Washer-Woman, The.

Braithwaite. Watchers, The.

Brooks, G. Mrs. Small went to the kitchen for her pocketbook.

Sunset of the City, A.

To Those of My Sisters Who Kept Their Naturals.

Brown, S. Choices.

Pardners.

Clark, C. Ode to a Beautiful Woman.

Clemmons. Freedom Song for the Black Woman, A.

Clifton, L. For de Lawd.

Harriet / if i be you.

In this garden.

She Is Dreaming.

There Is a Girl Inside.

Thirty-eighth year, The.

To Merle.

Way It Was, The.

Wishes for Sons.

Woman who loves, A.

Women You Are Accustomed To, The.

Coleman, W. Dear Mama.

Miss Jones.

Cook, W. Seth Bingham.

Cortez. Grinding Vibrato.

If the drum is a woman.

Cumbo. Black Sister.

Cuney. No Images.

Derricotte. Touching/Not Touching: My Mother.

Dove, R. For Kazuko.

Great Palaces of Versailles, The.

Spy.

Dunbar, P. Made to Order Smile, The.

On the Dedication of Dorothy Hall.

Turning of the Babies in the Bed, The.

Evans, M. I Am a Black Woman.

Forman, R. Up Sister.

You So Woman.

Franklin, C. Death of Days and Nights of Life.

Gee. By glistening, dancing seas.

Giovanni. All i gotta do.

Crutches.

Each Sunday.

Life I Led, The.

Linkage.

Poem Off Center, A.

Woman.

Woman Poem.

Women gather, The.

Wonder Woman, The.

Harper, F. Appeal to My Countrywomen, An.

Double Standard, A.

She's Free!

To White Ribbons of Maine Who Gave to Me Their Blessed Gifts.

Woman's Work.

Harper, M. Breaded Meat, Breaded Hands.

Harvey, Y. Sonia Told Them Women.

Hayden, R. Sphinx.

Hemphill. XXI.

Hughes, L. Addition: "Put 5 and 5 together."

As Befits a Man.

Gypsy Man.

Harlem Sweeties.

Jazzonia.

Preference.

Ruined Gal, A.

Troubled Woman.

When Sue Wears Red.

Jackson, G. Alice.

Jackson, R. 1973.

Johnson, G. Heart of a Woman, The.

Smothered Fires.

Jordan, J. Addenda to the Papal Bull.

Female and the Silence of a Man, The.

Gettin Down to Get over.

Memo.

Poem About My Rights.

Poem for South AFrican Women.

Jordan, N. When A Woman Gets Blue.

Knight, E. Genesis 11.

Lockett. This Poem for Black Women.

Loftin. Weeksville Women.

Lorde. Bazaar.

Beams.

Call.

Chain.

Coniagui women / wear their flesh like war, The.

Death Dance for a Poet.

For My Singing Sister.

For the Record.

Generation III.

Hard Love Rock #II.

Keyfoods.

Letter for Jan.

Need: A Chorale for Black Woman Voices.

NOW.

Outlines.

Party Time.

Poem for Women in Rage, A.

Portrait.

Question of *Essence*, A.

Scar.

Seventh Sign, The.

Stations.

To Marie, in Flight.

To the Poet Who Happens to Be Black and the Black Poet Who Happens to Be a Woman.

Vigil.

Woman.

Woman Speaks, A.

Woman Thing, The.

Women of Dan Dance with Swords in Their Hands to Mark the Time When They Were Warriors, The.

Women on Trains.

Mackey, N. Song of the Andoumboulou.

Madgett. Black Woman.

Woman with Flower.

Madhubuti. Big Momma.

Blackwoman.

Magnificent Tomorrows.

Poem Looking for a Reader, A.

Revolutionary Screw, The.

Womenblack: We Begin with You.

Major, C. Giant Red Woman.

Maroon. Neighbor.

Nude Woman Spotted in Cappuccino Cup as Advertising Dollar Co-Opts Another Life.

McClaurin. I, Woman.

McElroy, C. In My Mother's Room.

Woman's Song, A.

McKay, C. Wild Goat, The.

Miller, M. Scream, The.

Moss, T. Lessons from a Mirror.

Raising a Humid Flag.

Neal, L. For Our Women.

Nelson, M. Ballad of Aunt Geneva, The.

Seducing the Saint.

Sisters.

Ojenke. Amazon.

Parker, Dominique. Foxfire.

Parker, P. There Is a Woman in This Town.

Queen Latifah. Evil That Men Do, The.

Randall, D. Blackberry Sweet.

Reynolds, S. Moon/Light Quarter/Back Sack.

Open Letter to All Black Poets, An.

Rodgers, C. Feminism.

Poem for Some Black Women.

Rushing. Sent for You Yesterday.

Sanchez, S. Cause we are carving.

Kwa Mama Zetu Waliotuzaa.

Poem No. 8.

Present.

Who are you/ iden.

Woman. rocking her.

Woman who made, A.

Saunders, R. Hush Honey.

Sharp, S. In the Tradition of Bobbitt.

Tribal Marks.

Smith, P. Blonde White Women.

Snellings. Earth.

Spencer, A. Lady, Lady, I saw your face.

Letter to My Sister.

Wife-Woman, The.

Tallie. Karma's Footsteps.

Thomas, L. Electricity of Blossoms.

They Never Lose.

Thompson, D. Sister Lakin and Lally.

Thompson, P. Muse's Favor, The.

Toomer. Portrait in Georgia.

Walker, A. Pagan.

Well. / He was a poet.

Woman Is Not a Potted Plant, A.

Walker, M. My Truth and My Flame.

Watkins, N. Do You Know Me?

Williams, C. Gulf Coast Blues.
Williams, S. I Want Aretha to Set This to Music.
   She Had Known Brothers.
   Straight Talk from Plain Women.
   You Were Never Miss Brown to Me.
Young, A. Dear Old Stockholm.
   Head of a Woman.

Wood
Dunbar, P. To Pfrimmer.
Harper, M. Lathe: Shirl's Tree.

Woodpeckers
Weatherly, T. Blues for Franks Wooten.

Woods
Knight, E. Talking in the Woods with Karl Amorelli.
McClellan. April of Alabama, The.
Young, A. In the tender woodland.
See also **Forests**

Words
Alexander, E. Affirmative Action Blues.
Aubert, A. When the Wine Was Gone.
Baraka. From an Almanac.
   Ka 'Ba.
   Snake Eyes.
   Y's 18.
Beadle. Words are but leaves to the tree of mind.
Cortez. No Simple Explanations.
Cullen, C. Incident.
   Karenge Ya Marenge.
Dove, R. Ö.
Eady. Sherbet.
   Song.
   Why Do So Few Blacks Study Creative Writing?
Gilbert, C. Kite-Flying.
Giovanni. True Import of Present Dialogue, Black vs. Negro.
Harper, F. Careless Word, The.
   Only a word— a little word.
Hoagland, E. Anti-Semanticist, The.
Hughes, L. Refugee.
   Song After Lynching.
   Songs.
   Sweet Words on Race.
   To make words sing.
   Words Like Freedom.
Kaufman, B. Trip, Dharma Trip, Sangha Trip, The.
Kgositsile. To Mother.
   To My Daughter.
Komunyakaa. Safe Subjects.
   Tongue Is, The.
Lorde. Coal.
   Learning to Write.
Madhubuti. I ain't seen no poems stop a .38.
Major, C. Swallow the Lake.
Mullen, H. Momma Sayings.
Neal, L. Don't say goodbye to the Porkpie Hat that rolled.
Nelson, M. How I Discovered Poetry.
Patterson, R. "Word to the Wise Is Enough, A."
Reed, I. Beware: Do Not Read This Poem.
Sanchez, S. These words stained with red.
Tretheway. And Syllables Grow Wings There.
Troupe. Avalanche.
Weaver, M. Borders.
   Weekend Equestrian, The.
See also **Language**

Wordsworth, William
Grimké. Wordsworth.

Work
Angelou. One More Round.
   They Ask Why.
   Woman Work.
Dove, R. Great Palaces of Versailles, The.
   Satisfaction Coal Company, The.
   Zeppelin factory, The.
Dunbar, P. Not they who soar, but they who plod.
   Too Busy.
Forbes, C. Blue Monday.
Harper, F. Go work in my vineyard, said the

Lord.
   Little Builders, The.
Hughes, L. Buddy.
   Elevator Boy.
   Fired.
   Gone Boy.
   Necessity.
Shockley. Oseola McCarty.
Toomer. Cotton Song.
   Not for me—and may nothing enhance.
   Prayer (I): "How we have strained at our dark works."
Walker, M. Monologue.
See also **Labor and Laborers**

World
Spencer, A. Black man o' mine.
   White Things.
See also **Earth**

World War I
Dove, R. Passage, The.
Fauset. Christmas Eve in France.
Johnson, F. Soldiers of the Dusk, The.
Young, A. Sarajevo Moon.

World War II
African-American Oral Tradition. Hitler, You Lied to Me.
   Joe the Grinder and G.I. Joe.
   Pearl Harbor.
Christian. Go Down, Moses!
   Selassie at Geneva.
Cullen, C. La Belle, La Douce, La Grande.
Dodson, O. Conversation on V.
Dove, R. Aircraft.
   Aurora Borealis.
   Sightseeing.
Holman, M. Notes for a Movie Script.
Hughes, L. Bonds: In Memoriam.
   Dear Mr. President.
   Dimout in Harlem.
   Jim Crow's Last Stand.
   Salute to Soviet Armies.
   Song for Ourselves.
   Stalingrad: 1942.
   Underground, The.
   Will V-Day Be Me-Day Too?
   World War II.
Kaufman, B. War Memoir: Jazz, Don't Listen to It at Your Own Risk.
Lorde. Bicentennial Poem #21,000,000.
McKay, C. Look Within.
Nelson, M. Hurrah, Hurrah.
   Lonely Eagles.
   Three Men in a Tent.
   Tuskegee Airfield.
Shepherd, R. Lucky One, The.
Williams, N. For Lover Man, and All the Other Young Men Who Failed to Return from World War II.

Worldliness
Brooks, G. Mrs. Small went to the kitchen for her pocketbook.
Brown, S. Isaiah to Mandy.
Harper, F. Dialogue, A.
   Rallying Cry, The.
   Saved at Last.
Sanchez, S. Shedding my years and.
Williams, C. A. In Search of Aunt Jemima.

Worms
Danner, M. This Is an African Worm.
Redmond. Autumn God.
Toomer. Face.

Worry
Brown, S. Old Man Buzzard / Wid his bal' head.
Clifton, L. Island Mary.
Gee. By glistening, dancing seas.
Hughes, L. Gal's Cry for a Dying Lover.
Roberson. Sonnet.

Worship and Worshipers
Cannon, N. Ark, The.
Henderson, D. Song of Devotion to the Forest.
Hughes, L. Tambourines! / Tambourines!
   Testimonial.
McKay, C. St. Isaac's Church, Petrograd.
Wheatley, P. To the Rev. Dr. Thomas Amory

on Reading Sermons on Daily Devotion, in Which That Duty Is Recommended and Assisted.
See also **Churches; Faith; Religion**

Wrens
Thompson, P. Little Wren, A.

Wright, Richard
Harper, M. Afterword: a Film.
   Heartblow: Messages.
Medina, T. Big House Revisited, The.
Rivers, C. Mourning Letter from Paris, A.
   To Richard Wright.
Sanchez, S. Like bigger thomas.
Young, A. One Snapshot I Couldn't Take in France, The.

Writing and Writers
Alexander, K. Just Us.
Angelou. Artful Pose.
   Conceit, A.
   Impeccable Conception.
Aubert, A. All Singing in a Pie.
Baraka. Black Art.
   Bronze Buckaroo, The.
   From an Almanac (2).
   Gatsby's Theory of Aesthetics.
   Look for You Yesterday, Here You Come Today.
   Tone Poem.
Braxton, C. Say Hey Homeboy.
Brown, S. Against That Day.
Carroll, K. Short Poem.
Clifton, L. Adupe.
   Driving through New England.
   Eldridge.
   Lately / everybody i meet.
   Making of Poems, The.
   Poet, The.
   Speaking of Loss.
   Storm Poem, A.
Coffin, F. Harriet Beecher Stowe's Works.
Coleman, W. Word Game.
Corrothers. Me 'n' Dunbar.
Cortez. I and I.
   No Simple Explanations.
   Red Pepper Poet, The.
Cotter, Sr. On Hearing James W. Riley Read.
   Poet, The.
Cullen, C. To Certain Critics.
   Yet Do I Marvel.
Davis, F. Arthur Ridgewood, M.D.
Dove, R. At the German Writers Conference in Munich.
   Nexus.
Dunbar, P. Choice, A.
   Confirmation.
   Crumb, a crumb, and a little seed, A.
   Harriet Beecher Stowe.
   Inspiration.
   Lapse, The.
   Misapprehension.
   Poet, The.
   Poet and His Song, The.
   Poet and the Baby, The.
   Prometheus stole from Heaven the sacred fire.
   Then and Now.
   To a Poet and a Lady.
Eady. Why Do So Few Blacks Study Creative Writing?
Ellis, T. View of the Library of Congress from Paul Laurence Dunbar High School.
Evans, M. Writers, The.
Fabio. God's Trombone.
Finney, N. Fishing among the Learned.
Forbes, C. Poet's Shuffle, The.
Fordham. Pen, The.
Forman, R. This Poem.
Gilbert, C. And, Yes, Those Spiritual Matters.
Giovanni. And sometimes i sit.
   Beep Beep Poem, The.
   Boxes.
   For Saundra.
   Habits.
   How do you write a poem.
   I am she ... making rainbows.
   Kidnap Poem.
   Lorraine Hansberry: an Emotional View.
   Poem Off Center, A.

Poetry is a trestle.
Poetry is motion graceful.
Stardate Number 18628.190.
Toy Poem.
Harper, F.   To Mrs. Harriet Beecher Stowe.
Harper, M.   Alice.
Gains.
In Hayden's Collage.
Made Connections.
Hayden, R.   Paul Laurence Dunbar.
Hernton.   Distant Drum, The.
Young Negro poet / came from 'way down
South.
Horton, G.   Art of a Poet, The.
George Moses Horton, Myself.
On Hearing of the Intention of a Gentleman to
Purchase the Poet's Freedom.
Poet's Feeble Petition, The.
Hughes, L.   Anne Spencer's Table.
For Russell and Rowena Jelliffe.
My Beloved.
Not What Was.
Poet to Bigot.
Poet to Patron.
Theme for English B.
Jackson, A.   Why I Must Make Language.
Jackson, R.   After the Dance.
1973.
Joans.   Truth, The.
Johnson, A.   Our Days Are Numbered.
Johnson, J.   O Black and unknown bards of
long ago.
Jordan, J.   Free Flight.
Letter to My Friend the Poet Ntozake Shange.
Kaufman, B.   Abomunist Manifesto.
Afterwards, They Shall Dance.
Cincophrenicpoet.
Does the Secret Mind Whisper?
Enormous Gas Bill at the Dwarf Factory. A
Horror Movie to be Shot with Eyes, The.
Poet, The.
Suicide.
Terror is more certain than all the rare
desirable popular songs, A.
Unhistorical Events.
Why Write ABOUT.
Knight, E.   Apology for Apostasy?
Black Poet Leaps to His Death, A.
For Black Poets Who Think of Suicide.
Green Grass and Yellow Balloons.
Haiku: "Making jazz swing in."
Haiku: "To write a blues song."
Memo #9.
On the Projects Playground.
Poem to Galway Kinnell, A.
Komunyakaa.   Letter to Bob Kaufman.
Lane, P.   Midnight Song.
To a Woman Poet That I Know.
LeFlore.   This Poem.
Loftis.   Delirium.
In Memorium: Robert Hayden.
Lorde.   Learning to Write.
On the Edge.
Paperweight.
Poem for a Poet, A.
Question of Essence, A.
There Are No Honest Poems about Dead
Women.
To the Poet Who Happens to Be Black and
the Black Poet Who Happens to Be a
Woman.
Madhubuti.   Gwendolyn Brooks Elizabeth.
I ain't seen no poems stop a .38.
Poet: What Ever Happened to Luther?

McElroy, C.   Learning to Swim at
Forty-Five.
Odaro.   Alafia.
Pfister.   Granny Blak Poet (in Pastel).
Plumpp.   Poems are not places.
Redmond.   Aerolingual Poet of Prey.
Parapoetics.
Reed, I.   If My Enemy Is a Clown, a Natural
Born Clown.
Jacket Notes.
Reynolds, S.   Open Letter to All Black Poets,
An.
Rivera, E.   Elegy for a Martyred Poet.
Rodgers, C.   Brief Synopsis, A.
Rowe, G.   Mrs. Francis Ellen Harper.
Roy, L.   Bread Man, The.
Shange.   Inquiry.
Oh, I'm 10 Months Pregnant.
Pages for a Friend.
Smith, P.   Building Nicole's Mama.
Spencer, A.   Dunbar.
Troupe.   In Jimmy's Garden.
In Memoriam; for James Baldwin (1924–
1987).
My poems have holes sewn into them.
Walker, M.   For Gwen, 1969.
For Owen Dodson, 1983.
I want to write.
Warren-Moore.   For Etheridge Knight.
For Paula Cooper (The 18 Year Old Who
Waits on Death Row).
Wheatley, P.   Philis's Reply to the Answer in
Our Last by the Gentleman in the Navy.
To Mæcenas.
Whitman, A.   Poet hath a realm within, and
throne, The.
Young, A.   Boogie With O.O. Gabugah.
Election Night Pome.
Loneliness.
People of Letters.
Poetry.
Prestidigitator 1, The.
Realism.
Reggie's Version.
Some Spice for Jack Spicer.
Studio Up Over In Your Ear.
Yes, the Secret Mind Whispers.
Your Basic Black Poet.
Zu-Bolton.   Intro to My Final Book of Poems.

See also **Literature**

Wyoming (state)
Major, C.   I Was Looking for the University.

Y

Years
Dunbar, P.   King is Dead, The.
Hughes, L.   New Year.
Yoruba
Lorde.   Oya.
Winds of Orisha, The.
Young, Lester
Baraka.   Pres / spoke in a language.
Joans.   Lester Young.
Kaufman, B.   Walking Parker Home.
Young, A.   Lester Leaps In.
Young Men's Christian Association
Linden, M.   Y.M.C.A., The.
Youth
Baraka.   Vice.
Brooks, G.   We real cool. We.

Brown, S.   Challenge.
Memories of Salem.
Young Ones, The.
Clifton, L.   There Is a Girl Inside.
This morning / this morning.
Coleman, W.   At the Record Hop.
Cullen, C.   Uncle Jim.
Wisdom Cometh with the Years.
Youth Sings a Song of Rosebuds.
Dove, R.   Flash Cards.
Dunbar, P.   At Cheshire Cheese.
Ione.
Old Homestead, The.
Old Story, The.
Retrospection.
El-Hadi.   Drama, The.
Emanuel, J.   Treehouse, The.
Young Ones, Flip Side, The.
Fraser, A.   To the "J F K" Quintet.
Giovanni.   Age.
Grimké, A.   When the Green Lies over the
Earth.
Hayden, R.   Paul Laurence Dunbar.
Heard, J.   To Youth.
Henderson, D.   Boston Road Blues.
Horton, G.   Close of Life, The.
Hughes, L.   Being Old.
Comment on War.
Dark Youth of the U.S.A.
Man.
Poem for Youth.
Young Negro Girl.
Youth.
Johnson, G.   Lost Illusions.
Youth.
Jordan, J.   Unemployment Monologue.
Knight, E.   For Freckle-Faced Gerald.
Lorde.   Coping.
Generation.
Mentor.
Spring People.
Randall, D.   Green Apples.
Rite, The.
Sanchez, S.   Personal Letter No. 3.
Young Womanhood.
Toomer.   Delivered at the Knighting of Lord
Durgling by Great Bruce-Jean.
Troupe.   Reflections on Growing Older.
Walcott.   Glory Trumpeter, The.
Walker, M.   Dear are the names that charmed
me in my youth.
Jackson State, May 15, 1970.
Young, A.   Sweet Sixteen Lines.
Zu-Bolton.   Ain't No Spring Chicken.
Yugoslavia
Young, A.   Belgrade moon, where are you.
In a twinkling, the green.

Z

Zen Buddhism
Pritchard, N.   Love Poem.
See also **Buddhism and Buddhists**
Zimbabwe
Plumpp.   Zimbabwe.
Zinnias
Hayden, R.   Zinnias.
Zoos
Cullen, C.   Thoughts in a Zoo.
Zulus
Adisa.   Women at the Crossroad / (May
Elegba Forever Guard the Right Doors).